BUSINESS ENTERPRISES: LEGAL STRUCTURES, GOVERNANCE, AND POLICY
Cases, Materials, and Problems

BUSINESS ENTERPRISES: LEGAL STRUCTURES, GOVERNANCE, AND POLICY
Cases, Materials, and Problems

Douglas M. Branson
W. Edward Sell Chair in Business Law
University of Pittsburgh

Joan MacLeod Heminway
Associate Professor of Law
The University of Tennessee

Mark J. Loewenstein
Nicholas A. Rosenbaum Professor of Law
University of Colorado

Marc I. Steinberg
Radford Professor of Law & Senior Associate Dean for Research
Southern Methodist University

Manning Gilbert Warren III
Harold Edward Harter Chair of Commercial Law
University of Louisville

Library of Congress Cataloging-in-Publication Data

Business enterprises : legal structures, governance, and policy : cases, materials, and problems / Douglas M. Branson ... [et al.].

p. cm.

Includes index.

ISBN 978-0-8205-6467-8 (case bound)

1. Business enterprises--Law and legislation--United States. 2. Business enterprises--Law and legislation--United States--Cases. 3. Securities--United States. 4. Limited partnership--United States. 5. Private companies--United States. I. Branson, Douglas M.

KF1366.B87 2008

346.73'065--dc22

2008045293

NOTE TO USERS

To ensure that you are using the latest materials available in this area, please be sure to periodically check the LexisNexis Law School web site for downloadable updates and supplements at www.lexisnexis.com/lawschool.

Editorial Offices

744 Broad Street, Newark, NJ 07102 (973) 820-2000

201 Mission St., San Francisco, CA 94105-1831 (415) 908-3200

www.lexisnexis.com

MATTHEW◆BENDER

(2009-Pub.3213)

DEDICATIONS

Douglas M. Branson

I dedicate this book to my co-authors, who remained of good cheer throughout, and to my wife, Elizabeth Hurtt.

Joan MacLeod Heminway

I dedicate this book to Merrit, Helen, and Lou, who afforded me the time and knowledge I needed to accomplish this.

Mark J. Loewenstein

I dedicate this book to Louis Rosen, who took me under his wing when I first entered the practice of law and whose teachings I carry with me to this day.

Marc I. Steinberg

I dedicate this book to my wonderful family — my wife Laurie, my daughter Alexandra (Alex), and my sons Avram (Avi) and Phillip (Bear) — with all of my love.

Manning Gilbert Warren III

I dedicate this book to my former law partners at Ritchie, Rediker & Warren, Thomas A. Ritchie and J. Michael Rediker, for their creativity, their pragmatism and their professionalism in the practice of corporate law.

ACKNOWLEDGMENTS

I would like to acknowledge the support and understanding of my spouse, Elizabeth Hurtt. — Douglas Branson

I wish to acknowledge the more-than-capable research assistance of Rachel Kuipers Bates and Richard McDermott, both of whom read early (i.e., unpolished) versions of my text for this book. Thanks also are due to The University of Tennessee College of Law (which supported this project with research funding), to my coauthors (who have taught me so very much), and to my amazing administrative assistant, Sean Cary von Gunter (who manages to make me and my work look good regardless of the circumstances). And, finally, my family, especially Merrit, Scott, and Kate, deserves credit for putting up with my unavailability and moodiness when I work on intense projects like this. Without the assistance and support of all of these folks, I would not have been able to complete my work on this book. — Joan MacLeod Heminway

I thank my colleague, Professor Emeritus J. Dennis Hynes, who graciously allowed me to draw on our co-authored casebook for the materials in Chapters 2 and 3 of this book; my research assistants on this project, Jessica Lynn Broderick and Jennifer Kim, for their excellent work; the University of Colorado Law School for its financial support; and to my wonderful coauthors, who made this project a delightful one. — Mark J. Loewenstein

I thank the SMU Dedman School of Law for supporting this project. My gratitude is expressed to Dean John B. Attanasio, my former research assistant Mr. Aaron Rigby, and my administrative assistant Ms. Jan Spann. The strong support I receive from this superb law school is truly appreciated by me. I also wish to thank my coauthors for their friendship, support, diligence, and courtesy. — Marc I. Steinberg

I would like to acknowledge the outstanding work of my administrative assistant, Janet Gribbins Sullivan, in all aspects of this effort, including her critical review of the final drafts. I also would like to express special appreciation to my research assistant, Stacy Anne Hoehle, for her tireless editing, research, and dedication throughout the project. Last, I would like thank my wife, Judith, and the three of my children still at home during this work, my sons Marnix, Sebrand, and Marc, for their constant inspiration. — Manning Gilbert Warren III

PREFACE

In this book, five law professors from across the country have assembled cases, problems, and other materials for use in an introductory Business Associations, Business Organizations, Corporations, or similar law school course. Each author brings to the book his or her individual experience in the teaching and practice of the subject matter and his or her own voice.

This teaching and learning resource is designed to provide comprehensive coverage of state and federal law and policy governing the legal structures through which business is conducted in the United States, principally including unincorporated and incorporated business entities (as opposed to sole proprietorships). The authors generally anchor this law and policy in relevant theory and practice. In carrying out its objectives, the book covers foundational issues relating to agency and entity formation, corporate finance, internal governance, and legal liability to third parties. Moreover, the text covers fundamental state and federal rules governing corporate transactions and litigation and, in its final chapter, touchstone issues relating to the role of legal counsel in representing business enterprises. Importantly, the book focuses on privately held entities and also provides comprehensive coverage of the basics of public company theory, policy, law, and practice.

Each chapter begins with a title and a narrative that covers an introductory point or otherwise sets the stage for the materials that follow. Consideration is given to both legal analysis and practice issues. A number of chapters include significant descriptions of applicable theory and policy as framing devices for the chapter contents.

The materials in each chapter have been selected to afford adequate coverage of business law basics (including, for example, fundamental corporate finance and takeover nomenclature and other information necessary to an understanding of transactional business law). Law review articles, glossaries, charts, and textual citations to statutes and other materials supplement the standard fare of case law. Moreover, in key areas of study, the text allows for a comparison of laws and practices in other countries with those of the United States. These parts of the book are especially important, since more and more students must handle international contracts, transactions, or cases in the early years of their practice. To reinforce key principles and analysis, the book includes notes and problems that permit the integration of concepts and foster applied skills.

In short, this text allows for coverage of law, underlying theory and policy, and practice skills. In one volume, the book contains material sufficient to educate an emerging lawyer to function in general business law practice in a transactional or advocacy-oriented setting. In creating this resource, the five authors, all of whom have extensive academic and practical credentials, seek to create a comprehensive, introductory resource for students regardless whether they will subsequently practice in small, medium or large-sized firms here in the United States or abroad. In our increasingly electronic and global world, these students need wide-ranging, inclusive, applied knowledge of the legal aspects of business enterprises — structures, governance, and policy — and this book is designed to foster that knowledge.

TABLE OF CONTENTS

TABLE OF CONTENTS

TABLE OF CONTENTS

TABLE OF CONTENTS

TABLE OF CONTENTS

TABLE OF CONTENTS

TABLE OF CONTENTS

TABLE OF CONTENTS

TABLE OF CONTENTS

TABLE OF CONTENTS

TABLE OF CONTENTS

TABLE OF CONTENTS

TABLE OF CONTENTS

TABLE OF CONTENTS

Chapter 1

INTRODUCTION

A Short Essay on the History of Partnerships and Corporations

The Origins of Business Entity Law

Much of the theory of present-day commercial law can be traced back to medieval Italy, where both the ecclesiastical law and that of commercial associations contributed to later English and American ideas of partnership and incorporation.[1] By the thirteenth century, ecclesiastical law recognized the Roman Catholic Church as an entity: a singular institution instead of a plural group of people, with power conferred by the state. This entity theory transported easily to England, which at the time had quasi-institutions, but no legal theory to support them, and greatly influenced the growth of corporate law. Additionally, medieval Italy affected modern partnership law through two commercial associations, the *commenda*, and the *societas*.

The *commenda*, which gave partners investment opportunities with limited liability, influenced later forms of limited liability associations, particularly limited partnerships. The *societas*, meanwhile, was a form of contractual general partnership that established several key principles of partnership law: "firstly, that each partner represented the others, and could bind the others by his contracts made on behalf of the firm; and, secondly, that each partner was personally liable without any limitation to all the creditors of the firm."[2] The *societas* was common in Europe in the Middle Ages and was recognized by the law merchant, a uniform body of law applied internationally at the merchant fairs held throughout Europe, including England. At this time, the merchant courts in England almost exclusively handled partnership law cases. The law merchant, in addition to the principles of the *societas*, contributed the principle of partnership law that each partner has the right to an accounting from the other partners. One principle, not ultimately adopted by English law from the law merchant, was the idea of the partnership as an entity separate from its members; instead, partnerships were viewed as an aggregate of members. Because partnerships were considered an aggregate of individuals, as opposed to an entity, the withdrawal or death of any individual partner meant the dissolution of the partnership. The aggregate theory of partnerships persisted in the United States until 1994, as discussed below.

In the fifteenth and sixteenth centuries, merchant fairs became less common in England as businesses were established in urban areas, and the use of merchant courts decreased. The English equity courts assumed jurisdiction for commercial cases. They still applied the customs of the law merchant; little precedent was developed, and English treatises through the eighteenth century barely addressed the topic of partnership law. Despite lack of attention by the law, partnerships were a primary type of business association because of the requirement of royal charter or parliamentary approval for incorporation. Gradually, common law courts also decided cases involving partnerships, and as the number of partnership cases before the courts grew, a body of partnership law developed. Particularly significant in developing partnership law was the work of Chief Justice Lord Mansfield, who engrafted the mercantile customs into the English common law. In 1794, the first treatise on partnership law written in English was written by William Watson.

During this same time period, the English colonies were being established in

---

[1] C. T. Carr, The General Principles of the Law of Corporations 128 (1905); 8 W. S. Holdsworth, A History of English Law 207 (1926). Much of the historical material in this introduction is drawn from these two sources as well as Christopher Anglim, Joined in Common Enterprise: A Bibliography on the Origins of Early Anglo-American Partnership Law 22 (2005).

[2] Holdsworth, *supra* note 1 at 197.

America, and were home to many partnerships and other unincorporated business associations, such as "societies, groups of 'undertakers,' [and] 'companies,'" almost all of which were legally considered partnerships.[3] For instance, there were business associations organized for fishing and whaling, mining, and manufacturing. England's principles of law applied to its colonies in America, and even after independence and formation of the United States, English common law provided the foundation for state partnership law. American judges, at the beginning of the republic, also were influenced by civil law and maritime and admiralty cases, particularly applying them to commercial law.

Throughout the nineteenth century, as the partnership continued to be the leading form of business association, American partnership law remained, for the most part, a matter of state common law, with a few statutes codifying existing case law. But in the late nineteenth and early twentieth centuries, several states adopted statutory codes governing partnerships. In 1902, seeing the need to make commercial law uniform in the United States, the National Conference of Commissioners on Uniform State Laws (NCCUSL) began to work on the Uniform Partnership Act (UPA), which was completed in 1914. UPA, which codified common law partnership rules, was very successful, with the District of Columbia plus every state, except Louisiana, adopting it, with only minor variations. Among other things, it continued the common law rule of unlimited personal liability of each partner for the debts and obligations of the partnership.

Although this period also marked the beginning of liberal corporation statutes, as discussed below, the demand for entities that would protect investors from entity liabilities was strong, resulting in the drafting by NCCUSL of the Uniform Limited Partnership Act (ULPA), which was widely adopted following its promulgation in 1917. Under ULPA, only the "general partners" of the limited partnership would have liability for the obligations of the partnership. So long as the partners designated as "limited partners" remained inactive in the business, they would not be liable for the partnership's obligations.

Since the enactment of UPA by almost every state, partnership law has been derived from it and the common law that existed before its enactment (when needed to fill in the gaps), although UPA allows a partnership agreement to contract around its provisions. A Revised Uniform Limited Partnership Act (RULPA) was released in 1976, and in 1994, NCCUSL published an updated version of UPA called the Revised Uniform Partnership Act (RUPA). RUPA made partnerships more stable by treating them as an entity instead of an aggregate of individuals, thereby generally allowing the partnership to continue after a partner withdraws from the partnership. RUPA, or UPA in states that have not adopted RUPA, is the default law for unincorporated business entities: when parties "carry on as co-owners a business for profit," they have created a partnership and fall under the statute.

Starting in the 1970s, states began expanding the limited liability options for entrepreneurs. The limited liability company appeared on the scene, affording investors the option of participating in the business without fear of liability for entity obligations, and in short order, all states adopted enabling legislation. Soon thereafter, the idea of affording limited liability to all owners of an unincorporated entity was broadened to include general partnerships with the creation of the limited liability partnership (LLP). In 1997, RUPA was amended to include the Uniform Limited Liability Partnership Act (ULLPA). A partnership can receive LLP status, and thereby receive limited liability protection for all partners, with a simple filing with the state. Additionally, in 2001 NCCUSL published a new limited partnership act, commonly referred to as "Re-RULPA," which included a provision already the law in many states that allows for limited liability for the general partner(s) of a limited partnership if the

---

[3] 1 JOSEPH STANCLIFFE DAVIS, ESSAYS IN THE EARLIER HISTORY OF AMERICAN CORPORATIONS 91 (1917).

partnership files as a limited liability limited partnership (LLLP) with the state.

At the beginning of the twenty-first century, then, the entrepreneur has a dazzling number of entities from which to choose. In addition to the corporate form, discussed below, state law provides a general partnership, limited partnership, limited liability partnership, and limited liability company. The differences among these various entities are often subtle and confusing, and have given rise to a movement to rationalize (really, consolidate) these various entities. While the end of the twentieth century witnessed an increase in the number of choices of entities, the beginning of the twenty-first century is likely to witness a contraction.[4]

The Rise of Corporate Law

Of course, the limited liability protections offered by the new forms of unincorporated business association have existed for centuries in the corporation, first in England and then in the United States. Historically, entrepreneurs who wanted to join together in business had to choose between the ease of association offered by the partnership, founded on contract, and the limited liability offered by the corporation, founded on a grant of privilege from the state. At the end of the fourteenth century, kings began granting privileges to English merchants trading in foreign countries. For instance, in 1391, Richard II granted a royal charter to a group of English merchants trading in Prussia; the charter allowed the merchants to elect a governor to "rule over the traders, do speedy justice, settle disputes, and award compensation." The charter also allowed the merchants to pass ordinances. But even before this example of early business incorporation, there were signs of "corporateness" in England. For instance, kings had already been granting charters to towns in England, and the towns slowly began to be regarded as a separate entity, instead of a group of townspeople, aided by developments such as a common name for the town, a common seal, and the town being recognized as a party to a civil action. Before long, towns were thought to have "perpetual" existence, drawing a distinction between them and their "mortal members." Finally, the rise of guild merchants in English cities fostered the idea of voluntary association and membership.[5] The guilds were an early form of business association in England; they had bylaws, kept accounts, and had a governor and associates, and they influenced later corporations, such as the joint-stock companies.

The royal charters for merchants that began at the end of the fourteenth century often gave corporate form to business associations that already existed, such as the guilds, which would sometimes disband and then "reappear" as a corporation (although the companies were not necessarily called corporations). The corporate form gave these already-existing associations and new ones "governmental powers and trading privileges," which were especially important for explorers and merchants trading overseas, who were given an "exclusive right to traffic."[6] W. S. Holdsworth, in his *History of English Law*, lists the powers and privileges that these early corporations were granted by the crown:

> In the first place, they want a power to associate, as without some definite permission, associations were looked upon with suspicion by the government. In the second place, having got the right to associate, they want powers of self-government, powers to impose taxes on their members, powers to decide their own disputes, powers to take adequate measures to defend themselves against pirates and other enemies. They want the privilege of a monopoly of trade, dispensation from particular laws as to export and import, and other laws which might hinder their trade, remissions of customs duties. All these

---

[4] *See* Mark J. Loewenstein, *A New Direction for State Corporate Codes*, 68 U. Colo. L. Rev. 453 (1997).

[5] *Id.* at 147–48.

[6] Harold Joseph Laski, *The Early History of the Corporation in England*, 30 Harv. L. Rev. 561 (1917).

privileges the king, by virtue of his wide prerogatives to control foreign trade, could grant.[7]

In return, the king received control over the members and their trading activities, through the corporation. Other advantages of the corporate form over the partnership soon became apparent. The corporation had perpetual life, had greater continuity of management, had transferable shares, could bring suit against third parties, and could bring suit against its own members (a partnership could not legally bring suit against a partner). The common seal brought greater differentiation between the corporation and its members, and a majority vote was allowed for decision-making (partnerships required unanimity). Finally, there was separation between the corporation and its members when it came to corporate debt: an individual member was not personally liable for the debts of the corporation.

By the sixteenth and seventeenth centuries, one kind of corporation in particular rose to prominence in England — the joint-stock company. The principal goal of the joint-stock company was to make money for its members, and the method was to trade as a single entity using stock supplied by all members, paying out dividends of some kind later.[8] This form of corporation allowed a broad range of investment, and by the end of the seventeenth century, a paper published stock prices of these companies, investors became accustomed to the ups and downs of the market, and the occupation of the stockbroker had been born. Several problems soon arose out of the new stock market. One was that associations formed that acted like incorporated companies but did not have a charter, or associations bought a charter from another company and then used it for a completely different kind of business. Second, there was a lack of established law applicable to either corporate or unincorporated associations. Third, companies did not keep regular accounts or have solid ideas about how to distribute dividends. As a result, the risk of fraud to investors was high, and the legislature eventually passed the Bubble Act in 1720 after a large financial crash to try to correct the problem. The Bubble Act forbade business associations to act as a corporation without a charter, or to act under a previously issued charter in a way not expressly granted by the charter. The Act allowed for greater regulation of corporations by the state.

The laws applicable to corporations in England, both before and after the Bubble Act, also applied to corporate bodies in the English colonies, including the American colonies. In fact, "the first permanent English settlements, both in Virginia and in New England, were made on the initiative and at the expense of corporations modeled [sp] after the contemporary joint stock companies for foreign trade," under charter from the crown.[9] A few colonies, Massachusetts, Connecticut, and Rhode Island, were themselves corporations. The first corporations founded in the colonies also operated under charters granted by the crown under the same process used to acquire a charter in England. Eventually, though, as colonial governments were established, corporate charters were granted to most American corporations by the various branches of colonial government itself, including governors and legislative bodies, under express or implied delegated power from the king. No general act "permitting 'freedom of incorporation' in accordance with its provisions was known in America in the colonial days."[10]

While corporations were common in the colonies, corporations formed for business purposes were not; partnerships were the form of business enterprise utilized most often. Instead, corporations formed for public, religious, educational, and charitable purposes, and the law treated all kinds the same. Public corporations consisted of cities, including New York and Philadelphia; public educational institutions; and public charity

---

[7] HOLDSWORTH, *supra* note 1 at 201 (citations omitted).

[8] Famous examples of joint-stock companies include the South Sea Company and the East India Company.

[9] Davis, *supra* note 3 at 4.

[10] *Id.* at 106.

organizations. Religious corporations included the established churches of the colonies and missionary societies. Often, private educational corporations were also religious or charitable, such as orphan schools, but there were separate private charitable corporations as well, such as hospitals. Another important set of colonial corporations was the colleges, such as Harvard, William and Mary, Yale, and Princeton. A few business corporations did exist, including what is probably the first American business corporation, The New London Society United for Trade and Commerce, although, while the company was given many of the characteristics of a corporation, it was never officially "incorporated." A few businesses were incorporated to build wharves, sell insurance, and supply water. Business associations of other various kinds existed but were probably technically partnerships.

The main reason for the lack of business corporations at this time was the local and small-scale nature of enterprise, along with the lack of technical progress during a period spent trying to occupy a largely virgin landscape.[11] However, this situation changed somewhat after independence, partly because war allowed accumulation of capital and brought diverse groups of people into contact, and larger-scale businesses were increasingly seen as desirable. Of the three hundred charters for business corporations granted before 1801, ninety percent were granted after 1789.[12] Additionally, "a strong and growing prejudice in favor of equality" dissuaded Americans from the idea that corporate privilege should be granted only sparingly, "which led almost at once to the enactment of general incorporation acts for ecclesiastical, educational, and literary corporations."[13] While general incorporation acts passed for non-business corporations, businesses were still incorporated by special act of the legislature, but whether by general or special act, incorporation was viewed as a power belonging to the state.

The lack of general incorporation acts for businesses soon became problematic. Demand for corporate charters granted by the legislature outgrew the pace by which the legislature could enact each separate bill, and suspicions of favoritism prompted criticism. Therefore, states began passing broad general incorporation statutes and banning special incorporation acts. By the end of the 19th century, general acts of incorporation that mandated many terms of incorporation were common. Around this time, the country saw huge growth in infrastructure, population, and technology, leading to more opportunity for large corporations. This growth, along with influence from corporate managers and shareholders, drove states to liberalize their incorporation statutes and deregulate the corporate form, allowing corporations to own stock in other corporations, do business in any state, form for any lawful purpose, own land, and merge with other corporations.

New Jersey was the first state to liberalize its incorporation statutes through a series of legislative reforms in the early 1890s, culminating in a total revision of its corporate statutes in 1896.[14] The goal of the legislation was to attract firms from other states to incorporate in New Jersey, using incorporation fees as a source of revenue for the state. This strategy was successful and corporate fees facilitated the end of state property taxes in New Jersey. Other states soon followed New Jersey's lead: New York, Delaware, Maine, and West Virginia adopted similar statutes, and over the course of the twentieth century, all states moved to liberal "enabling" statutes. Meanwhile, first the states, and then, in the 1930s, the federal government started to regulate public corporations through securities law.

While every state enables the formation of corporations, Delaware, which has one of

---

[11] 2 Joseph Stancliffe Davis, Essays in the Earlier History of American Corporations 5–6 (1917).

[12] Id. at 8.

[13] Id. at 7.

[14] Christopher Grandy, New Jersey and the Fiscal Origins of Modern American Corporation Law 43 (1993).

the smallest populations of the fifty states, has become a hub of incorporations. In 2006, fifty percent of New York Stock Exchange and NASDAQ companies and sixty-one percent of Fortune 500 companies were incorporated in Delaware; overall, "[m]ore than 70 percent of all public offerings on U.S. exchanges in 2006 were incorporated in Delaware."[15] Delaware's supremacy over the incorporation market means that Delaware's corporate law is the most important corporate law in the United States, and "lawyers regularly look to Delaware case law for guidance if there is no binding precedent or controlling statute in the relevant state of incorporation."[16] How did Delaware become such a popular state for incorporation? The state's goal in deregulating its corporate law was the same as New Jersey's: to make money by attracting corporations. Because New Jersey was the most popular state for incorporation at the time, Delaware attempted to draw in companies by setting its corporate taxes a little lower than New Jersey's; soon, the number of corporations in Delaware began to grow steadily. Delaware has continued as a popular state for incorporation because its general corporation law is considered desirable by corporate management; its court of chancery (which adjudicates corporate disputes) is efficient and expert; the Delaware legislature is keen to keep its law current; and legal practitioners and sophisticated debt and equity providers have become comfortable with Delaware law. In short, what began in the early part of the twentieth century as a competition among the states to gain incorporation fees has dwindled as Delaware has become predominate, at least for large corporations.[17] This has allowed Delaware to raise its incorporation and annual franchise fees to the highest in the nation, by a wide margin.

Interestingly, while the influence of Delaware's corporate law is huge, its corporate statutes have not been widely copied—only three states, Kansas, Nevada, and Oklahoma, have statutes modeled after the Delaware General Corporation Law. Instead, many states have used the Model Business Incorporation Act as a guide for their corporate statutes, adopting all or most of the Model Act, although the Model Act and Delaware's statute are similar and have influenced each other. The Model Act is a project of the American Bar Association's Committee on Corporate Laws, which in 1940 began to draft a federal corporation act in case one was ever needed. After doing so, the Committee wrote a version for use by states, which it first promulgated in 1950. The Model Act has been periodically revised ever since, with major revisions in 1969, 1980 and 1984.

The Future of Business Entity Law

The impact of the limited liability company on new business formation has been dramatic. In 2006, for instance, Delaware reported that nearly 97,000 limited liability companies were formed under its statute. In that same year, about 35,000 corporations and 10,000 limited partnerships and limited liability partnerships were formed.[18] Since 2004, the number of limited liability companies formed in Delaware has grown by approximately forty-one percent, while the number of new corporations has grown by four percent. Clearly the limited liability company is the entity of choice for the vast majority of newly formed businesses. The flexibility of the limited liability company, which is discussed more fully in Chapter 3 below, is the main reason for its popularity. At the same time, businesses planning to "go public" are likely to continue to choose the corporate form and Delaware as the place of incorporation.

---

[15] Del. Dep't of State, Div. of Corps., 2006 Annual Report 1 (2006), http://corp.delaware.gov/2006%20Annual%20Report%20with%20Signature%20_2_.pdf.

[16] Michael P. Dooley & Michael D. Goldman, *Some Comparisons Between the Model Business Incorporation Act and the Delaware General Corporation Law*, 56 Bus. Law. 737, 738 (2001).

[17] *See generally* Mark J. Loewenstein, *Delaware as Demon: Twenty-Five Years After Professor Cary's Polemic*, 71 U. Colo. L. Rev. 497 (2000).

[18] Del. Dep't of State, Div. of Corps., 2006 Annual Report (2006), http://corp.delaware.gov/2006%20Annual%20Report%20with%20Signature%20_2_.pdf.

The growing popularity of the limited liability company and the movement toward rationalizing limited liability entity law may result in three choices: limited liability companies, general partnerships (which will remain the "default entity"), and corporations. It is possible that a statute will evolve that will govern all limited liability entities (other than corporations) and permit the organizer to choose to call the entity a partnership or limited liability company. In any case, a retrenchment on the number of entities seems inevitable.

Chapter 2
THE LAW OF AGENCY

A. DEFINING THE AGENCY RELATIONSHIP

The law of agency is ubiquitous in the law. The presence or absence of an agency relationship determines tort, contract, and criminal liability in numerous cases. An agent can bind his or her principal to a contract, subject that principal to tort liability and, in some circumstance, to criminal liability. The definition of an agency relationship is simple and intuitive and is captured in § 1.01 of Restatement (Third) of Agency:

> Agency is the fiduciary relationship that arises when one person (a "principal") manifests assent to another person (an "agent") that the agent shall act on the principal's behalf and subject to the principal's control, and the agent manifests assent or otherwise consents so to act.

In the typical agency relationship, the principal will hire or retain the agent to perform some service for the principal. The employment relationship is the most common principal-agent relationship. The difficult cases are those in which the relationship is less formal, as the next case aptly demonstrates.

THAYER v. PACIFIC ELECTRIC RAILWAY
Supreme Court of California
55 Cal. 2d 430, 360 P.2d 56, 11 Cal. Rptr. 560 (1961)

WHITE, J.

This is an appeal by the Pacific Electric Railway Company from a judgment for the plaintiff in the amount of $3,750 in an action for damages to freight of which defendant was the terminal carrier. The principal question raised is whether the plaintiff complied with the requirement of the bill of lading that in order to recover for damages to freight, a claim in writing must be filed with the carrier within nine months after delivery of the property.

The plaintiff is a Long Beach manufacturer of precision made aircraft parts. In 1955, he purchased a precision grinding machine that was then located in Illinois, and arranged to have the machine shipped to Artesia, California. The machine was in good condition when delivered to the originating carrier. On March 29, 1955, defendant's agent notified the plaintiff that the machine had arrived. Plaintiff contacted a firm of machinery movers and instructed them to remove it from the railroad car. When they went to pick up the machine on March 30, 1955, the movers observed that the machine was damaged. Before moving it from the railroad car, they contacted the plaintiff who made a personal inspection that same day.

The machine was severely damaged, even though it was bolted to heavy, wooden skids which in turn were bolted to the bottom of the box car. The boards on the bottom of the car had been jerked loose, breaking the blocks which were supporting the machine. The plaintiff had photographs taken of the damaged interior of the car and the damaged machine. After the plaintiff had returned to his office, he telephoned defendant's station agent, Carl Hileman, and complained about the condition of the machine. In response to the complaint, the agent visually inspected the machine and the box car and filled out a standard company form used for the inspection of damages. The plaintiff did not accompany the agent when the inspection was made or when the inspection form was filled out. Hileman's inspection report became a part of defendant's permanent files.

After completing the inspection, Hileman returned to plaintiff's office and there ensued a discussion over the condition of the machine. Before departing, the agent gave the plaintiff standard claim forms, explaining that they could be filled out and returned by plaintiff when the extent of the damage was ascertained. After the photographer had performed his function and Hileman had completed his inspection, plaintiff had the movers take the machine from the box car.

Representatives of the defendant negotiated with plaintiff over the amount due for freight charges, and after plaintiff rejected two bills because of the application of improper rate and weight standards, the freight charges were fixed at approximately $550. However, in spite of requests by defendant's agents, plaintiff refused to pay the charges. He insisted that the defendant owed him money because of the extensive damage to the machine.

On April 20, 1955, Hileman went to plaintiff's office in an attempt to collect the freight charges. He explained to plaintiff that the damage claim was a separate matter from the freight charges and that the freight bill had to be paid in spite of the damage. The plaintiff continued to object to payment, since he did not want to waive any of his rights to collect for the damages. Finally, while in plaintiff's office, the agent wrote on the freight bill, "Damage on this shipment, 4/20/55, C. D. Hileman." The plaintiff then wrote a check for the amount of the charge and received a copy of the annotated freight bill. Plaintiff testified that he would not have paid unless Hileman had made the above notation on the freight bill. A copy of the annotated freight bill was kept as a permanent record in defendant's offices. The latter's damage claim agent testified that claims for damaged freight are not always filed with his office and that they may be filed "With any agent of the company."

Determination by the plaintiff of the extent of damages to the machine took considerable time. It was necessary to secure cost estimates from machinery repairmen, and then, because of the extent of the damage, ascertain whether it would be cheaper to obtain another machine. After inquiry in the eastern machinery market, plaintiff had his machine repaired at an approximate cost of $3,500.

Plaintiff's attorney wrote to the defendant's claim agent on January 27, 1956, over nine months after the delivery of the machine, and detailed the extent of plaintiff's damages. . . . On June 29, 1956, the claim agent formally rejected plaintiff's claim, on the grounds that it had not been filed in writing within nine months, as required by a condition set forth on the bill of lading.

Section 2(b) of the bill of lading provided: "As a condition precedent to recovery, claims must be filed in writing with the receiving or delivering carrier, or carrier issuing this bill of lading, or carrier on whose line the loss, damage, injury or delay occurred, within nine months after delivery of the property . . . ."

However, even though as a rule the carrier must be given written notice of a claim within the period specified in the bill of lading, it has been said that the notice requirement, "does not require documents in a particular form. It is addressed to a practical exigency, and it is to be construed in a practical way." . . .

Defendant also contends that neither the inspection report nor the notation on the freight bill may be said to comply with the writing requirement of section 2(b) of the bill of lading, because both writings were made by defendant's agent, Hileman, and, defendant further contends, the claim in writing must be made by the claimant. While some of the cases indicate that the claim should emanate from the shipper, it is not settled law that the claim must be filed by the shipper personally. . . .

But even assuming that defendant is correct in its contention that the claim must emanate from the shipper, the trial court reached the conclusion that the notation on the freight bill was written by Hileman at plaintiff's insistence. Such a conclusion by the trier of fact finds support in the evidence and therefore, may not be disturbed on appeal. Thus, even though Hileman was employed by the defendant railway, he became plaintiff's agent for the purpose of noting on the freight bill that the plaintiff intended to claim damages because of the condition of his machine. Also, the plaintiff need not have expressly made Hileman his agent for the purpose of noting plaintiff's intention to claim damages. The existence of an agency is a question of fact, which may be implied from the conduct of the parties.

The judgment is affirmed.

GIBSON, C.J., and TRAYNOR, SCHAUER, McCOMB, PETERS, and DOOLING, J., concurred.

NOTES AND QUESTIONS

1. Note that the Restatement definition of agency refers to the relationship as "fiduciary." What does that mean? In general, a fiduciary owes to the person for whom he is a fiduciary (the "beneficiary") certain duties, called "fiduciary duties." These consist of, among other things, a duty on the part of the fiduciary to discharge his duties with care and with loyalty to the beneficiary. But these fiduciary duties imply an ongoing relationship, and an agency relationship may be limited to a single act, as the *Thayer* case so nicely illustrates. Even in that instance, however, fiduciary duties arise. If the station agent, who became for a very short time the agent of the plaintiff, had negligently recorded the date of the damage, and that negligence had, say, precluded plaintiff's claim, the station agent, in theory, could be held liable to the plaintiff. Fiduciary duties of agents are covered in greater detail below.

2. *The Dual Agency Rule.* The dual agency rule states that an agent cannot act on behalf of the adverse party to a transaction connected with the agency without the permission of the principal. *See Naviera Despina, Inc. v. Cooper Shipping Co.*, 676 F. Supp. 1134, 1141 (S.D. Ala. 1987) ("It is wrong, except where there is full disclosure and consent, for an agent to attempt to serve two masters with differing interests."). The reasoning behind the rule is expressed in *Atwood v. Chicago, Rock Island & Pac. Ry.*, 72 F. 447, 455 (W.D. Mo. 1896) ("It is a doctrine as old as the Bible itself, and the common law of the land follows it, that a man cannot serve two masters at the same time; he will obey the one and betray the other. He cannot be subject to two controlling forces which may at the time be divergent."). If the two principals are unaware of the double employment, the transaction between them is voidable. If one principal secretly employs the agent to act on its account knowing the other principal is unaware of the double employment, the defrauded principal can rescind or choose to affirm the transaction and recover damages from the other principal or the knowing agent. *See* RESTATEMENT (THIRD) OF AGENCY § 8.03, Comment d.

3. Is *Thayer* inconsistent with the dual agency rule? Can you make an argument that it is not, based on a common sense limitation to the rule? *See* Restatement (Second) of Agency § 391, Comments b and d, observing that the agent can deal with the other party "if such dealing is not inconsistent with his duties to his principal." *Accord Young v. Nevada Title Co.*, 744 P.2d 902 (Nev. 1987).

4. *Utah State Univ. v. Sutro & Co.*, 646 P.2d 715, 722 (Utah 1982), contains language relevant to this matter:

> It is not necessarily always true that a party acting as an agent in a transaction must be exclusively the agent of one party or the other. When he is requested and performs duties for each of the parties, with the knowledge and consent of both, he may very well be considered as an agent for each for the particular services he renders that principal.

This language makes clear what is suggested in note 2 above, that the dual agency rule does not apply when both principals consent to the situation. It is addressing a matter distinct from that raised in note 3, however.

A. GAY JENSON FARMS CO. v. CARGILL, INC.
Supreme Court of Minnesota
309 N.W.2d 285 (1981)

PETERSON, JUSTICE.

Plaintiffs, 86 individual, partnership or corporate farmers, brought this action against defendant Cargill, Inc. (Cargill) and defendant Warren Grain & Seed Co. (Warren) to recover losses sustained when Warren defaulted on the contracts made with plaintiffs for the sale of grain. After a trial by jury, judgment was entered in favor of plaintiffs, and Cargill brought this appeal. We affirm.

This case arose out of the financial collapse of defendant Warren and its failure to satisfy its indebtedness to plaintiffs. Warren, which was located in Warren, Minnesota, was operated by Lloyd Hill and his son, Gary Hill. Warren operated a grain elevator and as a result was involved in the purchase of cash or market grain from local farmers. The cash grain would be resold through the Minneapolis Grain Exchange or to the terminal grain companies directly. Warren also stored grain for farmers and sold chemicals, fertilizer and steel storage bins. In addition, it operated a seed business which involved buying seed grain from farmers, processing it and reselling it for seed to farmers and local elevators.

Lloyd Hill decided in 1964 to apply for financing from Cargill.[1] Cargill's officials from the Moorhead regional office investigated Warren's operations and recommended that Cargill finance Warren.

Warren and Cargill thereafter entered into a security agreement which provided that Cargill would loan money for working capital to Warren on "open account" financing up to a stated limit, which was originally set as $175,000.[2] Under this contract, Warren would receive funds and pay its expenses by issuing drafts drawn on Cargill through Minneapolis banks. The drafts were imprinted with both Warren's and Cargill's names. Proceeds from Warren's sales would be deposited with Cargill and credited to its account. In return for this financing, Warren appointed Cargill as its grain agent for transactions with the Commodity Credit Corporation. Cargill was also given a right of first refusal to purchase market grain sold by Warren to the terminal market.

A new contract was negotiated in 1967, extending Warren's credit line to $300,000 and incorporating the provisions of the original contract. It was also stated in the contract that Warren would provide Cargill with annual financial statements and that either Cargill would keep the books for Warren or an audit would be conducted by an independent firm. Cargill was given the right of access to Warren's books for inspection.

In addition, the agreement provided that Warren was not to make capital improvements or repairs in excess of $5,000 without Cargill's prior consent. Further, it was not to become liable as guarantor on another's indebtedness, or encumber its assets except with Cargill's permission. Consent by Cargill was required before Warren would be allowed to declare a dividend or sell and purchase stock.

Officials from Cargill's regional office made a brief visit to Warren shortly after the agreement was executed. They examined the annual statement and the accounts receivable, expenses, inventory, seed, machinery and other financial matters. Warren was informed that it would be reminded periodically to make the improvements

---

[1] Prior to this time, Atwood Larson had provided working capital for Warren, and Warren had used Atwood Larson as its commission agent for the sale of market grain on the grain exchange.

[2] Loans were secured by a second mortgage on Warren's real estate and a first chattel mortgage on its inventories of grain and merchandise in the sum of $175,000 with 7% interest. Warren was to use the $175,000 to pay off the debt that it owed to Atwood Larson.

recommended by Cargill.[3] At approximately this time, a memo was given to the Cargill official in charge of the Warren account, Erhart Becker, which stated in part: "This organization [Warren] needs *very strong* paternal guidance."

In 1970, Cargill contracted with Warren and other elevators to act as its agent to seek growers for a new type of wheat called Bounty 208. Warren, as Cargill's agent for this project, entered into contracts for the growing of the wheat seed, with Cargill named as the contracting party. Farmers were paid directly by Cargill for the seed and all contracts were performed in full. In 1971, pursuant to an agency contract, Warren contracted on Cargill's behalf with various farmers for the growing of sunflower seeds for Cargill. The arrangements were similar to those made in the Bounty 208 contracts, and all those contracts were also completed. Both these agreements were unrelated to the open account financing contract. In addition, Warren, as Cargill's agent in the sunflower seed business, cleaned and packaged the seed in Cargill bags.

During this period, Cargill continued to review Warren's operations and expenses and recommended that certain actions should be taken.[4] Warren purchased from Cargill various business forms printed by Cargill and received sample forms from Cargill which Warren used to develop its own business forms.

Cargill wrote to its regional office in 1970 expressing its concern that the pattern of increased use of funds allowed to develop at Warren was similar to that involved in two other cases in which Cargill experienced severe losses. Cargill did not refuse to honor drafts or call the loan, however. A new security agreement which increased the credit line to $750,000 was executed in 1972, and a subsequent agreement which raised the limit to $1,250,000 was entered into in 1976.

Warren was at that time shipping Cargill 90% of its cash grain. When Cargill's facilities were full, Warren shipped its grain to other companies. Approximately 25% of Warren's total sales was seed grain which was sold directly by Warren to its customers.

As Warren's indebtedness continued to be in excess of its credit line, Cargill began to contact Warren daily regarding its financial affairs. Cargill headquarters informed its regional office in 1973 that, since Cargill money was being used, Warren should realize that Cargill had the right to make some critical decisions regarding the use of the funds. Cargill headquarters also told Warren that a regional manager would be working with Warren on a day-to-day basis as well as in monthly planning meetings. In 1975, Cargill's regional office began to keep a daily debit position on Warren. A bank account was opened in Warren's name on which Warren could draw checks in 1976. The account was to be funded by drafts drawn on Cargill by the local bank.

In early 1977, it became evident that Warren had serious financial problems. Several farmers, who had heard that Warren's checks were not being paid, inquired or had their agents inquire at Cargill regarding Warren's status and were initially told that there would be no problem with payment. In April 1977, an audit of Warren revealed that Warren was $4 million in debt. After Cargill was informed that Warren's financial statements had been deliberately falsified, Warren's request for additional financing was refused. In the final days of Warren's operation, Cargill sent an official to supervise the elevator, including disbursement of funds and income generated by the elevator.

---

[3] Cargill headquarters suggested that the regional office check Warren monthly. Also, it was requested that Warren be given an explanation for the relatively large withdrawals from undistributed earnings made by the Hills, since Cargill hoped that Warren's profits would be used to decrease its debt balance. Cargill asked for written requests for withdrawals from undistributed earnings in the future.

[4] Between 1967 and 1973, Cargill suggested that Warren take a number of steps, including: (1) a reduction of seed grain and cash grain inventories; (2) improved collection of accounts receivable; (3) reduction or elimination of its wholesale seed business and its specialty grain operation; (4) marketing fertilizer and steel bins on consignment; (5) a reduction in withdrawals made by officers; (6) a suggestion that Warren's bookkeeper not issue her own salary checks; and (7) cooperation with Cargill in implementing the recommendations. These ideas were apparently never implemented, however.

After Warren ceased operations, it was found to be indebted to Cargill in the amount of $3.6 million. Warren was also determined to be indebted to plaintiffs in the amount of $2 million, and plaintiffs brought this action in 1977 to seek recovery of that sum. Plaintiffs alleged that Cargill was jointly liable for Warren's indebtedness as it had acted as principal for the grain elevator.

The jury found that Cargill's conduct between 1973 and 1977 had made it Warren's principal.[5] Warren was found to be the agent of Cargill with regard to contracts for:

1. The purchase and sale of grain for market.

2. The purchase and sale of seed grain.

3. The storage of grain.

The court determined that Cargill was the . . . principal of Warren. It was concluded that Cargill was jointly liable with Warren for plaintiffs' losses, and judgment was entered for plaintiffs. . . .

The major issue in this case is whether Cargill, by its course of dealing with Warren, became liable as a principal on contracts made by Warren with plaintiffs. Cargill contends that no agency relationship was established with Warren, notwithstanding its financing of Warren's operation and its purchase of the majority of Warren's grain. However, we conclude that Cargill, by its control and influence over Warren, became a principal with liability for the transactions entered into by its agent Warren.

. . . An agreement may result in the creation of an agency relationship although the parties did not call it an agency and did not intend the legal consequences of the relation to follow. The existence of the agency may be proved by circumstantial evidence which shows a course of dealing between the two parties. . . .

Cargill contends that the prerequisites of an agency relationship did not exist because Cargill never consented to the agency, Warren did not act on behalf of Cargill, and Cargill did not exercise control over Warren. We hold that all three elements of agency could be found in the particular circumstances of this case. By directing Warren to implement its recommendations, Cargill manifested its consent that Warren would be its agent. Warren acted on Cargill's behalf in procuring grain for Cargill as the part of its normal operations which were totally financed by Cargill.[6] Further, an agency relationship was established by Cargill's interference with the internal affairs of Warren, which constituted de facto control of the elevator.

A creditor who assumes control of his debtor's business may become liable as principal for the acts of the debtor in connection with the business. RESTATEMENT (SECOND) OF AGENCY § 14 O (1958).[7] It is noted in Comment a to section 14 O that:

> A security holder who merely exercises a veto power over the business acts of his debtor by preventing purchases or sales above specified amounts does not thereby become a principal. However, if he takes over the management of the

---

[5] [6] At trial, plaintiffs sought to establish actual agency by Cargill's course of dealing between 1973 and 1977 rather than "apparent" agency or agency by estoppel, so that the only issue in this case is one of actual agency.

[6] [7] Although the contracts with the farmers were executed by Warren, Warren paid for the grain with drafts drawn on Cargill. While this is not in itself significant — see *Lee v. Peoples Cooperative Sales Agency*, 201 Minn. 266, 276 N.W. 214 (1937) — it is one factor to be taken into account in analyzing the relationship between Warren and Cargill.

[7] The full text of § 14 O reads as follows:

> A creditor who assumes control of his debtor's business for the mutual benefit of himself and his debtor, may become a principal, with liability for the acts and transactions of the debtor in connection with the business.

debtor's business either in person or through an agent, and directs what contracts may or may not be made, he becomes a principal, liable as a principal for the obligations incurred thereafter in the normal course of business by the debtor who has now become his general agent. The point at which the creditor becomes a principal is that at which he assumes de facto control over the conduct of his debtor, whatever the terms of the formal contract with his debtor may be.

A number of factors indicate Cargill's control over Warren, including the following:

(1)   Cargill's constant recommendations to Warren by telephone;

(2)   Cargill's right of first refusal on grain;

(3)   Warren's inability to enter into mortgages, to purchase stock or to pay dividends without Cargill's approval;

(4)   Cargill's right of entry onto Warren's premises to carry on periodic checks and audits;

(5)   Cargill's correspondence and criticism regarding Warren's finances, officers' salaries, and inventory;

(6)   Cargill's determination that Warren needed "strong paternal guidance";

(7)   Provision of drafts and forms to Warren upon which Cargill's name was imprinted;

(8)   Financing of all Warren's purchases of grain and operating expenses; and

(9)   Cargill's power to discontinue the financing of Warren's operations.

We recognize that some of these elements, as Cargill contends, are found in an ordinary debtor-creditor relationship. However, these factors cannot be considered in isolation, but, rather, they must be viewed in light of all the circumstances surrounding Cargill's aggressive financing of Warren.

It is also Cargill's position that the relationship between Cargill and Warren was that of buyer-supplier rather than principal-agent. RESTATEMENT (SECOND) OF AGENCY § 14K (1958) compares an agent with a supplier as follows:

> One who contracts to acquire property from a third person and convey it to another is the agent of the other only if it is agreed that he is to act primarily for the benefit of the other and not for himself.

Factors indicating that one is a supplier, rather than an agent, are:

> (1)That he is to receive a fixed price for the property irrespective of [the] price paid by him. This is the most important. (2) That he acts in his own name and receives the title to the property which he thereafter is to transfer. (3) That he has an independent business in buying and selling similar property.

RESTATEMENT (SECOND) OF AGENCY § 14K, comment a (1958).

Under the Restatement approach, it must be shown that the supplier has an independent business before it can be concluded that he is not an agent. The record establishes that all portions of Warren's operation were financed by Cargill and that Warren sold almost all of its market grain to Cargill. Thus, the relationship which existed between the parties was not merely that of buyer and supplier.

In this case . . . Cargill furnished substantially all funds received by the elevator. Cargill did have a right of entry on Warren's premises, and it . . . required maintenance of insurance against hazards of operation. Warren's activities . . . formed a substantial part of Cargill's business that was developed in that area. In addition, Cargill did not think of Warren as an operator who was free to become Cargill's competitor, but rather conceded that it believed that Warren owed a duty of loyalty to Cargill. The decisions made by Warren were not independent of Cargill's interest or its control.

Further, we are not persuaded by the fact that Warren was not one of the "line" elevators that Cargill operated in its own name. The Warren operation, like the line elevator, was financially dependent on Cargill's continual infusion of capital. The arrangement with Warren presented a convenient alternative to the establishment of a line elevator. Cargill became, in essence, the owner of the operation without the accompanying legal indicia.

The amici curiae assert that, if the jury verdict is upheld, firms and banks which have provided business loans to county elevators will decline to make further loans. The decision in this case should give no cause for such concern. We deal here with a business enterprise markedly different from an ordinary bank financing, since Cargill was an active participant in Warren's operations rather than simply a financier. Cargill's course of dealing with Warren was, by its own admission, a paternalistic relationship in which Cargill made the key economic decisions and kept Warren in existence.

Although considerable interest was paid by Warren on the loan, the reason for Cargill's financing of Warren was not to make money as a lender but, rather, to establish a source of market grain for its business. As one Cargill manager noted, "We were staying in there because we wanted the grain." For this reason, Cargill was willing to extend the credit line far beyond the amount originally allocated to Warren. It is noteworthy that Cargill was receiving significant amounts of grain and that, notwithstanding the risk that was recognized by Cargill, the operation was considered profitable.

On the whole, there was a unique fabric in the relationship between Cargill and Warren which varies from that found in normal debtor-creditor situations. We conclude that, on the facts of this case, there was sufficient evidence from which the jury could find that Cargill was the principal of Warren within the definitions of agency set forth in Restatement (Second) of Agency §§ 1 and 14 O. . . .

It is also Cargill's position that the trial court erred in failing to submit certain requested jury instructions. . . .

Affirmed.

NOTES AND QUESTIONS

1. The court opinion quotes from and relies heavily upon § 14 O of the Restatement of Agency (Second). Do you think that the proposition set forth by the Restatement is undebatable? Certainly a party in control of an activity should be subject to standards of liability, such as requiring the exercise of due care. Negligence and dishonesty would be penalized by all courts under such circumstances. But should a party's liability be extended to full responsibility for all debts of a business, as if it were a co-owner of the business, solely as a result of its exercise of control as a creditor? What are the arguments on both sides of this? *See* J. Dennis Hynes, *Lender Liability: The Dilemma of the Controlling Creditor*, 58 TENN. L. REV. 635 (1991).

2. *Cargill* is an excellent example of a number of cases in which the courts focus on the control element of the agency relationship and pay less or little attention to other elements. The *Cargill* court did note that an agency relationship requires consent and that the agent act "on behalf of" the principal, but seemed to be persuaded by what it saw as the pervasive control that Cargill exercised over Warren.

PROBLEMS

1. Josephina, who suffered from dementia and other ailments, was admitted to the Evergreen Nursing Home. The necessary documents were signed by her husband, Luis. Evergreen typically required newly admitted patients to agree to arbitrate any disputes with it, and, in accordance with applicable state law, submitted to Luis a separate agreement providing for arbitration. Under the signature line, Luis circled the

word "agent" to indicate the capacity in which he was signing the agreement. Subsequently, Josephina was injured in a fall at the nursing home, and Luis and Josephina filed a claim in state court. Evergreen moved to dismiss the claim, on the grounds that it was subject to arbitration. Josephina argued that she had never authorized Luis to act as her agent and, therefore, she was not bound by the arbitration agreement. What arguments can be made on behalf of the parties?

2. HJH Food Products, Inc. imports various specialty food products and distributes those products through several regional wholesale distributors, who in turn sell to gourmet food stores. HJH's agreements with its distributors provides that HJH will pay the distributors a commission equal to 10% of the sales price of HJH products sold by the distributor to the stores. The distributors are prohibited by agreement from distributing products that compete with HJH imports and must periodically disclose to HJH what products they are carrying. Distributors must also advise HJH of the names of retailers to whom they distribute and must cease selling to any store that does not meet HJH's "standard of distinction and excellence." HJH terminated one of its distributors for breach of contract and the distributor claimed protection under a state statute that, if applicable, would limit HJH's ability to terminate the contract. The statute would only apply if the distributor was an agent of HJH. Was it?

B. CONTRACTUAL POWERS OF AN AGENT

A frequently litigated question in agency law is whether a contract or commitment made by an agent on behalf of a principal is binding on the principal. The resolution of this question turns on whether the agent had the authority to bind the principal. The courts have recognized at least two sources for an agent's authority: expressions made to the agent by the principal delineating the agent's authority, and representations made by the principal to the third party about the agent's authority. The former is characterized as "actual authority" and is frequently set forth in a written document, such as a contract between the principal and agent, in corporate bylaws, or in a written power of attorney. A writing is not, however, necessary; a principal can orally tell the agent what authority the agent has to bind the principal. The Restatement (Third) of Agency defines actual authority: "An agent acts with actual authority when, at the time of taking action that has legal consequences for the principal, the agent reasonably believes, in accordance with the principal's manifestations to the agent, that the principal wishes the agent so to act."

The second source of authority — which is based on representations made by the principal to third parties — is characterized as "apparent authority," on the theory that the agent "appears" to have certain authority to bind the principal even though the agent may not have the actual authority to do so. For instance, a corporate board of directors might appoint Alice as president of the corporation. To all the world, the president of a corporation has rather broad powers to represent the corporation and bind it to contracts, etc. In appointing Alice, however, the board might have decided to limit her authority in a way that is inconsistent with the normal authority of a corporate president. In that instance, Alice's apparent authority would exceed her actual authority and, unless a third party had notice of that disparity, Alice would be able to bind the corporation even though she lacked the actual authority to do so. Suppose, for example, that in the community in which the corporation does business corporate presidents have the authority to settle minor claims against the corporation, but Alice's contract with the corporation expressly denies her that authority. If Alice settled a minor claim on behalf of the corporation, and the claimant was unaware that Alice had been denied that authority by her corporation, the corporation would still be bound on the basis of her apparent authority to do so.

Judicial opinions are replete with references to other sources of authority for an agent: implied, incidental, and inherent authority are common. Implied and incidental authority are components of an agent's actual authority. At times, a principal will articulate authority, that is, describe an agent's actual authority, but that articulation suggests other authority that the principal must have implied. For instance, if a principal authorizes an agent to borrow money on its behalf, the agent's authority to execute a promissory note may be implied. The Restatement (Second) of Agency, § 7 observes that "most authority is created by implication."

Incidental authority is similar and is described in Restatement (Third) of Agency § 2.02, Comment d: "If a principal's manifestation to the agent expresses the principal's wish that something be done, it is natural to assume that the principal wishes, as an incidental matter, that the agent proceed in the usual and ordinary way if such has been established, unless the principal directs otherwise."

Inherent authority, however, is a bit murky. The Restatement (Second) of Agency § 8A defines the concept: "Inherent agency power is a term used . . . to indicate the power of an agent which is derived not from authority, apparent authority or estoppel, but solely from the agency relation and exists for the protection of persons harmed by or dealing with a servant or other agent." In practice, inherent agency authority is often indistinguishable from apparent authority. *See Cange v. Stotler & Co.*, 826 F.2d 581, 598 (7th Cir. 1987), where the court expresses skepticism as to whether inherent authority is different from express or apparent authority. The Restatement (Third) of Agency abandons the term entirely. RESTATEMENT (THIRD) OF AGENCY § 2.01, Comment b.

Finally, two other concepts are worth considering in regard to an agent's authority — estoppel and ratification. As to the former, courts have, at times, estopped a person to deny the authority of another to act on such person's behalf. For instance, if a client silently permits her attorney to settle an action on her behalf, the client might later be estopped to argue that the attorney lacked the authority to do so. *See Szymkowski v. Szymkowski*, 432 N.E.2d 1209, 1210 (Ill. App. 1982). Note that, generally, attorneys do not have the authority to settle litigation without the consent of their clients, so the settling attorney would lack the actual and apparent authority to do so. The Restatement (Third) provision on estoppel reads in part as follows:

§ 2.05 Estoppel To Deny Existence Of Agency Relationship

A person who has not made a manifestation that an actor has authority as an agent and who is not otherwise liable as a party to a transaction purportedly done by the actor on that person's account is subject to liability to a third party who justifiably is induced to make a detrimental change in position because the transaction is believed to be on the person's account, if

(1) the person intentionally or carelessly caused such belief, or

(2) having notice of such belief and that it might induce others to change their positions, the person did not take reasonable steps to notify them of the facts.

The concept of ratification, on the other hand, allows a person to ratify the actions of another undertaken on behalf of the person. Thus, a principal can ratify an unauthorized act of his agent and thereby be bound by such action. In addition, a person can ratify the very existence of an agency relationship. In the classic case of *Dempsey v. Chambers*, 28 N.E. 279 (Mass. 1891), for instance, McCullock delivered a load of coal to the plaintiff for the defendant. Although a member of defendant's household, McCullock was not in defendant's employ and had no authority to act on defendant's behalf. In the course of delivering the coal to plaintiff, McCullock damaged plaintiff's property. Defendant billed plaintiff for the coal. Subsequently, plaintiff sued for the damage to its property. The court held that by billing the plaintiff for the coal, defendant implicitly ratified an agency relationship between him and McCullock, thus rendering defendant liable for McCullock's negligent action.

1. An Agent's Express Authority

A principal may expressly authorize an agent to bind the principal contractually and often does so by means of a power of attorney or other written instrument. When the agent's authority is expressly set forth, whether in a power of attorney or otherwise, the agent acts with "express" authority. How should such documents be construed by the courts? Should those powers be read broadly or narrowly? The first case in this section grapples with those questions.

KING v. BANKERD

Court of Appeals of Maryland

303 Md. 98, 492 A.2d 608 (1985)

COLE, JUDGE.

The single issue presented in this case is whether a power of attorney authorizing the agent to "convey, grant, bargain and/or sell" the principal's property authorizes the agent to make a gratuitous transfer of that property.

The facts are uncomplicated. Howard R. Bankerd (Bankerd) and his wife, Virginia, owned, as tenants by the entirety, a home in Montgomery County, Maryland. They resided there until 1966 when Mrs. Bankerd moved out as a result of marital problems. Bankerd continued to live at the property until July 1968, when he "left for the west." Mrs. Bankerd thereupon resumed residency of the property. For the ensuing twelve years, Bankerd lived at various locations in Nevada, Colorado, and Washington, and he made no payments on the mortgage, for taxes, or for the maintenance and upkeep of the home.

Before Bankerd's departure, he executed a power of attorney to Arthur V. King, an attorney with whom he was acquainted. From 1971 to 1974, Bankerd did not communicate or correspond with King in any manner. In 1975, however, King sent Bankerd a letter enclosing an updated power of attorney because the Washington Suburban Sanitary Commission was about to put a sewer adjacent to the subject property, and King believed the new power would be beneficial. This power of attorney, which is the center of the instant litigation, was executed by Bankerd and returned to King. Dated October 30, 1975, this power of attorney provides:

> KNOW ALL MEN BY THESE PRESENTS, that I, Howard R. Bankerd, hereby make, constitute and appoint ARTHUR V. KING, my attorney for me, and in my name to convey, grant, bargain and/or sell the property designated in the Montgomery County land record as Lot 9 of an unrecorded subdivision as recorded in Liber 3027 at folio 293, situated at 14026 Travilah Road, Rockville, Maryland on such terms as to him may seem best, and in my name, to make, execute, acknowledge and deliver, good and sufficient deeds and conveyances for the same with or without covenants and warranties and generally to do and perform all things necessary pertaining to the future transfer of said property, and generally to do everything whatsoever necessary pertaining to the said property.

After granting this power of attorney, Bankerd had no further communication with King until 1978.

Mrs. Bankerd, who as noted above had been residing at and maintaining the subject property since 1968, requested King in September 1977 to exercise the power of attorney and to transfer Bankerd's interest in the property to her. King was aware that Mrs. Bankerd was nearing retirement and that she was "saddled" with a property she could neither sell nor mortgage. Consequently, King attempted to locate Bankerd. . . . King also made several other efforts, albeit unsuccessful, to obtain Bankerd's address.

Mrs. Bankerd informed King that her husband had once attempted to give the property away to a neighbor on the condition that the neighbor assume the mortgage payments. Consequently, King asserted that he believed Bankerd "didn't give a damn" about the property, that Bankerd had abandoned his interest in the property, and that given Bankerd's age (approximately sixty-nine years), King believed that Bankerd might even be deceased. King therefore conveyed Bankerd's interest in the property to Mrs. Bankerd by deed dated June 21, 1978. Mrs. Bankerd paid no consideration for the transfer and King received no compensation for the conveyance on behalf of Bankerd. Mrs. Bankerd thereafter sold the property to a third party for $62,500.

In 1981 Bankerd filed suit against King in the Circuit Court for Montgomery County alleging breach of trust and breach of fiduciary duty in King's conveyance of Bankerd's interest in the subject property in violation of the power of attorney. After the completion of the discovery proceedings each party moved for summary judgment. On August 12, 1982, the trial court granted summary judgment to Bankerd against King and awarded $13,555.05 in damages on the basis that King had negligently violated the fiduciary relationship that existed between those two parties. The Court of Special Appeals affirmed, holding that the broad language of the power of attorney did not authorize the conveyance without consideration in favor of Bankerd. *King v. Bankerd*, 55 Md. App. 619, 465 A.2d 1181 (1983).[8] We granted King's petition for certiorari to consider the issue of first impression presented in this case.

King basically contends that the language contained in a document granting a broad power of attorney be viewed in light of the surrounding circumstances to determine whether the attorney in fact had authority to transfer the property without consideration. Based on this contention, King concludes that the second power of attorney did not as a matter of law preclude him from gratuitously transferring Bankerd's property. We disagree.

Similar to other jurisdictions, Maryland appellate courts have had relatively few occasions to analyze powers of attorney. Because we last addressed the substantive law relating to powers of attorney over a half century ago, *see Kaminski v. Wladerek*, 149 Md. 548, 131 A. 810 (1926), we shall review the relevant rules relating to powers of attorney again.[9]

Broadly defined, a power of attorney is a written document by which one party, as principal, appoints another as agent (attorney in fact) and confers upon the latter the authority to perform certain specified acts or kinds of acts on behalf of the principal.

Various rules govern the interpretation of powers of attorney. As Chief Judge Murphy observed for this Court in *Klein v. Weiss*, 284 Md. 36, 61, 395 A.2d 126, 140 (1978), one "well settled" rule is that powers of attorney are "strictly construed as a general rule and [are] held to grant only those powers which are clearly delineated[.]" Although our predecessors recognized this rule over a century ago in *Posner v. Bayless*, 59 Md. 56 (1882), they were careful to note that the rule of strict construction "cannot override the general and cardinal rule" that the court determine the intention of the parties. To ascertain this intent, the *Posner* Court emphasized that the language used in the instrument and the object to be accomplished be viewed in light of the surrounding circumstances. Other courts of last resort have likewise embraced the rule of strict construction of powers of attorney. *See generally* Comment, *Construction of Written Powers of Attorney*, 18 OHIO ST. L.J. 129, 130 (1957) (indicating that American courts follow the strict construction principle).

---

8 [1] The Court of Special Appeals also rejected King's argument that Bankerd had abandoned his interest in the subject property and that summary judgment should have been denied on the basis of equitable estoppel.

9 [2] In this regard we note that MD. CODE (1981 Repl. Vol.), § 4-107 of the Real Property Article, which requires that an agent's authority to grant property be executed in the same manner as a deed, is not at issue here.

Another accepted rule of construction is to discount or disregard, as meaningless verbiage, all-embracing expressions found in powers of attorney. Restatement, *supra*, § 34 comment h. Because powers of attorney are ordinarily very carefully drafted and scrutinized, courts give the terms used a technical rather than a popular meaning. Restatement, *supra*, § 34 comment h. In addition, ambiguities in an instrument are resolved against the party who made it or caused it to be made, because that party had the better opportunity to understand and explain his meaning. Finally, general words used in an instrument are restricted by the context in which they are used, and are construed accordingly.

In accordance with these principles, nearly every jurisdiction that has considered the issue in the case *sub judice* has concluded that a general power of attorney authorizing an agent to sell and convey property, although it authorizes him to sell for such price and on such terms as to him shall seem proper, implies a sale for the principal's benefit. Such a power of attorney, however, does not authorize the agent to make a gift of the property, or to convey or transfer it without a present consideration inuring to the principal.

For the reasons below, we conclude that an agent holding a broad power of attorney lacks the power to make a gift of the principal's property, unless that power (1) is expressly conferred, (2) arises as a necessary implication from the conferred powers, or (3) is clearly intended by the parties, as evidenced by the surrounding facts and circumstances.

First, the power to make a gift of the principal's property is a power that is potentially hazardous to the principal's interests. Consequently, this power will not be lightly inferred from broad, all-encompassing grants of power to the agent. Accordingly, "the agent must be circumspect with regard to the powers created — or the lack of them." [Citation omitted.]

Second, the main duty of an agent is loyalty to the interest of his principal. *See* RESTATEMENT, *supra*, § 39 ("Unless otherwise agreed, authority to act as agent includes only authority to act for the benefit of the principal."); *id.* § 387 ("Unless otherwise agreed, an agent is subject to a duty to his principal to act solely for the benefit of the principal in all matters connected with his agency."). Thus, in exercising granted powers under a power of attorney, the attorney in fact is bound to act for the benefit of his principal and must avoid where possible that which is detrimental unless expressly authorized. We recognized these principles well over a century ago in *Adams' Express Co. v. Trego*, 35 Md. 47 (1872), where our predecessors quoted Judge Story's treatise on agency:

> Even if a general discretion is vested in the agent, it is not deemed to be unlimited. But it must be exercised in a reasonable manner, and cannot be resorted to in order to justify acts, which the principal could not be presumed to intend, or which would defeat, and not promote, the apparent end or purpose, for which the power was given.

Id. at 66–67 (quotation marks omitted). . . . In light of the duties of loyalty that arise from the fiduciary relation, it is difficult to imagine how a gift of the principal's real property would be to the benefit of the principal when the power of attorney does not authorize such a gift or the principal does not intend to authorize such a gift. In short, the agent is under a duty to serve his principal with only his principal's purposes in mind.

Third, "[i]t would be most unusual for an owner of property to grant a power of attorney authorizing the attorney in fact to give his property away. If a person has decided to make a gift of property, he or she usually decides as to who is going to be the donee." [214 N.Y.S.2d at 490.] . . .

The facts and surrounding circumstances presented in this case do not give rise to any fact or inference that King was authorized to make a gift of Bankerd's real property. In arguing that his conduct was reasonable under the circumstances, King points to his "beliefs" that Bankerd had abandoned the property, that Bankerd did not care about the property, and that Bankerd might be deceased. These arguments completely miss the mark. King's conduct could only be "reasonable" if Bankerd intended for King to give the property away. Although the facts and surrounding circumstances to which King points suggest reasons why he made the gift, they do not support an inference that Bankerd intended to authorize the gift.

Furthermore, the only evidence before the trial court that was relevant to this issue indicated that Bankerd did not intend to authorize King to give the subject property to Bankerd's wife or anyone else. In a letter Bankerd sent to King along with the executed power of attorney, Bankerd wrote that "[y]ou know if I outlive Va., [Bankerd's estranged wife] (and I'm ornery enough) you would certainly have a job on that Travilah Road (sic) [the subject property] bit *if* you would accept it, that is." [Emphasis in original.] Nothing could more clearly belie an assertion that Bankerd authorized any gift of the property. Bankerd, by virtue of this correspondence, notified King that he clearly anticipated maintaining his interest in the property. Furthermore, King wrote Bankerd assuring him that if the latter executed the new power of attorney he would do nothing detrimental to Bankerd's interests. Certainly, had King believed that he was acquiring the authority to give away Bankerd's property, King would not have made this representation.

In sum, there is no genuine dispute as to any material fact. Moreover, the facts are not susceptible of more than one permissible inference. We therefore hold that the trial court did not err in granting Bankerd's motion for summary judgment.

Judgment affirmed.

NOTE

A special sort of power of attorney is known as a "durable" power. Durable powers of attorney are made possible by statute, bypassing the common law rule that all agency powers, including powers of attorney, are revoked upon the incapacity of the principal. Durable powers can cover health care issues, if so drafted, as well as financial matters.

2.   An Agent's Apparent Authority

SMITH v. HANSEN, HANSEN & JOHNSON, INC.
Court of Appeals of Washington
818 P.2d 1127 (1991)

MORGAN, JUDGE.

The owner of a building hired Hansen, Hansen & Johnson, Inc. (HH & J) to renovate it. The renovation included design and construction of an exterior glass wall. A year or so, after the new wall was finished, it began to leak. The owner of the building sought redress from HH & J, which settled with the owner for $81,000. HH & J then sued Fentron, a corporation in the business of designing and installing glass walls. HH & J sought reimbursement plus other damages. [After a bench trial,] the trial court awarded damages, but we reverse. . . .

Fentron employed Everett Foster as a "manager of manufacturing services." Fentron furnished Foster with business cards, an office and a telephone. Foster's duties included purchasing material needed for manufacturing, but did not include selling products to customers. He was employed in the manufacturing department, and sales to customers were handled through the sales department.

In 1982, Foster visited Hansen [an architect and partner in HH & J, who was acquainted with Foster socially] at HH & J's offices. At this time, HH & J was the general contractor for construction of the Tacoma Dome Hotel, and Foster's purpose was to solicit sales for Fentron products and services in the construction of the hotel. In the course of the conversation Foster told Hansen that Fentron had salvage glass available and was trying to find a use for it. During this visit or at a later time, Foster "presented his business card showing that he was a manager of Fentron's manufacturing services division." Foster led Hansen to believe that Foster had authority to sell materials on behalf of Fentron, but in fact Foster's efforts were unknown to Fentron and contrary to its policies and direction.

Later, apparently in late 1982, Hansen called Foster at Fentron and inquired about salvage glass. Foster called back later and indicated that certain salvage glass, hereinafter called the ARCO glass, was available. In effect, Foster offered to sell the ARCO glass to HH & J at a reduced price, so that HH & J could use it on the 1111 Fawcett Building, the Tacoma office building that HH & J had been asked to renovate. Foster ostensibly made the offer on behalf of Fentron. The offer was oral, and HH & J did not request a written quotation from either Foster or Fentron. Foster told Hansen that the glass had been rejected from Fentron's ARCO project in Anchorage only because of its color, when in fact Fentron had rejected the glass for other manufacturing deficiencies. HH & J accepted the offer . . . [believing] it was dealing with Fentron. It would not have accepted had it known it was dealing with Foster individually. . . .

Starting on January 7, 1983, HH & J wrote a series of 29 checks, totaling about $20,000, in order to pay for the materials being delivered by Foster. According to the findings, the checks were made payable "to Foster," or "on his behalf," or "at his request." The first check, for $6,300, was dated January 7, 1983; the second, for $8,300, was dated February 16, 1983. At Foster's request, Roger Hansen, another principal in HH & J, made both checks payable to Foster personally. Foster said he needed the first check because the glass was at a salvage yard and was about to be destroyed. He said he needed the second check in order to obtain metal extrusions for the project. In mid-May, 1983, Foster absconded to California. . . . [The court turned to the issue whether Foster had apparent authority to bind Fentron to a contract for the sale of merchantable glass, among other things.]

Whether apparent authority exists in a particular case is a question of fact. The trial court resolved that question in favor of HH & J and against Fentron. On appeal, then, the issue is whether the court's finding of apparent authority is supported by substantial evidence. In deciding that issue, we view the evidence and the reasonable inferences therefrom in the light most favorable to HH & J, who was the prevailing party below.

Both actual and apparent authority depend upon objective manifestations.[10] The objective manifestations must be those of the principal. . . . With actual authority, the principal's objective manifestations are made to the agent; with apparent authority, they are made to a third person. . . . [11]

---

[10] [12] Although agency relationships do not always stem from contract, RESTATEMENT (SECOND) OF AGENCY, § 1, comment b, at 8, this objective manifestation requirement is similar to that which governs contract formation.

[11] [13] These rules are well summarized in the Restatement (Second) of Agency. With respect to actual authority, Restatement § 26 says in pertinent part:

> [A]uthority to do an act can be created by written or spoken words or other conduct of the principal which, reasonably interpreted, causes the agent to believe that the principal desires him so to act on the principal's account.

With respect to apparent authority, Restatement § 27 says in pertinent part:

> [A]pparent authority to do an act is created as to a third person by written or spoken words or any other conduct of the principal which, reasonably interpreted, causes the third person to believe that the principal consents to have the act done on his behalf by the person purporting to act for him.

Manifestations to a third person can be made by the principal in person or through anyone else, including the agent, who has the principal's actual authority to make them — e.g., an advertisement in the newspaper, provided it is placed by the principal or an agent with actual authority. However, such manifestations will support a finding of apparent authority only if they have two effects. First, they must cause the one claiming apparent authority to actually, i.e., subjectively, believe that the agent has authority to act for the principal. Second, they must be such that the claimant's actual, subjective belief is objectively reasonable.[12]

The Restatement of Agency summarizes some of the specific manifestations that can, in appropriate circumstances, support a finding of apparent authority. Restatement § 27, Comment a, says:

> The information received by the third person may come directly from the principal by letter or word of mouth, from authorized statements of the agent, from documents or other indicia of authority given by the principal to the agent, or from third persons who have heard of the agent's authority through authorized or permitted channels of communication. Likewise, as in the case of [actual] authority, apparent authority can be created by appointing a person to a position, such as that of manager or treasurer, which carries with it generally recognized duties; to those who know of the appointment there is apparent authority to do the things ordinarily entrusted to one occupying such a position, regardless of unknown limitations which are imposed upon the particular agent.

. . . The evidence is insufficient to support a reasonable inference that Foster had apparent authority to sell materials and designs on Fentron's behalf. Fentron did not represent to HH & J or anyone else that Foster had authority to contract, nor did it authorize Foster or anyone else to do so on its behalf. It did not furnish Foster with documents or other indicia of authority that could be shown to others, other than business cards and a telephone number. If it objectively manifested that Foster had authority, it did so because (1) it employed him as a "manager of manufacturing services," or (2) because it furnished him with an office, telephone number, and business cards that said he was a "manager of manufacturing services."

By employing Foster as a manager of manufacturing services, Fentron did not manifest that Foster had authority to sell materials and designs on its behalf. Although a general manager may have apparent authority to sell products, Fentron did not title Foster as its general manager, but instead titled him a "manager of manufacturing services." There is no evidence in the record that one titled "manager of manufacturing services" is customarily or generally understood in the business community to have the authority to sell, and we are unwilling to assume that the title is so understood. Therefore, the fact that Fentron employed and titled Foster as it did is not, by itself, sufficient to support the finding of apparent authority.

And with respect to how the creation of actual and apparent authority differs, comment a to Restatement § 27 says in pertinent part:

> Apparent authority is created by the same method as that which creates [actual] authority, except that the manifestation of the principal is to the third person rather than to the agent.

[12] [14] Again, these rules are well summarized in the Restatement. In § 8, comment c, it states:

> Apparent authority exists only to the extent that it is reasonable for the third person dealing with the agent to believe that the agent is authorized. Further, the third person must believe the agent to be authorized. In this respect, apparent authority differs from [actual] authority since an agent who is authorized can bind the principal to a transaction with a third person who does not believe the agent to be authorized. Obviously, manifestations must be communicated to the claimant before they can have either effect.

Even when the fact that Fentron furnished Foster with an office, telephone, and business cards is combined with his employment and qualified title, there is still insufficient evidence to support a reasonable inference that Fentron manifested that Foster had authority to sell products on its behalf. Taken in the light most favorable to HH & J, this combination of facts shows only that Foster was a Fentron employee whose authority was not apparent. Absent additional relevant evidence, it says nothing about whether he did or did not have Fentron's authority to sell products.[13] . . .

Finally, the evidence amply showed that HH & J subjectively believed that Foster [was] authorized by Fentron, but it is insufficient to support a reasonable inference that that belief was objectively reasonable. Before HH & J gave the first $6,300 check to Foster, it knew that Foster had requested that the check be made payable to him personally, that the glass was at a salvage yard instead of being in the control of Fentron, and that the glass was to be broken up and reprocessed almost immediately. Even if Fentron had engaged in more objective manifestations than it did, this knowledge by HH & J put it on notice as a matter of law that further inquiry of Fentron was needed.

Reversed with directions to dismiss the complaint.

Worswick, C.J., and Alexander, J., concur.

NOTES

1. The court quoted from the Restatement (Second) of Agency about the creation of apparent authority by appointing a person to a position that carries generally recognized powers. As one example of apparent authority by position, see *Bucher & Willis v. Smith*, 643 P.2d 1156, 1159 (Kan. App. 1982), involving the apparent authority of an estate's attorney (Johnson) to order a survey of the property owned by the estate. The court stated that in some situations

> the mere relationship between the agent and principal or the title conferred upon the agent by the principal is sufficient to constitute a representation of some authority. Illustrative cases include the so-called "powers of position," examples of which are: general manager [citations omitted]; president; and partner. Into this category, the relationship of attorney-client falls. In our view, the mere appointment of Johnson as attorney for the estate clothed him with sufficient apparent authority to obligate the estate for services, such as the survey, which were routinely and directly connected with the administration of the estate.

2. A power of position argument was made with regard to corporate officers in *Jennings v. Pittsburgh Mercantile Co.*, 202 A.2d 51, 54–55 (Pa. 1964), involving the apparent authority of the vice-president and treasurer-comptroller of a corporation to accept an offer of a sale and leaseback of all of the real property of the corporation for a period of 30 years. The court saw the issue as being "the apparent authority possessed *virtute officii* to consummate an extraordinary transaction." The court denied apparent authority, stating that "any other conclusion would improperly extend the usual scope of authority which attaches to the holding of various corporate offices, and would greatly undercut the proper role of the board of directors in corporate decision-making. . . . "

---

[13] [18] *Schoonover v. Carpet World, Inc.*, 91 Wash. 2d 173, 588 P.2d 729 (1978), and *Walker v. Pacific Mobile Homes, Inc.*, 68 Wash. 2d 347, 413 P.2d 3 (1966), contrast interestingly with the present case. In Schoonover, the principal, a carpet retailer, placed Rodriguez in sole control of one of its stores. The result was an appearance that Rodriguez had the authority to hire and fire persons to work at the store, and the plaintiff reasonably relied on that appearance. In *Walker*, the principal placed Stewart and Henderson in sole control of its mobile homes sales lot. The result was an appearance that they had the authority to receive the plaintiff's mobile home on consignment, and the plaintiff reasonably relied on that appearance. In the present case, Fentron employed a number of employees at its office, and other than what is discussed in the text, it did nothing to create an appearance that Foster was in control of its office or its operations.

We return to this topic in Chapter 7, *infra*.

Would it make any difference if the officer had falsely stated to the plaintiff (who was suing for a brokerage commission) that the board of directors had met and accepted the offer, and had authorized him to inform plaintiff of this? The fact situation in the case came close to this. The court denied apparent authority under this circumstance, stating: "An agent cannot, simply by his own words, invest himself with apparent authority." *See also Chase v. Consolidated Foods Corp.*, 744 F.2d 566, 569 (7th Cir. 1984) ("Even . . . the title of 'president' [does not invest the holder] with apparent authority to 'make a contract which is unusual and extraordinary,' that is, beyond the usual authority of a president, as a contract to sell a major corporate division would be."); *General Overseas Films, Ltd. v. Robin Int'l, Inc.*, 542 F. Supp. 684, 689 (S.D.N.Y. 1982), *aff'd without opinion*, 718 F.2d 1085 (2d Cir. 1983) (vice president-treasurer of a corporation, although "in a high and visible corporate position, with broad powers over financial affairs," does not have the apparent authority to issue a guarantee by the corporation of the debt of an unrelated corporation).

With regard to inferences that can be drawn from the agent's position, consider the language of Comment b of Restatement of Agency (Third) § 1.03:

> [A]n agent is sometimes placed in a position in an industry or setting in which holders of the position customarily have authority of a specific scope. Absent notice to third parties to the contrary, placing the agent in such a position constitutes a manifestation that the principal assents to be bound by actions by the agent that fall within that scope. A third party who interacts with the person, believing the manifestation to be true, need not establish a communication made directly to the third party by the principal to establish the presence of apparent authority as defined in § 2.03.

Consider, in light of Restatement (Third) § 1.03, *IOS Capital, LLC v. Allied Home Mortgage Capital Corp.*, 150 S.W.3d 148 (Mo. App. 2004), where the appellate court upheld a trial court judgment that a branch manager of a business that originated and processed home mortgage loans lacked the apparent authority to enter into a lease for a photocopy machine. The plaintiff failed to prove that it actually relied on the branch manager's apparent authority to enter into the lease. What evidence, beyond entering into the lease, would demonstrate plaintiff's reliance?

3. What effect does knowledge that an agent has a power of attorney have on apparent authority? See *Bayless v. Christie, Manson & Woods Int'l, Inc.*, 2 F.3d 347, 353 (10th Cir. 1993), noting that if the third party knows or has reason to know that the agent's authority is set forth in a written instrument, the party is under a duty to inspect that instrument.

4. Courts sometimes cite to a duty to inquire into an agent's apparent authority. *See, e.g., Link v. Kroenk* e, 909 S.W.2d 740, 745 (Mo. App. 1995) ("A person dealing with a supposed agent has a duty to ascertain for themselves the fact and scope of agency and must display that degree of common sense which distinguishes good faith from blind faith.").

5. Generally, an agent whose agency has been terminated has no power to bind the principal. An important exception to this general rule arises when the principal has provided the agent with a power of attorney or other indicia of authority. Under such circumstances, the principal may be held liable to third parties who deal with the agent on the basis of some such indicia of authority that the principal has failed to reacquire. See *Herbert Construction Co. v. Continental Ins. Co.*, 931 F.2d 989 (2d Cir. 1991), which discusses the duty on the principal to retrieve such indicia of authority.

6. When an agent misrepresents her authority, and the third party is unable to prevail on the issue of apparent authority, the agent will be liable to the third party for damages suffered by the third party who relied on the agent's purported authority. The theory for liability is that the agent, at least implicitly, if not explicitly, warranted her authority to bind the principal and should be liable for breach of this warranty. *See Husky Indus. v. Craig Indus.*, 618 S.W.2d 458 (Mo. Ct. App. 1981).

7. A principal may be held liable to a third party on a theory of estoppel if the principal is responsible for a misunderstanding that the third party has as to the agent's authority. *See, e.g., Szymkowski v. Szymkowski*, 432 N.E.2d 1209, 1210 (Ill. App. 1982), stating that, "Where a party silently stands by and permits her attorney to act in her behalf in [reaching a settlement of a property dispute], the party is estopped from denying the agent's apparent authority as to third persons." A closely related concept is agency by estoppel. Under this principle, a person is estopped to deny that another is her agent because she has mislead the third person into believing that to be the case. See, for example, *Gizzi v. Texaco*, 437 F.2d 308 (3d Cir. 1971), where the court held that Texaco might be liable for the alleged tortious conduct of an independent service station owner because its actions might have led the plaintiff to believe that the station owner was its agent.

8. Another term used in judicial opinions and some statutes is "ostensible authority." The Restatement (Third) of Agency includes this comment on the term:

> The doctrine in this section [§ 2.05 Estoppel To Deny Existence of Agency Relationship] encompasses definitions of "ostensible authority" that hold a principal accountable for an appearance of authority arising solely from the principal's failure to use ordinary care. Some statutes and cases so define "ostensible authority," while others use it as a synonym for "apparent authority" as defined in § 2.03.

PROBLEM

Katy Jacobs owned a retail store in Miami, Florida that specialized in selling kites. She hired her brother, Paul Jacobs, to run the shop and executed a power of attorney that read, in part, as follows:

> I hereby constitute and appoint Paul Jacobs as my attorney in fact in and throughout the State of Florida for me and in my name to purchase and to make and enter into, sign, and execute any contract or agreement with any persons, firm, company or companies for the purchase of any goods or merchandise in connection with the business carried on by me as aforesaid . . . and to make such purchase either for cash or for credit, as my attorney shall in his discretion think advisable. . . . And for me and on my behalf, and where necessary in connection with any purchases made on my behalf as aforesaid or in connection with my said business, to make, draw, sign, accept or indorse any bill or bills of exchange, promissory note or promissory notes, . . . and to sign my name or my trading name to any checks or orders for payment of money on my banking account in Miami, Florida.

Soon thereafter, Paul Jacobs, purporting to act on behalf of his principal, applied to Kites International, Inc., a firm that imported "stunt kites," for a loan of $50,000. Jacobs represented that he was authorized to borrow by the power of attorney which he had with him, and that his principal contemplated manufacturing traditional kites. Jacobs stated he wanted cash for machinery for this purposes. Without looking at the power of attorney, Kites International granted the loan, upon condition that Jacobs would push the sale of Kites International's stunt kites. Paul Jacobs applied the money "to his own purposes."

The loan by Kites International was not repaid and they are asserting a claim against Katy Jacobs. Describe what arguments you would make against Katy Jacobs if you were retained on behalf of Kites International after the true facts were discovered and the money lost. Would it have made any difference if Kites International had looked at the power of attorney, and then loaned the money?

C.   DUTIES OF PRINCIPALS AND AGENTS

1.   Duties of the Principal

The principal depends on the agent to achieve certain objectives or goals and, therefore, when we think of duties between a principal and agent, we normally think of what the agent must do. Nevertheless, some duties run in the other direction. For instance, the principal typically is required to compensate the agent and, of course, comply in good faith with any agreements that the parties have. The principal also has a duty to indemnify the agent against expenses incurred by the agent and claims arising in the normal course of the principal's business in which the agent finds itself embroiled. *See Admiral Oriental Line v. United States*, 86 F.2d 201 (2d Cir. 1936). The right to indemnification is subject to a few limitations. First, as provided in the Restatement (Third) of Agency § 8.14, Comment b, "A principal's duty to indemnify does not extend to losses that result from the agent's own negligence, illegal acts, or other wrongful conduct." Second, the right to indemnity depends on reasonable inferences drawn from the circumstances. Thus, a real estate broker, who is paid by commission, ordinarily is expected to bear certain expenses, like the cost of gasoline used in transporting potential purchasers to the property her principal is trying to sell. The general standard is expressed by Seavey: "[T]he principal bears the burdens to the extent that courts believe to be just, considering the customs of the business and the nature of the particular relation." WARREN A. SEAVEY, LAW OF AGENCY 266 (1964).

2.   Duties of the Agent

a.   Duty of Care

CARRIER v. MCLLARKY

Supreme Court of New Hampshire

693 A.2d 76 (1997)

JOHNSON, JUSTICE.

The defendant, Bruce M. McLlarky d/b/a Assured Plumbing & Heating, appeals an adverse judgment by the Derry District Court (Warhall, J.) in a small claims matter. We reverse.

The defendant installed a replacement hot water heater in the home of the plaintiff, Janet Carrier, in September 1994. The existing water heater had been installed by a different plumber approximately four years prior to its failure. When the defendant installed the new water heater, he told the plaintiff that he believed the old unit was under warranty, and that he would try to obtain a credit against the cost of the new water heater from the manufacturer. The defendant subsequently returned the defective unit to a supplier. The defendant has not given the plaintiff the desired credit and claims that he has failed to do so because he has not received payment from the manufacturer. The plaintiff sued the defendant in small claims court for the replacement value of the water heater and assorted costs. The district court rendered judgment in favor of the plaintiff, and this appeal followed.

[The appellate court approved the district court's determination that the parties had entered into an agency relationship and turned its attention to the duty of care defendant owed his principal, Carrier.]

The question thus becomes whether there is evidence in the record to support a finding of breach. Agents have a duty to conduct the affairs of the principal with a certain level of diligence, skill, and competence. "A determination that an agent was not sufficiently diligent is a question of fact that will not be disturbed unless it can be said that no rational trier of fact could come to the conclusion that the trial court has reached." 409 A.2d at 786. We find that in this case the trial court's findings were unreasonable and unsupported by the record.

"Under ordinary circumstances, the promise to act as an agent is interpreted as being a promise only to make reasonable efforts to accomplish the directed result." RESTATEMENT (SECOND) OF AGENCY § 377, comment b at 174 (1957). The court's own findings show that the defendant did make a reasonable attempt to obtain a refund for the plaintiff. Specifically, the court found that after agreeing to act on behalf of the plaintiff, "[t]he defendant then gave the old water [heater] to [a supplier] to return it to the manufacturer." The court's subsequent statement that "[t]he plaintiffs contacted the defendant numerous times regarding the credit and were told they would receive their money as soon as he received the credit," is insufficient to support a finding that the defendant breached his duty of diligence. This is especially true given that "[t]he duties of an agent toward his principal are always to be determined by the scope of the authority conferred." 3 Am. Jur. 2d *Agency* § 209; *see* Restatement (Second) of Agency § 376. The record shows only that the defendant was charged with returning the defective water heater for a possible credit; he did not guarantee that a credit would be obtained.

In addition, the degree of skill required by an agent in pursuit of the principal's objective is limited to the level of competence which is common among those engaged in like businesses or pursuits. *See* Restatement (Second) of Agency § 379, comment c at 179. There is no indication from the evidence on the record that more was required of the defendant in his agent capacity beyond executing the actual return and seeking the credit. The invoices and work orders provided to the court by the plaintiff do not indicate that the defendant guaranteed a refund. Rather, he merely promised to attempt to obtain a credit from the manufacturer. The invoice drawn up by the defendant and submitted as evidence by the plaintiff stated only that a refund under a warranty may be possible. Further, the record contains a letter from a supplier stating that the defendant "acted in a normal manner as any dealer would under these circumstances," and "was right to withhold credit . . . until the factory actually covered the unit."

Furthermore, an agent cannot be held liable to the principal simply "because he failed to procure for him something to which the latter is not entitled." 3 Am. Jur. 2d *Agency* § 215. The defendant correctly argues that any finding by the court that there was a valid warranty in place is unsupported by the record. The evidence submitted regarding the existence of a warranty included only two undated sales brochures claiming that a similar unit would be covered by a five to ten-year warranty and a letter dated approximately six months after the unit was replaced noting that a warranty currently offered to customers was valid for five to twelve years. Notably, the plaintiff did not produce a warranty for her actual unit. No evidence in the record established that the actual heater returned by the plaintiff was in fact covered by a warranty with terms identical to those described in the sales brochures or letter. Moreover, the defendant's supplier stated in a letter that the unit in question was not covered under a valid warranty.

There is also no support in the record for the holding that the defendant failed to turn over a refund actually received from the manufacturer. As noted above, the record contains a letter from a supplier stating that "[t]echnically, the unit was out of warranty." While the court did find the defendant to be less credible than the plaintiff, there is simply no evidence on the record that the defendant ever received the credit at all. Hence, there is no evidence to support a finding that the defendant breached his duty to remit funds actually received on behalf of the plaintiff. *Cf.* Restatement (Second) of Agency § 427 (agent who has received money on behalf of principal has duty to deliver it to principal on demand).

Consequently, because the district court's ruling was unsupported by the evidence, we reverse.

Reversed.

All concurred.

NOTES AND QUESTIONS

1. The Restatement (Third) of Agency § 8.08 sets forth the standard of care for agents, stating that an agent must act "with the care, competence, and diligence normally exercised by agents in similar circumstances."

2. A principal may recover from the agent any damages caused by the agent's negligence. The implications of this concept are significant: it means that an employer could recover for catastrophic losses caused by the simple negligence of a low-level employee. In practice, however, such losses are insured by the employer and the insurer would not pursue a claim against a judgment-proof employee. But the risk is there for employees in marginal cases where the employer or its insurer believes it can recover a loss from the employee. The parties can, of course, contract around this problem. *See Chemical Bank v. Security Pacific Nat'l Bank*, 20 F.3d 375, 377 (9th Cir. 1994) ("Beyond question [agent] acted negligently [by failing to file for $10 a financing statement, resulting in losses exceeding $1 million]. But there is no law against parties to a contract relieving themselves of liability by contract, particularly when they are sophisticated institutions represented by knowledgeable counsel. . . . According to the credit agreement, [agent] was liable only for its own gross negligence or willful misconduct; [the neglect of the agent] was insufficient to prove either willful misconduct or gross negligence.").

b.   Duty of Disclosure

OLSEN v. VAIL ASSOCIATES REAL ESTATE, INC.
Supreme Court of Colorado (en banc)
935 P.2d 975 (1997)

JUSTICE SCOTT delivered the Opinion of the Court.

Following the death of J. Perry Olsen in February 1988, his ranch (the estate property) was put on the market through an open listing.[14] Initially, the listing included an adjacent parcel of land (the children's property) owned by Janis O. Sterrett, James P. Olsen, Jr. and Valorie Olsen, the children of J. Perry Olsen. Valorie Olsen, individually and as personal representative of the estate of J. Perry Olsen, and James P. Olsen, Jr. (collectively the Olsens), are the petitioners before us. In March 1989, respondents, Vail Associates Real Estate, Inc., Daniel J. Leary, and Richard A. Kesler (collectively Vail Associates), introduced petitioners to a third party, Magnus Lindholm, who was interested in buying both properties.

The Olsens' attorney drafted a proposed land sale agreement that included both the estate property and the children's property. Lindholm counter-offered, after which the Olsens decided not to include the children's property in the sale and withdrew that parcel from the negotiations. Lindholm, however, felt that ownership of the estate property alone was not sufficient to ensure control over the development of the Lower Piney Valley, in which both properties were located. Lindholm's attorney therefore suggested that he explore the purchase of the only other parcel of land in the area, a ranch owned by Del Rickstrew (the Rickstrew property),[15] because that property had

---

[14] [2] An open listing solicits from any real estate agent the names of potential purchasers. The real estate agent is not the exclusive agent for the sale of the property and is only entitled to compensation upon the sale of property to a buyer that the agent has introduced to his selling principal.

[15] [3] The only private parcels of land in the Lower Piney Valley were the Olsen estate property, the children's property, and the Rickstrew property.

the primary access roads to both the estate property and the children's property and thus controlled any future development in the area.[16]

In December 1989, Lindholm requested that Vail Associates inquire whether the Rickstrew property was available for purchase. However, Rickstrew refused to negotiate the sale of his property through Vail Associates or any other real estate agent and demanded to negotiate personally with Lindholm. On January 5, 1990, Lindholm and Rickstrew commenced preliminary negotiations. During this time, Vail Associates performed certain tasks to facilitate the arrangement, such as introducing the parties, providing a model contract, and delivering a sealed package of unknown content to Rickstrew. However, Vail Associates did not directly participate in the discussions or negotiations between Rickstrew and Lindholm.

On January 13, 1990, Lindholm agreed to purchase the Rickstrew property, contingent upon a closing on the sale of the estate property. Although aware that negotiations were generally taking place, Vail Associates did not inform the Olsens that Lindholm was attempting to purchase the Rickstrew property. On January 18, 1990, Lindholm signed contracts to purchase both the estate property and the Rickstrew property. On March 20, 1990, the parties closed on the estate property, at which time the Olsens received $8,175,000, their asking price, and Vail Associates received their commission. The closing on the Rickstrew property occurred in June 1990, for a purchase price of $2,000,000, and Vail Associates did not receive a commission for that sale.

Upon learning of the sale of the Rickstrew property and the price Lindholm had paid for that property,[17] the Olsens sued Vail Associates, alleging a breach of fiduciary duty, fraudulent concealment, and negligence. After a bench trial, the trial court entered judgment for Vail Associates and against the Olsens. The court of appeals affirmed the trial court's judgment. . . .

A real estate broker, as any other agent, owes a fiduciary duty of good faith and loyalty to its principal, the seller. To discharge its fiduciary duty of good faith and loyalty, a real estate broker or agent must disclose all facts relative to the subject matter of the agency relationship that may be material to the decision the principal is about to make. Indeed, the law of agency imposes a strict duty of disclosure on a fiduciary. See generally Restatement (Second) of Agency § 381 (1958).

In the instant case, the Olsens contend that Vail Associates breached the fiduciary duty it owed to them by not revealing that Lindholm was negotiating to purchase the Rickstrew property and the ultimate sale price of that property.[18] . . . A breach of fiduciary duty occurs if the broker, as agent, conceals from the seller, as principal, "material" information, i.e., "information that bears upon the transaction in question." *Moore & Co. v. T-A-L-L*, 792 P.2d at 799 (Colo. 1990). An agent is thus required to disclose to the principal any facts "which might reasonably affect the principal's decision." *Wheeler v. Carl Rabe*, 599 P.2d at 904 (Colo. 1979). However, the burden is on the principal to demonstrate that the agent was aware of the nondisclosed fact, that the nondisclosed fact is material, and that the agent breached his or her fiduciary duty.

In terms of what constitutes "material" information in the present case, we find instructive . . . Restatement (Second) of Torts § 538(2)(a) (1977) ("The matter is

---

[16] [4] The easement through the Rickstrew property was limited at that time to agricultural purposes and the access road therefore could not be used for any other business purpose. Thus, by owning the Rickstrew property, Lindholm could maintain the limitations on the easement and be assured that the children's property would not be overly developed.

[17] [5] The record reveals that Lindholm paid $6,000 per acre for the Rickstrew property and $400 per acre for the estate property.

[18] [7] We treat the Olsens' argument as centered upon the nondisclosure of three particular facts: (1) that Lindholm was negotiating to purchase the Rickstrew property; (2) the purchase price to be paid by Lindholm for the Rickstrew property; and (3) the dual agency, if any, entered into by Vail Associates.

material if a reasonable [person] would attach importance to its existence or nonexistence in determining his choice of action in the transaction in question."). Thus, the question presented here is whether the information known to and withheld by Vail Associates would, if disclosed, have assumed actual significance in the deliberations of the Olsens in regard to the sale of the estate property or significantly altered the total mix of information available to them.

. . . [T]estimony in the record reveals that it was not knowledge of Lindholm's negotiations for the Rickstrew property that would have been valuable to the Olsens, but rather the actual price offered or paid for that property.[19] The Olsens' attorney testified that, in the past, other potential buyers' negotiations with Rickstrew had not caused the Olsens to alter their position in regard to the estate property and that only the fact of a contract for the sale of the Rickstrew property and the price to be paid under such contract would have been material to the deliberations of the Olsens in their dealings with Lindholm. The Olsens' attorney further testified that it was widely assumed that, for purposes of access, any potential purchaser of the estate property, including Lindholm, would also attempt to purchase the Rickstrew property. On this record, therefore, we do not consider failure to disclose the fact of preliminary negotiations between Lindholm and Rickstrew to be material to the Olsens.

. . . The Olsens testified and the trial court recognized that the per-acre price of the Rickstrew property would have been valuable information to the Olsens in their dealings with Lindholm.[20] Importantly, however, the trial court determined that Vail Associates did not have this information prior to the signing of the sale contract for the estate property and therefore could not have disclosed it to the Olsens.

Although it is undisputed that Vail Associates did not disclose this information regarding the sale price even after they learned of it,[21] the trial court noted that the Olsens failed to demonstrate how knowledge of the sale price after the contract for the estate property was signed would have in any way affected their decision-making as it related to the transaction. . . .

We therefore conclude that the trial court's determination that any omission by Vail Associates was not material is amply supported in the record and should not be disturbed on review.

The Olsens also assert that Vail Associates breached its fiduciary duty by engaging in a dual agency. . . . [A]lthough not directly pertinent to the question of a dual agency, we agree that Vail Associates did not act as agents for Lindholm in the sale of the Rickstrew property.

[T]he record reveals that, in connection with the sale of the estate property, Vail Associates only had contact with Lindholm which was necessary to facilitate the sale. Indeed, even Vail Associates' contact with Lindholm regarding the Rickstrew property was made in an effort to sell the estate property. . . .

[A]lthough Vail Associates had contact with Lindholm throughout the course of negotiations for the sale of the estate property, the record does not support a conclusion that it attempted to represent both the Olsens, as sellers, and Lindholm, as buyer, in the sale of the estate property. Also, the activities engaged in by Vail Associates for Lindholm in connection with his purchase of the Rickstrew property

---

[19] [8] . . . However, recognizing that materiality is a question of fact, we do not determine by our holding today that in every instance, negotiations are immaterial.

[20] [9] Counsel for Vail Associates conceded at oral argument before this court that if Vail Associates had known of the sale price of the Rickstrew property prior to the signing of the contract for the sale of the estate property, it would have had a duty to disclose such information.

[21] [10] By failing to disclose this information, Vail Associates may have violated the rules and standards promulgated by the Colorado Real Estate Commission. Indeed, the Chairman of the Commission testified that the actions of Vail Associates did not conform to its rules. . . .

amounted to no more than auxiliary or ministerial tasks, for which the agents received no commission. Thus, the trial court was correct in concluding, as a matter of law, that Vail Associates did not engage in a dual agency and did not breach its fiduciary duty of good faith and fair dealing by acting in such a capacity. . . . We therefore agree that no breach of fiduciary duty occurred and affirm the judgment of the court of appeals.

NOTE

Section 8.06 of the Restatement (Third) of Agency states that an agent acting as an adverse party with the principal's consent has a duty to deal fairly and to disclose all facts that the agent should know would reasonably affect the principal's judgment. Why doesn't the fact that the agent is openly acting as an adverse party transform the relationship to that of ordinary contracting parties, where no such burdens exist? That is, why continue to treat the relationship as if it were one of agency when the agent is not acting on the principal's behalf and the principal knows it? The Restatement (Second) of Agency § 390 appears to address this issue in Comment c: "If the agent is one upon whom the principal naturally would rely for advice, the fact that the agent discloses that he is acting as an adverse party does not relieve him from the duty of giving the principal impartial advice based upon a carefully informed judgment as to the principal's interests. If he cannot or does not wish to do so, he has a duty to see that the principal secures the advice of a competent and disinterested third person."

PROBLEM

Patty hired Arnold, a neighborhood boy, to mow her lawn using her old gas-powered mower. In the course of cutting the lawn, Arnold mowed over a sprinkler head and a cable for HD television. Is Arnold liable to Patty for the damages caused thereby?

c.   Duty of Loyalty

GELFAND v. HORIZON CORP.
United States Court of Appeals, Tenth Circuit
675 F.2d 1108 (10th Cir. 1982)

Before SETH, CHIEF JUDGE, DOYLE, CIRCUIT JUDGE, and ANDERSON, DISTRICT JUDGE.

WILLIAM E. DOYLE, CIRCUIT JUDGE.

Gelfand sued Horizon Corporation, a real estate concern, which was engaged in the owning and marketing of real estate around the country. Gelfand began working for Horizon in 1966. He served first as a real estate salesman and later as a sales manager. In recent times he was transferred to New Mexico and became the district manager in charge of Paradise Hills and Rio Communities which were located near Albuquerque. He had been paid a salary, but in 1977 it was decided by Horizon to pay him a lower salary, plus commissions and overrides based on real estate sales in his district. The percentages paid to the district manager were called overrides and were established by an inter-office memorandum in 1976.

Gelfand was terminated in January, 1979. Horizon's management apparently felt that Gelfand's success was benefiting him more than the company. Soon after that Gelfand claimed Horizon owed him commissions and overrides on some completed transactions. These Horizon refused to pay. Eventually, however, Gelfand filed suit in the Federal District Court in New Mexico, alleging that he was owed parts of some twelve different sales. Trial was to the court and it was concluded that Gelfand was entitled to commissions of eleven of the twelve sales, and judgment was entered in favor of Gelfand in the sum of $140,322.88.

On this appeal Horizon raises two points. First, that Gelfand was guilty of a breach of fiduciary duties with respect to one of the sales. There does not seem to be much controversy on this; it is the amount of the offset against Gelfand's claim which is in dispute. Horizon maintains that as a result of the breach of the fiduciary relationship, Horizon was entitled to an offset not only for profits accruing directly to the agent, but also for profits which accrued to third parties allied with the agent. The trial court gave damages based upon only those profits which had accrued directly to the agent. . . .

The Barranca Estates

This is the property which Gelfand sold to a corporation in which his wife had a one-third interest. Horizon was not apprised of the details of this transaction. The purchaser corporation was apparently formed for this particular conveyance; it was organized almost contemporaneously with the sale.

Horizon maintains that due to the breach of the fiduciary relationship, Gelfand was not entitled to a commission, but that Horizon was entitled to set off against Gelfand's other claims all of the profits that were made by the dummy corporation on the Barranca Estates transaction. The trial court, after hearing all the evidence, concluded that Horizon was entitled to an offset, but only as to the one-third share of the profits from the sale. On this appeal, Horizon contends that three-thirds should have been the award.

The Barranca Estates tract had been for sale for some time (one or two years) prior to Gelfand's arrival in New Mexico. The home office of Horizon in Tucson had set the sales price at $165,000. On November 10, 1977, Gelfand, working as an agent of Horizon, sold an option to buy the tract to B & C Enterprises, a New Mexico corporation, which is mentioned above, and in which Gelfand's wife and son were principals. B & C Enterprises had been incorporated October 27, 1977. Gelfand's wife had advanced the $2,500 price of the option herself. Within the ensuing month, B & C sold the option to Professional Homes, and received a $57,500 profit. Professional Homes paid B & C $60,000 for the option, and then exercised it, and paid Horizon $165,000 for the property. The profit was split three ways; $20,000 went to Mrs. Gelfand, and the balance was divided between Stewart Braums and David Simms, who were the other partners in B & C. B & C apparently went out of business immediately after this transaction.

The law regarding fiduciary relationships in New Mexico is generally similar to the laws throughout the United States. An agent occupies a relationship in which trust and confidence is the standard. When the agent places his own interests above those of the principal there is a breach of fiduciary duty to the principal. The fiduciary is duty bound to make a full, fair and prompt disclosure to his employer of all facts that threaten to affect the employer's interests or to influence the employee's actions in relation to the subject matter of the employment.

In the present case, the facts giving rise to the breach of the fiduciary relationship are undisputed. That Gelfand failed to disclose the relevant facts to Horizon at the time of the transaction cannot be questioned. Also, it is certain that the company would have objected to the sale to B & C Enterprises which had been formed the previous month. The violation of the fiduciary relationship was, indeed, blatant and the court was entirely correct in concluding that there was a breach of fiduciary duty owed by Gelfand to Horizon.

What should be the remedy for breach of fiduciary duty? The trial court refused to give Gelfand a commission on the sale. This was plainly correct. See *Canon v. Chapman*, 161 F. Supp. 104, 111 (D. Okla. 1958), holding that a broker is not entitled to compensation where he acts adversely to his principal's interest; *Craig v. Parsons*, 22 N.M. 293, 161 P. 1117, 1119 (1916). In this latter case, an agent's fraudulent conduct prevented him from receiving or retaining any benefit whatever from the transaction. Cf. *Iriart v. Johnson, supra*, 411 P.2d at 230, holding that a commission is a profit which the principal is entitled to recover. See also Douthwaite, *Profits and Their Recovery*, 15 VILLANOVA L. REV. 346, 373–74 (1970). Where an agent seeks to recover compensation growing out of the same transaction in which he was guilty of being disloyal to his principal, the court is justified in denying the compensation, and the equitable principle applicable to the fiduciary that he is not to profit from his own wrong comes into play.

We now turn to the issue whether the wife can be forced to return the $20,000 profit made in the transaction. We conclude that this is all part of the breach of fiduciary relationship, and that Gelfand was using his wife for the indirect purpose of gaining a profit which could not be given to him directly. Surely, the principal is entitled to recover that sum of money. . . . Bogert, Trusts and Trustees, Sec. 543, 543(A), 543(T), at 218, 225–26, 231–32 (rev. 2d ed. 1978) (profit made by fiduciary's wife is attributable to fiduciary and may be taken from him).

But the court's refusal to hold Gelfand liable for the profits made by the third parties is a more difficult problem.

It would appear from the cases that a fiduciary who has, by violating his obligation of loyalty, made it possible for others to make profits, can himself be held accountable for that profit regardless of whether he has realized it. There a trustee was surcharged for profits made by employees who traded in securities of trust subsidiaries. The theory is that the trustee is not to be free to authorize others to do what he is forbidden. There are a good many other cases which give support to this proposition. The liability of the fiduciary and of the profiting third party in such cases is said to be joint and several. The cases hold that the purpose for restoring profits is to discourage potential conflicts of interest and duty; the complaining principal or employer need not prove that any loss was caused by fiduciary's misconduct. This differs from the damages remedy, the purpose of which is to compensate the plaintiff for proven loss. The restitution of profits remedy serves primarily as a deterrent. Requiring the fiduciary to disgorge his own unjustly acquired gains serves a punitive as well as a compensatory function if no loss to the beneficiary is proven. To require him to account for the gains of others still more plainly operates to deter him and other fiduciaries from disloyalty.

So the trial court could have held Gelfand accountable for the $37,500 profit made by Braums and Simms. We do not hold that the trial court was incorrect in refusing to exercise its broad equity powers to this extent. Several reasons for the court's staying its own hand are suggested. First, the court is not obligated to compel a fiduciary to reimburse the beneficiary for third party profits. Thus, the authorization for such a remedy is not a mandatory one. Rather, it partakes of a discretionary equitable character. Second, the flexibility and concern for doing justice that are central to equity are another factor. It requires a case by case evaluation of all relevant circumstances whenever restitution of third party profits is sought.

From consideration of the evidence and the court's findings, it is our conclusion that the facts support the trial court's decision.

One factor which deserves prominent mention is that Horizon did not have a policy which forbade land purchases by employees or required disclosure in such situations. Other Horizon executives had bought property from Horizon for their own business interests. As a matter of fact, the evidence shows that Horizon employees could obtain a 20% discount on purchases of unimproved property. With respect to the sale of Barranca Estates to B & C Enterprises, Horizon's management executives were not wholly ignorant of the circumstances surrounding the transaction. The Tucson central office set the $165,000 sales price for the tract, and Horizon's Vice-President in Charge of Sales, S.P. Abrams, signed the B & C option purchase agreement himself.

Further elements supporting the trial court's decision are the non-existence of a strict trusteeship applicable to the two-thirds interest, see *Mosser v. Darrow*, 341 U.S. 267, 271 (1951) (trustee was held liable for profits made by employees, in part because the case involved "a strict trusteeship, not one of those quasi-trusteeships in which self-interest and representative interests are combined"), and the susceptibility of the other two B & C partners, Braums and Simms, to an action to recover profits (though Braums now lives in Florida). There are special rationales for holding fiduciaries liable for third-party profits, such as the possibility of reciprocal tipping arrangements. There is no evidence that Braums and Simms were in any position to return Gelfand's favor through questionable real estate transactions or other means. In addition, the Barranca Estates transaction appears to be an isolated incident in a long term of useful service by Gelfand to Horizon. See Douthwaite, *Profits and Their Recovery, supra*, at 374 (total forfeiture may be inappropriate where transaction complained of was isolable from fiduciary's conduct in general). . . .

It is our conclusion that substantial evidence supports the trial court's decision across the board. Accordingly, even if this court can find some support for the appellant's position, the ruling of the trial court should stand. "If, from established facts, reasonable men might draw different inferences, appellate courts may not substitute their judgment for that of the trial court."

Judgment . . . affirmed.

NOTES AND QUESTIONS

1. *Remedies.* In addition to the extensive discussion in *Gelfand* of the principal's remedies for breach of fiduciary duty, see *Tarnowski v. Resop*, 51 N.W.2d 801 (Minn. 1952), in which a principal in a suit against his agent recovered the agent's secret commission even though the principal had rescinded the underlying contract and recovered his down payment. He also recovered attorney's fees, all expenses, and loss of time devoted to the matter. *See also Moore & Co. v. T-A-L-L, Inc.*, 792 P.2d 794 (Colo. 1990) (agent forfeits commission retained by it even though principal unable to prove damages). With regard to the liability of the person who has aided the agent in breach of the fiduciary relation, see *Donemar, Inc. v. Molloy*, 169 N.E. 610 (N.Y. 1930), where the third party was ordered to pay a $4,555 "gratuity" to the principal, even though he had already paid it to the agent. In addition, the principal may obtain rescission of any agreements entered into by the agent. *See* RESTATEMENT (THIRD) OF AGENCY § 8.01, Comment d and *Mischke v. Mischke*, 530 N.W.2d 235, 241 (Neb. 1995) (transfers made by holder of durable power of attorney in breach of fiduciary duty void).

Does the remedy of forfeiture of profits include a right of the principal to recover whatever compensation was paid to the agent during the period of disloyalty? Courts are split on this. *See Phansalkar v. Andersen Weinroth & Co., L.P.*, 344 F.3d 184 (2d Cir. 2003) (all compensation forfeited during period of disloyalty, including investment opportunities); *Riggs Inv. Mgmt. v. Columbia Partners*, 966 F. Supp. 1250 (D.D.C. 1997) (all compensation forfeited from time disloyalty took place until termination of agent's employment, a period of six months); *Royal Carbo Corp. v. Flameguard, Inc.*, 645 N.Y.S.2d 18 (N.Y. App. Div. 1996) (all compensation forfeited during period of disloyalty, and agent held accountable to principal for profits lost on accounts agent diverted to others). But see *Hartford Elevator v. Lauer*, 289 N.W.2d 280 (Wis. 1980), rejecting a rule of per se forfeiture in favor of a consideration of all the circumstances, including the damage done to the employer and the value of the services of the employee. See also *Burg v. Miniature Precision Components*, 330 N.W.2d 192 (Wis. 1983), apparently narrowing the *Hartford Elevator* rule by placing the burden of proof on the employee under some circumstances to show that the agent's service during the period of disloyalty was of some value to the employer after deducting the damage done to the employer.

2. *The Economic Loss Rule.* The liability of an agent to the principal is also subject to the economic loss rule, which is recognized in many states and provides that "a party suffering only economic loss from the breach of a contractual duty may assert a tort claim for such a breach only if tort law provides an 'independent duty of care.' " *Tuchman v. Pell Rudman Trust Co., N.A.*, 245 F. Supp. 2d 1156, 1159 (D. Colo. 2003) (quoting from *Town of Alma v. AZCO Constr. Co.*, 10 P.3d 1256, 1264–66 (Colo. 2000)).

In *Tuchman*, the court held that if plaintiff established a contractual relationship with the defendant financial services firm, plaintiff could only recover damages for breach of contract, not for breach of fiduciary duty, as any duties that the defendant owed to the plaintiff would be governed by contract and there was no independent duty owed to the plaintiff. *Compare Lawyers Title Ins. Corp. v. Rex Title Corp.*, 282 F.3d 292 (4th Cir. 2002) (insurance agent owed independent duty of care to insurer, who could assert negligence claim against agent).

3. *Post Termination Competition.* One of the most difficult and frequently litigated questions involves what rights and duties continue between parties after termination of their relationship. Can an agent, after learning a particular skill, quit the principal's business and set up a competing business, assuming there is no agreement in her contract relating to this? In general, the common law will not stand in the way of competition, so long as it is fair. One factor that may prove important in assessing the fairness of the competition relates to the circumstances under which the employee left the business. See *Biever, Drees & Nordell v. Coutts*, 305 N.W.2d 33, 36 (N.D. 1981), a case where a former employee of an accounting partnership was enjoined from performing accounting services for certain clients of the partnership. There was no written employment agreement between the parties and therefore no covenant not to compete, nor was there an oral agreement with regard to competition after employment. Defendant had solicited certain clients of plaintiff for his business while still employed by plaintiff, however. The court quoted with approval the following language dealing with a similar situation: "While it is true that an employee may take steps to insure continuity in his livelihood in anticipation of resigning his position, he cannot feather his own nest at the expense of his employer while he is still on the payroll."

4. *Contractual Modification.* Another frequently litigated question is the extent to which the parties can contract around common law fiduciary duties. Consider this rule, as stated in § 8.06 of the Restatement (Third) of Agency:

§ 8.06 Principal's Consent

(1) Conduct by an agent that would otherwise constitute a breach of duty . . . does not constitute a breach of duty if the principal consents to the conduct, provided that

(a) in obtaining the principal's consent, the agent

(i) acts in good faith,

(ii) discloses all material facts that the agent knows, has reason to know, or should know would reasonably affect the principal's judgment unless the principal has manifested that such facts are already known by the principal or that the principal does not wish to know them, and

(iii) otherwise deals fairly with the principal; and

(b) the principal's consent concerns either a specific act or transaction, or acts or transactions of a specified type that could reasonably be expected to occur in the ordinary course of the agency relationship.

The topic of contracting around fiduciary duties is also taken up below, in connection with the fiduciary duties of partners to one another and of members in a limited liability company.

D. VICARIOUS LIABILITY FOR NEGLIGENT ACT

1. Introductory Note on Terminology

One of the most important consequences of finding that a person is an agent of another (the principal) is the imposition of vicarious liability on the principal for the tortious conduct of the agent. There are, generally speaking, two critical conditions to the imposition of vicarious liability:

1. *Control.* First, the principal must exercise, or at least have the right to exercise, a certain degree of control over the agent. At common law, if control was present, the relationship between the principal and agent was characterized as a master-servant relationship. Many courts, and the Restatement (Third) of Agency, have abandoned that terminology in favor of characterizing the relationship as employer-employee. This terminology is less than ideal, however, because a principal may exercise control over an agent and yet the agent is not, in *common usage*, an employee. Consider, for instance, a person who, gratuitously, assists another in a task, say repairing an automobile. Under such circumstances, the person providing the assistance might be characterized as the agent of the person being assisted (who would then be the principal) and, if the principal exercised a sufficient degree of control over the conduct of the agent, their relationship would be characterized as master-servant at common law. *See Heims v. Hanke*, 93 N.W.2d 455 (Wis. 1958) (nephew assisting uncle in washing car gave rise to master-servant relationship). The "servant" clearly would not be an employee, as that term is normally used, but would be so characterized under the Restatement (Third) of Agency. Moreover, in some true employment situations the employer does not exercise the degree of control over certain employees (typically licensed professionals such as physicians and lawyers) necessary to impose vicarious liability for the tortious conduct of those employees. In any event, the degree of control necessary to impose vicarious liability is the subject of *Kane Furniture Corp. v. Miranda*, set forth below. You will note from that case that if control is not present (as was the case there), so that the agent is not the servant or employee of the principal, the agent is characterized as an independent contractor.

2. *Scope of Employment.* The second condition to the imposition of vicarious liability is that the servant or employee be acting with the "scope of employment" at the time of the tortious conduct. The meaning of that term is, however, one of the most litigated questions in this area of the law and is explored in some depth below, in *Clover v. Snowbird Ski Resort*.

One final word about terminology is in order. The term vicarious liability is a broad one, signifying that one's liability is derived from the liability of another. In the context of agency law, we are concerned with a particular kind of vicarious liability, termed "respondeat superior" liability. This refers specifically to the liability of an employer (or master) for the conduct of its employee (or servant).

2.   The Control Test

KANE FURNITURE CORP. v. MIRANDA
Court of Appeals of Florida
506 So. 2d 1061 (1987), *review denied*, 515 So. 2d 230 (1988)

RYDER, ACTING CHIEF JUDGE.

Kane is a furniture store which also sells carpeting. Kane sold its carpet installation business to Perrone in 1975, and since that time, Kane has provided carpet installation services through Perrone's installation business (known as Service) as well as through other independent carpet installers.

For the past ten years, however, Perrone has been the principal carpet installer at Kane's St. Petersburg store. Initially, Kane put Perrone on a two-week probationary period during which Kane inspected Perrone's work to determine that Perrone was qualified. Thereafter, Perrone was given a small work area from which to assign installation jobs. Perrone hired other independent carpet installers, such as Kraus, to complete jobs which he could not perform.

On the morning of Saturday, August 6, 1983, Perrone assigned Kraus two installation jobs from Kane. Kraus completed the installation called for by the jobs around noon. Thereafter, Kraus, in his own truck, drove to a bar with his helper, Kevin Carleton, as a passenger. After drinking for approximately four hours, Kraus attempted to drive Carleton to Kane's warehouse parking lot in order that Carleton could retrieve his car. On the way to the parking lot, Kraus, traveling at a speed in excess of 50 m.p.h., ran a stop sign and collided broadside with the Miranda vehicle. Dr. Miranda's wife, Zenaida Quintos-Miranda, a passenger in the Miranda vehicle, died in a hospital soon after the accident.

This consolidated appeal arose from a wrongful death action which Dr. Romulo Miranda brought against Kane Furniture Corporation and Joseph P. Perrone for the death of Zenaida Quintos-Miranda. Kane appeals from the trial court's final summary judgment finding that Perrone was Kane's employee and that Kraus was Kane's subemployee. Kane also appeals the jury verdict award of 2.3 million dollars to Dr. Miranda.

We hold that the trial court erred in ruling that Perrone and Kraus were Kane's employees as a matter of law. We order the trial court to enter summary judgment for Kane finding that Perrone and Kraus are independent contractors.

Analysis of Restatement Factors

In *Cantor v. Cochran*, 184 So. 2d 173 (Fla. 1966), the Supreme Court of Florida approved the test set out in Restatement (Second) of Agency § 220 (1958) for determining whether one is an employee or independent contractor:

(2) In determining whether one acting for another is a servant or an independent contractor, the following matters of fact, among others, are considered:

(a) the extent of control which, by the agreement, the master may exercise over the details of the work;

(b) whether or not the one employed is engaged in a distinct occupation or business;

(c) the kind of occupation, with reference to whether, in the locality, the work is usually done under the direction of the employer or by a specialist without supervision;

(d) the skill required in the particular occupation;

(e) whether the employer or the workman supplies the instrumentalities, tools, and the place of work for the person doing the work;

(f) the length of time for which the person is employed;

(g) the method of payment, whether by the time or by the job;

(h) whether or not the work is a part of the regular business of the employer;

(i) whether or not the parties believe they are creating the relationship of master and servant; and

(j) whether the principal is or is not in business.

Upon applying the Restatement test to the facts before us, we come to the conclusion that Perrone and Kraus were independent contractors, not employees.

(a) *The extent of control which, by the agreement, the master may exercise over the details of the work*

It has been said that the extent of control is the most important factor in determining whether a person is an independent contractor or an employee. The right of control as to the mode of doing the work is the principal consideration. If a person is subject to the control or direction of another as to his results only, he is an independent contractor; if he is subject to control as to the means used to achieve the results, he is an employee. . . .

In *T & T Communications*, [460 So. 2d 996 (Fla. Ct. App. 1984)] the court found cable installers to be independent contractors primarily because the company's only concern was with the final product or result. Although the cable installers agreed with the cable company to complete the cable installations pursuant to the cable company's plans and specifications, the installers themselves determined the method by which to accomplish the installation. The court stated that further indicia that they were independent contractors were:

> The fact that cable installers are normally unsupervised . . . are skilled tradesmen . . . provide their own tools and transportation . . . are not employed for any length of time, are paid per installation, and receive no vacation and fringe benefits.

In the instant case, although Kane's salesmen diagrammed the installation layout plan, the carpet installers, Perrone and Kraus, had unbridled discretion in the physical performance of their tasks. Perrone did not report to anyone at Kane and had absolute discretion in contracting out installation jobs. The only instructions Kane gave Perrone were that he and the other carpet installers should be neatly attired and not intoxicated while on the job. Kane also instructed Perrone on customer satisfaction.

Once the carpet installer got the job, he was on his own. He performed his work completely without Kane's supervision or any other involvement. Upon completion of his task, the installer was free to go where he pleased: to another job or, unfortunately, to the local bar.

(b) *Whether or not the one employed is engaged in a distinct occupation or business*

Carpet installing can be viewed as a distinct occupation. Perrone and Kraus each had their own independent installation businesses. Perrone performed his services through a company which he purchased from Kane in 1975. Kraus performed his services through his own company, Mike's Carpet Service.

(c) *The kind of occupation with reference to whether, in the locality, the work is usually done under the direction of the employer or by a specialist without supervision*

Carpet installers are skilled workers who routinely perform without supervision. Perrone and Kraus performed work which emanated through Kane sales on an "as needed" basis. Both performed without Kane's supervision. Each was responsible for his own work. Kraus guaranteed his work for one year. Each, personally, was responsible for replacing carpeting he lost or damaged.

(d) *The skill required in the particular occupation*

Testimony at trial indicated that carpet installers are required to complete an apprenticeship in order to acquire the necessary skill to perform installation. As was aforementioned, Perrone also underwent a two-week probationary period at Kane.

(e) *Whether the employer or the workman supplies the instrumentalities, tools, and the place of work for the person doing the work*

Perrone and Kraus supplied their own installation equipment: knives, kickers, seaming irons, etc. They owned and insured their own trucks for work. Kane did not reimburse them for mileage and other expenses, such as gasoline.

While Kane supplied Perrone with a small space and a telephone from which to assign installation jobs, such accommodations did not make Perrone Kane's employee.

(f) *The length of time for which the person is employed*

Again, Perrone and Kraus worked for Kane on an "as needed" basis. The time spent on each job varied in length. The installation jobs were assigned on an "A.M. job or P.M.

job." Neither was obligated to work exclusively for Kane. Kane was not obligated to use only Perrone and Kraus.

(g) *The method of payment, whether by time or by job*

While Kane determined the amount Perrone was paid, Perrone was paid strictly on a per yard basis. Kane made its checks out to Perrone's company. Perrone, in turn, paid Kraus and the other installers to whom he had assigned jobs.

Independent contractors are normally paid "per installation" rather than "by time." For instance, in *VIP Tours*, [449 So. 2d 1307] a tour company was not deemed employer of tour guides using company vehicles who worked on a per job basis. In *T & T Communications*, cable splicers were found to be independent contractors where they were not employed for any length of time, were paid per installation and received no vacation or fringe benefits.

(h) *Whether or not the work is part of the regular business of the employer*

Kane is engaged in the retail furniture business. As a part of that business, Kane also sells carpeting and advertises installation as included in the purchase price. This is the only factor favoring the conclusion that Perrone and Kraus are employees. With all the other factors pointing to the conclusion that they are independent contractors, this factor alone is insufficient to sustain a holding that they are employees.

(i) *Whether or not the parties believe they are creating the relation of master and servant*

The parties' intent and course of dealing are important factors in determining their legal status. Clearly, the parties believed they were entering into an independent contractor relationship. Perrone and Kraus paid taxes as the owners of independent carpet installation businesses. Kane did not withhold social security or income taxes. Kane filed a Form "1099" for Perrone which is the IRS tax form a company files for nonemployees. A person who is responsible for paying all taxes due has been found to be an independent contractor.

Both Perrone and Kraus were free to accept or reject Kane's work. Perrone and Kraus were also able to work for companies in addition to Kane. Kane was not obligated to use Perrone or Kraus exclusively and, in fact, did not. Both Perrone and Kraus could hire their own employees.

Neither Perrone nor Kraus had employment agreements with Kane. Neither enjoyed the usual amenities associated with an employment relationship: fringe benefits, health care insurance, unemployment compensation, worker's compensation and paid vacations or holidays.

(j) *Whether the principal is or is not in business*

We concur that "the relevance of this factor is obscure, but for what it is worth, appellant is in business." [458 So. 2d at 898].

Measured against the Restatement criteria, we hold that Perrone and Kraus are independent contractors. Perrone and Kraus were independent contractors . . . just as the cable splicers were in *T & T Communications*.

Appellee argues that we should not hold that Perrone and Kraus were independent contractors as a matter of law. Rather, appellee contends that it is a question of fact for the jury. . . .

Even if the Restatement factors favored a finding of Perrone as Kane's employee, an application of the Restatement factors to Kraus and Kane's business relationship would indicate that Kraus was an independent contractor, not a subemployee. This alone would be sufficient to reverse the trial court's summary judgment finding of an employer/employee relationship. . . .

Reversed and remanded with instructions.

Lᴇʜᴀɴ and Fʀᴀɴᴋ, JJ., concur.

NOTE

The Restatement (Third) § 7.07, Comment f sets forth a list of similar factors:

Numerous factual indicia are relevant to whether an agent is an employee. These include: the extent of control that the agent and the principal have agreed the principal may exercise over details of the work; whether the agent is engaged in a distinct occupation or business; whether the type of work done by the agent is customarily done under a principal's direction or without supervision; the skill required in the agent's occupation; whether the agent or the principal supplies the tools and other instrumentalities required for the work and the place in which to perform it; the length of time during which the agent is engaged by a principal; whether the agent is paid by the job or by the time worked; whether the agent's work is part of the principal's regular business; whether the principal and the agent believe that they are creating an employment relationship; and whether the principal is or is not in business. Also relevant is the extent of control that the principal has exercised in practice over the details of the agent's work.

3.   The Scope of Employment

CLOVER v. SNOWBIRD SKI RESORT
Supreme Court of Utah
808 P.2d 1037 (1991)

Hᴀʟʟ, Cʜɪᴇꜰ Jᴜsᴛɪᴄᴇ.

Plaintiff Margaret Clover sought to recover damages for injuries sustained as the result of a ski accident in which Chris Zulliger, an employee of defendant Snowbird Corporation ("Snowbird"), collided with her. From the entry of summary judgment in favor of defendants, Clover appeals.

At the time of the accident, Chris Zulliger was employed by Snowbird as a chef at the Plaza Restaurant. Zulliger was supervised by his father, Hans Zulliger, who was the head chef at both the Plaza, which was located at the base of the resort, and the Mid-Gad Restaurant, which was located halfway to the top of the mountain. Zulliger was instructed by his father to make periodic trips to the Mid-Gad to monitor its operations. Prior to the accident, the Zulligers had made several inspection trips to the restaurant. On at least one occasion, Zulliger was paid for such a trip. He also had several conversations with Peter Mandler, the manager of the Plaza and Mid-Gad Restaurants, during which Mandler directed him to make periodic stops at the Mid-Gad to monitor operations.

On December 5, 1985, the date of the accident, Zulliger was scheduled to begin work at the Plaza Restaurant at 3 p.m. Prior to beginning work, he had planned to go skiing with Barney Norman, who was also employed as a chef at the Plaza. Snowbird preferred that their employees know how to ski because it made it easier for them to get to and from work. As part of the compensation for their employment, both Zulliger and Norman received season ski passes. On the morning of the accident, Mandler asked Zulliger to inspect the operation of the Mid-Gad prior to beginning work at the Plaza.

Zulliger and Norman stopped at the Mid-Gad in the middle of their first run. At the restaurant, they had a snack, inspected the kitchen, and talked to the personnel for approximately fifteen to twenty minutes. Zulliger and Norman then skied four runs before heading down the mountain to begin work. On their final run, Zulliger and Norman took a route that was often taken by Snowbird employees to travel from the top of the mountain to the Plaza. About mid-way down the mountain, at a point above the Mid-Gad, Zulliger decided to take a jump off a crest on the side of an intermediate run. He had taken this jump many times before. A skier moving relatively quickly is able to become airborne at that point because of the steep drop off on the downhill side of the crest. Due to this drop off, it is impossible for skiers above the crest to see skiers below the crest. The jump was well known to Snowbird. In fact, the Snowbird ski patrol often instructed people not to jump off the crest. There was also a sign instructing skiers to ski slowly at this point in the run. Zulliger, however, ignored the sign and skied over the crest at a significant speed. Clover, who had just entered the same ski run from a point below the crest, either had stopped or was traveling slowly below the crest. When Zulliger went over the jump, he collided with Clover, who was hit in the head and severely injured.

Clover brought claims against Zulliger and Snowbird, alleging that (1) Zulliger's reckless skiing was a proximate cause of her injuries, (2) Snowbird is liable for Zulliger's negligence because at the time of the collision, he was acting within the scope of his employment, (3) Snowbird negligently designed and maintained its ski runs, and (4) Snowbird breached its duty to adequately supervise its employees. Zulliger settled separately with Clover. Under two separate motions for summary judgment, the trial judge dismissed Clover's claims against Snowbird for the following reasons: (1) as a matter of law, Zulliger was not acting within the scope of his employment at the time of the collision, (2) Utah's Inherent Risk of Skiing Statute, Utah Code Ann. §§ 78-27-51 to -54 (Supp. 1986), bars plaintiff's claim of negligent design and maintenance, and (3) an employer does not have a duty to supervise an employee who is acting outside the scope of employment.

Under the doctrine of respondeat superior, employers are held vicariously liable for the torts their employees commit when the employees are acting within the scope of their employment. Clover's respondeat superior claim was dismissed on the ground that as a matter of law, Zulliger's actions at the time of the accident were not within the scope of his employment. In a recent case, *Birkner v. Salt Lake County*,[22] this court addressed the issue of what types of acts fall within the scope of employment. In *Birkner*, we stated that acts within the scope of employment are " 'those acts which are so closely connected with what the servant is employed to do, and so fairly and reasonably incidental to it, that they may be regarded as methods, even though quite improper ones, of carrying out the objectives of the employment.' "[23] The question of whether an employee is acting within the scope of employment is a question of fact. The scope of employment issue must be submitted to a jury "whenever reasonable minds may differ as to whether the [employee] was at a certain time involved wholly or partly in the performance of his [employer's] business or within the scope of employment."[24] In situations where the activity is so clearly within or without the scope of employment that reasonable minds cannot differ, it lies within the prerogative of the trial judge to decide the issue as a matter of law.

In *Birkner*, we observed that the Utah cases that have addressed the issue of whether an employee's actions, as a matter of law, are within or without the scope of employment have focused on three criteria.[25] "First, an employee's conduct must be of the general kind the employee is employed to perform. . . . In other words, the employee must be about the employer's business and the duties assigned by the employer, as opposed to being wholly involved in a personal endeavor."[26] Second, the

---

[22] [1] 771 P.2d 1053 (Utah 1989).

[23] [2] *Birkner v. Salt Lake County*, 771 P.2d at 1056 [quoting W. KEETON, *Prosser and Keeton on the Law of Torts* § 70, at 502 (5th ed. 1984)].

[24] [3] *Carter v. Bessey*, 97 Utah 427, 93 P.2d 490, 493 (1939).

[25] [4] *See* RESTATEMENT (SECOND) OF AGENCY § 228 (1958); W. KEETON, *Prosser and Keeton on the Law of Torts* § 70, at 502 (5th ed. 1984).

[26] [5] *Birkner v. Salt Lake County*, 771 P.2d 1053, 1056–57 (Utah 1989); *see also Keller v. Gunn Supply Co.*, 62 Utah 501, 220 P.2d 1063, 1064 (1923).

employee's conduct must occur substantially within the hours and ordinary spatial boundaries of the employment.[27] "Third, the employee's conduct must be motivated at least in part, by the purpose of serving the employer's interest."[28] Under specific factual situations, such as when the employee's conduct serves a dual purpose or when the employee takes a personal detour in the course of carrying out his employer's directions, this court has occasionally used variations of this approach. These variations, however, are not departures from the criteria advanced in *Birkner*. Rather, they are methods of applying the criteria in specific factual situations.

In applying the *Birkner* criteria to the facts in the instant case, it is important to note that if Zulliger had returned to the Plaza Restaurant immediately after he inspected the operations at the Mid-Gad Restaurant, there would be ample evidence to support the conclusion that on his return trip Zulliger's actions were within the scope of his employment. There is evidence that it was part of Zulliger's job to monitor the operations at the Mid-Gad and that he was directed to monitor the operations on the day of the accident. There is also evidence that Snowbird intended Zulliger to use the ski lifts and the ski runs on his trips to the Mid-Gad. It is clear, therefore, that Zulliger's actions could be considered to "be of the general kind that the employee is employed to perform."[29] It is also clear that there would be evidence that Zulliger's actions occurred within the hours and normal spatial boundaries of his employment. Zulliger was expected to monitor the operations at the Mid-Gad during the time the lifts were operating and when he was not working as a chef at the Plaza. Furthermore, throughout the trip he would have been on his employer's premises. Finally, it is clear that Zulliger's actions in monitoring the operations at the Mid-Gad, per his employer's instructions, could be considered "motivated, at least in part, by the purpose of serving the employer's interest."[30]

The difficulty, of course, arises from the fact that Zulliger did not return to the Plaza after he finished inspecting the facilities at the Mid-Gad. Rather, he skied four more runs and rode the lift to the top of the mountain before he began his return to the base. Snowbird claims that this fact shows that Zulliger's primary purpose for skiing on the day of the accident was for his own pleasure and that therefore, as a matter of law, he was not acting within the scope of his employment. In support of this proposition, Snowbird cites *Whitehead v. Variable Annuity Life Insurance*.[31] *Whitehead* concerned the dual purpose doctrine. Under this doctrine, if an employee's actions are motivated by the dual purpose of benefiting the employer and serving some personal interest, the actions will usually be considered within the scope of employment. However, if the primary motivation for the activity is personal, "even though there may be some transaction of business or performance of duty merely incidental or adjunctive thereto, the [person] should not be deemed to be in the scope of his employment."[32] In situations where the scope of employment issue concerns an employee's trip, a useful test in determining if the transaction of business is purely incidental to a personal motive is "whether the trip is one which would have required the employer to send another employee over the same route or to perform the same function if the trip had not been made."[33]

---

[27] [6] *Birkner v. Salt Lake County*, 771 P.2d at 1057; *see also Cannon v. Goodyear Tire & Rubber Co.*, 60 Utah 346, 208 P. 519, 520–21 (1922).

[28] [7] *Birkner v. Salt Lake County*, 771 P.2d at 1057; *see also, e.g., Whitehead v. Variable Annuity Life Ins.*, 801 P.2d at 936; *Stone v. Hurst Lumber Co.*, 15 Utah 2d 49, 386 P.2d 910, 911 (1963); *Combes v. Montgomery Ward & Co.*, 119 Utah 407, 228 P.2d 272, 274 (1951).

[29] [8] *Birkner v. Salt Lake County*, 771 P.2d at 1057.

[30] [9] *Id.*

[31] [10] 801 P.2d 934 (Utah 1989).

[32] [11] *Id.* [citing *Martinson v. W-M Ins. Agency*, 606 P.2d 256, 285 (Utah 1980)].

[33] [12] *Id.*

In *Whitehead*, we held that an employee's commute home was not within the scope of employment, notwithstanding the plaintiff's contention that because the employee planned to make business calls from his house, there was a dual purpose for the commute. In so holding, we noted that the business calls could have been made as easily from any other place as from the employee's home. The instant case is distinguishable from *Whitehead* in that the activity of inspecting the Mid-Gad necessitates travel to the restaurant. Furthermore, there is evidence that the manager of both the Mid-Gad and the Plaza wanted an employee to inspect the restaurant and report back by 3 p.m. If Zulliger had not inspected the restaurant, it would have been necessary to send a second employee to accomplish the same purpose. Furthermore, the second employee would have most likely used the ski lifts and ski runs in traveling to and from the restaurant.

There is ample evidence that there was a predominant business purpose for Zulliger's trip to the Mid-Gad. Therefore, this case is better analyzed under our decisions dealing with situations where an employee has taken a personal detour in the process of carrying out his duties. This court has decided several cases in which employees deviated from their duties for wholly personal reasons and then, after resuming their duties, were involved in accidents. In situations where the detour was such a substantial diversion from the employee's duties that it constituted an abandonment of employment, we held that the employee, as a matter of law, was acting outside the scope of employment. However, in situations where reasonable minds could differ on whether the detour constituted a slight deviation from the employee's duties or an abandonment of employment, we have left the question for the jury.

Under the circumstances of the instant case, it is entirely possible for a jury to reasonably believe that at the time of the accident, Zulliger had resumed his employment and that Zulliger's deviation was not substantial enough to constitute a total abandonment of employment. First, a jury could reasonably believe that by beginning his return to the base of the mountain to begin his duties as a chef and to report to Mandler concerning his observations at the Mid-Gad, Zulliger had resumed his employment. In past cases, in holding that the actions of an employee were within the scope of employment, we have relied on the fact that the employee had resumed the duties of employment prior to the time of the accident.[34] This is an important factor because if the employee has resumed the duties of employment, the employee is then "about the employer's business" and the employee's actions will be "motivated, at least in part, by the purpose of serving the employer's interest."[35] The fact that due to Zulliger's deviation, the accident occurred at a spot above the Mid-Gad does not disturb this analysis. In situations where accidents have occurred substantially within the normal spatial boundaries of employment, we have held that employees may be within the scope of employment if, after a personal detour, they return to their duties and an accident occurs.

Second, a jury could reasonably believe that Zulliger's actions in taking four ski runs and returning to the top of the mountain do not constitute a complete abandonment of employment. It is important to note that by taking these ski runs, Zulliger was not disregarding his employer's directions. In *Cannon v. Goodyear Tire & Rubber Co.*,[36] wherein we held that the employee's actions were a substantial departure from the course of employment, we focused on the fact that the employee's actions were in direct conflict with the employer's directions and policy. In the instant case, far from directing its employees not to ski at the resort, Snowbird issued its employees season ski passes as part of their compensation.

These two factors, along with other circumstances — such as, throughout the day

---

[34] [13] *See Burton v. La Duke*, 210 P. at 979–81.

[35] [14] *See id.* 210 P. at 981; *see also Birkner v. Salt Lake County*, 771 P.2d at 1057.

[36] [15] 60 Utah 346, 208 P. 519 (1922).

Zulliger was on Snowbird's property, there was no specific time set for inspecting the restaurant, and the act of skiing was the method used by Snowbird employees to travel among the different locations of the resort — constitute sufficient evidence for a jury to conclude that Zulliger, at the time of the accident, was acting within the scope of his employment.

Although we have held that Zulliger's actions were not, as a matter of law, outside the scope of his employment under the *Birkner* analysis, it is important to note that Clover also argues that Zulliger's conduct is within the scope of employment under two alternative theories. First, she urges this court to adopt a position taken by some jurisdictions that focuses, not on whether the employee's conduct is motivated by serving the employer's interest, but on whether the employee's conduct is foreseeable.[37] Such an approach constitutes a significant departure from the *Birkner* analysis.

Second, Clover urges this court to apply the premises rule, a rule developed in workers' compensation cases, to third-party tort-feasor claims. Under this rule, employees who have fixed hours and places of work will usually be considered to be acting outside of the scope of employment when they are traveling to and from work. However, they will be considered to be in the course of employment while traveling to and from work when they are on their employer's premises. In this instance, we decline to adopt such an approach. It is to be noted that the policies behind workers' compensation law differ from the policies behind respondeat superior claims. Furthermore, the premises rule departs from the analysis in *Birkner* in that it focuses entirely upon the second criterion discussed in *Birkner*, the hours and ordinary spatial boundaries of the employment, to the exclusion of the first and third criteria. Situations like the instant case, where the employee has other reasons aside from traveling to work to be on the employer's premises, demonstrate the need for a more flexible and intricate analysis in respondeat superior cases. In fact, it is not entirely clear that the premises rule would apply in a workers' compensation case if the only connection an employee had with work was that the employee, after some recreational skiing, was returning to work on the employer's ski runs. We therefore, in this instance, decline to adopt these approaches.

Reversed and remanded for further proceedings.

NOTE

In *Robarge v. Bechtel Power Corp.*, 131 Ariz. 280, 640 P.2d 211 (1982), the court held that an employee is not considered to be within the scope of employment when traveling to and from work. This is consistent with the prevailing view on the question. For a case contra to *Robarge*, see *Luth v. Rogers & Babler Constr. Co.*, 507 P.2d 761 (Alaska 1973), where a going and coming case was sent to the jury. The tortfeasor (Jack) was a flagman on a construction job, returning home from the jobsite at the end of the working day. The majority opinion found that the $8.50 per day additional remuneration paid to Jack (and all other employees) may have enabled laborers to commute to the job site, "thus benefiting Rogers," the defendant construction company. Under such circumstances, the court held, "It would not be unfair to require Rogers to pay for the [plaintiff's] resulting injuries."

The language in *Luth* of "benefit" to the employer is borrowed from the law of worker's compensation. Under worker's compensation, a far broader range of acts is included within the scope of employment (called "course of employment" in the language of worker's compensation) than under the law of respondeat superior. This difference between the two systems may be explained in part by the fact that in

---

37 [16] *See Bushey & Sons, Inc. v. United States*, 398 F.2d 167, 171 (2d Cir. 1968); *Hinman v. Westinghouse Elec. Co.*, 2 Cal. 3d 956, 471 P.2d 988, 990, 88 Cal. Rptr. 188, 190 (1970).

worker's compensation the exposure to liability for the employer is more confined. Liability extends only to the employer's workers. Also, payments to an injured worker are made according to a schedule and do not include pain and suffering, as noted earlier.

The exposure to liability under respondeat superior is much greater. The range of potential plaintiffs is undefined but potentially large, and the damages can be exceptionally high because pain and suffering and other open-ended features of tort damages are available to persons injured by an employee. Liability is strict under both systems, but the potential for severe loss for an innocent employer is far greater under vicarious tort liability. In addition, under worker's compensation, the injured party has only one defendant; under respondeat superior the injured person has two defendants: the tortfeasor and the tortfeasor's employer.

Perhaps for these reasons, most courts tend to draw tighter limits on what actions are within the scope of employment when dealing with vicarious tort liability. In most jurisdictions, courts look for some evidence of intent, at least in part, by the employee to serve the employer at the time of the loss, plus evidence meeting the other factors of time, place, and kind of work, with the objective of confining liability to acts that might fairly be said to have been performed as part of discharging the employee's obligation to the business. Admittedly, this distinction sometimes is lost sight of by courts when dealing with particularly troubling cases.

PROBLEM

Paul Carr was a lawyer in the firm of Murray & Carr. He had a part-time job as a municipal judge and did not share his income from this position with his firm. While driving from the firm's office to his judgeship, he negligently injured Adrienne O'Toole. The vehicle that Carr was driving was leased to him and paid for by him from distributions that he received from the law firm. O'Toole sued the law firm, claiming it was vicariously liable for Carr's negligence. Is it? Suppose O'Toole argued that the firm should be liable because it benefited indirectly from the prestige that attached to Carr's position? Would it make a difference if, immediately before the accident, Carr used his cell phone in the automobile and conducted firm business? (Assume alternatively that he completed the call before the accident and that he was on the phone at the time of the accident.)

E. VICARIOUS LIABILITY FOR INTENTIONAL MISCONDUCT

The imposition of vicarious liability for negligent conduct has been rationalized on the basis that negligent conduct by an employee can be anticipated by the employer and factored into the cost of doing business. Moreover, insurance can generally be obtained and imposing liability on the employer seems "fair." These rationales make less sense when the tortious conduct is intentional, and committed by an employee to further his own interests. The general rule was stated in *Bremen State Bank v. Hartford Accident & Indemnity Co.*, 427 F.2d 425 (7th Cir. 1970), where the court refused to hold a moving company liable for the theft committed by its employees that occurred when the company was moving a bank to a new locale: "the employer is liable for the negligent, wilful, malicious, or criminal acts of its employees when such acts are committed during the course of employment and in furtherance of the business of the employer; but when the act is committed solely for the benefit of the employee, the employer is not liable to the injured third party." Courts have been tempted by various arguments to abandon this bright-line rule, and the next case provides a leading example.

IRA S. BUSHEY & SONS v. UNITED STATES
United States Court of Appeals, Second Circuit
398 F.2d 167 (1968)

Before WATERMAN, FRIENDLY, and KAUFMAN, CIRCUIT JUDGES.

FRIENDLY, CIRCUIT JUDGE. While the United States Coast Guard vessel Tamaroa was being overhauled in a floating dry dock located in Brooklyn's Gowanus Canal, a seaman returning from shore leave late at night, in the condition for which seaman are famed, turned some wheels on the drydock wall. He thus opened valves that controlled the flooding of the tanks on one side of the drydock. Soon the ship listed, slid off the blocks and fell against the wall. Parts of the drydock sank, and the ship partially did — fortunately without loss of life or personal injury. The drydock owner sought and was granted compensation by the District Court for the Eastern District of New York in an amount to be determined, 276 F. Supp. 518; the United States appeals. . . .

The Tamaroa had gone into drydock on February 28, 1963; her keel rested on blocks permitting her drive shaft to be removed and repairs to be made to her hull. The contract between the Government and Bushey provided in part:

> (o) The work shall, whenever practical, be performed in such manner as not to interfere with the berthing and messing of personnel attached to the vessel undergoing repair, and provision shall be made so that personnel assigned shall have access to the vessel at all times, it being understood that such personnel will not interfere with the work or the contractor's workmen.

Access from shore to ship was provided by a route past the security guard at the gate, through the yard, up a ladder to the top of one drydock wall and along the wall to a gangway leading to the fantail deck, where men returning from leave reported at a quartermaster's shack.

Seaman Lane, whose prior record was unblemished, returned from shore leave a little after midnight on March 14. He had been drinking heavily; the quartermaster made mental note that he was "loose." For reasons not apparent to us or very likely to Lane,[38] he took it into his head, while progressing along the gangway wall, to turn each of three large wheels some twenty times; unhappily, as previously stated, these wheels controlled the water intake valves. After boarding ship at 12:11 a.m., Lane mumbled to an off-duty seaman that he had "turned some valves" and also muttered something about "valves" to another who was standing the engineering watch. Neither did anything; apparently Lane's condition was not such as to encourage proximity. At 12:20 a.m. a crew member discovered water coming into the drydock. By 12:30 a.m. the ship began to list, the alarm was sounded and the crew were ordered ashore. Ten minutes later the vessel and dock were listing over 20 degrees; in another ten minutes the ship slid off the blocks and fell against the drydock wall.

The Government attacks imposition of liability on the ground that Lane's acts were not within the scope of his employment. It relies heavily on § 228(1) of the Restatement of Agency 2d which says that "conduct of a servant is within the scope of employment if, but only if: . . . (c) it is actuated, at least in part by a purpose to serve the master." Courts have gone to considerable lengths to find such a purpose, as witness a well-known opinion in which Judge Learned Hand concluded that a drunken boatswain who routed the plaintiff out of his bunk with a blow, saying "Get up, you big son of a bitch, and turn to," and then continued to fight, might have thought he was acting in the interest of the ship. *Nelson v. American-West African Line*, 86 F.2d 730 (2d Cir. 1936), *cert. denied*, 300 U.S. 665, 57 S. Ct. 509, 81 L. Ed. 873 (1937). It would be going too far to find such a purpose here; while Lane's return to the Tamaroa was to serve his employer, no one

---

[38] [4] Lane disappeared after completing the sentence imposed by a court-martial and being discharged from the Coast Guard.

has suggested how he could have thought turning the wheels to be, even if — which is by no means clear — he was unaware of the consequences.

In light of the highly artificial way in which the motive test has been applied, the district judge believed himself obliged to test the doctrine's continuing vitality by referring to the larger purposes *respondeat superior* is supposed to serve. He concluded that the old formulation failed this test. We do not find his analysis so compelling, however, as to constitute a sufficient basis in itself for discarding the old doctrine. It is not at all clear, as the court below suggested, that expansion of liability in the manner here suggested will lead to a more efficient allocation of resources. As the most astute exponent of this theory has emphasized, a more efficient allocation can only be expected if there is some reason to believe that imposing a particular cost on the enterprise will lead it to consider whether steps should be taken to prevent a recurrence of the accident. Calabresi, *The Decision for Accidents: An Approach to Non-fault Allocation of Costs*, 78 Harv. L. Rev. 713, 725–34 (1965). And the suggestion that imposition of liability here will lead to more intensive screening of employees rests on highly questionable premises, see Comment, *Assessment of Punitive Damages Against an Entrepreneur for the Malicious Torts of His Employees*, 70 Yale L.J. 1296, 1301–04 (1961).[39] The unsatisfactory quality of the allocation of resource rationale is especially striking on the facts of this case. It could well be that application of the traditional rule might induce drydock owners, prodded by their insurance companies, to install locks on their valves to avoid similar incidents in the future,[40] while placing the burden on shipowners is much less likely to lead to accident prevention.[41] It is true, of course, that in many cases the plaintiff will not be in a position to insure, and so expansion of liability will, at the very least, serve *respondeat superior's* loss spreading function. See Smith, *Frolic and Detour*, 23 Colum. L. Rev. 444, 456 (1923). But the fact that the defendant is better able to afford damages is not alone sufficient to justify legal responsibility, see Blum & Kalven, Public Law Perspectives on a Private Law Problem (1965), and this overarching principle must be taken into account in deciding whether to expand the reach of *respondeat superior*.

A policy analysis thus is not sufficient to justify this proposed expansion of vicarious liability. This is not surprising since *respondeat superior*, even within its traditional limits, rests not so much on policy grounds consistent with the governing principles of tort law as in a deeply rooted sentiment that a business enterprise cannot justly disclaim responsibility for accidents which may fairly be said to be characteristic of its activities. It is in this light that the inadequacy of the motive test becomes apparent. Whatever may have been the case in the past, a doctrine that would create such drastically different consequences for the actions of the drunken boatswain in *Nelson* and those of the drunken seaman here reflects a wholly unrealistic attitude toward the risks characteristically attendant upon the operation of a ship. We concur in the statement of Mr. Justice Rutledge in a case involving violence injuring a fellow-worker, in this instance, in the context of workmen's compensation:

> Men do not discard their personal qualities when they go to work. Into the job they carry their intelligence, skill, habits of care, and rectitude. Just as inevitably they take along also their tendencies to carelessness and camaraderie, as well as emotional make-up. In bringing men together, work brings these qualities together, causes frictions between them, creates occasions for lapses

---

[39] [5] We are not here speaking of cases in which the enterprise has negligently hired an employee whose undesirable propensities are known or should have been.

[40] [6] The record reveals that most modern dry docks have automatic locks to guard against unauthorized use of valves.

[41] [7] Although it is theoretically possible that shipowners would demand that drydock owners take appropriate action, see Coase, *The Problem of Social Cost*, 3 J.L. & Econ. 1 (1960), this would seem unlikely to occur in real life.

into carelessness, and for fun-making and emotional flare-up. . . . These expressions of human nature are incidents inseparable from working together. They involve risks of injury and these risks are inherent in the working environment.

Put another way, Lane's conduct was not so "unforeseeable" as to make it unfair to charge the Government with responsibility. We agree with a leading treatise that "what is reasonably foreseeable in this context [of *respondeat superior*] . . . is quite a different thing from the foreseeably unreasonable risk of harm that spells negligence. . . . The foresight that should impel the prudent man to take precautions is not the same measure as that by which he should perceive the harm likely to flow from his long-run activity in spite of all reasonable precautions on his own part. The proper test here bears far more resemblance to that which limits liability for workmen's compensation than to the test for negligence. The employer should be held to expect risks, to the public also, which arise 'out of and in the course' of his employment of labor." 2 Harper & James, The Law of Torts 1377–78 (1956). See also Calabresi, *Some Thoughts on Risk Distribution and the Law of Torts*, 70 Yale L.J. 499, 544 (1961). Here it was foreseeable that crew members crossing the drydock might do damage, negligently or even intentionally, such as pushing a Bushey employee or kicking property into the water. Moreover, the proclivity of seamen to find solace for solitude by copious resort to the bottle while ashore has been noted in opinions too numerous to warrant citation. Once all this is granted, it is immaterial that Lane's precise action was not to be foreseen. . . .

Consequently, we can no longer accept our past decisions that have refused to move beyond the *Nelson* rule, since they do not accord with modern understanding as to when it is fair for an enterprise to disclaim the actions of its employees.

One can readily think of cases that fall on the other side of the line. If Lane has set fire to the bar where he had been imbibing or had caused an accident on the street while returning to the drydock, the Government would not be liable; the activities of the "enterprise" do not reach into areas where the servant does not create risks different from those attendant on the activities of the community in general.

We agree with the district judge that if the seaman "upon returning to the drydock, recognized the Bushey security guard as his wife's lover and shot him," 276 F. Supp. at 530, vicarious liability would not follow; the incident would have related to the seaman's domestic life, not to his seafaring activity, and it would have been the most unlikely happenstance that the confrontation with the paramour occurred on a drydock rather than at the traditional spot. Here Lane had come within the closed-off area where his ship lay, to occupy a berth to which the Government insisted he have access, cf. Restatement, Agency 2d, § 267, and while his act is not readily explicable, at least it was not shown to be due entirely to facets of his personal life. The risk that seamen going and coming from the Tamaroa might cause damage to the drydock is enough to make it fair that the enterprise bear the loss. It is not a fatal objection that the rule we lay down lacks sharp contours; in the end, as Judge Andrews said in a related context, "it is all a question [of expediency,] . . . of fair judgment, always keeping in mind the fact that we endeavor to make a rule in each case that will be practical and in keeping with the general understanding of mankind."

Affirmed.

NOTES AND QUESTIONS

1. *Ira S. Bushey & Sons* provides one theory for avoiding the "motive" test articulated in *Bremen State Bank* (above) and other courts have embraced other rationales. For instance, the Alaska court has adopted an "enterprise liability" test: "Employees' acts sufficiently connected with the enterprise are in effect considered as deeds of the enterprise itself." *Doe v. Samaritan Counseling Center*, 791 P.2d 344

(Alaska 1990). Of course, determining when an employee's acts are sufficiently connected poses a new set of problems.

2. Other courts have looked to § 219(2)(d) of the Restatement (Second) of Agency, which imposes liability on a master for the torts of a servant acting outside of the scope of employment where the servant "was aided in accomplishing the tort by the existence of the agency relationship." Although this section restates cases in which the servant or employee was able to defraud a third party because of the agency position, several courts have applied more broadly. See, for example, *Costos v. Coconut Island Corp.*, 137 F.3d 46 (1st Cir. 1998), where the owner of an inn was held vicariously liable for the rape of a guest committed by the night manager. The court based its decision on § 219(2)(d). The Restatement (Third) of Agency rejects this theory of liability and, instead, adopts the traditional motive test — if the employee was not motivated to serve the employer's interest in committing the intentional tort, then the employer is not liable. RESTATEMENT (THIRD) OF AGENCY § 7.07(2) ("An employee's act is not within the scope of employment when it occurs within an independent course of conduct not intended by the employee to serve any purpose of the employer.")

3. An employer is generally not liable for punitive damages when liability is vicarious unless the employer authorized or ratified the tortious behavior. See *Campen v. Stone*, 635 P.2d 1121, 1124 (Wyo. 1981) for a discussion of the doctrine. Similarly, there is no vicarious criminal liability unless (a) the employer authorized or consented to the criminal conduct of the employee, or (b) the criminal statute in question was enacted for "the public morals, health, peace and safety." *See People v. Travers*, 52 Cal. App. 3d 111, 124 Cal. Rptr. 728, 729–31 (1975) (affirming the criminal conviction of an otherwise innocent employer for an employee's sale of mislabeled motor oil).

PROBLEM

Alan was employed by Dominator Pizzas to deliver pizzas. Alan used his own car, but wore a Dominator Pizzas shirt when he made deliveries. While returning back to the store after delivering several pizzas, Bart negligently ran into Alan's car. In the course of exchanging information, Bart insulted Alan, prompting Alan to assault Bart, seriously injuring Bart. Bart has sued Dominator Pizzas. What result?

Chapter 3
THE LAW OF UNINCORPORATED BUSINESS ENTITIES

A. INTRODUCTION

Most businesses in the United States are unincorporated. That simple fact is often overlooked, as the vast majority of publicly held business entities are incorporated and they tend to grab most of the business headlines. But many privately held businesses, and most start-up businesses, elect not to incorporate. Once an entrepreneur makes that decision, a wide array of choices is available:

- *Sole proprietorship.* If an individual undertakes to engage in business without partners and without any organizational forethought, that individual is a sole proprietor. She will be personally liable for all of the debts of the business, including any tort liability, and will personally recognize the income or loss of the business on her personal income tax return. She may finance the business out of her personal accounts, freely commingling business with personal finances. No legal requirement exists for separate books and records, although the proprietor may wish to maintain separate books to determine how well, or poorly, the business is faring. There are probably more than 20 million sole proprietorships in the United States.

- *General partnership.* A general partnership is a default entity in the law. If two or more entrepreneurs join together to operate a business, they have thereby wittingly, or unwittingly, formed a general partnership. They need not file any document with the state to formalize or legitimize their undertaking. They will each be jointly and severally liable for all debts, including tort liability, of the business and each will be an agent for the other, with full agency authority to bind one another on obligations of the business. They can alter this by agreement, but in the absence of agreement, the common law, and today partnership statutes, provides these default rules. Like a sole proprietorship, partners will recognize a pro rata share of the business's income or loss on their personal income tax returns.

- *Limited liability partnership.* A limited liability partnership, or LLP, is a general partnership with an important modification: the partners are not personally liable for the debts and obligations of the business except to the extent they have agreed to be (for contractual obligations) or bear personal fault (for tort obligations). To obtain the advantages of limited liability, the partnership must file a document with the designated state office.

- *Limited partnership.* The limited partnership is a creature of statute formed by filing a document with a designated office in the state. The limited partnership in its simplest form has two classes of partners: general and limited. General partners in a limited partnership are like general partners in a conventional partnership, which includes having personal liability for the debts of the business.[1] For federal income tax purposes, limited and general partners are treated as partners in a general partnership. By statute the limited partners are not liable for the debts of the business, although care must be exercised in some states about their participation in control. They do not have agency authority as limited partners, although they can contract otherwise.

- *Limited liability limited partnership.* A limited liability limited partnership

---

[1] Often, a limited partnership will have a corporate general partner, as an "end run" around the liability issue.

(LLLP) is a limited partnership in which the general partner(s) has limited liability, akin to the liability of a partner in an LLP. To secure this limited liability, the partnership must file an election in a designated office in the state.

- *Limited liability company.* A limited liability company (LLC) is the newest option for our entrepreneur, offering the benefits of limited liability, taxation as a partnership, and management flexibility. Liability is limited in the sense that owners (called "members") are not liable as such for the debts of the business, in the same way that partners in an LLP are not liable. The LLC can elect to be "manager managed," in which case only those persons designated as managers have agency authority. Such an LLC is similar to a LLLP. Or, the LLC can elect to be "member managed," in which case all members have agency authority and participate in management. Such an LLC is akin to an LLP. As with LLPs and LLLPs, entrepreneurs forming an LLP must file a document with the state.

Each of the entities noted above, and the various statutes that govern them, is considered in greater detail in the materials that follow. A few general observations are, however, in order. First, in most states, the statutes related to general and limited partnerships are linked. The limited partnership statutes historically were an overlay on general partnership statutes in the sense that the latter governed the rights, obligations and liabilities of the general partners in the limited partnership. Therefore, a court considering, say, a governance problem related to a limited partnership would look to the general partnership statute. This tradition is changing, as the most recent uniform limited partnership statute (the Uniform Limited Partnership Act (2001)) is self-contained and de-links the limited partnership from the general partnership statute.

Second, parties forming any of the entities noted above should consider the applicability of the securities laws. Any passive investment may be deemed to be a "security," and the issuer of that security must register the sale with the Securities and Exchange Commission (and perhaps state regulators), or find an exemption from the registration requirement. The applicability of the securities laws is considered in greater detail in Chapter 5, *infra*.

Third, while the short introduction above suggests that the various entities are "pass-through" entities for purposes of federal income taxation, the organizers can elect to have the entity taxed as a corporation. Recent changes in the federal tax law — known as the "check-the-box" regulations — have allowed unincorporated entities to choose between pass-through taxation and corporate taxation. Prior to the adoption of these regulations, unincorporated entities often had to demonstrate to the IRS that they were more like partnerships than corporations if they sought pass-through taxation. The IRS employed a four-part test to make the determination. With the check-the-box regulations, that complexity has dropped out of business planning.

Fourth, recent legislative changes have facilitated conversions from one entity into another, and the merger of different kinds of entities. For instance, various statutes allow an easy conversion of, say, a corporation to a limited liability company or the merger of a limited liability partnership and a limited partnership. The National Conference of Commissioners on Uniform State Laws (NCCUSL) and the ABA have been developing a model act to deal with the conversions and mergers of business entities. See Model Entity Transactions Act, the most recent draft of which is available at http://www.law.upenn.edu/bll/archives/ulc/ueta/2005OctMETAfinal.htm.

At this point, the discerning reader may be asking himself or herself whether the proliferation of business entities makes sense. The short answer is no, it does not, but that something is being done about it. These entities came about as a result of lawyers seeking legislation to solve problems for their business clients, without being concerned too much about the "big picture." Now, however, a growing number of lawyers, legal scholars, and legislatures are concerned about this problem. Several years ago, the ABA appointed an ad hoc committee to study the question. (The Ad Hoc Committee on Entity Rationalization. *See* 57 Bus. Law. 1569 (2002).) A number of scholarly articles have appeared and several legislatures are seeking to streamline their business entity statutes. Progress is slow, however, and whether we will see a reduction in the number of entities remains to be seen. For a fuller discussion of this, see Mark J. Loewenstein, *A New Direction for State Corporate Codes*, 68 U. Colo. L. Rev. 453–73 (1997).

B.   GENERAL PARTNERSHIPS

1.   The Definition of a Partnership

If two or more persons associate together to carry on as co-owners a business for profit, they have formed a partnership, whether or not they intended to form a partnership. Thus, partnership is a default entity: the parties who fall within this definition do not need a written or even an oral agreement and need file no documents to form their partnership. Each state has adopted a partnership statute, generally tracking the Revised Uniform Partnership Act of 1997 (RUPA) or its predecessor, the Uniform Partnership Act (1914) (UPA), that describes the rights, duties and liabilities of partners, among other things. The definition set forth above is close paraphrase of the definition set forth in § 202(a) of RUPA.

Irrespective of whether UPA or RUPA applies, a partnership is primarily a contractual entity; that parties are free to shape their relationship in any way that they choose. The contractual nature of partnership was implicit in UPA and explicit in RUPA. RUPA § 103(b) sets forth an exclusive list of nonwaivable provisions in the Act; outside of those limitations, the parties are free to contract as they wish. The remaining provisions are then just default rules.

The consequences of determining that parties are partners of one another can be significant. As noted above, partners can bind one another to contracts and can be liable for one another's torts, among other things. Whether a partnership has been formed or not may be the most frequently litigated question in partnership law. The next case is a good example of how a court weighs the various elements.

ZIEGLER v. DAHL

Supreme Court of North Dakota

691 N.W.2d 271 (2005)

Sandstrom, Justice.

Michael Ziegler and Jack Kitsch appeal a summary judgment dismissing their claim that they were in a partnership with Steve Dahl, David Tronson, and James Legacie and are entitled to an accounting upon the winding up of the partnership. We affirm the district court's summary judgment.

Dahl, along with Tronson and Legacie, began marketing an ice fishing guide service on Devils Lake after the 1996–1997 ice fishing season. In the spring of 1997, Dahl conceived the name "Perch Patrol" for the guide service when he was asked by the local chamber of commerce to guide a camera crew from Midwest Outdoors Television. Dahl testified in his affidavit that each member of Perch Patrol agreed to be an independent contractor, each responsible for obtaining his own license and equipment. Dahl claimed they retained their own fees, but equally shared clients and marketing expenses.

Dahl asked Ziegler and Kitsch to help Perch Patrol guide ice fishermen on Devils Lake for the last part of the 1998–1999 ice fishing season. Ziegler testified in his affidavit that he considered Kitsch and himself employees of Perch Patrol for the remaining portion of the 1998–1999 season. They were paid for drilling holes in the ice, setting up shelters, and ensuring that the ice fishing clients were properly equipped. Neither Ziegler nor Kitsch had any client contact during that year.

Dahl presented Ziegler and Kitsch with a document titled "Perch Patrol Expansion" in the spring of 1999. The document contained sections called "Employee Proposal" and

"Partnership Proposal." Under the "Employee Proposal," Ziegler and Kitsch would receive 50 percent of the number of clients over six per day, and Dahl, Tronson, and Legacie would provide all of the fishing equipment. Under the "Partnership Proposal," Ziegler and Kitsch would "be their own separate entity under the Perch Patrol" and both parties would be "responsible for providing their own gear including fish houses, heaters, vexilars, augers, chairs, bait lunches, ect [sic]." The partnership proposal also provided that both "parties shall share equally in both the costs and the efforts in these endeavors." The parties did not adopt either proposal.

The parties later agreed, but never reduced their agreement to writing, that Dahl, Tronson, and Legacie had the right to guide and receive fees from the first six clients, Ziegler and Kitsch had the next four, and Dahl, Tronson, and Legacie had clients 11, 12, 15, 16, 19, and 20. The agreement was later changed to split the fees received from each client after the first ten, and they agreed to divide equally among the five members the tips received by the guides.

In November 1999, Dahl registered the trade name Perch Patrol with the North Dakota Secretary of State. On November 20, 1999, Ziegler and Kitsch each wrote a check payable to Dahl in the amount of $813.97. Ziegler and Kitsch claim the checks were an initial capital investment in a partnership, and Dahl claims they were for future marketing expenses. Dahl stated in his affidavit that he was responsible for all administrative activities for Perch Patrol, including establishing marketing agreements and plans with resorts, promoting the venture in promotional media, booking all reservations, distributing clients to guides, handling all funds, and planning each day's activities. All the parties attended at least some trade shows to promote the Perch Patrol guide service prior to the start of the 1999 ice fishing season.

On August 8, 2000, Dahl, Tronson, and Legacie informed Ziegler and Kitsch they could no longer guide with them. Dahl, Tronson, and Legacie continue to operate under the name Perch Patrol, which has been registered to Dahl with the Secretary of State as a Limited Liability Partnership since 2002.

The district court granted the motion for summary judgment dismissing Ziegler and Kitsch's claim that they were in a partnership, stating there was insufficient evidence to support a finding that a partnership was created . . .

. . . Ziegler argues the district court erred as a matter of law by requiring intent as an element of a partnership.

One of the most important tests of whether a partnership exists between two persons is the intent of the parties. North Dakota adopted the Revised Uniform Partnership Act in 1995, adding the words "whether or not the persons intend to form a partnership" to the definition of a partnership. 1995 N.D. Sess. Laws. ch. 430, § 4. The drafters of the uniform law did not intend any substantive changes in the current law when they added the additional phrase to the definition of a partnership. UNIFORM PARTNERSHIP ACT § 202, cmt. 1 (1997); *Byker v. Mannes*, 465 Mich. 637, 641 N.W.2d 210, 214 (2002). The addition of the phrase, "whether or not the persons intend to form a partnership," merely codifies the universal judicial construction of UPA Section 6(1) that a partnership is created by the association of persons whose intent is to carry on as co-owners a business for profit, regardless of their subjective intention to be "partners." Indeed, they may inadvertently create a partnership despite their expressed subjective intention not to do so. The new language alerts readers to this possibility.

. . . We have said participants in a business "must intend to be part of an association that includes *all* the essential elements of a partnership for that association to be a partnership." *Gangl v. Gangl*, 281 N.W.2d 574, 580 (N.D. 1979); *see also Tarnavsky v. Tarnavsky*, 147 F.3d 674 (8th Cir. 1998) (the actions of the parties evidence their intent to be partners). The existence of this element focuses "on the intent of the participants to be a part of a relationship which includes the other essential elements of [a] partnership." *Id.* Intent does not need to "be vocalized either in writing or orally, if it can be derived from the actions of the parties." *Id.*

Ziegler and Kitsch argue that both this Court and the federal [*sic*] district court failed to recognize the statutory change that incorporated into the definition of a partnership the language of whether or not a party intends to be a partner. They believe the language used in both *Tarnavsky* cases oversimplifies the meaning of intent of the parties and their holdings should be rejected. They argue, even if the district court correctly analyzed the intent element, the parties' intent to form a partnership is evidenced by Dahl's written "Partnership Proposal."

Their argument is misplaced. The addition of the phrase, "whether or not the persons intend to form a partnership," to North Dakota's statute does not change the elements of partnership formation. The purpose of the phrase was to clarify that a partnership could be created regardless of the parties' subjective intent, making it possible for individuals to inadvertently create a partnership despite their expressed subjective intent not to do so. We held in *Gangl* that parties must intend to be a part of a relationship that includes the other essential elements of a partnership, and to do things that further their co-ownership of a business for profit. The addition to the statutory definition did not change this requirement.

Dahl stated in his affidavit that neither he nor Tronson nor Legacie considered themselves, much less Ziegler or Kitsch, partners in Perch Patrol. Dahl said that he considered Perch Patrol to be an association of independent contractors and that Ziegler and Kitsch would be their own entities. The Perch Patrol expansion document given to Ziegler and Kitsch by Dahl did use the term partnership, but this proposal was never adopted. In Ziegler's affidavit, he said the parties did not accept the terms of the document, but contends the final agreement reflected the initial proposal. The terminology that parties give to their working arrangement is not determinative, "especially where the record indicates the parties did not intend to be a part of a relationship which included the other essential elements of a partnership." *Gangl*, 281 N.W.2d at 580. There was no evidence that Dahl or Tronson or Legacie intended to engage in activities that would form a partnership with Ziegler and Kitsch.

Other actions by the parties do not manifest an intent to form a relationship that constitutes a partnership. The parties did not file a partnership tax return, Dahl handled all of the administrative activities, each party provided his own equipment, and all of the major decisions were made without the input and direction of Ziegler and Kitsch. Ziegler and Kitsch argue the $813.97 checks written to Dahl were capital contributions showing their intent to buy into the partnership. Dahl, and even Ziegler in his affidavit, testified the checks were contributions toward meeting future partnership expenses. Because the parties never intended to engage in activities that would result in a partnership, the intent element is not satisfied.

Ziegler and Kitsch argue that the district court disregarded competent evidence when it concluded they had no right of control in the business and that the court incorrectly concluded a partner needs ultimate control in the partnership.

Co-ownership is the second necessary element to prove the existence of a partnership. *Tarnavsky*, 147 F.3d at 677–78. Co-ownership includes the "sharing of profits and losses as well as the power of control in the management of the business." *Id.* Control is an indispensable component of the co-ownership analysis. *Gangl*, 281 N.W.2d at 580. If partners are co-owners of a business, they each have the power of ultimate control. *Id.* (citing UNIFORM PARTNERSHIP ACT § 6, cmt. 1 (1914)). An important qualification to that rule, however, is that a person does not need to control the business but only needs to have the right to exercise control in the management of the business. *Id*

. . .

Ziegler and Kitsch argue the district court incorrectly sifted through evidence and became a fact finder, and the question of control should have gone to the jury to weigh the evidence and make a finding. Kitsch said in his affidavit that he participated in and made decisions regarding where to fish and that he provided other valuable knowledge and skill to Perch Patrol. He and Ziegler also claim Dahl contacted them daily to discuss business issues regarding Perch Patrol. Dahl said in his affidavit that no vote was ever taken on any issue relating to the operation and management of Perch Patrol and that he and Tronson and Legacie operated and managed all of the business functions. Dahl, in his affidavit, and Kitsch, in his deposition, said that Dahl was responsible for all of the administrative work for Perch Patrol. Ziegler and Kitsch stated in their depositions that they did what they were directed to do by Dahl, who told them which clients to guide and which ice, media, and trade shows to attend.

Ziegler and Kitsch failed to demonstrate that the discussions they had with Dahl were about the management and control of the business and that their discussions affected the activities of Perch Patrol . . .

There must be a "community of interest in the profits of the business, and an agreement or right to share profits, and, generally, an obligation to share losses as well." 59A Am. Jur. 2d *Partnership* § 149 (2003). The sharing of gross returns does not per se establish a partnership, because those returns could have been received in payment for "services as an independent contractor or of wages or other compensation to an employee." N.D.C.C. § 45-14-02(3)(b), (c)(2); *Tarnavsky*, 147 F.3d at 678.

Under the working agreement, Dahl, Tronson, and Legacie were entitled to the first six clients and Ziegler and Kitsch were allocated the next four. Each party received the fees generated by guiding his own clients, and they did not pool or divide these fees. Ziegler and Kitsch could have gone the entire winter without receiving any client fees had there been no more than six clients per day, because each guide received money only for services he actually performed. Ziegler testified in his affidavit that Dahl periodically collected the fees generated each day and distributed the revenues after deducting shared expenses for telephone bills and office supplies, and that each person was responsible for one-fifth of these expenses. Income used to pay partnership expenses is not profit. 59A Am. Jur. 2d *Partnership* § 152 (2003) (citing *Gangl*, 281 N.W.2d 574). A profit is the amount remaining after the expenses of the partnership are paid. *Id.* After Dahl deducted expenses, the money went directly to the individuals who guided the clients and was not shared with any other member of Perch Patrol. This fee structure used by Perch Patrol correlates more closely with an independent contractor payment system than with profit sharing among partners.

The final element of a partnership is the necessity of a profit motive. *Tarnavsky*, 147 F.3d at 678. Dahl testified during his deposition that his intent was to make a profit guiding, and there is no dispute that Perch Patrol was operated to generate client fees.

We conclude the district court did not err in ordering summary judgment, because Ziegler and Kitsch failed to show that the first two elements were present in their working agreement. . . . We therefore affirm the summary judgment.

QUESTION

Suppose the parties had agreed to share the fees from their guiding activities according to some formula based on the number of clients served. Would that have changed the outcome?

2. When a Partner Is Not a Partner

SERAPION v. MARTINEZ
United States Court of Appeals, First Circuit
119 F.3d 982 (1997)

Selya, Circuit Judge.

This appeal requires us to explore a gray area in the emerging jurisprudence of Title VII, 42 U.S.C. §§ 2000e to 2000e-17 (1994). Having completed that task, we conclude that while Title VII's employment-related shelter might in certain circumstances extend to a person who is a partner in a law firm, plaintiff-appellant Margarita Serapion, a partner in the now-disbanded law firm of Martinez, Odell, Calabria & Sierra (the Firm), is not entitled to such shelter here. Consequently, we affirm the lower court's entry of summary judgment in the defendants' favor.

In explaining our rationale, we take a slightly unorthodox course. We begin with the facts, then shift to a discussion of the statutory scheme, and then resume our historical account by describing the course of the litigation. In succession, we thereafter rehearse the summary judgment standard, limn the doctrinal parameters of the requisite Title VII inquiry, address the merits, iron out a procedural wrinkle, and at long last conclude.

I. THE FACTUAL PREDICATE

Serapion earned a distinguished reputation as a certified public accountant before deciding to switch careers. After graduating from the University of Puerto Rico Law School with honors in 1982, she joined the San Juan law firm of Colorado, Martinez, Odell, Calabria & Sierra as an associate. She left in 1983 for a stint in government service but returned in 1985. In the interim, Colorado had departed and the partnership had been reconstituted. Approximately one year later, the appellant was admitted into the Firm as a "junior" partner (sometimes termed a "non-proprietary" partner). While this status did not give her any equity position, it did give her some profit distribution units (PDUs) and enabled her to participate in meetings of the Board of Partners (a body which comprised all the partners, senior and junior — in the aggregate, roughly half the Firm's lawyers — and which had the ultimate responsibility for management and policymaking).

In 1990, Serapion became what is variously described as a "senior" or "proprietary" partner. Theretofore, the Firm's four name partners (all males) were the only other proprietary partners. They enjoyed equality among themselves in respect to compensation, PDUs, benefits, and equity, and they promised Serapion that she would be elevated to an equal partnership in three years. In the meantime, her status as a proprietary partner brought about several changes in her working conditions: she received a 4% equity interest in the Firm (ceded 1% by each name partner); she assumed *pro rata* liability for the Firm's debts, losses, and other obligations; and she became a voting member of the Executive Committee (a five-member group which was responsible for the Firm's day-to-day management). When the appellant became a proprietary partner, the Firm increased her allocation of PDUs to 75 units. Concomitantly, she began reaping a correspondingly larger share of the Firm's profits. Under the terms of the 1990 agreement, her allotment of PDUs (and, therefore, her share of the profits) was to continue to rise in increments until the end of 1992 when Serapion would achieve full parity with the four name partners.

Despite these emoluments, Serapion was not on an equal footing with the name partners. Each of them had a greater equity interest (24% apiece) and a more munificent compensation package (roughly one-third higher than hers in 1990, although the gap gradually closed). The difference in compensation was largely, if not entirely, a function of the disparate allocation of PDUs. Still, although her allotment of PDUs was less than that of the name partners, it was nonetheless significantly greater than that of even the most well-endowed junior partner.

Serapion alleges that three of her partners (Fred H. Martinez, Lawrence Odell, and Jose Luis Calabria) never intended that a woman would achieve parity. These partners, she says, connived to prevent her from reaping the fruits of her bargain, eventually demanding that she sign an agreement which would have significantly diminished her authority within the Firm. When Serapion stood her ground, the trio caused the Firm to dissolve in 1992 (shortly before the expiration of the three-year phase-in period) and simultaneously forged a new partnership called "Martinez, Odell & Calabria." The nascent firm included the three men, as well as most of the Firm's other lawyers. The founders did not invite either Serapion or Sierra (the remaining proprietary partner) to join.

II. THE STATUTORY SCHEME

We pause at this juncture to sketch the legal landscape. Title VII is one of the brightest stars in the firmament of this nation's antidiscrimination laws. Generally speaking, it bars certain employment-related actions undertaken on the basis of impermissible criteria (such as gender). . . .

The Firm is plainly an employer for Title VII purposes. After all, an employer is defined by statute as "a person engaged in an industry affecting commerce," and the statute makes clear that "a person" in this context can include a partnership. The rub is whether Serapion is an employee.

Although the language we have quoted speaks of "any individual," courts long ago concluded that Title VII is directed at, and only protects, employees and potential employees. We know, moreover, that a single individual in a single occupational setting cannot be both an employer and an employee for purposes of Title VII. Even so, the parameters of the term "employee" have proven elusive. Title VII defines an employee only as "an individual employed by an employer," 42 U.S.C. § 2000e(f), a turn of phrase which chases its own tail.

. . . There is a developing jurisprudence under Title VII. In it, we detect precedential value not only in cases which actually involve partnerships, but also in decisions which have determined the status of individuals by analogy to a partnership paradigm (even though the individuals involved were principals of entities other than partnerships). We do not, however, hitch our wagon to cases deciding whether a particular individual is an employee as opposed to an independent contractor. That distinction is between those who are part of an employer's business and those who are running their own businesses, and the factors central to that inquiry are inapposite here.

There are also a few cases which deal directly with whether a partner in a professional practice should be regarded as an employee for the purpose of Title VII (and, therefore, entitled to its safeguards). The seminal case is *Burke v. Friedman*, 556 F.2d 867, 869–70 (7th Cir. 1977), in which the court held that partners in an accounting firm were not employees vis-à-vis Title VII. This interpretation received a modicum of support in *Hishon v. King & Spalding*, 467 U.S. 69, 104 S. Ct. 2229, 81 L.Ed.2d 59 (1984). Although the *Hishon* Court answered a different question — holding that Title VII precluded a law firm from denying partnership consideration to an associate on the basis of her gender, *see id.* at 76–78, 104 S. Ct. at 2234–35 — Justice Powell cautioned that the majority opinion did "not require that the relationship among partners be characterized as an 'employment' relationship to which Title VII would apply." *Id.* at 79, 104 S. Ct. at 2236 (Powell, J., concurring). Since *Hishon*, several appellate courts have followed Justice Powell's lead and declared, with varying nuances, that partners are not protected as employees under federal antidiscrimination laws. *See Simpson v. Ernst & Young*, 100 F.3d 436, 443 (6th Cir. 1996), *cert. denied*, 520 U.S. 1248, 117 S. Ct.

1862, 137 L.Ed.2d 1062 (1997); *Wheeler*, 825 F.2d at 263; *accord* EEOC Decision No. 85-4, 2 Empl. Prac. Guide (CCH) ¶ 6846, at 7040–41 & n.4 (1985).

As we visualize it, the key inquiry is into the attributes of the relationship between the partnership and those whom it styles as partners. The method by which this inquiry is to be conducted — how a court determines whether an individual labelled as a partner is to be treated as an employee for purposes of Title VII — is an unresolved issue which lies at the epicenter of this appeal.

III. THE LITIGATION

When her three former partners folded the Firm and dashed her expectations of proprietary parity, Serapion sued them and their new firm (Martinez, Odell & Calabria) in Puerto Rico's federal district court. She charged in her complaint that the defendants had violated both Title VII and local law. After the defendants' early attempt to obtain summary judgment misfired, the parties engaged in pretrial discovery. Thereafter, the defendants renewed their quest for *brevis* disposition. Their new motion relied on alternative grounds. It averred that Serapion, as a partner in the Firm, was not an employee (and, therefore, had no recourse to Title VII). It also averred that Serapion had not adduced any competent proof that gender-based discrimination caused the Firm's disintegration (an event which the defendants attributed to irreconcilable differences between two warring factions of proprietary partners).

Judge Casellas granted the defendants' motion, holding that Serapion was not an employee as that term had been developed in federal jurisprudence and that she was thus ineligible for the prophylaxis of Title VII. See *Serapion v. Martinez*, 942 F. Supp. 80, 84–85 (D.P.R. 1996). The court held alternatively that Serapion had failed to make out a prima facie case of discrimination under Title VII. *See id.* at 85–87. Finally, the court refused to exercise supplemental jurisdiction over the pendent claim and dismissed that claim without prejudice to its pursuit in the courts of Puerto Rico. *See id.* at 88–89. This appeal followed.

IV. THE SUMMARY JUDGMENT STANDARD

. . . .

V. THE DOCTRINAL PARAMETERS

Putting this appeal into proper perspective requires us to articulate the doctrinal parameters which inform an inquiry into a partner's status vis-à-vis Title VII. We divide our discussion into two segments.

A.

Partnerships are mutable structures, and partners come in varying shapes and sizes. Consequently, attempting to delineate the circumstances in which a particular partner should be regarded as an employee for Title VII purposes is tricky business. Although one court has hinted at the desirability of a *per se* rule, saying in effect that all members of professional services corporations were employees for purposes of the antidiscrimination laws (there, the ADEA), no matter how significant a role they played in managing the affairs of the corporation, we reject the notion that labels can conclusively resolve status inquiries. We hold instead that the Title VII question cannot be decided solely on the basis that a partnership calls — or declines to call — a person a partner. A court must peer beneath the label and probe the actual circumstances of the person's relationship with the partnership. In other words, partnerships cannot exclude individuals from the protection of Title VII simply by draping them in grandiose titles which convey little or no substance. . . .

B.

Having determined that federal law controls the question of the appellant's status, we turn next to an analysis of those attributes of a partner's relationship to the partnership which may influence the decisional calculus. In this endeavor, we do not write on a pristine page. Two other courts of appeals have tried their hands at plotting the line which divides partners who may be treated as employees under federal antidiscrimination statutes from those who may not.

In *Simpson*, the Sixth Circuit considered the status for ADEA purposes of an individual denominated a partner by an international accounting firm. In attempting to ascertain whether the plaintiff, notwithstanding his title, qualified as a person protected by the ADEA, the court weighed factors such as:

> the right and duty to participate in management; the right and duty to act as an agent of other partners; exposure to liability; the fiduciary relationship among partners . . . participation in profits and losses; investment in the firm; partial ownership of firm assets; voting rights; the aggrieved individual's ability to control and operate the business; the extent to which the aggrieved individual's compensation was calculated as a percentage of the firm's profits; the extent of that individual's employment security; and other similar indicia of ownership.

Simpson, 100 F.3d at 443–44. Concluding that the plaintiff more closely resembled an employee than a proprietor — the court noted particularly that the plaintiff had no right either to participate in the partnership's management decisions or to vote for those who did, and that his compensation was not determined on the basis of the firm's profits — the court allowed the plaintiff to sue under the ADEA. *See id.* at 441–43.

The Tenth Circuit grappled with the same sort of conundrum in *Wheeler*, a case which also involved a partner in an accounting firm. In determining that the plaintiff was not an employee for purposes of either Title VII or the ADEA, the *Wheeler* court focused on her participation in firm profits and losses, her exposure to liability, her investment in the firm, and her voting rights under the partnership agreement. *See Wheeler*, 825 F.2d at 276. . . .

We think that these cases provide valuable guidance concerning the factors which courts must consider in making status determinations under Title VII. In large, the critical attributes of proprietary status involve three broad, overlapping categories: ownership, remuneration, and management. Within these categories, emphasis will vary depending on the circumstances of particular cases. Nonetheless, although myriad factors may influence a court's ultimate decision in a given case, we recount a non-exclusive list of factors that frequently will bear upon such determinations.

Under the first category, relevant factors include investment in the firm, ownership of firm assets, and liability for firm debts and obligations. To the extent that these factors exist, they indicate a proprietary role; to the extent that they do not exist, they indicate a status more akin to that of an employee.

Under the second category, the most relevant factor is whether (and if so, to what extent) the individual's compensation is based on the firm's profits. To the extent that a partner's remuneration is subject to the vagaries of the firm's economic fortunes, her status more closely resembles that of a proprietor; conversely, to the extent that a partner is paid on a straight salary basis, the argument for treating her as an ordinary employee will gain strength. A second potentially relevant factor in this regard relates to fringe benefits. An individual who receives benefits of a kind or in an amount markedly more generous than similarly situated employees who possess no ownership interest is more likely to be a proprietor.

Under the third category, relevant factors include the right to engage in policymaking; participation in, and voting power with regard to, firm governance; the ability to assign work and to direct the activities of employees within the firm; and the ability to act for the firm and its principals. Once again, to the extent that these factors exist, they indicate a proprietary role.

We add a note of caution. Status determinations are necessarily made along a continuum. The cases that lie at the polar extremes will prove easy to resolve. The close cases, however, will require a concerned court to make a case-specific assessment of whether a particular situation is nearer to one end of the continuum or the other. In performing this assessment, no single factor should be accorded talismanic significance. Rather, a status determination under Title VII must be founded on the totality of the circumstances which pertain in a particular case. Given these verities, any effort to formulate a hard-and-fast rule would likely result in a statement that was overly simplistic, or too general to be of any real help, or both.

VI. THE MERITS

To complete our journey, we must undertake a particularized analysis aimed at determining whether the lower court, *at the summary judgment stage*, appropriately could conclude that Serapion was not an employee of the Firm within the purview of Title VII. Consistent with the summary judgment protocol, we focus only on uncontested documentary proof, such as the provisions of the partnership agreement and the minutes of the Firm's Executive Committee meetings (every page of which bears the appellant's initials), supplemented by facts asserted by the appellant and those conceded by her.

The factors relevant to ownership and remuneration provide powerful indications that the appellant should not be treated as an employee for Title VII purposes. It is undisputed that Serapion received an equity interest in the Firm upon being named a proprietary partner. Her compensation was predicated in substantial measure on the Firm's profits,[2] and she would have been liable had the Firm sustained losses. In the ensuing months, she made substantial capital contributions to the Firm. She also received very generous fringe benefits, e.g., a car allowance in excess of $10,000 per annum and a discretionary expense allowance of $16,400 yearly. These benefits were comparable to those received by the other proprietary partners, but more extravagant than the benefits available to junior partners and associates.

The picture is only slightly less clear as to the management prong of the test. As a proprietary partner, the appellant participated meaningfully in the Firm's governance. Unlike non-proprietary partners (who were allowed to attend Board of Partners' meetings but could vote only on matters affecting their own interests), proprietary partners were guaranteed a vote in all matters brought before the Board. The partnership agreement describes this tribunal as "the highest policy and decision making body of the Firm." Furthermore, the appellant's vote had added significance: if an impasse developed between a majority of the Board and 4/5ths of the proprietary partners, the decision of the proprietary partners controlled. While the appellant belittles Board membership, voting status in a law firm's highest decisionmaking body is no small thing. The fact that the membership consisted of roughly half the lawyers in

---

[2] [6] Whereas associates in the Firm received fixed compensation (plus an occasional bonus based on performance), all partners (senior and junior) received a base salary supplemented by a share of the Firm's profits paid out periodically in proportion to each partner's allotment of PDUs. For example, when the appellant first ascended to proprietary partnership, her overall compensation was composed of a base salary ($60,183 per annum) plus a share of the firm's profits (amounting to approximately $30,000 during her first year as a proprietary partner). Her total compensation was pegged to 75% of what the four name partners received (resulting in gross remuneration appreciably higher than that earned by any non-proprietary partner). Her percentage allocation increased steadily during the period that followed, so that, at the time the Firm dissolved in 1992, her total compensation equalled 92% of the total compensation paid to each of the name partners.

the Firm dilutes, but does not dispel, the significance of such membership.[3]

Serapion's involvement in management went well beyond membership in the Board of Partners. She served as one of five voting members of the Executive Committee, which managed the Firm's day-to-day operations and regularly decided matters relating to salaries, finances, fee schedules, office space, employee performance, recruitment, admission of new partners, acceptance of business, work assignments, and the staffing of cases. In a period of about two years, the appellant attended no fewer than sixteen of these meetings and wrote up the minutes. A review of Serapion's handiwork shows her to have been a robust participant in important policy decisions; for example, the minutes reflect that she made several motions anent the admission of new partners. The Executive Committee was the nerve center of the Firm. The appellant's membership on it, coupled with her degree of involvement in management generally, strongly suggests that she was not an employee. So, too, does the fact that she had authority to act as an agent for the Firm and its partners; one manifestation of this authority was that, after she became a senior partner, the Firm empowered her to sign checks drawn on its accounts.

The appellant does not go gently into this dark night. For the most part, she strives to refocus our attention on the ways in which she possessed less power than the four name partners. She complains that her name was never added to the Firm's name; that neither her compensation nor her equity interest ever equalled that of the name partners; that she had less authority to assign matters within the Firm; and that she did not head any of the Firm's departments. But this constellation of complaints assumes that all partners except those equivalent in stature and authority to the most powerful partners of a law firm are employees for Title VII purposes. The assumption lacks any solid legal underpinning. A person with the requisite attributes of proprietary status is properly considered a proprietor, not an employee, regardless of the fact that others in the firm may wield more power.

The appellant also makes a closely related argument, noting that she rarely got her way on disputed matters and that she dissented from many decisions. But focusing on the fact that her views sometimes did not prevail confuses participation with control. Insofar as the management prong of the test is concerned, the hallmarks of proprietary status are the right to participate in decisionmaking and the right to have a meaningful say in governance. Within the structure of any organization, certain individuals tend to dominate others, and the dominators' viewpoints will more often be adopted. This phenomenon often occurs among equals (Adams reportedly wrote to Jefferson on November 12, 1813, describing Dickinson as "primus inter pares, the bellwether, the leader of the aristocratical flock") and, in all events, the exercise of hegemony by one partner does not automatically dislodge others in the hierarchy from proprietary status. Elsewise, all the partners in a law firm or an accounting practice, save only the managing partner(s), would be treated as employees for Title VII purposes regardless of the extent of their ownership or the correlation between their remuneration and the entity's profits. The law is to the contrary: it is not a necessary corollary of proprietary status that the views of the partner in question will always — or even usually — prevail.

In this case, all roads lead to Rome. The evidence is uncontradicted that the appellant had an ownership interest in the Firm; that her compensation depended substantially on the Firm's fortunes; and that she enjoyed significant voting rights in the Firm's two principal governing bodies. Given these undisputed facts, no reasonable factfinder could conclude that Margarita Serapion was other than a bona fide equity partner, and, as such, a person ineligible to claim the protection which Title VII reserves for those who are employees. Consequently, the district court did not err in granting summary

---

[3] [7] We take judicial notice of the fact that many law firms have partner/associate ratios near one-to-one, yet few lawyers working for these firms would deny that the partners enjoy a status fundamentally different from that of the associates.

judgment in the defendants' favor on the Title VII claim. . . .

Affirmed.

NOTES AND QUESTIONS

1. Courts look to several factors to determine whether the parties have formed a partnership. For instance, in *McDowell v. McDowell*, 143 S.W.3d 124, 129 (Tex. App. 2004), the court, citing RUPA, identified the following factors as relevant to whether a partnership or joint venture has been formed:

(1) receipt or right to receive a share of the profits of the business;

(2) expression of an intent to be partners in the business;

(3) participation or right to participate in the control of the business;

(4) sharing or agreeing to share:

　(A) losses of the business; or

　(B) liability for claims by third parties against the business; and

(5) contribution or agreeing to contribute money or property to the business.

The court stated that no one factor was dispositive and not all factors need be satisfied.

2. Many aspects of the spousal relationship resemble a partnership, particularly when one of the spouses conducts a business as a sole proprietor with the support of the other spouse. *Lampe v. Williamson*, 331 F.3d 750 (10th Cir. 2003), which arose in a bankruptcy setting, considered the claim by the Trustee in bankruptcy that a farm run by the husband was actually owned by a partnership consisting of both spouses when the wife argued that she co-owned the farm equipment. The court rejected the Trustee's arguments under § 202 of RUPA, focusing on the intent of the parties:

> The Lampes co-owned the farm equipment, jointly participated in the work, and shared the profits. Thus, their farm operation reflects some elements of a partnership. But the existence of a partnership where the alleged partners are spouses raises complex legal issues. The usual indicia of a partnership are blurred by the marital relationship. The co-owning of property, sharing of profits, and the apparent authority for one spouse to act on behalf of the other are all common to the marital relationship even absent a business. . . .
>
> The Trustee bears the burden of proving an exemption is improperly claimed. . . . Thus, the Trustee bears the burden of proving a partnership relationship existed between the Lampes in this case. Both Donald and Shelia Lampe testified that no partnership was intended, and they filed their joint tax returns reflecting that the farming business was a sole proprietorship. Although the Lampes deposited profits in a joint account, no evidence suggested this arrangement was required by an agreement to share profits as partners rather than the voluntary co-mingling of funds as spouses. The Trustee has not directed us to any evidence the Lampes held themselves out to creditors or customers as a legal partnership. Absent a showing of some other indicia of a partnership beyond those incident to the marital relationship, the Trustee has not met its burden of proving a partnership existed, and Shelia Lampe therefore is entitled to claim the "tools of the trade" exemption.

Does the court focus on the parties' subjective intent? Should it?

3. Partnership law recognizes a principle of "partnership by estoppel," meaning that a person may have the liabilities of partner if that person allows others to hold him out as a partner and that person may be able to bind the partnership as though a member of it. *See* UPA § 16, RUPA § 308.

PROBLEM

Betsy and Tom recently inherited some vacant land from their grandmother. The land is close to a growing city. They decide to hold onto the land and sell it in several years for a profit to be divided between them. In the meantime, they will split expenses, such as real estate taxes and liability insurance. Are Betsy and Tom partners concerning this project, thus owing each other fiduciary duties and each having the power to bind the other contractually in some situations?

Suppose Betsy and Tom decide to increase the value of their land by subdividing it and installing a sewer and water system and streets. In what way, if at all, would that affect your analysis of the facts cited above?

3. Partnership Property

As noted earlier, a partnership can be created and operated with considerable informality. This informality sometimes leads to confusion as to who owns what, particularly in small businesses. RUPA covers questions of partnership property in §§ 203 and 204. RUPA establishes two presumptions: one is that property purchased with partnership funds is partnership property, and the other that property acquired in the name of one or more of the partners without an indication of their status as partners and without use of partnership funds is presumed to be the partners' separate property, even if used for partnership purposes. This last principle was illustrated in *McCormick v. Brevig*, 96 P.3d 697 (Mont. 2004), where a mother deeded 10 head of Charolois cattle to her son Clark and his two sons. At the time, Clark had a ranching partnership with his sister Joan, who subsequently claimed that the cattle were partnership property, in part because these cattle were listed and treated as partnership property for all tax purposes, and proceeds from the sale of the cattle's offspring were placed into a partnership account. The Montana Supreme Court overruled a special master's treatment of the cattle as partnership assets in his accounting, a conclusion that had been endorsed by the Montana District Court. The Supreme Court's opinion read, in part, as follows:

> At trial, Clark argued that the Charolais cattle should be regarded as separate property due to the fact that his mother, who was not a partner, had gifted the cattle to Clark and his two sons, neither of whom are partners. The District Court concluded, however, that since Clark had signed tax returns indicating that the cattle were Partnership property, and had placed proceeds from the sale of calves into Partnership accounts, the cattle should be treated as Partnership assets.

> On cross-appeal, Clark challenges the District Court's characterization of the Charolais cattle as Partnership assets, and argues that the mere inclusion of the cattle in the Partnership tax returns is legally insufficient to transfer title of the cattle to the Partnership. We agree.

> As reflected in the statute [RUPA § 204], property purchased with partnership assets, or transferred in the partnership's name, or to one or more of the partners in their capacity as partners of the partnership, is presumed to be partnership property. On the other hand, property acquired in the name of a partner without an indication that the property is being transferred to that person in his or her capacity as a partner of the partnership is presumed to be separate property, even if used for partnership purposes.

> In the present case, [the] special master . . . included the cattle as partnership assets in his accounting because they were listed on the partnership tax returns. However, nothing in the record suggests that the Charolais cattle were purchased with Partnership assets or transferred to Clark and his two sons in

their capacity as partners of the Partnership. Nor has their [sic] been any assignment of the cattle to the Partnership. Therefore, despite the fact that the cattle were included in the Partnership tax returns, and proceeds from the sale of the cattle's offspring placed in Partnership accounts, the cattle are to be presumed separate property pursuant to [RUPA § 204(d)].

As Joan correctly points out, this presumption is a rebuttable one. Nonetheless, Joan did not introduce any evidence to overcome the presumption but, rather, has relied on appeal upon the District Court's findings that money from the sale of calves had been placed into Partnership accounts, and that the cattle had been listed on Partnership tax returns. However, we have previously considered and rejected arguments that a third party acquires an interest in cattle simply by feeding, watering, and pasturing them. . . . Joan has not demonstrated any equitable interest in the cattle by virtue of the Partnership's care and feeding of the cattle, nor has she provided any authority which would compel the conclusion that ownership of the cattle passed to the Partnership. Because the presumption established by [RUPA § 204(d)] has not been overcome by evidence to the contrary, we conclude the District Court erred in categorizing the Charolais cattle as Partnership assets, and reverse the court's determination in that regard.

Based on this excerpt, did the Montana Supreme Court consider the facts that Clark "had signed tax returns indicating that the cattle were Partnership property, and had placed proceeds from the sale of calves into Partnership accounts," evidence that the cattle were partnership property? Why might these facts be relevant?

4. The Authority of Partners

Not surprisingly, partnership draws heavily on the law of agency to determine the authority of partners to bind the partnership. Partnership statutes make clear that partners are agents of the partnership. UPA § 9, RUPA § 301. The next two cases demonstrate the extent of that authority.

a. Actual Authority

SUMMERS v. DOOLEY

Supreme Court of Idaho

94 Idaho 87, 481 P.2d 318 (1971)

Donaldson, Justice.

This lawsuit, tried in the district court, involves a claim by one partner against the other for $6,000. . . .

The pertinent facts leading to this lawsuit are as follows. Summers entered a partnership agreement with Dooley (defendant-respondent) in 1958 for the purpose of operating a trash collection business. The business was operated by the two men and when either was unable to work, the non-working partner provided a replacement at his own expense. . . . In July, 1966, Summers approached his partner Dooley regarding the hiring of an additional employee but Dooley refused. Nevertheless, on his own initiative, Summers hired the man and paid him out of his own pocket. Dooley, upon discovering that Summers had hired an additional man, objected, stating that he did not feel additional labor was necessary and refused to pay for the new employee out of the partnership funds. Summers continued to operate the business using the third man and in October of 1967 instituted suit in the district court for $6,000 against his partner, the gravamen of the complaint being that Summers has been required to pay out more than $11,000 in expenses, incurred in the hiring of the additional man, without any reimbursement from either the partnership funds or his partner. [The trial court denied Summers the reimbursement he sought for expenses related to hiring extra help, and he appealed.]

The principal thrust of appellant's contention is that in spite of the fact that one of the two partners refused to consent to the hiring of additional help, nonetheless, the non-consenting partner retained profits earned by the labors of the third man and therefore the non-consenting partner should be estopped from denying the need and value of the employee, and has by his behavior ratified the act of the other partner who hired the additional man.

The issue presented for decision by this appeal is whether an equal partner in a two man partnership has the authority to hire a new employee in disregard of the objection of the other partner and then attempt to charge the dissenting partner with the costs incurred as a result of his unilateral decision. . . .

An application of the relevant statutory provisions and pertinent case law to the factual situation presented by the instant case indicates that the trial court was correct in its disposal of the issue since a majority of the partners did not consent to the hiring of the third man. [UPA § 18(h)] provides:

> Any difference arising as to ordinary matters connected with the partnership business may be decided by a *majority of the partners*. . . . (emphasis supplied).

The intent of the legislature may be implied from the language used, or inferred on grounds of policy or reasonableness. A careful reading of the statutory provision indicates that [UPA § 18(e)] bestows *equal rights in the management and conduct of the partnership business* upon all of the partners.[4] The concept of equality between partners with respect to management of business affairs is a central theme and recurs throughout the Uniform Partnership law, which has been enacted in this jurisdiction. Thus the only reasonable interpretation of [UPA § 18(h)] is that business differences must be decided by a majority of the partners provided no other agreement between the partners speaks to the issues.

A noted scholar has dealt precisely with the issue to be decided.

> [I]f the partners are equally divided, those who forbid a change must have their way. Walter B. Lindley, A Treatise on the Law of Partnership, Ch. II, § III, ¶ 24-8, p. 403 (1924).

In the case at bar, one of the partners continually voiced objection to the hiring of the third man. He did not sit idly by and acquiesce in the actions of his partner. Under these circumstances it is manifestly unjust to permit recovery of an expense which was incurred individually and not for the benefit of the partnership but rather for the benefit of one partner.

Judgment affirmed. Costs to respondent.

McQUADE, C. J., and McFADDEN, SHEPARD and SPEAR, JJ., concur.

b. Apparent Authority

RNR INVESTMENTS LIMITED PARTNERSHIP v. PEOPLES FIRST COMMUNITY BANK
Court of Appeal of Florida
812 So. 2d 561 (2002)

VAN NORTWICK, J.

RNR Investments Limited Partnership (RNR) appeals a summary judgment of foreclosure granted in favor of appellee, Peoples First Community Bank (the Bank).

---

[4] In the absence of an agreement to the contrary. In the case at bar, there is no such agreement. . . .

RNR argues that the trial court erred in granting summary judgment because disputed issues of material fact remained with respect to one of RNR's affirmative defenses. In that affirmative defense, RNR alleged that the Bank was negligent in lending $960,000 to RNR without consent of the limited partners when, under RNR's Agreement of Limited Partnership, the authority of RNR's general partner was limited to obtaining financing up to $650,000. Under section 620.8301(a), Florida Statutes (2000), however, the Bank could rely upon the general partner's apparent authority to bind RNR, unless the Bank had actual knowledge or notice of his restricted authority. In opposing summary judgment, RNR produced no evidence showing that the Bank had actual knowledge or notice of restrictions imposed on the authority of RNR's general partner. Accordingly, no issues of material facts are in dispute and we affirm.

Factual and Procedural History

RNR is a Florida limited partnership formed pursuant to chapter 620, Florida Statutes, to purchase vacant land in Destin, Florida, and to construct a house on the land for resale. Bernard Roeger was RNR's general partner and Heinz Rapp, Claus North, and S.E. Waltz, Inc., were limited partners. The agreement of limited partnership provides for various restrictions on the authority of the general partner. Paragraph 4.1 of the agreement required the general partner to prepare a budget covering the cost of acquisition and construction of the project (defined as the "Approved Budget") and further provided, in pertinent part, as follows:

> The Approved Budget for the Partnership is attached hereto as Exhibit "C" and is approved by evidence of the signatures of the Partners on the signature pages of this Agreement. . . . In no event, without Limited Partner Consent, shall the Approved Budget be exceeded by more than five percent (5%), nor shall any line item thereof be exceeded by more than ten percent (10%). . . .

Paragraph 4.3 restricted the general partner's ability to borrow, spend partnership funds and encumber partnership assets, if not specifically provided for in the Approved Budget. Finally, with respect to the development of the partnership project, paragraph 2.2(b) provided:

> The General Partner shall not incur debts, liabilities or obligations of the Partnership which will cause any line item in the Approved Budget to be exceeded by more than ten percent (10%) or which will cause the aggregate Approved Budget to be exceed [sic] by more than five percent (5%) unless the General Partner shall receive the prior written consent of the Limited Partner.

In June 1998, RNR, through its general partner, entered into a construction loan agreement, note, and mortgage in the principal amount of $990,000. From June 25, 1998 through Mar. 13, 2000, the bank disbursed the aggregate sum of $952,699, by transfers into RNR's bank account. All draws were approved by an architect, who certified that the work had progressed as indicated and that the quality of the work was in accordance with the construction contract. No representative of RNR objected to any draw of funds or asserted that the amounts disbursed were not associated with the construction of the house.

RNR defaulted under the terms of the note and mortgage by failing to make payments due in July 2000 and all monthly payments due thereafter. The Bank filed a complaint seeking foreclosure. RNR filed an answer and affirmative defenses. In its first affirmative defense, RNR alleged that the Bank had failed to review the limitations on the general partner's authority in RNR's limited partnership agreement. RNR asserted that the Bank had negligently failed to investigate and to realize that the general partner had no authority to execute notes, a mortgage, and a construction loan agreement and was estopped from foreclosing. The Bank filed a motion for summary judgment with supporting affidavits attesting to the amounts due and owing and the amount of disbursements under the loan.

In opposition to the summary judgment motion, RNR filed the affidavit of Stephen E. Waltz, the president one of RNR's limited partners, S.E. Waltz, Inc. In that affidavit, Mr. Waltz stated that the partners anticipated that RNR would need to finance the construction of the residence, but that paragraph 2.2(b) of the partnership agreement limited the amount of any loan the general partner could obtain on behalf of RNR to an amount that would not exceed by more than 10% the approved budget on any one line item or exceed the aggregate approved budget by more than 5%, unless the general partner received the prior written consent of the limited partners. Waltz alleged that the limited partners understood and orally agreed that the general partner would seek financing in the approximate amount of $650,000. Further, Waltz stated:

> Even though the limited partners had orally agreed to this amount, a written consent was never memorialized, and to my surprise, the [Bank], either through its employees or attorney, . . . never requested the same from any of the limited partners at any time prior to [or] after the closing on the loan from the [Bank] to RNR.

Waltz alleged that the partners learned in the spring of 2000 that, instead of obtaining a loan for $650,000, Roeger had obtained a loan for $990,000, which was secured by RNR's property. He stated that the limited partners did not consent to Roeger obtaining a loan from the Bank in the amount of $990,000 either orally or in writing and that the limited partners were never contacted by the Bank as to whether they had consented to a loan amount of $990,000.

RNR asserts that a copy of the limited partnership agreement was maintained at its offices. Nevertheless, the record contains no copy of an Approved Budget of the partnership or any evidence that would show that a copy of RNR's partnership agreement or any partnership budget was given to the Bank or that any notice of the general partner's restricted authority was provided to the Bank.

. . .

[T]he trial court entered a summary final judgment of foreclosure in favor of the Bank. The foreclosure sale has been stayed pending the outcome of this appeal.

Apparent Authority of the General Partner

Although the agency concept of apparent authority was applied to partnerships under the common law, in Florida the extent to which the partnership is bound by the acts of a partner acting within the apparent authority is now governed by statute. Section [301(11)], a part of the Florida Revised Uniform Partnership Act (FRUPA), provides:

> Each partner is an agent of the partnership for the purpose of its business. An act of a partner, including the execution of an instrument in the partnership name, for apparently carrying on in the ordinary scope of partnership business or business of the kind carried on by the partnership, in the geographic area in which the partnership operates, binds the partnership unless the partner had no authority to act for the partnership in the particular manner and the person with whom the partner was dealing knew or had received notification that the partner lacked authority.

Thus, even if a general partner's actual authority is restricted by the terms of the partnership agreement, the general partner possesses the apparent authority to bind the partnership in the ordinary course of partnership business or in the business of the kind carried on by the partnership, unless the third party "knew or had received a notification that the partner lacked authority." Id. "Knowledge" and "notice" under FRUPA are defined in section [RUPA § 102]. That section provides that "[a] person knows a fact if the person has actual knowledge of the fact." Further, a third party has notice of a fact if that party: "(a) [k]nows of the fact; (b) [h]as received notification of the fact; or (c) [h]as reason to know the fact exists from all other facts known to the person at the time in question." [RUPA § 102(2)]. Finally, under [RUPA § 303], a partnership may file a statement of partnership authority setting forth any restrictions in a general partner's authority.

Commentators have described the purpose of these knowledge and notice provisions, as follows:

> Under RUPA, the term knew is confined to actual knowledge, which is cognitive awareness. . . . Therefore, despite the similarity in language, RUPA provides greater protection [than the Uniform Partnership Act (UPA)] to third persons dealing with partners, who may rely on the partner's apparent authority absent actual knowledge or notification of a restriction in this regard. RUPA effects a slight reallocation of the risk of unauthorized agency power in favor of third parties. That is consistent with notions of the expanded liability of principals since the UPA was drafted.
>
> RUPA attempts to balance its shift toward greater protection of third parties by providing several new ways for partners to protect themselves against unauthorized actions by a rogue partner. First, the partnership may notify a third party of a partner's lack of authority. Such notification is effective upon receipt, whether or not the third party actually learns of it. More significantly, the partnership may file a statement of partnership authority restricting a partner's authority.

Donald J. Weidner & John W. Larson, *The Revised Uniform Partnership Act: The Reporters' Overview*, 49 Bus. Law. 1, 31–32 (1993) (footnotes omitted). "Absent actual knowledge, third parties have no duty to inspect the partnership agreement or inquire otherwise to ascertain the extent of a partner's actual authority in the ordinary course of business, . . . even if they have some reason to question it." *Id.* at 32 n. 200. The apparent authority provisions of section [RUPA § 301(1)], reflect a policy by the drafters that "the risk of loss from partner misconduct more appropriately belongs on the partnership than on third parties who do not knowingly participate in or take advantage of the misconduct . . . " J. Dennis Hayes, *Notice and Notification Under the Revised Uniform Partnership Act: Some Suggested Changes*, 2 J. Small & Emerging Bus. L. 299, 308 (1998).

Analysis

Under [RUPA § 301(1)], the determination of whether a partner is acting with authority to bind the partnership involves a two-step analysis. The first step is to determine whether the partner purporting to bind the partnership apparently is carrying on the partnership business in the usual way or a business of the kind carried on by the partnership. An affirmative answer on this step ends the inquiry, unless it is shown that the person with whom the partner is dealing actually knew or had received a notification that the partner lacked authority. Here, it is undisputed that, in entering into the loan, the general partner was carrying on the business of RNR in the usual way. The dispositive question in this appeal is whether there are issues of material fact as to whether the Bank had actual knowledge or notice of restrictions on the general partner's authority.

RNR argues that, as a result of the restrictions on the general partner's authority in the partnership agreement, the Bank had constructive knowledge of the restrictions and was obligated to inquire as to the general partner's specific authority to bind RNR in the construction loan. We cannot agree. Under [RUPA § 301], the Bank could rely on the general partner's apparent authority, unless it had *actual knowledge* or *notice* of restrictions on that authority. While the RNR partners may have agreed upon restrictions that would limit the general partner to borrowing no more than $650,000 on behalf of the partnership, RNR does not contend and nothing before us would show that the Bank had actual knowledge or notice of any restrictions on the general partner's authority. Here, the partnership could have protected itself by filing a statement pursuant to [RUPA § 303] or by providing notice to the Bank of the specific restrictions on the authority of the general partner.

Because there is no disputed issue of fact concerning whether the Bank had actual knowledge or notice of restrictions on the general partner's authority to borrow, summary judgment was proper.

Affirmed.

MINER AND WOLF, JJ., concur

NOTES AND QUESTIONS

1. With regard to matters of authority, § 303 of RUPA provides for the filing of a statement of authority. If the statement is recorded in the appropriate office for recording interests in land, it can serve as notice of authority or the lack thereof to persons dealing with partnership real property.

2. With regard to the apparent authority of a partner, UPA and RUPA have similar, though not identical, language. Under UPA § 9(1), a partner binds the partnership when his act is "for apparently carrying on *in the usual way* the business of the partnership," while under RUPA § 301, the key language is, "for apparently carrying on *in the ordinary course* the partnership business or *business of the kind carried on by the partnership*" (emphasis added). RUPA thus makes two changes to UPA, but the comment to RUPA indicates that the change from "in the usual way" to "in the ordinary course" was not a substantive change, and the courts have treated the two phrases identically. *See* Baltrusch v. Baltrusch, 83 P.3d 256, 262 (Mont. 2003).

PROBLEM

Stroud and Freeman owned and operated a grocery store under the name S & F General Store as a general partnership. One of their suppliers was National Bread Co., which supplied baked breads. Stroud and Freeman disagreed on whether to continue to carry National Bread's products. Stroud did not like the quality, while Freeman thought the bread was a good value. Unable to resolve their differences, Stroud sent a written notice to National Bread Co. disclaiming liability for any amounts that might be due to National Bread for deliveries made after the date of the notice. Nonetheless, National Bread continued to deliver goods to S & F on Freeman's instructions. Several months later, S & F went out of business, owing National Bread $5,000 for bread deliveries. All of the bread was delivered after Stroud had contacted National Bread. S & F has no assets and Freeman is judgment proof. National Bread has decided to pursue Stroud for its unpaid bills. Is Stroud liable?

5. Liability for a Partner's Fraud

ROUSE v. POLLARD
Court of Errors & Appeals of New Jersey
130 N.J. Eq. 204, 21 A.2d 801 (1941)

CASE, JUSTICE.

This is an appeal by the complainant from a final decree in Chancery dismissing the bill as to all of the partners formerly of the law firm of Riker and Riker except Thomas E. Fitzsimmons against whom the decree ran as a judgment in the amount of $20,500 with interest and costs. The suit was to charge all of the members of the firm with liability for what was, in effect, an embezzlement of complainant's funds by the defendant Fitzsimmons in the above named amount. . . .

Complainant sought a separation from her husband. In or about the month of June, 1927, she went to the firm of Riker and Riker, stated her case and was referred to Fitzsimmons, a member of the firm. The separation agreement was signed, and there were a few other legal services rendered. In the course of the incidental conferences Fitzsimmons asked Mrs. Rouse what money she possessed and was informed by her of the amount thereof and the manner in which it was invested. According to Mrs. Rouse:

> He said the securities was a bad thing for a woman in my position to have and he suggested that I turn over my securities and sell them and turn the money over to the firm, that they dealt in gilt edge mortgage bonds, as he said. He said that they did that for their clients and it was perfectly secure. . . .

Mrs. Rouse wrote to her brokers directing them to sell her securities and to "forward a check for the same payable to me to my attorney, Mr. Thomas E. Fitzsimmons, c/o Riker & Riker, 24 Commerce Street, Newark, N.J." A check for $28,252.67 was sent as directed, was endorsed by Mrs. Rouse "Pay to the order of Thos. E. Fitzsimmons" and was deposited by Fitzsimmons in his personal bank account. No part ever came to the firm except $350, or thereabouts, which was paid by Fitzsimmons to the firm for the legal services rendered, and no member of the firm, other than Fitzsimmons, knew of the transaction. . . .

The experience of Mrs. Rouse is tragic and painful, but we must get, as best we may, at the facts. Her testimony reveals a faulty memory and a frail grasp upon the essentials of a business transaction. . . . Perhaps the initial respect which Mrs. Rouse entertained for Fitzsimmons' business sagacity and investment acumen was seeded in the fact that he was a member of the Riker firm; but he was a member of that firm for the practice of law, and that membership did not per se create liability by his partners for his acts outside the general scope of the practice of law. . . .

[I]f Fitzsimmons, as appellant now understands the fact to be, represented to her that the firm of Riker and Riker undertook to accept money in bulk from clients for future investment by and at the discretion of the attorneys in undesignated securities, and would do that for her, we are then confronted with the question whether Fitzsimmons, as a member of a firm of lawyers, bound together simply by an oral agreement "for the practice of law," could obligate his partners to such a venture. When Mrs. Rouse went to the offices of Riker and Riker in reliance upon their reputation as a law firm, stated the purpose of her visit, which was to obtain a legal service, and was introduced to Fitzsimmons as a member of the firm who would render the desired service, she had no justification therein for relying upon the responsibility of the partnership for any disconnected service assumed by Fitzsimmons outside one that was characteristically within the practice of law.

Appellant contends that the investment of the funds in mortgages was within the scope of the defendant law firm's practice or within the scope of Fitzsimmons' apparent authority. The proofs do not sustain the implication that the practice of this particular firm embraced the acceptance of clients' money to be placed at the firm's discretion in investments thereafter to be ascertained and selected, whether in first mortgages or otherwise. . . .

It has long been a recognized incident to the general practice of law, more extensively developed in some offices than in others, to make note of such clients as have moneys to invest on bond and mortgage, to bring the attention of those clients to the applications of proposed borrowers and, after the principals come to an agreement, to search the title, draw the necessary documents, even hold the money against the event, place the recordable papers on record and in general superintend the closing of the transaction. But we do not understand that it is a characteristic function of the practice of law to accept clients' money for deposit and future investment in unspecified securities at the discretion of the attorney, and we find to the contrary. It is possible that attorneys in isolated instances have done this; just as it is possible that a person of any profession or occupation has done so. It has not, however, been done by lawyers, in this jurisdiction at least, with such frequency or appropriateness as to become a phase of the practice. . . .

We have found that the incident sued upon, that is, the placing of money for the purposes named, is not a function of the practice of law and that it was not a part of any practice indulged in by the respondents; but beyond this appellant contends that it was within Fitzsimmons' apparent authority and so seeks to fasten liability upon respondents under that well known rule in the law of agency. The facts for the application of the principle do not exist. The respondents did nothing to indicate that Fitzsimmons had any authority to act in their behalf outside the practice of law.

Another point is that respondents should be made to answer for the loss upon the theory that inasmuch as they and the complainant were both innocent the burden should rest upon them because they put Fitzsimmons in the position where he was able to perpetrate the fraud upon complainant; and, yet another, that the respondents received a part of the funds and so are estopped from denying the authority of Fitzsimmons. These contentions also rest upon a warped view of the facts. The paying over of the money to Fitzsimmons not only was not an act in the practice of law, it was not a part of or connected with any transaction which Fitzsimmons was conducting or was authorized to conduct for the firm. The amount of $350 did not go to respondents as a participation in a tortious transaction but from money that belonged to Mrs. Rouse and in payment of legal services that were performed by the firm for her. The existence of the debt and the propriety of the charge were not in dispute. The money was paid to them in ignorance on their part, then and for many years thereafter, of any wrongdoing by Fitzsimmons, and without facts in their knowledge, or chargeable to their knowledge, which served to put them on notice. We find no element of estoppel.

The decree in the court below will be affirmed.

NOTES AND QUESTIONS

1. The law is not uniform in this area of partner fraud. See, for example, *Cook v. Brundidge, Fountain, Elliott & Churchill*, 533 S.W.2d 751 (Tex. 1976) (reversing summary judgment in favor of the defendant firm), *Roach v. Mead*, 722 P.2d 1229 (Or. 1986) (focusing on consumer's expectations as to what is carrying on in the usual way the business of the partnership); *Croisant v. Watrud*, 432 P.2d 799 (Or. 1967) (similar).

2. Partners can also incur liability as a result of the imputation of knowledge to them. RUPA § 102 and UPA § 12. Thus, if a partner is party to a breach of trust, knowledge of that breach may be imputed to the other partners, rendering them jointly liable. See *Federal Deposit Insur. Corp. v. Braemoor Assoc.*, 686 F.2d 550 (7th Cir. 1982), where the partnership benefited as a result of one partner's breach of fiduciary duty.

6. Rights and Duties Among Partners

a. Duty of Care

BANE v. FERGUSON
United States Court of Appeals, Seventh Circuit
890 F.2d 11 (1989)

POSNER, CIRCUIT JUDGE.

The question presented by this appeal from the dismissal of the complaint is whether a retired partner in a law firm has a . . . claim against the firm's managing council for acts of negligence that, by causing the firm to dissolve, terminate his retirement benefits. . . .

Charles Bane practiced corporate and public utility law as a partner in the venerable Chicago law firm of Isham, Lincoln & Beale, founded more than a century ago by

Abraham Lincoln's son, Robert Todd Lincoln. In August 1985 the firm adopted a noncontributory retirement plan that entitled every retiring partner to a pension, the amount depending on his earnings from the firm on the eve of retirement. The plan instrument provided that the plan, and the payments under it, would end when and if the firm dissolved without a successor entity, and also that the amount paid out in pension benefits each year could not exceed five percent of the firm's net income in the preceding year. Four months after the plan was adopted, the plaintiff retired, moved to Florida with his wife, and began drawing his pension (to continue until his wife's death if he died first) of $27,483 a year. Bane was 72 years old when he retired. So far as appears, he had, apart from social security, no significant source of income other than the pension.

Several months after Bane's retirement, Isham, Lincoln & Beale merged with Reuben & Proctor, another large and successful Chicago firm. The merger proved to be a disaster, and the merged firm was dissolved in April 1988 without a successor — whereupon the payment of pension benefits to Bane ceased and he brought this suit. The suit alleges that the defendants were the members of the firm's managing council in the period leading up to the dissolution and that they acted unreasonably in deciding to merge the firm with Reuben & Procter, in purchasing computers and other office equipment, and in leaving the firm for greener pastures shortly before its dissolution. The suit does not allege that the defendants committed fraud, engaged in self-dealing, or deliberately sought to destroy or damage the law firm or harm the plaintiff; the charge is negligent mismanagement, not deliberate wrongdoing. The suit seeks damages, presumably the present value of the pension benefits to which the Banes would be entitled had the firm not dissolved. . . .

Bane has four theories of liability. The first is that the defendants, by committing acts of mismanagement that resulted in the dissolution of the firm, violated the Uniform Partnership Act § 9(3)(c), which provides that "unless authorized by the other partners . . . one or more but less than all the partners have no authority to: Do any . . . act which would make it impossible to carry on the ordinary business of the partnership." This provision is inapplicable. Its purpose is not to make negligent partners liable to persons with whom the partnership transacts (such as Bane), but to limit the liability of the other partners for the unauthorized act of one partner. The purpose in other words is to protect partners. Bane ceased to be a partner when he retired in 1985.

Nor can Bane obtain legal relief on the theory that the defendants violated a fiduciary duty to him; they had none. A partner is a fiduciary of his partners, but not of his former partners, for the withdrawal of a partner terminates the partnership as to him. Bane must look elsewhere for the grounds of a fiduciary obligation running from his former partners to himself. The pension plan did not establish a trust, and even if, notwithstanding the absence of one, the plan's managers were fiduciaries of its beneficiaries (there are myriad sources of fiduciary duty besides a trust), the mismanagement was not of the plan but of the firm. There is no suggestion that the defendants failed to inform the plaintiff of his rights under the plan or miscalculated his benefits or mismanaged or misapplied funds set aside for the plan's beneficiaries; no funds were set aside for them. Even if the defendants were fiduciaries of the plaintiff, moreover, the business judgment rule would shield them from liability for mere negligence in the operation of the firm, just as it would shield a corporation's directors and officers, who are fiduciaries of the shareholders.

That leaves for discussion Bane's claims of breach of contract and of tort. [The court rejects both claims, which were made independently of the fiduciary duty claims.] We are sorry about the financial blow to the Banes but we agree with the district judge that there is no remedy under the law of Illinois.

Affirmed.

NOTES AND QUESTIONS

1. Courts are starting to apply the business judgment rule to decisions made by partners. The business judgment rule is discussed in Chapter 10, *infra*, as the standard by which judgments of the board of directors are reviewed by the courts. In the partnership context, see, for example, *Kuznik v. Bees Ferry Associates*, 538 S.E.2d 15, 27 (S.C. Ct. App. 2000); *Starr v. Fordham*, 648 N.E.2d 1261, 1265–66 (Mass. 1995). The South Carolina court in *Kuznik* set forth this formulation of the business judgment rule (although it may simply have been describing the applicable standard of conduct):

> We conclude the business judgment rule may apply to partnerships in South Carolina. When a partner alleges another has violated his fiduciary duty, the allegedly violating partner must show he acted: (1) in good faith; (2) with the care an ordinarily prudent person in a like position would exercise under similar circumstances; and (3) in a manner the partner reasonably believes to be in the best interests of the partnership. However, the rule will *not* apply if the partners have engaged in *self-dealing, fraud, or other unconscionable conduct.*

538 S.E.2d at 27 (emphasis in original). *See* Triem, *Judicial Schizophrenia in Corporate Law: Confusing the Standard of Care with the Business Judgment Rule*, 24 ALASKA L. REV. 23 (2007); Branson, *The Rule That Isn't a Rule: The Business Judgment Rule*, 36 VAL. U. L. REV. 631 (2002). If the business judgment rule applies, courts typically will not further review the decision in question. On the other hand, if the protection of the business judgment rule is inapplicable, for instance for any of the reasons stated in the *Kuznik* decision, then the burden shifts to the partner who made the decision to demonstrate that the decision was fair to the partners challenging it. Failing that, the decision maker is liable for damages resulting from the decision made. Under the Delaware corporate law formulation of the business judgment rule, the courts will presume that the directors acted in good faith, with due care and in the best interests of the corporation. The burden of proof is on those challenging the decision to overcome such presumptions. If the challengers meet that burden, then the directors bear the burden of proving the fairness of their decision. *See, e.g., Cede & Co. v. Technicolor, Inc.*, 634 A.2d 345, 361 (Del. 1993).

2. As noted above, a paid agent is subject to a duty to the principal to act with the standard of care and skill accepted in the locality for the kind of work involved and, in addition, to exercise any special skills the agent has or purports to have. As noted in *Bane*, this standard does not apply to partners. Instead, partners are not liable to other partners for mere negligence in the operation of the business. Why the different treatment for partners? Perhaps it can be explained in part by the special incentive partners have, stemming from personal liability for the debts of the business, to act with care and to monitor the behavior of fellow partners. If this explanation is accurate, should the standard of care be increased for partners in an LLP, where there is no liability for the debts of the business?

UPA does not specifically address the duty of care partners owe to each other. It specifies that, subject to contrary agreement, losses are shared according to the sharing of profits. Presumably this includes losses caused by a partner's negligence, unless agreed otherwise.

RUPA directly addresses a partner's standard of care, stating in § 404(c) that, "A partner's duty of care to the partnership and the other partners in the conduct and winding up of the partnership business is limited to refraining from engaging in grossly negligent or reckless conduct, intentional misconduct, or a knowing violation of law." By this approach, RUPA declined to create a special default rule for losses caused by the negligence of partners. Instead, such losses are treated in the same way as losses caused by the negligence of a nonpartner agent. (One would not want to push this analogy too far, however. The common law of agency requires an agent to indemnify the principal for losses caused by the agent's negligence, while partners generally do not have such an obligation, as developed in the *Moren* case below.) The drafters assumed that most partners would agree to share losses equally, reasoning that negligence is inevitable and likely to occur at random among partners. The Comments to § 404(c) are terse, but this point is made by the Reporter for RUPA in Donald J. Weidner, *Three Policy Decisions Animate Revision of Uniform Partnership Act*, 46 Bus. Law. 427, 464–68 (1991).

3. For a thoughtful commentary on the appropriateness of a gross negligence standard for a partner's duty of care, see J. William Callison, *"The Law Does Not Perfectly Comprehend": The Inadequacy of the Gross Negligence Duty of Care Standard in Unincorporated Business Organizations*, 94 Ky. L.J. 451 (2005–2006) (arguing that a gross negligence standard is inappropriate in some circumstances and that the RUPA drafters should not have attempted to articulate a single standard for all cases).

MOREN v. JAX RESTAURANT
Court of Appeals of Minnesota
679 N.W.2d 165 (2004)

Crippen, Judge.

FACTS

Jax Restaurant, the partnership, operates its business in Foley, Minnesota. One afternoon in October 2000, Nicole Moren, one of the Jax partners, completed her day shift at Jax at 4:00 p.m. and left to pick up her two-year-old son Remington from day care. At about 5:30, Moren returned to the restaurant with Remington after learning that her sister and partner, Amy Benedetti, needed help. Moren called her husband who told her that he would pick Remington up in about 20 minutes.

Because Nicole Moren did not want Remington running around the restaurant, she brought him into the kitchen with her, set him on top of the counter, and began rolling out pizza dough using the dough-pressing machine. As she was making pizzas, Remington reached his hand into the dough press. His hand was crushed, and he sustained permanent injuries.

Through his father, Remington commenced a negligence action against the partnership. The partnership served a third-party complaint on Nicole Moren, arguing that, in the event it was obligated to compensate Remington, the partnership was entitled to indemnity or contribution from Moren for her negligence. The district court's summary judgment was premised on a legal conclusion that Moren has no obligation to indemnify Jax Restaurant so long as the injury occurred while she was engaged in ordinary business conduct. The district court rejected the partnership's argument that its obligation to compensate Remington is diminished in proportion to the predominating negligence of Moren as a mother, although it is responsible for her conduct as a business owner. This appeal followed.

ISSUE

Does Jax Restaurant have an indemnity right against Nicole Moren in the circumstances of this case?

ANALYSIS

Under Minnesota's Uniform Partnership Act of 1994 (UPA), a partnership is an entity distinct from its partners, and as such, a partnership may sue and be sued in the name of the partnership. "A partnership is liable for loss or injury caused to a person . . . as a result of a wrongful act or omission, or other actionable conduct, of a partner acting in the ordinary course of business of the partnership or with authority of the partnership." [RUPA § 305] Accordingly, a "partnership shall . . . indemnify a partner for liabilities incurred by the partner in the ordinary course of the business of the partnership. . . . " [RUPA § 401(c)]. Stated conversely, an "act of a partner which is not apparently for carrying on in the ordinary course the partnership business or business of the kind carried on by the partnership binds the partnership only if the act was authorized by the other partners." [RUPA § 301(2)]. Thus, under the plain language of the [RUPA], a partner has a right to indemnity from the partnership, but the partnership's claim of indemnity from a partner is not authorized or required.

The district court correctly concluded that Nicole Moren's conduct was in the ordinary course of business of the partnership and, as a result, indemnity by the partner to the partnership was inappropriate. It is undisputed that one of the cooks scheduled to work that evening did not come in, and that Moren's partner asked her to help in the kitchen. It also is undisputed that Moren was making pizzas for the partnership when her son was injured. Because her conduct at the time of the injury was in the ordinary course of business of the partnership, under the [RUPA], her conduct bound the partnership and it owes indemnity to her for her negligence. [RUPA §§ 305(a) and 401(c)].

Appellant heavily relies on one foreign case for the proposition that a partnership is entitled to a contribution or indemnity from a partner who is negligent. See *Flynn v. Reaves*, 135 Ga. App. 651, 218 S.E.2d 661 (1975). In *Flynn*, the Georgia Court of Appeals held that "where a partner is sued individually by a plaintiff injured by the partner's sole negligence, the partner cannot seek contribution from his co-partners even though the negligent act occurred in the course of the partnership business." *Id.* at 663. But this case is inapplicable because the Georgia court applied common law partnership and agency principles and, like appellant, makes no mention of the RUPA, which is the law in Minnesota.

Appellant also claims that because Nicole Moren's action of bringing Remington into the kitchen was partly motivated by personal reasons, her conduct was outside the ordinary course of business. Because it has not been previously addressed, there is no Minnesota authority regarding this issue. But there are two cases from outside of Minnesota that address the issue in a persuasive fashion. *Grotelueschen v. Am. Family Ins. Co.*, 171 Wis. 2d 437, 492 N.W.2d 131, 137 (1992) (An "act can further part personal and part business purposes and still occur in the ordinary course of the partnership."); *Wolfe v. Harms*, 413 S.W.2d 204, 215 (Mo. 1967) ("[E]ven if the predominant motive of the partner was to benefit himself or third persons, such does not prevent the concurrent business purpose from being within the scope of the partnership."). Adopting this rationale, we conclude that the conduct of Nicole Moren was no less in the ordinary course of business because it also served personal purposes. It is undisputed that Moren was acting for the benefit of the partnership by making pizzas when her son was injured, and even though she was simultaneously acting in her role as a mother, her conduct remained in the ordinary course of the partnership business.

DECISION

Because Minnesota law requires a partnership to indemnify its partners for the result of their negligence, the district court properly granted summary judgment to respondent Nicole Moren. In addition, we conclude that the conduct of a partner may be partly motivated by personal reasons and still occur in the ordinary course of business of the partnership.

Affirmed.

NOTE AND QUESTION

In *Moren*, the court holds that a negligent partner is not liable to indemnify the partnership for the liability it incurred as a result of her negligence. Is the court's rationale convincing?

PROBLEM

Alpha Investment Co. is a partnership consisting of four partners engaged in the business of providing fee-based investment advice to wealthy individuals. One of the partners, Smith, is responsible for the day-to-day business operations of the company. Smith hired Cole to manage the company's computerized database. Smith did not check into Cole's background, nor did Smith call any previous employers or references. Had Smith done any checking, she would have learned that Cole had significant "character" problems and had been dismissed from a previous job because of suspicion of embezzlement. Cole used information from the database to defraud several Alpha clients. Does Smith have any potential liability for her conduct in hiring Cole?

b. Duty of Loyalty (Partnership Opportunity)

MEINHARD v. SALMON
Court of Appeals of New York
249 N.Y. 458, 164 N.E. 545, 62 A.L.R. 1 (1928)

Cardozo, Ch. J.

On April 10, 1902, Louisa M. Gerry leased to the defendant Walter J. Salmon the premises known as the Hotel Bristol at the northwest corner of Forty-second street and Fifth avenue in the city of New York. The lease was for a term of twenty years, commencing May 1, 1902, and ending April 30, 1922. The lessee undertook to change the hotel building for use as shops and offices at a cost of $200,000. Alterations and additions were to be accretions to the land.

Salmon, while in course of treaty with the lessor as to the execution of the lease, was in course of treaty with Meinhard, the plaintiff, for the necessary funds. The result was a joint venture with terms embodied in a writing. Meinhard was to pay to Salmon half of the moneys requisite to reconstruct, alter, manage and operate the property. Salmon was to pay to Meinhard 40 per cent of the net profits for the first five years of the lease and 50 per cent for the years thereafter. If there were losses, each party was to bear them equally. Salmon, however, was to have sole power to "manage, lease, underlet and operate" the building. There were to be certain pre-emptive rights for each in the contingency of death.

The two were coadventurers, subject to fiduciary duties akin to those of partners (*King v. Barnes*, 109 N.Y. 267). As to this, we are all agreed. The heavier weight of duty rested, however, upon Salmon. He was a coadventurer with Meinhard, but he was manager as well. During the early years of the enterprise, the building, reconstructed, was operated at a loss. If the relation had then ended, Meinhard as well as Salmon would have carried a heavy burden. Later the profits became large with the result that for each of the investors there came a rich return. For each, the venture had its phases of fair weather and of foul. The two were in it jointly, for better or for worse.

When the lease was near its end, Elbridge T. Gerry had become the owner of the reversion. He owned much other property in the neighborhood, one lot adjoining the Bristol Building on Fifth avenue and four lots on Forty-second street. He had a plan to lease the entire tract for a long term to some one who would destroy the buildings then existing, and put up another in their place. In the latter part of 1921, he submitted such a project to several capitalists and dealers. He was unable to carry it through with any of them. Then, in January, 1922, with less than four months of the lease to run, he approached the defendant Salmon. The result was a new lease to the Midpoint Realty Company, which is owned and controlled by Salmon, a lease covering the whole tract, and involving a huge outlay. The term is to be twenty years, but successive covenants for renewal will extend it to a maximum of eighty years at the will of either party. The existing buildings may remain unchanged for seven years. They are then to be torn down, and a new building to cost $3,000,000 is to be placed upon the site. The rental, which under the Bristol lease was only $55,000, is to be from $350,000 to $475,000 for the properties so combined. Salmon personally guaranteed the performance by the lessee of the covenants of the new lease until such time as the new building had been completed and fully paid for.

The lease between Gerry and the Midpoint Realty Company was signed and delivered on January 25, 1922. Salmon had not told Meinhard anything about it. Whatever his motive may have been, he had kept the negotiations to himself. Meinhard was not informed even of the bare existence of a project. The first that he knew of it was in February when the lease was an accomplished fact. He then made demand on the defendants that the lease be held in trust as an asset of the venture, making offer upon the trial to share the personal obligations incidental to the guaranty. The demand was followed by refusal, and later by this suit. A referee gave judgment for the plaintiff, limiting the plaintiff's interest in the lease, however, to 25 per cent. The limitation was on the theory that the plaintiff's equity was to be restricted to one-half of so much of the value of the lease as was contributed or represented by the occupation of the Bristol site. Upon cross-appeals to the Appellate Division, the judgment was modified so as to enlarge the equitable interest to one-half of the whole lease. With this enlargement of plaintiff's interest, there went, of course, a corresponding enlargement of his attendant obligations. The case is now here on an appeal by the defendants.

Joint adventurers, like copartners, owe to one another, while the enterprise continues, the duty of the finest loyalty. Many forms of conduct permissible in a workaday world for those acting at arm's length, are forbidden to those bound by fiduciary ties. A trustee is held to something stricter than the morals of the market place. Not honesty alone, but the punctilio of an honor the most sensitive, is then the standard of behavior. As to this there has developed a tradition that is unbending and inveterate. Uncompromising rigidity has been the attitude of courts of equity when petitioned to undermine the rule of undivided loyalty by the "disintegrating erosion" of particular exceptions (*Wendt v. Fischer*, 243 N.Y. 439, 444). Only thus has the level of conduct for fiduciaries been kept at a level higher than that trodden by the crowd. It will not consciously be lowered by any judgment of this court.

The owner of the reversion, Mr. Gerry, had vainly striven to find a tenant who would favor his ambitious scheme of demolition and construction. Baffled in the search, he turned to the defendant Salmon in possession of the Bristol, the keystone of the project. He figured to himself beyond a doubt that the man in possession would prove a likely customer. To the eye of an observer, Salmon held the lease as owner in his own right, for himself and no one else. In fact he held it as a fiduciary, for himself and another, sharers in a common venture. If this fact had been proclaimed, if the lease by its terms had run in favor of a partnership, Mr. Gerry, we may fairly assume, would have laid before the partners, and not merely before one of them, his plan of reconstruction. The pre-emptive privilege, or, better, the pre-emptive opportunity, that was thus an incident of the enterprise, Salmon appropriated to himself in secrecy and silence. He might have warned Meinhard that the plan had been submitted, and that either would be free to compete for the award. If he had done this, we do not need to say whether he would have been under a duty, if successful in the competition, to hold the lease so acquired for the benefit of a venture then about to end, and thus prolong by indirection its responsibilities and duties. The trouble about his conduct is that he excluded his coadventurer from any chance to compete, from any chance to enjoy the opportunity for benefit that had come to him alone by virtue of his agency. This chance, if nothing more, he was under a duty to concede. The price of its denial is an extension of the trust at the option and for the benefit of the one whom he excluded.

No answer is it to say that the chance would have been of little value even if seasonably offered. Such a calculus of probabilities is beyond the science of the chancery. . . . The very fact that Salmon was in control with exclusive powers of direction charged him the more obviously with the duty of disclosure, since only through disclosure could opportunity be equalized. If he might cut off renewal by a purchase for his own benefit when four months were to pass before the lease would have an end, he might do so with equal right while there remained as many years (cf. *Mitchell v. Reed*, 61 N.Y. 123, 127). He might steal a march on his comrade under cover of the darkness, and then hold the captured ground. Loyalty and comradeship are not so easily abjured. . . .

We have no thought to hold that Salmon was guilty of a conscious purpose to defraud. Very likely he assumed in all good faith that with the approaching end of the venture he might ignore his coadventurer and take the extension for himself. He had given to the enterprise time and labor as well as money. He had made it a success. Meinhard, who had given money, but neither time nor labor, had already been richly paid. There might seem to be something grasping in his insistence upon more. Such recriminations are not unusual when coadventurers fall out. They are not without their force if conduct is to be judged by the common standards of competitors. That is not to say that they have pertinency here. Salmon had put himself in a position in which thought of self was to be renounced, however hard the abnegation. He was much more than a coadventurer. He was a managing coadventurer. For him and for those like him, the rule of undivided loyalty is relentless and supreme. A different question would be here if there were lacking any nexus of relation between the business conducted by the manager and the opportunity brought to him as an incident of management. For this problem, as for most, there are distinctions of degree. If Salmon had received from Gerry a proposition to lease a building at a location far removed, he might have held for himself the privilege thus acquired, or so we shall assume. Here the subject-matter of the new lease was an extension and enlargement of the subject-matter of the old one. A managing coadventurer appropriating the benefit of such a lease without warning to his partner might fairly expect to be reproached with conduct that was underhand, or lacking, to say the least, in reasonable candor, if the partner were to surprise him in the act of signing the new instrument. Conduct subject to that reproach does not receive from equity a healing benediction.

A question remains as to the form and extent of the equitable interest to be allotted to the plaintiff. The trust as declared has been held to attach to the lease which was in the name of the defendant corporation. We think it ought to attach at the option of the defendant Salmon to the shares of stock which were owned by him or were under his control. The difference may be important if the lessee shall wish to execute an assignment of the lease, as it ought to be free to do with the consent of the lessor. On the other hand, an equal division of the shares might lead to other hardships. It might take away from Salmon the power of control and management which under the plan of the joint venture he was to have from first to last. The number of shares to be allotted to the plaintiff should, therefore, be reduced to such an extent as may be necessary to preserve to the defendant Salmon the expected measure of dominion. To that end an extra share should be added to his half. . . .

ANDREWS, J. (dissenting). . . . I am of the opinion that the issue here is simple. Was the transaction in view of all the circumstances surrounding it unfair and inequitable? I reach this conclusion for two reasons. There was no general partnership, merely a joint venture for a limited object, to end at a fixed time. The new lease, covering additional property, containing many new and unusual terms and conditions, with a possible duration of eighty years, was more nearly the purchase of the reversion than the ordinary renewal with which the authorities are concerned. . . .

Were this a general partnership between Mr. Salmon and Mr. Meinhard I should have little doubt as to the correctness of this result assuming the new lease to be an offshoot of the old. Such a situation involves questions of trust and confidence to a high degree; it involves questions of good will; many other considerations. As has been said, rarely if ever may one partner without the knowledge of the other acquire for himself the renewal of a lease held by the firm, even if the new lease is to begin after the firm is dissolved. Warning of such an intent, if he is managing partner, may not be sufficient to prevent the application of this rule. We have here a different situation governed by less drastic principles. . . .

It seems to me that the venture so inaugurated had in view a limited object and was to end at a limited time. There was no intent to expand it into a far greater undertaking lasting for many years. The design was to exploit a particular lease. Doubtless in it Mr. Meinhard had an equitable interest, but in it alone. This interest terminated when the joint adventure terminated. There was no intent that for the benefit of both any advantage should be taken of the chance of renewal — that the adventure should be continued beyond that date. Mr. Salmon has done all he promised to do in return for Mr. Meinhard's undertaking when he distributed profits up to May 1, 1922. Suppose this lease, non-assignable without the consent of the lessor, had contained a renewal option. Could Mr. Meinhard have exercised it? Could he have insisted that Mr. Salmon do so? Had Mr. Salmon done so could he insist that the agreement to share losses still existed or could Mr. Meinhard have claimed that the joint adventure was still to continue for twenty or eighty years? I do not think so. The adventure by its express terms ended on May 1, 1922. The contract by its language and by its whole import excluded the idea that the tenant's expectancy was to subsist for the benefit of the plaintiff. On that date whatever there was left of value in the lease reverted to Mr. Salmon, as it would had the lease been for thirty years instead of twenty. Any equity which Mr. Meinhard possessed was in the particular lease itself, not in any possibility of renewal. There was nothing unfair in Mr. Salmon's conduct.

I might go further were it necessary. Under the circumstances here presented had the lease run to both the parties I doubt whether the taking by one of a renewal without the knowledge of the other would cause interference by a court of equity. An illustration may clarify my thought. A and B enter into a joint venture to resurface a highway between Albany and Schenectady. They rent a parcel of land for the storage of materials. A, unknown to B, agrees with the lessor to rent that parcel and one adjoining it after the venture is finished, for an iron foundry. Is the act unfair? Would any general statements, scattered here and there through opinions dealing with other circumstance, be thought applicable? In other words, the mere fact that the joint venturers rent property together does not call for the strict rule that applies to general partners. Many things may excuse what is there forbidden. Nor here does any possibility of renewal exist as part of the venture. The nature of the undertaking excludes such an idea.

So far I have treated the new lease as if it were a renewal of the old. As already indicated, I do not take that view. Such a renewal could not be obtained. Any expectancy that it might be had vanished. What Mr. Salmon obtained was not a graft springing from the Bristol lease, but something distinct and different — as distinct as if for a building across Fifth avenue. I think also that in the absence of some fraudulent or unfair act the secret purchase of the reversion even by one partner is rightful. Substantially this is such a purchase. Because of the mere label of a transaction we do not place it on one side of the line or the other. Here is involved the possession of a large and most valuable unit of property for eighty years, the destruction of all existing structures and the erection of a new and expensive building covering the whole. No fraud, no deceit, no calculated secrecy is found. Simply that the arrangement was made without the knowledge of Mr. Meinhard. I think this not enough. . . .

Pound, Crane, and Lehman, JJ., concur with Cardozo, Ch. J., for modification of the judgment appealed from and affirmance as modified; Andrews, J., dissents in opinion in which Kellogg and O'Brien, JJ., concur.

NOTES AND QUESTIONS

1. It may be of interest to the reader that the building in the *Meinhard* case was not completed until after the stock market crash of 1929 and the resulting depression. As stated in *Salmon v. Commissioner*, 126 F.2d 203, 204 (2d Cir. 1942), this had the following consequences for Meinhard's estate:

> The old building had been profitable but by the time the new one was ready in 1931, the fall in the value of real estate made its operation impossible except at a loss, and Salmon and Meinhard were either compelled to pay the deficits, or to suffer the property to become unoccupied and perhaps to pass out of their hands. Meinhard had died and his estate paid to Salmon his part of the deficits. . . .

2. The duty of loyalty limits the ability of a partner to hire his or her spouse. The New York court explained that such a partner's "financial relationship with his wife conflicted with his duty to [his co-partners], and therefore violated the precept of undiluted trust at the core of his responsibilities as a fiduciary." The court said that full disclosure and consent were necessary under these circumstances. Birnbaum v. Birnbaum, 73 N.Y.2d 461, 539 N.E.2d 574, 541 N.Y.S.2d 746 (1989).

3. The court refers to Meinhard and Salmon as "coadventurers" who were "subject to fiduciary duties akin to those of partners." The term coadventurer is not often used by the courts or by lawyers drafting agreements and is probably synonymous with "joint venturer." Though not strictly a term of art, a joint venture is generally thought of as limited business undertaking by two, or at least a limited number, of participants. Inasmuch as the focus is on a particular undertaking, the formal structure the parties choose may be a corporation, partnership, or limited liability company. The most common form, however, is a partnership, and when the joint venture takes that form, all of the rules relating to partnerships apply, with possibly one exception. Because the business undertaking is a limited one, the courts may limit the venturers' duty of loyalty. It was on that basis that the dissenters in *Meinhard* would have found in favor of the defendant. Whether limited or not, joint venturers, coadventurers, and partners all owe fiduciary duties, and no case has been more widely cited for the extent of those duties than *Meinhard*. Applying the aspirational standard announced in *Meinhard* has proven to be difficult for the courts, as has been determining the extent to which the parties can contract around them. The materials below provide some guidance on these questions.

c. Duty of Loyalty (Conflict of Interest)

RUPA § 404(b) provides that a partner's duty of loyalty is *limited* to three specified duties: the duty to account for partnership property; the duty to refrain from dealing with the partnership as or on behalf of an adverse party; and the duty to refrain from competing with the partnership. Some states, including California, altered the language of § 404 to provide that a partner's duty of loyalty *included* those three duties, implying that the duty of loyalty may include other duties. The California Court of Appeals, in *Enea v. Superior Court*, 132 Cal. App. 4th 1559 (2005), so held in a case in which a partner leased partnership property to himself at less than fair market value. Analyzing the official and California versions of RUPA, the court wrote:

> Despite the numerous diversions offered by defendants, the case presents a very simple set of facts and issues. For present purposes it must be assumed that defendants in fact leased the property to themselves, or associated entities, at below-market rents. Defendants made no attempt to establish otherwise, let alone to establish the absence of triable issues of fact on the point. Therefore,

the sole question presented is whether defendants were categorically entitled to lease partnership property to themselves, or associated entities (or for that matter, to anyone) at less than it could yield in the open market. Remarkably, we have found no case squarely addressing this precise question. We are satisfied, however, that the answer is a resounding "No."

The defining characteristic of a partnership is the combination of two or more persons to jointly conduct business. It is hornbook law that in forming such an arrangement, the partners obligate themselves to share risks and benefits and to carry out the enterprise with the highest good faith toward one another — in short, with the loyalty and care of a fiduciary. "Partnership is a fiduciary relationship, and partners are held to the standards and duties of a trustee in their dealings with each other. . . . [I]n all proceedings connected with the conduct of the partnership, every partner is bound to act in the highest good faith to his copartner and may not obtain any advantage over him in the partnership affairs by the slightest misrepresentation, concealment, threat or adverse pressure of any kind. [Citations.]" (BT-I v. Equitable Life Assurance Society (1999) 75 Cal. App. 4th 1406, 1410–1411, 89 Cal. Rptr. 2d 811, *quoting* Leff v. Gunter (1983) 33 Cal. 3d 508, 514, 189 Cal. Rptr. 377, 658 P.2d 740.) Or to put the point more succinctly, "Partnership is a fiduciary relationship, and partners may not take advantages for themselves at the expense of the partnership." (Jones v. Wells Fargo Bank (2003) 112 Cal. App. 4th 1527, 1540, 5 Cal. Rptr. 3d 835; see Jones v. H. F. Ahmanson & Co. (1969) 1 Cal. 3d 93, 108, 111, 81 Cal. Rptr. 592, 460 P.2d 464.)

Here, the facts as assumed by the parties and the trial court plainly depict defendants taking advantages for themselves from partnership property *at the expense of the partnership*. The advantage consisted of occupying partnership property at below-market rates, i.e., less than they would be required to pay to an independent landlord for equivalent premises. The cost to the partnership was the additional rent thereby rendered unavailable for collection from an independent tenant willing to pay the property's value.

Defendants' objections to this reasoning ring hollow. Their main argument appears to be that their conduct was authorized by [the California version of RUPA § 404], which codifies the fiduciary duties of a partner under California law. The implication of such an argument is that [the California version of RUPA § 404] provides the *exclusive* statement of a partner's obligation to the partnership and to other partners. This premise would be correct if California had adopted, in its proposed form, the uniform law on which [the California version of RUPA § 404] is based. Section 404 of the Uniform Partnership Act (1997), also known as the Revised Uniform Partnership Act or RUPA, contains an explicitly exclusive enumeration of a partner's duties. After noting that a partner owes fiduciary duties of loyalty and care, the uniform Act declares that those duties are "limited to" obligations listed there. [RUPA § 404(b) and (c).] While [the California version of RUPA § 404] retains this language with respect to the duty of care, it repudiates it with respect to the duty of loyalty, stating instead that " . . . [a] partner's duty of loyalty to the partnership and the other partners *includes* all of the following: . . . " (Italics added.)

The leading treatise on RUPA confirms that by altering the proposed language, the California Legislature rejected one of the "fundamental" changes the drafters sought to bring to partnership law, i.e., "an exclusive statutory treatment of partners' fiduciary duties." (HILLMAN, ET AL., THE REVISED UNIFORM PARTNERSHIP ACT (2004 ed.), p. 202.) The proposed uniform version "[b]y its terms . . . comprises an exclusive statement of the fiduciary duties of partners among themselves and to the partnership. The formulation is exclusive in two ways; the duties of loyalty and care are the only components of the partners' fiduciary duties, and the duties themselves are exclusively defined." (*Ibid.*, fns. omitted.) But several states, *most clearly California*, balked at the latter restriction, leaving the articulation of the duty of loyalty to traditional common law processes. "Some adopting states . . . modified the RUPA language in ways which make, or arguably make, the fiduciary duty formulation non-exclusive. [Citation.] The available California legislative history states that: '[the California version of RUPA § 404] establishes a *comprehensive, but not exhaustive, definition* of partnership fiduciary duties. A partner owes *at least two* duties to other partners and the partnership: a duty of loyalty and a duty of care. In addition, an obligation of good faith and fair dealing is imposed on partners.' [Citation.] This reading is also supported by the drafters' conclusion in the legislative history that 'the new fiduciary duty section makes no substantive change from prior law.' [Citation.]" (*Ibid.*, fn. 5, quoting Senate Rules Com., Off. of Sen. Floor Analyses, 3d reading analysis of Assem. Bill No. 583 (1995–1996 Reg. Sess.) as amended Aug. 23, 1996, p. 6, some italics added.)

Further, even if the statutory enumeration of duties were exclusive, it would not entitle defendants to rent partnership property to themselves at below-market rates. The first duty listed in the statute is "[t]o account to the partnership and hold as trustee for it *any property, profit, or benefit* derived by the partner in the conduct . . . of the partnership business or *derived from a use by the partner of partnership property*. . . . "

Defendants persuaded the trial court that the conduct challenged by plaintiff was authorized by [the California version of RUPA § 404], which states, "A partner does not violate a duty or obligation under this chapter or under the partnership agreement merely because the partner's conduct furthers the partner's own interest." The apparent purpose of this provision, which is drawn verbatim from RUPA section 404(e), is to excuse partners from accounting for incidental benefits obtained in the course of partnership activities *without detriment to the partnership*.[5] It does not by its terms authorize the kind of conduct at issue here, which did not "merely" further defendants' own interests but did so by depriving the partnership of valuable assets, i.e., the space which would otherwise have been rented at market rates. Here, the statute entitled defendants to lease partnership property *at the same rent another tenant would have paid*. It did not empower them to occupy partnership property for their own exclusive benefit at partnership expense, in effect converting partnership assets to their own and appropriating the value it would otherwise have realized as distributable profits. Defendants' argument to the contrary seems conceptually indistinguishable from a claim that if a partnership's "primary purpose" is to purchase and hold investments, individual partners may freely pilfer its office supplies.

Defendants also persuaded the trial court that they had no duty to collect market rents in the absence of a contract expressly requiring them to do so.

---

[5] [3] The authors of the above-cited treatise note that this provision has received "two very different interpretations . . . , one rather narrow and the other quite broad. Under the narrow interpretation, Section 404(e) is essentially an evidentiary rule which could be paraphrased as 'the fact that a partner directly personally benefits from the partner's conduct in the partnership context does not, without more, establish a violation of the partner's duties or obligations under RUPA or the partnership agreement.' Under the broad interpretation, Section 404(e) means that partners are free to pursue their short-term, individual self-interest without notice to or the consent of the partnership, subject only to the specific restrictions contained in the Section 404(b) duty of loyalty — in effect that the pursuit of self-interest cannot be a violation of the non-fiduciary obligation of good faith and fair dealing." (HILLMAN, ET AL., *supra*, p. 207.) We need not decide which of these views, if either, prevails in California. Even under the broader reading, section 16404, subdivision (e), does not authorize a partner to exploit partnership property for personal advantage at partnership expense.

This argument turns partnership law on its head. Nowhere does the law declare that partners owe each other only those duties they explicitly assume by contract. On the contrary, the fiduciary duties at issue here are *imposed by law*, and their breach sounds in tort. We have no occasion here to consider the extent to which partners might effectively limit or modify those delictual duties by an explicit agreement or whether the partnership agreement in fact required market rents by its terms. There is no suggestion that it purported to affirmatively *excuse* defendants from the delictual duty not to engage in self-dealing. Instead, their argument is predicated on the wholly untenable notion that they were entitled to do so unless the agreement explicitly declared otherwise.

Defendants also assert, and the trial court found, that the "primary purpose" of the partnership was to hold the building for appreciation and eventual sale. This premise hardly justified summary adjudication. If the partners had explicitly agreed *not* to derive market rents from the property, but to let it be used for the exclusive advantage of some of them indefinitely, there would be some basis to contend that defendants were entitled to conduct themselves as they did — or at least that plaintiff was estopped to complain. But the mere anticipation of eventual capital gains as the main economic benefit to be derived from the venture has no tendency whatsoever to entitle individual partners to divert to their own advantage benefits that would otherwise flow to the partnership.

132 Cal. App. 4th at 1563–67.

d. Contracting Around Fiduciary Duties

In *Singer v. Singer*, 634 P.2d 766 (Okla. App. 1981), the court upheld a provision in a partnership agreement that permitted partners to compete with the partnership. The partnership in *Singer* was engaged in oil production and, during the term of the partnership, two of the partners acquired land that the partnership might have had an interest in acquiring. Absent the agreement, the conduct of the renegade partners might have run afoul of the fiduciary duty announced in *Meinhard*.

Section 103(b)(3) of RUPA states that the duty of loyalty may not be eliminated by the partnership agreement, but "the partners by agreement may identify specific types or categories of activities that do not violate the duty of loyalty, if not manifestly unreasonable." Would the *Singer* case likely come out the same in a RUPA jurisdiction?

In addition, in § 404(e), RUPA provides that, "A partner does not violate a duty or obligation under this Act or under the partnership agreement merely because the partner's conduct furthers the partner's own interest." Comment 1 to § 404 states that, "[a]rguably, the term 'fiduciary' is inappropriate when used to describe the duties of a partner because a partner may legitimately pursue self-interest and not solely the interest of the partnership and the other partners, as must a true trustee. Nevertheless, partners have long been characterized as fiduciaries." This idea is developed in Comment 5, which states, "That admonition [in § 404(e)] has particular application to the duty of loyalty and the obligation of good faith and fair dealing. It underscores the partner's rights as owner and principal in the enterprise, which must always be balanced against his duties and obligations as an agent and fiduciary."

This approach of RUPA has drawn fire from two different perspectives. One perspective is represented by Allan W. Vestal, *Fundamental Contractarian Error in the Revised Uniform Partnership Act of 1992*, 73 B.U. L. Rev. 523, 535 (1993) ("The Revised Act turns the world upside down with respect to the fiduciary relations of partners *inter se*. The engine of this error is the drafters' rejection of the fiduciary essence of the partnership relationship in favor of the contractarian premise. . . . This shift is breathtaking. In one stroke of the pen [referring to § 404(e)], the drafters have made the partners adversaries, whereas before they were bound by 'the duty of the finest loyalty' . . . ."). *See also* Claire Moore Dickerson, *Is It Appropriate to Appropriate Corporate Concepts: Fiduciary Duties and the Revised Uniform Partnership Act*, 64 U. Colo. L. Rev. 111, 155–56 (1993) ("Once the partnership form has been chosen, there would be no purpose in wasting time — and transaction costs — on negotiating the terms of a fiduciary duty. I do not agree with contractarian commentators who maintain that the traditional fiduciary duties are so vague and aspirational as to be meaningless. . . . Far from being naively aspirational, those duties serve to guide the parties to a standard of behavior that reduces the need to monitor.").

The other perspective is represented by Larry E. Ribstein, *The Revised Uniform Partnership Act: Not Ready for Prime Time*, 49 Bus. Law. 45, 52–54 (1993), stating in part as follows:

> *Fiduciary duty* is a type of contractual term courts supply because the parties themselves would have contracted for the duties if it were not so costly to contract in detail. . . . Because fiduciary duties are contractual 'gap-fillers,' the precise nature of the duties that exist in any particular contractual relationship depends on the express and implied terms of the relevant contract-
> . . . . The UPA prohibition on unilateral benefit without co-partners' consent [§ 21] gives courts the flexibility to fill gaps in partnership contracts by determining who owns what and the partners' duties regarding partnership property. Because the extensive case law under the UPA's simple language recognizes a full range of fiduciary duties, there was no need for further detail. Yet RUPA perversely attempts to spell out a set of duties that exists in all partnerships under all circumstances. . . . While partners may have a duty to act unselfishly in partnership affairs, RUPA errs in making this duty part of every partnership contract. Partners often do not contract to be strict fiducia-ries in the typical agency or trust sense of one who controls the property of another. In other words, partners are not necessarily comparable to directors or executives of publicly-held corporations. Instead, partners may be self-seeking co-venturers who are constrained from the worst kinds of misconduct by their contingent compensation, personal liability for debts, and their co-partners' close monitoring and power to withdraw at any time.

See also J. Dennis Hynes, *Freedom of Contract, Fiduciary Duties, and Partnerships: The Bargain Principle and the Law of Agency*, 54 Wash. & Lee L. Rev. 439 (1997); Allan W. Vestal, *Advancing the Search for Compromise: A Response to Professor Hynes*, 58 Law & Contemp. Probs. 55 (Spring 1995); J. William Callison, *Blind Men and Elephants: Fiduciary Duties Under the Revised Uniform Partnership Act, Uniform Limited Liability Company Act, and Beyond*, 1 J. Small & Emerging Bus. L. 109 (1997). Delaware has embraced a vigorous contractarian approach to partnership and LLC cases, as the materials below indicate. It is doubtful whether many other states would follow Delaware's lead; the fiduciary principles of partnership law are well-ingrained in the judicial decisions of most states.

7. Dissociation and Dissolution

a. The Dissolution Concept under UPA and RUPA

In the partnership materials thus far, we have noted various differences between UPA and RUPA, but for the most part RUPA did not change partnership law very significantly. In the area of dissolution, however, RUPA did implement an important change in the law. Under UPA, any time a partner left the partnership, for whatever reason, the partnership "dissolved." Unless the parties had an agreement that entitled the remaining partners to continue the business, the partnership was required to liquidate, discharge its debts, and distribute any remaining proceeds to the partners. Obviously, this made partnerships fairly "unstable" as a business entity. This lack of stability is consistent with an underlying philosophy of UPA — that partnerships were not separate legal entities but, rather, an aggregate of individuals. RUPA changed this, clearly declaring that a partnership is an entity in RUPA § 201. The departure of a partner under RUPA would not dissolve that partnership, except under certain limited circumstances. Rather, the departing partner is characterized as having "dissociated" from the partnership and the partnership continues without him. RUPA § 601 lists ten events that will cause dissociation, including the express will, expulsion, bankruptcy, or death of a partner. Most dissociations result in a buyout of the dissociating partner's interest under Article 7.[6]

The dissolution provisions of RUPA are contained in § 801. They are largely default in nature; with several narrow exceptions, they are not included in the list of mandatory terms in § 103. Thus, similar to UPA, partners under RUPA have the contractual freedom to avoid termination of the business. The way in which they accomplish this is different, however, because they can simply deny the event of dissolution, something unavailable under UPA. The end result is the same in many cases, however. The business continues and the departing partner is paid out.

b. Liquidation Rights

Unless otherwise agreed, dissolution creates liquidation rights in "each partner, as against his co-partners." UPA § 38(l). RUPA also recognizes the liquidation right. *See* § 807(a) (distribution "in cash" to partners) and (b) ("Each partner is entitled to a settlement of all partnership accounts upon winding up the partnership business."), which continue the rule of § 38(1) of UPA, although it applies to a narrower range of circumstances under RUPA. Not infrequently, one or more of the partners of a dissolved partnership desires to continue the business of the partnership and petition a court for a distribution of partnership assets in kind. Despite what appears to be clear language in UPA requiring a cash liquidation, the court split on whether, in fact, UPA demanded that. *Compare Dreifuerst v. Dreifuerst*, 280 N.W.2d 335 (Wis. Ct. App. 1979) (cash liquidation required) *with Rinke v. Rinke*, 48 N.W.2d 201 (Mich. 1951) (cash liquidation not required) *and Creel v. Lilly*, 729 A.2d 385 (Md. 1999) (same). Interestingly, the split of the courts in the interpretation of UPA, as reflected in the *Dreifuerst* and *Rinke* cases, has carried over to RUPA. In *McCormick v. Brevig*, 96 P.3d 697, 704 (Mont. 2004), the court held that under RUPA, when a dissolution results from a court order, "the partnership assets necessarily must be reduced to cash. . . . " *See also Pankratz Farms, Inc. v. Pankratz*, 95 P.3d 671 (Mont. 2004); *Mock v. Bigale*, 867 So. 2d 1259 (Fla. App. 2004). Taking a contrary view was the court in *Horne v. Aune*, 121 P.3d 1227, 1233–34 (Wash. App. 2005), a case involving a residence owned and occupied by two partners (Aune and Horne). One partner, Aune, moved out of the residence, dissolved the partnership, and sought to require a sale of the residence, while the other partner (Horne) desired to continue to reside there with her son. The court rejected Aune's argument that a sale was required:

> We decline Aune's invitation to follow the Montana Supreme Court's reasoning in *McCormick*. Instead, we adopt Maryland's approach in *Creel*. Contrary to *McCormick*, the winding-up statute does not plainly mean forced sale. Thus, in our view, the trial court's resort to the dictionary in *McCormick* was appropriate. According to Black's Law Dictionary, "liquidate" means:
>
> 1. To settle (an obligation) by payment or other adjustment; to extinguish (a debt). 2. To ascertain the precise amount of (debt, damages, etc.) by litigation or agreement. 3. To determine the liabilities and distribute the assets of (an entity), esp. in bankruptcy or dissolution. 4. To convert (a non-liquid asset) into cash. 5. To wind up the affairs of (a corporation, business, etc.).

---

[6] A partner's dissociation "will always result in either a buyout of the dissociated partner's interest or a dissolution and winding up of the partnership business." Comment 1 to § 603.

As used in [RUPA § 807(b)], the phrase "liquidation of the partnership assets," guarantees partners the right to receive, in cash, the fair value of their property interest upon winding up and dissolution of the partnership. But that result may be achieved by means other than forced sale. Historically, liquidation equaled forced sale because that was deemed the most accurate method of valuing partnership assets. But where, as here, the parties stipulate to the partnership assets' value, there is no reason to equate liquidation with forced sale. . . .

Although the court's equitable discretion is subject to partnership statutes, RUPA does not do away altogether with equitable considerations. "Unless displaced by particular provisions of this chapter, the principles of law and equity supplement this chapter." [RUPA § 104(a).] The court's exercise of equitable discretion to grant Horne the right to purchase the property is not inconsistent with the winding-up statute.

Opinions consistent with *Horne* include *Investment Management, Inc. v. Jordan Realty, Inc.*, 2002 Minn. App. LEXIS 925 (Minn. Ct. App. July 30, 2002). Were the *Investment Management* and *Horne* courts on solid ground citing equitable principles in the face of the statutory provision?

C.　LIMITED PARTNERSHIPS

1.　Organizational Requirements

The study of limited partnership law implicates at least three uniform acts: the Uniform Limited Partnership Act (1916) (ULPA), the Revised Uniform Limited Partnership Act (1976) (RULPA) and the Uniform Limited Partnership Act (2001) (often referred to in the literature as Re-RULPA). In addition, RULPA was significantly amended in 1985, and one can find many references to these amendments in the cases and limited partnership literature. Most states have adopted RULPA with those 1985 amendments. Re-RULPA, substantively, is very similar to RULPA with the 1985 amendments. As noted above, however, Re-RULPA integrates the provisions from general partnership law needed create a stand-alone limited partnership law.

RULPA, like its predecessors, requires the organizers of a limited partnership to make a filing with the state, usually the secretary of state. If the proper filing is made, and (under most statutes) the limited partners do not control the business, the limited partners will not be vicariously liable for the debts or obligations of the limited partnership, but the general partner will have vicarious liability. Several states have adopted legislation allowing the creation of a limited liability limited partnership (LLLP), under which the general partner enjoys the same limited liability as a partner in an LLP. In any case, if a filing is not made, the limited partner risks being treated as a general partner.

2.　The Agreement of Limited Partnership

The parties to a limited partnership typically set forth their understandings in a written agreement, although, strictly speaking, that is not necessary. RULPA acknowledges that the agreement may be oral. ["Partnership agreement means any valid agreement, written or oral, of the partners as to the affairs of a limited partnership and the conduct of its business." RULPA § 101(9)]. Under ULPA, the certificate of limited partnership required extensive disclosures of the arrangements of the parties, and could itself serve as an agreement. RULPA and its amendments severely reduced the amount of disclosure, so that a modern certificate of limited partnership includes very little information and could not serve as an agreement. This change in the law facilitates the use of limited partnerships for large undertakings with dozens and sometimes hundreds or even thousands of limited partners. Such partnerships are not uncommon in certain industries such as real estate and natural resources, although limited liability companies, considered below, are often the entity of choice for such businesses.

Assuming a written agreement is entered into, a question arises as to the rules that apply to interpreting that agreement. If ambiguous, for instance, is extrinsic evidence admissible? The Delaware Supreme Court addressed this issue in *SI Management L.P. v. Wininger*, 707 A.2d 37 (Del. 1998):

> Here, the setting in which the Limited Partnership came into existence appears on this record to be quite different from that in *Eagle* [*Industries, Inc. v. DeVilbiss Health Care*, 702 A.2d 1228 (Del. 1997)]. This was not a bilateral negotiated agreement. Rather, it appears that the General Partner solicited and signed on 1,850 investors to the Agreement that those investors had no hand in drafting. Based on that premise, the principle of *contra proferentem* applies. Accordingly, ambiguous terms in the Agreement should be construed against the General Partner as the entity solely responsible for the articulation of those terms. On remand and final hearing on a permanent injunction, the trial court should determine whether these plaintiffs actually did engage in negotiations with the General Partner on the issues in question here.

> A court considering extrinsic evidence assumes that there is some connection between the expectations of contracting parties revealed by that evidence and the way contract terms were articulated by those parties. Therefore, unless extrinsic evidence can speak to the intent of *all* parties to a contract, it provides an incomplete guide with which to interpret contractual language. Thus, it is proper to consider extrinsic evidence of bilateral negotiations when there is an ambiguous contract that was the product of those negotiations, as in *Eagle*.

> On the limited record before us in this case, however, it appears that the 1,850 investors comprising the limited partnership reacted to a "take it or leave it" proposal by the General Partner without meaningful individualized negotiations. Because the articulation of contract terms in this case appears to have been entirely within the control of *one party* — the General Partner — that party bears full responsibility for the effect of those terms. Accordingly, extrinsic evidence is irrelevant to the intent of *all* parties at the time they entered into the agreement.

QUESTION

Suppose the general partner involved in a dispute with the limited partners over the meaning of a provision in the partnership agreement became the general partner after the agreement was in existence. Would it make sense to construe the agreement against such a general partner? Suppose, instead, that the partnership agreement provided that the rule of *contra proferentem* would not apply to any disputes regarding the interpretation of the partnership agreement. Would such a provision be enforceable?

3. The Limited Partner

a. Participation in the Business of the Limited Partnership

One of the most vexing questions in the law of limited partnerships is whether limited partners lose their protected status of limited liability if they participate in the business of the partnership. Under ULPA, a limited partner would be liable if that limited partner "takes part in the control of the business." ULPA § 7. Under this standard, limited partners were well-advised not to participate in the business. RULPA, particularly the 1985 amendments, permitted greater activity by the limited partner without causing them to run the risk of incurring liability. Re-RULPA removed all limitations on limited partners; they can participate to any degree that they wish without running the risk of liability as partners. Re-RULPA, however, is not widely adopted; as of this writing, only a few states had adopted it. The next case is a good example of the complexity in terms of just what a limited partner may do in the business.

GATEWAY POTATO SALES v. G.B. INVESTMENT CO.
Court of Appeals of Arizona
822 P.2d 490 (1991)

TAYLOR, JUDGE.

Gateway Potato Sales (Gateway), a creditor of Sunworth Packing Limited Partnership (Sunworth Packing), brought suit to recover payment for goods it had supplied to the limited partnership. Gateway sought recovery from Sunworth Packing, from Sunworth Corporation as general partner, and from G.B. Investment Company (G.B. Investment) as a limited partner, pursuant to Arizona Revised Statutes Annotated, [RULPA § 303]. Under § [303], a limited partner may become liable for the obligations of the limited partnership under certain circumstances in which the limited partner has taken part in the control of the business.

G.B. Investment moved for summary judgment, urging that there was no evidence that the circumstances described in [§ 303] had occurred in this case. It argued that, as a limited partner, it was not liable to the creditors of the limited partnership except to the extent of its investment. The trial court agreed, granting G.B. Investment's motion for summary judgment.

Gateway appeals from the judgment and the denial of its motion for reconsideration, arguing the existence of conflicting evidence of material facts relating to the participation of the limited partner in the control of the partnership business. We agree and reverse the grant of summary judgment. . . .

In late 1985, Robert C. Ellsworth, the president of Sunworth Corporation, called Robert Pribula, the owner of Gateway, located in Minnesota, to see if Gateway would supply Sunworth Packing with seed potatoes. Pribula hesitated to supply the seed potatoes without receiving assurance of payment because Pribula was aware that Ellsworth had previously undergone bankruptcy. Pribula, however, decided to sell the seed potatoes to Sunworth Packing after being assured by Ellsworth that he was in partnership with a large financial institution, G.B. Investment Company, and that G.B. Investment was providing the financing, was actively involved in the operation of the business, and had approved the purchase of the seed potatoes. Thereafter, from February 1986 through April 1986, Gateway sold substantial quantities of seed potatoes to Sunworth Packing.

While supplying the seed potatoes, Pribula believed that he was doing business with a general partnership (i.e., Sunworth Packing Company, formed by Sunworth Corporation and G.B. Investment Company). The sales documents used by the parties specified "Sunworth Packing Company" as the name of the partnership. Pribula was neither aware of the true name of the partnership nor that it was a limited partnership.

All of Gateway's dealings were with Ellsworth. Pribula neither contacted G.B. Investment prior to selling the seed potatoes to the limited partnership nor did he otherwise attempt to verify any of the statements Ellsworth had made about G.B. Investment's involvement. The only direct contact between G.B. Investment and Gateway occurred some time after the sale of the seed potatoes. . . .

G.B. Investment's vice-president, Darl Anderson, testified in his affidavit that G.B. Investment had exerted no control over the daily management and operation of the limited partnership, Sunworth Packing. This testimony was contradicted, however, by the affidavit testimony of Ellsworth which was presented by Gateway in opposing G.B. Investment's motion for summary judgment. According to Ellsworth, G.B.

Investment's employees, Darl Anderson and Thomas McHolm, controlled the day-to-day affairs of the limited partnership and made Ellsworth account to them for nearly everything he did. This day-to-day contact included but was not limited to approval of most of the significant operational decisions and expenditures and the use and management of partnership funds without Ellsworth's involvement.[7]

Ellsworth testified further that he had described G.B. Investment's control of the business operation to Pribula. Pribula confirmed that Ellsworth had informed him that G.B. Investment's employees, McHolm and Anderson, were at the partnership's office on a frequent basis, that Ellsworth reported directly to them, that daily operations of the partnership were reviewed by representatives of G.B. Investment, and that Ellsworth had to get their approval before making certain business decisions. . . . [The court quotes RULPA § 303(a)]:

> [A] limited partner is not liable for the obligations of a limited partnership unless he is also a general partner or, in addition to the exercise of his rights and powers as a limited partner, he takes part in the control of the business. However, if the limited partner's participation in the control of the business is not substantially the same as the exercise of the powers of a general partner, he is liable only to persons who transact business with the limited partnership with actual knowledge of his participation in control.

. . . Gateway argued that the statute imposes liability on a limited partner whose participation in the control of the business is substantially the same as the exercised power of a general partner. Gateway further argued that even if the person transacting business with the limited partnership did not know of the limited partner's participation in control, there is liability. Alternatively, Gateway argued that the statute imposes liability when the powers exercised in controlling the business might fall short of being "substantially the same as the exercise of powers of a general partner," but the person transacting business with the limited partnership had actual knowledge of the participation in control. Gateway asserted that the evidence it was presenting in response to the motion for summary judgment raised issues of material fact as to whether either of these situations had occurred. If either had occurred, Gateway argued, it would be entitled to recover from the limited partner, G.B. Investment.

In granting G.B. Investment's motion for summary judgment, the trial court conclud[ed] that G.B. Investment could not be found liable under [§ 303] as a matter of law. [A]s we interpret the trial court's comments, it read the statute as having a threshold requirement — that is, under all circumstances, a creditor of the limited partnership must have contact with the limited partner in order to impose liability on the limited partner. The evidence before the trial court showed that Gateway merely relied upon the statements made by Ellsworth, president of the general partner, and that Gateway did not contact G.B. Investment prior to transacting business with the limited

---

[7] [1] Ellsworth described with some specificity the ways in which G.B. Investment's control was exerted:

a. During the early months of the Partnership, Thomas McHolm and/or Darl Anderson were at the Partnership's offices on a daily basis directing the operation of the Partnership, and thereafter, they were at the Partnership's offices at least 2–3 times per week reviewing the operations of the business, directing changes in operations, and instructing me to make certain changes in operating the Partnership's affairs. . . .

d. Prior to constructing improvements to the packaging facilities of the Partnership, Thomas McHolm and/or Darl Anderson had to approve all construction bids, individually selected some of the suppliers and subcontractors, and individually selected the equipment to be installed. . . .

f. During a great portion of the duration of the Partnership, Thomas McHolm and/or Darl Anderson oversaw the daily operations of the Partnership because I had to have all expenditures approved by Thomas McHolm and/or Darl Anderson and Darl Anderson had to approve and sign checks issued by the Partnership, including without limitation payroll checks and invoices for telephone charges, utilities, publications, interest payments, bank card charges, supplies, etc. Copies of a sampling of the invoices and the corresponding checks are attached hereto as Exhibit 2. . . .

partnership. Based upon these facts, the trial court concluded that liability could not be imposed upon G.B. Investment. . . .

To the extent that the trial court's ruling may have been based on a belief that a limited partner could never be liable under the statute unless the creditor had contact with the limited partner and learned directly from him of his participation and control of the business, we believe that ruling to be in error. In [§ 303] the legislature stopped short of expressly stating that if the limited partner's participation in the control of the business is substantially the same as the exercise of the powers of a general partner, he is liable to persons who transact business with a limited partnership even though they have no knowledge of his participation and control. It has made this statement by implication, though, by stating to the opposite effect that "if the limited partner's participation in the control of the business is not substantially the same as the exercise of the powers of a general partner, he is liable only to persons who transact business with the limited partnership with actual knowledge of his participation in control." [§ 303(a).]

We believe this interpretation is strengthened by an examination of the legislative history of Arizona's limited partnership statute. It is further strengthened by the legislature's refusal to modify this statute to correspond to the Revised Uniform Limited Partnership Act, as amended in 1985. . . . In 1985, the drafters of the RULPA backtracked from the position taken in section 303(a) of the 1976 Act. The new amendments reflect a reluctance to hold a limited partner liable if the limited partner had no direct contact with the creditor. The 1985 revised RULPA section 303(a) was amended to provide as follows:

> Except as provided in Subsection (d), a limited partner is not liable for the obligations of a limited partnership unless he is also a general partner or, in addition to the exercise of his rights and powers as a limited partner, he participates in the control of the business. *However, if the limited partner participates in the control of the business, he is liable only to persons who transact business with the limited partnership reasonably believing, based upon the limited partner's conduct, that the limited partner is a general partner.* (Emphasis added.)

The Arizona legislature, however, has not revised [RULPA] to correspond to the [1985] amendments. . . . It follows then that no contact between the creditor and the limited partner is required to impose liability.

Moreover, whereas section 303 of the RULPA [1985 amendments] states that the creditor's reasonable belief must be "based upon the limited partner's conduct," under [§ 303] the only requirement is that the creditor has had "actual knowledge of [the limited partner's] participation in control." The statute does not state that this knowledge must be based upon the limited partner's conduct. . . . Under the facts presented in this case, Gateway had no direct contact with G.B. Investment until after the sales were concluded. We conclude, therefore, that G.B. Investment would be liable only if the "substantially the same as" test was met.

Whether a limited partner has exercised the degree of control that will make him liable to a creditor has always been a factual question. This is so regardless of whether the particular statute involved is patterned after section 7 of the ULPA or after section 303 of the RULPA. Our current Arizona statute lists activities that a limited partner may undertake without participating in controlling the business. It also states that other activities may be excluded from the definition of such control. Where activities do not fall within the "safe harbor" of § 303(b), it is necessary for a trier-of-fact to determine whether such activities amount to "control." In the absence of actual knowledge of the limited partner's participation in the control of the partnership business, there must be evidence from which a trier-of-fact might find not only control, but control that is "substantially the same as the exercise of powers of a general partner." . . .

Viewing the facts in the light most favorable to Gateway, we cannot say as a matter of law that G.B. Investment was entitled to summary judgment. We conclude that Gateway is entitled to a determination by trial of the extent of control exercised by G.B. Investment over Sunworth Packing.

For the foregoing reasons, we reverse the judgment of the trial court and remand for further proceedings.

EHRLICH, P.J., and CLABORNE, J., concur.

b. The Limited Partner as Agent of the Corporate General Partner

Not infrequently, the general partner of a limited partnership is a corporation, the principals of which are also limited partners in their individual capacity. Should such individuals be treated as general partners? The next case grapples with that question.

ZEIGER v. WILF
Superior Court of New Jersey, Appellate Division
333 N.J. Super 258, 755 A.2d 608 (2000)

LESEMANN, J.A.D.

This case offers a virtual primer in the Byzantine relationships among various forms of business organizations employed in a modern venture capital project. It includes a limited partnership, a corporation, a general partnership and several sophisticated individuals all involved in the proposed redevelopment of a hotel/office building in downtown Trenton. It also demonstrates the significance of limited individual liability which is a key reason for employing some of those entities, and the inevitable risk that anticipated rewards from such a venture may not be realized.

At issue here is an agreement by which plaintiff, a seller of the property to be renovated, was to receive a "consultant fee" of $23,000 per year for sixteen years. The payments, however, ceased after two years. A jury found the redevelopers (a limited partnership and a corporation) liable for those payments, and an appeal by those entities has now been abandoned. As a result, the matter now focuses on plaintiff's claim that Joseph Wilf, the individual who led the various defendant entities, should be held personally liable for the consultant payments and that such liability should also be imposed on a general partnership owned by Wilf and members of his family.

There is no claim that Wilf personally, or his general partnership, ever guaranteed the consultant payments or that plaintiff ever believed Wilf had made such guarantees. Nor is there a claim that plaintiff did not understand at all times that he was contracting only with a limited partnership and/or a corporation, and not with Wilf personally or with his general partnership. For those reasons, and also because we find no merit in various other theories of individual liability advanced by plaintiff, we affirm the summary judgment entered in favor of Wilf individually, and we reverse the judgment against Wilf's family-owned general partnership. . . .

[The property was sold to Trenton, Inc., a corporation (the "corporation"), which was originally obligated on the consulting contract. That contract and the corporation's property rights were subsequently assigned to Trenton, L.P., a limited partnership (the "limited partnership"). The general partner of the limited partnership was Trenton, Inc. and the principle limited partner was CPA, a general partnership controlled by the defendant Wilf. CPA also owned 50% of the stock of Trenton, Inc. Wilf handled the renovations on behalf of the limited partnership as an officer of its corporate general partner.]

Eventually, the project failed. The limited partnership and the corporation filed bankruptcy. . . . On July 19, 1993, plaintiff sued Wilf, claiming that Wilf had become the "surviving partner and owner of the partnership assets" pertaining to the "purchase and transfer of" the hotel, and that he was in default respecting payment of plaintiff's consulting fees.

[The trial court granted summary judgment in favor of Wilf, dismissing the complaint as to him. Subsequently,] a jury returned a $456,801 verdict against the limited partnership and the corporation, to which sum the trial court added pre-judgment interest. However, while the trial court had submitted to the jury the liability issue as to the limited partnership and the corporation, it had withheld for determination by the court plaintiff's claim against CPA. On December 4, 1997, the court found that CPA was also liable to plaintiff for the aforesaid $456,801, and entered judgment against it for that amount.

This appeal was initially filed by plaintiff, seeking reversal of the judgment in favor of Joseph Wilf. A cross-appeal was then filed by CPA, by Trenton, L.P. and by Trenton, Inc. . . . [B]ecause of the intervening bankruptcy proceedings, defendants have advised that no "useful purpose is served by continuing to process this appeal" on behalf of the limited partnership or the corporation. Thus, defendants have argued for reversal only as against CPA while, of course, also maintaining that the dismissal as to defendant Wilf should be affirmed. . . .

[P]laintiff claims the limited partnership statute imposes general partner liability on Wilf because he functioned as the operating head of the parties' renovation project. We find the claim inconsistent with both the policy and the language of the statute.

A basic principle of [RULPA] is a differentiation between the broad liability of a general partner for the obligations of a limited partnership (see [RULPA § 404]), and the non-liability of a limited partner for such obligations. See [RULPA § 303(a)]. Preservation of that distinction and protection against imposing unwarranted liability on a limited partner has been a consistent concern of the drafters of the Uniform Act on which our New Jersey statute is based, and has been described as "the single most difficult issue facing lawyers who use the limited partnership form of organization." See Revised Unif. Limited Partnership Act, Prefatory Note preceding § 101, U.L.A. (1976) (hereinafter "Commissioners' Report"). Indeed, the history of the Uniform Limited Partnership Act, and thus the evolution of our New Jersey statute, shows a consistent movement to insure certainty and predictability respecting the obligations and potential liability of limited partners. The framers of the Act have accomplished that by consistently reducing and restricting the bases on which a general partner's unrestricted liability can be imposed on a limited partner. Under the present version of the Uniform Act, the imposition of such liability (absent fraud or misleading) is severely limited. Our New Jersey statute (as discussed below) reflects that same philosophy in the provisions of [RULPA § 303(a)].

The original version of the ULPA was adopted in 1916. That enactment dealt with the question of a limited partner's liability in one short provision. In Section 7 it said:

> A limited partner shall not become liable as a general partner unless, in addition to the exercise of his rights and powers as a limited partner, he takes part in the control of the business.

In 1976, the original ULPA was substantially replaced by a revised version (on which the New Jersey statute is based) which "was intended to modernize the prior uniform law." See Commissioners Report Prefatory Note preceding Section 101. One of the ways that modernization was effected was by a new Section 303, which replaced the old Section 7, and was adopted virtually verbatim as Section 27 of the New Jersey Statute. Section 303 reads as follows:

> [A] limited partner is not liable for the obligations of a limited partnership unless . . . , in addition to the exercise of his [or her] rights and powers as a limited partner, he [or she] takes part in the control of the business. However, if the limited partner's participation in the control of the business is not substantially the same as the exercise of the powers of a general partner, he [or

she] is liable only to persons who transact business with the limited partnership with actual knowledge of his participation in control.

The Commissioners' Report in the comment to Section 303 states:

Section 303 makes several important changes in Section 7 of the 1916 Act. . . . The second sentence of Section 303(a) reflects a wholly new concept. . . . It was adopted partly because . . . it was thought unfair to impose general partner's liability on a limited partner except to the extent that a third party had knowledge of his participation in control of the business . . . , but also (and more importantly) because of a determination that it is not sound public policy to hold a limited partner who is not also a general partner liable for the obligations of the partnership except to persons who have done business with the limited partnership reasonably believing, based on the limited partner's conduct, that he is a general partner.

Following that 1976 version, more limitations on a limited partner's liability came in 1988, with a series of "Safe Harbor" amendments, virtually all of which were adopted in New Jersey. See [RULPA § 303(b)]. The Commissioners' Report explained the reason for those additions to Section 303 of the Uniform Act:

Paragraph (b) is intended to provide a "Safe Harbor" by enumerating certain activities which a limited partner may carry on for the partnership without being deemed to have taken part in control of the business. This "Safe Harbor" list has been expanded beyond that set out in the 1976 Act to reflect case law and statutory developments and more clearly to assure that limited partners are not subjected to general liability where such liability is inappropriate.

Although plaintiff argues that [RULPA § 303] imposes a general partner's liability on Wilf (and CPA) because Wilf took "part in the control of the business," we are satisfied that the argument has no merit. To accept it, and impose such liability on the facts presented here, would reverse the evolution described above and create precisely the instability and uncertainty that the drafters of the RULPA (and the New Jersey Act) were determined to avoid.

Plaintiff's argument rests on Wilf's key role in the renovation project. Wilf acknowledges that role, but argues that his actions were taken as a vice president of Trenton, Inc. — the corporation which was the sole general partner of Trenton, L.P. Wilf argues that since the corporation is an artificial entity, it can only function through its officers, see *Printing Mart-Morristown v. Sharp Electronics Corp.*, 116 N.J. 739, 761, 563 A.2d 31 (1989), and that is precisely what he was doing at all times when he acted concerning this enterprise. Wilf also points to the "Safe Harbor" provisions of [RULPA § 303(b)] to reinforce his claim that his actions here did not impose general partner liability upon him.

We agree with that analysis. As noted, the 1988 "Safe Harbor" provisions set out a number of activities which, under the statute, do not constitute participating in "the control of" a business so as to impose a general partner's liability on a limited partner. The provision to which Wilf particularly refers is [RULPA § 303(b)(1)], which provides that,

b. A limited partner does not participate in the control of the business within the meaning of subsection a. solely by[,]

[1] Serving as an officer, director or shareholder of a corporate general partner;

That provision clearly applies here and essentially undercuts plaintiff's argument: while plaintiff claims that Wilf's activities constitute "control" of the activities of Trenton, L.P., the statute says, in just so many words, that those activities do *not* constitute the exercise of control.

In addition to the "Safe Harbor" protections, [RULPA § 303(a).] itself sharply limits the circumstances under which the exercise of "control" could lead to imposition of general partner liability on a limited partner. It first provides that if a limited partner's control activities are so extensive as to be "substantially the same as" those of a general partner, that control, by itself, is sufficient to impose liability: *i.e.*, if a limited partner acts "the same as" a general partner, he will be treated as a general partner. However, but for that extreme case, mere participation in control does not impose liability on a limited partner. Such liability may be imposed only as to "persons who," in essence, rely on the limited partner's participation in control, and thus regard him as a general partner.

That limitation of liability to those who rely on a limited partner's exercise of control is critical to a sound reading of the statute. It is consistent with the series of amendments from 1916 to now, which have been designed to insure predictability and certainty in the use of the limited partnership form of business organization. To reject plaintiff's claim of liability would be consistent with that view of the statute. To accept the claim would inject precisely the instability and uncertainty which the statute is designed to avoid.

Here, there was none of the "reliance" which is a necessary basis for a limited partner's liability. It bears repeating that plaintiff, an insider in the project, does not claim he was ever misled as to the entities with whom he was dealing. Plaintiff is described as a sophisticated, experienced developer and businessman. He does not deny that description. He does not claim that he ever sought or obtained any individual guarantee or promise of payment from Wilf, and certainly not from CPA. Nor does plaintiff deny that he understood completely that he was dealing with a limited partnership and a corporation. He does not deny his understanding that those entities, by their very nature, provide limited resources and limited recourse for parties with whom they contract. See *Frank Rizzo, Inc. v. Alatsas*, 27 N.J. 400, 402, 142 A.2d 861 (1958), where the court, speaking of a corporation but employing language equally applicable to a limited partnership, noted that:

> [o]rdinarily we do not think in terms of the possibility of individual liability of corporate officers for obligations incurred by the entity in the usual course of business. Such personal liability is inconsistent with the existence of a body corporate at common law and can emanate only from some positive legislative fiat.

In short, there is no claim that plaintiff was misled, or that he relied on some impression that Wilf was a general partner of Trenton, L.P., and thus there is no basis for any finding of personal liability against Wilf under [RULPA § 303(a)].

The only other possible statutory basis for imposing liability on Wilf is the provision which would impose such liability if Wilf's activities were "substantially the same as the exercise of the powers of a general partner" of Trenton, L.P. While that phrase is less than precise, and we are aware of no helpful decision interpreting or applying it, we see no basis for its application here.

First, recall that Wilf's activities as an officer of Trenton, Inc., are specifically sanctioned by the "Safe Harbor" provisions. With the other corporate officers having abrogated their responsibilities, it is difficult to see, first, what other choice was available to Wilf; and second, why his actions should have any adverse effect on him under the Limited Partnership Act.

Further, it is significant that plaintiff does not rest his argument so much on the powers and functions exercised by Wilf, as on the manner in which he exercised those functions. That is, the argument points mainly to Wilf's carelessness in not consistently and specifically identifying himself as an officer of Trenton, Inc., when he acted on behalf of Trenton, L.P. or signed documents on behalf of the limited partnership. The argument, in short, refers more to form than to substance. It lacks force because, regardless of Wilf's alleged carelessness, plaintiff was at all times fully aware of what Wilf was doing and how he was doing it. A failure to comply with some designated formality might have had some significance if, at any time or in any way, it misled plaintiff or prejudiced him. But, as we have noted several times, that is simply not the case.[8]

Plaintiff cites three out-of-state cases in support of his argument against Wilf and CPA. We find all of them either distinguishable or, for other reasons, non-persuasive. . . .

We are satisfied that, were we to find individual liability against Wilf because of his "control" here, we would be encouraging precisely the instability and uncertainty which are anathema to widespread use of the limited partnership as a business entity. The modern, sound view, epitomized by [RULPA], the New Jersey statute and the well-reasoned decisions discussed above is in the other direction: to curtail the threat of personal liability unless there is some "reliance on the part of the outsider dealing with the limited partnership." There was no such reliance here, and there is no basis for imposing personal liability on Wilf. . . .

The summary judgment in favor of defendant Wilf is affirmed, as is the judgment against Trenton, L.P. and Trenton, Inc. The judgment against defendant CPA is reversed. . . .

PROBLEM

Delta Contractors, L.P. was a limited partnership engaged in the business of home remodeling. The general partner was Betty Able, who ran the business. The limited partners consisted of 10 investors and Betty's husband, Churchill. Churchill was a high school teacher, whose involvement in the business was limited except for the summer periods, when school was not in session. During the summers, Churchill would frequently work in Delta's office, ordering materials, assisting with the bookkeeping, and engaging in other tasks as might be necessary. Churchill ordered a load of lumber from Western Lumber Supply Co. for a Delta job that proved to be Delta's undoing. Delta had underbid the job and it drove the company into bankruptcy. Western had filed a claim against Betty and Churchill individually for its unpaid invoice. Analyze Churchill potential liability under ULPA, RULPA, RULPA with the 1985 amendments, and Re-RULPA.

c. Limited Partner's Right to Maintain a Derivative Action

Among the rights that a limited partner does have is the right, under certain circumstances, to maintain an action on behalf of the limited partnership (a "derivative action") against the general partner(s). The theory that underlies this principle is that, if the limited partnership has a cause of action against the general partner for, say, breach of fiduciary duty to the limited partnership, the general partner is unlikely to pursue that claim; put simply, it will not sue itself. Unless the limited partners maintain the action, the injury to the partnership would be uncompensated. The action is "derivative" because it derives from an injury to the partnership; the injury suffered by the limited partners is only indirect. The law regarding derivative actions for limited partnerships is similar to the law relating to derivative actions maintained by

---

[8] [7] The 1976 version of the Uniform Act was amended in 1985, to eliminate entirely the reference to a limited partner's control activities being "substantially the same as the exercise of the powers of a general partner." Thus, the present version projects liability on a limited partner *only* if an outsider "reasonably [believed], based upon the limited partner's conduct, that the limited partner is a general partner." The purpose of the amendment, quite clearly, is to make even clearer the points noted in the comments quoted above: it "is not sound public policy" to hold a limited partner to a general partner's liability, unless he has misled others into believing he was a general partner. See REVISED UNIF. LIMITED PARTNERSHIP ACT, *supra*, Prefatory Note preceding Section 101.

Although, New Jersey has not (yet) adopted the 1985 amendment, neither has it rejected the proposal, and there is no reason to conclude that New Jersey's Section 27 is not consistent with both the presently existing Section 101 and its earlier version.

shareholders in the corporate setting. *See* Chapter 11, *infra*. RULPA expressly recognizes the right of limited partners to maintain derivative actions. *See* RULPA § 1001 *et seq.* The law regarding derivative actions for limited partnerships is not, however, identical to the law relating to corporations, because the nature of a partnership is different from a corporation. For instance, in *Anglo American Security Fund v. S.R. Global International Fund*, 829 A.2d 143 (Del. Ct. Ch. 2003), the court recognized that the limited partners could maintain a direct action for the improper withdrawal of funds by the general partner because the withdrawal resulted in an immediate reduction in the capital accounts of each of the partners. By contrast, if corporate officers improperly withdraw funds, the injury (and any recovery) would be that of the corporation and the action would be derivative.

4. The General Partner

The general partner of a limited partnership owes fiduciary duties of good faith, due care, and loyalty to the limited partnership. Because the ability of the limited partners to participate in the business is limited by statute, as noted above, and often by agreement as well, the limited partners are dependent on the general partner if they are to realize a return on their investment. The courts, therefore, generally have been protective of limited partners, as the *Appletree* case, below, demonstrates. However, like a general partnership, a limited partnership is basically contractual in nature, and, inevitably, the general partner will seek to limit its fiduciary duties. The *Brickell Partners* case, which follows *Appletree*, demonstrates the willingness of Delaware courts to enforce contractual limitations on fiduciary duties.

APPLETREE SQUARE I LIMITED PARTNERSHIP v. INVESTMARK, INC.
Court of Appeals of Minnesota
494 N.W.2d 889 (1993)

CRIPPEN, JUDGE.

Appletree Square One Limited Partnership purchased a commercial office building which is contaminated with asbestos fireproofing materials. Purchasers sued the sellers on various theories of fraud for failing to disclose the presence and hazards of asbestos. Purchasers appeal from summary judgment dismissing each of their claims. We reverse.

Appletree Square I Limited Partnership was formed September 21, 1981, to purchase and operate One Appletree Square, a 15-story office building. The partnership was organized under the 1976 Uniform Limited Partnership Act. Appellants represent the partnership and its affiliates who purchased the property (purchasers). Respondents represent the builders and sellers of the property (sellers), who held interests in the partnership when sale transactions occurred.

This suit is based on two transactions. The building sale occurred in 1981. In 1985, a further acquisition was made by sale of a 25 percent interest in the Appletree partnership. An affiliate of the purchasers, CRI, represented them in both transactions; CRI is a real estate syndication firm. During negotiations for the sale of the property in 1981, CRI wrote a letter to sellers requesting "any information that you have not already sent to us which would be material to our investors' participation in this development." In response, CRI was told to inspect the building and the records, because the sellers "ha[d] no way of knowing what information would be material to your investors' participation."

In 1986, the purchasers learned that the structural steel in the building had been coated with asbestos-based fireproofing, which was deteriorating and releasing fibers. The cost of abatement was estimated at ten million dollars. In their subsequent suit, the purchasers alleged that the sellers were liable for failing to disclose the presence and danger of asbestos. . . .

. . . The [trial] court stated that under [RULPA § 305] and the partnership agreement, the partners' fiduciary duties were only to render, on demand, true and full information. Because appellants had not demanded information about asbestos, respondents had not breached their fiduciary duty of disclosure. Additionally, the environmental liability statute [an additional claim made by plaintiffs] did not apply because it took effect after the 1981 transaction and because it applies to the sale of real estate, not partnership interests. . . .

This appeal turns on whether respondents had a fiduciary duty to disclose to appellants the presence and danger of asbestos. If such a fiduciary duty existed, the trial court must address triable issues on appellants' claims of breach of duty to disclose. . . .

Common Law Duty of Disclosure

Absent a fiduciary relationship, one party to a transaction has "no duty to disclose material facts to the other." In this case, appellants and respondents were partners in a limited partnership. The relationship of partners is fiduciary and partners are held to high standards of integrity in their dealings with each other. Parties in a fiduciary relationship must disclose material facts to each other. Where a fiduciary relationship exists, silence may constitute fraud. Under the common law, respondents had a duty to disclose information regarding asbestos if they knew about it.

Uniform Limited Partnership Act and Duties of Disclosure

The trial court held that the Uniform Limited Partnership Act changed the common law duties of disclosure. [RULPA § 305](2) states that limited partners have the right, "upon reasonable demand," to obtain information from the general partners. This statute mirrors the disclosure requirement in the Uniform Partnership Act and should be interpreted similarly. The trial court held that because appellants did not demand information about asbestos, respondents had no obligation to disclose the information.

The trial court's holding is contradicted by a proper interpretation of the disclosure statute. [RULPA § 305](2) addresses the narrow duty of partners to respond to requests for information. It does not negate a partner's broad common law duty to disclose all material facts. See H. Reuschlein & W. Gregory, Handbook on the Law of Agency and Partnership, 285 (1979) (the duty to render information is not the same as the duty to disclose). This view has been accepted by other jurisdictions that have adopted the uniform acts governing general and limited partnerships. See *Band v. Livonia Assocs.*, 439 N.W.2d 285, 294 (Mich. App. 1989) ("section 20 [of the Uniform Partnership Act] has been broadly interpreted as imposing a duty to disclose all known information that is significant and material to the affairs or property of the partnership"). . . . [RULPA § 305](2) did not eliminate respondents' common law duty to disclose material information to their partners.

Contractual Duties of Disclosure

The trial court also held that the parties limited their duties of disclosure in their contract. The contract stated that the general partners would "provide the partners with all information that may reasonably be requested." Again, appellants never requested information.

Partners may change their common law and statutory duties by incorporating such changes in their partnership agreement. However, where the major purpose of a contract clause is to shield wrongdoers from liability, the clause will be set aside as against public policy. Additionally, while "partners are free to vary many aspects of their relationship . . . they are not free to destroy its fiduciary character." H. Reuschlein and W. Gregory, Handbook on the Law of Agency and Partnership, 268 (1979).

To hold that partners may replace their broad duty of disclosure with a narrow duty to render information upon demand would destroy the fiduciary character of their relationship, and it would also invite fraud. Unless partners knew what questions to ask, they would have no right to know material information about the business. In this case, if respondents knew the building was contaminated with asbestos and if they reasonably should have known their partners did not know about the asbestos, they may have breached their fiduciary duty of disclosure. . . .

Justifiable Reliance

. . . The trial court held as a matter of law that appellants were not justified in relying on respondents to disclose the presence and danger of asbestos. The court based its decision on the fact that respondents told appellants to conduct their own investigation and on its finding that appellants were sophisticated buyers. A fiduciary's duty is defined "with reference to the experience and intelligence of the person to whom the duty is owed." *Perranoski*, 299 N.W.2d at 413. . . .

There is no compelling evidence that either the building specifications or a visual inspection of the building should have revealed the asbestos. Moreover, although the purchasers had partnership authority over management of the building prior to the 1985 partnership interest buyout, respondents were managers in fact from 1972 (when the building was constructed) to 1985. To discover asbestos on their own, appellants would have had to know enough to ask about it or know enough to have various building materials tested.

Finally, the fact that respondents told appellants to investigate did not make appellants' reliance unreasonable as a matter of law. Respondents' statement did not specifically tell appellants not to rely on them. Moreover, even if respondents had told appellants not to rely on them, that statement would not necessarily make reliance unreasonable. Evidence in the record permits a finding that respondents had superior knowledge and knew appellants did not know about the asbestos. These are fact questions which must be answered to determine whether respondents neglected their fiduciary duty to inform appellants. . . .

The trial court erred in holding that respondents' common law duties of disclosure were limited by the Uniform Limited Partnership Act and by the partnership agreement. The court also erred in determining issues of material fact regarding appellants' reliance on disclosures of respondents and in determining reasonable diligence. We reverse summary judgments for respondents. Further proceedings are to occur in accordance with this opinion.

Reversed.

NOTES AND QUESTIONS

1. Although the opinion is not entirely clear on the facts regarding the relationship of the parties, it can be read as a case involving the sale by general partners of partnership property to limited partners. With regard to the duty of general partners toward limited partners, all of the material in § 6, *supra*, regarding the fiduciary duties partners owe one another applies here, of course.

2. For a case discussing the duty of good faith of a general partner in a limited partnership, see *Desert Equities v. Morgan Stanley Leveraged Fund II*, 624 A.2d 1199 (Del. 1993). In that case, Desert Equities, a limited partner, sued the general partner alleging that it acted in bad faith in exercising its authority under the partnership agreement to exclude Desert from participating in investments of the partnership. Desert alleged that the general partner did this in retaliation for Desert's act of filing a suit against affiliates of the general partner in a different limited partnership. The court, in allowing the case to go to the finder of fact, stated that "a claim of bad faith hinges on a party's tortious state of mind." It quoted as follows from Black's Law Dictionary in support of its conclusion that bad faith is a state of mind: "[The] term 'bad faith' is not simply bad judgment or negligence, but rather it implies the conscious doing of a wrong because of dishonest purpose or moral obliquity; it is different from the negative idea of negligence in that it contemplates a state of mind affirmatively operating with furtive design or ill will." In *Della Ratta v. Larkin*, 856 A.2d 643 (Md. Ct. App. 2004), the court found that a general partner, who was presumed to have the authority to make a capital call on the limited partners, acted in bad faith when he made the call to "force out" the limited partners. The general partner had the opportunity to pursue third-party financing and good faith required that he do so.

3. While the trend of the law seems to allow parties to limit or waive fiduciary duties in their partnership agreement, and the Delaware courts generally enforce such waivers (*e.g.*, *Sonet v. Plum Creek Timber Co.*, 722 A.2d 319, 322 (Del. Ch. 1998) ("[P]rinciples of contract preempt fiduciary principles where the parties to a limited partnership have made their intentions to do so plain"), not all courts agree. *See, e.g.*, *BT-I v. Equitable Assurance Society of the United States*, 75 Cal. App. 4th 1406, 89 Cal. Rptr. 2d 811 (1999). In this case, the partnership was in default on its loan. The general partner bought the loan and subsequently foreclosed on the property. The limited partner claimed such actions breached the fiduciary duty of the general partner, who defended on the basis of a provision in the partnership agreement that gave it broad powers to refinance and restructure partnership debt. The general partner also relied on a provision of RUPA § 404(f), applicable in California, that states: "a partner may lend money to and transact other business with the limited partnership and, subject to applicable law, has the same rights and obligations with respect thereto as a person who is not a partner." The court was unconvinced and held in favor of the limited partner.

4. Delaware courts have embraced corporate notions in resolving fiduciary duty disputes between the general partner and limited partners. For instance, as in corporate law, if a majority of the limited partners approve, after full disclosure, a transaction in which the general partner has a conflict of interest, the Delaware courts will not examine the transaction to determine its fairness to the limited partners. *See, e.g.*, *R.S.M. Inc. v. Capital Management Holdings L.P.*, 790 A.2d 478, 498 (Del. Ch. 2001). *See* Chapter 10, *infra*.

5. Consistent with the philosophy of Re-RULPA to de-link UPA and ULPA, Re-RULPA contains a provision (§ 408) that tracks RUPA § 404, specifying the duties of a general partner.

BRICKELL PARTNERS v. WISE
Court of Chancery of Delaware
794 A.2d 1 (2001)

Strine, Vice Chancellor.

Plaintiff Brickell Partners brought this action challenging the acquisition of Crystal Gas Storage, Inc. by El Paso Energy Partners, L.P. ("El Paso" or the "Partnership"). Brickell Partners is a limited partner in El Paso and has sued derivatively on its behalf. Crystal Gas is owned by El Paso Energy Corp. ("Energy"), which also owns and controls El Paso's general partner, DeepTech International, Inc. Energy also holds 34.5% of El Paso's units, which are traded on the New York Stock Exchange.

El Paso purchased Crystal Gas for $170 million in newly issued El Paso preference units. The complaint alleges that this consideration exceeded "the value of Crystal Gas, its assets and businesses" and that the transaction is therefore substantively unfair to El Paso. By way of support for this assertion, the complaint simply notes that "for the quarter ended September 30, 1999, Crystal Gas reported a decline in revenues of $1.2 million and a decline for the nine months of that fiscal year of about $3.5 million."

The complaint also challenges the procedures used to effect this "conflict" transaction. The only procedural protection used by El Paso to ensure the interests of unit holders other than Energy was to subject the transaction to "Special Approval" by DeepTech's "Conflicts and Audit Committee." The two members of that Committee were defendant Michael B. Bracy, a director of DeepTech and a former employee of Energy, and defendant H. Douglas Church, another director of DeepTech.

The complaint alleges that the process was "irreparably impaired" because Bracy and Church owed fiduciary duties to DeepTech as DeepTech directors, and thus could not fairly opine on a transaction in which DeepTech and El Paso had conflicting interests. The complaint also charges that Bracy's former status as an employee in an unspecified position at Energy compromised him further.

The defendants — principally DeepTech and its directors — have filed a motion to dismiss the complaint. According to the defendants, the El Paso Partnership Agreement precludes the plaintiff's claims for breach of fiduciary duty in connection with the Crystal Gas acquisition. In particular, the defendants emphasize the following provision of the Partnership Agreement:

6.9 *Resolution of Conflicts of Interest.* (a) Unless otherwise expressly provided in this Agreement . . . *whenever a potential conflict of interest exists or arises between the General Partner or any of its Affiliates, on the one hand, and the Partnership,* the Operating Companies, any Partner or any Assignee, *on the other hand, any resolution or course of action in respect of such conflict of interest* shall be permitted and deemed approved by all Partners, *and shall not constitute a breach of this Agreement,* of the Operating Companies Agreements, of any agreement contemplated herein or therein, *or of any duty stated or implied by law or equity, if the resolution or course of action is or by operation of this Agreement, deemed to be fair and reasonable to the Partnership. The General Partner shall be authorized,* but not required in connection with its resolution of such conflict of interest, to seek *Special Approval of a resolution of such conflict or course of action. Any conflict of interest and any resolution of such conflict of interest shall be conclusively deemed fair and reasonable to the Partnership if such conflict of interest or resolution is (i) approved by Special Approval,* (ii) on whole, on terms no less favorable to the Partnership than those generally being provided to or available from unrelated third parties *or* (iii) fair to the Partnership, taking into account the totality of the relationships between the parties involved (including other transactions that may be particularly favorable or advantageous to the Partnership). . . . The General Partner (including the Conflicts and Audit Committee in connection with Special Approval) shall be authorized in connection with its determination of the "fair and reasonable" nature of any transaction or arrangement and in its resolution of any conflict of interest to consider (i) the relative interests of any party to such conflict, agreement, transaction or situation and the benefits and burdens relating to such interest; (ii) any customary or accepted industry practices and any customary or historical dealings with a particular Person; (iii) any applicable generally accepted accounting or engineering practices or principles; and (iv) such additional factors as the General Partner or such Conflicts and Audit Committee determines in its sole discretion to be relevant, reasonable or appropriate under the circumstances. Nothing contained in this Agreement, however, is intended to nor shall it be construed to require the General Partner or such Conflicts and Audit Committee to consider the interests of any Person other than the Partnership. In the absence of bad faith by the General Partner, the resolution, action or terms so made, taken or provided by the General Partner with respect to such matter shall not constitute a breach of this Agreement or any other agreement contemplated herein or a breach of any standard of care or duty imposed herein or therein or under the Delaware Act or any other law, rule or regulation.[9]

Pursuant to the Agreement, "Special Approval" means "approval of a majority of the members of the Conflicts and Audit Committee of the Partnership."[10] Such Special Approval was obtained for the Crystal Gas transaction.

The defendants argue that § 6.9 of the Agreement supplants the traditional default fiduciary duties that would otherwise apply to the Crystal Gas deal in the absence of contractual modification. The fiduciary duty of loyalty would, if unmodified, have required the defendants to demonstrate that the Crystal Gas acquisition was entirely fair. The defendants note that 6 Del. C. § 17-1101(c) statutorily authorized the parties to the Partnership Agreement to restrict the fiduciary duties owed to El Paso by DeepTech and the other defendants. As this court has noted many times in recent years, "principles of contract preempt fiduciary principles where the parties to a limited partnership have made their intentions to do so plain."[11]

Here, the plain and unambiguous language of § 6.9 of the Partnership Agreement displaces traditional fiduciary duty principles. In place of such principles, the Agreement provides limited partners solely with the protection of Conflicts and Audit Committee Review when DeepTech decides to seek "Special Approval" of a conflict transaction, as it did here. Such "Special Approval" is "conclusive [ ]" evidence of the "fair[ness] and reasonable[ness]" of a conflict transaction, and bars any challenge to the transaction based on the Agreement, other contracts, or default principles of law or equity.[12] As a result, the plain language of the Agreement appears to compel a dismissal of the complaint, assuming the plaintiff has not pled facts suggesting that the defendants did not comply with § 6.9 itself.

To meet this challenge, the plaintiff has argued that § 6.9 is ambiguous because the Agreement never defines precisely who shall serve on the Conflicts and Audit Committee. According to plaintiff, the reasonable expectation of a limited partner would be that the Committee would be comprised of persons with no relation or duty at all to DeepTech. Because the two members were both DeepTech directors, the plaintiff argues that the Committee process did not accord with that supposed expectation and therefore that the defendants may not rely upon the "Special Approval" safe harbor.

The problem for the plaintiff is that its argument (which sounds somewhat plausible in the abstract) has little force in the precise context governed by the Partnership Agreement. As this court has noted elsewhere, directors of corporate general partners occupy a strange and unsettling position. By definition, they find themselves in a position of on-going conflict because they owe fiduciary duties to the corporate general partner (on whose board they serve) and fiduciary duties to the limited partnership governed by the corporate general partner. Even when such directors have no material self-interest in the success of the corporate general partner as an entity or the partnership itself, they owe duties to two entities with potentially conflicting interests. Thus, their situation is subtly but critically different from the position of an outside, "independent" director of a corporation. An ideal corporate independent director owes her fidelity only to the corporation and its stockholders, to the exclusion of any potentially conflicting constituency. That can never be so with the director of a corporate general partner forced to opine on a transaction between an affiliate of the corporate general partner and the partnership.

This reality, however, dissipates the force of the plaintiff's argument. Although the Partnership Agreement does not define the Conflicts and Audit Committee of Deep-

---

[9] [4] Partnership Agreement § 6.9 (emphasis added).

[10] [5] *Id.* at A-10.

[11] [6] Sonet v. Timber Co., Del. Ch., 722 A.2d 319, 322 (1998).

[12] [7] Partnership Agreement § 6.9.

Tech, the very use of the term Committee implies that the group will be comprised of directors of DeepTech. It may be that the Agreement's use of the term Conflicts and Audit Committee and its conferral of certain types of authority on that Committee would lead a reasonable investor to conclude that the Committee would be comprised solely of *non-management directors* of DeepTech. What it cannot be reasonably read as implying is that the Committee would be comprised of members with no relationship to DeepTech at all.

Neither Bracy nor Church is alleged to be a current member of the management of DeepTech. Neither is alleged to be a stockholder of Energy (or even of DeepTech for that matter). At most, the plaintiff avers that Bracy used to work for Energy. When and for how long the plaintiff does not say. Even more important, the plaintiff does not allege facts from which it can be inferred that Bracy was beholden to Energy for material, personal reasons separate and apart from the structural conflict he inherently faced as a DeepTech director.[13]

Therefore, the plaintiff has failed to plead facts that indicate that the defendants' conduct is not insulated from challenge because of the Conflicts and Audit Committee's Special Approval of the Crystal Gas transaction. For that reason the plaintiff's complaint is dismissed with prejudice.

NOTES AND QUESTIONS

In *Brickell Partners*, a committee appointed by the corporate general partner approved the acquisition by the partnership of a corporation that was owned by an affiliate of the corporate general partner, a classic conflict of interest situation. The plaintiff limited partner challenged the transaction, but the court dismissed the action because the limited partnership agreement expressly permitted this process. Suppose, however, that the plaintiffs alleged that the members of the committee were significant shareholders of El Paso Energy Corp., the seller. Would that have affected the outcome of the case? What if committee members were corporate officers of DeepTech International, Inc., the corporate general partner, but not shareholders of El Paso Energy?

PROBLEM

The defendant was the general partner and a limited partner in a partnership that allowed limited partners, but not the general partner, to compete with the partnership (by acquiring licenses in areas adjoining the area in which the partnership had a license to operate a cellular telephone service). The general partner allegedly breached the agreement and its fiduciary duties by obtaining a license in an area that was prohibited to it. The general partner defended on the basis that it was also a limited partner and, as such, free to obtain the competing license. The general partner claimed to be relying on this provision of Delaware law:

> Unless otherwise provided in a partnership agreement, a partner or other person shall not be liable to a limited partnership or to another partner or to another person that is a party to or is otherwise bound by a partnership agreement for breach of fiduciary duty for the partner's or other person's good faith reliance on the provisions of the partnership agreement.

6 DEL. C. § 17-1101(e).

How should the court decide the case?

---

[13] [9] The complaint is also devoid of even a conclusory allegation that DeepTech or any other defendant tainted the Special Approval process by defrauding or otherwise tainting the work of the Conflicts and Audit Committee.

D. LIMITED LIABILITY COMPANIES

The limited liability company ("LLC") is a relatively new form of doing business. It was first created by statute in Wyoming in 1977, patterned on a European model. It is designed to offer co-owners of an unincorporated business who make a proper filing with the state freedom from personal liability for the debts of the business, the option to manage the business, and the tax advantage of partnership status.

The owners of an LLC enjoy limited liability. This means that owners, like limited partners in a limited partnership, are not vicariously liable for the contract or tort obligations of the business. When forming an LLC, most states require the organizers to elect a management structure. The LLC can be member-managed (and thus very similar in informality and flexibility to a limited liability partnership), or the LLC can be manager-managed, where the owners who are not also managers play a largely passive role, similar to limited partners in a limited liability limited partnership.

The proliferation of LLC legislation took place without the impetus of a model or uniform act promulgated by NCCUSL. This is unusual in modern law, as evidenced by the uniform partnership and limited partnership acts, which preceded and strongly influenced state legislation. A uniform act is now available, however. In 1995, NCCUSL promulgated the Uniform Limited Liability Company Act (1995) ("ULLCA"). ULLCA was amended in 1996 to reflect the check-the-box regulations described above. NC-CUSL recently completed a revision of ULLCA, which is likely to influence limited liability company acts across the country in the years to come. *See* http://www.law.upenn.edu/bll/archives/ulc/ullca/2006act_final.htm.

1. Formation; Operating Agreement

As noted above, a limited liability company is formed upon the filing of a document, generally called "articles of organization," with the secretary of state or some other designated state office. Alternatively, an existing entity (partnership or corporation) can convert into an LLC, if the state has a statute permitting such conversion.

Typically, the organizers of an LLC will enter into an "operating agreement" that delineates the obligations of the parties and any other provisions that the parties desire. As in a general partnership, an LLC is a contractual entity, with only a few mandatory, nonwaivable provisions. *See* ULLCA § 103(B). The contractual nature of an LLC and the effect of the operating agreement on the LLC are illustrated by the *Elf Atochem* case below, an early and important case in LLC law.

ELF ATOCHEM NORTH AMERICA, INC. v. JAFFARI
Supreme Court of Delaware
727 A.2d 286 (1999)

Veasey, Chief Justice:

This is a case of first impression before this Court involving the Delaware Limited Liability Company Act (the "Act"). The limited liability company ("LLC") is a relatively new entity that has emerged in recent years as an attractive vehicle to facilitate business relationships and transactions. The wording and architecture of the Act is somewhat complicated, but it is designed to achieve what is seemingly a simple concept — to permit persons or entities ("members") to join together in an environment of private ordering to form and operate the enterprise under an LLC agreement with tax benefits akin to a partnership and limited liability akin to the corporate form.

This is a purported derivative suit brought on behalf of a Delaware LLC calling into question whether: (1) the LLC, which did not itself execute the LLC agreement in this case ("the Agreement") defining its governance and operation, is nevertheless bound by the Agreement; and (2) contractual provisions directing that all disputes be resolved exclusively by arbitration or court proceedings in California are valid under the Act.

Resolution of these issues requires us to examine the applicability and scope of certain provisions of the Act in light of the Agreement.

We hold that: (1) the Agreement is binding on the LLC as well as the members; and (2) since the Act does not prohibit the members of an LLC from vesting exclusive subject matter jurisdiction in arbitration proceedings (or court enforcement of arbitration) in California to resolve disputes, the contractual forum selection provisions must govern.

Accordingly, we affirm the judgment of the Court of Chancery dismissing the action brought in that court on the ground that the Agreement validly predetermined the fora in which disputes would be resolved, thus stripping the Court of Chancery of subject matter jurisdiction.

Plaintiff below-appellant Elf Atochem North America, Inc., a Pennsylvania Corporation ("Elf"), manufactures and distributes solvent-based maskants to the aerospace and aviation industries throughout the world. Defendant below-appellee Cyrus A. Jaffari is the president of Malek, Inc., a California Corporation. Jaffari had developed an innovative, environmentally-friendly alternative to the solvent-based maskants that presently dominate the market.

For decades, the aerospace and aviation industries have used solvent-based maskants in the chemical milling process. Recently, however, the Environmental Protection Agency ("EPA") classified solvent-based maskants as hazardous chemicals and air contaminants. To avoid conflict with EPA regulations, Elf considered developing or distributing a maskant less harmful to the environment.

In the mid-nineties, Elf approached Jaffari and proposed investing in his product and assisting in its marketing. Jaffari found the proposal attractive since his company, Malek, Inc., possessed limited resources and little international sales expertise. Elf and Jaffari agreed to undertake a joint venture that was to be carried out using a limited liability company as the vehicle.

[After filing a Certificate of Formation], Elf, Jaffari and Malek, Inc. entered into a series of agreements providing for the governance and operation of the joint venture. Of particular importance to this litigation, Elf, Malek, Inc., and Jaffari entered into the Agreement, a comprehensive and integrated document of 38 single-spaced pages setting forth detailed provisions for the governance of Malek LLC, which is not itself a signatory to the Agreement. Elf and Malek LLC entered into an Exclusive Distributorship Agreement in which Elf would be the exclusive, worldwide distributor for Malek LLC. The Agreement provides that Jaffari will be the manager of Malek LLC. Jaffari and Malek LLC entered into an employment agreement providing for Jaffari's employment as chief executive officer of Malek LLC.

The Agreement is the operative document for purposes of this Opinion, however. Under the Agreement, Elf contributed $1 million in exchange for a 30 percent interest in Malek LLC. Malek, Inc. contributed its rights to the water-based maskant in exchange for a 70 percent interest in Malek LLC.

The Agreement contains an arbitration clause covering all disputes. The clause, Section 13.8, provides that "any controversy or dispute arising out of this Agreement, the interpretation of any of the provisions hereof, or the action or inaction of any Member or Manager hereunder shall be submitted to arbitration in San Francisco, California. . . . " Section 13.8 further provides: "No action . . . based upon any claim arising out of or related to this Agreement shall be instituted in any court by any Member except: (a) an action to compel arbitration . . . or (b) an action to enforce an award obtained in an arbitration proceeding. . . . " The Agreement also contains a forum selection clause, Section 13.7, providing that all members consent to: "exclusive jurisdiction of the state and federal courts sitting in California in any action on a claim arising out of, under or in connection with this Agreement or the transactions contemplated by this Agreement, provided such claim is not required to be arbitrated pursuant to Section 13.8"; and personal jurisdiction in California. The Distribution Agreement contains no forum selection or arbitration clause.

Elf's Suit in the Court of Chancery

On April 27, 1998, Elf sued Jaffari and Malek LLC, individually and derivatively on behalf of Malek LLC, in the Delaware Court of Chancery, seeking equitable remedies. Among other claims, Elf alleged that Jaffari breached his fiduciary duty to Malek LLC, pushed Malek LLC to the brink of insolvency by withdrawing funds for personal use, interfered with business opportunities, failed to make disclosures to Elf, and threatened to make poor quality maskant and to violate environmental regulations. Elf also alleged breach of contract, tortious interference with prospective business relations, and (solely as to Jaffari) fraud.

The Court of Chancery granted defendants' motion to dismiss based on lack of subject matter jurisdiction. The court held that Elf's claims arose under the Agreement, or the transactions contemplated by the agreement, and were directly related to Jaffari's actions as manager of Malek LLC. Therefore, the court found that the Agreement governed the question of jurisdiction and that only a court of law or arbitrator in California is empowered to decide these claims. Elf now appeals the order of the Court of Chancery dismissing the complaint. . . .

The phenomenon of business arrangements using "alternative entities" has been developing rapidly over the past several years. Long gone are the days when business planners were confined to corporate or partnership structures.

The Delaware Act was adopted in October 1992. . . . To date, the Act has been amended six times with a view to modernization. The LLC is an attractive form of business entity because it combines corporate-type limited liability with partnership-type flexibility and tax advantages. The Act can be characterized as a "flexible statute" because it generally permits members to engage in private ordering with substantial freedom of contract to govern their relationship, provided they do not contravene any mandatory provisions of the Act. . . .

The basic approach of the Delaware Act is to provide members with broad discretion in drafting the Agreement and to furnish default provisions when the members' agreement is silent. The Act is replete with fundamental provisions made subject to modification in the Agreement (*e.g.*, "unless otherwise provided in a limited liability company agreement . . . "). . . .

Section 18-1101(b) of the Act . . . provides that "[i]t is the policy of [the Act] to give the maximum effect to the principle of freedom of contract and to the enforceability of limited liability company agreements." . . .

In general, the commentators observe that only where the agreement is inconsistent with mandatory statutory provisions will the members' agreement be invalidated. Such statutory provisions are likely to be those intended to protect third parties, not necessarily the contracting members. As a framework for decision, we apply that principle to the issues before us, without expressing any views more broadly. . . .

Malek LLC's Failure to Sign the Agreement does not Affect the Members'
Agreement Governing Dispute Resolution

Elf argues that Malek LLC came into existence on October 29, 1996, when the parties filed its Certificate of Formation with the Delaware Secretary of State. The parties did not sign the Agreement until November 4, 1996. Elf contends that Malek LLC existed as an LLC as of October 29, 1996, but never agreed to the Agreement because it did not sign it. Because Malek LLC never expressly assented to the arbitration and forum selection clauses within the Agreement, Elf argues it can sue derivatively on behalf of Malek LLC pursuant to 6 Del. C. § 18-1001.[14]

We are not persuaded by this argument. Section 18-101(7) defines the limited liability company agreement as "any agreement, written or oral, *of the member or members* as to the affairs of a limited liability company and the conduct of its business." Here, Malek, Inc. and Elf, the members of Malek LLC, executed the Agreement to carry out the affairs and business of Malek LLC and to provide for arbitration and forum selection.

Notwithstanding Malek LLC's failure to sign the Agreement, Elf's claims are subject to the arbitration and forum selection clauses of the Agreement. The Act is a statute designed to permit members maximum flexibility in entering into an agreement to govern their relationship. It is the members who are the real parties in interest. The LLC is simply their joint business vehicle. This is the contemplation of the statute in prescribing the outlines of a limited liability company agreement.

Classification by Elf of its Claims as Derivative is Irrelevant

Elf argues that the Court of Chancery erred in failing to classify its claims against Malek LLC as derivative. Elf contends that, had the court properly characterized its claims as derivative instead of direct, the arbitration and forum selection clauses would not have applied to bar adjudication in Delaware.

In the corporate context, "the derivative form of action permits an individual shareholder to bring 'suit to enforce a corporate cause of action against officers, directors, and third parties.'" The derivative suit is a corporate concept grafted onto the limited liability company form. The Act expressly allows for a derivative suit, providing that "a member . . . may bring an action in the Court of Chancery in the right of a limited liability company to recover a judgment in its favor if managers or members with authority to do so have refused to bring the action or if an effort to cause those managers or members to bring the action is not likely to succeed." [§ 18-1001] Notwithstanding the Agreement to the contrary, Elf argues that [§ 18-1001] permits the assertion of derivative claims of Malek LLC against Malek LLC's manager, Jaffari.

Although Elf correctly points out that Delaware law allows for derivative suits against management of an LLC, Elf contracted away its right to bring such an action in Delaware and agreed instead to dispute resolution in California. That is, Section 13.8 of the Agreement specifically provides that the parties (*i.e.*, Elf) agree to institute "[n]o action at law or in equity based upon *any* claim arising out of or related to this Agreement" except an action to compel arbitration or to enforce an arbitration award. Furthermore, under Section 13.7 of the Agreement, each member (*i.e.*, Elf) "consent[ed] to the exclusive jurisdiction of the state and federal courts sitting in California in *any* action on a claim arising out of, under or in connection with this Agreement or the transactions contemplated by this Agreement."

Sections 13.7 and 13.8 of the Agreement do not distinguish between direct and derivative claims. They simply state that the members may not initiate *any* claims outside of California. Elf initiated this action in the Court of Chancery in contravention of its own contractual agreement. As a result, the Court of Chancery correctly held that all claims, whether derivative or direct, arose under, out of, or in connection with the Agreement, and thus are covered by the arbitration and forum selection clauses.

This prohibition is so broad that it is dispositive of Elf's claims (counts IV, V and VI of the amended complaint) that purport to be under the Distributorship Agreement that has no choice of forum provision. Notwithstanding the fact that the Distributorship

---

[14] [35] 6 Del. C. § 18-1001 provides: "Right to bring action. A member may . . . bring an action in the Court of Chancery in the right of a limited liability company to recover a judgment in its favor if managers or members with authority to do so have refused to bring the action or if an effort to cause those managers or members to bring the action is not likely to succeed."

Agreement is a separate document, in reality these counts are all subsumed under the rubric of the Agreement's forum selection clause for any claim "arising out of" and those that are "in connection with" the Agreement or transactions "contemplated by" or "related to" that Agreement under Sections 13.7 and 13.8. We agree with the Court of Chancery's decision that:

> plaintiff's claims arise under the LLC Agreement or the transactions contemplated by the Agreement, and are directly related to Jaffari's "action or inaction" in connection with his role as the manager of Malek. Plainly, all of plaintiff's claims revolve around Jaffari's conduct (or misconduct) as Malek's manager. Virtually all the remedies that plaintiff seeks bear directly on Jaffari's duties and obligations under the LLC Agreement. Plaintiff's complaint that "Jaffari . . . has totally disregarded his obligations under the *LLC Agreement*" also lends support to my conclusion.

The Court of Chancery was correct in holding that Elf's claims bear directly on Jaffari's duties and obligations under the Agreement. Thus, we decline to disturb its holding.

The Argument that Chancery Has "Special" Jurisdiction for Derivative Claims Must Fail

Elf claims that 6 Del. C. §§ 18-110(a), 18-111 and 18-1001 vest the Court of Chancery with subject matter jurisdiction over this dispute. According to Elf, the Act grants the Court of Chancery subject matter jurisdiction over its claims for breach of fiduciary duty and removal of Jaffari, even though the parties contracted to arbitrate all such claims in California. In effect, Elf argues that the Act affords the Court of Chancery "special" jurisdiction to adjudicate its claims, notwithstanding a clear contractual agreement to the contrary.

Again, we are not persuaded by Elf's argument. Elf is correct that 6 Del. C. §§ 18-110(a) and 18-111 vest jurisdiction with the Court of Chancery in actions involving removal of managers and interpreting, applying or enforcing LLC agreements respectively. As noted above, Section 18-1001 provides that a party may bring derivative actions in the Court of Chancery. Such a grant of jurisdiction may have been constitutionally necessary if the claims do not fall within the traditional equity jurisdiction. Nevertheless, for the purpose of designating a more convenient forum, we find no reason why the members cannot alter the default jurisdictional provisions of the statute and contract away their right to file suit in Delaware.

For example, Elf argues that Section 18-110(a), which grants the Court of Chancery jurisdiction to hear claims involving the election or removal of a manager of an LLC, applies to the case at bar because Elf is seeking removal of Jaffari. While Elf is correct on the substance of Section 18-110(a), Elf is unable to convince this Court that the parties may not contract to avoid the applicability of Section 18-110(a). We hold that, because the policy of the Act is to give the maximum effect to the principle of freedom of contract and to the enforceability of LLC agreements, the parties may contract to avoid the applicability of Sections 18-110(a), 18-111, and 18-1001. Here, the parties contracted as clearly as practicable when they relegated to California in Section 13.7 "any" dispute "arising out of, under or in connection with [the] Agreement or the transactions contemplated by [the] Agreement. . . . " Likewise, in Section 13.8: "*[n]o action* at law or in equity based upon *any claim arising out of or related to*" the Agreement may be brought, except in California, and then only to enforce arbitration in California.

Our conclusion is bolstered by the fact that Delaware recognizes a strong public policy in favor of arbitration. Normally, doubts on the issue of whether a particular issue is arbitrable will be resolved in favor of arbitration. In the case at bar, we do not believe there is any doubt of the parties' intention to agree to arbitrate *all* disputed matters in

California. If we were to hold otherwise, arbitration clauses in existing LLC agreements could be rendered meaningless. By resorting to the alleged "special" jurisdiction of the Court of Chancery, future plaintiffs could avoid their own arbitration agreements simply by couching their claims as derivative. Such a result could adversely affect many arbitration agreements already in existence in Delaware. . . .

We affirm the judgment of the Court of Chancery dismissing Elf Atochem's amended complaint for lack of subject matter jurisdiction.

NOTE

Following the decision in *Elf Atochem*, the Delaware legislature amended the LLC statute to codify the holding in the case. *See* 6 DEL. C. § 18-101(7) ("[a] limited liability company is not required to execute its limited liability company agreement. A limited liability company is bound by its limited liability company agreement whether or not the limited liability company executes the limited liability company agreement"). There is some authority contrary to *Elf Atochem. See Bubbles & Bleach, LLC v. Becker*, 1997 U.S. Dist. LEXIS 7471 (N.D. Ill. May 23, 1997) (an arbitration agreement not binding on an LLC because it was not a party to it).

2. The LLC as an Entity Apart from Its Members

ABRAHIM & SONS ENTERPRISES v. EQUILON ENTERPRISES, LLC
United States Court of Appeals, Ninth Circuit
292 F.3d 958 (2002)

Before PREGERSON, RYMER, and T.G. NELSON, CIRCUIT JUDGES.

T.G. NELSON, CIRCUIT JUDGE.

Appellants, a group of independent dealers who operate gas stations leased from Shell or Texaco, allege that the oil companies violated California law by transferring the gas stations to a limited liability company without first offering Appellants a chance to buy the stations. Appellees argue that California law does not apply to this situation because Appellees merely contributed their assets to a limited liability company that they controlled. The district court agreed with Appellees and granted their summary judgment motion. We reverse the district court.

I.

Appellants are forty-three independent dealers who operate Shell or Texaco gasoline stations in Southern California. All appellants leased their stations from, and had dealer agreements with, Shell or Texaco. In 1998, Shell and Texaco addressed growing concerns about declining oil prices, declining profits, and increased competition by combining their retail marketing and refining activities into a limited liability company, called Equilon Enterprises. They contributed all of their western refining and marketing assets to Equilon and assigned the gas station leases and dealer agreements to Equilon as well. In exchange, Shell and Texaco, as the sole members of Equilon, received 100% of the ownership interests in the limited liability company.[15] The individual gas stations continued to sell Shell and Texaco products under their same leases and agreements.

Appellants claim that Shell and Texaco violated California Business & Professions Code § 20999.25(a) by transferring the gas stations to Equilon without offering Appellants a chance to purchase the stations. Section 20999.25(a) prohibits a franchisor from selling, transferring, or assigning an interest in a premises to another person unless he or she first makes a bona fide offer to sell that interest to the franchisee.

---

[15] [1] Shell owns 56% of Equilon and Texaco owns 44% based on the value of the assets they contributed.

Alternatively, if the franchisor receives an acceptable offer from another party to buy the premises, the franchisor must offer the franchisee a right of first refusal.[16]

After Appellants filed their claim in state court, Appellees removed the case to federal district court on the basis of diversity and moved for summary judgment. The district court granted the motion, holding that Shell and Texaco's contribution of the gas stations to Equilon was not a sale, transfer, or assignment of the stations to another person. Appellants appeal that decision. . . .

II.

We review a grant of summary judgment de novo. We must determine, viewing the evidence in the light most favorable to the nonmoving party, whether any genuine issues of material fact exist and whether the district court correctly applied the relevant substantive law.

III.

This case involves the statutory interpretation of California Business & Professions Code § 20999.25(a), which reads in relevant part:

> In the case of leased marketing premises as to which the franchisor owns a fee interest, the franchisor *shall not sell, transfer, or assign to another person* the franchisor's interest in the premises unless the franchisor has first-
> . . . made a bona fide offer to sell, transfer, or assign to the franchisee the franchisor's interest in the premises. . . .[17]

No California cases interpret the phrase "sell, transfer, or assign to another person" within the meaning of this statute. Likewise, no cases interpret the identical language found in the Petroleum Marketing Practices Act,[18] after which the California statute is patterned. Therefore, we must decide how the California Supreme Court would interpret that phrase and whether the phrase encompasses the transaction at issue here.

When interpreting a statute, we attempt to "ascertain and effectuate legislative intent." In determining that intent, we must first look to the words of the statute, giving them their ordinary, common sense meaning. If the words of the statute are clear and unambiguous, there is no need to resort to other indicia of legislative intent. Only if the meaning is not clear will we turn to legislative history to help resolve the ambiguity.

California Business & Professions Code § 20999.25 indisputably governs the parties' relationship. The question here is whether Shell and Texaco's contribution of assets to Equilon falls under Section 20999.25(a). To decide this question, we must determine whether: (1) Equilon is "another person"; and (2) the contribution of assets was a sale, transfer, or assignment. We hold that the ordinary understanding of the words in Section 20999.25(a) encompasses the contribution of properties to Equilon in this case.

A. *Another Person*

We must first determine what types of entities fall within the meaning of "another person" under Section 20999.25(a). We believe that corporations and limited liability companies (LLCs) fall within that meaning. Corporations and LLCs are distinct legal entities, separate from their stockholders or members. The acts of a corporation or LLC are deemed independent of the acts of its members. For this reason, both corporations and LLCs are included within the definition of "person" in the California Corporations Code. The purpose of forming these types of businesses is to limit the liability of their shareholders and members.

---

[16]   [2] CAL. BUS. & PROF. CODE § 20999.25(a).

[17]   [6] CAL. BUS. & PROF. CODE § 20999.25(a) (emphasis added).

[18]   [7] 15 U.S.C. § 2802(b)(2)(E)(iii).

LLCs were not a form of business entity at the time the California legislature enacted Section 20999.25(a). However, the legislature had already enacted the California Corporations Code. Thus, when it enacted Section 20999.25(a), the legislature understood that corporations were considered distinct legal entities. Considering the legislature's understanding of corporations at the time it enacted Section 20999.25(a), and the fact that LLCs are also treated as distinct legal entities, both corporations and LLCs fit within the meaning of "another person" as stated in Section 20999.25(a). Because Equilon is an LLC, it is distinct from its members Shell and Texaco and is "another person" under Section 20999.25(a).

Shell and Texaco argue that Equilon is not a distinct entity because they own and control Equilon. In essence, they ask us to disregard the corporate form they themselves created because the form does not benefit them here. We refuse to do so. Members own and control most LLCs, yet the LLCs remain separate and distinct from their members. Indeed, the separate and distinct nature of LLCs is their reason for existence. Just because it happens not to benefit Shell and Texaco here is no reason to disregard the formation of this entity. Based on the common understanding of how an LLC works, Equilon fits within the meaning of "another person."

Finally, common sense dictates that Equilon is not the same entity as Shell or Texaco individually. Equilon is owned jointly by Shell and Texaco. The gas stations, which previously were owned by only one oil company, now will be controlled and influenced by both companies. Therefore, the current owner of the gas stations is not identical to the previous owners. We conclude that Equilon is "another person" under Section 20999.25(a).

B. *Sale, Transfer, or Assignment*

The second part of our analysis is whether the oil companies' contribution of assets to Equilon was a sale, transfer, or assignment. The district court focused on the fact that the transaction was a "tax-free exchange" in holding that it was not a sale, transfer, or assignment. While the tax-free nature of the transaction indicates that the transaction was not a sale, we see no reason why such a transaction could not be a transfer.

According to the rules of statutory construction, transfer must mean something different than sale or assignment. In common, everyday parlance, transfer has a broad meaning. Webster's Dictionary defines "transfer" as "[t]o convey or make over the possession or legal title of (e.g., property) to another." Because Shell and Texaco relinquished their title, possession, and control of the gas stations to Equilon, it makes perfect sense to say they transferred the properties to Equilon.

In support of the idea that the oil companies transferred the gas stations, we note that the record contains a copy of a corporate grant deed, which shows that Shell transferred title of its properties to Equilon. The deed states that Shell, as grantor, granted Equilon all of Shell's rights, title, and interest in the gas stations. We assume that Texaco executed a similar deed. In addition, the individual oil companies did not maintain control of their properties. Both companies submitted forms to the Securities Exchange Commission (SEC) documenting the formation of the limited liability company. In Shell's SEC form, the company admitted that it does not exercise control over Equilon. Texaco's SEC form stated that Texaco and Shell jointly control Equilon. Therefore, neither company maintained complete control over its former properties.

Finally, under the California Corporations Code, Shell and Texaco have no interest in the property of Equilon. Once members contribute assets to an LLC, those assets become capital of the LLC and the members lose any interest they had in the assets.[19]

---

[19] [21] CAL. CORP. CODE § 17001(g) (defining contribution as any money, property, or service rendered that a member contributes to an LLC as capital); *id.* § 17300 ("A member or assignee has no interest in specific limited liability company property."). See also *PacLink [Communications Int'l, Inc. v. Superior Court of Los Angeles County]*, 90 Cal. App. 4th 958, 964, 109 Cal. Rptr. 2d 436 (2001) ("Because members of the LLC hold

Thus, once Shell and Texaco contributed the gas stations to Equilon, they no longer had an interest in the stations and could not individually exert control over them. The oil companies no longer had title, possession, or control over the properties. Therefore, their contribution was a transfer to Equilon.

Because the plain language of the statute is unambiguous, we do not need to resort to the legislative history. We hold that the transaction at issue here was a transfer to another person, Equilon, which triggered the duty to offer the gas stations to the franchisees first. We therefore reverse the district court and remand for further proceedings.

Reversed and remanded.

NOTES AND QUESTIONS

1. Suppose that Texaco had assigned all of its fee interests to an LLC of which it was the sole member. Would that have triggered the right of first refusal? Should it have? Assuming that the right of first refusal would not have been triggered, suppose the LLC that received the fee interest and then became a member of an LLC together with a Shell-created LLC that did likewise. Would that have triggered the right of first refusal?

2. In *Frontier Traylor Shea, LLC v. Metropolitan Airports Commission*, 132 F. Supp. 2d 1193 (D. Minn. 2000), an LLC submitted the low bid on a construction project, but was not awarded the contract because in the pre-qualification materials the principals of the LLC represented that the "exact name" of the bidder was "Frontier/Traylor/Shea joint venture." The court held that the bidding authority did not abuse its discretion in determining that an LLC was not a joint venture because a joint venture is a "species of partnership" in which each of the venturers is liable for the debts of the undertaking. Thus, the actual bidder, an LLC, was substantially different from the entity represented in the pre-bid materials. The court's ruling might be questioned because, generically speaking, the principals were undertaking a joint venture, albeit in the form of an LLC. Moreover, the principals might have formed a joint venture of single member LLCs. Would that not have been consistent with the representation that the bidder would be a joint venture partnership?

3. Despite considerable authority that an LLC is a separate legal entity (e.g., § 201 of ULLCA states that an LLC is "a legal entity distinct from its members"), for purposes of diversity jurisdiction, most courts have held that an LLC is a citizen of the state or states of which its members are citizens. *Cosgrove v. Bartolotta*, 150 F.3d 729 (7th Cir. 1998). This follows the rule for limited partnerships. *Carden v. Arkoma Associates*, 494 U.S. 185 (1990). Corporations, however, are citizens of the state in which they are incorporated. 28 U.S.C. § 13329(c)(1). Does it make more sense to follow the rule for limited partnerships than corporations, especially considering how freely courts borrow from corporate law in the veil piercing cases?

4. Under § 501(a) of ULLCA, the property of the business of an LLC is owned by the LLC, not its members. An example of a court's failure to fully appreciate legal separateness is illustrated in the following case.

PREMIER VAN SCHAACK REALTY, INC. v. SIEG
Court of Appeals of Utah
51 P.3d 24 (2002)

GREENWOOD, JUDGE:

---

no direct ownership interest in the company's assets . . . , the members cannot be directly injured when the company is improperly deprived of those assets.")

Premier Van Schaack Realty, Inc. (Premier) seeks to enforce the brokerage fee payment provided in the listing agreement (the Agreement) it entered into with Thomas K. Sieg (Sieg) regarding the sale of real property located at 273 North East Capital, Salt Lake City, Utah (the Property). Premier appeals the trial court's grant of summary judgment to Sieg, arguing that: (1) a sale or exchange occurred pursuant to the Agreement; and (2) Sieg was not entitled to attorney fees. We affirm.

BACKGROUND

On February 7, 1997, Sieg entered into the Agreement with Coldwell Banker. Coldwell Banker subsequently assigned the Agreement to Premier. The Agreement provisions relevant to this appeal state:

> BROKERAGE FEE. If, during the Listing period, [12 months] [Premier], the Listing Agent, the Owner, another real estate agent, or anyone else locates a party who is ready, willing and able to buy, sell or exchange (collectively referred to as "acquire") the Property, or any part thereof, at the listing price and terms stated on the attached board/association property data information form, or any other price or terms to which the Owner may agree in writing, the Owner agrees to pay to [Premier] a brokerage fee in the amount of seven percent (7%) of such acquisition price. . . .

. . . .

In March 1997, Premier's real estate agent introduced Sieg to Michael Davis, Marion Vaughn, and Jane Johnson (DVJ), who offered to purchase the Property for $1.3 million. Sieg made a counter-offer that DVJ accepted. However, the anticipated sale never closed, and Sieg returned DVJ's earnest money.

In June 1997, DVJ proposed that they form a limited liability company (LLC) with Sieg. On September 26, 1997, DVJ and Sieg signed an operating agreement (the Operating Agreement), forming the LLC, MJTM. The Operating Agreement provided that Sieg would convey the Property to MJTM and Sieg would receive a 40% interest in MJTM and a preferential return of 9% on future profits. The Operating Agreement also provided that Sieg had a beginning balance of $670,000 in his initial capital contribution account and that MJTM assumed $580,000 of Sieg's debt. The other members of MJTM agreed not to encumber the Property without Sieg's approval. The Operating Agreement stated that the agreed value of the Property was $1.3 million. Furthermore, the Operating Agreement provided, "No Member shall be personally liable to any other Member for the return of any part of the Members' Capital Contributions." On January 21, 1998, Sieg transferred title to the Property to MJTM by warranty deed.

In January 1998, MJTM borrowed $1.413 million from Zions Bank secured by a lien on the Property. All of the members of MJTM personally guaranteed the loan. With the proceeds from this loan, MJTM paid off a $300,000 loan to Sieg secured by the Property.

When Premier discovered that Sieg had entered into this arrangement with MJTM, it demanded its commission of 7% of $1.3 million. Sieg refused to pay, claiming that his contribution of the Property was an investment and not a sale or exchange; thus Premier filed suit. On cross-motions for summary judgment the trial court ruled in favor of Sieg, holding that the transaction between Sieg and MJTM was not a sale or exchange pursuant to the Agreement because it lacked consideration. . . . This appeal followed.

ANALYSIS

I. Sale or Exchange

Premier argues that a sale or exchange occurred as defined in the Agreement; thus triggering the 7% commission provision. . . .

Because this court interprets contracts according to their plain meaning, Premier must show the following to prevail: (1) that there was a party who was ready, willing, and able to buy or exchange the Property; (2) that Sieg agreed to a sale or exchange; and (3) that the sale or exchange occurred during the term of the Agreement. For purposes of this appeal, we assume that the alleged sale or exchange occurred during the term of the Agreement. Indeed, there is no dispute that the transfer to MJTM took place during the term of the Agreement.

Consequently, we are left to decide whether a sale or exchange occurred between Sieg and MJTM triggering the commission provisions of the Agreement. Under Utah law, "sale" has been defined as, "the conveyance of title to the purchaser for a valuable consideration consisting of the purchase price, or the execution and delivery of a valid and enforceable contract of sale whereby some estate in land, legal or equitable, passes to the purchaser." *Lewis v. Dahl*, 161 P.2d 362, 365 (1945). While "exchange" has not been judicially defined in Utah, this court will apply its plain meaning when interpreting the Agreement. See *Dixon*, 987 P.2d 48. The plain meaning of "exchange" is, "the act of giving or taking one thing in return for another." Webster's Ninth New Collegiate Dictionary 432 (9th ed. 1986); see also Black's Law Dictionary 585 (7th ed. 1999). These definitions demonstrate that to have either a sale or an exchange, there must be consideration. . . .

Premier argues that Sieg received consideration from MJTM in several different ways. First, Sieg received a 40% interest in MJTM in exchange for the Property. Second, Sieg was entitled to a 9% preferential return from MJTM on all future profits. Third, Sieg had a beginning balance of $670,000 in his initial capital contribution account. Finally, MJTM promised to assume $580,000 of Sieg's debt.

Sieg contends that each of these alleged indicia of consideration fails for various reasons. Sieg argues that the interest in MJTM Premier relies on cannot serve as consideration because Sieg maintained an ownership interest in the Property. Additionally, Sieg argues that the alleged debt relief fails as consideration because Sieg was personally liable for his personal debt plus the debt of MJTM to Zions Bank.

To support his argument, Sieg cites *Cooley Investment Co. v. Jones*, 780 P.2d 29 (Colo. Ct. App. 1989), and *Dahdah v. Continent Realty, Inc.*, 434 So. 2d 997 (Fla. Dist. Ct. App. 1983) (per curiam), for the proposition that the 40% interest and 9% preferential return on future profits in exchange for the Property cannot be valuable consideration. In both *Cooley* and *Dahdah*, the property owner entered into a listing agreement with a realtor to sell his or her property. See *Cooley*, 780 P.2d at 30; *Dahdah*, 434 So.2d at 998. In both cases, the owner decided to convey the property to a partnership or joint venture in which the owner was a member in exchange for: (1) an interest in the joint venture; (2) a preferential interest in future profits; and (3) an initial capital contribution account balance that received no interest over time. See *Cooley*, 780 P.2d at 30–31; *Dahdah*, 434 So. 2d at 998. In each case, the court held that no sale or exchange occurred, [reasoning that the owner retained an ownership interest].

Like the property owners in *Cooley* and *Dahdah*, Sieg retained a substantial ownership interest in the Property that caused him to assume the risks of an investor instead of the risks of a seller. By illustration, when a person undertakes the risks of an investor, that person assumes the risk that the value of investment will increase or decrease over time, or that the investment may be completely lost. However, as a general rule, once a person sells property, appreciation, depreciation, or total loss of the property is of no concern since the sale severs the seller from any interest in the property. Sieg still retained a significant ownership interest in the Property, including the potential value of its future sale and the present right to prevent MJTM from encumbering the Property without his permission. Moreover, the value of Sieg's interest in MJTM is directly tied to the value of the Property because the Property is the only asset MJTM owned. Therefore, because Sieg retained such a substantial ownership interest in the Property, the transaction between Sieg and MJTM does not constitute a sale or exchange as contemplated in the Agreement.

Additionally, Premier's argument that the debt relief is consideration fails because Sieg personally guaranteed the $1.413 million loan that MJTM used to pay $300,000 of Sieg's debt. Simply stated, MJTM did not actually relieve Sieg of debt, but rather caused him to personally incur nearly three times more debt than he owed on the Property prior to joining MJTM. MJTM had no ability to pay Sieg's debt itself, without securing a loan secured by the Property, MJTM's only asset. Therefore, under the facts of this case, the debt relief promised in the Agreement was illusory.

Premier argues that, unlike the partnership and joint venture in *Cooley* and *Dahdah*, a limited liability company under Utah, Colorado, and Florida law is a separate legal entity that is able to buy property in its own name. Because a limited liability company is an entity distinct from its owners, Premier argues that if a seller of property transfers his property to a limited liability company or to a corporation of which he is the sole shareholder, such a transaction would constitute a sale or exchange. We believe, however, that focusing on the legal structure of the transferee averts attention from the critical question of whether there was valuable consideration.

Whether a sale or exchange for valuable consideration occurred is a fact-intensive inquiry that requires more than a mere showing that an owner transferred his property to a separate legal entity. In this case, Sieg's credit to his capital contribution account and debt assumption roughly approximate the $1.3 million value of the Property. The preferential interest in future profits and the Zions Bank loan reflect the investment nature of the transaction. Where the owner retains essentially the same ownership interest in the property as he had prior to the conveyance, with plans to develop the property by improving it with the possibility of future gains or losses, and can prevent the record owner from encumbering the property without his permission, such a transaction is not a sale or exchange. Therefore, because the facts in this case show Sieg continued to have substantially the same ownership interest in the Property after the deed to MJTM was executed, there was no consideration and a sale or exchange as contemplated in the Agreement did not occur.

CONCLUSION

In sum, the transfer of the Property from Sieg to MJTM was not supported by consideration so as to constitute a sale or exchange. Because no sale or exchange occurred, Sieg owes no commission under the Agreement. . . .

NOTES AND QUESTIONS

1. Compare to *Premier* the decision in *Gebhardt Family Investment, L.L.C. v. Nations Title Insurance of New York, Inc.*, 752 A.2d 1222 (Md. App. 2000). In *Gebhardt*, a husband and wife transferred real property to a limited liability company of which they were the sole members. The transfer was made for estate planning purposes, and no money changed hands. Subsequent to the transfer, the Gebhardts, in their individual capacities, made a claim under their title insurance policy when they learned of a cloud on title to the property. The title insurer defended on the basis that the Gebhardts no longer owned the property and, therefore, had no standing to maintain a claim. The court ruled in favor of the insurer, rejecting the Gebhardts' argument that because they were the sole members of the LLC., the conveyance was, in effect, to themselves and they still retained an interest in the property. Instead, the court found a transfer for value: "[U]pon executing the deed to the LLC, the Gebhardts reaped the limited liability and estate planning benefits conferred by the Virginia Limited Liability Company Act. Having accepted those benefits, it is disingenuous for the Gebhardts to now deny that the conveyance ever took place." *Id.* at 1227. See also *Hagan v. Adams Property Associates, Inc.*, 482 S.E.2d 805 (Va. 1997), where the court held that a transfer of real estate from the property owner to an LLC of which the transferor was one of three members was a "sale or exchange" for purposes of a brokerage agreement previously executed by the transferor. In response to the defendant's argument that there was no consideration, and thus no sale or exchange, the court ruled that the assumption by the limited liability company of the debt secured by a first deed of trust and the agreement of the limited liability company to place a second lien the property to secure a note due the transferor constituted consideration. (The court did not indicate the identity of the obligor on the note. Presumably, it was not the limited liability company, as that would more clearly indicate a sale to the limited liability company.) *See generally* 1 RIBSTEIN AND KEATINGE ON LIMITED LIABILITY COMPANIES § 3.8 (2006). Did the courts in *Gebhardt* and *Hagan* exalt form over substance, or should the *Premier* court be faulted for ignoring the separate legal identity of the limited liability company?

2. Creditors of an LLC will often try to reach the assets of its members when the LLC is insolvent. Courts have borrowed from corporate law and are willing to "pierce the veil" of the LLC as they would the veil of the corporation. See Chapter 7, *infra*, where corporate veil piercing is considered. For a case applying these principles in the context of an LLC, see *Litchfield Asset Man. Corp. v. Howell*, 799 A.2d 298 (Conn. Ct. App. 2002).

3.   Authority of Members

TAGHIPOUR v. JEREZ
Supreme Court of Utah
2002 UT 74, 52 P.3d 1252 (2002)

RUSSON, JUSTICE:

On a writ of certiorari, Namvar Taghipour, Danesh Rahemi, and Jerez, Taghipour and Associates, LLC, seek review of the decision of the court of appeals affirming the trial court's dismissal of their causes of action against Mount Olympus Financial, L.C. ("Mt. Olympus"). We affirm.

BACKGROUND

Namvar Taghipour, Danesh Rahemi, and Edgar Jerez ("Jerez") formed a limited liability company known as Jerez, Taghipour and Associates, LLC (the "LLC"), on August 30, 1994, to purchase and develop a particular parcel of real estate pursuant to a joint venture agreement. The LLC's articles of organization designated Jerez as the LLC's manager. In addition, the operating agreement between the members of the LLC provided: "No loans may be contracted on behalf of the [LLC] . . . unless authorized by a resolution of the [m]embers."

On August 31, 1994, the LLC acquired the intended real estate. Then, on January 10, 1997, Jerez, unbeknownst to the LLC's other members or managers, entered into a loan agreement on behalf of the LLC with Mt. Olympus. According to the agreement, Mt. Olympus lent the LLC $25,000 and, as security for the loan, Jerez executed and delivered a trust deed that conveyed the LLC's real estate property to a trustee with the power to sell the property in the event of default. Mt. Olympus then dispensed $20,000 to Jerez and retained the $5,000 balance to cover various fees. In making the loan, Mt. Olympus did not investigate Jerez's authority to effectuate the loan agreement beyond determining that Jerez was the manager of the LLC.

After Mt. Olympus dispersed the funds pursuant to the agreement, Jerez apparently misappropriated and absconded with the $20,000. Jerez never remitted a payment on the loan, and because the other members of the LLC were unaware of the loan, no loan payments were ever made by anyone, and consequently, the LLC defaulted. Therefore, Mt. Olympus foreclosed on the LLC's property. The members of the LLC, other than Jerez, were never notified of the default or pending foreclosure sale.

On June 18, 1999, Namvar Taghipour, Danesh Rahemi, and the LLC (collectively, "Taghipour") filed suit against Mt. Olympus and Jerez. Taghipour asserted three claims against Mt. Olympus: (1) declaratory judgment that the loan agreement and subsequent foreclosure on the LLC's property were invalid because Jerez lacked the authority to bind the LLC under the operating agreement, (2) negligence in failing to conduct proper due diligence in determining whether Jerez had the authority to enter into the loan agreement, and (3) partition of the various interests in the property at issue. In response, Mt. Olympus moved to dismiss all three claims, asserting that pursuant to Utah Code section 48-2b-127(2), the loan agreement documents are valid and binding on the LLC since they were signed by the LLC's manager. This section provides:

> Instruments and documents providing for the acquisition, mortgage, or disposition of property of the limited liability company shall be valid and binding upon the limited liability company if they are executed by one or more managers of a limited liability company having a manager or managers or if they are executed by one or more members of a limited liability company in which management has been retained by the members.

UTAH CODE ANN. § 48-2b-127(2) (1998). The trial court granted Mt. Olympus' motion and dismissed Taghipour's claims against Mt. Olympus, ruling that under the above section, "instruments and documents providing for the mortgage of property of a limited liability company are valid and binding on the limited liability company if they are executed by the manager," that the complaint alleges that Jerez is the manager of the LLC, and that therefore the loan documents Jerez executed are valid and binding on the LLC.

. . . The Utah Court of Appeals affirmed the trial court. . . .

. . .

ANALYSIS

The issue in this case is whether the loan agreement documents executed by Jerez, as manager of the LLC, are valid and binding on the LLC under section 48-2b-127(2) of the Utah Limited Liability Company Act (the "Act"), as the statute existed at the time Jerez executed the loan agreement[20] or whether the documents were not binding on the LLC because, consistent with section 48-2b-125(2)(b) of the Act, the operating agreement effectively denied Jerez the necessary authority to bind the LLC where the agreement provides: "No loans may be contracted on behalf of the [LLC] . . . unless authorized by a resolution of the [m]embers." Taghipour reasons that this operating agreement provision precludes Jerez from executing a loan without a resolution of the members since under section 48-2b-125(2)(b) of the Act a manager cannot bind a limited liability company if the articles of organization or operating agreement does not afford the manager the authority to do so.

---

[20] The court referred to footnote 1, which has been edited out of the case:

Since the occurrence of the facts giving rise to this suit, the legislature has revised the Utah Limited Liability Company Act, now entitled the Utah Revised Limited Liability Company Act, which is codified at Utah Code Ann. §§ 48-2c-101 to 1902 (Supp. 2001). The Utah Revised Limited Liability Company Act became effective on July 1, 2001. Because we apply the law as it existed at the time of the events giving rise to this suit, . . . we apply the Act as it existed before the revised act became effective. Further, because section 48-2b-127 was never amended from the time of its enactment until 2001, we simply cite the 1998 version of the statute for convenience although some of the pertinent facts occurred before that year.

— Eds.

I. COMPETING STATUTORY PROVISIONS

To determine whether the loan agreement in this case is valid and binding on the LLC, it must first be determined whether this case is governed by section 48-2b-127(2), which makes certain kinds of documents binding on a limited liability company when executed by a manager, or section 48-2b-125(2)(b), which provides that a manager's authority to bind a limited liability company can be limited or eliminated by an operating agreement.

When two statutory provisions purport to cover the same subject, the legislature's intent must be considered in determining which provision applies. *Jensen v. IHC Hosps., Inc.*, 944 P.2d 327, 331 (Utah 1997). To determine that intent, our rules of statutory construction provide that "when two statutory provisions conflict in their operation, the provision more specific in application governs over the more general provision." *Hall v. State Dep't of Corr.*, 2001 UT 34, 15, 24 P.3d 958; see also *Biddle v. Washington Terrace City*, 1999 UT 110, 14, 993 P.2d 875.

In this case, the Utah Court of Appeals, affirming the trial court, concluded that section 48-2b-127(2) was more specific than section 48-2b-125(2)(b), and therefore took precedence over it. However, Taghipour contends that in determining which of the two provisions is more specific, the more restrictive clause is more specific because it is more limiting and "would require authority in all situations." Accordingly, Taghipour contends that section 48-2b-125(2)(b) is the more restrictive, and consequently, the more specific, provision.

The question of which statute the legislature intended to apply in this case is determined by looking to the plain language of the statutes that purport to cover the same subject. . . . Section 48-2b-125(2)(b) provides in relevant part:

> If the management of the limited liability company is vested in a manager or managers, any manager has authority to bind the limited liability company, unless otherwise provided in the articles of organization or operating agreement.

In contrast, section 48-2b-127(2) provides:

> Instruments and documents providing for the acquisition, mortgage, or disposition of property of the limited liability company shall be valid and binding upon the limited liability company if they are executed by one or more managers of a limited liability company having a manager or managers or if they are executed by one or more members of a limited liability company in which management has been retained by the members.

Section 48-2b-127(2) is the more specific statute because it applies only to documents explicitly enumerated in the statute, i.e., the section expressly addresses "[i]nstruments and documents" that provide "for the acquisition, mortgage, or disposition of property of the limited liability company." Thus, this section is tailored precisely to address the documents and instruments Jerez executed, e.g., the trust deed and trust deed note. For example, a trust deed is similar to a mortgage in that it secures an obligation relating to real property, and a trust deed "is a conveyance" of title to real property, which is a disposition of property as contemplated by the statutory provision. Conversely, section 48-2b-125(2)(b) is more general because it addresses *every* situation in which a manager can bind a limited liability company.

Further, a statute is more specific according to the content of the statute, not according to how restrictive the statute is in application. Indeed, a specific statute may be either more or less restrictive than the statute more general in application, depending upon the intent of the legislature in enacting a more specific statute.

Moreover, if we were to hold that section 48-2b-125(2)(b) is the more specific provision, we would essentially render section 48-2b-127(2) "superfluous and inoperative," *Hall*, 2001 UT 34 at ¶ 15, 24 P.3d 958, because section 48-2b-127(2) would simply restate section 48-2b-125(2)(b) and would therefore be subsumed by section 48-2b-125(2)(b). Accordingly, the court of appeals correctly concluded that section 48-2b-127(2) is more specific, and therefore, the applicable statute in this case.

II. VALID AND BINDING LOAN AGREEMENT DOCUMENTS

Section 48-2b-127(2) must be applied to the facts of this case to determine whether the documents are valid and bind the LLC. At the time relevant to this case, section 48-2b-127(2), the statute applicable to the issue in this case provided:

> *Instruments and documents providing for the* acquisition, *mortgage,* or disposition *of property of the limited liability company shall be valid and binding upon the limited liability company if they are executed by one or more managers* of a limited liability company having a manager or managers or if they are executed by one or more members of a limited liability company in which management has been retained by the members.

UTAH CODE ANN. § 48-2b-127(2) (1998) (emphasis added). According to this section, the documents are binding if they are covered by the statute and if executed by a manager. There are no other requirements for such documents to be binding on a limited liability company.

In this case, as Taghipour acknowledges in the complaint and Taghipour's brief on appeal, Jerez was designated as the LLC's manager in the articles of organization. Jerez, acting in his capacity as manager, executed loan agreement documents, e.g., the trust deed and trust deed note, on behalf of the LLC that are specifically covered by the above statute. As such, these documents are valid and binding on the LLC under section 48-2b-127(2). Therefore, the court of appeals correctly concluded that the LLC was bound by the loan agreement and, consequently, that Mt. Olympus was not liable to Taghipour for Jerez's actions.

CONCLUSION

The court of appeals correctly determined that section 48-2b-127(2) (1998) governs this case, that under this statutory section the loan agreement is valid and binding on the LLC, and that Mt. Olympus did all that was required by statute. Therefore, the court of appeals correctly affirmed the trial court's dismissal of Taghipour's claims against Mt. Olympus. Accordingly, we affirm.

NOTES AND QUESTIONS

1. In a concurring opinion filed in the decision of the Utah court of appeals, Judge Orme said:

> I concur in the court's opinion. In so doing, I must note that I find the policy reflected in sections 48-2b-125(2)(b) and -127(2) to be quite curious. If, as in this case, there are restrictions in a limited liability company's organic documents on its managers' ability to unilaterally bind the company, those restrictions will be effective across the range of mundane and comparatively insignificant contracts purportedly entered into by the company, but the restrictions will be ineffective in the case of the company's most important contracts. Thus, if the articles of organization or operating agreement provide that the managers will enter into no contract without the approval of the company's members, as memorialized in an appropriate resolution, the company can escape an unauthorized contract for janitorial services, coffee supplies, or photocopying, but is stuck with the sale of its property for less than fair value or a loan on unfavorable terms. Surely, this is at odds with the expectations of the business community. A manager or officer typically can bind the company to comparatively unimportant contracts, but, as is provided in the Operating Agreement in this case, needs member or board

approval to borrow against company assets. Financial institutions know this and are able to protect themselves by insisting on seeing articles of incorporation, bylaws, and board resolutions — or the limited liability company equivalents — as part of the mortgage loan process. A cursory review of such documents in this case would have disclosed that Jerez lacked the authority to bind the company to the proposed loan agreement.

In short, I suspect that the strange result in this case is not so much the product of carefully weighed policy considerations as it is the product of a legislative oversight or lapse of some kind. That being said, I readily agree that the language of both statutory sections is clear and unambiguous and that it is not the prerogative of the courts to rewrite legislation. If the laws which dictate the result in this case need to be fixed, the repairs must come via legislative amendment rather than judicial pronouncement.

2001 UT App. 139, *21-23, 26 P.3d 885, 889 (Ct. App. 2001). Despite the view of the concurring judge that § 48-2b-127(2) was "the product of a legislative oversight or lapse of some kind," it is not an uncommon provision. Why might the legislature have decided to treat the execution of instruments and documents relating to real property with a different standard than all other instruments and documents?

2. The Uniform Act also distinguishes real property documents. Section 301(c) of ULLCA provides:

> Unless the articles of organization limit their authority, any member of a member-managed company or manager of a manager-managed company may sign and deliver any instrument transferring or affecting the company's interest in real property. The instrument is conclusive in favor of a person who gives value without knowledge of the lack of authority of person signing and delivering the instrument.

This provision seems internally inconsistent. The first sentence allows the LLC to limit the authority of a member or manager (provided it does so in the articles of organization, not just the operating agreement), while the second sentence seems to create apparent authority for the person signing the instrument. The Comment says that if a limitation is included in the articles of organization, it is effective "even as to persons without knowledge of the agent's lack of authority." The "lack of authority" reference in the second sentence of the quoted provision may simply refer to a limitation of authority included in the operating agreement. Thus, the drafters of the ULLCA have made the policy determination that those dealing with an LLC are on notice as to at least certain of the provisions in its articles of organization. The wisdom of this policy choice might be questioned; it means that persons dealing with an LLC must review the articles of organization or bear the risk of its limitations.

4.   Fiduciary Duty of Members

MCCONNELL v. HUNT SPORTS ENTERPRISES
Court of Appeals of Ohio
725 N.E.2d 1193 (1999)

TYACK, JUDGE.

In 1996, the National Hockey League ("NHL") determined it would be accepting applications for new hockey franchises. The deadline for applying for an NHL expansion franchise was November 1, 1996. [Lamar Hunt, John McConnell and others formed Columbus Hockey Limited, LLC ("CHL") for the purpose of seeking a franchise for Columbus, Ohio.] The members of CHL were McConnell, Wolfe Enterprises, Inc., Hunt Sports Group, Pizzuti Sports Limited, and Buckeye Hockey, L.L.C. Each member made an initial capital contribution of $25,000. CHL was subject to an operating agreement that set forth the terms between the members. Pursuant to section 2.1 of CHL's operating agreement, the general character of the business of CHL was to invest in and operate a franchise in the NHL.

On or about November 1, 1996, an application was filed with the NHL on behalf of the city of Columbus. In the application, the ownership group was identified as CHL. . . . A $100,000 check from CHL was included as the application fee. Also included within the application package was Columbus's plan for an arena to house the hockey games. There was no facility at the time, and the proposal was to build a facility that would be financed, in large part, by a three-year countywide one-half percent sales tax. The sales tax issue would be on the May 1997 ballot.

On May 6, 1997, the sales tax issue failed. . . . [O]n May 7, 1997, Dimon McPherson, chairman and chief executive officer of Nationwide Insurance Enterprise ("Nationwide"), met with Hunt, and they discussed the possibility of building the arena despite the failure of the sales tax issue. . . .

By May 28, 1997, Nationwide had come up with a plan to finance an arena privately and on such date, Nationwide representatives met with representatives of Hunt Sports Group. Hunt Sports Group did not accept Nationwide's lease proposal. [Hunt acted without consulting the other CHL investors. McPherson then approached McConnell.] McPherson told McConnell about [Hunt's] rejection of the lease proposal and discussed the NHL's [new] deadline. McConnell stated that if Hunt would not step up and lease the arena and, therefore, get the franchise, McConnell would. . . .

On June 9, 1997, a meeting [between Hunt, McConnell and other CHL investors] took place. . . . The NHL required that the ownership group be identified and that such ownership group sign a lease term sheet by June 9, 1997. [Hunt stated that he found Nationwide's lease offer unacceptable.] McConnell . . . accepted the term sheet and was signing it in his individual capacity. The term sheet contained a signature line for "Columbus Hockey Limited" as the franchise owner. [The name was eliminated.] McConnell then signed the term sheet as the owner of the franchise. . . .

On June 17, 1997, the NHL expansion committee recommended to the NHL board of governors that Columbus be awarded a franchise with McConnell's group as owner of the franchise. On the same date, the complaint in the case at bar was filed [by McConnell seeking a declaratory judgment that the ownership of the franchise by his group was proper]. On or about June 25, 1997, the NHL board of governors awarded Columbus a franchise with McConnell's group as owner.[21] Hunt Sports Group, Buckeye Hockey, L.L.C. and Ameritech have no ownership interest in the hockey franchise. . . . [The Hunt group filed an answer and counterclaim, in addition to a separate suit filed in New York.]

In their complaint, McConnell and Wolfe Enterprises, Inc. requested a declaration that section 3.3 of the CHL operating agreement allowed members of CHL to compete with CHL. Specifically, McConnell and Wolfe Enterprises, Inc. sought a declaration that under the operating agreement, they were permitted to participate in COLHOC and obtain the franchise. [A] second claim sought judicial dissolution of CHL. [The trial court rendered a judgment in favor of McConnell.] . . .

. . . Appellant [Hunt] asserts, in part, that the trial court's interpretation of section 3.3 was incorrect and that section 3.3 is ambiguous and subject to different interpretations. Therefore, appellant contends extrinsic evidence should have been considered, and such evidence would have shown the parties did not intend section 3.3 to mean members could compete against CHL and take away CHL's only purpose. . . .

Section 3.3 of the operating agreement states:

---

[21] [2] The ownership group is now formally known as COLHOC Limited Partnership ("COLHOC"). Portions of the record indicate COLHOC was formed before the June 9, 1997 meeting. JMAC, Inc. is the majority owner, and JMAC Hockey, L.L.C. is the general partner of COLHOC. JMAC Hockey, L.L.C. signed the general partnership agreement on June 26, 1997.

"*Members May Compete.* Members shall not in any way be prohibited from or restricted in engaging or owning an interest in any other business venture of any nature, including any venture which might be competitive with the business of the Company."

Appellant emphasizes the word "other" in the above language and states, in essence, that it means any business venture that is different from the business of the company. Appellant points out that under section 2.1 of the operating agreement, the general character of the business is "to invest in and operate a franchise in the National Hockey League." Hence, appellant contends that members may only engage in or own an interest in a venture that is not in the business of investing in and operating a franchise with the NHL.

Appellant's interpretation of section 3.3 goes beyond the plain language of the agreement and adds words or meanings not stated in the provision. Section 3.3, for example, does not state "[m]embers shall not be prohibited from or restricted in engaging or owning an interest in any other business venture that is different from the business of the company." Rather, section 3.3 states: "any other business venture *of any nature*." (Emphasis added.) It then adds to this statement: "including any venture which might be competitive with the business of the Company." The words "any nature" could not be broader, and the inclusion of the words "any venture which might be competitive with the business of the Company" makes it clear that members were not prohibited from engaging in a venture that was competitive with CHL's investing in and operating an NHL franchise. Contrary to appellant's contention, the word "other" simply means a business venture other than CHL. The word "other" does not limit the type of business venture in which members may engage.

Hence, section 3.3 did not prohibit appellees from engaging in activities that may have been competitive with CHL, including appellees' participation in COLHOC. Accordingly, . . . appellees were entitled to a declaration that section 3.3 of the operating agreement permitted appellees to request and obtain an NHL hockey franchise to the exclusion of CHL. . . .

Before we can review the propriety of the directed verdict in this case, the law on fiduciary duty and interference with a prospective business relationship must be addressed. The term "fiduciary relationship" has been defined as a relationship in which special confidence and trust is reposed in the integrity and fidelity of another, and there is a resulting position of superiority or influence acquired by virtue of this special trust. In the case at bar, a limited liability company is involved which, like a partnership, involves a fiduciary relationship. Normally, the presence of such a relationship would preclude direct competition between members of the company. However, here we have an operating agreement that by its very terms allows members to compete with the business of the company. Hence, the question we are presented with is whether an operating agreement of a limited liability company may, in essence, limit or define the scope of the fiduciary duties imposed upon its members. We answer this question in the affirmative.

A fiduciary has been defined as a person having a duty, *created by his or her undertaking*, to act primarily for the benefit of another in matters *connected with such undertaking*. . . . These principles support our conclusion that a contract may define the scope of fiduciary duties between parties to the contract.

. . . The operating agreement constitutes the undertaking of the parties herein. In becoming members of CHL, appellant and appellees agreed to abide by the terms of the operating agreement, and such agreement specifically allowed competition with the company by its members. As such, the duties created pursuant to such undertaking did not include a duty not to compete. Therefore, there was no duty on the part of appellees to refrain from subjecting appellant to the injury complained of herein.

We find further support for our conclusion in case law concerning close corporations and partnerships. . . . The *Cruz [v. S. Dayton Urological Assocs., Inc.*, 121 Ohio App.

3d 655, 700 N.E.2d 675 (1997)], case stands for the proposition that close corporation employment agreements may limit the scope of fiduciary duties that otherwise would apply absent certain provisions in such agreements. The same principle has been applied in situations involving partnerships that are subject to partnership agreements. See *Spayd v. Turner, Granzow & Hollenkamp* (1985), 19 Ohio St. 3d 55, 59, 19 OBR 54, 57–58, 482 N.E.2d 1232, 1236 (the respective rights of partnership members depend primarily on the specific provisions contained within the partnership contract as recognized in [UPA § 18] which states that the rights and duties of partners are subject to any agreement between the partners).

"Operating agreement" is defined in R.C. 1705.01(J) as all of the valid written or oral agreements of the members as to the affairs of a limited liability company and the conduct of its business. . . . Indeed, many of the statutory provisions in R.C. Chapter 1705 governing limited liability companies indicate they are, in various ways, subject to and/or dependent upon related provisions in an operating agreement. Here, the operating agreement states in its opening paragraph that it evidences the mutual agreement of the members in consideration of their contributions and promises to each other. Such agreement specifically allowed its members to compete with the company.

Given the above, we conclude as a matter of law that it was not a breach of fiduciary duty for appellees to form COLHOC and obtain an NHL franchise to the exclusion of CHL. In so concluding, we are not stating that *no* act related to such obtainment could be considered a breach of fiduciary duty. In general terms, members of limited liability companies owe one another the duty of utmost trust and loyalty. However, such general duty in this case must be considered in the context of members' ability, pursuant to operating agreement, to compete with the company.

[The court next considered the claim of tortuous interference, concluding that "there was not sufficient material evidence presented at trial so as to create a factual question for the jury on the issues of breach of fiduciary duty and tortious interference with business relationships. . . ."]

[McConnell] sought money damages for appellant's alleged breach of contract in unilaterally rejecting the Nationwide lease proposal, in failing to negotiate with Nationwide in good faith, in allowing Nationwide's deadline to expire without response, and in wrongfully and unlawfully usurping control of CHL. In granting appellees' motion for a directed verdict, the trial court found appellant violated the CHL operating agreement in failing to ask for and obtain the authorization of CHL members, other than appellees, prior to filing the answer and counterclaim in this action and the suit in New York. . . . The trial court awarded appellees $1.00 in damages.

. . . Appellant contends that under the operating agreement, it could only be liable for willful misconduct. In addition, appellant contends it was the "operating member" of CHL and, therefore, had full authority to act on CHL's behalf. For the reasons that follow, we conclude that a directed verdict in favor of appellees . . . was appropriate.

First, there was no evidence at trial that appellant was the operating member of CHL. The operating agreement, which sets forth the entire agreement between the members of CHL, does not name any person or entity the operating or managing member of CHL. Instead, all members of CHL had an equal number of units in CHL, as reflected by the amount of their capital contributions shown on Schedule A of the operating agreement. Pursuant to section 4.1 of the operating agreement, no member was permitted to take any action on behalf of the company unless such action was approved by the specified number of members, which was, at the very least, a majority of the units allocated.

This brings us to the question of whether appellant breached the operating agreement by failing to obtain the approval of the other CHL members prior to filing, in CHL's name, the answer and counterclaim in this suit [and] the suit in New York. . . . Again, section 4.1(b) of the operating agreement requires at least majority approval prior to taking any action on behalf of CHL. Further, the approval of the members as to any action on behalf of CHL must have been evidenced by minutes of a meeting properly noticed and held or by an action in writing signed by the requisite number of members. See section 4.2 of the operating agreement.

There is no evidence that appellant obtained the approval of CHL members prior to filing the actions listed above. Indeed, there is no evidence that appellant even asked permission of any member to file the actions, let alone held a meeting or requested approval in writing. . . . This was contrary to sections 4.1 and 4.2 of the operating agreement and constituted breach of such agreement.

Appellant points to section 4.4 of the operating agreement and contends appellees had to show willful misconduct on its part in filing such actions. Section 4.4 states:

> "*Exculpation of Members; Indemnity. In carrying out their duties hereunder*, the Members shall not be liable to the Company or to any other Member for their good faith actions, or failure to act, or for any errors of judgment, or for any act or omission believed in good faith to be within the scope of authority conferred by this Agreement, but only for their own willful misconduct in the performance of their obligations under this Agreement. Actions or omissions taken in reliance upon the advice of legal counsel as being within the scope of authority conferred by this Agreement shall be conclusive evidence of such good faith; however, good faith may be determined without obtaining such advice." (Emphasis added.)

Section 4.4's provisions are in the context of members carrying out their duties under the operating agreement. There was no duty on appellant's part to unilaterally file the actions at issue. Indeed, we have determined that appellant did not act properly under the operating agreement in filing such actions. Hence, the provision in section 4.4 indicating members were only liable to other members for their own willful misconduct in the performance of their obligations under the operating agreement does not even apply to the actions taken by appellant. However, even if we applied this provision, the evidence shows appellant engaged in willful misconduct in filing the actions at issue.

As indicated above, appellant was a member of CHL at the time of its formation. As a member of CHL, appellant agreed to be bound by the terms of the operating agreement. Hunt read the operating agreement prior to signing it. The agreement required a majority vote prior to taking any action on behalf of CHL, such as the filing of the actions at issue. Appellant nonetheless filed such actions without obtaining the required approval and, indeed, without even asking one member (other than itself) for such permission.

Appellant contends it filed such actions upon the advice of counsel and, therefore, good faith existed. However, there is no evidence that appellant took such actions in reliance upon advice from counsel that such actions were within the scope of authority conferred by the operating agreement. . . .

. . . The trial court found that appellant unlawfully usurped control of CHL by unilaterally rejecting the Nationwide lease proposal, by failing to disclose the proposal to CHL, and by commencing litigation. . . . The trial court found that such actions made it no longer feasible, profitable, advantageous, and reasonably practicable to operate the business of CHL. Based on these findings of fact, the trial court concluded that as a result of appellant's wrongful conduct, CHL should be judicially dissolved. . . . The trial court's determinations in this regard were erroneous because, while appellant did act wrongfully and breached the operating agreement in usurping control of CHL, such was not the reason it became no longer practicable to carry on the business of CHL. . . . Because [the] ownership group did not turn out to be CHL, there was no reason for CHL's existence anymore.

The fact that the franchise was owned by a group different from the ownership group originally contemplated made it no longer reasonably practicable to carry on the business of CHL, as CHL's only business was investing in and operating an NHL franchise. Appellant's wrongful actions taken in the weeks previous to the June 9, 1997 meeting had no effect on the ultimate outcome. . . .

Given the above, the evidence does not support the trial court's findings and conclusions that appellant wrongfully caused the dissolution of CHL. However, such was not reversible error. As stated above, the evidence supports the finding that it was not reasonably practicable to carry on the business of CHL in conformity with its articles of incorporation and operating agreement. Therefore, granting judgment in favor of appellees . . . and decreeing CHL judicially dissolved were proper. . . .

Judgment affirmed in part and reversed in part.

BOWMAN, J., concurs.

PEGGY L. BRYANT, J., concurs in part and dissents in part [concerning the reversal of the award of attorney fees].

NOTES AND QUESTIONS

1. Suppose that ULLCA §§ 409(b)(3) and 103(b)(2)(i) applied to the facts of *McConnell*. Would the provision permitting competition be deemed a "manifestly unreasonable" activity in light of the duty of loyalty? Would the case have been decided differently if the McConnell group had submitted a proposal simultaneously with the initial proposal by CHL (the original group)? Perhaps a provision that permitted competition under that scenario would be manifestly unreasonable, but not one construed to permit competition in the fact situation in this case.

2. In *KMK Factoring, L.L.C. v. McKnew (In re William McKnew)*, 270 B.R. 593 (Bankr. E.D. Va. 2001), the court was faced with the issue of whether a manager of an LLC is a fiduciary for purposes of the federal bankruptcy code. The issue in this case arose under § 523 of the Bankruptcy Code, which prohibits the discharge of an individual debtor from any debt for fraud or defalcation *while acting in a fiduciary capacity*. 11 U.S.C. § 523(a)(4) (2001) (emphasis added). After noting that the issue was one of federal law, the court concluded that for purposes of § 523, a manager of an LLC is not a fiduciary: "[T]he imposition of a fiduciary relationship here would unnecessarily stretch the long-imposed restriction of limiting such a relationship to an express or technical trust, and instead impose it to an instance where traditional concepts of embezzlement or larceny more nearly fit."

3. As *McConnell* indicates, parties to an LLC operating agreement can contract around or, at least in Delaware and possibly in other states, eliminate fiduciary duties. In this regard (as in many others), limited liability company law is parallel to the law of limited partnerships, developed in section 6(d) above. *See, generally,* Myron T. Steele, *Judicial Scrutiny of Fiduciary Duties in Delaware Limited Partnerships and Limited Liability Companies,* 32 DEL. J. CORP. L. 1 (2007).

KATRIS v. CARROLL
Appellate Court of Illinois
842 N.E.2d 221 (2005)

PRESIDING JUSTICE McNULTY delivered the opinion of the court:

This case concerns the applicability of fiduciary duties to a member of a manager-managed limited liability company under the Illinois Limited Liability Company Act (Act). Plaintiff-appellant Peter Katris, individually and in a derivative capacity on behalf of Viper Execution Systems, L.L.C. (the LLC), asserted a cause of action for collusion against defendants-appellees Patrick Carroll and Ernst & Company (Ernst). Katris, a manager of the LLC, contended that Carroll and Ernst colluded with a member of the LLC in the member's breach of his fiduciary duties to Katris and the LLC. The circuit court of Cook County granted summary judgment in favor of Carroll and Ernst, finding that the LLC member did not owe the LLC or Katris any fiduciary duty.

In affirming the circuit court's grant of summary judgment, we follow the plain meaning of section 15-3(g)(3) of the Act. This section imposes fiduciary duties only on a member of a manager-managed limited liability company who exercises some or all of the authority of a manager pursuant to the operating agreement. The facts in this case showed that the member did not exercise any such authority pursuant to the operating agreement. Accordingly, the member did not owe any fiduciary duties, and, as a result, the collusion claim fails and summary judgment was proper.

BACKGROUND

In the early to mid-1990s, Stephen Doherty wrote a software program called "Viper" for Lester Szlendak. Subsequently, Katris and William Hamburg, both Ernst employees, expressed interest in Viper, and on February 14, 1997, they joined Szlendak and Doherty in forming the LLC to exploit the capabilities of the software. On that date, they filed the LLC's articles of organization with the Secretary of State. In it, they indicated that management of the LLC was vested in its managers, Katris and Hamburg, and not retained by its members.

Pursuant to the LLC's operating agreement, signed by the four members on February 14, 1997, each member held a 25% interest, and as a condition of the operating agreement, Szlendak and Doherty assigned their rights, interest and title to Viper to the LLC. The operating agreement provided that the "business and affairs of the [LLC] shall be managed by its [m]anagers" and that the members agreed to elect Katris and Hamburg as the "sole [m]anagers" of the LLC. The operating agreement also enumerated the powers of the managers and set forth the rights and obligations of the members. However, none of the provisions setting forth the rights and obligations of the members provided the members with any managerial authority. Pursuant to its terms, the operating agreement could "not be amended except by the affirmative vote of [m]embers holding a majority of the [p]articipating [p]ercentages."

Also on February 14, 1997, Katris and Hamburg, as managers of the LLC, prepared a written consent adopting certain resolutions in lieu of holding an initial meeting of the managers. They resolved, *inter alia*, to adopt the operating agreement dated February 14, 1997, as the operating agreement of the LLC and to elect the following: Hamburg as chief executive officer, Katris as chief financial officer, Szlendak as director of marketing, and Doherty as director of technical services. The written consent contained signature lines for Hamburg and Katris, who were identified as "all of the [m]anagers" of the LLC.

Prior to and at the time of the LLC's formation, Doherty worked as an independent contractor for Hamburg and Carroll (also an Ernst employee); however, in late 1997, Ernst hired Doherty to work for Carroll. As part of his duties for Carroll, Doherty worked with a programmer hired by Ernst to adapt a software program ultimately called "Worldwide Options Web (WWOW)."

Katris initiated this action on January 16, 2002, and ultimately asserted a breach of fiduciary duty claim against Doherty and a claim for collusion against Doherty, Carroll and Ernst. He alleged that WWOW was functionally similar to Viper and contended that Doherty usurped a corporate opportunity of the LLC by working in secret with Carroll and the programmer hired by Ernst to develop competing software for Ernst. He further contended that Carroll and Ernst colluded with Doherty in the breach of Doherty's fiduciary duties to the LLC.

Doherty subsequently settled with Katris, providing Katris with an affidavit setting forth his involvement in the case in exchange for his dismissal. As a result of Doherty's dismissal from the case, only Katris' claim for collusion against defendants-appellees Carroll and Ernst remained.

Carroll and Ernst filed a motion for summary judgment asserting, *inter alia*, that Katris' collusion claim failed because Doherty, as a nonmanager member of the manager-managed LLC, did not owe Katris or the LLC a fiduciary duty under section 15-3(g) of the Act, and thus they could not collude with Doherty to breach a fiduciary duty under that section.

In response, Katris filed an affidavit attaching the February 14, 1997, written consent. Katris stated that the written consent constituted an amendment to the operating agreement and that, pursuant to the terms of that amendment, Doherty was named "Director of Technology" and "given the sole management responsibility for developing, writing, revising and implementing the Viper software." According to Katris' affidavit, Doherty "was in charge of adapting the software to route options orders, in addition to stock orders," and the "LLC relied on him totally to develop the Viper software." Katris contended that pursuant to section 15-3(g)(3) of the Act, Doherty was thus subject to the standards of conduct imposed upon managers under the Act and breached those duties by usurping a corporate opportunity belonging to the LLC.

On October 1, 2004, the circuit court entered an order granting Carroll and Ernst's motion for summary judgment. The court subsequently denied Katris' motion for reconsideration, and this appeal follows.

ANALYSIS

In this appeal, Katris contends that the trial court erred in granting summary judgment on his collusion claim against Carroll and Ernst.

Here, Katris asserted a cause of action for collusion against Carroll and Ernst. He contended that Carroll and Ernst colluded with Doherty in breaching Doherty's fiduciary duty to Katris and the LLC. Accordingly, Katris' claim against Carroll and Ernst depended upon a finding that Doherty owed Katris and the LLC a fiduciary duty. In this appeal, Katris contends that summary judgment was improper because Doherty owed Katris and the LLC such a fiduciary duty.

We look to the applicable provisions of the Act in determining the fiduciary duties owed by the managers and members of the LLC. The parties here agree that section 15-3(g) of the Act applies to determine Doherty's fiduciary duties.

Katris acknowledges that theirs was a manager-managed LLC and that, pursuant to the Act, a member of a manager-managed LLC "who is not also a manager owes no duties to the company or to the other members solely by reason of being a member." Katris thus concedes that Doherty did not owe any fiduciary duties solely by reason of being a member of the LLC.

Katris contends, however, that Doherty owed fiduciary duties to the LLC pursuant to section 15-3(g)(3) of the Act. Section 15-3(g)(3) provides:

> [A] member who pursuant to the operating agreement exercises some or all of the authority of a manager in the management and conduct of the company's business is held to the standards of conduct in subsections (b), (c), (d), and (e) of this Section to the extent that the member exercises the managerial authority vested in a manager by this Act[.]

Katris contends that Doherty exercised some of the authority of a manager in his capacity as director of technology for the LLC and thus falls within the ambit of this section. Carroll and Ernst disagree, contending that pursuant to the plain terms of the statute, Doherty was only subject to fiduciary duties if he exercised managerial authority pursuant to the operating agreement. They maintain that Doherty did not have any such managerial authority under the operating agreement. We agree.

" 'The cardinal rule of statutory construction is to ascertain and give effect to the intent of the legislature.' " *In re Application of the County Collector*, 826 N.E.2d 951 (2005). The plain meaning of the language used by the legislature is the best indication of legislative intent, and when the language is clear, this court should not look to extrinsic aids for construction. If possible, a statute should be construed so that no part is rendered superfluous or meaningless.

Looking at the plain language of section 15-3(g)(3) of the Act, Doherty was subject to fiduciary duties if he exercised some or all of the authority of a manager pursuant to the LLC's operating agreement. The Act provides for the creation of an operating agreement, stating that "[a]ll members of a limited liability company may enter into an operating agreement to regulate the affairs of the company and the conduct of its business and to govern relations among the members, managers, and company." The four members of the LLC here entered into such an operating agreement on February 14, 1997.

Looking to that operating agreement, it specifically provides that the business and affairs of the LLC "shall be managed by its [m]anagers," provides for the election of Katris and Hamburg as the "sole [m]anagers" of the LLC, and sets forth the powers of the managers of the LLC. Although the operating agreement also sets forth the rights and obligations of the members, these provisions do not provide for any managerial authority. Accordingly, Doherty did not exercise any managerial authority pursuant to the LLC's operating agreement.

Katris contends, however, that the managers amended the operating agreement by passing the February 14, 1997, written consent wherein they elected Doherty "Director of Technology." He contends that Doherty's designation as "Director of Technology" elevated him to a position beyond that of a mere member of the LLC and was sufficient to impart on him some managerial authority. This argument fails for two reasons.

First, Katris has provided no authority for his contention that the written consent constituted an amendment to the operating agreement. Pursuant to its own terms, an amendment to the operating agreement required the "affirmative vote of [m]embers holding a majority of the [p]articipating [p]ercentages." Katris and Hamburg were the sole participants to the February 14, 1997, written consent and held only a combined 50% interest in the LLC. They thus could not amend the operating agreement without an additional vote. Accordingly, the facts do not support Katris' contention that the written consent constituted an amendment to the operating agreement.

Second, even if the written consent were viewed as part of the operating agreement, it did not change and, indeed, it reaffirmed the terms of the operating agreement. Katris and Hamburg executed the written consent in their capacities as the managers of the LLC. In it, they specifically resolved to adopt the operating agreement the four members had executed that day as the operating agreement of the LLC. In the signature lines to the written consent, Katris and Hamburg designated themselves as "all of the [m]anagers" of the LLC. In light of these facts, something more than the managers' designation of Doherty as "Director of Technology" was required to change the terms of the operating agreement and grant Doherty managerial authority pursuant to it.

In reaching this conclusion, we find Katris' contentions in his affidavit, wherein he enumerates the managerial authority Doherty held as a result of being named "Director of Technology" in the written consent, inapposite under section 15-3(g)(3) of the Act. By its terms, that section applies where the nonmanager member exercises some or all of the authority of a manager *pursuant to the operating agreement*. To look beyond the operating agreement to Katris' affidavit would be to ignore the plain meaning of the statute and to render the express words used therein superfluous or meaningless. This we cannot do.

The undisputed facts of this case show that Doherty was a member of a manager-managed LLC and exercised no managerial authority pursuant to the LLC's operating agreement. Accordingly, the undisputed facts show that Doherty owed no fiduciary duties to Katris or the LLC pursuant to the Act and Katris' collusion claim against Carroll and Ernst fails as a matter of law. We therefore conclude that the circuit court properly granted the motion for summary judgment and affirm its judgment.

Affirmed.

QUESTION

While Doherty may not have had fiduciary duties to the LLC by virtue of being a nonmanaging member, might he not have had fiduciary duties as an employee or agent of the LLC?

5.　Fiduciary Duty of Managers

The managers of an LLC in a manager-managed limited liability company owe the same fiduciary duties of care and loyalty as a general partner owes to the limited partners of a limited partnership, and courts often draw on partnership precedents in LLC cases. Despite the obvious similarities between partnerships and LLCs, some courts look to corporate law to define the fiduciary duties of managers, perhaps because the management structure of limited liability companies is often similar to corporations, with boards of directors and officers. See, for instance, *Pinnacle Data Services, Inc. v. Gillen*, 104 S.W.3d 188, 198 (Tex. App. 2003). The courts apply the business judgment rule to actions of such directors, meaning that the courts will generally defer to the business judgments of the directors of an LLC unless the directors failed to act in good faith, acted without care (i.e., were allegedly grossly negligent), or had a conflict of interest. In *Blackmore Partners, L.P. v. Link Energy LLC*, 864 A.2d 80, 85–86 (Del. Ch. 2004), the unit holders, or members, of an LLC complained that the board of directors violated their fiduciary duties to the members when they sold all of the assets of the LLC (which they were empowered to do without a vote of the members) at a price that allowed the LLC to discharge its debts to its creditors, but provided no return to the unit holders. The plaintiffs did not specifically allege that the directors had a conflict of interest, acted with gross negligence or failed to act in good faith. Thus, it would seem that the directors' decision was "protected" by the business judgment rule. Nevertheless, the court declined to dismiss the action for failure to state a claim upon which relief may be granted:

> The complaint alleges, and for purposes of this motion the court assumes as true, that the Director Defendants approved a transaction that disadvantaged the holders of Link's equity units. Until the announcement of the transaction, the units had significant, if not substantial, trading value. Indeed, there is a basis in the complaint to infer that the value of Link's assets exceeded its liabilities by least $25 million. Moreover, the facts alleged support an inference that Link was neither insolvent nor on the verge of re-entering bankruptcy. Yet, as a result of the transaction at issue, those units were rendered valueless.
>
> In the circumstances, the allegation that the Defendant Directors approved a sale of substantially all of Link's assets and a resultant distribution of proceeds that went exclusively to the company's creditors raises a reasonable inference of disloyalty or intentional misconduct. Of course, it is also possible to infer (and the record at a later stage may well show) that the Director Defendants made a good faith judgment, after reasonable investigation, that there was no future for the business and no better alternative for the unit holders. Nevertheless, based only the facts alleged and the reasonable inferences that the court must draw from them, it would appear that no transaction could have been worse for the unit holders and reasonable to infer, as the plaintiff argues, that a properly motivated board of directors would not have agreed to a proposal that wiped out the value of the common equity and surrendered all of that value to the company's creditors.
>
> In an analogous case, Chancellor Allen recognized "[t]he broad principle that if directors take action directed against a class of securities, they should be required to justify" their action. Thus, while on a more complete record, it may

appear that the Director Defendants took no such action or were justified in acting as they did, this court cannot now conclude that the complaint does not state a claim for breach of the duty of loyalty or other misconduct not protected by the exculpatory provision in Link's operating agreement. For this reason, the Rule 12(b)(6) motion to dismiss must be denied.[22]

Is there any reason to treat the business judgments of the managers of an LLC different from the business judgments of corporate directors?

As the *McConnell* case, *supra*, indicates, the parties can vary fiduciary duties by contract, typically including the relevant provisions in the operating agreement. *McConnell* involved a contractual waiver of the fiduciary duties of members in a member-managed LLC, but similar waivers relating to the duties of managers in a manager-managed LLC are authorized in many LLC statutes. *See, e.g.*, Article 1528n of the Texas Limited Liability Company Act: "To the extent that at law or in equity, a member, manager, officer, or other person has duties (including fiduciary duties) and liabilities relating thereto to a limited liability company or to another member or manager, such duties and liabilities may be expanded or restricted by provisions in the regulations." (In Texas, the regulations are equivalent to the operating agreement.) Delaware permits not only expansion and restriction of fiduciary duties, but elimination as well. Delaware Limited Liability Company Act § 18-1101 (c).

6. Expulsion of a Member

Under the Uniform Limited Liability Company Act, a member can be expelled if the operating agreement so provides and, under certain defined circumstances, by unanimous consent of the members. *See* § 601. Some states that specifically authorize expulsion make that right nonwaivable in the operating agreement. *See CCD, L.C. v. Millsap*, 116 P.3d 366 (Utah 2005) (member's misappropriation of the LLC's trust fund warranted expulsion). What policy reasons would justify making the expulsion right nonwaivable?

7. Some Miscellaneous Issues

Dissolution. Limited liability companies are legal entities like partnerships formed under RUPA. The withdrawal, death, etc. of a member does not dissolve the limited liability company. Unless the operating agreement otherwise provides, the "dissociated" member is generally entitled to a buy-out of his interest. *See, e.g.*, ULLCA § 701.

Bankruptcy of a member. LLC statutes and operating agreements typically provide that a person ceases to be a member of the LLC if the member files a voluntary petition in bankruptcy. (*See, e.g.*, 6 DEL. CODE § 18-304). Such a provision, sometimes called an "ipso facto clause," raises a question under the federal bankruptcy code: "There is federal precedent that holds that an interest in an alternative entity — even a managing interest in a limited partnership — falls within the protective scope of § 365(e)(1) [the automatic stay provision] and that an ipso facto clause may not operate to divest a bankruptcy trustee from assuming that contract." *Milford Power Company, LLC v. PDC Milford Power*, LLC, 866 A.2d 738, 751 (Del. Ch. 2004) (citing *Summit Investment and Development Corp. v. Leroux*, 69 F.3d 608 (1st Cir. 1995)). In *Milford Power Company*, the Delaware Chancery Court upheld an ipso facto bankruptcy clause against a company that filed a Chapter 11 bankruptcy petition that was subsequently dismissed. However, the court held that while the member who filed the petition lost its membership interest and right to participate in the management of the LLC, it did not forfeit its economic interests, and would be treated as an assignee of a member's

---

[22] Ultimately, the defendants did prevail. Blackmore Partners, L.P. v. Link Energy LLC, 2005 Del. Ch. LEXIS 155 (Del Ch. Oct. 14, 2005). — Eds.

interest in the LLC. *See also In re Albright*, 291 B.R. 538 (Bankr. D. Colo. 2003) (the trustee in bankruptcy succeeded to all of the rights — economic and management — of the sole member of an LLC upon her filing a petition in bankruptcy).

Claims of a creditor of a member. Creditors of members of an LLC can obtain judicial relief through what is called a "charging order." *See, e.g.*, ULLCA § 504. This means that the creditor can get an order requiring the LLC to remit to the creditor any distributions that would otherwise be made by the LLC to the judgment debtor. This remedy precludes a judgment creditor of a member from obtaining a seizure and forced sale of the debtor-member's interest in the LLC. *Herring v. Keasler*, 563 S.E.2d 614 (N.C. Ct. App. 2002). A charging order will reach payments made to the owners of an LLC, even if characterized as compensation. *PB Real Estate, Inc. v. DEM II Properties*, 50 Conn. App. 741, 719 A.2d 73 (1998). Under certain circumstances, the creditor may be able to foreclose on the interest, requiring a judicial sale of the member's interest. The purchaser at such a foreclosure becomes a transferee of the member's interest, meaning that the purchaser is entitled to any distributions to which the member would be entitled, but may not participate in the management of the LLC or succeed to the voting rights, if any, of the member.

PROBLEM

Genesis, LLC, a manager-managed limited liability company, was formed to manufacture and market a telecommunications product developed by Carol, a member of the limited liability company. The other member was Don, who provided capital to the venture. Carol owned two-thirds of the equity and Don one-third. The operating agreement provided that Carol would appoint two of the three managers and Don would appoint the third manager. Don appointed himself, while Carol appointed herself and Ellen, a person with whom she worked at another company. Don and Ellen objected to many of the actions that Carol was taking and believed that she was jeopardizing the future of the company. They therefore engineered a plan. They executed a consent which merged Genesis, LLC into VGS, Inc., a corporation that Don formed and controlled. Carol did not learn of the merger until it was completed. Following the merger, Don would be in control and Carol would have a minority interest. The action that Don and Ellen took was valid under Delaware law. On what basis may Carol challenge the merger?

Chapter 4
THE PROCESS OF INCORPORATION

A. INTRODUCTION

This chapter deals with two subjects rather than one, but one subject, the process of incorporation, has a substantial impact on the other, what an English or Australian law student would call issues of legal personality.

The process of incorporation is relatively straight forward. The thornier issues, such as choice of entity (corporation, professional corporation, LLC, limited partnership, partnership, LLP, and so on), choice of the state of incorporation, or form of the capital structure, may be decided by the lawyer in charge, or by the lawyer and client. Thereafter, in many law firms, a young lawyer, or a non-lawyer paralegal, completes the process, including whether or not to include optional provisions in the articles of incorporation (certificate of incorporation in Delaware) and filing the necessary documents with the state (usually the Secretary of State but some times the Department of Corporations or other name). The more senior lawyer may then take over once again, after the Secretary of State stamps the articles "filed" and issues a certificate or charter, and the clients come into the law firm for the organizational meeting.

Most of those choices, and the orderliness of the process itself, affect the second set of issues, whether the separate legal personality of the corporation will be recognized — by customers, competitors, state officials and particularly, the courts.

The paralegal may lose the articles behind a filing cabinet. The client does business as if the law firm had filed the articles and the corporation duly formed. Will courts and others recognize the corporation as a separate entity liable for its own debts even though the letter of the law has not been complied with? Or, in order to avoid personal liability on the owners' parts, must the corporation have had a proper birth?

The same issue of defective incorporation (really defective existence) raises its head again at the other end of the spectrum. Officials may have declared the corporation dead (administratively dissolved) for failure to file annual reports or to pay the yearly fee for the privilege of corporate existence (the franchise tax). Can the corporation be brought back to life? If so, will the reinstatement relate back to the date of death?

In between birth and death, other issues of personality arise. Once it comes into being, will the corporation, or the persons who gave it birth (the promoters), or both, be liable on contracts a promoter entered into, ostensibly on behalf of a corporation to be formed ("promoter's liability on preincorporation contracts")? Further along, will the corporation alone be liable for its debts, or will the flesh and blood owners (the shareholders), or a parent corporation, also be held liable for the corporation's torts or breaches of contract. Chapter 7 devotes itself to this subject, among other names, known as the doctrine of corporate disregard or piercing the corporate veil. It, too, can be viewed as an issue of legal personality and whether corporateness will be held good across the board.

The ultra vires doctrine may permit recognition of the corporation's legal personality but permit challenges to the corporateness of an entity's activities, in at least two ways. One, strong form ultra vires, may permit challenges, whether as excuses for corporate nonperformance, or otherwise, to contracts as being "beyond the corporation's powers or purposes." Two, on a lesser scale, ultra vires may only permit suits inter se (shareholder verses director, director versus director) when allegedly the defendants have caused the corporation to exceed the purposes contained in its articles or certificate of incorporation.

These subjects, or some of them, may appear at times to have metaphysical components, especially the first time a student grapples with them. After some mastery, however, the same subjects become grist for the mill, part and parcel of every business lawyer's kit.

B. MECHANICS OF INCORPORATION

1. *Standard.* Over the last 30 years, the process of incorporating has become simpler and simpler. Since the first state adopted one in about 1870, all states have general incorporation acts. General incorporation connotes two things. One, any business may incorporate under them, save for special carve-outs, such as the businesses of banking and insurance. Two, the granting of corporate existence is a ministerial rather than a political act. Today a public official, the Secretary of State, issues the charter as a matter of course, rather than as of old when the legislature, parliament or sovereign issued the charter as a political act, under special incorporation acts.

Banking and insurance remain "affected with the public interest." Agencies other than the Secretary of State, such as the banking, financial institutions or insurance departments grant those charters, usually only after an approval process that amounts to more, often considerably more, than a ministerial act. Those areas call out for continuing regulation because consumers pay over funds (as deposits or for premiums) long before the quid pro quo (interest, payment of an insurance claim) becomes due. The thought is that in other businesses the consumer pays and receives goods or services in return, or shortly thereafter, so the need for continuing and special regulation is less. Most run-of-the mill corporations carry on a cash on the barrel head existence.

Blackstone, the leading nineteenth century author of commentaries upon the law, said that three was a corporation. Older statutes thus required at least three shareholders and three directors. The founders would often issue a single "qualifying share" to bring the number of owners up to three. *See, e.g., Minton v. Cavaney*, 56 Cal. 2d 576, 15 Cal. Rptr. 641, 364 P.2d 473 (1961) (Traynor, J.) (incorporating attorney, who accepted single qualifying share, rendered his estate liable on piercing the corporate veil grounds).

Modern statutes no longer require that or any other fiction. A corporation may have a single shareholder and a single director. An intermediate position is that several states require two directors if there are two shareholders and three directors if there 3 or more shareholders. The wisdom of having but a single director is a separate question, involving business rather than legal judgments.

A central feature of every set of articles or certificate has been the purpose clause. The whole body of doctrine on ultra vires grows out of activities that exceed the corporate purposes or powers. Corporations seek release from contracts; shareholders seek to enjoin corporate performance under contracts; or shareholders seek to hold directors liable for actions that fall outside of the purpose clause.

2. *Purpose Clauses.* Historically, corporations had to state one or more purposes. By the late nineteenth or early twentieth century, the practice had become to have long, prolix purpose clauses specifying undertakings the corporation could enter. In some more traditional English jurisdictions, corporate "objects clauses" still run on for several pages.

The later position became that promoters could form a corporation for any lawful purpose (statutes were general incorporation acts after all) but the incorporating papers had to state what that purpose would be (*e.g.,* operate a tavern, or build bridges).

Finally, state legislatures provided that the purpose of a corporation could be, *and could be stated to be,* any lawful purpose. *See, e.g.,* MBCA § 54(c) (1969).

The newest version of the Model Business Corporation Act (MBCA) (1984, but subject to continued revision) goes further. The Model Act provides for the "lawful limitless purpose corporation." The Act assumes that, if the articles say nothing about a corporate purpose, then the purpose is any lawful purpose. MBCA § 3.01(a).

In fact, under the newest Model Act version the draftsperson could fit "plain vanilla" articles of incorporation on a postcard. Gone, for instance, are requirements that articles state the corporation's duration (it is assumed to be perpetual) or purpose (it is assumed to be any lawful purpose). MBCA § 2.02(a) ("Articles of Incorporation") requires only four items:

(1) a corporate name for the corporation . . . ;

(2) the number of shares the corporation is authorized to issue;

(3) the street address [not post office box] of the corporation's registered office and the name of its registered agent at that office; and

(4) the name and address of each incorporator.

Del. Gen. Corp. Law § 102 is similar but requires statement of 5, and possibly 6, items rather than 4. To incorporate in Delaware, the certificate of incorporation must also state a purpose, but "[i]t shall be sufficient to state . . . that the purpose of the corporation is to engage in any lawful purpose or activity for which corporations may be organized under the General Corporation Law of Delaware."

3. *Board of Directors.* The Delaware certificate of incorporation must also state the "names and addresses of the persons who are to serve as directors until the first annual meeting of shareholders," but only "[i]f the powers of the incorporator or incorporators are to terminate upon the filing of the certificate of incorporation." Many attorneys do not, however, follow the latter course. They have the incorporators continue as the first directors until the organizational meeting, at which, in seriatim, incorporator by incorporator resigns, those incorporators still in office and the new directors filling the vacancy so created with a real party in interest.

4. *Name.* A comment (or two or three) about the name. The name the client or lawyer chooses must meet at least three requirements. One, traditionally, the name cannot be the same as, or deceptively similar to, the name of any other corporation incorporated or licensed to do business in the jurisdiction. Some statutes specify that such a name may be used if the corporation obtains written permission and, by use of the same or similar name, does not confuse the public. The Model Act now provides that the name chosen need only be "distinguishable on the records of the secretary of state," taken from the Delaware statute. *See* Del. Gen. Corp. Law § 102(1). Presumably, under that standard, a new corporation could add a letter or two to an existing name. The secretary of state would have to accept the articles for filing, leaving issues of passing off, unfair competition, and the like to courts. Many states, however, have not adopted the newest MBCA, or that provision, retaining the "deceptively similar test" and the authority of the secretary of state that goes with a more substantive test.

Two, the name a new corporation chooses cannot imply that the corporation is organized for other than a permitted purpose (*i.e.*, usually banking or insurance). Three, the name must contain word of corporateness ("corporation," "incorporated," "company," or "limited," or the abbreviation "corp.," "inc.," "co.," or "ltd.," or words or abbreviations of like import in another language). MBCA § 4.01.

There are also "house rules" that prevail in particular secretary of states' offices. For example, many house rules prohibit the use of profane or scatological words, or words similar thereto, in corporate names. The only manner in which to master those rules is through practice of law in a particular jurisdiction.

Statutes also contain a procedure whereby persons may pay a modest fee and reserve an available name, usually for 6 months or so. Most statutes do not permit renewals, as "name squatting" may take place in high tech, professional sports, and other fields.

Lawyers and paralegals have protocols for name clearances. Those protocols can include checking the name list in annual red book or on the electronic list the Secretary of State promulgates in many jurisdictions; researching the yellow pages in telephone directories in the city in which the corporation will locate, as well as adjoining or nearby cities, whether or not in the same state; or commissioning a full blown trademark search by an intellectual property attorney.

Articles or certificate no longer recite corporate powers, although they once did and may still do in other countries. Statutes contain long lists of powers corporations are deemed to have, e.g., to sue and be sued, to make and amend bylaws, to lend money, and so on. *See, e.g.*, MBCA § 3.02 (listing 15 broad powers); Del. Gen. Corp. Law § 122 (17 powers clauses). Statutes also contain a catchall that attempts to bestow upon corporations the legal abilities of flesh and blood persons ("the same power as an individual to do all things necessary or convenient to carry out its business and affairs, including without limitation. . . . " MBCA § 3.02). There exists no need to restate the powers, unless the participants which to curb or eliminate this or that power. Then, and only then, the parties may put a provision relating to powers in the articles of incorporation. A purpose clause, which may very well be included, will authorize a corporation to operate, or to engage in the business of, say, a laundry or a real estate business. By contract, powers are capabilities that in theory all businesses have, to lend money, issue shares, etc., across the board.

C. TAILORED ARTICLES OF INCOROPORATION (PRIVATE ORDERING)

1. *Optional "Charter" Provisions.* Both the MBCA and the Delaware General Corporation Law set out optional charter provisions which may be included in addition to the mandatory provisions discussed above. For example, MBCA § 2.02 lists:

a. The names and addresses of the initial directors;

b. A narrower purpose clause;

c. Provisions regarding management of the business and regulating the powers of the corporation;

d. Limitations or regulation of the powers of the corporation, its board of directors or its shareholders;

e. A par value for shares;

f. Classes of shares;

g. Imposition on shareholders of personal liability for the debt of the corporation to a specified extent and upon specified conditions;

h. "Elevation" of provisions the statute requires in the bylaws;

i. A limitation on director liability for damages (a raincoat, or tender mercy, or exculpatory provision);

j. Provisions permitting or making mandatory indemnification of directors and implementing the enabling authority the statute grants for indemnification.

Del. Gen. Corp. Law § 102(b) sets out another list. What is important to keep in mind is not what precisely is on the Delaware list, or how its differs from the MBCA list, but that these statutory lists are by way of example. They are not exhaustive.

Law firms will have lengthy specimen articles of incorporation, with numerous optional provisions and checkoffs, on their word processing or intranet. Specimen articles will have many more optional provisions than those listed above. Practitioners' advice books and manuals will also contain longer lists. Knowledge of which provisions to consider or whether or not to include them comes only with experience.

A second issue is whether, if the attorney decides to propose or adopt an alternative provision, she should elevate the provision to the articles, which become public records available for all, or incorporate then in bylaws or a comprehensive shareholders' agreement, which are the two alternative choices and which do not become publicly available. One school of thought is that articles should be as terse as possible. This school of thought militates toward keeping any optional provisions chosen semi-confidential, in bylaws or a governance agreement among the 3, 4 or 5 shareholders, rather than in articles or certificate.

The other school of thought is that clients do not pay attorneys to draft and file articles of incorporation which could fit on a post card. Most attorneys include some, or all, of the optional provisions chosen in more lengthy articles of incorporation which they then file with the secretary of state. Lawyers use provisions in the articles to implement power sharing arrangements or to memorialize parties' expectations in closely held incorporation situations. *See* Chapter 9 *infra.* They cause the directors to adopt stock bylaws which legal stationers often provide and which require the attorney to fill in a few blank spaces ("The annual meeting of shareholders will be held on the ___ day of ___ each year"). Lawyers do not even consider a hand tailored shareholders agreement because such agreements do not grow on trees; the economics of many situations do not justify the lawyer time that would be needed to negotiate and draft such an agreement. On the other hand, law firms that do a substantial business practice may have a specimen agreement on file, or on the intranet.

2. *Charter Provisions — Situational Use for a Particular Client.* That said and done, seven types of optional provisions which attorneys may hand tailor for the situation at hand and then include in the articles of incorporation or certificate are: (a) naming the initial board of directors; (b) including an article narrowing the purpose versus any lawful purpose; (c) capping or eliminating directory's duty of care liability (exculpatory clauses); (d) writing special governance provisions such as eliminating the board of directors altogether; (e) installing shareholders' preemptive rights; (f) electing treatment as a close corporation in the 15 or so jurisdictions that have special statutory chapters devoted to closely held entities; and (g) implementing (permitting or making obligatory) the indemnification of directors modern statutory schemes enable corporations to adopt.

a. Initial Board of Directors. Older statutes in a few jurisdictions required that articles of incorporation set out the names and addresses of the initial board of directors. Many attorneys continue to do so even though the statute no longer requires it. By so doing, they eliminate any absolute necessity for an organizational meeting. Organizational meetings do many things but a central task is election of the first board. Such meetings are usually positive, getting a corporation off to a proper start in life. But if the founders are quite experienced, or a face-to-face meeting is just not feasible, a board of directors will nonetheless be in place. Such a provision would have avoided the litigation in *Grant v. Mitchell*, 2001 WL 221509 (Del. Ch., Feb. 23, 2001), in which the parties had a full blown trial over whether the corporation had one director (Grant) or two (Grant and Mitchell). The corporation had never had an organizational meeting which, odds are, would have resolved the issue.

b. Including A Purpose Clause and Drafting It Narrowly. Some participants may be uncomfortable with an amorphous "any lawful purpose" clause. Regulatory schemes may require a corporation to list a purpose and to confine its activities to that sphere (e.g., operate a radio station, to engage in the small loan business). Last of all, participants may be uneasy with one another. They use the purpose clause to "box in" those who will be more active in the corporation. If the latter nonetheless leads the corporation astray, the other participants may have an action for damages under the ultra vires doctrine.

c. Exculpatory Clauses. Delaware crafted the first certificate option statute in June, 1986, as Del Gen. Corp. Law § 102(b)(7). Some practitioners refer to them as 102(b)(7) clauses. Thereafter statutory enactments swept the nation like wildfire, being adopted for not-for-profit, mutual benefit, insurance, banking, cooperative, specialized cooperative (e.g., fish marketing, agricultural, hospital, or other health care) corporate schemes as well as for business corporation acts. Early statutes allowed corporations to place in initial articles of incorporation, or later adopt by shareholder vote, provisions exculpating directors from duty of care liability or, short of exculpation, capping liability (e.g., to annual compensation) for duty of care violations. They do not eliminate the duty of care.

Plaintiffs, for instance, still may seek to enjoin a transaction emanating from a faulty process, on duty of care grounds.

Later statutes seek to enable corporations to adopt certificate or articles provisions exculpating directors on a wider basis. The current Model Act provision allows corporations to adopt:

> [A] provision eliminating or limiting the liability of a director to the corporation or its shareholders for money damages for any action taken, or any failure to take action, except liability for (A) the amount of a financial benefit received by a director to which he is not entitled; (B) an intentional infliction of harm on the corporation or its shareholders; (C) a violation of section 8.33 [authorizing illegal distributions]; or (D) an intentional violation of criminal law.

The full breadth of the provision would also eliminate liability for many duty of loyalty violations as well. Under the provision, a director would not be liable for having the corporation hire her son or his spouse because the director would receive no "financial benefit."

Well-schooled attorneys today frequently consider, and generally include, such an optional exculpatory, or 102(b)(7), article, in more sophisticated incorporation situations. Other attorneys may have the corporation seek some but not all the protections the option's breadth allows. By contrast, in the vast majority of incorporations, which involve closely held enterprises, smaller entities, and/or less specialized attorneys, the necessity of an exculpation article in articles of incorporation is not a central concern.

d. Special Governance Provisions. Older statues envision a corporation with four levels of persons: shareholders, who elect directors, who appoint officers, who hire employees who do the front line, day-to-day tasks. In smaller companies, the same persons wear all the hats. They think that the role playing the model requires is silly or, worse yet, a ploy by the attorney to garner additional fees. Modern statutes, for example, allow corporations to eliminate the board of directors altogether. *See, e.g.,* MBCA § 7.32 (by shareholder agreement). They may also do so by a provision in articles of incorporation.

Most states only permit, and no longer require, as they once did, cumulative voting for the election of directors. *See* Chapter 8, *infra*. At the least, if a board classification scheme is not also in effect, or if the board is other than quite small, cumulative voting permits substantial minorities to have a window on corporate affairs. The minority shareholders may never carry the day but they will have a representative director present at meetings of the board. So, if an outgrowth of preliminary planning is to have cumulative voting, the attorney must so provide in the articles or certificate of incorporation.

e. Provision for Preemptive Rights. The preemptive right is a right of first refusal which existing shareholders have in shares the corporation proposes to offer to third parties for cash. The preemptive right allows shareholders to maintain their proportionate ownership and voting interests. It does not apply, unless articles or the certificate otherwise provides, to shares issued for property, in merger, pursuant to the corporation's original plan of financing or, under some older statutes, for the first six months the corporation is in existence. The shareholder has the right to match the price the third party proposes to pay, not to receive shares at par value or some bargain basement price. *See, e.g., Stokes v. Continental Trust Co. of City of New York,* 186 N.Y. 285, 78 N.E. 1090 (1906).

Older statutes provided that the preemptive right existed, unless articles or certificate negated it. Newer statues set up a presumption that preemptive rights do not exist. *See, e.g.,* MBCA § 6.30(a) ("The shareholders of a corporation do not have a preemptive right to acquires the corporation's unissued shares except to the extent the articles of incorporation so provide"). Because the preemptive right is a high priority in many new incorporations, a common provision in articles is to provide for preemptive rights.

Remember, though, that to preserve proportionate interests among shareholders, not only a preemptive right, governing issuances by the corporation, but also a share transfer restriction (often called a buy-sell agreement), governing transfers by the shareholders, are both necessary.

f. Close Corporation Election. As time goes on, election to be treated under special chapters of the business corporations statute, which exist in approximately 15 states, has become less frequent. *See generally* Chapter 9, *infra.*

g. Indemnification Provisions. Corporate directors are sui generis. Directors are not, for example, agents of the corporation, so any contracts they attempt to make will not be binding and they are not entitled to the indemnity to which agents are entitled under common law. For that reason, corporate statutes had to enable corporations to provide for indemnification (if they wish to do so). MBCA §§ 8.50–8.59 and Del. Gen. Corp. Law § 145 do so, with one exception. MBCA § 8.52 makes indemnification mandatory (rather than merely permissive) in one instance, when the director has been "wholly successful, on the merits or otherwise." Del. Gen. Corp. Law § 145(c) does the same. In all other cases, the corporation must implement some or all of the authority the statute bestows upon it. Corporations routinely do so, often by provisions in the articles or certificate. Provisions may range from the very straight forward (indemnification to the fullest extent allowed by law) to the more complex (outlining the process by which the decisions to indemnify and to fund indemnification will be made). Chapter 14, *infra,* discusses indemnification and exculpation.

3. *Filing.* The filer prepares articles or certificate on ordinary paper (no forms are necessary any longer), or, indeed, on a computer screen. The Model Act includes "electronic transmission" in the terms "deliver" or "delivery." MBCA § 1.40(5). Certain legislatures have adopted the necessary provisions, allowing electronic filing, and more will do so in the future. In addition to filing by mail, or electronically, many secretary of state's offices also authorize counter filings, in which, for a small additional fee, a messenger or paralegal files articles over the counter at the state's offices and receives a certificate almost immediately.

Wishing to avoid even a few hours or days delay, a few law firms have generic corporations already formed, shelf corporations, that can be taken down off the shelf, adapted for use, and used immediately if a transaction requires it. At the other extreme, articles can specify a delayed effective date, under which corporate existence begins on the date specified rather than the date of filing. MBCA § 1.23. In the normal course, when nothing has been specified, corporate existence commences on the date and at the time the secretary of state accepts articles for filing. MBCA § 2.03.

A few states still require what all once did, a second filing with a local official such as the county recorder. The advent of the telecopier made it no longer necessary to have documents also available locally for examination. So, too, a handful of states require the new corporation to publish articles or certificate in a local or regional newspaper.

The filing of articles must be accompanied by a check representing a filing fee (e.g., $100) plus the franchise tax (e.g., $70) for the first year of corporate existence. Some states charge higher fees but, overall, the trend has been toward flat fees. By contrast, Delaware changes a variable fee, which can be quite high, based upon the authorized stock in the certificate. Del. Gen. Corp. Law § 391.

In days gone by, secretary of state's corporation division employees would closely examine articles proffered for filing, taking issue with certain provisions or the choice of name. They would refuse to file articles, returning them for what often were picayune corrections and wasting sometimes valuable time. Model Act § 1.25(d) attempts to change the practice, providing that "the duty to file documents under this section is a ministerial act." Over a dozen Model Act states have not adopted the provision, arguably because secretaries of states in those jurisdictions wished to retain their broader, traditional power to reject documents offered for filing.

D. CHOICE OF THE STATE OF INCORPORATION

State legislatures, assisted by bar association committees, keep corporate statutes relatively up-to-date. Secretary of states' offices run smoothly. In one version or another, the Model Business Corporation Act is the law of 39 states. 1 Model Bus. Corp. Act Ann. (Supp. 2007). For that reason, business lawyers stay at home in 95 percent of the cases. Two exceptions are, one that attorneys may incorporate in Delaware because the enterprise is already quite large, or will be used in a business combination with another large entity, or will embark immediately on an ambitions acquisition scheme. Sometimes, the founders have read a business magazine article praising Delaware, or want the bragging rights that they perceive come with having a Delaware corporation. Two, in California and other Western states many business attorneys advise a Nevada corporation. Although little has been written about it, in contrast to reams written about Delaware, Nevada has a reputation as the "Delaware of the West."

There used to be many more exceptions. New York law, for example, held directors liable for employee wage claims in certain instances. New York lawyers regularly formed New Jersey corporations for clients. All, or most all, of those local wrinkles are gone. There is no need, and costs, associated with going elsewhere, or running away as it sometimes called.

A remaining advantage of going elsewhere is that U.S. courts follow the internal affairs choice of law rule. Thus, although, a corporation may have its principal headquarters, most of its directors, officers, employees, and even shareholders, say, in Oregon, if Delaware is the state of incorporation, Delaware law governs conflicts among shareholders and officers or directors and other matters internal to the corporation. *See CTS Corp. v. Dynamics Corp. of America*, 481 U.S. 69 (1987) (Indiana law controls internal affairs of Indiana corporations, including shareholder voting rights); Richard Buxbaum, *The Threatened Constitutionalization of the Internal Affairs Doctrine in Corporate Law*, 75 Cal. L. Rev. 29 (1987). This is true even if a shareholder files suit in California, Illinois, or Oregon, rather than in Delaware. Thus, if Oregon owners perceive Delaware's rules to be pro-management, the internal affairs choice of law rules guarantees those owners that they will obtain the benefit of those rules by running away to Delaware, even if the corporation has no other contacts with Delaware.

A cost, though, is that if a shareholder files suit in Delaware, not only will the court apply Delaware law. The court will also uphold jurisdiction over corporate officers and directors for, by incorporation there, Delaware deems every officer and director of a Delaware corporation to have consented to suit there. *See* Del. Gen. Corp. Law § 3114. Armstrong v. Pomerance, 423 A.2d 174 (Del. 1980) (upholding statute). In the hypothetical, then, officers and directors may have to obtain counsel in Delaware and travel there from Oregon to participate in their defense.

Another cost is monetary. A pseudo foreign, or run away, corporation must maintain a registered agent and pay fees in the state of incorporation, which may be distant. Corporations such as CT Corporation or Prentice Hall provide those services for a yearly $100-150 fee. Then, however, the run away must come home again. The corporation will have to register as a foreign corporation licensed to do business in its real home state, maintain a registered agent there, and so on. So one cost of foreign incorporation is payment of 2 sets of fees (or 1 and 2/3) rather than 1. The amount may only be a few hundred dollars but the fees add up over several or more years. The advice then is to incorporate in the jurisdiction in which one practices in the vast majority of cases.

E. ETHICAL CONSIDERATIONS

The Rules of Professional Conduct (RPC) provide that the attorney's client is "the organization." RPC 1.13. If the attorney has any close or past connection with one of the participants (family relationship, past business dealings, past legal representation), the attorney may then, or later be accused of, favoring the interests of one participant over the others or the organization. In such a situation, in an ideal world, the other participants would seek separate counsel and the original attorney would cease representation of the business entity, at least at such time that its interests and the interests of the flesh and blood participant become adverse.

Alas, it is not an ideal world. The vast majority of business formations (including incorporations) can support only one attorney and the fee she is likely to charge. Each participant cannot afford having her own lawyer. Instead, an attorney should disclose any past connection with one of the participants and indicate that her intention is to represent the corporation and not any individual within it. Attorneys often make such disclosure in the engagement letter they send to clients. The attorney also has to be prepared to resign if, in the future, she finds herself favoring one participant, ceasing representation of everyone (the business entity and all of the participants).

PROBLEMS

1. Roy Bean's Exotic Food of All Nations is owned by Roy and his sister Gail, both well-to-do dentists. Gail has also become hostess of a popular cooking show on local television ("The Barefoot Bean"). Roy and Gail have an existing store that, after three years, has become profitable, at least in the busy months of the year. In the coming year, they plan to lease premises and open three new stores in the Indianapolis, Indiana metro area. The leases will have seven to eight year terms. The business plan, which they prepared for the bank, shows the stores breaking even in the fourth year. As they embark upon this expansion, they consult you, their attorney, for advice. Your advice to them?

2. Flee Baley practices law with six partners in a boutique litigation firm. Last year, Flee got hit with a malpractice claim in which the settlement exceeded the group's malpractice policy limits. Each partner had to chip in $40,000. They do not wish to see that happen again. What alternatives do they have?

3. Clare, Erika, and Rachel are women's golf professionals, who met late last year on the LPGA (Ladies Professional Golf Association) Tour. They have acquired 230 acres of land in central California, atop the Sierra Nevada foothills, upon which they plan to build a golf course, and paid a retainer to a golf course architect. They have each invested $500,000. They propose to sell 60-80 equity (voting) memberships for $40,000 each. Erika, Clare and Rachel will retain 51% control. Once the club has completed construction of the golf course, they will sell 200 non-equity memberships to the public.

What organizational form do you recommend? If a corporation is involved, what provisions would you recommend for inclusion in the articles of incorporation? Where would you incorporate?

F. TAXONOMY OF CORPORATIONS

There are not one but several taxonomies that may be applied. One is closely held versus other species of corporation. The sine qua non of a closely held corporation is a restriction on share transfer by which the owners put in place a device to keep shareholding close (e.g., among the members of one or two families, among employees, or among some other group of persons who will remain actively involved with the business). Close corporations are usually, but not necessarily, small, with three, five or perhaps ten members. They can be much larger (e.g., 50 shareholders) but keeping a share restriction in place becomes more difficult as the number grows.

Another is family versus merely family-owned. In a family corporation, the interests of the owners (members of the family) are by and large co-extensive with those of the corporation. The entity may have non-family members as employees but only two or three of them. By contrast, due to growth in revenues, size of facilities, number of employees, and so on, although still owned by family members, the corporation's interests are much larger than just those of the family.

A third taxonomy is size related: small (ten or fewer shareholders), quasi-public (11-299 shareholders), and public (300 or more shareholders). According to the Securities Exchange Act of 1934, public is over 500 holders of a class of equity securities and $10 million or more in assets. Congress added this classification of companies, known as 12(g) companies after the statutory section, in 1964. Distinguish carefully the company which has 400 holders of preferred shares and 400 holders of common shares. Although sizeable, the company is not a 12(g) corporation. There is a difference between holders of a class of shares and shareholders.

To fall back out of the SEC system, the number of holders of a corporation's class of equity securities must decline past 500, to below 300. For foreign issuers, as of 2007, the average value of a class of shares traded in the U.S. must fall to 5% or less of the total traded worldwide. *See* SEC Rule 12b-6, 17 CFR § 240.12b-6 (2006).

Prior to 1964, the Exchange Act, also known as the 34 Act, governed only 12(b) corporations, those which had a class of shares listed on a national stock exchange. The 1964 amendments brought under the SEC's aegis corporations whose shares were traded over-the-counter (OTC). Those corporations now had to file periodic reports with the SEC, obey the proxy rules in soliciting proxies (agencies to vote shares), and so on. The 1964 amendments vastly increased the number of corporations under the SEC's regulatory sway.

A fourth taxonomy is to classify corporation by how their shares are traded rather than size. The first rung of the ladder might be traded over-the-counter (OTC). Shares traded OTC are traded on a dealer basis. Trades are thus at arm's length. Brokerage firms make markets, that is, they maintain inventories of shares of certain corporations. When a customer wishes to buy, the brokerage firms check their inventories and mark up shares much like hardware stores used to sell hardware, over the counter.

Beginning in the 1970s, the National Association of Securities Dealers Automatic Quotation System (NASDAQ) computerized a portion of the OTC list. Among other things, NASDAQ made it easier to find market makers and to compare terms of trade various market makers offered.

The next classification in this taxonomy (how shares are traded) is exchange traded. Exchange trading is predominantly agency rather than dealer trading. When Mr. Smith in Seattle sells 1,000 Boeing, he places the order with the registered representative (his agent) who forwards the order to, say, the New York Stock Exchange (NYSE) where, by virtue of ownership of a seat, a sub agent is on the NYSE floor. The same is true of Mr. Jones who is in Atlanta and wishes to purchase 1,000 Boeing. These agents meet in the crowd, making the trade on behalf of far off traders. They charge commissions rather than markups, which they also must disclose, in part because they are functioning as agents. More and more, trades, even up to or over 1,000 shares, are executed electronically, with computers replacing flesh and blood traders, but the essential nature of the trading (centralized trading at an exchange) remains the same.

There used to be a progression, from local over-the-counter (advertised in the local newspaper), to regional OTC ("in the sheets," or pink sheets), to perhaps a regional stock exchange (the Pacific in Los Angeles and San Francisco, or the Midwest in Chicago). The company might then graduate to the American Stock Exchange (the AMEX or Curb, also on Wall Street, in New York, where the NYSE is located). Alternatively, the corporation might bypass the AMEX altogether, listing a class of shares on the NYSE (the Big Board).

In the 1980s, the NASDAQ not only computerized trading in many more stocks, it computerized trading in larger portions of the NYSE list. Today the NASDAQ lists approximately 3,200 issues. The NYSE lists shares of about 3,600 corporations. Overall, the SEC receives periodic reports (12(g) and 12(b)) from 16,500 corporations, more or less. It is estimated that there are 4.85 million corporation in the U.S.

Natural progressions take place less frequently. Principally because of the personal computer, many corporations feel that trading in their shares is just as visible on NASDAQ as it would be on the NYSE. Household name companies such as Microsoft, Cisco, or Starbucks remain traded OTC, on the NASDAQ. The NASDAQ now conducts about 13% of trading in the NYSE list. In fact, due to a number of factors, such as foreign trading, institutional investors trading directly with one another, NASDAQ, etc., the NYSE conducts only 70% or so of the trading in stocks of its own listed companies.

The AMEX has gotten smaller rather than larger and makes its way principally trading ETRs (exchange traded funds) and other baskets of stock. Regional exchanges now trade few regional stocks. Instead, they "dual list" corporations traded NYSE or NASDAQ. But it remains true that a frequently used taxonomy of corporations is how they are traded (in the sheets, NASDAQ, Amex, NYSE). Today, however, the taxonomy correlates less well with size than used to be the case.

A fifth, and last, classification correlates to size as well. Mutual funds, analysts, and others sort out publicly held companies according to the aggregate value of corporations' shares. Small cap companies have a market capitalization of less than $1 billion; mid cap companies have a market cap of $1-5 billion, or, under some schematics, $1-10 billion; and large cap stocks are those of corporations whose shares aggregate market cap exceed $5 or $10 billion. Mutual funds (open end investment funds) may publicize their niche as being small cap or medium cap corporations.

None of this is etched in stone. Different market participants use different classifications and rules of thumb. The taxonomies are not mutually exclusive either: a mid cap publicly held company may be traded NASDAQ, or an entity may be closely held but no longer a family corporation. There also are still other taxonomies of corporations but those related here are five widely used ones.

G.　DEFECTIVE INCORPORATION

In days gone-by, lawyers often got hung up on technicalities. Secretaries of state would return articles of incorporation, unfiled, after the attorney had told the clients to commence doing business in the corporate firm. The individuals would be left standing, with no protection against personal liability.

Today, the process of incorporation is simplified. Secretaries of state are supposed to perform only ministerial acts. Defective incorporations are far less frequent than they used to be. There is little excuse for lawyers and para-legals not to get it "right."

A fallback defense the common law recognized is that if the corporation were not *de jure*, good against all the world, it was at least *de facto*, good against all the world but the state. Thus, the flesh and blood owners should not personally be held liable to creditors, akin to partners in a general partnership.

The de facto corporation doctrine had three elements:

1. The existence of a law under which a corporation could be formed, not usually a problem in the era of general incorporation acts;

2. A good faith attempt to come under the law;

3. Conduct of the business by the putative shareholders as if the corporation existed (in the corporate name, etc.).

If the promoter had made no effort whatsoever, she could still point out to the defending attorney that the creditor had dealt with the business as if it were a corporation. Evidence might include invoices or correspondence addressed to a corporation. The attorney could invoke the corporation by estoppel doctrine, a liberal use of the estoppel concept which required no affirmative misrepresentation, reliance, or change of position. A leading case is *Cranson v. International Business Machines Corp.*, 200 A.2d 33 (Md. 1964), in which a creditor sued the president of a corporation that had never been formed, because the attorney had failed to file the articles of incorporation he had prepared. Nonetheless, the creditor had invoiced and sold typewriters to a corporation. It was held estopped to later deny that a corporation existed.

THOMPSON & GREEN MACHINERY CO. v. MUSIC CITY LUMBER CO.
Court of Appeals of Tennessee
683 S.W.2d 340 (1984)

LEWIS, J.: . . .

Joseph E. Walker is President of Music City Sawmill Co., Inc. . . . . Mr. Walker, supposedly on behalf of Sawmill, purchased a wheel loader from plaintiff. . . . However, on January 27, 1982 [the date of purchase] Sawmill was not a corporation . . . [T]he date of incorporation of Sawmill was actually January 28, 1982, one day after the sale of the wheel loader.

Sawmill . . . returned the wheel loader on August 27, 1982. On October 14, 1982, plaintiff sold the wheel loader for $15,303.83 and applied the proceeds to the note, leaving a balance of $17,925.81 . . .

Plaintiff brought suit against both Sawmill and Lumber [and later] amended it complaint to include Mr. Walker as a defendant after plaintiff learned that Sawmill was not a corporation on [the date of purchase]. . . .

Mr. Walker does not seriously assert that the doctrine of de facto corporation is still viable in Tennessee. He does forcefully insist that plaintiff is estopped to deny Sawmill's corporate existence because plaintiff (1) "dealt with Sawmill as a corporation" and (2) "did not intend to bind [Mr. Walker] personally on the promissory note."

It is the insistence of plaintiff that neither the doctrine of de facto corporation nor corporation by estoppel are viable in Tennessee since the passage of the Tennessee General Corporations Act. Plaintiff contends that defendant Walker is personally liable because of the interaction of Tenn. Code Ann. § 48-1-1405 [MBCA § 2.04] which provides that "[a]ll persons who assume to act as a corporation without authority so to do shall be jointly and severally liable for all debts and liabilities incurred or arising as a result thereof," and Tenn. Code Ann. § 48-1-204 which provides that "[a] corporation shall not . . . incur any indebtedness . . . until (a) The charter has been filed by the secretary of state, and (b) . . . there has been received the amount stated in the charter as being the minimum amount of consideration to be received for its shares before commencing business."

Plaintiff insists that since the charter was not filed by the Secretary of State when the promissory note was executed, the corporation neither had the authority to incur indebtedness nor the power to authorize any actions on its behalf and, therefore, pursuant to Tenn. Code Ann. § 48-1-1405, Mr. Walker is liable "for all debts and liabilities incurred" since he assumed to act as a corporation without authority.

It is conceded that Sawmill did not have a corporate existence on January 27th. It therefore follows that Mr. Walker could not and did not have authority to act for Sawmill on January 27th when he executed the promissory note to plaintiff. "[However] it is a general rule that one who deals with an apparent corporation as such and in such manner as to recognize its corporate existence de jure or de facto is thereby estopped to deny the fact thus admitted. . . . " 18 Am. Jur. 2d Corporations § 76.

Tennessee has long recognized the foregoing rule. Our Supreme Court, in Ingle System Co. v. Norris & Hall, . . . 178 S.W. 1113 [1114] (1915), stated:

When a private person enters into a contract with a body purporting to be a corporation, in which that body is described by the corporate name which it has assumed, such private person thereby admits the existence of the corporation for the purpose of the suit brought to enforce the obligations, and will not be permitted to deny the corporate existence of the plaintiff.

Courts in other jurisdictions which have considered the question of de facto corporations under statutes similar to Tenn. Code Ann. §§ 48-1-204 and 48- 1-1405 have held that under the act, de facto corporations no longer exist.

In Timberline Equipment Company, Inc. v. Davenport, 267 Ore. 64, 514 P.2d 1109 (1973), the Oregon Supreme Court, in interpreting ORS 57.321 and ORS 57.792 . . . This section is virtually identical to § 56 of the Model Act [1969]. The Comment to the Model Act . . . states: "Under the unequivocal provisions of the Model Act, any steps short of securing a certificate of incorporation would not constitute apparent compliance. Therefore a de facto corporation cannot exist under the Model Act."

ORS 57.793 provides:

"All persons who assume to act as a corporation without the authority of a certificate of incorporation issued by the Corporation Commissioner, shall be jointly and severally liable for all debts and liabilities incurred or arising as a result thereof."

. . . [The Oregon court concluded that:]

"Abolition of the concept of de facto incorporation, which at best was fuzzy, is a sound result. No reason exists for its continuance under general corporate laws, where the process of acquiring de jure incorporation is both simple and clear. . . .

[An]Alaska court upheld the cancellation of a special land-use permit upon the ground that the applicant had not yet been issued its certificate of incorporation at the time the permit was issued. Swindel v. Kelly, 499 P.2d 291 (Alaska 1972). Alaska has a statute similar to Oregon's. The court commented: "The concept of de facto corporations has been increasingly disfavored, and Alaska is among the states whose corporation statutes are designed to eliminate the concept." We hold the principle of de facto corporation no longer exists in Oregon.

. . . We hold that the Tennessee General Assembly, by passage of the Tennessee General Corporations Act of 1968, abolished the concept of de facto incorporation in Tennessee.

We have found only one jurisdiction which has considered corporation by estoppel- . . . Robertson v. Levy, 197 A.2d 443 (D.C. Ct. of App. 1964). In that case Levy and Robertson entered into an agreement whereby Levy was to form a corporation, Penn Ave. Record Shack, Inc., which was to purchase Robertson's business. Levy submitted articles of incorporation to the authority designated by statute on December 27, 1961, but no certificate of incorporation was issued at that time. Pursuant to the contract, an assignment of lease was entered into on December 31, 1961 between Robertson and Levy with Levy acting as president of Penn Ave. Record Shack, Inc. On January 2, 1962, the articles of incorporation were rejected by the designated authority. On that same day, however, Levy began to operate the business under the name Penn Ave. Record Shack, Inc. Robertson executed a bill of sale to Penn Ave. Record Shack, Inc. on January 8, 1962, disposing of the assets of his business to Penn Ave. Record Shack, Inc., and receiving in return a note providing for installment payments. The note was signed: "Penn Ave. Record Shack, Inc., by Eugene M. Levy, President." On January 17, 1962, the certificate of incorporation for Penn Ave. Record Shack, Inc. was issued. In June, 1962, Penn Ave. Record Shack, Inc. ceased to do any business, and, subsequently, Robertson sued Levy for the balance due on the note.

The trial court held that the District of Columbia Code § 29-950, which is identical to Tenn. Code Ann. § 48-1-1405, did not apply and "that Robertson was estopped to deny the existence of the corporation."

On appeal, the Court of Appeals for the District of Columbia held that, pursuant to § 29-921c, which is substantially the same as Tenn. Code Ann. § 48-1-203, courts must no longer inquire into the equities of a case to determine whether there has been "colorable compliance" with the statute, that before a certificate of incorporation issues, there "is no corporation de jure, de facto, or by estoppel." The Court went on to state: Under Section 29-950, if an individual or group of individuals assumes to act as a corporation before the certificate of incorporation has been issued, joint and several liability attaches. We hold, therefore, that the impact of these sections, when considered together, is to eliminate the concepts of estoppel and de facto corporatness under the Business Corporation Act of the District of Columbia. It is immaterial whether the third person believed he was dealing with a corporation or whether he intended to deal with the corporation. The certificate of incorporation provides the cutoff point; before it is issued, the individuals, and not the corporation, are liable.

. . . For this Court to hold that under the circumstances here Mr. Walker is not liable, it would be necessary that this Court rewrite the Tennessee General Corporations Act and hold that the Act does not mean what it says. We are not at liberty to do so. . . . To allow an estoppel would be to nullify Tenn. Code Ann. § 48-1-1405.

We are of the opinion that the doctrine of corporation by estoppel met its demise by the enactment of the Tennessee General Corporations Act of 1968.

It results that the judgment of the Chancellor is reversed and the cause remanded to the Chancery Court for the entry of judgment for plaintiff in the amount of $17,925.81 together with accrued interest and attorney's fees as provided by the note and for any other necessary proceedings. Costs are taxed to defendant Walker.

TODD, P.J., and KOCH, J., concur.

NOTES AND QUESTIONS

1. *Abolition of the De Facto Doctrine?* As the principle case reveals, in *Timberline Equip. Co. v. Davenport*, 267 Or. 64, 514 P.2d 1109 (1973), the Supreme Court of Oregon held that MBCA § 146 (1969) abolishes the de facto corporation doctrine. In Oregon, as well as jurisdictions which follow the case, corporations are either de jure or nothing. If a court finds an attempted incorporation to be defective, however, the Oregon court left some wiggle room. In that instance, only persons "who assume to act as a corporation" will be personally liable. That group "does not include those whose only connection with the organization is as an investor . . . [but does] include those persons who have an investment in the organization and who actively participate in the policy and operational decisions" of the enterprise.

MBCA § 2.04 reads: "All persons purporting to act as or on behalf of a corporation, knowing there was no incorporation under this act, are jointly and severally liable for all liabilities created while so acting." Does the more recent provision of the Model Business Corporation Act (1984) give more or less protection to the passive investor?

2. *De Jure or Nothing?* Would a rule of absolute liability (no wiggle room) make sense? After all, the process of incorporation is so simple that virtually no excuse exists for not complying.

3. *Corporations by Estoppel.* Could it be that while MBCA § 2.04 abolishes the de facto corporation doctrine, the doctrine of corporation by estoppel survives? The Official Comment to § 2.04 provides: "[T]he section does not foreclose the possibility that persons who urge defendants to execute contracts in the corporate name knowing that no steps to incorporate have been taken may be estopped to impose personal liability on individual defendants. This estoppel may be based upon the inequity perceived when persons, unwilling or reluctant to enter into a commitment under their own name, are persuaded to use the name of a nonexistent corporation, and then are sought to be held personally liable . . . by the party advocating the executive."

PROBLEM

Soupy Sales is forming a corporation with Smokey Robinson and Brenda Lee. The business of the corporation is to rent a hanger at local airfield in Eugene, Oregon, and operate a small (two airplane) charter service. Soupy visits lawyer Lash Lerue who tells Soupy that the articles were filed in state capital (Salem) days earlier.

Acting for the corporation, Soupy then buys a computer in installments from IBM, buys two airplanes from Cessna (again on time), and signs the lease for the hanger. Lash then telephones Soupy to say, "Whoa. It seems my secretary put the articles on top of the filing cabinet, from whence they fell between the cabinet and the wall. They were never filed in Salem. I am sorry to say you don't have a corporation after all." IBM, Cessna and Landlord sue Soupy, Smokey, and Brenda personally. The best defense?

I.   CORPORATE DEATH (INVOLUNTARY DISSOLUTION)

EQUIPTO DIVISION AURORA EQUIP. CO. v. YARMOUTH
Supreme Court of Washington
134 Wash. 2d 356, 359–73, 950 P.2d 451 (1998)

DOLLIVER, JUSTICE.

Petitioner Jerry Yarmouth seeks review of two summary judgments against him, both of which find him personally liable for debts incurred by Yarmouth in the name of J & R Interiors, Inc., a corporation which was dissolved at the time the contracts were made.

In 1990 a certificate of incorporation was issued to J & R Interiors, Inc. (hereinafter J & R). Jerry Yarmouth was the sole shareholder, director, and officer of the corporation. Thomas Farrow was the registered agent . . . [the] registered office was Farrow's law office.

Some time in 1991, the Secretary of State mailed notice of the due date for payment of J & R's annual license fee and filing of the annual report. Yarmouth alleges the 1991 notice was sent to J & R's registered office — Farrow's old business address — and was returned as undeliverable to the State.

As a result of J & R not receiving the notice, Yarmouth failed to pay J & R's annual fee and file the annual report. On August 19, 1991 . . . the Secretary of State administratively dissolved J & R. . . . Yarmouth, purportedly with the good faith belief that the corporation was intact, operated J & R as an ongoing business after its dissolution.

In fall 1992 J & R purchased a workbench from Equipto . . . The bill for the workbench, totaling nearly $20,000, became outstanding on December 20, 1992. J & R failed to pay the bill, so Equipto brought this action in February 1994 against Yarmouth personally. Yarmouth filed an answer in March 1994 claiming Equipto's cause of action was solely against the corporation. Equipto then filed a motion for summary judgment, to which it attached a sealed certificate from the Secretary of State showing J & R had been dissolved in 1991.

. . .

The trial court granted summary judgment to Equipto, against Yarmouth personally, for the outstanding debt. [T]he Court of Appeals affirmed. . . .

[D]raper Shade & Screen Co. v. Yarmouth, present[s] the identical issue. Draper Shade sued Yarmouth personally over outstanding bills for merchandise . . . received by J & R between October 1992 and December 1993 — again, while the corporation had been administratively dissolved. . . .

. . . Many states base their corporate statutes on the Model Business Corporation Act (MBCA). Washington's former Title 23A RCW, enacted in 1965, adopted most of the Model Act. Even though many states follow the MBCA, the case law from those jurisdictions varies greatly on the issue of post-dissolution liability, and there is little consistency in the analysis used to resolve the issue, or the results reached.

Further complicating research and analysis of the issue, the MBCA was significantly revised in 1984, when the American Bar Association adopted the Revised Model Business Corporation Act (RMBCA). Washington State completely revised its corporate act in 1989, repealing RCW 23A, and enacting RCW 23B, which is based primarily on the 1984 RMBCA. Most of the case law from all state jurisdictions, on the issue of postdissolution liability, relies on the old version of the MBCA. . . .

Our analysis must begin with a brief overview of administrative dissolution . . . . Once incorporated . . . a corporation has yearly responsibilities to maintain its corporate status. A domestic corporation must pay an annual $50 license fee, and it must file an annual report with the Secretary of State. . . .

A corporation's failure to pay its annual fee or file its annual report are grounds for administrative dissolution of the corporation by the Secretary of State. Once a cause for dissolution arises, the corporation is notified and has 60 days to correct the condition. If the corporation fails to correct the condition, the Secretary of State will administratively dissolve the corporation. Once dissolved, the corporation "continues its corporate existence but may not carry on any business except that necessary to wind up and liquidate its business and affairs under [MBCA § 14.05] and notify claimants under [MBCA § 14.06].

The statutory scheme allows for the reinstatement of an administratively dissolved corporation. Under [MBCA § 14.22(1)] . . . a corporation could apply for reinstatement within two years of dissolution. If the Secretary of State found that the grounds for dissolution had been corrected, the Secretary of State would reinstate the corporation. [MBCA § 14.22(2)]. Reinstatement related back to the effective date of the original dissolution, and the corporation resumed its business as if the dissolution had never occurred. [MBCA § 14.22(3)]. J & R was administratively dissolved in August 1991, and this two-year reinstatement window closed in 1993. When Yarmouth attempted to reinstate J & R in 1994, the Secretary of State required Yarmouth to form a new corporation because the two-year reinstatement period had passed.

. . .

[T]he Court of Appeals quotes [MBCA § 14.05] as limiting a dissolved corporation's activities to those necessary to wind up business. Since Yarmouth continued to conduct "ongoing" business after J & R was dissolved in August 1991, the Court of Appeals held his acts were ultra vires, and the corporation did not have the capacity to form the contract which gave rise to the debt. The court claimed no statutes addressed the question of Yarmouth's liability, so the court's analysis . . . applied the following common law agency principle:

> [A] person who purports to contract in the name of a principal that exists but lacks capacity to contract may be liable on the contract, but only if he or she . . . (b) knows or should know of the principal's lack of capacity, and the other contracting party does not.

The court found Yarmouth should have known J & R had been dissolved and should have known J & R could not carry on business after dissolution. Since he should have known of the principal's lack of capacity, the court found Yarmouth personally liable.

We decline to adopt the Court of Appeals' application of agency law to the issue of postdissolution liability. While the chapter on dissolution, [MBCA Ch.14], does not specifically address the question of a corporate officer's liability for conducting business as usual after the corporation has been dissolved, the WBCA does contain a general provision regarding personal liability. The main question presented in Yarmouth's petition for review is whether [MBCA § 2.04] resolves the legal question in this case, thereby precluding application of a common law agency analysis. . . .

Is Yarmouth's liability governed by [MBCA § 2.04]?

[MBCA § 2.04] states:

All persons purporting to act as or on behalf of a corporation, knowing there was no incorporation under this title, are jointly and severally liable for liabilities created while so acting except for any liability to any person who also knew that there was no incorporation.

As an initial matter, we decline to limit application of [MBCA § 2.04] exclusively to preincorporation situations. While [MBCA § 2.04] falls under the chapter entitled "Incorporation," and the title of the statute itself is "Liability for preincorporation transactions[,]" the section headings used in the title "do not constitute any part of the law." Our analysis must turn on the language within the statute.

The first phrase of the statute, "[a]ll persons purporting to act as or on behalf of a corporation," is straightforward. When Yarmouth conducted business with Equipto and Draper Shade, he purported to act as or for J & R, a corporation. The third phrase, "are jointly and severally liable for liabilities created while so acting," also applies to Yarmouth. . . .

The second phrase of the statute, "knowing there was no incorporation under this title," presents the greatest difficulty in this analysis. The first, and most obvious, scenario addressed by the phrase is a situation where one acts as a corporation before the corporation has been formed, or before "incorporation." This kind of liability usually involves a promoter's liability for preincorporation contracts. See, e.g., Goodman v. Darden, Doman & Stafford Assocs. [*infra*].

Yarmouth urges us to read the second phrase to encompass the situation where one acts after a corporation has been dissolved. This argument makes some sense. While it is obvious incorporation cannot exist prior to the filing of corporate papers, there must also be some point at the end of a corporation's existence where there ceases to be incorporation. One can act as a corporation . . . after the corporation ceases to exist. . . .

Does [MBCA § 2.04] require actual knowledge before imposing personal liability?

The courts [who have] construed the impact of the language have found the phrase "knowing there was no incorporation" requires actual knowledge. [*See, e.g.*, Sivers v. R & F Capital Corp., 123 Or. App. 35, 858 P.2d 895 (1993) ("[t]he wording of ORS 60.054 and the drafters' comments clearly indicate that the test for imposition of personal liability is one of actual knowledge."). *See also* Harris v. Looney, 43 Ark. App. 127, 862 S.W.2d 282, 285 (1993) (there must be a finding that the persons sought to be charged acted as or on behalf of the corporation and knew there was no incorporation); Weir v. Kirby Constr. Co., 446 S.E.2d 186, 188 (Ga. App. 1994) (statute "requires actual knowledge that there was no incorporation.")].

When we apply the actual knowledge requirement in RCW 23B.02.040 to this case, it becomes a question of fact as to whether Yarmouth knew J & R had been dissolved. The fact that he reestablished the corporation within days of allegedly learning of the dissolution supports his claim of lack of knowledge. On the other hand, the record is devoid of any documentary evidence supporting Yarmouth's claim that he never received any of the correspondence from the State . . .

If the trial courts find Yarmouth not liable for the debts under [MBCA § 2.04], Respondents' proper course of action is to pursue the "new" J & R for the debts of the dissolved corporation. . . .

DURHAM, C.J., and SMITH, GUY, TALMADGE and SANDERS, JJ., concur.

JOHNSON, JUSTICE, dissenting [omitted].

PROBLEM

The Fratelli brothers form a corporation, Mystic Pizza, Inc., hiring Julia Roberts as their manager. The articles list their lawyer as their registered agent and registered office to which the Secretary of State sends the annual report form. The Fratellis, however, lose contact with their lawyer, who eventually moves away. Annual reports are not filed. Franchise taxes are not paid for three years. As a result of a telephone call to the Secretary of State, "Chunk," the largest and nicest of the Fratellis, discovers that the corporation had been dissolved. He is worried that they might be personally liable on corporate obligations. He is worried that the IRS might seek back taxes from the Fratellis, treating corporate earnings as partnership earnings. Chunk wants Mystic Pizza, Inc., brought back to life. Can you do it?

J. PROMOTER'S LIABILITY ON PREINCORPORATION CONTRACTS

In cases of defective incorporation, *supra*, a founder or promoter signs contracts, thinking that the corporation exists and will be bound when, in reality, the corporation does not exist. By contrast, in this category of cases, the founder or promoter knows that the corporation has not yet come into being. Nonetheless, she signs contracts, making an attempt of one sort or another to provide that not only will the corporation be bound if and when it comes into existence but also, at that point, the promoter will no longer be liable. There are two approaches to this problem. One approach looks to the intent of the parties, as derived from all the facts and circumstances. Did the other party intend to look to the corporation, and the corporation alone, when it came into existence?

The second is the majority approach, which is rigid and formal. The promoter must do one of several well defined acts, dotting the i's and crossing the t's, or she remains liable.

To come even within the ambit of those preincorporation rules, however, the promoter must sign the contract with care. She must do two things. First, she must clearly indicate the non-existence of her principal. An agent warrants the existence of her principal. If it turns out that no principal existed, and it was not disclosed, she is liable for breach of warranty; therefore, she should sign "in formation," or "a corporation to be formed," for example.

Second, she must indicate her representative capacity. She may do so with further words, such as "promoter," "founder," "president-elect," or merely "by." Otherwise, a court may hold the contract should be construed so that both the corporation to be formed and the promoter will be bound.

In *Colonial Baking Co. v. Dowie*, 330 N.W.2d 279 (Iowa 1983), Frederick Dowie planned catering the pope's visit to Des Moines, Iowa. Dowie ordered 325,000 hot dog buns, which he paid for with a post dated check. "[D]reams of riches often turn to dust," meaning in this case that Dowie's company, Fred Dowie Enterprises, Inc., clearly indicated on the face of the check, sold only 300 hot dogs. Dowie stopped payment on the $28,640 check. Colonial Baking sued Dowie. The court found that, because the check failed to indicate that Dowie was acting in a representative capacity, both, Fred Dowie Enterprises, Inc., and Fred Dowie himself, and not just the corporation, were bound.

The Uniform Commercial Code (UCC) § 3-403(2) supports the result:

> An authorized representative who signs his own name to an instrument (a) is personally obligated if the instrument neither names the person represented nor shows that the representative signed in a representative capacity; (b) except as otherwise established between the immediate parties, is personally obligated

if the instrument names the person represented but does not show that the representative signed in a representative capacity.

An older case, *O'Rorke v. Geary*, 207 Pa. 240, 56 A. 541 (1903), held that, once within the ambit of the preincorporation rules, a promoter could do one of three things:

1. She could act merely as a go-between, accepting a contract offer which she would present to the corporation when and if it came into existence

2. She could obligate herself personally, looking to the corporation for indemnification if and when it came into existence

3. In the body of the contract, she could provide that when the corporation comes into existence, the other party will look to the corporation for performance.

Each of these courses of action has pitfalls:

1. An offeror can revoke a contract offer at any time until it is accepted, and may well do so. Despite the promoter's labors, the corporation may receive nothing

2. The promoter may look to the corporation for indemnity but the corporation may not wish to give it to her, especially if there has been a disagreement or falling out, or the corporation may not be able to, because it is broke, or needs its limited funds for other purposes

3. The contract may provide for a novation (the substitution of one party for another) or, more precisely, a novation in futuro. A novation requires three parties. Here, at the time of contracting, only two parties, the offeror and the promoter, exist.

This last reality leads to the first pitfall of the third course of action. If the corporation never comes into being, no novation will take place. The promoter, and the promoter alone, will remain obligated.

The second pitfall is that, even though this is a course of action promoters often chose, they seem seldom to get it right, and they wind up remaining liable on the contract. In *RKO-Stanley Warner Theaters, Inc. v. Graziano*, 467 Pa. 220, 355 A.2d 830 (1976), Jenofsky and Grazianno were forming a corporation to purchase a movie theater from RKO. The contract of purchase provided that:

> It is understood between the parties hereto that it is the intention of the Purchaser to incorporate. Upon condition that such incorporation be completed by closing [which it was], all agreements, covenants, and warranties contained herein shall be construed to have been made between Seller and the resultant corporation . . .

The court held the promoters liable nonetheless. They had provided that the corporation would become liable but they had not affirmatively provided that the promoter would drop out: "However, while Paragraph 19 does make provision for the recognition of the resultant corporation as to the closing documents, it makes no mention of any release of personal liability."

Goodman v. Darden, Doman & Stafford Associates, 100 Wash. 2d 476, 670 P.2d 648 (1983), appears slightly more forgiving but reaches the same result, holding the promoter bound by an agreement to arbitrate disputes. The promoter signed an agreement to renovate an apartment house "BUILDING DESIGN AND DEVELOPMENT INC. (In formation) John A. Goodman, President." The court opined that "release of the promoter depends on the intent of the parties." Although express language providing that the promoter would no longer be bound would be the best evidence, "[w]e do not believe the agreement to release a promoter from liability must say so in so many words, 'I agree to release.' . . . [E]xistence of an agreement to release him may be shown by circumstances." But the court then rejected the categories of circumstantial evidence offered, such as proof that the other party knew no corporation existed or evidence that the promoter expressed a desire not to be liable.

These rules are difficult for attorneys, let alone promoter clients. There is a subset of cases which do look to all the circumstances, divine the intention of the parties, and release or do not release a promoter accordingly. In *Quaker Hill, Inc. v. Parr*, 148 Colo. 45, 364 P.2d 1056 (1961), plaintiff, a New York Nursery, sold a quantity of nursery stock to defendants, who were to form a corporation which would purchase the stock, re-selling much if it to a cemetery corporation which the individual defendants owned. The nursery's salesman was the one who insisted that the time was short and the transaction go forward, even though a corporation had not yet been formed. The planting season was growing short, he testified. After the corporation had been formed, the nursery kept records in the name of Denver Memorial Nursery, Inc.

Due to the lateness of the day, the nursery stock died. The Denver corporation refused to pay. Following that refusal, the New York Nursery (Quaker Hill) sued the promoters individually. The court held them not liable. The intent to look to the corporation, and to the corporation alone, was clear from the circumstances of the case. *Sherwood & Roberts-Oregon, Inc. v. Alexander*, 269 Or. 389, 525 P.2d 135 (1974), is a similar "look to the intent" case.

Before the fact, however, no lawyer worth her salt is going to let the outcome depend upon judicial findings of intent (or as to the equities). Instead, at least before the fact, she is going to depend upon cases such as *Graziano* and *Goodman* and the old fashioned rules, strict as they may be. Cases such as *Quaker Hill v. Parr* may be useful in litigation but they have little use in a transactional context.

Thus, to work a novation in futuro, a promoter must be told to:

1. Indicate the non-existence of her principle
2. Sign in a representative capacity
3. Provide that when it comes into existence the corporation will be bound
4. Affirmatively provide that, also in that instance, the promoter no longer will be responsible.

As noted, these are tough rules, so a couple of other approaches might be mentioned:

1. Rather than an offer, take an assignable option which the promoter can then assign to the corporation when it comes into being. One difficulty is that if the project is aborted the consideration paid for the option is lost, with nothing to show in return for the expenditure. A second difficult is that option contracts are not standard. They may be viewed with trepidation by the other party to the proposed transaction. Their reaction may be, "Do you want it or not?"
2. Form the corporation first rather than simultaneously or later. In these days of electronic and counter filings, an attorney often is able to form a corporation in a few hours or, at most, in a day. If the attorney can convince the promoter to delay for that period of time, not signing anything, all of these complex issues of legal personality do not arise.

PROBLEM

For years, Gyro Gearloose has had his heart set on owning a Dunkin Donuts franchise in his home town of Altoona. When retail space became available across from the Altoona police station, a prime location for a donut shop, Gyro signed a five-year lease, as follows: "Altoona Dunkin Donuts, Inc., Gyro Gearloose." Alas, Gyro does not get the Dunkin Donuts franchise. He visits you to ascertain who is liable on the lease. What advice?

Now assume the opposite. Gyro is approved for the franchise by Dunkin Donuts and its area representative. As in the previous question, the prime space has become available but Gyro has not yet signed a lease. Gyro has surveyed the market. He wants quickly to place an order for a precise Swiss donut making machine. He is in a hurry and wants the machine to arrive before he opens the shop. Gyro visits your office. In very unsophisticated fashion, he asks "What paper work do I need from you as my lawyer before I can going on this thing?" How should you reply?

K. LIABILITY ON PREINCORPORATION CONTRACTS — THE CORPORATION'S VIEWPOINT

A somewhat counterintuitive teaching from a first year contracts course is that a defendant may have become bound by a contract to which he did not assent. If she accepts benefits under the contract, such as receiving copies of the magazine in the mail or letting the gardener cut his lawn, she may become bound.

Corporations are no different. They may become liable if they accept performance by the other party under a contract the corporation's promoter lays at the corporation's feet. They also may become bound through acquiescence. If the other party proves that the corporation had knowledge of the contract and allowed time to pass, even though it accepted no benefits from it, the corporation may become bound.

McArthur v. Times Printing, Inc., 48 Minn. 319, 51 N.W. 216 (1892), uses a finding of acquiescence to hold a newspaper corporation bound by an employment contract its promoter had negotiated on its behalf.

The practical upshot of this is that, one, at the organizational meeting the attorney or other person conducting the meeting should lay at the corporation's feet all of the contracts which the promoter has negotiated on the corporation's behalf. Two, the corporation's directors should then take action with regard to each contract, either accepting it, or affirmatively repudiating it. Otherwise, acquiescence may creep up, leaving the corporation responsible on a contract it otherwise might not wish to have.

L. ULTRA VIRES

1. Introduction

Historically, ultra vires is a legal term describing actions which are, or are alleged to be, beyond the powers or purposes of the corporation. Statutes today grant corporations all, or nearly all, the powers a natural person would have. *See, e.g.*, MBCA § 3.02. For the most part, then, modern corporate law cases deal with actions that exceed the permitted scope of operations described in the corporate purpose, or objects, clause. But that is not always the case. A shareholder might challenge the actions of a general business corporation that begins to do an insurance or banking business. The action might not exceed the purpose described (e.g., any lawful purpose) but the challenge to the line of endeavor would be ultra vires and the tenor of the charge is that the corporation has no power.

Distinguish illegal acts and frolic and detours by agents of the corporation. They may also be, but not necessarily are, ultra vires. Assume an airline that flies between Seattle and Los Angeles, on the West Coast. On a return flight, the pilot stops for a few hours in Las Vegas to see his or her significant other. The passengers play the slot machines in the airport lounge for a few hours. Everybody then flies on to Seattle. This is a classic frolic and detour by an agent. It could also be ultra vires if the airline's purpose clause states its objective is to fly between Seattle and Los Angeles but it is doubtful that the articles of incorporation would be that specific.

Assume instead that the pilot is intent on serving the corporation's best interests, stopping instead in Las Vegas (as well as Reno, Klamath Falls and Portland) to pick up additional fare paying passengers rather than to see a friend. The act is illegal. The airline is violating the Federal Aviation Act, as it is not certified on those routes. Again, it could also be ultra vires if the airline's purpose clause is to fly between Seattle and Los Angeles but it is doubtful that the articles of incorporation would be that specific. Distinguish then frolics and detours and illegal acts from ultra vires acts. They are different, although there may be overlap.

Text after text on business organizations law describes ultra vires as a dying doctrine. A Westlaw search (corporation/s ultra/s vires) produces 5310 law cases in the allstates database. A search in the allfeds database (last visited January 20, 2008) produces 1,162 additional appellate court opinions. Thus, although text writers opine that ultra vires is a dying doctrine, the word has not yet gotten through to law practitioners and judges.

The following section examines the reasons set out for the alleged decline in the doctrine. A later section devotes itself to the subject of statutes, which are ubiquitous and often controlling. The last three sections describe three areas (pigeonholes) in which the doctrine may retain some validity: gifts to charity; the law of municipal corporations (units of local government); and, in the area of business corporations, guaranty of the debts of another.

2. Reasons for the Decline of the Doctrine

1. *Judicial Hostility.* Too often corporations attempted to use the narrower wording of their purposes clauses as excuses for their non-performance of contracts they argued were beyond their purpose. Judges became wary, and then hostile, to such arguments, seeing then as ruses.

The fully rigorous common law doctrine is exemplified by *Ashbury Ry. Carriage & Iron Co. v. Riche*, 33 L.T.R. 450 (1875). Ashbury's objects clause authorized it "to sell or lend all kinds of railway plant [and] to carry on the business of mechanical engineers and general railway contractors." Riche procured a concession allowing him to build a railway line in Belgium. Instead of constructing the line, which arguably it could do, Ashbury bound itself to obtain the financing and, after completion, operate the railway. Ashbury sought to evade the contract which, because of intervening events, looked unprofitable. The House of Lords held the contract ultra vires, excusing Ashbury's non-performance. "The question is not the illegality of the contract but the competency and power of the company to make the contract."

Courts stopped permitting the defense of ultra vires when substantial performance on the other side had already occurred. Due to the strong common law interest in stability of land titles, courts never permitted the ultra vires defense in cases involving conveyancing. Logic dictated that law givers not apply the doctrine to cases of tort in which the victim had been hit by, say, a taxi cab owned by a corporation whose articles limited it to leasing trucks.

Little by little, spurred on by the result in cases such as *Ashbury Ry. Co. v. Riche*, courts so cabined the doctrine that its use was limited to the arena in which contracts remained wholly executory and a corporation had been one of the parties.

2. *Broad Purpose Clauses.* The advent of general corporation acts and the liberal use of broad (any lawful purpose) purpose clauses in articles and certificates of incorporation in the first place eliminated many opportunities to invoke the doctrine later.

Under general corporation acts, persons could form corporations for any lawful purpose, save for a few specific carve-outs, such as banking and insurance, and for activity which violates public policy or is illegal, such as transacting in narcotics or counseling on methods whereby businesses might evade environmental laws. Modern statutes also permitted corporations to have as their purpose any lawful purpose and so to state in articles or certificate. In fact, under the most recent version of the model act, corporations need not state a purpose at all. In that case, the law will assume that the corporation's purpose is broad, that is, any lawful purpose. *See* MBCA § 2.02(a) (no purpose clause required).

3. *Ease of Amendment.* Later on, in the life of the corporation, the ease of amendment of articles or certificate permitted companies, if they did not have a broad purpose clause in the first place, to broaden purpose clauses to remove strictures on pursuit of desired activities.

In days gone by, two-thirds of all the voting shares had to approve amendments to the articles of incorporation, 3/4trs in some systems (extraordinary resolution under English company law). Most U.S. states' laws relaxed the requirement to a majority of the shares entitled to vote on the amendment (a majority of the outstanding, not merely a majority of those present). In the late 1990s, the ABA Committee on Corporate Laws changed the Model Act to relax the vote requirement still further. A plurality can approve amendments to the articles, given the presence of a quorum, which for these purposes must be, and usually is, a majority. An amendment passes, then, if, given the presence of a quorum, the shares cast in favor of the amendment exceed the share votes cast against it (purality voting).

In theory then, a single vote may approve an amendment, if all the remaining shares abstain. MBCA § 10.03(e). This has proven a bit too raw: The ABA Committee is attempting to bolster the approval process back up, requiring a majority (50% plus 1) rather than a plurality (more votes in favor than against).

4. *Grants of Implied Powers.* Judicial and legislative grants of implied powers legitimated activities even though the corporation's purpose clause did not enumerate them specifically.

MBCA § 3.02 provides that "every corporation . . . has the same powers as an individual to do all things necessary or convenient to carry out its business and affairs . . . ." Del. Gen. Corp. Law § 111 is more verbose: "every corporation, its officers, directors, and stockholders shall possess and may exercise all of the powers and privileges granted by this chapter or by any other law . . . together with any powers incidental thereto, so far as such powers and privileges are necessary or convenient to the conduct, promotion, or attainment of the business or purposes set forth in its certificate of incorporation."

Judicially, the Supreme Court led the way. The corporation built a railway line down the East Coast of Florida. The corporation had a narrow purpose clause but the Court held that the business of leasing and operating a hotel was "incidental or auxiliary" to the stated purpose. The corporation had an implied power to engage in the challenged activity. *Jacksonville, M.P. Ry. & Nav. Co. v. Hooper*, 160 U.S. 514, 523 (1896).

5. *Statutes.* Legislatures adopted statutes that forbade use of an ultra vires defense in many cases.

All modern corporation statutory enactments have a provision reducing the occasions on which ultra vires may be raised. In Europe, the first directive on company law (1972) of the European Economic Community (EEC), now the European Union (EU), required member states to harmonize domestic law so that if one nation state's citizens contracted with an incorporated entity in another state, that citizen could rest assured that lack of authority or corporate capacity could not be asserted on the foreign entity's behalf to defeat the transaction. The directive was directed at English company law which had long held that ultra vires acts were not merely voidable but void ab initio (strict ultra vires doctrine). At the time the United Kingdom entered the Common Market, as it was then known, in 1973, England also amended Companies Act, 1948, to comply with the EEC directive. The most commonly seen form of statute in the United States is dealt with in the following section.

3.   Ultra Vires Statutes

TOTAL ACCESS, INC. v. CADDO ELECTRIC COOPERATIVE
Court of Civil Appeals of Oklahoma
9 P.3d 95 (2000)

HANSEN, VICE-CHIEF JUDGE:

Plaintiff, Total Access, Inc. (Total), seeks review of the trial court's order granting the motion to dismiss of Defendant Caddo Electric Cooperative). Total, an Internet service provider, sued Caddo for injunctive and declaratory relief, alleging the acts of Caddo in operating an Internet service provider were ultra-vires . . . . Caddo moved to dismiss on the grounds Total lacked standing to bring this action, [and] the trial court lacked subject matter jurisdiction. The trial court granted the motion and dismissed the action.

. . . .

An action in the nature of quo warranto may be brought when a corporation "abuses its power or intentionally exercises powers not conferred by law." The parties disagree as to who has standing to bring such an action. Caddo points to [MBCA § 3.04] as allowing only the corporation itself, a shareholder, or the Attorney General to assert a corporation's lack of power or capacity to do an act. Total does not allege it is a shareholder or member of Caddo. . . . Total argues it is a competitor and therefore has "an interest adverse to [Caddo's] illegal internet service provider" sufficient to provide standing.

. . . .

The Oklahoma General Corporations Act provides in § 1018 [MBCA § 3.04] that no act of a corporation shall be invalid because it was ultra vires, but the lack of capacity or power of a corporation to act may be asserted (1) by a shareholder in an action to enjoin the corporation from performing acts or transferring property, (2) by the corporation in an action against an officer or director for loss or damage due to unauthorized acts, and (3) by the Attorney General in an action to dissolve the corporation or enjoin it from transacting unauthorized business. The maxim of statutory construction, "expressio unius est exclusio alterius" means that the expression of one thing is the exclusion of another. It is "applicable only where in the natural association of ideas the contrast between a specific subject matter which is expressed and one which is not mentioned leads to an inference that the latter was not intended for inclusion in the statute." There is such a contrast between the situations where assertion of ultra vires acts is specifically authorized and those situations not mentioned as to lead to the inference the Legislature intended to exclude the authority to assert lack of corporate authority to act in any situation not expressly mentioned in § 1018. Total's action may only be brought by the Attorney General, a shareholder or member of Caddo, or Caddo itself. Total lacks standing to bring the action.

. . . Accordingly the trial court's order dismissing the case is AFFIRMED.

Adams, J., concurs; Joplin, J., dissents.

NOTES AND QUESTIONS

1. Just as a party is deemed to have no standing to use ultra vires in a challenge to a competitor's activities, a defendant in a contract action could not raise ultra vires as a defense for its non-performance or faulty performance.

2. Model Act MBCA § 3.04 provides:

(a) Except as provided in subsection (b), the validity of corporate action may not be challenged on the ground that the corporation lacks or lacked power to act;

(b) A corporation's power to act may be challenged:

(1) in a proceeding by a shareholder to enjoin the act;

(2) in a proceeding by the corporation, directly, derivatively, or through a receiver, trustee, or other legal representative, against an incumbent former director, officer, employee, or agent of the corporation; or

(3) in a proceeding by the attorney general.

(c) In a shareholder's proceeding . . . the court may enjoin or set aside the act, if equitable and if all affected persons are parties to the proceeding . . . .

Del. Gen. Corp. Law § 124 is in substance the same as MBCA § 3.04.

3. *Potential for Evasion.* What possibility might still exist which would enable a corporation to wiggle out of a contract (at least an executory one) on ultra vires grounds? *See, e.g., Inter-Continental Corp. v. Moody,* 411 S.W.2d 578 (Tex. App. 1966).

4. *Actions for Damages.* All jurisdictions allow use of ultra vires *inter se,* that is, among the participants in an incorporated venture. Such an action takes the form of a suit against officers and directors for losses the corporation has incurred because corporate officials caused the corporation to engage in activities afield of its purpose clause. *See, e.g., Lurie v. Arizona Fertilizer & Chemical Co.,* 101 Ariz. 482, 421 P.2d 330 (1966).

5. *Remaining Vitality — Municipal Law.* Citizens who form units, or subdivisions, of government form corporations. Whether they be cities, town or villages, or school, fire or irrigation districts, or health care organizations, units of local government are corporations. The city council functions essentially as a board of directors; the city manager in some cities, or the strong form mayor in others, functions much like a corporate president or CEO. In fact, the legal treatises devoted to local government law are corporation law treatises, or more accurately, municipal corporation law treatises. *See, e.g.,* EUGENE MCQUILLAN, A TREATISE ON THE LAW OF MUNICIPAL CORPORATIONS (3d ed. 1999) (15 volumes); EMMETT C. YOKLEY, MUNICIPAL CORPORATIONS (1956) (4 volumes).

One difference is the continued vitality of the ultra vires doctrine, and litigation based upon alleged violations of the doctrine, in municipal corporation law. The state's delegation to the unit of local government is strictly construed. Citizens, other governments, would-be competitors, and others use ultra vires to challenge government acts as beyond a governmental unit's purposes or powers. *See, e.g., City of Frederick v. Pickett,* 392 Md. 411, 897 A.2d 228 (2006) (condemnation of blighted property not ultra vires); *H.G. Brown Family Limited Partnership v. City of Villa Rica,* 278 Ga. 819, 607 S.E.2d 883 (Ga. 2005) (city contract to purchase land held ultra vires); and *Jeffrey Lake Development Co. v. Central Nebraska Power & Irrigation District,* 5 Neb. App. 974, 568 N.W.2d 585 (1997) (long term lease of lakefront lots held not to be ultra vires).

6. *Remaining Vitality — Gifts to Charity.* Corporation statutes today bestow upon corporations the power "to make donations for the public welfare or for charitable, scientific, or educational purposes." MBCA § 3.03(13). *See also* DEL. GEN. CORP. LAW § 122(9) ("[m]ake donations for the public welfare or for charitable, scientific or education purposes, and in time of war or other national emergencies in aid thereof"). Courts have held that corporations have power to make reasonable gifts. *See, e.g., A.P. Smith Manufacturing Co. v. Barlow,* 13 N.J. 145, 98 A.2d 581 (1952), discussed in Chapter 8 *infra* ($1,500 gift to Princeton University). Thus, from to power to make gifts *vel non* (ultra vires), the emphasis has switched to whether the gifts are reasonable in amount, related to the corporation's profitability, and related in some way to the corporation's business, at least if the gift is a larger one. The vehicle for mounting a challenge is a suit alleging breach of fiduciary duty against corporate officers and directors, who failed to exercise the requisite oversight (duty of care) or, alternatively favored the interests of a pet charity, etc., over the best interests of the corporation (self dealing, or a duty of loyalty violation). *See, e.g., Theodora Holding Co. v. Henderson,* 257 A.2d 398 (Del. Ch. 1969), shareholder challenge to a gift to a family foundation to a Colorado ranch for underprivileged children from New York; reasonableness applied as a yardstick); *Kahn v. Sullivan,* 594 A.2d 48 (Del. 1991) (Del. Gen. Corp. Law § 122(9) authorizes any reasonable gift by corporations). *See also* Chapter 8 *infra.*

8. *Remaining Vitality — Guarantee of the Debts of Another Person.*

a. Directly Beneficial Standard. Courts utilize demanding standards, such as a requirement that to be *intra vires* and enforceable such a guaranty must be "directly beneficial" to the corporation granting the guaranty or providing collateral for the debts of another. In *Woods Lumber Co. v. Moore,* 191 P. 905, 907 (Cal. 1920), the court held that the guaranty by a costume company of a movie production company's debt to a lumber firm "had to be directly connected with or beneficial to the authorized business carried on by the company." In the case at bar that could be demonstrated: the guaranteeing company would supply the costumes to the movie company once the movie company had used the lumber to construct a stage set.

   b. *Unanimous Shareholder Approval Standard. Cf. Real Estate Capital Corp. v. Thunder Corp.*, 31 Ohio Misc. 169, 287 N.E.2d 838 (1972), which uses ultra vires but a different test. The defendant corporation gave a second mortgage on its property to Real Estate Capital Corp. (RECC). The consideration ($105,000) went to Winthrop Homes, owned 100% by Julius Cohen. Defendant Thunder Bay had no visible relationship to Winthrop but was owned by Cohen (80%) and Berman (20%). Berman objected to RECC's attempts to collect from Thunder Bay. The court held the mortgage and supporting arrangements to be ultra vires and unenforceable. In determining the "validity of gratuitous guarantees and gifts by corporations," the court relied on earlier precedent holding that "[t]he voluntary transfer of property by a corporation to secure the individual indebtedness of one of its officers is binding upon the corporation only if all its stockholders assent there to . . . ." Berman had failed to consent.

   c. *Breach of Fiduciary Duty Versus Ultra Vires.* Plaintiffs could use breach of fiduciary duty grounds, alleging that rather than serving the best interests of the corporation, the corporate directors served the best interests of the debtor, or some person other than the corporation. For some reason, however, courts analyze these cases (guaranteeing or securing the debts of another) using the ultra vires doctrine. The area seems to be not only one of retained vitality but of vitality for the ultra vires doctrine.

   d. *Upstream Guarantees.* The guarantee of the debts of another or the furnishing of security for another's debts has particular relevance in corporate groups. For example, a parent corporation may fail in its attempt to obtain a bank loan for the reason that it is unable to provide collateral to the bank's satisfaction. The corporation may then offer a security interest in assets a subsidiary corporation owns. Or the parent corporation may offer to have the subsidiary, which has ample assets or cash flow, guarantee repayment of a loan to the parent corporation. Ordinarily, these type transactions (called "upstream" guarantees) present no problem if the parent owns 100% of the subsidiary's shares (a wholly owned subsidiary). But if minority shareholders exist (5%, 15%, 30%), they are prejudiced. They are entitled to have the subsidiary use its assets or cash flow for the benefit of the subsidiary, in which they own shares, and not the parent, in which they own no shares.

   The minority shareholders could sue the subsidiary's board of directors for breach of fiduciary duty. The gist of the complaint is that the directors are serving the best interests of the parent corporation rather than those of the subsidiary. Alternatively, the minority shareholders could sue the parent corporation in its capacity as controlling shareholder, alleging that it is breaching the fiduciary duty such a shareholder owes to the corporation whose shares it holds.

   These claims, however, are brought and analyzed in terms of ultra vires. Law firm attorneys spend countless hours structuring an upstream guarantee, making evident how it is "directly beneficial" to the guaranteeing corporation. They may even be asked to issue an opinion letter, analyzing the transaction and demonstrating why it is intra vires rather than ultra vires.

   e. *Crosstream and Downstream Guarantees.* When a subsidiary corporation guarantees a loan to another subsidiary corporation, or provides security for a loan to it, the transaction may be called a "cross stream" guaranty. *Real Estate Capital Corp. v. Thunder Corp., supra*, is a example of a cross stream guarantee. If a parent corporation guarantees a loan to a subsidiary corporation, etc, the transaction may be called a "downstream" guaranty. Subsidiaries which have a common owner (100% or controlling) are known as "brother," "sister," or "sibling" corporations.

PROBLEM

Brittany and Posh are to form a corporation to produce music. Posh suspects that Brittany, if given the chance, would use the corporation's resources to open a splashy new nightclub as a venue for her performances. In the past, Brittany has also used the music and lyrics of other recording artists, without permission, which, by all indications, she may do again, at least in her solo performances. In their preliminary meeting with their attorney (you), Posh voices her concerns and Brittany agrees to any reasonable measures that would rein in her tendencies. What steps would you take or documents might you draft?

M. THE ORGANIZATIONAL MEETING

At the time the drafter completes the articles of incorporation, or while the Secretary of State is processing them, the person in charge of the incorporation process will order a corporation starter kit from a legal stationer, several of which advertize in each local bar association magazine. The kit, costing $75 or so, will contain a minute book (bound in pseudo leather); pages of minute paper (extra weight); stock certificates bearing the corporate name and an appropriate logo (gowned woman holding a torch and standing atop the globe, etc); a stock set of bylaws for the particular jurisdiction; stock records upon which a person can enter the certificate number, number of shares, date when issued and (later) date when retired, etc.; and a corporate seal, similar to the metal seals notaries public use.

A paralegal or law firm associate will then prepare, often in advance, minutes of an organizational meeting. Delaware law provides that an organizational meeting "shall be held" but incorporators or directors, as the case may be, may sign "an instrument which states the action" taken without a meeting. *See* Del. Gen. Corp. Law § 108. MBCA § 2.05 is largely the same. Action by directors is necessary if the certificate of incorporation does not provide who the first directors will be. That is because otherwise a central item of business at organizational meetings is election of the first board of directors.

Many attorneys believe that a formal meeting, around a conference table, is highly desirable. It sets the right tone and gives the owners of the new corporation an opportunity to ask questions, etc. In fact, as stated before, the senior attorney, who often leaves the details of an incorporation to her subordinates, may come back into the picture to orchestrate the organizational meeting. At that meeting,

- One by one, the incorporators will resign. The incorporators remaining, along with the new directors who have just taken office, will appoint real parties in interest to the first board, unless, of course, articles or certificate already have named the first board.
- The directors will appoint the officers and fix their salaries.
- The attorney will offer an explanation of various provisions in the filed articles or certificate of incorporation, or at least call for questions that may exist.
- The directors will examine and adopt bylaws for the corporation (usually just the stock bylaws with the blanks filled in).
- Each subscription for shares should be viewed and accepted, or not, as may be the case.
- The directors must value all non-cash consideration to be issued for shares.
- The corporation, at the direction of the board, issues the shares. At some meetings, the certificates and stock records are filled out then and there, with the certificates physically delivered.
- The promoter(s) or attorney should lay at the feet of the new board all contracts

the promoters have entered into. The new board should accept or formally repudiate each one.

- Assignments of leases or other conveyances for any real property involved should be viewed, then (presumably) accepted.

- The chair of the meeting should exhibit to attendees a bill of sale for any personal property to be conveyed. It should be examined and formally accepted.

- The board should instruct a corporate officer to have the bookkeeper close the old books and open new ones in the corporate name.

- The board should further instruct an officer to change over telephone listings, letterheads, blank invoices, and so on, over into the corporate name.

- The attorney generally exhibits to the board, and has it adopt, a banking resolution. Banks insist that the corporate banking resolution be on a form the bank supplies.

- The lawyer will provide for view the form of stock certificate and the corporate seal, which the board of directors approves.

- Tax matters, such as a possible sub-chapter S election, or adoption of a so-called 1244 resolution, are discussed.

- The plan of further financing may be gone into, or it may be saved for a subsequent meeting.

- At this point, many attorneys deliver a caution. A corporation is a separate juridical (they don't use that word) person, or just a separate person. Owners (shareholders) may deal with it but, in doing so, they must be above board and document what they do. No longer can they skim funds off the till to buy groceries on their way home. No longer can they buy equipment, re-conveying it to the corporation at a markup. They must separate their affairs as owners or directors from those of the corporation. Failure to do so may result in, or contribute to, a calamity. The calamity is disregard of the corporation, or its separateness (piercing the corporate veil), or some variant, discussed Chapter 8 *infra*.

- A second lecture deals with the sale and issuance of securities. Usually, there exists an exemption for the initial subscribers. Down the road, any time a corporation offers, let alone sells, securities (e.g., common, preferred stock, bonds, warrants) it must register or have an exemption form registration. Securities laws are complicated and severe in the penalties levied upon those who violate them. *See, e.g.*, SECURITIES ACT OF 1933 § 24 (fine and prison term of up to five years for violations); SECURITIES EXCHANGE ACT OF 1934 § 32(a) (fines of up to $5 million and prison terms of up to 20 years for "willful violations"). The best course of action is to consult an attorney before even an offer of any kind whatsoever is made. *See generally* Chapter 5, *infra*.

Attorneys and law firms will have longer or differing lists of matters the participants do at the organization meeting. They will have sample sets of minutes to use as a template.

When the last of the attendees leaves the place of the meeting, a last question is what does all of this cost? Most attorneys charge a flat fee, ranging from $1,000 to $2,500. Only in more complicated matters do attorneys charge on an hourly basis for an incorporation.

Corporation service companies advertize in the *Wall Street Journal* and elsewhere for a Delaware or a Nevada incorporation for $500. Usually, the service consists of a bare bones incorporation. The biggest deficiency may be, however, that the corporation so created gets off on the wrong foot, without a relationship to a knowledgeable and objective advisor. Sometimes the old adage is true, "You get what you pay for."

Chapter 5

THE REGULATION OF SECURITIES OFFERINGS

A. WHAT IS A SECURITY?

The term "security" not only covers instruments commonly known in the investment world as securities, such as stocks and bonds, but may also include novel and unique instruments. Such instruments have included, for example, interests in "pyramid" sales schemes, chinchillas, and whiskey warehouse receipts. Ordinarily, these rather novel types of instruments come within the securities laws because they are held to be "investment contracts." *See* M. STEINBERG, UNDERSTANDING SECURITIES LAW 11–35 (4th ed. 2007).

Interpreted by the courts in an identical manner, the term "security" is defined in § 2(a)(1) of the Securities Act of 1933 and § 3(a)(10) of the Securities Exchange Act of 1934. Although it is evident that these definitions on their face are fairly broad, this is only the starting point. This is due to the language "unless the context otherwise requires" which precedes each of the provisions. This phrase, as will be seen, is very significant.

Failure on counsel's part to recognize that a "security" is present can be disastrous. As will be seen, absent an exemption, no sale of a security generally can take place unless a registration statement is in effect. Because the requirements for meeting any particular exemption may be complex, failure on counsel's part to perceive that his/her client's "deal" involves a security often means that the securities are being sold in violation of the securities laws. Under such circumstances, the Securities and Exchange Commission (SEC), state securities commissioner(s), and private parties may bring suit. Even criminal liability, depending on the circumstances, may be imposed. Hence, many deals have been scuttled, parties held liable, and lawyers sued for failure on counsel's part to recognize that a "security" was present. This point is brought home by the following case.

WARTZMAN v. HIGHTOWER PRODUCTIONS, LTD.

Court of Special Appeals of Maryland
53 Md. App. 656, 456 A.2d 82 (1983)

JAMES S. GETTY, JUDGE.

Woody Hightower did not succeed in breaking the Guinness World Record for flagpole sitting; his failure to accomplish this seemingly nebulous feat, however, did generate protracted litigation. . . .

Hightower Productions Ltd. (Hightower) . . . came into being in 1974 as a promotional venture conceived by Ira Adler, Frank Billitz and J. Daniel Quinn. The principals intended to employ a singer-entertainer who would live in a specially constructed mobile flagpole perch from April 1, 1975, until New Year's Eve at which time he would descend in Times Square in New York before a nationwide television audience having established a new world record for flagpole sitting.

The young man selected to perform this feat was to be known as "Woody Hightower". The venture was to be publicized by radio and television exposure, by adopting a theme song and by having the uncrowned champion make appearances from his perch throughout the country at concerts, state fairs, and shopping centers.

In November, 1974, the three principals approached Michael Kaminkow of the law firm of Wartzman, Rombro, Rudd and Omansky, P.A., for the specific purpose of incorporating their venture. Mr. Kaminkow, a trial attorney, referred them to his partner, Paul Wartzman.

The three principals met with Mr. Wartzman at his home and reviewed the promotional scheme with him. They indicated that they needed to sell stock to the public in order to raise the $250,000 necessary to finance the project. Shortly thereafter, the law firm prepared and filed the articles of incorporation and Hightower Productions Ltd. came into existence on November 6, 1974. The Articles of Incorporation authorized the issuance of one million shares of stock at the par value of 10 cents per share, or a total of $100,000.00.

Following incorporation, the three principals began developing the project. With an initial investment of $20,000, they opened a corporate account at Maryland National Bank and an office in the Pikesville Plaza Building. Then began the search for "Woody Hightower." After numerous interviews, twenty-three year old John Jordan emerged as "Woody Hightower".

After selecting the flagpole tenant, the corporation then sought a company to construct the premises to house him. This consisted of a seven foot wide perch that was to include a bed, toilet, water, refrigerator and heat. The accommodations were atop an hydraulic lift system mounted upon a flat bed tractor trailer.

. . . .

Hightower employed two public relations specialists to coordinate press and public relations efforts and to obtain major corporate backers. "Woody" received a proclamation from the Mayor and City Council of Baltimore and after a press breakfast at the Hilton Hotel on "All Fools Day" ascended to his home in the sky.

Within ten days, Hightower obtained a live appearance for "Woody" on the Mike Douglas Show, and a commitment for an appearance on the Wonderama television program. The principals anticipated a "snow-balling" effect from commercial enterprises as the project progressed with no substantial monetary commitments for approximately six months.

Hightower raised $43,000.00 by selling stock in the corporation. Within two weeks of "Woody's" ascension, another stockholders' meeting was scheduled, because the corporation was low on funds. At that time, Mr. Wartzman informed the principals that no further stock could be sold, because the corporation was "structured wrong", and it would be necessary to obtain the services of a securities attorney to correct the problem. Mr. Wartzman had acquired this information in a casual conversation with a friend who recommended that the corporation should consult with a securities specialist.

The problem was that the law firm had failed to prepare an offering memorandum and failed to assure that the corporation had made the required disclosures to prospective investors in accordance with the provisions of the Maryland Securities Act. . . . Mr. Wartzman advised Hightower that the cost of the specialist would be between $10,000.00 and $15,000.00. Hightower asked the firm to pay for the required services and the request was rejected.

Hightower then employed substitute counsel and scheduled a shareholders' meeting on April 28, 1975. At that meeting, the stockholders were advised that Hightower was not in compliance with the securities laws; that $43,000.00, the amount investors had paid for issued stock, had to be . . . placed in escrow; that the fee of a securities specialist would be $10,000.00 to $15,000.00 and that the additional work would require between six and eight weeks. In the interim, additional stock could not be sold, nor could "Woody" be exhibited across state lines. Faced with these problems, the shareholders decided to discontinue the entire project.

On October 8, 1975, Hightower filed suit [against the law firm] alleging breach of contract and negligence. . . .

The jury returned a verdict in favor of Hightower in the amount of $170,508.43.

. . . .

In conclusion, the final comment of Judge Lowe is equally apposite here.

> The unfortunate oversight on which this case was based was a costly one, but it was made by one who was hired precisely for the purpose of averting the consequent losses. It is he, and his firm, who must bear them.

Judgment affirmed.

1. Stock

In *Landreth Timber Co. v. Landreth*, 471 U.S. 681 (1985), and *Gould v. Ruefenacht*, 471 U.S. 701 (1985), the Supreme Court held that common stock having the attributes normally associated with this instrument is a security. In so holding, the Court rejected the approach embodied by the sale of business doctrine. That doctrine stood for the proposition that the incidental transfer of stock to manifest the sale of a closely-held business is not a security with respect to those who are entrepreneurs (namely, those who exercise control over critical entrepreneurial or managerial decisions of the corporation). In refusing to adopt the doctrine, the Supreme Court indicated that scrutiny of a transaction's economic substance is necessary only when the instruments involved are "unusual . . . not easily characterized as 'securities.' " Hence, the Court reasoned that the stock involved in the cases at bar bore all the characteristics traditionally associated with common stock, which the Court described as follows: "(i) the right to receive dividends contingent upon an apportionment of profits; (ii) negotiability; (iii) the ability to be pledged or hypothecated; (iv) the conferring of voting rights in proportion to the number of shares owned; and (v) the capacity to appreciate in value." Thereupon, looking to the "plain meaning" of the statutory definition of a "security," the Supreme Court held that traditional stock necessarily falls within the Acts' coverage.

2. Notes

In *Reves v. Ernst & Young*, 494 U.S. 56 (1990), the Court rejected the *Landreth Timber* rationale in the "note" context. Unlike "stock" which by its nature (if it has the attributes typically associated with such an instrument) is within the class of instruments Congress intended to regulate under the securities laws, the same cannot be said of "notes" which are used in a variety of settings, some of which are commercial and others of which involve investments. Hence, since "notes" are not necessarily securities, the Court, after searching for a proper standard to be applied, opted for the "family resemblance" test. This test encompasses the "motivations" of a reasonable buyer and seller to engage in the transaction, the plan of distribution, the reasonable expectations of the investing public, and the presence of a risk reducing factor. Applying the family resemblance test, the Court held that the notes at issue were securities.

3. Investment Contracts

The Supreme Court has construed the definition of a "security" several times in an attempt to clarify the statutory definitions contained in the securities acts. In its decisions, the Court has rejected a literal interpretation of the statutes, adopting instead a more flexible view which looks to the economic reality of the particular plan or scheme addressed. The *Howey* decision that follows focuses on the term "investment contract."

SECURITIES AND EXCHANGE COMMISSION v. W.J. HOWEY CO.
Supreme Court of the United States
328 U.S. 293, 66 S. Ct. 1100, 90 L. Ed. 1244 (1946)

Mr. Justice Murphy delivered the opinion of the Court.

This case involves the application of § 2(1) [today § 2(a)(1)] of the Securities Act of 1933 to an offering of units of a citrus grove development coupled with a contract for cultivating, marketing and remitting the net proceeds to the investor.

The Securities and Exchange Commission instituted this action to restrain the respondents from using the mails and instrumentalities of interstate commerce in the offer and sale of unregistered and non-exempt securities in violation of § 5(a) of the Act. . . .

Most of the facts are stipulated. The respondents, W. J. Howey Company and Howey-in-the-Hills Service, Inc., are Florida corporations under direct common control and management. The Howey Company owns large tracts of citrus acreage in Lake County, Florida. During the past several years it has planted about 500 acres annually, keeping half of the groves itself and offering the other half to the public "to help us finance additional development." Howey-in-the-Hills Service, Inc., is a service company engaged in cultivating and developing many of these groves, including the harvesting and marketing of the crops.

Each prospective customer is offered both a land sales contract and a service contract, after having been told that it is not feasible to invest in a grove unless service arrangements are made. While the purchaser is free to make arrangements with other service companies, the superiority of Howey-in-the-Hills Service, Inc., is stressed. Indeed, 85% of the acreage sold during the 3-year period ending May 31, 1943, was covered by service contracts with Howey-in-the-Hills Service, Inc.

The land sales contract with the Howey Company provides for a uniform purchase price per acre or fraction thereof, varying in amount only in accordance with the number of years the particular plot has been planted with citrus trees. Upon full payment of the purchase price the land is conveyed to the purchaser by warranty deed. Purchases are usually made in narrow strips of land arranged so that an acre consists of a row of 48 trees. During the period between February 1, 1941, and May 31, 1943, 31 of the 42 persons making purchases bought less than 5 acres each. The average holding of these 31 persons was 1.33 acres and sales of as little as 0.65, 0.7 and 0.73 of an acre were made. These tracts are not separately fenced and the sole indication of ownership is found in small land marks intelligible only through a plat book record.

The service contract, generally of a 10-year duration without option of cancellation, gives Howey-in-the-Hills Service, Inc., a leasehold interest and "full and complete" possession of the acreage. For a specified fee plus the cost of labor and materials, the company is given full discretion and authority over the cultivation of the groves and the harvest and marketing of the crops. The company is well established in the citrus business and maintains a large force of skilled personnel and a great deal of equipment, including 75 tractors, sprayer wagons, fertilizer trucks and the like. Without the consent of the company, the land owner or purchaser has no right of entry to market the crop; thus there is ordinarily no right to specific fruit. The company is accountable only for an allocation of the net profits based upon a check made at the time of picking. All the produce is pooled by the respondent companies, which do business under their own names.

The purchasers for the most part are non-residents of Florida. They are predominantly business and professional people who lack the knowledge, skill and equipment necessary for the care and cultivation of citrus trees. They are attracted by the expectation of substantial profits. . . . Many of these purchasers are patrons of a resort hotel owned and operated by the Howey Company in a scenic section adjacent to the groves. The hotel's advertising mentions the fine groves in the vicinity and the attention of the patrons is drawn to the groves as they are being escorted about the surrounding countryside. They are told that the groves are for sale; if they indicate an interest in the matter, they are then given a sales talk.

It is admitted that the mails and instrumentalities of interstate commerce are used in the sale of the land and service contracts and that no registration statement . . . has ever been filed with the Commission in accordance with the Securities Act of 1933 and the rules and regulations thereunder.[1]

Section 2(1) of the Act defines the term "security" to include the commonly known documents traded for speculation or investment. This definition also includes "securities" of a more variable character, designated by such descriptive terms as "certificate of interest or participation in any profit-sharing agreement," "investment contract" and "in general, any interest or instrument commonly known as a 'security.' " The legal issue in this case turns upon a determination of whether, under the circumstances, the land sales contract, the warranty deed and the service contract together constitute an "investment contract" within the meaning of § 2(1). . . .

The term "investment contract" is undefined by the Securities Act or by relevant legislative reports. But the term was common in many state "blue sky" laws in existence prior to the adoption of the federal statute and, although the term was also undefined by the state laws, it had been broadly construed by state courts so as to afford the investing public a full measure of protection. Form was disregarded for substance and emphasis was placed upon economic reality. An investment contract thus came to mean a contract or scheme for "the placing of capital or laying out of money in a way intended to secure income or profit from its employment." *State v. Gopher Tire & Rubber Co.*, 146 Minn. 52, 56, 177 N.W. 937, 938. This definition was uniformly applied by state courts to a variety of situations where individuals were led to invest money in a common enterprise with the expectation that they would earn a profit solely through the efforts of the promoter or of someone other than themselves.

By including an investment contract within the scope of § 2(1) of the Securities Act, Congress was using a term the meaning of which had been crystallized by this prior judicial interpretation. It is therefore reasonable to attach that meaning to the term as used by Congress, especially since such a definition is consistent with the statutory aims. In other words, an investment contract for purposes of the Securities Act means a contract, transaction or scheme whereby a person invests his money in a common enterprise and is led to expect profits solely from the efforts of the promoter or a third party, it being immaterial whether the shares in the enterprise are evidenced by formal certificates or by nominal interests in the physical assets employed in the enterprise. [Such a definition] permits the fulfillment of the statutory purpose of compelling full and fair disclosure relative to the issuance of "the many types of instruments that in our commercial world fall within the ordinary concept of a security." H. Rep. No. 85, 73d Cong., 1st Sess., p. 11. It embodies a flexible rather than a static principle, one that is capable of adaptation to meet the countless and variable schemes devised by those who seek the use of the money of others on the promise of profits.

The transactions in this case clearly involve investment contracts as so defined.

. . . .

This conclusion is unaffected by the fact that some purchasers choose not to accept the full offer of an investment contract by declining to enter into a service contract with the respondents. The Securities Act prohibits the offer as well as the sale of unregistered, non-exempt securities. Hence it is enough that the respondents merely offer the essential ingredients of an investment contract.

---

[1] [1] [To invoke jurisdiction under the federal securities laws, there must be some use of the mails or of the instrumentalities of interstate commerce. This requirement is normally met without difficulty. Use of the telephone in connection with the subject action, for example, is sufficient. — Ed.]

We reject the suggestion of the Circuit Court of Appeals that an investment contract is necessarily missing where the enterprise is not speculative or promotional in character and where the tangible interest which is sold has intrinsic value independent of the success of the enterprise as a whole. The test is whether the scheme involves an investment of money in a common enterprise with profits to come solely from the efforts of others. If that test be satisfied, it is immaterial whether the enterprise is speculative or non-speculative or whether there is a sale of property with or without intrinsic value. The statutory policy of affording broad protection to investors is not to be thwarted by unrealistic and irrelevant formulae.

Reversed.

NOTE

The factual setting presented to the Supreme Court in *Howey* has been repeated numerous times. Courts repeatedly look beyond a strict statutory construction and examine the economic reality of the transaction to determine whether a property interest combined with some form of service contract constitutes a security (termed the "aggregation approach"). The *Howey* analysis applied by the courts in these cases can usually be broken down into three issues: First, are the investors' interests interwoven with those of other investors and/or the promoter for a return on their investment ("common enterprise")? Second, is the interest bought in order to obtain a financial return or for other reasons ("expectation of profits")? And third, does the investor participate in the venture to such a degree that he or she is not dependent essentially or "solely on the efforts of others" for profits?

For a more recent U.S. Supreme Court decision interpreting the term "investment contract," see *SEC v. Edwards*, 540 U.S. 389 (2004) (holding that contractual entitlement to a fixed rate of return in a payphone package investment met the *Howey* test, and hence, was a security).

B.   THE EXEMPTION-REGISTRATION QUERY

The general rule is that, absent an exemption, all offers or sales of securities must be registered pursuant to § 5 of the U.S. Securities Act of 1933 ("Securities Act" or "1933 Act"). Note, importantly, that the securities law antifraud provisions apply irrespective of whether an exemption from registration exists.

There are two general types of exemptions: transactional exemptions and securities exempt from registration. The latter covers specific securities or categories of securities which are never required to be registered under § 5, largely due to the intrinsic character or nature of the issuer itself. These exempt securities include, for example, certain short-term promissory notes or bills of exchange, securities issued or guaranteed by municipalities, state or federal governments, and securities issued by nonprofit, religious, educational, or charitable organizations.

Moreover, some securities, although exempt from the Securities Act's registration requirements, come under the supervision of another federal or state governmental authority. For example, with respect to securities issued by national banks, the Comptroller of the Currency has developed a regulatory framework somewhat similar, yet many feel not as rigorous, as that developed by the Securities and Exchange Commission ("SEC"). On the other hand, the securities of bank holding companies are not exempt securities under the federal securities laws.

Even if a transactional exemption has been perfected, thereby obviating the need to register the offering, the antifraud provisions of the securities acts nonetheless fully apply. The antifraud provisions most frequently invoked are § 17(a) of the Securities Act, § 10(b) of the Securities Exchange Act, and Rule 10b-5 promulgated by the SEC pursuant to its § 10(b) rulemaking authority. In addition, the antifraud provisions of the state securities laws may be invoked.

Significantly, federal law thus is not the only source of regulation in this setting. The state "blue sky" laws also frequently apply and present additional dilemmas for the corporate practitioner and his or her client. With certain exceptions, to perfect an exemption, in addition to satisfying the requirements of federal law, the securities regulations of *each* state (or territory) where *any* offer or sale is made also must be satisfied. To the credit of the SEC and the states, significant progress has been made in coordinating the federal and state transactional exemption scheme, thereby alleviating much of the burden in complying with this multi-faceted regulatory framework. Moreover, federal legislation enacted in 1996 preempts state regulation of certain exempt offerings.

It is the transactional exemptions which play an important role in this context. Before delving into the pertinent issues, one may ask: What's the "big deal"? Why not simply register the offer or sale under § 5 of the 1933 Act? The answers are several. In order to register an offer or sale under § 5, and have what is called a "public offering" or "to go public,"[2] a registration statement must be filed with the Securities and Exchange Commission (SEC). The registration statement (the prospectus which is a part thereof) is no ordinary document. The disclosures required are detailed and complex, the document's length is massive, and the costs of preparing the registration statement, including accountant, attorney, investment banker, and printer fees, can easily run into the hundreds of thousands of dollars.

The costs and nature of the registration statement are due largely to § 11 of the 1933 Act, which in practical effect, imposes a "due diligence" requirement upon certain parties, including the issuer's directors and certain of its executive officers, the underwriters, and experts, including accountants (with respect to those portions of the registration statement which an accountant "expertises"). Attorneys, unless they act as experts,[3] are not subject to § 11 liability. Counsel, nonetheless, is integrally involved in the registration process. He or she frequently is delegated by the issuer, underwriter, or other parties potentially liable under § 11 to perform the requisite "due diligence" on their behalf. Other fundamental aspects of counsel's role in this process involve the drafting of the language contained in the registration statement, advising whether certain disclosures should or must be made, and acting as informal mediator between the various parties involved.

In theory, "due diligence" is a defense that may be asserted by the subject party rather than an affirmative obligation. It is certainly true that if the statements made in the registration statement are true or if no lawsuit is ultimately brought, no liability will be incurred for failure to exercise due diligence. If an action is instituted and a material misstatement or omission is shown, however, liability often may be avoided under § 11 only by proving the performance of due diligence. In the realities of corporate practice, therefore, due diligence is a necessity rather than a discretionary function.

Hence, the "due diligence" requirement is given "teeth" by the liability consequences. In general, if there is a material misrepresentation or nondisclosure in the registration statement, parties subject to § 11 liability, except the issuer, can avoid such liability only by showing that they had exercised "due diligence," i.e., that they had conducted a reasonable investigation and, after such investigation, had no reason to believe and did not believe that the registration statement contained any materially false or misleading

---

[2] The terms "public offering" and "going public" are often not synonymous. In short, the initial public offering ("IPO") made by an enterprise constitutes "going public." On the other hand, a successful corporation which has gone public decades ago may make public offerings of its securities on a periodic basis.

[3] Counsel acts as an expert, for example, if he or she proffers an opinion contained or referred to in the registration statement. An accountant, by certifying financial statements contained in the registration statement, is a party who frequently is sued as an expert under § 11.

statement.[4] While the issuer is the only party subject to strict liability, it may well be insolvent. The result is that aggrieved plaintiffs seek redress against the "deep pockets," frequently the underwriters and the accountants. Because of the severe financial ramifications that can amount to several million dollars, parties potentially subject to § 11 liability seek to ensure that abundant due diligence is performed and extensive disclosure made, including the potentially negative consequences and risks of the venture.

Accordingly, the costs of having a "registered" offering under the Securities Act frequently will be substantial. For a start-up venture or a business in severe financial difficulty, the costs of a public offering normally will prove prohibitive. Moreover, it is next to impossible successfully to consummate a registered offering unless receptive investment bankers can be retained to underwrite the offering and the financial markets are favorable. These conditions are exacerbated in cases where enterprises with little or no previous earnings history seek to "go public."

Even if a financially successful registered offering can be made, it may be advisable for the client nonetheless to perfect a transactional exemption. By refraining from "going public," the enterprise essentially is keeping its financial affairs and related matters private among its various participants. By "going public," however, the enterprise, pursuant to the disclosure requirements of the securities laws, will be hanging its dirty linen out for public viewing.[5] The enterprise, pursuant to certain provisions of the Securities Exchange Act, such as § 12(g) or § 15(d), will be required to file annual, quarterly, and other periodic reports with the SEC as well as to provide periodic reports to its shareholders and the pertinent self regulatory organizations. Note that an enterprise having at least 500 shareholders of record and $10 million in net assets must become a public reporting company irrespective of whether it has a registered offering.

By "going public," other sections of the Exchange Act, such as the record keeping and internal accounting control provisions,[6] also will become applicable. Moreover, the certification, internal control, and other mandates of the Sarbanes-Oxley Act of 2002 must be implemented.[7] Hence, the enterprise, by having a registered offering, will be faced not only with public scrutiny but saddled with high accounting and legal fees as well as the persistent threat of litigation due to the consequences of public disclosure.

For the above reasons as well as others (such as, by taking the corporation public, the insiders may potentially risk loss of control through a hostile takeover), it may well be advisable and indeed necessary to procure a transactional exemption. It should not be surprising that, given the above, the vast majority of offerings are made under a transactional exemption rather than a registered offering pursuant to § 5 of the Securities Act. In most situations, therefore, counsel will seek the viability of a transactional exemption before advising that a registered offering go forward. Hence, we begin our study of the offering process with the transactional exemptions.

---

[4] With respect to expertise portions of the registration statement, nonexperts are not required to investigate. They need show only that they had no reason to believe and did not believe that the expertise portions of the registration statement contained any materially false or misleading statement. Moreover, experts are liable under § 11 only for those portions of the registration statement which they "expertised."

[5] *See, e.g.*, Schlick v. Penn-Dixie Cement Corp., 507 F.2d 374, 384 (2d Cir. 1974).

[6] Section 13(b) of the 1934 Act, also known as the accounting provisions of the Foreign Corrupt Practices Act of 1977 which were enacted as an amendment to the Exchange Act, generally requires subject registrants to maintain reasonably accurate books and records and internal accounting controls. The provisions were passed by Congress in the aftermath of the revelation that several hundred American corporations had paid millions of dollars into domestic political slush funds and as bribes to foreign officials for the purpose of procuring or retaining business in the particular foreign country.

[7] The Sarbanes-Oxley Act is covered later in this Chapter.

C. EXEMPTIONS FROM REGISTRATION

The following discussion focuses on certain key exemptions from Securities Act registration. The onus of ensuring that a company perfects such an exception, depending on the circumstances, may fall on corporate counsel. For example, in *In re Google*, Securities Act Release No. 8523 (2004), the SEC brought an enforcement action against Google's General Counsel based on his alleged conduct which contributed to registration violations by Google. The case was settled (with the attorney neither admitting nor denying wrongdoing).

1. The Statutory Private Offering Exemption — § 4(2)

Section 4(2) of the Securities Act exempts from the registration requirements "transactions by an issuer not involving any public offering." There is no monetary limit to the amount of funds that can be raised under this exemption. The provision's legislative history expresses Congress' intent to exempt those transactions from registration "where there is no practical need for [such] application . . . [or] where the public benefits are too remote." H.R. REP. No. 85, 73d Cong., 1st Sess. 5 (1933).

As construed, federal courts have looked to a number of factors in determining the availability of the § 4(2) private offering exemption. Undoubtedly, the starting point is the Supreme Court's seminal decision in *Securities and Exchange Commission v. Ralston Purina Co.*

SECURITIES AND EXCHANGE COMMISSION v. RALSTON PURINA CO.
Supreme Court of the United States
346 U.S. 119, 73 S. Ct. 981, 97 L. Ed. 2d 1494 (1953)

MR. JUSTICE CLARK delivered the opinion of the Court.

Section 4(1) [now Section 4(2)] of the Securities Act of 1933 exempts "transactions by an issuer not involving any public offering" from the registration requirements of § 5. We must decide whether Ralston Purina's offerings of treasury stock to its "key employees" are within this exemption. On a complaint brought by the Commission under § 20(b) of the Act seeking to enjoin respondent's unregistered offerings, the District Court held the exemption applicable and dismissed the suit. The Court of Appeals affirmed. The question has arisen many times since the Act was passed; an apparent need to define the scope of the private offering exemption prompted certiorari.

Ralston Purina manufactures and distributes various feed and cereal products. Its processing and distribution facilities are scattered throughout the United States and Canada, staffed by some 7,000 employees. At least since 1911 the company has had a policy of encouraging stock ownership among its employees; more particularly, since 1942 it has made authorized but unissued common shares available to some of them. Between 1947 and 1951, the period covered by the record in this case, Ralston Purina sold nearly $2,000,000 of stock to employees without registration and in so doing made use of the mails.

In each of these years, a corporate resolution authorized the sale of common stock "to employees . . . who shall, without any solicitation by the Company or its officers or employees, inquire of any of them as to how to purchase common stock of Ralston Purina Company." A memorandum sent to branch and store managers after the resolution was adopted advised that "[t]he only employees to whom this stock will be available will be those who take the initiative and are interested in buying stock at present market prices." Among those responding to these offers were employees with the duties of artist, bakeshop foreman, chow loading foreman, clerical assistant, copywriter, electrician, stock clerk, mill office clerk, order credit trainee, production trainee, stenographer, and veterinarian. The buyers lived in over fifty widely separated communities scattered from Garland, Texas, to Nashua, New Hampshire, and Visalia,

California. The lowest salary bracket of those purchasing was $2,700 in 1949, $2,435 in 1950 and $3,107 in 1951. The record shows that in 1947, 243 employees bought stock, 20 in 1948, 414 in 1949, 411 in 1950, and the 1951 offer, interrupted by this litigation, produced 165 applications to purchase. No records were kept of those to whom the offers were made; the estimated number in 1951 was 500.

The company bottoms its exemption claim on the classification of all offerees as "key employees" in its organizations. Its position on trial was that

> A key employee . . . is not confined to an organization chart. It would include an individual who is eligible for promotion, an individual who especially influences others or who advises others, a person whom the employees look to in some special way, an individual, of course, who carries some special responsibility, who is sympathetic to management and who is ambitious and who the management feels is likely to be promoted to a greater responsibility.

That an offering to all of its employees would be public is conceded.

The Securities Act nowhere defines the scope of § 4[(2)'s] private offering exemption. Nor is the legislative history of much help in staking out its boundaries. . . .

Decisions under comparable exemptions in the English Companies Acts and state "blue sky" laws, the statutory antecedents of federal securities legislation, have made one thing clear — to be public an offer need not be open to the whole world. . . .

Exemption from the registration requirements of the Securities Act is the question. The design of the statute is to protect investors by promoting full disclosure of information thought necessary to informed investment decisions. The natural way to interpret the private offering exemption is in light of the statutory purpose. Since exempt transactions are those as to which "there is no practical need for [the bill's] application," the applicability of § 4[(2)] should turn on whether the particular class of persons affected needs the protection of the Act. An offering to those who are shown to be able to fend for themselves is a transaction "not involving any public offering."

The Commission would have us go one step further and hold that "an offering to a substantial number of the public" is not exempt under § 4[(2)]. We are advised that "whatever the special circumstances, the Commission has consistently interpreted the exemption as being inapplicable when a large number of offerees is involved." But the statute would seem to apply to a "public offering" whether to few or many. It may well be that offerings to a substantial number of persons would rarely be exempt. Indeed nothing prevents the Commission, in enforcing the statute, from using some kind of numerical test in deciding when to investigate particular exemption claims. But there is no warrant for superimposing a quantity limit on private offerings as a matter of statutory interpretation.

The exemption, as we construe it, does not deprive corporate employees, as a class, of the safeguards of the Act. We agree that some employee offerings may come within § 4[(2)], e.g., one made to executive personnel who because of their position have access to the same kind of information that the Act would make available in the form of a registration statement. Absent such a showing of special circumstances, employees are just as much members of the investing "public" as any of their neighbors in the community. . . .

Keeping in mind the broadly remedial purposes of federal securities legislation, imposition of the burden of proof on an issuer who would plead the exemption seems to us fair and reasonable. Agreeing, the court below thought the burden met primarily because of the respondent's purpose in singling out its key employees for stock offerings. But once it is seen that the exemption question turns on the knowledge of the offerees, the issuer's motives, laudable though they may be, fade into irrelevance. The focus of inquiry should be on the need of the offerees for the protections afforded by registration. The employees here were not shown to have access to the kind of information which registration would disclose. The obvious opportunities for pressure and imposition make it advisable that they be entitled to compliance with § 5.

Reversed.

NOTE

The lower federal courts subsequent to *Ralston Purina* have had numerous occasions to construe the § 4(2) exemption. Although the principles emerging from these cases are not crystal clear, the following points can be made:

First, as construed by some courts, the § 4(2) exemption turns on whether *all offers* (rather than actual purchases) are made in accordance with the exemption. A single noncomplying offer may invalidate the entire offering. For example, the Fifth Circuit has stated: "[W]e have held that the defendant must establish that each and every offeree either had the same information that would have been available in a registration statement or had access to such information."[8]

Second, although the courts and the SEC have not placed a finite number on how many offers can be permissibly made under the § 4(2) exemption, it is clear that certain limits, depending on the circumstances, apply.

Third, related to the above point, is that, pursuant to the § 4(2) exemption, the issuer cannot engage in general solicitation or advertising. The limits of what conduct constitutes general solicitation so as to make unavailable the § 4(2) exemption (as well as the Rule 505 and Rule 506 exemptions of Regulation D) at times are unclear. For example, a seminar held for an offering where twenty-five existing clients of adequate sophistication attend should be permitted while a seminar for a particular offering open to all clients of a major broker-dealer (e.g., Merrill Lynch) should be deemed general solicitation.

Fourth, an issuer should take certain precautions against resales, such as obtaining written commitments by purchasers that they are acquiring for investment purposes (called an investment letter), placing appropriate legends on the certificates, and issuing stop transfer instructions. These procedures help the issuer perfect the § 4(2) exemption in the event that purchasers subsequently resell their stock. It may well be, however, that the absence of these steps does not nullify an otherwise valid Section 4(2) exemption if no distribution in fact takes place.

Fifth, all offerees must be financially sophisticated or be advised by someone who has the requisite acumen (called an offeree representative). Under case law, individual wealth does not make one sophisticated for Section 4(2) private placement purposes.[9] An example is the Fifth Circuit's decision in *Doran v. Petroleum Management Corp.,* 545 F.2d 893, 903 (5th Cir. 1977).

Sixth, irrespective of whether an offeree (or offeree representative) has financial acumen, "[s]ophistication is not a substitute for access to the [type of] information that a registration statement would disclose."[10] In short, if offerees have not received the type of information that registration would elicit, they cannot bring any alleged "sophistication" to bear in deciding whether or not to invest.[11] Hence, all offerees must be provided with the type of information (not necessarily identical) that would be contained in a registration statement or have access to such information.

Ascertaining which offerees have "access" to registration-type information may be

---

[8] Swenson v. Engelstad, 626 F.2d 421, 425–26 (5th Cir. 1980). *See* Mark v. FSC Securities Corp., 870 F.2d 331, 334 (6th Cir. 1989).

[9] For a more relaxed standard, see *Acme Propane, Inc. v. Tenexco, Inc.*, 844 F.2d 1317, 1321 (7th Cir. 1988).

[10] *Doran,* 545 F.2d at 902. *See* United States v. Custer Channel Wing Corp., 376 F.2d 675, 678 (4th Cir. 1967).

[11] *See* Hill York Corp. v. American International Franchises, Inc., 448 F.2d 680, 690 (5th Cir. 1971).

problematic. Relevant factors include promoter or high level executive status in the enterprise, family ties, a privileged relationship based upon prior business dealings between the parties, and economic bargaining power that enables an offeree effectively to obtain the registration-type information.[12]

Note that, with respect to § 4(2) offerings, state regulation also applies. In addition, states have authority to prosecute or to provide redress for fraud. Interestingly, enactment of the National Securities Markets Improvement Act of 1996 preempts state regulation of SEC "rules or regulations issued under section 4(2)." *See* § 18(b)(4)(D) of the Securities Act. Nonetheless, states may continue to impose their own requirements for private offerings that are exempt under the statute itself (namely, the § 4(2) *statutory* exemption).

2. Rule 506 of Regulation D

As seen from the preceding discussion, perfecting a § 4(2) exemption is no easy matter. In addition, the alleged vagueness of judicial decisions, setting forth relevant Section 4(2) criteria, resulted in the securities bar clamoring for an SEC "safe harbor" rule. In an effort to facilitate capital formation, the SEC promulgated Regulation D in 1982. Rule 506, one of the rules promulgated by the Commission pursuant to Regulation D, is a "safe harbor" to the § 4(2) exemption. Compliance with Rule 506 thus may be viewed as an alternative method to perfect the § 4(2) private offering exemption. Moreover, federal legislation enacted in 1996 preempts state regulation of Rule 506 offerings (but does not preempt § 4(2) offerings).

Generally, Rule 506 is available to any issuer. There is no limit to the aggregate price of the securities offered. Although Rule 506 does not limit the number of offerees, no advertising or general solicitation is permitted under the rule. Hence, depending on the circumstances, offers to a large number of offerees may be viewed as general solicitation, resulting in loss of the exemption. The number of non-accredited purchasers is limited to thirty-five plus an unlimited number of accredited investors. If any of the purchasers are not accredited, then specified disclosure must be made to all non-accredited purchasers. As addressed later, a substantial compliance standard applies to Rule 506 offerings.

There is no requirement under Rule 506 that the issuer determine that the purchaser can bear the economic risk of the investment. Suitability determinations, however, must be made for all non-accredited purchasers. Except for accredited investors, the issuer prior to sale must "reasonably believe" that each non-accredited purchaser either alone or with his or her "purchaser" representative has such knowledge and experience in financial and business matters that he or she is capable of evaluating the merits and risks of the prospective investment. Moreover, the issuer must take certain actions to guard against resales (e.g., obtaining purchaser investment letters) in order to help ensure that a "distribution" does not occur. In addition, the issuer is required to provide written disclosure to all non-accredited purchasers regarding limitations on resale.

An important concept under Rule 506 is that of an "accredited investor." Under Regulation D, accredited investors irrebuttably are deemed to have access to registration-type information and to possess investment sophistication. Under Rule 501, accredited investors include not only certain institutional investors but also "fat cat" individual investors. These persons include those whose net worth at the time of the purchase exceeds $1 million (including the value of one's residence) and those who had an individual income exceeding $200,000 in each of the two most recent years (or $300,000 joint income with one's spouse) and who reasonably anticipate such an income

---

[12] *See* Doran v. Petroleum Management Corp., 545 F.2d 893, 903 (5th Cir. 1977).

for the current year.[13] Importantly, in a Rule 505 or 506 offering involving accredited investors, there is no mandated delivery of information to such accredited investors as Regulation D presumes that these investors can fend for themselves.

It is noteworthy that Rule 506 expands the § 4(2) private offering exemption in at least two ways. First, unlike § 4(2) which applies to both offers and sales, Rule 506 focuses on purchaser (rather than offeree) qualification. Hence, for example, Rule 506, unlike § 4(2), requires that only purchasers meet the sophistication standards. Second, institutions and wealthy individuals irrebuttably are deemed under Regulation D to be sophisticated and to have access to the type of information that a registration statement would provide. Case law under § 4(2), particularly with respect to wealthy individual investors, disagrees with the SEC's position.

Significantly, federal legislation enacted in 1996 preempts state regulation of offerings coming within Rule 506 (*see* § 18(b)(4)(D) of the Securities Act). States nonetheless may set forth notice filing requirements and collect fees with respect to such offerings. States also retain their authority to bring enforcement actions for fraudulent conduct in connection with such offerings. However, with respect to the requisite parameters of the Rule 506 exemption, once an issuer shows that it has met the requirements for this exemption, the states no longer have any role.[14]

3. The Limited Offering Exemptions

The statutory limited offering exemptions are contained in §§ 3(b) and 4(6) of the Securities Act. These exemptions reflect Congressional concern that small enterprises should not be unduly burdened in raising capital. The limited offering exemptions discussed at this point are § 4(6), Rule 504 of Regulation D, and Regulation A.

a. The Section 4(6) Exemption

Generally, § 4(6) exempts from registration under the Securities Act offers and sales by any issuer solely to one or more "accredited investors" if the total offering price does not exceed the amount permitted under § 3(b) of the Act (currently $5 million). No advertising or public solicitation is permitted in connection with a § 4(6) offering, and the issuer must file a notice of such sales made pursuant to the exemption with the SEC.

b. The Section 3(b) Exemptions

Generally, § 3(b) contains an exemption for small offerings, empowering the Commission to exempt from registration any offering of securities where the aggregate amount of such offering does not exceed $5,000,000. The most significant rules that the SEC has promulgated pursuant to this authority are Regulation A and Rules 504.

The SEC adopted Rule 504 to facilitate the capital raising needs for the small start-

---

[13] *See* Securities Act Release Nos. 6389 (1982), 6758 (1988).

[14] Note that Rule 508 provides a "substantial compliance" defense in private actions:

   Rule 508 provides that an exemption from the registration requirements will be available for an offer or sale to a particular individual or entity, despite failure to comply with a requirement of Regulation D, if the requirement is not designed to protect specifically the complaining person; the failure to comply is insignificant to the offering as a whole; and there has been a good faith and reasonable attempt to comply with all requirements of the regulation. Rule 508 specifies that the provisions of Regulation D relating to general solicitation, the dollar limits of Rules 504 and 505 and the limits on non-accredited investors in Rules 505 and 506 are deemed significant to every offering and therefore not subject to the Rule 508 defense. Further, the rule specifies that any failure to comply with a provision of Regulation D is actionable by the Commission under the Securities Act.

Securities Act Release No. 6825 (1989).

up company. The exemption is not available for investment companies and reporting entities under the Exchange Act (i.e. those registrants which must file periodic reports with the SEC). In a Rule 504 offering, the issuer need not determine whether the purchaser is sophisticated; nor does the issuer need to provide a purchaser representative for the unsophisticated. There are no specified federal disclosure requirements in a Rule 504 offering and there is no express limit on the number of offerees and purchasers. Offerings made pursuant to the Rule 504 exemption (in aggregation with all other securities sold in reliance on any exemption under § 3(b) or in violation of § 5) during any twelve-month period have a ceiling of $1 million.[15]

In fact, the Rule 504 offering exemption permits the issuer to conduct, in essence, a "mini-public" offering where general solicitation is permitted and purchasers in such offerings acquire freely transferable securities. In order for general solicitation to be permitted and the securities acquired to be freely transferable, one of two conditions must be met:

- the transactions are registered under a state law requiring public filing and delivery of a disclosure document before sale. For sales to occur in a state without this sort of provision, the transactions must be registered in another state with such a provision and the disclosure document filed in that state must be delivered to all purchasers before sale in both states; *or*

- the securities are issued under a state law exemption that permits general solicitation and general advertising so long as sales are made only to "accredited investors" as that term is defined in Regulation D.[16]

Where neither of these conditions is satisfied, Rule 504 prohibits advertising and general solicitation and deems the securities acquired restricted. Imposing these limitations, according to the SEC, was necessary in order to curb abuse of the Rule 504 exemption in the markets for "microcap" enterprises.[17]

Turning to Regulation A, although Regulation A is an exemption from registration for non-reporting companies, it in fact permits generalized interstate public offerings of up to $5 million during any 12-month period, including up to $1.5 million in non-issuer resales. The Regulation imposes no limit on the number of offerees or purchasers and authorizes the use of broker-dealers to advertise and distribute the securities. Purchasers of securities acquired in a Regulation A offering generally may resell such securities without being subject to restrictions on resale imposed by such SEC rules as 147 and 505–506. In addition, like Rule 508 in Regulation D, Regulation A contains a "substantial compliance" standard.

An offering pursuant to Regulation A may very much resemble a "mini-public" offering. Indeed, the filing with the SEC of an "offering statement" (like a registration statement in a registered offering) is required. Note, however, that because Regulation A offerings are exempt from registration, there is no § 11 liability (for materially false or misleading statements contained in the registration statement) and no requirement for the company to file with the SEC periodic reports under the Exchange Act.

4. Intrastate Offerings

Section 3(a)(11) of the Securities Act provides an exemption from registration with respect to "[a]ny security which is a part of an issue offered and sold only to persons resident within a single State or Territory, where the issuer of such security is a person resident and doing business, or, if a corporation, incorporated by and doing business

---

[15] Securities Act Release Nos. 6389 (1982), 6758 (1988).

[16] Securities Act Release No. 7644 (1999).

[17] *Id.* Offerings involving securities of microcap enterprises often are associated with low prices per share, limited public information, thin capitalization, and little, if any, analyst coverage.

within, such State or Territory." The rationale underlying the intrastate offering exemption is based on "the probability that investors in local enterprise will have adequate familiarity with [such enterprises] and an acknowledgment that [local] issuers will be relatively small and thus less able to bear the burden of federal registration,"[18] thereby leaving the respective states as the principal regulators in such offerings. In 1974, the SEC, in order to establish more definitive standards regarding the intrastate exemption, promulgated Rule 147 to serve as a safe harbor.[19] If the conditions of the rule have not been met, the party still may assert the availability of the Section 3(a)(11) statutory exemption. Unlike the exemption provided by Rule 147 and unlike those exemptions provided by Rules 504–506 of Regulation D as well as Section 4(2) of the Securities Act which are available only to the issuer, the Section 3(a)(11) exemption also may be used under certain circumstances by shareholders seeking to resell their stock.

D. OVERVIEW OF THE REGISTRATION PROCESS

To protect investors and the integrity of the securities markets, the Securities Act of 1933 (Securities Act or 1933 Act) has two basic objectives: (1) to provide investors with adequate and accurate material information concerning securities offered for sale; and (2) to prohibit fraudulent practices in the offer or sale of securities. The registration framework of the Securities Act seeks to meet these goals by imposing certain obligations and limitations upon persons engaged in the offer or sale of securities. For the Securities Act's registration framework to apply, the interstate commerce requirement must be met. This normally is satisfied without difficulty.

Under federal law, the main purpose of registration is to provide adequate and accurate disclosure of material information concerning the issuer (as well as affiliates and certain other parties) and the securities the issuer (which, for example, may be common stock in a corporation or interests in a limited partnership) proposes to offer. The disclosure of this information enables investors to evaluate the securities offered and thus make informed investment decisions.

The registration of a securities offering with the SEC does not mean that the offering is considered to be a good risk. The Commission does not have the authority to prevent an offering from going to market because it considers the investment to be of a speculative nature. Rather, the main role of the federal securities laws in this setting is to require the accurate disclosure of material information.

On the other hand, a number of states apply "merit" regulation to certain securities offerings. Under this standard, the pertinent state securities administrator can prevent an offering from going forward because it is not "fair, just and equitable." Under merit regulation, therefore, adequate disclosure is not the only criterion. The substantive fairness of the offering also may be scrutinized.

It also should be pointed out that neither the SEC nor the states verify the truthfulness of the disclosures made in the registration statement. That a registration statement becomes effective in no way vouches for the veracity of the information contained therein. In this regard, both federal and state law prohibits materially false and misleading statements, with civil and criminal remedies available to redress such violations.

---

[18] Deaktor, *Integration of Securities Offerings*, 31 U. FLA. L. REV. 465, 481 (1979).

[19] *See* Securities Act Release No. 5450 (1974). *See generally* Morrissey, *Think Globally, Act Locally: It's Time to Reform the Intrastate Exemption*, 20 SEC. REG. L.J. 59 (1992).

E. "GOING PUBLIC" — PROS AND CONS

Briefly, the *advantages* of an enterprise going public and having its initial public offering (IPO) include:

1. The funds obtained from the offering may be used for capital formation purposes as well as for retiring existing indebtedness;

2. The insiders may sell a substantial portion of their stock and thereby become (if they are not already) millionaires;

3. A public offering, by improving the company's financial position, will enable the company to have access to capital on more favorable terms;

4. The funds desired from the offering may enable the company to expand by acquiring other businesses;

5. By offering stock remuneration packages tied to a public market, the enterprise will be in a better position to hire and retain quality personnel; and

6. By having a public market for its stock, the company may become better known, thereby possibly resulting in improved profits.

On the other hand, perceived *disadvantages* of going public include:

1. The costs of an IPO, particularly when compared to other methods of procuring funds, are high;

2. Due to shareholder concern for the short-term, management may discount long-term strategies in order to put emphasis on the company's stock price;

3. Management, through its sale of stock, may lose control of the enterprise and become subject to a hostile takeover; and

4. By going public, the enterprise becomes a reporting company under the Securities Exchange Act. Such a consequence may be viewed as having several disadvantages to insiders including:

    a. The company now must file periodic and annual reports, comply with the internal accounting controls and recordkeeping mandates of the Foreign Corrupt Practices Act (even if all of the company's operations are domestic), be subject to the federal proxy provisions, as well as a number of other requirements;

    b. The company becomes subject to the rigors of the Sarbanes-Oxley Act (SOX). For example, SOX: requires chief executive officer and chief financial officer certification of the subject company's periodic reports with the SEC; mandates the implementation of sufficient internal controls; delineates the composition and functions of audit committees; bars company loans to directors and executive officers; and bars an auditor from performing certain non-audit services for a corporate audit-client;

    c. The expenses of complying with Exchange Act and SOX requirements will be substantial;

    d. Insiders lose some of their privacy as their salaries, perquisites, and transactions with the issuer must be disclosed pursuant to SEC rules;

    e. Due to such mandated disclosure, there is a greater risk of shareholder litigation; and

    f. Insiders are subject to the short-swing six-month trading provisions of § 16 of the Exchange Act, thereby resulting in some loss of liquidity and potential liability.

Given the above, the decision to go public may not be an easy one. Moreover, the registration process, including the planning, preparation, structuring, and timing of a public offering, is a major undertaking for all parties concerned.

F. A BRIEF LOOK AT THE PROCESS OF A PUBLIC OFFERING

In brief, and put simplistically, the process of a public offering may be analogized to the sale of commercial goods. In a public offering, the distribution chain normally is as follows: Issuer — Underwriters — Participating Dealers — Investors or Purchasers (who may be individuals or institutions). Generally speaking, the larger in dollar size and the greater the geographical area where the selling activity takes place, the larger the number of underwriters and dealers who will comprise the distribution chain to effectuate the offering. Note the similarity to the sale of commercial goods: Manufacturer — Wholesalers — Retailers — Consumers. As with the sale of commercial goods where wholesalers may sell directly to the public, underwriters also may bypass the "dealer-link" and sell the securities directly to investors. This may occur, for example, when an underwriter (such as Merrill Lynch) has a national retail brokerage capacity with which to market the securities directly to investors.

Underwriting agreements for the most part are on a "firm commitment" basis. This means that the underwriters agree to purchase the securities from the issuer (at a discount) with the intent to resell them to participating dealers and/or investors. Although the underwriters incur the risk of "being stuck" with the securities if there is insufficient buyer interest, this risk is minimized due to that, during the "waiting" period (when, regardless of the status of the subject issuer, offers can be made), purchaser interest can be estimated with a fair degree of accuracy. And, importantly, the underwriters' obligations normally are subject to several conditions, including various "outs" to not close should certain adverse developments arise prior to the closing date. Thus, the underwriters customarily are not obligated until the "eve" of the offering's effective date when the underwriting agreement is finalized to, inter alia, determine the desired number of shares to be offered and fix the offering price per share. By that time, there exists a strong indication of the market's likely response to the offering.[20]

Another type of underwriting agreement is on a "best efforts" basis. In this situation, the underwriters act as agents for the issuer. Rather than purchasing the securities outright from the issuer and incurring the risk of insufficient investor interest in such securities or the specter of a "bear" market, the underwriters, acting as agent for the issuer, locate buyers utilizing their "best efforts." This type of offering may be used for start-up or financially troubled enterprises where there is a substantial degree of uncertainty regarding the offering, as well as the company's ultimate success. Because investors may wish some degree of comfort when they part with their money in these types of offerings, such offerings frequently may be made on "a part or none" or "an all or nothing" basis. This means that, unless the requisite number of shares as stated in the registration statement are sold to bona fide purchasers and the proceeds are received by a specified date, all funds must be returned to the prospective investors.[21]

In either a "firm commitment" or "best efforts" underwriting arrangement, the obligations of the underwriters normally are subject to various contractual conditions, called "outs." Pursuant to such an arrangement, for example, underwriters may have the right not to close the "deal" if specified adverse developments arise before the closing date (such as the presence of adverse market conditions) or if the issuer fails to comply with its specified representations and warranties. Moreover, the underwriters condition their obligations by bargaining for the receipt of certain legal opinions and/or representations from counsel for the issuer.[22]

---

[20] *See* C. Johnson & J. McLaughlin, Corporate Finance and the Securities Laws 65–117 (3d ed. 2004); Schneider, Manko, & Kant, *Going Public: Practice, Procedure and Consequences*, 27 Vill. L. Rev. 1, 24 (1981).

[21] *See* Rule 10b-9, 17 C.F.R. § 240.10b-9; Securities Act Release No. 11532 (1975). *See generally* Frelich & Janvey, *Understanding "Best Efforts" Offerings*, 17 Sec. Reg. L.J. 151 (1989).

[22] *See* Schneider, Manko, & Kant, *Going Public: Practice, Procedure and Consequences*, 27 Vill. L. Rev.

G. STATE "BLUE SKY" LAW

Generally, under state securities (also known as "blue sky") law, as under the federal securities laws, every security offered to be sold in the applicable state must be registered or exempt from registration. Note one important caveat: If the securities offered are or will be listed on the New York or American Stock Exchange or traded on the NASDAQ National Market System, offerings of such securities are exempt from state registration requirements. Hence, companies whose stock is or will be listed on a major stock exchange or traded on the NASDAQ National Market System are exempt from the states' registration requirements.[23]

Although many states reject merit regulation, a number of others adhere to this approach. In states adopting merit regulation, full and fair disclosure alone is not enough. Rather, the offering also must be deemed "fair, just, and equitable." The debate over merit regulation generally has focused on whether full disclosure of material information concerning an offering is sufficient to protect investors, the propriety of paternalistic government regulation, and the economic costs versus benefits of such a system of regulation.[24] Generally, merit regulation is used to describe the securities laws of those states which, "in addition to requiring full disclosure, have granted their administrators power to analyze the securities to be offered, the terms of the offering, and the business of the issuer for purposes of determining, according to certain formal and informal rules, whether the securities are too speculative for public sale."[25]

In general, "tough" merit regulation states may deny registration or impose conditions (such as requiring escrow of insider proceeds for a certain period of time or until specified contingencies are met) where insiders or promoters have invested relatively little in relation to the amount of capital sought by the offering or if the promoters or insiders have received "cheap stock" (namely, stock received at significantly lower prices than the proposed public offering price). Further, registration may be denied in such states if the proposed offering price is deemed too high (e.g., the issuer's earnings history is not reflected in the proposed offering price), if the voting rights sought to be issued to the public are inequitable, or if the underwriter's commissions are unreasonable for the proposed offering.[26]

H. THE REGISTERED OFFERING — FRAMEWORK OF SECTION 11

As discussed in the foregoing materials, a registered offering under the Securities Act requires that a registration statement be utilized. A key policy underlying this requirement is to enable prospective purchasers to make informed investment decisions based upon the disclosure of adequate and truthful information regarding the issuer, its associated persons, and the offering. This policy is frustrated when a registration statement (including the statutory prospectus which comprises part of the registration statement) contains materially false or misleading statements.

1, 24 (1981). *See generally* L. Loss & J. Seligman, Securities Regulation 315–595 (3d ed. 1989). Such opinions, representations, or statements from counsel raise serious liability concerns. *See generally* Glaser, FitzGibbon, & Weise, Legal Opinions (2d ed. 2001 & 2006 supp.); Rice & Steinberg, *Legal Opinions in Securities Transactions*, 16 J. Corp. L. 375 (1991).

[23] *See* T. Hazen, The Law of Securities Regulation § 8.2 (5th ed. 2005). *See generally* J. Long, Blue Sky Law § 1.04 (2007).

[24] *See generally* Campbell, *An Open Attack on the Nonsense of Blue Sky Regulation*, 10 J. Corp. L. 553 (1985); Sargent, *The Challenge to Merit Regulation*, 12 Sec. Reg. L.J. 276, 367 (1984); Tyler, *More About Blue Sky*, 39 Wash. & Lee L. Rev. 899 (1982); American Bar Association, *Report on State Regulation of Securities Offerings*, 41 Bus. Law. 785 (1986).

[25] J. Mofsky, Blue Sky Restrictions on New Business Promotions 7–8 (1971).

[26] *See* J. Long, Blue Sky Law §1.05 (2007)

In view of the above, investors under certain conditions may recover their losses if they purchase securities pursuant to a registration statement which contains a material misrepresentation or nondisclosure. The federal law provision most likely to be invoked in this context is § 11 of the Securities Act.

Although handed down four decades ago, the seminal case on due diligence in the § 11 context is *Escott v. BarChris Construction Corporation*. This case is contained in Chapter 12, *infra*. While reading the decision, consider whether the court's approach adequately takes into account business realities. Does *BarChris* reflect an accommodation between the interests of entrepreneurs and investors? What due diligence steps should potential § 11 defendants routinely take to help guard against their being held liable for a materially false or misleading registration statement?

ESCOTT v. BARCHRIS CONSTRUCTION CORPORATION

United States District Court, Southern District of New York

283 F. Supp. 643 (1968)

[This case is contained in Chapter 12, infra.]

I.   THE SARBANES-OXLEY ACT

After the enactment of three major acts of federal legislation in 1995, 1996, and 1998, seeking to foster capital formation and redress perceived abuses associated with class actions, the election of President George W. Bush portended the continued deregulation of the securities markets and affected players in the process. Instead, the very opposite occurred: After the revelation of major financial debacles that impaired the very foundation of the U.S. capital markets, Congress enacted the most pro-regulatory securities legislation since the passage of the Securities Exchange Act in 1934.

The Sarbanes-Oxley Act of 2002 (SOX) federalizes state corporation law in several ways, going far beyond the disclosure framework that serves as the foundation to federal securities regulation.[27] Regulation of auditors now is at a level never envisioned even in the worst nightmares of the accounting profession. Moreover, chief executive and chief financial officers must "certify" with prudence, taking care to have effective controls in place to help assure the accuracy of their assessments. Overlooked to some degree, yet a surprising mandate in light of previous law, is Congress' direction for the SEC to oversee a continuous issuer disclosure regime.[28]

The U.S. securities markets traditionally have been viewed as premier, serving a vital role in the stability of our economy. Hopefully, the enactment of the Sarbanes-Oxley Act as well as vigorous implementation and enforcement of its provisions will help restore investor confidence in the integrity of our financial markets.

The following discussion focuses on a number of the Act's key provisions.

---

[27] For example, directors who serve on an audit committee must be independent (Sarbanes-Oxley Act § 301(m)(3)), CEOs and CFOs must forfeit bonuses if an issuer financial restatement is prepared under certain circumstances (Sarbanes-Oxley Act § 304), and company loans to directors and executive officers are generally prohibited (Sarbanes-Oxley Act § 402).

[28] *See* Sarbanes-Oxley Act § 409, *amending*, § 13(l) of the Exchange Act (requiring publicly-held companies to "disclose to the public on a rapid and current basis such additional information concerning material changes in the financial condition or operations of the issuer in plain English . . . as the Commission determines, by rule . . . .") This provision is a marked contrast to the previously established periodic disclosure framework. *See* Securities Act Release No. 8090 (2002); Steinberg, *Insider Trading, Selective Disclosure, and Prompt Disclosure: A Comparative Analysis*, 22 U. PA. J. INT'L L. 635 (2001).

1.   CEO and CFO Certifications

The Sarbanes-Oxley Act enhanced senior corporate management's responsibility to the investing public by requiring that the chief executive officer (CEO) and the chief financial officer (CFO) each certify, among other items, that the company's financial disclosures are a fair and accurate representation of such company's financial position. Under the Act, the CEO and the CFO of all publicly-held companies each must provide two separate certifications (pursuant to SOX Sections 302 and 906). Section 302 of the Act covers each registrant annual (Form 10-K) and quarterly (Form 10-Q) report required to be filed under the Exchange Act. The § 302 certification mandates that the CEO and CFO each certify as follows:

1. I have reviewed this annual report on Form 10-K [or periodic report on Form 10-Q] of the Registrant;

2. Based on my knowledge, this report does not contain any untrue statement of a material fact or omit to state a material fact necessary to make the statements made, in light of the circumstances under which such statements are made, not misleading with respect to the period covered by this report;

3. Based on my knowledge, the financial statements, and other financial information included in this report, fairly present in all material respects the financial condition, results of operations and cash flows of the Registrant as of, and for, the periods presented in this report;

4. The Registrant's other certifying officer and I are responsible for establishing and maintaining disclosure controls and procedures and internal control over financial reporting for the Registrant and have:

(a) Designed such disclosure controls and procedures, or caused such disclosure controls and procedures to be designed under our supervision, to ensure that material information relating to the Registrant, including its consolidated subsidiaries, is made known to us by others within those entities, particularly during the period in which this report is being prepared;

(b) Designed such internal control over financial reporting, or caused such internal control over financial reporting to be designed under our supervision, to provide reasonable assurance regarding the reliability of financial reporting and the preparation of financial statements for external purposes in accordance with generally accepted accounting principles;

(c) Evaluated the effectiveness of the Registrant's disclosure controls and procedures and presented in this report our conclusions about the effectiveness of the disclosure controls and procedures, as of the end of the period covered by this report based on such evaluation; and

(d) Disclosed in this report any change in the Registrant's internal control over financial reporting that occurred during the Registrant's most recent fiscal quarter (the Registrant's fourth fiscal quarter in the case of an annual report) that has materially affected, or is reasonably likely to materially affect, the Registrant's internal control over financial reporting; and

5. The Registrant's other certifying officer and I have disclosed, based on our most recent evaluation of internal control over financial reporting, to the Registrant's auditors and the audit committee of the Registrant's board of directors (or persons performing the equivalent functions):

(a) All significant deficiencies and material weaknesses in the design or operation of internal control over financial reporting which are reasonably likely to adversely affect the Registrant's ability to record, process, summarize and report financial information; and

(b) Any fraud, whether or not material, that involves management or other employees who have a significant role in the Registrant's internal control over financial reporting.[29]

The § 906 certification, adding § 1350 to the criminal statutes, applies to each Exchange Act report containing financial statements and provides for significant criminal penalties for knowingly false certification. Pursuant to § 906, the CEO and CFO certification each must state "that the periodic report containing the financial statements fully complies with the [Exchange Act periodic reporting] requirements and that information contained in the [subject] periodic report fairly presents, in all material respects, the financial condition and results of operations of the issuer."[30]

These provisions in SOX place CEOs and CFOs in a potentially precarious situation, such as where a company restates its audited financials. Clearly, a CEO or CFO who, with knowledge, falsely certifies any such report is subject to severe penalties. As a defense, the officer may claim that he or she did not know that a statement in the report was materially incorrect. Even assuming that this defense is meritorious, the officer nevertheless is subject to other civil liability based on SOX's mandate that the certifying officer engage in specified affirmative conduct for the establishment and implementation of reasonably effective disclosure controls and procedures. Such liability may arise, for example: in a private § 10(b) action (where recklessness is sufficient scienter); in an SEC enforcement action (where depending on the provision violated, negligence is sufficient); or in a state court suit for breach of fiduciary duty.

2. Audit Committee

Under the Sarbanes-Oxley Act, the audit committee is defined as a committee established by the board of directors for the purpose of overseeing the accounting and financial reporting processes of the company and the audits of such company's financial statements. Under SOX, if no such committee exists, then the entire board of directors is considered the audit committee; however, all members of the audit committee must be independent.[31] The audit committee is given the direct responsibility of engaging the auditing firm, preapproving audit as well as non-audit services, and overseeing the auditor's work. Under SOX, the independent auditor is required to directly report to the audit committee. In addition, the audit committee must establish procedures for dealing with internal corporate "whistle-blower" complaints concerning accounting or auditing matters. The audit committee also is vested with the power to employ its own legal counsel and other advisers as the committee deems is necessary to carry out its duties.[32]

3. Forfeiture of Bonuses and Profits

In the event that a publicly-held company must prepare an accounting restatement due to the material noncompliance of such registrant as a result of misconduct, the CEO and the CFO must reimburse the company for any bonus or other incentive-based compensation. Moreover, under such circumstances, any profits realized from the sale of the registrant's securities received by the subject officer within the twelve-month period following the filing with the SEC of the misleading report(s) must be disgorged to the company. Unfortunately, the statute does not explain when an accounting restatement is considered to be "as a result of misconduct." Therefore, determination of the meaning of this term will be left to judicial resolution.

---

[29] Rule 13a-14(a)/15d-14(a) Certification. *See* Sarbanes-Oxley Act § 302(a)(1)–(a)(6).

[30] 18 U.S.C. § 1350.

[31] Sarbanes-Oxley Act §§ 205(a)(58)(A)–(B), *amending*, §§ 3(a)(58)(A)–(B), 10A(m)(3) of the Exchange Act; Securities Act Release No. 8220 (2003).

[32] Sarbanes-Oxley Act §§ 201(h), 202(i), 301(m), *amending*, § 10A(h), (i), (m) of the Exchange Act. Note that the auditors are precluded from engaging in specified non-audit services. SOX §§ 201–203.

4. Officer and Director Bars

SOX lowers the standard for barring individuals from being officers and directors of publicly-held companies. Previously, a court had authority to bar a securities law violator from serving as a director or officer of a publicly-held enterprise who was found liable for securities fraud and held to be "substantially unfit." SOX lowers that standard to "unfitness." Accordingly, upon a finding that the subject violator engaged in securities fraud and is deemed unfit to serve as a director or officer of a publicly-held company, a bar order is to be entered.[33]

5. Prohibition of Loans to Directors and Officers

The Sarbanes-Oxley Act prohibits loans by a publicly-held company to its executive officers and directors. Certain limited types of loans are permitted if they are extended in the ordinary course of business by the company and are granted to the fiduciary on the same basis as loans provided to the general public.

6. Management Assessment of Internal Controls

SOX requires management to create, maintain, and assess internal controls. Management also must report on the effectiveness of the internal controls. In addition, the Act requires the independent auditor to report on whether the company has adequate internal controls.[34] Subsequently, the SEC adopted rules mandating that each Exchange Act reporting company include in its Form 10-K a report of management addressing the subject company's internal control over financial reporting. The Commission stated:

> As directed by Section 404 of the Sarbanes-Oxley Act of 2002, we are adopting rules requiring companies subject to the reporting requirements of the Securities Exchange Act of 1934, other than registered investment companies, to include in their annual reports a report of management on the company's internal control over financial reporting. The internal control report must include: a statement of management's responsibility for establishing and maintaining adequate internal control over financial reporting for the company; management's assessment of the effectiveness of the company's internal control over financial reporting as of the end of the company's most recent fiscal year; a statement identifying the framework used by management to evaluate the effectiveness of the company's internal control over financial reporting; and a statement that the registered public accounting firm that audited the company's financial statements included in the annual report has issued an attestation report on management's assessment of the company's internal control over financial reporting. Under [these] rules, a company is required to file the registered public accounting firm's attestation report as part of the annual report. Furthermore, . . . management [must] evaluate any change in the company's internal control over financial reporting that occurred during a fiscal quarter that has materially affected, or is reasonably likely to materially affect, the company's internal control over financial reporting.[35]

---

[33] Sarbanes-Oxley Act § 305, *amending*, § 20(e) of the Securities Act & § 21(d)(2) of the Exchange Act. *See* Barnard, *Rule 10b-5 and the "Unfitness" Question*, 47 ARIZ. L. REV. 9 (2005).

[34] Sarbanes-Oxley Act § 404.

[35] Securities Act Release No. 8238 (2003). The SEC has undertaken the task of redesigning Section 404 implementation with the goal of making this process more efficient and cost effective. *See* Securities Act Release Nos. 8730, 8731 (2006); Fed. Sec. L. Rep. (CCH) No. 2239, at 3–4 (2006).

7.   Real-Time Disclosure

SOX requires publicly-held companies, as set forth by SEC rules, to make rapid and current disclosure of material changes in their financial condition or operations. These disclosures must be in plain English.[36] Under this provision, the Commission has added several items to be promptly disclosed pursuant to Form 8-K.[37]

8.   Accounting Oversight Board

The Sarbanes-Oxley Act established the Public Accounting Oversight Board (PCAOB or Board). The Board's fundamental purpose is to oversee the auditing of public companies in order to help ensure accurate and independent financial reporting by public companies subject to the federal securities laws. The PCAOB is not an agency of the federal government; it is a non-profit corporation formed under the laws of the District of Columbia. The Board has sweeping powers to establish quality control, ethical, and auditing standards for accounting firms. The PCAOB also has the power and authority to inspect, investigate, and bring disciplinary proceedings against public auditing firms.[38]

---

[36] Sarbanes-Oxley Act § 409, *amending*, § 13(l) of the Exchange Act.

[37] *See* Securities Exchange Act Release No. 49424 (2004). *See generally* Horwich, *New Form 8-K and Real-Time Disclosure*, 37 Rev. Sec. & Comm. Reg. 109 (2004).

[38] Sarbanes-Oxley Act § 101(a)–(b). *See* M. Steinberg, Understanding Securities Law 142–58 (4th ed. 2007); Nagy, *Playing Peekaboo with Constitutional Law: The PCAOB and Its Public or Private Status*, 80 Notre Dame L. Rev. 975 (2005).

Chapter 6

BASIC CORPORATE FINANCE, ACCOUNTING, AND DISTRIBUTIONS

A. INTRODUCTION AND GLOSSARY

This chapter provides an overview of corporate finance, certain fundamental accounting principles, and the law related to dividends and other corporate distributions. In order to represent their clients competently in virtually unlimited contexts and across legal fields, all lawyers should develop basic familiarity with these principles. Understandably, many may have chosen the legal field precisely because of their disdain for "numbers." However, lawyers must understand their clients' business and financial fundamentals, as well as corporate legal principles, in order to advise clients as to the applicability of those principles in particular business contexts. This obligation begins in the formative stages of the clients' businesses and continues throughout their operations. This is critical both to the structuring process and to recognition of a multitude of legal issues. The following glossary contains a number of the more essential terms.

Glossary of Terms

Authorized Shares: The number of shares prescribed in the articles of incorporation. The corporation can only issue shares that have been authorized in the articles. *See, e.g.,* MBCA § 6.01.

Balance Sheet: An accounting statement that provides a financial photograph of a business at a particular point in time, generally at year-end. It has three sections: (1) assets, listed at cost on the left-hand side; (2) liabilities or debts owed, listed on the right-hand side; and (3) equity or net worth, which is the difference between the amounts of assets and liabilities. The two sides balance because assets must always equal liabilities and equity.

Bond: A long-term debt security typically secured or collateralized and issued under a contract known as an indenture, which provides the governing terms and conditions. The bond itself is a financial instrument in which the corporate borrower (the seller of the security) promises to pay specified principal and interest to the lender (the buyer of the security) at specified dates. The indenture is a contract between the corporate borrower and an independent trustee empowered to act on behalf of the bondholders, as third-party beneficiaries, to administer payment of principal and interest and to protect bondholder interests in the event of default.

Capital Surplus: Generally referred to as paid-in surplus, that component of shareholders' equity that consists of amounts paid to a corporation for its shares in excess of stated capital. Also commonly referred to as paid-in capital in excess of par value.

Classified Stock: Stock, whether preferred or common, that is issued in separate classes having different voting, dividend, liquidation, or other rights. *See, e.g.,* MBCA §§ 6.01, 6.02.

Common Stock: Equity security representing the residual ownership interests in the corporation after the senior financial claims of general and secured creditors — including bond, note, and debenture holders and preferred shareholders have been satisfied. Common stock generally provides voting rights and, hence, collective control of the corporation. It typically does not have any conversion right, a right to convert into another type of security, or redemption rights, including an option for the shareholder to put the stock back to the corporation or for the corporation to call the stock for cash surrender.

Conversion Rights: Options, often granted to shareholders or other security holders by the corporation at the time of the issuance of the security, to convert such security into another security of the corporation. They are commonly granted to both preferred shareholders and debt holders at time of issuance, permitting conversion of the preferred shares or debt securities into common stock within a prescribed period of time or upon the occurrence of specified conditions. *See, e.g.*, MBCA § 6.01(c)(2).

Debenture: A long-term debt security that is not secured by real estate, a pledge of revenues, or other collateral.

Debt: Fixed claims against the corporation for principal and interest. The primary types of corporate debt are: (1) trade debt, recorded on the balance sheet as accounts payable; (2) bank debt, recorded as loans payable; and (3) bonds, debentures, and notes.

Distribution: A direct or indirect transfer of money or other property (except its own shares) or incurrence of indebtedness by a corporation to or for the benefit of its shareholders in respect of any of its shares. A distribution may be in the form of a declaration or payment of a dividend; a repurchase, redemption, or other acquisition of shares; a distribution of indebtedness; or otherwise. *See* MBCA § 1.40(6). Distributions are generally subject to statutorily imposed restraints designed to protect corporate creditors by prohibiting distributions that would render the corporation insolvent. *See, e.g.*, MBCA §§ 6.40(c), 8.33. They may also be subject to restrictions in the corporation's articles of incorporation, indentures, loan agreements, and shareholder agreements.

Dividend: A type of distribution involving the pro rata payment or transfer of cash, common and preferred stock, debt or other property to equity shareholders based on corporate earnings. Dividends are subject to statutory restraints on distribution.

Earned Surplus: Generally referred to as retained earnings, that component of shareholders' equity that results from the cumulative profits and losses of a corporation minus total distributions. Where the cumulative result produces a negative balance, it is referred to as accumulated deficit rather than retained earnings.

Income Statement: An accounting statement providing a view of a business's financial position over a period of time — generally a quarter or year — rather than at one point in time. It has three sections: revenues, expenses, and net income (or net loss), with the latter being the difference between the amounts of revenues and expenses.

Note: A financial instrument in which the borrower promises to pay principal and interest to the lender at specified dates or interest at specified dates and principal on demand. It is a debt that may or may not be a security, may be long-term or short-term, secured or unsecured, and payable on demand, in periodic installments of principal and interest, or payable in periodic payments of interest only and principal at maturity.

Par Value: Although no longer required by statute, an arbitrarily set dollar amount that has to be paid for common shares before they can be deemed fully paid and non-assessable. Its original purposes were to set a minimum price for shares and to provide an equity cushion for creditors that could not be impaired through distributions to shareholders. Although par value stock remains permissible, most common stock is issued without par value. *See, e.g.*, MBCA § 6.21. When par value is used, it typically is set very low, at $.01 per share or less, thereby providing little or no value upon which creditors can be presumed to rely.

Preemptive Rights: Generally, the right accorded to shareholders to buy any newly issued shares necessary to maintain their proportionate equity interest in the corporation. Under most modern corporate statutes, shareholders do not have preemptive rights unless the articles of incorporation specifically grant those rights to shareholders. *See, e.g.*, MBCA § 6.30.

Preferred Stock: A hybrid security between debt and common stock legally classified as an equity security. It typically earns a fixed dividend and is entitled to fixed rights on liquidation. The preferred shareholder has priority at liquidation over common shareholders, i.e., the preferred shareholder is entitled to a fixed payment before any net assets are distributed to common shareholders. Similarly, the preferred shareholder must be paid the agreed dividend before any dividends may be paid to common shareholders. However, since he holds an equity security, the preferred shareholder is subject to the board of directors' discretion on the payment of dividends. The board's failure to pay the contracted amount does not constitute default and provides no debt claim against the corporation. If the preferred shares are made cumulative, by providing for unpaid dividends to accumulate, any unpaid dividends will carry forward until declared and paid by the board. Preferred stock, unlike common shares, typically is redeemable by the corporation at a fixed price and has no voting rights. Preferred stock may also have conversion rights, giving preferred stockholders the right to convert their shares into common stock under specified terms. It may also be granted participation rights, giving preferred shareholders the right to participate in any distributions of dividends to common shareholders. Given the breadth of contractual terms that may be negotiated by the parties, preferred stock is often defined by the creativity of the parties and their lawyers.

Redemption: A distribution of assets to some or all of a corporation's shareholders through an involuntary buyback of its outstanding shares. *See, e.g.*, MBCA § 6.01(c)(2). Redemption rights may be provided pursuant to terms in the articles of incorporation authorizing the shares, through other contractual provisions granting an option to the corporation to call the shares for surrender, or by granting an option to the shareholder to put the shares back to the corporation. Redemptions are generally subject to statutory restraints on distributions. *See, e.g.*, MBCA § 6.03(b). Such reacquired shares constitute authorized but unissued shares. *See, e.g.*, MBCA § 6.31(a).

Reduction Surplus: The amount by which stated capital has been reduced by the corporation, generally through amendment to the articles of incorporation reducing or eliminating par value. It is recorded on the corporate balance sheet as a subcategory of capital surplus.

Repurchase: A corporate distribution of assets to some or all shareholders through a voluntary buyback of a portion of its outstanding shares. Repurchases are generally subject to statutory restraints on distributions. *See, e.g.*, MBCA § 6.03(b). Such reacquired shares constitute authorized but unissued shares. *See, e.g.*, MBCA § 6.31(a).

Retained earnings: See Earned Surplus.

Revaluation Surplus: The amount by which shareholders' equity has been increased through a revaluation or reappraisal of the corporation's assets to reflect actual market value rather than historical cost less depreciation. Although prohibited by some statutes, good faith revaluation of assets by a corporation's board of directors is allowed by many corporate statutes. *See, e.g.*, MBCA § 6.40(d); DEL. GEN. CORP. LAW § 172.

Share Dividend: A pro rata issue of additional authorized shares to equity shareholders. The issuance only divides corporate ownership among a greater number of shares. *See, e.g.*, MBCA § 6.23. Shares issued as a share dividend do not change the equity or the proportionate ownership of the corporation.

Shareholders' Equity: The difference in value between the assets and liabilities of the corporation, as recorded on the corporate balance sheet. The three primary components of shareholders' equity are: (1) stated capital or capital stock; (2) capital surplus or paid-in surplus; and (3) earned surplus or retained earnings.

Stated Capital: Often referred to as capital stock, this is that component of shareholders' equity that consists of the total or aggregate par value of the common stock, if any, and any other amounts that may be allocated by the board of directors to the stated capital account on the corporate balance sheet.

Treasury Stock: Now infrequently used, authorized and validly issued shares of a corporation's stock which have been reacquired by the corporation. Once denominated as equity on the corporate balance sheet, such reacquired shares are now simply redesignated as authorized but unissued shares. *See, e.g.*, MBCA § 6.31(a).

Watered Stock: Broadly viewed to include bonus stock, discount stock, and watered stock. Bonus stock are shares issued without consideration; discount stock are shares issued for less than par value; and watered stock are shares issued for property of overstated value.

Working Capital: Often referred to as net current assets, the excess of current assets (cash, marketable securities, accounts receivable, and inventory) over current liabilities (accounts payable, notes payable, interest, wages, and taxes). Where a corporation has no or insufficient working capital, it would be unable to pay its debts as they fall due and, hence, be insolvent in the equity sense.

B. BASIC CORPORATE FINANCE

1. Corporate Securities

The corporation must have capital to finance its organization, development, and operations, at least until such time as the business is generating sufficient income to provide that capital. The basic types of corporate securities issued by the corporation in exchange for capital are equity securities — namely common and preferred stock — and debt securities. Normally, corporations at the time of formation are capitalized with equity securities in the form of common stock. Normally, the board of directors issues this common stock to the promoters and perhaps others who are or will be engaged in the management of the business. The offer and sale of the shares to these insiders would usually be exempt from federal securities registration under § 4(2) of the Securities Act of 1933, and from state registration under similar statutory exemptions. It should be noted that these shares may be subject to restrictions on transfer, discussed later in this chapter and, in any event, generally may not be offered or sold to others without registration or an exemption from registration.

Common stock and preferred stock are the primary types of equity securities. The term "equity" refers to shareholders' equity or the amount of the difference in value between the assets and liabilities of the corporation, as determined at a particular point in time. After the corporation's debts have been deducted, the equity shareholders own what is left over. Holders of equity securities have no debt claims against the corporation for the amount of their capital investment and are fully subordinate to the corporation's debtholders. Debt may take the form of a non-security, such as a bank loan or trade debt, or, for well-established companies, may actually be offered and sold as debt securities in the marketplace, such as bonds and debentures. Debt securities are also subject to federal and state registration requirements and generally may not be offered or sold without registration or an exemption from registration. The following discussion should provide a general understanding of the equity and debt sources of capital for the corporate enterprise.

a. Equity Securities

The issuance of a class of equity securities, normally in the form of common stock, is mandatory under modern corporate statutes. Under modern corporate statutes, a corporation's articles of incorporation must authorize one or more classes of shares that have unlimited voting rights and that are entitled to receive the net assets upon dissolution. *See, e.g.,* MBCA § 6.03(b). Moreover, at least one such share must be outstanding at all times. *See, e.g.,* MBCA § 6.03(c). Of course, all equity securities must be authorized in the articles of incorporation. The articles of incorporation generally must set forth the following: (1) the number of shares the board of directors is authorized to issue; (2) the classes or types of shares, including any classes of common stock and series of preferred stock; and (3) the preferences, rights, and limitations relative to each class and series, which normally must be identical within each class or series. These preferences, rights, and limitations are basically as extensive as the creativity of the lawyers in crafting provisions for the benefit of the corporation or its investors. *See, e.g.,* MBCA § 6.01(a) and (e). When one class of equity is authorized with a specified preference or priority over the common stock in the payment of dividends and in the distribution of assets should the corporation dissolve, it is generally referred to as preferred stock. Rights and limitations that may be provided for any particular class of equity security include voting rights, conversion rights, redemption rights, and preemptive rights, among others.

i. Common Stock

Common stock represents the residual ownership interests in the corporation after the senior financial claims of general and secured creditors, and of preferred shareholders, if any, have been satisfied. In other words, should the corporation liquidate its assets, the common shareholders are entitled to what is left over after the company's debts have been paid and preferences of any preferred shareholders are satisfied. These net assets are often referred to as the residuary or net equity owned by the common shareholders.

The customary attributes of common stock include the following:

1. *Voting Rights.* The statutory norm of voting rights is one share, one vote, on each matter voted on at a shareholders' meeting. Although at least one class must have voting rights, the articles of incorporation may provide for classes of stock with limited or no voting rights or for classes of stock with super-voting rights, e.g., ten votes per share. *See, e.g.,* MBCA § 6.01(c). Note, only shares are entitled to vote under most corporate statutes. *See, e.g.,* MBCA § 7.21(a). Moreover, the exercise of common stockholders' voting rights may be subject to shareholder agreements that mandate certain outcomes, as discussed in Chapter 9. Shareholder voting rights are the most important shareholder power and are the fundamental tenet of corporate governance. Common stockholders exercise voting rights to elect the corporation's board of directors and to approve major organic changes in the corporation's affairs. These include, among others, amendments to the articles of incorporation, mergers, and voluntary dissolution.

2. *Liquidation Rights.* Common stockholders normally have the right to a pro rata distribution of the corporation's net assets upon dissolution. However, as stated previously, their liquidation rights may be subordinate to other classes of equity securities, generally preferred stock, that have priority of payment.

3. *Dividends.* Generally, common stockholders are not entitled to dividends, which are periodic pro rata distributions of cash or other assets to holders of equity securities. Under modern corporate law, the board of directors generally has broad discretion in setting dividend policy and in the declaration of dividends. In addition, the payment of dividends or other corporate distributions is subject to statutory restraints, as discussed later in this chapter. *See, e.g.,* MBCA § 6.40. Assuming those statutory restraints are not invoked, once the board of directors declares a dividend, it may not be rescinded, and the shareholders become corporate creditors with a debt claim against the corporation.

4. *Conversion Rights.* Normally, common stockholders are not granted conversion rights, which provide an option to convert their shares into some other corporate security.

5. *Redemption Rights.* Normally, common stockholders are not granted redemption rights, which provide an option to sell or put the shares to the corporation. Conversely, they are normally not subject to a corporate right to buy or call the shares.

6. *Preemptive Rights.* Under modern corporate statutes, shareholders do not have preemptive rights to maintain their proportionate equity interests in the corporation. *See, e.g.,* MBCA § 6.30. However, the articles of incorporation may include provisions that grant these rights to common stockholders. If so, the common stockholders would be entitled to a rights offering before the corporation could issue shares to new investors.

ii. Preferred Stock

The terms common stock and preferred stock are not specifically reflected in many corporate statutes, but they are integral to corporate finance. Although common stock is virtually always issued as part of the company's capitalization, another type of equity security, preferred stock, may also be issued. Preferred stock basically means stock that is preferred or has preferences over the common stock, largely in terms of dividend payments and fixed payments upon the corporation's liquidation. The customary attributes of preferred stock are as follows:

1. *Voting Rights*. Normally, preferred stock has no voting rights, although these rights may be conferred by statute or by the articles of incorporation. However, when the preferred stock is created, contractual provisions often grant voting rights if the agreed dividends have not been declared and paid after a substantial period of time.

2. *Liquidation Rights*. Preferred stockholders are generally entitled to a liquidation preference over the common stockholders upon corporate dissolution. The preference is normally a fixed price per share, equal to stated capital or par value, often together with a relatively small liquidation premium, that must be paid before the distribution of the remaining net assets to common stockholders. In addition, if the preferred stock was made cumulative at the time of its issuance, then the liquidation preference extends to dividends in arrears.

3. *Dividends*. Similar to common stockholders, preferred stockholders are not entitled to dividends, despite contractual provisions that state the dividend rate, e.g., "$10 preferred, $100 par value," which represents an intended ten percent rate of return. Again, the declaration of a dividend generally remains within the board of directors' discretion and subject to statutory restraints on distributions. However, the preferred stockholder does have a dividend preference requiring that the agreed dividend rate must be paid prior to any dividend payment to common shareholders. If the preferred stock was made *cumulative* at the time of its issuance, the preferred stockholders' dividend preference extends to all unpaid dividends from prior years. Any arrearages from prior years, as well as the current year, must be paid to the preferred stockholders before payment of dividends to common stockholders. In addition, the preferred stock may have contractual provisions deeming it *participating*, in which event, it would be entitled to share in any dividends declared on the common stock.

4. *Conversion Rights*. Preferred stockholders may be granted conversion rights by contractual provisions at time of issuance. Normally, these rights provide preferred stockholders the option to convert preferred shares to common stock within a prescribed period of time or upon the occurrence of specified conditions. The provisions granting these rights typically specify a ratio for the exchange and often include antidilution clauses that adjust the ratio if the corporation subsequently issues additional common shares. Conversion rights can prove quite valuable since conversion may give the preferred stockholders voting power and possible control, as well as a larger proportion of shareholders equity.

5. *Redemption Rights*. Generally, preferred stockholders do not have redemption rights that provide them an option to sell or "put" the shares to the corporation at a specified price. However, it is not uncommon for the corporation itself to retain an option to buy or "call" the shares. The corporation would consider exercise of its call option in the event the fixed dividend rate on the preferred became higher than market rates for capital.

6. *Preemptive Rights*. Preferred stockholders normally do not have preemptive rights. Even where common stockholders have been granted preemptive rights in the articles of incorporation, preferred stockholders are typically excluded. *See, e.g.*, MBCA § 6.30(b)(4).

2. Debt Securities

The capitalization of virtually all corporations involves both equity capital and debt capital. In addition to the capital provided by the sale of common stock to the initial shareholders, additional capital is frequently obtained through bank loans, usually collateralized by corporate assets and personally guaranteed by the initial shareholders. The shareholders themselves may directly loan money to the new business, taking back the corporation's interest bearing promissory notes, normally uncollateralized since the company's assets are likely to have already secured its bank loans. From another perspective, shareholders and other noncommercial lenders in such transactions are offeree-purchasers of the corporation's notes and the corporation is the issuer-offeror-seller of those notes. This view may prove useful in identifying the issue whether these notes are securities subject to state and federal registration requirements. In addition to bank and shareholder loans, another major source of capital is the extension of credit by suppliers and other trade creditors. This type of debt capital is generally referred to as *trade debt* or *open account indebtedness*, and is normally unsecured and not evidenced by a promissory note or other debt instrument. This source is often crucial to newly formed corporations since the absence of such credit would significantly increase the amount of working capital necessary for operations. Finally, corporations that are well established financially may be positioned to issue and sell debt securities in securities markets.

C. THE BASICS OF FINANCIAL STATEMENTS

1. Introduction

All lawyers must understand the basics of financial statements and must possess at least a rudimentary knowledge of fundamental accounting principles. Basic accounting knowledge has become integral to the lawyer's duty of competence under modern rules of professional responsibility. The host of legal issues faced by lawyers today often involves contractual, valuation, or disclosure issues that may present themselves as accounting issues. For example, whether to recognize a tract of real estate as an asset on the corporate balance sheet may be dependent on questions of equitable or legal title to that real estate. Whether to recognize revenue from the sale of goods on the corporation's income statement may be dependent on questions regarding the existence of a binding contract or agreements that would render the contract illusory. Similarly, otherwise valid contracts are misdated to manipulate the timing of revenue recognition, thus evidencing intent to deceive or outright fraud. Again, it cannot be overemphasized that these questions are legal issues often disguised as solely accounting issues.

The corporation's balance sheets and income statements are not only used to measure the corporation's financial position and results of operations for internal purposes. They are also used to secure capital from others, including equity capital from new investors and, more frequently, debt capital from banks and other lending institutions. The use of deceptive financial statements to obtain capital constitutes garden-variety fraud, as to which lawyers and not accountants are the established experts. *See, e.g.*, RESTATEMENT (SECOND) OF TORTS § 552(1). Certainly, business lawyers cannot feign ignorance of these legal issues and simply abdicate their responsibilities to the accounting profession. *See generally*, Manning G. Warren III, *Revenue Recognition and Corporate Counsel*, 56 SMU L. REV. 885 (2003). Moreover, the business lawyer is significantly more effective, and appreciated, when he develops a fundamental understanding of his corporate client's business and a continual awareness of its financial position.

The section provides a very general overview of the basic financial statements, the balance sheet and the income statement, as well as double-entry bookkeeping, the methodology used in their construction. It should be sufficient to enhance understanding of many of the issues presented in important case law set forth in this text, especially those cases involving the propriety of dividend declarations and other distributions, as well as those involving valuation, insolvency, and financial fraud. It is not intended as a substitute for more detailed and substantive treatment of this area in accounting for lawyers courses.

2.   Double-Entry Bookkeeping

Double-entry bookkeeping is the methodology used in the construction of basic financial statements. It requires that every transaction be reflected in equal and offsetting entries to a corporation's accounting records. For example, if a corporation obtains a bank loan for $10,000, two accounting changes have occurred, and each must be accounted for on the corporation's balance sheet. First, the balance in the corporation's cash account has increased by $10,000. Second, the balance in the corporation's liabilities, under notes payable, has increased by $10,000. The two entries are offsetting, ensuring that the balance sheet *balances*. Similarly, if a corporation then buys a used forklift for $5,000, two accounting changes must be made. First, the balance in the corporation's cash account must be reduced by $5,000. Second, a new asset account, equipment, must be created, or an existing equipment account increased, in the amount of $5,000. Again, the offsetting entries balance each other. In the first example, new debt on the liability side of the balance sheet results in a corresponding increase on the asset side of the balance sheet. In the second example, one type of asset, cash, was simply converted to a different type of asset, equipment, both on the asset side of the balance sheet. In both examples, the double-entry bookkeeping methodology ensured that the corporation's financial statements would balance.

3.   Balance Sheets

The balance sheet is a basic accounting statement that provides a financial photograph of a business at a particular point in time, generally at year-end. Balance sheets have three sections, Assets, Liabilities, and Shareholders' Equity. Assets, including cash and other property, generally listed at historical cost, are set forth on the left-hand side of the balance sheet under the heading, Assets. Liabilities, including bank loans, trade debts, and other liabilities, are set forth at the top of the right-hand side of the balance sheet under the heading, Liabilities. Shareholders' Equity, which includes the amounts the shareholders have invested in a corporation's equity securities, as well as any retained earnings, is set forth on the right-hand side of the balance sheet below the Liabilities section. The Shareholders' Equity section must always equal the difference between the assets total on the left-hand side and the liabilities total on the upper right-hand side. This difference is the corporation's equity, often referred to as net worth.

The fundamental balance sheet equation is Assets (A) equals Liabilities (L) and Shareholders' Equity (E) or $A = L + E$. By definition, the left- and right-hand sides of the balance sheet must always balance. To illustrate balance sheet construction, we can utilize a fictional, but typical, start-up company. Joan Pitt and Kent Coltex have formed Colorado Consultations, Inc. to provide business management advice. Pitt invested $100,000 in cash and an additional $50,000 in-kind through the contribution of computer and telephone equipment valued in that amount. Coltex invested $50,000 in cash and an additional $100,000 in-kind through the transfer of improved real estate to be used as the corporate offices. Pitt and Coltex each received 100 shares of the corporation's authorized 300 shares. The asset side of the corporation's balance sheet would reflect $150,000 in the cash account, $50,000 in the equipment account and $100,000 in the real estate account, totaling $300,000. The liability and shareholders' equity side of the balance sheet would reflect $0.00 in liabilities and $300,000 in shareholders equity. If the corporation then borrowed $100,000 from a bank to finance a marketing campaign, $100,000 would be booked under liabilities, as a note payable, on the right-hand side of the balance sheet, and $100,000 would be added to the cash account under assets on the left-hand side of the balance sheet. The following balance sheet reflects the effects of these hypothetical transactions:

Colorado Consultations, Inc.
Balance Sheet
As of December 31, 2007

Assets			Liabilities and Shareholders' Equity		
	Cash	$250,000	Liabilities		
				Notes Payable	$100,000
				Accounts Payable	0
	Equipment	50,000	Shareholders' Equity		
	Building	100,000		Stated Capital	300,000
				Earned Surplus	0
Total		$400,000	Total		$400,000

You should note that this hypothetical balance sheet *balances*, based on the fundamental equation discussed above, A = L + E. In addition, E = A − L: E = $400,000 (A) − $100,000 (L), or E = $300,000. Again, this hypothetical balance sheet presents a static, one point in time, financial photograph reflecting the sum of corporate financial activity as of its date.

4. Income Statements

The income statement is a basic accounting statement that provides a view of the corporation's financial operations over a period of time, generally a quarter or year, rather than at one particular point in time. In effect, it is more like a documentary than a photograph. Income statements have three sections, Revenues, Expenses, and Net Income (or Net Loss), with the latter reflecting the difference between the amounts of revenues and expenses. Revenues are the assets, cash or in-kind, received by the corporation in exchange for its goods or services. Expenses are the costs or assets that the corporation has used in producing the revenues. Net Income (Net Loss) simply states the difference between the corporation's revenues and its expenses. To illustrate the construction of the income statement, we can return to our fictional start-up company, Colorado Consultations, Inc. Let's assume that during the corporation's first three months of operations, it received $35,000 in revenues for its consulting services and $5,000 in interest paid on its cash on hand. During that same period, its expenses included $3,000 for utilities, $500 for insurance, $1,500 for entertainment, and $5,000 for office supplies, including marketing brochures. The following income statement reflects these revenues and expenses in the operations of the corporation during the subject period:

Colorado Consultations, Inc.
Income Statement
For the Quarter Ending March 31, 2008

Revenues:		
Services	$35,000	
Investments	5,000	
Total Revenues		$40,000
Expenses:		
Utilities	$ 3,000	
Insurance	500	
Entertainment	1,500	
Supplies	5,000	
Total Expenses		$10,000
Net Income Before Taxes		$30,000

Although this income statement is quite elemental, it is illustrative of corporate businesses generally, from the smallest closely held corporations to publicly held *Fortune* 500 companies.

NOTES AND QUESTIONS

1. Could you update the hypothetical Colorado Consulting, Inc.'s balance sheet to March 31, 2008, using its income statement as of that date? What additional information, if any, would be required?

2. Note that the hypothetical Colorado Consulting, Inc.'s income statement reflects the *cash basis* of accounting, rather than the *accrual basis* of accounting. The cash basis of accounting recognizes or books revenues and expenses in the accounting period in which the cash revenues are received or the expenses are paid. This is done even where certain revenues and expenses are prepaid for goods and services to be provided in other accounting periods. The accrual basis of accounting attempts to match revenues and expenses to the accounting period to which they pertain through the process of accrual and deferral. An accrual of revenues occurs when revenues are recognized in the period that the services were performed even if the bill for those services has not yet been paid. A deferral of revenues occurs when cash paid in advance of performance is not recognized as revenue until the services are actually performed. Accrual and deferral of expenses operate in the same manner. Most medium-sized and large businesses use the accrual method of accounting in constructing their income statements. This method tends to provide a more accurate view of the corporation's financial operations.

3. Suppose that the hypothetical Colorado Consulting, Inc.'s income statement reflects utilities expenses for the first *two* quarters of 2008 or $1,500 in prepaid utilities expense. If the corporation were using accrual basis accounting, the balance sheet would be adjusted to add an asset account, prepaid utilities. How would you adjust the income statement?

D.   DIVIDENDS AND OTHER DISTRIBUTIONS TO SHAREHOLDERS

1.   Introduction

The vast majority of corporations are closely held, having a small number of founding shareholders who typically serve as both directors and officers of the company. As officers, they are employees of the corporation and are paid salaries, often supplemented by bonuses, for their services. Shareholders who are not so employed by the corporation more than likely have income from other employment, other investments, or both, and similarly may have no additional need for monetary distributions from the corporation. Shareholders of closely held corporations generally prefer that the corporation retain its annual earnings and reinvest that capital in the enterprise. Since they may have no compelling need for corporate distributions, asset growth becomes their primary investment objective that will be reflected in the board of directors' distribution policy. The corporate distribution policy becomes more problematic when the relationships among the small group of shareholders begin to fracture. One or more of the founding shareholders may be terminated as corporate officers, and hence, be denied their reasonably expected salaries. And, of course, over time, the founding shareholders' shares may be devised or otherwise passed on to others who have no expectations of employment but who nevertheless would very much appreciate some periodic return on their ownership interests. Since no active market exists for the shares of closely held corporate securities, not to mention the existence of practical and regulatory barriers to their offer and sale, only a change in the corporation's distribution policy could provide a return on these investments. Consequently, tension develops, friction ensues, and litigation may be commenced. This section first addresses the types of distributions that corporations are typically empowered to make. It then explores the extent of the corporate board of directors' discretion in setting distribution policy. Finally, it explains the statutory and contractual limitations that have been designed to offer some protection to creditors against distributions to shareholders that would undermine the collectibility of the creditors' debt claims.

2. Basic Types of Distributions

Corporations, through action of their boards of directors, can distribute money or other assets in kind to shareholders through a number of mechanisms. The most commonly recognized distribution is the board's declaration of a dividend, normally payable in cash to shareholders who are shareholders of record as of a set record date. Technically, a dividend is a distribution of past or current earnings, but the term is frequently used in a more general sense to include all selective or pro rata distributions of corporate assets to shareholders. The board may also distribute corporate assets by effecting a redemption or by taking other action to enable the corporation to repurchase its own shares from shareholders on a pro rata or selective basis. Distributions can also be made to shareholders in disguised forms, through the payment of excessive salaries, consulting fees, and other non-arm's length contractual payments, which can and often should be recharacterized as dividends. Finally, on liquidation, distributions are made on a pro rata basis to shareholders of all remaining corporate assets after the claims of creditors have been satisfied.

3. The Board of Directors' Discretion

Generally, the declaration of dividends and other distributions of corporate assets are within the board of directors' discretion, subject to any applicable statutory or contractual restrictions, as discussed later in this section. The board's exercise of this discretion is largely sacrosanct where publicly held corporations are concerned. However, courts have been far less deferential to boards of directors' discretion where those boards have refused to declare dividends to shareholders of closely held corporations. They have increasingly accorded credence to the *reasonable expectations* of shareholders, often through application of the fiduciary duty of loyalty or its subsumed duty of good faith.

GOTTFRIED v. GOTTFRIED
Supreme Court of New York
73 N.Y.S.2d 692 (1947)

CORCORAN, J.

This action was brought in the early part of 1945 by minority stockholders of Gottfried Baking Corporation (hereinafter called 'Gottfried'), to compel the Board of Directors of that corporation to declare dividends on its common stock. The defendants are Gottfried itself, its directors, and Hanscom Baking Corporation (hereinafter called 'Hanscom'), a wholly owned subsidiary of Gottfried. Gottfried is a closely held family corporation. All of its stockholders, with minor exceptions, are children of the founder of the business, Elias Gottfried, and their respective spouses.

Both corporations are engaged in the manufacture and sale of bakery products; Gottfried for distribution (sic) at wholesale, and Hanscom for distribution at retail in its own stores. . . .

At the end of 1946 the outstanding capitalization of Gottfried consisted of 4500 shares of 'A' stock, without nominal or par value, and 20,862 shares of common stock without par value. The 'A' stock is entitled to dividends of $8 per share before any dividends may be paid upon the common stock, as well as a further participation in earnings. At the end of 1944, immediately before this action was commenced, Gottfried also had outstanding preferred stock in the face amount of $79,000, and Hanscom had outstanding $86,000 face amount of preferred stock. The plaintiffs in the aggregate owned approximately 38% of each of these classes of securities. The individual defendants owned approximately 62 per cent.

From 1931 until 1945 no dividends had been paid upon the common stock, although dividends had been paid regularly upon the outstanding preferred stock and intermittently upon the 'A' stock. There seems to be no question with respect to the policy of the Board of Directors in not declaring dividends prior to 1944. An analysis of the financial statements of the corporation shows a net working capital deficit at the end of 1941, in which year a consolidated loss of $109,816 had been incurred. Moreover, until the end of 1943 the earned surplus was relatively small in relation to the volume of business done and the growing requirements of the business.

Although the action was brought in the early part of 1945 to compel the declaration of dividends upon the common stock, dividends actually were declared and paid upon said stock in 1945, and subsequently. The purpose of the action now, therefore, is to compel the payment of dividends upon the common stock in such amount as under all the circumstances is fair and adequate.

The action is predicated upon the claim that the policy of the Board of Directors with respect to the declaration of dividends is animated by considerations other than the best welfare of the corporations or their stockholders. The plaintiffs claim that bitter animosity on the part of the directors, who own the controlling stock, against the plaintiff minority stockholders, as well as a desire to coerce the latter into selling their stock to the majority interests at a grossly inadequate price, and the avoidance of heavy personal income taxes upon any dividends that might be declared, have been the motivating factors that have dominated the defendants. Plaintiffs contend, moreover, that the defendants, by excessive salaries, bonuses and corporate loans to themselves or some of them, have eliminated the immediate need of dividends in so far as they were concerned, while at the same time a starvation dividend policy with respect to the minority stockholders-not on the payroll-operates designedly to compel the plaintiffs to sacrifice their stock by sale to the defendants.

There is no essential dispute as to the principles of law involved. If an adequate corporate surplus is available for that purpose, directors may not withhold the declaration of dividends in bad faith. But the mere existence of an adequate corporate surplus is not sufficient to invoke court action to compel such a dividend. There must also be bad faith on the part of the directors. . . .

There are no infallible distinguishing earmarks of bad faith. The following facts are relevant to the issue of bad faith and are admissible in evidence: intense hostility of the controlling faction against the minority; exclusion of the minority from employment by the corporation; high salaries, or bonuses or corporate loans made to the officers in control; the fact that the majority group may be subject to high personal income taxes if substantial dividends are paid; the existence of a desire by the controlling directors to acquire the minority stock interests as cheaply as possible. But if they are not motivating causes they do not constitute 'bad faith' as a matter of law.

The essential test of bad faith is to determine whether the policy of the directors is dictated by their personal interests rather than the corporate welfare. Directors are fiduciaries. Their cestui que trust comprises the corporation and the stockholders as a body. Circumstances such as those above mentioned and any other significant factors, appraised in the light of the financial condition and requirements of the corporation, will determine the conclusion as to whether the directors have or have not been animated by personal, as distinct from corporate, considerations.

The court is not concerned with the direction which the exercise of the judgment of the Board of Directors may take, provided only that such exercise of judgment be made in good faith. It is axiomatic that the court will not substitute its judgment for that of the Board of Directors.

It must be conceded that closely held corporations are easily subject to abuse on the part of dominant stockholders, particularly in the direction of action designed to compel minority stockholders to sell their stock at a sacrifice. But close corporation or not, the court will not tolerate directorate action designed to achieve that or any other wrongful purpose. Even in the absence of bad faith, however, the impact of dissension and hostility among stockholders falls usually with heavier force in a closely held corporation. In many such cases, a large part of a stockholder's assets may be tied up in the corporation. It is frequently contemplated by the parties, moreover, that the respective stockholders receive their major livelihood in the form of salaries resulting from employment by the corporation. If such employment be terminated, the hardship suffered by the minority stockholder or stockholders may be very heavy. Nevertheless, such situations do not in themselves form a ground for the interposition of a court of equity.

There is no doubt that in the present case bitter dissension and personal hostility have existed for a long time between the individual plaintiffs and defendants. The plaintiffs Charles Gottfried and Harold Gottfried have both been discontinued from the corporate payrolls.

It is true too that several of the defendants have in recent years received as compensation substantial sums. In the case of Maurice K. Gottfried this has taken the form of ten per cent of the gross annual profits of Hanscom before corporate income taxes. During the period from January 1, 1943 to December 21, 1946, he received, in addition to a fixed salary of $15,600, an aggregate sum of $220,528.91, or an average of $45,105.78 per annum. The evidence in this connection discloses, however, that he has been the chief executive officer of Hanscom since its acquisition by Gottfried in 1933. The stock of Hanscom had been purchased in 1933 at a cost of $10,000 plus the assumption of liabilities amounting to $18,000. At that time Hanscom had 12 retail stores, a basement bakery, and a volume of sales of around $300,000. By way of contrast, for the year 1945 its net sales aggregated $4,614,000. For the year 1946, they had increased to $5,907,500. The number of stores had grown to 63, and operations had been expanded from the Washington Heights district of Manhattan to all the boroughs of the City of New York except Richmond. . . .

Plaintiff Charles Gottfried testified that Benjamin Gottfried, one of the defendants, told him that he and the other minority stockholders would never get any dividends because the majority could freeze them out and that the majority had other ways than declaring dividends of getting money out of the companies. Benjamin Gottfried denied that he had ever made such statements. There is no evidence, moreover, that such statements were made by any of the other defendants. The court does not believe that this disputed testimony carries much weight upon the question of a concerted policy on the part of the directors to refrain from declaring dividends for the purpose of 'freezing out' the plaintiffs.

Nor does the evidence with respect to the financial condition of the corporation and its business requirements sustain the plaintiffs' claims. The action was started in the early part of 1945. The financial condition of Gottfried at the end of the immediately preceding year is of fundamental importance in determining the validity of plaintiffs' claim at the time that suit was brought. The consolidated balance sheet for the year ended December 30, 1944 discloses current assets of $1,055,844 against current liabilities of $468,438, or a working capital of $587,407. Of the current assets, cash represented $523,691 and inventory $357,347. The ratio of current assets to current liabilities at that time was, therefore, slightly above 2 to 1. The gross volume of business done in 1944 was $8,737,475. The net working capital, therefore, was less than 7 per cent of the volume of business transacted. The net earnings for this year were $174,415.28, somewhat less than those for the two preceding war years. The earned surplus was $867,141.

The evidence discloses that at the end of 1944 expenditures in the amount of approximately $564,220 were contemplated to be made, and actually were made in 1945 in addition to ordinary operating expenses and in addition to other normal use of working capital. This sum included the retirement of the then outstanding preferred stocks of Gottfried and Hanscom in the sum of $165,000. Since all the parties held these preferred stocks in the same ratio as they held Gottfried 'A' stock and common stock, each of the stockholders, including the plaintiffs, participated proportionately in the benefits of such retirement. After said retirement their respective pro rata interests in Gottfried were precisely the same as before these distributions were made. From this point of view the plaintiffs were in at least as good a position as a result of this preferred stock retirement as though dividends had been paid upon the common stock in the sum of $165,000, which is almost equivalent to the entire net earnings for the year 1944. It is noteworthy in this connection, moreover, that the retirement of the preferred stock was urged by both Charles and Harold Gottfried, two of the plaintiffs, at the annual meeting of the stockholders of Gottfried held on December 5, 1944. Harold went so far as to request that funds be borrowed from a bank in order to effect such retirement. These stockholders certainly cannot complain because a sum almost equivalent to the prior year's entire net income was defrayed, in accordance with their own request, in the form of retirement of preferred stock rather than by payment of dividends on the common stock.

Under these circumstances, it may not be said that the directorate policy regarding common stock dividends at the time the suit was brought was unduly conservative. It certainly does not appear to have been inspired by bad faith.

The testimony discloses that many general considerations affected the policy of the Board of Directors in connection with dividend payments. Some of the major factors were as follows: the recognition that earnings during the war years might be abnormal and not representative of normal earning capacity; the pressing need for heavy expenditures for new equipment and machinery, replacement of which had been impossible during the war years; heavy expenditures required to finance the acquisition and equipment of new Hanscom stores in harmony with the steady growth of the business; the increased initial cost of opening new stores because, under present conditions, it has been difficult to lease appropriate sites necessitating actual acquisition by ownership of locations; the erection of a new bakery for Hanscom at a cost of approximately $1,000,000 inasmuch as the existing plant is incapable of producing the requirements of Hanscom sales which are running at the rate of approximately

$6,000,000 per annum; unstable labor conditions with actual and threatened strikes; several pending actions involving large sums of money under the Federal Fair Labor Standards Act; a general policy of financing expansion through earnings requiring long-term debt.

The plaintiffs oppose many of these policies of expansion. There is no evidence of any weight to the effect that these policies of the Board of Directors are actuated by any motives other than their best business judgment. If they are mistaken, their own stock holdings will suffer proportionately to those of the plaintiffs. With the wisdom of that policy the court has no concern. It is this court's conclusion that these policies and the expenditures which they entail are undertaken in good faith and without relation to any conspiracy, scheme or plan to withhold dividends for the purpose of compelling the plaintiffs to sell their stock or pursuant to any other sinister design.

The plaintiffs have failed to prove that the surplus is unnecessarily large. They have also failed to prove that the defendants recognized the propriety of paying dividends but refused to do so for personal reasons.

The complaint is dismissed and judgment directed for the defendants.

DODGE v. FORD MOTOR CO.
[*See* Chapter 8, *infra*]

MILLER v. MAGLINE, INC.
Court of Appeals of Michigan
76 Mich. App. 284, 256 N.W.2d 761 (1977)

BEFORE DANHOF, C. J., AND BASHARA AND MAHER, JJ.

DANHOF, CHIEF JUDGE.

On December 27, 1967, plaintiffs, minority shareholders, brought this action to compel the declaration and payment of dividends and to recover allegedly excessive compensation paid to named corporate officers. [After trial], the chancellor concluded that a dividend should be declared, but denied the excess compensation claim, finding the compensation paid to defendant officers to have been reasonable. [The Chancellor] ordered defendant Magline's directors to declare and pay a dividend of $75 per share for the period of July 1, 1963 to June 30, 1968, dismissed plaintiffs' excessive compensation claim, and retained jurisdiction to determine whether dividends should be awarded for the period from July 1, 1968 to June 30, 1973. Magline has appealed from the dividend award and the chancellor's retention of jurisdiction. . . .

Plaintiff Miller and defendant Law incorporated Magline. Law has served as president to the present, but Miller is no longer a corporate officer. Within a few months after Magline's incorporation, plaintiff Thorpe joined the company as an officer and director. By 1959 defendants Schilling, Graves, Monroe, Mortenson, and See had joined the company. The board presently consists of plaintiffs Miller and Thorpe, Raymond G. Miller (plaintiff Miller's son), and the individual defendants Law, Schilling, See, Graves and Monroe.

Plaintiffs own approximately 41% of the 4,138 shares of Magline stock issued and outstanding; defendants own the remaining 59%. . . . By virtue of their majority holdings and executive offices, defendants control all aspects of corporate activity. . . .

Magline has experienced considerable success in the field of commercial and defense related applications of magnesium and related light metals. Up to the time of trial Magline had consistently shown a profit on its overall operations, but it had never paid a dividend. Instead, the board has adhered to the policy adopted in 1950 by Law, Miller, and Thorpe of compensating corporate managers by means of a low base salary coupled with an incentive bonus plan based on a percentage of earnings. The remaining profits were to be retained by the corporation to be used as working capital. This policy was satisfactory to all concerned so long as the principal shareholders were actively participating in management and sharing in the incentive bonus compensation plan.

In 1962, however, important changes occurred. Plaintiff Miller was seriously injured and thereafter ceased to play an active role in corporate management. In the same year, plaintiff Thorpe resigned as vice president of Magline. Both Thorpe and Miller continued as directors and shareholders of Magline, however.

On November 10, 1962, the board adopted resolutions confirming defendants Law, Monroe, See, Schilling, and Graves in their respective offices of president and general manager, vice president in charge of engineering, vice president in charge of sales, secretary, and treasurer and assistant secretary. Whereas previous resolutions had provided for employment "during the fiscal year," the 1962 resolutions provided for employment "during the fiscal year ending June 30, 1963 and until his successor be duly elected and qualify," thereby rendering annual resolutions unnecessary. The employment resolutions provided for low base salaries and fixed the incentive bonuses for Law, Monroe, See, and Graves at an aggregate of 23% of net earnings before taxes and profit sharing. . . . Because Miller and Thorpe were no longer officers, they were excluded from the incentive bonus program. . . .

As a result, the employment resolutions adopted at the 1962 meeting remained in effect until February, 1966. During that time corporate earnings, and hence incentive bonuses, increased dramatically. . . . These increases stemmed primarily from Magline's increased production under government defense procurement contracts during the Viet Nam War years.

Magline's earnings surplus increased from $459,710 to $2,492,156 during the period from 1963 to 1968.

At the February 19, 1966 meeting the board reduced the percentages by which the incentive bonuses of Law, Monroe, See, Graves, Mortenson, and Schilling were computed to an aggregate of 14 ½ % of net earnings before profit sharing and taxes. . . . The board rejected plaintiffs' motion to declare a $10 dividend at the October, 1966 meeting, and like motions at the 1967 and 1968 board meetings were also defeated.

Law testified that the fiscal years from 1964 through 1969 were the most profitable in Magline's history. In 1963 Magline had net income of $55,760 on gross sales of $2,024,901 with earned surplus of $226,620. In 1968, Magline had net income of $569,670 on gross sales of $10,429,988 with earned surplus of $2,492,156.

Plaintiffs alleged that in withholding a dividend defendants had violated the fiduciary duty which they owed, as majority stockholders and directors, to the minority stockholders, and that defendants' refusal to declare a dividend was an arbitrary, capricious, and unwarranted abuse of their discretion. In the landmark case on court-compelled dividends for closed corporations, *Dodge v. Ford Motor Co.*, 204 Mich. 459, 500, 170 N.W. 668, 682, 3 A.L.R. 413 (1919), the Court adopted the following statements:

> " 'It is a well-recognized principle of law that the directors of a corporation, and they alone, have the power to declare a dividend of the earnings of the corporation, and to determine its amount. 5 Am. & Eng. Enc. Law (1st Ed.), p. 725. Courts of equity will not interfere in the management of the directors unless it is clearly made to appear that they are guilty of fraud or misappropriation of the corporate funds, or refuse to declare a dividend when the corporation has a surplus of net profits which it can, without detriment to its business, divide among its stockholders, and when a refusal to do so would amount to such an abuse of discretion as would constitute a fraud, or breach of that good faith which they are bound to exercise towards the stockholders.'

Dodge v. Ford Motor Co., *supra*, at 500, 170 N.W. at 682, quoting *Hunter v. Roberts, Throp & Co.*, 83 Mich. 63, 71, 47 N.W. 131 (1890). Breach of this fiduciary duty amounts to a breach of trust, and has consistently been recognized in Michigan as a ground for court intervention. . . . The Courts have also been sensitive to the "special problems inherent in the close corporation, and have applied corporate doctrine accordingly." *Darvin v. Belmont Industries, Inc.*, 40 Mich. App. 672, 677, 199 N.W.2d 542, 544, 64 A.L.R.3d 349 (1972). In *Thompson v. Walker, supra*, 253 Mich. at 135, 234 N.W. at 147, the Court said, "It is especially true, where one man or family controls and dominates a corporation, that he, or they, must act in the utmost good faith in the control and management of the corporation as to minority stockholders.". . .

The chancellor concluded that plaintiffs were entitled to a dividend:

"It is our opinion that under all of the circumstances of the case, that the directors of the management group were placed in the impossible situation of trying to give an impartial answer to the determination as to whether dividends should be granted. They already were taking a profit distribution via a percentile of profits before taxes. Therefore, we deem it an untenable position to argue that non payment of dividends is justified on the basis that such a concept of profit distribution would imperil the continued well being of the corporation. If such retention of profits were indicated they should have been more diligent in seeing that distributions based upon percentage of profits also should be curtailed.

"We are of the opinion that a dividend should be declared for the years up to the time of the trial of this cause based upon the accumulated net undivided profits. To the extent that the management group, as directors, has adopted a non-dividend policy, we are of the opinion that it has defeated one of the major purposes of a profit corporation, that is, to accumulate profits and divide them amongst the corporate owners when that is reasonable and proper. Under the circumstances here, their participating in a distribution to them of those profits and a squirreling away of the balance to meet future needs is, in our opinion, inequitable in not giving consideration properly to the needs and requirements of all of the stockholders of the corporation."

It is apparent that the chancellor found for plaintiffs on the basis of their breach of fiduciary duty theory. Accordingly, the question presented is whether the chancellor's conclusion that defendants' actions constituted a breach of their fiduciary duties was clearly erroneous.

Defendants contend that a dividend is inappropriate in light of the evidence that the corporation had working capital shortages, particularly in view of the provisions of Magline's by-laws with regard to the declaration of dividends.[1]

. . .

Plaintiffs' expert testified that Magline had "a plethora of working capital, an overabundance of working capital," . . . and the chancellor correctly found that Magline has used "very little borrowed capital." The chancellor's finding that defendants' admitted nondividend policy defeated one of the major purposes of a profit corporation, the accumulation and distribution of profits to corporate owners, . . . and

---

[1] [14] The by-laws provide that the directors shall have power,

"Subject to any and all provisions and restrictions of the Articles of Incorporation or the laws of the State of Michigan, to declare dividends out of the net profits or earned surplus of the corporation at such time and in such amounts as the Directors may from time to time designate; provided, however, that nothing herein contained shall require the Directors to declare dividends from the net profits accruing to the corporation from time to time if, in the judgment of the Directors, such net profits should properly be retained for use as further working capital or to further the purposes of the corporation."

M.C.L.A. § 450.22; M.S.A. § 21.22, in effect at the time of trial, provided in part that "Nothing contained in this section shall prevent the directors of any corporation . . . from setting apart out of any of the funds of the corporation available for dividends a reserve or reserves for any proper purpose."

his conclusion that, in view of the handsome distributions to defendants under the incentive bonus plan, their argument that a dividend would imperil the corporation was untenable, are supported by the record. Such findings justified the chancellor's interference with the discretion entrusted to the directors under the by-laws and M.C.L.A. § 450.22; M.S.A. § 21.22, in effect at the time of trial. *See Dodge v. Ford Motor Co., supra*, 204 Mich. at 507, 170 N.W. 668. The company's by-laws cannot be used as a shield behind which breaches of the directors' fiduciary duty to the stockholders can be carried on with impunity. Our review of the record satisfies us that a dividend is not only "possible as a business proposition," but will also be made out of a "plain and abundant surplus."

. . .

Defendant next contends that a dividend should not have been declared because there was testimony predicting losses for the fiscal year ending in 1970. In *Barrows v. J.N. Fauver Co., supra*, 280 Mich. at 556, 274 N.W. at 327, the Court said that "relief, particularly as to distribution of surplus, (must) be based upon present, actual and probable future conditions and needs of the company, and it cannot be resolved back to a situation which no longer exists." The chancellor observed:

> "So long as the corporation continues to be successful it is suggested that the earnings and profits retained are needed for the corporation, that they are not going to waste, but that the corporation will be able to use them. On the other hand, it is suggested to us that the future is bleak and that there will come a time when the corporation will not be able to earn a profit and that it will need all of its accumulated profits to meet the needs of the lean years. As the Plaintiffs ask, when if ever will a return be made to stockholders?"[2]

Defendant also claims that the cyclical and highly competitive nature of Magline's government contract business rendered a dividend inappropriate. The chancellor considered this factor, . . . along with the possibility of future losses, and, balancing these reasons for concern about the company's future against defendants' participation in the handsome incentive distributions, concluded that a dividend should be decreed. We find no abuse of the chancellor's discretion in this regard. Nor did the chancellor err in ordering a dividend despite evidence that the corporation's failure to do so was motivated in part by its sense of community responsibility to the "depressed" area where Magline conducts its operations, a factor which the chancellor also considered. A sense of community responsibility, however laudable, cannot justify the withholding of dividends that otherwise ought to be declared. *Dodge v. Ford Motor Co., supra*, 204 Mich. at 504–507, 170 N.W. 668.

Similarly without merit are defendant's contentions that the chancellor failed to relate the amount of the dividend to specific financial information for any single fiscal year, and that the dividend award was therefore arbitrary. Plaintiffs relied on defendants' own financial statements to establish the amount of earned surplus available for distribution, and defendant did not dispute the accuracy of its own figures. . . . Adopting these figures, the chancellor found that the book value of Magline stock was $2,725,246 in 1968, and that of this $2,492,156 represented earned surplus, equivalent to approximately $600 per share. Noting that defendants had received an average of $196,000 per year in salary and bonuses over the base period from 1958 to 1968, during which sales increased six times, book value four times, and net income before taxes more than 41 times, and taking into consideration that "no prior distribution had been made or was contemplated by the management group," the chancellor found that "distribution of a substantial portion of the retained earnings would be unwarranted." He concluded that "the history of the corporation and all of its surrounding circumstances warrant a

---

[2] [24] Defendants Law and Schilling could not foresee a time when a dividend might be paid.

dividend distribution of $75.00 per share." There is no precise formula for computing a dividend; in each case the amount must be determined with regard to all of the relevant circumstances. *See Dodge v. Ford Motor Co., supra*, 204 Mich. at 508–509, 170 N.W. 668. Our review of the chancellor's discursive opinion satisfies us that he did in fact consider all such circumstances in arriving at his determination, and we find no abuse of his discretion.

. . .

The chancellor retained jurisdiction to determine whether an additional dividend should be awarded for the period from July 1, 1968 to June 30, 1973, provided plaintiffs filed a petition for such purpose within 90 days after the decree entered. Plaintiffs did so, and defendant now contends that the chancellor erred in retaining jurisdiction.

We recognize that courts are, and should be, most reluctant to interfere with the business judgment and discretion of the directors in the conduct of corporate affairs. Here, however, the chancellor has found that the defendant board members were in a position in which it was "impossible" for them to give "an impartial answer to the determination as to whether dividends should be granted." The facts of the instant case present a study in the oppression of minority shareholders of a closed corporation by the majority, see 2 O'Neal, *supra*, at s 8.07, p. 44, s 8.08, pp. 58–60, and it was not improper for the chancellor to observe that the circumstances that led him to conclude that the dividend should be ordered remained unchanged at the time he entered his decree. The shape of equitable relief is not of necessity controlled by the prayer; it is fashioned by the chancellor according to the conditions and equities existing at the time the decree is made. . . .

The decree is affirmed.

NOTES AND QUESTIONS

1. Do you agree with the Michigan Court of Appeals' decision in *Miller v. Magline, Inc.* to compel the declaration and payment of dividends or do you believe the court should have deferred to the business judgment of the corporation's board of directors?

2. *Miller v. Magline, Inc.* is one of many cases in the last several decades that have developed special common law protection for shareholders in closely held corporations. Courts have generally recognized that corporate shareholders are in a fiduciary relationship, and, accordingly, have fiduciary duties to each other in addition to any fiduciary duties they may owe to the corporation as directors, officers, employees, or majority shareholders. The fiduciary duties of these shareholders to each other are analogous of those owed by general partners to each other in partnerships. With increasing frequency, these shareholders often pursue claims for breach of fiduciary duty in order to reform the distribution policies of closely held corporations to better satisfy their expectations. In addition, these shareholders also pursue actions for involuntary dissolution on grounds that continuing failure to pay dividends constitutes a form of oppression. See Chapter 9, Problems in Closely Held Corporations, for a more thorough discussion of distribution issues that arise in the closely held corporation context.

4. Limitations on Corporate Distributions Under Corporate Statutes

a. Policies Supporting Limitations

Distributions by the corporation to its shareholders, whether through dividends, share repurchases, or other methods, obviously could create serious concerns for trade creditors, banks, and others who have extended credit to the business. When the business is operated in the general partnership form, these creditors may be somewhat less concerned because they can also pursue the general partners individually, based on those partners' unlimited personal liability. The corporate debtor's shareholder-owners have limited liability, and, unless they have personally cosigned or guaranteed the debts, generally have no liability to the corporate creditors. In the closely held corporation context, where the shareholders may also be the directors and officers, it is quite conceivable that the corporate debtor could distribute to its shareholders the total amount of their investment, and, even worse, the funds borrowed by the corporation from its creditors. Moreover, once the shareholders have been given back their original investment, they may have less incentive, as corporate officers and directors, to manage the business effectively with appropriate avoidance of unreasonable risks. Indeed, they may take the money and run, sometimes referred to metaphorically as "jumping ship," leaving the other suppliers of corporate capital adrift on stormy seas. In any event, the corporation, its assets having been substantially dissipated through distribution to its shareholder-owners, would be unable to satisfy the claims of its creditors. The creditors, in turn, would have no viable remedy. Corporate statutes imposing restrictions upon corporate distributions to shareholders were enacted in response to these concerns. As you review the various types of statutory restrictions, you should consider whether any of them provide meaningful protection to creditors.

b.   Balance Sheet or Capital Impairment Restrictions

The balance sheet or capital impairment limitation reflects the traditional statutory approach followed in addressing creditor concerns about corporate distributions to shareholders. This approach is exemplified by the Delaware General Corporation Law §§ 160 and 170(a), addressing share repurchases and dividends, respectively. In essence, the Delaware corporate provisions state that distributions generally cannot exceed the amount of the corporation's *surplus*. As you will recall from the discussion of equity securities, *shareholders' equity* or *net worth* is the amount of the difference between total assets and total liabilities. In turn, shareholders' equity has three primary components that are generally set forth as accounts on the corporate balance sheet. The first is *stated capital*, which is the arbitrarily set par value, if any, and an amount arbitrarily allocated by the board to the stated capital account. Under the Delaware provisions, it is this category of shareholders' equity that provides the equity cushion for creditors — it cannot be *impaired* by distributions. The second component of shareholders' equity is *paid-in surplus*, which is the consideration paid for the shares in excess of stated capital. The third component is *earned surplus*, which is the amount of earnings from operations retained by the corporation. The sum of these last two components constitutes the *surplus* available for distribution under Delaware's balance sheet approach. As set forth in the Delaware statute, the "surplus" available for distributions is "the excess, if any, at any given time, of the net assets of the corporation [shareholders' equity] over the amount so determined to be [stated] capital." DEL. GEN. CORP. LAW § 154. The obvious weakness in this approach is that the "capital" referred to does not represent the total consideration paid by the shareholders for their shares, but some fractional amount of that investment arbitrarily designated as capital in the corporation's articles of incorporation, or, if the shares have no par value, some fractional amount arbitrarily determined by the board of directors. The board of directors makes this arbitrary decision under Delaware law to avoid the statute's default provision that would otherwise designate as stated capital all consideration paid for the shares. For example, if 1,000 shares were issued, without par, for $1,000 each, or, for total consideration of $1,000,000, the board of directors could allocate $1,000 to stated capital and, thus would provide virtually none of the protection to creditors ostensibly afforded by the balance sheet approach.

c. Earned Surplus Restrictions

The earned surplus approach was followed in an earlier version of the Model Business Corporation Act and has been incorporated into many state corporation statutes. This approach provides that a corporation may make distributions out of its *earned surplus*, which refers to the sum of its net profits and gains over the years, less its losses and prior distributions to shareholders. In other words, statutes following this approach ostensibly restricted distributions to the third component of shareholders' equity, earned surplus, as opposed to the balance sheet approach that allowed both paid-in surplus and earned surplus to be utilized for distributions. However, the prior version of the Model Act also permitted dividends to be paid out of capital surplus, the functional equivalent of paid-in capital, if expressly authorized by a company's articles of incorporation. Consequently, both surplus components of shareholders' equity could be used for distributions after all. In the end, the balance sheet and earned surplus approach converged, providing only illusory protection to creditors.

d. Solvency Restriction

The current version of the Model Business Corporation Act abandons both the balance sheet and the earned surplus approaches. Instead, it follows a *double solvency* test that prohibits distributions if their payment would render the corporation insolvent under the *equity* or *bankruptcy* definitions of the term. The equitable concept of insolvency turns on whether a corporation is able to pay its debts as they become due. The bankruptcy concept of insolvency is based on whether a corporation's assets at least equal the amount of its liabilities. Under the Model Act, a corporation may not make a distribution to its shareholders if, after giving it effect, the corporation would not be able to pay its debts in the usual course of business or the corporation's total assets would be less than the sum of its liabilities (as well as any liquidation preferences). MBCA § 6.40(c). In other words, the Model Act permits a corporation to make distributions to its shareholders of all three components of its shareholders' equity: stated capital, paid-in surplus, and earned surplus, leaving no remaining equity cushion for the protection of its creditors.

5. Director Liability for Improper Distributions

Most state corporate statutes set forth specific provisions imposing direct personal liability on directors who voted for or assented to an improper distribution. However, strict liability is not imposed. The Model Business Corporation Act requires the party asserting liability to establish that the directors did not comply with the directors' statutory standards of conduct, including good faith and due care. Moreover, the statute further protects directors by protecting their good faith reliance on reports from corporate officers and employees, lawyers and accountants, and board committees. MBCA §§ 8.33, 8.30. Corporate statutes often provide directors who are held liable a right of contribution from other directors who voted for or assented to the improper distribution. *See, e.g.*, MBCA § 8.33(b)(1) and DEL. GEN. CORP. LAW § 174(b). In addition, directors may also be permitted to obtain recoupment from each shareholder who received the distribution with knowledge of its illegality. *See, e.g.*, MBCA § 8.33(b)(2); N.Y. BUS. CORP. LAW § 719(d). In any event, directors of corporations that are insolvent or near insolvent, the so-called zone of solvency, should exercise caution before making any transfer of corporate assets. Indeed, their decisions may be subjected to heightened scrutiny without the protection traditionally afforded by the business judgment rule. *See, e.g.*, Richard M. Cieri & Michael J. Riela, *Protecting Directors and Officers of Corporations That Are Insolvent or in the Zone of Insolvency: Important Considerations, Practical Solutions*, 2 DEPAUL BUS. & COMM. L.J. 295 (2004).

KLANG v. SMITH'S FOOD & DRUG CENTERS, INC.
Supreme Court of Delaware
702 A.2d 150 (1997)

BEFORE VEASEY, C.J., WALSH, HOLLAND, HARTNETT AND BERGER, JJ., constituting the Court en Banc.

VEASEY, CHIEF JUSTICE:

This appeal calls into question the actions of a corporate board in carrying out a merger and self-tender offer. Plaintiff in this purported class action alleges that a corporation's repurchase of shares violated the statutory prohibition against the impairment of capital. . . .

No corporation may repurchase or redeem its own shares except out of "surplus," as statutorily defined, or except as expressly authorized by provisions of the statute not relevant here. Balance sheets are not, however, conclusive indicators of surplus or a lack thereof. Corporations may revalue assets to show surplus, but perfection in that process is not required. Directors have reasonable latitude to depart from the balance sheet to calculate surplus, so long as they evaluate assets and liabilities in good faith, on the basis of acceptable data, by methods that they reasonably believe reflect present values, and arrive at a determination of the surplus that is not so far off the mark as to constitute actual or constructive fraud.

We hold that, on this record, the Court of Chancery was correct in finding that there was no impairment of capital and there were no disclosure violations. Accordingly, we affirm.

Facts

Smith's Food & Drug Centers, Inc. ("SFD") is a Delaware corporation that owns and operates a chain of supermarkets in the Southwestern United States. Slightly more than three years ago, Jeffrey P. Smith, SFD's Chief Executive Officer, began to entertain suitors with an interest in acquiring SFD. At the time, and until the transactions at issue, Mr. Smith and his family held common and preferred stock constituting 62.1% voting control of SFD. Plaintiff and the class he purports to represent are holders of common stock in SFD.

On January 29, 1996, SFD entered into an agreement with The Yucaipa Companies ("Yucaipa"), a California partnership also active in the supermarket industry. Under the agreement, the following would take place:

> (1) Smitty's Supermarkets, Inc. ("Smitty's"), a wholly-owned subsidiary of Yucaipa that operated a supermarket chain in Arizona, was to merge into Cactus Acquisition, Inc. ("Cactus"), a subsidiary of SFD, in exchange for which SFD would deliver to Yucaipa slightly over 3 million newly issued shares of SFD common stock;

> (2) SFD was to undertake a recapitalization, in the course of which SFD would assume a sizable amount of new debt, retire old debt, and offer to repurchase up to fifty percent of its outstanding shares (other than those issued to Yucaipa) for $36 per share; and

> (3) SFD was to repurchase 3 million shares of preferred stock from Jeffrey Smith and his family.

SFD hired the investment firm of Houlihan Lokey Howard & Zukin ("Houlihan") to examine the transactions and render a solvency opinion. Houlihan eventually issued a report to the SFD Board replete with assurances that the transactions would not endanger SFD's solvency, and would not impair SFD's capital in violation of 8 Del. C. § 160. On May 17, 1996, in reliance on the Houlihan opinion, SFD's Board determined that there existed sufficient surplus to consummate the transactions, and enacted a resolution proclaiming as much. On May 23, 1996, SFD's stockholders voted to approve the transactions, which closed on that day. The self-tender offer was oversubscribed, so SFD repurchased fully fifty percent of its shares at the offering price of $36 per share.

Disposition in the Court of Chancery

This appeal came to us after an odd sequence of events in the Court of Chancery. On May 22, 1996, the day before the transactions closed, plaintiff Larry F. Klang filed a purported class action in the Court of Chancery against Jeffrey Smith and his family, various members of the SFD Board, Yucaipa, Yucaipa's managing general partner Ronald W. Burkle, Smitty's and Cactus. . . . [Plaintiff] contended that the stock repurchases violated 8 Del. C. § 160[3] by impairing SFD's capital. . . .

The Court of Chancery heard plaintiff's motion to have the transactions rescinded, and released a Memorandum Opinion dismissing plaintiff's claims in full. . . .

Plaintiff's Capital-Impairment Claim

A corporation may not repurchase its shares if, in so doing, it would cause an impairment of capital, unless expressly authorized by Section 160. . . . A repurchase impairs capital if the funds used in the repurchase exceed the amount of the corporation's "surplus," defined by 8 Del. C. § 154 to mean the excess of net assets over the par value of the corporation's issued stock.[4]

Plaintiff asked the Court of Chancery to rescind the transactions in question as violative of Section 160. As we understand it, plaintiff's position breaks down into two analytically distinct arguments. First, he contends that SFD's balance sheets constitute conclusive evidence of capital impairment. He argues that the negative net worth that appeared on SFD's books following the repurchase compels us to find a violation of Section 160. Second, he suggests that even allowing the Board to "go behind the balance sheet" to calculate surplus does not save the transactions from violating Section 160. In connection with this claim, he attacks the SFD Board's off-balance-sheet method of calculating surplus on the theory that it does not adequately take into account all of SFD's assets and liabilities. Moreover, he argues that the May 17, 1996 resolution of the SFD Board conclusively refutes the Board's claim that revaluing the corporation's assets gives rise to the required surplus. We hold that each of these claims is without merit.

SFD's balance sheets do not establish a violation of 8 Del. C. § 160

In an April 25, 1996 proxy statement, the SFD Board released a pro forma balance sheet showing that the merger and self-tender offer would result in a deficit to surplus on SFD's books of more than $100 million. A balance sheet the SFD Board issued

---

[3] [1] Section 160(a) provides:

(a) Every corporation may purchase, redeem, receive, take or otherwise acquire, own and hold, sell, lend exchange, transfer or otherwise dispose of, pledge, use and otherwise deal in and with its own shares; provided, however, that no corporation shall:

(1) Purchase or redeem its own shares of capital stock for cash or other property when the capital of the corporation is impaired or when such purchase or redemption would cause any impairment of the capital of the corporation, except that a corporation may purchase or redeem out of capital any of its own shares which are entitled upon any distribution of its assets, whether by dividend or in liquidation, to a preference over another class or series of its stock, or, if no shares entitled to such a preference are outstanding, any of its own shares, if such shares will be retired upon their acquisition and the capital of the corporation reduced in accordance with §§ 243 and 244 of this title.

[4] [5] Section 154 provides, "Any corporation may, by resolution of its board of directors, determine that only a part of the consideration . . . received by the corporation for . . . its capital stock . . . shall be capital. . . . The excess . . . of the net assets of the corporation over the amount so determined to be capital shall be surplus. Net assets means the amount by which total assets exceed total liabilities. Capital and surplus are not liabilities for this purpose."

shortly after the transactions confirmed this result. Plaintiff asks us to adopt an interpretation of 8 Del. C. § 160 whereby balance sheet net worth is controlling for purposes of determining compliance with the statute.[5] Defendants do not dispute that SFD's books showed a negative net worth in the wake of its transactions with Yucaipa, but argue that corporations should have the presumptive right to revalue assets and liabilities to comply with Section 160.

Plaintiff advances an erroneous interpretation of Section 160. We understand that the books of a corporation do not necessarily reflect the current values of its assets and liabilities. Among other factors, unrealized appreciation or depreciation can render book numbers inaccurate. It is unrealistic to hold that a corporation is bound by its balance sheets for purposes of determining compliance with Section 160. Accordingly, we adhere to the principles of Morris v. Standard Gas & Electric Co.[6] allowing corporations to revalue properly its assets and liabilities to show a surplus and thus conform to the statute.

It is helpful to recall the purpose behind Section 160. The General Assembly enacted the statute to prevent boards from draining corporations of assets to the detriment of creditors and the long-term health of the corporation.[7] That a corporation has not yet realized or reflected on its balance sheet the appreciation of assets is irrelevant to this concern. Regardless of what a balance sheet that has not been updated may show, an actual, though unrealized, appreciation reflects real economic value that the corporation may borrow against or that creditors may claim or levy upon. Allowing corporations to revalue assets and liabilities to reflect current realities complies with the statute and serves well the policies behind this statute.

The SFD Board appropriately revalued corporate assets to comply with 8 Del. C. § 160.

Plaintiff contends that SFD's repurchase of shares violated Section 160 even without regard to the corporation's balance sheets. Plaintiff claims that the SFD Board was not entitled to rely on the solvency opinion of Houlihan, which showed that the transactions would not impair SFD's capital given a revaluation of corporate assets. The argument is that the methods that underlay the solvency opinion were inappropriate as a matter of law because they failed to take into account all of SFD's assets and liabilities. In addition, plaintiff suggests that the SFD Board's resolution of May 17, 1996 itself shows that the transactions impaired SFD's capital, and that therefore we must find a violation of 8 Del. C. § 160. We disagree, and hold that the SFD Board revalued the corporate assets under appropriate methods. Therefore the self-tender offer complied with Section 160, notwithstanding errors that took place in the drafting of the resolution.

On May 17, 1996, Houlihan released its solvency opinion to the SFD Board, expressing its judgment that the merger and self-tender offer would not impair SFD's capital. Houlihan reached this conclusion by comparing SFD's "Total Invested Capital" of $1.8 billion — a figure Houlihan arrived at by valuing SFD's assets under the "market multiple" approach — with SFD's long-term debt of $1.46 billion. This comparison yielded an approximation of SFD's "concluded equity value" equal to $346 million, a figure clearly in excess of the outstanding par value of SFD's stock. Thus, Houlihan concluded, the transactions would not violate 8 Del. C. § 160.

Plaintiff contends that Houlihan's analysis relied on inappropriate methods to mask a violation of Section 160. Noting that 8 Del. C. § 154 defines "net assets" as "the amount by which total assets exceeds total liabilities," plaintiff argues that Houlihan's analysis is erroneous as a matter of law because of its failure to calculate "total assets" and "total liabilities" as separate variables. In a related argument, plaintiff claims that the analysis

---

[5] [6] *See, e.g., Wright v. Heizer Corp.*, 503 F. Supp. 802, 810 (N.D. Ill. 1980); *In re Kettle Fried Chicken of America, Inc.*, 513 F.2d 807, 811 (6th Cir. 1975).

[6] [7] *Morris v. Standard Gas & Electric Co.*, 63 A.2d 577 (Del. Ch. 1949).

[7] [8] *See Pasotti v. United States Guardian Corp.*, 156 A. 255, 257 (Del. Ch. 1931).

failed to take into account all of SFD's liabilities, i.e., that Houlihan neglected to consider current liabilities in its comparison of SFD's "Total Invested Capital" and long-term debt. Plaintiff contends that the SFD Board's resolution proves that adding current liabilities into the mix shows a violation of Section 160. The resolution declared the value of SFD's assets to be $1.8 billion, and stated that its "total liabilities" would not exceed $1.46 billion after the transactions with Yucaipa. As noted, the $1.46 billion figure described only the value of SFD's long-term debt. Adding in SFD's $372 million in current liabilities, plaintiff argues, shows that the transactions impaired SFD's capital.

We believe that plaintiff reads too much into Section 154. The statute simply defines "net assets" in the course of defining "surplus." It does not mandate a "facts and figures balancing of assets and liabilities" to determine by what amount, if any, total assets exceeds total liabilities.[8] The statute . . . does not require any particular method of calculating surplus, but simply prescribes factors that any such calculation must include. Although courts may not determine compliance with Section 160 except by methods that fully take into account the assets and liabilities of the corporation, Houlihan's methods were not erroneous as a matter of law simply because they used Total Invested Capital and long-term debt as analytical categories rather than "total assets" and "total liabilities."

We are satisfied that the Houlihan opinion adequately took into account all of SFD's assets and liabilities. Plaintiff points out that the $1.46 billion figure that approximated SFD's long-term debt failed to include $372 million in current liabilities, and argues that including the latter in the calculations dissipates the surplus. In fact, plaintiff has misunderstood Houlihan's methods. The record shows that Houlihan's calculation of SFD's Total Invested Capital is already net of current liabilities. Thus, subtracting long-term debt from Total Invested Capital does, in fact, yield an accurate measure of a corporation's net assets.

The record contains, in the form of the Houlihan opinion, substantial evidence that the transactions complied with Section 160. Plaintiff has provided no reason to distrust Houlihan's analysis. In cases alleging impairment of capital under Section 160, the trial court may defer to the board's measurement of surplus unless a plaintiff can show that the directors "failed to fulfill their duty to evaluate the assets on the basis of acceptable data and by standards which they are entitled to believe reasonably reflect present values."[9] In the absence of bad faith or fraud on the part of the board, courts will not "substitute [our] concepts of wisdom for that of the directors."[10] Here, plaintiff does not argue that the SFD Board acted in bad faith. Nor has he met his burden of showing that the methods and data that underlay the board's analysis are unreliable or that its determination of surplus is so far off the mark as to constitute actual or constructive fraud.[11] Therefore, we defer to the board's determination of surplus, and hold that SFD's self-tender offer did not violate 8 Del. C. § 160.

On a final note, we hold that the SFD Board's resolution of May 17, 1996 has no bearing on whether the transactions conformed to Section 160. The record shows that the SFD Board committed a serious error in drafting the resolution: the resolution states that, following the transactions, SFD's "total liabilities" would be no more than $1.46 billion. In fact, that figure reflects only the value of SFD's long-term debt. Although the SFD Board was guilty of sloppy work, and did not follow good corporate practices, it does not follow that Section 160 was violated. The statute requires only that

---

[8] [9] *See Farland v. Wills*, 1 DEL. J. CORP. L. 467, 475 (Del. Ch. 1975).

[9] [10] *Morris*, 63 A.2d at 582.

[10] [11] *Id.* at 583.

[11] [12] We interpret 8 Del. C. § 172 to entitle boards to rely on experts such as Houlihan to determine compliance with 8 Del. C. § 160. Plaintiff has not alleged that the SFD Board failed to exercise reasonable care in selecting Houlihan, nor that rendering a solvency opinion is outside Houlihan's realm of competence. Compare 8 Del. C. § 141(e) (providing that directors may rely in good faith on records, reports, experts, etc.).

there exist a surplus after a repurchase, not that the board memorialize the surplus in a resolution. The statute carves out a class of transactions that directors have no authority to execute, but does not, in fact, require any affirmative act on the part of the board. The SFD repurchase would be valid in the absence of any board resolution. A mistake in documenting the surplus will not negate the substance of the action, which complies with the statutory scheme.

The judgment of the Court of Chancery is affirmed.

6.   Shareholder Liability for Improper Distributions

Shareholders who have received distributions in violation of balance sheet or earned surplus restrictions are generally not liable to the corporation or creditors of the corporation so long as they had no knowledge of the distribution's illegality. However, under common law, the shareholder may be held liable to the extent of the distribution, without regard to fault, where the distribution was from an insolvent corporation. In effect, the shareholder has received funds impressed with a constructive trust for the benefit of creditors of an insolvent estate. *See, e.g., Woods v. National City Bank*, 24 F.2d 661 (2d Cir. 1928). Moreover, the Uniform Fraudulent Conveyance Act (UFTA) may provide an additional basis for liability. This statute treats as fraudulent any transfer without a reasonably equivalent exchange by a transferor who at the time was, or by virtue of the transfer became, insolvent. UFTA § 5. It also renders such transfers fraudulent where the transferor's assets were unreasonably small, given the nature of the transaction or business involved. UFTA § 4. Creditors of the corporation are given the right to avoid such fraudulent transfers to satisfy their claims and to attachment of assets and other collection remedies against the transferee's property. UFTA § 7. Moreover, these remedies can be exercised by a trustee in bankruptcy under federal bankruptcy laws. *See* 11 U.S.C.A. §§ 544(b), 548, and 541(a).

7.   Contractual Restrictions on Corporate Distributions

Given the illusory protections afforded creditors under state corporate law, it is understandable that those creditors with the power to do so have turned to contract law to protect themselves against potentially harmful distributions to the corporate debtors' shareholders. Although trade creditors are not usually positioned to exercise such power, it is quite common for institutional lenders to do so. Banks and other lending institutions often impose outright prohibitions or substantial limitations on the payment of dividends, share repurchases, and other forms of corporate distributions. Accordingly, in determining the propriety of any corporate distribution, it is critically important to review the corporation's loan agreements, trust indentures, underwriting agreements, and other agreements that could contain contractual restrictions on distributions. In addition, it is not uncommon for shareholders themselves, particularly preferred shareholders and investors in other debt or equity securities, to insist that provisions limiting corporate distributions to common shareholders be included in the corporation's articles or by-laws. As a practical matter, it should be noted that the restrictions on distributions discussed above are often supplemental to the creditor's security interests in corporate property and personal guarantees demanded by creditors from the corporate debtors' shareholders.

Chapter 7
LIMITATIONS ON LIMITED LIABILITY

A. INTRODUCTION

It is a well-settled principle of corporate law in this country that as a general proposition those who own stock in a corporation, either as individuals or enterprises, are not personally liable for the debts and obligations of the corporation. Considered one of the most attractive aspects of incorporation, shareholder limited liability affords corporations the growth potential and access to monetary resources required to compete in the marketplace while providing risk averse shareholders the protection necessary to invest without being personally subject to the company's creditors.

Limited liability is the status granted to businesses that file for and satisfy certain state law requirements. Generally, limited liability status is available to, for example, corporations, limited liability partnerships and limited liability companies. Shareholder limited liability serves to cap the monetary amount of an investor's risk exposure to the amount contributed by such shareholder in the enterprise; i.e., no personal liability for the investor. Phrased another way, an investor is only liable to the corporation's creditors up to the amount of his/her investment, including any unrealized gains or capital appreciation.

The principal reason for allowing limited liability is that it promotes capital formation by providing investors with the assurance that ordinarily only the assets voluntarily invested in the corporation will be available to corporate creditors and subject to the company's liabilities. From a public policy standpoint, limited liability encourages expansion, reduces the costs of monitoring managers or other shareholders, promotes the transferability of shares, and enables market prices to more accurately reflect information about the value of firms. Additionally, due to limited investor liability, a corporation's management will likely be more willing to take on certain ventures or make decisions that otherwise would be deemed too risky if unlimited personal liability was at stake.

Like almost every legal doctrine, there are exceptions to the general rule of limited shareholder liability. For example, criminal or civil liability may exist for shareholders, directors or officers who act improperly. The subject of this Chapter is another exception to the general rule of limited shareholder liability: an equitable doctrine known as "alter ego" or "piercing the corporate veil," in which courts impose personal liability on active shareholders of corporations for the debts of their corporations. Because of the potential for abuse created by shareholder limited liability, the judicial response has been to create the veil-piercing doctrine as an equitable mode of compensating claimants and holding the responsible shareholders personally liable. " 'Piercing the corporate veil' refers to the judicially imposed exception to this [limited liability] principle by which courts disregard the separateness of the corporation and hold a shareholder responsible for the corporation's action as if it were the shareholder's own."[1] When applying this doctrine, generally only active (and not passive) shareholders are at risk of personal liability.

As we examine the material in this Chapter, query whether a number of cases explored here would have been more successful if agency theory had been invoked, particularly in situations where a principal-agent relationship could have been shown.

---

[1] Thompson, *Piercing the Corporate Veil: An Empirical Study*, 76 CORNELL L. REV. 1036 (1991). The Empirical Study is discussed later in this Chapter. *See generally* A. PINTO & D. BRANSON, UNDERSTANDING CORPORATE LAW, 37–68 (2d ed. 2004); Millon, *Piercing the Corporate Veil, Financial Responsibility, and the Limits of Limited Liability*, 56 EMORY L.J. 1305 (2007); Morrissey, *Piercing All the Veils: Applying an Established Doctrine to a New Business Order*, 32 J. CORP. L. 530 (2007).

Note, moreover, that if an owner/shareholder engaged in the tortious conduct, such person would incur direct liability as a tortfeasor.

PROBLEMS

1. Jack, a sole proprietor, runs a small internet business out of his house selling vintage baseball memorabilia, including baseball cards, autographs and apparel, through websites like Ebay.com. He takes appropriate precautions to ensure the authenticity of each item he sells and his business has steadily increased over the last few years. However, after recently purchasing a baseball autographed by Mickey Mantle from Jack, one customer complained that it was fake, demanded a refund and threatened to sue Jack for fraud. Unbeknownst to Jack, the autograph turned out to be a forgery and he refunded the purchaser's money, narrowly averting a lawsuit. Up until this point Jack had taken no steps to avail himself of the protection of his state's business corporation laws and he is now worried that future business dealings may expose his family's personal assets, including his possessions and personal investments, to his business' creditors. Jack seeks your advice to help limit his personal liability and protect his personal assets from any future corporate creditors. In addition to increasing his memorabilia authentication procedures, Jack plans on incorporating his business under the laws of his state and would like to know what steps he needs to take in running his business to ensure that he is not personally liable for debts and liabilities of his company.

2. Jack's baseball memorabilia business, Jack's Inc., is now ten years old and it has grown to become one of the largest independent internet memorabilia businesses in the country. As a result, Jack has decided to sell his company to The On-Deck Company, Inc., one of the largest baseball card manufacturers in the country. As part of the purchase agreement, On-Deck agreed to assume all of Jack's Inc.'s present and future liabilities. After the acquisition, On-Deck decided to run Jack's Inc. as a wholly-owned subsidiary, with Jack's Inc. having no bank account and holding no shareholder or board of director meetings. Upon receipt by Jack's Inc. of revenue from the sale of memorabilia, such revenue was promptly placed into On-Deck's bank account. On-Deck dispersed half of Jack's vast inventory of valuable memorabilia to its other subsidiaries for sale to the public. On-Deck also purchased an insurance policy to cover all of Jack Inc.'s current and future liabilities, including foreseeable litigation costs. The insurance policy provided a maximum coverage of $3,000 per item with the maximum total coverage of $100,000 for all claims.

Six months after Jack sold his business to On-Deck, a group of plaintiffs instituted a lawsuit seeking $800,000 in damages against Jack's Inc., now a subsidiary of On-Deck, alleging multiple claims, including breach of contract, misrepresentation and fraud. The lawsuit also seeks to hold On-Deck and its other subsidiaries liable on an alter ego, single business enterprise, or piercing the corporate veil basis. It appears that while a vast majority of Jack's inventory was original and extremely valuable, one of the ways that Jack made a name for himself was by blatantly forging rare autographs and selling them as originals.

As a result of the threatened class action lawsuit, Jack's Inc. filed for bankruptcy. On-Deck and its wholly-owned subsidiaries have come to you, their outside corporate counsel, for advice on the likely effect of the lawsuit. Will the plaintiffs be able to pierce the corporate veil of Jack's Inc. and hold On-Deck and/or affiliates of On-Deck liable if Jack's Inc.'s assets are insufficient to cover the damages?

B.   GENERAL CHARACTERISTICS OF PIERCING THE CORPORATE VEIL

The rationalization for the veil piercing doctrine is that shareholder limited liability is a privilege of incorporation and, if abused, liability for wrongdoing should flow through the legally created veils to the culpable party, usually either an individual shareholder or related corporate entity. The foundation for veil-piercing is stated in the oft-quoted case of *United States v. Milwaukee Refrigerator Transit Co.*:

> [A] corporation will be looked upon as a legal entity as a general rule, and until sufficient reason to the contrary appears; but when the notion of legal entity is used to defeat public convenience, justify wrong, protect fraud, or defend crime, the law will regard the corporation as an association of persons.[2]

A favorite among litigators, the "piercing" doctrine is frequently invoked when privately-held corporations have assets that are insufficient to satisfy a claim or judgment. Although it is theoretically conceivable to pierce the corporate veil of publicly-held corporations, the doctrine has only been successfully invoked in the context of privately held corporations whose stock is owned by another business enterprise (which may be a publicly-held corporation) or whose stock is held by individual equity holders. The doctrine is almost entirely the manifestation of judge-made law and thus the inquiry into its application is a fact-based, case-by-case analysis. In fact, nearly all state corporation statutes avoid the veil-piercing doctrine altogether.[3]

While the number of veil-piercing cases is abundant, the justifications provided by courts for either piercing the veil or upholding shareholder limited liability vary by jurisdiction, are often inconsistent in analysis, and hard to predict in terms of the relative weight given to different factual determinations. However, two general factors are evident in nearly every instance in which the veil of a corporation is pierced: (1) domination or control by a shareholder, whether an individual or another corporate entity, over the subject corporation; and (2) some type of fraud, wrong or injustice. As will be seen in the following sections, the type of control and degree of harm needed to find personal shareholder liability varies depending on the context and type of case in which veil piercing is sought. As a result, practicing attorneys and law students alike often find that the doctrine of piercing the corporate veil may lead to uncertain results in application.[4]

The importance of limited liability for investors should not be overlooked in light of the relatively few instances in which shareholders may be held personally liable for corporate acts. However, as will be clear when considering the factors that lead to piercing the corporate veil, piercing the veil has proven an important tool in compensating injured plaintiffs who otherwise would be left without adequate recourse.[5]

C.   FACTORS TO PIERCE THE CORPORATE VEIL

When a court allows a plaintiff to pierce the corporate veil of a corporation (or other limited liability enterprise) and recover from the equity holders that own the subject enterprise, the court is placing the interests of creditors above those of the equity holders. As stated above, veil-piercing is largely a judge-made doctrine consisting of a fact-based inquiry in which its application and outcome may differ from case to case. As a result, there is not a step-by-step test with which to apply the doctrine and the factors relevant to piercing the corporate veil are not consistent in every case. While it appears

---

[2] United States v. Milwaukee Refrigerator Transit Co., 142 F. 247 (E.D. Wis. 1905).

[3] Model Bus. Corp. Act § 6.22(b) (providing that a shareholder may become personally liable for corporate debts "by reason of his own acts or conduct").

[4] *See* J. Cox & T. Hazen, Corporations §§ 7.01–7.09 (2d ed. 2003).

[5] *Id. See* A. Pinto & D. Branson, Understanding Corporate Law 66–67 (2d ed. 2004).

that the context in which the doctrine is invoked appears to matter when applying the following veil-piercing factors, courts that have pierced the veil of limited liability have typically found the presence of at least two (and often more) of the following factors discussed in this Section. Judges often require that multiple factors be proven because of the extreme consequence of lifting the limited liability enjoyed by shareholders. Exposing investors' personal assets to the claims of corporate creditors is a result that courts do not take lightly.[6] As will be evident in the case law discussed later in this Chapter, no single factor has proven to be uniformly determinative in allowing the corporate veil to be pierced. Depending on the particular situation in which veil piercing is sought, the following factors are often assigned varying significance.

1. Lack of Corporate Formalities

One of the most common factors discussed in veil piercing cases is whether the corporation exercised traditional corporate formalities and upheld the governing structure of the entity. Corporate formalities often include holding regular board and shareholder meetings, documenting meeting minutes, issuing stock certificates, electing officers and directors and documenting corporate transactions.[7] The absence of these fundamental corporate functions evinces a lack of respect for the corporate form and a mentality that a separate identity has not been implemented for the subject corporation. However, the lack of corporate formalities alone is rarely, if ever, sufficient to pierce the corporate veil and courts have generally required the presence of an equitable reason to find shareholder liability.[8]

Plaintiffs often advance arguments that the failure to observe corporate formalities is a prime example of shareholders using the corporation as their "alter ego" by disregarding their corporate obligations.[9] Additionally, by ignoring corporate procedures, third parties, depending on the circumstances, may be able to show that they were deceived as to the actual entity with whom they were dealing. When evidence of the lack of corporate formalities is coupled with proof of misrepresentation or undercapitalization, a greater likelihood exists that a court will rule in favor of piercing the corporate veil.[10]

In contrast, state statutes like the Texas Business Corporation Act, Art. 2.21, foreclose the lack of corporate formalities as a consideration in piercing the corporate veil. Article 2.21(A)(3) states:

> A holder of shares . . . shall be under no obligation to the corporation or to its obligees with respect to . . . any obligation of the corporation on the basis of the failure of the corporation to observe any corporate formality, including without limitation: (a) the failure to comply with any requirement of this Act or of the articles of incorporation or bylaws of the corporation; or (b) the failure to observe any requirement prescribed by this Act or by the articles of incorpo-

---

[6] *See* De Witt Truck Brokers, Inc. v. W. Ray Flemming Fruit Co., 540 F.2d 681, 683 (4th Cir. 1976) (stating that "power to pierce the corporate veil, though, is to be exercised 'reluctantly' and 'cautiously' "); Krivo Indus. Sup. Co. v. Nat'l Distillers & Chemical Corp., 483 F.2d 1098, 1102 (5th Cir. 1973) (concluding that the "corporate form . . . is not lightly disregarded, since limited liability is one of the principal purposes for which the law has created the corporation").

[7] J. COX & T. HAZEN, CORPORATIONS at § 7.04.

[8] *Id.* at §§ 7.23–7.25; *see also* Pepsi-Cola Metro. Bottling Co. v. Checkers, Inc., 754 F.2d 10 (1st Cir. 1985); K-Mart Corp. v. Knitjoy Mfg., 542 F. Supp. 1189 (E.D. Mich. 1982).

[9] *See* A. PINTO & D. BRANSON, UNDERSTANDING CORPORATE LAW 43–44 (2d ed. 2004).

[10] *See, e.g., De Witt Truck Brokers, Inc.*, 540 F.2d at 687 (concluding that "undercapitalization, coupled with disregard of corporate formalities, lack of participation on the part of the other stockholders, and the failure to pay dividends while paying substantial sums . . . to the dominant stockholder, all fitting into a picture of basic unfairness, has been regarded fairly uniformly to constitute a basis for an imposition of individual liability under the doctrine").

ration or bylaws for acts to be taken by the corporation, its board of directors, or its shareholders.[11]

2. Commingling of Corporate Affairs

Another factor that plays heavily into courts allowing a plaintiff to pierce the corporate veil is the failure to keep personal and corporate assets separate. When assets of the corporation and its owners become commingled, it may become difficult for third party creditors to identify the assets and liabilities of the corporation. Commingling may occur when, among other things, two corporate entities use the same bank accounts for business transactions, make monetary transfers to one another, or make cross-corporate loans. The commingling issue also may arise when two business enterprises share the same employees, office space and real or personal property. The rationale that the commingling of corporate affairs should lead to personal liability is based on the theory that creditors should have a clear idea which assets are going to be available to meet their claims and should not have to endure the risk that corporate assets will be used for personal reasons.[12] As seen by the cases that follow in this Chapter, commingling of corporate affairs is a common argument made by plaintiffs seeking to pierce the corporate veil.

The determination whether commingling of corporate assets exists to hold the parent responsible for the actions of the subsidiary is a factual analysis. To pierce the corporate veil in this context often requires the presence of misrepresentation, inadequate capitalization or fraud.[13] For example, in *American Trading and Production Corp. v. Fischbach & Moore*, the plaintiff sued both the parent and the subsidiary based on the mere instrumentality doctrine. The court found that the degree of commingling between the two entities was inadequate to pierce the corporate veil of the subsidiary:

> [A]ll four of the subsidiary's directors were also directors of the parent, and four of the Subsidiary's directors were also officers of the Parent. However, the corporations maintain separate offices and conduct separate directors' meetings. The financial books and records of the Subsidiary are maintained by its employees . . . [and] [t]he Subsidiary has its own bank accounts and negotiates its own loans . . . [and] these loans are evidenced by notes and . . . interest at the prime rate.[14]

As opposed to the parent-subsidiary context, commingling of corporate assets can also be a factor in piercing the corporate veil to hold individual owners liable for the actions of the corporation. When individual owners enlist corporate personnel and assets for their own personal benefit, commingling often occurs. Examples of commingling by individual owners are shareholders skimming off the corporate till, purchasing equipment or raw materials which the owners then sell to the corporation at a mark-up, receiving loans or making cash withdrawals from corporate accounts with no interest, utilizing corporate equipment for personal ventures, or requiring that company employ-

---

[11] Tex. Bus. Corp. Act Ann. art. 2.21.

[12] *See* NLRB v. W. Dixie Enterprises, 190 F.3d 1191 (11th Cir. 1999) (piercing the corporate veil because the owners of the company used personal checks to pay for corporate expenses, the corporation paid individual expenses and the entity failed to keep separate corporate records); *but see* Gardemal v. Westin Hotel Co., 186 F.3d 588 (5th Cir. 1999) (refusing to pierce the corporate veil when there was alleged inadequate capitalization and commingling of assets).

[13] *See* American Trading & Prod. Corp. v. Fischbach & Moore, Inc., 311 F. Supp. 412, 416 (N.D. Ill. 1970) (stating that "[s]ome element of unfairness, something akin to fraud or deception, or the existence of a compelling public interest must be present in order to disregard the corporate fiction").

[14] *American Trading & Prod. Corp.*, 311 F. Supp. at 414 (N.D. Ill. 1970).

ees complete personal tasks unrelated to their employment.[15] The case of *NLRB v. West Dixie Enterprises, Inc.*, in which the full opinion appears below, is one notable example in which individual personal liability was levied on this basis. In *West Dixie Enterprises*, individuals were held liable for corporate improprieties (discriminatory hiring practices) on a piercing theory where they used personal checks to pay for corporate expenses, the corporation paid certain individual expenses, and separate corporate records were not maintained.

The fact that a corporation and its assets are used to benefit its owners does not conclusively mean that piercing will occur and that shareholders will be personally liable. Nonetheless, to minimize this possibility, corporations and their owners should be careful to fully document their transactions with each other so as to create the impression that all dealings are at arms-length. To rebut or avoid commingling allegations, at a minimum corporations should maintain distinct corporate bank accounts, seek to minimize cross-utilization of corporate assets and employees, and document the purpose for and details of related party dealings.

3. Undercapitalization

Courts have accepted proof of the undercapitalization of a business as sufficient justification to pierce the corporate veil and hold the shareholders personally liable. The theory behind undercapitalization is that, if owners either initially incorporated or continued to run their business with capital levels insufficient to cover ordinary risks of loss inherent in the business, then the owners themselves should be personally liable for claims against the corporation. Authority for piercing the corporate veil based on insufficient corporate assets is seen from the following:

> It is coming to be recognized as the policy of the law that shareholders should in good faith put at the risk of the business unencumbered capital reasonably adequate for its prospective liabilities. If the capital is *illusory or trifling compared with the business to be done and the risks of loss, this is a ground for denying the separate entity privilege.*

H. BALLANTINE, CORPORATIONS 303 (rev. ed. 1946) (emphasis added).

However, as case law shows, inadequate capitalization alone is rarely sufficient to pierce the corporate veil of the subject corporation. One example involves the case of *Baatz v. Arrow Bar* in which the court refused to pierce the corporate veil even after explicitly finding evidence of significant undercapitalization.[17] The *Baatz* court discounted the fact that an uninsured restaurant was capitalized only with borrowed money in determining if the shareholders should be personally liable beyond the assets of the company. Nevertheless, when combined with other factors, a finding of undercapitalization is a significant factor in favor of veil-piercing.[18]

Like the other factors analyzed when determining if a corporate veil should be pierced, determining what exactly qualifies as undercapitalization is a case-by-case factual analysis. In addition, common problems exist in the undercapitalization analysis, including how foreseeable potential claims/losses are and how much capitalization is adequate. Also, with respect to tort claimants, most courts generally include proceeds from insurance policies carried by the corporation in the definition of capital when

---

[15]   *See* NLRB v. W. Dixie Enters., 190 F.3d 1191 (11th Cir. 1999).

[17]   Baatz v. Arrow Bar, 452 N.W.2d 138 (S.D. 1990).

[18]   *See* Bendix Home Sys. v. Hurston Enterprises, 566 F.2d 1039 (5th Cir. 1978) (finding undercapitalization only one of many factors that must be considered when disregarding the limited liability of a corporation); *but see* Minton v. Cavaney, 364 P.2d 473 (Cal. 1961) (representing the minority of decisions in which the court found undercapitalization alone sufficient to pierce the corporate veil). The *Minton v. Cavaney* decision is contained later in this Chapter.

determining capitalization levels.[19] Stated somewhat differently, a company's capital in the tort context includes not only traditional equity capital but also liability insurance coverage.

Many courts considering undercapitalization inquire into the occurrence of reasonably foreseeable losses and the corresponding magnitude of such losses as compared with the capital balances maintained to cover the foreseeable losses. Regardless of the tests articulated by different courts to determine the sufficiency of capitalization, the general crux of available precedent centers on the extent to which the enterprise is deemed to have operated with financial responsibility. As such, evident from the following case law, the amount of insurance maintained by the corporation and other precautions taken against risk of loss are relevant to the inquiry into the adequacy of capital.

4. Tort vs. Creditor

While public policy and numerous commentators argue that it should be far easier for a plaintiff to pierce the corporate veil of a corporation when alleging a tort rather than a breach of contract, the results of the Empirical Study by Professor Thompson (discussed below) evidence a different reality. The public policy argument follows that a voluntary creditor, one who purposefully deals with a corporation through a contract, chooses to deal with the corporation and has the opportunity to investigate the capitalization levels of the company. For example, in negotiating a contract, the contract claimant has the opportunity to bargain for protection in the event of inadequate capital by seeking personal guarantees from shareholders, seeking prohibition on the paying of dividends or other distributions, securing the debt against the company's physical assets or requiring the corporation to maintain certain levels of liquid assets. Thus, it is often argued that the absence of such provisions in the contract is indicative of the limits of the agreement negotiated between the parties, thereby resulting in the plaintiff assuming the risk of loss flowing from inadequate capitalization. If, however, the defendant, while negotiating the subject contract, made material misrepresentation that induced the plaintiff to enter the contract with lesser minimum capitalization protections (e.g., false financial statements provided to creditors), courts are more willing to pierce the corporate veil and attach liability to shareholders.[20]

Conversely, when a plaintiff becomes an involuntary creditor of a corporation because the corporation commits a tort, the tort claimant did not have the opportunity to bargain for protections from the corporation. Public policy accordingly more often supports piercing the corporate veil when a tort is proven. The argument follows that tort claimants were not able to foresee the defendant corporation's undercapitalization and thus should be able to recover from the shareholder's assets if recovery from the limited liability entity is inadequate.

Note that the situation where the individual shareholder, officer or director actually participated in the tortious conduct must be distinguished from the corporation committing the tort. If an individual in the company commits a tort or participates/directs the corporation to purposely commit a tort, the individual is always liable and it is unnecessary to invoke the piercing the corporate veil doctrine in order to

---

[19] *See* Walkovszky v. Carlton, 18 N.Y.2d 414 (N.Y. 1966) (holding that carrying the minimum amount of insurance required by law was adequate capitalization of the corporation against potential tort claims). The *Walkovszky v. Carlton* decision is set forth later in this Chapter.

[20] *See generally* Baker v. Kulczyk, 732 P.2d 386, 389 (Idaho Ct. App. 1987) (stating that the court would have been inclined to pierce the corporate veil if the plaintiff had introduced evidence to show that they were induced to contract with the undercapitalized corporation because of misrepresentations regarding financial stability).

recover.[21] Thus, the issue of piercing in the tort setting typically arises where an agent of a limited liability entity commits a tort and the plaintiff seeks to hold the shareholder(s) personally liable. It is important to keep in mind that because virtually all piercing cases involve closely-held corporations (or privately-held subsidiaries of publicly-held companies), the directors and officers sought to be held personally liable through piercing also normally have a substantial ownership interest in the limited liability entity.

5. Misrepresentation/Fraud

In order to successfully implement the veil-piercing doctrine, many courts require plaintiffs to show a degree of commingling or lack of corporate formalities along with another equitable factor like misrepresentation or fraud.[22] In addition to varying on the issue of whether fraud alone is sufficient to pierce the corporate veil in absence of other veil-piercing factors, courts and state statutes are also inconsistent on the issue of what type of fraud is sufficient to pierce — actual or constructive fraud.[23] When actual fraud is required to be shown, the plaintiff must show that the culpable party made "a representation of fact, which is either untrue and known to be untrue or recklessly made, and which was offered to deceive the other party and to induce him to act upon it, causing injury."[24] In addition to affirmative misrepresentations being the foundation of actual fraud, courts also accept silence when one has a duty to speak as constituting actual fraud.[25]

Additionally, as stated above, some courts accept constructive fraud, when coupled with other piercing factors, as sufficient grounds to pierce the corporate veil.[26] Generally, constructive fraud may be defined as acts or practices that, although disclosed to the complainant, are extremely unfair and which may have a capacity to mislead.[27] However, while the definition of fraud is given a broad interpretation by some courts in the veil-piercing context, states like Texas have legislatively restricted the veil-piercing doctrine in the contractual context by requiring that actual fraud, not constructive fraud, be shown in order to disregard a corporation's limited liability.[28]

6. An Empirical Study

Professor Robert B. Thompson conducted an in-depth analysis in the late 1980s of more than 1,600 cases ("Empirical Study") involving the concept of piercing the corporate veil and observed significant trends regarding the judicial handling of the doctrine.[29] Professor Thompson recognized the confusion and frustration felt by many

---

[21] *See, e.g.,* S. PRESSER, PIERCING THE CORPORATE VEIL 1–6 (2004).

[22] *See, e.g., De Witt,* 540 F.2d at 681.

[23] *Compare* Bergh v. Mills, 763 P.2d 214 (Wyo. 1988) (stating that fraud alone is sufficient and looking for actual fraud in order to invoke the doctrine); TEX. BUS. CORP. ACT ANN. art. 2.21(A) (Vernon 2003) (altering prior Texas common law that accepted constructive fraud and requiring actual fraud in the contractual context be shown in order to disregard the limited liability afforded corporations); *with* @Wireless Enters., Inc. v. AI Consulting, LLC, 2006 U.S. Dist. LEXIS 79874 (W.D.N.Y. Oct. 30, 2006) (analyzing constructive fraud as a possible basis for piercing the corporate veil).

[24] Klembczyk v. Di Nardo, 705 N.Y.S.2d 743, 744 (N.Y. App. Div. 4th Dep't 1999).

[25] *See Bergh,* 763 P.2d at 214.

[26] *See* F. GEVURTZ, CORPORATIONS § 1.5 (2000).

[27] *See* BLACK'S LAW DICTIONARY 686 (8th ed. B. Garner editor-in-chief 2004) (defining constructive fraud as "[u]nintentional deception or misrepresentation that causes injury to another" or conduct "by which one person obtains an advantage against conscience over another, or which equity or public policy forbids as being to another's prejudice").

[28] *See* TEX. BUS. CORP. ACT ANN. art. 2.21(A).

[29] Thompson, *Piercing the Corporate Veil: A Empirical Study,* 76 CORNELL L. REV. 1036 (1991).

legal commentators in interpreting judicial opinions analyzing the veil-piercing doctrine. Citing vague and inconclusive language used in piercing cases as a probable cause of conflicting decisions, Professor Thompson found numerous decisions invoking the veil-piercing doctrine to have directly analogous facts yet completely opposite conclusions. He pointed out that despite the negative commentary and somewhat inconsistent case law regarding the doctrine, "many believe that beneath this layer of unhelpful language courts are getting it right."[30]

One product of a review of the entire set of 1,600 cases involves the conclusion that, without exception, piercing the corporate veil only occurs in small to mid-sized, close corporations:

> Piercing the corporate veil is limited to close corporations and corporate groups (parent/subsidiary or sibling corporations). In the entire data set, piercing did not occur in a publicly held corporation. This universal respect for the separateness of the corporate entity in publicly held corporations reflects the different role that limited liability plays in larger corporations. All corporations can use the corporate form to allocate risk. Limited liability performs the additional function in larger corporations of facilitating the transferability of shares and making possible organized securities markets with the increased liquidity and diversification benefits that these markets make possible. The absence of these market-related benefits for close corporations explains, in part, why courts are more willing to pierce the veil of close corporations. . . .[31]

The Empirical Study also provides evidence that refutes previously drawn conclusions regarding the realities of the veil-piercing doctrine. For example, contrary to other commentators' suggestions, courts are more likely to pierce the corporate veil to reach an individual shareholder than to reach other corporate entities, whether parent or sister companies. Additionally, as discussed above, contrary to many public policy arguments, courts actually pierce corporations' veils more often when the underlying suit involves a claim based on contract rather than tort. This is one of the most surprising results of the study; namely, the premise that contract claimants voluntarily choose to deal with corporations and, thus, are able to evaluate credit risks and negotiate for contractual provisions that protect against undercapitalization; absent fraud or other disclosure deficiency, if the corporation is ultimately unable to adequately compensate for debts or liabilities, then the risk of loss should fall on the claimant. Conversely, regarding involuntary tort claimants who did not choose to deal with the undercapitalized corporation, when harmed, they supposedly should be able to more often pierce the corporate veil and recover from shareholders. However, as the statistics in the study evidence, this is not the situation.

Other general observations from the study tend to reinforce previous thoughts on the piercing doctrine. For example, the likelihood of a court piercing the corporate veil increases as the number of shareholders decrease. Additionally, courts do not appear to be permitting more piercing now than in previous decades and federal courts pierce the veil in about the same percentage as state courts. As the next section illustrates, courts analyze the general piercing factors of undercapitalization, commingling of corporate assets, and lack of corporate formalities in different ways depending on the facts of each case.

---

[30] *Id.* at 1037.

[31] *Id.* at 1047–48.

D. CONTEXT MATTERS WHEN PIERCING THE CORPORATE VEIL

Courts afford the aforementioned general veil-piercing factors in varying degrees of significance depending on the circumstances in which the veil is sought to be pierced. Thus, most veil-piercing cases can be divided into two general situations in which the likelihood of affirmatively piercing the corporate veil is contingent on either: (1) the type of shareholder from whom personal liability is sought, whether an individual share-holder or parent corporation; or (2) whether the alleged injury suffered by the plaintiff stems from a contract or tort claim. It is important to remember that the veil-piercing doctrine is an equitable remedy in which to hold active shareholders personally liable for corporate liabilities; it has no application to passive shareholders.

1. Individual Shareholder Liability

As previously mentioned, the shareholders of large, publicly-held corporations are not held personally liable for the debts and liabilities of the corporation through the veil-piercing doctrine discussed herein. Therefore, piercing the corporate veil occurs solely in closely-held corporations where personal liability is sought to be imposed against the active owners of the corporation.

a. Individual Shareholder Piercing: Tort

MINTON v. CAVANEY
Supreme Court of California
364 P.2d 473

TRAYNOR, J.

The Seminole Hot Springs Corporation, hereinafter referred to as Seminole, was duly incorporated in California on March 8, 1954. It conducted a public swimming pool that it leased from its owner. On June 24, 1954, plaintiffs' daughter drowned in the pool, and plaintiffs recovered a judgment for $10,000 against Seminole for her wrongful death. The judgment remains unsatisfied.

On January 30, 1957, plaintiffs brought the present action to hold defendant Cavaney personally liable for the judgment against Seminole. Cavaney died on May 28, 1958, and his widow, the executrix of his estate, was substituted as defendant. The trial court entered judgment for plaintiffs for $10,000. Defendant appeals.

Plaintiffs introduced evidence that Cavaney was a director and secretary and treasurer of Seminole and that on November 15, 1954, about five months after the drowning, Cavaney as secretary of Seminole and Edwin A. Kraft as president of Seminole applied for permission to issue three shares of Seminole stock, one share to be issued to Kraft, another to F. J. Wettrick and the third to Cavaney. The Commissioner of Corporations refused permission to issue these shares unless additional information was furnished. The application was then abandoned and no shares were ever issued. There was also evidence that for a time Seminole used Cavaney's office to keep records and to receive mail. Before his death Cavaney answered certain interrogatories. He was asked if Seminole "ever had any assets?" He stated that "insofar as my own personal knowledge and belief is concerned said corporation did not have any assets." Cavaney also stated in the return to an attempted execution that "[I]nsofar as I know, this corporation had no assets of any kind or character. The corporation was duly organized but never functioned as a corporation."

Defendant introduced evidence that Cavaney was an attorney at law, that he was approached by Kraft and Wettrick to form Seminole, and that he was the attorney for Seminole. Plaintiffs introduced Cavaney's answer to several interrogatories that he held the post of secretary and treasurer and director in a temporary capacity and as an accommodation to his client.

Defendant contends that the evidence does not support the court's determination that Cavaney is personally liable for Seminole's debts and that the "alter ego" doctrine is inapplicable because plaintiffs failed to show that there was " '(1) . . . such unity of interest and ownership that the separate personalities of the corporation and the individual no longer exist and (2) that, if the acts are treated as those of the corporation alone, an inequitable result will follow.' "

The figurative terminology "alter ego" and "disregard of the corporate entity" is generally used to refer to the various situations that are an abuse of the corporate privilege. The equitable owners of a corporation, for example, are personally liable when they treat the assets of the corporation as their own and add or withdraw capital from the corporation at will; when they hold themselves out as being personally liable for the debts of the corporation; or when they provide inadequate capitalization and actively participate in the conduct of corporate affairs.

In the instant case the evidence is undisputed that there was no attempt to provide adequate capitalization. Seminole never had any substantial assets. It leased the pool that it operated, and the lease was forfeited for failure to pay the rent. Its capital was " 'trifling compared with the business to be done and the risks of loss. . . .' " The evidence is also undisputed that Cavaney was not only the secretary and treasurer of the corporation but was also a director. The evidence that Cavaney was to receive one-third of the shares to be issued supports an inference that he was an equitable owner and the evidence that for a time the records of the corporation were kept in Cavaney's office supports an inference that he actively participated in the conduct of the business. The trial court was not required to believe his statement that he was only a "temporary" director and officer "for accommodation." In any event it merely raised a conflict in the evidence that was resolved adversely to defendant. Moreover, . . . the business and affairs of every corporation shall be controlled by, a board of [directors]. Defendant does not claim that Cavaney was a director with specialized duties. It is immaterial whether or not he accepted the office of director as an "accommodation" with the understanding that he would not exercise any of the duties of a director. A person may not in this manner divorce the responsibilities of a director from the statutory duties and powers of that office.

There is no merit in defendant's contentions that the "alter ego" doctrine applies only to contractual debts and not to tort claims . . . .

NATIONAL LABOR RELATIONS BOARD v. WEST DIXIE ENTERPRISES, INC.
Court of Appeals of United States
190 F.3d 1191 (11th Cir. 1999)

Before EDMONDSON, BIRCH and CARNES, CIRCUIT JUDGES.

PER CURIAM:

West Dixie Enterprises, Inc. and Carole Ann and Paul Paolicelli appeal the National Labor Relations Board's (NLRB) order holding them liable for violating sections 8(a)(1) and 8(a)(3) of the National Labor Relations Act (NLRA), 29 U.S.C. §§ 158(a)(1) and 158(a)(3), respectively. For the reasons set forth below, we affirm the NLRB's order.

Beginning in 1993, West Dixie was a Florida corporation doing business as an electrical contractor. Carole Ann Paolicelli was the company's owner, sole shareholder, and president. Her husband, Paul Paolicelli, directed all of West Dixie's daily operations.

At times, Mr. Paolicelli made personal loans to West Dixie and used his personal credit card to order materials and equipment for the company. In addition, the Paolicellis often issued checks from their personal joint checking account to meet the payroll, and Mrs. Paolicelli allowed employees to use her personal car for company business. For approximately six months, West Dixie funds were used to pay the rent on Mr. Paolicelli's apartment.

The NLRB found that in July, August, and September of 1994, West Dixie refused to hire three job applicants because of their union membership; created the impression that union activities were under surveillance; interrogated employees about union membership; prohibited employees from discussing the union; and threatened to assign union supporters more burdensome job duties. The respondents do not dispute these findings for purposes of the appeal. The respondents also do not dispute that from the beginning of May 1994 to the end of October 1994, West Dixie made interstate purchases of supplies totaling more than $50,000.

West Dixie was administratively dissolved on August 26, 1994 for failure to file an annual report under Florida law. The Paolicellis continued to operate the business as usual under the name West Dixie until it was reinstated as a corporation on October 25, 1995. West Dixie has not operated as a business since its reinstatement.

The International Brotherhood of Electrical Workers, Local Union No. 728 filed a charge of unfair labor practices against West Dixie on October 31, 1994. The NLRB conducted an investigation and filed a complaint against West Dixie on February 28, 1995. The complaint was later amended to add the Paolicellis as alter egos of the corporation. After a hearing in October 1996, an Administrative Law Judge ("ALJ") concluded that . . . the Paolicellis were alter egos of West Dixie and were therefore also liable for the violations. The respondents filed exceptions to the ALJ's decision, but the NLRB entered a Final Order in November 1997 affirming the ALJ's decision. West Dixie and the Paolicellis appealed, raising the . . . alter ego issues.

The Paolicellis argue that they are not personally liable for the NLRA violations under Florida Statutes § 607.1421(4), which sets forth the state law conditions for piercing the corporate veil and holding individuals personally liable for corporate misdeeds. It is clear, however, that "personal liability for remedial obligations arising from corporate unfair labor practices under the National Labor Relations Act is a question of Federal law because it arises in the context of a Federal labor dispute." . . . .

In *White Oak Coal* [318 N.L.R.B. 734], the NLRB adopted the Tenth Circuit's two-pronged test for determining whether owners or operators of a corporation are personally liable for the unfair labor practices of the corporation. Under that test:

> the corporate veil may be pierced when: (1) there is such unity of interest, and lack of respect given to the separate identity of the corporation by its shareholders, that the personalities and assets of the corporation and the individuals are indistinct; and (2) adherence to the corporate form would sanction a fraud, promote injustice, or lead to an evasion of legal obligations.

Under the first prong, courts should consider "(a) the degree to which the corporate legal formalities have been maintained, and (b) the degree to which individual and corporate funds, other assets, and affairs have been commingled." In this case, there is substantial evidence of commingling of funds and assets and of a failure to maintain corporate formalities. The Paolicellis often used personal checks or credit cards to pay for West Dixie's supplies and payroll. In addition, West Dixie paid six months' rent for Mr. Paolicelli's personal apartment. The Paolicellis produced no records indicating that any of these payments were bona fide loans or repayments, or that the individual and corporate identities were kept separate. The failure to keep adequate records itself may evidence a lack of arm's-length dealing between the individuals and the corporation. . . .

With regard to the second prong of the test, whether a finding of no personal liability "would sanction a fraud, promote injustice, or lead to an evasion of legal obligations," we acknowledge that in this case most of the payments flowed from the individual owners and operators to the corporation instead of in the opposite direction. But it is undisputed that West Dixie funds were used to pay rent on Mr. Paolicelli's personal apartment for six months, and the Paolicellis have failed to produce records showing that this arrangement constituted anything but a diversion of corporate assets for personal use. As a result, those funds are unavailable to meet West Dixie's remedial obligations under the NLRA.

In addition, the Paolicellis continued to operate their electrical contracting business under the name West Dixie after the corporation was administratively dissolved under Florida law on August 26, 1994 until it was reinstated on October 25, 1995. The continued operation of the business cuts in favor of piercing the corporate veil under both prongs of the test. It not only demonstrates a failure to adhere to corporate formalities and maintain separate identities, but also could have affected the corporation's ability to meet its remedial obligations resulting from the unfair labor practices.

For these reasons, we hold that the NLRB did not err in concluding that the Paolicellis are personally liable for West Dixie's violations of the NLRA.

AFFIRMED.

BAATZ v. ARROW BAR
Supreme Court of South Dakota
452 N.W.2d 138 (1989)

SABERS, JUSTICE.

Kenny and Peggy Baatz (Baatz), appeal from summary judgment dismissing Edmond, LaVella, and Jacquette Neuroth, as individual defendants in this action.

Facts

Kenny and Peggy were seriously injured in 1982 when Roland McBride crossed the center line of a Sioux Falls street with his automobile and struck them while they were riding on a motorcycle. McBride was uninsured at the time of the accident and apparently is judgment proof.

Baatz alleges that Arrow Bar served alcoholic beverages to McBride prior to the accident while he was already intoxicated. Baatz commenced this action in 1984, claiming that Arrow Bar's negligence in serving alcoholic beverages to McBride contributed to the injuries they sustained in the accident. Baatz supports his claim against Arrow Bar with the affidavit of Jimmy Larson. Larson says he knew McBride and observed him being served alcoholic beverages in the Arrow Bar during the afternoon prior to the accident, while McBride was intoxicated.

Edmond and LaVella Neuroth formed the Arrow Bar, Inc. in May 1980. During the next two years they contributed $50,000 to the corporation pursuant to a stock subscription agreement. The corporation purchased the Arrow Bar business in June 1980 for $155,000 with a $5,000 down payment. Edmond and LaVella executed a promissory note personally guaranteeing payment of the $150,000 balance. In 1983 the corporation obtained bank financing in the amount of $145,000 to pay off the purchase agreement. Edmond and LaVella again personally guaranteed payment of the corporate debt. Edmond is the president of the corporation, and Jacquette Neuroth serves as the manager of the business. . . . [T]he corporation did not maintain dram shop liability insurance at the time of the injuries to Kenny and Peggy.

In 1987 the trial court entered summary judgment in favor of Arrow Bar and the individual defendants. Baatz appealed that judgment and we reversed and remanded to the trial court for trial. Shortly before the trial date, Edmond, LaVella, and Jacquette moved for and obtained summary judgment dismissing them as individual defendants. Baatz appeals. We affirm.

Individual liability by piercing the corporate veil.

Baatz claims that even if Arrow Bar, Inc. is the licensee, the corporate veil should be pierced, leaving the Neuroths, as the shareholders of the corporation, individually liable. A corporation shall be considered a separate legal entity until there is *sufficient reason* to the contrary. When continued recognition of a corporation as a separate legal entity would "produce injustices and inequitable consequences," then a court has sufficient reason to pierce the corporate veil. Factors that indicate injustices and inequitable consequences and allow a court to pierce the corporate veil are:

(1)   fraudulent representation by corporation directors;

(2)   undercapitalization;

(3)   failure to observe corporate formalities;

(4)   absence of corporate records;

(5)   payment by the corporation of individual obligations; or

(6)   use of the corporation to promote fraud, injustice, or illegalities.

When the court deems it appropriate to pierce the corporate veil, the corporation and its stockholders will be treated identically.

Baatz advances several arguments to support his claim that the corporate veil of Arrow Bar, Inc. should be pierced, but fails to support them with facts, or misconstrues the facts.

First, Baatz claims that since Edmond and LaVella personally guaranteed corporate obligations, they should also be personally liable to Baatz. However, the personal guarantee of a loan is a contractual agreement and cannot be enlarged to impose tort liability. Moreover, the personal guarantee creates individual liability for a corporate obligation, the opposite of factor (5), above. As such, it supports, rather than detracts from, recognition of the corporate entity.

Baatz also argues that the corporation is simply the alter ego of the Neuroths, and, [that accordingly] the corporate veil should be pierced. Baatz' discussion of the law is adequate, but he fails to present evidence that would support a decision in his favor in accordance with that law. When an individual treats a corporation "as an instrumentality through which he [is] conducting his personal business," a court may disregard the corporate entity. Baatz fails to demonstrate how the Neuroths were transacting personal business through the corporation. In fact, the evidence indicates the Neuroths treated the corporation separately from their individual affairs.

Baatz next argues that the corporation is undercapitalized. Shareholders must equip a corporation with a reasonable amount of capital for the nature of the business involved. Baatz claims the corporation was started with only $5,000 in borrowed capital, but does not explain how that amount failed to equip the corporation with a reasonable amount of capital. In addition, Baatz fails to consider the personal guarantees to pay off the purchase contract in the amount of $150,000, and the $50,000 stock subscription agreement. There simply is no evidence that the corporation's capital in whatever amount was inadequate for the operation of the business. Normally questions relating to individual shareholder liability resulting from corporate undercapitalization should not be reached until the primary question of corporate liability is determined. Questions depending in part upon other determinations are not normally ready for summary judgment. However, simply asserting that the corporation is undercapitalized does not make it so. Without some evidence of the inadequacy of the capital, Baatz fails to present specific facts demonstrating a genuine issue of material fact.

Finally, Baatz argues that Arrow Bar, Inc. failed to observe corporate formalities because none of the business' signs or advertising indicated that the business was a corporation. Baatz cites SDCL 47-2-36 as requiring the name of any corporation to contain the word corporation, company, incorporated, or limited, or an abbreviation for such a word. In spite of Baatz' contentions, the corporation is in compliance with the statute because its corporate name — Arrow Bar, Inc. — includes the abbreviation of the word incorporated. Furthermore, the "mere failure upon occasion to follow all the forms prescribed by law for the conduct of corporate activities will not justify" disregarding the corporate entity. Even if the corporation is improperly using its name, that alone is not a sufficient reason to pierce the corporate veil. This is especially so where, as here, there is no relationship between the claimed defect and the resulting harm.

In addition, the record is void of any evidence which would support imposition of individual liability by piercing the corporate veil under any of the other factors listed above in (1), (4) or (6).

In summary, Baatz fails to present specific facts that would allow the trial court to find the existence of a genuine issue of material fact. There is no indication that any of the Neuroths personally served an alcoholic beverage to McBride on the day of the accident. Nor is there any evidence indicating that the Neuroths treated the corporation in any way that would produce the injustices and inequitable consequences necessary to justify piercing the corporate veil. In fact, the only evidence offered is otherwise. Therefore, we affirm summary judgment dismissing the Neuroths as individual defendants.

b.   Individual Shareholder Piercing: Contract

BRUNSWICK CORP. v. WAXMAN
United States Court of Appeals
599 F.2d 34 (2d Cir. 1979)

MULLIGAN, CIRCUIT JUDGE:

Brunswick Corporation (Brunswick) appeals from an order and judgment of the Hon. John R. Bartels, United States District Court for the Eastern District of New York, dismissing the complaint and entering judgment for the defendants after a trial without a jury. Brunswick brought this diversity action against the individual defendants seeking over a million dollars in damages. This amount represents the deficiency due under conditional sales contracts entered into between Brunswick and the Waxman Construction Corporation (Construction Corp.) whereby the latter entity purchased bowling lanes and pinsetters. The individual defendants, Harry Waxman and the late Sydney Waxman, signed the contracts as president and secretary of the Construction Corp. The theory of the plaintiff is that the corporate veil of the Construction Corp. should be pierced and the Waxmans held personally liable for the deficiency.

The fact findings of the trial court indicate that in August 1960, the Waxmans formed the Construction Corp. as a no-asset New York corporation to act as signatory and obligor on a series of conditional sales agreements for the purchase of bowling equipment to be operated in five new bowling alleys. The five alleys and the Brunswick equipment were operated by the Waxmans through five separate partnerships, which owned the non-Brunswick equipment and fixtures in the alleys. The Waxmans owned or leased the real property on which the bowling alleys were located, but charged the Construction Corp. no rent for the use of the premises. Nor did the Waxmans pay rent to the Construction Corp. for the use of the bowling equipment. In addition, the Waxmans owned in their individual or partnership capacities all the licenses and permits necessary to operate the alleys. Proceeds from the daily operation of the businesses were deposited in individual bowling alley accounts and later transferred into a central Waxman enterprises bank account from which funds were withdrawn to meet the necessary operating expenses of the alleys. It was from this central bank account that amounts due on the sales contracts with Brunswick were withdrawn and deposited in the Construction Corp. account. The court below found that the

Construction Corp.'s sole corporate activity was the transfer of funds into and out of its bank account for the purpose of meeting the installment payments under the Brunswick contracts. The Construction Corp. held no stockholders' or directors' meetings, adopted no bylaws, and issued no stock. While it filed federal and New York State income tax returns, none of these returns showed any income, nor did any report the Brunswick equipment as corporate assets.

Due to a general decline in the bowling industry [when bowling was no longer "kingpin"], the Construction Corp. was unable to meet its payment obligations under the sales contracts. Pursuant to a 1963 extension agreement, title to the Brunswick equipment was transferred from Construction Corp. to five new corporations, which were also to receive an additional $375,000 in non-Brunswick assets. However, the Waxmans never transferred the additional assets to the five corporations. In addition, these newly formed corporations were as inactive as the Construction Corp. had been. By late 1965, two of the five corporations, Bruckner Lanes, Inc. and Pike Lanes, Inc., were in default. In 1966, Brunswick repossessed its equipment held by Bruckner Lanes and sold it at a substantial deficiency. Although an extension agreement was reached with Pike Lanes in 1966, that corporation continued in substantial default and its equipment was also repossessed and sold by Brunswick at a substantial deficiency.

Although we are persuaded that the district judge reached the proper result here in dismissing the complaint, we cannot subscribe entirely to his views on the law of New York in the field of "piercing the corporate veil" and the disregard of the corporate fiction. New York law in this area is hardly as clear as a mountain lake in springtime. Since Professor Wormser's initial discussion of the topic in *Piercing the Veil of Corporate Entity*, 12 Colum. L. Rev. 496 (1912), there have been scores of articles and hundreds of cases discussing the problem, advancing and espousing various theories. In particular we are dubious that, as suggested by the district court, the plaintiff need establish that the Waxmans committed a fraud on Brunswick and that there be a causal connection between the fact that the Waxmans conducted business individually and the contract losses suffered by Brunswick. . . .

The district judge who tried the case found that Brunswick had knowingly entered into the conditional sales contracts involved in this litigation with a no-asset corporation which was created for the sole purpose of taking title to the equipment which Brunswick sold. Brunswick knew or should be charged with the knowledge that the Waxmans wished to avoid personal liability and that the sole obligor on the sales contract was to be the corporate dummy created for that purpose. Further Brunswick investigated to determine whether the alleys themselves were likely to generate revenues sufficient to make the payments for the equipment purchased by the Construction Corp. Thus, Brunswick was aware or should have known that the dummy corporation was created for the limited purpose of purchase, that the property and buildings in which the equipment was to be installed were owned by the Waxmans in their individual capacities, and that the Waxmans would personally conduct the bowling alley business.Under these circumstances Brunswick obtained precisely what it bargained for, and it did not bargain for or contemplate the individual liability of the Waxmans which it now seeks to enforce. To pierce the corporate veil here would not in our view accomplish justice or equity but would in fact thwart that end. We therefore refuse to disregard the corporate entity in this case. The creation of the dummy corporation under these circumstances to eliminate personal responsibility should be respected.

AFFIRMED.

NOTES AND QUESTIONS

1. Another oft-cited individual shareholder liability case, *Kinney Shoe Corporation v. Polan*, 939 F.2d 209 (4th Cir. 1991), illustrates the uncertainty of result in veil-piercing contract cases. The court reasoned:

Piercing the corporate veil is an equitable remedy, and the burden rests with the party asserting such claim. A totality of the circumstances test is used in determining whether to pierce the corporate veil, and each case must be decided on its own facts. The district court's findings of facts may be overturned only if clearly erroneous.

Kinney seeks to pierce the corporate veil of Industrial so as to hold [the individual shareholder] Polan personally liable on the sublease debt. The Supreme Court of Appeals of West Virginia has set forth a two prong test to be used in determining whether to pierce a corporate veil in a breach of contract case. This test raises two issues: first, is the unity of interest and ownership such that the separate personalities of the corporation and the individual shareholder no longer exist; and second, would an equitable result occur if the acts are treated as those of the corporation alone. Laya v. Erin Homes, Inc., 352 S.E.2d 93 (W. Va. 1986). Numerous factors have been identified as relevant in making this determination. "The following factors were identified in *Laya:* (1) commingling of funds and other assets of the corporation with those of the individual shareholders; (2) diversion of the corporation's funds or assets to noncorporate uses (to the personal uses of the corporation's shareholders); (3) failure to maintain the corporate formalities necessary for the issuance of or subscription to the corporation's stock, such as formal approval of the stock issue by the board of directors; (4) an individual shareholder representing to persons outside the corporation that he or she is personally liable for the debts or other obligations of the corporation; (5) failure to maintain corporate minutes or adequate corporate records; (6) identical equitable ownership in two entities; (7) identity of the directors and officers of two entities who are responsible for supervision and management (a partnership or sole proprietorship and a corporation owned and managed by the same parties); (8) failure to adequately capitalize a corporation for the reasonable risks of the corporate undertaking; (9) absence of separately held corporate assets; (10) use of a corporation as a mere shell or conduit to operate a single venture or some particular aspect of the business of an individual or another corporation; (11) sole ownership of all the stock by one individual or members of a single family; (12) use of the same office or business location by the corporation and its individual shareholder(s); (13) employment of the same employees or attorney by the corporation and its shareholder(s); (14) concealment or misrepresentation of the identity of the ownership, management or financial interests in the corporation, and concealment of personal business activities of the shareholders (sole shareholders do not reveal the association with a corporation, which makes loans to them without adequate security); (15) disregard of legal formalities and failure to maintain proper arm's length relationships among related entities; (16) use of a corporate entity as a conduit to procure labor, services or merchandise for another person or entity; (17) diversion of corporate assets from the corporation by or to a stockholder or other person or entity to the detriment of creditors, or the manipulation of assets and liabilities between entities to concentrate the assets in one and the liabilities in another; (18) contracting by the corporation with another person with the intent to avoid risk of nonperformance by use of the corporate entity; or the use of a corporation as a subterfuge for illegal transactions; (19) the formation and use of the corporation to assume the existing liabilities of another person or entity."[33]

The district court found that the two prong test of *Laya* had been satisfied. The court concluded that Polan's failure to carry out the corporate formalities with respect to Industrial, coupled with Industrial's gross undercapitalization,

---

[33] *Id.* at 211 (quoting *Laya*, 352 S.E.2d at 98–99).

resulted in damage to Kinney. We agree.

It is undisputed that Industrial was not adequately capitalized. Actually, it had no paid in capital. Polan had put nothing into this corporation, and it did not observe any corporate formalities. As the West Virginia court stated in *Laya*, '[i]ndividuals who wish to enjoy limited personal liability for business activities under a corporate umbrella should be expected to adhere to the relatively simple formalities of creating and maintaining a corporate entity.' " . . . This, the court stated, is "a relatively small price to pay for limited liability." Another important factor is adequate capitalization. "[G]rossly inadequate capitalization combined with disregard of corporate formalities, causing basic unfairness, are sufficient to pierce the corporate veil in order to hold the shareholder(s) actively participating in the operation of the business personally liable for a breach of contract to the party who entered into the contract with the corporation." . . . .

In this case, Polan bought no stock, made no capital contribution, kept no minutes, and elected no officers for Industrial. . . . Polan was obviously trying to limit his liability and the liability of Polan Industries, Inc. by setting up a paper curtain constructed of nothing more than Industrial's certificate of incorporation. These facts present the classic scenario for an action to pierce the corporate veil so as to reach the responsible party and produce an equitable result. Accordingly, we hold that the district court correctly found that the two prong test in *Laya* [for veil piercing] had been satisfied.

Can the foregoing decision be reconciled with the Second Circuit's decision in Brunswick? In both situations, a no-asset corporation was set up, failing to adhere to corporate formalities. No misrepresentation was communicated to creditors in either case. Which result do you favor and why?

2. Some states, however, are more restrictive in recognizing the veil-piercing doctrine and expressly require a showing of actual fraud in order to successfully hold active shareholders liable for the contractual debts of the corporation. For example, Article 2.21 of the Texas Business Corporation Act states that:

(A) A holder of shares . . . shall be under no obligation to the corporation or to its obligees with respect to:

. . . . (2) any contractual obligation of the corporation or any matter relating to or arising from the obligation on the basis that the holder . . . is or was the alter ego of the corporation, or on the basis of actual fraud or constructive fraud, a sham to perpetrate a fraud, or other similar theory, unless the obligee demonstrates that the holder . . . caused the corporation to be used for the purpose of perpetrating and did perpetrate an actual fraud on the obligee primarily for the direct personal benefit of the holder . . . ; or (3) any obligation of the corporation on the basis of the failure of the corporation to observe any corporate formality, including without limitation: (a) the failure to comply with any requirement of this Act or of the articles of incorporation or bylaws of the corporation; or (b) the failure to observe any requirement prescribed by this Act or by the articles of incorporation or bylaws for acts to be taken by the corporation, its board of directors, or its shareholders.

(B) The liability of a holder . . . of shares of a corporation . . . for an obligation that is limited by Section A of this article is exclusive and preempts any other liability imposed on a holder . . . of a corporation . . . for that obligation under common law or otherwise, except that nothing contained in this article shall limit the obligation of a holder . . . when: (1) the holder . . . has expressly assumed, guaranteed, or agreed to be personally liable to the obligee for the obligation; or (2) the holder . . . is otherwise liable to the obligee for the obligation under this Act or another applicable statute.[34]

2.   Business Enterprise Liability Doctrine

In addition to seeking personal liability from individual shareholders/owners for the actions of a corporate entity, an alternative is to allege that the corporation in question is actually part of a larger corporate organization and that the assets of other related corporate entities should be used to satisfy the debts of the entity accused of wrongdoing. This principle is called the Business Enterprise Liability Doctrine and it seeks to pool the assets of related corporate entities to cover the liabilities of the undercapitalized corporation. The Business Enterprise Liability Doctrine is invoked in two different instances: (1) when a corporation owns many subsidiaries all of which are related as brother-sister sibling corporations or (2) when one corporation owns another in a parent-subsidiary relationship. In the former example, a plaintiff will attempt to recover damages from the related sibling corporations that may have more sizable assets than either the entity that caused the injury or the parent corporation. In the latter case, a plaintiff will seek to pierce the veil of the subsidiary and reach the assets of the well-capitalized parent corporation.

a.   Business Enterprise Liability: Tort

WALKOVSZKY v. CARLTON
Court of Appeals of New York
18 N.Y.2d 414 (1966)

FULD, J.

This case involves what appears to be a rather common practice in the taxicab industry of vesting the ownership of a taxi fleet in many corporations, each owning only one or two cabs.

The complaint alleges that the plaintiff was severely injured four years ago in New York City when he was run down by a taxicab owned by the defendant Seon Cab Corporation and negligently operated at the time by the defendant Marchese. The individual defendant, Carlton, is claimed to be a stockholder of 10 corporations, including Seon, each of which has but two cabs registered in its name, and it is implied that only the minimum automobile liability insurance required by law (in the amount of $10,000) is carried on any one cab. Although seemingly independent of one another, these corporations are alleged to be "operated . . . as a single entity, unit and enterprise" with regard to financing, supplies, repairs, employees and garaging, and all are named as defendants. The plaintiff asserts that he is also entitled to hold their stockholders personally liable for the damages sought because the multiple corporate structure constitutes an unlawful attempt "to defraud members of the general public" that might be injured by the cabs.

The defendant Carlton has moved to dismiss the complaint on the ground that as to him it "fails to state a cause of action." . . .

The law permits the incorporation of a business for the very purpose of enabling its proprietors to escape personal liability but, manifestly, the privilege is not without its limits. Broadly speaking, the courts will disregard the corporate form, or, to use accepted terminology, "pierce the corporate veil," whenever necessary "to prevent fraud or to achieve equity". . . .

. . . .

In the case before us, the plaintiff has explicitly alleged that none of the corporations

---

[34]   TEX. BUS. CORP. ACT ANN. art. 2.21. *See* Steinberg, *Alter Ego and Single Business Enterprise in the Texas Contractual Debt Context*, 41 TEX. J. BUS. L. 1 (2005).

"had a separate existence of their own" and, as indicated above, all are named as defendants. However, it is one thing to assert that a corporation is a fragment of a larger corporate combine which actually conducts the business. It is quite another to claim that the corporation is a "dummy" for its individual stockholders who are in reality carrying on the business in their personal capacities for purely personal rather than corporate ends. Either circumstance would justify treating the corporation as an agent and piercing the corporate veil to reach the principal but a different result would follow in each case. In the first, only a larger *corporate* entity would be held financially responsible while, in the other, the stockholder would be personally liable. Either the stockholder is conducting the business in his individual capacity or he is not. If he is, he will be liable; if he is not, then, it does not matter — insofar as his personal liability is concerned — that the enterprise is actually being carried on by a larger "enterprise entity." . . .

Reading the complaint in this case most favorably and liberally, we do not believe that there can be gathered from its averments the allegations required to spell out a valid cause of action against the defendant Carlton.

The individual defendant is charged with having "organized, managed, dominated and controlled" a fragmented corporate entity but there are no allegations that he was conducting business in his individual capacity. Had the taxicab fleet been owned by a single corporation, it would be readily apparent that the plaintiff would face formidable barriers in attempting to establish personal liability on the part of the corporation's stockholders. The fact that the fleet ownership has been deliberately split up among many corporations does not ease the plaintiff's burden in that respect. The corporate form may not be disregarded merely because the assets of the corporation, together with the mandatory insurance coverage of the vehicle which struck the plaintiff, are insufficient to assure him the recovery sought. If Carlton were to be held individually liable on those facts alone, the decision would apply equally to the thousands of cabs which are owned by their individual drivers who conduct their businesses through corporations organized pursuant to the Business Corporation Law and carry the minimum insurance required by the Vehicle and Traffic Law. These taxi owner-operators are entitled to form such corporations and we agree . . . that, if the insurance coverage required by statute "is inadequate for the protection of the public, the remedy lies not with the courts but with the Legislature." It may very well be sound policy to require that certain corporations must take out liability insurance which will afford adequate compensation to their potential tort victims. However, the responsibility for imposing conditions on the privilege of incorporation has been committed by the Constitution to the Legislature and it may not be fairly implied, from any statute, that the Legislature intended, without the slightest discussion or debate, to require of taxi corporations that they carry automobile liability insurance over and above that mandated by the Vehicle and Traffic Law.

. . . .

This is not to say that it is impossible for the plaintiff to state a valid cause of action against the defendant Carlton. However, the simple fact is that the plaintiff has just not done so here. While the complaint alleges that the separate corporations were undercapitalized and that their assets have been intermingled, it is barren of any "sufficiently particular[ized] statements" that the defendant Carlton and his associates are actually doing business in their individual capacities, shuttling their personal funds in and out of the corporations "without regard to formality and to suit their immediate convenience." Such a "perversion of the privilege to do business in a corporate form" would justify imposing personal liability on the individual stockholders. Nothing of the sort has in fact been charged. . . .

In point of fact, the principle relied upon in the complaint to sustain the imposition of personal liability is not agency but fraud. Such a cause of action cannot withstand analysis. If it is not fraudulent for the owner-operator of a single cab corporation to take out only the minimum required liability insurance, the enterprise does not become either illicit or fraudulent merely because it consists of many such corporations. The plaintiff's injuries are the same regardless of whether the cab which strikes him is owned by a single corporation or part of a fleet with ownership fragmented among many corporations. . . .

In sum, then, the complaint falls short of adequately stating a cause of action against the defendant Carlton in his individual capacity.

KEATING, J., Dissenting

The defendant Carlton, the shareholder here sought to be held for the negligence of the driver of a taxicab, was a principal shareholder and organizer of the defendant corporation which owned the taxicab. The corporation was one of 10 organized by the defendant, each containing two cabs and each cab having the "minimum liability" insurance coverage mandated by the Vehicle and Traffic Law. The sole assets of these operating corporations are the vehicles themselves and they are apparently subject to mortgages.

From their inception these corporations were intentionally undercapitalized for the purpose of avoiding responsibility for acts which were bound to arise as a result of the operation of a large taxi fleet having cars out on the street 24 hours a day and engaged in public transportation. And during the course of the corporations' existence all income was continually drained out of the corporations for the same purpose. The issue presented by this action is whether the policy of this State, which affords those desiring to engage in a business enterprise the privilege of limited liability through the use of the corporate device, is so strong that it will permit that privilege to continue no matter how much it is abused, no matter how irresponsibly the corporation is operated, no matter what the cost to the public. I do not believe that it is.

Under the circumstances of this case the shareholders should all be held individually liable to this plaintiff for the injuries he suffered. At least, the matter should not be disposed of on the pleadings by a dismissal of the complaint. If a corporation is organized and carries on business without substantial capital in such a way that the corporation is likely to have no sufficient assets available to meet its debts, it is inequitable that shareholders should set up such a flimsy organization to escape personal liability. The attempt to do corporate business without providing any sufficient basis of financial responsibility to creditors is an abuse of the separate entity and will be ineffectual to exempt the shareholders from corporate debts. It is coming to be recognized as the policy of law that shareholders should in good faith put at the risk of the business unencumbered capital reasonably adequate for its prospective liabilities. If capital is illusory or trifling compared with the business to be done and the risks of loss, this is a ground for denying the separate entity privilege.

. . . .

The defendant Carlton claims that, because the minimum amount of insurance required by the statute was obtained, the corporate veil cannot and should not be pierced despite the fact that the assets of the corporation which owned the cab were "trifling compared with the business to be done and the risks of loss" which were certain to be encountered. I do not agree.

The Legislature in requiring minimum liability insurance of $10,000, no doubt, intended to provide at least some small fund for recovery against those individuals and corporations who just did not have and were not able to raise or accumulate assets sufficient to satisfy the claims of those who were injured as a result of their negligence. It certainly could not have intended to shield those individuals who organized corporations, with the specific intent of avoiding responsibility to the public, where the operation of the corporate enterprise yielded profits sufficient to purchase additional insurance. Moreover, it is reasonable to assume that the Legislature believed that those individuals and corporations having substantial assets would take out insurance far in excess of the minimum in order to protect those assets from depletion. Given the costs of hospital care and treatment and the nature of injuries sustained in auto collisions, it would be unreasonable to assume that the Legislature believed that the minimum provided in the statute would in and of itself be sufficient to recompense "innocent victims of motor vehicle accidents . . . for the injury and financial loss inflicted upon them".

. . . .

What I would merely hold is that a participating shareholder of a corporation vested with a public interest, organized with capital insufficient to meet liabilities which are certain to arise in the ordinary course of the corporation's business, may be held personally responsible for such liabilities. Where corporate income is not sufficient to cover the cost of insurance premiums above the statutory minimum or where initially adequate finances dwindle under the pressure of competition, bad times or extraordinary and unexpected liability, obviously the shareholder will not be held liable.

The only types of corporate enterprises that will be discouraged as a result of a decision allowing the individual shareholder to be sued will be those such as the one in question, designed solely to abuse the corporate privilege at the expense of the public interest.

GARDEMAL v. WESTIN HOTEL CO.
United States Court of Appeals
186 F.3d 588 (5th Cir. 1999)

DeMoss, Circuit Judge:

Plaintiff-appellant, Lisa Cerza Gardemal ("Gardemal"), sued defendants-appellees, Westin Hotel Company ("Westin") and Westin Mexico, S.A. de C.V. ("Westin Mexico"), under Texas law, alleging that the defendants were liable for the drowning death of her husband in Cabo San Lucas, Mexico. The district court dismissed the suit in accordance with the magistrate judge's recommendation that the court grant Westin's motion for summary judgment, and Westin Mexico's motion to dismiss for lack of personal jurisdiction. We affirm the district court's rulings.

I.

In June 1995, Gardemal and her husband John W. Gardemal, a physician, traveled to Cabo San Lucas, Baja California Sur, Mexico, to attend a medical seminar held at the Westin Regina Resort Los Cabos ("Westin Regina"). The Westin Regina is owned by Desarollos Turisticos Integrales Cabo San Lucas, S.A. de C.V. ("DTI"), and managed by Westin Mexico. Westin Mexico is a subsidiary of Westin, and is incorporated in Mexico. During their stay at the hotel, the Gardemals decided to go snorkeling with a group of guests. According to Gardemal, the concierge at the Westin Regina directed the group to "Lovers Beach" which, unbeknownst to the group, was notorious for its rough surf and strong undercurrents. While climbing the beach's rocky shore, five men in the group were swept into the Pacific Ocean by a rogue wave and thrown against the rocks. Two of the men, including John Gardemal, drowned.

Gardemal, as administrator of her husband's estate, brought wrongful death and survival actions under Texas law against Westin and Westin Mexico, alleging that her husband drowned because Westin Regina's concierge negligently directed the group to Lovers Beach and failed to warn her husband of its dangerous condition. Westin then moved for summary judgment, alleging that although it is the parent company of Westin Mexico, it is a separate corporate entity and thus could not be held liable for acts committed by its subsidiary. The magistrate judge agreed with Westin, and recommended that Westin be dismissed from the action. In reaching its decision the magistrate judge rejected Gardemal's assertion that the state-law doctrines of alter-ego and single business enterprise allowed the court to disregard Westin's separate corporate identity. . . .

In this action Gardemal seeks to hold Westin liable for the acts of Westin Mexico . . . because Westin Mexico functioned as the alter ego of Westin. . . . Gardemal next contends that Westin may be held liable on the theory that Westin Mexico operated a single business enterprise. We consider first the issue of whether Westin may be held liable on an alter-ego theory.

1.

Under Texas law [in the tort context] the alter ego doctrine allows the imposition of liability on a corporation for the acts of another corporation when the subject corporation is organized or operated as a mere tool or business conduit. It applies "when there is such unity between the parent corporation and its subsidiary that the separateness of the two corporations has ceased and holding only the subsidiary corporation liable would result in injustice." . . . Alter ego is demonstrated "by evidence showing a blending of identities, or a blurring of lines of distinction, both formal and substantive, between two corporations." . . . An important consideration is whether a corporation is under-funded or undercapitalized, which is an indication that the company is a mere conduit or business tool.

On appeal Gardemal points to several factors which, in her opinion, show that Westin is operating as the alter ego of Westin Mexico. She claims, for example, that Westin owns most of Westin Mexico's stock; that the two companies share common corporate officers; that Westin maintains quality control at Westin Mexico by requiring Westin Mexico to use certain operations manuals; that Westin oversees advertising and marketing operations at Westin Mexico through two separate contracts; and that Westin Mexico is grossly undercapitalized. Gardemal places particular emphasis on the last purported factor, that Westin Mexico is undercapitalized. She insists that this factor alone is sufficient evidence that Westin Mexico is the alter ego of Westin. We are not convinced.

The record, even when viewed in a light most favorable to Gardemal, reveals nothing more than a typical corporate relationship between a parent and subsidiary. It is true, as Gardemal points out, that Westin and Westin Mexico are closely tied through stock ownership, shared officers, financing arrangements, and the like. But this alone does not establish an alter-ego relationship. As we explained in *Jon-T Chemicals, Inc.*, [768 F. 2d 686 (5th Cir. 1985)], there must be evidence of complete domination by the parent.

> The control necessary . . . is not mere majority or complete stock control but such domination of finances, policies and practices that the controlled corporation has, so to speak, no separate mind, will or existence of its own and is but a business conduit for its principal.

Thus, "one-hundred percent ownership and identity of directors and officers are, even together, an insufficient basis for applying the alter ego theory to pierce the corporate veil." . . .

In this case, there is insufficient record evidence that Westin dominates Westin Mexico to the extent that Westin Mexico has, for practical purposes, surrendered its corporate identity. In fact, the evidence suggests just the opposite that Westin Mexico functions as an autonomous business entity. There is evidence, for example, that Westin Mexico banks in Mexico and deposits all of the revenue from its six hotels into that account. The facts also show that while Westin is incorporated in Delaware, Westin Mexico is incorporated in Mexico and faithfully adheres to the required corporate formalities. Finally, Westin Mexico has its own staff, its own assets, and even maintains its own insurance policies.

Gardemal is correct in pointing out that undercapitalization is a critical factor in our alter-ego analysis, especially in a tort case like the present one. But as noted by the district court, there is scant evidence that Westin Mexico is in fact undercapitalized and unable to pay a judgment, if necessary. This fact weighs heavily against Gardemal because the alter ego doctrine is an equitable remedy which prevents a company from avoiding liability by abusing the corporate form. "We disregard the corporate fiction . . . when the corporate form has been used as part of a basically unfair device to achieve an inequitable result." . . . In this case, there is insufficient evidence that Westin Mexico is undercapitalized or uninsured. Moreover, there is no indication that Gardemal could not recover by suing Westin Mexico directly. As a result, equity does not demand that we merge and disregard the corporate identities of Westin and Westin Mexico. We reject Gardemal's attempt to impute liability on Westin based on the alter-ego doctrine.

2.

Likewise, we reject Gardemal's attempt to impute liability to Westin based on the single business enterprise doctrine. Under that doctrine, when corporations are not operated as separate entities, but integrate their resources to achieve a common business purpose, each constituent corporation may be held liable for the debts incurred in pursuit of that business purpose. Like the alter-ego doctrine, the single business enterprise doctrine is an equitable remedy which applies when the corporate form is "used as part of an unfair device to achieve an inequitable result."

On appeal, Gardemal attempts to prove a single business enterprise by calling our attention to the fact that Westin Mexico uses the trademark "Westin Hotels and Resorts." She also emphasizes that Westin Regina uses Westin's operations manuals. Gardemal also observes that Westin allows Westin Mexico to use its reservation system. Again, these facts merely demonstrate what we would describe as a typical, working relationship between a parent and subsidiary. Gardemal has pointed to no evidence in the record demonstrating that the operations of the two corporations were so integrated as to result in a blending of the two corporate identities. Moreover, Gardemal has come forward with no evidence that she has suffered some harm, or injustice, because Westin and Westin Mexico maintain separate corporate identities.

Reviewing the record in the light most favorable to Gardemal, we conclude that there is insufficient evidence that Westin Mexico was Westin's alter ego. Similarly, there is insufficient evidence that the resources of Westin and Westin Mexico are so integrated as to constitute a single business enterprise. Accordingly, we affirm the district court's grant of Westin's motion for summary judgment on that issue. . . .

[The court also affirmed the district court's decision granting Westin Mexico's motion to dismiss for lack of personal jurisdiction.]

AFFIRMED.

b. Business Enterprise Liability: Contract

OTR ASSOCIATES v. IBC SERVICES, INC.
Superior Court of New Jersey, Appellate Division
801 A.2d 407 (2002)

PRESSLER, P.J.A.D.

The single dispositive issue raised by this appeal is whether the trial court, based on its findings of fact following a bench trial, was justified, as a matter of law, in piercing the corporate veil and thus holding a parent corporation liable for the debt incurred by its wholly owned subsidiary. We are satisfied that the facts, both undisputed and as found, present a textbook illustration of circumstances mandating corporate-veil piercing.

Plaintiff OTR Associates, a limited partnership, owns a shopping mall in Edison, New Jersey, in which it leased space in 1985 for use by a Blimpie franchisee, Samyrna, Inc., a corporation owned by Sam Iskander and his wife. The franchise agreement, styled as a licensing agreement, had been entered into in 1984 between Samyrna and the parent company, then known as International Blimpie Corporation, whose name was changed in 1985 to Astor Restaurant Group, Inc., and again in 1991 or 1992 to Blimpie International, Inc. Thus the three names denote the same corporation at different stages of its existence, and we refer to it hereafter as Blimpie. Blimpie was the sole owner of a subsidiary named IBC Services, Inc. (IBC), created for the single purpose of holding the lease on premises occupied by a Blimpie franchisee. Accordingly, it was IBC that entered into the lease with OTR in July 1985 and, on the same day and apparently with OTR's consent, subleased the space to the franchisee. The history of the tenancy was marked by regular and increasingly substantial rent arrearages, and it was terminated by a dispossess judgment and warrant for removal in 1996. In 1998 OTR commenced this action for unpaid rent, then in the amount of close to $150,000, against Blimpie under both its present name and its former name, International Blimpie Corporation. It also joined as defendants the leasing subsidiary, IBC, as well as Garden State Blimpie, Inc., another wholly-owned leaseholding subsidiary of Blimpie to whom IBC had assigned the lease in 1991 without notice to the landlord in violation of the terms of the lease requiring such notice. The action was tried in December 2000, and judgment was entered in favor of OTR against Blimpie as well as the two judgment-proof subsidiaries in the full amount of the rent arrearages plus interest thereon, then some $208,000. Blimpie appeals, and we affirm.

. . . .

[T]he basic finding that must be made to enable the court to pierce the corporate veil is "that the parent so dominated the subsidiary that it had no separate existence but was merely a conduit for the parent." . . . But beyond domination, the court must also find that the "parent has abused the privilege of incorporation by using the subsidiary to perpetrate a fraud or injustice, or otherwise to circumvent the law." And the hallmarks of that abuse are typically the engagement of the subsidiary in no independent business of its own but exclusively the performance of a service for the parent and, even more importantly, the undercapitalization of the subsidiary rendering it judgment-proof.

Blimpie concedes that it formed IBC for the sole purpose of holding the lease on the premises of a Blimpie franchisee. It is also clear that IBC had virtually no assets other than the lease itself, which, in the circumstances, was not an asset at all but only a liability since IBC had no independent right to alienate its interest therein but was subject to Blimpie's exclusive control. It had no business premises of its own, sharing the New York address of Blimpie. It had no income other than the rent payments by the franchisee, which appear to have been made directly to OTR. It does not appear that it had its own employees or office staff. We further note that Blimpie not only retained the right to approve the premises to be occupied by the franchisee and leased by IBC, but itself, in its Georgia headquarters, managed all the leases held by its subsidiaries on franchisee premises. . . .

Domination and control by Blimpie of IBC is patent and was not, nor could have been, reasonably disputed. The question then is whether Blimpie abused the privilege of incorporation by using IBC to commit a fraud or injustice or other improper purpose. We agree with the trial judge that the evidence overwhelmingly requires an affirmative answer. The testimony of plaintiff's partners who were involved in the dealings with IBC was that they believed that they were dealing with Blimpie, the national and financially responsible franchising company, and never discovered the fact of separate corporate entities until after the eviction. While it is true that IBC never apparently expressly claimed to be Blimpie, it not only failed to explain its relationship to Blimpie as a purported independent company but it affirmatively, intentionally, and calculatedly led OTR to believe it was Blimpie. Illustratively, when OTR was pre-leasing space in the mall, the first approach to it was the appearance at its on-site office of two men in Blimpie uniforms who announced that they wanted to open a Blimpie sandwich shop. One of the men was the franchisee, Iskander. The other was never identified but presumably was someone with a connection to Blimpie. It is also true that the named tenant in the lease was IBC Services, Inc., but the tenant was actually identified in the first paragraph of the lease as "IBC Services, Inc. having an address at c/o International Blimpie Corporation, 1414 Avenue of the Americas, New York, New York." It hardly required a cryptographer to draw the entirely reasonable inference that IBC stood for International Blimpie Corporation, Blimpie's corporate name when the lease was executed. . . .

Beyond the circumstances surrounding the commencement of the tenancy relationship, the correspondence through the years between plaintiff and the entity it believed to be its tenant confirmed plaintiff's belief that Blimpie was its tenant. Blimpie's letters to OTR were on stationary headed only by the Blimpie logo. There is nothing in any of that correspondence that would have suggested the existence of an independent company standing between the franchisor and the franchisee, and, indeed, the correspondence received by OTR from its lessee typically referred to the sub-tenant, Samyrna, as "our franchisee."

We agree with the trial judge that the inference is ineluctable and virtually conceded by Blimpie that IBC was created as a judgment-proof corporation for the sole purpose of insulating Blimpie from any liability on the lease in the event of the franchisee's default, a purpose found by the trial judge to have been deliberately concealed by Blimpie by its conduct in creating the impression from the outset of the tenancy relationship and throughout its duration that it and IBC were one and the same. . . .

As we understand Blimpie's defense and its argument on this appeal, it asserts that it is entitled to the benefit of the separate corporate identities merely because IBC observed all the corporate proprieties — it had its own officers and directors albeit interlocking with Blimpie's, it filed annual reports, kept minutes, held meetings, and had a bank account. But that argument begs the question. The separate corporate shell created by Blimpie to avoid liability may have been mechanistically impeccable, but in every functional and operational sense, the subsidiary had no separate identity. It was moreover not intended to shield the parent from responsibility for its subsidiary's obligations but rather to shield the parent from its own obligations. And that is an evasion and an improper purpose, fraudulently conceived and executed. The corporate veil was properly pierced.

. . . .

The judgment appealed from is affirmed.

NOTE

Traditional veil piercing requires, for example, that each veil be pierced to reach from a fourth or fifth tier subsidiary, through intermediate subsidiaries, to reach the publicly-held, and visible, parent or multinational parent corporation. Such an approach is said to be a manifestation of the "entity theory" of veil piercing, going entity by entity. Under the "enterprise theory," advocated by many commentators but only hesitatingly adopted by courts, a court would regard all of the subsidiaries, plus any brother-sister corporations who had any involvement in the alleged wrongdoing, as well as the parent corporation, to be a single entity for liability purposes. Professor Phillip Blumberg has been a persistent advocate of an enterprise rather than entity by entity approach to the liability of corporate groups. *See* P. BLUMBERG & K. STRASSER, THE LAW OF CORPORATE GROUPS: ENTERPRISE LIABILITY (1998).

F.   REVERSE VEIL PIERCING

It is well-settled, as this Chapter has previously discussed, that in certain situations courts will disregard the corporate fiction of limited liability that separates the assets of the subject corporation from its shareholders and impose personal liability on active shareholders through the doctrine of piercing the corporate veil. In the same vein, many jurisdictions also hold that the opposite is available as an equitable remedy on the theory of reverse veil-piercing in which a claimant is allowed to reach the assets of the corporation to satisfy a claim against a corporate director/officer or shareholder. In the case of a reverse veil-piercing claim, a plaintiff with a claim against a shareholder or insider of the corporation attempts to have the insider and the limited liability entity treated as a single person so the assets of the corporation can be used to compensate for the injury caused by the corporate insider. Moreover, reverse piercing can be sought to be invoked by a controlling shareholder against third parties.[35] The following case decided by the Colorado Supreme Court provides a recent example of reverse veil-piercing.

PHILLIPS v. ENGLEWOOD POST NO. 322 VETERANS OF FOREIGN WARS OF THE UNITED STATES, INC.

Supreme Court of Colorado

139 P.3d 639 (2006)

JUSTICE MARTINEZ delivered the Opinion of the Court.

[W]e agreed to answer a certified question of law posed to us by the United States District Court for the District of Colorado. The federal district court requested a determination of whether Colorado law recognizes the so-called reverse piercing of the corporate veil doctrine. Reverse piercing occurs when a claimant seeks to disregard the separate existence of a corporation and obtain the assets of the entity due to the actions of a dominant shareholder or other corporate insider.

We have not previously considered whether reverse piercing is appropriate under Colorado law. Colorado does permit traditional piercing of the corporate veil, however, in extraordinary circumstances. Traditional piercing occurs when a trial court disregards the corporate form and attaches liability on individual shareholders for the obligations of the corporation.

While some different considerations color the unique types of piercing, traditional veil piercing and allowing a corporate outsider to reverse pierce the corporate form are substantially similar and both serve the purpose of achieving an equitable result.

---

[35] Crespi, *The Reverse Pierce Doctrine: Applying Appropriate Standards*, 16 J. CORP. L. 33 (1990).

Accordingly, we determine that a corporation, in limited circumstances, may be liable for the debts of a controlling shareholder or other corporate insider where the shareholder or insider treated the corporation as his alter ego to perpetuate a fraud or defeat a rightful claim and an equitable result is achieved by piercing.

. . . .

To prevent abuse, Colorado law permits trial courts to disregard the corporate form and pierce the corporate veil when a corporation and a shareholder are alter egos of each other. Here, we are asked to expand this principle to disregard the corporate fiction and allow liability to be imposed on the corporation for acts of a dominant shareholder or other corporate insider.

Reverse piercing occurs when a claimant seeks to hold a corporation liable for the obligations of an individual shareholder. Two types of reverse piercing exist: inside and outside claims.

Inside claims involve a "controlling insider who attempts to have the corporate entity disregarded to avail the insider of corporate claims against third parties" or to protect corporate assets "from third party claims . . . ." Gregory S. Crespi, *The Reverse Pierce Doctrine: Applying Appropriate Standards*, 16 J. Corp. L. 33, 37 (1990); . . . Inside reverse piercing claims allow a shareholder to disregard the corporate form of which he or she is a part.

Outside reverse piercing claims occur when a corporate outsider "pressing an action against a corporate insider seeks to disregard the corporate entity [and] seeks to subject corporate assets to the claim" or when an outsider "with a claim against a corporate insider seeks to assert that claim against the corporation in an action between the claimant and the corporation." Crespi, *supra* at 55; . . . Outside reverse piercing actions involve a corporate outsider seeking to obligate a corporation for the debts of a dominant shareholder or other corporate insider.

Although the certified question of law could be read to encompass both inside and outside reverse piercing claims, we limit our review to outside claims due to the facts presented in this case. Here, Appellant, an outsider to Philsax, Inc., seeks to hold the corporation liable for the obligations of Debtor. Accordingly, we turn to whether Colorado law permits outside reverse piercing of the corporate veil.

Admittedly, the corporate interests at stake in traditional and outside reverse piercing differ, as does the entity pierced. In traditional veil piercing, the veil shields a shareholder who is abusing the corporate fiction to perpetuate a wrong. In outside reverse piercing, however, the corporate form protects the corporation which, through the acts of a dominant shareholder or other corporate insider, uses the legal fiction to perpetuate a fraud or defeat a rightful claim of an outsider. While traditional and outside reverse piercing affect diverse corporate interests, the purposes sought to be achieved are similar.

Both types of piercing strive to achieve an equitable result. In traditional piercing, equity requires the veil be pierced to impose liability on a shareholder who has abused the corporate form for his or her own advantage. Similarly, in outside reverse piercing, an equitable result is achieved by ignoring the corporate fiction to attach liability to the corporation. "Indeed, it is particularly appropriate to apply the alter ego doctrine in 'reverse' when the controlling party uses the controlled entity to hide assets or secretly to conduct business to avoid the preexisting liability of the controlling party." . . . Thus, the purpose of obtaining a just result is furthered by permitting outside reverse piercing in Colorado.

Due to the similarities and parallel goals achieved in outside reverse piercing and traditional piercing, we hold that Colorado law permits outside reverse piercing when justice so requires.

We recognize that some jurisdictions refuse to allow outside reverse piercing of the corporate form because, when inartfully performed, outside reverse piercing has the potential to prejudice innocent shareholders and creditors, and to bypass normal judgment procedures. As will be explained fully [below], this concern is effectively alleviated by the requirement that piercing obtain an equitable result.

. . . .

Having concluded that outside reverse piercing is appropriate, we proceed to discuss the limitations of the doctrine. A court may reverse pierce the corporate veil and obtain the assets of a corporation for the obligations of a controlling shareholder or other corporate insider only upon a clear showing that (1) the controlling insider and the corporation are alter egos of each other, (2) justice requires recognizing the substance of the relationship over the form because the corporate fiction is utilized to perpetuate a fraud or defeat a rightful claim, and (3) an equitable result is achieved by piercing. Only when a claimant makes a clear showing of each factor may the corporate form be disregarded.

Generally, in determining whether to outside reverse pierce the corporate veil, a court should review the same factors utilized in determining whether traditional veil piercing is appropriate.

Here, the first factor to consider is whether Debtor and Philsax, Inc. [Philsax] were alter egos of each other. In making this determination, our analysis suggests the Debtor's control over Philsax is relevant. Debtor removed and added directors without board approval and used the sale of corporate property to pay for his personal expenses. Margaret M. Phillips, the other shareholder [of Philsax], could not explain her role in the corporation. Also significant is Philsax's failure to operate as a distinct business entity, including the lack of a bank account and intermingling . . . . Furthermore, Philsax's failure to observe many of the corporate formalities is germane; specifically the entity had no written bylaws, did not provide notice to directors or shareholders of board meetings, and did not maintain any written financial statements.

The second factor to review is whether justice requires recognizing the substance of the relationship between Debtor and Philsax over the form. Relevant to this inquiry is whether Philsax transferred its assets to defeat a third party judgment against Debtor.

The third determination is whether an equitable result would be achieved by piercing. As previously alluded to, some additional equitable considerations apply in the outside reverse piercing context.

When innocent shareholders or creditors would be prejudiced by outside reverse piercing, an equitable result is not achieved. Innocent shareholders possess legitimate expectations that corporate assets will be insulated from the claims of a controlling insider's creditors. Similarly, secured and unsecured creditors of the corporation have a cognizable legal interest in corporate assets, upon which they relied in lending money and selling goods and services to the corporation. Accordingly, equity requires that innocent shareholders and creditors be adequately protected before outside reverse piercing is appropriate under Colorado law.

As pertinent here, Debtor identified the creditors of Philsax as identical to his personal creditors. The corporation has no other creditors. As the creditors of the entity are those of the Debtor, no creditors would be injured by outside reverse piercing. Our analysis does suggest, however, that if innocent shareholders would be prejudiced, piercing would not be warranted.

Furthermore, as piercing the corporate veil is an extraordinary remedy, the availability of alternative, adequate remedies must be considered by the trial court. These remedies may include, but are not limited to, conversion, fraudulent conveyance of assets, respondeat superior, and agency law. When a less invasive, adequate remedy is available, outside reverse piercing is discouraged.

In summation, we conclude that outside reverse piercing is appropriate when a claimant demonstrates that a controlling insider and a corporation are alter egos of each other and justice requires recognizing the substance of that relationship over the form to achieve an equitable result. An equitable result is not achieved when innocent shareholders or creditors are prejudiced by outside reverse piercing. Additionally, a court should avoid outside reverse piercing when alternative, adequate remedies are available. In light of these limitations, this decision is unlikely to impact many business entities other than a limited number of closely held corporations with few shareholders or only a single shareholder.

. . . .

G. EQUITABLE SUBORDINATION: THE DEEP ROCK DOCTRINE

The Deep Rock Doctrine, taken from the name of the subsidiary in the 1939 Supreme Court case of first impression,[36] is invoked when a corporation is in bankruptcy and its general creditors ask the court to subordinate the debt of the corporation's shareholders so the creditors can recover first. It is an equitable doctrine in which courts readjust the order of payments during a bankruptcy proceeding relegating shareholders of the bankrupt company that hold debt "to go to the back of the line,"ultimately making it unlikely that they will receive any payment after the general creditors are paid. If shareholder loans are subordinated to the claims of other general creditors, they will be reclassified as an infusion of equity (e.g., common stock) into the company and reimbursed in the bankruptcy in the same order as other common stockholders. The general creditors thus benefit when a court is persuaded to invoke the doctrine because they share the liquidated assets of the bankrupt corporation with fewer claimants and potentially receive larger recoveries.[37]

The Deep Rock doctrine may be imposed by courts when some kind of improper conduct surrounds a loan made to a corporation by a controlling shareholder. Section 501(c) of the Bankruptcy Act of 1978 states that "after notice and a hearing, the court may . . . under principles of equitable subordination, subordinate for purposes of distribution all or part of an allowed claim to all or part of another allowed claim . . . ."[38] Courts have used a number of factors to subordinate the position of claims by controlling shareholders. Often the Deep Rock Doctrine is invoked when a parent corporation has extended loans as the controlling shareholder of an insolvent subsidiary. Although normally not sufficient by itself to invoke the Deep Rock Doctrine, undercapitalization of the insolvent corporation is often the primary reason offered by creditors when asking for equitable subordination. Courts often employ a version of the reasonable person standard when analyzing the level of undercapitalization of a corporation when a shareholder advanced the loan. If an informed outside source would have provided the loan to the corporation knowing its financial condition, then the shareholder should be allowed to provide the loan and not have it subordinated and reclassified as equity. However, if a bank or other unaffiliated party would not have given the loan because of the precarious financial condition of the company and the shareholder provided the loan anyway, the company may well be considered undercapitalized.[39]

In addition to undercapitalization, some degree of suspicious conduct by the directors, officers or active shareholders that made the loans is evident in cases employing the Deep Rock Doctrine.[40] In *Costello v. Fazio*, for example, the Ninth Circuit considered

---

[36] Taylor v. Standard Gas & Elec. Co., 306 U.S. 307 (1939).

[37] *See* J. Cox & T. Hazen, Corporations § 7.10 (2d ed. 2003).

[38] 11 U.S.C.A. § 510(c).

[39] *See* J. Cox & T. Hazen, Corporations § 7.10 (2d ed. 2003). *see also*, Pepper v. Litton, 308 U.S. 295 (1939).

[40] *See* Costello v. Fazio, 256 F.2d 903 (9th Cir. 1958); *In re* Fett Roofing & Sheet Metal Co., 438 F. Supp 726 (E.D. Va. 1977).

more than the undercapitalization of the corporation in determining that the promissory notes of controlling partners should be subordinated to claims of general unsecured creditors.[41] The Ninth Circuit found it suspicious, significantly contributing to a finding of equitable subordination, that the stockholders "stripped the business of 88% of its stated capital at a time when it had a minus working capital and had suffered substantial business losses."[42] Additionally, in *In re Fett Roofing and Sheet Metal Co., Inc.*, the court reclassified the plaintiff's monetary transfers to the corporation as capital contributions instead of loans based, in part, on the plaintiff's conduct in making advances and withdrawals of money to the enterprise.[43] The plaintiff in *In re Fett* transferred money and assets worth less than $5,000 in exchange for 100% of the corporate stock. Years later, the plaintiff transferred over $75,000 to the company in exchange for demand promissory notes. After the corporation became insolvent, the plaintiff recorded deeds of trust to secure his promissory notes with the company's assets and backdated the deeds to the original dates he made monetary transfers to the corporation. The court found the plaintiff's lending activities suspicious in light of the 80 to 1 debt-to-equity ratio of the company, his daily control over the company's affairs, the backdating of the deeds, and the lack of corporate formalities in providing the secured promissory notes. Concluding that the plaintiff actually provided the corporation with capital instead of extending secured loans, the court subordinated the plaintiff's claims to those of other creditors of the bankrupt corporation.[44]

H. PIERCING THE VEIL OF THE LIMITED LIABILITY COMPANY

The limited liability company ("LLC") is a relatively new corporate vehicle. Members of a LLC ordinarily are not held personally liable for the debts of the firm. While LLCs can either be manager-managed or member-managed, state statutes allow members to participate in management. As § 303 of the Uniform Limited Liability Company Act provides:

> Except as otherwise provided . . . , the debts, obligations, and liabilities of a limited liability company, whether arising in a contract, tort, or otherwise, are solely the debts, obligations, and liabilities of the company. A member or manager is not personally liable for a debt, obligation, or liability of the company solely by reason of being or acting as a member or manager.

With respect to the LLC, the question arises whether the corporate veil-piercing doctrine applies.

While a number of states like Minnesota expressly provide that common-law corporate veil-piercing doctrines apply with the same strength and frequency to LLCs,[45] numerous other state statutes are silent on the effect of the doctrine on LLCs. One example of a statute being silent as to LLC veil-piercing is the Wyoming LLC statute. However, this did not stop the Wyoming Supreme Court from expressly likening a LLC to a corporation, analyzing the doctrine's applicability as such and finding the LLC and its members vulnerable to veil-piercing:

> We have long recognized that piercing the corporate veil is an equitable doctrine. The concept of piercing the corporate veil is a judicially created remedy for situations where corporations have not been operated as separate entities as contemplated by statute and, therefore, are not entitled to be treated

---

[41] *Costello*, 256 F.2d at 910.

[42] *Id.*

[43] *In re* Fett Roofing & Sheet Metal Co., 438 F. Supp at 726.

[44] *Id.* at 731.

[45] Minn. Stat. Ann. § 322B.303(2).

as such. The determination of whether the doctrine applies centers on whether there is an element of injustice, fundamental unfairness, or inequity . . . . [B]ecause it is an equitable doctrine, "[t]he paucity of statutory authority for LCC piercing should not be considered a barrier to its application." . . . Lack of explicit statutory language should not be considered an indication of the legislature's desire to make LLC members impermeable . . . We can discern no reason, in either law or policy, to treat LLCs differently than we treat corporations. If the members and officers of an LLC fail to treat it as a separate entity as contemplated by statute, they should not enjoy immunity from individual liability for the LLC's acts that cause damage to third parties.[46]

Conversely, a number of commentators advocate abolishing the veil-piercing doctrine in the LLC context. Although conceding that there is "little direct evidence that legislatures intended to treat LLCs and corporations differently, [nonetheless] . . . if legislatures had intended to incorporate the corporate law doctrines, they easily could have done so explicitly [in LLC statutes.]"[47] Professor Stephen M. Bainbridge concludes that:

> [T]he emerging doctrines for piercing the LLC veil are hopelessly dysfunctional. They encourage inefficient investment in irrelevant precautions, while encouraging expensive and complex litigation. They may discourage capital formation in small businesses by exposing those businesses to a disproportionate share of the burden from the tort liability system, which in turn undermines the valuable democratic contribution — at the risk of being too corny, the American dream — of small business ownership and entrepreneurship.[48]

Nonetheless, thus far, as a general proposition, courts treat LLCs the same as corporations for veil-piercing purposes.[49]

I. SHAREHOLDER LIABILITY UNDER FEDERAL LAW: ENVIRONMENTAL VEIL PIERCING

Corporations are established and governed largely by state law. However, in recent decades there has been a significant increase in the amount of federal law that gives federal courts a basis to hold corporate shareholders personally liable. One such example is the Comprehensive Environmental Response, Compensation and Liability Act ("CERCLA").[50]

CERCLA was enacted to protect communities and hold liable those parties that contaminated and then abandoned real property that contained significant levels of toxic waste. Under CERCLA, broad federal authority is provided to hold liable four distinct groups of "potential responsible parties" that may be liable for contamination: (1) the current owner or operator of the contaminated site; (2) the previous owner or operator responsible for the site at the time the contamination occurred; (3) a person who

---

[46] Kaycee Land & Livestock v. Flahive, 46 P.3d 323, 326–27 (Wyo. 2002), relying on, Gelb, *Liabilities of Members and Managers of Wyoming Limited Liability Companies*, 31 LAND & WATER L. REV. 133 (1996).

[47] Bainbridge, *Abolishing LLC Veil Piercing*, 2005 U. ILL. L. REV. 77, 92 (2005). *But see* Morrissey, *Piercing All the Veils: Applying an Established Doctrine to a New Business Order*, 32 J. CORP. L. 530 (2007).

[48] Bainbridge, *supra* note 47, at 106.

[49] *See* MINN. STAT. ANN. § 322B.303(2) (stating that LLCs may have their veil of limited liability pierced the same as corporations); CONN. GEN. STAT. § 34-133(a) (remaining silent on the express application of the veil-piercing doctrine on LLCs). However, the judiciary in Connecticut has interpreted its silent statute as not foreclosing the application of the veil-piercing doctrine in LLCs. Bastan v. RJM & Assocs., 2001 Conn. Super. LEXIS 1605 (Conn. Super. Ct. June 4, 2001).

[50] Comprehensive Environmental Response, Compensation, and Liability Act, 42 U.S.C §§ 9601–9675 (2000). We already have seen veil piercing in the federal statutory context in the NLRB-West Dixie case set forth earlier in this Chapter.

arranged for the disposal of toxic waste at the site; and (4) the person who transported the contaminant to the site. CERCLA has provided numerous unique opportunities for federal courts to determine if corporate shareholders are "owners" or "operators" of polluted sites and, therefore, liable for the clean-up costs of the toxic waste. Prior to the following United States Supreme Court case, many lower federal courts adopted varied and inconsistent definitions of "owner" and "operator" as they applied to limited liability entities.

UNITED STATES v. BESTFOODS
United States Supreme Court
524 U.S. 51 (1998)

JUSTICE SOUTER delivered the Opinion of the Court

. . . .

It is a general principle of corporate law deeply "ingrained in our economic and legal systems" that a parent corporation (so-called because of control through ownership of another corporation's stock) is not liable for the acts of its subsidiaries. Douglas & Shanks, *Insulation from Liability Through Subsidiary Corporations*, 39 Yale L.J. 193 (1929). . . . Thus it is hornbook law that "the exercise of the 'control' which stock ownership gives to the stockholders . . . will not create liability beyond the assets of the subsidiary. That 'control' includes the election of directors, the making of by-laws . . . and the doing of all other acts incident to the legal status of stockholders. Nor will a duplication of some or all of the directors or executive officers be fatal." . . . Although this respect for corporate distinctions when the subsidiary is a polluter has been severely criticized in the literature, . . . nothing in CERCLA purports to reject this bedrock principle, and against this venerable common-law backdrop, the congressional silence is audible. . . . The Government has indeed made no claim that a corporate parent is liable as an owner or an operator under § 107 simply because its subsidiary is subject to liability for owning or operating a polluting facility.

But there is an equally fundamental principle of corporate law, applicable to the parent-subsidiary relationship as well as generally, that the corporate veil may be pierced and the shareholder held liable for the corporation's conduct when, inter alia, the corporate form would otherwise be misused to accomplish certain wrongful purposes, most notably fraud, on the shareholder's behalf. . . . Nothing in CERCLA purports to rewrite this well-settled rule, either. CERCLA is thus like many another congressional enactment in giving no indication that "the entire corpus of state corporation law is to be replaced simply because a plaintiff's cause of action is based upon a federal statute," . . . and the failure of the statute to speak to a matter as fundamental as the liability implications of corporate ownership demands application of the rule that "[i]n order to abrogate a common-law principle, the statute must speak directly to the question addressed by the common law" . . . . The Court of Appeals was accordingly correct in holding that when (but only when) the corporate veil may be pierced, may a parent corporation be charged with derivative CERCLA liability for its subsidiary's actions.

. . . .

If the Act rested liability entirely on ownership of a polluting facility, this opinion might end here; but CERCLA liability may turn on operation as well as ownership, and nothing in the statute's terms bars a parent corporation from direct liability for its own actions in operating a facility owned by its subsidiary. As Justice (then-Professor) Douglas noted almost 70 years ago, derivative liability cases are to be distinguished from those in which "the alleged wrong can seemingly be traced to the parent through the conduit of its own personnel and management" and "the parent is directly a participant in the wrong complained of." . . . In such instances, the parent is directly liable for its own actions. See H. HENN & J. ALEXANDER, LAWS OF CORPORATIONS 347 (3d ed. 1983) ("Apart from corporation law principles, a shareholder, whether a natural person or a corporation, may be liable on the ground that such shareholder's activity resulted in the liability"). The fact that a corporate subsidiary happens to own a polluting facility operated by its parent does nothing, then, to displace the rule that the parent "corporation is [itself] responsible for the wrongs committed by its agents in the course of its business," . . . and whereas the rules of veil piercing limit derivative liability for the actions of another corporation, CERCLA's "operator" provision is concerned primarily with direct liability for one's own actions. . . . It is this direct liability that is properly seen as being at issue here.

Under the plain language of the statute, any person who operates a polluting facility is directly liable for the costs of cleaning up the pollution. This is so regardless of whether that person is the facility's owner, the owner's parent corporation or business partner, or even a saboteur who sneaks into the facility at night to discharge its poisons out of malice. If any such act of operating a corporate subsidiary's facility is done on behalf of a parent corporation, the existence of the parent-subsidiary relationship under state corporate law is simply irrelevant to the issue of direct liability. . . .

This much is easy to say: the difficulty comes in defining actions sufficient to constitute direct parental "operation." Here of course we may again rue the uselessness of CERCLA's definition of a facility's "operator" as "any person . . . operating" the facility, which leaves us to do the best we can to give the term its "ordinary or natural meaning." . . . In a mechanical sense, to "operate" ordinarily means "[t]o control the functioning of; run: operate a sewing machine." American Heritage Dictionary 1268 (3d ed. 1992); see also Webster's New International Dictionary 1707 (2d ed. 1958) ("to work; as, to operate a machine"). . . . So, under CERCLA, an operator is simply someone who directs the workings of, manages, or conducts the affairs of a facility. To sharpen the definition for purposes of CERCLA's concern with environmental contamination, an operator must manage, direct, or conduct operations specifically related to pollution, that is, operations having to do with the leakage or disposal of hazardous waste, or decisions about compliance with environmental regulations.

. . . .

Chapter 8

MANAGEMENT AND CONTROL OF THE CORPORATION

A. SOCIAL RESPONSIBILITY

A seemingly timeless issue in corporate law is whether, or the extent to which, a corporation has a "social responsibility." See, for example, C.A. Harwell Wells, *The Cycles of Corporate Social Responsibility: An Historical Retrospective for the 21st Century*, 51 U. KAN. L. REV. 77 (2002); Douglas M. Branson, *Corporate Governance "Reform" and the New Corporate Social Responsibility*, 62 U. PITT. L. REV. 605, 608–17 (2001), reviewing this history. What commentators mean by this phrase is whether a corporation has some sort of obligation to contribute to society beyond making a profit for its shareholders and following the law. Those who believe that the corporation does have such an obligation do not specify the extent of that obligation by, for instance, arguing what portion of corporate profits should be sacrificed "for the common good," or given to charity. Indeed, quantifying a corporate social responsibility in this sense would be difficult, if not impossible. Rather, the debate tends to center more around justifying corporate behavior that does not maximize corporate profits on the basis that such behavior furthers other, laudable ends (if, in fact, that is the case). For instance, a business might install antipollution devices limiting carbon emissions and announce that it is doing so because of its concern for global warming. A shareholder complaining that the board's decision to do so wasted corporate assets might be faced with an argument that the action was protected by the business judgment rule because the favorable publicity that accompanied the announcement served a corporate purpose. But even if the corporation did not announce its altruistic action, the directors might defend their actions as consistent with the corporation's social responsibility and, therefore, appropriate. One can see from this simple hypothetical how difficult it would be to police the conduct of directors who rely on social responsibility as the source of their authority. Nonetheless, the debate rages on.

Corporate charitable contributions represent a particular application of the notion of social responsibility. The next case presents a discussion of the issue in the context of a corporate contribution to a private university. As you read this case, consider whether the outcome would have been different if the contribution had been made anonymously. In other words, to what extent is the board's decision a simple business judgment with the benefit to the corporation coming in the form of favorable publicity?

A.P. SMITH MFG. CO. v. BARLOW
Supreme Court of New Jersey
13 N.J. 145, 98 A.2d 581 (1953)

JACOBS, J.

[The shareholders of A.P. Smith Mfg. Co. challenged the corporation's gift of $1500 to Princeton University. In response, the corporation filed a declaratory judgment action and the Chancery Court held in favor of the corporation after a trial.]

Mr. Hubert F. O'Brien, the president of the company, testified that he considered the contribution to be a sound investment, that the public expects corporations to aid philanthropic and benevolent institutions, that they obtain good will in the community by so doing, and that their charitable donations create favorable environment for their business operations. In addition, he expressed the thought that in contributing to liberal arts institutions, corporations were furthering their self-interest in assuring the free flow of properly trained personnel for administrative and other corporate employment. Mr. Frank W. Abrams, chairman of the board of the Standard Oil Company of New Jersey, testified that corporations are expected to acknowledge their public responsibilities in support of the essential elements of our free enterprise system. He indicated that it was not 'good business' to disappoint 'this reasonable and justified public expectation,' nor was it good business for corporations 'to take substantial benefits from their membership in the economic community while avoiding the normally accepted obligations of citizenship in the social community.' Mr. Irving S. Olds, former chairman of the board of the United States Steel Corporation, pointed out that corporations have a self-interest in the maintenance of liberal education as the bulwark of good government. He stated that 'Capitalism and free enterprise owe their survival in no small degree to the existence of our private, independent universities' and that if American business does not aid in their maintenance it is not 'properly protecting the long-range interest of its stockholders, its employees and its customers.' Similarly, Dr. Harold W. Dodds, President of Princeton University, suggested that if private institutions of higher learning were replaced by governmental institutions our society would be vastly different and private enterprise in other fields would fade out rather promptly. Further on he stated that 'democratic society will not long endure if it does not nourish within itself strong centers of non-governmental fountains of knowledge, opinions of all sorts not governmentally or politically originated. If the time comes when all these centers are absorbed into government, then freedom as we know it, I submit, is at an end.'

The objecting stockholders have not disputed any of the foregoing testimony nor the showing of great need by Princeton and other private institutions of higher learning and the important public service being rendered by them for democratic government and industry alike. Similarly, they have acknowledged that for over two decades there has been state legislation on our books which expresses a strong public policy in favor of corporate contributions such as that being questioned by them. Nevertheless, they have taken the position that (1) the plaintiff's certificate of incorporation does not expressly authorize the contribution and under common-law principles the company does not possess any implied or incidental power to make it . . . .

In his discussion of the early history of business corporations Professor Williston refers to a 1702 publication where the author stated flatly that 'The general intent and end of all civil incorporations is for better government.' And he points out that the early corporate charters, particularly their recitals, furnish additional support for the notion that the corporate object was the public one of managing and ordering the trade as well as the private one of profit for the members . . . . However, with later economic and social developments and the free availability of the corporate device for all trades, the end of private profit became generally accepted as the controlling one in all businesses other than those classed broadly as public utilities. As a concomitant the common-law rule developed that those who managed the corporation could not disburse any corporate funds for philanthropic or other worthy public cause unless the expenditure would benefit the corporation. During the 19th Century when corporations were relatively few and small and did not dominate the country's wealth, the common-law rule did not significantly interfere with the public interest. But the 20th Century has presented a different climate. Berle & Means, The Modern Corporation and Private Property (1948). Control of economic wealth has passed largely from individual entrepreneurs to dominating corporations, and calls upon the corporations for reasonable philanthropic donations have come to be made with increased public support. In many instances such contributions have been sustained by the courts within the common-law doctrine upon liberal findings that the donations tended reasonably to promote the corporate objectives.

. . . The foregoing authorities illustrate how courts, while adhering to the terms of the common-law rule, have applied it very broadly to enable worthy corporate donations with indirect benefits to the corporations. In State ex rel. Sorensen v. Chicago B. & Q.R. Co., 112 Neb. 248, 199 N.W. 534, 537 (1924), the Supreme Court of Nebraska, through Justice Letton, went even further and without referring to any limitation based on economic benefits to the corporation said that it saw 'no reason why if a railroad company desires to foster, encourage and contribute to a charitable enterprise, or to one designed for the public weal and welfare, it may not do so' . . . .

When the wealth of the nation was primarily in the hands of individuals they discharged their responsibilities as citizens by donating freely for charitable purposes. With the transfer of most of the wealth to corporate hands and the imposition of heavy burdens of individual taxation, they have been unable to keep pace with increased philanthropic needs. They have therefore, with justification, turned to corporations to assume the modern obligations of good citizenship in the same manner as humans do. Congress and state legislatures have enacted laws which encourage corporate contributions, and much has recently been written to indicate the crying need and adequate legal basis therefore . . . .

. . . It seems to us that just as the conditions prevailing when corporations were originally created required that they serve public as well as private interests, modern conditions require that corporations acknowledge and discharge social as well as private responsibilities as members of the communities within which they operate. Within this broad concept there is no difficulty in sustaining, as incidental to their proper objects and in aid of the public welfare, the power of corporations to contribute corporate funds within reasonable limits in support of academic institutions. But even if we confine ourselves to the terms of the common-law rule in its application to current conditions, such expenditures may likewise readily be justified as being for the benefit of the corporation; indeed, if need be the matter may be viewed strictly in terms of actual survival of the corporation in a free enterprise system . . . .

. . . In the light of all of the foregoing [statutes enacted in 1930 and 1950 that expressly authorize corporate charitable contributions] we have no hesitancy in sustaining the validity of the donation by the plaintiff. There is no suggestion that it was made indiscriminately or to a pet charity of the corporate directors in furtherance of personal rather than corporate ends. On the contrary, it was made to a preeminent institution of higher learning, was modest in amount and well within the limitations imposed by the statutory enactments, and was voluntarily made in the reasonable belief that it would aid the public welfare and advance the interests of the plaintiff as a private corporation and as part of the community in which it operates. We find that it was a lawful exercise of the corporation's implied and incidental powers under common-law principles and that it came within the express authority of the pertinent state legislation. As has been indicated, there is now widespread belief throughout the nation that free and vigorous non-governmental institutions of learning are vital to our democracy and the system of free enterprise and that withdrawal of corporate authority to make such contributions within reasonable limits would seriously threaten their continuance. Corporations have come to recognize this and with their enlightenment have sought in varying measures, as has the plaintiff by its contribution, to insure and strengthen the society which gives them existence and the means of aiding themselves and their fellow citizens. Clearly then, the appellants, as individual stockholders whose private interests rest entirely upon the well-being of the plaintiff corporation, ought not be permitted to close their eyes to present-day realities and thwart the long-visioned corporate action in recognizing and voluntarily discharging its high obligations as a constituent of our modern social structure.

The judgment entered in the Chancery Division is in all respects

Affirmed.

NOTES AND QUESTIONS

1. In an omitted portion of the opinion, the court dealt with the question of whether a change in the state's corporate code could affect the relationship between the corporation and the shareholders and between shareholders inter se, concluding that it could. This implicates the "reserved power," pursuant to which the state reserves the power to amend or repeal all or any part of the corporate code. See, e.g., MBCA § 1.02.

The court noted that the application of the reserve clause has been upheld under the federal constitution.

2. Corporate codes all contain provisions expressly authorizing corporations to make charitable donations. *See, e.g.*, MBCA § 3.02(13): "[A corporation has the power] to make donations for the public welfare or for charitable, scientific or educational purposes." Some codes, however, are broader, making it clear that there need be no benefit to the corporation from the donation. See for example, the New York Business Corporation Law, § 202(a)(12), which includes among the powers of a corporation the power "to make donations, *irrespective of corporate benefit*, for the public welfare or for community fund, hospital, charitable, educational, scientific, civic or similar purposes, and in time of war or other national emergency in aid thereof." (emphasis added) Juxtaposing the MBCA and New York provision gives rise to the implication that corporations operating under the MBCA must demonstrate a corporate benefit to justify a charitable donation. Courts, however, have been deferential to boards and have considered charitable contributions as an exercise of the board's business judgment. Finally, consider the American Law Institute's Principles of Corporate Governance, § 2.10(b)(3), which provides that a corporation may "devote a reasonable amount of resources to public welfare, humanitarian, educational, and philanthropic purposes" even if "corporate profit and shareholder gain are not thereby enhanced."

3. The board's power to make charitable contributions is enhanced if the state has enacted an "other constituency" statute. Under these statutes, which have been enacted in roughly 30 states, the board may take into account the effects of its actions on various constituencies of the corporation, including shareholders, employees, suppliers, customers, creditors, and the communities in which the corporation has offices or other facilities. Such a provision, of course, provides another basis for making charitable contributions, as well as resisting a possible change of control of the corporation, a topic covered in Chapter 16 below.

4. One possible basis to challenge a charitable contribution is that the directors who approved the contribution were conflicted. Suppose, for instance, that the CEO of Mega Corp. was a director of the local opera company and persuaded the Mega Corp. board to make a contribution to it. Assuming that the opera is a charitable organization (i.e., exempt from federal income taxation and donations are deductible under the Internal Revenue Code), could a shareholder successfully challenge the contribution?

B.   CORPORATE PURPOSE

The preceding case suggests that a corporation can make charitable contributions even if it does not benefit directly thereby. But how far can a corporate board take this principle? Are charitable contributions an exception to notion that corporate action should benefit the corporation, or just a manifestation of the freedom that directors have to conduct corporate business? The next case, a "nugget" of corporate law, addresses the issue.

DODGE v. FORD MOTOR CO.
Supreme Court of Michigan
204 Mich. 459, 170 N.W. 668 (1919)

OSTRANDER, J.

[The Ford Motor Co. was organized in 1903 and, by any measure, was wildly successful in the ensuing years. It paid regular monthly dividends at the rate of 5% on its $2,000,000 capital and special dividends between 1911 and 1915 amounting to $41,000,000 in the aggregate. Despite these large dividends, the company's surplus increased markedly, amounting to $112 million by July 31, 1916. The company followed a practice of steadily decreasing the price of its cars, so that while the original model sold for $900, by 1916, the price was $360 which, of course, greatly increased unit sales.

The plaintiffs owned 10% of the company's stock, but Henry Ford owned 58% and dominated the board of directors. The plaintiffs' complaint was prompted by Ford's decision to discontinue the payment of special dividends.

The plaintiffs also complained of Ford's announced intention to reinvest profits so that the company would become vertically integrated. He suggested that the company would purchase iron ore mines, build ships to transport the iron ore, and build the factories necessary to produce steel for the cars. The plaintiffs sought (a) to enjoin this business plan, (b) a decree requiring the distribution to the stockholders of at least 75% of the accumulate cash surplus, and (c) an order that, in the future, earnings be distributed to the stockholders "except as may be reasonably required for emergency purposes in the conduct of the business." The lower court ordered the company to declare a dividend equal to one-half of the accumulated cash surplus on hand at the July 31, 1916. The company appealed.]

. . . The case for plaintiffs must rest upon the claim, and the proof in support of it, that the proposed expansion of the business of the corporation, involving the further use of profits as capital, ought to be enjoined because inimical to the best interests of the company and its shareholders, and upon the further claim that in any event the withholding of the special dividend asked for by plaintiffs is arbitrary action of the directors requiring judicial interference.

The rule which will govern courts in deciding these questions is not in dispute. It is, of course, differently phrased by judges and by authors, and, as the phrasing in a particular instance may seem to lean for or against the exercise of the right of judicial interference with the actions of corporate directors, the context, or the facts before the court, must be considered. This court, in Hunter v. Roberts, Throp & Co., 83 Mich. 63, 71, 47 N.W. 131, 134, recognized the rule in the following language: 'It is a well-recognized principle of law that the directors of a corporation, and they alone, have the power to declare a dividend of the earnings of the corporation, and to determine its amount. 5 Amer. & Eng. Enc. Law, 725. Courts of equity will not interfere in the management of the directors unless it is clearly made to appear that they are guilty of fraud or misappropriation of the corporate funds, or refuse to declare a dividend when the corporation has a surplus of net profits which it can, without detriment to its business, divide among its stockholders, and when a refusal to do so would amount to such an abuse of discretion as would constitute a fraud, or breach of that good faith which they are bound to exercise towards the stockholders.'

. . . When plaintiffs made their complaint and demand for further dividends, the Ford Motor Company had concluded its most prosperous year of business. The demand for its cars at the price of the preceding year continued. It could make and could market in the year beginning August 1, 1916, more than 500,000 cars. Sales of parts and repairs would necessarily increase. The cost of materials was likely to advance, and perhaps the price of labor; but it reasonably might have expected a profit for the year of upwards of $60,000,000. It had assets of more than $132,000,000, a surplus of almost $112,000,000, and its cash on hand and municipal bonds were nearly $54,000,000. Its total liabilities, including capital stock, was a little over $20,000,000. It had declared no special dividend during the business year except the October, 1915, dividend. It had been the practice, under similar circumstances, to declare larger dividends. Considering only these facts, a refusal to declare and pay further dividends appears to be not an exercise of discretion on the part of the directors, but an arbitrary refusal to do what the circumstances required to be done. These facts and others call upon the directors to justify their action, or failure or refusal to act. In justification, the defendants have offered testimony tending to prove, and which does prove, the following facts: It had been the policy of the corporation for a considerable time to annually reduce the selling price of cars, while keeping up, or improving, their quality. As early as in June, 1915, a general plan for the expansion of the productive capacity of the concern by a practical duplication of its plant had been talked over by the executive officers and directors and agreed upon; not all of the details having been settled, and no formal action of directors having been taken. The erection of a smelter was considered, and engineering and other data in connection therewith secured. In consequence, it was determined not to reduce the selling price of cars for the year beginning August 1, 1915, but to maintain the price and to accumulate a large surplus to pay for the proposed expansion of plant and equipment, and perhaps to build a plant for smelting ore. It is hoped, by Mr. Ford, that eventually 1,000,000 cars will be annually produced. The contemplated changes will permit the increased output.

The plan, as affecting the profits of the business for the year beginning August 1, 1916, and thereafter, calls for a reduction in the selling price of the cars. It is true that this price might be at any time increased, but the plan called for the reduction in price of $80 a car. The capacity of the plant, without the additions thereto voted to be made (without a part of them at least), would produce more than 600,000 cars annually. This number, and more, could have been sold for $440 instead of $360, a difference in the return for capital, labor, and materials employed of at least $48,000,000. In short, the plan does not call for and is not intended to produce immediately a more profitable business, but a less profitable one; not only less profitable than formerly, but less profitable than it is admitted it might be made. The apparent immediate effect will be to diminish the value of shares and the returns to shareholders.

It is the contention of plaintiffs that the apparent effect of the plan is intended to be the continued and continuing effect of it, and that it is deliberately proposed, not of record and not by official corporate declaration, but nevertheless proposed, to continue the corporation henceforth as a semi-eleemosynary institution and not as a business institution. In support of this contention, they point to the attitude and to the expressions of Mr. Henry Ford.

Mr. Henry Ford is the dominant force in the business of the Ford Motor Company. No plan of operations could be adopted unless he consented, and no board of directors can be elected whom he does not favor . . . . A business, one of the largest in the world, and one of the most profitable, has been built up. It employs many men, at good pay. 'My ambition,' said Mr. Ford, 'is to employ still more men, to spread the benefits of this industrial system to the greatest possible number, to help them build up their lives and their homes. To do this we are putting the greatest share of our profits back in the business.'

With regard to dividends, the company paid sixty per cent. on its capitalization of two million dollars, or $1,200,000, leaving $58,000,000 to reinvest for the growth of the company. This is Mr. Ford's policy at present, and it is understood that the other stockholders cheerfully accede to this plan.[1]

He had made up his mind in the summer of 1916 that no dividends other than the regular dividends should be paid, 'for the present.'

'Q. For how long? Had you fixed in your mind any time in the future, when you were going to pay — A. No.

'Q. That was indefinite in the future? A. That was indefinite; yes, sir.'

The record, and especially the testimony of Mr. Ford, convinces that he has to some extent the attitude towards shareholders of one who has dispensed and distributed to them large gains and that they should be content to take what he chooses to give. His testimony creates the impression, also, that he thinks the Ford Motor Company has made too much money, has had too large profits, and that, although large profits might be still earned, a sharing of them with the public, by reducing the price of the output of the company, ought to be undertaken. We have no doubt that certain sentiments,

---

[1] In the report of the case, this paragraph is in quotation marks. They have been removed here because this appears to be the court's observation, not a quote from Ford's testimony.

philanthropic and altruistic, creditable to Mr. Ford, had large influence in determining the policy to be pursued by the Ford Motor Company-the policy which has been herein referred to. . . .

. . . The difference between an incidental humanitarian expenditure of corporate funds for the benefit of the employees, like the building of a hospital for their use and the employment of agencies for the betterment of their condition, and a general purpose and plan to benefit mankind at the expense of others, is obvious. There should be no confusion (of which there is evidence) of the duties which Mr. Ford conceives that he and the stockholders owe to the general public and the duties which in law he and his co directors owe to protesting, minority stockholders. A business corporation is organized and carried on primarily for the profit of the stockholders. The powers of the directors are to be employed for that end. The discretion of directors is to be exercised in the choice of means to attain that end, and does not extend to a change in the end itself, to the reduction of profits, or to the nondistribution of profits among stockholders in order to devote them to other purposes.

There is committed to the discretion of directors, a discretion to be exercised in good faith, the infinite details of business, including the wages which shall be paid to employees, the number of hours they shall work, the conditions under which labor shall be carried on, and the price for which products shall be offered to the public.

It is said by appellants that the motives of the board members are not material and will not be inquired into by the court so long as their acts are within their lawful powers. As we have pointed out, and the proposition does not require argument to sustain it, it is not within the lawful powers of a board of directors to shape and conduct the affairs of a corporation for the merely incidental benefit of shareholders and for the primary purpose of benefiting others, and no one will contend that, if the avowed purpose of the defendant directors was to sacrifice the interests of shareholders, it would not be the duty of the courts to interfere.

We are not, however, persuaded that we should interfere with the proposed expansion of the business of the Ford Motor Company. In view of the fact that the selling price of products may be increased at any time, the ultimate results of the larger business cannot be certainly estimated. The judges are not business experts. It is recognized that plans must often be made for a long future, for expected competition, for a continuing as well as an immediately profitable venture. The experience of the Ford Motor Company is evidence of capable management of its affairs. It may be noticed, incidentally, that it took from the public the money required for the execution of its plan, and that the very considerable salaries paid to Mr. Ford and to certain executive officers and employees were not diminished. We are not satisfied that the alleged motives of the directors, in so far as they are reflected in the conduct of the business, menace the interests of shareholders. It is enough to say, perhaps, that the court of equity is at all times open to complaining shareholders having a just grievance.

. . . The decree of the court below fixing and determining the specific amount to be distributed to stockholders is affirmed. In other respects, except as to the allowance of costs, the said decree is reversed. . . .

NOTES AND QUESTIONS

1. The published opinion in this case is relatively long, and includes considerable discussion of the company's income and balance sheets. Such a review is necessary, of course, if the court is to make a business decision. Studying this opinion might lead a jurist to eschew such an analysis and embrace the business judgment rule. Nevertheless, one must ask whether there are any circumstances in which a court should become embroiled in the typical business decisions at issue here — dividend policy and expansion plans. Was the court on firm ground in affirming the order for a special dividend?

2. Suppose that Ford testified that he disfavored future special dividends because the plaintiffs planned to use the money to compete with Ford Motor. Would this have changed the result in the case?

3. Assuming that the court reached the conclusion that the directors were badly motivated in deciding not to declare a dividend, how should the court go about deciding how large a dividend should be declared?

4. Suppose that the court declined to intervene, stating categorically that deciding whether the corporation should declare a dividend, or how much that dividend should be, is beyond the competence of the court. What would the consequence of such a ruling be?

A Comparative Perspective

Traditionally, the debate surrounding corporate social responsibility has focused on the extent to which corporate boards can, should, or must consider the impact of their decisions on communities or constituents other than their shareholders. Does the board violate its fiduciary duty if it fails to maximize profits because it wishes to avoid a plant closure in an economically distressed city? *Dodge v. Ford Motor Co.* did not put that question to rest. As corporations have grown in size and influence, they have become tempting targets for critics, who see such corporations both as a source of many societal problems and vehicles for positive social change. In the most recent iteration of this debate, the impact of large multinational corporations on developing countries has garnered much attention. These corporations comply with local law, but local law does not adequately protect the local labor force, the environment or cultural traditions, to name just a few impacts. How can these corporations be encouraged to do more? In *The Social Responsibility of Large Multinational Corporations*, 16 TRANSNAT'L LAW. 121, 139 (2002), Professor Branson identifies several sources of "soft law" that might play a role: "aspirational codes of best practices . . . ; voluntary codes of conduct and vendor standards; non-governmental organizations, their standards, and their monitoring activities; trade agreements and treaties that also attempt to influence internal corporate affairs; international organizations such as the OECD . . . ; and stock exchanges that will compete amongst each other in devising optimal governance standards."

C. CORPORATE GOVERNANCE

The term "corporate governance" generally refers to the allocation of power between and among the corporate board and shareholders. The Delaware Supreme Court captured the idea in *MM Companies, Inc. v. Liquid Audio, Inc.*, 813 A.2d 1118, 1126 (Del. 2003) (footnotes omitted):

> The most fundamental principles of corporate governance are a function of the allocation of power within a corporation between its stockholders and its board of directors. The stockholders' power is the right to vote on specific matters, in particular, in an election of directors. The power of managing the corporate enterprise is vested in the shareholders' duly elected board representatives. Accordingly, while these "fundamental tenets of Delaware corporate law provide for a separation of control and ownership," the stockholder franchise has been characterized as the "ideological underpinning" upon which the legitimacy of the directors managerial power rests.

While the Delaware court, in this excerpt, envisions a minimalist role for shareholders, that need not be the case. The articles of incorporation can allocate greater power to the shareholders, such as approving particular transactions, or the exclusive power to amend the bylaws, etc. In structuring a closely-held corporation, the initial investors may protect their interests by appropriately drafted articles of incorporation. In the modern publicly-held corporation, however, rarely do shareholders have more than the statutorily prescribed powers.

The passive role of shareholders in publicly-held corporations has given rise to the observation that there is a "separation" between ownership and control. Professors Adolf Berle, Jr. and Gardiner Means made this observation in *The Modern Corporation and Private Property* (1932), arguing that this separation had given rise to a class of professional managers who would not be responsive to the shareholders because the shareholders lacked an effective way to remove or replace them. Moreover, the managers were not dependent on the shareholders for capital, as expansion could be achieved through re-investment of corporate earnings. Freed from accountability to shareholders, managers could become more "socially responsible," as Professor Berle later argued. ADOLF BERLE, JR., POWER WITHOUT PROPERTY 2–8 (1959). However, managers also could act in a more self-interested fashion. Encouraging socially responsible behavior and restraining self-interested behavior has, as noted above, occupied the thoughts of legal scholars since Berle and Means launched the debate.

The drafters of federal securities laws have not given up on the possibility of effective shareholder participation, and section 14 of the Securities and Exchange of 1934 reflects considerable efforts to enhance shareholder democracy. That effort has continued in the twenty-first century, as the Securities and Exchange Commission has considered giving shareholders direct access to the company's proxy statement to nominate directors and increased ability to include shareholder proposals in the proxy statement. In addition, Congress has considered legislation that would give shareholders an advisory vote on executive compensation. These initiatives, which are limited to "reporting companies," that is, large publicly held companies registered with the SEC, are covered in more detail below. We now turn our attention to issues of control in a closely held corporation.

MOUNTAIN MANOR REALTY, INC. v. BUCCHERI

Court of Appeals of Maryland
55 Md. App. 185, 461 A.2d 45 (1983)

WILNER, J.

[Mountain Manor, Inc. (MMI) had three shareholders — Conway (22 shares), Leatherman (22 shares) and Roby (12 shares), each of whom was a director of the corporation. MMI operated an alcoholic rehabilitation facility on property owned by Mountain Manor Realty, Inc. (Realty), a corporation controlled by Conway. As a result of a shareholders agreement, MMI had a right of first refusal if Roby sought to sell his shares. Roby and Leatherman sold their shares to Buccheri and then resigned as directors of MMI. Roby did not first offer his shares to MMI.]

Conway challenged the sale of Roby's 12 shares, contending that it was in contravention of the 1974 stockholders' agreement, to which Roby was a party. He dutifully called a special stockholders meeting for October 23, 1981, however, stating in the notice that the meeting was called "for the purpose of electing directors of the Corporation and such other business as may properly come before the meeting, it being understood that the matter of ownership of the stock of the corporation will be addressed at such special meeting."

In an effort to retain control of the corporation, which control he was likely to lose on October 23, Conway, without notice to Buccheri, Leatherman, or Roby, called a special meeting of directors for October 22, 1981, in Easton, Maryland. At the time, of course, by reason of the resignations of Leatherman and Roby, he was the only remaining director. He invited to this meeting his attorney and two acquaintances-Margaret Faulstich, who had been one of MMI's initial stockholders, and William C. Widman, an insurance agent who had placed some insurance for MMI.

. . . The "upshot" of the meeting was that

(1) Conway, as sole surviving director, elected Faulstich and Widman as directors to fill the vacancies created by the resignations of Leatherman and Roby;

(2) Conway then presented to this newly constituted board an offer by Realty to purchase 13 shares of MMI stock at a price of $7,000 a share, the purchase price to be paid by means of a credit of $91,000 against the arrearage of rent due by MMI to Realty on the lease. The price was subject to upward adjustment to match the price paid by Buccheri for Roby's stock if that price was more than $7,000 a share;

(3) The board accepted the offer and authorized the issuance of the 13 shares to Realty; and

(4) Realty executed a "Credit Toward Rent," which was delivered to MMI, and MMI issued stock certificate no. 14, evidencing 13 shares to Realty.

At the stockholders meeting the next day, which was attended by Buccheri and Roby, Conway announced first that the company did not recognize the sale of Roby's 12 shares. He then distributed copies of the minutes of the October 22 directors meeting showing the sale of the 13 shares to Realty. Purporting to vote 35 shares (his 22 and Realty's 13), Conway thereupon nominated himself, Faulstich, and Widman as directors. Counsel for Buccheri, who was also in attendance, disputed the validity of Realty's 13 shares; and, on the authority of the 34 shares owned by Buccheri, or by Buccheri and Roby, Buccheri nominated a different slate. The vote was either 35-34 in favor of Conway's slate or 34-22 in favor of the Buccheri slate, depending upon the validity of the 13 shares sold to Realty.[2] Upon the assumption that he had won, Conway declared the meeting adjourned.

Conway's confidence in his victory was apparently not complete. On November 5, 1981, he filed an action in the Circuit Court for Frederick County seeking a declaratory judgment that (1) because it contravened the 1974 stockholders agreement, the sale of Roby's 12 shares to Buccheri was invalid and Buccheri was therefore not the lawful owner of those 12 shares, (2) 13 shares of MMI stock were validly issued to Realty on October 22, 1981, and (3) the corporate directors were Conway, Faulstich, and Widman.

On August 3, 1982, the court gave Conway a meaningless partial victory. It declared that Roby had in fact signed the 1974 stockholders agreement, that his 12 shares were subject to it, that the sale of those shares to Buccheri was not in accordance with the agreement, and that Buccheri therefore did not own those shares. The court also declared, however, that the 13 shares "were not legally issued to the Realty Company on October 22, 1981, because the transaction of [Conway] at the meeting of October 22, 1981, was completely illegal." It explained:

"Sec. 2-408B of the Corporations and Associations Article of the *Annotated Code of Maryland* provides as follows:

'b. Quorum-(1) Unless the By-Laws of the corporation provide otherwise, majority of the entire board of directors constitutes a quorum for transaction of business.

(2) Notwithstanding any provision of the By-Laws to the contrary, a quorum may not be less than:

(i) One-third of the entire board of directors or

(ii) Two directors.'

Dr. Conway individually could not transact any business of the corporation as a sole stockholder because he would be in violation of the above statute. Furthermore, Dr. Conway's action at the meeting on October 22, 1981, was not in the best interest of the

---

[2] As Roby was present and voted the 12 shares that Conway claimed had never been properly sold to Buccheri, there is no question but that 34 votes were properly cast for the Buccheri slate.

corporation for the reason that the control of the corporation was manipulated by sale of the stock to himself without regard of [*sic*] a stockholders meeting to be held in a couple of days for the purpose of electing new directors. It is inconceivable to this Court that such action would be orchestrated and then ask the Court to apply its stamp of approval."

From that conclusion, the court declared that Conway, Faulstich, and Widman did not constitute the directors of MMI.

Conway's appeal attacks both reasons advanced by the court for declaring the October 22 transaction invalid. He argues:

"I. Conway, as the sole remaining director of Mountain Manor, had the right to elect two directors to fill the vacancies on the Mountain Manor Board of Directors.

II. The transaction by which Realty acquired 13 shares of Mountain Manor stock complied with Md. Corp. & Ass'ns Code Ann., § 2-419 which governs interested director transactions, and thus the stock was validly issued to Realty."

Although we do not necessarily recommend the procedures employed by Conway to retain control of the company (any more than we recommend the secret double-dealing between Roby and Buccheri), we think, for the reasons that follow, that the court may have erred in declaring the October 22 transaction to be invalid.[3]

The court's action with respect to the 13 shares issued to Realty rested, as we have seen, on two bases: (1) that Conway "could not transact any business of the corporation as a sole stockholder" because of the quorum requirements of Md.Code Ann.Corp. and Ass'ns art., § 2-408(b);[4] and (2) that the transaction was not in the best interest of MMI because "control of the corporation was manipulated by sale of the stock to himself without regard of [*sic*] a stockholders meeting to be held in a couple days . . . ."

As to the first of these reasons, we note initially that Conway did not purport to act as "a sole stockholder," which, of course, he was not, but rather as the sole surviving director, which, of course, he was. More important, § 2-408(b) is not the only relevant statute.

Section 2-402(a) requires that a corporation "shall have at least three directors at all times." The number of directors may be greater than three, as established in the charter or the by-laws, but it may not be less than three. MMI, it was agreed, had three directors. As the court correctly observed, § 2-408(b) provides that, absent a contrary provision in the by-laws, a majority of the entire board of directors constitutes a quorum for the transaction of business, but that in no event may a quorum be less than "(i) One third of the entire board of directors; or (ii) Two directors."

What the court omitted to consider, however, was § 2-407(a)(2)(i), dealing with vacancies on the board of directors. That subsection states: "Unless the bylaws provide otherwise: . . . [a] majority of the remaining directors, *whether or not sufficient to constitute a quorum*, may fill a vacancy on the board of directors which results from any cause except an increase in the number of directors." (Emphasis supplied.)

MMI's by-laws are not contrary to that provision; indeed, they track it. Article II, § 9, dealing with vacancies on the board of directors, provides, in relevant part, that, "If any director shall die or resign . . . a majority of the remaining directors (*although such majority is less than a quorum*) may elect a successor to hold office for the unexpired portion of the term of the director whose place shall so become vacant, and until his successor shall have been duly chosen and qualified." (Emphasis supplied.)

With the resignations of Roby and Leatherman, Conway, being the only remaining

---

[3] No appeal was taken from that part of the judgment dealing with Roby's 12 shares.

[4] The court's reference to § 2-408B is evidently a typographical error. The language quoted appears in § 2-408(b).

director and thus necessarily "a majority of the remaining directors," had the authority under § 2-407(a)(2)(i) and art. II, § 9 of the by-laws to fill the two vacancies, notwithstanding that under § 2-408(b) there was the lack of a quorum. There being no challenge here to the qualifications of Faulstich and Widman, or *otherwise* to the procedure of their election, we perceive no legal impropriety in their election on October 22 as successor directors.

[The court then considered whether the lower court correctly set aside the sale of shares to Realty, holding that the lower court utilized an incorrect standard. The court of appeals remanded the case ordering the trial court to apply the proper standard under Maryland law: "If the court finds that the transaction was, on the whole, motivated by a legitimate corporate purpose, it should declare the sale to be valid; if it finds to the contrary — that the purpose of the transaction was primarily one of management's self-perpetuation and that that purpose outweighed any other legitimate business purpose — it should declare the sale to be invalid."]

NOTES AND QUESTIONS

1. If Leatherman and Roby had not resigned, Conway would not have been in a position to replace them and appoint directors friendly to him. On the other hand, if they had not resigned, Buccheri could not have taken control of the corporation. Assuming that Leatherman and Roby had no interest in remaining as directors, and Buccheri in any event did not wish them to remain, how should Buccheri have proceeded to gain control?

2. How likely do you think it is that Conway would succeed on remand in establishing that the issuance of stock to Realty was legitimate?

3. Assuming that the court sets aside the issuance of the shares to Realty, what then?

4. *A Larger Role for Shareholders (of Publicly-held Corporations)?* As noted above, the SEC from time to time has considered an increased role for shareholders of publicly-held corporations. In recent years, that has translated into a proposal to allow shareholder direct access to the company's proxy statement for the purpose of nominating individuals to serve as directors of the company. In 2003, the SEC proposed Rule 14a-11, which, if adopted, would require corporations to include the names of shareholder nominees in the corporate proxy materials in either one of two instances: First, if at least 35% of shareholders withheld support for a board nominee in an election; or second, if a majority of shareholders vote to be governed by Rule 14a-11. Only shareholders holding at least 5% of outstanding shares for at least two years would be eligible to nominate board members. The proposal was highly criticized, in part because it was considered too inflexible and did not allow for differences according to the differing needs of corporations. *See,* Brett H. McDonnell, *Shareholder Bylaws, Shareholder Nominations, and Poison Pills,* 3 BERKELEY BUS. L.J. 205 (2005). At this writing, the SEC had not yet approved the rule.

While the SEC has been pondering whether to change its rules to permit shareholders access to the proxy statement, shareholders have been taking matters into their own hands by proposing amendments to their company's bylaws and then using SEC Rule 14a-8 to require the company to include the proposed amendment in the company's proxy statement. While these efforts have been somewhat successful, the Commission recently amended its rules to limit this strategy. This is covered in greater detail below. In a somewhat related development, Congress recently proposed that shareholders be given an advisory vote on executive compensation. Under a bill passed by the House of Representatives in 2007, the SEC would be required to adopt rules under with shareholders could express their approval, or disapproval, on executive pay, starting in 2009. This idea was developed in a 1996 law review article. Mark J. Loewenstein, *Reflections on Executive Compensation and a Modest Proposal for (Further) Reform,* 50 SMU L. REV. 201 (1996).

Finally, the role of shareholders and the protection of minority shareholders are enhanced when the articles or bylaws require a supermajority approval for specified corporate action. For instance, the articles might provide that in lieu of the typical majority requirement to approve a merger, an 80% vote is necessary. Such provisions are enforceable if they are clear and unambiguous. Centaur Partners, IV v. National Intergroup, Inc., 582 A.2d 923 (Del. 1990).

5. *A Comparative Law Perspective.* Shareholders of European companies tend to have a greater role in corporate governance than do their American counterparts. For instance, European shareholders typically have the right to approve dividends and greater access to the company's proxy statement. In France, the ability of shareholders to include matters on the agenda of the annual meeting is roughly coextensive with management's power. One scholar recently summed up the effect of shareholder power in Europe:

> In Continental Europe, the law generally confers much more authority upon stockholders, in fact, so much more that the board cannot possibly ignore their point of view. A board that is determined to run the corporation independently and without unforeseen interventions by others must retain or act in concert with — which may be understood as being appointed by — a majority shareholder. The result — and partially also the cause — is a prevailing concentrated ownership structure in Continental Europe, while ownership is usually dispersed in the United States.

Sofie Cools, *The Real Difference in Corporate Law Between the United States and Continental Europe: Distribution of Powers*, 30 DEL. J. CORP. L. 697, 765–66 (2005).

D.   THE BOARD OF DIRECTORS AND ITS COMMITTEES

1.   The Function of the Board

The board of directors is responsible for managing the business and affairs of the corporation. Its function was well stated in the case of *Manson v. Curtis*, 119 N.E. 559, 562 (1918) (citations omitted):

> While the ordinary rules of law relating to an agent are applicable in considering the acts of a board of directors in behalf of a corporation when dealing with third persons, the individual directors making up the board are not mere employees, but a part of an elected body of officers constituting the executive agents of the corporation. They hold such office charged with the duty to act for the corporation according to their best judgment, and in so doing they cannot be controlled in the reasonable exercise and performance of such duty. As a general rule, the stockholders cannot act in relation to the ordinary business of the corporation, nor can they control the directors in the exercise of the judgment vested in them by virtue of their office. The relation of the directors to the stockholders is essentially that of trustee and cestui que trust . . . . The corporation is the owner of the property, but the directors in the performance of their duty possess it, and act in every way as if they owned it. Directors are the exclusive, executive representatives of the corporation, and are charged with the administration of its internal affairs and the management and use of its assets.

This common law assessment of the role and function of the board of directors is consistent with its statutory formulations. Consider, for instance, Model Act § 8.01(b):

> All corporate powers shall be exercised by or under the authority of the board of directors of the corporation, and the business and affairs of the corporation shall be managed by or under the direction, and subject to the oversight, of its board of directors, subject to any limitation set forth in the articles of incorporation or in an agreement authorize under section 7.32.

The Model Act, in the next subsection, delineates the board's oversight responsibilities in a public corporation. *See also* PRINCIPLES OF CORPORATE GOVERNANCE § 3.02. Directors of a corporation are not agents of the corporation; unless specifically authorized by the board of directors, individual directors have no authority to bind the corporation to contracts or otherwise commit the corporation to a course of action. Directors can only act in consort with their fellow directors.

2. Board Structures

In recent years, increasing attention has been given to how boards, particularly the boards of publicly-held companies, are populated and structured. The strong trend in corporate law over the past several decades has been to increase the representation, and power, of so-called independent directors. The prevailing philosophy has been that independent directors would better protect the interests of shareholders and more effectively oversee the corporation. There is, however, no single definition of independent director. For instance, under NASDAQ Rule 4350(c), a majority of the directors on a listed company's board must be independent. A board member is *not* independent if:

- The director has been employed by the company in the last three years.

- The director or any member of their family has received compensation in excess of $120,000 during any one of the last three years from the company.

- The director has a family member who is an executive officer of the company.

- The director is, or has a family member who is, a partner or controlling shareholder or executive officer of an organization the company did business with and the transaction(s) represented 5% or more (or $200,000, whichever is more) of the recipient's revenues.

- The director or family member is employed as an executive officer at a company where the issuer's executive officer is on the compensation committee.

- The director or family member is a current partner of the issuer's auditor.

- In the case of an investment company, an "interested person" under the ICA.

The New York Stock Exchange has adopted a similar rule. *See* NYSE Rule 303A.

What these various definitions omit, however, are non-quantitative factors that may affect the independence of a director. The case of *In re Oracle Corp. Derivative Litig.*, 824 A.2d 917 (Del. Ch. 2003) explored that question in the context of whether the members of a special litigation committee, established to consider whether the corporation should pursue a derivative action against certain of its senior executive officers for insider trading, were independent. The trial court stated that, "[a]t bottom, the question of independence turns on whether a director is, for any substantial reason, incapable of making a decision with only the best interests of the corporation in mind. That is, the Supreme Court cases ultimately focus on impartiality and objectivity." 824 A.2d at 938. The court continued that "a director may be compromised if he is beholden to an interested person. Beholden in this sense does not mean just owing in the financial sense, it can also flow out of 'personal and other relationships' to the interested party." *Id.* at 938–39. Following a careful, fact-intensive analysis, the court ultimately determined that the board members in the Oracle case were not sufficiently independent of those on whom they were to pass judgment. Interestingly, they would have been deemed independent for purposes of the various stock exchange rules set forth above.

Beyond the search for independence, reformers of corporate governance have sought to restructure corporate boards to give these independent directors greater authority in the management of the corporation. For instance, the NYSE adopted Rule 303A.03: "To empower non-management directors to serve as a more effective check on management, the non-management directors of each listed company must meet at regularly scheduled executive sessions without management." The commentary to this rule states that an independent director must preside over these meetings, and if it is the same person at all the meetings, their name must be disclosed in the company's proxy statement. This person is commonly referred to as the "lead director." If the same person is not the lead director at all such meetings, then the company must disclose the process used to select a lead director for each executive session. Alternatively, the company may elect a non-executive Chairman of the Board. These rules appear to have led most companies to identify a specific person as lead director. In 2005, nearly 17% of Fortune 500 companies had a non-executive Chair and nearly 62% designated a Lead Director. Executive Compensation Trends, Equilar Inc. (January 2007), *available at* http://www.equilar.com/newsletter/january_2007/ect_jan_2007_pv.html.

The corporate governance reforms of the Sarbanes-Oxley Act require publicly-held companies to have an independent audit committee that "shall be directly responsible for the appointment, compensation, and oversight of the work of any registered public accounting firm employed [to audit the company]." In terms of independence, the Act provides that the audit committee members cannot "accept any consulting, advisory, or other compensatory fee" from the company or "be an affiliated person" of the company or any of its subsidiaries. Securities Exchange Act of 1934, § 10A(m). The stock exchanges have similarly emphasized the importance of independent nominating and compensation committees for the board. Whether this movement to independence will improve corporate performance is an open question, but not one that is foremost in the minds of the reformers. *See* Sanjai Bhagat & Bernard Black, *The Non-Correlation Between Board Independence and Long-Term Firm Performance*, 27 J. Corp. L. 231 (2002). Rather, the main concern of these reforms seems to be reining in the excesses and abuses of corporate management so evident in the corporate scandals that marked the beginning of the twenty-first century.

3. Removal of Directors

One element of control that shareholders do maintain over the board of directors is the power to remove directors. At common law, directors could be removed only for cause, a rule which is somewhat counter-intuitive inasmuch as any interest that a person has in continuing as a director should pale in comparison to the interest of shareholders in being able to remove directors with whom they are displeased. Not surprisingly, modern statutes permit shareholders to remove directors with or without cause, unless the articles require cause. There are exceptions to this rule when the board of directors is classified and when cumulative voting is in effect. In the case of the former, generally directors can only be removed for a cause. In the case cumulative voting, no director may be removed without cause if the votes cast against his removal would be sufficient to elect him. *See, e.g.,* Del. Gen. Corp. Law § 141(k). In any case, what constitutes cause, and the extent to which a director is entitled to some sort of "due process" before being removed for cause, has arisen from time to time, as the following materials indicate.

SUPERWIRE.COM, INC. v. HAMPTON
Court of Chancery of Delaware
805 A.2d 904 (2002)

Lamb, V.C.

[This case involved a struggle for the control of Entrata Communications Corporation, a Delaware corporation. Its principal shareholder was Superwire.com, Inc., which was also a major creditor of Entrata. A dispute arose between the parties, and Superwire sought to exercise its voting power to remove the Entrata directors and replace them with its nominees. It sought to do so by circulating written consents to various shareholders of Entrata. Under applicable Delaware law, if shareholders holding a majority of the outstanding shares execute a written consent to the proposed action, the action is effective when such consents are delivered to the corporation.

Entrata sought to counter Superwire.com's efforts by issuing additional shares to dilute Superwire's voting power and by asking shareholders (other than Superwire) to revoke the consents, dated November 8, that they had executed to remove Hampton, one of Entrata's directors, for cause. Superwire brought an action under § 225 of the Delaware Code for a determination of whose slate of nominees legally constituted the Entrata board and, in particular, that its removal of Hampton was proper.]

The defendants' motion to dismiss the claim relating to the November 8 consent raises both legal issues that can be resolved at this time and factual issues that must await trial, if there is to be one.

The November 8 consent purports to remove Hampton "for cause." Defendants move to dismiss because the complaint does not allege facts showing that Hampton was afforded notice of specific charges and an opportunity to be heard. Superwire responds that (a) the consent is valid even if no notice or opportunity to be heard was afforded to Hampton because the certificate of incorporation permitted his removal without cause and, (b) in any case, it is not obligated to allege those facts in order to survive a motion to dismiss.

Superwire misstates the law in contending that the fact that it might have proceeded "without cause" can serve to validate an otherwise invalid attempt to remove Hampton "for cause." Directors of Delaware corporations can be removed "for cause" or, where permitted by the governing documents and the law, "without cause." But there are additional requirements that must be observed when doing so "for cause." A "for cause" removal of a director requires that the individual be given (i) specific charges for his removal, (ii) adequate notice, and (iii) a full opportunity to meet the accusation. The same is true whether the action is taken at a meeting of stockholders or by written consent.

These procedural safeguards are of some importance. In many cases, there are substantial collateral affects of being removed "for cause" that do not attend a removal "without cause." These can include differences in the treatment of rights flowing from contracts or other terms of employment. There are also likely to be significant reputational affects flowing from a "for cause" removal. These consequences alone might justify the conclusion that one choosing to act "for cause" must follow the prescribed procedures.

Moreover, it is a fallacy to suppose that a stockholder who succeeds in obtaining enough consents to remove a director "for cause" without affording the director notice and an opportunity to be heard would necessarily obtain the requisite number of consents if it complies with the law, or even if it seeks to remove the director "without cause." In this case, for example, the complaint reflects a contention that the stockholders who joined with Superwire in executing the November 8 consent promptly executed revocations of those consents, claiming that Superwire misled them into agreeing to remove Hampton. Those revocations may not have been legally effective, since they were expressed after the November 8 consent was delivered to Entrata. But they do serve to illustrate the point that compliance with established legal standards can affect the outcome.

Thus, the validity of the November 8 consent will depend on whether it was solicited in compliance with the procedural safeguards articulated in *Campbell v. Loew's*, [134 A.2d 852, 859 (Del.Ch.1957)] and specifically applied to actions taken by written consent in *Bossier v. Connell* [1986 Del. Ch. Lexis 511, at 15 (Del.Ch.)].

For the purposes of the motion to dismiss, however, the question is whether Superwire was obliged to include in its complaint factual allegations that would support a finding that it gave Hampton notice of the charges against him and an opportunity to be heard. The answer to this question must be "no" because it is sufficient under the general notice pleading standard found in Court of Chancery Rule 8(a) that the complaint "contain . . . a short and plain statement of the claim showing that the pleader is entitled to relief." The allegations found in paragraph 22 of the complaint are sufficient for this purpose because they identify the consent, allege that it was executed by holders of the requisite number of shares, that it was delivered to the corporation and that it was effective on the date of its delivery. These are the elements described in Section 228 of the DGCL. The defense is free to show that the November 8 consent was invalid for whatever reason or reasons may exist. However, there is no requirement that the complaint allege facts sufficient to disprove any of those matters. . . .

The motion to dismiss the claim relating to the November 8 consent is denied.

NOTES AND QUESTIONS

1. If Superwire obtained sufficient consents to remove Hampton, of what use would a hearing be, inasmuch as the consenting shareholders would not be present to hear Hampton's defense? Or does the court's holding mean that the consents are not valid until after Hampton has had an opportunity to respond?

2. A board of directors lacks the authority to remove a director with or without cause, unless a statute so provides. See Indiana Code § 23-1-33-8, an unusual statute that permits the shareholders or the board of directors to remove directors with or without cause, unless the articles of incorporation provide otherwise or the director whose removal is sought was elected by a voting group. The statute was applied in *Murray v. Conseco, Inc.*, 795 N.E.2d 454 (Ind. 2003). In addition, some statutes permit removal of a director by a court for cause. See, e.g., CAL. CORP. CODE § 304. The courts have recognized a common law right to remove directors for cause, an action called "amotion." See *Bruch v. National Guarantee Credit Corporation*, 116 A. 738 (Del. Ch. 1922) (holding that the right of amotion is lodged in the corporation, but cannot be exercised by the directors; i.e, directors have no power to remove fellow directors).

3. Not all gatherings of directors are "meetings" for legal purposes. In *Fogel v. U.S. Energy Systems, Inc.*, 2007 Del. Ch. LEXIS 178 (Del. Ch. Dec. 13, 2007), the court noted that "[t]he mere fact that directors are gathered together does not a meeting make. There was no formal call to the meeting, and there was no vote whatsoever. The independent directors caucused on their own in what they admit was not a meeting and informally decided among themselves how they would proceed."

PROBLEM

Assume that you have been asked to form a corporation for four individuals, Able, Baker, Carr, and Dean. Able will provide financing but otherwise not take part in the business, Baker will be responsible for general operations, Carr will be responsible for sales, and Dean will be responsible for manufacturing operations. The initial board will consist of Able, Baker, and Carr, each of whom will own 30 shares. Dean will own 90 shares. The applicable state law provides that directors may be removed with or without cause, unless the articles require cause. Would you recommend that the articles require cause for removal?

4.   Equitable Restraints on Board Action

Action taken by the board of directors is effective and binding on the corporation if a quorum of the board is present and the action is approved by the affirmative vote of a majority of directors present. See, e.g., MBCA § 8.24. The articles of incorporation can vary the quorum and voting requirements. Assuming that the board acts consistently with the articles, bylaws, and statute, in general, its actions may not be challenged by the shareholders or third parties, unless, in the case of shareholders, the claim is made that the action is in violation of the board's fiduciary duties of loyalty and care. This deferential standard, sometimes characterized as the business judgment rule is covered in greater detail in Chapter 10, *infra*. As the next cases indicate, however, the Delaware courts have also imposed equitable constraints on board action. These widely-cited and respected cases are particularly remarkable because the Delaware courts are also recognized as supporting freedom of contract. To the extent that the Delaware corporate law and the corporation's articles and bylaws form the basis for a contract between the shareholders and directors, the intervention of equitable doctrines imposes external terms that the parties might not have a factored into their analysis. As you read these cases, consider whether this added cost is justified.

SCHNELL v. CHRIS-CRAFT INDUSTRIES, INC.
Supreme Court of Delaware
285 A.2d 437 (1971)

HERMANN, J.

This is an appeal from the denial by the Court of Chancery of the petition of dissident stockholders for injunctive relief to prevent management from advancing the date of the annual stockholders' meeting from January 11, 1972, as previously set by the by-laws, to December 8, 1981.

It will be seen that the Chancery Court considered all of the reasons stated by management as business reasons for changing the date of the meeting; but that those reasons were rejected by the Court below in making the following findings:

> I am satisfied, however, in a situation in which present management has disingenuously resisted the production of a list of its stockholders to plaintiffs or their confederates and has otherwise turned a deaf ear to plaintiffs' demands about a change in management designed to lift defendant from its present business doldrums, management has seized on a relatively new section of the Delaware Corporation Law for the purpose of cutting down on the amount of time which would otherwise have been available to plaintiffs and others for the waging of a proxy battle. Management thus enlarged the scope of its scheduled October 18 directors' meeting to include the by-law amendment in controversy after the stockholders committee had filed with the S.E.C. its intention to wage a proxy fight on October 16.
>
> Thus plaintiffs reasonably contend that because of the tactics employed by management (which involve the hiring of two established proxy solicitors as well as a refusal to produce a list of its stockholders, coupled with its use of an amendment to the Delaware Corporation Law to limit the time for contest), they are given little chance, because of the exigencies of time, including that required to clear material at the S.E.C., to wage a successful proxy fight between now and December 8. * * *.

In our view, those conclusions amount to a finding that management has attempted to utilize the corporate machinery and the Delaware Law for the purpose of perpetuating itself in office; and, to that end, for the purpose of obstructing the legitimate efforts of dissident stockholders in the exercise of their rights to undertake a proxy contest against management. These are inequitable purposes, contrary to established principles of corporate democracy. The advancement by directors of the by-law date of a stockholders' meeting, for such purposes, may not be permitted to stand. Compare Condec Corporation v. Lunkenheimer Company, Del. Ch., 230 A.2d 769 (1967).

When the by-laws of a corporation designate the date of the annual meeting of stockholders, it is to be expected that those who intend to contest the reelection of incumbent management will gear their campaign to the by-law date. It is not to be expected that management will attempt to advance the date in order to obtain an inequitable advantage in the contest.

Management contends that it has complied strictly with the provisions of the new Delaware Corporation Law in changing the by-law date. The answer to that contention, of course, is that inequitable action does not become permissible simply because it is legally possible.

Management relies upon American Hardware Corp. v. Savage Arms Corp., 37 Del.Ch. 10, 135 A.2d 725, aff'd, 37 Del.Ch. 59, 136 A.2d 690 (1957). The case is inapposite for two reasons: It involved an effort by stockholders, engaged in a proxy contest, to have the stockholders' meeting adjourned and the period for the proxy contest enlarged; and there was no finding there of inequitable action on the part of management. We agree with the rule of *American Hardware* that, in the absence of fraud or inequitable conduct, the date for a stockholders' meeting and notice thereof, duly established under the by-laws, will not be enlarged by judicial interference at the request of dissident stockholders solely because of the circumstance of a proxy contest. That, of course, is not the case before us.

We are unable to agree with the conclusion of the Chancery court that the stockholders' application for injunctive relief here was tardy and came too late. The stockholders' learned of the action of management unofficially on Wednesday, October 27, 1971; they filed this action on Monday, November 1, 1971. Until management changed the date of the meeting, the stockholders had no need of judicial assistance in that connection. There is no indication of any prior warning of management's intent to take such action; indeed, it appears that an attempt was made by management to conceal its action as long as possible. Moreover, stockholders may not be charged with the duty of anticipating inequitable action by management, and of seeking anticipatory injunctive relief to foreclose such action, simply because the new Delaware Corporation Law makes such inequitable action legally possible.

Accordingly, the judgment below must be reversed and the cause remanded, with instruction to nullify the December 8 date as a meeting date for stockholders; to reinstate January 11, 1972 as the sole date of the next annual meeting of the stockholders of the corporation; and to take such other proceedings and action as may be consistent herewith regarding the stock record closing date and any other related matters.

BLASIUS INDUSTRIES, INC. v. ATLAS CORP.
Court of Chancery of Delaware
564 A.2d 651 (1988)

ALLEN, Chancellor.

[Blasius acquired a 9.1% interest in Atlas in the late summer and early fall of 1987. Michael Lubin and Warren Delano, representatives of Blasius, then approached the Atlas board and proposed a restructuring plan pursuant to which Atlas would sell substantial assets and distribute the proceeds to its shareholders. By the end of the year, it was clear that Atlas was strongly opposed to Blasuis's proposal. At that point, Blasius delivered to Atlas a written consent that, if approved by a majority of Atlas shareholders, would amend the Atlas bylaws to increase the size of the board from seven to fifteen members, the maximum number under Atlas's charter, and elect eight named persons to fill the new directorships. Within a few days, the Atlas board met and voted to amend the bylaws to increase the size of the board from seven to nine and appointed two individuals, friendly to management, to fill those newly created positions. The motive and effect of the action of the Atlas board was to preclude the holders of a majority of the company's shares from installing a board that included a majority of new directors.]

[This case] was filed on December 30, 1987. As amended, it challenges the validity of board action taken at a telephone meeting of December 31, 1987 that added two new members to Atlas' seven member board. That action was taken as an immediate response to the delivery to Atlas by Blasius the previous day of a form of stockholder consent that, if joined in by holders of a majority of Atlas' stock, would have increased the board of Atlas from seven to fifteen members and would have elected eight new members nominated by Blasius.

As I find the facts of this . . . case, [it] present[s] the question whether a board acts consistently with its fiduciary duty when it acts, in good faith and with appropriate care, for the primary purpose of preventing or impeding an unaffiliated majority of shareholders from expanding the board and electing a new majority. For the reasons that follow, I conclude that, even though defendants here acted on their view of the corporation's interest and not selfishly, their December 31 action constituted an offense to the relationship between corporate directors and shareholders that has traditionally been protected in courts of equity. As a consequence, I conclude that the board action taken on December 31 was invalid and must be voided.

. . .

Plaintiff attacks the December 31 board action as a selfishly motivated effort to protect the incumbent board from a perceived threat to its control of Atlas. Their conduct is said to constitute a violation of the principle, applied in such cases as *Schnell v. Chris-Craft Industries*, Del.Supr., 285 A.2d 437 (1971), that directors hold legal powers subjected to a supervening duty to exercise such powers in good faith pursuit of what they reasonably believe to be in the corporation's interest. The December 31 action is also said to have been taken in a grossly negligent manner, since it was designed to preclude the recapitalization from being pursued, and the board had no basis at that time to make a prudent determination about the wisdom of that proposal, nor was there any emergency that required it to act in any respect regarding that proposal before putting itself in a position to do so advisedly.

Defendants, of course, contest every aspect of plaintiffs' claims. They claim the formidable protections of the business judgment rule. *See, e.g., Aronson v. Lewis*, Del.Supr., 473 A.2d 805 (1983); *Grobow v. Perot*, Del.Supr., 539 A.2d 180 (1988); *In re J.P. Stevens & Co., Inc. Shareholders Litigation*, Del.Ch., 542 A.2d 770 (1988).

They say that, in creating two new board positions and filling them on December 31, they acted without a conflicting interest (since the Blasius proposal did not, in any event, challenge their places on the board), they acted with due care (since they well knew the persons they put on the board and did not thereby preclude later consideration of the recapitalization), and they acted in good faith (since they were motivated, they say, to protect the shareholders from the threat of having an impractical, indeed a dangerous, recapitalization program foisted upon them). Accordingly, defendants assert there is no basis to conclude that their December 31 action constituted any violation of the duty of the fidelity that a director owes by reason of his office to the corporation and its shareholders.

Moreover, defendants say that their action was fair, measured and appropriate, in light of the circumstances. Therefore, even should the court conclude that some level of substantive review of it is appropriate under a legal test of fairness, or under the intermediate level of review authorized by Unocal Corp. v. Mesa Petroleum Co., Del.Supr., 493 A.2d 946 (1985), defendants assert that the board's decision must be sustained as valid in both law and equity.

One of the principal thrusts of plaintiffs' argument is that, in acting to appoint two additional persons of their own selection, including an officer of the Company, to the board, defendants were motivated not by any view that Atlas' interest (or those of its shareholders) required that action, but rather they were motivated improperly, by selfish concern to maintain their collective control over the Company. That is, plaintiffs say that the evidence shows there was no policy dispute or issue that really motivated this action, but that asserted policy differences were pretexts for entrenchment for selfish reasons. If this were found to be factually true, one would not need to inquire further. The action taken would constitute a breach of duty. Schnell v. Chris Craft Industries, Del.Supr., 285 A.2d 437 (1971); Guiricich v. Emtrol Corp., Del.Supr., 449 A.2d 232 (1982). . . .

While I am satisfied that the evidence is powerful, indeed compelling, that the board was chiefly motivated on December 31 to forestall or preclude the possibility that a majority of shareholders might place on the Atlas board eight new members sympathetic to the Blasius proposal, it is less clear with respect to the more subtle motivational question: whether the existing members of the board did so because they held a good faith belief that such shareholder action would be self-injurious and shareholders needed to be protected from their own judgment.

On balance, I cannot conclude that the board was acting out of a self-interested motive in any important respect on December 31. I conclude rather that the board saw the "threat" of the Blasius recapitalization proposal as posing vital policy differences between itself and Blasius. It acted, I conclude, in a good faith effort to protect its incumbency, not selfishly, but in order to thwart implementation of the recapitalization that it feared, reasonably, would cause great injury to the Company.

The real question the case presents, to my mind, is whether, in these circumstances, the board, even if it *is* acting with subjective good faith (which will typically, if not always, be a contestable or debatable judicial conclusion), may validly act for the principal purpose of preventing the shareholders from electing a majority of new directors. The question thus posed is not one of intentional wrong (or even negligence), but one of authority *as between the fiduciary and the beneficiary* (not simply legal authority, *i.e.*, as between the fiduciary and the world at large).

It is established in our law that a board may take certain steps-such as the purchase by the corporation of its own stock-that have the effect of defeating a threatened change in corporate control, when those steps are taken advisedly, in good faith pursuit of a corporate interest, and are reasonable in relation to a threat to legitimate corporate interests posed by the proposed change in control. *See Unocal Corp. v. Mesa Petroleum Co.*, Del.Supr., 493 A.2d 946 (1985); *Kors v. Carey*, Del.Ch., 158 A.2d 136 (1960); *Cheff v. Mathes*, Del.Supr., 199 A.2d 548 (1964); *Kaplan v. Goldsamt*, Del.Ch., 380 A.2d 556 (1977). Does this rule-that the reasonable exercise of good faith and due care generally validates, in equity, the exercise of legal authority even if the act has an entrenchment effect-apply to action designed for the primary purpose of interfering with the effectiveness of a stockholder vote? Our authorities, as well as sound principles, suggest that the central importance of the franchise to the scheme of corporate governance, requires that, in this setting, that rule not be applied and that closer scrutiny be accorded to such transaction.

1. *Why the deferential business judgment rule does not apply to board acts taken for the primary purpose of interfering with a stockholder's vote, even if taken advisedly and in good faith.*

A. *The question of legitimacy.*

The shareholder franchise is the ideological underpinning upon which the legitimacy of directorial power rests. Generally, shareholders have only two protections against perceived inadequate business performance. They may sell their stock (which, if done in sufficient numbers, may so affect security prices as to create an incentive for altered managerial performance), or they may vote to replace incumbent board members.

It has, for a long time, been conventional to dismiss the stockholder vote as a vestige or ritual of little practical importance. It may be that we are now witnessing the emergence of new institutional voices and arrangements that will make the stockholder vote a less predictable affair than it has been. Be that as it may, however, whether the vote is seen functionally as an unimportant formalism, or as an important tool of discipline, it is clear that it is critical to the theory that legitimates the exercise of power by some (directors and officers) over vast aggregations of property that they do not own. Thus, when viewed from a broad, institutional perspective, it can be seen that matters involving the integrity of the shareholder voting process involve consideration not present in any other context in which directors exercise delegated power.

B. *Questions of this type raise issues of the allocation of authority as between the board and the shareholders.*

The distinctive nature of the shareholder franchise context also appears when the matter is viewed from a less generalized, doctrinal point of view. From this point of view, as well, it appears that the ordinary considerations to which the business judgment rule originally responded are simply not present in the shareholder voting context. That is, a decision by the board to act for the primary purpose of preventing the effectiveness of a shareholder vote inevitably involves the question who, as between the principal and the agent, has authority with respect to a matter of internal corporate governance. That, of course, is true in a very specific way in this case which deals with the question who should constitute the board of directors of the corporation, but it will be true in every instance in which an incumbent board seeks to thwart a shareholder majority. A board's decision to act to prevent the shareholders from creating a majority of new board positions and filling them does not involve the exercise of *the corporation's power* over its property, or with respect to *its* rights or obligations; rather, it involves allocation, between shareholders as a class and the board, of effective power with respect to governance of the corporation. This need not be the case with respect to other forms of corporate action that may have an entrenchment effect-such as the stock buybacks present in *Unocal, Cheff* or *Kors v. Carey.* Action designed principally to interfere with the effectiveness of a vote inevitably involves a conflict between the board and a shareholder majority. Judicial review of such action involves a determination of the legal and equitable obligations of an agent towards his principal. This is not, in my opinion, a question that a court may leave to the agent finally to decide so long as he does so honestly and competently; that is, it may not be left to the agent's business judgment.

2. *What rule does apply: per se invalidity of corporate acts intended primarily to thwart effective exercise of the franchise or is there an intermediate standard?*

Plaintiff argues for a rule of *per se* invalidity once a plaintiff has established that a board has acted for the primary purpose of thwarting the exercise of a shareholder vote. . . .

In my view, our inability to foresee now all of the future settings in which a board might, in good faith, paternalistically seek to thwart a shareholder vote, counsels against the adoption of a *per se* rule invalidating, in equity, every board action taken for the sole or primary purpose of thwarting a shareholder vote, even though I recognize the transcending significance of the franchise to the claims to legitimacy of our scheme of corporate governance. It may be that some set of facts would justify such extreme action. This, however, is not such a case.

3. *Defendants have demonstrated no sufficient justification for the action of December 31 which was intended to prevent an unaffiliated majority of shareholders from effectively exercising their right to elect eight new directors.*

The board was not faced with a coercive action taken by a powerful shareholder against the interests of a distinct shareholder constituency (such as a public minority). It was presented with a consent solicitation by a 9% shareholder. Moreover, here it had time (and understood that it had time) to inform the shareholders of its views on the merits of the proposal subject to stockholder vote. The only justification that can, in such a situation, be offered for the action taken is that the board knows better than do the shareholders what is in the corporation's best interest. While that premise is no doubt true for any number of matters, it is irrelevant (except insofar as the shareholders wish to be guided by the board's recommendation) when the question is who should comprise the board of directors. The theory of our corporation law confers power upon directors as the agents of the shareholders; it does not create Platonic masters. It may be that the Blasius restructuring proposal was or is unrealistic and would lead to injury to the corporation and its shareholders if pursued. Having heard the evidence, I am inclined to think it was not a sound proposal. The board certainly viewed it that way, and that view, held in good faith, entitled the board to take certain steps to evade the risk it perceived. It could, for example, expend corporate funds to inform shareholders and seek to bring them to a similar point of view. But there is a vast difference between expending corporate funds to inform the electorate and exercising power for the primary purpose of foreclosing effective shareholder action. A majority of the shareholders, who were not dominated in any respect, could view the matter differently than did the board. If they do, or did, they are entitled to employ the mechanisms provided by the corporation law and the Atlas certificate of incorporation to advance that view. They are also entitled, in my opinion, to restrain their agents, the board, from acting for the principal purpose of thwarting that action.

I therefore conclude that, even finding the action taken was taken in good faith, it constituted an unintended violation of the duty of loyalty that the board owed to the shareholders. I note parenthetically that the concept of an unintended breach of the duty of loyalty is unusual but not novel. *See Lerman v. Diagnostic Data, supra;* AC Acquisitions Corp. v. Anderson, Clayton & Co., Del.Ch., 519 A.2d 103 (1986). That action will, therefore, be set aside by order of this court.

QUESTION

What alternative courses of conduct could the Atlas board have pursued? Could they, for instance, have undertaken a recapitalization, say a self-tender, that would have made the Blasius restructuring moot?

PROBLEM

Walter had effective voting control of Spectru Co., Delaware corporation, and was its Chairman and CEO. While Walter was a brilliant engineer, and responsible for developing Spectru's key products, he was a poor manager. As a result of Walter's poor direction, the company was insolvent and in jeopardy of losing several key employees. In addition, a recent investigation had confirmed the accusations of a female employee that Walter had sexually harassed her. In a desperate situation, the board of directors, without Walter's knowledge, approached an outside investor, who agreed to invest $1 million in the company, provided he was given voting control and certain other assurances. The board convened a meeting at which Walter understood various matters would be considered, but he did not know that the board of directors would also consider and vote upon the investor's proposal and Walter's ouster as director and officer of the company. Unwittingly, Walter attended the meeting and the board, over his objections, removed him as an officer and issued stock giving voting control to the outside investor, who promptly delivered a written consent to the company removing Walter as a director. Walter has filed an action under the Delaware Code asserting that the action taken at the meeting was invalid. What outcome?

5. Board Committees

Corporate boards, particularly those of large corporations, typically operate through committees. Corporate codes allow such committees to have broad authority; under the MBCA, for instance, the only authorities denied to board committees are authorizing distributions, proposing actions requiring shareholder approval, filling vacancies on the board, or amending the bylaws. *See* MBCA § 8.25(e). The corporate scandals that marked the beginning of the twenty-first century, and the ongoing controversy surrounding executive compensation, have brought renewed interest in the use of committees that are independent of corporate management. As a result, independent audit and compensation committees are the norm in publicly-held corporations. This reality is, however, the culmination of developments over a number of years.

The SEC first recommended the use of committees composed of independent directors in 1940. However, it was not until 1972 that the SEC issued a formal release stating their support for such a committee. Finally, in 1976, the Chairman of the SEC recommended the SROs take the lead in this area and in 1977, the NYSE implemented rules requiring listed companies to have audit committees composed of independent directors. *See* Roberta S. Karmel, *American Law Institute's Corporate Governance Project: Independent Directors: The Independent Corporate Board: A Means to What End?*, 52 Geo. Wash. L. Rev. 534 (1984).

Following the report of a Blue Ribbon Committee appointed by the SEC in the late 1990s, the SEC and SROs promulgated rules that elevated the audit committee's ability to actively monitor management. Specifically, the rules had three primary requirements. First, companies must maintain audit committees composed of only independent board members. Second, the committee must have at least three directors, must be composed of directors who are financially literate, and at least one director must have financial management or accounting expertise. Third, the company must adopt a written charter for the committee outlining the scope of the committee's responsibilities and processes for fulfilling those responsibilities and specifying that the committee is "ultimately responsible for selecting, evaluating, overseeing the independence of, and, when need be, replacing the outside auditors." Gregory S. Rowland, *Earnings Management, the SEC, and Corporate Governance Director Liability Arising from the Audit Committee Report*, 102 Colum. L. Rev. 168, 176 (2002).

With regard to compensation committees, the SROs have implemented rules requiring that companies have compensation committees composed of only independent directors. *See, e.g.*, NYSE Corporate Governance Standards, Rule 303A.05. These committees typically approve the compensation of the company's top executives and certify whether performance goals in incentive compensation plans have been satisfied. *See* Nathan Knutt, Note: *Executive Compensation Regulation: Corporate America, Heal Thyself*, 47 Ariz. L. Rev. 493, 499 (2005).

6.   The Role of Officers

While the business and affairs of the corporation are "managed by or under the direction of" the board of directors (MBCA § 8.01(b)), it is the corporate officers who manage the day-to-day business of the corporation. Like all agents, corporate officers have the duty to act with diligence, in good faith, and with loyalty. The latter includes a duty of candor. *See* Melvin Aron Eisenberg, *The Duty of Good Faith*, 31 Del. J. Corp. L. 1, 46–51 (2006). The authority of a corporate officer can be found in several different sources: the corporation code, the corporate bylaws, the officer's employment contract, relevant board resolutions, the authorized direction of a superior officer, and the common law of agency. It is possible, but unusual, to include provisions regarding the authority of officers in the articles of incorporation. In any case, a lawyer rendering a legal opinion on whether a corporate officer has the authority to take certain action would be well-advised to consult all of these sources.

The next case illustrates an important limitation on the authority of a corporate CEO.

GRIMES v. ALTEON, INC.
Supreme Court of Delaware
804 A.2d 256 (2002)

Veasey, C.J.

Alteon Inc., defendant below and appellee, is a pharmaceutical company specializing in drugs for cardiovascular and renal diseases. Charles L. Grimes, plaintiff below and appellant, is a lawyer and an investor who, along with his wife, Jane Gillespie Grimes, often purchases large blocks of stock (but below 10% to avoid insider obligations) in small technology-based companies. Grimes and his wife had held approximately 9.9% of Alteon's stock at the time of the events that have given rise to this litigation. Those events, as set forth in the complaint, may be summarized as follows.

Kenneth I. Moch, the President and Chief Executive Officer of Alteon, told Grimes that Alteon needed additional funds, and that Alteon was considering a private placement stock offering. Grimes told Moch that he was concerned about his holdings being diluted, and that he would buy 10% of any such offering. According to Grimes, Moch promised orally that he would offer Grimes 10% of the offering. In return, Grimes promised orally to buy 10% of the offering. Grimes admits that there is no writing memorializing these promises. He also admits that Alteon's board did not approve this transaction.

Subsequently, Alteon publicly announced a private placement offering. It did not allow Grimes to participate in this private placement, which presumably was fully taken by other purchasers. The stock market reacted positively to the placement, and Alteon's stock price increased from $3 to as high as $5-5/16 per share. [The Court of Chancery ruled in favor of the defendant, dismissing the complaint.]

Grimes has appealed to this Court the judgment of the Court of Chancery dismissing his complaint. We agree with the essential holding of the Court of Chancery that the agreement is invalid because it was not approved by the board of directors and was not memorialized in a written instrument. We do so based on the statutory scheme of the Corporation Law pertaining to stock issuance, with particular emphasis on Sections 152 and 157.

Stock Issuance and the Delaware General Corporation Law Statutory Scheme

Grimes argues that his arrangement with Moch does not constitute a "right" within the meaning of 8 Del. C. § 157 and, therefore, need not be approved by the board or evidenced by a written instrument as required by that statute. Alteon argues that it does. Grimes argues that Section 157 applies only to options and "option like" rights. The fatal defect in Grimes' claim is that the agreement purports to grant a right that was not expressly approved by the board of directors as required by the statutory scheme of the Delaware General Corporation Law exemplified by Section 152 and Section 157.

The agreement purports to bind the corporation to issue to Grimes 10% of a future issuance of stock. Grimes' right to require the issuance of stock to him arises only if and when there is a public or private offering of newly issued stock. Because Grimes claims a right to require the issuance to him of 10% of any such offering, the Corporation Law applies and requires that the agreement and the issuance of the stock must be approved by the board of directors and evidenced by a written instrument.

One must read in pari materia the relevant statutory provisions of the Corporation Law. First there is the fundamental corporate governance principle set forth in 8 Del. C. § 141(a) that the "business and affairs of every corporation . . . shall be managed by and under the direction of" the board of directors. One then turns to the board's role in stock issuance set forth in the relevant sections of Subchapter V of Title 8. The provisions in this Subchapter relate to the issuance of capital stock, subscriptions for additional shares, options and rights agreements. Taken together, they are calculated to advance two fundamental policies of the Corporation Law: (1) to consolidate in its board of directors the exclusive authority to govern and regulate a corporation's capital structure; and (2) to ensure certainty in the instruments upon which the corporation's capital structure is based.

As this Court has stated in requiring strict adherence to statutory formality in matters relating to the issuance of capital stock, the "issuance of corporate stock is an act of fundamental legal significance having a direct bearing upon questions of corporate governance, control and the capital structure of the enterprise. The law properly requires certainty in such matters."[5] Delaware's statutory structure implements these policies through a "clear and easily followed legal roadmap" of statutory provisions.[6] This statutory scheme consistently requires board approval and a writing.

Various provisions in Subchapter V set forth the formal requirements for the issuance of capital stock, the establishment of classes of stock, the consideration for the issuance of stock, and formalities regarding rights, options and subscriptions relating to capital stock. The statutes relating to the issuance of stock that provide the policy context that is relevant here are 8 *Del. C.* §§ 151, 152, 153, 157, 161, and 166. Taken together, these provisions confirm the board's exclusive authority to issue stock and regulate a corporation's capital structure. To ensure certainty, these provisions contemplate board approval and a written instrument evidencing the relevant transactions affecting issuance of stock and the corporation's capital structure.

Section 151(a), relating to classes and series of stock, states that "the resolution or resolutions providing for the issue of such stock [must be] adopted by the board of directors pursuant to authority expressly vested in it by the provisions of its certificate of incorporation." Section 152, relating to the issuance of stock, states, "The consideration . . . for subscriptions to, or the purchase of, the capital stock to be issued by a corporation shall be paid in such form and in such manner as the board of directors shall determine." Section 153, relating to the consideration for the issuance of stock, requires that such consideration shall be determined from time to time by the board of directors. Section 157, relating to rights and options respecting stock, requires board approval and a written instrument to create such rights or options. Section 161, relating to the issuance of additional stock, allows the directors to "issue or take subscriptions for additional shares of its capital stock up to the amount authorized in its certificate of incorporation." Section 166, relating to the formalities required of stock subscriptions, provides that subscription agreements are not enforceable against the subscriber unless in writing and signed by the subscriber.

The requirement of board approval for the issuance of stock is not limited to the act of transferring the shares of stock to the would-be stockholder, but includes an antecedent transaction that purports to bind the corporation to do so. As noted, Section 152 requires the directors to determine the "consideration . . . for subscriptions to, or the purchase of, the capital stock" of a corporation. Thus, director approval of the transaction fixing such consideration is required. Moreover, it is well established in the case law that directors must approve a sale of stock. This duty is considered so important that the directors cannot delegate it to the corporation's officers. . . .

Section 152

This transaction fixed the "form" and "manner" of the consideration Alteon could receive from Grimes, thereby implicating 8 *Del. C.* § 152. That provision states, "The consideration . . . for subscriptions to, or the purchase of, the capital stock to be issued by a corporation shall be paid in such form and in such manner as the board of directors shall determine." Regardless of what label is put on the transaction entered into between Grimes and Moch, the transaction contemplated that Grimes would eventually "purchase" the "capital stock" of Alteon, and the agreement constrains the board's determination of the consideration for the issuance of the stock.

This transaction has two features fixing "consideration." First, Alteon bound itself to offer 10% of its stock to Grimes as part of any offering. Second, Alteon could not charge

---

[5] [7] *STAAR Surgical Co. v. Waggoner*, 588 A.2d 1130, 1136 (Del. 1991); *accord Kalageorgi*, 750 A.2d at 538.

[6] [8] *Kalageorgi* [v. Victor Kamkin, Inc.], 750 A.2d at 538.

Grimes any more for this 10% than it charged other investors for the remainder.

Both of these features of the transaction served to "cap" the value of the cash consideration Grimes was to give Alteon on the transfer of the stock. This transaction restricted the manner of payment of consideration for Alteon's stock, because it required that it come from Grimes. Because Grimes was a 10% stockholder already, such a commitment could well have tangible negative effects for Alteon's raising of capital from sources other than Grimes. In essence, the promise to Grimes cost Alteon a certain freedom in raising capital, and could well have lowered the ultimate price Alteon could have charged for its capital stock. Section 152 mandates board approval for such promises relating to consideration, and that approval was absent in this case.

Section 157

Section 157(a) permits a corporation to "create and issue, whether or not in connection with the issue and sale of any shares of stock or other securities of the corporation, rights or options entitling the holders thereof to purchase from the corporation any shares of its stock," provided that "such rights or options [are] evidenced by or in such instrument or instruments as shall be approved by the board of directors." [8 DEL. C. § 157]. Because it is indisputable that Alteon's board of directors never passed any such resolution approving this transaction, this agreement is invalid if it is a "right" or an "option."

[The Court went on to conclude that Grimes's oral contract embodied such a "right."] This reading of Section 157, to require all stock transactions not specifically dealt with in other provisions of the Corporation Law to require board approval under Section 157, serves two complementary purposes that Delaware Courts have found in the statutory scheme of our Corporation Law. The first is that the corporation should have the freedom to enter into new and different forms of transactions. Indeed, that was exactly the purpose for which Section 157 was originally created. The second is that, to the extent such transactions obligate the board concerning stock issuance, the board must approve them in writing. Certainty in investor expectations emphasizes the need for written board approval of any such transaction. Grimes' contention that his transaction, because of its sui generis nature, need not receive board approval does not comport with this policy.

Conclusion

We agree with the conclusion of the Court of Chancery that the Grimes agreement is unenforceable for lack of both board approval and a written agreement. . . .

NOTES AND QUESTIONS

1. Although the term was rejected by the drafters of the Restatement (Third) of Agency, the term "inherent authority" is often used by courts to describe the authority of corporate officers. *See, e.g., Autoxchange.Com, Inc. v. Dreyer & Reinbold, Inc.*, 815 N.E.2d 1064 (Ind. Ct. App. 2004) (corporate officer and minority shareholder had the "inherent agency authority" to direct purchaser of corporate property to pay corporate creditor directly); *Menard, Inc. v. Dage-MTI, Inc.*, 726 N.E.2d 1206 (Ind. 2000) (corporate president had the inherent agency authority to sell real estate owned by corporation).

2. Suppose that the Alteon board knew of the deal that Moch had made with Grimes. Should that change the outcome of the case?

E. THE ROLE OF SHAREHOLDERS

As noted above, the shareholders' statutory role in the scheme of corporate governance is a limited one: they elect and, under some circumstances can remove, directors; they can vote on certain fundamental changes to the corporation (mergers, sale of substantially all of the corporation's assets, amendments to the articles of incorporation) proposed by the board of directors; under SEC Rule 14a-8 shareholders in publicly-held corporations can propose various resolutions to be voted on by their fellow shareholders; and, subject to certain limitations, they can amend the bylaws. The shareholders' Rule 14a-8 prerogatives are taken up at the end of this chapter. For now, we turn our attention to the shareholders' role in bylaw amendments, which has been an increasingly important issue because of its potential impact on corporate governance.

INTERNATIONAL BROTHERHOOD OF TEAMSTERS GENERAL FUND v. FLEMING COMPANIES, INC.
Supreme Court of Oklahoma
975 P.2d 907 (1999)

Simms, J.

The United States Court of Appeals, Tenth Circuit, John C. Porfilio, Presiding Judge, pursuant to 20 O.S.1991, § 1601, certified to the Oklahoma Supreme Court the following question of law:

Does Oklahoma law [A] restrict the authority to create and implement shareholder rights plans exclusively to the board of directors, or [B] may shareholders propose resolutions requiring that shareholder rights plans be submitted to the shareholders for vote at the succeeding annual meeting?

We answer the first part of the question in the negative and the second part affirmatively. We hold under Oklahoma law there is no exclusive authority granted boards of directors to create and implement shareholder rights plans, where shareholder objection is brought and passed through official channels of corporate governance. We find no Oklahoma law which gives exclusive authority to a corporation's board of directors for the formulation of shareholder rights plans and no authority which precludes shareholders from proposing resolutions or bylaw amendments regarding shareholder rights plans. We hold shareholders may propose bylaws which restrict board implementation of shareholder rights plans, assuming the certificate of incorporation does not provide otherwise.

The International Brotherhood of the Teamsters General Fund [Teamsters] owns sixty-five shares of Fleming Companies, Inc. [Fleming or the company] stock. In 1986, Fleming implemented a shareholder's rights plan with the term of the plan to expire in 1996. The rights plan implemented by Fleming is an anti-takeover mechanism . . . . The defensive plans usually result in entrenching existing management, making a takeover without the approval of incumbent management more difficult. These rights plans can make it far more expensive to effect a takeover. Because the rights plans make the merger of companies more painful for the suitor and assist incumbent management in maintaining control, the plans are often called "poison pill rights plans" or "poison pills."

. . . In 1997, Teamsters mounted an organized effort to change the continued implementation of the rights plan. Teamsters prepared a proxy statement for inclusion in the proxy materials for the 1997 annual shareholder's meeting. With the proxy effort, the Teamsters proposed an amendment to the company's bylaws which would require any rights plan implemented by the board of directors to be put to the shareholders for a majority vote.[7] The proposal was essentially a ratification procedure wherein the

---

[7] [3] The 1997 proxy proposal provided:

shareholders would force the board to formulate a rights plan both the board and shareholders could agree on or do away with such a plan altogether.

Fleming refused to include the resolution in its 1997 proxy statement, declaring the proposal was not a subject for shareholder action under Oklahoma law. Teamsters then brought an action in the Federal District Court for the Western District of Oklahoma. The district court ruled in favor of the Teamsters, the court finding that "shareholders, through the devise of bylaws, have a right of review." Fleming appealed to the 10th Circuit Court of Appeals, which submitted the certified question to this Court.

Fleming sought to postpone any shareholder vote on the 1997 proxy issue until after the resolution of this case. But the U.S. District Court and later the 10th Circuit denied Fleming's motion to suspend the injunction. Fleming was then forced to allow its shareholders to vote on the Teamsters' proxy. The Teamsters' resolution passed with approximately 60% of the voted shares.

Fleming's position is that 18 O.S.1991, § 1038 gives the board of directors authority to create and issue shareholder rights plans, subject only to limits which might exist in the corporation's certificate of incorporation; and that shareholders cannot through bylaws restrict the board's powers to implement a rights plan.[8] The Teamsters' position is that 18 O.S.1991, § 1013 gives shareholders of a publicly traded corporation, such as Fleming, the authority to adopt bylaws addressing a broad range of topics from a corporation's business, corporate affairs, and rights and powers of shareholders and

---

Resolved, That shareholders hereby exercise their right under 18 O.S.A. Sec. 1013 to amend the bylaws of Fleming Companies, Inc. to add the following Article:

Article X

Poison Pills (Shareholder Rights Plans)

A. The Corporation shall not adopt or maintain a poison pill, shareholder rights plan, rights agreement or any other form of "poison pill" which is designed to or has the effect of making acquisition of large holdings of the Corporation's shares of stock more difficult or expensive (such as the 1986 "Rights Agreement"), unless such plan is first approved by a majority shareholder vote. The Company shall redeem any such rights now in effect. The affirmative vote of a majority of shares voted shall suffice to approve such a plan.

B. This article shall be effective immediately and automatically as of the date it is approved by the affirmative vote of the holders of a majority of the shares, present, in person or by proxy at a regular or special meeting of shareholders.

C. Notwithstanding any other provision of these bylaws, this Article may not be amended, altered, deleted or modified in any way by the Board of Directors without prior shareholder approval.

---

[8] [5] 18 O.S.1991, § 1038:

Rights and options respecting stock

Subject to any provisions in the certificate of incorporation, every corporation may create and issue, whether or not in connection with the issue and sale of any shares of stock or other securities of the corporation, rights or options entitling the holders thereof to purchase from the corporation any shares of its capital stock of any instrument or instruments as shall be approved by the board of directors. The terms upon which, including the time or times, which may be limited or unlimited in duration, at or within which, and the price or prices at which any such shares may be purchased from the corporation upon the exercise of any such right or option, shall be such as shall be stated in the certificate of incorporation, or in a resolution adopted by the board of directors providing for the creation and issue of such rights or options, and, in every case, shall be set forth or incorporated by reference in the instrument or instruments evidencing such rights or options. In the absence of actual fraud in the transaction, the judgment of the directors as to the consideration for the issuance of such rights or options and the sufficiency thereof shall be conclusive. In case the shares of stock of the corporation to be issued upon the exercise of such rights or options shall be shares having a par value, the price or prices so to be received therefor shall not be less than the par value thereof. In case the shares of stock so to be issued shall be shares of stock without par value, the consideration therefor shall be determined in the manner provided for in Section 34 of this act.

directors.[9] It is this apparent conflict which brings this federal certified question to this Court.

This is a case of first impression in Oklahoma and there is little guidance from other states. Oklahoma and Delaware have substantially similar corporation acts, especially with regard to Title 18, §§ 1013 & 1038 which are of primary concern here. 8 Del.C. § 109(a) & (b); 8 Del.C. § 157. However, a review of Delaware decisions revealed no comparable case from that state.

The 10th Circuit's question is ultimately one of corporate governance and what degree of control shareholders can exact upon the corporations in which they own stock.

In the scheme of corporate governance the role of shareholders has been purposefully indirect. Shareholders' direct authority is limited. This is true for obvious reasons. Large corporations with perhaps thousands of stockholders could not function if the daily running of the corporation was subject to the approval of so many relatively attenuated people. However, the authority given a board of directors under the Oklahoma General Corporation Act, 18 O.S.1991, § 1027, is not without shareholder oversight, 18 O.S.1991, § 1013(B).

Fleming's argument relies on this passage, 18 O.S.1991, § 1038 (emphasis added):

Subject to any provisions in the certificate of incorporation, *every corporation* may create and issue . . . rights or options entitling the holders thereof to purchase from the corporation any shares of its capital stock of any class or classes, such rights or options to be evidenced by or in such instrument or instruments as shall be approved by the board of directors.

In making its argument, Fleming asserts that the word "corporation" is synonymous with "board of directors" as the term is used in 18 § 1038. Therefore, according to Fleming, "every corporation may create and issue . . . rights and options[.]", can actually be read to say "[every corporation's board of directors] may create and issue . . . rights and options[.]" However, in light of the fact that both terms, "corporation" and "board of directors", are used distinctly throughout the General Corporation Act and within the text of 18 § 1038 itself, this assertion is flawed. Further, the Former Business Corporation Act, 18 § 1.2(1) and (23), defines "corporation" and "director" differently. The statutes indicate our legislature has an understanding of the distinct definitions it assigns to these terms, and we find it unlikely the legislature would interchange them as Fleming contends.

While this Court would agree with Fleming that a corporation may create and issue rights and options within the grant of authority given it in 18 § 1038, it does not

---

[9] [6] 18 O.S. 1991, § 1013(A) & (B):

Bylaws

A. The original or other bylaws of a corporation may be adopted, amended or repealed by the incorporators, by the initial directors if they were named in the certificate of incorporation, or, before a corporation has received any payment for any of its stock, by its board of directors. After a corporation has received any payment for any of its stock, the power to adopt, amend or repeal bylaws shall be in the shareholders entitled to vote, or, in the case of a nonstock corporation, in its members entitled to vote; provided, however, any corporation, in its certificate of incorporation, may confer the power to adopt, amend or repeal bylaws upon the directors or, in the case of a nonstock corporation, upon its governing body by whatever name designated. The fact that such power has been so conferred upon the directors or governing body, as the case may be, shall not divest the shareholders or members of the power, nor limit their power to adopt, amend or repeal bylaws.

B. The bylaws may contain any provision, not inconsistent with law or with the certificate of incorporation, relating to the business of the corporation, the conduct of its affairs, and its rights or powers or the rights or powers of its shareholders, directors, officers or employees.

automatically translate that the board of directors of that corporation has in itself the same breadth of authority.

A shareholder rights plan is essentially a variety of stock option plan. Its use as an anti-takeover mechanism does not change its essential character. While shareholder ratification of poison pills has not been tested in the courts, the same cannot be said for stock option plans as a whole. There is authority supporting shareholder ratification of stock option plans.

. . . We find nothing in the Oklahoma General Corporation Act, 18 O.S.1991 § 1001 et seq., or existing case law which indicates the shareholder rights plan is somehow exempt from shareholder adopted bylaws. Fleming argues that only the certificate of incorporation can limit the board's authority to implement such a plan, relying on § 1038. While this Court might agree that a certificate of incorporation, which somehow precludes bylaw amendments directed at shareholder rights plans, could preclude the Teamsters from seeking the bylaw changes which are proposed in this case, neither party has indicated Fleming's certificate speaks in any way to the board's authority or shareholder constraints regarding shareholder rights plans. We find no authority to support the contention that a certificate of incorporation which is silent with regard to shareholder rights plans precludes shareholder enacted bylaws regarding the implementation of rights plans.

A number of states have taken affirmative steps to ensure their domestic corporations, and in many instances the board of directors itself, are able to implement shareholder rights plans to protect the company from takeover. The legislation is typically called a shareholders rights plan endorsement statute. However, the Oklahoma legislature has not passed such legislation. There are at least twenty-four states with these share rights plan endorsement statutes.[10]

These statutes demonstrate that a board of directors can operate with relative autonomy when a rights plan endorsement statute applies. This does not suggest the absence of a share rights plan endorsement statute in Oklahoma precludes the implementation of such a takeover defense. We merely find that without the authority granted in such an endorsement statute, the board may well be subject to the general procedures of corporate governance, including the enactment of bylaws which limit the board's authority to implement shareholder rights plans.

This Court understands much of the reasoning behind the enactment of rights plan endorsement statutes and why so many state legislatures are inclined to facilitate this takeover protection for their domestic corporations. In addition, we understand Fleming's desire to have a rights plan available for quick, and more effective, implementation. However, if, as in this case, the certificate of incorporation does not offer directors this broad authority to protect against mergers and takeover, corporations must look to Oklahoma's legislature, not this Court, which is more properly vested with the means to offer boards such authority.

In answering this certified question, we do not suggest all shareholder rights plans

---

[10] [7] John H. Matheson & Brent A. Olson, *Shareholder Rights and Legislative Wrongs: Toward Balanced Takeover Legislation*, 59 Geo. Wash. L.Rev. 1425, 1554–58 (August 1991).

Examples of states with shareholder rights plan endorsement statutes are as follows:

Colorado, Co. Stat. § 7-106-208; Georgia, Ga. Stat. § 14-2-624; Hawaii, Haw. Stat. § 415-20; Idaho, Idaho Stat. §§ 30-1610, 30-1706; Illinois, Ill. Stat. Ch. 805 § 5/6.05(f); Indiana, Ind. Stat. §§ 23-1-35-1(f), 23-1-26-5; Iowa, Iowa Stat. § 490.624A; Kentucky, Ky. Stat. § 271B.12-210(5); Massachusetts, Mass. Stat. 156B § 32A; Michigan, Mich. Stat. Ch. 450 § 1342a; Nevada, Nev. Stat. 78.378; New Jersey, N.J. Stat. 14A:7-7(1) & (3); New York, McKinney's Bus. Corp. Law Ch. 4, Art. 5, § 505(2)(a)(i) & (ii); North Carolina, N.C. Stat. § 55-6-24(a) & (b); Ohio, Ohio Stat. § 1701.16; Oregon, Or. Stat. § 60.157(1) & (2); Pennsylvania, Pa. Stat. 15 Pa. C.S.A. §§ 1525, 2513; Rhode Island, R.I. Stat. § 7-5.2-7; South Dakota, S.D. Stat. § 47-33-5; Tennessee, Tenn. Stat. § 48-16-205; Utah, Utah Stat. § 16-10a-624; Virginia, Va. Stat. § 13.1-646; Wyoming, Wyo. Stat. § 17-16-624; Wisconsin, Wis. Stat. 180.0624.

are required to submit to shareholder approval, ratification or review; this is not the question presented to us. Instead, we find shareholders may, through the proper channels of corporate governance, restrict the board of director's authority to implement shareholder rights plans.

NOTES AND QUESTIONS

1. Note that the Oklahoma statute permits both directors and shareholders to amend the bylaws, but the directors' authority to do so must be set forth in the articles of incorporation. In the MBCA, the directors and shareholders also share the power, unless the articles reserve the power exclusively to the shareholders. (MBCA § 10.20). As a matter of policy, which approach is preferable? In forming a new corporation under, say, the MBCA, would you recommend drafting the articles of incorporation so as to reserve the power exclusively to the shareholders?

2. In the *Fleming* case, the Oklahoma Supreme Court noted that Oklahoma, unlike several other states it mentioned, does not have a statute that specifically authorizes the board to adopt a so-called shareholders rights plan. Suppose that a state had a statute similar to the Nevada statute. Would the power of the shareholders to adopt bylaw amendments be precluded by such a statute?

3. In the *Blasius* case, we saw an example of shareholders acting by written consent, in lieu of a formal meeting. The ability to act by written consent has been around for a number of years, but only relatively recently have statutes permitted shareholders to act by less than unanimous written consent. (If directors seek to act outside of a meeting, it must be by unanimous written consent.) Delaware was among the first to permit shareholder action by less than unanimous written consent, requiring that the consent or consents "be signed by the holders of outstanding stock having not less than the minimum number of votes that would be necessary to authorize or take such action at a meeting at which all shares entitled to vote thereon were present and voted. . . ." DEL. CODE § 228(a). The articles of incorporation can limit the ability of shareholders to act by written consent. Under the MBCA, shareholders may act by less than unanimous consent (with same voting requirements in the Delaware code) if so permitted in the articles of incorporation. MBCA § 7.04(b). If forming a corporation under the MBCA, would you recommend including a provision permitting action by less than unanimous written consent?

4. The Delaware Supreme Court recently issued an opinion on the validity of a bylaw in the context of a referral from the Securities and Exchange Commission. *CA, Inc. v. AFSCME Employees Pension Plan*, __ A.2d __ (Del. 2008). [11] At issue was a proposed bylaw amendment that a shareholder (AFSCME Employees Pension Plan) requested the company (CA, Inc.) to include in its annual proxy statement so that shareholders could decide whether to adopt it. The proposed bylaw amendment would have required the CA board of directors to reimburse the reasonable expenses of a shareholder who successfully proposed the election of one or more directors, provided that number was fewer than 50% of the directors to be elected (a so-called "short slate"). The issues before the court were whether, under Delaware law, the proposed bylaw amendment was a proper subject for action by shareholders and whether, if adopted, the bylaw would cause CA to violate any Delaware law to which it is subject. The court answered both questions in the affirmative. Because the bylaw would potentially cause CA to violate Delaware law, under SEC Rule 14a-8 (considered below), CA could exclude the proposal from its proxy statement.

As to the first issue, the court recognized that there are limits to the kinds of bylaws that shareholders may adopt. In short, such bylaws must be "process based," which the court defined quite broadly. This proposal was process based because it related to the

---

[11] Under a 2007 amendment to the Delaware state constitution, the Court is authorized to decide questions of law certified to it by the SEC.

selection of contestants for election to the board, a right that shareholders possess and may facilitate: "The shareholders are entitled to facilitate the exercise of [the right to participate in selecting nominees of the board] by proposing a bylaw that would encourage candidates other than board-sponsored nominees to stand for election. The [bylaw proposed by AFSCME] would accomplish that by committing the corporation to reimburse the election expenses of shareholders whose candidates are successfully elected."

As to the second issue, the court noted that in all circumstances when the directors act, they must act consistently with their fiduciary duties. As there may be circumstances in which the proper exercise of the board's fiduciary duties would counsel against the reimbursement of election expenses, the bylaw, if adopted, was invalid. The court pointed to a situation in which the election contest was not over competing views of proper corporate policy, but rather was motivated by "personal or petty concerns." When that is the case, reimbursement should be denied, because no corporate purpose would be served by such an expenditure.

PROBLEM

Dapoint Co., a Delaware corporation, became concerned that Smith, a large shareholder, would solicit consents from Dapoint's shareholders that would result in the removal and replacement of Dapoint's incumbent directors. To give the board an opportunity to respond to such a consent solicitation, the Dapoint board adopted a bylaw that delayed the effectiveness of any such consent solicitation until 60 days after the consents are received by the corporation. Smith has challenged the legality of the bylaw. Assume that the Dapoint articles contain no provisions relating to consent solicitations. Is Smith on firm ground?

F.   DUTY TO CREDITORS

Whether directors owe fiduciary duties to creditors is an issue that arises often in litigation. The general rule is that creditors can protect themselves by contracting for the protections that they desire. They could, in theory, contract for the creation of fiduciary duties between them and the board of directors. At the least, they could expressly limit the actions that the corporation can take so as to protect their interests. Nevertheless, the conventional wisdom, drawn in part from the well known case of *Francis v. United Jersey Bank*, which is set forth in Chapter 10, is that under some circumstances directors do owe fiduciary duties to creditors. The duties, if any, that directors owe to creditors are considered there.

G.   SHAREHOLDER VOTING

1.   Proxy Voting

Proxy voting is virtually indispensable for public corporations when shareholder voting takes place. Shareholders whose stake is small generally do not take the time to attend meetings of shareholders; it is just not cost efficient to do so. In those corporations in which shareholdings are widely disbursed, that is, where no shareholder owns more than, say, five percent, obtaining a quorum for the meeting can be difficult. Proxy voting solves some of the problem, as shareholders are often willing to execute a "proxy card" authorizing someone else (generally corporate management) to vote their shares. (Even this can be a chore in some corporations, which hire proxy solicitation firms to encourage shareholders to give their proxies.) Technically, the shareholder "gives a proxy" to someone who then "holds a proxy" and can vote the shareholder's shares. All of this is provided for in state corporation statutes, which also typically provide that such proxies are revocable (with certain exceptions) and expire after a set period of time. Note that proxy voting is not, technically, absentee voting, which must be authorized in the bylaws. Under SEC rules, however, the shareholder can direct how the holder of the proxy should vote the shares, thus turning the proxy into a form of absentee voting.

The difficulties of obtaining shareholder proxies is compounded somewhat by the growing practice of nominee ownerships. Corporations issue stock certificates to evidence the share ownership, but increasingly shareholders are electing to "leave" their shares with their stockbroker, to facilitate subsequent transfer and to avoid the necessity of keeping track of their stock certificates. Stockbrokers, in turn, register such shares in the name of a nominee (typically Cede & Co.) and leave the shares on deposit with Depositary Trust Co. Therefore, when a corporation examines its list of shareholders, it often finds that a large percentage of its shares are held in nominee name and it is unaware of the identity of the beneficial owners of those shares. It is possible for it to learn those names, but only if the beneficial owners do not object to disclosure (and most do not). The resulting list of beneficial owners it referred as a NOBO list — non-objecting beneficial owners. In any event, when the corporation finds it necessary to obtain, or solicit, proxies from such shareholders, it can send materials to the stockbrokers, who then forward the materials on to the beneficial owners. On routine matters (such as uncontested election of directors), the stockbrokers may vote the shares of the beneficial owners.

As noted in the *Blasius* case, shareholder voting holds an exalted place in the hierarchy of corporate governance. In publicly-held corporations, federal law, particularly § 14(a) of the Securities Exchange Act of 1934 and the rules and regulations adopted by the SEC thereunder, is of paramount importance. For the most part, however, § 14(a) regulates the *process* of soliciting proxies from shareholders, including some of the matters discussed in the preceding paragraph. One non-procedural rule is Rule 14a-9, which, in language similar to Rule 10b-5, prohibits fraud in connection with the solicitation of a proxy. (Rule 14a-9 is covered in more detail below.) Despite the influence of federal law, state law continues to play an important role in protecting the shareholder's franchise. We will look first at the continuing role that state law plays in proxy voting and then turn to federal regulation.

2. State Regulation

LACOS LAND COMPANY v. ARDEN GROUP, INC.
Delaware Court of Chancery
517 A.2d 271 (1986)

ALLEN, CHANCELLOR.

This action constitutes a multi-pronged attack upon a proposed recapitalization of defendant Arden Group, Inc., authorized by a vote of Arden's shareholders at their June 10, 1986 annual meeting. The recapitalization, if effectuated, will create a new Class B Common Stock possessing ten votes per share and entitled, as a class, to elect seventy-five percent of the members of Arden's board of directors. This new stock is, pursuant to the terms of a presently pending exchange offer, available on a share-for-share basis to all holders of Arden's Class A Common Stock. It is, however, acknowledged by defendants that the new Class B Common Stock has been deliberately fashioned to be attractive mainly to defendant Briskin-Arden's principal shareholder and chief executive officer. Thus, the recapitalization is not itself a device to raise capital but rather is a technique to transfer stockholder control of the enterprise to Mr. Briskin.

Plaintiff is an Arden stockholder owning approximately 4.5% of Arden's Class A Common Stock; an additional stockholder owning approximately 4.6% of that stock has moved to intervene in this action as a plaintiff. Defendants are the members of Arden's board of directors. Pending is an application to preliminarily enjoin the issuance of Class B Common Stock which was originally scheduled to occur on July 18, 1986, but which has been voluntarily delayed by defendants . . .

I.

The new supervoting common stock whose issuance is sought to be enjoined will differ from Arden's other authorized class of common stock, Class A Common Stock, most importantly, in its enhanced voting power, its diminished dividend rights and in restrictions upon its transfer.

Specifically, with respect to voting rights, the recent charter amendment provides that "on every matter submitted to a vote or consent of the stockholder, every holder of Class A Common Stock shall be entitled to one vote . . . for each share . . . and every holder of Class B Common Stock shall be entitled to 10 votes . . . for each share. . . ."

As to the election of directors, the restated certificate provides that Class A shares, together with the Company's preferred stock, voting as a class shall "be entitled to elect 25% of the total number of directors to be elected" rounded up to the nearest whole number. The Class B shares are entitled to vote as a separate class and to elect the remaining 75% of directors to be elected . . .

With respect to dividend rights, Class A Common Stock will, following the initial issuance of Class B shares, have the right to receive a one-time dividend of $.30 per share; Class B shares are to have no right to participate to any extent in that cash dividend. Excepting this one-time $.30 dividend, each share of Class B stock is to be entitled to participate in all dividends declared and paid with respect to a share of Class A stock but only to the extent of 90% of such dividend.

Class B shares may be transferred only to a Permitted Transferee,[12] but under certain circumstances may be converted on a share-for-share basis into Class A stock. A transfer of Class B to a person other than a Permitted Transferee at a time when conversion to Class A would be permitted would convert the transferred stock into Class A stock. Generally, Class B stock may, at the option of the holder, be converted to Class A stock on a share-for-share basis at the earlier of (i) the third anniversary of its issuance or (ii) the death of the holder.

Defendant Briskin owns or controls 16.9% of Arden's Class A Common Stock (21.1% were he to exercise certain presently exercisable stock options). The proxy statement states (at p. 20):

> Based on Mr. Briskin's expressed intention to exchange all of the Briskin Shares for Class B Common Stock, the Briskin Shares would represent approximately 67.7% of the combined voting power of the capital stock of the Company if no shares of Class A Common Stock other than the Briskin Shares were exchanged for Class B Common Stock.

In view of the lack of transferability and reduced dividend rights of the Class B Common Stock, the Board of Directors does not anticipate that any significant number of holders of Class A Common Stock other than Mr. Briskin will accept the Exchange Offer.

II.

. . . In instigating the dual common stock voting structure, Mr. Briskin was apparently not responding to any specific threat to existing policies or practices of Arden posed by a specific takeover threat. Rather, he apparently was motivated to protect his

---

[12] [2] For a natural person Permitted Transferees include (1) the holder's spouse or any lineal descendant of a grandparent of the holder or the holder's spouse, (2) the trustee of any trust for the benefit of the holder or a Permitted Transferee, (3) charitable organizations, (4) a corporation or partnership under majority control of the holder or a Permitted Transferee and (5) the holder's estate.

power to control Arden's business future. Such a motivation, while it may be suspect — since it may reflect not a desire to protect business policies and capabilities for the benefit of the corporation and its shareholders but rather a wish simply to retain the benefits of office — does not itself constitute a wrong.

In this instance, Briskin initially took his idea to the board of directors at its November 22, 1985 meeting. The Board established a three member committee of non-officer directors to consider the matter . . . The special committee retained neither independent counsel nor an independent financial advisor. At its first meeting, held on April 7, 1986, the chairman of this group distributed to the committee a draft report that he had previously prepared which gave approval to a supervoting stock plan. The committee reviewed this draft and suggested changes. The chairman noted the suggested changes and prepared a final three page report which was signed four days later at the committee's second, and final, meeting.

The committee's report was presented to the board at its April 22 meeting at which time the board approved the supervoting stock plan.

At that meeting the board fixed the date of the Company's annual meeting for June 10, 1986. Management of the Company prepared a proxy statement describing the proposed charter amendments authorizing the new supervoting Class B Common Stock, describing the Exchange Offer by which it was proposed that such new stock be distributed and setting out the background of, and the reasons for, this proposal.

At the June 10 annual meeting the Arden stockholders approved the proposed certificate amendments. Of 2,303,170 shares outstanding, 1,463,155 voted in favor (64%) and 325,004 (14%) voted to reject the proposal. Of the affirmative votes, 427,347 were voted by Briskin or his family and 388,493 were voted by a trustee as directed by Arden's management. As to the preferred stock, 74.4% of the 136,359 shares outstanding voted in favor of the proposal, more than half of which were voted by a trustee as directed by Arden's management.

As a consequence of the stockholders' approval of the proposal, the Company, on June 18, 1986, distributed to all holders of its Class A Common Stock an Offering Circular offering to exchange for each share of such common stock one share of Class B Common Stock with the rights, preferences, etc. described above.

III.

Our corporation law provides great flexibility to shareholders in creating the capital structure of their firm. Differing classes of stock with differing voting rights are permissible under our law; restriction on transfers are possible, and charter provisions requiring the filling of certain directorates by a class of stock are, if otherwise properly adopted, valid. Thus, each of the significant characteristics of the Class B Common Stock is in principle a valid power or limitation of common stock. The primary inquiry therefore is whether the Arden shareholders have effectively exercised their will to amend the Company's restated certificate of incorporation so as to authorize the implementation of the dual class common stock structure. The charge is that they have not done so — despite the report of the judge of elections that the proposed amendments carried — in part because the proxy statement upon which the vote was solicited was materially misleading and in part because the entire plan to put in place the Class B stock constitutes a breach of duty on the part of a dominated board.

For the reasons that follow I conclude that plaintiff has demonstrated a reasonable probability that on final hearing it will be demonstrated that the June 10, 1986 vote of the Arden shareholders has been fundamentally and fatally flawed and that, therefore, the amendments to Arden's restated certificate of incorporation purportedly authorized by that vote are voidable. In summary, the basis for this conclusion is two-fold. First, I conclude provisionally on the basis of the record now available, that the June 10 vote was inappropriately affected by an explicit threat of Mr. Briskin that unless the proposed amendments were approved, he would use his power (and not simply his power *qua* shareholder) to block transactions that may be in the best interests of the Company, if those transactions would dilute his ownership interest in Arden. I use the word threat because such a position entails, in my opinion, the potential for a breach of Mr. Briskin's duty, as the principal officer of Arden and as a member of its board of directors, to exercise corporate power unselfishly, with a view to fostering the interests of the corporation and all of its shareholders. Second, I conclude provisionally, that the proxy statement presents a substantial risk of misleading shareholders on a material point concerning Mr. Briskin's status as a "Restricted Person" under Article Twelfth of the Company's certificate of incorporation.

IV.

Judging from what is stated in the proxy materials, Arden's board in recommending the charter amendments and Arden's shareholders in approving them were both placed, inappropriately, in a position that made it significantly less likely than it might otherwise have been that approval of the plan to effectively transfer all shareholder power to Mr. Briskin would have been given.

To a shareholder who wondered why his board of directors was recommending a plan expected to place all effective shareholder power in a single shareholder, the proxy statement gives a clear answer: Mr. Briskin is demanding it; it's not such a big deal anyway since, as a practical matter, he has great power already; and if he doesn't get these amendments, he may exercise his power to thwart corporate transactions that may be in the Company's best interests. Thus, in order for the board to be "permitted to consider" (proxy p. 20) certain transactions that might threaten to reduce Mr. Briskin's control, the board approved the proposal. This story is disclosed more or less straight forwardly in the proxy solicitation materials.

As to Mr. Briskin's position, the proxy statement states (emphasis added throughout):

Purpose and Effects of the Proposal

1. *Purpose.* . . . Arden shareholders were unmistakably told that should they fail to approve the proposed amendments, Mr. Briskin "would not give his support to any transaction [that might make the Company vulnerable to an unsolicited or hostile takeover attempt] for which his approval might be required . . . ". Using the term in the vague way which we ordinarily do, a vote in such circumstances as these could be said to be "coerced." But that label itself supplies no basis to conclude that the legal effect of the vote is impaired in any way. As stated in Katz v. Oak Industries, Inc., Del. Ch., 508 A.2d 873, 880 (1986):

> . . . [F]or purposes of legal analysis, the term "coercion" itself — covering a multitude of situations — is not very meaningful. For the word to have much meaning for purposes of legal analysis, it is necessary in each case that a normative judgment be attached to the concept ("inappropriately coercive" or "wrongfully coercive," etc.). But, it is then readily seen that what is legally relevant is not the conclusory term "coercion" itself but rather the norm that leads to the adverb modifying it.

The determination of whether it was inappropriate for Mr. Briskin to structure the choice of Arden's shareholders (and its directors), as was done here, requires, first, a determination of which of his hats — shareholder, officer or director — Mr. Briskin was wearing when he stated his position concerning the possible withholding of his "support" for future transactions unless steps were taken "to secure his voting position." If he spoke only as a shareholder, and should have been so understood, an evaluation of the propriety of his position might be markedly different than if the "support" referred to could be or should be interpreted as involving the exercise of his power as either an officer or director of Arden.

On this point defendants' position at oral argument confirms that which the proxy language itself indicates — that, in taking this position, Mr. Briskin did not limit, and could not be understood to have limited, himself to exercising only stockholder power. Defendants have emphasized that Briskin's "practical" power derives in part from his notable success as a chief executive officer; his history of success, I was reminded, creates influence and his position confers power to initiate board consideration of important matters. Moreover, the proxy statement made clear that the approval that Briskin threatened to withhold included approval of transactions that did not require a vote of stockholders. . . . Accordingly, the conclusion seems inescapable that, in announcing an intent to withhold support for corporate action that might entail, for instance, the issuance of stock, even if that act might be in the best interests of the corporation, unless "steps were taken to preserve his voting position," Mr. Briskin could not be understood to have been acting only as a shareholder.

As a director and as an officer, of course, Mr. Briskin has a duty to act with complete loyalty to the interests of the corporation and its shareholders. His position as stated to the shareholders in the Company proxy statement seems inconsistent with that obligation. In form at least, the statement by a director and officer that he will not give his support to a corporate transaction unless steps are taken to confer a personal power or benefit, suggests an evident disregard of duty. However, the nature of the *quid pro quo* sought by Mr. Briskin in this case is at least consistent with a benign or selfless motive. The Class B stock he sought to have the board recommend and the stockholders approve would transfer complete control of the enterprise to him for an indefinite period, but it is a control that may not be transferred generally and so it is unlikely that Mr. Briskin was motivated to gain access to a control premium for his stock by insisting on a device of this kind as a price of his supporting certain types of future action. . . .

Mr. Briskin's motivation in fact, however, need not be determined in order to conclude that the stockholder vote of June 10, 1986 was fatally flawed by the implied (indeed, the expressed) threats that unless the proposed amendments were authorized, he would oppose transactions "which could be determined by the Board of Directors to be in the best interests of all of the stockholders." As a corporate fiduciary, Mr. Briskin has no right to take such a position, even if benevolently motivated in doing so. Shareholders who respect Mr. Briskin's ability and performance — and who are legally entitled to his undivided loyalty — were inappropriately placed in a position in which they were told that if they refused to vote affirmatively, Mr. Briskin would not support future possible transactions that might be beneficial to the corporation. A vote of shareholders under such circumstances cannot, in the face of a timely challenge by one of the corporation's shareholders, be said, in my opinion, to satisfy the mandate of Section 242(b) of our corporation law requiring shareholder consent to charter amendments.

V.

I turn now to the alternative basis for my finding of a probability of ultimate success. It also relates to the integrity of the stockholder vote approving the amendments; in this case, however, it relates to the quality of the disclosure. [The court went on to conclude that shareholders would likely be misled by the proxy statement.]

For the foregoing reasons, plaintiff's motion shall be granted.

NOTES AND QUESTIONS

1. Note how the court characterized the defect in the conduct of the defendant: That the conduct rendered ineffective shareholder consent to an amendment to the corporate charter. No statute in Delaware rendered ineffective a proxy obtained by virtue of a misrepresentation or as a result of coercion, yet the court reads those limitations as an implicit part of the statute requiring shareholder approval. On what basis does the court reach this conclusion?

2. Of what significance is it that the shareholders were allegedly coerced into approving the plan? In other words, if the plan were not approved, and an attractive offer was made for Arden, would not Briskin's fiduciary duties require him to act in the best interests of the company, at least to the extent he would be acting as a director or officer? Is it different from the situation in which Briskin would find himself if that plan was approved?

SCHREIBER v. CARNEY
Delaware Court of Chancery
447 A.2d 17 (1982)

HARTNETT, VICE CHANCELLOR.

[Texas International Airlines, Inc. developed a plan of reorganization to convert itself into a holding company and create a new subsidiary, Texas Air Corporation, to be the operating company. Technically, this was accomplished by way of a share for share merger between Texas International and Texas Air. As a result of the merger, shareholders of Texas International would end up owning equivalent shares of the new holding company. One of Texas International's preferred shareholders, Jet Capital Corporation, effectively had a veto over the transaction. Jet Capital considered exercising that veto because otherwise it faced serious adverse tax consequences. It held warrants to acquire Texas International stock and the automatic conversion of those warrants in connection with the reorganization would result in taxable income to Jet Capital. One way for Jet Capital to avoid that would be to exercise the warrants, but it lacked the capital to do so. Texas International and Jet Capital developed a solution under which Texas International would loan Jet Capital the funds necessary to exercise the warrants and avoid the adverse tax consequences. The arrangement was approved by independent directors of Texas International and by a majority of its unaffiliated stockholders after full disclosure. Plaintiff challenged the reorganization plan on various grounds.]

Next to be considered is plaintiff's motion for summary judgment on the grounds that vote-buying existed and, therefore, the entire transaction including the merger was void because Jet Capital, in consideration for being extended an extremely advantageous loan, withdrew its opposition to the proposed merger. Thus, it is alleged that in substance and effect, Texas International purchased Jet Capital's necessary vote in contravention of settled law and public policy. As a consequence, plaintiff urges that the less than unanimous shareholder consent was insufficient to ratify a void act and its illegality permeated the entire transaction rendering the merger itself void. The critical inquiry, therefore, is whether the loan in question was in fact vote-buying and, if so, whether vote-buying is illegal, *per se.*

It is clear that the loan constituted vote-buying as that term has been defined by the courts. Vote-buying, despite its negative connotation, is simply a voting agreement supported by consideration personal to the stockholder, whereby the stockholder divorces his discretionary voting power and votes as directed by the offerer. The record clearly indicates that Texas International purchased or "removed" the obstacle of Jet Capital's opposition. Indeed, this is tacitly conceded by the defendants. However, defendants contend that the analysis of the transaction should not end here because the legality of vote-buying depends on whether its object or purpose is to defraud or in some manner disenfranchise the other stockholders. Defendants contend that because the loan did not defraud or disenfranchise any group of shareholders, but rather enfranchised the other shareholders by giving them a determinative vote in the proposed merger, it is not illegal *per se*. Defendants, in effect, contend that vote-buying is not void *per se* because the end justified the means. Whether this is valid depends upon the status of the law.

The Delaware decisions dealing with vote-buying leave the question unanswered. See *Macht v. Merchants Mortgage & Credit Co.*, Del.Ch., 194 A. 19 (1937); *Hall v. Isaacs*, Del.Ch., 146 A.2d 602 (1958), *aff'd*, Del.Supr., 163 A.2d 288 (1960); and *Chew v. Inverness Mgt. Corp.*, Del. Ch., 352 A.2d 426 (1976). In each of these decisions, the Court summarily voided the challenged votes as being purchased and thus contrary to public policy and in fraud of the other stockholders. However, the facts in each case indicated that fraud or disenfranchisement was the obvious purpose of the vote-buying.

. . . The present case presents a peculiar factual setting in that the proposed vote-buying consideration was conditional upon the approval of a majority of the disinterested stockholders after a full disclosure to them of all pertinent facts and was purportedly for the best interests of all Texas International stockholders. It is therefore necessary to do more than merely consider the fact that Jet Capital saw fit to vote for the transaction after a loan was made to it by Texas International . . .

A review of the present controversy, therefore, must go beyond a reading of *Macht v. Merchants Mortgage & Credit Co.*, supra, and consider the cases cited therein: *Dieckmann v. Robyn*, Mo.App., 162 Mo.App. 67, 141 S.W. 717 (1911); *Brady v. Bean*, 221 Ill. 279 (1921); *Smith v. San Francisco, etc.*, 115 Cal. 584, 47 P. 582 (1897); and *Cone v. Russell*, 48 N.J.Eq. 208, 21 A. 847 (1891). There are essentially two principles which appear in these cases. The first is that vote-buying is illegal *per se* if its object or purpose is to defraud or disenfranchise the other stockholders. A fraudulent purpose is as defined at common law, as a deceit which operates prejudicially upon the property rights of another.

The second principle which appears in these old cases is that vote-buying is illegal *per se* as a matter of public policy, the reason being that each stockholder should be entitled to rely upon the independent judgment of his fellow stockholders. Thus, the underlying basis for this latter principle is again fraud but as viewed from a sense of duty owed by all stockholders to one another. The apparent rationale is that by requiring each stockholder to exercise his individual judgment as to all matters presented, "[t]he security of the small stockholders is found in the natural disposition of each stockholder to promote the best interests of all, in order to promote his individual interests." *Cone v. Russell*, 48 N.J.Eq. 208, 21 A. 847, 849 (1891). In essence, while self interest motivates a stockholder's vote, theoretically, it is also advancing the interests of the other stockholders. Thus, any agreement entered into for personal gain, whereby a stockholder separates his voting right from his property right was considered a fraud upon this community of interests.

The often cited case of *Brady v. Bean*, 221 Ill.App. 279 (1921), is particularly enlightening. In that case, the plaintiff-an apparently influential stockholder-voiced his opposition to the corporation's proposed sale of assets. The plaintiff feared that his investment would be wiped out because the consideration for the sale appeared only sufficient enough to satisfy the corporation's creditors. As a result and without the knowledge of the other stockholders, the defendant, also a stockholder as well as a director and substantial creditor of the company, offered to the plaintiff in exchange for the withdrawal of his opposition, a sharing in defendant's claims against the corporation. In an action to enforce this contract against the defendant's estate, the Court refused relief stating:

> "Appellant being a stockholder in the company, any contract entered into by him whereby he was to receive a personal consideration in return for either his action or his inaction in a matter such as a sale of all the company's assets, involving, as it did, the interests of all the stockholders, was contrary to public policy and void, it being admitted that such contract was not known by or assented to by the other stockholders. *The purpose and effect of the contract*

was apparently to influence appellant, in his decision of a question affecting the rights and interests of his associate stockholders, by a consideration which was foreign to those rights and interests and would likely to induce him to disregard the consideration he owed them and the contract must, therefore, be regarded as a fraud upon them. Such an agreement will not be enforced, as being against public policy. *Teich v. Kaufman*, 174 Ill.App. 306; *Guernsey v. Cook*, 120 Mass. 501; *UPalmbaum [Palmbaum] v. Magulsky*, 217 Mass. 306 [104 N.E. 746]." (emphasis added) 221 Ill.App. at 283.

In addition to the deceit obviously practiced upon the other stockholders, the Court was clearly concerned with the rights and interests of the other stockholders. Thus, the potential injury or prejudicial impact which might flow to other stockholders as a result of such an agreement forms the heart of the rationale underlying the breach of public policy doctrine.

An automatic application of this rationale to the facts in the present case, however, would be to ignore an essential element of the transaction. The agreement in question was entered into primarily to further the interests of Texas International's other shareholders. Indeed, the shareholders, after reviewing a detailed proxy statement, voted overwhelmingly in favor of the loan agreement. Thus, the underlying rationale for the argument that vote-buying is illegal *per se*, as a matter of public policy, ceases to exist when measured against the undisputed reason for the transaction.

Moreover, the rationale that vote-buying is, as a matter of public policy, illegal *per se* is founded upon considerations of policy which are now outmoded as a necessary result of an evolving corporate environment. According to 5 Fletcher *Cyclopedia Corporation* (Perm. Ed.) § 2066:

"The theory that each stockholder is entitled to the personal judgment of each other stockholder expressed in his vote, and that any agreement among stockholders frustrating it was invalid, is obsolete because it is both impracticable and impossible of application to modern corporations with many widely scattered stockholders, and the courts have gradually abandoned it."

. . . Delaware has discarded the presumptions against voting agreements. Thus, under our present law, an agreement involving the transfer of stock voting rights without the transfer of ownership is not necessarily illegal and each arrangement must be examined in light of its object or purpose. To hold otherwise would be to exalt form over substance. . . . More than the mere form of an agreement relating to voting must be considered and voting agreements in whatever form, therefore, should not be considered to be illegal *per se* unless the object or purpose is to defraud or in some way disenfranchise the other stockholders. This is not to say, however, that vote-buying accomplished for some laudible purpose is automatically free from challenge. Because vote-buying is so easily susceptible of abuse it must be viewed as a voidable transaction subject to a test for intrinsic fairness.

. . . I therefore hold that the agreement, whereby Jet Capital withdrew its opposition to the proposed merger in exchange for a loan to fund the early exercise of its warrants was not void *per se* because the object and purpose of the agreement was not to defraud or disenfranchise the other stockholders but rather was for the purpose of furthering the interest of all Texas International stockholders. The agreement, however, was a voidable act. Because the loan agreement was voidable it was susceptible to cure by shareholder approval. *Michelson v. Duncan*, Del.Supr., 407 A.2d 211 (1979). Consequently, the subsequent ratification of the transaction by a majority of the independent stockholders, after a full disclosure of all germane facts with complete candor precludes any further judicial inquiry of it.

NOTES AND QUESTIONS

1. While allegations of vote-buying are not uncommon, see, for example, *Hewlett v. Hewlett-Packard Co.*, 2002 Del. Ch. LEXIS 35 (Del. Ch. Apr. 30, 2002), a chapter in the proxy fight over the HP-Compaq Computer Corp. merger, in recent years a new issue has emerged — "empty voting." This term refers to the phenomenon in which a shareholder has more votes than shares or, put differently, shares are voted by persons who have no economic interest in the underlying shares that they are voting. For instance, a party may borrow shares immediately before the record date, vote those shares and then immediately return the shares to the lender, usually paying a small fee for the privilege. A related example is one in which an investor acquires shares but simultaneously hedges that acquisition (and the economic risk of share ownership) with derivative transactions. The investor is left with voting power but no underlying economic interest in the shares. These and other transactions, which are complicated and somewhat exotic, are possible because of increasingly sophisticated derivatives markets, which allow investors to "decouple" economic risks from voting power. Does the doctrine established in *Schreiber* limit the ability of investors to vote such shares? *See generally*, Henry T.C. Hu and Bernard Black, *Empty Voting and Hidden (Morphable) Ownership: Taxonomy, Implications, and Reforms*, 61 Bus. Law 101 (2006).

2. In proxy contests, where corporate management and an outsider vie for the proxies of the shareholders, management draws on the corporate treasury to fund its solicitation of proxies. The outsiders, of course, have to fund their expenses from their own resources, thus creating an unfair advantage for management. The ability of management to tap corporate resources to support the re-election of incumbent directors is not, however, without limits. The courts have said that management can only use corporate funds in an election contest when there are "policy differences" between its nominees and those of the insurgents, as opposed to mere "personality conflicts." *Levin v. Metro-Goldwyn-Mayer, Inc.*, 264 F. Supp. 797 (S.D.N.Y 1979). Second, the expenses for which management seeks reimbursement must be "reasonable and proper expenses for the solicitation of proxies." *Rosenfeld v. Fairchild Engine & Airplane Corp.*, 128 N.E.2d 291, 293 (N.Y. 1955). In this context, of course, expenses for "vote buying" could not be deemed "reasonable." Finally, if the insurgents do prevail in an election contest, they can obtain reimbursement for their expenses from the corporate treasury, provided the shareholders approve. Why is shareholder approval necessary if the insurgents seek reimbursement, but not if the incumbents do?

PROBLEM

Barney & Smith Co. is an investment partnership that owns shares in several publicly-held companies. Among its portfolio companies is Craft Co., a conglomerate with many different operating companies. The partners of Barney & Smith believe that Craft Co. should sell off several of its underperforming operating companies to private equity partnerships and distribute the proceeds in the form of a dividend to Craft's long-suffering shareholders. The Craft board is resistant to the idea, asserting that the market is undervaluing Craft shares, but will someday see its value. Barney & Smith is not that patient and has decided to launch a proxy fight to take control of Craft's board. In response, Craft has undertaken an aggressive campaign to persuade its shareholders that current management is best suited to realize the long term potential of the company. Craft management has hired a proxy solicitation firm and authorized it to "wine and dine" Craft's largest shareholders — several large pension funds. Craft is also placing daily, full page advertisements in the Wall Street Journal and the New York Times urging shareholders to vote for its slate of nominees. Barney & Smith wishes to enjoin these practices. Can it?

3. Federal Regulation: Proxy Solicitations

As noted above, federal law generally regulates the process of proxy voting. Section 14(a) of the Securities Exchange Act of 1934 makes it unlawful for any person to solicit any proxy in contravention of the rules and regulations adopted by the SEC "as necessary or appropriate in the public interest or for the protection of investors." With this broad rulemaking authority, the SEC has adopted a series of rules in Regulation 14A, including rules that specify what information must be furnished to stockholders, the form of the proxy that may solicited, etc.

A rule that has figured frequently in litigation is Rule 14a-9, which prohibits solicitations "containing any statement which . . . is false or misleading with respect to any material fact, or which omits to state any material fact necessary in order to make the statements therein not false or misleading. . . . " Neither § 14(a) nor Rule 14a-9 provides for a private right of action to remedy violations of the statute or rules thereunder; however, the U.S. Supreme Court, in *J. I. Case v. Borak*, 377 U.S. 426 (1964) held that a shareholder may maintain both direct and derivative actions for violations of § 14(a). The Court reasoned that among the chief purposes of § 14(a) was the protection of investors, "which certainly implies the availability of judicial relief where necessary to achieve that result." *Id.* at 432. Noting the large number of proxy statements received by the SEC, the Court provided an additional rationale for allowing private enforcement: it "provides a necessary supplement to Commission action." *Id.*

Whenever the Court recognizes an "implied private right of action," it must then provide the elements of that action. The materials that follow discuss the most significant elements of a private cause of action under Rule 14a-9.

MILLS v. ELECTRIC AUTO-LITE CO.
United States Supreme Court
396 U.S. 375 (1970)

Mr. Justice Harlan delivered the opinion of the Court.

This case requires us to consider a basic aspect of the implied private right of action for violation of § 14(a) of the Securities Exchange Act of 1934, recognized by this Court in J. I. Case Co. v. Borak, 377 U.S. 426, 84 S. Ct. 1555, 12 L. Ed. 2d 423 (1964). As in Borak the asserted wrong is that a corporate merger was accomplished through the use of a proxy statement that was materially false or misleading. The question with which we deal is what causal relationship must be shown between such a statement and the merger to establish a cause of action based on the violation of the Act.

I.

Petitioners were shareholders of the Electric Auto-Lite Company until 1963, when it was merged into Mergenthaler Linotype Company. They brought suit on the day before the shareholders' meeting at which the vote was to take place on the merger against Auto-Lite, Mergenthaler, and a third company, American Manufacturing Company, Inc. The complaint sought an injunction against the voting by Auto-Lite's management of all proxies obtained by means of an allegedly misleading proxy solicitation; however, it did not seek a temporary restraining order, and the voting went ahead as scheduled the following day. Several months later petitioners filed an amended complaint, seeking to have the merger set aside and to obtain such other relief as might be proper.

In Count II of the amended complaint, which is the only count before us, petitioners predicated jurisdiction on § 27 of the 1934 Act, 15 U.S.C. § 78aa. They alleged that the proxy statement sent out by the Auto-Lite management to solicit shareholders' votes in favor of the merger was misleading, in violation of § 14(a) of the Act and SEC Rule 14a-9 thereunder. Petitioners recited that before the merger Mergenthaler owned over 50%

of the outstanding shares of Auto-Lite common stock, and had been in control of Auto-Lite for two years. American Manufacturing in turn owned about one-third of the outstanding shares of Mergenthaler, and for two years had been in voting control of Mergenthaler and, through it, of Auto-Lite. Petitioners charged that in light of these circumstances the proxy statement was misleading in that it told Auto-Lite shareholders that their board of directors recommended approval of the merger without also informing them that all 11 of Auto-Lite's directors were nominees of Mergenthaler and were under the 'control and domination of Mergenthaler.' Petitioners asserted the right to complain of this alleged violation both derivatively on behalf of Auto-Lite and as representatives of the class of all its minority shareholders.

On petitioners' motion for summary judgment with respect to Count II, the District Court for the Northern District of Illinois ruled as a matter of law that the claimed defect in the proxy statement was, in light of the circumstances in which the statement was made, a material omission. The District Court concluded, from its reading of the Borak opinion, that it had to hold a hearing on the issue whether there was 'a causal connection between the finding that there has been a violation of the disclosure requirements of § 14(a) and the alleged injury to the plaintiffs' before it could consider what remedies would be appropriate.

After holding such a hearing, the court found that under the terms of the merger agreement, an affirmative vote of two-thirds of the Auto-Lite shares was required for approval of the merger, and that the respondent companies owned and controlled about 54% of the outstanding shares. Therefore, to obtain authorization of the merger, respondents had to secure the approval of a substantial number of the minority shareholders. At the stockholders' meeting, approximately 950,000 shares, out of 1,160,000 shares outstanding, were voted in favor of the merger. This included 317,000 votes obtained by proxy from the minority shareholders, votes that were 'necessary and indispensable to the approval of the merger.' The District Court concluded that a causal relationship had thus been shown, and it granted an interlocutory judgment in favor of petitioners on the issue of liability, referring the case to a master for consideration of appropriate relief.

. . . The Court of Appeals for the Seventh Circuit affirmed the District Court's conclusion that the proxy statement was materially deficient, but reversed on the question of causation. The court acknowledged that, if an injunction had been sought a sufficient time before the stockholders' meeting, 'corrective measures would have been appropriate.' 403 F.2d 429, 435 (1968). However, since this suit was brought too late for preventive action, the courts had to determine 'whether the misleading statement and omission caused the submission of sufficient proxies,' as a prerequisite to a determination of liability under the Act. If the respondents could show, 'by a preponderance of probabilities, that the merger would have received a sufficient vote even if the proxy statement had not been misleading in the respect found,' petitioners would be entitled to no relief of any kind. Id., at 436.

The Court of Appeals acknowledged that this test corresponds to the common-law fraud test of whether the injured party relied on the misrepresentation. However, rightly concluding that '(r)eliance by thousands of individuals, as here, can scarcely be inquired into' (id., at 436 n. 10), the court ruled that the issue was to be determined by proof of the fairness of the terms of the merger. If respondents could show that the merger had merit and was fair to the minority shareholders, the trial court would be justified in concluding that a sufficient number of shareholders would have approved the merger had there been no deficiency in the proxy statement. In that case respondents would be entitled to a judgment in their favor.

II.

. . . As we stressed in Borak, § 14(a) stemmed from a congressional belief that '(f) air corporate suffrage is an important right that should attach to every equity security bought on a public exchange.' H.R.Rep.No.1383, 73d Cong., 2d Sess., 13. The provision was intended to promote 'the free exercise of the voting rights of stockholders' by ensuring that proxies would be solicited with 'explanation to the stockholder of the real nature of the questions for which authority to cast his vote is sought.' Id. at 14; S.Rep.No.792, 73d Cong., 2d Sess., 12; see 377 U.S., at 431, 84 S. Ct. 1555, 1559. The decision below, by permitting all liability to be foreclosed on the basis of a finding that the merger was fair, would allow the stockholders to be by-passed, at least where the only legal challenge to the merger is a suit for retrospective relief after the meeting has been held. A judicial appraisal of the merger's merits could be substituted for the actual and informed vote of the stockholders.

The result would be to insulate from private redress an entire category of proxy violations — those relating to matters other than the terms of the merger. Even outrageous misrepresentations in a proxy solicitation, if they did not relate to the terms of the transaction, would give rise to no cause of action under § 14(a). Particularly if carried over to enforcement actions by the Securities and Exchange Commission itself, such a result would subvert the congressional purpose of ensuring full and fair disclosure to shareholders.

Further, recognition of the fairness of the merger as a complete defense would confront small shareholders with an additional obstacle to making a successful challenge to a proposal recommended through a defective proxy statement. The risk that they would be unable to rebut the corporation's evidence of the fairness of the proposal, and thus to establish their cause of action, would be bound to discourage such shareholders from the private enforcement of the proxy rules that 'provides a necessary supplement to Commission action.' J. I. Case Co. v. Borak, 377 U.S., at 432, 84 S. Ct. at 1560.[13]

Such a frustration of the congressional policy is not required by anything in the wording of the statute or in our opinion in the Borak case. Section 14(a) declares it 'unlawful' to solicit proxies in contravention of Commission rules, and SEC Rule 14a-9 prohibits solicitations 'containing any statement which. . . is false or misleading with respect to any material fact, or which omits to state any material fact necessary in order to make the statements therein not false or misleading . . ..' Use of a solicitation that is materially misleading is itself a violation of law, as the Court of Appeals recognized in stating that injunctive relief would be available to remedy such a defect if sought prior to the stockholders' meeting. In Borak, which came to this Court on a dismissal of the complaint, the Court limited its inquiry to whether a violation of § 14(a) gives rise to 'a federal cause of action for rescission or damages,' 377 U.S., at 428, 84 S.Ct. at 1558. Referring to the argument made by petitioners there 'that the merger can be dissolved only if it was fraudulent or non-beneficial, issues upon which the proxy material would not bear,' the Court stated: 'But the causal relationship of the proxy material and the merger are questions of fact to be resolved at trial, not here. We

---

[13] [5] The Court of Appeals' ruling that 'causation' may be negated by proof of the fairness of the merger also rests on a dubious behavioral assumption. There is no justification for presuming that the shareholders of every corporation are willing to accept any and every fair merger offer put before them; yet such a presumption is implicit in the opinion of the Court of Appeals. That court gave no indication of what evidence petitioners might adduce, once respondents had established that the merger proposal was equitable, in order to show that the shareholders would nevertheless have rejected it if the solicitation had not been misleading. Proof of actual reliance by thousands of individuals would, as the court acknowledged, not be feasible, see R. Jennings & H. Marsh, Securities Regulation, Cases and Materials 1001 (2d ed. 1968); and reliance on the nondisclosure of a fact is a particularly difficult matter to define or prove, see 3 L. Loss, Securities Regulation 1766 (2d ed. 1961). In practice, therefore, the objective fairness of the proposal would seemingly be determinative of liability. But, in view of the many other factors that might lead shareholders to prefer their current position to that of owners of a larger, combined enterprise, it is pure conjecture to assume that the fairness of the proposal will always be determinative of their vote. Cf. Wirtz v. Hotel, Motel & Club Employees Union, 391 U.S. 492, 508, 88 S. Ct. 1743, 1752, 20 L. Ed. 2d 763 (1968).

therefore do not discuss this point further.' Id., at 431, 84 S.Ct. at 1559. In the present case there has been a hearing specifically directed to the causation problem. The question before the Court is whether the facts found on the basis of that hearing are sufficient in law to establish petitioners' cause of action, and we conclude that they are.

Where the misstatement or omission in a proxy statement has been shown to be 'material,' as it was found to be here, that determination itself indubitably embodies a conclusion that the defect was of such a character that it might have been considered important by a reasonable shareholder who was in the process of deciding how to vote. This requirement that the defect have a significant propensity to affect the voting process is found in the express terms of Rule 14a-9, and it adequately serves the purpose of ensuring that a cause of action cannot be established by proof of a defect so trivial, or so unrelated to the transaction for which approval is sought, that correction of the defect or imposition of liability would not further the interests protected by § 14(a).

. . . There is no need to supplement this requirement, as did the Court of Appeals, with a requirement of proof of whether the defect actually had a decisive effect on the voting. Where there has been a finding of materiality, a shareholder has made a sufficient showing of causal relationship between the violation and the injury for which he seeks redress if, as here, he proves that the proxy solicitation itself, rather than the particular defect in the solicitation materials, was an essential link in the accomplishment of the transaction. This objective test will avoid the impracticalities of determining how many votes were affected, and, by resolving doubts in favor of those the statute is designed to protect, will effectuate the congressional policy of ensuring that the shareholders are able to make an informed choice when they are consulted on corporate transactions.[14]

III.

Our conclusion that petitioners have established their case by showing that proxies necessary to approval of the merger were obtained by means of a materially misleading solicitation implies nothing about the form of relief to which they may be entitled. We held in Borak that upon finding a violation the courts were 'to be alert to provide such remedies as are necessary to make effective the congressional purpose,' noting specifically that such remedies are not to be limited to prospective relief. 377 U.S., at 433, 434, 84 S.Ct. at 1560. In devising retrospective relief for violation of the proxy rules, the federal courts should consider the same factors that would govern the relief granted for any similar illegality or fraud. One important factor may be the fairness of the terms of the merger. Possible forms of relief will include setting aside the merger or granting other equitable relief, but, as the Court of Appeals below noted, nothing in the statutory policy 'requires the court to unscramble a corporate transaction merely because a violation occurred.' 403 F.2d, at 436. In selecting a remedy the lower courts should exercise "the sound discretion which guides the determinations of courts of equity," keeping in mind the role of equity as 'the instrument for nice adjustment and reconciliation between the public interest and private needs as well as between competing private claims.' Hecht Co. v. Bowles, 321 U.S. 321, 329–330, 64 S.Ct. 587, 591–592, 88 L.Ed. 754 (1944), quoting from Meredith v. Winter Haven, 320 U.S. 228, 235, 64 S.Ct. 7, 11, 88 L.Ed. 9 (1943).

. . . Monetary relief will, of course, also be a possibility. Where the defect in the proxy solicitation relates to the specific terms of the merger, the district court might appropriately order an accounting to ensure that the shareholders receive the value

---

[14] [7] We need not decide in this case whether causation could be shown where the management controls a sufficient number of shares to approve the transaction without any votes from the minority. Even in that situation, if the management finds it necessary for legal or practical reasons to solicit proxies from minority shareholders, at least one court has held that the proxy solicitation might be sufficiently related to the merger to satisfy the causation requirement, see Laurenzano v. Einbender, 264 F.Supp. 356 (D.C.E.D.N.Y.1966).

that was represented as coming to them. On the other hand, where, as here, the misleading aspect of the solicitation did not relate to terms of the merger, monetary relief might be afforded to the shareholders only if the merger resulted in a reduction of the earnings or earnings potential of their holdings. In short, damages should be recoverable only to the extent that they can be shown. If commingling of the assets and operations of the merged companies makes it impossible to establish direct injury from the merger, relief might be predicated on a determination of the fairness of the terms of the merger at the time it was approved. These questions, of course, are for decision in the first instance by the District Court on remand, and our singling out of some of the possibilities is not intended to exclude others.

IV.

Although the question of relief must await further proceedings in the District Court, our conclusion that petitioners have established their cause of action indicates that the Court of Appeals should have affirmed the partial summary judgment on the issue of liability. The result would have been not only that respondents, rather than petitioners, would have borne the costs of the appeal, but also, we think, that petitioners would have been entitled to an interim award of litigation expenses and reasonable attorneys' fees. Cf. Highway Truck Drivers & Helpers Local 107 v. Cohen, 220 F.Supp. 735 (D.C.E.D.Pa.1963). We agree with the position taken by petitioners, and by the United States as amicus, that petitioners, who have established a violation of the securities laws by their corporation and its officials, should be reimbursed by the corporation or its survivor for the costs of establishing the violation.

. . . The absence of express statutory authorization for an award of attorneys' fees in a suit under § 14(a) does not preclude such an award in cases of this type . . .

. . . While the general American rule is that attorneys' fees are not ordinarily recoverable as costs, both the courts and Congress have developed exceptions to this rule for situations in which overriding considerations indicate the need for such a recovery. A primary judge-created exception has been to award expenses where a plaintiff has successfully maintained a suit, usually on behalf of a class, that benefits a group of others in the same manner as himself. To allow the others to obtain full benefit from the plaintiff's efforts without contributing equally to the litigation expenses would be to enrich the others unjustly at the plaintiff's expense. This suit presents such a situation. The dissemination of misleading proxy solicitations was a 'deceit practiced on the stockholders as a group,' J. I. Case Co. v. Borak, 377 U.S., at 432, 84 S.Ct. at 1560, and the expenses of petitioners' lawsuit have been incurred for the benefit of the corporation and the other shareholders.

The fact that this suit has not yet produced, and may never produce, a monetary recovery from which the fees could be paid does not preclude an award based on this rationale. Although the earliest cases recognizing a right to reimbursement involved litigation that had produced or preserved a 'common fund' for the benefit of a group, nothing in these cases indicates that the suit must actually bring money into the court as a prerequisite to the court's power to order reimbursement of expenses . . .

. . . In many suits under § 14(a), particularly where the violation does not relate to the terms of the transaction for which proxies are solicited, it may be impossible to assign monetary value to the benefit. Nevertheless, the stress placed by Congress on the importance of fair and informed corporate suffrage leads to the conclusion that, in vindicating the statutory policy, petitioners have rendered a substantial service to the corporation and its shareholders. Whether petitioners are successful in showing a need for significant relief may be a factor in determining whether a further award should later be made. But regardless of the relief granted, private stockholders' actions of this sort 'involve corporate therapeutics,'[15] and furnish a benefit to all shareholders by providing an important means of enforcement of the proxy statute. To award attorneys' fees in such a suit to a plaintiff who has succeeded in establishing a cause of action is not to saddle the unsuccessful party with the expenses but to impose them on the class that has benefited from them and that would have had to pay them had it brought the suit.

For the foregoing reasons we conclude that the judgment of the Court of Appeals should be vacated and the case remanded to that court for further proceedings consistent with this opinion.

It is so ordered . . .

NOTES AND QUESTIONS

1. What elements of a private cause of action under Rule 14a-9 were established in *Mills*?

2. What effect do you suppose the Court's ruling has had in terms of private enforcement of Rule 14a-9?

3. Suppose the proxy statement in *Mills* clearly disclosed the share ownership of Auto-Lite, making it clear that Mergenthaler owned a majority of the outstanding voting shares of Auto-Lite and the power to elect all of its directors, but failed to state that, in fact, Mergenthaler had elected the directors. Would the shareholders have been able to state a cause of action under Rule 14a-9?

4. The Court returned to the issue of causation in *Virginia Bankshares, Inc. v. Sandberg*, 501 U.S. 1083 (1991), where it held that if the votes of the minority are not required by law or corporate bylaw to authorize an action subject to the proxy solicitation, plaintiff cannot demonstrate causation. The Court also held in that case that if the proxy statement includes a misrepresentation regarding the directors' motives for recommending shareholder approval, that misrepresentation, standing alone, is an insufficient basis to maintain an action under Rule 14a-9. So, if the proxy statement recites that the directors recommend approval of a merger because they "believe" that the merger "is in the best interest of the shareholders," but the directors do not believe that statement, the misrepresentation is not actionable unless, in fact, the merger was not in the best interests of the shareholders.

5. As we will see in Chapter 12, scienter, or proof that the defendant intended to defraud the plaintiff, is a necessary element in actions based on Rule 10b-5. Is the same true when the action is based on Rule 14a-9? The Sixth Circuit has held that scienter is a necessary element for private actions under Rule 14a-9, at least in the context of a claim against a company's accountant. *Adams v. Standard Knitting Mills, Inc.*, 623 F.2d 422, 431 (6th Cir. 1980). However, two other circuits have held that only negligence is required for actions against the corporation itself. *Gould v. American-Hawaiian S.S. Co.*, 535 F.2d 761, 777–78 (3d Cir. 1978); *Gerstle v. Gamble-Skogmo, Inc.*, 478 F.2d 1281, 1300–01 (2d Cir. 1973).

PROBLEM

Alpha, Inc. proposed to merge its partially-owned subsidiary, Beta Co., into itself. Alpha owned 75% of the outstanding common shares of Beta, the only class of stock outstanding. The balance of the shares was held by approximately 1,000 shareholders, who would receive cash in the merger. Under the relevant corporate statute, a vote of shareholders owning, in the aggregate, a majority of the outstanding shares of Beta was needed to approve such a transaction. Alpha caused Beta to issue a proxy statement to the Beta shareholders soliciting their proxies to be voted by the Beta executive committee in favor of the merger. The proxy statement disclosed that Beta's

---

[15] [23] Murphy v. North American Light & Power Co., 33 F. Supp. 567, 570 (D.C.S.D. N.Y. 1940).

net worth was materially less than what it actually was, or at least that is what some shareholders believe. Is there any basis for those shareholders to challenge the merger under Rule 14a-9, assuming the merger was consummated but that the complaining shareholders never gave a proxy to vote their shares?

3. Federal Regulation: Shareholder Proposals

One unusual area of federal regulation is found in Rule 14a-8 (also part of Regulation 14A), which enables shareholders, subject to certain limitations, to propose resolutions for consideration by the shareholders at any annual or special meeting of shareholders and requires a registered company to include those proposals in its proxy statement and on the proxy card. What is unusual about this rule is the extent to which is it substantive — it requires publicly-held companies to give access to its proxy statement and to allow shareholders to vote on shareholder proposals with which the board might disagree. One court has rationalized the rule on the theory that "the corporate circulation of proxy materials which fail to make reference to a shareholder's intention to present a proper proposal at the annual meeting renders the solicitation inherently misleading." *New York City Employees' Retirement System v. American Brands, Inc.*, 634 F. Supp. 1382, 1386 (S.D.N.Y. 1986). The Rule is also unusual in that it is set forth in a question and answer format. The Rule has been a part of Regulation 14A since 1942 and has become increasingly important in recent years as various shareholder groups have become more active in corporate governance.

Any shareholder who has owned $2,000 worth of stock (or 1% of the outstanding shares) for at least a year may submit a proposal subject to Rule 14a-8. This low threshold has meant that the Rule is often used by social activists seeking to change corporate practices that they consider immoral or otherwise objectionable (e.g., a challenge to the company's doing business with an undesirable regime). Shareholders meeting the eligibility requirement can submit a proposal and supporting statement (which together may not exceed 500 words) and, subject to certain exceptions, the company must include the proposal on the proxy card and the supporting statement in the proxy statement. The four principal exceptions (of 13 set forth in the rule) are that: the proposal is improper under state law; the proposal is not significantly related to the company's business; the proposal relates to the company's ordinary business operations; or the proposal relates to the election of directors.

If the company believes that the proposal falls within one of the exceptions, it may seek guidance from the staff of the SEC. If the staff agrees that the proposal is excludable, it will send the company a "no action" letter; that is, a letter advising the company that if it excludes the proposal from its proxy statement, the staff will not recommend that the Commission take any action against the company. On the other hand, if the staff does not agree with the company's assessment, it will so advise the company. Either the company or the proposing shareholder can appeal to the Commission from an adverse determination from the staff. A further appeal to the U.S. Court of Appeals for the District of Columbia is possible. Alternatively, if the company excludes a shareholder proposal, the shareholder may seek relief from the U.S. District Court. Needless to say, there has been much litigation over this issue, and the materials that follow touch upon a few of the significant cases in this area.

a. The "Not Significantly Related" Exception

LOVENHEIM v. IROQUOIS BRANDS, LTD.
U.S. District Court for the District of Columbia
618 F. Supp. 554 (1985)

GASCH, District Judge.

I. BACKGROUND

This matter is now before the Court on plaintiff's motion for preliminary injunction.

Plaintiff Peter C. Lovenheim, owner of two hundred shares of common stock in Iroquois Brands, Ltd. (hereinafter "Iroquois/Delaware"), seeks to bar Iroquois/Delaware from excluding from the proxy materials being sent to all shareholders in preparation for an upcoming shareholder meeting information concerning a proposed resolution he intends to offer at the meeting. Mr. Lovenheim's proposed resolution relates to the procedure used to force-feed geese for production of paté de foie gras in France,[16] a type of paté imported by Iroquois/Delaware. Specifically, his resolution calls upon the Directors of Iroquois/Delaware to:

> form a committee to study the methods by which its French supplier produces paté de foie gras, and report to the shareholders its findings and opinions, based on expert consultation, on whether this production method causes undue distress, pain, or suffering to the animals involved and, if so, whether further distribution of this product should be discontinued until a more humane production method is developed.

Mr. Lovenheim's right to compel Iroquois/Delaware to insert information concerning his proposal in the proxy materials turns on the applicability of section 14(a) of the Securities Exchange Act of 1934, 15 U.S.C. § 78n(a) ("the Exchange Act"), and the shareholder proposal rule promulgated by the Securities and Exchange Commission ("SEC"), Rule 14a-8.

. . . Iroquois/Delaware has refused to allow information concerning Mr. Lovenheim's proposal to be included in proxy materials being sent in connection with the next annual shareholders meeting. In doing so, Iroquois/Delaware relies on an exception to the general requirement of Rule 14a-8, Rule 14a-8(c)(5). That exception provides that an issuer of securities "may omit a proposal and any statement in support thereof" from its proxy statement and form of proxy:

> if the proposal relates to operations which account for less than 5 percent of the issuer's total assets at the end of its most recent fiscal year, and for less than 5 percent of its net earnings and gross sales for its most recent fiscal year, and is not otherwise significantly related to the issuer's business.

Rule 14a-8(c)(5), 17 C.F.R. § 240.14a-8(c)(5).

. . . Iroquois/Delaware's reliance on the argument that this exception applies is based on the following information contained in the affidavit of its president: Iroquois/Delaware has annual revenues of $141 million with $6 million in annual profits and $78 million in assets. In contrast, its paté de foie gras sales were just $79,000 last year, representing a net loss on paté sales of $3,121. Iroquois/Delaware has only $34,000 in assets related to paté. Thus none of the company's net earnings and less than .05 percent

---

[16] [2] Paté de foie gras is made from the liver of geese. According to Mr. Lovenheim's affidavit, force-feeding is frequently used in order to expand the liver and thereby produce a larger quantity of paté. Mr. Lovenheim's affidavit also contains a description of the force-feeding process:

> Force-feeding usually begins when the geese are four months old. On some farms where feeding is mechanized, the bird's body and wings are placed in a metal brace and its neck is stretched. Through a funnel inserted 10–12 inches down the throat of the goose, a machine pumps up to 400 grams of corn-based mash into its stomach. An elastic band around the goose's throat prevents regurgitation. When feeding is manual, a handler uses a funnel and stick to force the mash down.

Affidavit of Peter C. Lovenheim at ¶ 7. Plaintiff contends that such force-feeding is a form of cruelty to animals. *Id.*

Plaintiff has offered no evidence that force-feeding is used by Iroquois/Delaware's supplier in producing the paté imported by Iroquois/Delaware. However his proposal calls upon the committee he seeks to create to investigate this question.

of its assets are implicated by plaintiff's proposal. These levels are obviously far below the five percent threshold set forth in the first portion of the exception claimed by Iroquois/Delaware.

Plaintiff does not contest that his proposed resolution relates to a matter of little economic significance to Iroquois/Delaware. Nevertheless he contends that the Rule 14a-8(c)(5) exception is not applicable as it cannot be said that his proposal "is not otherwise significantly related to the issuer's business" as is required by the final portion of that exception. In other words, plaintiff's argument that Rule 14a-8 does not permit omission of his proposal rests on the assertion that the rule and statute on which it is based do not permit omission merely because a proposal is not economically significant where a proposal has "ethical or social significance."[17]

Iroquois/Delaware challenges plaintiff's view that ethical and social proposals cannot be excluded even if they do not meet the economic or five percent test. Instead, Iroquois/Delaware views the exception solely in economic terms as permitting omission of any proposals relating to a de minimis share of assets and profits. Iroquois/Delaware asserts that since corporations are economic entities, only an economic test is appropriate.

The Court would note that the applicability of the Rule 14a-8(c)(5) exception to Mr. Lovenheim's proposal represents a close question given the lack of clarity in the exception itself. In effect, plaintiff relies on the word "otherwise," suggesting that it indicates the drafters of the rule intended that other non-economic tests of significance be used. Iroquois/Delaware relies on the fact that the rule examines other significance in relation to the issuer's business. Because of the apparent ambiguity of the rule, the Court considers the history of the shareholder proposal rule in determining the proper interpretation of the most recent version of that rule. Prior to 1983, paragraph 14a-8(c)(5) excluded proposals "not significantly related to the issuer's business" but did not contain an objective economic significance test such as the five percent of sales, assets, and earnings specified in the first part of the current version. Although a series of SEC decisions through 1976 allowing issuers to exclude proposals challenging compliance with the Arab economic boycott of Israel allowed exclusion if the issuer did less than one percent of their business with Arab countries or Israel, [18]the Commission stated later in 1976 that it did "not believe that subparagraph (c)(5) should be hinged solely on the economic relativity of a proposal." Securities Exchange Act Release No. 12,999, 41 Fed. Reg. 52, 99 4, 52,997 (1976). Thus the Commission required inclusion "in many situations in which the related business comprised less than one percent" of the company's revenues, profits or assets "where the proposal has raised *policy questions* important enough to be considered 'significantly related' to the issuer's business."[19]

As indicated above, the 1983 revision adopted the five percent test of economic significance in an effort to create a more objective standard. Nevertheless, in adopting

---

[17] [8] The assertion that the proposal is significant in an ethical and social sense relies on plaintiff's argument that "the very availability of a market for products that may be obtained through the inhumane force-feeding of geese cannot help but contribute to the continuation of such treatment." Plaintiff's brief characterizes the humane treatment of animals as among the foundations of western culture and cites in support of this view the Seven Laws of Noah, an animal protection statute enacted by the Massachusetts Bay Colony in 1641, numerous federal statutes enacted since 1877, and animal protection laws existing in all fifty states and the District of Columbia. An additional indication of the significance of plaintiff's proposal is the support of such leading organizations in the field of animal care as the American Society for the Prevention of Cruelty to Animals and The Humane Society of the United States for measures aimed at discontinuing use of force-feeding.

[18] [10] C.F.R. § 240.14a-8(c)(5) (1983).

[19] [11] Comment, *1983 Amendments, supra* note 10 at 185 (emphasis supplied). For example, "[p]roposals requesting the cessation of further development, planning and construction of nuclear power plants and proposals requesting shareholders be informed as to all aspects of the company's business in European communist countries have been included in this way." *Id.* (footnotes omitted).

this standard, the Commission stated that proposals will be includable notwithstanding their "failure to reach the specified economic thresholds if a significant relationship to the issuer's business is demonstrated on the face of the resolution or supporting statement." Securities Exchange Act Release No. 19,135, 47 Fed. Reg. 47,420, 47,428 (1982). Thus it seems clear based on the history of the rule that "the meaning of 'significantly related' is not *limited* to economic significance." Comment, *1983 Amendments, supra* note 10 at 183 (emphasis in original).

The only decision in this Circuit cited by the parties relating to the scope of section 14 and the shareholder proposal rule is *Medical Committee for Human Rights v. SEC,* 432 F.2d 659 (D.C.Cir.1970). That case concerned an effort by shareholders of Dow Chemical Company to advise other shareholders of their proposal directed at prohibiting Dow's production of napalm. Dow had relied on the counterpart of the 14a-8(c)(5) exemption then in effect to exclude the proposal from proxy materials and the SEC accepted Dow's position without elaborating on its basis for doing so. In remanding the matter back to the SEC for the Commission to provide the basis for its decision, *id.* at 682, the Court noted what it termed "substantial questions" as to whether an interpretation of the shareholder proposal rule "which permitted omission of [a] proposal as one motivated primarily by *general* political or social concerns would conflict with the congressional intent underlying section 14(a) of the [Exchange] Act." 432 F.2d at 680 (emphasis in original).

Iroquois/Delaware attempts to distinguish *Medical Committee for Human Rights* as a case where a company sought to exclude a proposal that, unlike Mr. Lovenheim's proposal, was economically significant merely because the motivation of the proponents was political. The argument is not without appeal given the fact that the *Medical Committee* Court was confronted with a regulation that contained no reference to economic significance. Yet the *Medical Committee* decision contains language suggesting that the Court assumed napalm was not economically significant to Dow:

> The management of Dow Chemical Company is repeatedly quoted in sources which include the company's own publications as proclaiming that the decision to continue manufacturing and marketing napalm was made not *because* of business considerations, but *in spite* of them; that management in essence decided to pursue a course of activity which generated little profit for the shareholders. . . .

Id. at 681 (emphasis in original).

This Court need not consider, as the *Medical Committee* decision implied, whether a rule allowing exclusion of all proposals not meeting specified levels of economic significance violates the scope of section 14(a) of the Exchange Act. *See* 432 F.2d at 680. Whether or not the Securities and Exchange Commission could properly adopt such a rule, the Court cannot ignore the history of the rule which reveals no decision by the Commission to limit the determination to the economic criteria relied on by Iroquois/Delaware. The Court therefore holds that in light of the ethical and social significance of plaintiff's proposal and the fact that it implicates significant levels of sales, plaintiff has shown a likelihood of prevailing on the merits with regard to the issue of whether his proposal is "otherwise significantly related" to Iroquois/Delaware's business.[20]

---

[20]   [16] The result would, of course, be different if plaintiff's proposal was ethically significant in the abstract but had no meaningful relationship to the business of Iroquois/Delaware as Iroquois/Delaware was not engaged in the business of importing paté de foie gras.

. . . For the reasons discussed above, the Court concludes that plaintiff's motion for preliminary injunction should be granted.

NOTE ON "ORDINARY BUSINESS" EXCEPTION AND SOCIALLY SIGNIFICANT ISSUES

Under 14a-8(i)(7), a company may exclude a shareholder proposal if it "deals with a matter relating to the company's ordinary business operations." The policy behind the exclusion is to keep proposals consistent with state corporate law, which relegates ordinary business matters to a corporation's board of directors and management. As the SEC has explained, shareholder oversight of some business matters is not practical because the matters involve day-to-day management. Also impractical are shareholder attempts to micromanage company operations.

In the 1970s, shareholder proposals involving social responsibility issues became more common, and many of the proposals could arguably be excluded under the "ordinary business" exception (for instance, a proposal recommending the corporation stop buying from a low-cost, but environmentally destructive, company). This caused the SEC to examine how to distinguish between routine and important business matters. In 1976, the Commission chose not to amend the exception to make the distinction more clear and instead changed the way it would interpret "ordinary business," keeping proposals about matters "which have significant policy, economic, or other implications inherent in them" outside the purview of the exception. Whether proposals implicated socially significant issues was determined on a case-by-case basis.

Over the years, the staff of the Commission considered many proposals concerning employment practices, allowing most to be excluded under the "ordinary business" exception, but allowing some proposals related to equal employment. Then, in 1992, shareholders of the Cracker Barrel Old Country Store, Inc. submitted a proposal requesting that the company implement non-discrimination policies and include a prohibition against discrimination based on sexual orientation in the company's employment policy statement. The proposal was in response to a press release Cracker Barrel had issued the year before explaining its policy of not employing homosexuals, after which several gay and lesbian employees were fired. In its no-action letter to Cracker Barrel, the SEC allowed exclusion of the proposal and announced a bright-line rule: it would consider any employment-related proposal excludable under the "ordinary business" exception unless the proposal concerned compensation of senior executives or directors.

The SEC's decision was immediately controversial. In 1998, in response to the criticisms, the SEC reversed its position, returning to a case-by-case determination of social significance in employment-related proposals and other sorts of proposals. More recently, then SEC Chairman Harvey Pitt suggested that the Rule ought to be amended to delete the ordinary business exception entirely. *See* http://www.socialfunds.com/news/article.cgi/article934.html. As of this writing, however, the exception remains intact.

b.   The "Election of Directors" Exception

One longstanding controversy in corporate law is whether shareholders should have access to their corporation's proxy statement in order to nominate candidates of their choice. Shareholder activists have argued that in the absence of access to the proxy statement, contesting the board's nominees is prohibitively expensive. Giving shareholders access, it is argued, would enhance shareholder democracy, presumably a good thing. Nevertheless, Rule 14a-8 (i)(8) allows a company to omit a shareholder proposal that relates to the election of directors. The Commission rationalized this rule in part on the basis that shareholders using Rule 14a-8 to nominate directors could circumvent the proxy rules and undercut their usefulness in contested election contests. Stifled by this rule, then, shareholder activists tried another strategy: submit a proposal under Rule 14a-8 to amend the company's bylaws to require the company to publish the names of shareholder-nominated candidates for director positions together with any candidates nominated by the company's board of directors. This tactic met with varying success and in *AFSCME v. American Intn'l Group, Inc.*, 462 F.3d 121 (2d Cir. 2006), the court held that the company could not exclude such a proposal. In response to this decision, the Commission amended the rule in December, 2007 to make clear its position that such a proposal is excludable. The rule now provides that a company may omit a proposal that "relates to a nomination or an election for membership on the company's board of directors . . . or a procedure for such nomination or election." In its release adopting the amendment, the Commission expressly mentioned the Second Circuit's decision in *AFSCME* and explained why it believed that the amendment disposed of the issue.

PROBLEM

Schaf is a shareholder in NGN Casino Co., which operates a large casino in Las Vegas, Nevada. Schaf is also an enthusiastic, though largely unsuccessful, gambler. He sought, but was denied, "comps" (complimentary casino services) when he gambled at NGN's casino and he has had an ongoing dispute with NGN management over its denial of comps to him.

Schaf presented a timely proposal to NGN management for inclusion in its proxy statement. The proposal essentially would ask shareholders to adopt a company policy that patrons either be excluded entirely from the casino's premises or be awarded comps on an equal basis.

May NGN omit Schaf's proposal from its proxy statement? If so, on what basis? If you were advising Schaf, in what way might he structure his proposal to assure compliance with Rule 14a-8?

H. SHAREHOLDER INSPECTION RIGHTS

At common law, the courts recognized the right of shareholders to inspect corporate books and records as an incident of ownership, and that right, with certain limitations, is included in all corporate codes. The Model Business Corporation Act, for instance, recognizes two categories of records which shareholders may inspect. The first category is characterized by the fact that the information is readily available and not particularly valuable to the corporation: the articles of incorporation, bylaws, board resolutions relating classes or series of shares, names and addresses of directors and officers, etc. *See* MBCA § 16.01(e). For publicly-held corporations, this information is generally available from public filings. Not surprisingly, shareholders wishing to inspect this first category of information need only make a written demand at least five days in advance of the date of inspection.

The second category of information subject to inspection is quite different. This is information that may not be easily assembled and that, often, the corporation wishes to keep private, such as director minutes, accounting records and the list of shareholders. To inspect this category of information, the shareholder's demand must be made "in good faith and for a proper purpose." MBCA § 16.02(c). In addition, the shareholder must describe "with reasonable particularity his purpose and the records he desires to inspect." *Id.* Finally, the records that the shareholder wishes to inspect must be "directly connected with his purpose." *Id.* These qualifications to inspection are often the subject of litigation, as the following materials indicate.

STATE EX. REL. PILLSBURY v. HONEYWELL, INC.
Minnesota Supreme Court
191 N.W.2d 406 (1971)

KELLY, J.

. . . Petitioner attended a meeting on July 3, 1969, of a group involved in what was known as the 'Honeywell Project.' Participants in the project believed that American involvement in Vietnam was wrong, that a substantial portion of Honeywell's production consisted of munitions used in that war and that Honeywell should stop this production of munitions. Petitioner had long opposed the Vietnam War, but it was at the July 3rd meeting that he first learned of Honeywell's involvement. He was shocked at the knowledge that Honeywell had a large government contract to produce anti-personnel fragmentation bombs. Upset because of knowledge that such bombs were produced in his own community by a company which he had known and respected, petitioner determined to stop Honeywell's munitions production.

On July 14, 1969, petitioner ordered his fiscal agent to purchase 100 shares of Honeywell. He admits that the sole purpose of the purchase was to give himself a voice in Honeywell's affairs so he could persuade Honeywell to cease producing munitions. Apparently not aware of that purpose, petitioner's agent registered the stock in the name of a Pillsbury family nominee-Quad & Co. Upon discovering the nature of the registration, petitioner bought one share of Honeywell in his own name on August 11, 1969. In his deposition testimony petitioner made clear the reason for his purchase of Honeywell's shares: 'q . . . (D)o I understand that you requested Mr. Lacey to buy these 100 shares of Honeywell in order to follow up on the desire you had to bring to Honeywell management and to stockholders these theses that you have told us about here today? 'A Yes. That was my motivation.'

The 'theses' referred to are petitioner's beliefs concerning the propriety of producing munitions for the Vietnam War.

. . . Prior to the instigation of this suit, petitioner submitted two formal demands to Honeywell requesting that it produce its original shareholder ledger, current shareholder ledger, and all corporate records dealing with weapons and munitions manufacture. Honeywell refused.

. . . In the deposition petitioner outlined his beliefs concerning the Vietnam War and his purpose for his involvement with Honeywell. He expressed his desire to communicate with other shareholders in the hope of altering Honeywell's board of directors and thereby changing its policy. To this end, he testified, business records are necessary to insure accuracy.

. . . The trial court dismissed the petition, holding that the relief requested was for an improper and indefinite purpose. Petitioner contends in this appeal that the dismissal was in error.

Honeywell is a Delaware corporation doing business in Minnesota. Both petitioner and Honeywell spent considerable effort in arguing whether Delaware or Minnesota law applies. The trial court, applying Delaware law, determined that the outcome of the case rested upon whether or not petitioner has a proper purpose germane to his interest as a shareholder. This test is derived from the common law and is applicable in Minnesota . . .

. . . The trial court ordered judgment for Honeywell, ruling that petitioner had not demonstrated a proper purpose germane to his interest as a stockholder. Petitioner contends that a stockholder who disagrees with management has an absolute right to inspect corporate records for purposes of soliciting proxies. He would have this court rule that such solicitation is per se a 'proper purpose.' Honeywell argues that a 'proper purpose' contemplates concern with investment return. We agree with Honeywell.

. . . Several courts agree with petitioner's contention that a mere desire to communicate with other shareholders is, per se, a proper purpose. This would seem to confer an almost absolute right to inspection. We believe that a better rule would allow inspections only if the shareholder has a proper purpose for such communication . . .

. . . Petitioner had utterly no interest in the affairs of Honeywell before he learned of Honeywell's production of fragmentation bombs. Immediately after obtaining this knowledge, he purchased stock in Honeywell for the sole purpose of asserting ownership privileges in an effort to force Honeywell to cease such production. We agree with the court in Chas. A. Day & Co. v. Booth, 123 Maine 443, 447, 123 A. 557, 558 (1924) that 'where it is shown that such stockholding is only colorable, or solely for the purpose of maintaining proceedings of this kind, (we) fail to see how the petitioner can be said to be a 'person interested,' entitled as of right to inspect . . ..' But for his opposition to Honeywell's policy, petitioner probably would not have bought Honeywell stock, would not be interested in Honeywell's profits and would not desire to communicate with Honeywell's shareholders. His avowed purpose in buying Honeywell stock was to place himself in a position to try to impress his opinions favoring a reordering of priorities upon Honeywell management and its other shareholders. Such a motivation can hardly be deemed a proper purpose germane to his economic interest as a shareholder.

. . . We do not mean to imply that a shareholder with a bona fide investment interest could not bring this suit if motivated by concern with the long- or short-term economic effects on Honeywell resulting from the production of war munitions. Similarly, this suit might be appropriate when a shareholder has a bona fide concern about the adverse effects of abstention from profitable war contracts on his investment in Honeywell.

In the instant case, however, the trial court, in effect, has found from all the facts that petitioner was not interested in even the long-term well-being of Honeywell or the enhancement of the value of his shares. His sole purpose was to persuade the company to adopt his social and political concerns, irrespective of any economic benefit to himself or Honeywell. This purpose on the part of one buying into the corporation does not entitle the petitioner to inspect Honeywell's books and records . . .

SEINFELD v. VERIZON COMMUNICATIONS, INC.
Delaware Supreme Court
909 A.2d 117 (2006)

Before Steele, Chief Justice, Holland, Berger, Jacobs and Ridgely, Justices, constituting the Court en Banc.

Holland, Justice.

The plaintiff-appellant, Frank D. Seinfeld ("Seinfeld"), brought suit under section 220 of the Delaware General Corporation Law to compel the defendant-appellee, Verizon Communications, Inc. ("Verizon"), to produce, for his inspection, its books and records related to the compensation of Verizon's three highest corporate officers from 2000 to 2002. Seinfeld claimed that their executive compensation, individually and collectively, was excessive and wasteful . . .

Facts

Seinfeld asserts that he is the beneficial owner of approximately 3,884 shares of Verizon, held in street name through a brokerage firm. His stated purpose for seeking Verizon's books and records was to investigate mismanagement and corporate waste regarding the executive compensations of Ivan G. Seidenberg, Lawrence T. Babbio, Jr. and Charles R. Lee. Seinfeld alleges that the three executives were all performing in the same job and were paid amounts, including stock options, above the compensation provided for in their employment contracts. Seinfeld's section 220 claim for inspection is further premised on various computations he performed which indicate that the three executives' compensation totaled $205 million over three years and was, therefore, excessive, given their responsibilities to the corporation.

During his deposition, Seinfeld acknowledged he had no factual support for his claim that mismanagement had taken place. He admitted that the three executives did not perform any duplicative work. Seinfeld conceded he had no factual basis to allege the executives "did not earn" the amounts paid to them under their respective employment agreements. Seinfeld also admitted "there is a possibility" that the $205 million executive compensation amount he calculated was wrong.

The issue before us is quite narrow: should a stockholder seeking inspection under section 220 be entitled to relief without being required to show some evidence to suggest a credible basis for wrongdoing? We conclude that the answer must be no.

. . . The qualified inspection rights that originated at common law are now codified in Title 8, section 220 of the Delaware Code, which provides, in part:

(b) Any stockholder, in person or by attorney or other agent, shall, upon written demand under oath stating the purpose thereof, have the right during the usual hours for business to inspect for any proper purpose . . .

More than a decade ago, we noted that "[s]urprisingly, little use has been made of section 220 as an information-gathering tool in the derivative [suit] context."[21] Today, however, stockholders who have concerns about corporate governance are increasingly making a broad array of section 220 demands. The rise in books and records litigation is directly attributable to this Court's encouragement of stockholders, who can show a proper purpose, to use the "tools at hand" to obtain the necessary information before filing a derivative action. Section 220 is now recognized as "an important part of the corporate governance landscape."[22]

Seinfeld Denied Inspection

The Court of Chancery determined that Seinfeld's deposition testimony established only that he was concerned about the large amount of compensation paid to the three executives. That court concluded that Seinfeld offered "no evidence from which [it] could evaluate whether there is a reasonable ground for suspicion that the executive's compensation rises to the level of waste."[23] It also concluded that Seinfeld did not "submit any evidence showing that the executives were not entitled to [the stock] options."[24] The Court of Chancery properly noted that a disagreement with the business judgment of Verizon's board of directors or its compensation committee is not evidence of wrongdoing and did not satisfy Seinfeld's burden under section 220. The Court of Chancery held:

viewing the evidence in the light most favorable to Seinfeld, the court must conclude that he has not carried his burden of showing that there is a credible basis from which the court can infer that the Verizon board of directors committed waste or mismanagement in compensating these three executives during the relevant period of time. Instead, the record clearly establishes that Seinfeld's Section 220 demand was made merely on the basis of suspicion or curiosity.[25]

. . . In a section 220 action, a stockholder has the burden of proof to demonstrate a proper purpose by a preponderance of the evidence. It is well established that a stockholder's desire to investigate wrongdoing or mismanagement is a "proper purpose." Such investigations are proper, because where the allegations of mismanagement

---

[21] [11] *Rales v. Blasband*, 634 A.2d 927, 934–35 n. 10 (Del.1993) (quoted in *Grimes v. Donald*, 673 A.2d 1207, 1216 n. 11 (Del.1996)).

[22] [14] *Security First Corp. v. U.S. Die Casting & Dev. Co.*, 687 A.2d 563, 571 (Del.1997). *See also* E. Norman Veasey & Christine T. DiGuglielmo, *What Happened in Delaware Corporate Law and Governance from 1992–2004? A Retrospective on Some Key Developments*, 153 U. Pa. L.Rev. 1399, 1466–69 (2005) (discussing the use of section 220 and cases that have applied it).

[23] [15] *Seinfeld v. Verizon Commc'ns, Inc.*, 2005 WL 3272365 at *3 (Del.Ch.).

[24] [16] *Id.*

[25] [17] *Id.* (footnote omitted).

prove meritorious, investigation furthers the interest of all stockholders and should increase stockholder return.

The evolution of Delaware's jurisprudence in section 220 actions reflects judicial efforts to maintain a proper balance between the rights of shareholders to obtain information based upon credible allegations of corporation mismanagement and the rights of directors to manage the business of the corporation without undue interference from stockholders. In *Thomas & Betts*, this Court held that, to meet its "burden of proof, a stockholder must present some *credible basis* from which the court can infer that waste or mismanagement may have occurred."[26] Six months later, in *Security First*, this Court held "[t]here must be *some evidence* of possible mismanagement as would warrant further investigation of the matter."[27]

Our holdings in *Thomas & Betts* and *Security First* were contemporaneous with our decisions that initially encouraged stockholders to make greater use of section 220. In *Grimes v. Donald*, decided just months before *Thomas & Betts*, this Court reaffirmed the salutary use of section 220 as one of the "tools at hand" for stockholders to use to obtain information. When the plaintiff in *Thomas & Betts* suggested that the burden of demonstrating a proper purpose had been attenuated by our encouragement for stockholders to use section 220, we rejected that argument:

> Contrary to plaintiff's assertion in the instant case, this Court in *Grimes* did not suggest that its reference to a Section 220 demand as one of the "tools at hand" was intended to eviscerate or modify the need for a stockholder to show a proper purpose under Section 220.

In *Security First* and *Thomas & Betts*, we adhered to the Court of Chancery's holding in *Helmsman Mgmt. Servs., Inc. v. A & S Consultants, Inc.* that:

> A mere statement of a purpose to investigate possible general mismanagement, without more, will not entitle a shareholder to broad § 220 inspection relief. There must be *some evidence* of possible mismanagement as would warrant further investigation of the matter.[28]

Standard Achieves Balance

Investigations of meritorious allegations of possible mismanagement, waste or wrongdoing, benefit the corporation, but investigations that are "indiscriminate fishing expeditions" do not.[29] "At some point, the costs of generating more information fall short of the benefits of having more information. At that point, compelling production of information would be wealth-reducing, and so shareholders would not want it produced."[30] Accordingly, this Court has held that an inspection to investigate possible wrongdoing where there is no "credible basis," is a license for "fishing expeditions" and thus adverse to the interests of the corporation:

> Stockholders have a right to at least a limited inquiry into books and records when they have established some credible basis to believe that there has been

---

26 [27] *Thomas & Betts Corp. v. Leviton Mfg. Co.*, 681 A.2d [1026] at 1031 [Del. 1996] (emphasis added).

27 [28] *Security First Corp. v. U.S. Die Casting & Dev. Co.*, 687 A.2d [563] at 568 [Del. 1997] (original emphasis omitted; emphasis added)(quoting *Helmsman Mgmt. Servs., Inc. v. A & S Consultants, Inc.*, 525 A.2d 160, 166 (Del.Ch. 1987)).

28 [31] *Helmsman Mgmt. Servs., Inc. v. A & S Consultants, Inc.*, 525 A.2d at 166 (emphasis added); *see also Security First Corp. v. U.S. Die Casting & Dev. Co.*, 687 A.2d at 568; *Thomas & Betts Corp. v. Leviton Mfg. Co.*, 681 A.2d at 1031.

29 [32] *Security First Corp. v. U.S. Die Casting & Dev. Co.*, 687 A.2d 563, 571 (Del.1997).

30 [33] Fred S. McChesney, *"Proper Purpose,"* Fiduciary Duties, and Shareholder-Raider Access to Corporate Information, 68 U. Cin. L.Rev. 1199, 1207–08 (2000).

wrongdoing. . . . Yet it would invite mischief to open corporate management to indiscriminate fishing expeditions.[31]

A stockholder is "not required to prove by a preponderance of the evidence that waste and [mis]management are actually occurring."[32] Stockholders need only show, by a preponderance of the evidence, a credible basis from which the Court of Chancery can infer there is possible mismanagement that would warrant further investigation[33] — a showing that "may ultimately fall well short of demonstrating that anything wrong occurred."[34] That "threshold may be satisfied by a credible showing, through documents, logic, testimony, or otherwise, that there are legitimate issues of wrongdoing."[35]

Although the threshold for a stockholder in a section 220 proceeding is not insubstantial, the "credible basis" standard sets the lowest possible burden of proof. The only way to reduce the burden of proof further would be to eliminate any requirement that a stockholder show *some evidence* of possible wrongdoing. That would be tantamount to permitting inspection based on the "mere suspicion" standard that Seinfeld advances in this appeal. However, such a standard has been repeatedly rejected as a basis to justify the enterprise cost of an inspection.

The judgment of the Court of Chancery is affirmed.

NOTES AND QUESTIONS

1. Why is it not a proper purpose to inspect the corporate records to determine whether or not executive compensation is appropriate?

2. Compare *Haywood v. Ambase Corp.*, 2005 Del. Ch. LEXIS 131 (Del. Ch. Aug. 22, 2005), to *Seinfeld*, where the plaintiff, who also was questioning executive compensation, hired a compensation expert to compare the CEO's compensation to the compensation of similarly situated CEOs and, on that basis, convinced the court that there was a credible basis from which to infer mismanagement.

3. The Delaware courts have held that a shareholder has a proper purpose to inspect the shareholder list if the shareholder seeks to (a) communicate with other shareholders about joining in a suit against the corporation (either as a direct action or a derivative action), *Compaq Computer Corp. v. Horton*, 631 A.2d 1 (Del. 1993); or (b) solicit proxies from fellow shareholders in an election of directors, *Credit Bureau Reports, Inc. v. Credit Bureau of St. Paul, Inc.*, 290 A.2d 691 (Del. 1972). In an omitted portion of the *Honeywell* decision, however, the court rejected the plaintiff's demand to inspect the shareholder list to communicate with other shareholders with the hope of electing one or more directors sympathetic to the plaintiff's perspective. The court noted that the plaintiff did not seek to elect directors who would further the plaintiff's

---

[31] [35] *Security First Corp. v. U.S. Die Casting & Dev. Co.*, 687 A.2d at 571.

[32] [36] *Thomas & Betts Corp. v. Leviton Mfg. Co. Inc.*, 681 A.2d 1026, 1031 (Del.1996) ("In order to meet that burden of proof, a stockholder must present some credible basis from which the court can infer that waste or mismanagement may have occurred.").

[33] [37] *Security First Corp. v. U.S. Die Casting & Dev. Co.*, 687 A.2d at 567–69. Accord *Brehm v. Eisner*, 746 A.2d 244, 267 n. 75 (Del.2000).

[34] [38] *Khanna v. Covad Commc'ns Group, Inc.*, 2004 WL 187274 at *6 n. 25 (Del.Ch.). *See also Forsythe v. CIBC Employee Private Equity Fund (U.S.) I.L.P.*, 2005 WL 1653963, at *5 (Del.Ch.) (finding that "[w]hile the facts fall well short of actually proving wrongdoing, they do provide a credible basis for inferring mismanagement").

[35] [39] *Security First Corp. v. U.S. Die Casting & Dev. Co.*, 687 A.2d at 568.

economic interest and therefore did not have a proper purpose. 191 N.W.2d at 412–13.

PROBLEM

The Conservative Research Foundation, Inc. (CRF) is a shareholder of International Oil, Inc. (IO) and it has submitted a shareholder proposal to IO requesting that the corporation inform the government of Sudan, where it does business, that it will terminate operations in Sudan unless the government takes certain specified measures to end the violence in Darfur. CRF has now made a demand on IO seeking to inspect IO's shareholder list for the purpose of communicating with fellow shareholders about the economic risks of IO's business activities in Sudan, seeking shareholder support for the resolution that CRF has submitted to the IO board and bringing to the attention of the IO shareholders the possibility that IO may refuse to submit the resolution to the shareholders. IO has refused to provide CRF the list, claiming that its purpose is not proper. Is IO correct?

Chapter 9

PROBLEMS IN CLOSELY HELD CORPORATIONS

A. INTRODUCTION

This chapter addresses many of the special problems commonly encountered by shareholders of closely held corporations. Closely held corporations are generally defined as corporations having a small number of shareholders, who normally expect to be involved in the day-to-day management and operations of the corporation's business, and who have shares that are not registered with the SEC, listed on a stock exchange, or otherwise regularly traded on a securities market. As specifically defined in *Donahue v. Rodd Electrotype Co., infra*, a closely held corporation is one with (1) a small number of shareholders, (2) no ready market for its stock, and (3) substantial majority shareholder participation in the management, direction, and operation of the business.

As noted by the *Donahue* court, closely held corporations resemble partnerships that were incorporated by the owners primarily to secure limited liability for the owners and not to change the nature of the fiduciary relationship among those owners in providing their capital, skills, experience, and labor to the enterprise. That relationship was expected to continue as one of mutually-reposed trust and confidence, with each shareholder-owner subject to duties of utmost good faith and loyalty to his fellow shareholders. Consequently, a vast majority of state courts have held that shareholders of closely held corporations are not only fiduciaries to the corporation by virtue of their positions as officers, directors or majority shareholders, but are also fiduciaries of each other. *See* Shannon W. Stevenson, *The Venture Capital Solution to the Problem of Close Corporation Shareholder Fiduciary Duties*, 51 DUKE L. REV. 1139, 1147 (1997). According to *Donahue*, the strict duty of loyalty owed by those shareholders to each other is even more exacting than their position-related duties of loyalty to the corporation.

Many of the problems of closely held corporations stem from the very closeness of the shareholder-owners' relationships and their expectations of personal involvement in management and operations. They typically expect to serve as directors, setting corporate policies and monitoring implementation of those policies. They also expect to serve as officers or as other primary employees, executing corporate policies on a day-to-day basis for compensation. As observed in Chapter 6's discussion of distributions to shareholders, closely held corporations generally do not distribute cash or other assets to their shareholders, but instead, provide compensation to their shareholders in the form of salaries and bonuses as compensation for their services as officers and employees. Moreover, this distribution policy is particularly attractive for its tax advantages since reasonable salaries are business expenses deductible from the corporation's income, while dividends are not. But, in the closely held corporation, familiarity often breeds contempt. When the close relationship fractures, one or more of the shareholders may be terminated as a corporate officer or employee and, consequently, denied their reasonably anticipated salaries. Unlike the shareholder in a publicly held corporation who can simply follow the *Wall Street Rule* and sell his shares in an actively-traded securities market, the unemployed shareholder of the closely held corporation is frozen in with no prospect of any return on his illiquid investment. The remaining shareholders, benefiting from their continuing salaries, have no compunction to change distribution policies and begin declaring dividends. They are also likely to be the only market for the excluded shareholder's stock and, even assuming their willingness to buy that stock, are often unlikely to pay fair value. Indeed, as the court in *Donahue* notes, majority freeze-out schemes which deny employment and withhold dividends are often designed to compel the minority shareholder to relinquish his stock at an inadequate price. Although the excluded shareholder may be able to bring a lawsuit against the other shareholders for breach of fiduciary duty, or for involuntary dissolution, discussed *infra*, this course of action is likely to be time consuming, very expensive, and not necessarily successful.

Moreover, even in the absence of freeze-out schemes, a shareholder in a closely held corporation who simply needs the cash represented by his investment, perhaps due to unanticipated personal problems, faces potentially serious obstacles in trying to liquidate his investment. Lawyers representing closely held corporations or their shareholders should foresee both these and other contextual dilemmas by advising the client about the practicability of shareholders agreements providing for the acquisition of the shares by the corporation or the remaining shareholders at a predetermined price or at a price based on a predetermined valuation formula. Moreover, like partners who can keep out newcomers through the common law default rule of *delectus personae* (a black ball rule), the shareholder-owners of closely held corporations normally have an understandable fear of strangers as would-be fellow owners. They, too, generally prefer to maintain their closeness by restricting transfer of the shares to the corporation or the remaining shareholders. Again, lawyers should recognize these common expectations and anticipate potential dilemmas by advising the client about lawful restrictions on transfers of shares, including pricing options for share acquisitions, that may be set forth in shareholder agreements.

Many other issues arising from the closeness of shareholders in closely held corporations may also be addressed by shareholder agreements or by provisions in a corporation's articles of incorporation or bylaws. Again, these issues arise from the closely held shareholder's reasonable expectations of continued participation in and control of the corporate enterprise. These include not only his expectations of employment, resale opportunities and restrictions on taking on new shareholder "partners," but also expectations regarding maintenance of proportionate voting power through preemptive rights, classified stock, and voting agreements. As will be seen, many of these control devices conflict with the traditional statutory norm of corporate governance, which reposes managerial power and responsibility in the board of directors rather than with the shareholders.

Despite this conflict, courts have recognized the special dynamics of the close relationships of shareholders in closely held corporations. Similar to their imposition of fiduciary duties on these shareholders, as opposed to shareholders of publicly held corporations, the courts have again distinguished closely held corporations by allowing significant deviations from statutory norms. Although most state legislatures responded with close corporation statutes authorizing broad deviations from the traditional norm of corporate governance, they have seldomly been used. Instead, corporate lawyers and their clients continue to look largely to the common law developed by the courts in resolving the special problems of closely held corporations.

B.   FIDUCIARY DUTIES AMONG SHAREHOLDERS

DONAHUE v. RODD ELECTROTYPE CO. OF NEW ENGLAND, INC.
Supreme Judicial Court of Massachusetts
367 Mass. 578, 328 N.E.2d 505 (1975)

BEFORE TAURO, C.J., AND REARDON, QUIRICO, BRAUCHER, KAPLAN AND WILKINS, JJ.

TAURO, CHIEF JUSTICE.

The plaintiff, Euphemia Donahue, a minority stockholder in the Rodd Electrotype Company of New England, Inc. (Rodd Electrotype), a Massachusetts corporation, brings this suit against the directors of Rodd Electrotype, Charles H. Rodd, Frederick I. Rodd and Mr. Harold E. Magnuson, against Harry C. Rodd, a former director, officer, and controlling stockholder of Rodd Electrotype and against Rodd Electrotype (hereinafter called defendants). The plaintiff seeks to rescind Rodd Electrotype's purchase of Harry Rodd's shares in Rodd Electrotype and to compel Harry Rodd to repay to the corporation the purchase price of said shares, $36,000, together with interest from the date of purchase. The plaintiff alleges that the defendants caused the corporation to purchase the shares in violation of their fiduciary duty to her, a minority stockholder of Rodd Electrotype.[1]

The trial judge, after hearing oral testimony, dismissed the plaintiff's bill on the merits. He found that the purchase was without prejudice to the plaintiff and implicitly found that the transaction had been carried out in good faith and with inherent fairness. The Appeals Court affirmed with costs. . . . The case is before us on the plaintiff's application for further appellate review. . . .

[The facts may be summarized as follows: During the mid-1930's, Harry Rodd and Joseph Donahue had become employees of Royal Electrotype, later renamed Rodd Electrotype. Rodd rapidly advanced within the company, first becoming a director, then general manager and treasurer, and, by 1955, president of the company. In contrast, Donahue's duties were confined to operational matters within the plant. Although he became the plant superintendent and, by 1955, vice president, Donahue never participated in the management of the corporation. In the years preceding 1955, Rodd acquired 200 shares and Donahue 50 shares of the corporation's stock at $20 per share, giving them, respectively, 80% and 20% interests. As the dominant shareholder, Rodd installed his sons, Charles and Frederick, as corporate officers in the early 1960's. In 1964, Frederick replaced Donahue as plant superintendent, and, in 1965, Charles succeeded his father as president and general manager. From 1959 to 1967, Harry Rodd gave 117 of his 200 shares to his sons and his daughter, Phyllis, and returned two shares to the corporate treasury.

In 1970, Harry Rodd, at 77 and suffering continual health problems, agreed with his sons that he should retire. However, he insisted that some financial arrangements be made as to his remaining 81 shares. His son Charles, acting on the company's behalf, negotiated for the purchase of 45 of the 81 shares for $800 per share ($36,000), reflecting book value, which was then approved at a special meeting of the board of directors, comprising Charles, Frederick and a lawyer. Subsequently, Harry Rodd sold six shares to his children at $800 per share and gave them his remaining 30 shares. Meanwhile, Donahue had died and passed his 50 shares to his wife and son. When the Donahue's discovered at a subsequent shareholders' meeting that the company had purchased 45 of Harry Rodd's shares, they offered their 50 shares to the corporation on the same terms. Their offer was rejected, resulting in this litigation.]

In her argument before this court, the plaintiff has characterized the corporate purchase of Harry Rodd's shares as an unlawful distribution of corporate assets to controlling stockholders. She urges that the distribution constitutes a breach of the fiduciary duty owed by the Rodds, as controlling stockholders, to her, a minority stockholder in the enterprise, because the Rodds failed to accord her an equal opportunity to sell her shares to the corporation. The defendants reply that the stock purchase was within the powers of the corporation and met the requirements of good faith and inherent fairness imposed on a fiduciary in his dealings with the corporation. They assert that there is no right to equal opportunity in corporate stock purchases for the corporate treasury. For the reasons hereinafter noted, we agree with the plaintiff and reverse the decree of the Superior Court. However, we limit the applicability of our holding to 'close corporations,' as hereinafter defined. Whether the holding should apply

---

[1] [4] In form, the plaintiff's bill of complaint presents, at least in part, a derivative action, brought on behalf of the corporation, and, in the words of the bill, 'on behalf of . . . (the) stockholders' of Rodd Electrotype. Yet . . . the plaintiff's bill, in substance, was one seeking redress because of alleged breaches of the fiduciary duty owed to her, a minority stockholder, by the controlling stockholders. We treat that bill of complaint (as have the parties) as presenting a proper cause of suit in the personal right of the plaintiff. . . . The case was tried on the plaintiff's theory. The evidence introduced was consistent with litigation of the personal right presented in the bill. The issue of the duty owed by controlling stockholders to minority stockholders was sufficiently before the trial court.

to other corporations is left for decision in another case, on a proper record.

A. *Close Corporations.* In previous opinions, we have alluded to the distinctive nature of the close corporation (e.g., *Brigham v. M. & J. Corp.*, 352 Mass. 674, 678, 227 N.E.2d 915 (1967); see *Samia v. Central Oil Co. of Worcester*, 339 Mass. 101, 112–113, 158 N.E.2d 469 (1959)), but have never defined precisely what is meant by a close corporation. There is no single, generally accepted definition. Some commentators emphasize an 'integration of ownership and management' (Note, Statutory Assistance for Closely Held Corporations, 71 Harv. L. Rev. 1498 (1958)), in which the stockholders occupy most management positions. . . . Others focus on the number of stockholders and the nature of the market for the stock. In this view, close corporations have few stockholders; there is little market for corporate stock. The Supreme Court of Illinois adopted this latter view in *Galler v. Galler*, 32 Ill.2d 16, 203 N.E.2d 577 (1964). . . . We accept aspects of both definitions. We deem a close corporation to be one typified by: (1) a small number of stockholders; (2) no ready market for the corporate stock; and (3) substantial majority stockholder participation in the management, direction and operations of the corporation.

As thus defined, the close corporation bears striking resemblance to a partnership. Commentators and courts have noted that the close corporation is often little more than an 'incorporated' or 'chartered' partnership.[2] . . . The stockholders 'clothe' their partnership 'with the benefits peculiar to a corporation, limited liability, perpetuity and the like.' . . . In essence, though, the enterprise remains one in which ownership is limited to the original parties or transferees of their stock to whom the other stockholders have agreed,[3] in which ownership and management are in the same hands, and in which the owners are quite dependent on one another for the success of the enterprise. Many close corporations are 'really partnerships between two or three people who contribute their capital, skills, experience and labor.' . . . Just as in a partnership, the relationship among the stockholders must be one of trust, confidence and absolute loyalty if the enterprise is to succeed. Close corporations with substantial assets and with more numerous stockholders are no different from smaller close corporations in this regard. All participants rely on the fidelity and abilities of those stockholders who hold office. Disloyalty and self-seeking conduct on the part of any stockholder will engender bickering, corporate stalemates, and, perhaps, efforts to achieve dissolution. . . .

Although the corporate form provides. . . . advantages for the stockholders (limited liability, perpetuity, and so forth), it also supplies an opportunity for the majority stockholders to oppress or disadvantage minority stockholders. The minority is vulnerable to a variety of oppressive devices, termed 'freezeouts,' which the majority may employ. See, generally, Note, *Freezing Out Minority Shareholders*, 74 HARV. L.

---

[2] [12] The United States Internal Revenue Code given substantial recognition to the fact that close corporations are often merely incorporated partnerships. The so-called Subchapter S, 26 U.S.C. §§1371–1379 (1970), enables 'small business corporations,' defined by the statute (26 U.S.C. § 1371(a) (1970)), to make an election which generally exempts the corporation from taxation (26 U.S.C. § 1372(b)(1) (1970)) and causes inclusion of the corporation's undistributed, as well as distributed, taxable income in the gross income of the stockholders for the year (26 U.S.C. § 1373(a) (1970)). This is essentially the manner in which partnership earnings are taxed. See 26 U.S.C. § 701 (1970).

[3] [13] The original owners commonly impose restrictions on transfers to stock designed to prevent outsiders who are unacceptable to the other stockholders from acquiring an interest in the close corporation. These restrictions often take the form of agreements among the stockholders and the corporation or bylaws which give the corporation or the other stockholders a right of 'first refusal' when any stockholder desires to sell his shares. See *Albert E. Touchet, Inc. v. Touchet*, 264 Mass. 499, 502, 163 N.E. 184 (1928); Hornstein, *Stockholders' Agreements in the Closely Held Corporation*, 59 YALE L.J. 1040, 1048–1049 (1950). In a partnership, of course, a partner cannot transfer his interest in the partnership so as to give his assignee a right to participate in the management or business affairs of the continuing partnership without the agreement of the other partners. G.L.C. 108A, § 27. See *Hazen v. Warwick*, 256 Mass. 302, 308, 152 N.E. 342 (1926).

Rev. 1630 (1961). An authoritative study of such 'freeze-outs' enumerates some of the possibilities: 'The squeezers . . . may refuse to declare dividends; they may drain off the corporation's earnings in the form of exorbitant salaries and bonuses to the majority shareholder-officers and perhaps to their relatives, or in the form of high rent by the corporation for property leased from majority shareholders . . . ; they may deprive minority shareholders of corporate offices and of employment by the company; they may cause the corporation to sell its assets at an inadequate price to the majority shareholders. . . . ' In particular, the power of the board of directors, controlled by the majority, to declare or withhold dividends and to deny the minority employment is easily converted to a device to disadvantage minority stockholders. . . .

The minority can, of course, initiate suit against the majority and their directors. Self-serving conduct by directors is proscribed by the director's fiduciary obligation to the corporation. . . . However, in practice, the plaintiff will find difficulty in challenging dividend or employment policies. Such policies are considered to be within the judgment of the directors. This court has said: 'The courts prefer not to interfere . . . with the sound financial management of the corporation by its directors, but declare as general rule that the declaration of dividends rests within the sound discretion of the directors, refusing to interfere with their determination unless a plain abuse of discretion is made to appear.' . . . Judicial reluctance to interfere combines with the difficulty of proof when the standard is 'plain abuse of discretion' or bad faith . . . to limit the possibilities for relief. . . .

Thus, when these types of 'freeze-outs' are attempted by the majority stockholders, the minority stockholders, cut off from all corporation related revenues, must either suffer their losses or seek a buyer for their shares. Many minority stockholders will be unwilling or unable to wait for an alteration in majority policy. Typically, the minority stockholder in a close corporation has a substantial percentage of his personal assets invested in the corporation. The stockholder may have anticipated that his salary from his position with the corporation would be his livelihood. Thus, he cannot afford to wait passively. He must liquidate his investment in the close corporation in order to reinvest the funds in income producing enterprises.

At this point, the true plight of the minority stockholder in a close corporation becomes manifest. He cannot easily reclaim his capital. In a large public corporation, the oppressed or dissident minority stockholder could sell his stock in order to extricate some of his invested capital. By definition, this market is not available for shares in the close corporation. In a partnership, a partner who feels abused by his fellow partners may cause dissolution by his 'express will . . . at any time' . . . and recover his share of partnership assets and accumulated profits. . . . If dissolution results in a breach of the partnership articles, the culpable partner will be liable in damages. . . . By contrast, the stockholder in the close corporation or 'incorporated partnership' may achieve dissolution and recovery of his share of the enterprise assets only by compliance with the rigorous terms of the applicable chapter of the General Laws. . . .

Thus, in a close corporation, the minority stockholders may be trapped in a disadvantageous situation. No outsider would knowingly assume the position of the disadvantaged minority. The outsider would have the same difficulties. To cut losses, the minority stockholder may be compelled to deal with the majority. This is the capstone of the majority plan. Majority 'freeze-out' schemes which withhold dividends are designed to compel the minority to relinquish stock at inadequate prices. . . . When the minority stockholder agrees to sell out at less than fair value, the majority has won.

Because of the fundamental resemblance of the close corporation to the partnership, the trust and confidence which are essential to this scale and manner of enterprise, and the inherent danger to minority interests in the close corporation, we hold that stockholders[4] in the close corporation owe one another substantially the same fiduciary duty in the operation of the enterprise[5] that partners owe to one another. In our previous decisions, we have defined the standard of duty owed by partners to one another as the 'utmost good faith and loyalty.' *Cardullo v. Landau*, 329 Mass. 5, 8, 105 N.E.2d 843 (1952); *DeCotis v. D'Antona*, 350 Mass. 165, 168, 214 N.E.2d 21 (1966). Stockholders in close corporations must discharge their management and stockholder responsibilities in conformity with this strict good faith standard. They may not act out of avarice, expediency or self-interest in derogation of their duty of loyalty to the other stockholders and to the corporation.

We contrast this strict good faith standard with the somewhat less stringent standard of fiduciary duty to which directors and stockholders of all corporations must adhere in the discharge of their corporate responsibilities. Corporate directors are held to a good faith and inherent fairness standard of conduct . . . and are not 'permitted to serve two masters whose interests are antagonistic.' . . . 'Their paramount duty is to the corporation, and their personal pecuniary interests are subordinate to that duty.' . . .

The more rigorous duty of partners and participants in a joint adventure, here extended to stockholders in a close corporation, was described by then Chief Judge Cardozo of the New York Court of Appeals in *Meinhard v. Salmon*, 249 N.Y. 458, 164 N.E. 545 (1928): 'Joint adventurers, like copartners, owe to one another, while the enterprise continues, the duty of the finest loyalty. Many forms of conduct permissible in a workaday world for those acting at arm's length, are forbidden to those bound by fiduciary ties. . . . Not honesty alone, but the punctilio of an honor the most sensitive, is then the standard of behavior.' *Id.* at 463–464, 164 N.E. at 546.

Application of this strict standard of duty to stockholders in close corporations is a natural outgrowth of the prior case law. In a number of cases involving close corporations, we have held stockholders participating in management to a standard of fiduciary duty more exacting than the traditional good faith and inherent fairness standard because of the trust and confidence reposed in them by the other stockholders. In *Silversmith v. Sydeman*, 305 Mass. 65, 25 N.E.2d 215 (1940), the plaintiff brought suit for an accounting of the liquidation of a close corporation which he and the defendant had owned. In assessing their relative rights in the discount of a note, we had occasion to consider the defendant's fiduciary duty with respect to the financial affairs of the company. We implied that, in addition to the fiduciary duty owed by an officer to the corporation, a more rigorous standard of fiduciary duty applied to the defendant by virtue of the relationship between the stockholders: ' . . . it could be found that the plaintiff and the defendant were acting as partners in the conduct of the company's business and in the liquidation of its property even though they had adopted a corporate form as the instrumentality by which they should associate in the furtherance of their joint venture.' *Id.* at 68, 25 N.E.2d at 217.

In *Samia v. Central Oil Co. of Worcester*, 339 Mass. 101, 158 N.E.2d 469 (1959), sisters alleged that their brothers had systematically excluded them from management, income and partial ownership of a close corporation formed from a family partnership. In rejecting arguments that the plaintiffs' suit was barred by the statute of limitations or laches, we stressed the familial relationship among the parties, which should have

---

[4] [14] We do not limit our holding to majority stockholders. In the close corporation, the minority may do equal damage through unscrupulous and improper 'sharp dealings' with an unsuspecting majority. See *Helms v. Duckworth*, 101 U.S. App. D.C. 390, 249 F.2d 482 (1957).

[5] [15] We stress that the strict fiduciary duty which we apply to stockholders in a close corporation in this opinion governs only their actions relative to the operations of the enterprise and the effects of that operation on the rights and investments of other stockholders. We express no opinion as to the standard of duty applicable to transactions in the shares of the close corporation when the corporation is not a party to the transaction. . . .

given rise to a particularly scrupulous fidelity in serving the interests of all of the stockholders: 'All three brothers . . . were directors of Central, a small family corporation, not a large publicly owned organization, and as such were in a special position of family trust.' *Id.* at 112, 158 N.E.2d at 476.

In *Wilson v. Jennings*, 344 Mass. 608, 184 N.E.2d 642 (1962), the plaintiffs, stockholders in a close corporation, brought suit on their own behalf and on behalf of the corporation against a number of defendants, including the third stockholder who was generally in charge of corporate operations. The corporation had been organized to exploit a 'plastic top' for containers invented by the plaintiffs and another. The [court entered] a final decree which, *inter alia*, cancelled shares of stock issued to the operating stockholder after the original issue, voided an employment contract between the operating stockholder and the corporation, and ordered transfer to the corporation of stock in and dividends from a corporation the operating stockholder had established to manufacture the container tops. Although the decree [was modified on appeal, the appellate court] sustained the judge's finding that the operating stockholder had violated his duty to the other stockholders in causing other shares to be issued to himself . . .

In these and other cases . . . we have imposed a duty of loyalty more exacting than that duty owed by a director to his corporation . . . or by a majority stockholder to the minority in a public corporation because of facts particular to the close corporation in the cases. In the instant case, we extend this strict duty of loyalty to all stockholders in close corporations. The circumstances which justified findings of relationships of trust and confidence in these particular cases exist universally in modified form in all close corporations . . .

B. *Equal Opportunity in a Close Corporation.* Under settled Massachusetts law, a domestic corporation, unless forbidden by statute, has the power to purchase its own shares. . . . An agreement to reacquire stock [is] enforceable, subject, at least, to the limitations that the purchase must be made in good faith and without prejudice to creditors and stockholders.' . . . When the corporation reacquiring its own stock is a close corporation, the purchase is subject to the additional requirement, in the light of our holding in this opinion, that the stockholders, who, as directors or controlling stockholders, caused the corporation to enter into the stock purchase agreement, must have acted with the utmost good faith and loyalty to the other stockholders.

To meet this test, if the stockholder whose shares were purchased was a member of the controlling group, the controlling stockholders must cause the corporation to offer each stockholder an equal opportunity to sell a ratable number of his shares to the corporation at an identical price.[6] Purchase by the corporation confers substantial benefits on the members of the controlling group whose shares were purchased. These benefits are not available to the minority stockholders if the corporation does not also offer them an opportunity to sell their shares. The controlling group may not, consistent with its strict duty to the minority, utilize its control of the corporation to obtain special advantages and disproportionate benefit from its share ownership. . . .

The benefits conferred by the purchase are twofold: (1) provision of a market for shares; (2) access to corporate assets for personal use. By definition, there is no ready market for shares of a close corporation. The purchase creates a market for shares which previously had been unmarketable. It transforms a previously illiquid investment into a liquid one. If the close corporation purchases shares only from a member of the controlling group, the controlling stockholder can convert his shares into cash at a time

---

[6] [16] Of course, a close corporation may purchase shares from one stockholder without offering the others an equal opportunity if all other stockholders give advance consent to the stock purchase arrangements through acceptance of an appropriate provision in the articles of organization, the corporation by-laws (*see Brown v. Little Brown & Co. Inc.*, 269 Mass. 102, 168, N.E. 521 (1929)), or a stockholder's agreement. Similarly, all other stockholder may ratify the purchase. . . .

when none of the other stockholders can. Consistent with its strict fiduciary duty, the controlling group may not utilize its control of the corporation to establish an exclusive market in previously unmarketable shares from which the minority stockholders are excluded. . . .

The purchase also distributes corporate assets to the stockholder whose shares were purchased. Unless an equal opportunity is given to all stockholders, the purchase of shares from a member of the controlling group operates as a *preferential* distribution of assets. In exchange for his shares, he receives a percentage of the contributed capital and accumulated profits of the enterprise. The funds he so receives are available for his personal use. The other stockholders benefit from no such access to corporate property and cannot withdraw their shares of the corporate profits and capital in this manner unless the controlling group acquiesces. Although the purchase price for the controlling stockholder's shares may seem fair to the corporation and other stockholders under the tests established in the prior case law, . . . the controlling stockholder whose stock has been purchased has still received a relative advantage over his fellow stockholders, inconsistent with his strict fiduciary duty — an opportunity to turn corporate funds to personal use.

The rule of equal opportunity in stock purchases by close corporations provides equal access to these benefits for all stockholders. We hold that, in any case in which the controlling stockholders have exercised their power over the corporation to deny the minority such equal opportunity, the minority shall be entitled to appropriate relief.[7] . . .

C. *Application of the Law to this Case.* We turn now to the application of the learning set forth above to the facts of the instant case.

The strict standard of duty is plainly applicable to the stockholders in Rodd Electrotype. Rodd Electrotype is a close corporation. Members of the Rodd and Donahue families are the sole owners of the corporation's stock. In actual numbers, the corporation, immediately prior to the corporate purchase of Harry Rodd's shares, had six stockholders. The shares have not been traded, and no market for them seems to exist. Harry Rodd, Charles Rodd, Frederick Rodd, William G. Mason (Phyllis Mason's husband), and the plaintiff's husband all worked for the corporation. The Rodds have retained the paramount management positions.

Through their control of these management positions and of the majority of the Rodd Electrotype stock, the Rodds effectively controlled the corporation. In testing the stock purchase from Harry Rodd against the applicable strict fiduciary standard, we treat the Rodd family as a single controlling group. We reject the defendants' contention that the Rodd family cannot be treated as a unit for this purpose. From the evidence, it is clear that the Rodd family was a close-knit one with strong community of interest. . . . Harry Rodd had hired his sons to work in the family business, Rodd Electrotype. As he aged, he transferred portions of his stock holdings to his children. Charles Rodd and Frederick Rodd were given positions of responsibility in the business as he withdrew from active management. In these circumstances, it is realistic to

---

[7] [17] Under the Massachusetts law, '(n)o stockholder shall have any pre-emptive right to acquire stock of the corporation except to the extent provided in the articles of organization or in a by-law adopted by and subject to amendment only by the stockholders.' G.L.C. 156B, § 20. We do not here suggest that such pre-emptive rights are required by the strict fiduciary duty applicable to the stockholders of close corporations. However, to the extent that a controlling stockholder or other stockholder, in violation of his fiduciary duty, causes the corporation to issue stock in order to expand his holdings or to dilute holdings of other stockholders, the other stockholders will have a right to relief in court. Even under the traditional standard of duty applicable to corporate directors and stockholders generally, this court has looked favorably upon stockholder challenges to stock issues which, in violation of a fiduciary duty, served personal interests of other stockholder/directors and did not serve the corporate interest. . . .

assume that appreciation, gratitude, and filial devotion would prevent the younger Rodds from opposing a plan which would provide funds for their father's retirement.

Moreover, a strong motive of interest requires that the Rodds be considered a controlling group. When Charles Rodd and Frederick Rodd were called on to represent the corporation in its dealings with their father, they must have known that further advancement within the corporation and benefits would follow their father's retirement and the purchase of his stock. The corporate purchase would take only forty-five of Harry Rodd's eighty-one shares. The remaining thirty-six shares were to be divided among Harry Rodd's children in equal amounts by gift and sale. Receipt of their portion of the thirty-six shares and purchase by the corporation of forty-five shares would effectively transfer full control of the corporation to Federick Rodd and Charles Rodd, if they chose to act in concert with each other or if one of them chose to ally with his sister . . . Although the defendants are correct when they assert that no express agreement involving a quid pro quo — subsequent stock gifts for votes from the directors — was proved, no express agreement is necessary to demonstrate the identity of interest which disciplines a controlling group acting in unison. . . .

On its face, then, the purchase of Harry Rodd's shares by the corporation is a breach of the duty which the controlling stockholders, the Rodds, owed to the minority stockholders, the plaintiff and her son. The purchase distributed a portion of the corporate assets to Harry Rodd, a member of the controlling group, in exchange for his shares. The plaintiff and her son were not offered an equal opportunity to sell their shares to the corporation. In fact, their efforts to obtain an equal opportunity were rebuffed by the corporate representative. . . .

Because of the foregoing, we hold that the plaintiff is entitled to relief. Two forms of suitable relief are set out hereinafter. The judge below is to enter an appropriate judgment. The judgment may require Harry Rodd to remit $36,000 with interest at the legal rate from July 15, 1970, to Rodd Electrotype in exchange for forty-five shares of Rodd Electrotype treasury stock. This, in substance, is the specific relief requested in the plaintiff's bill of complaint. Interest is manifestly appropriate. A stockholder, who, in violation of his fiduciary duty to the other stockholders, has obtained assets from his corporation and has had those assets available for his own use, must pay for that use. . . . In the alternative, the judgment may require Rodd Electrotype to purchase all of the plaintiff's shares for $36,000 without interest. In the circumstances of this case, we view this as the equal opportunity which the plaintiff should have received. Harry Rodd's retention of thirty-six shares, which were to be sold and given to his children within a year of the Rodd Electrotype purchase, cannot disguise the fact that the corporation acquired one hundred per cent of that portion of his holdings (forty-five shares) which he did not intend his children to own. The plaintiff is entitled to have one hundred per cent of her forty-five shares similarly purchased. . . . The case is remanded to the Superior Court for entry of judgment in conformity with this opinion.

WILKES v. SPRINGSIDE NURSING HOME, INC.
Supreme Judicial Court of Massachusetts
370 Mass. 842, 353 N.E.2d 657(1976)

BEFORE HENNESSEY, C.J., AND REARDON, QUIRICO, BRAUCHER AND KAPLAN, JJ.

HENNESSEY, CHIEF JUSTICE.

In 1951 Wilkes acquired an option to purchase a building and lot located on the corner of Springside Avenue and North Street in Pittsfield, Massachusetts, the building having previously housed the Hillcrest Hospital. Though Wilkes was principally engaged in the roofing and siding business, he had gained a reputation locally for profitable dealings in real estate. Riche, an acquaintance of Wilkes, learned of the option, and interested Quinn (who was known to Wilkes through membership on the draft board in Pittsfield) and Pipkin (an acquaintance of both Wilkes and Riche) in joining Wilkes in his investment. The four men met and decided to participate jointly in the purchase of the building and lot as a real estate investment which, they believed, had good profit potential on resale or rental.

The parties later determined that the property would have its greatest potential for profit if it were operated by them as a nursing home. Wilkes consulted his attorney, who advised him that if the four men were to operate the contemplated nursing home as planned, they would be partners and would be liable for any debts incurred by the partnership and by each other. On the attorney's suggestion, and after consultation among themselves, ownership of the property was vested in Springside, a corporation organized under Massachusetts law.

Each of the four men invested $1,000 and subscribed to ten shares of $100 par value stock in Springside. At the time of incorporation it was understood by all of the parties that each would be a director of Springside and each would participate actively in the management and decision making involved in operating the corporation. It was, further, the understanding and intention of all the parties that, corporate resources permitting, each would receive money from the corporation in equal amounts as long as each assumed an active and ongoing responsibility for carrying a portion of the burdens necessary to operate the business.

The work involved in establishing and operating a nursing home was roughly apportioned, and each of the four men undertook his respective tasks. Initially, Riche was elected president of Springside, Wilkes was elected treasurer, and Quinn was elected clerk. Each of the four was listed in the articles of organization as a director of the corporation.

At some time in 1952, it became apparent that the operational income and cash flow from the business were sufficient to permit the four stockholders to draw money from the corporation on a regular basis. Each of the four original parties initially received $35 a week from the corporation. As time went on the weekly return to each was increased until, in 1955, it totaled $100.

In 1959, after a long illness, Pipkin sold his shares in the corporation to Connor . . . after which Connor received a weekly stipend from the corporation equal to that received by Wilkes, Riche and Quinn.

In 1965, the stockholders decided to sell a portion of the corporate property to Quinn who, in addition to being a stockholder in Springside, possessed an interest in another corporation which desired to operate a rest home on the property. Wilkes was successful in prevailing on the other stockholders of Springside to procure a higher sale price for the property than Quinn apparently anticipated paying or desired to pay. After the sale was consummated, the relationship between Quinn and Wilkes began to deteriorate.

The bad blood between Quinn and Wilkes affected the attitudes of both Riche and Connor. As a consequence of the strained relations among the parties, Wilkes, in January of 1967, gave notice of his intention to sell his shares for an amount based on an appraisal of their value. In February of 1967 a directors' meeting was held and the board exercised its right to establish the salaries of its officers and employees. A schedule of payments was established whereby Quinn was to receive a substantial weekly increase and Riche and Connor were to continue receiving $100 a week. Wilkes, however, was left off the list of those to whom a salary was to be paid. . . .

At the annual meeting in March, Wilkes was not reelected as a director, nor was he reelected as an officer of the corporation. He was further informed that neither his services nor his presence at the nursing home was wanted by his associates.

The meetings of the directors and stockholders in early 1967, the master found, were used as a vehicle to force Wilkes out of active participation in the management and operation of the corporation and to cut off all corporate payments to him. Though the board of directors had the power to dismiss any officers or employees for misconduct or neglect of duties, there was no indication in the minutes of the board of directors' meeting of February, 1967, that the failure to establish a salary for Wilkes was based on either ground. The severance of Wilkes from the payroll resulted not from misconduct or neglect of duties, but because of the personal desire of Quinn, Riche and Connor to prevent him from continuing to receive money from the corporation. Despite a continuing deterioration in his personal relationship with his associates, Wilkes had consistently endeavored to carry on his responsibilities to the corporation in the same satisfactory manner and with the same degree of competence he had previously shown. Wilkes was at all times willing to carry on his responsibilities and participation if permitted so to do and provided that he receive his weekly stipend.

1. We turn to Wilkes's claim for damages based on a breach of the fiduciary duty owed to him by the other participants in this venture. In light of the theory underlying this claim, we do not consider it vital to our approach to this case whether the claim is governed by partnership law or the law applicable to business corporations. This is so because, as all the parties agree, Springside was at all times relevant to this action, a close corporation as we have recently defined such an entity in *Donahue v. Rodd Electrotype Co. of New England, Inc.* . . .

In *Donahue*, we held that 'stockholders in the close corporation owe one another substantially the same fiduciary duty in the operation of the enterprise that partners owe to one another.' . . . As determined in previous decisions of this court, the standard of duty owed by partners to one another is one of 'utmost good faith and loyalty.' . . . Thus, we concluded in *Donahue*, with regard to 'their actions relative to the operations of the enterprise and the effects of that operation on the rights and investments of other stockholders,' '(s)tockholders in close corporations must discharge their management and stockholder responsibilities in conformity with this strict good faith standard. They may not act out of avarice, expediency or self-interest in derogation of their duty of loyalty to the other stockholders and to the corporation. . . . '

In the *Donahue* case we recognized that one peculiar aspect of close corporations was the opportunity afforded to majority stockholders to oppress, disadvantage or 'freeze out' minority stockholders. In *Donahue* itself, for example, the majority refused the minority an equal opportunity to sell a ratable number of shares to the corporation at the same price available to the majority. The net result of this refusal, we said, was that the minority could be forced to 'sell out at less than fair value . . . since there is by definition no ready market for minority stock in a close corporation.'

'Freeze outs,' however, may be accomplished by the use of other devices. One such device which has proved to be particularly effective in accomplishing the purpose of the majority is to deprive minority stockholders of corporate offices and of employment with the corporation. . . . .

The denial of employment to the minority at the hands of the majority is especially pernicious in some instances. A guaranty of employment with the corporation may have been one of the 'basic reason(s) why a minority owner has invested capital in the firm. . . . The minority stockholder typically depends on his salary as the principal return on his investment, since the 'earnings of a close corporation . . . are distributed in major part in salaries, bonuses and retirement benefits.' F.H. O'Neal, Close Corporations § 1.07 (1971). Other noneconomic interests of the minority stockholder are likewise injuriously affected by barring him from corporate office. See {4Remove}F.H. O'Neal, Squeeze-Outs of Minority Shareholders 79 (1975). Such action severely restricts his participation in the management of the enterprise, and he is relegated to enjoying those benefits incident to his status as a stockholder. . . . In sum, by terminating a minority stockholder's employment or by severing him from a position as an officer or director, the majority effectively frustrate the minority stockholder's purposes in entering on the corporate venture and also deny him an equal return on his investment.

The *Donahue* decision acknowledged, as a 'natural outgrowth' of the case law of this Commonwealth, a strict obligation on the part of majority stockholders in a close corporation to deal with the minority with the utmost good faith and loyalty. On its face, this strict standard is applicable in the instant case. The distinction between the majority action in *Donahue* and the majority action in this case is more one of form than of substance. Nevertheless, we are concerned that untempered application of the strict good faith standard enunciated in *Donahue* to cases such as the one before us will result in the imposition of limitations on legitimate action by the controlling group in a close corporation which will unduly hamper its effectiveness in managing the corporation in the best interests of all concerned. The majority, concededly, have certain rights to what has been termed 'selfish ownership' in the corporation which should be balanced against the concept of their fiduciary obligation to the minority. . . .

Therefore, when minority stockholders in a close corporation bring suit against the majority alleging a breach of the strict good faith duty owed to them by the majority, we must carefully analyze the action taken by the controlling stockholders in the individual case. It must be asked whether the controlling group can demonstrate a legitimate business purpose for its action. . . . In asking this question, we acknowledge the fact that the controlling group in a close corporation must have some room to maneuver in establishing the business policy of the corporation. It must have a large measure of discretion, for example, in declaring or withholding dividends, deciding whether to merge or consolidate, establishing the salaries of corporate officers, dismissing directors with or without cause, and hiring and firing corporate employees.

When an asserted business purpose for their action is advanced by the majority, however, we think it is open to minority stockholders to demonstrate that the same legitimate objective could have been achieved through an alternative course of action less harmful to the minority's interest. . . . If called on to settle a dispute, our courts must weigh the legitimate business purpose, if any, against the practicability of a less harmful alternative.

Applying this approach to the instant case it is apparent that the majority stockholders in Springside have not shown a legitimate business purpose for severing Wilkes from the payroll of the corporation or for refusing to reelect him as a salaried officer and director. . . . There was no showing of misconduct on Wilkes's part as a director, officer or employee of the corporation which would lead us to approve the majority action as a legitimate response to the disruptive nature of an undesirable individual bent on injuring or destroying the corporation. On the contrary, it appears that Wilkes had always accomplished his assigned share of the duties competently, and that he had never indicated an unwillingness to continue to do so.

It is an inescapable conclusion from all the evidence that the action of the majority stockholders here was a designed 'freeze out' for which no legitimate business purpose has been suggested. Furthermore, we may infer that a design to pressure Wilkes into selling his shares to the corporation at a price below their value well may have been at the heart of the majority's plan.

In the context of this case, several factors bear directly on the duty owed to Wilkes by his associates. At a minimum, the duty of utmost good faith and loyalty would demand that the majority consider that their action was in disregard of a longstanding policy of the stockholders that each would be a director of the corporation and that employment with the corporation would go hand in hand with stock ownership; that Wilkes was one of the four originators of the nursing home venture; and that Wilkes, like the others, had invested his capital and time for more than fifteen years with the expectation that he would continue to participate in corporate decisions. Most important is the plain fact that the cutting off of Wilkes's salary, together with the fact that the corporation never declared a dividend, . . . assured that Wilkes would receive no return at all from the corporation.

2. The question of Wilkes's damages at the hands of the majority has not been thoroughly explored on the record before us. Wilkes, in his original complaint, sought damages in the amount of the $100 a week he believed he was entitled to from the time his salary was terminated up until the time this action was commenced. However, the record shows that, after Wilkes was severed from the corporate payroll, the schedule of salaries and payments made to the other stockholders varied from time to time. In addition, the duties assumed by the other stockholders after Wilkes was deprived of his share of the corporate earnings appear to have changed in significant respects.[8] Any resolution of this question must take into account whether the corporation was dissolved during the pendency of this litigation.

The case is remanded to the Probate Court for Berkshire County for further proceedings concerning the issue of damages. Thereafter a judgment shall be entered declaring that Quinn, Riche and Connor breached their fiduciary duty to Wilkes as a minority stockholder in Springside, and awarding money damages therefor. Wilkes shall be allowed to recover from Riche, the estate of T. Edward Quinn and the estate of Lawrence R. Connor, ratably, according to the inequitable enrichment of each, the salary he would have received had he remained an officer and director of Springside. In considering the issue of damages the judge on remand shall take into account the extent to which any remaining corporate funds of Springside may be diverted to satisfy Wilkes's claim.

NOTES AND QUESTIONS

1. The court in *Donahue* held that all shareholders in closely held corporations owe fiduciary duties directly to each other similar to those owed among partners. It then specifically adopted an equal opportunity rule applicable to *controlling* shareholders in closely-held corporations. Accordingly, the court held, these shareholders "must cause the corporation to offer each shareholder an equal opportunity to sell a ratable number of his shares to the corporation at an identical price." You should consider whether controlling shareholders of all corporations, closely held or not, owe fiduciary duties to the corporation itself, even if not to their fellow shareholders individually. The courts have generally found that they do. *See, e.g., Kahn v. Lynch Communication Systems, Inc.*, 638 A.2d 1110 (Del. 1994). Consequently, you should consider further whether the equal opportunity rule should be extended beyond the closely-held corporation setting to shareholders in any corporation where a controlling person has caused a corporation to repurchase his own shares. Both affirmative and negative positions have been cogently advanced. *See, e.g.*, William B. Andrews, *The Stockholder's Right to Equal Opportunity in the Sale of Shares*, 78 Harv. L. Rev. 505 (1965); George B. Javaras, *Equal Opportunity in the Sale of Controlling Shares: A Reply to Professor Andrews*, 32 U. Chi. L. Rev. 420 (1965).

2. In both the *Donahue* and *Wilkes* cases, the court found breaches of fiduciary duty by shareholders in closely held corporations who happened to be majority or controlling shareholders. However, you should recognize that the fiduciary duties owed among fellow shareholders in closely held corporations are not limited to those who happen to have majority or controlling shareholder status. It is true that in many decisions the breaching shareholder is, in fact, the majority shareholder, but this obviously is the natural result of the power held by that shareholder over his minority shareholder colleagues. In other words, the majority is virtually always positioned to harm the minority, subject to the fiduciary restraint. However, the other shareholders, when positioned to harm their fellow shareholders in widely-varying contexts, are also

---

[8] [15] In fairness to Wilkes, who, as the master found, was at all times ready and willing to work for the corporation, it should be noted that neither the other stockholders nor their representatives may be heard to say that Wilkes's duties were performed by them and the Wilkes's damages should, for that reason, be diminished.

subject to the fiduciary restraint generally applicable to shareholders in closely held corporations. In *Smith v. Atlantic Properties, Inc.*, below, the breaching shareholder was a minority shareholder, although he was found to have been an "ad hoc controlling shareholder" due to the corporation's supermajority voting provisions. And in *Sletteland*, which follows, the breaching shareholder had no controlling position, ad hoc or otherwise, but, rather, caused harm to his fellow shareholders through his power to litigate.

SMITH v. ATLANTIC PROPERTIES, INC.
Appeals Court of Massachusetts
12 Mass. App. Ct. 201, 422 N.E.2d 798 (1981)

BEFORE HALE, C. J., AND CUTTER AND BROWN, JJ.

CUTTER, JUSTICE.

In December, 1951, Dr. Louis E. Wolfson agreed to purchase land in Norwood for $350,000. . . . Dr. Wolfson offered a quarter interest each in the land to Mr. Paul T. Smith, Mr. Abraham Zimble, and William H. Burke. . . . Mr. Smith, an attorney, organized the defendant corporation (Atlantic) in 1951 to operate the real estate. Each of the four subscribers received twenty-five shares of stock. Mr. Smith included, both in the corporation's articles of organization and in its by-laws, a provision reading, "No election, appointment or resolution by the Stockholders and no election, appointment, resolution, purchase, sale, lease, contract, contribution, compensation, proceeding or act by the Board of Directors or by any officer or officers shall be valid or binding upon the corporation until effected, passed, approved or ratified by an affirmative vote of eighty (80%) per cent of the capital stock issued outstanding and entitled to vote." This provision (hereafter referred to as the 80% provision) was included at Dr. Wolfson's request and had the effect of giving to any one of the four original shareholders a veto in corporate decisions. . . .

After the first year, Atlantic became profitable and showed a profit every year prior to 1969, ranging from a low of $7,683 in 1953 to a high of $44,358 in 1954.

For various reasons, which need not be stated in detail, disagreements and ill will soon arose between Dr. Wolfson, on the one hand, and the other stockholders as a group. Dr. Wolfson wished to see Atlantic's earnings devoted to repairs and possibly some improvements in its existing buildings and adjacent facilities. The other stockholders desired the declaration of dividends. Dr. Wolfson fairly steadily refused to vote for any dividends. Although it was pointed out to him that failure to declare dividends might result in the imposition by the Internal Revenue Service of a penalty under the Internal Revenue Code, I.R.C. § 531, *et seq.* (relating to unreasonable accumulation of corporate earnings and profits), Dr. Wolfson persisted in his refusal to declare dividends. The other shareholders did agree over the years to making at least the most urgent repairs to Atlantic's buildings, but did not agree to make all repairs and improvements which were recommended in a 1962 report by an engineering firm retained by Atlantic to make a complete estimate of all repairs and improvements which might be beneficial.

The fears of an Internal Revenue Service assessment of a penalty tax were soon realized. Penalty assessments were made in 1962, 1963, and 1964. These were settled by Dr. Wolfson for $11,767.71 in taxes and interest. Despite this settlement, Dr. Wolfson continued his opposition to declaring dividends. The record does not indicate that he developed any specific and definitive schedule or plan for a series of necessary or desirable repairs and improvements to Atlantic's properties. At least none was proposed which would have had a reasonable chance of satisfying the Internal Revenue Service that expenditures for such repairs and improvements constituted "reasonable needs of the business," I.R.C. § 534(c), a term which includes (see I.R.C. § 537) "the reasonably anticipated needs of the business." Predictably, despite further warnings by Dr. Wolfson's shareholder colleagues, the Internal Revenue Service assessed further penalty taxes for the years 1965, 1966, 1967, and 1968. These taxes were upheld by the United States Tax Court. . . . An examination of these decisions makes it apparent that Atlantic has incurred substantial penalty taxes and legal expense largely because of Dr. Wolfson's refusal to vote for the declaration of sufficient dividends to avoid the penalty, a refusal which was . . . attributed in some measure to a tax avoidance purpose on Dr. Wolfson's part.

On January 30, 1967, the shareholders, other than Dr. Wolfson, initiated this proceeding in the Superior Court. . . . The plaintiffs sought a court determination of the dividends to be paid by Atlantic, the removal of Dr. Wolfson as a director, and an order that Atlantic be reimbursed by him for the penalty taxes assessed against it and related expenses. . . .

The trial judge made findings . . . of essentially the facts outlined above and concluded that Dr. "Wolfson's obstinate refusal to vote in favor of . . . dividends was . . . caused more by his dislike for other stockholders and his desire to avoid additional tax payments than . . . by any genuine desire to undertake a program for improving . . . [corporate] property." She also determined that Dr. Wolfson was liable to Atlantic for taxes and interest amounting to "$11,767.11 plus interest from the commencement of this action, plus $35,646.14 plus interest from August 11, 1975," the date of the First Circuit decision affirming the second penalty tax assessment. The latter amount includes an attorney's fee of $7,500 in the Federal tax cases. She also ordered the directors of Atlantic to declare "a reasonable dividend at the earliest practical date and reasonable dividends annually thereafter consistent with good business practice." . . .

1. The trial judge, in deciding that Dr. Wolfson had committed a breach of his fiduciary duty to other stockholders, relied greatly on broad language in *Donahue v. Rodd Electrotype Co.*, 367 Mass. 578, 586–597, 328 N.E.2d 505 (1975), in which the Supreme Judicial Court afforded to a minority stockholder in a close corporation equality of treatment (with members of a controlling group of shareholders) in the matter of the redemption of shares. The court . . . relied on the resemblance of a close corporation to a partnership and held that "stockholders in the close corporation owe one another substantially the same fiduciary duty in the operation of the enterprise that partners owe to one another." That standard of duty, the court said, was the "utmost good faith and loyalty." The court went on to say that such stockholders "may not act out of avarice, expediency or self-interest in derogation of their duty of loyalty to the other stockholders and to the corporation." Similar principles were stated in *Wilkes v. Springside Nursing Home, Inc.*, 370 Mass. 842, 848–852, 353 N.E.2d 657 (1976). . . .

In the *Donahue* case . . . the court recognized that cases may arise in which, in a close corporation, majority stockholders may ask protection from a minority stockholder. Such an instance arises in the present case because Dr. Wolfson has been able to exercise a veto concerning corporate action on dividends by the 80% provision . . . [which] may have substantially the effect of reversing the usual roles of the majority and the minority shareholders. The minority, under that provision, becomes an *ad hoc controlling interest.* . . .

The provision is only one of several methods which have been devised to protect minority shareholders in close corporations from being oppressed by their colleagues and, if the device is used reasonably, there may be no strong public policy considerations against its use . . . In the present case, Dr. Wolfson testified that he requested the inclusion of the 80% provision "in case the people [the other shareholders] whom I knew, but not very well, ganged up on me." The possibilities of shareholder disagreement on policy made the provision seem a sensible precaution. A question is presented, however, concerning the extent to which such a veto power possessed by a minority stockholder may be exercised as its holder may wish, without a violation of the "fiduciary duty" referred to in the *Donahue* case, . . . as modified in the *Wilkes* case.

The decided cases in Massachusetts do little to answer this question. The most pertinent guidance is probably found in the *Wilkes* case, . . . essentially to the effect that in any judicial intervention in such a situation there must be a weighing of the business interests advanced as reasons for their action (a) by the majority or controlling group and (b) by the rival persons or group. It would obviously be appropriate, before a court-ordered solution is sought or imposed, for both sides to attempt to reach a sensible solution of any incipient impasse in the interest of all concerned after consideration of all relevant circumstances. . . .

2. With respect to the past damage to Atlantic caused by Dr. Wolfson's refusal to vote in favor of any dividends, the trial judge was justified in finding that his conduct went beyond what was reasonable. The other stockholders shared to some extent responsibility for what occurred by failing to accept Dr. Wolfson's proposals with much sympathy, but the inaction on dividends seems the principal cause of the tax penalties. Dr. Wolfson had been warned of the dangers of an assessment under the Internal Revenue Code. . . . He had refused to vote dividends in any amount adequate to minimize that danger and had failed to bring forward, within the relevant taxable years, a convincing, definitive program of appropriate improvements which could withstand scrutiny by the Internal Revenue Service. Whatever may have been the reason for Dr. Wolfson's refusal to declare dividends (and even if in any particular year he may have gained slight, if any, tax advantage from withholding dividends) we think that he recklessly ran serious and unjustified risks of precisely the penalty taxes eventually assessed, risks which were inconsistent with any reasonable interpretation of a duty of "utmost good faith and loyalty." The trial judge (despite the fact that the other shareholders helped to create the voting deadlock and despite the novelty of the situation) was justified in charging Dr. Wolfson with the out-of-pocket expenditure incurred by Atlantic for the penalty taxes and related counsel fees of the tax cases.

3. The trial judge's order to the directors of Atlantic, "to declare a reasonable dividend at the earliest practical date and reasonable dividends annually thereafter," presents difficulties. . . . It . . . fails to order the directors to exercise similar business judgment with respect to Dr. Wolfson's desire to make all appropriate repairs and improvements to Atlantic's factory properties. . . .

Although the [trial court's] reservation of jurisdiction is appropriate in this case, . . . its purpose should be stated more affirmatively. It should be revised to provide: (a) a direction that Atlantic's directors prepare promptly financial statements and copies of State and Federal income and excise tax returns for the five most recent calendar or fiscal years, and a balance sheet as of as current a date as is possible; (b) an instruction that they confer with one another with a view to stipulating a general dividend and capital improvements policy for the next ensuing three fiscal years; (c) . . . if such a stipulation is not filed within sixty days . . . the court . . . may direct the adoption (and carrying out), if it be then deemed appropriate, of a specific dividend and capital improvements policy adequate to minimize the risk of further penalty tax assessments for the then current fiscal year of Atlantic. The court also may reserve jurisdiction to take essentially the same action for each subsequent fiscal year until the parties are able to reach for themselves an agreed program.

MEROLA v. EXERGEN CORPORATION
Supreme Judicial Court of Massachusetts
423 Mass. 461, 668 N.E.2d 351 (1996)

Before LIACOS, C. J., and WILKINS, LYNCH, O'CONNOR, and GREANEY, JJ.

LYNCH, JUSTICE.

The plaintiff, a former vice president of Exergen Corporation (Exergen) and a former minority stockholder of that corporation, brought suit in the Superior Court against Exergen and the president and majority stockholder, Francesco Pompei, because of his termination as an officer and employee of Exergen. . . .

We summarize the facts found by the judge. Exergen was formed in May, 1980, as a corporation in the business of developing and selling infrared heat detection devices. From Exergen's inception to the date of trial, Pompei, the founder, was the majority shareholder in the corporation, as well as its president, owning over sixty per cent of the shares issued. At all relevant times, Pompei actively participated in and controlled the management of Exergen and, as the majority shareholder, had power to elect and change Exergen's board of directors. The plaintiff began working for Exergen on a part-time basis in late 1980 while he was also employed full time by Analogic Corporation. In the course of conversations with Pompei in late 1981, and early 1982, the plaintiff was offered full-time employment with Exergen, and he understood that, if he came to work there and invested in Exergen stock, he would have the opportunity to become a major shareholder of Exergen and for continuing employment with Exergen.

As of March 1, 1982, the plaintiff resigned from Analogic and began working full time for Exergen. He also then began purchasing shares in Exergen when the company made periodic offerings to its employees. From March, 1982, through June, 1982, the plaintiff purchased 4,100 shares. . . . By late 1983, the plaintiff had exercised his option to purchase an additional 1,200 shares. The plaintiff was not offered additional stock options after late 1983.

In response to special questions the jury made the following findings which were adopted by the judge: (1) the plaintiff did not receive an opportunity to become a major shareholder of Exergen; (2) there was a legitimate business purpose for not providing the plaintiff an opportunity to become a major shareholder of Exergen; (3) this business purpose could have been accomplished through an alternative course of action less harmful to the plaintiff's interests; and (4) the plaintiff suffered no damages by not being able to become a major shareholder of Exergen.

With regard to the alleged breach of fiduciary duty for terminating the plaintiff's employment with Exergen, the judge adopted the following findings by the jury: (1) the plaintiff was terminated by Pompei on April 16, 1987, and therefore did not receive continuing employment by Exergen; (2) there was no legitimate business purpose for not continuing the plaintiff's employment by Exergen; and (3) the plaintiff suffered damages in lost wages, reduced by income from other employment, in the total amount of $50,000. . . .

Based on these findings, the judge ruled that, as matter of law, Pompei breached a fiduciary duty to the plaintiff to honor the reasonable expectations that the plaintiff had concerning investments of time and resources in Exergen, and awarded the plaintiff $50,000 in damages.

Breach of fiduciary duty. In *Donahue v. Rodd Electrotype Co.*, 367 Mass. 578, 593, 328 N.E.2d 505 (1975), this court recognized a fiduciary duty by a majority shareholder of "utmost good faith and loyalty" toward shareholders of a close corporation. A claim based on this duty is an equitable claim against individual stockholders. . . . The determination whether a breach of this fiduciary duty has occurred is a matter of law for the court, as is the remedy for such breach.

We agree with the judge's conclusion that Exergen was a close corporation, and that stockholders in a close corporation owe one another a fiduciary duty of "utmost good faith and loyalty." *Donahue v. Rodd Electrotype Co.*, *supra* at 593, 328 N.E.2d 505. We, therefore, look to see whether the plaintiff has established a breach of that duty under the principles of *Donahue*. Even in close corporations, the majority interest "must have a large measure of discretion, for example, in declaring or withholding dividends, deciding whether to merge or consolidate, establishing the salaries of corporate officers, dismissing directors with or without cause, and hiring and firing corporate employees." *Wilkes v. Springside Nursing Home, Inc.*, 370 Mass. 842, 851, 353 N.E.2d 657 (1976).

Principles of employment law permit the termination of employees at will, with or without cause excepting situations within a narrow public policy exception. . . . However, the termination of a minority shareholder's employment may present a situation where the majority interest has breached its fiduciary duty to the minority interest. . . . *Wilkes v. Springside Nursing Home, Inc., supra* at 852–853, 353 N.E.2d 657. There the court concluded that the majority stockholders had attempted unfairly to "freeze out" a minority stockholder by terminating his employment, in part because their policy and practice was to divide the available resources of the corporation equally by way of salaries to the shareholders who all participated in the operation of the enterprise. *Id.* at 846, 353 N.E.2d 657. As the investment became more profitable, the salaries were increased. *Id.* The court recognized that "[t]he minority stockholder typically depends on his salary as the principal return on his investment, since the 'earnings of a close corporation . . . are distributed in major part in salaries, bonuses and retirement benefits.'" *Id.* at 850, 353 N.E.2d 657, quoting 1 F.H. O'Neal, Close Corporations § 1.07 (1971). Given those facts, this court concluded that the other shareholders did not show a legitimate business purpose for terminating the minority stockholder and that the other parties acted "in disregard of a longstanding policy of the stockholders that each would be a director of the corporation and that employment with the corporation would go hand in hand with stock ownership." *Id.* at 853, 353 N.E.2d 657.

Here, although the plaintiff invested in the stock of Exergen with the reasonable expectation of continued employment, there was no general policy regarding stock ownership and employment, and there was no evidence that any other stockholders had expectations of continuing employment because they purchased stock. The investment in the stock was an investment in the equity of the corporation which was not tied to employment in any formal way. The plaintiff acknowledged that he could have purchased 5,000 shares of stock while he was working part time before resigning from his position at Analogic Corporation and accepting full-time employment at Exergen. He testified that he was induced to work for Exergen with the promise that he could become a major stockholder. There was no testimony that he was ever required to buy stock as a condition of employment.

Unlike the *Wilkes* case, there was no evidence that the corporation distributed all profits to shareholders in the form of salaries. On the contrary, the perceived value of the stock increased during the time that the plaintiff was employed. The plaintiff first purchased his stock at $2.25 per share and, one year later, he purchased more for $5 per share. This indicated that there was some increase in value to the investment independent of the employment expectation. Neither was the plaintiff a founder of the business, his stock purchases were made after the business was established, and there was no suggestion that he had to purchase stock to keep his job.

The plaintiff testified that, when he sold his stock back to the corporation in 1991, he was paid $17 per share. This was a price that had been paid to other shareholders who sold their shares to the corporation at a previous date, and it is a price which, after consulting with his attorney, he concluded was a fair price. With this payment, the plaintiff realized a significant return on his capital investment independent of the salary he received as an employee.

We conclude that this is not a situation where the majority shareholder breached his fiduciary duty to a minority shareholder. "[T]he controlling group in a close corporation must have some room to maneuver in establishing the business policy of the corporation." *Wilkes v. Springside Nursing Home, Inc., supra* at 851, 353 N.E.2d 657. Although there was no legitimate business purpose for the termination of the plaintiff, neither was the termination for the financial gain of Pompei or contrary to established public policy. Not every discharge of an at-will employee of a close corporation who happens to own stock in the corporation gives rise to a successful breach of fiduciary duty claim. The plaintiff was terminated in accordance with his employment contract and fairly compensated for his stock. He failed to establish a sufficient basis for a breach of fiduciary duty claim under the principles of *Donahue v. Rodd Electrotype Co.,* *supra.* . . .

Judgment reversed.

NOTES AND QUESTIONS

1. In the *Donahue, Wilkes, Smith,* and *Merola* cases, the Massachusetts courts addressed the fiduciary duties owed by majority or controlling shareholders (including *ad hoc* controlling shareholders) to the other shareholders in closely held corporations. As previously discussed, it is important that you distinguish their fiduciary duties as shareholders of closely held corporations from the fiduciary duties owed by majority or controlling shareholders generally. To whom are their respective fiduciary duties owed? What is the difference in the scope of their respective fiduciary duties? And, lastly, do these differences have practical consequences? The opinions in *Rosenthal* and *Hagshenas* which follow provide useful discussions of these issues.

2. In the *Sletteland* case below, the Montana Supreme Court addresses the fiduciary duties of a single shareholder in a closely held corporation who was neither a majority nor a controlling shareholder. The court correctly concluded that the fiduciary duty of utmost good faith and loyalty among shareholders of closely held corporations extends not only to majority or controlling shareholders but to minority shareholders as well. Whenever a minority shareholder has the power to do damage to the corporation or his fellow shareholders, he must strictly observe utmost good faith and loyalty standards. Do you agree with the court's holding that filing a disruptive lawsuit constituted a breach of the minority shareholder's fiduciary duties?

SLETTELAND v. ROBERTS
Supreme Court of Montana
304 Mont. 21, 16 P.3d 1062 (2000)

Justice William E. Hunt, Sr.

Facts

James P. Sletteland, the appellant, was a shareholder in a closely held Montana corporation called Billings Generation, Inc. (BGI). The four other shareholders in BGI were Jeff Smith, Ron Blendu, Owen Orndorff and R. Lee Roberts. The five shareholders each have expertise and experience in the area of power production in different capacities. As a group, they have been involved with several projects, corporations, and partnerships. Each shareholder owned 20% of the shares in BGI. At the time of the litigation, all five were directors of BGI; Orndorff, Roberts and Smith were officers. Blendu and Sletteland had both been removed as officers by vote of 60 percent of the shareholders, *i.e.*, Orndorff, Roberts and Smith.

Orndorff and Roberts are both attorneys practicing in Boise with experience in the area of cogeneration. Neither is licensed to practice in the state of Montana. Sletteland has been employed for over 18 years as an investment banker, and is a law school graduate who is licensed to practice law in New York.

A variety of corporate entities and partnerships were discussed at trial and in the District Court's findings, but the relevant entities are as follows: BGI; Exxon Billings Cogeneration, Inc. (EBCI), a Montana Corporation which is a solely owned subsidiary of Exxon U.S.A., Inc. Corporation; and the Yellowstone Energy Limited Partnership (YELP), which is a partnership between BGI and EBCI. The purpose of the YELP partnership was to acquire, design, construct, invest in, own, maintain, develop, improve, manage and otherwise operate a qualified cogeneration or small power production facility under the Public Utility Regulatory Policy Act (PURPA) to be constructed and developed near Billings, Montana. In this partnership, BGI is the general partner and holds a 35% interest in YELP. EBCI is the limited partner with a 65% interest in YELP. YELP owns and operates a cogeneration plant in Billings, Montana that generates steam and electric power.

In the process of establishing this plant, Orndorff and Roberts rendered legal services and billed YELP for these services. YELP paid a total of $633,000 to the two of them between mid 1993 and February 1996. Each charged a rate of $225 per hour.

James Sletteland . . . brought an action individually and on behalf of BGI and YELP seeking recovery of excessive legal fees charged by Roberts and Orndorff and for removal of Roberts and Orndorff from the board of directors of BGI. Roberts, Orndorff and Smith filed a counterclaim alleging that the filing of the initial lawsuit by Sletteland derailed the financing of an energy project of the partnership in which all parties are involved. Orndorff, Roberts and Smith argue that this action amounted to a breach of fiduciary duty and negligence. . . .

At the time the initial lawsuit was filed, the project was having financial trouble due to technical problems with the plant and high interest debts. The YELP project was attempting to refinance these high interest debts with lower interest financing. The window of opportunity for the financing being attempted was short, and Orndorff, Roberts and Smith alleged that the timing of the lawsuit by Sletteland was specifically intended to derail financing. Ultimately, the refinancing fell through.

On the original claim, the District Court found that the attorneys had overcharged and required repayment based on a reduced hourly rate, but did not find evidence of fraud and did not remove them as directors. On the counterclaim the District Court found that Sletteland was negligent and breached his fiduciary duties to BGI and his fellow shareholders by the timing of his filing of the main action. Sletteland was found liable to the other three shareholders in the amount of $3,027,939. Sletteland appeals from this judgment and Orndorff, Roberts and Smith cross-appeal.

Discussion

Issue 1

Whether the District Court erred in holding that the hourly rate for legal fees charged by Orndorff and Roberts to the partnership had not been agreed upon and was excessive.

. . .

The YELP partnership agreement specified that the limited partner had the authority to approve legal expenses. It was up to the limited partner to modify the procedure for approving legal work, or to demand repayment if the work was found to be unacceptable. The rate was approved in advance and all parties were aware of it. We find that the District Court has abused its discretion in modifying the rate for legal work. We reverse on this issue.

We note that as part of his appeal, Sletteland argues that Orndorff and Roberts should have been removed as directors of BGI. . . . In light of our discussion and decision in the first issue, we find this contention to be without merit.

Issue 2

Whether the District Court erred in finding that Sletteland breached his fiduciary duties to the other shareholders of the corporation and the partnership, causing damage to the corporation and the other shareholders.

At the time the lawsuit was filed, BGI and EBCI were attempting to obtain additional tax exempt financing for the project. The physical facility was in need of repair, and the project owed large amounts to its creditors, at a high interest rate. BGI was among the parties that would have received payment as a creditor of the YELP project. Due to certain federal tax requirements, it was necessary that the refinancing be completed by June 25, 1997.

The District Court found that there were two causes delaying the refinancing. First, there were some business issues that had not been agreed upon. According to testimony, these were not "deal breakers," but some changes needed to be made before financing could go ahead. Second, the lawsuit became an issue hampering the refinancing. . . .

The District Court noted that a letter from the President of EBCI to Orndorff in November of 1996 indicates that the lawsuit was a major cause to the failure of refinancing, stating:

> EBCI is willing and eager to recommence all activities related to refinancing. As was communicated to you, we believe that the dispute among the owners of BGI has created a serious impediment to YELP's ability to move forward with refinancing. This belief is underscored by the letter from the partnership's bond counsel indicating that where fraud has been alleged against the senior officers of the general partner, underwriters are unlikely to take up the bonds until the litigation is resolved. It appears to us that BGI and its owners have, in effect, caused termination of the refinancing effort.

In addition, bond counsel indicated that until the litigation was resolved, underwriters or purchasers were unlikely to take up the bonds.

The District Court applied the "substantial factor" test in determining whether Sletteland's actions caused the refinancing to fail, and as a result caused damage to BGI. This was the appropriate standard under these circumstances . . .

Sletteland breached his duty of care to his fellow shareholders. The fiduciary duty between stockholders of a close corporation is one of the "utmost good faith and loyalty." *Daniels v. Thomas, Dean & Hoskins, Inc.* (1990), 246 Mont. 125, 137, 804 P.2d 359, 366. Sletteland makes the argument that this standard only applies to a majority shareholder. On the contrary, this duty of good faith cannot be limited where a minority shareholder has power to do damage to the corporation.

We agree with the District Court that Sletteland, in filing his suit, "did not use the care an ordinarily prudent person would in a similar position." Sletteland admittedly knew of the refinancing. The District Court noted that he is "an attorney and an investment banker who is quite knowledgeable in financial matters." In that capacity, he would have been aware of the effect that a lawsuit, alleging misconduct of the board members, would have on a refinancing effort. The District Court concluded that Sletteland "either intentionally decided to derail the refinancing, since the other parties would not do the refinancing on his terms, or was so careless in his activities that no reasonable person could be expected to act in a similar manner." The record supports this conclusion.

There was clearly animosity in the relationship between the business partners. In March of 1996, Sletteland had submitted a bill to BGI for $39,000, charging $325 an hour with no documentation to substantiate any work done. BGI did not want to pay the bill, but the limited partner wanted to close financing and directed that the bill be paid. Ultimately, in June of 1996, Sletteland was removed as an officer of BGI. According to Roberts and Orndorff, Sletteland and Blendu wanted the other three shareholders to purchase their interests, and warned that "unpleasant things would happen" if their demands were not met.

It appears that the suit was brought specifically to derail refinancing of the project. Sletteland admitted at trial that the timing of the suit was up to him and that he was not faced with any statute of limitations problem. The initial law suit was filed by Sletteland on October 2, 1996. This was immediately before the individuals involved in the refinancing were to meet to discuss the refinancing. He did no investigation to see what the effect of the lawsuit would be on the refinancing. The court concluded that "it only makes sense that he would be expected to know that the filing of his suit alleging director fraud would delay or derail the refinancing . . . there was no particular reason to file this suit when he did. He was asked to withdraw the suit so that the refinancing could conclude, but he refused to do so."

J. A. TURNAGE, C. J., KARLA M. GRAY, TERRY N. TRIEWEILER, AND JIM REGNIER, JJ. concur.

ROSENTHAL v. ROSENTHAL
543 A.2d 348 (Me. 1988)

[The court addressed the scope and character of the fiduciary obligations owed among shareholders in a closely held corporation, here a complex of family businesses:]

Against [the only] remaining claim that [Robert and Rona Rosenthal] wrongfully froze Theodore [Rosenthal] out of the family enterprises, defendants raise a number of objections concerning the presiding justice's jury instructions on the general fiduciary obligations owed to each other by Robert, Rona, and Theodore in the context of their dealings in the Rosenthal business complex. The presiding justice set forth the following four specific fiduciary duties owed by the business associates to each other:

(1) To act with that degree of diligence, care and skill which ordinarily prudent persons would exercise under similar circumstances in like positions;

(2) To discharge the duties affecting their relationship in good faith with a view to furthering the interests of one another as to the matters within the scope of the relationship;

(3) To disclose and not withhold from one another relevant information affecting the status and affairs of the relationship;

(4) To not use their position, influence or knowledge respecting the affairs and organization that are subject to the relationship to gain any special privilege or advantage over the other person or persons involved in the relationship.

This delineation of fiduciary obligations reflects accurately the duties of care and loyalty owed under Maine law by a corporate director to the corporation and its shareholders, as well as the duties of a partner to the partnership and his fellow partners. . . .

For the first time on appeal defendants object to the presiding justice's definition of the scope of the Rosenthals' duties as including "furthering the interests *of one another*," rather than being restricted to furthering the interests of the business enterprise. We can find no clear error in that instruction, however, given the special nature of the Rosenthal family business, which most closely resembles a single complex family partnership doing business through numerous entities of varied legal forms.. . . The duties owed in the circumstances here presented necessarily flowed to the other business associates, as well as to the Rosenthal enterprise as a whole and the component entities.

HAGSHENAS v. GAYLORD
Appellate Court of Illinois, Second District
557 N.E.2d 316 (1990)

JUSTICE DUNN delivered the opinion of the court:

This case was initiated on April 29, 1982, when Bruce Hagshenas (Bruce) sued for dissolution of Imperial based on the dissension and corporate deadlock between himself, a 50% shareholder, and Robert Gaylord (Robert) and Virginia Gaylord (Virginia), the other 50% shareholders. The Gaylords filed a counterclaim alleging breach of fiduciary duties and sought damages. . . .

On October 2, 1982, Bruce and his wife, Barbara, resigned from Imperial as officers and directors. The following day they purchased a new agency and began competing with Imperial. On November 1, 1982, the Gaylords moved for a preliminary injunction to stop Bruce from competing with Imperial. On February 16, 1983, the court entered a preliminary injunction that ordered Bruce to deliver an irrevocable voting proxy of his stock and barred him from personally soliciting travel business from Imperial for one year.

In April 1983, the cause proceeded on Bruce's amended complaint for dissolution and the Gaylords' amended complaint for damages for breach of fiduciary duty. On October 1, 1987, the trial court ruled Bruce failed to prove his case and found in favor of the Gaylords on their complaint for breach of fiduciary duty. The court found that damages were too inexact to be determined and therefor fashioned an equitable remedy, ordering Bruce to transfer his Imperial stock to Imperial to be held in constructive trust as treasury stock and voted on by the Gaylords. Bruce was also ordered to pay court costs.

. . .

Bruce argues the court erred in finding he owed a fiduciary duty to the Gaylords after he resigned as a director and officer of Imperial. He contends he was free to compete with Imperial once he resigned. Ordinarily, after a director or officer resigns from a corporation, he or she owes no fiduciary duty to that corporation. . . . The Gaylords contend, however, that Bruce continued to owe a fiduciary duty similar to that of a partner since he continued to own half the stock of Imperial, a company that was essentially a close corporation.

In general, a mere owner of stock in a company does not owe a fiduciary duty to that company. The Business Corporation Act provides that "[a] holder of or subscriber to shares of a corporation shall be under no obligation to the corporation or its creditors with respect to such shares other than the obligation to pay the corporation the full consideration for which said shares were issued or to be issued." . . . In contrast to the Business Corporation Act, the Close Corporation Act provides that, where the articles of incorporation provide that the business of the corporation shall be managed by the shareholders of the corporation rather than by a board of directors, shareholders shall be deemed to be directors for purposes of the Business Corporation Act, and shareholders shall be subject to all liabilities of directors. . . . Bruce asserts that Imperial was not organized under the Close Corporation Act and does not fall under the Close Corporation Act definitions. The Gaylords have not argued otherwise. The record does not include the articles of incorporation or the shares of stock. Thus, we accept the assertion that Imperial is not a close corporation under the Close Corporation Act, and we do not apply this act to this case.

This conclusion does not, however, end our inquiry on the subject of a fiduciary duty owed by a 50% shareholder in a small corporation such as Imperial. The Close Corporation Act provides that its provisions "shall not be deemed to repeal, amend or modify any statute or rule of common law which is or would be applicable to any corporation which is not a close corporation as herein defined." . . . We believe that, though Imperial was not organized or registered as a close corporation under the Close Corporation Act, for all practical purposes it acted as a close corporation. In *Galler v. Galler* (1964), 32 Ill.2d 16, 27, 203 N.E.2d 577, the supreme court defined a close corporation as "one in which the stock is held in a few hands, or in a few families, and wherein it is not at all, or only rarely, dealt in by buying or selling." Imperial meets this test. Its stock was equally split between Bruce and the Gaylords, and there was no buying or selling of this stock. We also find it significant that the shareholders elected themselves directors and officers and participated in the day-to-day operations.

Therefore, though we do not apply the Close Corporation Act to this case, we will consider this case under common law principles which have been applied to closely held corporations. In *Illinois Rockford Corp. v. Kulp* (1968), 41 Ill.2d 215, 242 N.E.2d 228, the supreme court found that 50% shareholders of a company owed a fiduciary duty to each other similar to that of partners. In this case, plaintiff and defendant were each 50% shareholders of a small furniture company. The company fell on hard times, and defendant negotiated a sale of the company. He assured plaintiff they were both getting the same amount for their shares. It was clear, however, that defendant had negotiated a better deal for himself and had intentionally left plaintiff with the impression he was getting the same deal as defendant. . . . In finding defendant breached a fiduciary duty, the court first stated that it has consistently refused to set out the precise boundaries of whether a fiduciary duty exists. . . . It then stated:

> A fiduciary relation exists in all cases in which a confidential relationship has been acquired. The origin of the confidence is immaterial. It may be moral, social, domestic, or purely personal. [Citation.] In *Tilley v. Shippee*, 12 Ill.2d 616, at page 624 [147 N.E.2d 347], we said: 'Their decision to form and operate as a corporation rather than a partnership does not change the fact that they were embarking on a joint enterprise, and their mutual obligations were similar to those of partners.' See also *Helms v. Duckworth* (D.C.Cir.), 249 F.2d 482; *Sher v. Sandler*, 325 Mass. 348, 90 N.E.2d 536.

Kulp demonstrates that, in a closely held corporation, the mere fact that a business is run as a corporation rather than a partnership does not shield the business venturers from a fiduciary duty similar to that of true partners.

Kulp cited *Helms v. Duckworth* (D.C. Cir. 1957), 249 F.2d 482, a case that explicitly held that shareholders in a closely held corporation owe a fiduciary duty to the other shareholders. In *Helms*, the court found that defendant, a 49% shareholder who had equal voting rights in a close corporation, misrepresented himself in negotiating an agreement with plaintiff, a 51% shareholder in the corporation. The court held that, in an intimate business venture such as this, the stockholders of a close corporation occupy a position similar to joint adventurers and partners. *Helms*, 249 F.2d at 486. The court continued:

> While courts have sometimes declared stockholders 'do not bear toward each other that same relation of trust and confidence which prevails in partnerships,' this view ignores the practical realities of the organization and functioning of a small 'two man' corporation organized to carry on a small business enterprise in which the stockholders, directors and managers are the same persons. A distinguishing characteristic of such a corporation is the absence of a division between the stockholder-owners and the director-managers, for the former either personally manage and direct the business or so dominate the directors as to render the latter agents. Yet the fiduciary capacity of directors and dominant or controlling shareholders is unquestioned. *Pepper v. Litton*, 1939, 308 U.S. 295, 306, 60 S.Ct. 238, 245, 84 L.Ed. 281. We believe that the holders of closely held stock in a corporation such as shown here owe a fiduciary duty to deal fairly, honestly, and openly with their fellow stockholders and to make disclosure of all essential information. 249 F.2d at 486–87.

The Supreme Court of Massachusetts has also held that shareholders in a closely held corporation owe a fiduciary duty toward each other similar to that of partners. (*Donahue v. Rodd Electrotype Co. of New England* (1975), 367 Mass. 578, 328 N.E.2d 505; see also Farnsworth, Recent Developments, Close Corporations: Donahue v. Rodd Electrotype Co. of New England, Inc., 367 Mass. 578, 328 N.E.2d 505 (1975), 61 Cornell L. Rev. 986 (1976).) . . .

We find the positions stated in *Kulp, Helms* and *Donahue* persuasive in this case. In this case the facts demonstrate that, though Imperial was purchased as a corporation, it clearly was an enterprise closely resembling a partnership. Hagshenas and the

Gaylords were not only equal 50% shareholders; they were the directors and officers of the company; they oversaw the day-to-day operations. A partner owes a duty to exercise the highest degree of honesty and good faith in the dealings and in handling of business assets, thereby prohibiting enhancement of personal interests at the expense of the interests of the enterprise. *Jaffe Commercial Finance Co. v. Harris* (1983), 119 Ill.App.3d 136, 143, 74 Ill.Dec. 722, 456 N.E.2d 224.

We find Bruce, as a 50% shareholder in this closely held corporation, owed a fiduciary duty similar to a partner to Imperial and its shareholders. He violated his fiduciary duty when he opened a competing business and hired away all of Imperial's employees. The sales employees were of great significance to Imperial's success. It was obvious Imperial would lose the majority of its customers if the sales people left. This action clearly benefited Bruce at the expense of Imperial.

We are not persuaded that Bruce's resignation as an officer and director relieved him of his fiduciary duty. We recognize that, after his resignation, Bruce was not involved in sales, management, or other Imperial day-to-day operations. By maintaining his 50% ownership interest, however, Bruce retained significant control over Imperial. Though the record does not contain the articles of incorporation or the by-laws, we presume Bruce maintained half the voting power of the corporation up until the time the court ordered him to file a voting proxy. He did not purport to give up this control when he resigned. After his resignation, he objected to Imperial buying a new agency, and, moreover, he continued his suit for dissolution.

In finding Bruce owed a fiduciary duty as a 50% shareholder in this closely held corporation, we recognize a significant difference between a shareholder of a closely held corporation and a shareholder of public stock. Unlike the holders of public stock, who can sell their stock when disagreements over management arise, shareholders in a small corporation do not usually have an available market to sell their shares. *Galler*, 32 Ill.2d at 27, 203 N.E.2d 577. We find it implicit that people who enter into a small business enterprise, as in this case, place their trust and confidence in each other. Thus, we find support for finding a fiduciary duty from *Kulp*, 41 Ill.2d at 215, 242 N.E.2d 228, which held that a fiduciary relation exists in all cases in which a confidential relationship has been acquired. Bruce argues there can be no finding of trust and confidence in this case because the parties were openly hostile to each other by the time he resigned. The important point in time is not the time at which the parties' differences became irreconcilable but, rather, the time in which they entered into the business relationship. We find no evidence of hostility or mistrust between the parties when they entered this business.

The fact that the parties were in disagreement when Bruce began competing with Imperial does not excuse his conduct. The parties, being equal shareholders, were at each other's mercy. If there were problems that could not be resolved, then the proper course of action would have been to negotiate a sale or buy out of the shares or file for dissolution. . . .

In summary, we affirm the trial court's decision on liability, and we reverse the trial court's award of equitable damages and remand the cause for a determination of damages based on the evidence.

Affirmed in part; reversed in part and remanded.

C. OPPRESSION, DEADLOCK, AND DISSOLUTION

As observed in the previous section, shareholders in closely held corporations, at least those who have had a falling out with those shareholders comprising the majority, are not in an enviable position. They may be subjected to freeze-outs in which they are not reelected to the board of directors, fired from their corporate employment and denied dividends. Holding an illiquid investment with no return, their only option may be to try to sell their shares to the majority on unfavorable terms. The majority shareholders, despite their leverage in this context, may simply spurn the minority shareholder's overtures. Assuming no mandatory buyout provision has been imposed by a shareholders agreement, the minority shareholder will have no recourse but litigation. In most jurisdictions, the minority shareholder can bring a direct action against the majority shareholders for breach of their common law fiduciary duties, as established by the case law addressed in the previous section. The filing of this litigation, if not noisy threats to do so, may trigger the majority's decision to reacquire the shares themselves or to cause the corporation to do so (assuming it can accomplish this selective distribution lawfully).

Alternatively, the minority shareholder can bring a statutory action against the corporation itself for involuntary dissolution on the grounds of oppression. *See, e.g.,* MBCA § 14.30(a)(2)(ii). Given the increasing tendency of the courts to grant relief in these proceedings to shareholders of closely held corporations, the filing of a suit for involuntary dissolution may lead the majority shareholders to acquisition negotiations. If the action proceeds, the plaintiff shareholder must prove that oppression has occurred, generally viewed not as a single instance of misconduct, but as a course of misconduct intended to harm the interests of the minority shareholder or to otherwise frustrate his expectations. If the court finds the plaintiff has shown oppression, the court may dissolve the corporation, which would extinguish its legal existence. This event would then require the *winding up* of the corporation's affairs, including *liquidation* of its assets to cash, satisfaction of creditor claims, and the distribution of remaining assets to the shareholders based on their proportionate equity ownership. Given the extreme nature of the dissolution remedy, courts have increasingly exercised their equitable authority to condition orders of dissolution on the majority's purchase of the minority shareholder's shares at a fair price. Moreover, modern corporate statutes have been amended to permit majority shareholders in closely held corporations to avoid dissolution by electing to buy out at *fair value* the shares of the complaining minority shareholder. *See, e.g.,* MBCA § 14.34.

Modern corporate statutes vary in the grounds they provide for involuntary dissolution of corporations in shareholder proceedings. However, they typically include the following:

(1) the directors are deadlocked in the management of the corporation, the shareholders are unable to break the deadlock and irreparable injury is threatened,

(2) the shareholders are deadlocked in voting power and have failed in two or more annual meetings to elect successor directors,

(3) the directors or those in control of the corporation have engaged in conduct that is illegal, oppressive, or fraudulent, and

(4) the corporate assets are being misapplied or wasted.

See, e.g., MBCA § 14.30(a)(2).

The following cases illustrate the various issues that commonly arise when shareholders pursue the involuntary dissolution remedy.

MEISELMAN v. MEISELMAN
Supreme Court of North Carolina
309 N.C. 279, 307 S.E.2d 551 (1983)

[The court, in addressing a shareholder's petition for involuntary dissolution of a closely held corporation, interpreted the statutory provision permitting dissolution on grounds that "liquidation is reasonably necessary for the protection of the rights or interests of the complaining shareholder."] "[W]e hold that a complaining shareholder's "rights or interests" in a close corporation include the 'reasonable expectations' the complaining shareholder has in the corporation. These 'reasonable expectations' are to be ascertained by examining the entire history of the participants' relationship. That history will include the 'reasonable expectations' created at the inception of the participants' relationship; those 'reasonable expectations' as altered over time; and the 'reasonable expectations' which develop as the participants engage in a course of dealing in conducting the affairs of the corporation. The interests and views of the other participants must be considered in determining 'reasonable expectations.' The key is '*reasonable.*' In order for plaintiff's expectations to be reasonable, they must be known to or assumed by the other shareholders and concurred in by them. Privately held expectations which are not made known to the other participants are not 'reasonable.' Only expectations embodied in understandings, express or implied, among the participants should be recognized by the court. . . .

In so holding, we recognize the rule that Professor O'Neal suggests should be applied in a corporation based on a "personal relationship":

> [A] court should give relief, dissolution or some other remedy to a minority shareholder whenever corporate managers or controlling shareholders act in a way that disappoints the minority shareholder's reasonable expectations, even though the acts of the managers or controlling shareholders fall within the literal scope of powers or rights granted them by the corporation act or the corporation's charter or bylaws.

> The reasonable expectations of the shareholders, as they exist at the inception of the enterprise, and as they develop thereafter through a course of dealing concurred in by all of them, is perhaps the most reliable guide to a just solution of a dispute among shareholders, at least a dispute among shareholders in the typical close corporation. In a close corporation, the corporation's charter and bylaws almost never reflect the full business bargain of the participants. O'Neal, *Close Corporations: Existing Legislation and Recommended Reform,* 33 Bus. Law. 873, 886 (1978).

After articulating the 'rights or interests' of the complaining shareholder, the trial court is then to determine if liquidation is 'reasonably necessary' for the protection of those 'rights or interests.' Although a literal reading of the statute would suggest that liquidation is the only relief which may be given if a remedy is 'reasonably necessary' for the protection of the shareholder's 'rights or interests,' this is not the case. This statute granting trial courts the power to dissolve a corporation is not to be read in isolation. The trial court is given the power to order alternative forms of relief. . . . "

IN THE MATTER OF KEMP & BEATLEY, INC.
Court of Appeals of New York
64 N.Y.2d 63, 473 N.E.2d 1173, N.Y.S.2d 799 (1984)

COOKE, CHIEF JUDGE.

When the majority shareholders of a close corporation award *de facto* dividends to all shareholders except a class of minority shareholders, such a policy may constitute "oppressive actions" and serve as a basis for an order made pursuant to section 1104-a of the Business Corporation Law dissolving the corporation. In the instant matter, there is sufficient evidence to support the lower courts' conclusion that the majority shareholders had altered a longstanding policy to distribute corporate earnings on the basis of stock ownership, as against petitioners only. Moreover, the courts did not abuse their discretion by concluding that dissolution was the only means by which petitioners could gain a fair return on their investment.

I

The business concern of Kemp & Beatley, incorporated under the laws of New York, designs and manufactures table linens and sundry tabletop items. The company's stock consists of 1,500 outstanding shares held by eight shareholders. Petitioner Dissin had been employed by the company for 42 years when, in June 1979, he resigned. Prior to resignation, Dissin served as vice president and a director of Kemp & Beatley. Over the course of his employment, Dissin had acquired stock in the company and currently owns 200 shares.

Petitioner Gardstein, like Dissin, had been a longtime employee of the company. Hired in 1944, Gardstein was for the next 35 years involved in various aspects of the business including material procurement, product design, and plant management. His employment was terminated by the company in December 1980. He currently owns 105 shares of Kemp & Beatley stock.

Apparent unhappiness surrounded petitioners' leaving the employ of the company. Of particular concern was that they no longer received any distribution of the company's earnings. Petitioners considered themselves to be "frozen out" of the company; whereas it had been their experience when with the company to receive a distribution of the company's earnings according to their stockholdings, in the form of either dividends or extra compensation, that distribution was no longer forthcoming.

Gardstein and Dissin, together holding 20.33% of the company's outstanding stock, commenced the instant proceeding in June 1981, seeking dissolution of Kemp & Beatley pursuant to section 1104-a of the Business Corporation Law. Their petition alleged "fraudulent and oppressive" conduct by the company's board of directors such as to render petitioners' stock "a virtually worthless asset." . . .

Upon considering the testimony of petitioners and the principals of Kemp & Beatley, the referee concluded that "the corporate management has by its policies effectively rendered petitioners' shares worthless, and . . . the only way petitioners can expect any return is by dissolution." . . .

The involuntary dissolution statute (Business Corporation Law, § 1104-a) permits dissolution when a corporation's controlling faction is found guilty of "oppressive action" toward the complaining shareholders. The referee considered oppression to arise when "those in control" of the corporation "have acted in such a manner as to defeat those expectations of the minority stockholders which formed the basis of [their] participation in the venture." The expectations of petitioners that they would not be arbitrarily excluded from gaining a return on their investment and that their stock would be purchased by the corporation upon termination of employment, were deemed defeated by prevailing corporate policies. Dissolution was recommended in the referee's report, subject to giving respondent corporation an opportunity to purchase petitioners' stock.

Supreme Court confirmed the referee's report. It, too, concluded that due to the corporation's new dividend policy petitioners had been prevented from receiving any return on their investments. Liquidation of the corporate assets was found the only means by which petitioners would receive a fair return. The court considered judicial dissolution of a corporation to be "a serious and severe remedy." Consequently, the order of dissolution was conditioned upon the corporation's being permitted to purchase petitioners' stock. The Appellate Division affirmed, without opinion. . . .

Specifically, this court must determine whether the provision for involuntary dissolution when the "directors or those in control of the corporation have been guilty of . . . oppressive actions toward the complaining shareholders" was properly applied in the circumstances of this case. We hold that it was, and therefore affirm.

II

[T]he Legislature has shown a special solicitude toward the rights of minority shareholders of closely held corporations by enacting section 1104-a of the Business Corporation Law. That statute provides a mechanism for the holders of at least 20% of the outstanding shares of a corporation whose stock is not traded on a securities market to petition for its dissolution "under special circumstances" (citation omitted). The circumstances that give rise to dissolution fall into two general classifications: mistreatment of complaining shareholders, . . . or misappropriation of corporate assets . . . by controlling shareholders, directors or officers.

Section 1104-a . . . describes three types of proscribed activity: "illegal," "fraudulent," and "oppressive" conduct. The first two terms are familiar words that are commonly understood at law. The last, however, does not enjoy the same certainty gained through long usage. As no definition is provided by the statute, it falls upon the courts to provide guidance. . . .

The statutory concept of "oppressive actions" can, perhaps, best be understood by examining the characteristics of close corporations and the Legislature's general purpose in creating this involuntary dissolution statute. It is widely understood that, in addition to supplying capital to a contemplated or ongoing enterprise and expecting a fair and equal return, parties comprising the ownership of a close corporation may expect to be actively involved in its management and operation. . . .

As a leading commentator in the field has observed: "Unlike the typical shareholder in a publicly held corporation, who may be simply an investor or a speculator and cares nothing for the responsibilities of management, the shareholder in a close corporation is a co-owner of the business and wants the privileges and powers that go with ownership. His participation in that particular corporation is often his principal or sole source of income. As a matter of fact, providing employment for himself may have been the principal reason why he participated in organizing the corporation. He may or may not anticipate an ultimate profit from the sale of his interest, but he normally draws very little from the corporation as dividends. In his capacity as an officer or employee of the corporation, he looks to his salary for the principal return on his capital investment, because earnings of a close corporation, as is well known, are distributed in major part in salaries, bonuses and retirement benefits." O'Neal, Close Corporations [2d ed.], § 1.07, at pp. 21–22 [n. omitted].

Shareholders enjoy flexibility in memorializing these expectations through agreements setting forth each party's rights and obligations in corporate governance. . . . In the absence of such an agreement, however, ultimate decision making power respecting corporate policy will be reposed in the holders of a majority interest in the corporation. . . . A wielding of this power by any group controlling a corporation may serve to destroy a stockholder's vital interests and expectations.

As the stock of closely held corporations generally is not readily salable, a minority shareholder at odds with management policies may be without either a voice in protecting his or her interests or any reasonable means of withdrawing his or her investment. This predicament may fairly be considered the legislative concern underlying the provision at issue in this case; inclusion of the criteria that the corporation's stock not be traded on securities markets and that the complaining shareholder be subject to oppressive actions supports this conclusion.

Defining oppressive conduct as distinct from illegality in the present context has been considered in other forums. The question has been resolved by considering oppressive actions to refer to conduct that substantially defeats the "reasonable expectations" held by minority shareholders in committing their capital to the particular enterprise. . . . This concept is consistent with the apparent purpose underlying the provision under review. A shareholder who reasonably expected that ownership in the corporation would entitle him or her to a job, a share of corporate earnings, a place in corporate management, or some other form of security, would be oppressed in a very real sense when others in the corporation seek to defeat those expectations and there exists no effective means of salvaging the investment.

Given the nature of close corporations and the remedial purpose of the statute, this court holds that utilizing a complaining shareholder's "reasonable expectations" as a means of identifying and measuring conduct alleged to be oppressive is appropriate. A court considering a petition alleging oppressive conduct must investigate what the majority shareholders knew, or should have known, to be the petitioner's expectations in entering the particular enterprise. Majority conduct should not be deemed oppressive simply because the petitioner's subjective hopes and desires in joining the venture are not fulfilled. Disappointment alone should not necessarily be equated with oppression.

Rather, oppression should be deemed to arise only when the majority conduct substantially defeats expectations that, objectively viewed, were both reasonable under the circumstances and were central to the petitioner's decision to join the venture. It would be inappropriate, however, for us in this case to delineate the contours of the courts' consideration in determining whether directors have been guilty of oppressive conduct. As in other areas of the law, much will depend on the circumstances in the individual case.

The appropriateness of an order of dissolution is in every case vested in the sound discretion of the court considering the application. . . . Under the terms of this statute, courts are instructed to consider both whether "liquidation of the corporation is the only feasible means" to protect the complaining shareholder's expectation of a fair return on his or her investment and whether dissolution "is reasonably necessary" to protect "the rights or interests of any substantial number of shareholders" not limited to those complaining. . . . Implicit in this direction is that once oppressive conduct is found, consideration must be given to the totality of circumstances surrounding the current state of corporate affairs and relations to determine whether some remedy short of or other than dissolution constitutes a feasible means of satisfying both the petitioner's expectations and the rights and interests of any other substantial group of shareholders. *See, also,* Business Corporation Law, § 1111, subd. [b], par. [1].

By invoking the statute, a petitioner has manifested his or her belief that dissolution may be the only appropriate remedy. Assuming the petitioner has set forth a prima facie case of oppressive conduct, it should be incumbent upon the parties seeking to forestall dissolution to demonstrate to the court the existence of an adequate, alternative remedy. . . . A court has broad latitude in fashioning alternative relief, but when fulfillment of the oppressed petitioner's expectations by these means is doubtful, such as when there has been a complete deterioration of relations between the parties, a court should not hesitate to order dissolution. Every order of dissolution, however, must be conditioned upon permitting any shareholder of the corporation to elect to purchase the complaining shareholder's stock at fair value. *See* Business Corporation Law, § 1118.

III

There was sufficient evidence presented at the hearing to support the conclusion that Kemp & Beatley had a longstanding policy of awarding *de facto* dividends based on stock ownership in the form of "extra compensation bonuses." . . . [T]here was uncontroverted proof that this policy was changed either shortly before or shortly after petitioners' employment ended. . . . It was not unreasonable for the fact finder to have determined that this change in policy amounted to nothing less than an attempt to exclude petitioners from gaining any return on their investment through the mere recharacterization of distributions of corporate income. Under the circumstances of this case, there was no error in determining that this conduct constituted oppressive action within the meaning of section 1104-a of the Business Corporation Law.

Nor may it be said that Supreme Court abused its discretion in ordering Kemp & Beatley's dissolution, subject to an opportunity for a buyout of petitioners' shares. After the referee had found that the controlling faction of the company was, in effect, attempting to "squeeze-out" petitioners by offering them no return on their investment and increasing other executive compensation, respondents, in opposing the report's confirmation, attempted only to controvert the factual basis of the report. They suggested no feasible, alternative remedy to the forced dissolution. In light of an apparent deterioration in relations between petitioners and the governing shareholders of Kemp & Beatley, it was not unreasonable for the court to have determined that a forced buyout of petitioners' shares or liquidation of the corporation's assets was the only means by which petitioners could be guaranteed a fair return on their investments.

JASEN, JONES, WACHTLER, MEYER and SIMONS, JJ., concur.

GIMPEL v. BOLSTEIN

Supreme Court, Queens County, New York

125 Misc. 2d 45, 477 N.Y.S.2d 1014 (1984)

ARTHUR W. LONSCHEIN, JUSTICE.

Robert Gimpel is a shareholder in Gimpel Farms, Inc. Believing himself oppressed by the conduct of his fellow shareholders, he has brought a petition to dissolve the corporation pursuant to section 1104-a of the Business Corporation Law and a derivative action pursuant to section 626 of the Business Corporation Law. . . .

The essential facts may be simply stated:

Gimpel Farms is a family corporation engaged in the dairy business. It was founded in 1931 by Louis Gimpel, and control has now passed through his heirs of the second generation (his son and Robert's father, David Gimpel, and his son-in-law, Moe Bolstein) to his heirs of the third generation (Robert, his brother George, and his cousin Diane Bolstein Kaufman). David Gimpel died in 1980, leaving his voting stock to Robert and George and his non-voting stock to his wife Shirley. Moe Bolstein is still alive, but has sold all of his shares to his daughter Diane.

The family members have always participated actively in the management and daily operations of the company and have taken their recompense in the form of salary and perquisites. Moe Bolstein continues to be employed by the corporation as an officer and executive, and draws a substantial salary, although the amount of work he actually does is in dispute. Diane Kaufman's husband, Charles, and George Gimpel also are employed by the corporation in executive capacities and draw substantial salaries. It appears that no dividends have ever been paid.

Robert owns his stock by gift and bequest from his father. He was employed by the company in an important and sensitive managerial position until 1974, when he was discharged due to allegations that he had embezzled some $85,000. The defendants put forth substantial evidence to support these allegations. Robert rebuts them with a form of artful evasion properly characterized as a "non-denial denial," that is, he never actually states that he did not embezzle the funds. He says, instead, that he was never prosecuted for any crime and that the statute of limitations for such a prosecution has passed. Further, as he delicately phrases it, his father "adjusted any disputed financial transaction." This is insufficient to controvert the point, and for the purposes of this motion the court deems it established that in 1975 Robert was, in fact, a thief, that he stole from the family company, and was discharged from all company employment when his theft became known.

Since that time, Robert has received no benefits from his ownership position with this obviously profitable company. The company has continued to adhere to its policy of not paying dividends and, while the other shareholders have received substantial sums as salary, benefits and perquisites, Robert has received not a penny. Not surprisingly, he has also been excluded from all managerial decisions (there have been no formal shareholders' meetings) and has received the barest minimum of information concerning company affairs. The only opportunity Robert has had to gain from his interest came in 1980, when, after his father's death, the other shareholders offered to buy out his shares at a figure which he rejected as inadequate.

THE PETITION FOR DISSOLUTION

The court has the power to order the dissolution of a corporation where "the directors or those in control of the corporation have been guilty of illegal, fraudulent or oppressive actions toward the complaining shareholders" (BCL § 1104-a[a][1]) or where "the property or assets of the corporation are being looted, wasted or diverted for non-corporate purposes by its directors, officers or those in control." (BCL § 1104-a[a][2].) Dissolution under this section is discretionary. (*Topper v. Park Sheraton Pharmacy, Inc.*, 107 Misc.2d 25, 28, 433 N.Y.S.2d 359.) It is a "drastic" remedy, and before ordering it the court must consider whether it is the only means by which the complaining shareholders can reasonably expect to receive a fair return on their investment or whether it is reasonably necessary to protect their rights and interests (BCL § 1104-a[b]; *Muller v. Silverstein*, 92 A.D.2d 455, 458 N.Y.S.2d 597). The corporation or any of its shareholders may avoid the proceeding by electing to purchase the petitioner's shares at their fair value (BCL § 1118).

Robert alleges numerous acts by the majority which he claims constitute "oppressive" conduct. Stripped of the legal interpretations and conclusory language with which they are presented, the allegations fall into three categories:

(1) He has been excluded from "corporate participation";

(2) The profits of the corporation are distributed to the majority interests in the form of salaries, benefits and perquisites, with no dividends being declared; whereby Robert derives no benefit whatsoever from his ownership interest; and

(3) He has been excluded from examination of the corporate books and records which he is entitled to examine, completing his "freeze-out" from the corporation. Robert expressly disclaims, as well he should, any claim that his dismissal in 1975 constituted "oppression" in any sense. Clearly, it was proper to dismiss a thief. Yet, he claims that his *continued* exclusion from "corporate participation" does constitute oppression.

The first question presented is whether the conduct of the majority can be said to be "oppressive" within the meaning of section 1104-a of the Business Corporation Law. The term is not defined within the statute. Two definitions have gained currency in New York and in the numerous reported decisions across the country construing similar statutes.

The most prominent of these stems from the writings of F. Hodge O'Neal, and defines "oppression" as a violation by the majority of the "reasonable expectations" of the minority. This definition has been accepted by the leading New York cases dealing with "oppression," *Topper v. Park Sheraton Pharmacy (supra)* and *Matter of Gene Barry One Hour Photo Process v. Taines*, 111 Misc.2d 559, 444 N.Y.S.2d 540.

The second definition is derived from British law, and describes "oppressive conduct" as burdensome, harsh and wrongful conduct; a lack of probity and fair dealing in the affairs of a company to the prejudice of some of its members; or a visible departure from the standards of fair dealing, and a violation of fair play on which every shareholder who entrusts his money to a company is entitled to rely. . . .

This definition, too, has found support in New York cases. . . .

These two approaches are, of course, not mutually exclusive, and will frequently be found to be equivalent. Often, however, it will be found that one or the other lends itself more nearly to the facts of the case as an appropriate analytical framework.

Here, the "reasonable expectations" test seems to be inappropriate, given the corporation's advanced stage of existence and the plaintiff's place and record. It is frequently said that the relationship between the founders of a close corporation approximates that between partners, and the "reasonable expectations" test is indeed an examination into the spoken and unspoken understanding upon which the founders relied when entering into the venture. Here, however, we have a corporation in its fifty-third year of existence. The sole founder, Louis, transferred ownership and control to his son and son-in-law (David and Moe) many years ago, and they ran the business as essentially equal partners until the death of David in 1980. To the extent that Louis adopted the corporate form in cooperation with David and Moe in order to facilitate their takeover of the business, the "reasonable expectations" test could be said to apply to the relationship between them. However, David is dead, and his sons now own his voting shares. Moe's shares, voting and non-voting, have all been sold to his daughter.

Thus, all present holders of the voting shares of the corporation are two generations removed from the adoption of the corporate form. While the manner of their dealing with each other may in some respects resemble that of partners, it cannot fairly be said that they entered into the business with the same "reasonable expectations" as partners do. Since they all acquired their shares by bequest or gift from other parties, they in no sense chose each other as business associates. The original participants in a close corporation enter into their agreement on the basis of the assessments of each other's talents, assets, intentions and characters and their agreement must, therefore, be regarded as personal in nature. Unless there is an unmistakable expression of their intent to the contrary, the agreement will not "run with the shares." Hence, the present shareholders are not bound by whatever unwritten agreements may have existed between Louis, David and Moe, and did not form any agreement among themselves which could inure to Robert's benefit.

Also, it must be recognized that "reasonable expectations" do not run only one way. To the extent that Robert may have entertained "reasonable expectations" of profit in 1975, the other shareholders also entertained "reasonable expectations" of fidelity and honesty from him. All such expectations were shattered when Robert stole from the corporation. His own acts broke all bargains. . . . Since then, the only expectations he could reasonably entertain were those of a discovered thief: ostracism and prosecution. To the extent that the majority has refrained from prosecuting him, they have dealt with him more kindly than he had reason to expect, not less.

Even though Robert may not lay claim to the reasonable expectation of any specific benefits, it does not necessarily follow that the majority shareholders may treat him as shabbily as they please. Where the question of oppressiveness cannot be resolved by comparing the conduct of the majority to the "reasonable expectations" of the parties, the court must look to the alternative test described above, and consider whether that conduct was inherently oppressive. Although a minority shareholder may be in the position of a stranger to them, the majority must still act with "probity and fair dealing," and if their conduct becomes "burdensome, harsh and wrongful," they may be found to have been guilty of oppression and the corporation may be subject to dissolution.

Under this test, Robert's discharge, as well as his subsequent exclusion from corporate management, were not oppressive. It was clearly not wrongful for the corporate victim of a theft to exclude the thief from the councils of power. . . . Thus, the only forms of participation which may fairly be said to be open to Robert are those open to a shareholder in the position of a stranger: possible entitlement to dividends, voting at shareholders' meetings, and access to corporate records. (BCL § 624.) Robert has received none of these.

Turning first to the failure to declare dividends, it seems that from the beginning of the corporation until Robert's fall from favor in 1975, the corporation had declared no dividends, apparently by consent of all shareholders, but in any event without objection from anyone. All concerned received all income from the corporation in the form of salary for their corporate positions. This policy was basic to the financial structure of the business. . . .

Robert's claim that it was wrongful for them to continue that policy after his discharge amounts to an assertion that they were bound to change the basic structure of the business for his sole benefit and to their detriment. This assertion cannot stand.

As to his other allegations of oppression, the failures to hold shareholders' meetings, to issue proper stock certificates reflecting his actual interest in the corporation, or to allow him access to stock ledgers may all have been improper, but do not, individually or collectively, constitute oppressive conduct such as would justify dissolution.

Having considered and rejected dissolution of the corporation, the court is nonetheless constrained to recognize that Robert cannot be forever compelled to remain an outcast. Even Cain was granted protection from the perpetual vengefulness of his fellow man. (Genesis 4:12–15.) While his past misdeeds provided sufficient justification for the majority's acts to date, there is a limit to what he can be forced to bear, and that limit has been reached. The other shareholders need not allow him to return to employment with the corporation, but they must by some means allow him to share in the profits.

The court is not without jurisdiction to fashion a remedy here. While the statute itself makes explicit mention of only one remedy, that being liquidation, the court is also charged to consider whether that is the only means available to protect the rights of the petitioning shareholder. BCL § 1104-a[2][a]. Clearly, this gives the court discretion in a proper case, to fashion an appropriate remedy. . . . . A number of states have recognized a panoply of alternative remedies, to which a court may turn where relief is warranted, short of dissolution.[9]

To begin with, the corporation must immediately allow Robert full access to corporate records. . . . . If the administration of David Gimpel's estate has progressed to the point where stock certificates may properly be issued to Robert under David's will, this must be done promptly.

Most importantly, the majority must make an election: they must either alter the corporate financial structure so as to commence payment of dividends, or else make a reasonable offer to buy out Robert's interest. The election must be made within six months of the order to be entered hereon, and must be made known at a shareholders' meeting within that time. If the corporation chooses to commence payment of dividends, the dividends must be substantial (consistent with sound business judgment) and not a sham. To the extent that the salaries paid to majority shareholders have been fixed so as to include amounts in lieu of dividends, the salaries must be adjusted downward. . . . .

---

[9] [11] The following list was set forth in *Baker v. Commercial Body Builders*, 264 Or. 614, 507 P.2d 387 and cited with approval in *Fix v. Fix Material Co.*, 538 S.W.2d 351 and *Masinter v. Webco*, 262 S.E.2d 433:

(a) The entry of an order requiring dissolution of the corporation at a specified future date, to become effective only in the event that the stockholders fail to resolve their differences prior to that date;

(b) The appointment of a receiver, not for the purposes of dissolution, but to continue the operation of the corporation for the benefit of all the stockholders, both majority and minority, until differences are resolved or "oppressive" conduct ceases;

(c) The appointment of a "special fiscal agent" to report to the court relating to the continued operation of the corporation, as a protection to its minority stockholders, and the retention of jurisdiction of the case by the court for that purpose;

(d) The retention of jurisdiction of the case by the court for the protection of the minority stockholders without appointment of a receiver or "special fiscal agent";

(e) The ordering of an accounting by the majority in control of the corporation for funds alleged to have been misappropriated;

(f) The issuance of an injunction to prohibit continuing acts of "oppressive" conduct and which may include the reduction of salaries or bonus payments found to be unjustified or excessive;

(g) The ordering of affirmative relief by the required declaration of a dividend or a reduction and distribution of capital;

(h) The ordering of affirmative relief by the entry of an order requiring the corporation or a majority of its stockholders to purchase the stock of the minority stockholders at a price to be determined according to a specified formula or at a price determined by the court to be a fair and reasonable price;

(i) The ordering of affirmative relief by the entry of an order permitting minority stockholders to purchase additional stock under conditions specified by the court;

(j) An award of damages to minority stockholders as compensation for any injury suffered by them as the result of "oppressive" conduct by the majority in control of the corporation.

If the election is made to buy out Robert's shares, the offer again must be substantial and made in good faith. . . . The court's order herein will be phrased as a mandatory injunction, with dissolution being one of the remedies for contempt. . . .

For the reasons stated above, therefore, the court grants summary judgment to the petitioner on the petition for dissolution only to the extent that an injunction will issue governing the future conduct of the corporation. . . .

D. SHAREHOLDER AGREEMENTS AND OTHER CONTROL DEVICES

1. Introduction

Shareholders in closely held corporations whose expectations are frustrated by the other shareholders may, as previously discussed, pursue the remedies of breach of fiduciary duty against fellow shareholders or seek involuntary dissolution against the corporation. However, many of the common difficulties experienced by those shareholders can be either avoided or resolved by careful corporate planning. This requires consideration of the usual and reasonable expectations of the shareholders of closely held corporations and the development of control devices to prevent their frustration. Typically, those expectations include the following:

1. membership in the board of directors;

2. voting rights proportionate to investment that cannot be diluted by the issuance of additional authorized shares;

3. the right to veto material changes to the structure and purposes of the venture;

4. the right to veto or at least approve new owner-shareholders of the enterprise;

5. employment by the corporation as an officer or other primary employee with reasonable salary and bonuses;

6. liquidity rights that facilitate the fair value redemption of shares by the corporation or other shareholders upon the occurrence of certain triggering events, including loss of employment through discharge or retirement, deadlock, involuntary dispositions, and death;

7. the equal opportunity to participate in corporate benefits, including distributions through redemptions and other favorable treatment accorded other shareholders; and

8. various limitations on the purposes or powers of the corporation, including prohibitions against entry into unrelated businesses and against entry into partnerships.

Each of these expectations can be addressed by specially crafted control devices, set forth as provisions in either the articles of incorporation, the bylaws, a shareholders' agreement, or some combination of these. The more common control devices include agreements relating to preemptive rights, supermajority voting requirements, vote pooling agreements and voting trusts, irrevocable proxies, multiple classes of stock (with equal or disparate voting rights), limitations on the purposes and powers of the corporation, limitations on transfers of shares, shareholder agreements restricting management discretion, and provisions facilitating liquidity of shares upon the occurrence of certain events. This section generally addresses each of these devices and the manner in which they are implemented.

2. Preemptive Rights, Supermajority Voting, and Classified Stock

a. Preemptive Rights

The shareholders of closely held corporations will generally prefer preemptive rights to purchase their pro rata share of any additional shares offered by the corporation that would otherwise dilute the shareholders' voting power. Indeed, the board of directors' subsequent issuance of previously authorized shares to other shareholders or third parties could substantially diminish the excluded shareholders' equity interest in the enterprise. Consequently, their preemptive rights to participate in subsequent equity offerings should be granted and thereafter continuously guarded. Under most modern corporate statutes, shareholders do not have preemptive rights unless the articles of incorporation specifically grant those rights to shareholders. *See, e.g.*, MBCA § 6.30(a). To secure these rights, the articles should include a statement to the effect that "the corporation elects to have preemptive rights." MBCA § 6.30(b). This statement triggers the applicability of a number of Model Business Corporation Act provisions unless the articles specifically state otherwise. For example, preemptive rights do not apply to shares issued as compensation to directors, officers, or employees of the corporation, authorized shares issued within the first six months of incorporation or "shares sold otherwise than for money." MBCA § 6.30(b)(3). These provisions should be carefully reviewed, and, if unacceptable, the articles should provide otherwise. Shareholders in closely held corporations normally would prefer preemptive rights that are significantly broader than the limited rights provided by the statute's opt-in provisions. In addition, shareholders should be made aware that preemptive rights are waivable by conduct, and, consequently, when the corporation undertakes to issue additional shares, the affected shareholders should act promptly to protect their rights. *See, e.g., Dingus v. FADA Serv. Co.*, 856 S.W.2d 45 (Ky. App. 1993). On the other hand, should special circumstances occur, shareholders may waive preemptive rights by a writing not supported by any consideration. *See, e.g.*, MBCA § 6.30(b)(1).

b. Supermajority Voting and Quorum Provisions

The minority shareholder in a closely held corporation, at the time of his investment, should have a basic understanding of the business and its governance structure, as reflected in the corporation's articles and bylaws. But, as emphasized previously, the minority shareholder after making his investment in the deal is potentially at the mercy of the majority shareholders or a group of minority shareholders who may combine forces to form a majority. The majority, for any number of reasons, objective or subjective, may determine to change the deal in some fundamental way. For example, let us assume that the intended business of a corporation was wholesale wine distribution. Quite appropriately, the founding shareholders, in drafting the articles of incorporation, may reject the statutory default provision permitting the corporation to engage in any lawful business. *See, e.g.*, MBCA § 3.01(a). Instead, they may insert a provision that restricts the business to the distribution of wine at wholesale. However, the majority shareholders may subsequently decide that the corporation should leave this business and establish an Italian restaurant. Of course, to do so would be *ultra vires* of the corporation's powers under its articles of incorporation. However, to surmount this obstacle, the majority may simply cause the board to propose an amendment deleting the restriction related to wholesale wine distribution. Because the action to be taken by the shareholders is an amendment to the articles of incorporation, special formalities are required by statute. *See, e.g.*, MBCA §§ 10.01–10.09. These include, among others, special notice to all shareholders and a minimum quorum of a majority of the shares entitled to be cast, i.e., a majority of the voting shares outstanding must be present to convene the meeting. *See, e.g.*, MBCA § 10.03. Unless the articles have provided for a greater vote, the proposed amendment under many corporate statutes may be approved by only a plurality of the votes, i.e., the votes actually cast in favor must only exceed the votes cast in opposition. *See, e.g.*, MBCA § 7.25(c). Consequently, the minority shareholder who invested in one business may now find himself outvoted and invested in another business with more extensive risks.

This outcome can be avoided by inclusion of supermajority voting or supermajority quorum provisions in the articles of incorporation. *See, e.g.*, MBCA §§ 7.27, 8.24. For example, let us assume that a corporation has four shareholders, each with twenty-five percent of the voting shares. Each shareholder could be provided a veto power over any proposed amendment by including a provision in the articles requiring approval of any amendments by at least eighty percent of the shares entitled to be cast. Similarly, typical statutory quorum requirements for shareholders meetings could be increased from a majority of votes entitled to be cast to eighty percent, thereby precluding any action from being taken when the objecting shareholder in our example fails to attend. *See, e.g.*, MBCA § 7.27. However, if that shareholder should attend, but then departs before the vote, the supermajority quorum provision would be ineffective. This is because of the rule that once a share is represented at a shareholders' meeting, it is deemed present for quorum purposes for the remainder of the meeting. *See, e.g.*, MBCA § 7.25(b). Supermajority voting provisions are generally more effective than supermajority quorum provisions, which by reason of a shareholder's absence, preclude opportunities for compromise on contested issues. Moreover, a court might not accord supermajority quorum provisions their intended effect. *See, e.g.*, *Gearing v. Kelly*, 182 N.E.2d 391 (N.Y. 1962).

Supermajority voting and quorum provisions for meetings of boards of directors may also be prescribed in the articles of incorporation. *See, e.g.*, MBCA § 8.24. Absent such provisions, most corporate statutes set the quorum as a simple majority of the fixed number of directors and the required vote as a majority of the directors present. These default rules can work a perversion of corporate democracy not generally desired by shareholders. For example, assuming a five-member board of directors, board action could be effected by the affirmative vote of two directors at a meeting attended by three. Consequently, all closely held corporations should consider inclusion of supermajority voting provisions for both shareholders and directors meetings.

Consideration should also be given to inclusion in the articles of supermajority voting provisions for amendments to the bylaws. Generally, the initial bylaws of the corporation are adopted by the board of directors and set forth detailed provisions regarding the structure and management of the corporate business. Under must corporate statutes, both the board of directors and the shareholders are empowered to amend the corporation's bylaws. *See, e.g.*, MBCA § 10.20. Although supermajority voting provisions for both board and shareholders' meetings likely provide sufficient control, consideration might also be given to a provision in the articles of incorporation reserving the power to amend the bylaws exclusively to the shareholders.

Another important issue to be considered in adopting supermajority voting provisions is how high the required voting percentage should be set. Extremely high percentages and, particularly, unanimity requirements, may prove disadvantageous to the shareholders generally. As a practical matter, they can readily produce deadlock, stagnation and complete frustration of corporate purposes. They have also been challenged on public policy grounds as antithetical to established corporate democracy principles. *See, e.g.*, *Sutton v. Sutton*, 637 N.E.2d 260 (N.Y. 1994). Although the court in *Sutton* did not invalidate the subject provisions, other courts may view the issue differently.

c.   Classification of Stock

The minority shareholder's preference for veto power can also be realized through the use of classified stock. *See, e.g.*, MBCA § 6.01. Although one class of voting common stock is the norm for closely held corporations, the creation in the articles of incorporation of multiple classes of stock and a classified board of directors may be used to ensure membership on the board of each minority shareholder to ensure board representation of various groups of minority shareholders. For example, as illustrated by *Lehrman v. Cohen, infra,* classification of separate groups of shares issued to different shareholder families, with each class entitled to elect one or more directors, can ensure fair representation. If each class differs only as to voting rights, the issuing corporation should not be disqualified from electing Subchapter S passthrough status under the Internal Revenue Code. *See* Chapter 4. In addition to allocating control among minority shareholders, classification can also be used to allocate dividends and asset distributions (although potentially fatal to a Subchapter S election). Generally, the founding shareholders of a closely held corporation prefer equal voting representation, even where they contribute different amounts of capital to the new enterprise. For example, if two of the new corporation's founders contributed 25 percent of the capital and the third 50 percent, their voting and distribution expectations could be preserved through the classification of the corporation's shares into voting and non-voting shares. Each shareholder could be issued 100 shares of the voting class, for a total of 300 shares, to accommodate their desire for equal voting representation. Non-voting shares could then be issued to ensure distributions proportionate to each shareholder's actual capital investment. In this example, 150 non-voting shares could be issued to each of the 25 percent investors and 400 non-voting shares could be issued to the 50 percent investor. The 25 percent investors would then have a total of 250 shares each and the 50 percent investor would have a total of 500 shares. If structured so that dividends are paid equally on shares of both classes of stock, the investors will have equal voting rights but with distribution rights proportionate to their respective capital investments. This particular use of classified stock is only one of many that can be creatively employed to resolve control, distribution and other issues among shareholders in closely held corporations.

LEHRMAN v. COHEN
Supreme Court of Delaware
43 Del. Ch. 222, 222 A.2d 800 (1966)

WOLCOTT, CHIEF JUSTICE, AND CARY AND HERRMANN, JJ., SITTING.

HERRMANN, JUSTICE.

The primary problem presented on this appeal involves the applicability of the Delaware Voting Trust Statute. . . .

These are the material facts:

Giant Food Inc. (hereinafter the 'Company') was incorporated in Delaware in 1935 by the defendant N. M. Cohen and Samuel Lehrman, deceased father of the plaintiff Jacob Lehrman. From its inception, the Company was controlled by the Cohen and Lehrman families, each of which owned equal quantities of the voting stock, designated Class AC (held by the Cohen family) and Class AL (held by the Lehrman family) common stock. The two classes of stock have cumulative voting rights and each is entitled to elect two members of the Company's four-member board of directors.

Over the years, as may have been expected, there were differences of opinion between the Cohen and Lehrman families as to operating policies of the Company. Samuel Lehrman died in 1949; each of his children inherited part of his stock in the Company; but a dispute arose among the children regarding an Inter vivos gift of certain shares made to the plaintiff by his father shortly before his death. To eliminate the Lerhman family dispute and its possible disruption of the affairs of the Company, an arrangement was made which settled the dispute. . . . An essential part of the arrangement, upon the insistence of the Cohens, was the establishment of a fifth directorship to obviate the risk of deadlock which would have continued if the equal division of voting power between AL and AC stock were continued.

To implement the arrangement, on December 31, 1949, the Company's certificate of incorporation was amended, Inter alia, to create a third class of voting stock, designated Class AD common stock, entitled to elect the fifth director. Article Four of the amendment to the certificate of incorporation provided for the issuance of one share of Class AD stock, having a par value of $10. and the following rights and powers:

'The holder of Class AD common stock shall be entitled to all of the rights and privileges pertaining to common stock without any limitations, prohibitions restrictions or qualifications except that the holder of said Class AD stock shall not be entitled to receive any dividends declared and paid by the corporation, shall not be entitled to share in the distribution of assets of the corporation upon liquidation or dissolution either partial or final, except to the extent of the par value of said Class AD common stock, and in the election of Directors shall have the right to vote for and elect one of the five Directors hereinafter provided for. 'The corporation shall have the right, at any time, to redeem and call in the Class AD stock by paying to the holder thereof the par value of said stock, provided however, that such redemption or call shall be authorized and directed by the affirmative vote of four of the five Directors hereinafter provided for.'

By resolution of the board of directors, the share of Class AD stock was issued forthwith to the defendant Joseph B. Danzansky, who had served as counsel to the Company since 1944. All corporate action regarding the creation and the issuance of the Class AD stock was accomplished by the unanimous vote of the AC and AL stockholders and of the board of directors. In April 1950, pursuant to the arrangement, Danzansky voted his share of AD stock to elect himself as the Company's fifth director; and he served as such until the institution of this action in 1964. During that entire period, the AC and AL stock have been voted to elect two directors each. From 1950 through 1964, Danzansky regularly attended board meetings, raised and discussed general items of business, and voted on all issues as they came before the board. He was not obliged to break any deadlock among the directors prior to October 1, 1964 because no such deadlock arose before that date.

Beginning in December 1959, 200,000 shares of non-voting common stock of the Company were sold in a public issue for over $3,000,000. . . .

From the outset and until October 1, 1964, the defendant N. M. Cohen was president of the Company. On that date, a resolution was adopted at the Company's annual stockholders' meeting to give Danzansky a fifteen year executive employment contract at an annual salary of $67,600, and options for 25,000 shares of the non-voting common stock of the Company. The AC and AD stock were voted in favor and the AL stock was voted against the resolution. At a directors meeting held the same day, Danzansky was elected president of the Company by a 3-2 vote, the two AL directors voting in opposition. On December 11, 1964, Danzansky resigned as director and voted his share of AD stock to elect as the fifth director, Millard F. West, Jr., a former AL director and investment banker whose firm was one of the underwriters of the public issue of the Company's stock. The newly constituted board ratified the election of Danzansky as president; and, on January 27, 1965, after the commencement of this action and after a review and report by a committee consisting of the new AD director and one AL director, Danzansky's employment contract was approved and adopted with certain modifications.

The plaintiff brought this action on December 11, 1964. . . . The First Claim charges that the creation, issuance, and voting of the one share of Class AD stock resulted in an arrangement illegal under the law of this State. . . . The Court of Chancery . . . granted summary judgment in favor of the defendants and denied the plaintiff's motion for summary judgment. The plaintiff appeals.

I

The plaintiff's primary contention is that the Class AD stock arrangement is, in substance and effect, a voting trust; that, as such, it is illegal because not limited to a ten year period as required by the Voting Trust Statute. The defendants deny that the AD stock arrangement constitutes a disguised voting trust; but they concede that if it is, the arrangement is illegal for violation of the Statute. . . .

The criteria of a voting trust under our decisions have been summarized by this Court in Abercrombie v. Davies, 36 Del.Ch. 371, 130 A.2d 338 (1957). The tests there set forth, accepted by both sides of this cause as being applicable,[10] are as follows: (1) the voting rights of the stock are separated from the other attributes of ownership; (2) the voting rights granted are intended to be irrevocable for a definite period of time; and (3) the principal purpose of the grant of voting rights is to acquire voting control of the corporation.

Adopting and applying these tests, the plaintiff says, as to the first element, that the AD arrangement provides for a divorcement of voting rights from beneficial ownership of the AC and AL stock; that the creation and issuance of the share of AD stock is tantamount to a pooling by the AC and AL stockholders of a portion of their voting stock and giving it to a trustee, in the person of the AD stockholder, to vote for the election of the fifth director; that after the creation of the AD stock, the AC and AL stockholders each hold but 40% of the voting power, and the AD stockholder holds the controlling balance of 20%; that the AD stock has no property rights except the right to a return of the $10 paid as the par value; and that, therefore, there has been a transfer of the voting rights devoid of any participating property rights. So runs the argument of the plaintiff in support of his contention that the first of the Abercrombie criteria for a voting trust is met.

The contention is unacceptable. The AD arrangement did not separate the voting rights of the AC or the AL stock from the other attributes of ownership of those classes of stock. Each AC and AL stockholder retains complete control over the voting of his stock; each can vote his stock directly; no AL or AC stockholder is divested of his right to vote his stock as he sees fit; no AL or AC stock can be voted against the shareholder's wishes; and the AL and AC stock continue to elect two directors each.

The AD stock arrangement, as we view it, became a part of the capitalization of the Company. The fact that there is but a single share, or that the par value is nominal, is of no legal significance; the one share and the $10. par value might have been multiplied many times over, with the same consequence. It is true that the creation of the separate class of AD stock may have diluted the voting power which had previously existed in the AC and AL stock-the usual consequence when additional voting stock is created-but the creation of the new class did not divest and separate the voting. Rights which remain vested in each AC and AL shareholder, together with the other attributes of the ownership of that stock. The fallacy of the plaintiff's position lies in his premise that since the voting power of the AC and AL stock was reduced by the creation of the AD stock, the percentage of reduction became the Res of a voting trust. In any recapitalization involving the creation of additional voting stock, the voting power of the previously existing stock is diminished; but a voting trust is not necessarily the result.

Since the holders of the Class AC and Class AL stock of the Company did not

---

[10] [3] While the tests and criteria set forth in the Abercrombie case prevail, its facts are entirely different. There, several stockholders, each representing a minority interest, agreed to place their stock in escrow for a period of ten years, in exchange for stock receipts, for the purpose of acquiring voting control of the corporation. Agents were appointed and, by irrevocable proxies, the agents were given joint and several voting rights and sole power of decision; no stockholder retained the right to vote his own stock. On those facts, an attempt having been thus made to separate the vote from the stock, this Court held that the stockholders had created a voting trust subject to the controls and limitations of § 218.

separate the voting rights from the other attributes of ownership of those classes when they created the Class AD stock, the first Abercrombie test of a voting trust is not met.

This conclusion disposes of the second and third Abercrombie tests, i.e., that the voting rights granted are irrevocable for a definite period of time, and that the principal object of the grant of voting rights is voting control of the corporation. Having held that the AC and AL stockholders have not divested themselves of their voting rights, although they may have diluted their voting powers, we do not reach the remaining Abercrombie tests, both of which assume the divestiture of voting rights.

In the final analysis, the essence of the question raised by the plaintiff in this connection is this: Is the substance and purpose of the AD stock arrangement sufficiently close to the substance and purpose of § 218 to warrant its being subjected to the restrictions and conditions imposed by that Statute? The answer is negative not only for the reasons above stated, but also because § 218 regulates trusts and pooling agreements amounting to trusts, not other and different types of arrangements and undertakings possible among stockholders. Compare *Ringling Bros.-Barnum & Bailey Combined Shows, Inc. v. Ringling*, 29 Del.Ch. 610, 53 A.2d 441 (1947); *Abercrombie v. Davies, supra*. The AD Stock arrangement is neither a trust nor a pooling agreement. We hold, therefore, that the Class AD stock arrangement is not controlled by the Voting Trust Statute.

II

The plaintiff's second point is that even if the Class AD stock arrangement is not a voting trust in substance and effect, the AD stock is illegal, nevertheless, because the creation of a class of stock having voting rights only, and lacking any substantial participating proprietary interest in the corporation, violates the public policy of this State as declared in § 218.

The fallacy of this argument is twofold: First, it is more accurate to say that what the law has disfavored, and what the public policy underlying the Voting Trust Statute means to contol [sic], is the separation of the vote from the stock — not from the stock ownership. . . . Clearly, the AD stock arrangement is not violative of that public policy. Secondly, there is nothing in § 218, either expressed or implied, which requires that all stock of a Delaware corporation must have both voting rights and proprietary interests. Indeed, public policy to the contrary seems clearly expressed by 8 Del. C. § 151(a) which authorizes, in very broad terms, such voting powers and participating rights as may be stated in the certificate of incorporation. Non-voting stock is specifically authorized by § 151(a); and in the light thereof, consistency does not permit the conclusion, urged by the plaintiff, that the present public policy of this State condemns the separation of voting rights from beneficial stock ownership. . . .

We conclude that the plaintiff's contention in this regard cannot withstand the force and effect of § 151(a). In our view, that Statute permits the creation of stock having voting rights only, as well as stock having property rights only. The voting powers and the participating rights of the Class AD stock being specified in the Company's certificate of incorporation, we are of the opinion that the Class AD stock is legal by virtue of § 151(a).

We are told that if the AD stock arrangement is allowed thus to stand, our Voting Trust Statute will become a 'dead letter' because it will be possible to evade and circumvent its purpose simply by issuing a class of non-participating voting stock, as was done here. We have three negative reactions to this argument:

First, it presupposes a divestiture of the voting rights of the AC and AL stock — an untenable supposition as has been stated. Secondly, it fails to take into account the main purpose of a Voting Trust Statute: to avoid secret, uncontrolled combinations of stockholders formed to acquire voting control of the corporation to the possible detriment of non-participating shareholders. . . . It may not be said that the AD stock arrangement contravenes that purpose. Finally on this point, if we misconceive the legislative intent, and if the AD stock arrangement in this case reveals a loophole in § 218 which should be plugged, it is for the General Assembly to accomplish — not for us to attempt by interstitial judicial legislation.

III

The plaintiff advances yet another reason for invalidating the AD stock. The essence of this argument is that the only function of that class of stock is to break directorial deadlocks; that the issuance of the AD stock is merely a technical divice [sic] to permit that result; that, as such, it is illegal because it permits the AC and AL directors of the Company to delegate their statutory duties to the AD director as an arbitrator.

We see nothing inherently wrong or contrary to the public policy of this State, as plaintiff seems to suggest, about a device, otherwise lawful, designed by the stockholders of a corporation to break deadlocks of directors. The plaintiff says in this connection, that if public policy sanctioned such device, our General Corporation Law would provide for it. The fallacy of this argument lies in the assumption that legislative silence is a dependable indicator of public policy. . . . We know of no reason, either under our statutes or our decisions, which would prevent the stockholders of a Delaware corporation from protecting themselves and their corporation, by a plan otherwise lawful, against the paralyzing and often fatal consequences of a stalemate in the directorate of the corporation. We hold, therefore, that the AD stock arrangement had a proper purpose.

As to the means adopted for the accomplishment of that purpose, we find the AD stock arrangement valid by virtue of § 141(a) of the Delaware Corporation Law which provides: 'The business of every corporation organized under the provisions of this chapter shall be managed by a board of directors, except as hereinafter or in its certificate of incorporation otherwise provided.' The AD stock arrangement was created by the unanimous action of the stockholders of the Company by amendment to the certificate of incorporation. The stockholders thereby provided how the business of the corporation is to be managed, as is their privilege and right under § 141(a). It was this stockholder action which delegated to the AD director whatever powers and duties he possesses; they were not delegated to him by his fellow directors, either out of their own powers and duties, or otherwise.

It is settled, of course, as a general principle, that directors may not delegate their duty to manage the corporate enterprise. *Adams v. Clearance Corporation*, 35 Del. 459, 121 A.2d 302 (1956). But there is no conflict with that principle where, as here, the delegation of duty, if any, is made not by the directors but by stockholder action under § 141(a), via the certificate of incorporation.

In our judgment, therefore, the AD stock arrangement is not invalid on the ground that it permits the AC and AL directors of the Company to delegate their statutory duties to the AD director. . . .

Finding no error in the judgment below, it is affirmed.

3. Shareholder Voting Agreements and Irrevocable Proxies

a. Pooling Agreements

Frequently, in a closely held corporation, no single shareholder has voting control. Instead, a shareholder must combine with one or more additional shareholders to form a control block. Rather than having to develop informal voting coalitions on a continual basis, shareholders of like minds may enter into an agreement in which they pool their shares as a voting block. *See, e.g.*, MBCA § 7.31. Generally, these pooling agreements set forth an agreement to vote in board of directors elections for specified individuals or for the nominees of the parties to the agreement. They may also provide for the affirmative or negative vote by the parties on certain designated policy issues. Some of these agreements provide for the appointment of an irrevocable proxy, as discussed below, for the life of the agreement, authorizing a third party to vote the shares in accordance with the agreement. *See, e.g.*, MBCA § 7.22. Other agreements designate an arbitrator to vote the parties' shares, pursuant to a revocable or irrevocable proxy, where the parties have been unable to reach consensus. *See, e.g., Ringling Bros.- Barnum & Bailey Combined Shows, Inc. v. Ringling*, 53 A.2d 441 (Del. 1947). Generally, pooling agreements are specifically enforceable, especially given the difficulty in calculating monetary damages for breach. *See, e.g.*, MBCA § 7.31.

b. Voting Trusts

Voting trusts are a control device much less frequently used than the far less formal pooling agreements. They do achieve the similar result of combining shares to form a voting block. However, with voting trusts, shareholders forming the coalition actually transfer legal title to their shares to the trustee who they designate in the agreement. Generally, they are provided voting trust certificates as evidence of their equitable ownership interests in the trust. Once the voting trust is lawfully formed, the trustee will have exclusive power to vote the shares. The requirements for creating a voting trust are quite formal. *See, e.g.*, MBCA § 7.30. The voting trust agreement must be signed by each of the party shareholders, the agreement and a detailed list of beneficial owners delivered to the corporation's principal offices, and the transferred shares registered in the trustee's name. Unless extended, it is valid for not more than ten years after its effective date. For a general discussion of the voting trust and its operation, see *Abercrombie v. Davies*, 130 A.2d 338 (Del. 1957); *Oceanic Exploration Co. v. Grynberg*, 428 A.2d 1 (Del. 1981).

c. Irrevocable Proxies

Irrevocable proxies often complement shareholder agreements that relate to the parties' voting of their shares. They are a commonly used control device by which shareholders agree to grant another person or each other binding authority to vote their shares. Normally, a shareholder's appointment of a proxy to vote his shares is revocable at any time, like any other agency relationship. *See* RESTATEMENT (THIRD) AGENCY § 310. However, under modern corporate statutes, the appointment will be irrevocable if the appointment form expressly states that it is irrevocable and the appointment is coupled with an interest. *See, e.g.*, MBCA § 7.22(d); DEL. GEN. CORP. LAW § 212(e). These statutes have simply codified the co-existing common law. *See, e.g.*, RESTATEMENT (THIRD) AGENCY § 3.12. The underlying policy is that the proxy holder should have an economic interest in the viability of the corporation that motivates him to vote in a manner that advances the corporation's best interests. Otherwise, the separation of the voting right from ownership could pervert the objectives of corporate democracy. Proxy holders having appointments coupled with an interest commonly include pledgees, persons who have purchased or agreed to purchase shares, creditors who have required proxy appointments in loan agreements, employees with employment contracts that require the appointment, and parties to voting agreements. *See, e.g.*, MBCA § 7.22(d); N.Y. GEN. BUS. CORP. LAW §§ 609(f), (g) and 620(a). It should be noted that when this interest is extinguished, the proxy appointment becomes revocable. *See* MBCA § 7.22(f). In creating irrevocable proxies, counsel to the parties should precisely state in the appointment form or agreement that the proxy is irrevocable and specify any limitations on the authority of the proxy holder.

4. Shareholder Agreements Restricting Board Discretion

Many of the expectations of minority shareholders in a closely held corporation can be satisfied by shareholder agreements addressing a wide number of issues normally within the discretion of the board of directors. For example, these shareholders, as discussed previously, often have expectations regarding membership on the board of directors, salaried employment as corporate officers or as other primary employees of the enterprise, and investment returns through corporate distributions. These expectations obviously conflict with the core principle of the corporate statutory norm that "all corporate powers shall be exercised by or under the authority of the board of directors." *See*, MBCA § 8.01(b). Corporate statutes have traditionally reflected a desirable symmetry, granting enormous power to the board while imposing corresponding fiduciary responsibilities of care, loyalty and good faith. However, to the extent boards of directors are stripped of this power by shareholders, the power and responsibility symmetry of the public policy is lost. The board's power, and hence, control would be usurped without a corresponding decrease in their fiduciary responsibilities. Corporate governance, now out of kilter, could inevitably lead to organizational chaos.

The cases that follow illustrate how the courts have struggled with this dilemma. These cases illustrate how courts have become increasingly cognizant of the special dynamics of the closely held corporation and, accordingly, more permissive of shareholder agreements that control various management decisions. State legislatures followed suit, with close corporation acts, to permit closely held corporations to opt in to more informal corporate governance schemes. However, these statues were rarely used. More importantly, general incorporation statutes were amended to add provisions authorizing shareholder agreements restricting board discretion. *See, e.g.*, N.Y. Bus. Corp. Law § 620; Cal. Corp. Code §§ 158, 300(b); and MBCA § 7.32. The Model Business Corporation Act's recitation of the core principal of corporate governance, that all corporate powers must be exercised by the board, is now followed by the language, "subject to any limitation set forth in the articles of incorporation *or in an agreement authorized under section 7.32.*" MBCA § 8.01. Section 7.32 reflects a truly remarkable departure from the traditional statutory norms with which courts had struggled for decades.

Section 7.32 of the Model Business Corporation Act provides for the effectiveness of shareholder agreements despite their inconsistency with other provisions of the statute. If authorized in the articles or bylaws by unanimous vote or in a written agreement signed by all shareholders at the time, an agreement is effective even if by its terms it has any of the following results:

1. eliminates the board or restricts its discretion or powers;

2. governs corporate distributions (subject to § 6.40);

3. establishes who shall be directors and officers;

4. governs the exercise of voting power by shareholders and directors;

5. establishes the terms of transfers of property or the provision of services between the corporation and its shareholders, directors, officers or employees;

6. transfers to one or more shareholders the authority to manage the corporation, including the power to resolve deadlocks;

7.   requires dissolution at the request of shareholders or upon certain events; and

8. otherwise governs the exercise of corporate powers or the management of the corporation or the relationships among the shareholders, the directors and the corporation, so long as not contrary to public policy. MBCA § 7.32(a)

Statutory recognition of these agreements has greatly enhanced the opportunities for shareholders in closely held corporations to ensure their expectations are fulfilled.

MCQUADE v. STONEHAM

Court of Appeals of New York

263 N.Y. 323, 189 N.E. 234 (1934)

POUND, CHIEF JUDGE.

The action is brought to compel specific performance of an agreement between the parties, entered into to secure the control of National Exhibition Company, also called the Baseball Club (New York Nationals or Giants). This was one of Stoneham's enterprises which used the New York polo grounds for its home games. McGraw was manager of the Giants. McQuade was at the time the contract was entered into a city magistrate. He resigned December 8, 1930.

Defendant Stoneham became the owner of 1,306 shares, or a majority of the stock of National Exhibition Company. Plaintiff and defendant McGraw each purchased 70 shares of his stock. Plaintiff paid Stoneham $50,338.10 for the stock he purchased. As a part of the transaction, the agreement in question was entered into. It was dated May 21, 1919. Some of its pertinent provisions are:

'VIII. The parties hereto will use their best endeavors for the purpose of continuing as directors of said Company and as officers thereof the following:

'Directors:

'Charles A. Stoneham, 'John J. McGraw, 'Francis X. McQuade' — with the right to the party of the first part [Stoneham] to name all additional directors as he sees fit:

'Officers:

'Charles A. Stoneham, President, 'John J. McGraw, Vice-President, 'Francis X. McQuade, Treasurer.

'IX. No salaries are to be paid to any of the above officers or directors, except as follows:

"President	$45,000
"Vice-President	7,500
"Treasurer	7,500

'X. There shall be no change in said salaries, no change in the amount of capital, or the number of shares, no change or amendment of the by-laws of the corporation or any matters regarding the policy of the business of the corporation or any matters which may in anywise affect, endanger or interfere with the rights of minority stockholders, excepting upon the mutual and unanimous consent of all of the parties hereto.

'XIV. This agreement shall continue and remain in force so long as the parties or any of them or the representative of any, own the stock referred to in this agreement, to wit, the party of the first part, 1,166 shares, the party of the second part 70 shares and the party of the third part 70 shares, except as may otherwise appear by this agreement.

In pursuance of this contract Stoneham became president and McGraw vice president of the corporation. McQuade became treasurer. In June 1925, his salary was increased to $10,000 a year. He continued to act until May 2, 1928, when Leo J. Bondy was elected to succeed him. The board of directors consisted of seven men. The four outside of the parties hereto were selected by Stoneham and he had complete control over them. At the meeting of May 2, 1928, Stoneham and McGraw refrained from voting, McQuade voted for himself, and the other four voted for Bondy. Defendants did not keep their agreement with McQuade to use their best efforts to continue him as treasurer. On the contrary, he was dropped with their entire acquiescence. At the next stockholders' meeting he was dropped as a director although they might have elected him.

. . .

The cause for dropping McQuade was due to the falling out of friends. McQuade and Stoneham had disagreed. The trial court has found in substance that their numerous quarrels and disputes did not affect the orderly and efficient administration of the business of the corporation; that plaintiff was removed because he had antagonized the dominant Stoneham by persisting in challenging his power over the corporate treasury and for no misconduct on his part. The court also finds that plaintiff was removed by Stoneham for protecting the corporation and its minority stockholders. We will assume that Stoneham put him out when he might have retained him, merely in order to get rid of him.

Defendants say that the contract in suit was void because the directors held their office charged with the duty to act for the corporation according to their best judgment and that any contract which compels a director to vote to keep any particular person in office and at a stated salary is illegal. Directors are the exclusive executive representatives of the corporation, charged with administration of its internal affairs and the management and use of its assets. They manage the business of the corporation. General Corporation Law, Consol. Laws, c. 23, § 27. 'An agreement to continue a man as president is dependent upon his continued loyalty to the interests of the corporation.' *Fells v. Katz*, 256 N.Y. 67, 72, 175 N.E. 516, 517. So much is undisputed.

Plaintiff contends that the converse of this proposition is true and that an agreement among directors to continue a man as an officer of a corporation is not to be broken so long as such officer is loyal to the interests of the corporation and that, as plaintiff has been found loyal to the corporation, the agreement of defendants is enforceable.

Although it has been held that an agreement among stockholders whereby it is attempted to divest the directors of their power to discharge an unfaithful employee of the corporation is illegal as against public policy (*Fells v. Katz, supra*), it must be equally true that the stockholders may not, by agreement among themselves, control the directors in the exercise of the judgment vested in them by virtue of their office to elect officers and fix salaries. Their motives may not be questioned so long as their acts are legal. The bad faith or the improper motives of the parties does not change the rule. *Manson v. Curtis*, 223 N.Y. 313, 324, 119 N.E. 559, Ann. Cas. 1918E, 247. Directors may not by agreements entered into as stockholders abrogate their independent judgment. *Creed v. Copps*, 103 Vt. 164, 152 A. 369, 71 A.L.R. 1287, annotated.

Stockholders may, of course, combine to elect directors. That rule is well settled. As Holmes, C. J., pointedly said (*Brightman v. Bates*, 175 Mass. 105, 111, 55 N.E. 809, 811): 'If stockholders want to make their power felt, they must unite. There is no reason why a majority should not agree to keep together.' The power to unite is, however, limited to the election of directors and is not extended to contracts whereby limitations are placed on the power of directors to manage the business of the corporation by the selection of agents at defined salaries.

The minority shareholders whose interests McQuade says he has been punished for protecting, are not, aside from himself, complaining about his discharge. He is not acting for the corporation or for them in this action. It is impossible to see how the corporation has been injured by the substitution of Bondy as treasurer in place of McQuade. As McQuade represents himself in this action and seeks redress for his own wrongs, 'we prefer to listen to [the corporation and the minority stockholders] before any decision as to their wrongs.' *Faulds v. Yates*, 57 Ill. 416, 417, 11 Am. Rep. 24.

It is urged that we should pay heed to the morals and manners of the market place to sustain this agreement and that we should hold that its violation gives rise to a cause of action for damages rather than base our decision on any outworn notions of public policy. Public policy is a dangerous guide in determining the validity of a contract and courts should not interfere lightly with the freedom of competent parties to make their own contracts. We do not close our eyes to the fact that such agreements, tacitly or openly arrived at, are not uncommon, especially in close corporations where the stockholders are doing business for convenience under a corporate organization. We know that majority stockholders, united in voting trusts, effectively manage the business of a corporation by choosing trustworthy directors to reflect their policies in the corporate management. Nor are we unmindful that McQuade has, so the court has found, been shabbily treated as a purchaser of stock from Stoneham. We have said: 'A trustee is held to something stricter than the morals of the market place' (*Meinhard v. Salmon*, 249 N.Y. 458, 464, 164 N.E. 545, 546, 62 A.L.R. 1), but Stoneham and McGraw were not trustees for McQuade as an individual. Their duty was to the corporation and its stockholders, to be exercised according to their unrestricted lawful judgment. They were under no legal obligation to deal righteously with McQuade if it was against public policy to do so.

The courts do not enforce mere moral obligations, nor legal ones either, unless some one seeks to establish rights which may be waived by custom and for convenience. We are constrained by authority to hold that a contract is illegal and void so far as it precludes the board of directors, at the risk of incurring legal liability, from changing officers, salaries, or policies or retaining individuals in office, except by consent of the contracting parties. On the whole, such a holding is probably preferable to one which would open the courts to pass on the motives of directors in the lawful exercise of their trust.

The judgment of the Appellate Division and that of the Trial Term should be reversed and the complaint dismissed, with costs in all courts.

[Concurring opinion omitted]

CRANE, KELLOGG, O'BRIEN, and HUBBS, JJ., concur with POUND, C. J.

CLARK v. DODGE
Court of Appeals of New York
269 N.Y. 410, 199 N.E. 641 (1936)

CROUCH, JUDGE.

The action is for the specific performance of a contract between the plaintiff, Clark, and the defendant Dodge, relating to the affairs of the two defendant corporations. . . .

Th[e] facts, briefly stated, are as follows: The two corporate defendants are New Jersey corporations manufacturing medicinal preparations by secret formulae. The main office, factory, and assets of both corporations are located in the state of New York. In 1921, and at all times since, Clark owned 25 per cent and Dodge 75 per cent of the stock of each corporation. Dodge took no active part in the business, although he was a director, and through ownership of their qualifying shares, controlled the other directors of both corporations. He was the president of Bell & Co., Inc., and nominally general manager of Hollings-Smith Company, Inc. The plaintiff, Clark, was a director and held the offices of treasurer and general manager of Bell & Co., Inc., and also had charge of the major portion of the business of Hollings-Smith Company, Inc. The formulae and methods of manufacture of the medicinal preparations were known to him alone. Under date of February 15, 1921, Dodge and Clark, the sole owners of the stock of both corporations, entered into a written agreement under seal, which after reciting the stock ownership of both parties, the desire of Dodge that Clark should continue in the efficient management and control of the business of Bell & Co., Inc., so long as he should 'remain faithful, efficient and competent to so manage and control the said business'; and his further desire that Clark should not be the sole custodian of a specified formula, but should share his knowledge thereof and of the method of manufacture with a son of Dodge, provided, in substance, as follows: That Dodge during his lifetime and, after his death, a trustee to be appointed by his will, would so vote his stock and so vote as a director that the plaintiff (a) should continue to be a director of Bell & Co., Inc.; and (b) should continue as its general manager so long as he should be 'faithful, efficient and competent'; (c) should during his life receive one-fourth of the net income of the corporations either by way of salary or dividends; and (d) that no unreasonable or incommensurate salaries should be paid to other officers or agents which would so reduce the net income as materially to affect Clark's profits. Clark on his part agreed to disclose the specified formula to the son and to instruct him in the details and methods of manufacture; and, further, at the end of his life to bequeath his stock — if no issue survived him — to the wife and children of Dodge.

It was further provided that the provisions in regard to the division of net profits and the regulation of salaries should also apply to the Hollings-Smith Company.

The complaint alleges due performance of the contract by Clark and breach thereof by Dodge in that he has failed to use his stock control to continue Clark as a director and as general manager, and has prevented Clark from receiving his proportion of the income, while taking his own, by causing the employment of incompetent persons at excessive salaries, and otherwise.

The relief sought is reinstatement as director and general manager and an accounting by Dodge and by the corporations for waste and for the proportion of net income due plaintiff, with an injunction against further violations.

The only question which need be discussed is whether the contract is illegal as against public policy within the decision in *McQuade v. Stoneham*, 263 N.Y. 323, 189 N.E. 234, upon the authority of which the complaint was dismissed by the Appellate Division.

'The business of a corporation shall be managed by its board of directors.' General Corporation Law (Consol. Laws, c. 23) § 27. That is the statutory norm. Are we committed by the *McQuade* case to the doctrine that there may be no variation, however slight or innocuous, from that norm, where salaries or policies or the retention of individuals in office are concerned? There is ample authority supporting that doctrine. . . . Apart from its practical administrative convenience, the reasons upon which it is said to rest are more or less nebulous. Public policy, the intention of the Legislature, detriment to the corporation, are phrases which in this connection mean little. Possible harm to bona fide purchasers of stock or to creditors or to stockholding minorities have more substance; but such harms are absent in many instances. If the enforcement of a particular contract damages nobody — not even, in any perceptible degree, the public — one sees no reason for holding it illegal, even though it impinges slightly upon the broad provision of section 27. Damage suffered or threatened is a logical and practical test, and has come to be the one generally adopted by the courts. See 28 Colum. L. Rev. 366, 372. Where the directors are the sole stockholders, there seems to be no objection to enforcing an agreement among them to vote for certain people as officers. There is no direct decision to that effect in this court, yet there are strong indications that such a rule has long been recognized. The opinion *in Manson v. Curtis*, 223 N.Y. 313, 325, 119 N.E. 559, 562, Ann.Cas. 1918E, 247, closed its discussion by saying: 'The rule that all the stockholders by their universal consent may do as they choose with the corporate concerns and assets, provided the interests of creditors are not affected, because they are the complete owners of the corporation, cannot be invoked here.' That was because all the stockholders were not parties to the agreement there in question. So, where the public was not affected, 'the parties in interest, might, by their original agreement of incorporation, limit their respective rights and powers,' even where there was a conflicting statutory standard. *Ripin v. United States Woven Label Co.*, 205 N.Y. 442, 448, 98 N.E. 855, 857. 'Such corporations were little more (though not quite the same as) than chartered partnerships.' . . . The rule recognized in *Manson v. Curtis* . . . was thus stated by Blackmar, J., in *Kassel v. Empire Tinware Co.*, 178 App. Div. 176, 180, 164 N.Y.S. 1033, 1035: 'As the parties to the action are the complete owners of the corporation, there is no reason why the exercise of the power and discretion of the directors cannot be controlled by valid agreement between themselves, provided that the interests of creditors are not affected.'

. . .

[T]here can be no doubt that the agreement here in question was legal and that the complaint states a cause of action. There was no attempt to sterilize the board of directors, as in the *Manson* and *McQuade* cases. The only restrictions on Dodge were (a) that as a stockholder he should vote for Clark as a director — a perfectly legal contract; (b) that as director he should continue Clark as general manager, so long as he proved faithful, efficient, and competent — an agreement which could harm nobody; (c) that Clark should always receive as salary or dividends one-fourth of the 'net income.' For the purposes of this motion, it is only just to construe that phrase as meaning whatever was left for distribution after the directors had in good faith set aside whatever they deemed wise; (d) that no salaries to other officers should be paid, unreasonable in amount or incommensurate with services rendered — a beneficial and not a harmful agreement.

If there was any invasion of the powers of the directorate under that agreement, it is so slight as to be negligible; and certainly there is no damage suffered by or threatened [sic] to anybody. The broad statements in the *McQuade* opinion, applicable to the facts there, should be confined to those facts.

The judgment of the Appellate Division should be reversed and the order of the Special Term affirmed, with costs in this court and in the Appellate Division.

CRANE, C. J., and LEHMAN, O'BRIEN, HUBBS, LOUGHRAN, and FINCH, JJ., concur.

GALLER v. GALLER
Supreme Court of Illinois
32 Ill.2d 16, 203 N.E.2d 577 (1964)

UNDERWOOD, JUSTICE.

Plaintiff, Emma Galler, sued in equity for an accounting for specific performance of an agreement made in July, 1955, between plaintiff and her husband, of one part, and defendants, Isadore A. Galler and his wife, Rose, of the other. Defendants appealed from a decree of the superior court of Cook County granting the relief prayed. The First District Appellate Court reversed the decree and denied specific performance, affirming in part the order for an accounting, and modifying the order awarding master's fees. . . . That decision is appealed here on a certificate of importance.

There is no substantial dispute as to the facts in this case. From 1919 to 1924, Benjamin and Isadore Galler, brothers, were equal partners in the Galler Drug Company, a wholesale drug concern. In 1924 the business was incorporated under the Illinois Business Corporation Act, each owning one half of the outstanding 220 shares of stock. In 1945 each contracted to sell 6 shares to an employee, Rosenberg, at a price of $10,500 for each block of 6 shares, payable within 10 years. . . . Rosenberg was not involved in this litigation either as a party or as a witness, and in July of 1961, prior to the time that the master in chancery hearings were concluded, defendants Isadore and Rose Galler purchased the 12 shares from Rosenberg. A supplemental complaint was filed by the plaintiff, Emma Galler, asserting an equitable right to have 6 of the 12 shares transferred to her and offering to pay the defendants one half of the amount that the defendants paid Rosenberg. The parties have stipulated that pending disposition of the instant case, these shares will not be voted or transferred.

In March, 1954, Benjamin and Isadore, on the advice of their accountant, decided to enter into an agreement for the financial protection of their immediate families and to assure their families, after death of either brother, equal control of the corporation. . . . Between the execution of the agreement in July, 1955, and Benjamin's death in December, 1957, the agreement was not modified. . . . It appears from the evidence that some months after the agreement was signed, the defendants Isadore and Rose Galler and their son, the defendant, Aaron Galler sought to have the agreements destroyed. The evidence is undisputed that defendants had decided prior to

Benjamin's death they would not honor the agreement, but never disclosed their intention to plaintiff or her husband.

. . . .

Shortly after Benjamin's death, Emma went to the office and demanded the terms of the 1955 agreement be carried out. Isadore told her that anything she had to say could be said to Aaron, who then told her that his father would not abide by the agreement. He offered a modification of the agreement by proposing the salary continuation payment but without her becoming a director. When Emma refused to modify the agreement and sought enforcement of its terms, defendants refused and this suit followed.

During the last few years of Benjamin's life both brothers drew an annual salary of $42,000. Aaron, whose salary was $15,000 as manager of the warehouse prior to September, 1956, has since the time that Emma agreed to his acting as president drawn an annual salary of $20,000. In 1957, 1958, and 1959 a $40,000 annual dividend was paid. Plaintiff has received her proportionate share of the dividend.

The July, 1955, agreement in question here, entered into between Benjamin, Emma, Isadore and Rose, recites that Benjamin and Isadore each own 47 ½% of the issued and outstanding shares of the Galler Drug Company, an Illinois corporation, and that Benjamin and Isadore desired to provide income for the support and maintenance of their immediate families. No reference is made to the shares then being purchased by Rosenberg. The essential features of the contested portions of the agreement are substantially as set forth in the opinion of the Appellate Court: (2) that the bylaws of the corporation will be amended to provide for a board of four directors; that the necessary quorum shall be three directors; and that no directors' meeting shall be held without giving ten days notice to all directors. (3) The shareholders will cast their votes for the above named persons (Isadore, Rose, Benjamin and Emma) as directors at said special meeting and at any other meeting held for the purpose of electing directors. (4, 5) In the event of the death of either brother his wife shall have the right to nominate a director in place of the decedent. (6) Certain annual dividends will be declared by the corporation. The dividend shall be $50,000 payable out of the accumulated earned surplus in excess of $500,000. If 50% of the annual net profits after taxes exceeds the minimum $50,000, then the directors shall have discretion to declare a dividend up to 50% of the annual net profits. If the net profits are less than $50,000, nevertheless the minimum $50,000 annual dividend shall be declared, providing the $500,000 surplus is maintained. Earned surplus is defined. (9) The certificates evidencing the said shares of Benjamin Galler and Isadore Galler shall be a legend that the shares are subject to the terms of this agreement. (10) A salary continuation agreement shall be entered into by the corporation which shall authorize the corporation upon the death of Benjamin Galler or Isadore Galler, or both, to pay a sum equal to twice the salary of such officer, payable monthly over a five-year period. Said sum shall be paid to the widow during her widowhood, but should be paid to such widow's children if the widow remarries within the five-year period. The parties to this agreement further agree and hereby grant to the corporation the authority to purchase, in the event of the death of either Benjamin or Isadore, so much of the stock of Galler Drug Company held by the estate as is necessary to provide sufficient funds to pay the federal estate tax, the Illinois inheritance tax and other administrative expenses of the estate. If as a result of such purchase from the estate of the decedent the amount of dividends to be received by the heirs is reduced, the parties shall nevertheless vote for directors so as to give the estate and heirs the same representation as before (2 directors out of 4, even though they own less stock), and also that the corporation pay an additional benefit payment equal to the diminution of the dividends. In the event either Benjamin or Isadore decides to sell his shares he is required to offer them first to the remaining shareholders and then to the corporation at book value, according each six months to accept the offer.

The Appellate Court found the 1955 agreement void because 'the undue duration, stated purpose and substantial disregard of the provisions of the Corporation Act outweigh any considerations which might call for divisibility' and held that 'the public policy of this state demands voiding this entire agreement.'

While the conduct of defendant towards plaintiff was clearly inequitable, the basically controlling factor is the absence of an objecting minority interest, together with the absence of public detriment. . . .

At this juncture it should be emphasized that we deal here with a so-called close corporation. . . . For our purposes, a close corporation is one in which the stock is held in a few hands, or in a few families, and wherein it is not at all, or only rarely, dealt in by buying or selling . . . Moreover, it should be recognized that shareholder agreements similar to that in question here are often, as a practical consideration, quite necessary for the protection of those financially interested in the close corporation. While the shareholder of a public issue corporation may readily sell his shares on the open market should management fail to use, in his opinion, sound business judgment, his counterpart of the close corporation often has a large total of his entire capital invested in the business and his no ready market for his shares should he desire to sell. He feels, understandably, that he is more than a mere investor and that his voice should be heard concerning all corporate activity. Without a shareholder agreement, specifically enforceable by the courts, insuring him a modicum of control, a large minority shareholder might find himself at the mercy of an oppressive or unknowledgeable majority. Moreover, as in the case at bar, the shareholders of a close corporation are often also the directors and officers thereof. With substantial shareholding interests abiding in each member of the board of directors, it is often quite impossible to secure, as in the large public issue corporation, independent board judgment free from personal motivations concerning corporate policy. For these and other reasons too voluminous to enumerate here, often the only sound basis for protection is afforded by a lengthy, detailed shareholder agreement securing the rights and obligations of all concerned. For a discussion of these and other considerations, see Note, A Plea for Separate Statutory Treatment of the Close Corporation, 33 N.Y.U.L. Rev. 700 (1958). . . .

[T]here has been a definite, albeit inarticulate, trend toward eventual judicial treatment of the close corporation as *sui generis*. Several shareholder-director agreements that have technically 'violate' the letter of the Business Corporation Act have nevertheless been upheld in the light of the existing practical circumstances, i.e., no apparent public injury, the absence of a complaining minority interest, and no apparent prejudice to creditors. However, we have thus far not attempted to limit these decisions as applicable only to close corporations and have seemingly implied that general considerations regarding judicial supervision of all corporate behavior apply . . .

It is therefore necessary, we feel, to discuss the instant case with the problems peculiar to the close corporation particularly in mind.

It would admittedly facilitate judicial supervision of corporate behavior if a strict adherence to the provisions of the Business Corporation Act were required in all cases without regard to the practical exigencies peculiar to the close corporation . . . However, courts have long ago quite realistically, we feel, relaxed their attitudes concerning statutory compliance when dealing with close corporate behavior, permitting 'slight deviations' from corporate 'norms' in order to give legal efficacy to common business practice (citations omitted).

Again, 'As the parties to the action are the complete owners of the corporation, there is no reason why the exercise of the power and discretion of the directors cannot be controlled by valid agreement between themselves, provided that the interests of creditors are not affected.' *Clark v. Dodge*, 199 N.E. 641, 643, quoting from *Kassel v. Empire Tinware Co.*, 178 App.Div. 176, 180, 164 N.Y.S. 1033, 1035. . . .

This court has recognized, albeit *sub silentio*, the significant conceptual differences between the close corporation and its public issue counterpart in, among other cases, *Kantzler v. Bensinger*, 214 Ill. 589, 73 N.E. 874, where an agreement quite similar to the one under attack here was upheld. Where, as in *Kantzler* and here, no complaining minority interest appears, no fraud or apparent injury to the public or creditors is present, and no clearly prohibitory statutory language is violated, we can see no valid reason for precluding the parties from reaching any arrangements concerning the management of the corporation which are agreeable to all. . . .

Since the question as to the duration of the agreement is a principal source of controversy, we shall consider it first. The parties provided no specific termination date, and while the agreement concludes with a paragraph that its terms 'shall be binding upon and shall inure to the benefits of' the legal representatives, heirs and assigns of the parties, this clause is, we believe, intended to be operative only as long as one of the parties is living. It further provides that it shall be so construed as to carry out its purposes, and we believe these must be determined from a consideration of the agreement as a whole. Thus viewed, a fair construction is that its purposes were accomplished at the death of the survivor of the parties. While these life spans are not precisely ascertainable, and the Appellate Court noted Emma Galler's life expectancy at her husband's death was 26.9 years, we are aware of no statutory or public policy provision against stockholder's agreements which would invalidate this agreement on that ground. . . . While defendants argue that the public policy evinced by the legislative restrictions upon the duration of voting trust agreements . . . should be applied here, this agreement is not a voting trust, but . . . is a straight contractual voting control agreement which does not divorce voting rights from stock ownership. . . . In view of the history of decisions of this court generally upholding, in the absence of fraud or prejudice to minority interests or public policy, the right of stockholders to agree among themselves as to the manner in which their stock will be voted, we do not regard the period of time within which this agreement may remain effective as rendering the agreement unenforceable.

The clause that provides for the election of certain persons to specified offices for a period of years likewise does not require invalidation. In *Kantzler v. Bensinger*, 214 Ill. 589, 73 N.E. 874, this court upheld an agreement entered into by all the stockholders providing that certain parties would be elected to the offices of the corporation for a fixed period. In *Faulds v. Yates*, 57 Ill. 416, we upheld a similar agreement among the majority stockholders of a corporation, notwithstanding the existence of a minority which was not before the court complaining thereof [citation omitted].

We turn next to a consideration of the effect of the stated purpose of the agreement upon its validity. The pertinent provision is: 'The said Benjamin A. Galler and Isadore A. Galler desire to provide income for the support and maintenance of their immediate families.' Obviously, there is no evil inherent in a contract entered into for the reason that the persons originating the terms desired to so arrange their property as to provide post-death support for those dependent upon them. Nor does the fact that the subject property is corporate stock alter the situation so long as there exists no detriment to minority stock interests, creditors or other public injury. . . .

The terms of the dividend agreement require a minimum annual dividend of $50,000, but this duty is limited by the subsequent provision that it shall be operative only so long as an earned surplus of $500,000 is maintained. It may be noted that in 1958, the year prior to commencement of this litigation, the corporation's net earnings after taxes amounted to $202,759 while its earned surplus was $1,543,270, and this was increased in 1958 to $1,680,079 while earnings were $172,964. The minimum earned surplus requirement is designed for the protection of the corporation and its creditors, and we take no exception to the contractual dividend requirements as thus restricted. . . .

The salary continuation agreement is a common feature, in one form or another, of corporate executive employment. It requires that the widow should receive a total benefit, payable monthly over a five-year period, aggregating twice the amount paid her deceased husband in one year. This requirement was likewise limited for the protection of the corporation by being contingent upon the payments being income tax deductible by the corporation. The charge made in those cases which have considered the validity of payments to the widow of an officer and shareholder in a corporation is that a gift of its property by a noncharitable corporation is in violation of the rights of its shareholders and ultra vires. Since there are no shareholders here other than the parties to the contract, this objection is not here applicable, and its effect, as limited, upon the corporation is not so prejudicial as so require its invalidation. . . .

We hold defendants must account for all monies received by them from the corporation since September 25, 1956, in excess of that theretofore authorized. . . .

Affirmed in part and reversed in part, and remanded with directions.

NOTES AND QUESTIONS

1. The courts historically have been restrictive in their refusal to uphold significant deviations from the traditional statutory norms of corporate governance, particularly in the absence of shareholder unanimity. After all, these traditional statutory norms were established for publicly held corporations long before the corporation became a popular form of choice for small, closely held corporations. *See* MBCA § 7.32, Official Comment. State legislatures sought to relax traditional restrictions by enacting close corporation statutes that would permit corporations held by a modest number of shareholders to opt in to more flexible and informal corporate governance schemes. These statutes authorized shareholders to enter agreements on corporate management and related matters that might otherwise be challenged as invalid departures from statutory norms. It should be noted that close corporation statutes defined close corporations much more broadly than the courts in cases like *Donahue v. Rodd Electrotype, Inc.*, *supra*, which defined closely held corporations, in part, as corporations with substantial majority stockholder participation in the management, direction and operations of the businesses. Instead, these statutory close corporations are generally defined quantitatively, e.g., as corporations held by a certain number of shareholders regardless of majority participation in management. *See, e.g.*, DEL. GEN. CORP. LAW § 342 (corporations held by less than 30 shareholders).

While these statutes had theoretical appeal, statutory close corporations were never generally accepted in practice. From the beginning, attorneys were reluctant to cause their corporate clients to opt in. This was possibly due to their unfamiliarity with the concept and numerous uncertainties regarding judicial interpretation, particularly issues related to subsequent business combinations and conversions to *normal* corporation status. Moreover, the general incorporation statutes were later broadly revised to permit shareholders in many non-publicly held corporations to enter shareholder agreements that substantially departed from traditional corporate governance norms. *See, e.g.*, MBCA § 7.32, discussed *supra*, at page 352; N.Y. BUS. CORP. LAW § 620. Consequently, only a small fraction of newly formed corporations have elected treatment as statutory close corporations. *See generally*, 1 O'NEAL AND THOMPSON'S CLOSE CORPORATIONS AND LLCS § 1.20 (3d ed. 2004).

2. Today, only a small minority of jurisdictions require corporations to opt in to statutory close corporation status before shareholders are permitted to develop their own private agreements concerning corporate governance. The question has arisen in several of those jurisdictions as to the effect of a closely held corporation's failure to opt in formally to become a statutory close corporation. For example, in *Ramos v. Estrada*, 8 Cal. App. 4th 1070, 10 Cal. Rptr. 2d 833 (1992), the court did not invalidate a shareholders' agreement that significantly impinged shareholder voting rights despite the corporation's failure to elect close corporation status. This was a likely result because California Corporation Code § 706 specifically provided that its close corporation provisions allowing such agreements would not invalidate otherwise legal shareholder voting agreements.

The Delaware court in *Nixon v. Blackwell*, 626 A.2d 1366 (Del. 1993) reached the opposite result. Under the Delaware General Corporation Law § 341, only corporations that satisfy the criteria and actually elect close corporation status may avail themselves of the special provisions authorizing broad shareholder flexibility in crafting corporate governance arrangements. However, the court in *Nixon* went considerably further by holding that the Delaware statute's special provisions for close corporations preempted the field in the areas covered. Consequently, the court refused to fashion any additional judicial rules for the protection of minority shareholders in a corporation that failed to elect close corporation status. In this case, the minority shareholders sued the directors, who were employee shareholders, and the corporation for breach of fiduciary duty for providing shareholder liquidity, through employee stock ownership plans (ESOPs) and key man life insurance, only to employee shareholders of the corporation. In essence, the plaintiffs wanted *Donahue's* equal opportunity rule to be fashioned and applied by the Delaware court to the non-employee shareholders. In refusing to do so, the Delaware court noted that the same result might have been reached even if the corporation actually had been a "statutory" close corporation. *Nixon*, 626 A.2d at 1380.

It should be noted that even the *Donahue* court may have reached the same result if it had been confronted with facts similar to those presented in *Nixon*. First, while the Delaware corporation in *Nixon* was non-publicly held, it did not have substantial majority shareholder participation in the business' management, direction, and operations. Moreover, the plaintiffs were neither founders nor employees and had no frustrated expectations from the time of their investments. And, perhaps most importantly, the plaintiffs in *Nixon* did not assert that they and all their fellow shareholders were fiduciaries of each other. Certainly, the facts did not suggest such a reposal of trust and confidence. Accordingly, the quasi-partnership fiduciary duties of shareholders in closely held corporations were not at issue.

3. Modern statutes, in providing greater contractual freedom to shareholders of non-publicly held corporations, have followed the basic legal maxim that greater power should be accompanied by greater responsibility. Where shareholders have entered agreements granting themselves managerial power while depriving the board of directors of its traditional managerial authority, these shareholders properly assume the fiduciary duties of those directors. This works the restoration of the power and responsibility symmetry previously discussed.

The Model Act expressly relieves directors from liability for breach of fiduciary duties and imposes that liability on shareholders to the extent those shareholders have been granted directorial power under a shareholders' agreement. *See* MBCA § 7.32(e). Similarly Delaware's close corporation provisions "relieve the directors and impose upon the shareholders who are parties to the agreement the liability for managerial acts or omissions which is imposed on directors to the extent and so long as the discretion or powers of the board in its management of corporate affairs is controlled by such agreement." DEL. GEN. CORP. LAW § 350. These modern corporate statutes have developed a recalibrating symmetry of power and responsibility, imposing directorial fiduciary duties on shareholders to the extent that managerial powers have been assumed. It should be noted that these duties have been statutorily imposed independently of any preexisting duties owed to the corporation as officers, directors, or controlling shareholders, or owed to fellow shareholders by shareholders of closely held corporations. To what extent do you believe courts would judicially impose similar directorial duties on shareholders assuming directorial power even in the absence of statutory provisions?

5.   Restrictions on Transfers of Shares

a.   Introductory Note

Restrictions on the transfer of shares in a closely held corporation may be set forth in a corporation's articles of incorporation, bylaws or in a shareholders' agreement among all or certain shareholders or among the corporation and all or certain of its shareholders. *See, e.g.*, MBCA § 6.27(a). The major purposes of these restrictions is to limit transfers to third parties and, accordingly, control the entry of new participants in the enterprise. This is especially important for closely held corporations, as incorporated partnerships, whose shareholders are unlikely to desire new co-owners with difficult personalities or different business objectives. Moreover, they do not want the corporation's shares to fall into the hands of competitors who would gain access to the corporate books and records. Transfer restrictions are particularly important to family-owned businesses, whose shareholders usually prefer the business to remain in the family. The other primary purpose of these restrictions is to provide liquidity for the shareholders of closely held corporations. Stock transfer restrictions can be structured to create a private contractual market for the shares through various types of specially designed provisions. These include, among others, mandatory buy-out agreements, which require the corporation to buy and the shareholder to sell upon termination of his employment, require his spouse to sell shares held prior to or a result of divorce, or require his estate to sell upon his death.

Restrictions on transfer of shares, though an essential control device for shareholders in closely held corporations, historically collided with the core common law principles favoring the free transfer of personal property, abhorring restraints on alienation, strictly construing such constraints, and invalidating them if determined to be unreasonable. Today, most state corporation statutes have provisions permitting the imposition of transfer restrictions if for "any reasonable purpose." The Model Business Corporation Act provides that share transfer restrictions are authorized (1) to maintain the corporation's status, when it is dependent on the number or identity of its shareholders, e.g., IRC Subchapter S eligibility; (2) to preserve exemptions under federal or state securities laws, e.g., SEC Regulation D; and (3) *for any other reasonable purpose*. MBCA § 6.27(c). The Model Act then expressly authorizes, without limitation, the following kinds of restrictions on the transfer of shares:

1.   first offer restrictions that obligate the shareholder to *first offer* the corporation or other persons (separately, consecutively, or simultaneously) an opportunity to buy the shares;

2.   mandatory buy-out restrictions that obligate the corporation or other persons to acquire the shares;

3.   consent restrictions that require the corporation or other persons to approve any proposed transfer of shares, if not *manifestly unreasonable;* and

4.   marketability restrictions that prohibit the transfer of the shares to designated persons or classes of persons, if not *manifestly unreasonable*. MBCA § 6.27(d).

The Model Act further provides that transfer restrictions do not effect shareholders who purchased the shares *before* the restriction was adopted unless such shareholders voted in favor of the restriction or are parties to the shareholder agreement that imposed them. MBCA § 6.27(a). The transfer restriction is valid against shareholders who purchased the shares *after* the restriction was adopted if the restriction is conspicuously noted on the share certificate. Unless the restriction is noted on the certificate (or an information statement if uncertificated), the restriction cannot be enforced against a person without knowledge of the restriction. MBCA § 6.27(b).

b. First Options and Refusals

The "first offer" restriction expressly authorized by the Model Act, § 6.27(d)(1), actually includes two basic types of stock transfer restrictions, *first refusals* and *first options*. First refusals prohibit the sale of shares to a third party unless first offered to the corporation or its shareholders on the same terms, including price, offered to that third party. This is the least restrictive type of transfer restraint and is virtually always upheld by the courts. *See, e.g., Groves v. Pickett*, 420 F.2d 1119 (9th Cir. 1970). First options prohibit the sale of the shares to a third party unless first offered to the corporation or its shareholders at a specific *price* or at a price determined by a formula set forth in the restriction. This type of restriction is generally upheld as a reasonable restraint on alienation. *See, e.g., In re Estate of Mather, infra; Lash v. Lash Furniture Co., infra.*

IN RE ESTATE OF MATHER
Supreme Court of Pennsylvania
189 A.2d 586 (1963)

BELL, CHIEF JUSTICE.

The Executors of the Estate of Gilbert Mather took this appeal from a decree which entered judgment on the pleadings and ordered specific performance of a written stock option agreement. The Executors claim the agreement was invalid as *an unreasonable restraint on alienation*, because the optional purchase price was fixed at $1.00 per share, which was only a small fraction of the stock's actual value.

. . . .

The . . . written agreement[] . . . [was] made between mature members of a close family and it is conceded that there was no overreaching or fraud or deceit. The facts and the lawfulness of the purpose were admitted by appellants. However, appellants argue that the agreement was *an invalid restraint on alienation* because the price was clearly very *unfair* and *unchangeable*. . . . Moreover, we repeat, the agreement clearly and expressly set forth the *intention* of all the parties — they wanted to keep the family business in the Mather family and to give each other and their personal representatives the options, rights and obligations hereinabove recited. There was a limited but not an absolute restriction on sale, since if the option was not exercised by a living signatory to the family agreement 'the holder of said stock or his personal representatives shall have the right to sell same upon the open market without restrictions.' In this free land of ours where even a State can not impair the obligations of a contract, we cannot understand how it can be seriously contended that this written family agreement, and family agreements are always favored in the law — when made by adult business men without any overreaching or fraud, is 'a scrap of paper.'

. . . .

'The question posed, therefore, is whether the provision, according the corporation a right or first option to purchase the stock at the price which it originally received for it, amounts to an unreasonable restraint. In our judgment, it does not.

'The courts have almost uniformly held valid and enforcible [sic] the first option provision, in charter or by-law, whereby a shareholder desirous of selling his stock is required to afford the corporation, his fellow stockholders or both an opportunity to buy it before he is free to offer it to outsiders [citations omitted]. The courts have often said that this first option provision is 'in the nature of a contract' between the corporation and its stockholders and, as such, binding upon them [citations omitted]. In *Doss v. Yingling*, . . . 95 Ind. App. 494, 172 N.E. 801, a leading case on the subject and one frequently cited throughout the country, a by-law provision against transfer by any stockholder — there were three — of any shares until they had first been offered for sale to other stockholders at *book value*, was sustained as reasonable and valid, 95 Ind. App. at page 500, 172 N.E. at page 803: 'The weight of authority is to the effect that a corporate by-law which requires the owner of the stock to give the other stockholders of the corporation . . . *an option to purchase the same at an agreed price or the then-existing book value before offering the stock for sale to an outsider, is a valid and reasonable restriction and binding upon the stockholders.*"

Another familiar example of the application of the restraint on alienation principle, is an attempted fettering of an absolute gift or grant of a fee, by a restraint on alienation or sale [citations omitted]. More recently the principle has been applied, on Constitutional grounds, to restraints on alienation to persons except those of the Caucasian race. *Shelley v. Kraemer*, 334 U.S. 1, 68 S.Ct. 836, 92 L.Ed. 1161; *Barrows v. Jackson*, 346 U.S. 249, 73 S.Ct. 1031, 97 L.Ed. 1586.

. . . .

To summarize: We find no merit in appellants' contention that where there is no overreaching or fraud, the great difference between the sale price and the actual value of the stock is sufficient, alone or with the aforesaid additional facts, to invalidate the agreement or defeat specific performance.

Decree affirmed, costs to be paid by appellants.

MR. JUSTICE COHEN files a dissenting opinion.

COHEN, JUSTICE (dissenting).

The majority here fails to recognize, and hence does not discuss, the manner in which this agreement differs from the usual first option agreement. Here, the agreement creates an absolute restraint against transfers and provides for a first refusal price which is unconscionably nominal in relation to the value of the shares *at the time the arrangement was made*. I would hold where an agreement entered into at a time when the actual value of the stock is $50 or more a share, which agreement prohibits the sale of shares by any party during his life-time without first offering the same to the other shareholders at a price of $1.00 per share, that the imposition of this nominal and unvariable pre-emption price creates an unreasonable restraint upon the alienability of the shares and imposes an invalid restriction on their transfer. See Sparks, '*Future Interests*' 32 N.Y.U. Law Rev. 1434 (1957); Baker and Cary, Cases and Materials on Corporations, 322–26 (3d ed. 1958).

The fact that the parties have entered into the agreement of their own free will cannot validate provisions which are void as against public policy; nor does the fact that there was no overreaching or that Gilbert Mather himself bought shares at $1.00 per share from Victor Mather's executors legalize an unreasonable restraint on alienation.

I dissent.

LASH v. LASH FURNITURE COMPANY OF BARRE
Supreme Court of Vermont
130 Vt. 517, 296 A.2d 207 (1972)

BARNEY, JUSTICE.

This is an action in equity relating to stock transfers and management of a corporation. It is also a family dispute involving one of the furniture stores established by the late Myron Lash of Burlington. This particular store is in Barre and, at the time with which this equity action is concerned, three Lash Brothers owned all of the voting stock of that Barre store, the Lash Furniture Company of Barre, Inc., in equal shares. . . .

The dispute arose as a consequence of the sale, by Wallace Lash, of his stock holdings in the Barre operation. Ralph Lash was the ultimate purchaser. The transfer was challenged because of a corporate bylaw requiring that any stock sold be first offered to the corporation at the proposed price. This offer was, in fact, made, but under circumstances which generated an attack on the transaction by the plaintiff.

The corporation, by vote, rejected the opportunity to purchase. Each brother had four voting shares. Wallace, as seller, did not vote. Ralph voted against purchase of the stock by the corporation and Herman voted in favor of accepting the offer. Thus, the transaction was not authorized and was lost to the corporation. This was in April or May, 1967.

In June, 1967, Ralph Lash bought Wallace's stock. This gave him effective control of the Barre corporation, since he then held two-thirds of the voting stock. . . .

This lawsuit seeks to reverse that acquisition of Wallace's stock. . . .

The chancellor, by his judgment order, found that the facts supported a determination that Ralph Lash's fiduciary duty toward Lash Furniture Company of Barre, Inc. barred him from retaining his rights to the purchased shares of stock. Ralph disputes this ruling by pointing to a number of cases that say, in substance, that there is nothing by way of fiduciary duty, without more, that precludes officers and directors from buying and selling stock in the corporation which they direct or manage. . . .

This Court does not see that as the true issue. The problem originates with the vote by the stockholders and directors, they being identical in this case, to reject the purchase of Wallace's stock. The price was concededly fair, and, with admirable sensitivity for his own position as seller, Wallace did not vote on the question of purchase then before them. As has been noted, Ralph opposed it, while Herman took the opposite side. . . .

There is a fiduciary duty in directors of corporations not to let outside commitments, personal or otherwise, divert them from their duty to further the interests of the company they represent. The presence of competing interests may disqualify the directors from acting in a representative capacity. . . . The interest of Ralph in purchasing the stock himself conflicted with his obligation to evaluate the purchase or non-purchase of such stock from the standpoint of benefit to the corporation.

The facts found by the master determined that Ralph's concern with the disposition of the stock was based, not on his fiduciary responsibilities, but on his personal interests, including his desire to acquire control of the Barre corporation. This was, of course, a rejection by Ralph of the duty to decide the question on the basis of proper corporate policy. *Creed v. Copps*, 103 Vt. 164, 168, 152 A. 369 (1930). This finding and the other facts in the case thus, in our view, differentiate it from the circumstances of *Boss v. Boss*, 98 R.I. 146, 200 A.2d 231 (1964). The order requiring the transfer of the stock to the corporation is affirmed. . . .

c. Mandatory Buy-Outs

The second restriction expressly authorized by the Model Business Corporation Act, § 6.27(d)(2), refers to another basic type of transfer restraint, mandatory buy-out agreements. There are several variations of mandatory buy-out agreements. Where the *shareholders* agree to a mandatory obligation to buy a shareholder's shares upon the termination of employment, death, or other prescribed triggering event, it is generally referred to as a *buy-sell* or *cross-purchase agreement*. Where the shareholders and the corporation agree to a mandatory obligation to buy a shareholders' shares upon a triggering event, it is generally referred to as a *redemption agreement*. Redemption agreements are generally funded by life insurance policies maintained by the corporation on the lives of each of the shareholders. Both these agreements are particularly advantageous to the selling shareholder or deceased shareholder's estate by providing liquidity for shares which otherwise have no market. Another variation of the mandatory buy-out agreement is the reciprocal put or Russian roulette buy-out provision. It is especially useful in resolving deadlock where two shareholders or voting blocks owning equal voting rights are fundamentally opposed to each other. The provision permits either shareholder to offer to sell his shares to the other shareholder on specific terms and at a certain price, but on the condition that, if the offer is refused, the offeror shareholder is obligated to buy and the offeree shareholder is obligated to sell his shares on the offered terms and price. This variation is commonly used by shareholders in closely held corporations, although it does advantage the shareholder with the greater financial resources.

d.   Consent Restraints

The third restriction specifically approved and identified in the Model Business Corporation Act, § 6.27(d)(3), is that type of share transfer restraint that has encountered the greatest resistance from the courts, the so-called *consent restraint.* *See, e.g., Rafe v. Hindin*, 288 N.Y.S.2d 662, *aff'd*, 296 N.Y.S.2d 955, 244 N.E.2d 649 (1968). Its requirement that shareholders desiring to sell their shares to a third party must first obtain the approval of the corporation's board of directors or shareholders is, to say the least, highly restrictive of the shareholder's right to transfer the shares. Although courts have become more tolerant of consent restraints in recent years, considerable uncertainly remains. Obviously, their legality is dependent in Model Act states on a given court's interpretation of the statutory phrase, "manifestly unreasonable."

e.   Marketability Restraints

The final restriction approved in the Model Business Corporation Act, § 6.27(d)(4) are those that prohibit a shareholder's sale of his shares to designated persons or types of persons so long as not manifestly unreasonable. This type of share transfer restraint generally is used to restrict resales to competitors and their affiliates. However, courts are likely to view them with suspicion if they arbitrarily single out specific potential buyers or if they so narrowly limit potential buyers that the opportunity to sell the shares is virtually eliminated. Again, the legality of this type of restraint depends on a given court's view of whether it is unreasonable under the circumstances.

f.   Judicial Interpretation

Restrictions on transfers of shares, because they cut across the grain of the common law, present continual interpretive dilemmas for the courts. Although legislatures have enacted corporate laws approving the broad use of stock transfer restrictions, the courts continue to construe them as narrowly as possible to promote free transferability. Some courts have held that restrictions on transfer are inapplicable to transfers among existing shareholders. *See, e.g., Remillong v. Schneider*, 185 N.W.2d 493 (N.D. 1971). Other courts have been reluctant to apply stock transfer restrictions to transfers incident to divorce, at least where the divorced spouse was not made a party to the agreement that imposed the restrictions. *See, e.g., Durkee v. Durkee-Mower Co.*, 428 N.E.2d 139 (Mass. 1981); *Castonguary v. Castonguary*, 306 N.W.2d 143 (Minn. 1981). Similar resistance has occurred with respect to testamentary transfers. Frequently, this judicial resistance is explained by a failure of the drafters to explicitly state the breadth of the restriction. Any ambiguities will be interpreted in favor of free transferability. To help further ensure enforceability, many lawyers incorporate restrictions in the articles of incorporation. Some impose a condition to any permitted transfer, whether to another shareholder, employee, divorcee, donee, devisee, legatee, or other transferee, that the acquiring shareholder join in the transfer restriction agreement, agreeing that the acquired shares, with appropriate legend, continue to be subject to the terms of that agreement.

g.   Pricing Provisions

One of the more critical provisions in any type of share transfer restraint is the provision that sets the price or pricing formula to be applied when a triggering event occurs. It is vital that the provision be tightly drafted to eliminate any ambiguities and that the parties fully understand the pricing terms. Each of the parties should concur, at a time when they remain objective, that the pricing mechanism is fair and reasonable. In order to preempt conflict when the provision is ultimately utilized, the pricing term should reflect an approach that would achieve an arm's length bargain among unrelated parties. Although pricing itself should not be determinative of the share transfer restraint's validity, a manifestly unreasonable price often impacts a court's willingness to enforce the restraint. In one case, a court found that a requirement that a terminated employee sell his shares back to the corporation at the price he paid for the shares constituted an impermissible forfeiture and excessive liquidated damages. *See Man O War Restaurants, Inc. v. Martin*, 932 S.W.2d 366 (Ky. 1996). That court emphasized that the price set should bear some relation to its actual current value. Most courts have been far more tolerant of pricing terms that result in large discrepancies between the price set and fair value. *See, e.g., In re Estate of Mather, supra.* However, caution still favors an arm's length pricing mechanism. The following pricing alternatives are among the more commonly used in presetting prices in share transfer restraints:

(i) Book Value

Perhaps the most common approach to pricing shares under share transfer restraints is to value the shares based on their book value or net asset value. It is a readily ascertainable number because it is reflected in the corporation's financial statements and is generally familiar to the parties. The inherent weakness in this approach is that book value, reflecting asset values at their historical cost, may significantly undervalue the current worth of the corporation's assets. This approach is also particularly harsh in pricing shares of companies engaged in providing services, since much of their value is represented by goodwill rather than hard assets typical of more capital intensive manufacturing companies. *See, e.g., Jones v. Harris*, 388 P.2d 539 (Wash. 1964).

(ii) Capitalized Earnings

Another common approach to valuation of shares under share transfer restraints is to develop a formula based on the corporation's earnings. Of course, this formula must be accompanied by a clear definition of earnings to be calculated and an appropriate capitalization rate to be applied. For the closely held corporation, this approach has several major disadvantages. First, it is very difficult to devise a formula that takes into account abnormal years and non-recurring profits and losses. Second, the corporation's earnings are often distributed to employee-shareholders in the form of salaries, thereby significantly reducing the amount of earnings and their reliability as a factor in valuation. Third, the corporation's future earnings may be adversely impacted by the departure of the selling shareholder. And lastly, for closely held businesses still in the development stage, earnings are unlikely to provide a reliable gauge of the corporation's future earnings potential.

(iii) Periodic Revisions

A third approach to valuation of shares that is commonly used is to set a price per share at the time the provision is approved, subject to re-evaluation at regular intervals. Another variation is to establish a formula, e.g., two times book value, subject to review and possible revisions at periodic intervals. The disadvantage of this approach is that the parties fail to monitor the price or formula at periodic intervals or become deadlocked in their attempts at revision.

(iv) Appraisals

A fourth common approach to valuation of shares is to provide for the appointment of an appraiser. This approach may also be used in conjunction with the periodic revisions approach where, triggered, for example, by a failure of the parties to agree on a revised price within a set period of time following the re-evaluation date. This approach sometimes involves the appointment of several appraisers, with the price to be established by consensus.

6. Fiduciary Duties in Implementing Restrictions on Transfer

This chapter began with an extensive review of the common law fiduciary duties applicable to shareholders in closely held corporations, duties that each shareholder owes to the other. Moreover, it has long been established that majority shareholders have common law fiduciary duties independent of their shareholder status as quasi-partners of an incorporated partnership. The following opinions reflect the recurring issue of whether and to what extent these fiduciary duties are invoked in the creation and implementation of share transfer restraints, particularly mandatory buy-outs. Some courts have been more deferential to contract, perhaps inappropriately elevating contractual considerations over fiduciary responsibilities. *See, e.g., Gallagher v. Lambert*, below. Other courts have responded more sympathetically to minority shareholders subjected to unreasonable hardship. *See, e.g., Pedro v. Pedro*, which follows.

GALLAGHER v. LAMBERT
Court of Appeals of New York
549 N.E.2d 136 (1989)

Bellacosa, Judge.

Plaintiff Gallagher purchased stock in the defendant close corporation with which he was employed. The purchase of his 8.5% interest was subject to a mandatory buy-back provision: if the employment ended for any reason before January 31, 1985, the stock would return to the corporation for book value. The corporation fired plaintiff prior to the fulcrum date, after which the buy-back price would have been higher.

We must decide whether plaintiff's dismissed causes of action, seeking the higher repurchase price based on an alleged breach of a fiduciary duty, should be reinstated. We think not and affirm, concluding that the Appellate Division did not err in dismissing these causes of action by summary judgment because there was no cognizable breach of any fiduciary duty owed to plaintiff under the plain terms of the parties' repurchase agreement.

Gallagher was employed by defendant Eastdil Realty as a mortgage broker from 1968 to 1973. Three years later, in 1976, he returned to the company as a broker, officer and director, serving additionally as president and chief executive officer of defendant's wholly owned subsidiary, Eastdil Advisors, Inc. Gallagher was at all times an employee at will. Still later, in 1981, Eastdil offered all its executive employees an opportunity to purchase stock subject to a mandatory buy-back provision, which provided that upon "voluntary resignation or other termination" prior to January 31, 1985, an employee would be required to return the stock for book value. After that date, the formula for the buy-back price was keyed to the company's earnings. Plaintiff accepted the offer and its terms.

On January 10, 1985, Gallagher was fired by Eastdil Realty. He did not and does not now contest the firing. But he demanded payment for his shares calculated on the post-January 31, 1985 buy-back formula. Eastdil refused and Gallagher sued, asserting eight causes of action. Only three claims, based on an alleged breach of fiduciary duty of good faith and fair dealing, are before us. The trial court denied defendants' motion for summary judgment on these claims, stating that factual issues were raised relating to defendants' motive in firing plaintiff. The Appellate Division, by divided vote, reversed, dismissed those claims and ordered payment for the shares at book value. 143 A.D.2d 313, 532 N.Y.S.2d 255. That court then granted leave and certified the following question to us: "Was the order of this Court, which modified the order of the Supreme Court, properly made?"

The parties negotiated a written contract containing a common and plain buy-back provision. Plaintiff got what he bargained for — book value for his minority shares if his employment in the corporation ended before January 31, 1985. There being no basis presented for the courts to interfere with the operation and consequences of this agreement between the parties, the order of the Appellate Division granting summary judgment to defendants, dismissing the first three causes of action, should be affirmed and the certified question answered in the affirmative.

Earlier this year, in *Ingle v. Glamore Motor Sales*, 73 N.Y.2d 183, 538 N.Y.S.2d 771, 535 N.E.2d 1311, we expressly refrained from deciding the precise issue presented by this case. There, the challenge was directed to the at-will discharge from employment and was predicated on a claimed fiduciary obligation flowing from the shareholder relationship. Relying principally on *Sabetay v. Sterling Drug*, 69 N.Y.2d 329, 335–336, 514 N.Y.S.2d 209, 506 N.E.2d 919, and *Murphy v. American Home Prods. Corp.*, 58 N.Y.2d 293, 300, 461 N.Y.S.2d 232, 448 N.E.2d 86, we held that "[a] minority shareholder in a close corporation, by that status alone, who contractually agrees to the repurchase of his shares upon termination of his employment for any reason, *acquires no right from the corporation or majority shareholders against at-will discharge.*" *Ingle v. Glamore Motor Sales*, 73 N.Y.2d, *supra*, at 188, 538 N.Y.S.2d 771, 535 N.E.2d 1311 [emphasis added]. However, we cautioned that "[i]t is necessary . . . to appreciate and keep distinct the duty a corporation owes to a minority shareholder *as a shareholder* from any duty it might owe him as an *employee.*" *Id.* at 188, 538 N.Y.S.2d 771, 535 N.E.2d 1311.

The causes before us on this appeal are based on an alleged departure from a fiduciary duty of fair dealing existing independently of the employment and arising from the plaintiff's simultaneous relationship as a minority shareholder in the corporation. Plaintiff claims entitlement to the higher price based on a breach flowing from Eastdil's premature "bad faith" termination of his at-will employment because, he asserts, the sole purpose of the firing at that time was to acquire the stock at a contractually and temporally measured lower buy-back price formula.

The claim seeking a higher price for the shares cannot be neatly divorced, as the dissent urges, from the employment because the buy-back provision links them together as to timing and consequences. Plaintiff not only agreed to the particular buy-back formula, he helped write it and he reviewed it with his attorney during the negotiation process, before signing the agreement and purchasing the minority interest. These provisions, which require an employee shareholder to sell back stock upon severance from corporate employment, are designed to ensure that ownership of all of the stock, especially of a close corporation, stays within the control of the remaining corporate owners-employees; that is, those who will continue to contribute to its successes or failures. *See* Kessler, *Share Repurchases Under Modern Corporation Laws*, 28 Fordham L. Rev. 637, 648 (1959–1960). These agreements define the scope of the relevant fiduciary duty and supply certainty of obligation to each side. They should not be undone simply upon an allegation of unfairness. This would destroy their very purpose, which is to provide a certain formula by which to value stock in the future. *Allen v. Biltmore Tissue Corp.*, 2 N.Y.2d 534, 542–543, 161 N.Y.S.2d 418, 141 N.E.2d 812. Indeed, the dissenters in *Ingle* itself acknowledged that employee shareholders would be precluded from complaining about the terms of an otherwise enforceable buy-back provision. *Ingle v. Glamore Motor Sales*, 73 N.Y.2d, *supra*, at 192, n. 1, 538 N.Y.S.2d 771, 535 N.E.2d 1311.

Gallagher accepted the offer to become a minority stockholder, but only for the period during which he remained an employee. The buy-back price formula was designed for the benefit of both parties precisely so that they could know their respective rights on certain dates and avoid costly and lengthy litigation on the "fair value" issue. *See Coleman v. Taub*, 3d Cir., 638 F.2d 628, 637. Permitting these causes to survive would open the door to litigation on both the value of the stock and the date of termination, and hinder the employer from fulfilling its contractual rights under the agreement. This would frustrate the agreement and would be disruptive of the settled principles governing like agreements where parties contract between themselves in advance so that there may be reliance, predictability and definitiveness between themselves on such matters. There being no dispute that the employer had the unfettered discretion to fire plaintiff at any time, we should not redefine the precise measuring device and scope of the agreement. Defendant agreed to abide by these terms and thus fulfilled its fiduciary duty in that respect. . . .

Accordingly, the order of the Appellate Division should be affirmed, with costs, and the certified question answered in the affirmative. . . .

KAYE, JUDGE (dissenting).

By proceeding, as if inexorably, from *Sabetay* to *Ingle* to *Gallagher*, the court avoids confronting plaintiff's true claims and unnecessarily weakens traditional protections afforded minority shareholders in close corporations. I therefore respectfully dissent.

I

To begin at a point of agreement, this case is significantly different from *Ingle v. Glamore Motor Sales*, 73 N.Y.2d 183, 538 N.Y.S.2d 771, 535 N.E.2d 1311. As the majority acknowledges, this case presents "an alleged departure from a fiduciary duty of fair dealing existing independently of the employment" that was not present in *Ingle* (majority opn., at 566, at 946 of 549 N.Y.S.2d, at 137 of 549 N.E.2d).

In *Ingle* we reached only the corporation's duty to plaintiff as *an employee*, carving out and reserving for another day any question of the duty a corporation might owe an employee as *a shareholder*, which was not in issue. The court was careful to note that Mr. Ingle had already accepted full payment for his shares without reservation; while his complaint referred to a fiduciary duty owed him as a shareholder, the only interest he asserted in the litigation was in his job. In its succinct opinion the court took pains to emphasize at least six separate times that its concern was only with Mr. Ingle's employment, not in any sense with the duty a corporation owes to a minority shareholder, or with undervaluation of shares (73 N.Y.2d, at 187, 188, 189, 538 N.Y.S.2d 771, 535 N.E.2d 1311).

Here, plaintiff *does* question the duty the corporation owes him as a shareholder. He *does* contend that the corporation undervalued his shares and that it did not offer a fair price for his equity interest. Indeed, that is the only question he raises; he does not challenge defendant's absolute right to terminate his employment. Yet despite careful identification and recognition in *Ingle* of the different considerations such a question would present, now that the question is before us the court finds that the very same answer and the very same rationale are wholly dispositive, with no analysis of the fiduciary obligation owed plaintiff.

The court's insistence that the rationale of *Ingle* and the other at-will employment cases must be carried over-lock, stock and barrel — even to the fiduciary obligations owed minority shareholders in close corporations, plainly represents an extension of the law to a different jural relationship. I believe this is wholly unwarranted.

II

A fuller statement of the facts portrays both plaintiff's true claims and the error of summary dismissal of his complaint.

Before he was dismissed on January 10, 1985, plaintiff (James V. Gallagher) was an officer and director of both defendant Eastdil Realty, Inc. and its wholly owned subsidiary, Eastdil Advisers, Inc. Eastdil Realty is a closely held real estate investing banking firm. Defendant Lambert is its founder, principal shareholder and chief executive officer. The other defendants are officers and shareholders of the corporation.

Gallagher was first employed by Eastdil Realty as vice-president, from 1968 to 1973, when he left to start his own firm. He returned as a consultant in 1976, and was soon offered a full-time position as vice-president at a base salary of $60,000. In 1978, Gallagher was appointed president and chief executive officer of the newly created Eastdil Advisors, and he was elected to Eastdil's board of directors in 1980. As Gallagher's responsibilities increased, his salary and bonuses rose commensurately and steadily — from $135,000 in 1979 to more than a million dollars for the fiscal year ending on January 31, 1984.

In 1981, a number of executives of Eastdil Realty were offered the opportunity to purchase shares of class B nonvoting stock in the company. Gallagher bought 4% — 40 shares — at $100 a share. Lambert continued to own all of the voting stock. In connection with his purchase of shares, Gallagher executed a stockholders' agreement that contained a mandatory repurchase provision. For a period of two years "commencing with the voluntary resignation or other termination of any class B stockholder's employment with the company," the company had a right to reacquire the shares. The agreement set the repurchase price at book value.

In mid-1983, Eastdil implemented a recapitalization plan. All of the voting stock was to be retired, and the nonvoting shares increased and redistributed, and then converted into voting common stock. As Gallagher alleges, the recapitalization was no act of charity by the corporation; it was a response to a mass exodus of valued employees, and an effort to forestall further defections by offering financial incentives to continue with the corporation at least to year-end.

In summer 1984, Gallagher received 8.5% of Eastdil's stock, becoming the third largest shareholder, and he executed an amended stockholders' agreement. The agreement continued to provide for mandatory repurchase at book value upon "voluntary resignation or other termination" of employment. But it also stipulated that after January 31, 1985, the buy-out price would be calculated by an escalating formula based on the company's earnings and the length of the shareholder's employment. According to Gallagher, the new buy-out price represented "golden handcuffs" designed to induce employees to remain on, at least until January 31, 1985.

On January 10, 1985 — just 21 days before the new valuation formula became effective — Gallagher was fired and Eastdil invoked its right to repurchase his stock at book value. According to Gallagher, book value for the shares was $89,000; the price under the new valuation formula would have been around $3,000,000. . . .

III

Gallagher alleges that defendants had no bona fide, business-related reason to terminate his employment when they did — assertions we must accept as true on this summary judgment motion. He charges that defendants fired him for the sole purpose of recapturing his shares at an unfairly low price and redistributing them among themselves.

These claims put in issue an aspect of the employee-shareholder relationship that we have not previously considered in our at-will employment cases. Plaintiff claims that defendants, the holders of a majority of the corporate stock, breached distinctly different duties to him by manipulating his termination so as to deprive him of the opportunity to reap the benefits of a "golden handcuffs" agreement, and for no other reason than to effect repurchase of his shares at less than their fair value. In short, plaintiff claims defendants breached two duties related to each other but conceptually unrelated to his at-will employment status: (1) a duty of good faith in the performance of the shareholders' agreement, and (2) a fiduciary obligation owed to him as a minority shareholder by the controlling shareholders to refrain from purely self-aggrandizing conduct. Neither claim is foreclosed by plaintiff's status as an at-will employee.

If plaintiff were a minority shareholder, but not an employee, defendants would be barred from acting selfishly and opportunistically, for no corporate purpose, as he alleges they did. The controlling stockholders in a close corporation stand, in relation to minority owners, in the same fiduciary position as corporate directors generally, and are held "to the extreme measure of candor, unselfishness and good faith." *Kavanaugh v. Kavanaugh Knitting Co.*, 226 N.Y. 185, 193, 123 N.E. 148. Although, without more, the courts will not interfere when parties have set the repurchase price at book value, *Allen v. Biltmore Tissue Corp.*, 2 N.Y.2d 534, 542–543, 161 N.Y.S.2d 418, 141 N.E.2d 812, here plaintiff asserts there was more. The corporation agreed, commencing January 31, 1985, to pay a higher price, said to be more reflective of the true value of defendant's shares. Defendants' invocation of the pre-January 31 repurchase price was adverse to plaintiff's interests as a minority stockholder, and therefore subject to a standard of good faith under the foregoing principles.

Directors and majority shareholders may not act "for the aggrandizement or undue advantage of the fiduciary to the exclusion or detriment of the [minority] stockholders." *Alpert v. 28 Williams St. Corp.*, 63 N.Y.2d 557, 569, 483 N.Y.S.2d 667, 473 N.E.2d 19 [citing cases]. Nor is it considered a legitimate corporate interest if the sole purpose is reduction of the number of profit-sharers, or ultimately "to increase the individual wealth of the remaining shareholders." *Id.* at 573, 483 N.Y.S.2d 667, 473 N.E.2d 19. Yet that is precisely what we must assume defendants' motive was, and this court now sanctions such conduct. . . .

Moreover, defendants' interpretation denies that defendants themselves had any duty of good faith in connection with the shareholders' agreement. We have said that "there is an implied covenant that neither party shall do anything which will have the effect of destroying or injuring the right of the other party to receive the fruits of the contract, which means that in every contract there exists an implied covenant of good faith and fair dealing." *Kirke La Shelle Co. v. Armstrong Co.*, 263 N.Y. 79, 87, 188 N.E. 163. This general rule does not apply to at-will employment relationships, as "it would be incongruous to say that an inference may be drawn that the employer impliedly agreed to a provision which would be destructive of his right of termination." *Murphy v. American Home Prods. Corp.*, 58 N.Y.2d 293, 304–305, 461 N.Y.S.2d 232, 448 N.E.2d 86. It does not follow, however, that there can be no covenant of good faith implicit in the shareholders' agreement that gives rise to obligations surviving termination of the employment relationship.

Assuming plaintiff's claims about the purpose of the amendments to be true, the expectations and relationship of the parties, as structured by the shareholders' agreement, dictate an implied contractual obligation of good faith, notwithstanding that there is none in their employment relationship. *See, Wakefield v. Northern Telecom*, 769 F.2d 109 (2d Cir.) A covenant of good faith is anomalous in the context of at-will employment because performance and entitlement to benefits are simultaneous. Termination even without cause does not operate to deprive the employee of the benefits promised in return for performance.

But the alleged "golden handcuffs" agreement is different. An implied covenant of good faith *is* necessary to enable the employee to receive the benefits promised for performance. As one court noted, "an unfettered right to avoid payment . . . creates incentives counterproductive to the purpose of the contract itself in that the better the performance by the employee, the greater the temptation to terminate." *Wakefield v. Northern Telecom, supra*, at 112–113; Note, *Exercising Options to Repurchase Employee-Held Stock: A Question of Good Faith*, 68 Yale L.J. 773, 779 (1959).

. . .

IV

Denial of summary judgment would deprive defendants of no legitimate expectation or right, contractual or otherwise. Under the law, they remain free to terminate plaintiff's employment as agreed; they remain free to buy back his stock at book value as agreed-so long as there is a corporate purpose for their conduct. What controlling shareholders cannot do to a minority shareholder is take action against him solely for the self-aggrandizing, opportunistic purpose of themselves acquiring his shares at the low price, and they cannot do this because in the law it means something to be a shareholder, particularly a minority shareholder.

Because the majority gives no credence whatever to plaintiff's independent status as a shareholder, and because the majority now needlessly extends the at-will employment doctrine yet another notch, to diminish the long-recognized duties owed minority shareholders, I must dissent.

Order affirmed.

PEDRO v. PEDRO

Court of Appeals of Minnesota
489 N.W.2d 798 (1992)

NORTON, JUDGE.

After a request for dissolution of The Pedro Companies by respondent, Alfred Pedro, appellants, Carl and Eugene Pedro and The Pedro Companies, moved that the action proceed as a buyout pursuant to Minn. Stat. § 302A.751 (1990).

After a jury awarded damages, this court determined the jury's verdict was merely advisory and remanded the case to the trial court to make findings. *Pedro v. Pedro*, 463 N.W.2d 285 (Minn. App. 1990) (*Pedro 1*), *pet. for rev. denied* (1991). On remand, the trial court awarded damages for breach of fiduciary duty and for wrongful termination of lifetime employment. In addition to other issues, appellants challenge the propriety of the trial court's rulings on these matters.

FACTS

Alfred, Carl, and Eugene Pedro are brothers who each owned a one-third interest in The Pedro Companies ("TPC"), a closely held Minnesota corporation, which manufactures and sells luggage and leather products. All three brothers worked in the business for all or most of their adult lives. TPC has annual sales of approximately $6 million. Carl has worked for TPC since 1940 and he is currently employed by the company. Eugene has worked for TPC since 1939 and is also currently employed by the company. Alfred worked for TPC for 45 years and was fired in 1987 at the age of 62. Each brother, as an equal shareholder, received the same benefit and compensation as the others. Each shareholder had an equal vote in the management of the company.

In 1968, all of the company's shareholders (the three brothers and their father) entered into a stock retirement agreement ("SRA") which was designated to facilitate the purchase of the shareholder's stock upon death, or when a living shareholder wished to sell his stock. In 1975, the father died and the company purchased his stock from his estate, pursuant to the terms of the SRA.

In 1979, the remaining shareholders (the three brothers) modified and re-executed the SRA, reducing the purchase price of the shares. The agreement provided in part:

Until and unless changed the value of each share of stock shall be as follows:
75% of net book value at the end of the preceding calendar year. It is the intent

of the parties that the value of a Stockholder's interest as herein determined does include good will.

The relationship between respondent and the other two shareholders deteriorated through 1987 and 1988, after Alfred discovered an apparent discrepancy of almost $330,000 between the internal accounting records and the TPC checking account. Approximately $40,000 was discovered in an emergency investigation, yet about $270,000 of the discrepancy remained unexplained.

Alfred was very concerned and insisted that an independent accountant be retained to locate the source of the discrepancy. In May 1987, Carl and Eugene agreed to retain an accountant to investigate the cash shortage. After a month with no results, TPC dismissed the accountant. Alfred testified that soon afterwards, the corporate accountant admitted in a meeting with all three brothers that there was a $140,000 to $147,000 discrepancy which was unexplainable.

Alfred testified that during this time, Eugene would interfere with his area of responsibility in the TPC plant and undermine his management authority. Alfred testified that he was told to cooperate, resign or be fired. He was told if he did not forget about the apparent discrepancy, his brothers would fire him. Alfred again repeated his demand that the corporation hire an independent accountant to investigate the situation.

In October 1987, a second independent accountant was hired to investigate the shortage. After concluding his investigation, the accountant issued a report identifying a $140,000 discrepancy which could not be reconciled. He testified that throughout his investigation, he was refused access to numerous documents. He also stated there were over 20 leads never followed up before he ended his investigation.

Alfred was placed on a mandatory leave of absence from TPC on October 27, 1987. In December 1987, Alfred received a written notice that he was fired and all of his pay and benefits were discontinued. Employees were informed that Alfred had a nervous breakdown.

Alfred commenced this action in February 1988. Upon remand from this court on the earlier appeal, the trial court made the following findings of fact and conclusions of law. The court awarded Alfred $766,582.33 as damages for his one-third ownership in TPC which was determined by the terms of the SRA. Alfred was awarded $58,260.69 for prejudgment interest on this award.

The trial court also awarded Alfred $563,417.67 based on its finding that the individual defendants had breached their fiduciary duties to Alfred. The award represented the difference between the fair market value of Alfred Pedro's stock as determined by the trial court and the value provided by the SRA. In addition, the trial court awarded $68,690.05 for prejudgment interest on this award.

The trial court further found that Alfred had a contract of lifetime employment with TPC. The court found wrongful termination and awarded him $256,740 as compensation for lost wages. Because the contract was for lifetime employment, the award represented lost wages until he reached the age of 72. The court reduced this award by payments made to Alfred since December 1989. Moreover, the court awarded prejudgment interest in the sum of $31,750.37 on this award.

The trial court also awarded Alfred $200,000 for attorney fees and expenses incurred by him. This award was based on the trial court's finding that appellants had acted in a manner which was "arbitrary, vexatious and otherwise not in good faith . . . prior to and during this action." The court awarded Alfred an additional $6,063 for attorney fees for having to respond to appellants' motion to recuse the trial judge and for the preparation of Findings of Fact, Conclusions of Law and Order for Judgment.

ISSUES

1. Was the evidence sufficient to support the trial court's finding of breach of fiduciary duty?

2. Did the trial court properly determine Alfred Pedro had a reasonable expectation of lifetime employment, thereby awarding him damages for lost wages following the buyout until he reached age 72?

3. Did the trial court make proper determinations regarding joint and several liability, prejudgment interest, recusal of the trial judge, and attorney fees?

ANALYSIS

I

Respondent claims appellants' challenge to the sufficiency of the finding of breach of fiduciary duty is improperly before this court. Respondent asserts appellants waived the issue by failing to challenge the jury's determination on this issue. We disagree. In *Pedro 1*, we remanded for independent findings by the trial court with the jury's verdict being merely advisory. It would be inequitable to hold that appellants are not bound by the jury verdict and then decide they have waived an issue by not challenging that nonbinding determination. Because this is appellants' first opportunity to challenge the sufficiency of the trial court findings as to breach of fiduciary duty, we must address that issue.

The relationship among shareholders in closely held corporations is analogous to that of partners. *See Westland Capital Corp. v. Lucht Eng'g, Inc.*, 308 N.W.2d 709, 712 (Minn. 1981) (close corporation has been described as partnership in corporate guise). Shareholders in closely held corporations owe one another a fiduciary duty. *Evans v. Blesi*, 345 N.W.2d 775, 779 (Minn. App.1984). In a fiduciary relationship "the law imposes upon them highest standards of integrity and good faith in their dealings with each other." *Prince v. Sonnesyn*, 222 Minn. 528, 535, 25 N.W.2d 468, 472 (1946) [citation omitted]. Owing a fiduciary duty includes dealing "openly, honestly and fairly with other shareholders." *Evans*, 345 N.W.2d at 779.

The court's findings of fact contain many examples where appellants did not act openly, honestly, and fairly with respondent Alfred Pedro. The trial court found that at no time since the action was commenced, did appellants ever implement payments admittedly due under the SRA. Appellants interfered with respondent's responsibilities in TPC and hired a private investigator to follow him when he was not in the office. The court found appellants fabricated accusations of neglect and malfeasance which were not substantiated during the trial.

Moreover, an employee testified that after respondent was terminated, employees were informed that he had a nervous breakdown. Also, respondent testified he was told if he did not forget about the discrepancies in the financial records, his brothers would fire him. Finally, appellants admitted in their motion requesting a buyout, that they were acting "in a manner unfairly prejudicial" toward respondent pursuant to Minn. Stat. § 302A.751, subd. 1(b)(2) (1990). This admission supports a finding of breach of fiduciary duty.

Appellants claim no breach of fiduciary duty can exist because there has been no diminution in the value of the corporation or the stock value of respondent's shares. In support of this assertion, appellants cite several cases where actions by an officer or director did reduce the value of the corporation, constituting a breach of fiduciary duty. *See e.g., Jordan v. Duff and Phelps, Inc.*, 815 F.2d 429 (7th Cir. 1987); *Coleman v. Taub*,

638 F.2d 628 (3rd Cir. 1981); *Harris v. Mardan Business Sys., Inc.*, 421 N.W.2d 350 (Minn. App.1988).

However, an action depleting a corporation's value is not the exclusive method of breaching one's fiduciary duties. *See Evans*, 345 N.W.2d at 779–80 (majority shareholders breached fiduciary duty to minority shareholder by forcing his resignation). Moreover, loss in value of a shareholder's stock is not the only measure of damages. *See Pavlidis v. New England Patriots Football Club, Inc.*, 675 F.Supp. 701, 703 (D. Mass. 1987) (damages for corporate director's breach of fiduciary duty was either profits made by director or value of property at time of breach plus interest).[11]

Moreover, the measure of damages for the buyout was proper. In *Pedro 1*, this court stated:

> If the fair value of the shares is greater than the purchase price for the buyout as calculated from the formula in the SRA, the difference is the measure of respondent's damage resulting from having been forced to sell his shares in the company. *Pedro*, 463 N.W.2d at 288.

Here there was evidence in the record that the fair market value of respondent's shares equalled $1,330,000. After subtracting the undisputed purchase price set forth under the SRA of $766,582.33, the trial court properly awarded damages for breach of fiduciary duty of $563,417.67.

II

Appellants claim the evidence was insufficient for the court to find a contract for lifetime employment. They also assert damages for lost wages following the buyout were improper. Again, we are unable to set aside findings of fact unless they are clearly erroneous. Minn .R. Civ. P. 52.01. Based upon the unique facts in this case, we affirm the trial court's award of damages for lost wages.

Trial courts have broad equitable powers in fashioning relief for the buyout of shareholders in a closely held corporation. Minn. Stat. § 302A.751, subd. 3a provides:

> In determining whether to order equitable relief, dissolution, or a buy-out, the court shall take into consideration the duty which all shareholders in a closely held corporation owe one another to act in an honest, fair and reasonable manner in the operation of the corporation and the reasonable expectations of the shareholders as they exist at the inception and develop during the course of the shareholders' relationship with the corporation and with each other.

This section allows courts to look to respondent's reasonable expectations when awarding damages. In addition to an ownership interest, [t]he reasonable expectations of such a shareholder are a job, salary, a significant place in management, and economic security for his family. Joseph E. Olson, *A Statutory Elixir for the Oppression Malady*, 36 Mercer L. Rev. 627, 629 (1985) (footnote omitted).

In *Pine River State Bank v. Mettille*, 333 N.W.2d 622 (Minn. 1983), the supreme court explained that the court must ascertain the intent of the parties to the employment contract. *Id.* at 628. When ascertaining the intent, trial courts must consider the written and oral negotiations of the parties as well as the parties' situation, the type of employment and the particular circumstances of the case. *Eklund v. Vincent Brass and Aluminum Co.*, 351 N.W.2d 371, 376 (Minn. App.1984), *pet. for rev. denied* (1984).

In a closely held corporation the nature of the employment of a shareholder may create a reasonable expectation by the employee-owner that his employment is not

---

[11] [1] This court recognized in *Pedro 1* that damages were appropriate even where there was no diminution of respondent's stock value by stating: "Inasmuch as appellants' breaches of fiduciary duty forced the buyout, they cannot benefit from wrongful treatment of their fellow shareholder and must disgorge any such gain." *Pedro*, 463 N.W.2d at 288.

terminable at will. *Pedro,* 463 N.W.2d at 289.

The unique facts in the record support the trial court's finding of an agreement to provide lifetime employment to respondent. Carl Pedro, Sr. worked at the corporation until his death. Eugene Pedro, who worked for over 50 years at TPC, testified that he intended to always work for the company. Carl Pedro, Jr. worked at TPC for over 34 years. Alfred Pedro testified of his expectation of a lifetime job like his father. He had already been employed by TPC for 45 years. Even the corporate accountant testified regarding Carl's and Eugene's expectations that they would work for the corporation as long as they wanted. Based upon this evidence it was reasonable for the trial court to determine that the parties did in fact have a contract that was not terminable at will.

Appellants claim a grant of damages for both lost wages and breach of fiduciary duty under § 302A.751, subd. 3a allows respondent a double recovery. In support of this assertion, appellants misquote *Pedro 1* in their brief by connecting, within one block quotation, sentences from entirely different sections of the opinion. In any event, section 302A.751, subd. 3a, allows the trial court to consider respondent's reasonable expectations. Even appellants concede respondent has two separate interests, as owner and employee. Thus, allowing recovery for each interest is appropriate and will not be considered a double recovery.

Finally, appellants dispute the trial court's award of damages for lost wages following the buyout. They claim once respondent's ownership interest is severed, he has no right to damages for lost wages. We believe the trial court's award of future damages for lost wages is wholly consistent with the court's broad equitable powers found in § 302A.751, subd. 3a and is warranted based upon its finding of a contract for lifetime employment. . . .

The facts of this case support the trial court's findings that appellants breached their fiduciary duties to respondent and wrongfully terminated his contract for lifetime employment.

Affirmed.

JENSEN v. CHRISTENSEN & LEE INSURANCE, INC.
Court of Appeals of Wisconsin
157 Wis.2d 758, 460 N.W.2d 441 (1990)

BROWN, JUDGE.

This is an appeal by Dean A. Jensen, a minority stockholder and former employee of a close corporation known as Christensen & Lee Insurance, Inc. He claims that the directors of the corporation violated the public policy of this state by terminating his employment, thus triggering a stock buyout at a low purchase price which redounded to the financial benefit of the directors. He made a claim for relief which he now argues is based upon secs. 180.307 and 180.355, Stats. He asserts that these statutes prohibit such a "squeeze out" because it is a willful failure to deal fairly with a stockholder. He made a further claim that when such a "squeeze out" is brought about by the termination of employment, there is a basis for a wrongful discharge cause of action . . .

We agree with the trial court that the complaint failed to state the elements necessary for a wrongful discharge claim. However, the complaint sufficiently states a claim by a shareholder against the directors for willfully failing to deal fairly with shareholders in a matter in which the directors had a material conflict of interest. We affirm in part, reverse in part and remand.

Jensen sued Christensen & Lee Insurance, Inc. He also sued its directors and majority shareholders: Ejner J. Lie, Christian A. Lie and Joseph G. Lipari.

Jensen was an employee of Christensen & Lee Insurance for twenty years. It was alleged and not denied that Jensen was the top salesman in the company. At the time of his termination, Jensen also had a substantial minority stockholder interest and was a director of the company. In December 1988, the defendants voted to terminate Jensen's employment with the company. In January 1989, the defendants removed Jensen as a director. The termination of Jensen as employee and director triggered the purchase of Jensen's stock under a stock retirement agreement and a deferred compensation agreement (collectively "the agreements").

Jensen alleges that the terminations were made so that the company could pay him a lower amount for his stock than it would have to pay if he continued his employment until he reached normal retirement age in 1991. Jensen further alleges that by the terms of the agreements, the stock purchase was to be triggered only when Jensen voluntarily elected a retirement date or when he reached the mandatory retirement age of sixty-five. Following his termination, Jensen elected a retirement date of 1991. Thus, he claims that his stock should be purchased at the 1991 price. Jensen also alleges that because he was wrongfully discharged, he is owed compensation for lost salary benefits from December 1988 to his elected retirement date in 1991. . . .

We initially discuss Jensen's allegation that the defendants breached their duty to a minority shareholder. Section 180.307, Stats., provides that a director of a corporation is liable for a breach of duty to a shareholder in two instances relevant to this case. First is where there is willful failure to deal fairly with the stockholder in a matter in which the director has a material conflict of interest. Sec. 180.307(1)(a). The second is where the director derives an improper personal profit in the transaction involving the stockholder. Sec. 180.307(1)(c). Additionally, sec. 180.355, Stats., provides that there must be full disclosure when directors of a corporation vote on a matter in which they have a financial conflict of interest and that the votes of the interested directors cannot be counted in approving the transaction.

Jensen argues in effect that the other directors received financial gain by terminating his employment prior to either his voluntary or mandatory retirement because the corporation would have to pay a higher price for his stock at the time of his retirement than it had to pay at the time of his termination. Thus, the directors breached their fiduciary duty to Jensen. . . .

Jensen's complaint makes the following allegations. The defendants were directors and Jensen was a stockholder of the corporation. The directors voted to terminate Jensen's employment and to remove him as a stockholder. The action of the directors violated the agreements which were based on Jensen continuing to work until age sixty-five. The corporation understated the purchase price of Jensen's stock because the accountant had a financial conflict of interest. The directors' breach of fiduciary duty caused a decrease in the payments Jensen should have received under the terms of the agreements. The directors had a conflict of interest and they used their positions to benefit financially.

We hold that there are sufficient allegations to plead a claim that the defendants breached their fiduciary duty to Jensen as a minority shareholder of the close corporation. The defendants' argument that the agreements provide for discharge as a legitimate triggering mechanism for the company's purchase of stock may be a proper issue in later proceedings. However, it is not controlling to whether this complaint states a valid claim for relief under the statute. We reverse on this issue. . . .

We affirm the trial court's dismissal of Jensen's wrongful discharge cause of action for failure to state a claim for which relief can be granted. We reverse the trial court's dismissal of Jensen's cause of action alleging breach of fiduciary duty to a minority shareholder. We remand for trial on the issue of breach of fiduciary duty.

PROBLEM

Two weeks ago you received a telephone call from a friend you know at your tennis club. He related that his brother-in-law, Bill Bentley, had invested $1,000,000 in cash eighteen months ago to acquire fifty percent of the common stock of SDM, Inc., from the then 100 percent owners, the Pizzario family. The stock purchase agreement between Bentley and the Pizzario family, as negotiated by the parties' respective lawyers, contains the following provision: "In matters regarding the election of directors the parties shall vote their shares as a unit in favor of the three nominees of the Pizzario family and the three nominees of Mr. Bentley. The salaries of the President and the Chief Executive Officer, adjusted on July 1 of each year based on the Consumer Price Index, shall be, respectively, $200,000 and $250,000 annually, exclusive of prerequisites to be determined by the board of directors." Consequently, there are six directors, three of whom were elected by the Pizzario family and three by Bill Bentley. The Pizzario family has retained the key management positions in the company, including the offices of President and Chief Executive Officer.

At the time of Bentley's investment, SDM was engaged solely in the men's retail apparel business. He is now upset by management's recent opening of a "wholesale" men's clothing store, fearing that it will lessen SDM's upscale image. Bentley also suspects gross mismanagement and perhaps self-dealing by the Pizzarios. Bentley's requests for corporate information have been summarily rejected by management. Bentley now wants out of these arrangements and would like to recover his investment.

1.   Did Bentley receive faulty advice from his former lawyer? If so, in what regard?

2.   What advice would you provide Bentley in his efforts to recover his investment?

3.   What substantive legal claims, if any, should Bentley assert against the controlling shareholders?

Chapter 10
FIDUCIARY DUTY

A. INTRODUCTION

There are many different categories of persons whom either the law denominates, or plaintiffs seek to have denominated, fiduciaries. Recognition of a relationship denominated as fiduciary means that credible legal authority has found that the person (the fiduciary) has control over and responsibility for the well being and destiny of another. Mr. Justice Frankfurter stated: "But to say that a [person] is a fiduciary only begins analysis; it gives direction to further inquiry." *Chenery Corp. v. SEC*, 318 U.S. 80, 86–7 (1943). From a finding that a person had fiduciary status, differing legal consequences may flow.

Be that as it may, denomination as a fiduciary requires that person exercise a certain degree of selflessness (other regarding behavior). Among the categories of persons the law traditionally has denominated fiduciary, under one way of looking at it, law can require a high degree of selfless behavior, a relatively low degree of selfless behavior, or something in between. The law requires a great degree of self abnegation from persons found to be trustees (toward the beneficiary of the trust) or guardians (toward the ward of the guardianship). By contrast, a court may find that a franchisor is a fiduciary only if there is a holding out, a promise, that the franchisor will look out for the interests of the franchisee. Otherwise the relationship adheres strictly to what the contract provides.

In some jurisdictions (California, for instance), courts hold a stock broker (registered representative) always to be a fiduciary. In other jurisdictions, courts hold a stock broker to be a ministerial agent ("Buy 500 shares of IBM"), with minimal fiduciary duties, in some cases, but full-fledged fiduciaries in instances in which there has been a holding out ("I will act as your financial advisor").

By and large, plaintiffs have failed to obtain rulings that certain categories of persons occupy positions as fiduciaries. Rabbis and pastors have escaped denomination (at least as fiduciaries), outside a one-on-one counseling role. So, too, teachers and professors have eluded plaintiffs' attempts to hold those persons fiduciaries, as have physicians and psychiatrists. Not to be denied, plaintiffs' lawyers continue to seek to have wide circles of persons denominated as fiduciaries (hair dressers, fashion consultants, insurance agents, financial advisors, etc.).

This chapter deals with five types of persons the law invariably denominates as fiduciaries: partners, LLC managers, corporate directors, corporate officers, and controlling stockholders. The first four categories of persons all have duties registering on the up hill half of the spectrum, approaching but not reaching, say, the level of selflessness required of trustees and guardians. Arguably, partners' duties ("the utmost good faith and loyalty") exceed those of directors and officers but debaters who would argue the other side would not be hard to find.

By contrast, early case law found controlling shareholders to have no duties. Share owners owned shares precisely for the purpose of pursuing their own selfish economic interests. *Northwest Transportation Co. v. Beatty*, 12 App. Cas. 589 (Privy Council 1887); *Boss v. Boss*, 98 R.I. 146, 200 A.2d 231 (R.I. 1964). Later corporate law cases put some brakes on that principle. In pursuing their self interest, controlling shareholders could not go so far as to work a fraud, commit an illegality, or reap a benefit to the detriment or exclusion of the other shareholders. Courts, however, stopped way short of imposing an all purpose duty on shareholders as they had done on corporate directors. Nonetheless, still later cases denominate the duty a fiduciary one even though critics find the notion of a stockholder having duties denominated as fiduciary to be oxymoronic.

The duties to be examined for what they require in specified instances include those of care ("that amount of care exercised by like persons in similar circumstances") and loyalty (place the "best interests of the corporation" over those of self, family, friends, associates, or other businesses in which the director holds an interest). Even though directors may exercise due care, and believe fervently that what they approve is in the entity's best interests, it may violate the law. So a third duty, the duty to act lawfully, is necessary, although it seldom needs to be invoked.

For many years, authoritative sources declined to adumbrate sub duties. Over and above care and loyalty, for example, they declined to promulgate a duty that directors attend meetings. Recently, that has changed. Courts have posited a state law duty of disclosure, sometimes known as the duty of candor, apart from the federal securities law duty to disclose which traditionally has ruled the roost. Others purport to find and argue the need for a separate fiduciary duty of good faith, to act as a catchall, for example, in cases in which revenge or spite rather than greed causes fiduciaries to stray from the proper path, or as an alternative to a separate duty, in cases in which directors oversee unlawful action.

The chapter thus deals with questions Mr. Justice Frankfurter posited in *Chenery Corp. v. SEC, supra,* more than 60 years ago: "To whom is he a fiduciary? What obligations does he owe as a fiduciary? In what respect has he failed to discharge those obligations? [W]hat are the consequences of his deviation?"

B. THE DUTY OF CARE

BRANE v. ROTH
Court of Appeal of Indiana
590 N.E.2d 587 (1993)

RATLIFF, CHIEF JUDGE . . . This case involves a shareholders' action against the directors of a rural grain elevator cooperative for losses Co-op suffered in 1980 due to the directors' failure to protect its position by adequately hedging in the grain market. Paul Brane, Kenneth Richison, Ralph Dawes, and John Thompson were directors of Co-op in 1980. Eldon Richison was Co-op's manager that year who handled the buying and selling of grain. [N]inety percent of Co-op's business was buying and selling grain. The directors met on a monthly basis reviewing the manager's general report and financial reports prepared by Virginia Daihl, Co-op's bookkeeper. The directors also discussed maintenance and improvement matters and authorized loan transactions for the Co-op. Requests for additional information on the reports were rare. The directors did not make any specific inquiry as to losses sustained in 1980.

The records show that Co-op's gross profit had fallen continually from 1977. After a substantial loss in 1979, Co-op's CPA, Michael Matchette, recommended that the directors hedge Co-op's grain position to protect itself . . . . The directors authorized the manager to hedge for Co-op. Only a minimal amount was hedged, specifically $20,050 in hedging contracts were made, whereas Co-op had $7,300,000 in grain sales.

On February 3, 1981, Matchette presented the 1980 financial statement to the directors, indicating a net profit of only $68,684. In 1982, Matchette informed the directors of errors in his 1980 financial statement and that Co-op had actually experienced a gross loss of $227,329. The directors consulted another accounting firm to review the financial condition of Co-op. CPA Rex E. Coulter found additional errors in Matchette's 1980 financial statement, which increased the gross loss to $424,038. Coulter opined that the primary cause of the gross loss was the failure to hedge.

The court entered specific findings and conclusions determining that the directors breached their duties by retaining a manager inexperienced in hedging; failing to maintain reasonable supervision over him; and failing to attain knowledge of the basic fundamentals of hedging to be able to direct the hedging activities and supervise the manager properly; and that their gross inattention and failure to protect the grain profits caused the resultant loss of $424,038.89.

The directors contend that the trial court applied the wrong standard of care to their actions. The trial court utilized the standard of care set forth in IND. CODE § 23-1-2-11. [Repealed in 1986, now IND. CODE § 23 1 35 1.] In 1980, I.C. § 23-1-2-11 provided that a director shall perform his duties in good faith in the best interest of the corporation and with such care as an ordinarily prudent person in a like position would use in similar circumstances. The statute allows the director to rely upon information, reports, and opinions of the corporation's officers and employees which he reasonably believes to be reliable and competent, and public accountants on matters which he reasonably believes to be within such person's professional competence. Id. A director has no liability if he meets this standard of care. Id.

I.C. § 23-1-2-11 was repealed and replaced by IND. CODE § 23-1-35-1, which preserved the former standard of care but narrowed liability by adding that a director is not liable unless he has breached or failed to perform his duties and such breach or failure to perform constitutes willful misconduct or recklessness. The directors assert that I.C. 23-1-35-1 should be applied retroactively to this case.

Generally, statutes are not given retroactive effect unless expressly stated by the legislature. Even when amendments are remedial, retroactive application is disfavored when existing rights would be infringed. Because I.C. § 23-1-35-1 narrows director liability, the statute affects existing rights shareholders had against directors.

Therefore, we refuse to grant the directors' request to apply I.C. § 23-1-35-1 retroactively. We find that the trial court applied the correct standard of care upon the directors . . . .

. . . .

The directors argue . . . that the trial court's decision is contrary to law because the shareholders failed to show proximate cause and specific damages. [W]e find that there was probative evidence that Co-op's losses were due to a failure to hedge. Coulter testified that grain elevators should engage in hedging to protect the co-op from losses from price swings. One expert in the grain elevator business and hedging testified that co-ops should not speculate and that Co-op's losses stemmed from the failure to hedge.

Further evidence in the record supports the court's findings and its conclusions that the directors breached their duty by their failure to supervise the manager and become aware of the essentials of hedging to be able to monitor the business which was a proximate cause of Co-op's losses. Although the directors argue that they relied upon their manager and should be insulated from liability, the business judgment rule protects directors from liability only if their decisions were informed ones. See Hanson Trust PLC v. ML SCM Acquisitions, Inc. (2d Cir. 1986), 781 F.2d 264, 275 (director's decision must be an informed one); Aronson v. Lewis (1984), Del., 473 A.2d 805, 812 (business judgment rule is the presumption that directors acted on an informed basis, in good faith and in honest belief that the action taken was in the best interest of the company; the rule does not protect directors who have abdicated their functions or absent a conscious decision, failed to act; directors have a duty to inform themselves of all material information reasonably available to make their decision).

In W & W Equipment Co. v. Mink (1991), Ind. App., 568 N.E.2d 564, we stated that "a director cannot blindly take action and later avoid the consequences by saying he was not aware of the effect of the action he took. A director has some duty to become informed about the actions he is about to undertake." Here, the evidence shows that the directors made no meaningful attempts to be informed of the hedging activities and their effects upon Co-op's financial position. Their failure to provide adequate supervision of the manager's actions was a breach of their duty of care to protect Co-op's interests in a reasonable manner. See Tower Recreation, Inc. v. Beard (1967), 141 Ind. App. 649, 651, 231 N.E.2d 154, 155 (directors have a duty to reasonably protect the interests of the company). The business judgment rule does not shield the directors from liability.

In conclusion no. 4, the trial court noted the statutory standard of care in I.C. § 23-1-2-11. [T]he court [also] cited Coddington v. Canaday (1901), 157 Ind. 243, 61 N.E. 567 . . . . In Coddington, our supreme court held that directors are not liable for mere errors of judgment, but that they are liable for losses occurring through their gross inattention to the business or their willful violation of their duties. We perceive the directors' argument to be that the court erred in referring to both Coddington and I.C. § 23-1-2-11 because the Coddington language and the standard in I.C. § 23-1-2-11 are irreconcilable. We disagree.

The Coddington case points out particular duties which were breached by bank directors, such as the duties of: knowing the company's general financial condition, knowing its solvency position, checking or preventing improvident or dishonest conduct of managers, examining corporate records and knowing the manner in which business is conducted, and supervising managers. The trial court cited the duties in Coddington . . . , after commenting . . . that I.C. § 23-1-2-11 is in harmony with and supported by Coddington. The court then proceeded to list the duties which Co-op's directors had breached, which were similar to those listed in Coddington . . . .

In Coddington, the court determined the bank directors were grossly inattentive to the business and willfully violated their duties. The directors argue that this language requires "gross negligence" before liability is exacted. We disagree with the directors' interpretation and also note that as discussed in Issue Two, the proper standard of care is that set forth in I.C. § 23-1-2-11, which is not a gross negligence standard. The trial court's reference to Coddington reinforces the findings of the particular breaches of duties here and does not imply that a finding of gross negligence by Co-op's directors was necessary. . . . It was necessary that the trial court here decide whether the directors acted as ordinarily prudent persons in like positions in similar circumstances would have acted. The trial court applied that standard correctly.

. . . .

Affirmed.

GARRARD, J., concurs.

SULLIVAN, J., concurs in result.

NOTES

1. *Objective or Quasi Subjective Standard?* The tort law standard is an objective one: the degree of care a reasonable person would exercise. Evidence of what is always done, or usually done, in a community or within a profession is not dispositive, for the whole profession or community may be comprised of fools. *See The T. J. Hooper*, 60 F.2d 737 (2d Cir. 1932) (Learned Hand, J.) ("[I]n most cases reasonable prudence is in fact common prudence; but strictly it is never its measure: a whole calling may have been laggard in the adoption of new and available devices"). In contrast, what officers and directors do, or have done, in similar size corporations engaged in similar businesses is not only relevant evidence. It can be dispositive. Thus, the testimony of five automobile drivers in the same or similar community may not even be admissible while the evidence of five directors of what boards of directors do in mid-sized banks not only is admissible but may be determinative of the case. *Litwin v. Allen*, 25 N.Y.S.2d 667 (Sup. Ct. 1940). MBCA § 8.30(b) ("The members of the board of directors or a committee of the board . . . shall discharge their duties with the care that a person *in like position* would reasonably believe appropriate *under similar circumstances*") (emphasis added).

2. *Legislative Legerdemain.* As the principal cases demonstrates, legislatures in several states have amended statutes, making the standard of care either more subjective, more forgiving, or both. Thus, in 1986, Indiana narrowed the standard of

care's effect by providing that a director who has breached the traditional standard "is not liable unless he has breached or failed to perform his duties and such a breach or failure to perform constitutes wilful misconduct or recklessness." IND. CODE § 23-1-35-1. Virginia provides that "A director shall discharge his duties . . . in accordance with his good faith business judgment of the best interests of the corporation." CODE OF VA.. § 13.1-690(A) (1985). The statute has been held to adopt a wholly subjective "empty head but warm heart" standard. *See, e.g., Willard v. Moneta Bldg. Supply, Inc.*, 258 Va. 140, 515 S.E.2d 277 (1999) ("A director's discharge of his duties is not measured by what a reasonable person would do . . . instead, a director must act in accordance with his good faith business judgment of what is in the best interests of the corporation"). The statute has been called a "radical departure from the former common law." *WLR Foods, Inc. v. Tyson Foods, Inc.*, 155 F.R.D. 142 (W.D. Va. 1994), *affirmed* 65 F.3d 1172 (4th Cir. 1995).

In addition, as this chapter discusses *infra*, in 1985 Delaware enacted Del. Gen. Corp. L. 102(b)(7), which provided that a corporation may adopt a provision for its certificate of incorporation which provides for the elimination or limitation of breach of due care monetary damage liability by its directors. The corporation may not eliminate liability of duty of loyalty breaches, knowing misconduct, authorization of illegal distributions, or improper receipt of a personal benefit. All jurisdictions have followed Delaware in permitting corporations to opt out of duty of care money damages liability of the type *Brane v. Roth* analyzes.

3. *The Model Business Corporation Act.* The American Bar Association's Committee on Corporate Laws also has injected a subjective element into the Act. Rather than a common denominator standard ("care of a reasonable person in like position in similar circumstances"), as the Model Act traditionally has contained, the Act now contains a more variable and subjective standard ("the care that a person in a like position would reasonably believe appropriate . . . ."). It is important to remember that the model statute is not law but an authoritative body's view of what the law should provide. On the other hand, legislatures generally will adopt model statutes if a state bar association committee urges them to do so.

4. *Gross Negligence or Ordinary Care?* Following *Smith v. Von Gorkom, infra,* advocates often contend that the standard of conduct for directors had become only slight care (recklessness) rather than some version of ordinary care. *See* note 1. In *Smith*, a celebrated 1985 Delaware Supreme Court case, Mr. Justice Horsey stated that "We think the concept of gross negligence is also the proper standard for determining whether a business judgment reached by the board of directors was an informed one." 488 A.2d 858, 873. The court did not change the underlying standard of conduct, as many contend, but only its role in the business judgment rule context. In the words of an intermediate Louisiana appellate court, "the standard of conduct is that set forth by the plain language of the statute — the care of an ordinarily prudent person in like position in similar circumstances. It is not gross negligence." *Theriot v. Bourg*, 691 So. 2d 213, 222–234 (La. App. 1997). That said and done, in most instances, that is, those in which boards undertaken some action, including a decision to take no action, under the interaction of the business judgment rule and the standard of care, the operative standard is gross negligence. But in cases in which directors do absolutely nothing, as alleged in *Brane v. Roth, supra,* the standard is still the common denominator negligence standard.

5. *Skill as an Ingredient.* Older formulations of the corporate director's duty of care sometimes referred to that amount of "care and skill" exercised by like persons in similar circumstances. *See, e.g.,* N.Y. BUS. CORP. LAW § 717 (1963); GA. BUS. CORP. CODE ANN. § 713 (1968); N.C. GEN. STAT. § 35 (1955); PA. STAT. ANN. § 408 (1968). Older cases also intimated that the director of a business corporation had to have a modicum, if not more, of business acumen. *See Hun v. Cary*, 82 N.Y. 65 (1880). These statements have all but disappeared from formulations of the standard of conduct. The Model Act specifically rejects skill as now or ever having been part of the legal standard. Comment to MBCA § 8.30, 3 MODEL BUS. CORP. ACT ANN. § 8.30, at 929 (standard never has called for "some undefined degree of expertise"). The care of "an ordinarily prudent person in like position . . . in similar circumstances" is intended to focus on "the basic attributes of common sense, practical wisdom, and informed judgment." E, Norman Veasey & Bayless Manning, *Codified Standard — Safe Harbor or Uncharted Reef? An Analysis of the Model Act Standard of Care Compared with Delaware Law*, 35 BUS. LAW. 919, 942 (1980).

6. *Knowledge and Skill after Becoming a Director.* Although the prevailing view now is that no special knowledge or skill are required in order for a person to become a corporate director, the topography changes once a person assumes her seat. Thereafter, she must quickly assimilate the knowledge of the company and its business necessary for her to perform their duties. Long ago, a director may have been excused from duty of care liability because she did not quickly "get up to speed." *See, e.g.*, Allied Freightways, Inc. v. Cholfin, 91 N.E.2d 765 (Mass. 1950) ("She might have been an ordinary housewife with no business experience"; director spouse of male director held not liable). Today "officers and directors have an affirmative duty to be aware of the companies they serve and they can be held liable for activities of other officers and directors they should know about." Senn v. Northwest Underwriters, Inc., 875 P.2d 637, 640 (Wash. App. 1994) (spouse director held liable for husband director's defalcations of insurance premia) (citing cases). The advice for a director who, after becoming a director, feels she has been unable to acquire the necessary skill and background is to resign.

7. *Elements of Negligence.* Many of the commentators pointedly announce that the standard of conduct applicable to corporate directors is not negligence. Instead, they contend for some *sui generis* categorization of the applicable standard, or for gross negligence. Nonetheless, while the duty applicable to officers and directors may differ from the usual tort law standard, *see* note 1 *supra*, application of the remainder of the negligence rubric learned in first year torts may be helpful. Thus, a violation of the duty of care claim against a corporate official requires not only a demonstration of what the standard of conduct is but also of what the standard may or may not require in particular circumstances (violation of duty), legal or proximate cause, and damage. Usually, the front line defense will be the business judgment rule, discussed *infra*. In addition, the protestation of the experts to the contrary, an attorney can bring to the table much of the bag of tricks she learned in first year torts, such as an intervening and superceding cause, or the absence of damage to the corporation (negligence in the air, so to speak). It is to those subjects that this treatment now briefly turns.

8. *Does the Corporation Owe Fiduciary Duties?* In *Hyman v. New York Stock Exchange*, 848 N.Y.S.2d 51 (2007), the Supreme Court, Appellate Division, said "no": "As the Exchange correctly argues, to recognize a fiduciary relationship between the corporation and its shareholders would lead to the confounding possibility that a shareholder of a corporation could bring a derivative action on behalf of the corporation against the corporation itself." Other courts have disdained such reasoning as legal formalism. *See, e.g.*, Jordan v. Duff & Phelps, Inc., 815 F.2d 429 (7th Cir. 1987) (Easterbook, J.). *See generally* DOUGLAS M. BRANSON, CORPORATE GOVERNANCE § 10.06, at 559 (1993) ("Does the Corporation Owe Fiduciary Duties?").

PROBLEM

Alan Associate is second chairing a trial. Alan's law firm represents plaintiff shareholders suing over the failure of Old Line Insurance, a regional medical malpractice carrier. The defendants are the directors of Old Line. At their meetings, the directors never discussed or otherwise inquired in the adequacy of Old Line's reserves. When malpractice claims increased, and the payout per claim also increased, Old Line had insufficient reserves to carry it through the tough times and until it could increase its premium revenue. When Old Line began to fail, the state insurance commissioner put the company into receivership. The shareholders lost the entire value of their investment.

The defense is about to put on the stand directors from three or four other insurance carriers. The tenor of their testimony is that, in companies of this size, insurance company directors do not concern themselves with the adequacy of reserves, relying entirely upon management and the company's actuary.

Alan rises to object to the testimony. His best objection is:

A.   Irrelevant. What other insurance carriers do is of no moment because they are not defendants in this case.

B.   Irrelevant. The custom in the trade or profession is irrelevant, or of limited relevance, because the whole trade or profession may have been laggard in the adoption of acts and practices that could have prevented the harm.

C.   Hearsay. The testimony is offered to prove what a collegial group does in board meetings and other board members are not present and therefore, cannot be cross-examined.

D.   None. The testimony is relevant.

C.   VIOLATION OF DUTY

FRANCIS v. UNITED JERSEY BANK
Supreme Court of New Jersey
87 N.J. 15, 432 A.2d 814 (1981)

POLLOCK, J. . . . The primary issue on this appeal is whether a corporate director is personally liable in negligence for the failure to prevent the misappropriation of trust funds by other directors who were also officers and shareholders of the corporation.

Plaintiffs are trustees in bankruptcy of Pritchard & Baird Intermediaries Corp. (Pritchard & Baird), a reinsurance broker or intermediary. At the time of her death, Mrs. Pritchard was a director and the largest single shareholder of Pritchard & Baird. Because Mrs. Pritchard died after the institution of suit but before trial, her executrix was substituted as a defendant. United Jersey Bank is joined as the administrator of the estate of Charles Pritchard, Sr., who had been president, director, and majority shareholder of Pritchard & Baird.

This litigation focuses on payments made by Pritchard & Baird to Charles Pritchard, Jr. and William Pritchard, who were sons of Mr. and Mrs. Charles Pritchard.

The trial court, sitting without a jury, characterized the payments as fraudulent conveyances within N.J.S.A. 25:2-10 and entered judgment of $10,355,736.91 plus interest against the estate of Mrs. Pritchard. . . .

The Appellate Division affirmed, but found that the payments were a conversion of trust funds, rather than fraudulent conveyances of the assets of the corporation. . . .

Although we accept the characterization of the payments as a conversion of trust funds, the critical question is not whether the misconduct of Charles, Jr. and William should be characterized as fraudulent conveyances or acts of conversion. Rather, the initial question is whether Mrs. Pritchard was negligent in not noticing and trying to prevent the misappropriation of funds held by the corporation in an implied trust. A further question is whether her negligence was the proximate cause of the plaintiffs' losses. . . .

The matrix for our decision is the customs and practices of the reinsurance industry and the role of Pritchard & Baird as a reinsurance broker. Reinsurance involves a contract under which one insurer agrees to indemnify another for loss sustained under the latter's policy of insurance. Insurance companies that insure against losses arising out of fire or other casualty seek at times to minimize their exposure by sharing risks with other insurance companies. Thus, when the face amount of a policy is comparatively large, the company may enlist one or more insurers to participate in that risk. Similarly, an insurance company's loss potential and overall exposure may be reduced by reinsuring a part of an entire class of policies (e.g., 25% of all of its fire insurance policies). The selling insurance company is known as a ceding company. The entity that assumes the obligation is designated as the reinsurer.

. . . .

The reinsurance business was described by an expert at trial as having "a magic aura around it of dignity and quality and integrity." A telephone call which might be confirmed by a handwritten memorandum is sufficient to create a reinsurance obligation. Though separate bank accounts are not maintained for each treaty, the industry practice is to segregate the insurance funds from the broker's general accounts. Thus, the insurance fund accounts would contain the identifiable amounts for transmittal to either the reinsurer or the ceder. . . .

The corporate minute books reflect only perfunctory activities by the directors, related almost exclusively to the election of officers . . . . None of the minutes for any of the meetings contain a discussion of the loans to Charles, Jr. and William or of the financial condition of the corporation. Moreover, upon instructions of Charles, Jr. that financial statements were not to be circulated to anyone else, the company's statements for the fiscal years beginning February 1, 1970, were delivered only to him.

. . . .

The "loans" to Charles, Jr. and William far exceeded their salaries and financial resources. If the payments to Charles, Jr. and William had been treated as dividends or compensation, then the balance sheets would have shown an excess of liabilities over assets. If the "loans" had been eliminated, the balance sheets would have depicted a corporation not only with a working capital deficit, but also with assets having a fair market value less than its liabilities.

. . . .

The pattern that emerges from these figures is the substantial increase in the monies appropriated by Charles Pritchard, Jr. and William Pritchard after their father's withdrawal from the business and the sharp decline in the profitability of the operation after his death. This led ultimately to the filing in December, 1975, of an involuntary petition in bankruptcy . . . .

Mrs. Pritchard was not active in the business of Pritchard & Baird . . . . She briefly visited the corporate offices in Morristown on only one occasion, and she never read or obtained the annual financial statements. She was unfamiliar with the rudiments of reinsurance and made no effort to assure that the policies and practices of the corporation, particularly pertaining to the withdrawal of funds, complied with industry custom or relevant law. Although her husband had warned her that Charles, Jr. would "take the shirt off my back," Mrs. Pritchard did not pay any attention to her duties as a director or to the affairs of the corporation.

After her husband died in December 1973, Mrs. Pritchard became incapacitated and was bedridden for a six-month period. She became listless at this time and started to drink rather heavily. Her physical condition deteriorated, and in 1978 she died. The trial court rejected testimony seeking to exonerate her because she "was old, was grief-stricken at the loss of her husband, sometimes consumed too much alcohol and was psychologically overborne by her sons." That court found that she was competent to act and that the reason Mrs. Pritchard never knew what her sons "were doing was because she never made the slightest effort to discharge any of her responsibilities as a director of Pritchard & Baird."

. . . .

As a general rule, a director should acquire at least a rudimentary understanding of the business of the corporation. Accordingly, a director should become familiar with the fundamentals of the business in which the corporation is engaged. Campbell, supra, 62 N.J. Eq. at 416, 50 A. 120. Because directors are bound to exercise ordinary care, they cannot set up as a defense lack of the knowledge needed to exercise the requisite degree of care. If one "feels that he has not had sufficient business experience to qualify him to perform the duties of a director, he should either acquire the knowledge by inquiry, or refuse to act." Ibid.

Directors are under a continuing obligation to keep informed about the activities of the corporation. Otherwise, they may not be able to participate in the overall management of corporate affairs. Barnes v. Andrews, 298 F. 614 (S.D.N.Y. 1924) (director guilty of misprision of office for not keeping himself informed about the details of corporate business). . . .

Directorial management does not require a detailed inspection of day-to-day activities, but rather a general monitoring of corporate affairs and policies. Accordingly, a director is well advised to attend board meetings regularly. Indeed, a director who is absent from a board meeting is presumed to concur in action taken on a corporate matter, unless he files a "dissent with the secretary of the corporation within a reasonable time after learning of such action." N.J.S.A. 14A:6-13 (Supp. 1981-1982) [MBC § 8.24(d)]. Regular attendance does not mean that directors must attend every meeting, but that directors should attend meetings as a matter of practice. . . .

While directors are not required to audit corporate books, they should maintain familiarity with the financial status of the corporation by a regular review of financial statements. . . . The review of financial statements . . . may give rise to a duty to inquire further into matters revealed by those statements.

. . . .

A director is not an ornament, but an essential component of corporate governance. Consequently, a director cannot protect himself behind a paper shield bearing the motto, "dummy director." Campbell, supra, 62 N.J. Eq. at 443, 50 A. 120. ("The directors were not intended to be mere figure-heads without duty or responsibility"); Williams v. McKay, supra, 46 N.J. Eq. at 57–58, 18 A. 824 (director voluntarily assuming position also assumes duties of ordinary care, skill and judgment). The New Jersey Business Corporation Act, in imposing a standard of ordinary care on all directors, confirms that dummy, figurehead, and accommodation directors are anachronisms with no place in New Jersey law. Similarly . . . the New York courts have not exonerated a director who acts as an "accommodation." Barr v. Wackman, 36 N.Y.2d 371, 329 N.E.2d 180, 188 . . . . Thus, all directors are responsible for managing the business and affairs of the corporation.

. . . .

As a reinsurance broker, Pritchard & Baird received annually as a fiduciary millions of dollars of clients' money which it was under a duty to segregate. To this extent, it resembled a bank rather than a small family business. Accordingly, Mrs. Pritchard's relationship to the clientele of Pritchard & Baird was akin to that of a director of a bank to its depositors. All parties agree that Pritchard & Baird held the misappropriated funds in an implied trust. That trust relationship gave rise to a fiduciary duty to guard the funds with fidelity and good faith.

. . . .

In summary, Mrs. Pritchard was charged with the obligation of basic knowledge and supervision of the business of Pritchard & Baird. Under the circumstances, this obligation included reading and understanding financial statements, and making reasonable attempts at detection and prevention of the illegal conduct of other officers and directors. She had a duty to protect the clients of Pritchard & Baird against policies and practices that would result in the misappropriation of money they had entrusted to the corporation. She breached that duty.

Nonetheless, the negligence of Mrs. Pritchard does not result in liability unless it is a proximate cause of the loss. . . . Analysis of proximate cause requires an initial determination of cause-in-fact. Causation-in-fact calls for a finding that the defendant's act or omission was a necessary antecedent of the loss, i.e., that if the defendant had observed his or her duty of care, the loss would not have occurred. Ibid., W. Prosser, Law of Torts § 41 at 238 (4 ed. 1971). Further, the plaintiff has the burden of establishing the amount of the loss or damages caused by the negligence of the defendant. H. Henn, Law of Corporations § 234 at 456 (2 ed. 1970). . . .

Cases involving nonfeasance present a much more difficult causation question than those in which the director has committed an affirmative act of negligence leading to the loss. Analysis in cases of negligent omissions calls for determination of the reasonable steps a director should have taken and whether that course of action would have averted the loss.

Usually a director can absolve himself from liability by informing the other directors of the impropriety and voting for a proper course of action. Conversely, a director who votes for or concurs in certain actions may be "liable to the corporation for the benefit of its creditors or shareholders, to the extent of any injuries suffered by such persons, respectively, as a result of any such action." N.J.S.A. 14A:6-12 (Supp. 1981–1982). A director who is present at a board meeting is presumed to concur in corporate action taken at the meeting unless his dissent is entered in the minutes of the meeting or filed promptly after adjournment. N.J.S.A. 14:6-13 [MBCA § 8.24(d)]. In many, if not most, instances an objecting director whose dissent is noted . . . would be absolved after attempting to persuade fellow directors to follow a different course of action. . . .

Even accepting the hypothesis that Mrs. Pritchard might not be liable if she had objected and resigned, there are two significant reasons for holding her liable. First, she did not resign until just before the bankruptcy. Consequently, there is no factual basis for the speculation that the losses would have occurred even if she had objected and resigned. Indeed, the trial court reached the opposite conclusion: "The actions of the sons were so blatantly wrongful that it is hard to see how they could have resisted any moderately firm objection to what they were doing." . . .

. . . .

In assessing whether Mrs. Pritchard's conduct was a legal or proximate cause of the conversion, "(l)egal responsibility must be limited to those causes which are so closely connected with the result and of such significance that the law is justified in imposing liability." Prosser, supra, § 41 at 237. Such a judicial determination involves not only considerations of causation-in-fact and matters of policy, but also common sense and logic.

. . . .

Within Pritchard & Baird, several factors contributed to the loss of the funds: commingling of corporate and client monies, conversion of funds by Charles, Jr. and William, and dereliction of her duties by Mrs. Pritchard. The wrongdoing of her sons, although the immediate cause of the loss, should not excuse Mrs. Pritchard from her negligence which also was a substantial factor contributing to the loss. RESTATEMENT (SECOND) OF TORTS, supra, § 442B, comment b. *Her sons knew that she, the only other director, was not reviewing their conduct; they spawned their fraud in the backwater of her neglect.* Her neglect of duty contributed to the climate of corruption; her failure to act contributed to the continuation of that corruption. Consequently, her conduct was a substantial factor contributing to the loss.

. . . .

To conclude, by virtue of her office, Mrs. Pritchard had the power to prevent the losses sustained by the clients of Pritchard & Baird. With power comes responsibility. She had a duty to deter the depredation of the other insiders, her sons. She breached that duty and caused plaintiffs to sustain damages.

The judgment of the Appellate Division is affirmed.

For affirmance Justices SULLIVAN, PASHMAN, CLIFFORD, SCHREIBER, HANDLER and POLLOCK.

NOTES AND QUESTIONS

1. *Duty to Whom?* In a partnership, partners owe duties one to another. By contrast, in a corporation, an officer or director owes her duties to the entity (the corporation), and not any one person within it. *Percival v. Wright*, 2 Ch. 421 (1902) (fiduciary duty claim against corporate official for insider trading would not lie because fiduciary owed his duty to the corporation and not to anyone in it). In most instances, shareholders cannot bring an action directly against officers or directors for the reason that those persons owe no duties to shareholders. Instead, utilizing a device known as the derivative action, see Chapter 11, *infra*, the shareholder must satisfy a number of prerequisites (verification, record ownership, security for costs, demand on the board of directors) to be able to step into the shoes of the corporation, to whom the duties are owed. The shareholder can then continue the action but with any recovery going to the corporate treasury. In fact, one option of a board of directors, as the representative of the party to whom the duty is owed, is to accept demand and take over the action for itself, in which case the parties will be realigned. *See* Introduction, *supra*.

2. *Duty to Shareholders?* Nonetheless, one of the most frequently encountered misstatements, by laypersons, corporate directors, lawyers, and even judges, is that directors owe their fiduciary duties to shareholders, or to the corporation and its shareholders. *See, e.g., Francis v. United Jersey Bank, supra*. It usually causes little mischief, as shareholders' interests are considered closely to be congruent with the "best interests of the corporation." Since at least the 1970s, however, a growing number of scholars have urged abandonment of the shareholder-centric model. They urge that, as a matter of corporate law, corporations, and those who operate them, would owe duties to a number of constituencies (stakeholders) other than shareholders (just one of many stakeholder groups), namely, employees, consumers, suppliers, communities in which the corporation has facilities, regional, state, and national economies, and so on. One term frequently used is the "communitarian model" of the corporation. *See, e.g.,* Kent Greenfield, *There's A Forest in Those Trees: Teaching About the Role of Corporations in Society*, 34 GA. L. REV. 1011 (2000); David Millon, *New Game Plan or Business As Usual?: A Critique of the Team Production Model of Corporation Law*, 86 VA. L. REV. 1001 (2000).

3. *Duty to Depositors?* One subgroup of creditors, depositors in financial institutions, may have duties owed directly to them. There exists a line of older cases which hold that directors of banks and other deposit institutions owe duties of care and loyalty to depositors. In *Francis v. United Jersey Bank, supra*, the court struggled with those precedents, on the ground that a reinsurance brokerage firm operates much like a bank.

4. *Use of Advisory Boards of Directors.* In the eyes of the law, there exists no such thing as an honorary, figurehead, or specialized director. In a high tech business, the financial, marketing and business aspects may have far outstripped the technical aspects with which the founders and certain of the directors are conversant. Founders may realize that, as directors, they are over their head. If they are anything, they are specialized, or figurehead, directors who should resign. Yet they want the emoluments of office: meetings in a paneled room, annual retainers and meeting fees, the status of being a director, and so on. One solution has been to create a second board of directors which has the same emoluments and may even meet some of the time with the original board of directors. These advisory boards have become quite common in high tech, real estate, and banking. In the latter two, it is not uncommon to have an advisory board for each region in which the corporation operates. Courts have held that a corporation must have a "real" or official board of directors. *See, e.g.,* MBCA § 8.01(a) ("Except as provided in section 7.32 [shareholder agreements] each corporation must have a board of directors"). If the issue arise, which of several is the "real" board of directors is an issue of fact.

5. *Sub-duties of the Duty of Care.* The original American Bar Association Corporate Director's Guidebook (1978) frowned on all but the most general attempt to adumbrate sub duties of the duty of care. *See* 33 Bus. Law. 1595, 1600. Nonetheless, over the years, courts and commentators have proffered various lists of sub duties. The Committee on Corporate Laws' attempt at a list is contained in a recently promulgated MBCA § 8.01 (c):

> In the case of a public company, the board's oversight responsibilities include attention to:
>
> (i) business performance and plans;
>
> (ii) major risks to which the corporation may be exposed;
>
> (iii) the performance and compensation of senior officers;
>
> (iv) policies and practices to foster the corporation's compliance with law and ethical conduct;
>
> (v) preparation of the corporation's financial statements;
>
> (vi) the effectiveness of the corporation's internal controls;
>
> (vii) arrangements for providing adequate and timely information to directors; and
>
> (viii) the composition of the board and its committees, taking into account the important role of independent directors.

6. Caremark *Duties.* One principal sub duty most do agree exists today is that, as part of their duty of care, in the larger modern corporation, directors must insure that corporations and their senior managers have in place a preventive law system (an "information and reporting system") which insures that all the corporation's businesses comply with the law and which gives off early warning signals where danger of noncompliance might exist. This has become known as directors' *Caremark* duties, after *In re Caremark Int'l Derivative Litig.*, 698 A.2d 959 (Del. Ch. 1996), in which Chancellor Allen approved the settlement of the derivative suit and commented how directors' duties have changed over the decades. Many corporations elevate the importance of this particular sub duty by forming a separate committee of directors, often called the Risk Management Committee, to oversee its implementation. In conjunction with legal counsel, committees and senior managers often oversee a legal auditing process which examines each area or business in which the corporation may have exposure and puts in place an information and reporting system to hinder and to give early warning if the risk of exposure increases.

7. *Duty to Creditors?* In *Credit Lyonnais Bank Nederland N.V. v. Pathe Comm. Corp.*, 17 Del. J. Corp. L. 1099, 1155 (Del. Ch. 1992), an influential judge (Chancellor William Allen, now professor at NYU School of Law)) posited that fiduciaries of corporations owe their duties directly to creditors when the corporation "is operating on the brink of insolvency." For at least several decades prior to *Credit Lyonnais*, corporate law was perceived as having little or no role in protecting creditors. Instead, fraudulent conveyance and bankruptcy laws protected creditors. Plaintiff creditors sometimes plead a *Credit Lyonnaise* type claim but the number of final resolutions is small because bankruptcy frequently has intervened. *See also Angelo Gordon & Co. v. Allied Riser Communications Corp.*, 822 A.2d 1065 (Del. Ch. 2002) (when is an entity "in the vicinity of insolvency?" and other questions discussed).

While *Credit Lyonaise* and its "vicinity of insolvency" (aka "zone of insolvency") theory often has been invoked, Chancellor Allen's statements are dictum, as the suit *sub judice* was not a suit by directors seeking to hold directors accountable but rather one by a shareholder. Nonetheless, the *Credit Lyonaise* and zone of insolvency theory became the stuff of urban legend, at least until 2007, when the Supreme Court of Delaware resolved the issue once and (hopefully) for all.

NORTH AMERICAN CATHOLIC EDUCATIONAL PROGRAMMING FOUNDATION [NACEPF], INC. v. GHEEWALLA
Supreme Court of Delaware
930 A.2d 92 (Del. 2007)

HOLLAND, JUSTICE: . . . NACEPF holds certain radio wave spectrum licenses regulated by the Federal Communications Commission. In March 2001, NACEPF, together with other similar spectrum license-holders, entered into the Master Use and Royalty Agreement with Clearwire Holdings, Inc. . . . . Under the Master Agreement, Clearwire could obtain rights to those licenses as then-existing leases expired and the then-current lessees failed to exercise rights of first refusal.

The defendant-appellees are Rob Gheewalla, Gerry Cardinale, and Jack Daly, who served as directors of Clearwire at the behest of Goldman Sachs & Co. NACEPF's Complaint alleges that the Defendants, even though they comprised less than a majority of the board, were able to control Clearwire because its only source of funding was Goldman Sachs. According to NACEPF, they used that power to favor Goldman Sachs' agenda in derogation of their fiduciary duties as directors of Clearwire. In addition to bringing fiduciary duty claims, NACEPF's Complaint also asserts that the Defendants fraudulently induced it to enter into the Master Agreement with Clearwire and that the Defendants tortiously interfered with NACEPF's business opportunities.

NACEPF is not a shareholder of Clearwire. Instead, NACEPF filed its Complaint in the Court of Chancery as a putative creditor of Clearwire. The Complaint alleges direct, not derivative, fiduciary duty claims against the Defendants, who served as directors of Clearwire while it was either insolvent or in the "zone of insolvency."

. . . .

[T]he Court of Chancery concluded: (1) that creditors of a Delaware corporation in the "zone of insolvency" may not assert direct claims for breach of fiduciary duty against the corporation's directors; [and] (2) that the Complaint failed to state a claim for the narrow, if extant, cause of action for direct claims involving breach of fiduciary duty brought by creditors against directors of insolvent Delaware corporations . . . .

In this opinion, we hold that the creditors of a Delaware corporation that is either insolvent or in the zone of insolvency have no right, as a matter of law, to assert direct claims for breach of fiduciary duty against the corporation's directors. Accordingly, we have concluded that the judgments of the Court of Chancery must be affirmed.

. . . .

According to the Complaint, the Defendants represented to NACEPF and the other [Spectrum Development] Alliance members that Clearwire's stated business purpose was to create a national system of wireless connections to the internet. Between 2000 and March 2001, Clearwire negotiated a Master Agreement with the Alliance, which Clearwire and the Alliance members entered into in March 2001. NACEPF asserts that it negotiated the terms of the Master Agreement with . . . the Defendants. NACEPF submits that all of the Defendants purported to be acting on the behalf of Goldman Sachs and the entity that became Clearwire.

Under the terms of the Master Agreement, Clearwire was to acquire the Alliance members' . . . spectrum licenses when those licenses became available. To do so, Clearwire was obligated to pay NACEPF and other Alliance members more than $24.3 million. The Complaint alleges that the Defendants knew but did not tell NACEPF that Goldman Sachs did not intend to carry out the business plan that was the stated rationale for asking NACEPF to enter into the Master Agreement, i.e., by funding Clearwire.

In June 2002, the market for wireless spectrum collapsed when WorldCom announced its accounting problems. It appeared that there was or soon would be a surplus of spectrum available from WorldCom. Thereafter, Clearwire began negotiations with the members of the Alliance to end Clearwire's obligations to the members. Eventually, Clearwire paid over $2 million to HITN and ITF to settle their claims and; according to NACEPF, was only able to limit its payments to that amount by otherwise threatening to file for bankruptcy protection. These settlements left the NACEPF as the sole remaining member of the Alliance. The Complaint alleges that, by October 2003, Clearwire "had been unable to obtain any further financing and effectively went out of business."

. . . [N]ACEPF alleges that because, at all relevant times, Clearwire was either insolvent or in the "zone of insolvency," the Defendants owed fiduciary duties to NACEPF "as a substantial creditor of Clearwire," and that the Defendants breached those duties by:

(1) not preserving the assets of Clearwire for its benefit and that of its creditors when it became apparent that Clearwire would not be able to continue as a going concern and would need to be liquidated and (2) holding on to NACEPF's license rights when Clearwire would not use them, solely to keep Goldman Sachs's investment in play.

. . . .

The Defendants moved to dismiss the Complaint . . . for NACEPF's failure to state a claim upon which relief can be granted under Court of Chancery Rule 12(b)(6).

Allegations of Insolvency and Zone of Insolvency

In support of its claim that Clearwire was either insolvent or in the zone of insolvency during the relevant periods, NACEPF alleged that Clearwire needed "substantially more financial support than it had obtained in March 2001." The Complaint alleges Goldman Sachs had invested $47 million in Clearwire, which "represent[ed] 84% of the total sums invested in Clearwire in March 2001, when Clearwire was otherwise virtually out of funds."

After March 2001, Clearwire had financial obligations related to its agreement with NACEPF and others that potentially exceeded $134 million, did not have the ability to raise sufficient cash from operations to pay its debts as they became due and was dependent on Goldman Sachs to make additional investments to fund Clearwire's operations for the foreseeable future.

The Complaint also alleges . . . upon the closing of the Master Agreement, Clearwire had approximately $29.2 million in cash and of that, $24.3 million would be needed for future payments for spectrum to the Alliance members. Clearwire's "burn" rate was $2.1 million per month and it had then no significant revenues. . . .

Additionally, in the Complaint, NACEPF alleges that, "[b]y October 2003, Clearwire had been unable to obtain any further financing and effectively went out of business. Except for money advanced to it as a stopgap measure by Goldman Sachs in late 2001, Clearwire was never able to raise any significant money."

The Court of Chancery opined that insolvency may be demonstrated by either showing (1) "a deficiency of assets below liabilities with no reasonable prospect that the business can be successfully continued in the face thereof," or (2) "an inability to meet maturing obligations as they fall due in the ordinary course of business." Applying the standards applicable to review under Rule 12(b)(6), the Court of Chancery concluded that NACEPF had satisfactorily alleged facts which permitted a reasonable inference that Clearwire operated in the zone of insolvency during at least a substantial portion of the relevant periods for purposes of this motion to dismiss. The Court of Chancery also concluded that insolvency had been adequately alleged in the Complaint, for Rule 12(b)(6) purposes, for at least a portion of the relevant periods following execution of the Master Agreement.

Corporations in the Zone of Insolvency Direct Claims for Breach of Fiduciary Duty May Not Be Asserted by Creditors

In order to withstand the Defendant's Rule 12(b)(6) motion to dismiss, the Plaintiff was required to demonstrate that the breach of fiduciary duty claims set forth in Count II are cognizable under Delaware law. This procedural requirement requires us to address a substantive question of first impression that is raised by the present appeal: as a matter of Delaware law, can the creditor of a corporation that is operating within the zone of insolvency bring a direct action against its directors for an alleged breach of fiduciary duty?

It is well established that the directors owe their fiduciary obligations to the corporation and its shareholders. While shareholders rely on directors acting as fiduciaries to protect their interests, creditors are afforded protection through contractual agreements, fraud and fraudulent conveyance law, implied covenants of good faith and fair dealing, bankruptcy law, general commercial law, and other sources of creditor rights. [See Production Res. Group v. NCT Group, Inc., 863 A.2d at 790]. Delaware courts have traditionally been reluctant to expand existing fiduciary duties. [*See, e.g.*, Wal-Mart Stores, Inc. v. AIG Life Ins. Co., 872 A.2d 611, 625 (Del. Ch. 2005), aff'd in part and rev'd in part on other grounds, 901 A.2d 106 (Del. 2006).] Accordingly, "the general rule is that directors do not owe creditors duties beyond the relevant contractual terms." [See, e.g., Simons v. Cogan, 549 A.2d 300, 304 (Del. 1988); Katz v. Oak Indus., Inc., 508 A.2d 873, 879 (Del. Ch. 1986); Geyer v. Ingersoll Publ'ns Co., 621 A.2d 784, 787 (Del. Ch. 1992); Production Res. Group v. NCT Group, Inc., 863 A.2d 772, 787 (Del. Ch. 2004)].

In this case, NACEPF argues that when a corporation is in the zone of insolvency, this Court should recognize a new direct right for creditors to challenge directors' exercise of business judgments as breaches of the fiduciary duties owed to them. This Court has never directly addressed the zone of insolvency issue . . . . That subject has been discussed, however, in several judicial opinions [Credit Lyonnais Bank Nederland N.V. v. Pathe Commc'ns Corp., 1991 WL 277613 (Del. Ch.); Production Resources Group, L.L.C. v. NCT Group, Inc., 863 A.2d 772 (Del. Ch. 2004); Trenwick America Litig. Trust v. Ernst & Young, L.L.P., 906 A.2d 168 (Del. Ch. 2006); Big Lots Stores, Inc. v. Bain Capital Fund VII, LLC, 922 A.2d 1169 (Del. Ch. 2006)] and many scholarly articles [multiple citations omitted].

In Production Resources, the Court of Chancery remarked that recognition of fiduciary duties to creditors in the "zone of insolvency" context may involve: "using the law of fiduciary duty to fill gaps that do not exist. Creditors are often protected by strong covenants, liens on assets, and other negotiated contractual protections. The implied covenant of good faith and fair dealing also protects creditors. So does the law of fraudulent conveyance. With these protections, when creditors are unable to prove that a corporation or its directors breached any of the specific legal duties owed to them, one would think that the conceptual room for concluding that the creditors were somehow, nevertheless, injured by inequitable conduct would be extremely small, if extant. Having complied with all legal obligations owed to the firm's creditors, the board would, in that scenario, ordinarily be free to take economic risk for the benefit of the firm's equity owners, so long as the directors comply with their fiduciary duties to the firm by selecting and pursuing with fidelity and prudence a plausible strategy to maximize the firm's value."

In this case, the Court of Chancery noted that creditors' existing protections-among which are the protections afforded by their negotiated agreements, their security instruments, the implied covenant of good faith and fair dealing, fraudulent conveyance law, and bankruptcy law-render the imposition of an additional, unique layer of protection through direct claims for breach of fiduciary duty unnecessary. It also noted that "any benefit to be derived by the recognition of such additional direct claims appears minimal . . . ." The Court of Chancery reasoned that "an otherwise solvent corporation operating in the zone of insolvency is one in most need of effective and proactive leadership — as well as the ability to negotiate in good faith with its creditors — goals which would likely be significantly undermined by the prospect of individual liability arising from the pursuit of direct claims by creditors." We agree.

. . . The directors of Delaware corporations have "the legal responsibility to manage the business of a corporation for the benefit of its shareholders owners." . . . This Court has endeavored to provide the directors with clear signal beacons and brightly lined channel markers as they navigate with due care, good faith, and loyalty on behalf of a Delaware corporation and its shareholders. This Court has also endeavored to mark the safe harbors clearly.

In this case, the need for providing directors with definitive guidance compels us to hold that no direct claim for breach of fiduciary duties may be asserted by the creditors of a solvent corporation that is operating in the zone of insolvency. When a solvent corporation is navigating in the zone of insolvency, the focus for Delaware directors does not change: directors must continue to discharge their fiduciary duties to the corporation . . . .

Insolvent Corporations Direct Claims For Breach of Fiduciary Duty May Not Be Asserted by Creditors

It is well settled that directors owe fiduciary duties to the corporation. When a corporation is solvent, those duties may be enforced by its shareholders, who have standing to bring derivative actions on behalf of the corporation because they are the ultimate beneficiaries of the corporation's growth and increased value. When a corporation is insolvent, however, its creditors take the place of the shareholders as the residual beneficiaries of any increase in value.

Consequently, the creditors of an insolvent corporation have standing to maintain derivative claims against directors on behalf of the corporation for breaches of fiduciary duties. The corporation's insolvency "makes the creditors the principal constituency injured by any fiduciary breaches that diminish the firm's value."

. . . .

[T]he Court of Chancery has never recognized that a creditor has the right to assert a direct claim for breach of fiduciary duty against the directors of an insolvent corporation. However, prior to this opinion, that possibility remained an open question because of the "arguendo assumption" in this case and the dicta in Production Resources. . . . In this opinion, we recognize "the pragmatic conduct-regulating legal realms . . . calls for more precise conceptual line drawing."

Recognizing that directors of an insolvent corporation owe direct fiduciary duties to creditors, would create uncertainty for directors who have a fiduciary duty to exercise their business judgment in the best interest of the insolvent corporation. To recognize a new right for creditors to bring direct fiduciary claims against those directors would create a conflict between those directors' duty to maximize the value of the insolvent corporation for the benefit of all those having an interest in it, and the newly recognized direct fiduciary duty to individual creditors. Directors of insolvent corporations must retain the freedom to engage in vigorous, good faith negotiations with individual creditors for the benefit of the corporation. Accordingly, we hold that individual creditors of an insolvent corporation have no right to assert direct claims for breach of fiduciary duty against corporate directors. Creditors may nonetheless protect their interest by bringing derivative claims on behalf of the insolvent corporation . . . .

Conclusion

The creditors of a Delaware corporation that is either insolvent or in the zone of insolvency have no right, as a matter of law, to assert direct claims for breach of fiduciary duty against its directors. Therefore, Count II of NACEPF's Complaint failed to state a claim upon which relief could be granted. Consequently, the final judgment of the Court of Chancery is affirmed.

NOTES AND QUESTIONS

1. *Zone of Insolvency?* In light of its opinion, that no creditor cause of action existed when an incorporated debtor was merely in the vicinity or zone, the court found it unnecessary to resolve the long vexed question of when exactly corporations are in the "zone of insolvency." *See* 930 A.2d 92, at 98 & n.20.

2. *Clearwire Survives.* Clearwire may not have been near bankruptcy after all. The company is the brainchild of cellular telephone king Craig O. McCaw, who is attempting to create a nationwide WiMax system. The stock ticker symbol is CLWR.

PROBLEM

The Cambridge Bank is an old fashioned bank. It has one office, three tellers, a cashier, a president, and a seven-person board of directors, which meets quarterly, but after the bank has closed for the day. Cambridge Bank also has no computers. All record keeping is done by hand. The cashier takes slips from the tellers, makes entries in the journal and ledgers by hand, and counts the cash at the end of each day.

The cashier is a young fellow. The last two years he has arrived at work in a new SAAB convertible. He has taken to wearing Armani and Versace suits. No one has taken particular notice of these events.

While in the last three years the bank has seemed very busy, deposits have continued to drop. Finally, the outside auditors call in all of the depositors' passbooks. The passbooks show deposits exceeding those recorded in the ledger by over $250,000 annually. Deposits actually have increased but the cash is gone.

The cashier breaks down and confesses. Alas, he has spent all the money on wild Club Med "sophisticated singles" vacations and first class air tickets. The bank is defunct.

Disgruntled shareholders sue the cashier, the president, and the directors.

Which would you rather defend? Why?

Two other directors of Old Line Insurance, *supra*, defend on other grounds. John Bares Fortippton was the former CEO of Big Time Insurance. He now lives most of the year at his farm house in Vermont. What meetings he participates in, he participates by conference telephone call. In his deposition, he testified that he allowed his name to be added to the Old Line board to enhance Old Line's prestige.

Bob Knight, a retired university administrator and coach in Bloomington, Indiana, attends meetings but only when they concern the company's business in Indiana. He testifies that he was added to the board to help it drum up and service business in the Hoosier State.

Does either have a shot at a valid defense?

D. *CAREMARK* DUTIES

STONE EX REL. AMSOUTH BANCORPORATION v. RITTER
Supreme Court of Delaware
911 A.2d 362 (2006)

Before STEELE, CHIEF JUSTICE, HOLLAND, BERGER, JACOBS, and RIDGELY, JUSTICES (constituting the Court en Banc).

HOLLAND, JUSTICE:

. . . .

The Court of Chancery characterized the allegations in the derivative complaint as a "classic Caremark claim," a claim that derives its name from In re Caremark Int'l Deriv. Litig. In Caremark, the Court of Chancery recognized that: "[g]enerally where a claim of directorial liability for corporate loss is predicated upon ignorance of liability creating activities within the corporation . . . only a sustained or systematic failure of the board to exercise oversight — such as an utter failure to attempt to assure a reasonable information and reporting system exists — will establish the lack of good faith that is a necessary condition to liability" [In re Caremark Int'l Inc. Deriv. Litig., 698 A.2d at 971; see also David B. Shaev Profit Sharing Acct. v. Armstrong, 2006 WL 391931, at 5 (Del. Ch.); Goodman v. Huang, 823 A.2d 492, 506 (Del. Ch. 2003)].

In this appeal, the plaintiffs acknowledge that the directors neither "knew [n]or should have known that violations of law were occurring," i.e., that there were no "red flags" before the directors. Nevertheless, the plaintiffs argue that the Court of Chancery erred by dismissing the derivative complaint which alleged that "the defendants had utterly failed to implement any sort of statutorily required monitoring, reporting or information controls that would have enabled them to learn of problems requiring their attention." The defendants argue that the plaintiffs' assertions are contradicted by the derivative complaint itself and by the documents incorporated therein by reference.

Consistent with our opinion in In re Walt Disney Co. Deriv Litig, we hold that Caremark articulates the necessary conditions for assessing director oversight liability. [906 A.2d 27 (Del. 2006)] We also conclude that the Caremark standard was properly applied to evaluate the derivative complaint in this case. Accordingly, the judgment of the Court of Chancery must be affirmed.

This derivative action is brought on AmSouth's behalf by William and Sandra Stone, who allege that they owned AmSouth common stock "at all relevant times." The nominal defendant, AmSouth, is a Delaware corporation with its principal executive offices in Birmingham, Alabama. During the relevant period, AmSouth's wholly-owned subsidiary, AmSouth Bank, operated about 600 commercial banking branches in six states throughout the southeastern United States and employed more than 11,600 people.

In 2004, AmSouth and AmSouth Bank paid $40 million in fines and $10 million in civil penalties to resolve government and regulatory investigations pertaining principally to the failure by bank employees to file "Suspicious Activity Reports" ("SARs"), as required by the federal Bank Secrecy Act ("BSA") . . .

The government investigations arose originally from an unlawful "Ponzi" scheme operated by Louis D. Hamric, II and Victor G. Nance. In August 2000, Hamric, then a licensed attorney, and Nance, then a registered investment advisor with Mutual of New York, contacted an AmSouth branch bank in Tennessee to arrange for custodial trust accounts to be created for "investors" in a "business venture." That venture (Hamric and Nance represented) involved the construction of medical clinics overseas. In reality, Nance had convinced more than forty of his clients to invest in promissory notes bearing high rates of return, by misrepresenting the nature and the risk of that investment. Relying on similar misrepresentations by Hamric and Nance, the AmSouth branch employees in Tennessee agreed to provide custodial accounts for the investors and to distribute monthly interest payments to each account upon receipt of a check from Hamric and instructions from Nance.

The Hamric-Nance scheme was discovered in March 2002, when the investors did not receive their monthly interest payments. Thereafter, Hamric and Nance became the subject of several civil actions brought by the defrauded investors in Tennessee and Mississippi (and in which AmSouth also was named as a defendant), and also the subject of a federal grand jury investigation in the Southern District of Mississippi. Hamric and Nance were indicted on federal money-laundering charges, and both pled guilty.

. . . .

On October 12, 2004, the Federal Reserve and the Alabama Banking Department concurrently issued a Cease and Desist Order against AmSouth, requiring it, for the first time, to improve its BSA/AML program. That Cease and Desist Order required AmSouth to (among other things) engage an independent consultant "to conduct a comprehensive review of the Bank's AML Compliance program and make recommendations, as appropriate, for new policies and procedures to be implemented by the Bank." KPMG Forensic Services ("KPMG") performed the role of independent consultant and issued its report on December 10, 2004 (the "KPMG Report").

Also on October 12, 2004, FinCEN and the Federal Reserve jointly assessed a $10 million civil penalty against AmSouth for operating an inadequate anti-money-laundering program and for failing to file SARs. . . . FinCEN found that "AmSouth violated the suspicious activity reporting requirements of the Bank Secrecy Act," and that "[s]ince April 24, 2002, AmSouth has been in violation of the anti-money-laundering program requirements of the Bank Secrecy Act." Among FinCEN's specific determinations were its conclusions that "AmSouth's [AML compliance] program lacked adequate board and management oversight," and that "reporting to management for the purposes of monitoring and oversight of compliance activities was materially deficient." AmSouth neither admitted nor denied FinCEN's determinations in this or any other forum.

The standard for assessing a director's potential personal liability for failing to act in good faith in discharging his or her oversight responsibilities has evolved beginning with our decision in Graham v. Allis-Chalmers Manufacturing Company, [188 A.2d 125 (Del. 1963)] through the Court of Chancery's Caremark decision to our most recent decision in Disney. A brief discussion of that evolution will help illuminate the standard that we adopt in this case.

Graham and Caremark

Graham was a derivative action brought against the directors of Allis-Chalmers for failure to prevent violations of federal anti-trust laws by Allis-Chalmers employees. There was no claim that the Allis-Chalmers directors knew of the employees' conduct that resulted in the corporation's liability. Rather, the plaintiffs claimed that the Allis-Chalmers directors should have known of the illegal conduct by the corporation's employees. In Graham, this Court held that "absent cause for suspicion there is no duty upon the directors to install and operate a corporate system of espionage to ferret out wrongdoing which they have no reason to suspect exists."

In Caremark, the Court of Chancery reassessed the applicability of our holding in Graham when called upon to approve a settlement of a derivative lawsuit brought against the directors of Caremark International, Inc. The plaintiffs claimed that the Caremark directors should have known that certain officers and employees of Caremark were involved in violations of the federal Anti-Referral Payments Law. That law prohibits health care providers from paying any form of remuneration to induce the referral of Medicare or Medicaid patients. The plaintiffs claimed that the Caremark directors breached their fiduciary duty for having "allowed a situation to develop and continue which exposed the corporation to enormous legal liability and that in so doing they violated a duty to be active monitors of corporate performance."

In evaluating whether to approve the proposed settlement agreement in Caremark, the Court of Chancery narrowly construed our holding in Graham "as standing for the proposition that, absent grounds to suspect deception, neither corporate boards nor senior officers can be charged with wrongdoing simply for assuming the integrity of employees and the honesty of their dealings on the company's behalf." The Caremark Court opined it would be a "mistake" to interpret this Court's decision in Graham to mean that: corporate boards may satisfy their obligation to be reasonably informed concerning the corporation, without assuring themselves that information and reporting systems exist in the organization that are reasonably designed to provide to senior management and to the board itself timely, accurate information sufficient to allow management and the board, each within its scope, to reach informed judgments concerning both the corporation's compliance with law and its business performance.

To the contrary, the Caremark Court stated, "it is important that the board exercise a good faith judgment that the corporation's information and reporting system is in concept and design adequate to assure the board that appropriate information will come to its attention in a timely manner as a matter of ordinary operations, so that it may satisfy its responsibility." The Caremark Court recognized, however, that "the duty to act in good faith to be informed cannot be thought to require directors to possess detailed information about all aspects of the operation of the enterprise." The Court of Chancery then formulated the following standard for assessing the liability of directors where the directors are unaware of employee misconduct that results in the corporation being held liable:

> Generally where a claim of directorial liability for corporate loss is predicated upon ignorance of liability creating activities within the corporation, as in Graham or in this case, . . . only a sustained or systematic failure of the board to exercise oversight — such as an utter failure to attempt to assure a reasonable information and reporting system exists — will establish the lack of good faith that is a necessary condition to liability.

[In re Caremark Int'l Inc. Deriv. Litig., 698 A.2d at 971.]

Caremark Standard Approved

As evidenced by the language quoted above, the Caremark standard for so-called "oversight" liability draws heavily upon the concept of director failure to act in good faith [discussed *infra*]. That is consistent with the definition(s) of bad faith recently approved by this Court in its recent Disney decision, where we held that a failure to act in good faith requires conduct that is qualitatively different from, and more culpable than, the conduct giving rise to a violation of the fiduciary duty of care (i.e., gross negligence). In Disney, we identified the following examples of conduct that would establish a failure to act in good faith:

> A failure to act in good faith may be shown, for instance, where the Fiduciary intentionally acts with a purpose other than that of advancing the best interests of the corporation, where the fiduciary acts with the intent to violate applicable positive law, or where the fiduciary intentionally fails to act in the face of a known duty to act, demonstrating a conscious disregard for his duties. There may be other examples of bad faith yet to be proven or alleged, but these three are the most salient.

The third of these examples describes, and is fully consistent with, the lack of good faith conduct that the Caremark court held was a "necessary condition" for director oversight liability, i.e., "a sustained or systematic failure of the board to exercise oversight — such as an utter failure to attempt to assure a reasonable information and reporting system exists. . . . " Indeed, our opinion in Disney cited Caremark with approval for that proposition. Accordingly, the Court of Chancery applied the correct standard in assessing whether demand was excused in this case where failure to exercise oversight was the basis or theory of the plaintiffs' claim for relief.

It is important, in this context, to clarify a doctrinal issue that is critical to understanding fiduciary liability under Caremark as we construe that case. The phraseology used in Caremark and that we employ here — describing the lack of good faith as a "necessary condition to liability" — is deliberate. The purpose of that formulation is to communicate that a failure to act in good faith is not conduct that results, ipso facto, in the direct imposition of fiduciary liability. The failure to act in good faith may result in liability because the requirement to act in good faith "is a subsidiary element[,]" i.e., a condition, "of the fundamental duty of loyalty." It follows that because a showing of bad faith conduct, in the sense described in Disney and Caremark, is essential to establish director oversight liability, the fiduciary duty violated by that conduct is the duty of loyalty.

This view of a failure to act in good faith results in two additional doctrinal consequences. First, although good faith may be described colloquially as part of a "triad" of fiduciary duties that includes the duties of care and loyalty, the obligation to act in good faith does not establish an independent fiduciary duty that stands on the same footing as the duties of care and loyalty. Only the latter two duties, where violated, may directly result in liability, whereas a failure to act in good faith may do so, but indirectly. The second doctrinal consequence is that the fiduciary duty of loyalty is not limited to cases involving a financial or other cognizable fiduciary conflict of interest. It also encompasses cases where the fiduciary fails to act in good faith. As the Court of Chancery aptly put it in Guttman, "[a] director cannot act loyally towards the corporation unless she acts in the good faith belief that her actions are in the corporation's best interest." [Guttman v. Huang, 823 A.2d 492, 506 n.34 (Del. Ch. 2003)].

We hold that Caremark articulates the necessary conditions predicate for director oversight liability: (a) the directors utterly failed to implement any reporting or information system or controls; or (b) having implemented such a system or controls, consciously failed to monitor or oversee its operations thus disabling themselves from being informed of risks or problems requiring their attention. In either case, imposition of liability requires a showing that the directors knew that they were not discharging their fiduciary obligations. Where directors fail to act in the face of a known duty to act, thereby demonstrating a conscious disregard for their responsibilities, they breach their duty of loyalty by failing to discharge that fiduciary obligation in good faith.

Chancery Court Decision

. . . The Court of Chancery found that the plaintiffs did not plead the existence of "red flags" — "facts showing that the board ever was aware that AmSouth's internal controls were inadequate, that these inadequacies would result in illegal activity, and that the board chose to do nothing about problems it allegedly knew existed." In dismissing the derivative complaint in this action, the Court of Chancery concluded: "This case is not about a board's failure to carefully consider a material corporate decision that was presented to the board. This is a case where information was not reaching the board because of ineffective internal controls. . . . With the benefit of hindsight, it is beyond question that AmSouth's internal controls with respect to the Bank Secrecy Act and anti-money laundering regulations compliance were inadequate. Neither party disputes that the lack of internal controls resulted in a huge fine — $50 million, alleged to be the largest ever of its kind. The fact of those losses, however, is not alone enough for a court to conclude that a majority of the corporation's board of directors is disqualified from considering demand that AmSouth bring suit against those responsible."

Reasonable Reporting System Existed

The KPMG Report evaluated the various components of AmSouth's longstanding BSA/AML compliance program. The KPMG Report reflects that AmSouth's Board dedicated considerable resources to the BSA/AML compliance program and put into place numerous procedures and systems to attempt to ensure compliance [including a full time BSA Offcier, a BSA/AML Compliance Department, and a Suspicious Activity Oversight Committee]. According to KPMG, the program's various components exhibited between a low and high degree of compliance with applicable laws and regulations.

. . . .

The KPMG Report reflects that the directors not only discharged their oversight responsibility to establish an information and reporting system, but also proved that the system was designed to permit the directors to periodically monitor AmSouth's compliance with BSA and AML regulations. For example, as KPMG noted in 2004, AmSouth's designated BSA Officer "has made annual high-level presentations to the Board of Directors in each of the last five years." Further, the Board's Audit and Community Responsibility Committee (the "Audit Committee") oversaw AmSouth's BSA/AML compliance program on a quarterly basis. The KPMG Report states that "the BSA Officer presents BSA/AML training to the Board of Directors annually," and the "Corporate Security training is also presented to the Board of Directors."

The KPMG Report shows that AmSouth's Board at various times enacted written policies and procedures designed to ensure compliance with the BSA and AML regulations. For example, the Board adopted an amended bank-wide "BSA/AML Policy" on July 17, 2003 — four months before AmSouth became aware that it was the target of a government investigation. That policy was produced to plaintiffs in response to their demand to inspect AmSouth's books and records pursuant to section 220 and is included in plaintiffs' appendix. Among other things, the July 17, 2003, BSA/AML Policy directs all AmSouth employees to immediately report suspicious transactions or activity to the BSA/AML Compliance Department or Corporate Security.

Complaint Properly Dismissed

In this case, the adequacy of the plaintiffs' assertion that demand is excused depends on whether the complaint alleges facts sufficient to show that the defendant directors are potentially personally liable for the failure of non-director bank employees to file SARs. Delaware courts have recognized that "[m]ost of the decisions that a corporation, acting through its human agents, makes are, of course, not the subject of director attention." Consequently, a claim that directors are subject to personal liability for employee failures is "possibly the most difficult theory in corporation law upon which a plaintiff might hope to win a judgment."

The KPMG Report — which the plaintiffs explicitly incorporated by reference into their derivative complaint — refutes the assertion that the directors "never took the necessary steps . . . to ensure that a reasonable BSA compliance and reporting system existed." KPMG's findings reflect that the Board received and approved relevant policies and procedures, delegated to certain employees and departments the responsibility for filing SARs and monitoring compliance, and exercised oversight by relying on periodic reports from them. Although there ultimately may have been failures by employees to report deficiencies to the Board, there is no basis for an oversight claim seeking to hold the directors personally liable for such failures by the employees.

With the benefit of hindsight, the plaintiffs' complaint seeks to equate a bad outcome with bad faith. The lacuna in the plaintiffs' argument is a failure to recognize that the directors' good faith exercise of oversight responsibility may not invariably prevent employees from violating criminal laws, or from causing the corporation to incur significant financial liability, or both, as occurred in Graham, Caremark and this very case. In the absence of red flags, good faith in the context of oversight must be measured by the directors' actions "to assure a reasonable information and reporting system exists" and not by second-guessing after the occurrence of employee conduct that results in an unintended adverse outcome. Accordingly, we hold that the Court of Chancery properly applied Caremark and dismissed the plaintiffs' derivative complaint for failure to excuse demand by alleging particularized facts that created reason to doubt whether the directors had acted in good faith in exercising their oversight responsibilities. [Affirmed]

NOTE

In late 2006, AmSouth mergered with a larger regional bank, Regions Financial Corp., also based in Birmingham, Alabama, and no longer exists as a stand alone corporation.

PROBLEM

CB Foods, Inc. is a large publicly-held company in the fruit, frozen vegetable, and canned meat business. CB's annual sales exceed $1 billion. The company has 6,000 employees, many of whom operate 42 plants located in various parts of the United States. In its business, the company generates large amounts of waste products (vegetable and animal matter), solvents (de-greasing agents used on its machinery), and waste water (especially in processing fruits and vegetables).

You are the newest lawyer in the CB law department, which has four lawyers. The CLO (Chief Legal Officer) calls you into her office. She says, "Our outside law firm thinks we need a legal and environmental audit of all our operations. You are newly out of law school. Is this necessary (it will cost a lot of money) or is it just a ruse to get more legal fees out of us?" She adds, "What are steps should or can we take to lessen our exposure?"

What is your reply?

E.   PROXIMATE CAUSATION

BARNES v. ANDREWS
District Court, Southern District of New York
298 F. 614, 616 (1924)

LEARNED HAND, J.

[Defendant served 2 years as a director of a corporation formed to manufacture starters for Ford automobiles and airplanes. Of only 2 directors' meetings held, defendant missed one because of his mother's death. The corporation failed, in part due to the incompetency of the factory manager. Nonetheless, Learned Hand refused to hold defendant liable because the plaintiff had failed to establish a causal link between the corporate loss and the defendant's general nonfeasance]

[T]he plaintiff must accept the burden of showing that the performance of the defendant's duties would have avoided the loss, and what loss it would have avoided. . . .

When the corporate funds have been illegally lent, it is a fair inference that a protest would have stopped the loan. But when a business fails from general mismanagement, business incapacity, or bad judgment, how is it possible to say that a single director could have made the company successful? [T]he plaintiff must show that, had Andrews done this full duty, he could have made the company prosper, or at least broken its fall. He must show what sum he could have saved the company. Neither of these he made any effort to do.

NOTES AND QUESTIONS

1. *Nonfeasance Cases.* Plaintiff's burden seems clearer in a transactional setting than in a general nonfeasance context. *See, e.g., FDIC v. Bierman*, 2 F.3d 1424, 1437 (7th Cir. 1993) ("[I]f a Board member objected to a loan, members 'weren't going to cram anything down anyone's throat,' " finding liable board members who remained silent). *See also Resolution Trust Corp. v. Franz*, 909 F. Supp. 1128, 1143 (N.D. Ill. 1995) (failure by directors to heed documented Federal Home Loan Bank Board criticisms can be both the "but for" and "substantial factor" elements in proximate cause analysis). *Cf. FDIC v. Bober*, 2002 U.S. Dist. LEXIS 13231 (S.D.N.Y. July 18, 2002) (director failed to attend 13 of 17 board meetings: whether the losses may have been avoided had he attended rests on disputed facts, precluding summary judgment).

2. *Superceding Causes.* A defendant may avert liability by demonstrating that an intervening cause superceded any proximate or "legal" cause that otherwise may have existed. An older, illustrative case is *Martin v. Hardy*, 251 Mich. 413, 232 N.W. 197 (1930), in which directors' nonfeasance would have resulted in failure of "an old fashioned dry goods store." The court found that what otherwise may have caused the loss, directors' inattention, had been superceded by an intervening cause, the advent of "chain store competition" in Ludington, Michigan. A more recent decision, *Smith v. Pacific Pools of Washington, Inc.*, 12 Wash. App. 578, 530 P.2d 658 (1975), found that the corporate president's alcoholism might have caused the corporation's losses but the intervention of a regional economic malaise in the Pacific Northwest had superceded the corporate official's duty of care violations. The severe decline in incomes and housing prices had ultimately lead to a severe decrease in swimming pool construction.

3. *Requirement of Damage.* Unlike in a duty of loyalty case, in which either damage to the corporation, or an illicit gain to the officer or director will ground an action, *see infra*, a duty of care case requires that the directors' actions have proximately caused damage to the entity. *See, e.g., Cede & Co. v. Technicolor, Inc.*, 634 A.2d 345, 368 (Del. 1993) (mistakenly referring to *Barnes v. Andrews* as a "seventy year old obscure decision"); *Diamond v. Oreamuno*, 301 N.Y.S.2d 78, 248 N.E.2d 910 (N.Y. 1969) (violation of duty of care allegation requires showing of damage while duty of loyalty claim does not: nonetheless finding that insider trading damages the corporation); Baker v. Mutual Loan & Investment Co., 50 S.E.2d 692, 696 (S.C. 1948) (finding damage to the corporation in an unlawful distribution, which all shareholders had received, because "[t]he capital of the corporation was then seriously impaired"). An issue revolves around whether or not impairment of the corporation's profitability (the corporation is not otherwise as profitable as it might have been) rather than affirmative harm to the corporation will suffice. Aren't earnings that might have been foregone too speculative upon which to premise a finding of harm or damage?

F. THE BUSINESS JUDGMENT RULE

SMITH v. VAN GORKOM
Supreme Court of Delaware
488 A.2d 858 (1985)

Before HERRMANN, C.J., and McNEILLY, HORSEY, MOORE, AND CHRISTIE, JJ., constituting the Court en banc.

HORSEY, Justice (for the majority):

This appeal from the Court of Chancery involves a class action brought by shareholders of the defendant Trans Union Corporation, originally seeking rescission of a cash-out merger of Trans Union . . ..

Following trial, the former Chancellor granted judgment for the defendant directors . . .. Judgment was based [on a finding] that the Board of Directors had acted in an informed manner so as to be entitled to protection of the business judgment rule in approving the cash-out merger . . ..

Speaking for the majority of the Court, we conclude that both rulings of the Court of Chancery are clearly erroneous. Therefore, we reverse and direct that judgment be entered in favor of the plaintiffs and against the defendant directors for the fair value of the plaintiffs' stockholdings in Trans Union . . .

We hold . . . that the Board's decision, reached September 20, 1980, to approve the proposed cash-out merger was not the product of an informed business judgment . . . .

Beginning in the late 1960's, and continuing through the 1970's, Trans Union pursued a program of acquiring small companies in order to increase available taxable income [against which it could use the investment tatx credit (ITC) and depreciation deductions its rail car leasing business generated].

On August 27, 1980, [Chairperson and Chief Executive Officer Jerome] Van Gorkom met with Senior Management of Trans Union. Van Gorkom reported on his lobbying efforts in Washington and his desire to find a solution to the tax credit problem more permanent than a continued program of acquisitions. Various alternatives were suggested and discussed preliminarily, including the sale of Trans Union to a company with a large amount of taxable income.

Donald Romans, Chief Financial Officer of Trans Union, stated that his department had done a "very brief bit of work on the possibility of a leveraged buy-out." This work had been prompted by a media article which Romans had seen regarding a leveraged buy-out by management. The work consisted of a "preliminary study" of the cash which could be generated by the Company if it participated in a leveraged buy-out. As Romans stated, this analysis "was very first and rough cut at seeing whether a cash flow would support what might be considered a high price for this type of transaction."

On September 5, at another Senior Management meeting which Van Gorkom attended, Romans again brought up the idea of a leveraged buy-out as a "possible strategic alternative" to the Company's acquisition program. Romans and Bruce S. Chelberg, President and Chief Operating Officer of Trans Union, had been working on the matter in preparation for the meeting. According to Romans: They did not "come up" with a price for the Company. They merely "ran the numbers" at $50 a share and at $60 a share with the "rough form" of their cash figures at the time. Their "figures indicated that $50 would be very easy to do but $60 would be very difficult to do under those figures." This work did not purport to establish a fair price for either the Company or 100% of the stock. It was intended to determine the cash flow needed to service the debt that would "probably" be incurred in a leveraged buy-out, based on "rough calculations" . . ..

At this meeting, Van Gorkom stated that he would be willing to take $55 per share for his own 75,000 shares. He vetoed the suggestion of a leveraged buy-out by Management, however, as involving a potential conflict of interest for Management. Van Gorkom, a certified public accountant and lawyer, had been an officer of Trans Union for 24 years, its Chief Executive Officer for more than 17 years, and Chairman of its Board for 2 years. It is noteworthy in this connection that he was then approaching 65 years of age and mandatory retirement.

. . . .

Van Gorkom decided to meet with Jay A. Pritzker, a well-known corporate takeover specialist and a social acquaintance. However, rather than approaching Pritzker simply to determine his interest in acquiring Trans Union, Van Gorkom assembled a proposed per share price for sale of the Company and a financing structure by which to accomplish the sale. Van Gorkom did so without consulting either his Board or any members of Senior Management except one: Carl Peterson, Trans Union's Controller.

Telling Peterson that he wanted no other person on his staff to know what he was doing, but without telling him why, Van Gorkom directed Peterson to calculate the feasibility of a leveraged buy-out at an assumed price per share of $55. [T]he record is devoid of any competent evidence that $55 represented the per share intrinsic value of the Company.

Having thus chosen the $55 figure, based solely on the availability of a leveraged buy-out, Van Gorkom multiplied the price per share by the number of shares utstanding to reach a total value of the Company of $690 million. Van Gorkom told Peterson to use this $690 million figure and to assume a $200 million equity contribution by the buyer. Based on these assumptions, Van Gorkom directed Peterson to determine whether the debt portion of the purchase price could be paid off in five years or less if financed by Trans Union's cash flow as projected in the Five Year Forecast, and by the sale of certain weaker divisions identified in a study done for Trans Union by the Boston Consulting Group ("BCG study"). Peterson reported that, of the purchase price, approximately $50-80 million would remain outstanding after five years. Van Gorkom was disappointed, but decided to meet with Pritzker nevertheless.

Van Gorkom arranged a meeting with Pritzker at the latter's home on Saturday, September 13, 1980. Van Gorkom prefaced his presentation by stating to Pritzker: "Now as far as you are concerned, I can, I think, show how you can pay a substantial premium over the present stock price and pay off most of the loan in the first five years. * * * If you could pay $55 for this Company, here is a way in which I think it can be financed."

Van Gorkom then reviewed with Pritzker his calculations based upon his proposed price of $55 per share. Although Pritzker mentioned $50 as a more attractive figure, no other price was mentioned. However, Van Gorkom stated that to be sure that $55 was the best price obtainable, Trans Union should be free to accept any better offer. Pritzker demurred, stating that his organization would serve as a "stalking horse" for an "auction contest" only if Trans Union would permit Pritzker to buy 1,750,000 shares of Trans Union stock at market price which Pritzker could then sell to any higher bidder. After further discussion on this point, Pritzker told Van Gorkom that he would give him a more definite reaction soon.

On Monday, September 15, Pritzker advised Van Gorkom that he was interested in the $55 cash-out merger proposal and requested more information on Trans Union. . . .

On Thursday, September 18, Van Gorkom met again with Pritzker. At that time, Van Gorkom knew that Pritzker intended to make a cash-out merger offer at Van Gorkom's proposed $55 per share. Pritzker instructed his attorney, a merger and acquisition specialist, to begin drafting merger documents. There was no further discussion of the $55 price. However, the number of shares of Trans Union's treasury stock to be offered to Pritzker was negotiated down to one million shares; the price was set at $38-75 cents above the per share price at the close of the market on September 19. At this point, Pritzker insisted that the Trans Union Board act on his merger proposal within the next three days . . .

. . . .

On Friday, September 19, Van Gorkom called a special meeting of the Trans Union Board for noon the following day. He also called a meeting of the Company's Senior Management to convene at 11:00 a.m., prior to the meeting of the Board. No one, except Chelberg and Peterson, was told the purpose of the meetings. Van Gorkom did not invite Trans Union's investment banker, Salomon Brothers or its Chicago-based partner, to attend.

[A]t the Senior Management meeting on September 20 . . . Van Gorkom disclosed the offer and described its terms, but he furnished no copies of the proposed Merger Agreement. Romans announced that his department had done a second study which showed that, for a leveraged buy-out, the price range for Trans Union stock was between $55 and $65 per share. Van Gorkom neither saw the study nor asked Romans to make it available for the Board meeting.

Senior Management's reaction to the Pritzker proposal was completely negative. No member of Management, except Chelberg and Peterson, supported the proposal. Romans objected to the price as being too low [and] took the position that the agreement to sell Pritzker one million newly-issued shares at market price would inhibit other offers, as would the prohibitions against soliciting bids and furnishing inside information to other bidders. Romans argued that the Pritzker proposal was a "lock up" . . .. Nevertheless, Van Gorkom proceeded to the Board meeting as scheduled without further delay.

Ten directors served on the Trans Union Board, five inside (defendants Bonser, O'Boyle, Browder, Chelberg, and Van Gorkom) and five outside (defendants Wallis, Johnson, Lanterman, Morgan and Reneker). All directors were present at the meeting, except O'Boyle who was ill. Of the outside directors, four were corporate chief executive officers and one was the former Dean of the University of Chicago Business School. None was an investment banker or trained financial analyst. All members of the Board were well informed about the Company and its operations as a going concern. . . ..

Van Gorkom began the Special Meeting of the Board with a twenty-minute oral presentation. Copies of the proposed Merger Agreement were delivered too late for study before or during the meeting. He reviewed the Company's ITC and depreciation problems and the efforts theretofore made to solve them. He discussed his initial meeting with Pritzker and his motivation in arranging that meeting. Van Gorkom did not disclose to the Board, however, the methodology by which he alone had arrived at the $55 figure, or the fact that he first proposed the $55 price in his negotiations with Pritzker.

[F]or a period of 90 days, Trans Union could receive, but could not actively solicit, competing offers; the offer had tobe acted on by the next evening, Sunday, September 21 . . .. Trans Union was required to sell Pritzker one million newly-issued shares of Trans Union at $38 per share,

Van Gorkom took the position that putting Trans Union "up for auction" through a 90-day market test would validate a decision by the Board that $55 was a fair price. He told the Board that the "free market will have an opportunity to judge whether $55 is a fair price." Van Gorkom framed the decision before the Board not as whether $55 per share was the highest price that could be obtained, but as whether the $55 price was a fair price . . ..

Attorney Brennan advised the members of the Board that they might be sued if they failed to accept the offer and that a fairness opinion was not required as a matter of law.

Romans told the Board that, in his opinion, $55 was "in the range of a fair price," but "at the beginning of the range."

. . . .

The Board meeting of September 20 lasted about two hours. Based solely upon Van Gorkom's oral presentation . . . Romans' oral statement, Brennan's legal advice, and their knowledge of the market history of the Company's stock, the directors approved the proposed Merger Agreement.

. . . .

[On] October 9, Trans Union issued a press release announcing: (1) that Pritzker had obtained "the financing commitments necessary to consummate" the merger with Trans Union; (2) that Pritzker had acquired one million shares of Trans Union common stock at $38 per share; (3) that Trans Union was now permitted to actively seek other offers and had retained Salomon Brothers for that purpose; and (4) that if a more favorable offer were not received before February 1, 1981, Trans Union's shareholders would thereafter meet to vote on the Pritzker proposal.

Salomon Brothers' efforts over a three-month period from October 21 to January 21 produced only one serious suitor for Trans Union-General Electric Credit Corporation ("GE Credit"), a subsidiary of the General Electric Company. However, GE Credit was unwilling to make an offer for Trans Union unless Trans Union first rescinded its Merger Agreement with Pritzker. When Pritzker refused, GE Credit terminated further discussions with Trans Union in early January.

In the meantime, in early December, the investment firm of Kohlberg, Kravis, Roberts & Co. ("KKR"), the only other concern to make a firm offer for Trans Union, withdrew its offer under circumstances hereinafter detailed.

On December 19, this litigation was commenced . . . .. On January 26, Trans Union's Board met and, after a lengthy meeting, voted to proceed with the Pritzker merger. The Board also approved for mailing, "on or about January 27," a Supplement to its Proxy Statement. . . .

On February 10, the stockholders of Trans Union approved the Pritzker merger proposal. Of the outstanding shares, 69.9% were voted in favor of the merger; 7.25% were voted against the merger; and 22.85% were not voted.

II.

We turn to the issue of the application of the business judgment rule to the September 20 meeting of the Board.

The Court of Chancery concluded from the evidence that the Board of Directors' approval of the Pritzker merger proposal fell within the protection of the business judgment rule. The Court found that the Board had given sufficient time and attention to the transaction, since the directors had considered the Pritzker proposal on three different occasions, on September 20, and on October 8, 1980 and finally on January 26, 1981. On that basis, the Court reasoned that the Board had acquired, over the four-month period, sufficient information to reach an informed business judgment on the cash-out merger proposal. The Court ruled:

> . . . that given the market value of Trans Union's stock, the business acumen of the members of the board of Trans Union, the substantial premium over market offered by the Pritzkers and the ultimate effect on the merger price provided by the prospect of other bids for the stock in question, that the board of directors of Trans Union did not act recklessly or improvidently in determining on a course of action which they believed to be in the best interest of the stockholders of Trans Union.

The Court of Chancery made but one finding; i.e., that the Board's conduct over the entire period from September 20 through January 26, 1981 was not reckless or improvident, but informed. This ultimate conclusion was premised upon three subordinate findings, one explicit and two implied. The Court's explicit finding was that Trans Union's Board was "free to turn down the Pritzker proposal" not only on September 20 but also on October 8, 1980 and on January 26, 1981. The Court's implied, subordinate findings were: (1) that no legally binding agreement was reached by the parties until January 26; and (2) that if a higher offer were to be forthcoming, the market test would have produced it . . . ..

. . . ..

[W]e conclude that the Court's ultimate finding that the Board's conduct was not "reckless or imprudent" is contrary to the record and not the product of a logical and deductive reasoning process.

The plaintiffs contend that the Court of Chancery erred as a matter of law by exonerating the defendant directors under the business judgment rule without first determining whether the rule's threshold condition of "due care and prudence" was satisfied. . . .

Under Delaware law, the business judgment rule is the offspring of the fundamental principle, codified in 8 Del.C. s 141(a), that the business and affairs of a Delaware corporation are managed by or under its board of directors. Pogostin v. Rice, Del.Supr., 480 A.2d 619, 624 (1984); Aronson v. Lewis, Del.Supr., 473 A.2d 805, 811 (1984) . . .. In carrying out their managerial roles, directors are charged with an unyielding fiduciary duty to the corporation and its shareholders. The business judgment rule exists to protect and promote the full and free exercise of the managerial power granted to Delaware directors. The rule itself "is a presumption that in making a business decision, the directors of a corporation acted on an informed basis, in good faith and in the honest belief that the action taken was in the best interests of the company." Thus, the party attacking a board decision as uninformed must rebut the presumption that its business judgment was an informed one.

The determination of whether a business judgment is an informed one turns on whether the directors have informed themselves "prior to making a business decision, of all material information reasonably available to them."

Under the business judgment rule there is no protection for directors who have made "an unintelligent or unadvised judgment." A director's duty to inform himself in preparation for a decision derives from the fiduciary capacity in which he serves the corporation and its stockholders. Since a director is vested with the responsibility for the management of the affairs of the corporation, he must execute that duty with the recognition that he acts on behalf of others. Such obligation does not tolerate faithlessness or self-dealing. But fulfillment of the fiduciary function requires more than the mere absence of bad faith or fraud. Representation of the financial interests of others imposes on a director an affirmative duty to protect those interests and to proceed with a critical eye in assessing information of the type and under the circumstances present here.

Thus, a director's duty to exercise an informed business judgment is in the nature of a duty of care, as distinguished from a duty of loyalty. Here, there were no allegations of fraud, bad faith, or self-dealing, or proof thereof. Hence, it is presumed that the directors reached their business judgment in good faith, and considerations of motive are irrelevant to the issue before us.

The standard of care applicable to a director's duty of care has also been recently restated by this Court. In Aronson, supra, we stated:

> While the Delaware cases use a variety of terms to describe the applicable standard of care, our analysis satisfies us that under the business judgment rule director liability is predicated upon concepts of gross negligence.

We again confirm that view. We think the concept of gross negligence is also the proper standard for determining whether a business judgment reached by a board of directors was an informed one.

In the specific context of a proposed merger of domestic corporations, a director has a duty under 8 Del.C. s 251(b), along with his fellow directors, to act in an informed and deliberate manner in determining whether to approve an agreement of merger before submitting the proposal to the stockholders. Certainly in the merger context, a director may not abdicate that duty by leaving to the shareholders alone the decision to approve or disapprove the agreement.

It is against those standards that the conduct of the directors of Trans Union must be tested, as a matter of law and as a matter of fact, regarding their exercise of an informed business judgment in voting to approve the Pritzker merger proposal.

. . . .

On the record before us, we must conclude that the Board of Directors did not reach an informed business judgment on September 20, 1980 in voting to "sell" the Company for $55 per share pursuant to the Pritzker cash-out merger proposal. Our reasons, in summary, are as follows:

The directors (1) did not adequately inform themselves as to Van Gorkom's role in forcing the "sale" of the Company and in establishing the per share purchase price; (2) were uninformed as to the intrinsic value of the Company; and (3) given these circumstances, at a minimum, were grossly negligent in approving the "sale" of the Company upon two hours' consideration, without prior notice, and without the exigency of a crisis or emergency.

As has been noted, the Board based its September 20 decision to approve the cash-out merger primarily on Van Gorkom's representations. None of the directors . . . had any prior knowledge that the purpose of the meeting was to propose a cash-out merger of Trans Union. No members of Senior Management were present, other than Chelberg, Romans and Peterson; and the latter two had only learned of the proposed sale an hour earlier. . . .

Without any documents before them concerning the proposed transaction, the members of the Board were required to rely entirely upon Van Gorkom's 20-minute oral presentation of the proposal. No written summary of the terms of the merger was presented; the directors were given no documentation to support the adequacy of $55 price per share for sale of the Company; and the Board had before it nothing more than Van Gorkom's statement of his understanding of the substance of an agreement which he admittedly had never read, nor which any member of the Board had ever seen.

[T]here is no evidence that any "report," as defined under s 141(e), concerning the Pritzker proposal, was presented to the Board on September 20. Van Gorkom's oral presentation of his understanding of the terms of the proposed Merger Agreement, which he had not seen, and Romans' brief oral statement of his preliminary study regarding the feasibility of a leveraged buy-out of Trans Union do not qualify as "reports" for these reasons: The former lacked substance because Van Gorkom was basically uninformed as to the essential provisions of the very document about which he was talking. Romans' statement was irrelevant to the issues before the Board since it did not purport to be a valuation study. At a minimum for a report to enjoy the status conferred by s 141(e), it must be pertinent to the subject matter upon which a board is called to act, and otherwise be entitled to good faith, not blind, reliance. Considering all of the surrounding circumstances-hastily calling the meeting without prior notice of its subject matter, the proposed sale of the Company without any prior consideration of the issue or necessity therefor, the urgent time constraints imposed by Pritzker, and the total absence of any documentation whatsoever-the directors were duty bound to make reasonable inquiry of Van Gorkom and Romans, and if they had done so, the inadequacy of that upon which they now claim to have relied would have been apparent.

The defendants rely on the following factors to sustain the Trial Court's finding that the Board's decision was an informed one: (1) the magnitude of the premium or spread between the $55 Pritzker offering price and Trans Union's current market price of $38 per share; (2) the amendment of the Agreement as submitted on September 20 to permit the Board to accept any better offer during the "market test" period; (3) the collective experience and expertise of the Board's "inside" and "outside" directors; and (4) their reliance on Brennan's legal advice that the directors might be sued if they rejected the Pritzker proposal. We discuss each of these grounds seriatim:

A substantial premium may provide one reason to recommend a merger, but in the absence of other sound valuation information, the fact of a premium alone does not provide an adequate basis upon which to assess the fairness of an offering price.

. . . .

[B]y their own admission [the directors] could not rely on the stock price as an accurate measure of value. Yet, also by their own admission, the Board members assumed that Trans Union's market price was adequate to serve as a basis upon which to assess the adequacy of the premium for purposes of the September 20 meeting.

The parties do not dispute that a publicly-traded stock price is solely a measure of the value of a minority position and, thus, market price represents only the value of a single share. Nevertheless, on September 20, the Board assessed the adequacy of the premium over market, offered by Pritzker, solely by comparing it with Trans Union's current and historical stock price.

Indeed, as of September 20, the Board had no other information on which to base a determination of the intrinsic value of Trans Union as a going concern. As of September 20, the Board had made no evaluation of the Company designed to value the entire enterprise, nor had the Board ever previously considered selling the Company or consenting to a buy-out merger. Thus, the adequacy of a premium is indeterminate unless it is assessed in terms of other competent and sound valuation information that reflects the value of the particular business.

Despite the foregoing facts and circumstances, there was no call by the Board, either on September 20 or thereafter, for any valuation study or documentation of the $55 price per share as a measure of the fair value of the Company in a cash-out context. . . .

We do not imply that an outside valuation study is essential to support an informed business judgment; nor do we state that fairness opinions by independent investment bankers are required as a matter of law. Often insiders familiar with the business of a going concern are in a better position than are outsiders to gather relevant information; and under appropriate circumstances, such directors may be fully protected in relying in good faith upon the valuation reports of their management.

Here, the record establishes that the Board did not request its Chief Financial Officer, Romans, to make any valuation study or review of the proposal to determine the adequacy of $55 per share for sale of the Company. On the record before us: The Board rested on Romans' elicited response that the $55 figure was within a "fair price range" within the context of a leveraged buy-out. No director sought any further information from Romans. No director asked him why he put $55 at the bottom of his range. No director asked Romans for any details as to his study, the reason why it had been undertaken or its depth. No director asked to see the study; and no director asked Romans whether Trans Union's finance department could do a fairness study within the remaining 36-hour period available under the Pritzker offer.

. . . .

The record also establishes that the Board accepted without scrutiny Van Gorkom's representation as to the fairness of the $55 price per share for sale of the Company-a subject that the Board had never previously considered. The Board thereby failed to discover that Van Gorkom had suggested the $55 price to Pritzker and, most crucially, that Van Gorkom had arrived at the $55 figure based on calculations designed solely to determine the feasibility of a leveraged buy-out. . . .

We do not say that the Board of Directors was not entitled to give some credence to Van Gorkom's representation that $55 was an adequate or fair price. Under s 141(e), the directors were entitled to rely upon their chairman's opinion of value and adequacy, provided that such opinion was reached on a sound basis. Here, the issue is whether the directors informed themselves as to all information that was reasonably available to them. Had they done so, they would have learned of the source and derivation of the $55 price and could not reasonably have relied thereupon in good faith.

None of the directors, Management or outside, were investment bankers or financial analysts. Yet the Board did not consider recessing the meeting until a later hour that day (or requesting an extension of Pritzker's Sunday evening deadline) to give it time to elicit more information as to the sufficiency of the offer, either from inside Management (in particular Romans) or from Trans Union's own investment banker, Salomon Brothers, whose Chicago specialist in merger and acquisitions was known to the Board and familiar with Trans Union's affairs.

Thus, the record compels the conclusion that on September 20 the Board lacked valuation information adequate to reach an informed business judgment as to the fairness of $55 per share for sale of the Company

(2)

This brings us to the post-September 20 "market test" upon which the defendants ultimately rely to confirm the reasonableness of their September 20 decision to accept the Pritzker proposal. In this connection, the directors present a two-part argument: (a) that by making a "market test" of Pritzker's $55 per share offer a condition of their September 20 decision to accept his offer, they cannot be found to have acted impulsively or in an uninformed manner on September 20; and (b) that the adequacy of the $17 premium for sale of the Company was conclusively established over the following 90 to 120 days by the most reliable evidence available-the marketplace. Thus, the defendants impliedly contend that the "market test" eliminated the need for the Board to perform any other form of fairness test either on September 20, or thereafter.

Again, the facts of record do not support the defendants' argument. There is no evidence: (a) that the Merger Agreement was effectively amended to give the Board freedom to put Trans Union up for auction sale to the highest bidder; or (b) that a public auction was in fact permitted to occur. The minutes of the Board meeting make no reference to any of this. . . .

. . . .

Van Gorkom states that the Agreement as submitted incorporated the ingredients for a market test by authorizing Trans Union to receive competing offers over the next 90-day period. However, he concedes that the Agreement barred Trans Union from actively soliciting such offers and from furnishing to interested parties any information about the Company other than that already in the public domain. . . .

. . . .

The defendants attempt to downplay the significance of the prohibition against Trans Union's actively soliciting competing offers by arguing that the directors "understood that the entire financial community would know that Trans Union was for sale upon the announcement of the Pritzker offer, and anyone desiring to make a better offer was free to do so." Yet, the press release issued on September 22, with the authorization of the Board, stated that Trans Union had entered into "definitive agreements" with the Pritzkers; and the press release did not even disclose Trans Union's limited right to receive and accept higher offers. Accompanying this press release was a further public announcement that Pritzker had been granted an option to purchase at any time one million shares of Trans Union's capital stock at 75 cents above the then-current price per share.

Thus, notwithstanding what several of the outside directors later claimed to have "thought" occurred at the meeting, the record compels the conclusion that Trans Union's Board had no rational basis to conclude on September 20 or in the days immediately following, that the Board's acceptance of Pritzker's offer was conditioned on . . . a "market test" of the offer . . ..

The directors' unfounded reliance on both the premium and the market test as the basis for accepting the Pritzker proposal undermines the defendants' remaining contention that the Board's collective experience and sophistication was a sufficient basis for finding that it reached its September 20 decision with informed, reasonable deliberation. [Trans Union's five "inside" directors had backgrounds in law and accounting, 116 years of collective employment by the Company and 68 years of combined experience on its Board. Trans Union's five "outside" directors included four chief executives of major corporations and an economist who was a former dean of a major school of business and chancellor of a university. The "outside" directors had 78 years of combined experience as chief executive officers of major corporations and 50 years of cumulative experience as directors of Trans Union. Thus, defendants argue that the Board was eminently qualified to reach an informed judgment on the proposed "sale" of Trans Union notwithstanding their lack of any advance notice of the proposal, the shortness of their deliberation, and their determination not to consult with their investment banker or to obtain a fairness opinion]. Compare Gimbel v. Signal Companies, Inc., Del. Ch., 316 A.2d 599 (1974), aff'd per curiam, Del.Supr., 316 A.2d 619 (1974). There, the Court of Chancery preliminary enjoined a board's sale of stock of its wholly-owned subsidiary for an alleged grossly inadequate price. It did so based on a finding that the business judgment rule had been pierced for failure of management to give its board "the opportunity to make a reasonable and reasoned decision." The Court there reached this result notwithstanding the board's sophistication and experience . . .. The Court found those factors denoting competence to be outweighed by evidence of gross negligence; that management in effect sprang the deal on the board by negotiating the asset sale without informing the board; that the buyer intended to "force a quick decision" by the board; that the board meeting was called on only one-and-a-half days' notice; that its outside directors were not notified of the meeting's purpose; that during a meeting spanning "a couple of hours" a sale of assets worth $480 million was approved; and that the Board failed to obtain a current appraisal of its oil and gas interests. The analogy of Signal to the case at bar is significant.

Several defendants testified that [attorney] Brennan advised them that Delaware law did not require a fairness opinion or an outside valuation of the Company before the Board could act on the Pritzker proposal. If given, the advice was correct. However, that did not end the matter. Unless the directors had before them adequate information regarding the intrinsic value of the Company, upon which a proper exercise of business judgment could be made, mere advice of this type is meaningless . . ..

We conclude that Trans Union's Board was grossly negligent in that it failed to act with informed reasonable deliberation in agreeing to the Pritzker merger proposal on September 20; and we further conclude that the Trial Court erred as a matter of law in failing to address that question before determining whether the directors' later conduct was sufficient to cure its initial error. A second claim is that counsel advised the Board it would be subject to lawsuits if it rejected the $55 per share offer. It is, of course, a fact of corporate life that today when faced with difficult or sensitive issues, directors often are subject to suit, irrespective of the decisions they make. However, counsel's mere acknowledgement of this circumstance cannot be rationally translated into a justification for a board permitting itself to be stampeded into a patently unadvised act. While suit might result from the rejection of a merger or tender offer, Delaware law makes clear that a board acting within the ambit of the business judgment rule faces no ultimate liability. Thus, we cannot conclude that the mere threat of litigation, acknowledged by counsel, constitutes either legal advice or any valid basis upon which to pursue an uninformed course.

Since we conclude that Brennan's purported advice is of no consequence to the defense of this case, it is unnecessary for us to invoke the adverse inferences which may be attributable to one failing to appear at trial and testify.

. . . .

To summarize: we hold that the directors of Trans Union breached their fiduciary duty to their stockholders . . . by their failure to inform themselves of all information reasonably available to them and relevant to their decision to recommend the Pritzker merger . . ..

We hold, therefore, that the Trial Court committed reversible error in applying the business judgment rule in favor of the director defendants in this case.

On remand, the Court of Chancery shall conduct an evidentiary hearing to determine the fair value of the shares represented by the plaintiffs' class, based on the intrinsic value of Trans Union on September 20, 1980. . . .. Thereafter, an award of damages may be entered to the extent that the fair value of Trans Union exceeds $55 per share.

REVERSED and REMANDED for proceedings consistent herewith.

MᶜNEILLY, Justice, dissenting (omitted).

NOTES AND QUESTIONS

1. *Legislative Trump Card.* The result in this case rocked the corporate world. Beset already by great difficulties in procuring Director & Officer (D & O) liability insurance, corporate directors and insurers felt that the principal case represented daunting amounts of future liability. D & O insurance became unavailable for some corporate directors at any price, and prohibitively expensive for others. Moreover, as Justice McNeilly elaborated upon in his dissent, Trans Union's Board was as distinguished and accomplished a board of directors as could be found. In June 1985, the Delaware General Assembly adopted Del. Gen. Corp. L. §102(b)(7), which virtually every state quickly followed. Section 102(b) lists permissible option provisions for a certificate of incorporation in Delaware. The raincoat provision (b(7)) enables corporations and drafters to add "[a] provision eliminating or limiting the personal liability of a director to the corporation or its stockholders for monetary damages for breach of fiduciary duty as a director, provided that any such provision shall not eliminate of limit the liability of a director: (i) For any breach of the director's duty of loyalty to the corporation or its stockholders; (ii) for acts or omissions not in good faith or which involve intentional misconduct or a knowing violation of law; (iii) under §174 of this title [liability for knowingly authorizing illegal distributions]; or (iv) for any transaction from which the director derived an improper personal benefit." The legislature intended the enactment to overrule *Smith v. Van Gorkom*. Two-thirds of publicly held corporations have amended their articles of incorporation, as have countless numbers of non-public ones, to add such exculpatory or §102(b)(7) provisions to their articles or certifcates.

2. *Reverse Roadmap Case.* The student or the practitioner can use *Smith v. Van Gorkom* as a guide for what not to do in advising a board of directors considering a sale of the company or other major transaction or, in a reverse approach, do everything the opposite of what Van Gorkom and the Trans Union Board did. Thus, an attorney might advise the board to:

- Consult internal corporate personnel, requesting copies of any reports or studies they may have crafted and insisting upon a forum in which directors can ask questions and explore alternatives with the senior managers.

- Utilize outside experts. Many believe the opinion to stand for the opposite of what it says. In a transaction of any size, directors may be well-advised to seek the services of an outside expert, such as an investment banker, financial analyst, or valuation expert.

- Meet in executive session. The insiders (CEO, President, COO, etc.) should absent themselves for part or all of a meeting so that directors may have, and may be recorded as having had, a free, unimpeded discussion of the issues.

- Insist on provision of some written documents. Only a few directors, if any, will plow through the written agreement of sale or merger but all directors should receive a draft, along with the letter of intent, term sheet and/or executive summary. When a corporation is buying another company or asset, many practitioners prefer to keep writings to a minimum. Writings can lead to leaks which may lead to insider trading which may derail a proposed transaction. By contrast, when directors are considering sale of the entire kit and caboodle, rather than purchase of what will only become part of it, they should have documents.

- Directors should be advised to insist upon adjournments, which will give them time to mull things over, or talk among themselves. If one adjournment is advisable, two or three may be better evidence that directors took their responsibilities seriously.

3. *"Intrinsic Value" or "Inherent Value."* Mr. Justice Horsey refers to these concepts throughout his opinion. Prospectors may make the argument that gold or silver has an intrinsic value but a share or stock, or even gold and silver? Isn't a share of stock, or any other assets, worth what numerous and willing buyers and sellers say it is worth?

4. *Case for the Ages.* Legal scholars still debate the ramifications, doctrinal significance, practical setting, and every other aspect of *Smith v. Van Gorkom. See, e.g.,* Symposium, Van Gorkom *and the Corporate Board: Problem, Solution or Placebo?*, 96 Nw. U. L. Rev. 447 (2002).

5. *Pritzker Paid?* Jay Pritzker (from a family of wealthy Chicago attorneys who, inter alia, developed the Hyatt luxury hotel chain) got Jerome Van Gorkom to, in effect, bid against himself; negotiated a leg up option that amounted to "heads I win, tails you lose"; and obtained an agreement to obtain a company that has become one of the three large credit reporting companies which dominate that business in the United States. Needless to say, he had a strong incentive to keep the deal he had negotiated alive. After the opinion, Trans Union's directors faced the prospect of up to $133,577,580 in liability ($65 per share minus $55 times the number of shares outstanding). To keep his deal intact, Pritzker reportedly paid a portion of the $23.5 million which settled the case. D & O insurers paid the rest. *See* Bayless Manning, *Reflections and Practical Tips on Life in the Boardroom After* Van Gorkom," 41 Bus. Law. 1 (1985).

Lyman Johnson, *The Modest Business Judgment Rule*
55 Bus. Law. 625, 626–31 (2000)[*]

Beginning in 1984 [Aronson v. Lewis, 473 A.2d 805, 812], and continuing today [Parnes v. Bally Entertainment Corp., 722 A.2d 1243, 1247 (1999)], the Delaware Supreme Court formulates the business judgment rule as "a presumption that in making a business decision the directors of a corporation acted on an informed basis, in good faith, and in the honest belief that the action taken was in the best interests of the company." In 1993 and 1995 decisions . . . [t]he court first noted that, by statute [Del. Code Ann. Tit. 8, § 141(a) (1991) . . .], the business and affairs of a corporation are managed by or under the direction of its board of directors. The court next observed that, in exercising these statutory powers, directors "are charged with an unyielding fiduciary duty to protect the interests of the corporation and to act in the best interests of the corporation" [Cede & Co. v. Techincolor, Inc., 634 A.2d 345, 360 (1993)].

. . . .

. . . Properly understood, the business judgment rule should not be regarded as a generalized liability shield for directors and their decisions. The rule, likewise, is not designed to perform a host of other functions it frequently is assigned. It is not, for example, "essentially a presumption that directors did not breach their duty of care"; nor is it a watered-down duty of care (. . . "Care Light"). Also, the business judgment rule is not usefully regarded as either a substantive standard for affirmatively guiding judicial conduct or a process-oriented standard for guiding judicial review . . . .

Properly understood, the business judgment rule is simply a policy of judicial *non-review.* Recall the . . . statement that "our courts will not second guess these business judgments" [*Cede, supra,* at 361]. A more modest expression of the sound statutory and policy bases underlying this judicial deference to director decisions . . . is as follows:

"[W]here money damages or equitable relief is sought, the business judgement rule is a judicial policy of not reviewing the substantive merits of a board of directors decision for the purpose of deciding whether directors breached or fulfilled their duty of care."

Conversely, [not applying the business judgment rule in the first place] courts may

---

review challenged board decisions: (i) for fraud, illegality, ultra vires, or waste; (ii) under a reasonableness test, to ascertain (a) director compliance with the duty of due care; (b) director compliance with the *Unocal* standard [applicable to adoption of takeover defenses]; or (c) whether director action was taken in bad faith [out of revenge, spite, etc.]; and (iii) under an entire fairness test, for the substantive merits of business decisions, where director loyalty is implicated [*See* Nixon v. Blackwell, 626 A.2d 1366, 1376 (Del. 1993); Weinberger v. UOP, Inc., 457 A.2d 701, 710–11 (Del. 1983)].

American Law Institute
Principles of Corporate Governance and Structure § 4.01(c) (1994)

(c) A director or officer who makes a business judgment in good faith fulfills the [duty of care] if the director or officer:

(1) is not interested in the subject matter of his business judgment;

(2) is informed with respect to the subject of the business judgment to the extent the director or officer reasonable believes to be appropriate under the circumstances; and

(3) rationally believes that the business judgment is in the best interests of the corporation.

Douglas M. Branson, *The Rule That Isn't a Rule — The Business Judgment Rule*
36 VAL. L. REV. 631, 645 (2002)*

Presumption or Prerequisite?

Delaware Courts . . . phrase the business judgment rule as a "presumption" that "in making a decision, the directors of a corporation acted on an informed basis and in good faith" [*See, e.g.*, Aronson v. Lewis, 473 A.2d 805 (1984)]. In his treatise, the late Professor Ed Cleary found no concept in the law of evidence more slippery than the concept of presumption, save perhaps the concept burden of proof [EDWARD W. CLEARY, MCCORMICK ON EVIDENCE § 342 (3d ed. 1984)]. . . .

The most frequent understanding of presumption is the . . . "bursting bubble" theory of presumptions. That is to say, a party's proof of circumstances A, B, and C (here, a judgment or decision, by duly elected directors, who exercised some care) leads to a presumption of the ultimate fact, D (reasonable care was in fact exercised). If the opposing party can poke a hole in the foundational facts (conflicts of interest, were woefully under-informed . . .), then the bubble bursts and the presumption of the ultimate fact dissipates, or, indeed, evaporates altogether. This theory of presumption predominates in American law and is the version the Federal Rules of Evidence adopted [*See* Fed. R. Evid. 301; Cleary, *supra*, at 974–75].

. . . .

Delaware courts' lack of deliberation on the use and misuse of presumptions may be of little significance in Delaware but could affect outcomes elsewhere. The courts of many states look to the law of Delaware in processing corporate law cases. Blending the Delaware business judgment rule with the accepted wisdom about presumptions, other state courts could come to a result opposite that which Delaware courts would reach, holding corporate directors for trial on breach of the duty of care allegations.

The American Law Institute states its version of the rule as a safe harbor rather than a presumption. Although the ALI version has been criticized as a movement "from presumption to prerequisite," [William Carney, *Section 4.01 of the American Law Institute's Corporate Governance Project; Restatement or Misstatement?*, 66 WASH. U. L.Q. 239, 273 (1988)] the ALI version offers greater protection and clarity than the presumption formulation of the business judgment rule [but] the ALI version requires a greater quantum of proof by directors.

NOTES

1. *See also* Lyman P.Q. Johnson, *Corporate Officers and the Business Judgment Rule*, 60 Bus. Law. 439 (2005) (examining doctrinal support for business judgment rule protection for corporate officers and their decisions).

2. *Contexts.* The rule is a many-faceted stone. The rule protects both directors and decisions from plenary judicial scrutiny. This may take the form of dismissal by a court at the summary judgment stage, based upon business judgment rule. If the directors lose a motion for summary judgment, they may nonetheless defend on the merits, invoking the business judgment rule. The rule has become the measuring stick by which courts evaluate directors' adoption of takeover defenses. *See* Chapter 16 *infra.* Courts also review independent directors' conclusions that shareholder derivative suits are not in the best interests of the corporation, using either a business judgment rule analysis or a modified form of analysis that may permit the court, in its discretion, to review directorial conclusions on the merits. *See* Chapter 11, *infra.*

3. *In the Office or Boardroom.* In a transactional, or preventive law context, the business law advisor to a board of directors, or the managers of a manager managed LLC, or the general partners of a limited partnership, and so on, has as her primary task shaping the decision making process so that, if a shareholder challenge later arises, directors are able to invoke the business judgment rule. They may do so both to protect the decision made and themselves from personal liability. The advisor, thus, must have in mind the following elements, or components of the rule.

4. *There Must Have Been a Decision or Judgment.* This requirement includes decisions to make no decision at all. Sometimes it is said that there must be an *independent* decision or judgment. Rubber stamping the CEO's or controlling shareholder's wish or command will not suffice. *See, e.g., McMullin v. Beran*, 765 A.2d 910, 916–20, 924 (Del. 2000) (finding that directors of a subsidiary were not entitled to business judgment rule protection because they delegated the decision to the parent corporation when they "had an ultimate statutory duty and fiduciary responsibility to make an informed and independent decision"); *Miller v. Schreyer*, 683 N.Y.S.2d 51, 54 (N.Y. App. Div. 1999) ("when the wrong alleged is inaction of the board rather than a conscious decision . . . the business judgement rule is inapplicable"); *Brane v. Roth*, 590 N.E.2d 587, 592 (Ind. App. 1992) ("[T]he rule does not protect directors who have abdicated their position or absent a conscious decision, have failed to act"). Veteran corporate directors maintain that boards often act by consensus and consensuses build by a process of accretion. The modern business judgment rule requires instead that boards of directors put matters to motions and vote them up or down, which encourages confrontation inconsistent with the collegial manner in which boards operate. The rule forces boards to act like legislative bodies or faculty meetings at universities.

5. *Component of the Rule — An Informed Decision (Some Care).* The decision or judgment must have been an informed one but it is incorrect to say that it must have been "duly informed" one, or made in the exercise of reasonable care. If being fully informed, or having had acted with reasonable care, were necessary, all such cases would require trials, at which finders of fact would determine if in fact due care was exercised. But the purpose of the business judgement rule is to dispense with a need for trials in most cases and to give flesh to the concept that it is directors, and not courts, who oversee management of corporation's business and affairs.

This is the meaning of the Supreme Court of Delaware in *Smith v. Van Gorkom*, 488 A.2d 858, 873 (Del. 1985), when Justice Horsey stated that "[w]e think the concept of gross negligence is also the proper standard for determining whether a business judgment reached by a board of directors was an informed one." Gross negligence is not the standard of care overall. The statute requires due care. But exercise of some care, rather that due care, is the standard applicable to the process of making a judgment or decision.

In *Brehm v. Eisner*, 746 A.2d 244, 259 (Del. 2000), Chief Justice Veasey concluded that "[t]he Board is responsible for considering only *material* facts that are *reasonably available*, not those that are immaterial or out of the board's reasonable reach." Some commentators state that how much information is enough information is itself a business judgment, to be shielded from judicial inquiry if the process demonstrates that the board exercised some care.

6. *Component of the Rule — Absence of Disabling Conflicts of Interest.* Receipt of normal directors' fees does not disable. *Marx v. Akers*, 666 N.Y.S.2d 1034 (N.Y. 1996) (prospect of $80,000 per year at IBM does not disable). That a director was a former neighbor of an executive on the other side of a transaction did not disable the director. *Odyssey Partners v. Fleming Cos.*, 735 A.2d 386, 409–10 (Del. Ch. 1999). Conversely, receipt of a $150,000 finder's fee disabled a director. *Cede & Co. v. Technicolor, Inc.*, 634 A.2d 345, 362 (Del. 1993). A further question, however, is whether a disabling conflict on one or more decision makers' parts, though less than a majority, taints a collegial decision making process. The latter is a question of fact.

When a critical mass of directors wore second hats as high paid consultants, hired by the controlling shareholder, their decision was not entitled to business judgment rule protection. *Clark v. Lomas & Nettleton Fin. Corp.*, 581 F.2d 516 (5th Cir. 1978).

Structural bias, the predilection of directors to favor those of the same social or economic class, such as fellow directors or corporate officers, in the eyes of most courts does not disable, as a matter of law. A universal principle is that if a single decision maker seeks the business judgment rule's protection she must, "like Caesar's wife, be above reproach." *Kahn v. Tremont Corp.*, 694 A.2d 422, 430 (Del. Ch. 1997); *Lewis v. Fuqua*, 502 A.2d 962, 967 (Del. Ch. 1985).

7. *Component of the Rule — A Rational Basis for the Decision Made.* Some judges and commentators say that the directors are entitled to the rule's protection if their decision was other than "manifest folly." By contrast, the statement that all directors' decisions must have a sound business purpose goes too far in the other direction. *See* ALI CORP. GOV. PROJ. § 4.01(c)(4). Professor Lyman Johnson disputes the ALI version, denying that a rational basis was ever a component of the rule. Johnson, *supra*, at 632–33. *See also WLR Foods, Inc. v. Tyson Foods, Inc.*, 65 F.3d 1172, 1182–83 (4th Cir. 1995) (rationality of decision made is irrelevant; only good faith of directors making the decision is at issue). *Cf. Parnes v. Bally Entertainment Corp.*, 722 A.2d 1243, 1246 (Del. 1999) (rule does not protect "inexplicable decisions"); *Gimbel v. Signal Cos.*, 316 A.2d 599, 610 (Del. Ch.), *aff'd*, 316 A.2d 619 (Del. 1974) ("There are limits on the business judgment rule which fall short of intentional or inferred fraudulent misconduct and which are based simply on gross inadequacy of price").

8. *Umbrella Requirement of Good Faith.* An attorney advising a board might run through the rule's components as a checklist; judgment or decision, absence of disabling conflicts, some care exercised, and a rational basis. Even if all the law's formal requirements have been met, however, seasoned lawyers still apply a "smell test." In the business judgment rule context, the good faith element serves as a surrogate for a smell test. *See, e.g., Harhen v. Brown*, 710 N.E.2d 224, 234–35 (Mass. App. 1999) (cryptic peremptory denial of shareholder derivative action demand not in good faith).

Good faith also has particular utility in several delimited areas. One is when the decision maker's decision making process has been infected by base motives other than greed: revenge, spite, hatred, pride, or some other motive could be found to have dominated the process. *See, e.g., In re RJR Nabisco Shareholders Litig.*, 1999 WL 7036, slip op. at 15 (Del. Ch. 1989).

PROBLEMS

1. The board of Borgen Stanley had noted that the corporation had on hand excess cash of $500 million. Desiring to lie low for a year, after a quick canvas of the markets and a report from one of the corporation's financial advisors, the board directed the CFO to invest the cash in tax-free municipal bonds earning 5 percent interest. Uncertainty in the markets, occasioned by the impending invasion of a Middle Eastern country by an allied force, soon thereafter pushed interest rates to 16 percent in the short term bond market. With all of that excess cash, Borgen Stanley could have earned considerably more in the high yield bond market.

A shareholder has sued the board, seeking to hold liable its members for the hurried decision they made. The judge asks you, his law clerk, what decision he should make and why on the board members' motion for summary judgment.

2. The Birmingham Barons are a class AAA (one level below the major leagues) minor league baseball team. They play their home games at beautiful Black Warrior field which sits on the banks of the Black Warrior River. The Baron's majority shareholder, Wimp Borchers, a successful local car dealer, fervently believes that "God intended baseball games to be played outdoors in the afternoon." Black Warrior Stadium thus has no lights; it cannot accommodate night time baseball.

Recently, a celebrated athlete (some say the most celebrated of all time) has decided to try his hand at baseball, with the Barons no less. His presence on the team would triple attendance, that is, if the Barons played night baseball.

Instead, the Barons continue to lose money each year. Year after year, the Baron's board summarily votes to continue to have the team play day baseball only.

Shlensky, a rabid baseball fan, is a minority shareholder in the Barons, who has given upon on the major league team he formerly supported and moved to Birmingham. He has sued Sanders and the other board members for breach of the duty of care.

Shlensky says that if the directors only conducted the most perfunctory market study they would see that the team could make considerably more money playing night time baseball, especially given the presence of the aforesaid celebrated athlete. Does Shlenksy's suit have a chance?

3. Assume that, in the previous problem, the seven directors of the Birmingham Barons include the following: the outside lawyer whose firm does $300,000 in legal work for the Barons each year; Wimp's long time Saturday morning golf partner; the owner of the radio station that broadcasts the Baron's games; a senior vice president of the Barons in charge of marketing; an accounting professor who chairs the audit committee; and Wimp's nephew, Sany Borchers. The seventh director is Wimp himself, of course.

Assume further that the directors did discuss and deliberate the question of night baseball over three successive meetings, culminating in a formal 6-0 vote, Wimp abstaining. Can you nonetheless challenge (that is, pass a red face test) the failure to commence play of night time baseball?

4. Change the hypothetical once again. The directors are not as described in the previous problem. Instead, they are all pillars of the Birmingham business community. None has financial ties to the Barons or its controlling shareholder. They are CEOs and business leaders. Only one or two have social ties to Wimp Sanders.

When confronted by the shareholder demand to consider playing night baseball, the directors hire a consultant, Reggie Doby. Reggie quickly renders onto the board a written report. The report purports to find a trend back to day time baseball, at least by minor league teams operating in cities with more than 400,000 inhabitants. Reggie also openly discloses that he is the president of a not-for-profit organization named "Daytime Baseball Boosters, Inc."

Following receipt and review of the report, the Barons directors now vote 6-0, Wimp abstaining, to continue playing day time baseball only.

Would you as a plaintiff's attorney still take the case of the complaining Barons shareholder?

5. Now, assume that the relatively disinterested Barons board receives the consultant's report and decides to do it one better. The board votes 6-0, Wimp abstaining, to have their baseball club play only early morning baseball. Among other things, in order to avoid the afternoon heat, the Barons will commence games at 7:00 am. Double headers (successive games played back-to-back) will commence at 5:45 am. The twilight double header of old will be replaced by the "dawn double header." Reporting on these developments, sports writer Lash Larue writes of the Barons board of directors, "Where are they coming from?"

Can a plaintiff shareholder's attorney argue for non-application of the business judgment rule?

G. THE DUTY OF LOYALTY

State Ex Rel. Hayes Oyster Co. v. Keypoint Oyster Co.
Supreme Court of Washington
64 Wash. 2d 375, 391 P.2d 979 (1964)

DENNEY, JUDGE.

. . . .

[Verne] Hayes was one of the founders of Coast which, over the years, became a public corporation and acquired several large oyster property holdings, among which were oyster beds and facilities for harvesting oysters located at Allyn and Poulsbo, Washington. . . . Hayes was an officer and director of Coast from its incorporation and was president and manager and owner of 23 percent of its stock . . . .

On October 21, 1958, Coast and Hayes entered into a full employment contract by which Hayes was to act as president and manager of Coast for a 10-year period and to refrain directly or indirectly from taking part in any business which would be in competition with the business of Coast, except Hayes Oyster.

Hayes Oyster was a family-owned corporation in which Sam Hayes owned about 75 percent and Verne Hayes about 25 percent of its stock.

In the spring of 1960, Coast owed substantial amounts to several creditors and it became apparent that the corporation must have cash . . . . Several alternatives were considered by the directors of Coast, among them Hayes' suggestion to sell Allyn and Poulsbo. In June 1960, Hayes inquired of Engman, a long-time employee of Coast . . . if Engman would be interested in purchasing Allyn and Poulsbo. Engman was interested but needed capital with which to commence operations. Engman then asked Hayes if he would 'come in' with him. Hayes replied that his full-employment contract with Coast might forbid it, but he would consult Ward Kumm, attorney for and long-time director of Coast.

Hayes testified that in July 1960, he told Engman that he had consulted with Kumm and his brother Sam Hayes and that Hayes Oyster could aid Engman . . . . (Kumm denied that he ever talked to Hayes on the matter.) At this time, Engman told Hayes he would attempt to secure a loan from relatives.

On August 4, 1960, an informal meeting was held in Long Beach, California, attended by Hayes, Kumm, and representatives of Van Camp Seafoods Company, owner of 23 percent of Coast stock . . . . Hayes' plan to sell Allyn and Poulsbo was approved and a meeting of Coast's board of directors was called. On August 11, 1960, the board of directors of Coast approved the sale of Allyn and Poulsbo to Engman at a price of $250,000, nothing down, payment of $25,000 a year, interest at 5 percent on unpaid balance. . . . Hayes informed Engman of the action of the board of directors and put him in possession of Allyn and Poulsbo on August 16, 1960.

Engman instructed Kumm to draw the necessary documents to incorporate the new enterprise to be known as Keypoint Oyster Company, which was to enter into the contract with Coast for the purchase of Allyn and Poulsbo. Engman, his wife, and Sam Hayes were the incorporators, directors and officers of Keypoint. Certificate No. 1 for 250 shares of stock was issued to Engman, certificate No. 2 for 249 shares to Engman's wife, and certificate No. 3 for one qualifying share to Sam Hayes. Kumm forwarded the stock certificates to Engman, accompanied by a separate assignment in blank . . . .

Shortly thereafter, Engman delivered to Verne Hayes Keypoint certificate of stock No. 2, issued to Edith Engman, together with the separate assignment signed by her in which the name of the assignee was left blank. It is undisputed that the words 'Hayes Oyster Company' as assignee were not typed in said assignment until July 5, 1962.

The trial court found that, on September 1, 1960, Hayes and Engman agreed that Hayes Oyster would acquire 50 percent interest in Keypoint in consideration of Hayes co-signing the note. . . .

Hayes made no mention at the meeting in Long Beach on August 4, 1960, or at the Coast directors' meeting on August 11, 1960, that Hayes or Hayes Oyster might acquire some interest in Keypoint. Hayes made no disclosure to any officer, director, stockholder or employee of Coast at the shareholders' meeting or at the time Hayes signed the contract for Coast on October 21, 1960, that Hayes or Hayes Oyster were to participate in or have a financial interest in Keypoint. Indeed, Coast acquired no knowledge of the Engman-Hayes deal until subsequent to the termination of Hayes' administrative duties as president and general manager of Coast in May, 1961 . . .

. . . .

[H]ayes was required to divulge his interest in Keypoint. His obligation to do so arises from the possibility, even probability that some controversy might arise between Coast and Keypoint relative to the numerous provisions of the executory contract. Coast shareholders and directors had the right to know of Hayes' interest in Keypoint in order to intelligently determine the advisability of retaining Hayes as president and to determine whether or not it was wise to enter into the contract at all, in view of Hayes' conduct. In all fairness, they were entitled to know that their president and director might be placed in a position where he must choose between the interest of Coast and Keypoint in conducting Coast's business with Keypoint.

. . . .

It is true that Hayes hypothecated his stock in Coast to one of Coast's creditors in early August 1960. Undoubtedly, this aided Coast in placating its creditors at that time and showed absence of an intent to defraud Coast. It is not necessary, however, that an officer or director of a corporation have an intent to defraud or that any injury result to the corporation for an officer or director to violate his fiduciary obligation in secretly acquiring an interest in corporate property.

In the case of Lycette v. Green River Gorge, Inc., 21 Wash.2d 859, p. 865, 153 P.2d 873, p. 876, we said: "Actual injury is not the principle upon which the law proceeds in condemning such contracts. Fidelity in the agent is what is aimed at, and as a means of securing it, the law will not permit the agent to place himself in a situation in which he may be tempted by his own private interest to disregard that of his principal."

. . . .

Coast had the option to affirm the contract or seek rescission. It chose the former and can successfully invoke the principle that whatever a director or officer acquires by virtue of his fiduciary relation, except in open dealings with the company, belongs not to such director or officer, but to the company. Nothing less than this satisfies the law.

. . . .

The decree and judgment of the trial court denying Engman any right or interest in the disputed stock is affirmed. . . . The decree ordering issuance of a new certificate of stock for 250 shares of Keypoint Oyster Company to Hayes Oyster Company is reversed with direction to order Keypoint Oyster Company to issue a new certificate for 250 shares of its stock to Coast Oyster Company and cancel the certificates heretofore standing in the name of or assigned to Hayes Oyster Company.

WEAVER, HUNTER, HAMILTON, and HALE, JJ., concur.

NOTES AND QUESTIONS

1. *Harm to the Principal or Illicit Gain to the Director or Officer?* As the principal case indicates, a gain incurred while serving the best interests of a competitor or of one's self may be sufficient to ground an action. The gain need not necessarily be secret, even though often it is, as with Verne Hayes in the principal case. When the American Law Institute adopted Part V of its Principles of Corporate Governance and Structure, a major controversy was that the reporters had titled the part the "Duty of Fair Dealing." Fairness has as its obverse harm, or the likelihood of harm, less inclusive than the prevention of illicit gain, in some cases of which harm will be absent. The reporters denied any such intention. *See* ALI PRINCIPLES OF CORPORATE GOVERNANCE AND STRUCTURE, INTRODUCTION TO PART V, DUTY OF FAIR DEALING, at 199–200 (1994) (hereinafter ALI CORP. GOV. PROJ.) ("Courts have traditionally analyzed the obligation of a director or office who acts with a pecuniary interest in a matter in terms of a 'duty of loyalty' to the corporation. . . . [P]art V avoids use of the term . . . and instead uses the term 'duty of fair dealing.' ").

2. *Mechanical Rules.* In the Nineteenth Century, dealings in which a director was found to have violated his duty of loyalty were declared void. *See, e.g., Wardell v. Union Pacific RR*, 103 U.S. 651 (1881). Sometime early in the twentieth century, courts began taking a softer line: contracts and other dealings tainted with a duty of loyalty violation were voidable, not void *ab initio*, at the corporation's election. *See* Harold Marsh, Jr., *Are Directors Trustees? Conflicts of Interest and Corporate Morality*, 22 BUS. LAW. 35, 36–38 (1966).

Older mechanical rules, for instance, declared that the vote of a single director with divided loyalties tainted the entire board process, even if the board had approved the transaction 8-1. *See, e.g., Tefft v. Schaefer*, 239 P. 837 (Wash. 1925). Courts have now abolished the old rule, bifurcating the process. The question of whether the interested director's participation tainted the deliberations of a collegial body is a further and separate inquiry, not an automatic result.

3. *Pedestrian Cases.* Duty of loyalty issues can be complex, involving as they do interested director transactions, usurpation of corporate opportunities, executive compensation, and so on. At the other end of the spectrum, however, the duty of loyalty also is the legal vehicle, criminal prosecutions aside, whereby cases of brazen thievery, outright conversion, and destruction of corporate property are vindicated. *See, e.g., Enstar Group, Inc. v. Grassgreen*, 812 F. Supp. 1562, 1566 (M.D. Ala. 1993) (officers of Kinder-Care, Inc., used commitment fees paid by Drexel-Burnham in return for commitment of Kinder-Care funds to prospective junk bond financing to service their personal investments); *A & P's Hole-In-One, Inc. v. Moskop*, 832 S.W.2d 860, 862 (Ark. App. 1992) (half-owner of incorporated business held liable on duty of loyalty grounds to account for use of corporate funds to pay personal expenses); *Genesis Respiratory Servs., Inc. v. Hall*, 649 N.E.2d 1266, 1268 (Ohio App. 1994) (director unilaterally used corporate funds to pay himself increased salary, other payments and rent on building he owned); *Venizelos v. Oceania Maritime Agency, Inc.*, 702 N.Y.S.2d 17, 18 (A.D. 2000) ($26 million in damages upheld against defendant corporate officer, the court finding that "the sole purpose and effect of his transactions . . . was to steal from "his aunt and female cousins"); Douglas M. Branson, Corporate Governance § 8.01, at 392, n.3 (1993).

4. *NonShareholder Constituency Statutes.* The director and officer's duty was to place the "best interests" of the corporation before those of herself, family friends, or other entities in which the director had an interest. Coyly, the law has never with precision defined what precisely is subsumed in the best interests of the corporation, although it has come close. *See, e.g., Dodge v. Ford Motor Co.*, 170 N.W. 668 (N.J. 1919) ("A business corporation is organized and carried on primarily [not exclusively] for the profit of its stockholders"). Beginning with Pennsylvania in 1985, 15 Pa. Cons. Stat. § 1715(d), over 30 states adopted statutes to permit directors to consider interests other than shareholder interests in decisions they make. The statutes expressly mention interests of suppliers, employees, customers, local communities in which the corporation operates, state and regional economies, as well as the national economy. *See, e.g.*, Iowa Code § 490.1108; Mo. Ann. Stat. § 351.357; Or. Rev. Stat. § 60.357(5); Tenn. Code Ann. § 48-35-204. Only Connecticut's statute is mandatory: directors *must* consider the interests of nonshareholder constituencies. Conn. Gen. Stat. § 33-313(e). About one third of the statutes limit themselves to the adoption of defenses against takeover bids. Some are worded very strongly. The Pennsylvania statute, for example, relieves directors from any obligation "to regard any corporate interest or interests of any particular group affected by such action as a dominant or controlling interest or factor." There are very few, if any, cases interpreting such statutes. *See, e.g.*, Stephen Bainbridge, *Interpreting Nonshareholder Constituency Statutes*, 19 Pepp. L. Rev. 971 (1992); Marleen O'Connor, *Restructuring the Corporation's Nexus of Contracts: Recognizing a Fiduciary Duty to Protect*, 60 N.C. L. Rev. 1189 (1991). Many codes of best practices, as well as the literature, now refer to such constituencies as "stakeholders," with shareholders being merely another constituency, along with employees, customers, or suppliers.

PROBLEM

El Cid, Inc., is a publicly-held steel producer located in Toledo, Ohio. El Cid has modern plants but has had losses for four consecutive years, mainly due to foreign competition. El Cid's board of directors has recently been approached by a Scottish consortium that wishes to purchase El Cid's facilities, which consist of five plants employing 4200 individuals. The directors' due diligence reveals that the Scots have broken up and sold off two similarly situated steel producing companies in Europe.

While the El Cid directors deliberate, the El Cid employees propose a purchase ("leveraged buyout") to be financed by a major Toledo bank. The offer is firm and in writing, but is for 15 percent less than the Scots's offer.

El Cid director Chuck Heston consults you. What do you tell him?

Note that Ohio has a so-called "nonshareholder constituency" statute which provides that directors may consider the "interests of employees, suppliers, creditors, or customers, the economy of the State and the nation, and the long term, as well as the short term interests of the corporation, including the possibility that these interests may best be served by the continued independence of the corporation."

H.   INTERESTED DIRECTOR TRANSACTIONS

Del. Gen. Corp. Law § 144
Interested Directors; Quorum

(a) No contract or transaction between a corporation and 1 or more of its directors or officers, or between a corporation and any other corporation, partnership, association, or other organization in which 1 or more of its directors or officers, are directors or officers, or have a financial interest, shall be void or voidable solely for this reason, or solely because the director or officer is present at or participates in the meeting of the board or committee which authorizes the contract or transaction, or solely because any such director's or officer's votes are counted for such purpose, if:

(1) The material facts as to the director's or officer's relationship or interest and as to the contract or transaction are disclosed or are known to the board of directors or the committee, and the board or committee in good faith authorizes the contract or transaction by the affirmative votes of a majority of the disinterested directors, even though the disinterested directors be less than a quorum; or

(2) The material facts as to the director's or officer's relationship or interest and as to the contract or transaction are disclosed or are known to the shareholders entitled to vote thereon, and the contract or transaction is specifically approved in good faith by vote of the shareholders; or

(3) The contract or transaction is fair as to the corporation as of the time it is authorized, approved or ratified, by the board of directors, a committee or the shareholders.

(b) Common or interested directors may be counted in determining the presence of a quorum at a meeting of the board of directors or of a committee which authorizes the contract or transaction.

NOTES AND QUESTIONS

1. *Not Mandatory.* These statutes, which exist in every U.S. jurisdiction, represent a safe harbor. They have no mandatory content. *Ex ante* astute practitioners will attempt to structure approval (or disapproval) of an interested director transaction so as to come within the safe harbor. If, however, for some reason the transaction has not been approved in one of the specified ways, what then? In *Marciano v. Nakash*, 535 A.2d 400, 403 (Del. 1987), the court "provided that the interested director statute "does not provide the only validation standard for interested director transactions." Two families owned the company which manufactured *Guess* jeans and other denim clothing. One family stayed away from board meetings, making invocation of the statutory safe harbor impossible. The second family proceeded with a necessary loan to the corporation, at defensible rates of interest. When payment became due, the second family was allowed to collect it, over the objection of the other family. The court held that the directors could defend on ground that the transaction had been fair, or "intrinsically fair." The only shortcoming of reliance on the common law, the Delaware court noted, was that "the sole forum for demonstrating fairness may be a judicial one."

2. *Effect of Compliance.* On their face, such statutes seems to be self implementing, precluding all judicial review. Court have not given them such impregnable effect. The more modest view is that compliance with the statute shifts the burden of proof, to the one (shareholder) who alleges that the transaction was unfair, if the interested director has followed the statutory procedure. Conversely, if the interested corporate official has not followed the procedure, the burden of proving fairness remains with her. CAL. CORP. CODE § 310(a)(3), as well as cases such as *Lewis v. S. L. & E., Inc.*, 629 F.2d 764, 768 (2d Cir. 1980), makes such burden shifting express. The effect is not insignificant: proving fairness *vel non* often involves expensive appraisers, expert witnesses, and attorneys. The ALI pursues a course designed to give advance approval greater effect: compliance with the safe harbor statute shifts the burden and results in review under a business judgment rather than fairness standard. *See* ALI CORP. GOV. PROJ. § 502(a)(2) ("the transaction is authorized in advance, following . . . disclosure, by disinterested directors who reasonably have concluded that the transaction was fair to the corporation at the time it was approved").

3. *Obvious Unfairness.* What would happen if a group of disinterested directors received full disclosure and then approved a transaction that had a high likelihood of resulting in harm to the corporation or an illicit gain to the corporate official? In *Fliegler v. Lawrence*, 361 A.2d 218 (Del. 1976), the court faced such a case. The corporate president acquired an antimony property which the corporation was unable to develop. The president deeded the property to a private company that was able to develop the mining property, but also arranged a long term option to the public company. The defendant directors contended that board approval of the transaction precluded judicial review. Mr. Justice McNeilly responded:

> We do not read the statute as providing the broad immunity for which defendants contend. It merely removes an "interested director" cloud when its terms are met and provides against the invalidation of an agreement "solely" because such director or officer is involved. Nothing in the statute sanctions unfairness to [the corporation] or removes the transaction form judicial scrutiny.

In *Remillard Brick Co. v. Remillard-Dandini Co.*, 241 P.2d 66, 74 (Cal. App. 1952), the Supreme court of California had reached a similar result, permitting the court in its discretion to review the transaction for fairness, despite disinterested director approval:

> The section does not permit an officer or director, by abuse of his power, to obtain an unfair advantage or profit for himself, at the expense of the corporation. The director cannot, by reason of his position, drive a harsh and unfair bargain with the corporation he is supposed to represent. . . . Even though the requirements of section 820 are technically met, transactions that are unfair and unreasonable to the corporation may be avoided. It would be a shocking concept of corporate morality to hold that because the majority shareholders or directors disclose their purpose and interest, they may strip of its assets to their own financial advantage . . . .

4. *Model Business Corporation Act Subchapter F.* In 1988, and in revised form in 2004, the ABA Committee on Corporate Laws adopted a lengthy and convoluted four section subchapter which has an avowed purpose the elimination of even the infrequent judicial review that cases such as *Fliegler* and *Remillard Brick* presage. MBCA § 8.60 introduces the new term "conflicting interest" transaction, which has yet to achieve (or not achieve — it is too early to tell) wide circulation. Substantive treatment begins with a narrow definition of what a "conflicting interest" transaction is and therefore is within the section in the first place. Through a narrow definition of "related party," for example, transactions with a director's in-law or first cousin do not constitute conflicting interest transactions, as a matter of law, even though common sense would indicate that in such transactions directors often would have divided loyalties. Official Comment to § 8.60 provides that "[t]he definition of 'conflicting interest is exclusive." It further provides that "The definition operates preclusively: it not only designates the area within which the rules of Subchapter F are to be applied but also denies the power of the court to act with respect to conflict of interest claims against directors in circumstances that lie outside the statutory definition . . . ."

Along those lines, MBCA § 8.62(a) provides that "[a] transaction . . . that is not a director's conflicting interest transaction may not be enjoined, set aside, or give rise to an award of damages . . . " MBCA § 8.62(b) holds that conflicting interest transactions also may not be set aside, etc.: if (1) director's action pursuant to § 8.63 has been taken; (2) shareholder action pursuant to § 8.63 has been taken; or (3) "the transaction . . . is established to have been fair to the corporation."

MBCA § 8.63 makes director action easy to achieve. A transaction is approved if it has received "the affirmative vote of a majority (but no less than two) of those qualified directors on the board . . . " Those qualified [disinterested] directors also constitute a valid quorum if they number two, or more. Thus, if 11 of 13 directors have divided loyalties in transaction with the corporation, the other two directors may approve it and, if they do so, their actions (and the transaction itself) are unassailable.

Approximately 16 of the 40 Model Business Corporation Act jurisdictions have adopted subchapter F.

5. *Shareholder Approval.* MBCA § 8.63 holds an interested director transaction unassailable if a majority of the qualified shares have approved, but the section excludes from the definition qualified shares held "by a director who has a conflicting interest respecting the transaction or by a related person of the director."

In bygone days, a board of directors might refer an interested director matter for consideration at the shareholder level because, due to conflicts on the part of a critical mass of directors, or a majority, a quorum of directors could not be achieved. By providing that interested directors count for quorum purposes, DEL. GEN. CORP. LAW § 144, or that the qualified directors, whatever their number, providing it is more than two, constitute a quorum, MBCA § 862, assembling a quorum is seldom, if ever, a problem today.

Nonetheless, boards of directors may refer certain interested director transactions to shareholders' meetings for consideration, for at least three reasons: (1) political: a transaction approved by shareholders is easier still to defend than is one approved by directors alone; (2) at the shareholder level, majority approval may be easier to obtain, as shareholders, even those who are also directors, have much more latitude to vote their selfish interests, at least if they do not work a fraud or illegality or attempt to reap a benefit to the exclusion of the minority, *see, e.g., North West Transp. Co., Ltd. v. Beatty*, 12 App. Cas. 589 (Privy Council 1887), and *Boss v. Boss*, 200 A.2d 231 (R.I. 1964), although this is often modified by statute; and (3) shareholder approval may result in a standard of judicial review even more deferential than business judgment rule (but not as beneficial as the no review whatsoever of the MBCA subchapter F). For instance, under ALI CORP. GOV. PROJ. § 5.02(a)(2)(D) provides that not only does a shareholder vote shift the burden of proof it also ratchets up the burden of proof, and thus, the standard of review for a court, to one of waste. Waste has been defined as a transaction in which "the consideration the corporation receives no person of ordinary sound business judgment would deem it worth that which the corporation has paid." *Michelson v. Duncan*, 407 A.2d 211, 214 (Del. 1979); *Schreiber v. Carney*, 447 A.2d 17, 26 (Del. Ch. 1982). A waste standard is as deferential a standard of review, and uphill battle for a plaintiff, as could be imagined.

6. *Interlocking Directorates.* The same individual may serve as a director on two boards of directors of two corporations. This type of arrangement is often referred to as an interlocking (sometimes overlapping) directorship or directorate. The corporations may do business with each other in other than standardized or routine, and therefore defensible, terms. The question that arises is whether each such transaction, even if small in size or significance, should receive consideration for treatment as an interested director transaction, when the only actual conflict is one or more shared directors. At larger corporations at least, the board may have a crowded agenda for meetings and may be loathe to take time to deal with such issues.

The common law said "yes." Although the conflict is less than the case in which a director has an actual pecuniary interest, courts stated that transactions involving corporations with a common director should be carefully scrutinized and reviewed for fairness. *See, e.g., Shlensky v. South Parkway Bldg. Corp.*, 166 N.E.2d 793 (Ill. 1960). A handful of corporation codes singled out the interlocking director situation for special treatment. In California, disclosure and disinterested director approval of the transaction precluded all judicial review. CAL. CORPS. CODE § 310(b). A Connecticut statute changed the standard of judicial review to "manifest unfairness," when the only conflict was an overlapping director. CONN. GEN. STAT. § 33-323(b) (repealed 1989).

MBCA Subchapter F excludes most such transactions from a need to "be passed through the board." First, the transaction must be "of such character and significance to the corporation that in the normal course [it would be] bought before the board of directors." MBCA § 8.60(1)(ii). Second, only if the director is an actual party to the transaction, or has a material beneficial interest (ownership) in a party, is the transaction a candidate for board treatment. *See* Official Comment to § 8.60(2)(3) ("Party to the Transaction").

7. *Independence.* The disinterested, or qualified, directors should be free of conflicts of interest. Courts also state that they should be of independent, that is, relatively free of the influence of a controlling shareholder or dominating director. If such is the case, as pointed out *supra*, the disinterested director approval is often then protected from plenary judicial review by the business judgment rule. Some courts subsume this requirement under the umbrella good faith element of the business judgment rule.

In *Orman v. Cullman*, 794 A.2d 5 (Del. Ch. 2002), a case involving the acquisition of General Cigar, Inc., by a subsidiary of Swedish Match AB, Delaware Chancellor Chandler discoursed at length on disinterestedness and independence and the difference between them. He held a director who received a $75,000 consulting payment to be disinterested because, although he would receive a benefit not offered to rank-and-file shareholders, he would not "receive a personal financial benefit *from a transaction* that is not shared equally by the stockholders. Under his contract, the director would receive the same annual fee both prior to and after the merger. He received nothing "from a transaction."

Independence, according to Chancellor Chandler (a former law professor at the University of Alabama),

> [d]oes not involve a question of whether the challenged director derives a benefit *from a transaction* that is not generally shared with the other shareholders. Rather, it involves an inquiry into whether the director's decision resulted from that director being *controlled* by another. A director can be controlled if in fact he is *dominated* by that other . . . . A director may be considered beholden to (and thus controlled by another where the alleged controlling entity has unilateral power . . . to decide whether the challenged director continues to receive a benefit . . . .

Chancellor Chandler held that, at least for purposes of summary judgment, questions of fact existed as to whether a majority of the General Cigar directors were disinterested and independent. Thus, they, and their decision, were not entitled to business judgment rule protection. *See also Aronson v. Lewis*, 473 A.2d 805 (Del. 1984) (a leading case outlining elements of the business judgment rule in Delaware, defining "interest" as "meaning that directors can neither appear on both sides of a transaction nor expect to derive any personal financial benefit from it . . . as opposed to a benefit which devolves upon the corporation or all stockholders generally").

8. *Sarbanes-Oxley Provisions.* Sarbanes-Oxley Provisions § 301 (exchanges and NASDAQ to amend listing standards) (2002) requires that all members of the audit committee of a publicly held corporation be independent. By the statute's terms, receipt of any fees, directly as in *Orman*, or through a firm of which the audit committee is a member, renders the particular director non-independent. Lawyers, bankers, and the like then may serve on the board but may not serve on the audit committee if their firm does work for the corporation.

9. *Loans to Officers and Directors.* Loans of funds and of use of the corporation's credit, which the Sarbanes-Oxley Act forbids in publicly held corporations, are discussed *infra*.

10. *Duty of Loyalty, Not Conflicts of Interest.* What the law forbids of officers, directors, or partners, is duty of loyalty violations. A conflict of interest alone is at most a red flag, indicating that special treatment of the transaction may be in order. Unlike public officials, who may have a legal duty to avoid even the appearance of a conflict of interest, a corporate official may have a conflict of interest. And, unlike a trustee, a director or officer may be able "to purchase at his own sale." She just has to do it right.

Take for example, a director who discovers that her son in a candidate for vice-president of marketing at the corporation on whose board she sits. She certainly could resign her board seat, eliminating the conflict altogether, and that is one piece of advice that may sometimes be given. Alternatively, though, she may recuse herself, allowing her fellow directors to evaluate the proposed hire. With full disclosure, a vote of the disinterested directors, and arguable (ball park) fairness to the corporation, the son's employment may not be successfully challenged. Add the ingredient that often the transaction is more than fair to the corporation (e.g., the son has an MBA from Northwestern and 15 years marketing experience with other companies). What the law ultimately forbids is violations of the duty of loyalty, not conflicts of interest, which, for corporate and similar officials, and unlike trustees, for example, can be "engineered around." Advising on proper processess to engineer around conflicts of interest, and thereby avoid duty of loyalty claims, is a principal task of business lawyers.

11. *Presence or Absence of the Interested Director.* Only a single state's statute, Vermont's, required that, in order to receive safe harbor protection the interested director has to absent herself from review of the proposed transaction. To remove any inference of "back scratching," however, many experienced practitioners recommend that the interested director absent herself from the room and that the record (corporate minutes) reflect that absence. She should not stray too far, though, remaining reasonably available should questions arise.

PROBLEMS

1. Amelia Earheart sits on the boards of both Otter Aircraft, Ltd., and Owens Corning Composites, Inc. (OCC). Otter has been purchasing from OCC composite wing assemblies for its new Tri Otter commuter airliner. The Otter purchasing department has been purchasing approximately $900,000 of wing assemblies per year. Otter's annual sales are $100 million. Amelia has discovered these facts. Need she take any action?

2. Bob Sole is a director and CEO of Sunsweet Juice Co. The corporation processes fruit for its own brand of juice and for other labels as well. The corporation has now decided to divest itself of the bottling plant and vehicle fleet utilized for the latter endeavor.

Sarah Sole, first cousin and childhood friend of Bob Sole, bids at the appraised market price. Or, more accurately, she bids in the name of a corporation she has formed for purposes of acquiring the assets.

The jurisdiction has adopted the Model Business Corporation Act in its entirety. Does the transaction require any special scrutiny or treatment?

3. Three directors of the Blue Moon Motel Co., Ltd., (there are five altogether) own a parcel of property which they believe to be a prime motel site, located as it is just off a major interstate highway. They have had the property appraised. They now propose to convey to Blue Moon at the appraised value. At the directors' meeting convened to approve the land transaction, one of the directors looks up and notes, "A quorum of disinterested directors would be three. There are only two of us without any interest in this transaction. Counsel, what do we do?" Your reply? Structure consideration and, probably approval, of the transaction, from start to finish.

I.   USURPATION OF A CORPORATE OPPORTUNITY

TODAY HOMES, INC. v. WILLIAMS
Supreme Court of Virginia
272 Va. 462, 634 S.E.2d 737 (2006)

Justice G. STEVEN AGEE

Chesapeake is a property developer and builder of single-family homes. Like other companies in the home building industry, Chesapeake "needed land . . . to build houses on." [Emma] Williams served as Chesapeake's vice president of operations . . . and [George] Woodhouse was Chesapeake's vice president of production. . . .

In the course of her employment, Williams was "responsible for all purchasing activities and customer service," but not the acquisition of land. Woodhouse supervised the actual construction work of the homes Chesapeake built. Neither person's job description involved finding or purchasing lots for buildings.

At the beginning of 2003, Frank Grossman, a realtor with Long & Foster Realtors, told Woodhouse about certain property he had listed for sale in Hampton ("the Sinclair Property"). Woodhouse mentioned the Sinclair Property to Williams and showed her a site plan. At that time, the development plan for the Sinclair Property included a "55 and older active adult communit[y]." Woodhouse testified that he did not believe Chesapeake would be interested in the property because Chesapeake "didn't do any 55 and older active adult communities." Williams also believed Chesapeake would not be interested in purchasing the property.

. . . .

Woodhouse prepared a letter resigning from his employment with Chesapeake the day Williams was terminated [March 13], but did not submit the letter until April 24, 2003, when he gave his two weeks' notice. . . . John M. Barnes, president of Chesapeake, asked Woodhouse to continue his employment with Chesapeake through at least May 20 because Woodhouse held the company's only North Carolina contractor's license, and Chesapeake's subcontractors were dependent on the license. . . .

After Williams' termination, but while Woodhouse remained employed by Chesapeake, the two discussed going into business together and caused Majestic to be incorporated on March 27, 2003. Williams and Woodhouse were listed as president and secretary, respectively, of Majestic. . . .

After forming Majestic, Williams searched for properties to purchase by contacting real estate companies. Near the end of March 2003, Woodhouse put [Frank] Grossman in contact with Williams, and discussed the Sinclair Property with her. When Grossman showed Williams the Sinclair Property, she recognized it as "the same property that [she] had heard about from [Woodhouse]" earlier in the year when she was working for Chesapeake.

On April 15, 2003, Majestic entered into a contract with Marlyn to purchase 27 lots on the Sinclair Property. Williams, but not Woodhouse, was a signatory to the agreement on behalf of Majestic. In 2004, Majestic had gross profit from the sale of homes on the Sinclair Property of $4,469,585.00. There is no dispute that neither Williams nor Woodhouse ever disclosed the Sinclair Property to Chesapeake or received Chesapeake's consent to acquire it.

. . . .

After a one-day bench trial, the trial court dismissed Chesapeake's amended bill of complaint and entered a final decree on September 27, 2005, stating that Chesapeake "failed to meet its burden of proof . . . .

The Defendants argue that Chesapeake's threshold burden was not met because the trial court did not find the Sinclair Property to be a corporate opportunity for Chesapeake. . . . [T]he Defendants argue they learned of the Sinclair Property in their individual capacities, and not in their role as officers of Chesapeake. Thus, they argue there was no duty of disclosure on their part and no corresponding breach of fiduciary duty.

CHESAPEAKE'S PRIMA FACIE CASE

We first address the question of whether the Sinclair Property was a corporate opportunity for Chesapeake, because if there was no corporate opportunity, then there was no fiduciary duty to breach in that regard. [T]he trial court did conclude that the Sinclair Property was a corporate opportunity for Chesapeake: "[I]t's clear to the Court that these lots, any lots, were important to [Chesapeake], that they were, in fact, seeking other business opportunities." No reasonable reading of the trial court's determination could lead to a conclusion other than that it found the Sinclair Property to be a corporate opportunity for Chesapeake.

. . . .

The trial court specifically found Williams to be "an officer of [Chesapeake]." While the trial court did not use the same words regarding Woodhouse, it found he "was the vice president involving production" of Chesapeake . . . . The Defendants do not contest on appeal that they were officers of Chesapeake, and in that capacity, had a fiduciary relationship to Chesapeake.

Neither is there any dispute that Woodhouse or Williams did not disclose the Sinclair Property to Chesapeake or seek Chesapeake's consent to take the Sinclair Property. Accordingly, Chesapeake did prove its prima facie case . . . .

BREACH OF FIDUCIARY DUTY

Our inquiry now turns to what duty, if any, the Defendants owed Chesapeake regarding the Sinclair Property. It is a fundamental principle that a corporate officer or director is under a fiduciary obligation not to divert a corporate business opportunity for personal gain because the opportunity is considered the property of the corporation. . . . As long as an individual remains a corporate officer, he "owes an undivided duty to [the corporation], and cannot place himself in any other position which would subject him to conflicting duties, or expose him to the temptation of acting contrary to [its] best interests."

The "unbending rule" that a fiduciary "entrusted with the business of another cannot be allowed to make that business an object of interest to himself," is abrogated if the fiduciary obtains the "consent of the [corporation]" after "full disclosure." As this Court has observed, "[t]he motive of self-interest is so natural and the danger of temptation to secure private advantage so great," that "good faith alone is not sufficient in the absence of full disclosure and consent of the interested parties . . . to make an exception to the general rule that a [corporate fiduciary] cannot enter into any relation or do any act inconsistent with the interest of the [corporation]."

. . . .

Once a plaintiff has shown that a corporate opportunity existed and the corporate fiduciary appropriated it without disclosure and the consent of the corporation, a prima facie case has been shown. Under our jurisprudence, the burden shifts to the defendant fiduciary to show why the taking of the corporate opportunity was not a breach of his fiduciary duty. "[W]hen transactions have occurred between fiduciaries and [the corporation], the burden of proof lies upon the [fiduciary] to show that the transaction has been fair." Giannotti v. Hamway, 239 Va. 14, 24, 387 S.E.2d 725, 731 (1990). "The burden of proof lies, in all cases, upon the party who fills the position of active confidence to show the transaction has been fair." Waddy v. Grimes, 154 Va. 615, 648, 153 S.E. 807, 817 (1930).

It is true that "[r]esignation or termination does not automatically free a director or employee from his or her fiduciary obligations." Liability post-termination continues only for those "transactions completed after termination of the officer's association with the corporation, but which began during the existence of the relationship or that were founded on information gained during the relationship." . . .

The record for purposes of appeal establishes that Williams' purchase of the Sinclair Property through Majestic was not "founded on information gained during" her employment with Chesapeake. Prior to her termination, Williams had no intention of leaving Chesapeake and starting her own development company. There is no evidence in the record that she used any of Chesapeake's resources to establish Majestic or regarding the Sinclair Property. Williams' casual knowledge of the Sinclair Property before her termination triggered no duty to disclose because her relationship with the Sinclair Property as a corporate opportunity occurred only after March 13th. After March 13th, Williams was under no fiduciary duty to Chesapeake because she was no longer an officer. [In contrast to Williams, Woodhouse did continue as an officer of Chesapeake for at least two months after March 13th and took certain actions in regard to the Sinclair Property].

There was thus no basis for liability on Williams' part after March 13 for breach of a fiduciary duty to Chesapeake as she had no duty. [T]he trial court did not err in dismissing the amended bill of complaint as to Williams.

For the foregoing reasons, we will reverse the trial court's judgment dismissing the amended bill of complaint as to Woodhouse and affirm the trial court's judgment as to Williams and Majestic. We will remand the case to the trial court for further proceedings to determine whether Woodhouse breached a fiduciary duty to Chesapeake, in conformance with the principles expressed in this opinion.

BRANDT v. SOMERVILLE
Supreme Court of North Dakota
692 N.W.2d 144 (2005)

KAPSNER, JUSTICE. . . . In 1978, David Brandt and Dean Somerville incorporated Posilock as a closely-held corporation to manufacture and market a [patented] bearing puller developed and patented by Dean Somerville and David Brandt's deceased father, Paul Brandt. . . .

The Somerville and the Brandt families initially did most of the work to manufacture and sell the bearing pullers, and Posilock operated out of a building in McHenry, North Dakota. After a 1984 fire destroyed that building, Somervilles purchased property in Cooperstown, which they leased to Posilock to continue operations. Although the Brandts collectively retained half of Posilock's stock and David Brandt served as a director and secretary for Posilock, Brandts' involvement with the day-to-day operations of Posilock gradually diminished after the 1984 fire and move to Cooperstown. . . .

In 1998, Posilock's supplier of component parts for the bearing puller announced a large price increase for those parts, and Somervilles formed PL MFG as a division of Dynamics 360 to produce the component parts for the bearing puller. PL MFG also makes products for other manufacturers, but about half of its production consists of the parts for Posilock's bearing puller. The startup cost for PL MFG included a $450,000 loan to Posilock from Sheyenne Valley Electric Cooperative. . . . The loan process required . . . a personal guarantee by Dean and Margaret Somerville. . . .

In October 2000, Brandts sued Somervilles and Posilock, alleging Somervilles operated Posilock without regard to their duties and obligations to the corporation and to Brandts, and Somervilles breached numerous fiduciary duties to Brandts . . . .

After a bench trial, the court found . . . Somervilles' involvement with PL MFG was conducted in a manner "unfairly prejudicial" to Brandts and constituted a wrongful appropriation of Posilock's corporate opportunity to produce its own parts. . . .

. . . .

[B]randts claim two of Somervilles' family-owned corporations, Dynamics 360 and DMI, appropriated Posilock's corporate opportunities. They argue Dynamics 360, through its PL MFG division, misappropriated Posilock's corporate opportunity to manufacture parts for the bearing puller and DMI misappropriated Posilock's corporate opportunity for marketing products. Brandts claim they should have been awarded damages for both misappropriations, or the court should have granted them equitable relief for Somervilles' actions.

. . . .

[T]he trial court's findings indicate Somervilles' conduct regarding the $450,000 loan formed a significant part of the court's decision that Somervilles' conduct was "unfairly prejudicial" toward Brandts. The court analyzed those claims as a misappropriation of Posilock's corporate opportunity, and the court effectively found a breach of Somervilles' fiduciary duties for the misappropriation of Posilock's corporate opportunity. See Jundt v. Jurassic Res. Dev., 2003 ND 9, 656 N.W.2d 15 (stating fiduciary obligation imposed upon corporate officers and directors precludes them from appropriating business opportunity that belongs to corporation). . . .

. . . .

[S]omervilles assert the trial court erred as a matter of law in concluding they wrongfully appropriated Posilock's corporate opportunity. Somervilles argue there was no corporate opportunity that Posilock had the financial ability to pursue. They claim, as a matter of law, Posilock did not have the financial ability to pursue the opportunity to manufacture parts for the bearing puller and would have had to rely on the personal guarantee of Dean Somerville to pursue that opportunity.

. . . .

"What constitutes the usurpation of a corporate 'opportunity' is the subject of considerable litigation. . . . [H]owever, a single definitive test has not yet emerged." Four tests have been established as standards for identifying a corporate opportunity: the "line of business" test, the "interest or expectancy" test, the "fairness" test, and the "ALI" test. Under any test, a corporate opportunity exists when a proposed activity is reasonably incident to the corporation's present or prospective business and is one in which the corporation has the capacity to engage. Whether or not a given opportunity meets the requisite relationship is largely a question of fact to be determined from the objective facts and surrounding circumstances existing at the time the opportunity arises. Whether or not an officer has misappropriated a corporate opportunity does not depend on any single factor. "[However] [A] director is not required to use his or her own money or credit to finance the business of the company."

. . . .

Here, the trial court concluded Posilock had a corporate opportunity to manufacture its own parts, which was reasonably incident to its present or prospective business, and it had the capacity to engage in that opportunity. . . . The court also found Posilock, with the personal guarantee of Dean Somerville, had the financial ability to expend necessary capital to manufacture its own parts as demonstrated by the fact that Posilock obtained the $450,000 loan, the proceeds of which were transferred to Dynamics 360. [T]here was evidence Posilock was substantially debt free and was profitable and had been experiencing growth. There was also evidence Posilock was a financially stable company and had sufficient accounts receivable and cash reserves to pursue this corporate opportunity.

We affirm the judgment and the post-judgment order.

GERALD W. VANDE WALLE, C.J., MARY MUEHLEN MARING, WILLIAM A. NEUMANN, and DALE V. SANDSTROM, JJ., concur.

NOTES AND QUESTIONS

1. *"Unfairly Prejudicial" Conduct.* MBCA § 14.30, and similar statutes in most jurisdictions, permit courts to grant dissolution, or some form of lesser included relief, on grounds that minority shareholders have been subjected to "oppression." In turn,

one line of court cases equates oppression with highly unfair or unfairly prejudicial acts and practices. The principal case raises the issue but treatment of the subject is contained in the chapter dealing with closely held corporations Chapter 9, *supra*.

2. *Scenario.* If a corporate director consults an attorney as to a favorable opportunity that the fiduciary has discovered, the easiest advice the attorney can give may be for the fiduciary to present the opportunity first to the corporation, making full disclosure both of her interest and of the corporation's interests in a potential transaction. Next, the director should procure two (not merely one) votes by a disinterested decisionmaker (usually the disinterested directors): one, that the corporation does not wish to avail itself of the opportunity and, two, that is fair for the director or other fiduciary to pursue it. The transaction (really non-transaction) should then receive the safe harbor protection of an interested director statute such as MBCA Subchapter F, §§ 8.60–8.63. So it is untrue that a corporate officer or director may never usurp a corporate (or partnership) opportunity: with the proper procedural steps, they may be able to do so. *See also* ALI Corp. Gov. Project § 505(a).

The rub is that the fiduciary may not wish to present the opportunity to the corporation, especially if she views it as very favorable opportunity, or a "sure thing." Her fear is that, should she present the opportunity to the corporation, the corporation may well take it. On the other hand, if her attorney can render an opinion (informal at least) that business proposition is not a "corporate opportunity," she may have little worry about any procedural hoops.

Thus it is that the issue, which opportunities are corporate opportunities, looms large in advising an individual director. Moreover, the issue may loom larger in an increasing number of cases. In days of yore, it was not realistic that a corporate director would divert to herself the opportunity to build a steel plant, for development of the opportunity took a great deal of capital. In today's world, in which much more value inures in intellectual property (ideas, information, etc., in the "knowledge based economy") the ease with which an opportunity can be diverted may be less and the temptation to do so resultingly greater.

3. *Interest or Expectancy Test.* The earliest test, still in use, deems opportunities of the corporation "property wherein the corporation has an interest already existing or in which it has an expectancy growing out of an existing right," *Lagarde v. Anniston Lime & Stone Co.*, 28 So. 199 (Ala. 1899). The corporation owned 1/3 of a gravel pit, had a contract to acquire 1/3, and had a strong interest in 1/3. Despite the latter, the corporation had no opportunity: the director had been free to acquire it because inherent in the contract to acquire the middle 1/3 the corporation had an interest or expectancy but it had no contractual rights whatsoever in the third 1/3.

4. *Line of Business Test.* Needless to say, interest or expectancy constitutes an extremely narrow test. The Delaware Supreme Court thought so in a famous case, *Guth v. Loft, Inc.*, 5 A.2d 503, 511 (1939). The board of directors sent president Charles Guth to prospect for a new soft drink syrup, other than Coca Cola. The president found Pepsi but formed a new corporation with one Megargel, which corporation acquired the Pepsi-Cola formula and trademark out of bankruptcy. Luft, Inc., was successful in imposing a constructive trust on Guft's interest in Pepsi, even though Guft had subsequently resigned from Loft and had spent years building up the Pepsi Cola trademark. "[I]f there is presented to a corporate officer or director a business opportunity which the corporation is financially able to undertake [and which] is in the line of the corporation's business, and is of practical advantage to it," then it is a corporate opportunity. Loft, Inc., would have had no opportunity under the interest or expectancy test but did so under the line of business test. The test is often broadened to "the line of business in which the corporation is engaged, or may reasonably be expected to engage." *See, e.g., Ellzey v. Fyr Pruf, Inc.*, 376 So. 2d 1328, 1333 (Miss. 1979) (flexible line of business test); *Imperial Group (Texas), Inc. v. Scholnick*, 709 S.W.2d 358, 365 (Tex. App. 1986) (same). As one can see, the remedy for usurpation of a corporate opportunity (constructive trust) can be quite severe.

5. *Fairness Test.* Some cases ask merely whether it is fair that the corporate director be required to present the opportunity to the corporation. *See Durfee v. Durfee*, 80 N.E.2d 522 (Mass. 1948); *Miller v. Miller*, 222 N.W.2d 71 (Minn. 1974).

6. *"By Virtue of the Position" Test.* A controlling factor is the setting (loosely defined) in which the fiduciary learned of the business proposition. If she became aware of it because of her corporate affiliation, "even though the executive had not used corporate assets, the corporation has no interest or expectancy in the opportunity, and the opportunity lies well afield of the corporation's line of business," it is a corporate opportunity. BRANSON, CORPORATE GOVERNANCE § 8.26, at 467. *See also Boyd v. Howard*, 556 S.E.2d 337, 339 (N.C. App. 2001); *Today Homes, Inc. v. Williams, supra.*

7. *Use of Corporate Assets or Information Test.* A little noticed test, or sub test, in most jurisdictions is that if the fiduciary uses anything beyond a de minimus amount of corporate assets or information to develop the opportunity, she may be found to have diverted a corporate opportunity. This can be true even though the corporation has previously rejected the opportunity. *See, e.g., Banks v. Bryant*, 497 So. 2d 460 (Ala. 1986) (use of corporate aircraft and accounting systems to develop a opportunity which the corporation had once rejected).

8. *Layering of Tests. Broz v. Cellular Info. Sys.*, 673 A.2d 148, 155 (Del. 1996), is a recent Delaware foray into the area. It stands for the unremarkable proposition that in determining the scope of a corporation's business, and therefore which opportunities are in the line of business, the trial court need not consider the business interests of the corporation's prospective merger partner. The court took most of ten pages to engage in confused, doctrinal overkill, holding that:

> [A] corporate officer or director may not take a corporate opportunity for his own if: (1) the corporation is financially able to exploit the opportunity; (2) the opportunity is within the corporation's line of business; (3) the corporation has an interest or expectancy in the opportunity; and (4) by taking the opportunity for his own, the corporate fiduciary will thereby be placed in a position inimicable to his duties to the corporation.

The medium may be more important than the message. The Delaware decision, as well as opinions by other courts, make clear that under modern analysis the task is not to apply this or that test of corporate opportunity. Rather, the task is to layer various test one upon another, akin to drawing ever larger concentric circles, rather than applying only one single test of what opportunities are corporate opportunities.

9. *The ALI Test.* The American Law Institute test utilizes the layering approach. The ALI schematic has been adopted by several state's highest courts as the test of which opportunities are corporate opportunities. *See, e.g., Demoulas v. Demoulas Super Markets, Inc.*, 677 N.E.2d 159 (Mass. 1997); *Northeast Harbor Golf Club, Inc. v. Harris*, 661 A.2d 1146 (Me. 1995); *Klinicki v. Lundgren*, 695 P.2d 906 (Or. 1985); *Brandt v. Sommerville, supra.* ALI Corp. Gov. Proj. § 5.05(b) provides:

> [A] corporate opportunity means:

> (1) Any opportunity to engage in a business activity of which the officer or senior executive becomes aware, either:

> (A) In connection with the performance of functions as a director or senior executive, or under circumstances that should reasonably lead the director . . . to believe that the person offering the opportunity expects it to be offered to the corporation; or

> (B) Through the use of corporate information or property, if the resulting opportunity is one that the director . . . should reasonable be expected to believe would be of interest to the corporation; or

> (2) Any opportunity to engage in a business activity of which a senior

executive becomes aware and knows is closely related to a business in which the corporation is engaged or expects to engage.

The ALI thus layers by virtue of the position, use of corporate assets or information, and line of business (senior executives only) tests of which opportunities are corporate opportunities.

10. *Lack of Financial Ability.* As may be deduced from the discussion above, Delaware seems to include lack of wherewithal as a ground upon which a court could base a finding that a business proposition is not an opportunity for a corporation. The law charges the directors with the task of raising capital sufficient for a corporation to meet its needs. If, however, lack of wherewithal means an attractive proposition may not become an opportunity in the first place, and thus, potentially available to them, directors have an incentive to maintain the corporation in reduced circumstances. For those reasons, courts hold that lack of wherewithal is, if anything, a matter in defense of a charge of usurpation. *See, e.g., Graham v. Mimms*, 444 N.E.2d 549 (Ill. App. 1982). Some courts never accept lack of wherewithal as a defense. *Irving Trust Co. v. Deutsch*, 73 F.2d 121 (2d Cir. 1934), is a leading case. Other courts accept the matter as a defense only if the corporation is insolvent, along the lines that directors have no duty to raise new money to throw after bad. *See, e.g., Nicholson v. Evans*, 642 P.2d 727, 731 (Utah 1982). Other defenses, similar to lack of wherewithal in that it may be the board of directors' mission to remove the obstacle, include lack of corporate legal capacity or earlier abandonment by the corporation of the opportunity.

11. *The MBCA Provision.* In 2005–06, the Committee on Corporate Laws added § 8.70, "Business Opportunities" to the end of MBCA Chapter 8, "Officers and Directors." The section prohibits a court from granting either equitable relief or an award of damages for a "director taking advantage, directly or indirectly, of a business opportunity" if the director has received board or shareholder approval in accordance with the section and MBCA § 8.62, *supra.* MBCA § 8.70(b) goes on to provide that, in any judicial proceeding, "the fact that the director did not employ the procedure described in subsection (a) before taking advantage of the opportunity shall not create an inference that the opportunity should have been first presented to the corporation or alter the burden of proof otherwise applicable that the director breached a duty to the corporation in the circumstances." The new section seems an attempt to curb the uncurbable: in some cases, such an inference may be inescapable.

PROBLEMS

1. Celeste is vice-president (information technology) for Hemlock Forest Products, Inc. While at a fundraiser for the school her children attend, Celeste is approached by John Barbar, whose conversational opening is, "Say, you're with Hemlock Forest Products, aren't you?" Barbar then describes a process he has developed for re-cycling used lumber into wood chips. The breakthrough is that the process removes nails and other impurities.

Celeste telephones several acquaintances in the industry. They are extremely skeptical that is can be done but emphasize the potential if it can. Celeste also speaks with a banker and a Small Business Administration (SBA) counselor. She has one additional conversation with Barbar.

Celeste resigns from Hemlock. She and Barbar form a new corporation, obtain an SBA guaranteed loan from the bank, and build a prototype. In no time, they are licensing the technology to all the major forest products and paper producing companies, except Hemlock. Hemlock hauls Celeste into court. You are defending. What is the theory of your defense? What pitfalls must you avoid?

2. Miss Jean Brody has her own company (Brody Prime, Ltd), which has speculated in Federal Communications Commission (FCC) cellular telephone licenses. She holds licenses for several service areas in South central Wisconsin. She also sits on the board of the Yelm telephone company in Southern Minnesota. Yelm is an old fashioned local service provider with copper wire running from customers' homes and businesses to Yelm's exchanges.

Several cellular licenses along the Minnesota-Wisconsin border come onto the market. Jean asks all of her Yelm director colleagues whether Yelm has an interest, but individually rather than at a board meeting. They all say "no," the CEO adding that Yelm has little cash right now because it has been building out a cable television system. Miss Jean Brody and Brody Prime then sign a contract to purchase the licenses from various holders.

Before Miss Brody closes on the deal, FirstWave Communications, an Illinois full service telecommunications company (cellular, internet access, cable television, and traditional telephone service) announces a merger with Yelm.

FirstWave sues Brody Prime and Miss Jean, asking that a constructive trust be placed on the contract to purchase the cellular licenses. Is there a corporate opportunity? What test should you apply? Do you need to research Wisconsin law?

3. Brothers Hector and Ajax operate a successful business which exports scrap metal. Each owns 35 percent. The former manager, Rosen, comes into the office one day. Rosen owns 20 percent. Friends and employees own the remaining 10 percent.

Rosen is moving to Bisbee, Arizona. He inquires if the corporation will buy back his shares. The brothers confer. They respond that the corporation has no interest but it would give Rosen $5 per share. Rosen departs on friendly terms.

Ajax then excuses himself, saying he has an errand to run. He intercepts Rosen in the parking lot. He offers Rosen $12 per share. Rosen accepts.

Using his newly acquired majority control, Ajax puts his business associates on the board. They promote Ajax to CEO, at a greatly increased salary. Meanwhile, Hector languishes. His salary increases, but only slightly. He moves down the hall, to a distant office.

Hector consults you. Weren't the Rosen shares a corporate opportunity? Didn't Ajax usurp it?

J. COMPETITION WITH THE CORPORATION

ALI, Corporate Governance Project
§ 5.06 Competition with the Corporation

General Rule. Directors and senior executives may not advance their pecuniary interest by engaging in competition with the corporation, unless either:

1. Any reasonably foreseeable harm to the corporation from such competition is outweighed by the benefit that the corporation may reasonably be expected to derive from allowing the competition to take place, or there is no reasonably foreseeable harm to the corporation from such competition;

2. The competition is authorized in advance or ratified, following disclosure concerning the conflict of interest and the competition, by disinterested directors . . . in a manner that satisfies the business judgment rule; or

3. The competition is authorized in advance or ratified, following such disclosure, by disinterested shareholders and the shareholders' action is not equivalent to a waste of corporate assets.

NOTES

1. *Middle Test.* The ALI describes itself as a "middle ground." Usually, the test of when a corporate official may compete with the corporation he serves is phrased permissively (and is next to meaningless): he may compete as long as he is in "good faith" or engaged in "healthy competition." An especially permissive test is that a corporate officer or director may compete until such time as "additional circumstances show a course of conduct of causing deliberate injury to the business and reputation of the corporation." *Atkinson v. Marquart*, 541 P.2d 556, 558 (Ariz. 1975). Few courts go that far, as duty of loyalty violations can be grounded either in harm to the corporation or illicit gain to the officer or director. But the business world demonstrates that competition occurs every day: software company executives serve on the boards of other software providers, or owners and directors of small or family owned lumber companies serve on the boards of large forest products concerns. Such service most always satisfies the first prong of the ALI test: the benefit to the corporation outweighs any reasonably foreseeable harm.

2. *Alternative Phrasing.* A corporate director may compete with the corporation on whose board he sits so long as he does not engage in bad faith, or prohibited, competition. Bad faith competition includes:

- Use of confidential or proprietary information, but not "general experience, knowledge, memory, and skill."

- Use of customer lists which show not just names and contact but additional information as well (customer preferences, past orders, future plans, etc.).

- Dispargement of the corporation or its manner of doing business (defamation of the corporation, its products, or its services).

- Other forms of tortious conduct, such as interference with the corporation's existing or prospective business advantage.

- Use of more than nominal amounts of the corporation's assets, facilities or time.

3. *Relationship to Usurpation of Corporate Opportunities.* If a director or his family had been engaged in the competing business before he became a director, he usually continues as before, refraining only from bad faith acts. By contrast, if the director desires to enter a competing business after he became a director, competition may also constitute diversion of a corporate opportunity. That is especially true in a jurisdiction which makes line of business part of the test of which opportunities constitute corporate opportunities. He must therefore submit the proposition of potential competition to the board of directors, just to be safe.

4. *The "Inevitable Disclosure" Argument.* In *PepsiCo, Inc. v. Redmond*, 54 F.3d 1262 (7th Cir. 1995), defendant had been Pepsi's manager in California. Quaker Oats recruited him to manage its Snapple and Gatoraide brands. Despite the absence of a covenant not to compete, the Seventh Circuit enjoined him from performance of his new duties on grounds that not the actual but the "threatened inevitable" disclosure of trade secrets constituted unfair competition. The only defense against the inevitable disclosure argument seems a lobotomy for the departing officer or director. *Cf. Dangeles v. Muhlenfeld*, 548 N.E.2d 45 (Ill. App. 1989) ("one who works for another cannot be compelled to erase from his mind all of the general skills, knowledge, acquaintances, and overall experience he acquired during the course of his employment").

5. *Plans or Preparation for Competition after Cessation of the Fiduciary Relationship.* Render on to Caesar what is Caesar's. Courts will wink at de minimus use of corporate time, assets, and the like. Otherwise, the executive must:

- Be truthful especially when asked ("I hear you might be leaving. Is that true?");

- Do not recruit agents or employees of the corporation while still a fiduciary;

- Meet with architects, potential investors, and the like on the officer's or director's own time, not the corporation's time;

- In professional settings, solicit customers or clients only in accordance with the profession's rules, and be prepared to pay a fair charge for work already done on client cases which depart with the fiduciary.

By contrast, if "[t]heir activities with respect to the competing corporation prior to their actual termination were confined to the planning stage," no consequences will follow. *Voss Eng'g, Inc. v. Voss Indus.*, 481 N.E.2d 63, 65 (Ill. App. 1985); *Today Homes, Inc., supra. See also Dwyer Costello & Knox, P.C. v. Diak*, 846 S.W.2d 742, 747 (Mo. App. 1993). Remember as well, "[T]here is an off-setting policy . . . of safeguarding society's interest in fostering free and vigorous competition. . . . [Courts recognize] a privilege in favor of employees which enables them to make arrangements to compete with their employers prior to leaving the employ of their prospective rivals . . . " *Science Accessories v. Summagraphics*, 425 A.2d 957, 963 (Del. 1980).

PROBLEM

John Waters owns the movie rights to "Teenage Mutants." Michael Eisner asks Waters to join the Walt Disney Company board of directors. Waters thinks it would be "divine" to do so.

Shortly thereafter, the Disney board discusses another property, "Nail Polish," but declines the movie rights. Mr. Waters acquires "Nail Polish."

Waters then forms his own production company, Sparkling Waters, Inc. employing his children, Rickey Waters and Victoria Waters. They successfully produce "Mutants" and "Polish." Waters then has a falling out with Disney and resigns from the Disney board. Michael Eisner demands a cut of Sparking Waters's profits for the Disney treasury. What result?

K. DIRECTORS' AND OFFICERS' COMPENSATION

RYAN v. GIFFORD
Court of Chancery of Delaware
918 A.2d 341, 345–355 (2007)

CHANDLER, CHANCELLOR.

On March 18, 2006, *The Wall Street Journal* sparked controversy throughout the investment community by publishing a one-page article . . . which revealed an arguably questionable compensation practice. Commonly known as backdating, this practice involves a company issuing stock options to an executive on one date while providing fraudulent documentation asserting that the options were actually issued earlier. These options may provide a windfall for executives because the falsely dated stock option grants often coincide with market lows. Such timing reduces the strike prices and inflates the value of stock options, thereby increasing management compensation. This practice allegedly violates any stock option plan that requires strike prices to be no less than the fair market value on the date on which the option is granted by the board. Further, this practice runs afoul of many state and federal common and statutory laws that prohibit dissemination of false and misleading information.

After the article appeared in the Journal, Merrill Lynch issued a report demonstrating that officers of numerous companies, including Maxim Integrated Products, Inc., had benefitted from so many fortuitously timed stock option grants that backdating seemed the only logical explanation. The report engendered this action.

Plaintiff Walter E. Ryan alleges that defendants breached their duties of due care and loyalty by approving or accepting backdated options that violated the clear letter of the shareholder-approved Stock Option Plan and Stock Incentive Plan ("option plans"). Individual defendants move to stay this action in favor of earlier filed federal actions in California ("federal actions"). In the alternative, they move to dismiss this action on its merits.

In this Opinion, I grant individual defendants' motion to dismiss all claims arising *before* April 11, 2001. I deny the remainder of the individual defendants' motion to stay or dismiss.

Facts

Maxim Integrated Products, Inc. is a technology leader in design, development, and manufacture of linear and mixed-signal integrated circuits used in microprocessor-based electronic equipment. From 1998 to mid-2002, Maxim's board of directors and compensation committee granted stock options for the purchase of millions of shares of Maxim's common stock to John F. Gifford, founder, chairman of the board, and chief executive officer, pursuant to shareholder-approved stock option plans filed with the Securities and Exchange Commission. Under the terms of these plans, Maxim contracted and represented that the exercise price of all stock options granted would be no less than the fair market value of the company's common stock, measured by the publicly traded closing price for Maxim stock on the date of the grant. Additionally, the plan identified the board or a committee designated by the board as administrators of its terms.

Ryan is a shareholder of Maxim . . . . He filed this derivative action on June 2, 2006, against Gifford; James Bergman, B. Kipling Hagopian, and A.R. Frank Wazzan, members of the board and compensation committee at all relevant times; Eric Karros, member of the board from 2000 to 2002, and M.D. Sampels, member of the board from 2001–2002. Ryan alleges that nine specific grants were backdated between 1998 and 2002, as these grants seem too fortuitously timed to be explained as simple coincidence. All nine grants were dated on unusually low (if not the lowest) trading days of the years in question, or on days immediately before sharp increases in the market price of the company.

The allegations in this case involve backdating option grants and whether such practice violates one or more of Delaware's common law fiduciary duties. This question is one of great import to the law of corporations. It encompasses numerous issues, including the propriety of this type of executive compensation, requisite disclosures that must accompany such compensation, and the legal implications of intentional non-compliance with shareholder-approved plans (if such practices are deemed noncompliant), to name only a few. Investors are challenging this very practice in many courts throughout the United States, including this Court. . . .

A director who approves the backdating of options faces at the very *least* a substantial likelihood of liability, if only because it is difficult to conceive of a context in which a director may simultaneously lie to his shareholders (regarding his violations of a shareholder-approved plan, no less) and yet satisfy his duty of loyalty. Backdating options qualifies as one of those "rare cases [in which] a transaction may be so egregious on its face that board approval cannot meet the test of business judgment, and a substantial likelihood of director liability therefore exists." Plaintiff alleges that three members of a board *approved* backdated options, and another board member accepted them. These are sufficient allegations to raise a reason to doubt the disinterestedness of the current board and to suggest that they are incapable of impartially considering demand.

. . . .

Defendants assert that plaintiff fails to state a claim for breach of fiduciary duty. This defense, stripped to its essence, states that in order to survive a motion to dismiss on a fiduciary duty claim, the complaint must rebut the business judgment rule. That is, plaintiff must raise a reason to doubt that the directors were disinterested or independent. Where the complaint does not rebut the business judgment rule, plaintiff must allege waste. Plaintiff here, argue the defendants, fails to do either. Further, there is no evidence that the defendants acted intentionally, in bad faith, or for personal gain. Therefore, so the argument goes, plaintiff fails to plead facts sufficient to rebut the business judgment rule and cannot maintain an action for breach of fiduciary duties.

The Business Judgment Rule and Bad Faith

[T]he complaint here alleges bad faith and, therefore, a breach of the duty of loyalty sufficient to rebut the business judgment rule and survive a motion to dismiss. The business affairs of a corporation are to be managed by or under the direction of its board of directors. In an effort to encourage the full exercise of managerial powers, Delaware law protects the managers of a corporation through the business judgment rule. This rule "is a presumption that in making a business decision the directors of a corporation acted on an informed basis, in good faith and in the honest belief that the action taken was in the best interest of the company." Nevertheless, a showing that the board breached either its fiduciary duty of due care or its fiduciary duty of loyalty in connection with a challenged transaction may rebut this presumption. Such a breach may be shown where the board acts intentionally, in bad faith, or for personal gain.

In *Stone v. Ritter* [*supra*], the Supreme Court of Delaware held that acts taken in bad faith breach the duty of loyalty. Bad faith, the Court stated, may be shown where "the fiduciary intentionally acts with a purpose other than that of advancing the best interests of the corporation, where the fiduciary acts with the intent to violate applicable positive law, or where the fiduciary intentionally fails to act in the face of known duty to act, demonstrating a conscious disregard for his duties." Additionally, other examples of bad faith might exist. These examples include any action that demonstrates a faithlessness or lack of true devotion to the interests of the corporation and its shareholders.

Based on the allegations of the complaint, and all reasonable inferences drawn therefrom, I am convinced that the intentional violation of a shareholder approved stock option plan, coupled with fraudulent disclosures regarding the directors' purported compliance with that plan, constitute conduct that is disloyal to the corporation and is therefore an act in bad faith. Plaintiffs allege the following conduct: Maxim's directors affirmatively represented to Maxim's shareholders that the exercise price of any option grant would be no less than 100% of the fair value of the shares, measured by the market price of the shares on the date the option is granted. Maxim shareholders, possessing an absolute right to rely on those assurances when determining whether to approve the plans, in fact relied upon those representations and approved the plans. Thereafter, Maxim's directors are alleged to have deliberately attempted to circumvent their duty to price the shares at no less than market value on the option grant dates by surreptitiously changing the dates on which the options were granted. To make matters worse, the directors allegedly failed to disclose this conduct to their shareholders, instead making false representations regarding the option dates in many of their public disclosures.

I am unable to fathom a situation where the deliberate violation of a shareholder approved stock option plan and false disclosures, obviously intended to mislead shareholders into thinking that the directors complied honestly with the shareholder-approved option plan, is anything but an act of bad faith. It certainly cannot be said to amount to faithful and devoted conduct of a loyal fiduciary. . . .

. . . .

Conclusion

For the foregoing reasons, I grant defendants' motion to dismiss all claims arising before April 11, 2001 [on statute of limitations grounds]. I deny defendants' motion to stay or dismiss with respect to all other claims.

IT IS SO ORDERED.

IN RE TYSON FOODS, INC., CONSOLIDATED SHAREHOLDER LITIGATION

Court of Chancery of Delaware

919 A.2d 563, 576 & 592–93 (2007)

CHANDLER, CHANCELLOR

. . . .

Plaintiffs allege that the Compensation Committee, at the behest of several Defendant board members, "spring-loaded" these options. Days before Tyson would issue press releases that were very likely to drive stock prices higher, the Compensation Committee would award options to key employees. [A compensation committee that "spring loads" options grants them to executives before the release of material information reasonably expected to drive the shares of such options higher. (An opposite effect, "bullet dodging," is achieved by granting options to employees after the release of materially damaging information)]. Around 2.8 million shares of Tyson stock bounced from the corporate vaults to various defendants in this manner. Plaintiffs specifically identify four instances of allegedly well-timed option grants.

The Compensation Committee (then Massey, Vorsanger, and Cassady) granted John Tyson, former — CEO Wayne Britt, and then — COO Greg Lee options on 150,000 shares, 125,000 shares and 80,000 Class A shares, respectively, at $15 per share on September 28, 1999. The next day, Tyson informed the market that Smithfield Foods, Inc. had agreed to acquire Tyson's Pork Group. The announcement propelled the price upwards to $16.53 per share in less than six days, and to $17.50 per share by December 1, 1999.

Once again, the Compensation Committee (then Massey, Hackley, and Allen) granted options on 200,000 Class A shares to John Tyson, 100,000 to Lee, and 50,000 to then — CFO Steven Hankins at $11.50 per share on March 29, 2001. A day later, Tyson publicly cancelled its $3.2 billion deal to acquire IBP, Inc. By the close of that day, the stock price had shot up to $13.47.

The Compensation Committee (then Hackley, Allen, and Massey) granted options on 200,000 Class A shares to John Tyson, 60,000 to Lee, and 15,000 to Hankins sometime in October 2001. Within two weeks, Tyson publicly announced its 2001 fourth-quarter earnings would be more than double those expected by analysts, catapulting the stock price to $11.90 by the end of November.

The Compensation Committee (then Smith, Jones, and Hackley) granted stock options to a number of executives and directors, including 500,000 to John Tyson, 280,000 to Bond, and 160,000 to Lee, at $13.33 per share on September 19, 2003. On September 23, 2003, Tyson publicly announced that earnings were to exceed Wall Street's expectations, propelling the price to $14.25.

. . . .

[P]laintiffs must demonstrate that the grant of the 2003 options could not be within the bounds of the Compensation Committee's business judgment. A severe test faces those seeking to overcome this presumption: "[W]here a director is independent and disinterested, there can be no liability for corporate loss, unless the facts are such that no person could possibly authorize such a transaction if he or she were attempting in good faith to meet their duty." [Gagliardi v. TriFoods Int'l, Inc., 683 A.2d 1049, 1052–1053 (Del. Ch.1996)]

Whether a board of directors may in good faith grant spring-loaded options is a somewhat more difficult question than that posed by options backdating, a practice that has attracted much journalistic, prosecutorial, and judicial thinking of late. . . .

At their heart, all backdated options involve a fundamental, incontrovertible lie: directors who approve an option dissemble as to the date on which the grant was actually made. Allegations of springloading implicate a much more subtle deception. [The touchstone of disloyalty or bad faith in a spring-loaded option remains deception, not simply the fact that they are (in every real sense) "in the money" at the time of issue. A board of directors might, in an exercise of good faith business judgment, determine that in the money options are an appropriate form of executive compensation. Recipients of options are generally unable to benefit financially from them until a vesting period has elapsed, and thus an option's value to an executive or employee is of less immediate value than an equivalent grant of cash. A company with a volatile share price, or one that expects that its most explosive growth is behind it, might wish to issue options with an exercise price below current market value in order to encourage a manager to work hard in the future while at the same time providing compensation with a greater present market value. One can imagine circumstances in which such a decision, were it made honestly and disclosed in good faith, would be within the rational exercise of business judgment. But the facts alleged in this case are different.]

Granting spring-loaded options, without explicit authorization from shareholders, clearly involves an indirect deception. A director's duty of loyalty includes the duty to deal fairly and honestly with the shareholders for whom he is a fiduciary. It is inconsistent with such a duty for a board of directors to ask for shareholder approval of an incentive stock option plan and then later to distribute shares to managers in such a way as to undermine the very objectives approved by shareholders. This remains true even if the board complies with the strict letter of a shareholder-approved plan as it relates to strike prices or issue dates.

[The court held that Count II of the Complaint, "Grant of Options Between 1999 and 2001," "survives as to the seven members of the compensation committee."]

NOTES AND QUESTIONS

1. *Subsequent Developments.* The court also noted that as of the time it was writing, "between 120–170 [publicly held] companies were implicated in lawsuits or investigations" involving backdating stock option grants to senior executives. 918 A.2d 341, n.15. That number quickly exceeded 200, with over 90 corporate officers losing their positions.

2. *Legal Test.* As the principal cases illustrate, judicial review of compensation decisions is under the duties of care and loyalty. Before the fact, officer and director compensation decisions generally are treated as but an instance of interested director transaction, with full disclosure and vote by disinterested decision-makers, usually directors assisted by a compensation consultant (whose report furnishes the rational basis). If approval of compensation has been by directors disinterested in the matter, after the fact, the analysis becomes duty of care, the safe harbor statute, and the business judgment rule. If the director or officer exercised tangible influence over the decision-making process, and the directors were rendered thereby not independent, compensation decisions and their review are a duty of loyalty issue. *See generally* DOUGLAS M. BRANSON, CORPORATE GOVERNANCE § 8.18, at 442.

3. *Statutory Provisions — Directors.* It has been traditional to provide that directors are able to fix their own compensation *qua* director (annual retainer and meeting fees) even though technically they have a conflict of interest in the matter. *See, e.g.,* DEL. GEN. CORP. LAW § 141(h) ("Unless otherwise restricted by the certificate of incorporation or bylaws, the board of directors shall have the authority to fix the compensation of directors.").

4. *Statutory Provisions — Officers.* The board of directors appoints, and if necessary, removes persons from officer positions. It is also common in board minutes to fix, opposite their names, and on a prospective basis, the compensation of officers. In addition, or in the alternative, officers will have free standing contracts fixing their compensation. Otherwise, officers are not entitled to compensation by virtue of being an officer alone. Some express prospective provision is as necessary because of the presumption against retroactive compensation. *See, e.g., Stevens, By and For the*

Benefit of Park View Corp. v. Richardson, 755 P.2d 389, 392 (Alaska 1988); ALI Corp. Gov. Proj. § 5.03, at 330 (courts should give "especially close scrutiny to the payment of compensation for past services.").

With that background in mind, it becomes possible to explain another type common statutory provision. MBCA § 8.44 (a), for example, provides that "[t]he appointment of an officer does not itself create contract rights." Someone, usually the attorney, must affirmatively provide for compensation, and other contract rights, by one or other means outlined.

On the opposite end of an officer's tenure, "removal does not affect the officer's contract rights, if any, with the corporation. An officer's resignation does not affect the corporation's contract rights, if any, with the officers. MBCA § 8.44(b).

5. *Special Rules for Performance Based Compensation (Stock Options).* Such compensation has become ubiquitous, in part because since 1993 IRC § 162(m) requires that, to be deductible as a business expense, all cash compensation over $1 million per year must be performance based. The types of plan are numerous: qualified stock options, non-qualified options, restricted stock grants, employee stock purchase plans, zero cost options, phantom stock plans, stock appreciation rights, and participating unit plans (PUPs). Delaware cases in the 1950s questioned stock option plans which allowed covered executives to exercise their options, pocket the profits, and leave the corporation's employ. The absence of any requirement for further employment or other performance resulted in an absence of consideration and, hence, waste or gifting of corporate assets. *See* Kerbs v. California Eastern Airways, Inc., 90 A.2d 652 (Del. 1952). *See also* Beard v. Elster, 160 A.2d 731 (Del. 1960) (stock option plan contained conditions tending to insure that corporation received the benefit). For several decades, attorneys drafting such plans included provisions conducive to the performance being actually received, including requirements for continuing service and vesting of options only over a period of time, typically 5 or more years.

6. *Reasonable Relationship Test.* In *Rogers v. Hill*, 289 U.S. 582 (1933), the Supreme Court struck down large bonus payments to officers and directors of American Tobacco Co., which were based upon profits and uncapped in any other manner, as excessive and bearing "no reasonable relationship" to the services rendered. More recently, the Arkansas Supreme Court applied the reasonable relationship test to strike down $500,685 annual salaries for three investors who acquired 50.5% of small drug store chain but who performed little in the way of services. *Hall v. Staha*, 858 S.W.2d 672, 674–75 (1993). The decision is devoid of citation or discussion. And, on a wider scale, for the most part, any requirement of a reasonable relation has been lost in the mists of time.

7. *Delaware — Business Judgment Rule Only.* In the halcyon days of the 1990s, with corporate profits ever increasing, Delaware courts threw out any tests of executive compensation other than business judgment rule, including *Kerbs* and *Beard* analysis as well as, *sub silento*, the reasonable relationship test. In *Lewis v. Vogelstein*, 699 A.2d 327 (Del. Ch. 1997) (Allen Ch.), the court upheld a grant by Mattel Toy Co. of options on 15,000 shares to sitting directors of the corporation, with no conditions attached. In *Zupnick v. Goizueta*, 698 A.2d 384 (Del. Ch. 1997) (Jacobs, V.C.), solely on business judgment rule grounds, the court upheld an option grant of five million Coca-Cola shares to the CEO in gratitude for *past* services and accomplishments. Under previous analysis, such compensation would have amounted to a waste or gift of corporate assets. Under current Delaware analysis, gifts are permissible if the board of directors observes the proper procedural formalities. Experts in the compensation field assume that the courts of other states would follow the Delaware courts' lead.

8. *Sarbanes Oxley Act (2002) Provisions.* In Enron, CEO Kenneth Lay did not even take out bank loans in order to pay the strike price on options he exercised. Wags called the Enron treasury "Ken Lay's ATM." In WorldCom, mostly to meet margin calls in a rapidly falling stock market, WorldCom lent CEO Bernard Ebbers $405 million of corporate funds. Because of these abuses, in its first foray into the matter of corporate governance, theretofore a matter previously committed to state law, Congress included a number of provisions which impact executives' compensation at publicly held corporations:

a. SOX § 402 prohibits, with limited exceptions for financial institutions, loans of corporate funds or lending of the corporation's credit to directors and officers. Advances of defense costs under indemnification arrangements, excessive perks (personal use of corporate airplane, ski lodge, country club memberships), and other payments on executive's behalf must be re-examined to determine if de facto they are loans or uses of corporate funds or credit for the benefit of executives.

The original MBCA (1950) forbade loans to officers and directors of corporate funds. A subsequent restatement of the act (1969) permitted such transactions, but only after a shareholder vote (often 2/3rds). Abolishing any special treatment whatsoever, later versions of the MBCA (1984 onward) treated such extensions of credit as merely another interested director transaction, which as few as two qualified directors could approve (under Subchapter F). SOX returns to the original 1950 MBCA provision, at least for public corporations.

b. If a corporation has to re-state its financial statements, and the cause of restatement is "misconduct" in fashioning the original financials, the CEO and the CFO must forfeit all incentive (performance) based and equity pay for the previous 12 months. SOX § 304. Had such a provision been in force in 2001, when Enron had to re-state its financial statements, the CEO and CFO would have had to forfeit over $200 million. In *Neer v. Pelino*, 389 F. Supp. 2d 648, 652–57 (E.D. Pa. 2005), the court held that no private right of action exists under the section, although the corporation itself may seek "disgorgement." *See also In re Goodyear Tire & Rubber Co. Derivative Lit.*, 2007 WL 43557 (N.D. Ohio 2007) (same).

c. Corporate pension funds often have blackout periods, when traditional or 401(k) plan participants cannot trade in the shares of the sponsoring corporation. Plan administrators may impose a blackout for administrative purposes or surrounding earnings announcements. In Enron, corporate officers sold millions of Enron shares while plan participants could not, due to imposition of a backout period. SOX § 306 makes it illegal for corporate officers or directors to sell shares received as compensation during any blackout period. In contrast to the earnings restatement provision, *supra*, the section also provides an express cause of action. If, after 60 days the corporation had failed to take action, "an action . . . by the owner of any security of the issuer in the name and in behalf of the issuer may go forward."

d. The SEC may seek escrow of any "extraordinary payments," such as termination payments or bonuses, made to corporate executives. The escrow remains in place, pending the outcome of any investigation or charges against the executive. SOX § 1103. In *SEC v. Gemstar-TV Guide Int'l, Inc.*, 401 F.3d 1031 (9th Cir. 2005), a U.S. Court of Appeals upheld imposition of such an escrow on termination payments for insiders.

9. *Typical Compensation Arrangements.* Executives will receive a salary, due to Internal Revenue Code considerations, *supra*, in the vicinity of $1 million. They will also receive a "medium term" benefit, often in the form of a bonus, with the first year guaranteed. Such bonuses regularly amount to 2–3 times salary. Longer term compensation may take the form of grants of stock options, although the Financial Accounting Standards Board determination that corporations must expense the estimate value of options at the time the corporation grants them has caused many corporations to turn to restricted stock grants and other forms of long term compensation. The long term compensation plan sets one or more types of "performance hurdles," usually achievable with little effort. The executive will also receive an array of fringe benefits, such as health insurance for the executive and her family, life insurance, use of corporate airplanes, condominiums, or ski lodges, and so. A committee of the board of directors, denominated the compensation (remuneration) committee, negotiates the "package" and recommends its approval by the full board of directors.

10. *"Say on Pay" Statutes, Bylaws, and Proxy Proposals.* Although the numbers vary slightly from study to study, the average CEO of a public corporation in the U.S. earned $14 million in 2007. The kings of compensation have been CEOs Michael Eisner ($585 million in 1998 at Walt Disney Co.) and Larry Ellison ($725 million in 2002 at Oracle Co.), mostly through the exercise of stock options with low strike prices. U.S. style executive compensation has been a scandal in many other countries, although simultaneously many executives in those countries connive to receive some, if not all, the benefits of U.S. style compensation. To hold those executives in check, at least in part, nations such as Australia and Britain enacted legal requirements for an advisory shareholder vote on executive's pay. The U.S. Congress has not enacted any such provision but both it and the SEC have various proposals under consideration. Regardless, in 2007 and other recent proxy seasons, shareholders of more than several large U.S. corporations have adopted recommendations that, as an internal governance matter, corporations and their boards of directors adopt "say on pay" bylaw provisions providing or advisory votes.

PROBLEMS

1. Dunhill Pharmaceuticals is a profitable corporation that produces generic drugs. The corporation's shares are traded OTC. The class of shares is also registered with the SEC under Securities Exchange Act of 1934 § 12(g).

Dunhill, Soha, and Hall increase their collective ownership of Dunhill to 50.5%. They then cause to board of directors to be downsized from 7 to 3 directors. As directors, they then vote themselves annual compensation of $10 million each. They also authorize personal lines of credit for themselves from the corporate treasury. They each may borrow from the corporation up to $10 million.

They are capable managers but can they do this? What prevents them from such a power play?

2. Assume that Dunhill Pharmaceuticals directors do not take excessive salaries, as in the previous problem. Nor do they put in place the line of credit arrangement. Instead, the company proposes to adopt a qualified stock-option plan for the key executives. The exercise, or "strike" price is the same as the current market price, so the plan is for "qualified" options which will not result in income to the executive until such time as he exercises the option and sells the stock.

You are asked to review the option plan from a corporate law standpoint. Is there anything special you examine?

IN RE THE WALT DISNEY COMPANY DERIVATIVE LITIGATION
Supreme Court of Delaware
906 A.2d 27 (2006)

Before STEELE, CHIEF JUSTICE, HOLLAND, BERGER, JACOBS and RIDGELY, JUSTICES, constituting the Court en Banc.

JACOBS, JUSTICE. In August 1995, Michael Ovitz and The Walt Disney Company entered into an employment agreement under which Ovitz would serve as President of Disney for five years. In December 1996, only fourteen months after he commenced employment, Ovitz was terminated without cause, resulting in a severance payout to Ovitz valued at approximately $130 million.

In January 1997, several Disney shareholders brought derivative actions in the Court of Chancery, on behalf of Disney, against Ovitz and the directors of Disney who served at the time of the events complained of. . . . After the disposition of several pretrial motions and an appeal to this Court, the case was tried before the Chancellor over 37 days between October 20, 2004 and January 19, 2005. In August 2005, the

Chancellor handed down a well-crafted 174 page Opinion and Order, determining that "the director defendants did not breach their fiduciary duties or commit waste." . . .

I. THE FACTS

. . . .

In 1994 Disney lost in a tragic helicopter crash its President and Chief Operating Officer, Frank Wells, who together with Michael Eisner, Disney's Chairman and Chief Executive Officer, had enjoyed remarkable success at the Company's helm. Eisner temporarily assumed Disney's presidency, but only three months later, heart disease required Eisner to undergo quadruple bypass surgery. Those two events persuaded Eisner and Disney's board of directors that the time had come to identify a successor to Eisner.

Eisner's prime candidate for the position was Michael Ovitz, who was the leading partner and one of the founders of Creative Artists Agency ("CAA"), the premier talent agency . . . .

Eisner and Ovitz had enjoyed a social and professional relationship that spanned nearly 25 years. Although in the past the two men had casually discussed possibly working together, in 1995 . . . Eisner became seriously interested in recruiting Ovitz to join Disney. Eisner shared that desire with Disney's board members on an individual basis.

A. Negotiation Of The Ovitz Employment Agreement

Eisner and Irwin Russell, who was a Disney director and chairman of the compensation committee, first approached Ovitz about joining Disney. . . .

Both Russell and Eisner negotiated with Ovitz, over separate issues and concerns. From his talks with Eisner, Ovitz gathered that Disney needed his skills and experience to remedy Disney's current weaknesses . . . . [A]t some point during the negotiations Ovitz came to believe that he and Eisner would run Disney, and would work together in a relation akin to that of junior and senior partner. . . .

Russell assumed the lead in negotiating the financial terms of the Ovitz employment contract. In the course of negotiations, Russell learned . . . that Ovitz owned 55% of CAA and earned approximately $20 to $25 million a year from that company. From the beginning Ovitz made it clear that he would not give up his 55% interest in CAA without "downside protection." . . .

Under the proposed OEA [Ovitz Employment Agreement], Ovitz would receive a five-year contract with two tranches of options. The first tranche consisted of three million options vesting in equal parts in the third, fourth, and fifth years, and if the value of those options at the end of the five years had not appreciated to $50 million, Disney would make up the difference. The second tranche consisted of two million options that would vest immediately if Disney and Ovitz opted to renew the contract.

The proposed OEA . . . provided that absent defined causes, neither party could terminate the agreement without penalty. If Ovitz, for example, walked away, for any reason other than those permitted under the OEA, he would forfeit any benefits remaining under the OEA . . . . Likewise, if Disney fired Ovitz for any reason other than gross negligence or malfeasance, Ovitz would be entitled to a non-fault payment ("NFT"), which consisted of his remaining salary, $7.5 million a year for unaccrued bonuses, the immediate vesting of his first tranche of options and a $10 million cash out payment for the second tranche of options.

[R]ussell also expressed his concern that the negotiated terms represented an extraordinary level of executive compensation. Russell acknowledged, however, that Ovitz was an "exceptional corporate executive" and "highly successful and unique entrepreneur "who merited "downside protection and upside opportunity." . . . [R]ussell . . . caution[ed] that Ovitz's salary would be at the top level for any corporate officer and significantly above that of the Disney CEO. Moreover, the stock options granted under the OEA would exceed the standards applied within Disney and corporate America and would "raise very strong criticism." Russell shared this original case study only with Eisner and Ovitz. . . .

. . . .

On August 10, Russell, [Raymond] Watson [former board chair] and [Graef] Crystal [compensation specialist] met. . . . Two days later, Crystal faxed to Russell a memorandum concluding that the OEA would provide Ovitz with approximately $23.6 million per year for the first five years, or $23.9 million a year over seven years if Ovitz exercised a two year renewal option. Those sums, Crystal opined, would approximate Ovitz's current annual compensation at CAA.

. . . .

While Russell, Watson and Crystal were finalizing their analysis of the OEA, Eisner and Ovitz reached a separate agreement. Eisner told Ovitz that . . . Ovitz would join Disney only as President, not as a co-CEO with Eisner. [O]vitz accepted those terms, and that evening Ovitz, Eisner, Sid Bass [a major shareholder] and their families celebrated Ovitz's decision to join Disney.

. . . The next day, August 13, Eisner met with Ovitz, Russell, Sanford Litvack (an Executive Vice President and General Counsel), and Stephen Bollenbach (Chief Financial Officer) to discuss the decision to hire Ovitz. Litvack and Bollenbach were unhappy with that decision, and voiced concerns that Ovitz would disrupt the cohesion that existed between Eisner, Litvack and Bollenbach. Litvack and Bollenbach were emphatic that they would not report to Ovitz, but would continue to report to Eisner. . . .

On August 14, Eisner and Ovitz signed a letter agreement (the "OLA"), which outlined the basic terms of Ovitz's employment, and stated that the agreement (which would ultimately be embodied in a formal contract) was subject to approval by Disney's compensation committee and board of directors. Russell called Sidney Poitier, a Disney director and compensation committee member, to inform Poitier of the OLA . . . . Poitier believed that hiring Ovitz was a good idea because of Ovitz's reputation and experience. Watson called Ignacio Lozano, another Disney director and compensation committee member, who felt that Ovitz would successfully adapt from a private company environment to Disney's public company culture. Eisner also contacted each of the other board members by phone to inform them of the impending new hire . . . .

. . . .

On September 26, 1995, the Disney compensation committee (which consisted of Messrs. Russell, Watson, Poitier and Lozano) met for one hour to consider, among other agenda items, the proposed terms of the OEA. A term sheet was distributed at the meeting, although a draft of the OEA was not. The topics discussed were historical comparables, such as Eisner's and Wells' option grants, and also the factors that Russell, Watson and Crystal had considered in setting the size of the option grants and the termination provisions of the contract. Watson testified that he provided the compensation committee with the spreadsheet analysis that he had performed in August . . . .

B. Ovitz's Performance As President of Disney

Ovitz's tenure as President of the Walt Disney Company officially began on October 1, 1995, the date that the OEA was executed. When Ovitz took office, the initial reaction was optimistic . . . . By the fall of 1996, however, it had become clear that Ovitz was "a poor fit with his fellow executives." By then the Disney directors were discussing that the disconnect between Ovitz and the Company was likely irreparable and that Ovitz would have to be terminated.

. . . .

. . . In mid-September [1996], Litvack, with Eisner's approval, told Ovitz that he was not working out at Disney and that he should start looking for a graceful exit from Disney and a new job. Litvack reported this conversation to Eisner, who sent Litvack back to Ovitz to make it clear that Eisner no longer wanted Ovitz . . . . Ovitz responded by telling Litvack that he was not leaving and that if Eisner wanted him to leave Disney, Eisner could tell him that to his face.

. . . .

C. Ovitz's Termination At Disney

. . . Eisner and Ovitz met several times. During those meetings they discussed Ovitz's future, including Ovitz's employment prospects at Sony. Eisner believed that . . . Sony would be willing to take Ovitz in "trade" from Disney. Eisner favored such a trade, which would not only remove Ovitz from Disney, but also would relieve Disney of any obligation to pay Ovitz under the OEA. [N]egotiations [with Sony] did not prove fruitful, however. On November 1, Ovitz wrote a letter to Eisner . . . that Ovitz had decided to recommit himself to Disney . . . .

In response to this unwelcome news, Eisner wrote (but never sent) a letter to Ovitz on November 11, in which Eisner attempted to make it clear that Ovitz was no longer welcome at Disney. Instead . . . Eisner met with Ovitz personally on November 13, and discussed much of what the letter contained. Eisner left that meeting believing that "Ovitz just would not listen . . . Ovitz insisted that he would stay at Disney, going so far as to state that he would chain himself to his desk."

During this period Eisner was also working with Litvack to explore whether they could terminate Ovitz under the OEA for cause. If so, Disney would not owe Ovitz the NFT payment. From the very beginning, Litvack advised Eisner that he did not believe there was cause to terminate Ovitz under the OEA. Litvack's advice never changed.

At the end of November 1996, Eisner again asked [attorney] Litvack if Disney had cause to fire Ovitz and thereby avoid the costly NFT payment. Litvack proceeded to examine that issue more carefully. He studied the OEA, refreshed himself on the meaning of "gross negligence" and "malfeasance," and reviewed all the facts concerning Ovitz's performance of which he was aware. Litvack also consulted Val Cohen, co-head of Disney's litigation department and Joseph Santaniello, in Disney's legal department. Cohen and Santaniello both concurred in Litvack's conclusion that no basis existed to terminate Ovitz for cause. Litvack . . . believed that it "was not a close question . . . 'a no brainer.' " Eisner testified that after Litvack notified Eisner that he did not believe cause existed, Eisner "checked with almost anybody that [he] could find that had a legal degree, and there was just no light in that possibility. It was a total dead end from day one."

Litvack also believed that it would be inappropriate, unethical and a bad idea to attempt to coerce Ovitz (by threatening a for-cause termination) into negotiating for a smaller NFT package than the OEA provided. The reason was that when pressed by Ovitz's attorneys, Disney would have to admit that in fact there was no cause, which could subject Disney to a wrongful termination lawsuit. Litvack believed that attempting to avoid legitimate contractual obligations would harm Disney's reputation as an honest business partner . . . .

The Disney board next met . . . An executive session took place after the board meeting, from which Ovitz was excluded. [E]isner informed the directors who were present that he intended to fire Ovitz . . . and that he had asked Gary Wilson, a board member and friend of Ovitz, to speak with Ovitz while Wilson and Ovitz were together on vacation during the upcoming Thanksgiving holiday.

[T]he Ovitz and Wilson families left on their yacht for a Thanksgiving trip to the British Virgin Islands. Ovitz hoped that if he could manage to survive at Disney until

Christmas, he could fix everything with Disney and make his problems go away. Wilson quickly dispelled that illusion, informing Ovitz that Eisner wanted Ovitz out . . . . Reporting back his conversation with Ovitz, Wilson told Eisner that Ovitz was a "loyal friend and devastating enemy," and he advised Eisner to "be reasonable and magnanimous, both financially and publicly, so Ovitz could save face."

On December 10, the Executive Performance Plan Committee met . . . . Russell informed those in attendance that Ovitz was going to be terminated, but without cause.

On December 11, Eisner met with Ovitz to agree on the wording of a press release . . . Eisner and Ovitz agreed that neither Ovitz nor Disney would disparage each other in the press, and that the separation was to be undertaken with dignity and respect for both sides. After his December 11 meeting with Eisner, Ovitz never returned to Disney.

. . . Before the press release was issued, Eisner attempted to contact each of the board members by telephone to notify them that Ovitz had been officially terminated. None of the board members at that time, or at any other time, objected to Ovitz's termination . . . . Although the board did not meet to vote on the termination, the Chancellor found that most, if not all, of the Disney directors trusted Eisner's and Litvack's conclusion that there was no cause to terminate Ovitz, and that Ovitz should be terminated without cause even though that involved making the costly NFT payment.

II. SUMMARY OF APPELLANTS' CLAIMS OF ERROR

[T]he Court of Chancery rejected all of the plaintiff-appellants' claims on the merits . . . . On appeal, the appellants claim that the adverse judgment rests upon multiple erroneous rulings and should be reversed, because the 1995 decision to approve the OEA and the 1996 decision to terminate Ovitz on a non-fault basis, resulted from various breaches of fiduciary duty by Ovitz and the Disney directors.

. . . . It is notable that the appellants do not contend that the Disney defendants are directly liable as a consequence of those fiduciary duty breaches. Rather, appellants' core argument is indirect, i.e., that those breaches of fiduciary duty deprive the Disney defendants of the protection of business judgment review, and require them to shoulder the burden of establishing that their acts were entirely fair to Disney. That burden, the appellants contend, the Disney defendants failed to carry. [The plaintiff-appellants appear to have structured their liability claim in this indirect way because Article Eleventh of the Disney Certificate of Incorporation contains an exculpatory provision modeled upon 8 Del. C. s 102(b)(7). That provision precludes a money damages remedy against the Disney directors . . . . For that reason the plaintiffs are asserting their due care claim as the basis for shifting the standard of review from business judgment to entire fairness, rather than as a basis for direct liability. Presumably for the sake of consistency the appellants are utilizing their good faith fiduciary claim in a like manner.] . . .

Alternatively, the appellants claim that even if the business judgment presumptions apply, the Disney defendants are nonetheless liable, because the NFT payout constituted corporate waste . . . .

. . . .

IV. THE CLAIMS AGAINST THE DISNEY DEFENDANTS

. . . Those claims are subdivisible into two groups: (A) claims arising out of the approval of the OEA and of Ovitz's election as President; and (B) claims arising out of the NFT severance payment to Ovitz . . . .

A. *Claims Arising From The Approval Of The OEA And Ovitz's Election As President*

. . . [T]he appellants' core argument in the trial court was that the Disney defendants' approval of the OEA and election of Ovitz as President were not entitled to business judgment rule protection, because those actions were either grossly negligent or not performed in good faith.

. . . .

(a) TREATING DUE CARE AND BAD FAITH AS SEPARATE GROUNDS FOR DENYING BUSINESS JUDGMENT RULE REVIEW

This argument is best understood against the backdrop of the presumptions that cloak director action being reviewed under the business judgment standard. Our law presumes that "in making a business decision the directors of a corporation acted on an informed basis, in good faith, and in the honest belief that the action taken was in the best interests of the company." Those presumptions can be rebutted if the plaintiff shows that the directors breached their fiduciary duty of care or of loyalty or acted in bad faith. If that is shown, the burden then shifts to the director defendants to demonstrate that the challenged act or transaction was entirely fair to the corporation and its shareholders.

Because no duty of loyalty claim was asserted . . . the only way to rebut the business judgment rule presumptions would be to show that the Disney defendants had either breached their duty of care or had not acted in good faith. At trial, the plaintiff-appellants attempted to establish both grounds, but the Chancellor determined that the plaintiffs had failed to prove either.

. . . .

(b) RULING THAT THE FULL DISNEY BOARD WAS NOT REQUIRED TO CONSIDER AND APPROVE THE OEA

. . . This challenge also cannot survive scrutiny.

As the Chancellor found, under the Company's governing documents the board of directors was responsible for selecting the corporation's officers, but under the compensation committee charter, the committee was responsible for establishing and approving the salaries, together with benefits . . . . The compensation committee also had the charter-imposed duty to "approve employment contracts, or contracts at will" for "all corporate officers who are members of the Board of Directors regardless of salary." That is exactly what occurred here. The full board ultimately selected Ovitz as President, and the compensation committee considered and ultimately approved the OEA, which embodied the terms of Ovitz's employment, including his compensation.

The Delaware General Corporation Law (DGCL) [8 Del. C. s 141(c)] expressly empowers a board of directors to appoint committees and to delegate to them a broad range of responsibilities, which may include setting executive compensation. Nothing in the DGCL mandates that the entire board must make those decisions. At Disney, the responsibility to consider and approve executive compensation was allocated to the compensation committee, as distinguished from the full board. . . .

. . . .

(c) WHETHER THE BOARD MEMBERS' OBSERVANCE OF THEIR DUTY OF CARE SHOULD HAVE BEEN DETERMINED ON A DIRECTOR-BY-DIRECTOR BASIS OR COLLECTIVELY

[T]he appellants argued that the board had failed to exercise due care, using a director-by-director, rather than a collective analysis. In this Court, however, the appellants argue that the Chancellor erred in following that very approach. An about-face, the appellants now claim that in determining whether the board breached its duty of care, the Chancellor was legally required to evaluate the actions of the old board collectively.

The argument fails because nowhere do appellants identify how this supposed error caused them any prejudice. The Chancellor viewed the conduct of each director individually, and found that no director had breached his or her fiduciary duty of care (as members of the full board) in electing Ovitz as President or (as members of the compensation committee) in determining Ovitz's compensation. If, as appellants now argue, a due care analysis of the board's conduct must be made collectively, it is incumbent upon them to show how such a collective analysis would yield a different result. The appellants' failure to do that dooms their argument on this basis as well.

(d) HOLDING THAT THE COMPENSATION COMMITTEE MEMBERS DID NOT FAIL TO EXERCISE DUE CARE IN APPROVING THE OEA

The appellants next challenge the Chancellor's determination that although the compensation committee's decision-making process fell far short of corporate governance "best practices," the committee members breached no duty of care in considering and approving the NFT terms of the OEA. . . .

The appellants advance five reasons why a reversal is compelled: (i) not all committee members reviewed a draft of the OEA; (ii) the minutes of the September 26, 1995 compensation committee meeting do not recite any discussion of the grounds for which Ovitz could receive a non-fault termination; (iii) the committee members did not consider any comparable employment agreements . . . . (iv) Crystal did not attend the September 26, 1995 committee meeting . . .; and (v) Poitier and Lozano did not review the spreadsheets generated by Watson. . . .

[T]he overall thrust of that claim is that the compensation committee approved the OEA with NFT provisions that could potentially result in an enormous payout, without informing themselves of what the full magnitude of that payout could be. Rejecting that claim, the Court of Chancery found that the compensation committee members were adequately informed. . . .

In a "best case" scenario, all committee members would have received, before or at the committee's first meeting on September 26, 1995, a spreadsheet or similar document prepared by (or with the assistance of) a compensation expert (in this case, Graef Crystal). Making different, alternative assumptions, the spreadsheet would disclose the amounts that Ovitz could receive under the OEA in each circumstance that might foreseeably arise. One variable in that matrix of possibilities would be the cost to Disney of a non-fault termination for each of the five years of the initial term of the OEA. [The] spreadsheet . . . ultimately would become an exhibit to the minutes of the compensation committee meeting . . . .

Had that scenario been followed, there would be no dispute (and no basis for litigation) over what information was furnished to the committee members or when it was furnished. . . .

The Disney compensation committee met twice: on September 26 and October 16, 1995. The minutes of the September 26 meeting reflect that the committee approved the terms of the OEA. . . . except for the option grants, which were not approved until October 16 . . . . [T]he compensation committee considered a "term sheet" which, in summarizing the material terms of the OEA, relevantly disclosed that in the event of a non-fault termination, Ovitz would receive: (i)the present value of his salary ($1 million per year) for the balance of the contract term, (ii) the present value of his annual bonus payments (computed at $7.5 million) for the balance of the contract term, (iii) a $10 million termination fee, and (iv) the acceleration of his options for 3 million shares, which would become immediately exercisable at market price.

Thus, the compensation committee knew that in the event of an NFT, Ovitz's severance payment alone could be in the range of $40 million cash, plus the value of the accelerated options. Because the actual payout to Ovitz was approximately $130 million, of which roughly $38.5 million was cash, the value of the options at the time of the NFT payout would have been about $91.5 million. Thus, the issue may be framed as whether the compensation committee members knew, at the time they approved the OEA, that the value of the option component of the severance package could reach the $92 million order of magnitude if they terminated Ovitz without cause after one year. The evidentiary record shows that the committee members were so informed. On this question the documentation is far less than what best practices would have dictated. There is no exhibit to the minutes that discloses, in a single document, the estimated value of the accelerated options in the event of an NFT termination after one year. . . .

. . . .

The OEA was specifically structured to compensate Ovitz for walking away from $150 million to $200 million of anticipated commissions from CAA over the five-year OEA contract term. This meant that if Ovitz was terminated without cause, the earlier in the contract term the termination occurred the larger the severance amount would be to replace the lost commissions. . . . Accordingly, the Court of Chancery had a sufficient evidentiary basis in the record from which to find that . . . the compensation committee members were adequately informed . . . .

[T]he appellants argue that not all members of the compensation committee reviewed the then-existing draft of the OEA. The Chancellor properly found that that was not required . . .

[C]ontrary to the appellants' position, the compensation committee members did consider comparable employment agreements. . . .

Finally, the appellants contend that Poitier and Lozano did not review the spreadsheets generated by Watson at the September 26 meeting. The short answer is that even if Poitier and Lozano did not review the spreadsheets themselves, Russell and Watson adequately informed them of the spreadsheets' contents. . . .

(e) HOLDING THAT THE REMAINING DISNEY DIRECTORS DID NOT FAIL TO EXERCISE DUE CARE IN APPROVING THE HIRING OF OVITZ AS THE PRESIDENT OF DISNEY

. . . .

[T]he appellants argue that the Disney directors breached their duty of care by failing to inform themselves of all material information reasonably available with respect to Ovitz's employment agreement. We need not dwell on the specifics of this argument, because in substance they repeat the gross negligence claims previously leveled at the compensation committee-claims . . . . The only properly reviewable action of the entire board was its decision to elect Ovitz as Disney's President. [T]he sole issue . . . is "whether [the remaining members of the old board] properly exercised their business judgment and acted in accordance with their fiduciary duties when they elected Ovitz to the Company's presidency." The Chancellor determined that . . . the directors were informed of all information reasonably available and, thus, were not grossly negligent. We agree.

. . . .

2. The Good Faith Determinations

The Court of Chancery held that the business judgment rule presumptions protected the decisions of the compensation committee and the remaining Disney directors, not only because they had acted with due care but also because they had not acted in bad faith. . . .

In its Opinion the Court of Chancery defined bad faith as follows:

> Upon long and careful consideration, I am of the opinion that the concept of *intentional dereliction of duty, a conscious disregard for one's responsibilities,* is an appropriate (although not the only) standard for determining whether fiduciaries have acted in good faith. Deliberate indifference and inaction *in the face of a duty to act* is, in my mind, conduct that is clearly disloyal to the corporation. It is the epitome of faithless conduct.

The appellants contend that . . . that the trial court had adopted a different definition in its 2003 [Disney] decision . . . [that for bad faith to be extant] the directors must have "*consciously and intentionally disregarded their responsibilities,* adopting a 'we don't care about the risks' attitude concerning a material corporate decision." . . .

. . . .

The appellants' first argument-that there is a real, significant difference between the Chancellor's pre-trial and post-trial definitions of bad faith-is plainly wrong. We perceive no substantive difference . . . .

. . . .

[T]his case . . . is one in which the duty to act in good faith has played a prominent role, yet to date is not a well-developed area of our corporate fiduciary law. Although the good faith concept has recently been the subject of considerable scholarly writing [multiple citations omitted] . . . the duty to act in good faith is, up to this point relatively uncharted. Because of the increased recognition of the importance of good faith, some conceptual guidance to the corporate community may be helpful. For that reason we proceed to address the [the subject] [*see* the discussion in Kerr *infra*] [lengthy discussion by the court omitted] . . . .

. . . .

Having sustained the Chancellor's finding that the Disney directors acted in good faith when approving the OEA and electing Ovitz as President, we next address the claims arising out of the decision to pay Ovitz the amount called for by the NFT provisions of the OEA.

B. Claims Arising From The Payment Of The NFT Severance Payout To Ovitz

[The] overall thrust [of plaintiff's claims] is that even if the OEA approval was legally valid, the NFT severance payout to Ovitz pursuant to the OEA was not. . . .

1. Was Action By The New Board Required
To Terminate Ovitz As The President of Disney?

The Chancellor determined that although the board as constituted upon Ovitz's termination (the "new board") had the authority to terminate Ovitz, neither that board nor the compensation committee was required to act, because Eisner also had, and properly exercised, that authority. The new board, the Chancellor found, was not required to terminate Ovitz under the company's internal documents. . . .

Article Tenth of the Company's certificate of incorporation in effect at the termination plainly states that:

The officers of the Corporation shall be chosen in such a manner, shall hold their offices for such terms and shall carry out such duties as are determined solely by the Board of Directors, subject to the right of the Board of Directors to remove any officer or officers at any time with or without cause.

Article IV of Disney's bylaws provided that the Board Chairman/CEO "shall, subject to the provisions of the Bylaws and the control of the Board of Directors, have general and active management, direction, and supervision over the business of the Corporation and over its officers. . . . "

The issue is whether the Chancellor's interpretation of these instruments, as giving the board and the Chairman/CEO concurrent power to terminate a lesser officer, is legally permissible. . . . Disney's governing instruments do not vest the removal power exclusively in the board, nor do they expressly give the Board Chairman/CEO a concurrent power to remove officers. Read together, the governing instruments do not yield a single, indisputably clear answer, and . . . are ambiguous.

. . . .

Here, the extrinsic evidence clearly supports the conclusion that the board and Eisner understood that Eisner, as Board Chairman/CEO had concurrent power with the board to terminate Ovitz as President. In that regard, the Chancellor credited the testimony of new board members that Eisner, as Chairman and CEO, was empowered to terminate Ovitz without board approval or intervention . . . .

. . . .

2. In Concluding That Ovitz Could Not Be Terminated For Cause, Did Litvack or Eisner Breach Any Fiduciary Duty?

It is undisputed that Litvack and Eisner . . . both concluded that if Ovitz was to be terminated, it could only be without cause, because no basis existed to terminate Ovitz for cause. The appellants argued in the Court of Chancery that the business judgment presumptions do not protect that conclusion, because by permitting Ovitz to be terminated without cause, Litvack and Eisner acted in bad faith and without exercising due care. . . . . . . [L]itvack and Eisner did not breach their fiduciary duty of care or their duty to act in good faith.

. . . .

3. Were The Remaining Directors Entitled To Rely Upon Eisner's And Litvack's Advice That Ovitz Could Not Be Fired For Cause?

The appellants' third claim of error challenges the Chancellor's conclusion that the remaining new board members could rely upon Litvack's and Eisner's advice that Ovitz could be terminated only without cause. The short answer to that challenge is that, for the reasons previously discussed, the advice the remaining directors received and relied upon was accurate. Moreover, the directors' reliance on that advice was found to be in good faith. Although formal board action was not necessary, the remaining directors all supported the decision to terminate Ovitz based on the information given by Eisner and Litvack. . . .

V. THE WASTE CLAIM

. . . This claim is rooted in the doctrine that a plaintiff who fails to rebut the business judgment rule presumptions is not entitled to any remedy unless the transaction constitutes waste [*In re* J.P. Stevens & Co., Inc. S'holders Litig., 542 A.2d 770, 780 (Del. Ch. 1988)]. . . .

To recover on a claim of corporate waste, the plaintiffs must shoulder the burden of proving that the exchange was "so one sided that no business person of ordinary, sound judgment could conclude that the corporation has received adequate consideration." [Brehm v. Eisner, 746 A.2d 244, at 263 (Del. 2000)]. A claim of waste will arise only in the rare, "unconscionable case where directors irrationally squander or give away corporate assets." This onerous standard for waste is a corollary of the proposition that where business judgment presumptions are applicable, the board's decision will be upheld unless it cannot be "attributed to any rational business purpose." [Sinclair Oil Corp. v. Levien, 280 A.2d 717, 720 (Del. 1971); see also Unocal Corp. v. Mesa Petroleum Co., 493 A.2d 946, 954 (Del. 1985)].

The claim that the payment of the NFT amount to Ovitz, without more, constituted waste is meritless on its face, because at the time the NFT amounts were paid, Disney was contractually obligated to pay them. The payment of a contractually obligated amount cannot constitute waste, unless the contractual obligation is itself wasteful.

VI. CONCLUSION

For the reasons stated above, the judgment of the Court of Chancery is affirmed.

NOTES

1. *Best Seller.* A business book recounting these events, and more, is James B. Stewart, *Disney Wars* (2006).

2. De Facto *Director or Officer Concept.* Omitted from the opinion (which is highly excerpted) is any discussion of the claims plaintiff shareholders made against Michael Ovitz, *inter alia*, for return of some or all of $130 million plus severance payment. Plaintiffs had to make a case based upon violations of fiduciary duty, rather than arms' length dealing between Disney and Ovitz. Plaintiffs tired to make the case that Ovitz had been a *de facto* officer, and therefore a fiduciary, in the period in which negotiation and formation of the contract had occurred, *viz.*, before October 1, 1995, the date when the Disney Board formally approved hiring Ovitz as president. Plaintiffs relied upon the *de facto* director or officer concept (what the English term a "shadow director" — when a person has a measure of control over the policies and practices of the corporation but formally is not listed as being a member of the board).

In *Disney*, 906 A.2d 27, 48–49, the court found that "the *de facto* argument lacks merit, both legally and factually":

> A *de facto* officer is one who actually assumes possession of an office under the claim and color of an election or appointment and who is actually discharging the duties of that office, but for some legal reason lacks *de jure* legal title to that office. Here, Ovitz did not assume, or purport to assume the duties of the Disney presidency before October 1, 1995.

3. *Options Valuation.* Compensation specialists often must value stock options, received now, but to be exercised in the future, when the stock price presumably will be higher, but could be lower. They do so using mathematical formulae. One such formula is the widely used Black-Scholes method. Another is the aptly named Monte Carlo formula. Valuations are doubly necessary now because, under Generally Accepted Accounting Principles, corporations must deduct the present value of options as an expense, at the time the corporation grants the option.

L. AIDING AND ABETTING BREACHES OF FIDUCIARY DUTY

KOKEN v. STEINBERG
Commonwealth Court of Pennsylvania
825 A.2d 723, 725–26 & 731 (2003)

COLLINS, PRESIDING JUDGE.

Deloitte & Touche, L.L.P. and [Deloitte partner] Jan A. Lomelle have filed preliminary objections in the nature of a demurrer to the complaint filed against them by the Liquidator [Diane Koken]. For the reasons set forth below the Court overrules those objections.

Deloitte provided auditing and actuarial services to Reliance Insurance Company (Reliance) for a number of years up to and including 1999. Deloitte provided statements of actuarial opinion regarding the loss reserves carried by Reliance, conducted audits of Reliance's financial statements, and issued reports on those audits. Deloitte's services were performed pursuant to engagement letters countersigned by Reliance.

In October 2002, the Liquidator filed this action against Deloitte, alleging that Deloitte had committed various torts and breaches of contract in connection with its audit and actuarial duties . . . . [T]he Liquidator alleges that Deloitte "propped up Reliance's reported financial position, deflected regulatory scrutiny, and permitted Reliance to pay out cash to its unregulated parent companies and undertake additional policyholder obligations when Deloitte . . . knew or should have known that Reliance was seriously financially troubled and was or would shortly be insolvent." The result, according the Liquidator, was a one billion dollar overstatement of Reliance's financial condition that was a direct and proximate cause of harm to Reliance, its policyholders, and creditors.

. . . .

[D]eloitte argues that Count VII, which claims that Deloitte aided and abetted breaches of fiduciary duty by executives of Reliance, must be dismissed because no Pennsylvania court has recognized the tort and, in addition, because the Complaint fails to set forth the elements of the tort.

Section 876 of the Restatement (Second) of Torts, Persons Acting In Concert, provides that one is subject to liability for harm to a third person arising from the tortious conduct of another if he a) does a tortious act in concert with the other or pursuant to a common design with him; b) knows that the other's conduct constitutes a breach of duty and gives substantial assistance or encouragement to the other so to conduct himself; or c) gives substantial assistance to the other in accomplishing a tortious result and his own conduct, separately considered, constitutes a breach of duty to the third person.

Our Supreme Court addressed Section 876 in Skipworth by Williams v. Lead Industries Association, Inc., 547 Pa. 224, 690 A.2d 169 (1997), and this Court is convinced by this language in Skipworth that Section 876 is a viable cause of action in Pennsylvania.

. . . .

[T]he Liquidator has clearly identified the wrong, a breach of fiduciary duty, the wrongdoer, Reliance, and the party that acted in concert with the wrongdoer, Deloitte. Accordingly, this Court concludes that the Liquidator has stated a cause of action against Deloitte for aiding and abetting a breach of fiduciary duty pursuant to Section 876 of the Restatement (Second) of Torts.

[D]eloitte's argues that even if the tort of aiding and abetting should exist in Pennsylvania, the Complaint fails to allege the necessary elements of the tort. In order for this cause of action to be viable, there must be acts of a tortious character pursuant to a common design or plan. RESTATEMENT (SECOND) OF TORTS s 876 comment (b) (1977). In the alternative, a defendant must render substantial assistance to another to accomplish a tortious act. As specifically stated in comment (d) to s 876(b), "in determining liability, the factors are the same as those used in determining the existence of legal causation when there has been negligence. . . .

. . . .

In Pierce v. Rossetta Corp., Civil Action No. 88-5873, 1992 WL 165817 (E.D. Pa. June 12, 1992) . . . the district court held: the elements for a claim for aiding and abetting breach of a fiduciary duty under Pennsylvania law would be: (1) a breach of a fiduciary duty owed to another; (2) knowledge of the breach by the aider and abettor; and (3) substantial assistance or encouragement by the aider and abettor in effecting that breach. Id. at 8 (citing, Restatement (Second) Torts s 876 (1979)).

In her Complaint at paragraph 162 the Liquidator alleges, "The officers and directors of Reliance owed Reliance, its policyholders and other creditors fiduciary duties, including the duties of care, loyalty, candor, and disclosure." In paragraphs 163 to 172 the Liquidator details how the officers and directors of Reliance breached those fiduciary duties. The Liquidator pleads Deloitte's knowledge of the officers' and directors' duties and its knowledge of their breach of those duties in paragraph 173, that Deloitte rendered substantial assistance or encouragement in effecting the breach is plead in paragraph 174, and, in paragraph 175, that that assistance and encouragement were the cause of damage to Reliance.

. . . .

Accordingly, the Court will dismiss the preliminary objections filed by Deloitte & Touche, L.L.P. and Jan A. Lomelle in their entirety.

NOTES AND QUESTIONS

1. *Strategy.* In the securities area, class action plaintiffs often named 10-12-14 collateral participants as defendants. *See, e.g.,* Douglas M. Branson, *Collateral Participant Liability Under the Securities Laws — Charting the Proper Course,* 65 OR. L. REV. 327, 327–29 (1986) (42 defendants in one typical case and 700 in another). The roster of defendants could include accountants, as in the principal case, lawyers, tax lawyers, architects, engineers, individual directors, celebrity spokespersons, banks, business consultants, and others, all alleged to be secondarily liable because they had assisted a primary violator, usually the issuer of the securities, who had violated the securities laws. The allegations of secondary liability were usually made more poignant because the primary violator had become bankrupt or could not be found. Plaintiff's counsel would then work the prisoners' dilemma against the defendants, achieving settlements beginning with the less culpable. Fattening his war chest, the lawyer was able to continue against those defendants whose culpability was greater and whose pockets were deeper.

2. *After* Central Bank. In *Central Bank of Denver v. First Interstate Bank,* 511 U.S. 164 (1994), the Court unequivocally closed the door on aiding and abetting allegations under the federal securities law, finding no authority therefore in the federal securities statutes. Despite, or because of, *Central Bank,* aiding and abetting breaches of fiduciary duty allegations under state corporate law have flourished, while aiding and abetting allegations under the federal securities laws have disappeared, with one difference.

3. *State of Mind ("Scienter") Requirement.* Under the pre *Central Bank* decisions, an aiding and abetting charge required an allegation that the secondary violator (the collateral participant) should have, in the exercise of the slightest care, been aware that the primary violator was violating, or had violated, the law. State law claims ratchet this element up; they uniformly require actual knowledge. *See, e.g., Brasseur v. Speranza,* 800 N.Y.S.2d 669, (A.D. 2005) ("To state a claim under this theory a plaintiff must allege that the defendant had actual knowledge of [the primary violator's] breach of fiduciary duty; constructive knowledge will not suffice": claim that managing director of condominium should have known that board members breached duties dismissed). Of course, actual knowledge seldom proves itself directly (except on television) because we cannot read persons' minds. Instead, in the usual cases, the circumstantial evidence mounts until the inference arises that, more probable than not, defendant must have known.

4. *Substantial Assistance.* Another question, which also existed under the federal securities law decisions, was whether mere inaction, or silence, could constitute the aider and abettor's substantial assistance, required to ground a claim. A leading case was *Brennan v. Midwestern Life Ins. Co.*, 417 F.2d 147 (7th Cir. 1969) (issuer of stock did nothing when alerted to failure of securities firm to deliver shares). State courts have held that silence or inaction cannot amount to the substantial assistance required, absent a fiduciary duty to the plaintiff which required the aider and abettor to have spoken to the plaintiff (e.g., an attorney or an accountant in certain circumstances). *See Global Minerals and Metals Corp. v. Holme*, 824 N.Y.S.2d 210, 217 (A.D. 2006) (aiding and abetting violation alleged against wife of faithless fiduciary dismissed). *See also Williams v. Sidley Austin Brown & Woo* d, 832 N.Y.S.2d 9, 11 (A.D. 2007) (aiding and abetting allegations against selling agent and law firm upheld, holding that review of tax opinions and other documents and in helping obtain loans, secondary defendants must have known that "opinion letters contained false representations" and also had rendered substantial assistance to the primary violator, the promoter and issuer of the tax shelters).

5. *Leading Cases.* The Delaware courts authored some of the earliest, and still leading, decisions on the state law claim of aiding and abetting. *See Laventhol, Krekstein, Horwath & Horwath v. Tuckman*, 372 A.2d 168 (Del. 1976); *Penn Mart Realty Co. v. Becker*, 298 A.2d 349 (Del. Ch. 1972). *See also HMG/Courtland Properties v. Gray*, 749 A.2d 94 (Del. Ch. 1999); *Jackson National Life Ins. Co. v. Kennedy*, 741 A.2d 377 (Del. Ch. 1999). *See also Sample v. Morgan*, 935 A.2d 1046 (Del. Ch. 2007) (long arm jurisdiction upheld over out-of-state lawyer alleged to have aided and abetted breach of fiduciary duty).

M.   THREE ADDITIONAL (INCHOATE) FIDUCIARY DUTIES

1.   The Duty of Candor

TURNER v. BERNSTEIN
Court of Chancery of Delaware
776 A.2d 530, 531–535, 542, 545, 547 (2000)

STRINE, VICE CHANCELLOR.

. . . The plaintiffs allege that the GenDerm directors breached their fiduciary duties by failing to provide the GenDerm stockholders with information material to the decision whether to approve a merger of GenDerm into a wholly-owned subsidiary of Medicis Pharmaceutical Corporation in December 1997. In particular, the plaintiffs allege that the GenDerm directors deprived the company's stockholders of the information necessary to make an informed decision whether to accept the consideration offered in the Medicis merger or to seek appraisal.

[T]he GenDerm board provided the GenDerm stockholders with extremely cursory information in connection with the Medicis merger. For example, the GenDerm board did not give the stockholders any current financial information or explain why the merger was in the best interests of the GenDerm stockholders. While the board did tell stockholders they could call the company if they had any questions, the board essentially defaulted on its affirmative obligation to disclose the information material to the decisions it was asking the GenDerm stockholders to make.

Factual Background

[G]enDerm was a non-public corporation that sold topically applied pharmaceutical products, such as an arthritis pain relieving cream. Dr. Joel E. Bernstein founded GenDerm and served as its Chairman of the Board during the entire thirteen-year period preceding the merger. . . . [G]enDerm was owned by a fairly broad group of stockholders. It had over eleven and half million issued shares held by in excess of 150 record holders. But voting control of the company was not dispersed. Rather, the GenDerm board of directors controlled a majority of the company's stock.

. . . .

[In October, 1997] GenDerm entered into a letter of intent contemplating an acquisition of the company by Medicis . . . As GenDerm explained to its shareholders, the merger consideration consisted on a per share basis of:

1. Approximately $3.64 in cash at closing.

2. Contingent cash payments totaling up to approximately $0.89 upon the release of escrow funds, expected to occur over the 32 months after closing (the exact amount and timing of the payments will depend on the amount of claims, if any, against the escrow . . .)

3. Contingent cash "earnout" payments of up to approximately $1.44 expected to be paid in the year 2000, based on GenDerm's 1999 sales.

. . . .

On or about December 1, 1997, the GenDerm board sought written consents approving the Medicis merger. On its face, the solicitation appears to have been addressed to all GenDerm stockholders. But the solicitation was apparently not sent to all the stockholders. Plaintiffs claim that they never received it, and the defendants have produced no evidence that it was sent to them. Furthermore, to the extent that the solicitation was genuinely one of all stockholders, the timing of its mailing was breathtakingly risky. The package was dated December 1, 1997 but indicates that "[t]he closing of the transaction is expected to occur on or about next Wednesday December 3, 1997."

The solicitation materials consisted solely of a one-page letter, a consent form, and a copy of the merger agreement and of 8 Del. C. s 262 [the appraisal provision]. Aside from a paragraph describing the merger consideration, the only substantive portions of the solicitation letter stated: *The Board of Directors has approved the transaction and recommends that the Company's stockholders approve the transaction. . . .*

. . . .

What is anomalous about this case is the total dearth of information provided to the GenDerm stockholders. They did not even receive the company's most recent financial results for the periods proximate to the vote. They did not receive any projections of future company performance or any explanation of why the GenDerm board believed that the merger consideration was more worthwhile to the stockholders than the returns that could be expected if the company were to pursue its existing business plan.

[T]he Seller's Report provided to Medicis by GenDerm in October 1997 contained a great deal of information that GenDerm stockholders would have found material in determining whether to accept the merger consideration or seek appraisal. Some excerpts:

GenDerm Corporation (the Company) is a very different and a much healthier company than it was one year ago. Gross sales for the U.S. in 1997 are now expected to be in excess of the $26.1 million upon which the attached pro forma 1997 Income statement was based. . . . As can be seen from the 1997 September YTD Preliminary (based on actual September gross sales and high confidence expense estimates) Income Statement, the Company has been profitable since May 1997.

With growth driven by new products — particularly OVIDE® Cream Shampoo and ZONACORT™ Cream, GenDerm gross sales are expected to reach $100 million by the year 2002.

. . . .

The fiduciary duty of disclosure flows from the broader fiduciary duties of care and loyalty. That disclosure duty is triggered (inter alia) where directors (as GenDerm's former directors did here) present to stockholders for their consideration a transaction that requires them to cast a vote and/or make an investment decision, such as whether or not to accept a merger or demand appraisal. Stockholders confronted with that choice are entitled to disclosure of the available material facts needed to make such an informed decision. Specifically in the merger context, the directors of a constituent corporation whose shareholders are to vote on a proposed merger, have a fiduciary duty to disclose to the shareholders the available material facts that would enable them to make an informed decision, pre-merger, whether to accept the merger consideration or demand appraisal.

. . . .

Without belaboring the obvious, the defendant directors did not discharge their obligation to provide the GenDerm stockholders with "the available material facts that would enable them to make an informed decision . . . whether to accept the merger consideration or demand appraisal." . . . . [See] O'Malley v. Boris, Del. Supr., 742 A.2d 845, 851 (1999) (. . . "[investors should not be required to 'correctly read between the lines' to learn all of the material facts relating to the transaction at issue"); Sealy Mattress Co. of N.J., Inc. v. Sealy, Inc., Del. Ch., 532 A.2d 1324, 1340 (1987) ("The duty of candor must be discharged by the fiduciary directly to the beneficiary stockholder in the transaction itself. . . . "]

. . . .

Certainly, an allegation that directors totally ignored their fiduciary duty to disclose material facts in connection with a cash-out merger would seem to raise a serious question of director fidelity "unrelated to judgmental factors of valuation" [. . . Wacht v. Continental Hosts, Ltd., Del. Ch., C.A. No. 7954, mem. op. at 6, 9, 1986 WL 4492, Berger, V.C. (Apr. 11, 1986) (duty of fair dealing includes "the duty of complete candor," and where complaint states a claim for breach of that disclosure duty, the "complaint adequately states a claim for unfair dealing and is not subject to dismissal on the ground that appraisal is plaintiff's exclusive remedy"). In view of the importance our law places on full disclosure, it would be difficult to reconcile allowing equitable unfair dealing cases to proceed with barring equitable actions based on inadequate disclosures.

[T]he plaintiffs are entitled to summary judgment on the liability aspect of their disclosure claim.

NOTES AND QUESTIONS

1. *Genesis.* The duty of candor first received mention in *Lynch v. Vickers*, 383 A.2d 278 (Del. 1978). Commentary did not appear until the 1990s. *See* Douglas M. Branson, *Emergence of a New Duty — The Duty of Candor, in* CORPORATE GOVERNANCE § 10.07 (1993). Later commentary includes Lawrence Hamermesh, *Calling Off the Lynch Mob: The Corporate Directors' Duty of Candor*, 49 VAND. L. REV. 1087 (1996). Previously, attorneys and others had always thought of disclosure duties as emanating principally from federal and state securities law. With *Lynch*, the Delaware courts began making clear that state corporate law (the duties of care and loyalty, or an independent duty known as candor), require certain disclosures, regardless of what securities laws may require.

2. *Like the Artist Formerly Known as Prince.* After 20 or so Delaware decisions, the Supreme Court of Delaware decreed abandonment of the duty formerly known as candor, insisting that the duty, if it was an independent duty, should be referred to as the "duty of disclosure." *Stroud v. Grace*, 606 A.2d 75, 84 (Del. 1992) ("[i]t is more appropriate for our courts to speak of a duty of disclosure . . . rather than the unhelpful terminology . . . 'duty of candor' "). Just as with the musical artist's name, as the principal case illustrates, however, the candor terminology crept back into the decisions. *See also McMullin v. Beran*, 765 A.2d 910, 917 (Del. 2000).

3. *History.* As with many features of Delaware corporate law making, in its first decisions the Delaware Supreme Court let the "genie out of the bottle." For example, in *In re Tri-Star Pictures, Inc.*, 634 A.2d 319, 333 (Del. 1993), the court held that a violation gives rise to an independent right to seek damages ("a virtual per se rule of damages for breach of the fiduciary duty of disclosure"). Faced then with an ever growing array of class actions over disclosure violations, the court quickly had to adumbrate features of the duty, in the process cutting back on its application. First, as recounted in the principal case, the court held that the duty of candor or disclosure does not replicate the federal securities laws; also, the duty only applies in those instances in which the corporation and its board of directors seeks a shareholder permission or consent. *See Arnold v. Society for Sav. Bancorp*, 678 A.2d 533, 539 (Del. 1996). Then, in *Loudon v. Archer-Daniels-Midland*, 700 A.2d 135, 142 (Del. 1997), among instances in which shareholder consents are sought, the court held that the duty does not extend to the election of directors unless the directors have been finally adjudicated to have committed an offence. "[T]he circumstances recognized in *Tristar* — disclosure violations and deprivation of stockholders' economic or voting rights — that would give rise to a damages remedy are absent here" (failure to disclose criminal antitrust charges pending against ADM officials).

4. *Intentional or Knowing Conduct.* With *Malone v. Brincat*, 722 A.2d 5 (Del. 1998), the duty of candor took another twist. *Malone* created an exception to the rule that the duty of candor operates only when shareholder consent is sought. In *Malone*, plaintiff alleged that directors of Mercury Finance had knowingly permitted overstatement of Mercury's earnings to the tune of $2 billion. The "seeking shareholder consent" requirement goes out the window, the court held, if directors have acted knowingly or intentionally permitted the circulation of false or misleading information. "We hold that directors who knowingly disseminate false information that results in corporate injury or damage to an individual violate their fiduciary duty and may be held accountable . . . ."

5. *Other Applications.* Directors may have no duty to disclose all information in their possession to fellow directors. But when a director "seeks board approval of a transaction," the director's duty of candor operates, as a matter of state law requiring that she make full disclosure. *Benihana of Tokyo, Inc. v. Benihana, Inc.*, 891 A.2d 150, 181 & n.187 (Del. Ch. 2005).

6. *Importance.* Events of the last 20 years have given the duty of candor added importance. Specifically, the widespread adoption by the states of provisions allowing corporations in articles of incorporation to limit or exclude damages for duty of care provisions (exculpatory, "rain coat" or 102(b)(7) provisions), and Delaware's treatment of such articles in litigation contexts, and the adoption of the State Uniform Standards Act (SUSA) in 1998, heighten the importance of the duty of candor.

The Delaware court has held that if a corporation has adopted exculpatory provisions, upon proof thereof, a trial court is to dismiss all duty of care damage allegations against corporate directors. *See Arnold v. Soc. for Savings Bancorp.*, 650 A.2d 1270 (Del. 1994) (articles of incorporation can result in exculpation and dismissal of duty of candor violations, at least if no self dealing or "intentional misconduct or a knowing violation of law was involved"). *Cf. Zirn v. VLI Corp.*, 621 A.2d 773 (Del. 1993) (exculpatory provision did not relieve directors from potential duty of candor liability). Simultaneously, the court has been somewhat coy pinning down whether the duty of candor springs from the duty of care, the duty of loyalty, or is a free standing obligation. Thus, insofar as a duty of candor violation allegation is based upon the duty of loyalty rather than care, or upon some other duty, the allegation can escape dismissal under *Arnold* or *Zirn* grounds. *See, e.g., In re Reliance Securities Litigation*, 91 F. Supp. 2d 706, 731–32 (D. Del. 2000).

Congress enacted SUSA in 1998 because, in order to evade the harsh mandates of the Private Securities Litigation Reform Act of 1995 (PSLRA), *see infra*, many plaintiff's attorneys were filing class actions, including actions under the Securities Act of 1933, under which there is concurrent jurisdiction, in state court. In state court, the PSLRA pleading, certification, strict discovery limitation, and other provisions did not apply. SUSA provides that in any disclosure class or group action purporting to represent more than 50 shareholders a defendant may remove it to federal court where, of course, the PSLRA will apply. *See* Chapter 12, *infra*.

SUSA, however, contains what has been termed the "Delaware carveout." Essentially, state courts may retain subject matter jurisdiction over duty of candor cases. State actions are preserved in state court if they involve "the purchase or sale of securities by the issuer . . . exclusively from or to holders of equity securities in the issuer," or "any recommendation, statement of position, or other communication with respect the sale of securities of the issuer . . . made by or on behalf of the issuer . . . and concerns decisions of those equity holders with respect to voting their securities . . . or exercising dissenters' or appraisal rights." SUSA § 16(d). *See also Gibson v. PS Group Holdings, Inc.*. 2000 U.S. Dist. LEXIS 3158 (S.D. Cal. Mar. 8, 2000) (applying Delaware carveout in remanding shareholder class action to state court).

7. *Other Jurisdictions.* Courts in states other than Delaware have recognized the right and utilized the duty of candor terminology. *See, e.g., Persinger v. Carmazzi*, 441 S.E.2d 646, 652 (W. Va. 1994); *Potter v. Pohlad*, 560 N.W.2d 389, 395 (Minn. App. 1997).

2. The Duty of Good Faith

Janet E. Kerr, *Developments in Corporate Governance: The Duty of Good Faith and Its Impact on Director Conduct*
13 GEO. MASON L. REV. 1037, 1040–58, 1080–81 (2006)[*]

. . . .

A. *Defining Good Faith*

Although the duty of good faith has long been important in fiduciary duty analysis, courts have yet to explain its meaning concisely and consistently.[1] In practice, the duty of good faith "works as part of the articulation of the business judgment rule that applies to the directors' decision-making process and . . . is part of the directors' oversight responsibility . . . . [A] director who flunks the 'good faith' test has not lived up to her currently expected standard of conduct."[2] Moreover, a director's behavior arguably implicates the duty of good faith if it is "reckless, disingenuous, irresponsible, or irrational." Such behavior could lead to personal liability for directors even where the actions are not necessarily self-dealing in nature.

Historically, the duty of good faith did not impose upon directors a duty to operate a "corporate system of espionage" to ferret out wrongdoing, absent suspicion such wrongdoing existed. In a move toward increased director responsibility, the Delaware Supreme Court stated in 1996 that a sustained or systematic failure of the board of directors to exercise oversight — such as an utter failure to attempt to assure that a reasonable information and reporting system exits — would establish a lack of good faith. . . . [R]ecently, the following have been considered potential violations of the

---

[1] *See* Lyman P.Q. Johnson & Mark A. Sides, *The Sarbanes-Oxley Act and Fiduciary Duties*, 30 WM. MITCHELL L. REV. 1149, 1200 (2004).

[2] E. Norman Veasey, *Counseling Directors in the New Corporate Culture*, 59 BUS. LAW. 1447, 1454–56 (2004).

duty of good faith: intentional or unintentional misconduct;[3] reckless behavior given a certain duration or magnitude; conscious disregard of known risks;[4] and behavior that cannot rationally be explained on any other grounds.[5] According to the latest cases, directors may be liable for a good faith violation if they act as if they simply do not care about the risks inherent in the transaction at hand.[6]

Other undefined aspects of the duty of good faith include whether bad faith in the corporate context can be inferred and whether recklessness constitutes bad faith. Such concepts are ripe for litigation and are highly fact sensitive. [C]ourts generally agree that a finding of bad faith requires proof of an illicit motive or bad faith state of mind. Both the Delaware Supreme Court and the Delaware Court of Chancery have stated that a bad faith state of mind and even recklessness can be inferred if there are sufficiently specific and particularized allegations of fact. To be clear, Delaware courts have not expressly equated recklessness with bad faith. But several decisions indicate that even where there is no explicit bad faith intent or motive, Delaware courts could conclude that particular behavior, reckless or otherwise, was so inappropriate that it must have been undertaken in bad faith. Because of the uncertainty surrounding these concepts, future litigation addressing the question of whether a director acted in good faith will likely include discussions of whether or not reckless behavior amounts to a breach of the duty of good faith and whether or not bad faith can be inferred in the absence of an explicit bad faith intent or motive. As a consequence of the uncertainty, courts will likely refrain from constructing bright line rules with regard to the good faith analysis. Director liability will hinge upon judicial interpretation of these ambiguous concepts.

B. *Recent Developments*

. . . .

Several recent cases illustrate a judicial willingness to entertain the possibility of a more expansive definition of the duty of good faith. *In re Abbott Laboratories Derivative Shareholders Litigation*[7] involved a complaint by shareholders that the board of directors failed to act when the Food and Drug Administration raised concerns over a six-year period about one of the company's manufacturing facilities.[8] The failure to take action presented a typical due care scenario.[9] The court found that if the allegations in the complaint were true, they evidenced a "sustained and systematic failure of the board to exercise oversight . . . ."[10] Since this failure to exercise oversight was a recurring problem over the course of a significant amount of time, the court, citing *Caremark*, found that the behavior "indicat[ed] that the directors' decision

---

[3] *See* McCall v. Scott, 239 F.3d 808, 818 (6th Cir. 2001), *amended by*, 250 F.3d 997 (refusing to conclude that only intentional conduct could implicate the duty of good faith).

[4] *McCall*, 239 F.3d at 818–19 (quoting Franklin R. Balotti & Jesse A. Finkelstein, Delaware Law of Corporations and Business Organizations § 4.29, at 4-116 to 4-116.1 (3d ed. Supp. 2000), for the proposition that a conscious disregard of known risks could be considered a violation of the duty of good faith).

[5] McGowan v. Ferro, 859 A.2d 1012, 1031 (Del. Ch. 2004) (citing *In re* J.P. Stevens & Co. S'holders Litig., 542 A.2d 770, 780 (Del. Ch. 1988), *aff'd*, 873 A.2d 1099 (Del. 2005); Reed & Neiderman, *supra* note 5, at 140).

[6] *In re* Walt Disney Co. Derivative Litig., 825 A.2d 275, 289 (Del. Ch. 2003).

[7] 325 F.3d 795 (7th Cir. 2003).

[8] *Abbott*, 325 F.3d at 798. . . .

[9] A typical due care scenario involves a director who is entirely disinterested but whose actions have failed to meet an acceptable level of carefulness or attentiveness. David A. Drexler Et Al., 1 Delaware Corporation Law and Practice § 15.06 (2005).

[10] *Abbott*, 325 F.3d at 809 (quoting *Caremark*, 698 A.2d at 971) (internal quotation marks omitted). *See* Mark J. Loewenstein, *The Quiet Transformation of Corporate Law*, 57 SMU L. Rev. 353 (2004), for further discussion of this case.

to not act was not made in good faith and was contrary to the best interests of the company." The court noted that the magnitude and duration of the alleged wrongdoing were important factors in determining whether there had been a violation of the duty of good faith. The board's "conscious inaction" over a six-year period led to the imposition of the highest fine ever imposed by the FDA. The court found that the plaintiff's allegations, if true, indicated a breach of the duty of good faith such that the directors would not be protected by the business judgment rule. The "conscious disregard" of known risks, if proven, amounted to conduct that could not have been undertaken in good faith. The court in *Abbott* changed its focus of analysis from breach of the duty of due care to breach of the duty of good faith.[11]

In *McCall v. Scott*,[12] shareholders brought suit against certain directors of Columbia/HCA Healthcare Corporation ("Columbia") alleging "widespread and systematic health care fraud by Columbia's hospitals, home health agencies, and other facilities." The plaintiffs alleged that a violation of the duty of good faith could be inferred from the directors' failure to act in the face of an ongoing federal investigation and a *New York Times* investigation into the company's billing practices, among other things. The court agreed that, if the allegations were true, such intentional misconduct and reckless behavior could result in a violation of the duty of good faith. Because the court found that the plaintiffs' allegations were adequate, the exculpatory provision in Columbia's articles was not applicable. Most significantly, the court did not limit a finding of bad faith to instances of intentional conduct but indicated that bad faith could be *inferred.* Also noteworthy is the court's indication that the defendants should have been more aware of the employee misconduct because the directors possessed a specialized knowledge and background. Consequently, some have cautioned that *McCall* potentially represents a substantial source of director liability.

. . . [discussion of *Stockbridge v. Gemini Air Cargo, Inc.*, 611 S.E.2d 600 (Va. 2005), omitted]

A recent case from the District of Kansas considered the definition of good faith for purposes of Delaware Code, Title 8, Section 102(b)(7), which serves to limit or eliminate a director's personal liability for breaches of fiduciary duty in certain circumstances.[13] One count of the plaintiff's complaint charged the directors with corporate waste. The complaint asserted that the company could have sold an asset for a substantially higher return than it received. The directors argued that the corporation's exculpatory provision barred the plaintiff's claim. Indicating a willingness to infer bad faith, the court stated that to sufficiently plead a claim for corporate waste *or bad faith*, the "plaintiff must show that the board's decision was so egregious or irrational that it could not have been based on a valid assessment of the corporation's best interests." The court ruled against the board of directors, finding that if the plaintiff's allegations were true, "the board did not have any valid business reason to choose such a transaction, particularly when an alternative transaction . . . would have yielded 90 [percent] of fair market value." . . .

In re Walt Disney Co. Derivative Litigation[14] [the opinion of the Delaware Supreme Court is reproduced *supra*] involved a challenge to the decision of Disney's board to approve a contract for Michael Ovitz, which resulted in a $140,000,000 payout after just one year of employment. The plaintiffs' basic claim exemplified a typical duty of due

---

[11] One writer claims that the analysis in Abbott was flawed in a couple of ways and that the conclusion that the *Abbott* board acted in bad faith was conclusory. Nevertheless, the author reasoned that "[o]ne might conclude from Abbott . . . that [because] the court was skeptical of the combined effect of the business judgment rule and the provision in the company's articles limiting the directors' liability . . . [t]he avenue for review was the good faith exception." Loewenstein, *supra* note [11], at 375.

[12] 239 F.3d 808 (6th Cir. 2001), *amended by* 250 F.3d 997 (6th Cir. 2001).

[13] Grogan v. O'Neil, 292 F. Supp. 2d 1282, 1293 (D. Kan. 2003); *see* DEL. CODE ANN. tit. 8, § 102(b)(7) (2003).

[14] 825 A.2d 275 (Del. Ch. 2003).

care situation: they claimed that the board had not done its job in adequately informing itself about Ovitz's employment contract. The facts alleged that the defendant directors were essentially absent from the negotiation and adoption of Ovitz's employment agreement. It was further alleged that the compensation committee spent less than one hour reviewing the terms in the draft agreement, and that the defendant directors failed to review the final agreement, which contained terms materially different from those in the draft agreement. Finally, the directors neither questioned the no-fault termination of Ovitz nor considered alternatives. As alleged, it appears that the directors placed the entire process of negotiation of Ovitz's employment agreement, and later his termination, within the hands of Michael Eisner, Disney's Chief Executive Officer at that time and Ovitz's long-time friend.

When moving for a motion to dismiss, the board contended that it could not be liable for a due care violation because of an exculpatory provision in its articles exempting it from liability for due care violations. The Delaware Court of Chancery proceeded to find that the facts of the case "[gave] rise to a reason to doubt whether the board's actions were taken honestly and in good faith." The court reasoned that the facts suggest more than a failure to become informed about an issue of material importance, but portrayed a conscious and intentional "we don't care about the risks" attitude. Thus, the plaintiffs' allegations convinced the court to deny the motion to dismiss and recast the case as one involving a breach of the duty of good faith.[15] Significantly, exculpatory provisions do not protect actions not taken in good faith. . . .

More than two years later, the Delaware Court of Chancery ruled upon the merits of the case.[16] . . . The court found that the board of directors did not act in bad faith when it hired Ovitz and approved his employment agreement, but may have been "ordinarily negligent." According to the business judgment rule, ordinary negligence alone is insufficient to constitute a violation of the duty of due care. Although Eisner made no effort to notify the board of his agreement to hire Ovitz, he informed himself of all material information reasonably available when making this employment decision, thereby exercising good faith.[17] Likewise, other directors also informed themselves of all material information reasonably available.

Although Judge Chandler ruled in favor of the defendant directors, he was clear in pointing out that the "defendants' conduct . . . fell *significantly* short of the best practices of ideal corporate governance" and Eisner's conduct in particular was not consistent with how fiduciaries of Delaware corporations are expected to act.[18] Judge Chandler criticized that by making the decision regarding Ovitz's hiring without board input, Eisner "enthroned himself as the omnipotent and infallible monarch of his personal Magic Kingdom . . . ." [and, on appeal, Justice Jacobs held, *inter alia*, that good faith is a separate and independent duty rather than implicit in the duties of care or loyalty].

. . . .

Historically, the duty of good faith has been an important component of corporate law. But the duty remains largely undefined. It is unclear whether recklessness amounts to bad faith, or whether director action that is so egregious that it cannot be explained on any other grounds may very well be seen as a breach of that director's

---

[15] [Hillary] Sale, [*Delaware's Good Faith*, 89 CORNELL L. REV. 456'] at 48–81 [2004].

[16] See *In re* Walt Disney Co. Derivative Litig., No. CIV. A. 15452, 2005 WL 2056651, at *1 (Del. Ch. Aug. 9, 2005).

[17] *Id.* at 41. The court clarified that by acting in good faith, Eisner acted "with the subjective belief that those actions were in the best interests of the Company . . . ." *Id.*

[18] *Id.* at 1, 41 (emphasis added). Judge Chandler noted that the ideals of corporate governance have evolved because of recent corporate scandals, including the debacles involving Enron and World-Com. *Id.* at 1. However, Delaware law does not hold fiduciaries liable for a failure to comply with the ideals of director conduct. *Id.*

duty of good faith. Likewise, fiduciary action portraying a "we don't care about the risks" attitude will likely be deemed a violation of the duty of good faith.

3. The Duty to Act Lawfully

PROBLEM

Local state telephone company in the state of Clinton (Clinton Bell) equips the State Democratic Committee (SDC) with banks of telephones for phonethons and provides a myriad of other telecommunications services. After the elections, SDC has a huge $4 million telephone bill which it cannot pay.

SDC seeks forgiveness of the debt. Clinton Bell's board of directors deliberates. Forgiveness of the debt might well serve the company's best interests as the both the new governor of Clinton and the house and senate leaders are newly elected Democrats. The company has several important measures on its legislative agenda.

None of the directors serves on the SDC or otherwise has a interest in the subject matter of the decision. The board receives reports from the CFO and the company's attorneys. The CFO opines that forgiveness of the debt will not put the company in any financial strait. Only the attorney has a caveat. She reports that the forgiveness of the debt may be construed as an indirect gift to partisan campaigns for political office and, hence, illegal. She indicates that she will do further research on the question. The board, however, is impatient. They decide to vote. They forgive the debt.

An irate Clinton Bell shareholder consults you. Did the Clinton Bell directors violate their fiduciary duties? Is the Clinton Bell board's decision shielded from judicial scrutiny by the business judgment rule?

NOTE

A Third Duty? The Duty to Act Lawfully. Directors may act with due care. They may honestly believe that they are serving the best interests of the corporation. Yet the course upon which they cause the corporation to embark is illegal. For that reason, some commentators posit the necessity for a third fiduciary duty, in addition to duties of care and loyalty, the duty to act lawfully. *See, e.g.*, ARTHUR PINTO & DOUGLAS BRANSON, UNDERSTANDING CORPORATE LAW § 8.06, at 219 (2d ed. 2004). In *Miller v. American Telephone & Telegraph Co.*, 507 F.2d 759 (3d Cir. 1974), the court found such a duty to exist and applied it to facts similar to those in the problem.

Two other approaches are possible. A court could posit the existence of an independent duty of good faith and that it had been violated. Or a court could refuse to apply the business judgment rule, leaving directors open to the charge that in forgiving the debt the directors had violated their duty of care. Along such lines, articulated as an independent duty or not, directors have always had a duty to see that they, and the corporate managers over whom they have supervision, act lawfully.

Chapter 11
DERIVATIVE LITIGATION

A. INTRODUCTION

The modern history of the derivative suit began with the revival, based upon several older cases, of the Special Litigation Committee (SLC) of the board of directors, from the late 1970s onward. Prior to that time, a number of legislative enactments labeled "reforms" dated from the strike suit era of the 1920s and 1930s. Some of those reforms are still on the books while others have been repealed but no pattern exists. Instead, the survival of the older set of reforms is a bit of a crazy quilt, which necessitates that all or most all, of those incidents of the derivative action be reviewed as well. They are reviewed *infra*, following discussion of the SLC device.

U.S. courts of equity invented the derivative action in the 1870s as a means for aggrieved shareholders to step into the corporation's shoes in order to vindicate its rights. Courts thought such a procedural device necessary because those ordinarily in control of the corporation's business and affairs, which includes litigation in its behalf, namely, the board of directors, in the typical derivative suit are the alleged perpetrators of any wrongdoing that has occurred. Because directors may be very hesitant to sue their brethren or, indeed, themselves, equity had to invent a device which would enable others to vindicate the corporation's interests.

Derivative action plaintiffs name the corporation as a nominal defendant but any recovery or settlement, less attorney's fees, goes to the corporate treasury. Laws require that, in most instances, the shareholder plaintiff make demand on the corporation's board of directors. *See infra.* If the board accepts the demand, and proceeds in some way with the suit, the shareholder plaintiff drops out and the corporation is actually re-aligned as a plaintiff. *See, e.g., Valeant Pharms. Int'l v. Jerney*, 921 A.2d 732 (Del. Ch. 2007); *Powell v. Western Illinois Elec. Coop.*, 536 N.E.2d 231 (Ill. App. 1989).

To avoid unjust enrichment, the plaintiffs' attorney's fees come out of any judgment or settlement (common fund) her efforts have created for shareholders as a class or, in some cases, for any common benefit (bylaw amendments, adoption of corporate policy) her efforts have produced, even in cases in which the plaintiff has not prevailed, on the merits or otherwise. *See, e.g., Crandon Capital Partners v. Shelk*, 157 P.3d 176 (Or. 2007) ("actions by the corporate defendant [Willamette Industries] that moot the shareholder's substantive claims [removal of takeover defenses and merger with Weyerhaeuser Co.] do not necessarily moot the shareholder's claim for attorney fees"); *Seattle Trust & Sav. Bank v. McCarthy*, 617 P.2d 1023 (Wash. 1980) (shareholder lost case but recovered fees because holding that preemptive right was no longer a vested right benefitted all shareholders).

Derivative litigation presents problems other species of litigation do not present: multiple lawsuits, as there may be hundreds or thousands of shareholders who may be aggrieved; unfaithful champions, that is, lawyers, intent on reaping a large fee from a corporate fisc rather than insuring that justice is done; and strike suits in which plaintiff shareholders know little of the suit's merits and attorneys are the true parties in interest. Because problems are endemic, derivative suits have always been subject to close judicial scrutiny and legislative control. The latest of the latter, which approximately half the states have adopted, is a requirement of universal demand under which demand on the board of directors is no longer ever excused as "futile." *See In re Guidant Shareholders Derivative Litigation, infra.*

The potential "shows stopper" for derivative litigation, however, rather than universal demand, has been the advent of the SLC, under whose aegis derivative litigation can be sidetracked, or derailed altogether, as not "in the corporation's best interest." A seminal piece is George Dent, *The Power of Directors to Terminate Shareholder*

Litigation: The Death of the Derivative Suit?, 75 Nw. U. L. R. 96 (1980).

Some room exists to avoid the SLC device through bringing a direct rather than derivative action. Also, a few other exceptions to the demand requirement (close corporation, irreparable injury, undue delay exceptions) exist. But in cases in which counsel is present, and is able to script it correctly, use of the SLC device has had a negative effect on derivative litigation in the United States.

Therefore, in the late 1980s, increasingly plaintiffs turned away from derivative litigation to class action suits alleging material omissions or disclosure in a misleading way under the federal securities laws. *See* Chapter 12, *infra.* Then, too, the derivative suit has seen a revival as, *inter alia*, the stock option back dating suits have been bought, in whole or in part, as derivative actions. Many shareholder complaints in small and medium size corporations always have gone forward as derivative suits. Knowledge of the in's and out's of the derivative action, and the theories behind the principal ones, have always been a part of every lawyer's tool kit.

PROBLEM

David Falconer is a disgruntled shareholder in Roadstar, Inc., a manufacturer of truck bodies. Roadstar is a small, publicly held company with 150 or so shareholders and a five person board. David is disgruntled because a truck fabricator just breached a contract for delivery of 1,000 truck bodies over two years.

The fabricator, Drummond Co., Falconer has learned, is owned by cousins of Reid Manley, Roadstar's CEO and largest shareholder. Reid's brother, Mark Manley, also sits on the Roadstar board, as does their father, John Manley. Cancellation of the order means that Roadstar will have a loss rather than a healthy projected profit this year, as well as next year. The other two directors, a banker named Baker and a law professor at State U named Andreen, seldom attend board meetings.

Falconer is incensed because the Manleys have done nothing regarding the breach, allowing it to happen with nary a protest. What is the nature of his claim, against whom would he file his claims, and what is the nature of the action overall?

B. THE SPECIAL LITIGATION COMMITTEE AND THE SCOPE OF JUDICIAL REVIEW

ZAPATA CORP. v. MALDONADO
Supreme Court of Delaware
430 A.2d 779 (1981)

Before DUFFY, QUILLEN and HORSEY, JJ.

QUILLEN, JUSTICE:

In June, 1975, William Maldonado, a stockholder of Zapata, instituted a derivative action in the Court of Chancery on behalf of Zapata against ten . . . directors of Zapata, alleging breaches of fiduciary duty. Maldonado did not first demand that the board bring this action, stating instead such demand's futility because all directors were named as defendants and allegedly participated in the acts specified. In June, 1977, Maldonado commenced an action in the United States District Court for the Southern District of New York against the same defendants, save one, alleging federal security law violations as well as the same common law claims . . . .

By June, 1979 . . . the remaining directors appointed two new outside directors to the board. The board then created an "Independent Investigation Committee," composed solely of the two new directors, to investigate Maldonado's actions to determine whether the corporation should continue any or all of the litigation. The Committee's determination was stated to be "final, . . . not . . . subject to review by the Board of Directors and . . . in all respects . . . binding upon the Corporation."

Following an investigation, the Committee concluded, in September, 1979, that each action should "be dismissed forthwith as their continued maintenance is inimical to the Company's best interests . . . ." Consequently, Zapata moved for dismissal or summary judgment . . . . On January 24, 1980, the District Court for the Southern District of New York granted Zapata's motion for summary judgment, Maldonado v. Flynn, S.D.N.Y., 485 F. Supp. 274 (1980), holding, under its interpretation of Delaware law, that the Committee had the authority, under the "business judgment" rule, to require the termination of the derivative action. . . .

On March 18, 1980, the Court of Chancery . . . denied Zapata's motions, holding that Delaware law does not sanction this means of dismissal. More specifically, it held that the "business judgment" rule is not a grant of authority to dismiss derivative actions and that a stockholder has an individual right to maintain derivative actions . . . . Maldonado v. Flynn, Del. Ch., 413 A.2d 1251 (1980). . . .

. . . .

The "business judgment" rule is a . . . judicial creation that presumes propriety, under certain circumstances, in a board's decision. Viewed defensively, it does not create authority. In this sense the "business judgment" rule is not relevant in corporate decision making until after a decision is made. It is generally used as a defense to an attack on the decision's soundness. The board's managerial decision making power, however, comes from § 141(a) ["The business and affairs of every corporation organized under this chapter shall be managed by or under the direction of a board of directors . . . ."]. The judicial creation and legislative grant are related because the "business judgment" rule evolved to give recognition and deference to directors' business expertise when exercising their managerial power under § 141(a).

[T]he focus in this case is on the power to speak for the corporation as to whether the lawsuit should be continued . . . . [W]e turn first to the Court of Chancery's conclusions concerning the right of a plaintiff stockholder in a derivative action. We find that its determination that a stockholder, once demand is made and refused, possesses an independent, individual right to continue a derivative suit for breaches of fiduciary duty over objection by the corporation, as an absolute rule, is erroneous.

. . . .

[M]cKee v. Rogers, Del. Ch., 156 A. 191 (1931), stated "as a general rule" that "a stockholder cannot be permitted . . . to invade the discretionary field committed to the judgment of the directors and sue in the corporation's behalf when the managing body refuses. This rule is a well settled one."

The McKee rule, of course, should not be read so broadly that the board's refusal will be determinative in every instance. Board members, owing a well-established fiduciary duty to the corporation, will not be allowed to cause a derivative suit to be dismissed when it would be a breach of their fiduciary duty. Generally disputes pertaining to control of the suit arise in two contexts.

Consistent with the purpose of requiring a demand, a board decision to cause a derivative suit to be dismissed as detrimental to the company, after demand has been made and refused, will be respected unless it was wrongful. [I]n other words, when stockholders, after making demand and having their suit rejected, attack the board's decision as improper, the board's decision falls under the "business judgment" rule and will be respected if the requirements of the rule are met. A claim of a wrongful decision not to sue is thus the first exception and the first context of dispute. Absent a wrongful refusal, the stockholder in such a situation simply lacks legal managerial power.

But it cannot be implied that, absent a wrongful board refusal, a stockholder can never have an individual right to initiate an action. For, as is stated in McKee, a "well settled" exception exists to the general rule.

"(A) stockholder may sue in equity in his derivative right to assert a cause of action in behalf of the corporation, without prior demand upon the directors to sue, when it is apparent that a demand would be futile, that the officers are under an influence that sterilizes discretion and could not be proper persons to conduct the litigation."

156 A. at 193. This exception [is] the second context for dispute . . .

These comments in McKee . . . make obvious sense. A demand, when required and refused (if not wrongful), terminates a stockholder's legal ability to initiate a derivative action. But where demand is properly excused, the stockholder does possess the ability to initiate the action on his corporation's behalf.

. . . We see no inherent reason why the "two phases" of a derivative suit, the stockholder's suit to compel the corporation to sue and the corporation's suit, should automatically result in the placement in the hands of the litigating stockholder sole control of the corporate right throughout the litigation. To the contrary, it seems to us that such an inflexible rule would recognize the interest of one person or group to the exclusion of all others within the corporate entity. . . .

The question to be decided becomes: When, if at all, should an authorized board committee be permitted to cause litigation, properly initiated by a derivative stockholder in his own right, to be dismissed? . . . Even when demand is excusable, circumstances may arise when continuation of the litigation would not be in the corporation's best interests. Our inquiry is whether, under such circumstances, there is a permissible procedure under § 141(a) by which a corporation can rid itself of detrimental litigation. If there is not, a single stockholder in an extreme case might control the destiny of the entire corporation. This concern was bluntly expressed by the Ninth Circuit in Lewis v. Anderson, 9th Cir., 615 F.2d 778, 783 (1979): "To allow one shareholder to incapacitate an entire board of directors merely by leveling charges against them gives too much leverage to dissident shareholders. "But, when examining the means, including the committee mechanism examined in this case, potentials for abuse must be recognized. This takes us to the second and third aspects of the issue on appeal.

. . . .

The corporate power inquiry then focuses on whether the board, tainted by the self-interest of a majority of its members, can legally delegate its authority to a committee of two disinterested directors. We find our statute clearly requires an affirmative answer to this question. As has been noted, under an express provision of the statute, § 141(c), a committee can exercise all of the authority of the board to the extent provided in the resolution of the board. . . .

We do not think that the interest taint of the board majority is per se a legal bar to the delegation of the board's power to an independent committee composed of disinterested board members. The committee can properly act for the corporation to move to dismiss derivative litigation that is believed to be detrimental to the corporation's best interest.

Our focus now switches to the Court of Chancery which is faced with a stockholder assertion that a derivative suit, properly instituted, should continue . . . and a corporate assertion, properly made by a board committee acting . . . that the same derivative suit should be dismissed as inimical to the best interests of the corporation.

[T]he problem is relatively simple. If, on the one hand, corporations can consistently wrest bona fide derivative actions away from well-meaning derivative plaintiffs through the use of the committee mechanism, the derivative suit will lose much, if not all, of its generally-recognized effectiveness . . . If, on the other hand, corporations are unable to rid themselves of meritless or harmful litigation . . . , the derivative action, created to benefit the corporation, will produce the opposite, unintended result. It thus appears desirable to us to find a balancing point where bona fide stockholder power to bring corporate causes of action cannot be unfairly trampled on by the board of directors, but the corporation can rid itself of detrimental litigation.

As we noted, the question has been treated by other courts as one of the "business judgment" of the board committee. The issues become solely independence, good faith, and reasonable investigation [by the committee]. The ultimate conclusion of the committee, under that view, is not subject to judicial review.

We are not satisfied, however, that acceptance of the "business judgment" rationale at this stage of derivative litigation is a proper balancing point. [I]t seems to us that there is sufficient risk in the realities of a situation like the one presented in this case to justify caution beyond adherence to the theory of business judgment.

The context here is a suit against directors where demand on the board is excused. We think some tribute must be paid to the fact that the lawsuit was properly initiated. It is not a board refusal case. . . .

[N]otwithstanding our conviction that Delaware law entrusts the corporate power to a properly authorized committee, we must be mindful that directors are passing judgment on fellow directors in the same corporation and fellow directors, in this instance, who designated them to serve both as directors and committee members. The question naturally arises whether a "there but for the grace of God go I" empathy might not play a role. And the further question arises whether inquiry as to independence, good faith and reasonable investigation is sufficient safeguard against abuse . . . .

. . . .

. . . There is some analogy to a settlement in that there is a request to terminate litigation without a judicial determination of the merits.

. . . .

After an objective and thorough investigation of a derivative suit, an independent committee may cause its corporation to file a pretrial motion to dismiss in the Court of Chancery. The basis of the motion is the best interests of the corporation, as determined by the committee. The motion should include a thorough written record of the investigation and its findings and recommendations. [A]kin to proceedings on summary judgment, each side should have an opportunity to make a record on the motion.

First, the Court should inquire into the independence and good faith of the committee and the bases supporting its conclusions. Limited discovery may be ordered to facilitate such inquiries. The corporation should have the burden of proving independence, good faith and a reasonable investigation, rather than presuming independence, good faith and reasonableness. If the Court determines either that the committee is not independent or has not shown reasonable bases for its conclusions, or, if the Court is not satisfied for other reasons relating to the process, including but not limited to the good faith of the committee, the Court shall deny the corporation's motion. If, however, the Court is satisfied under Rule 56 standards that the committee was independent and showed reasonable bases for good faith findings and recommendations, the Court may proceed, in its discretion, to the next step.

The second step provides, we believe, the essential key in striking the balance between legitimate corporate claims as expressed in a derivative stockholder suit and a corporation's best interests as expressed by an independent investigating committee. The Court should determine, applying its own independent business judgment, whether the motion should be granted . . . The second step is intended to thwart instances where corporate actions meet the criteria of step one, but the result does not appear to satisfy its spirit, or where corporate actions would simply prematurely terminate a stockholder grievance deserving of further consideration in the corporation's interest. The Court of Chancery of course must carefully consider and weigh how compelling the corporate interest in dismissal is when faced with a non-frivolous lawsuit.

The interlocutory order of the Court of Chancery is reversed and the cause is remanded for further proceedings consistent with this opinion.

NOTES AND QUESTIONS

1. *Disability.* On a question the federal district court had certified to it, the Supreme Court of Iowa dealt with a situation in which a majority of directors colorably were defendants in a derivative suit. In *Miller v. Register & Tribune Syndicate, Inc.*, 336 N.W. 2d 709, 716 (Iowa 1983), the court held that "directors who are parties to a derivative action may not confer upon a special litigation committee . . . the power to bind the corporation as to its conduct of the litigation." The court did hold that in such a case the directors could apply to a court of equity "to make appointments to enable corporate functions to be carried out." In Delaware, the outcome probably would depend not on a majority vel non, but whether a critical mass of directors existed who, while perhaps named as defendants, were not colorably implicated in the alleged wrongdoing. Merely having been named as defendants does not, without more, disable directors from creating a litigation committee (SLC) and appointing directors (usually expansion directors) to it. *See, e.g.*, ALI Corp. Gov. Proj. §1.23.

2. *No Makeweight Factors.* Loss of executive time, real or alleged, negative impacts on employee and managerial morale, impact on public relations, and other factors are likely to be present in any case in which a derivative action based upon apparently sufficient grounds, has been filed. Judge Winter cautioned against committees and courts using such factors in their analysis of whether continuation of a derivative suit was in the corporation's best interest or not. In *Joy v. North*, 692 F.2d 880, 892-96 (2d Cir. 1982), *cert. denied*, 103 S. Ct. 1498 (1983), Judge Winter developed a blueprint for SLCs to follow:

> [T]he burden is on the moving party, as in motions for summary judgment generally. . . . The showing is to be based upon the underlying data developed in the course of discovery and of the committee's investigation [and] not simply naked conclusions. The weight to be given certain evidence is to be determined by conventional analysis, such as whether testimony is under oath and subject to cross examination ... The court's [and the committee's] function is not unlike a lawyer's determining what a case is "worth" for purposes of settlement.

Judge Winter went into even greater detail:

> Judicial scrutiny of special litigation committee recommendations should thus be limited to a comparison of the direct costs imposed upon the corporation by the litigation with the potential benefits [likely recovery]. We are mindful that other less direct costs may be incurred, such as negative impact on morale and upon the corporate image. Nevertheless, such factors ... should [never] be taken into account. Quite apart from the elusiveness of attempting to predict such effects, they are quite likely to be related to the degree of corporate wrongdoing, a spectacular fraud being generally more newsworthy and damaging to morale than a mistake in judgment.

DESIGOUDAR v. MEYERCORD
Court of Appeals, Sixth District, California
108 Cal. App. 4th 173, 133 Cal. Rptr. 2d 408 (2003)

PREMO, ACTING P.J.

We hold that judicial review of the decision of a special litigation committee is governed by the business judgment rule. When asserted in connection with a summary judgment motion the material issues of fact relevant to the special litigation committee defense are the independence of the committee members and their good faith in conducting their investigation. Neither the merits of the derivative claim nor the substance of the committee's decision to reject the claim is subject to judicial review . . .

This case revolves around an agreement between CMD, a publicly traded California corporation, and CellAccess, a small Silicon Valley start-up. Chan Desaigoudar was the founder, chief executive officer, and chairman of the board of CMD. Himanshu Vaishnev was . . . one of the four founders of CellAccess. Vaishnev approached Chan Desaigoudar about investing in CellAccess and Desaigoudar brought the opportunity to the CMD board. In September 1994 CMD finalized an agreement with CellAccess under which CMD would fund CellAccess . . . . In exchange, CMD received a 56 percent interest in the new company.

Very shortly after . . . CMD became embroiled in accusations of accounting irregularities. The [SEC] and the Department of Justice began investigating reports that CMD had been falsely reporting its revenue. Several lawsuits were filed against the company and its stock price plummeted 40 percent. Allegations surfaced implicating Chan Desaigoudar in the wrongdoing. The board relieved him of his positions as CEO and chairman and hired defendant Jeffrey Kalb to be CEO.

In January 1995 CMD disclosed that for the fiscal year ending June 1994 it had overstated earnings by around $20 million, or 70 percent. The company was facing an indisputably serious business and financial crisis. Kalb decided, with the board's approval, to terminate several projects, including the agreement with CellAccess. Kalb negotiated an agreement under which CellAccess gave CMD a promissory note for the $300,000 . . . and a warrant for the purchase of CellAccess stock. In November 1995 FORE Systems, Inc. acquired CellAccess in a stock-for-stock transaction valued at more than $37 million.

The heart of plaintiffs' derivative claim is their allegation that if CMD had not terminated the original agreement with CellAccess it would have had a 56 percent interest in that company worth around $20 million . . . . Instead, CMD had a warrant exercised for a return of $1.6 million.

The Chan Desaigoudar Foundation is a a major CMD shareholder. Plaintiffs, in their capacity as trustees of the Chan Desaigoudar Foundation, filed an amended complaint in the form of a shareholders' derivative action. They named eight individuals as defendants and included CMD as a nominal defendant. Defendants Angel Jordan, Wade Meyercord, C. Kumar N. Patel, Stuart Schube, and John Sprague were CMD directors at the time of the alleged wrongdoing. Defendant Scott Hover-Smoot was CMD general counsel and defendant Jeffrey Kalb was president and CEO.

The amended complaint included [allegations that] the individual defendants had wasted corporate assets because they had not investigated the value of CellAccess before disposing of CMD's interest in it [and] . . . that the defendants had concealed . . . that they had disposed of corporate assets for less than fair market value in order to increase earnings for the pertinent fiscal quarter and thereby secure shareholder approval of stock options for themselves. The amended complaint also alleged that because a majority of the board was involved in the wrongdoing, it was futile to present a pre-complaint demand to the board. . . .

The Committee's Investigation and the Stay of Proceedings

In February 2000, the CMD board of directors appointed a special litigation committee consisting of two directors who had joined the board after the alleged wrongdoing (the Committee). The board charged the Committee with assessing the merits of the amended complaint . . . . Plaintiffs attempted to pursue discovery . . . . CMD moved for an order staying the lawsuit until the Committee completed its investigation. The trial court granted the motion . . . .

At the conclusion of its investigation in April 2001, the Committee produced a detailed report in which it concluded that the various decisions pertaining to the termination of CMD's investments in CellAccess and other projects were " 'valid exercise[s] of business judgment' based on 'multiple valid business purposes, including the need to conserve cash at a time when the Company's financial resources were limited, the need to focus resources on CMD's core business, and the need to reduce management and resource diversion.' " The Committee found no credible evidence of self-dealing. . . . The Committee's ultimate conclusion was that the derivative suit "would be unlikely to succeed on the merits, unlikely to result in any monetary recovery to CMD, and wholly opposed to the best interests of CMD."

. . . The court granted defendants' motion for summary judgment, stating: "Plaintiffs have failed to present evidence sufficient to raise a triable issue of fact with respect to whether or not the members of the Special Litigation Committee, J. Daniel McCranie and Donald L. Waite, were 'disinterested' or whether or not the Special Litigation Committee conducted an 'adequate' investigation of the claims presented in the Amended Complaint . . . .

Questions Presented

1. In considering the defense motion for summary judgment, which was brought on the basis of the special litigation committee defense, was the trial court required to consider the merits of the derivative claim?

2. Did the trial court err by granting summary judgment even though the derivative lawsuit and all discovery connected with it had been stayed?

. . . .

The Special Litigation Committee Defense

In order to put the issue in context, we begin with some basic principles of corporate law. First among these is the nature of the shareholders' derivative lawsuit. Because a corporation is a legal entity separate from its shareholders, when a corporation has suffered an injury to its property the corporation is the party that possesses the right to sue for redress. If a corporation fails to pursue redress of an injury, a shareholder may file a derivative action on behalf of the corporation. The "derivative" action is so called because the rights of the plaintiff shareholders derive from the primary corporate right to redress the wrongs against it.

Another principle is the "business judgment rule." The business judgment rule is premised on the notion that management of the corporation is best left to those to whom it has been entrusted, not to the courts. The rule requires judicial deference to the business judgment of corporate directors so long as there is no fraud or breach of trust, and no conflict of interest exists. . . .

Finally, there is the demand requirement. Unless there are reasons for not doing so, a shareholder must first demand that the company's board of directors pursue the proposed action before the shareholder may undertake the prosecution of a derivative claim. If the board refuses to pursue the claim, that refusal is protected by the business judgment rule and constitutes a defense to a shareholder's derivative lawsuit.

Findley v. Garrett (1952) 109 Cal. App. 2d 166 [240 P.2d 421] illustrates the interplay of these rules. Findley . . . involved a shareholder's claim that officers and directors of Douglas Aircraft Company had fraudulently organized a second company and utilized the new company for their own profit at the expense of Douglas. A disinterested majority of the board concluded that it was not in the interests of the company to prosecute the lawsuit. As a result, the case was dismissed on demurrer. The appellate court affirmed, explaining: "It was a question of business whether the transactions over a 12-year period should be investigated and prosecuted. Directors have the same discretion with respect to the prosecution of claims on behalf of the corporation as they have in other business matters." "Where a board of directors, in refusing to commence an action to redress an alleged wrong against a corporation, acts in good faith within the scope of its discretionary power and reasonably believes its refusal to commence the action is good business judgment in the best interest of the corporation, a stockholder is not authorized to interfere with such discretion by commencing the action."

Although the business judgment rule protects a board's good faith decision to reject a derivative lawsuit, the board cannot avail itself of the protection of the rule if a majority of the board has a personal interest in the outcome. (§ 204, subbed. (a) (10) (iii).) Therefore, when the shareholder alleges wrongdoing on the part of a majority of directors, as plaintiffs have alleged in this case, the common practice is for the board to appoint a special litigation committee of independent directors to investigate the challenged transaction. The parties do not dispute that a decision of a special litigation committee not to prosecute a lawsuit, like the decision of the full board, is a defense to a shareholder's derivative action in California.

The special litigation committee defense has been recognized in some form or other in almost every state. The traditional version of the defense requires the trial court to determine, "as a matter of fact, whether the committee members were disinterested and whether they conducted an adequate investigation. If it answers yes to both questions . . . it must dismiss the derivative action." The New York case of Auerbach v. Bennett (1979) 47 N.Y.2d 619, 633 is typically cited as standing for this approach.

A modified version of the defense was described in Zapata Corp. v. Maldonado [*supra*]. Zapata adopts the Auerbach analysis but adds a second, discretionary step in which the court applies its own business judgment to the committee's conclusion. Courts following the Zapata approach all require this two-step analysis but vary as to the degree of scrutiny the court may apply to the merits of the committee's decision. [Defendants refer to the *Auerbach* version as the "majority" rule and the *Zapata* approach as the "minority" version. In fact, with few exceptions the precise elements of the common law defense vary from state to state]. (See Houle v. Low (1990) 407 Mass. 810, 814–826 [trial court must determine whether committee's decision was "reasonable and principled"]; Alford v. Shaw (1987) 320 N.C. 465, 468–474 [trial court [may in its discretion] consider totality of circumstances to determine whether decision was "just and reasonable"]; Lewis v. Boyd (Tenn. Ct. App. 1992) 838 S.W.2d 215, 222–226 [trial court must determine whether decision was "reasonable and principled"]; In re PSE & G Shareholder Lit. (2002) 173 N.J. 258, 286 [initial burden is on corporation to prove independence, good faith, due care, and reasonableness of decision].)

A number of states have codified the defense, the majority adhering to section 7.44 of the American Bar Association's 1984 Model Business Corporations Act, which uses the traditional approach. (See . . . Ariz. Rev. Stat. Ann. § 10-3634; Conn. Gen. Stat. Ann. § 33-724; Fla. Stat. Ann. § 607.07401, subbed. (3); Ga. Code Ann. §§ 14-2-744, 14-3-744 [taking a position midway between the model act and the Zapata line of cases]; Idaho Code § 30-1-744; Me. Rev. Stat. Ann. tit. 13-A, § 632; Miss. Code Ann. § 79-4-7.44; Mont. Code Ann. §§ 35-1-545, 35-2-1304; Neb. Rev. Stat. Ann. § 21-2074; N.H. Rev. Stat. Ann. § 293-A: 7.44; N.C. Gen. Stat. § 55-7-44; Tex. Bus. Corp. Act Ann. art. 5.14, subds. F, H; Va. Code Ann. § 13.1-672.4; Wis. Stat. Ann. §§ 180.0744, 181.0744.)

. . . Decisions of the Ninth Circuit Court of Appeals in California have utilized the Auerbach approach. (See Lewis v. Anderson (9th Cir. 1979) 615 F.2d 778 (Lewis); Gaines v. Haughton (9th Cir. 1981) 645 F.2d 761.) . . .

[T]he [SLC] defense is intended "to further the fundamental principle that those best suited to make decisions for a corporation-including the decision to file suit on its behalf-are its directors, not its stockholders or the courts. To serve this purpose, the defense must be allowed whenever it is shown that a committee of disinterested directors acting in good faith has determined a derivative action is not in the best interests of the corporation — if possible, on motion, but if necessary, in a full trial." [T]he substance of the derivative claim was not an element of the defense. We agree with that conclusion.

The primary rationale advanced in support of the two-step approach is that judicial scrutiny of the reasonableness of a business decision not to prosecute a derivative claim (which necessarily includes review of the merits of the claim), minimizes the possibility that the result will have been affected by "structural bias." That is, "[a] derivative action invokes a response of group loyalty," so that even a "maverick" director may feel compelled to close ranks and protect his fellows from the attack of the "strike suiter." . . . Hasan v. CleveTrust Realty Investors (6th Cir. 1984) 729 F.2d 372, 377 . . .

The problem of structural bias was the reason for Zapata's two-step review: "[W]e must be mindful that directors are passing judgment on fellow directors in the same corporation and fellow directors, in this instance, who designated them to serve both as directors and as committee members. The question naturally arises whether a 'there but for the grace of God go I' empathy might not play a role. . . . Zapata added the second step of its analysis in order to "strik[e] the balance between legitimate corporate claims as expressed in a derivative stockholder suit and a corporation's best interests as expressed by an independent investigating committee."

The rationale for engaging in the Auerbach analysis is the courts' reluctance to make business decisions. Auerbach recognized that corporate management is best suited to make business judgments . . . .

We acknowledge that the potential for structural bias requires the court to be " 'mindful of the need to scrutinize carefully the mechanism by which directors delegate to a minority committee the business judgment authority to terminate derivative litigation, particularly when the lawsuit is directed against some or a majority of the directors.' (Gaines v. Haughton, supra, 645 F.2d at p. 772 . . . .) In our view, however, careful scrutiny of a committee's independence and its decision-making process strikes an acceptable balance between legitimate shareholder claims and corporate directors' judgment.

. . . .

The trial court therefore did not err in failing to consider the merits of plaintiffs' derivative claim.

WE CONCUR: ELIA and BAMATTRE-MANOUKIAN, JJ.

THOMPSON v. SCIENTIFIC ATLANTA, INC.
Court of Appeals of Georgia
275 Ga. App. 680, 621 S.E.2d 796 (2005)

ANDREWS, PRESIDING JUDGE. . . . SA [now part of Cisco, Inc.] is a Gwinnett County corporation engaged in the design, development, and manufacturing of networks used by cable operators to distribute video . . . . In 1998, SA began shipping newly developed digital set-tops . . . that replaced analog set-tops and equipment previously sold by SA.

In its Third Quarter Fiscal Year 2001 earnings release on April 19, 2001, SA reported record financial results, but indicated it expected to sustain business performance at the present level rather than expand the business at growth rates previously achieved. During SA's Fourth Quarter Fiscal Year 2001, certain officers and directors traded their stock in the company during SA's open trading window and these sales were in line with their previous trading histories.

On July 19, 2001, financial results for the Fourth Quarter Fiscal Year 2001 and for the entire fiscal year were released by SA, reflecting a record year for SA in many ways. The announcement also indicated, however, that new orders and sales declined in the Fourth Quarter from the Third Quarter. Following this announcement, SA's stock price dropped as numerous analysts expressed concern about the apparent declining demand for digital set-tops in the cable industry . . . .

On December 10, 2001, SA received a "derivative demand" letter from [Plaintiff Paul] Thompson in which he alleged that the stock price drop had been due to breaches of fiduciary duty by members of the Board of Directors and demanded that SA sue the defendants for unspecified damages. SA responded by letter . . . . No response was received from Thompson.

On February 16, 2002, the Board of Directors held a special meeting and appointed three members of the Board who had not sold stock in the questioned transactions to serve as the Special Litigation Committee (SLC) provided for in OCGA § 14-2-744(a). The SLC was to conduct an investigation of Thompson's allegations. On May 15, 2002, the Board approved a resolution that provided the SLC with full power and authority to make final binding determinations on the Board's behalf . . . The SLC had full access to all SA personnel, advisors, and records, and SA directed all officers and employees to cooperate with the SLC. The SLC retained independent legal counsel and a special accounting advisor.

On November 14, 2003, Thompson filed his complaint, naming as defendants all members of the Board of Directors . . . claiming breaches of fiduciary duties by these individuals, including releasing inaccurate financial information and then engaging in stock sales based on alleged insider information.

[A]fter interviewing numerous witnesses, reviewing voluminous documents, and consulting with independent legal counsel and financial advisors, the SLC issued its report, which determined that Thompson's claims were without merit and contrary to the best interests of SA and its shareholders. Pursuant to this report, the Board of Directors adopted the SLC's recommendations and a motion to dismiss Thompson's lawsuit was filed on March 18, 2004. . . .

Thompson's sole enumeration of error is that the court erred by dismissing the action under OCGA § 14-2-744 "without allowing Plaintiff and his counsel a fair opportunity to conduct discovery to aid the court in determining whether the SLC was independent, thorough, and came to reasonable conclusions."

OCGA § 14-2-744, Dismissal, provides, in pertinent part, that

(a) The court may dismiss a derivative proceeding if, on motion by the corporation, the court finds that one of the groups specified in subsection (b) of this Code section has made a determination in good faith after conducting a reasonable investigation upon which its conclusions are based that the maintenance of the derivative suit is not in the best interests of the corporation. The corporation shall have the burden of proving the independence and good faith of the group making the determination and the reasonableness of the investigation.

(b) The determination in subsection (a) of this Code section shall be made by: . . .

(2) A majority vote of a committee consisting of two or more independent directors appointed by a majority vote of independent directors present at a meeting of the board of directors, whether or not such independent directors constitute a quorum; . . . .

(c) None of the following shall by itself cause a director to be considered not independent for purposes of subsection (b) of this Code section:

(1) The nomination or election of the director by directors who are not independent;

(2) The naming of the director as a defendant in the derivative proceeding; or

(3) The fact that the director approved the action being challenged in the derivative proceeding so long as the director did not receive a personal benefit as a result of the action.

Here, the over 900-page report of the SLC reflected a detailed and documented investigation, including the backgrounds and qualifications of its members. Having received a copy of the report, Thompson failed to initiate any discovery pursuant to OCGA § 9-11-26 et seq. in an effort to show that the SLC did not make a determination in good faith after conducting a reasonable investigation. As stated in Millsap v. American Family Co., 430 S.E.2d 385, "[t]he Delaware court in Zapata [Corp. v. Maldonado] recognized that the motion to dismiss under these circumstances 'is perhaps best considered as a hybrid summary judgment motion for dismissal because the stockholder plaintiff's standing to maintain the suit has been lost.' "

[Plaintiff Thompson] made no request of the trial court to allow the limited discovery appropriate in such a context. As stated in Kaplan v. Wyatt, 499 A.2d 1184, 1192(IV) (Del. 1985), "[i]n the Zapata context, discovery may be ordered to facilitate inquiries into independence, good faith, and the reasonableness of the investigation. This discovery is not by right, but by order of the Court, with the type and extent of discovery left totally to the discretion of the Court."

. . . .

Judgment affirmed.

PHIPPS and MIKELL, JJ., concur.

NOTES AND QUESTIONS

1. *Routine Cases.* The principal cases demonstrate how routine employment of the SLC device has become. Moreover, as the principal cases indicate, the pro director approach of *Auerbach v. Bennett*, although not ubiquitous, has been the template for several states' decisions. *See, e.g.*, *Curtis v. Nevens*, 31 P.3d 146 (Colo. 2001); *Hirsch v. Jones Intercable Inc.*, 984 P.2d 629, 637 (Colo. 1999); *Black v. NuAire, Inc.*, 426 N.W.2d 203 (Minn. App. 1988). Under *Auerbach*, the trial court performs a straight business judgment type review of the SLC directors' recommendation. The only difference is that the board of directors and the SLC must put forth evidence that they were in good faith and disinterested and that they conducted a diligent investigation of the allegations. In a straight business judgment rule context, under Delaware law, independence and care by directors would be presumed.

2. *Background — Demand.* Federal Rules of Civil Procedure 23.1, "Derivative Actions By Shareholders," and their state analogs, require a derivative action plaintiff to "allege with particularity the efforts, if any, made by the plaintiff to obtain the action the plaintiff desires from the directors or comparable authority and, if necessary, from the shareholders or members, and the reasons for the plaintiff's failure to obtain the action or for not making the effort." It is state substantive law, not procedural law, which determines when demand will be required and when it will not be. Thus, the law of the state of incorporation and not the law of the forum governs questions relating to demand.

For plaintiffs, traditional demand may lead to several unfavorable outcomes. The board of directors may reject demand, in which case rejection may be subject to a very summary, truncated review. Or, it may be accepted, in which case the plaintiff's suspicion is that, aligned as plaintiff, the corporation may enter into a sweetheart settlement with the wrongdoers. *But see Valeant Pharms. Int'l v. Jerney*, 921 A.2d 732 (Del. Ch. 2007) (as objector to a proposed settlement, the former derivative action plaintiff re-entered the picture, intervening to protest a settlement (successfully) that would have allowed a corporate executive to retain a $3 million bonus alleged to have been wrongful)

3. *Demand Accepted.* Not all cases resemble *Valeant Pharmaceuticals* in which the parties proffer the settlement to the court for its approval. There exists no affirmative requirement that they do so. Often the corporation and the defendants do so because they wish to be able to erect the bar of *res judicata* against any later shareholder action challenging the same acts. *Wolf v. Barkes*, 348 F.2d 994 (2d Cir.), *cert. denied*, 382 U.S. 941 (1965). If the statute of limitations has run, or shareholder interest has dwindled, however, the corporation could enter into a settlement, lopsided or otherwise, never proffering the settlement to any one, including the court, for approval. The possibility of a sub silento sweetheart settlement, following acceptance of demand, is a principal reason plaintiffs' attorneys find the demand accepted branch of the demand doctrine as not favorable.

4. *Early Precedents.* The earliest modern case is *Gall v. Exxon Corp.*, 418 F. Supp. 508 (S.D.N.Y. 1976) (SLC recommendation that suit not continue against officers and directors of Italian subsidiary based upon illegal payments). The device gained added credence in 1979 when New York's highest court, the Court of Appeals, decided *Auerbach v. Bennett, supra.* Last of all, in *Burks v. Lasker*, 441 U.S. 471 (1979), the Supreme Court held that no impediment under federal securities law or the Investment Company Act of 1940 prevented use of an SLC to terminate a derivative action against directors of a mutual fund, if the governing state law (all investment companies begin life as a corporation or trust chartered under state law) permitted it.

5. *Standard of Review for the SLC.* An SLC can report that, based upon the SLC's investigation, the shareholder action should not proceed because none of the suspect officers or directors have violated the law. But that would be icing on the cake. All the SLC's recommendation need do is make a finding that, law breaking vel non, pursuance of the alleged wrong is not "in the corporation's best interests." Using make weight factors (factors present in nearly every case, such as drain on executive time, adverse impact on employee morale, adverse impact on public relations), though, SLCs could find that actions never, or only very rarely, should go forward. An early case, *Joy v. North, supra,* by and large, but not completely, rejected use of such factors.

6. *Educated* Erie *Guesses and Delaware's Response.* Many of the early cases were by federal courts, applying state law, which in most instances federal judges opined would be the same as the New York approach articulated in *Auerbach.* *See, e.g., Lewis v. Anderson*, 615 F.2d 778 (9th Cir. 1979); *Abbey v. Control Data Corp.*, 603 F.2d 724 (8th Cir. 1979). Delaware, therefore surprised everyone, when, somewhat belatedly, in *Zapata Corp. v. Maldonado, supra,* the court held that, in its discretion, a Delaware trial court could review the merits of the SLC's recommendation and, impliedly, the plaintiffs' complaint. This discretionary review quickly became known as the "Zapata second step."

After several years, the Delaware Court stuffed the genie back into the bottle, in part. The court held that there could be no *Zapata* second step, i.e., discretionary review on the merits in demand refused, as opposed to demand excused, cases. See *Levine v. Smith*, 591 A.2d 194, 211 (Del. 1991), a result which federal Judge Frank Easterbrook has characterized as "illogical at best." *Kamen v. Kemper Fin. Serv., Inc.*, 908 F.2d 1338, 1343 (7th Cir.), *reversed,* 111 S.Ct. 1711 (1991).

7. *Demand Excused.* Under this branch (the three branches are demand accepted, demand excused, and demand refused), plaintiff seeks to bypass the board of directors, filing immediately in court. She usually will allege that demand is excused as futile, in the main because he alleges that a majority of the directors, or perhaps a critical mass of them, are implicated in the wrongdoing or in the cover-up which followed. Demand can also be excused as futile for other reasons, such as: (a) lack of response from the corporation; (b) inability of directors to take a position with respect to the demand (e.g., directors are evenly split); (c) threat to the corporation of irreparable harm; or (d) the corporation is a 2–3 shareholder closely held corporation, in which some jurisdictions and the ALI Corp. Gov. Proj. § 7.01 allow the court to dispense with demand. These other grounds for futility, including demand futility, are discussed below.

8. *Demand Refused.* In this scenario, the shareholder contacts the corporation's board of directors. In cases of colorable allegations, boards may well form an SLC at this earlier temporal stage (before suit has been filed) and follow a procedure similar to that in demand excused cases. In *Harhen v. Brown*, 730 N.E.2d 859 (Mass. 2000), a case involving illegal acts by a lobbyist for John Hancock Life Ins. Co., the court held that, although temporally at an early stage, the SLC procedure and review thereof is the same in a demand rejected as it is a demand excused case.

Under Delaware precedent, however, by making a demand, a shareholder concedes the disinterestedness of the board and its ability to deal with a demand: "a shareholder acknowledges the absence of facts to support a finding of demand futility," *Spiegel v. Buntrock*, 571 A.2d 767, 776 (Del. 1990). So the fork in the road is a pronounced one. The shareholder must seek an intracorporate resolution, or he must go to court. He cannot "mix and match." By doing anything that might be construed as having made a demand, such as engaging in preliminary talks, etc., the shareholder forfeits his right to a potential review on the merits *in futuro. See Levine v. Smith, supra.* He has lost part of his case without even thinking about it, motivated perhaps to attempt a non-judicial resolution of the issues.

9. *Scope of Review — Discretionary Review in Demand Rejected as Well as Demand Refused Cases.* In *Alford v. Shaw*, 358 S.E.2d 323 (1987), the Supreme Court of North Carolina agreed with Judge Easterbrook, holding that in her discretion a trial judge may examine the merits of an SLC recommendation and report in all cases. *Lewis v. Boyd*, 838 S.W.2d 215, 224 (Tenn. App. 1992), in similar fashion observes that "the depth of review should not depend on whether or not the shareholder made a demand prior to filing suit." *See also Brady v. Calcote*, 2005 Tenn. App. LEXIS 8 (Tenn. Ct. App. Jan. 11, 2005) (taxing costs against shareholder-former-director).

10. *Mandatory Review of SLC Recommendations.* The Supreme Judicial Court of Massachusetts decided that a trial court should always conduct a review. *Houle v. Low*, 556 N.E.2d 51 (Mass. 1990). *See also Harhen v. Brown, supra.* New Jersey seems to fall in this camp as well. In *Fink v. Codey (In re PSE & G Shareholder Litig.)*, 801 A.2d 295 (N.J. 2002), four separate derivative suits, later consolidated, complained of mismanagement of the defendant's nuclear power plants. The Supreme Court of New Jersey did not follow *Auerbach v. Bennett*:

> Instead, we shall apply a modified business judgment rule that imposes an initial burden on the corporation to demonstrate that in deciding to reject or terminate a shareholder's suit the members of the board: (1) were independent and disinterested; (2) acted in good faith and with due care in their investigation of the shareholder's allegations, and that (3) the board's decision was reasonable. All three elements must be satisfied. Moreover, shareholders in these circumstances must be permitted access to corporate documents and other [limited] discovery . . .

801 A.2d at 312 (affirming trial court's rejection of all plaintiffs' claims).

11. *The American Law Institute Approach.* Under the ALI schematic, a court should follow the *Auerbach v. Bennett* approach in cases which raise duty of care violations. In cases which allege duty of loyalty violations, the trial court may proceed to a Zapata second step, both in demand refused and well as demand excused cases. ALI Corp. Gov. Proj. §7.10. Pennsylvania became the first jurisdiction to follow that approach to review of an SLC's determination, adopting the ALI provisions *en masse. Cuker v. Mikalauskas*, 692 A.2d 1042, 1049 (Pa. 1997) ("We specifically adopt §§ 7.02–7.10 and 7.13 of the ALI Principles," including its universal demand requirement).

PROBLEM

Richie and Potsie have a rapidly growing nine store Happy Days CD and video chain in Milwaukee, Wisconsin. Richie, who owns 52 percent, has just gone through a divorce. Potsie, who owns 25 percent, relates to you that Richie has used corporate funds to purchase a new home in Whitefish Bay (for cash), a 32 foot sailboat (for cash), and a luxury automobile (for cash). Potsie is concerned that Happy Days will no longer be able to pay suppliers, who demand cash on delivery already because Happy Days has made late payments recently.

Representing Potsie, you have been downtown to see Arthur Fonzerelli, the attorney who represents Happy Days and Richie Cunningham. You had a seemingly productive meeting, with Arthur showing sympathy for Potise's plight. When you return to your office, a fax from Arthur is waiting. The fax from Fonzerelli states that if you dare file a lawsuit without first making a demand on the Happy Days board of directors (Potsie, Richie, Mr. C, Big Al, and Chachi), Fonzerelli will seek sanctions against you.

Potsie pleads that something must be done quickly. Should you file suit and seek a preliminary injunction against Richie's use of corporate funds?

Potsie then proceeds to court, filing a complaint. The corporation, by its attorney (Fonzerelli), appears. First, he moves for dismissal on grounds that no demand has been made and that demand was not excused. Assume that the court rules against him, holding that demand was indeed "excused."

Fonzerelli then requests a lengthy continuance, pending the corporation's formation of a special litigation committee (SLC) of the board of directors and an investigation by it of the alleged wrongdoing. Will the court grant the continuance?

C.   WHEN IS DEMAND EXCUSED AS FUTILE?

ARONSON v. LEWIS
Supreme Court of Delaware
473 A.2d 805 (1984)

Before MCNEILLY, MOORE and CHRISTIE, JJ.

MOORE, JUSTICE: . . . [W]hen is a stockholder's demand upon a board of directors, to redress an alleged wrong to the corporation, excused as futile [?]

. . . .

In our view demand can only be excused where facts are alleged with particularity which create a reasonable doubt that the directors' action was entitled to the protections of the business judgment rule.

The issues of demand futility rest upon the allegations of the complaint. The plaintiff, Harry Lewis, is a stockholder of Meyers [Parking Systems, Inc.]. The defendants are Meyers and its ten directors . . . .

In 1979, Prudential Building Maintenance Corp. (Prudential) spun off its shares of Meyers to Prudential's stockholders. Prior thereto Meyers was a wholly owned subsidiary of Prudential. Meyers provides parking lot facilities and related services throughout the country. Its stock is actively traded over-the-counter.

This suit challenges certain transactions between Meyers and one of its directors, Leo Fink, who owns 47% of its outstanding stock. Plaintiff claims that these transactions were approved only because Fink personally selected each director . . . of Meyers.

Prior to January 1, 1981, Fink had an employment agreement with Prudential which provided that upon retirement he was to become a consultant to that company for ten years. This provision became operable when Fink retired in April 1980. Thereafter, Meyers agreed with Prudential to share Fink's consulting services and reimburse Prudential for 25% of the fees paid Fink. Under this arrangement Meyers paid Prudential $48,332 in 1980 and $45,832 in 1981.

On January 1, 1981, the defendants approved an employment agreement between Meyers and Fink for a five year term with provision for automatic renewal each year thereafter, indefinitely. Meyers agreed to pay Fink $150,000 per year, plus a bonus of 5% of its pre-tax profits over $2,400,000. Fink could terminate the contract at any time, but Meyers could do so only upon six months' notice. At termination, Fink was to become a consultant to Meyers and be paid $150,000 per year for the first three years, $125,000 for the next three years, and $100,000 thereafter for life. Death benefits were also included. The agreement also provided that Fink's compensation was not to be affected by any inability to perform services on Meyers' behalf. Fink was 75 years old when his employment agreement with Meyers was approved by the directors. . . .

Additionally, the Meyers board approved . . . interest-free loans to Fink totaling $225,000. These loans were unpaid . . . when the complaint was filed. At oral argument defendants' counsel represented that these loans had been repaid . . . .

The complaint charges that these transactions had "no valid business purpose," and were a "waste of corporate assets" because the amounts to be paid are "grossly excessive," that Fink performs "no or little services," and because of his "advanced age" cannot be "expected to perform any such services". . . . Finally, it is alleged that the loans to Fink were in reality "additional compensation" . . . .

The complaint alleged that no demand had been made on the Meyers board because:

[S]uch attempt would be futile for the following reasons:

(a) All of the directors in office are named as defendants herein and they have participated in, expressly approved and/or acquiesced in, and are personally liable for, the wrongs complained of herein.

(b) Defendant Fink, having selected each director, controls and dominates every member of the Board . . . .

(c) Institution of this action by present directors would require the defendant-directors to sue themselves, thereby placing the conduct of this action in hostile hands and preventing its effective prosecution.

The relief sought included the cancellation of the Meyers-Fink employment contract and an accounting by the directors, including Fink, for all damage sustained . . . .

Defendants moved to dismiss for plaintiff's failure to make demand on the Meyers board prior to suit, or to allege with factual particularity why demand is excused.

[T]he trial judge noted that the demand requirement of Rule 23.1 is a rule of substantive right designed to give a corporation the opportunity to rectify an alleged wrong without litigation, and to control any litigation which does arise. According to the Vice Chancellor, the test of futility is "whether the Board, at the time of the filing of the suit, could have impartially considered and acted upon the demand."

[A] plaintiff need not allege that the challenged transaction could never be deemed a product of business judgment. Rather, the Vice Chancellor maintained that a plaintiff "must only allege facts which, if true, show that there is a reasonable inference that the business judgment rule is not applicable for purposes of considering a pre-suit demand."

The Vice Chancellor . . . dealt with plaintiff's contention that Fink, as a 47% shareholder of Meyers, dominated and controlled each director, thereby making demand futile. Plaintiff also argued that Fink's interest, when combined with the shareholdings of four other defendants, amounted to 57.5% of Meyers' outstanding shares. After noting the presumptions under the business judgment rule that a board's actions are taken in good faith and in the best interests of the corporation, the Court of Chancery ruled that mere board approval of a transaction benefitting a substantial, but non-majority, shareholder will not overcome the presumption of propriety. Specifically, the court observed that:

A plaintiff, to properly allege domination of the Board, particularly domination based on ownership of less than a majority of the corporation's stock, in order to excuse a pre-suit demand, must allege ownership plus other facts evidencing control to demonstrate that the Board could not have exercised its independent business judgment.

As to the combined 57.5% control claim . . . there were no factual allegations regarding the alignment of the four directors with Fink, such as a claim that they were beneficiaries of the Meyers-Fink agreement. Because it was not alleged in the complaint, the court rejected plaintiff's argument that, as evidence of alignment with Fink, two of the directors have "similar" compensation agreements with Meyers.

Turning to plaintiff's allegations of board approval, participation in, and/or acquiescence in the wrong, the trial court focused on the underlying transaction to determine whether the board's action was wrongful and not protected by the business judgment rule. The Vice Chancellor indicated that if the underlying transaction supported a reasonable inference that the business judgment rule did not apply, then the directors who approved the transaction were potentially liable for a breach of their fiduciary duty, and thus, could not impartially consider a stockholder's demand.

The defendants make two arguments, one policy-oriented and the other, factual. First, they assert that the demand requirement embraces the policy that directors, rather than stockholders, manage the affairs of the corporation. . . . Second, the defendants point to . . . plaintiff's basic allegations and argue that they lack the factual particularity necessary to excuse demand. Concerning the allegation that Fink dominated and controlled the Meyers board, the defendants point to the absence of any facts explaining how he "selected each director." With respect to Fink's 47% stock interest, the defendants say that absent other facts this is insufficient to indicate domination and control. Regarding the claim of hostility to the plaintiff's suit, because defendants would have to sue themselves, the latter assert that this bootstrap argument ignores the possibility that the directors have other alternatives, such as cancelling the challenged agreement. As for the allegation that directorial approval of the agreement excused demand, the defendants reply that such a claim is insufficient, because it would obviate the demand requirement in almost every case. The effect would be to subvert the managerial power of a board of directors. Finally, . . . defendants conclude that the plaintiff's allegations fall far short of the factual particularity required by Rule 23.1.

A cardinal precept of the General Corporation Law of the State of Delaware is that directors, rather than shareholders, manage the business and affairs of the corporation. 8 Del. C. § 141(a). Section 141(a) states in pertinent part: "The business and affairs of a corporation organized under this chapter shall be managed by or under the direction of a board of directors . . . ."

The existence and exercise of this power carries with it certain fundamental fiduciary obligations to the corporation and its shareholders. Moreover, a stockholder is not powerless to challenge director action which results in harm to the corporation. The machinery of corporate democracy and the derivative suit are potent tools to redress the conduct of a torpid or unfaithful management. The derivative action developed in equity to enable shareholders to sue in the corporation's name where those in control of the company refused to assert a claim belonging to it. The nature of the action is two-fold. First, it is . . . a suit by the shareholders to compel the corporation to sue. Second, it is a suit by the corporation, asserted by the shareholders on its behalf, against those liable to it.

By its very nature the derivative action impinges on the managerial freedom of directors. Hence, the demand requirement . . . exists at the threshold, first to insure that a stockholder exhausts his intracorporate remedies, and then to provide a safeguard against strike suits. Thus, by promoting this form of alternate dispute resolution, rather than immediate recourse to litigation, the demand requirement is a recognition of the fundamental precept that directors manage the business and affairs of corporations.

In our view the entire question of demand futility is inextricably bound to issues of business judgment and the standards of that doctrine's applicability. The business judgment rule is an acknowledgment of the managerial prerogatives of Delaware directors under Section 141(a). . It is a presumption that in making a business decision the directors of a corporation acted on an informed basis, in good faith and in the honest belief that the action taken was in the best interests of the company. Kaplan v. Centex Corp., Del. Ch., 284 A.2d 119, 124 (1971); Robinson v. Pittsburgh Oil Refinery Corp., Del. Ch., 126 A. 46 (1924). Absent an abuse of discretion, that judgment will be respected by the courts. The burden is on the party challenging the decision to establish facts rebutting the presumption. See Puma v. Marriott, Del. Ch., 283 A.2d 693, 695 (1971).

The function of the business judgment rule is of paramount significance in the context of a derivative action. It comes into play in several ways — in addressing a demand, in the determination of demand futility, in efforts by independent disinterested directors to dismiss the action as inimical to the corporation's best interests, and generally, as a defense to the merits of the suit. However, in each of these circumstances there are certain common principles governing the application and operation of the rule.

First, its protections can only be claimed by disinterested directors whose conduct otherwise meets the tests of business judgment. From the standpoint of interest, this means that directors can neither appear on both sides of a transaction nor expect to derive any personal financial benefit from it in the sense of self-dealing, as opposed to a benefit which devolves upon the corporation or all stockholders generally. Sinclair Oil Corp. v. Levien, Del. Supr., 280 A.2d 717, 720 (1971); Cheff v. Mathes, Del.Supr., 199 A.2d 548, 554 (1964); David J.Greene & Co. v. Dunhill International, Inc., Del. Ch., 249 A.2d 427, 430 (1968). . . .

Second, to invoke the rule's protection directors have a duty to inform themselves, prior to making a business decision, of all material information reasonably available to them. Having become so informed, they must then act with requisite care in the discharge of their duties. While the Delaware cases use a variety of terms to describe the applicable standard of care, our analysis satisfies us that under the business judgment rule director liability is predicated upon concepts of gross negligence.

However, it should be noted that the business judgment rule operates only in the context of director action. Technically speaking, it has no role where directors have either abdicated their functions, or absent a conscious decision, failed to act. . . .

The gap in our law, which we address today, arises from this Court's decision in Zapata Corp. v. Maldonado [*supra*]. There, the Court restricted application of the business judgment rule in a factual context similar to this action. . . . We also concluded that where demand is excused a shareholder possesses the ability to initiate a derivative action, but the right to prosecute it may be terminated upon the exercise of applicable standards of business judgment. The thrust of Zapata is that in either the demand-refused or the demand-excused case, the board still retains its Section 141(a) managerial authority to make decisions regarding corporate litigation. Moreover, the board may delegate its managerial authority to a committee of independent disinterested directors. Thus, even in a demand-excused case, a board has the power to appoint a committee of one or more independent disinterested directors to determine whether the derivative action should be pursued or dismissal sought. [T]he Court of Chancery, in passing on a committee's motion to dismiss a derivative action in a demand excused case, must apply a two-step test. First, the court must inquire into the independence and good faith of the committee and review the reasonableness and good faith of the committee's investigation. Second, the court must apply its own independent business judgment to decide whether the motion to dismiss should be granted.

After Zapata numerous derivative suits were filed without prior demand upon boards of directors. The complaints in such actions all alleged that demand was excused because of board interest, approval or acquiescence in the wrongdoing. In any event, the Zapata demand-excused/demand-refused bifurcation, has left a crucial issue unanswered: when is demand futile and, therefore, excused?

. . . .

[Earlier] cases cannot be taken to mean that any board approval of a challenged transaction automatically connotes "hostile interest" and "guilty participation" by directors, or some other form of sterilizing influence upon them. Were that so, the demand requirements of our law would be meaningless . . .

The trial court . . . stated the test to be based on allegations of fact, which, if true, "show that there is a reasonable inference" the business judgment rule is not applicable for purposes of a pre-suit demand.

The problem with this formulation is [that] demand futility becomes virtually automatic under such a test. Bearing in mind the presumptions with which director action is cloaked, we believe that the matter must be approached in a more balanced way.

Our view is that in determining demand futility the Court of Chancery in the proper exercise of its discretion must decide whether, under the particularized facts alleged, a reasonable doubt is created that: (1) the directors are disinterested and independent and [sic — or] (2) the challenged transaction was otherwise the product of a valid exercise of business judgment. Hence, the Court of Chancery must make two inquiries, one into the independence and disinterestedness of the directors and the other into the substantive nature of the challenged transaction and the board's approval thereof. As to the latter inquiry the court does not assume that the transaction is a wrong to the corporation requiring corrective steps by the board. Rather, the alleged wrong is substantively reviewed against the factual background alleged in the complaint. As to the former inquiry, directorial independence and disinterestedness, the court reviews the factual allegations to decide whether they raise a reasonable doubt, as a threshold matter, that the protections of the business judgment rule are available to the board.

However, the mere threat of personal liability for approving a questioned transaction, standing alone, is insufficient to challenge either the independence or disinterestedness of directors, although in rare cases a transaction may be so egregious on its face that board approval cannot meet the test of business judgment, and a substantial likelihood of director liability therefore exists. See Gimbel v. Signal Cos., Inc., Del.Ch., 316 A.2d 599, aff'd, 316 A.2d 619 (1974); Cottrell v. Pawcatuck Co., Del.Supr., 128 A.2d 225 (1956). In sum the entire review is factual in nature. The Court of Chancery in the exercise of its sound discretion must be satisfied that a plaintiff has alleged facts with particularity which, taken as true, support a reasonable doubt that the challenged transaction was the product of a valid exercise of business judgment. Only in that context is demand excused.

Plaintiff's claim that Fink dominates and controls the Meyers' board is based on: (1) Fink's 47% ownership of Meyers' outstanding stock, and (2) that he "personally selected" each Meyers director. Plaintiff also alleges that mere approval of the employment agreement illustrates Fink's domination and control of the board. In addition, plaintiff argued on appeal that 47% stock ownership, though less than a majority, constituted control given the large number of shares outstanding, 1,245,745.

Such contentions do not support any claim under Delaware law that these directors lack independence. In Kaplan v. Centex Corp., Del.Ch., 284 A.2d 119 (1971), the Court of Chancery stated that "[s]tock ownership alone, at least when it amounts to less than a majority, is not sufficient proof of domination or control". . . .

The requirement of director independence inhers in the conception and rationale of the business judgment rule. The presumption of propriety that flows from an exercise of business judgment is based in part on this unyielding precept. Independence means that a director's decision is based on the corporate merits of the subject before the board rather than extraneous considerations or influences. While directors may confer, debate, and resolve their differences through compromise, or by reasonable reliance upon the expertise of their colleagues and other qualified persons, the end result, nonetheless, must be that each director has brought his or her own informed business judgment to bear with specificity upon the corporate merits of the issues without regard for or succumbing to influences which convert an otherwise valid business decision into a faithless act.

Thus, it is not enough to charge that a director was nominated by or elected at the behest of those controlling the outcome of a corporate election. That is the usual way a person becomes a corporate director. It is the care, attention and sense of individual responsibility to the performance of one's duties, not the method of election, that generally touches on independence.

We conclude that in the demand-futile context a plaintiff charging domination and control of one or more directors must allege particularized facts manifesting "a direction of corporate conduct in such a way as to comport with the wishes or interests of the corporation (or persons) doing the controlling." Kaplan, 284 A.2d at 123. The shorthand shibboleth of "dominated and controlled directors" is insufficient. . . .

Here, plaintiff has not alleged any facts sufficient to support a claim of control. The personal-selection-of-directors allegation stands alone, unsupported. At best it is a conclusion devoid of factual support. The causal link between Fink's control and approval of the employment agreement is alluded to, but nowhere specified. . . .

Turning to the board's approval of the Meyers-Fink employment agreement, plaintiff's argument is simple: all of the Meyers directors are named defendants, because they approved the wasteful agreement; if plaintiff prevails on the merits all the directors will be jointly and severally liable; therefore, the directors' interest in avoiding personal liability automatically and absolutely disqualifies them from passing on a shareholder's demand.

Such allegations are conclusory at best. In Delaware mere directorial approval of a transaction . . . is insufficient to excuse demand. Here, plaintiff's suit is premised on the notion that the Meyers-Fink employment agreement was a waste of corporate assets. So, the argument goes, by approving such waste the directors now face potential personal liability . . . . The complaint does not allege particularized facts indicating that the agreement is a waste of corporate assets. Indeed, the complaint as now drafted may not even state a cause of action, given the directors' broad corporate power to fix . . . compensation . . . .

[T]he plaintiff alleged a lack of consideration flowing from Fink to Meyers, since the employment agreement provided that compensation was not contingent on Fink's ability to perform any services. The bare assertion that Fink performed "little or no services" was plaintiff's conclusion based solely on Fink's age and the existence of the Fink-Prudential employment agreement. As for Meyers' loans to Fink, beyond the bare allegation that they were made, the complaint does not allege facts indicating the wastefulness of such arrangements. Again, the mere existence of such loans, given the broad corporate powers conferred by Delaware law, does not even state a claim.

In sum, we conclude that the plaintiff has failed to allege facts with particularity indicating that the Meyers directors were tainted by interest, lacked independence, or took action contrary to Meyers' best interests in order to create a reasonable doubt as to the applicability of the business judgment rule. Only in the presence of such a reasonable doubt may a demand be deemed futile. . . .

REVERSED AND REMANDED.

NOTES AND QUESTIONS

1. *Leading Business Judgment Rule Case in Delaware.* An earlier precedent, *Warshaw v. Calhoun*, 221 A.2d 487 (Del.1966), had been the leading Delaware decision on the business judgment rule, discussed in Chapter 10 *supra*. Apart from its teachings about derivative actions, Delaware courts now cite *Aronson v. Lewis* for business judgment rule purposes more than any other case.

2. *Criticisms.* Although *Aronson* announces a seemingly lenient standard as to when demand will be excused as futile ("reasonable doubt"), it leans toward not excusing demand in the case at bar. Some find disturbing its findings that, as a matter of law, a 47% shareholder cannot control the composition of the board in a publicly held corporation. On its facts, *Aronson* is, according to some, a very pro-management and anti-derivative suit decision.

3. *Topographical Error: Disjunctive ("or") Rather than Conjunctive ("and").* In *Aronson*, the court used the conjunctive: namely, that a shareholder plaintiff must show a reasonable doubt countered by showing "that (1) the directors are disinterested and

independent and (2) the challenged transaction was otherwise the product of a valid business judgment." Subsequent decisions, such as *Levine v. Smith*, 591 A.2d 194, 205 (1991), make clear that "or" rather than "and" was intended.

SHOEN v. SAC HOLDING CO.
Supreme Court of Nevada
137 P.2rd 1171 (2006)

Before the Court En Banc.

In resolving this appeal, we clarify when the demand for corrective action that a shareholder must make upon a company's board of directors before filing a derivative suit may be excused as futile. Appellants . . . are shareholders in AMERCO, a Nevada holding company whose main subsidiary is U-Haul International, Inc. In 2002 and 2003, appellants filed four separate derivative suits.. . .

The district court dismissed appellants'. . . consolidated complaints, finding that they did not sufficiently allege that such a demand would be futile.

We conclude that, when a shareholder's demand would be made to the same board that voted to take (or reject) an action, so that the allegedly improper action constitutes a business decision by the board, a shareholder asserting demand futility must allege, with particularity, facts that raise a reasonable doubt as to the directors' independence or their entitlement to protection under the business judgment rule. However, when a board does not affirmatively make a business decision or agree to the subject action, the demand requirement will be excused as futile only when particularized pleadings show that at least fifty percent of the directors considering the demand for corrective action would be unable to act impartially.. . .

U-Haul was founded by Leonard Samuel Shoen in 1945, and its business concerns include wholly owned U-Haul centers and a network of independent dealers that sell moving products and rent trucks, trailers, and self-storage units to "do-it-yourself" movers. In addition to its U-Haul concerns, AMERCO acquires and develops real property for self-storage facilities through a subsidiary called AMERCO Real Estate Corporation (AREC). Ultimately, Leonard transferred most of his AMERCO stock to his thirteen children, including sons Paul, Edward J. (Joe), James, and Mark, which led, in the 1980s, to an unfortunate and well-documented family feud . . . .

The derivative suits allege that, in addition to owning AMERCO stock, each of the four sons is or has at relevant times served as an AMERCO director and/or officer. Joe and James have served on AMERCO's board of directors since 1986. Mark served as a director between 1990 and 1997 and is also employed as an AMERCO executive officer. While Paul no longer participates as an AMERCO officer or director, he served on the board of directors for several years before 1991, and from 1997 to 1998.

In the 1990s, Joe, James, and Mark formed SAC Holding Corporation and various SAC Self-Storage Corporations and partnerships to operate as real estate holding companies (the SAC entities). In 1994, however, before filing for personal bankruptcy, Joe and James [A 1994 lawsuit in Arizona, arising out of the corporate in-fighting, resulted in a jury award of $461 million in compensatory damages against Joe and James and $7 million in punitive damages against Joe.] transferred their shares in the SAC entities to Mark. Ever since that time, Mark has been the SAC entities' sole shareholder.

According to appellants, Joe, James, and Mark have formed an "insider group." Through board domination, appellants claim, the "insider group" brothers have engaged in acts to further their own interests, to the detriment of AMERCO shareholders, by building a competing business in the SAC entities. This operation was accomplished, they assert, through the transfer of AMERCO's self-storage business and assets to the SAC entities at unfair terms.

Consequently, appellants filed derivative suits seeking, among other things, to "halt and unwind" the AMERCO-SAC entities transactions. But none of the appellants made any pre-suit demand on the AMERCO board of directors or the other shareholders to obtain the corrective action. Instead, appellants alleged in their complaints that any such demand would be futile, in large part because several board members, while not voting for the challenged transactions, participated in the wrongdoing and because the board is dominated and controlled by the interested "insider group" and in particular, by Joe.

. . . .

The proposed consolidated complaint asserts eight causes of action, involving alleged breaches of fiduciary duties and violations of corporate and tort laws. In that complaint, appellants assert that, before the SAC entities were formed, AMERCO aggressively pursued opportunities to add self-storage facilities to its portfolio. Since then, . . . they claim, those efforts have been refocused to benefit Mark and the SAC entities, rather than AMERCO.

In particular, the proposed consolidated complaint asserts that Mark and the SAC entities have improperly profited in the following three ways. First, appellants allege that AMERCO's public filings show that AMERCO or its subsidiaries sold self-storage properties to the SAC entities at "acquisition cost plus capitalized expenses," or at prices ultimately determined by Joe. The prices were allegedly unfairly low because they did not include added value resulting from AMERCO having leased the property, goodwill associated with use of the U-Haul name, and the properties' locations near U-Haul centers where customers can obtain and return moving vehicles.

Second, appellants allege that AMERCO financed the self-storage property transactions by giving the SAC entities over $400 million in nonrecourse loans. As a result, AMERCO was left with the financial risk, while the SAC entities reaped appreciation, tax benefits, and net cash flow.

For instance, appellants assert that, in 1995, when AMERCO needed capital itself, it loaned the SAC entities $54,671,000 to purchase forty-four self-storage properties, twenty-four of which were purchased from AMERCO or AREC at the profitless price of $26,287,000. . . .

And third, the proposed complaint alleges that the SAC entities profited from the use of AREC's employee resources to locate, purchase, develop, and lease self-storage facilities, without, "on information and belief," justly compensating AREC or AMERCO.

According to the proposed complaint, none of the AMERCO-SAC entities transactions, or the use of AREC employees, was presented to or ever approved by AMERCO's board of directors.. . .

Ordinarily, under Nevada's corporations laws, a corporation's "board of directors has full control over the affairs of the corporation." The board's power to act on the corporation's behalf is governed by the directors' fiduciary relationship with the corporation and its shareholders, which imparts upon the directors duties of care and loyalty. In essence, the duty of care consists of an obligation to act on an informed basis; the duty of loyalty requires the board and its directors to maintain, in good faith, the corporation's and its shareholders' best interests over anyone else's interests.

Balancing these duties, however, is the protection generally afforded directors in conducting the corporation's affairs by the business judgment rule. The business judgment rule is a "presumption that in making a business decision the directors of a corporation acted on an informed basis, in good faith and in the honest belief that the action taken was in the best interests of the company." In 1991, the Nevada Legislature codified the business judgment rule at NRS 78.138 [("Directors and officers, in deciding upon matters of business, are presumed to act in good faith, on an informed basis and with a view to the interests of the corporation.")].

In managing the corporation's affairs, the board of directors may generally decide whether to take legal action on the corporation's behalf. Nonetheless, when the board fails to appropriately act, individual shareholders may file a suit in equity to enforce the corporation's rights. Thus, so-called derivative suits allow shareholders to "compel the corporation to sue" and to thereby pursue litigation on the corporation's behalf against the corporation's board of directors and officers, in addition to third parties. But because the power to manage the corporation's affairs resides in the board of directors, a shareholder must, before filing suit, make a demand on the board, or if necessary, on the other shareholders, to obtain the action that the shareholder desires [NRS 41.520(2) ("The complaint must also set forth with particularity the efforts of the plaintiff to secure from the board of directors or trustees and, if necessary, from the shareholders such action as he desires, and the reasons for his failure to obtain such action or the reasons for not making such effort.")

This demand requirement recognizes the corporate form in two ways. First, a demand informs the directors of the complaining shareholder's concerns and gives them an opportunity to control any acts needed to correct improper conduct or actions, including any necessary litigation The demand requirement also acknowledges that "the acts in question may be subject to ratification by a majority of the shareholders, thus precluding the necessity of suit." [Wolgin v. Simon, 722 F.2d 389, 392 (8th Cir.1983)]. Second, the demand requirement protects clearly discretionary directorial conduct and corporate assets by discouraging unnecessary, unfounded, or improper shareholder actions. Thus, in "promoting . . . alternate dispute resolution, rather than immediate recourse to litigation, the demand requirement is a recognition of the fundamental precept that directors manage the business and affairs of corporations."

Pleading demand satisfaction or futility

In light of the demand requirement, NRCP 23.1 imposes heightened pleading imperatives in shareholder derivative suits. Under this rule, a derivative complaint must state, with particularity, the demand for corrective action that the shareholder made on the board of directors (and, possibly, other shareholders) and why he failed to obtain such action, or his reasons for not making a demand. Thus, as the Delaware Supreme Court has recognized in a similar shareholder demand context, a shareholder must "set forth . . . particularized factual statements that are essential to the claim" that a demand has been made and refused, or that making a demand would be futile or otherwise inappropriate. [Brehm [v. Eisner], 746 A.2d [244] at 254 [Del.2000] (noting that the "with particularity" pleading required in shareholder derivative suits in Delaware is similar to the heightened pleading required for claims involving fraud or mistake . . . .)]. We note, however, that NRCP 8(e) requires pleadings to be "simple, concise, and direct." Accordingly, "the pleader is not required to plead evidence." Nonetheless, mere conclusory assertions will not suffice.. . .

A shareholder's failure to sufficiently plead compliance with the demand requirement deprives the shareholder of standing and justifies dismissal of the complaint for failure to state a claim upon which relief may be granted. .

Demand futility

In Johnson v. Steel, Incorporated [100 Nev. 181, 184, 678 P.2d 676, 679 (1984)], this court stated that "[w]here the board participated in the wrongful act or is controlled by the principal wrongdoer, it is generally held that no demand is needed." For instance, there is no point in requiring a party to make a demand for corrective action to officers and directors who are swayed by outside interests, which contaminates their ability to conduct the corporation's affairs.

However, the directive previously articulated in Johnson is insufficient. The Johnson directive, broadly interpreted, suggests that the demand prerequisite could be excused with a mere allegation of participation. Such a broad reading could subject the board to immediate litigation . . . .We agree with the Delaware Supreme Court's observation in Aronson v. Lewis that "[b]earing in mind the presumptions with which director action is cloaked, . . . the matter must be approached in a more balanced way." [473 A.2d 805, 814 (Del.1984)] Accordingly, to the extent that Johnson suggests that the demand requirement is excused as to the board of directors merely because the shareholder derivative complaint alleges that a majority of the directors participated in wrongful acts, without regard to their impartiality or to the protections of the business judgment rule, it is overruled.

The business judgment rule, however, pertains only to directors whose conduct falls within its protections. Thus, it applies only in the context of valid interested director action, or the valid exercise of business judgment by disinterested directors in light of their fiduciary duties. But the subject of shareholder derivative complaints is not necessarily always a business decision by the directors, and the directors to whom a demand must be made are not always the same directors as those against whom the allegations are made. Thus, it is not enough to say that the court must always look to the business judgment rule in deciding whether demand futility has been sufficiently pleaded.

Facing this same quandary, the Delaware Supreme Court has developed, in a series of decisions, two associated analyses to be conducted depending on whether the board that would consider a demand is (1) potentially protected by the business judgment rule when its direct action is in question, or (2) can be disinterested and independent in its evaluation of the demand for corrective action.

When the alleged wrongs constitute a business decision by the board of directors

In Aronson . . . , the Delaware Supreme Court examined whether making a demand on a board of directors was excused merely because the shareholder plaintiff alleged that the board participated in the wrongdoing and consequently was automatically considered partial or "guilty." That court concluded that allegations of mere participation in the wrongdoing are insufficient to excuse the demand requirement because, in making a business decision, disinterested directors may invoke the business judgment rule's protections. In other words, even a bad decision is generally protected by the business judgment rule's presumption that the directors acted in good faith, with knowledge of the pertinent information, and with an honest belief that the action would serve the corporation's interests.

In explaining how the business judgment rule presumption operates, the Aronson court first noted that only disinterested directors can claim its protections. Then, if that threshold is met, the business judgment rule presumes that the directors have complied with their duties to reasonably inform themselves of all relevant, material information and have acted with the requisite care in making the business decision. Consequently, a plaintiff challenging a business decision and asserting demand futility must sufficiently show that either the board is incapable of invoking the business judgment rule's protections (e.g., because the directors are financially or otherwise interested in the challenged transaction) or, if the board is capable of invoking the business judgment rule's protections, that that rule is not likely to in fact protect the decision (i.e., because there exists a possibility of overcoming the business judgment rule's presumptions that the requisite due care was taken when the business decision was made). Of course, since approval of a transaction by the majority of a disinterested and independent board usually "bolsters" the presumption that the transaction was carried out with the requisite due care "[i]n such cases, a heavy burden falls on a plaintiff to avoid presuit demand." [See Grobow v. Perot, 539 A.2d, 180, 190 (Del.1988); see also Rales v. Blasband, 634 A.2d 927, 934 (Del.1993) (recognizing that demand futility analyses are "designed, in part, . . . [to require] derivative plaintiffs to make a threshold showing, through the allegation of particularized facts, that their claims have some merit")]..

The Aronson court accordingly concluded that a two-pronged demand futility analysis applies to determine if a complaint has created a reasonable doubt as to whether the directors, having made a business decision, were disinterested and independent, or likely entitled to the business judgment rule's protection:.

[I]n determining demand futility[,] the [trial court] . . . must decide whether, under the particularized facts alleged, a reasonable doubt is created that: (1) the directors are disinterested and independent [or] (2) the challenged transaction was otherwise the product of a valid exercise of business judgment. [Although the two-pronged Aronson analysis was originally articulated in the conjunctive, . . . the Delaware Supreme Court, in quoting this analysis in a 1993 case, replaced that conjunctive with the disjunctive "or." [Rales v. Blasband, 634 A.2d 927, 933 (Del.1993) . . . Levine v. Smith, 591 A.2d 194, 206 (Del.1991) ("The point is that in a claim of demand futility, there are two alternative hurdles, either of which a derivative shareholder complainant must overcome to successfully withstand a Rule 23.1 motion.")].

Under the Aronson test's first prong, the demand requirement is excused without further inquiry if the complaint's allegations, taken as true . . . show that the protection afforded by "the business judgment rule is inapplicable to the board majority approving the transaction" because those directors are interested, or are controlled by another who is interested, in the subject transaction (that has not been otherwise approved by the shareholders). . . .

The second prong of the Aronson test for demand futility is implicated only if the business judgment rule remains applicable because a majority of directors are disinterested or independent of one who is interested under the first prong. When undertaking analysis under the second prong of the Aronson test to determine if the complaint's particularized facts raise a reasonable doubt as to the challenged transaction constituting a valid exercise of business judgment, "the alleged wrong is substantively reviewed against the factual background alleged in the complaint."

When the alleged wrongs do not result from a business decision by the board of directors

The Aronson test examines whether the board considering the demand would likely be entitled to the business judgment rule's protection with regard to the challenged act, but the business judgment rule technically applies only in the context of a board of directors' decision. However, the business judgment rule's protections would not apply, for example, when the board members who decided the challenged act have since changed or when the challenged act does not constitute a business decision by the board.

Nonetheless, the demand requirement is not automatically excused just because the business judgment rule's protections technically would not apply to a particular set of circumstances. The Delaware court, in Rales v. Blasband, [634 A.2d at 933–34 (pointing out three situations that most often give cause to apply the Rales test: (1) where the majority of the directors who made the challenged business decision have been replaced, (2) where the complaint's subject matter is not a business decision of the board, and (3) where the challenged decision was made by a different company)] expounded upon language in Aronson to develop a different demand futility analysis for when the board considering a demand is not implicated in a challenged business transaction. In those circumstances, "the demand futility analysis considers only whether a majority of the directors had a disqualifying interest in the [demand] matter or were otherwise unable to act independently" at the time the complaint was filed. Thus, while the Rales test for alleged wrongs that do not implicate the business judgment rule directly is similar to that of the Aronson test's first prong, it looks not at whether the board majority approving the alleged transaction is entitled to the business judgment rule's protection for that action, but rather at "whether the board that would be addressing the demand can impartially consider its merits without being influenced by improper considerations," such that it could "properly exercise its independent and disinterested business judgment in responding to a demand."

Thus, as with the Aronson test, under the Rales test, directors' independence can be implicated by particularly alleging that the directors' execution of their duties is unduly influenced, manifesting "a direction of corporate conduct in such a way as to comport with the wishes or interests of the [person] doing the controlling. A lack of independence also can be indicated with facts that show that the majority is "beholden to" directors who would be liable [Beam ex rel. M. Stewart Living v. Stewart (Beam II), 845 A.2d 1040, 1056 (Del.2004)] or for other reasons is unable to consider a demand on its merits, for directors' discretion must be free from the influence of other interested persons [Seminaris v. Landa, 662 A.2d 1350, 1354 (Del.Ch.1995)].

And again, to show interestedness, a shareholder must allege that a majority of the board members would be "materially affected, either to [their] benefit or detriment, by a decision of the board, in a manner not shared by the corporation and the stockholders." [We note that, depending on the circumstances, allegations of close familial ties might suffice to show interestedness or partiality. Compare Harbor Finance Partners v. Huizenga, 751 A.2d 879, 889 (Del.Ch.1999) ("Close familial relationships between directors can create a reasonable doubt as to impartiality."); In re Oracle Corp. Derivative Litigation, 824 A.2d 917, 937-938 (Del.Ch.2003), and Beam ex rel. Martha Stewart Living Omnimedia, Inc. v. Stewart, 833 A.2d 961, 979 (Del.Ch.2003), aff'd, 845 A.2d at 1051; Grimes v. Donald, 673 A.2d 1207, 1216 (Del.1996) (noting that "material . . . familial interest" may be a basis for claiming demand futility), overruled in part on other grounds by Brehm v. Eisner, 746 A.2d 244 (Del. 2000), with In re Walt Disney Co. Derivative Lit., 731 A.2d 342, 355 (Del.Ch. 1998), rev'd in part on other grounds sub nom. Brehm v. Eisner, 746 A.2d 244, Danielewicz v. Arnold, 137 Md. App. 601, 769 A.2d 274, 289 (2001) (recognizing that appellant had failed to establish that demand futility merely by asserting that two board members of a three-member board of directors were related), and Siegman v. Maloney, 65 N.J. Eq. 372, 54 A. 405 (1903) (stating that, alone, "[n]either the existence of blood nor of business relationship justifies a presumption of dishonesty"). Thus, generally, to show partiality based on familial relations, the particularized pleadings must demonstrate why the relationship creates a reasonable doubt as to the director's disinterestedness.] Allegations of mere threats of liability through approval of the wrongdoing or other participation, however, do not show sufficient interestedness to excuse the demand requirement. [See Pogostin v. Rice, 480 A.2d 619, 624–25 (Del.1984) . . . .] Instead, as the Delaware courts have indicated, interestedness because of potential liability can be shown only in those "rare case[s] . . . where defendants' actions were so egregious that a substantial likelihood of director liability exists." [Seminaris, 662 A.2d at 1354 (citing Aronson, 473 A.2d at 815); see also Baxter Intern., Inc. Shareholders Lit., 654 A.2d 1268, 1269 (Del.Ch.1995) ("Directors who are sued for failure to oversee subordinates have a disabling interest when 'the potential for liability is not 'a mere threat' but instead may rise to "a substantial likelihood." (quoting Rales, 634 A.2d at 936)); McCall v. Scott, 239 F.3d 808, 824 (6th Cir.2001) (concluding that particularized facts raised a reasonable doubt as to disinterestedness by presenting a substantial likelihood of director liability).

With regard to the duty of care, the business judgment rule does not protect the gross negligence of uninformed directors and officers. And directors and officers may only be found personally liable for breaching their fiduciary duty of loyalty if that breach involves intentional misconduct, fraud, or a knowing violation of the law. Accordingly, interestedness through potential liability is a difficult threshold to meet.

The Delaware court's approach is a well-reasoned method for analyzing demand futility and is highly applicable in the context of Nevada's corporations law. Hence, we adopt the test described in Aronson, as modified by Rales, above. When evaluating demand futility, Nevada courts must examine whether particularized facts demonstrate: (1) in those cases in which the directors approved the challenged transactions, a reasonable doubt that the directors were disinterested or that the business judgment rule otherwise protects the challenged decisions; or (2) in those cases in which the challenged transactions did not involve board action or the board of directors has changed since the transactions, a reasonable doubt that the board can impartially consider a demand.

Making a demand on AMERCO's board of directors

Appellants essentially allege that the AMERCO board members knew or should have known of the challenged acts, at times through their participation therein, but nonetheless failed to prevent or remedy the wrongs. Appellants also assert that a majority of the board intentionally signed false and misleading public disclosure statements designed to conceal the substance of the transactions from the AMERCO shareholders. Since, for the most part, appellants have alleged a failure to properly supervise or a willful disregard of duties, they do not challenge any board-considered business decision. Therefore, the Rales test applies. [See McCall v. Scott, 239 F.3d 808, 816 (6th Cir. 2001) (applying the Rales test to claims challenging not a "conscious Board decision to refrain from acting," but the board's failure to take action out of nonfeasance-intentional ignorance and willful blindness), amended in part, 250 F.3d 997 (6th Cir.2001); In re Xcel Energy, 222 F.R.D. at 607 (explaining that, even when defendant directors also serve on finance and audit committees, particularized facts must "link a majority of the directors to . . . concerted board action" before the Aronson test becomes appropriate under allegations of misconduct in light of committee knowledge but board inaction); Kohls v. Duthie, 791 A.2d 772, 777, 781 (Del.Ch.2000) (analyzing a demand futility claim under the Rales test rather than the Aronson test since the allegations indicated that, while the board's directors knew of a possible corporate opportunity and discussed taking advantage of it personally, they never met to consider it on behalf of the corporation). . .].

The Rales test inquires whether the complaint's particularized facts show that the board is incapable of impartially considering a demand — i.e., that a majority of the board members are interested in the decision to act on the demand or dependent on someone who is interested in that decision. Consistent with that test, appellants contend that the proposed consolidated complaint raises a reasonable doubt that the current board of directors would be able to exercise its independent and disinterested business judgment in responding to a demand.

. . . .

CONCLUSION

Today, we clarify the pleading requirements for shareholder derivative suits .... By extending this court's holding in Johnson to incorporate the approaches enunciated by the Delaware Supreme Court in Aronson and Rales for determining demand futility, we conclude that when it is asserted that a demand upon the corporation's board of directors or shareholders would be futile and should be excused, the shareholder must plead, with sufficient particularity, that a reasonable doubt exists that the directors are independent and disinterested or entitled to the protections of the business judgment rule. However, where the contested corporate transaction is not the result of director action, the demand futility analysis is limited to whether a majority of the directors had a disqualifying interest in the matter or were otherwise unable to act on the demand with impartiality.

Rose, C.J., Becker, Maupin, Gibbons, Douglas and Parraguirre, JJ., concur.

NOTES

1. *Failure to Exercise Oversight.* The principal case indicates that, while not impossible, the threshold is "very high" for a plaintiff who wishes to establish lack of disinterest and therefore demand futility by reason of potential liability. An added reason is that it is so easy for a derivative action plaintiff to name all, or most all, director defendants, then alleging that because of a fear of liability the directors are not disinterested. Along related lines, plaintiffs also have a hard row to hoe when they allege that directors lack disinterest because they failed to exercise oversight over the principal wrongdoers. One court has opined that "failure of oversight" is possibly the most difficult theory on corporate law upon which a plaintiff might hope to win a judgment" or procure a finding that directors lacked independence. *Coca-Cola Enters. Inc. Derivative Litig.*, 478 F. Supp. 2d 1369 (N.D. Ga. 2007). *See also Brehm v. Eisner*, 746 A.2d 244 (Del. 2000).

2. *Consultantships.* The principal case deals at length with precedents disabling, or not disabling, directors because of family relationships. Note 1 deals with the threat of potential liability or allegations of failure of oversight, either of which very seldom disable. By contrast, direct or indirect pecuniary interest in the matter under consideration usually does disable. One form of indirect pecuniary interest, which may neuter a director's independence, is receipt by him of consulting fees in addition to his usual and customary director's stipend. In *Enron*, in addition to generous yearly fees, each of 14 "outside" directors had either a consulting arrangement with Enron or was affiliated with a charity which received substantial yearly gifts from Enron. In *Clark v. Lomas & Nettleton Fin. Corp.*, 625 F.2d 49 (5th Cir. 1980), the court found that a majority of the board lacked independence because each outside director had a generous consulting arrangement for the company.

3. *Other Forms of Remuneration.* Post *Enron*, the New York Stock Exchange listing rules make a director *per se* non-independent if either she or her firm receives $100,000 or more, annually from the corporation. NASDAQ sets the bar lower, at $60,000 per director per year. Of course a director who alone, or through her firm, receives less may also be determined to lack independence in a given case.

4. *Employment.* Controlling shareholders may staff the board of directors and an SLC with employees whose impartiality may be compromised. On balance, directors find that such boards lack independence. *See Gries Sports Enters., Inc. v. Cleveland Browns Football Co.*, 496 N.E.2d 959 (Ohio 1986) (employee, attorney and advertising executive on board of directors).

5. *Friendship.* Courts have held that friendship or social relationships are insufficient to disable or to render not independent. *See, e.g., Beam ex rel. Martha Stewart Living Omnimedia v. Stewart*, 845 A.2d 1040 (Del. 2004).

6. *Former Employee and Former Neighbor.* A court found that whether a former employee who had resigned his corporate office but remained on the board of directors was independent was an issue of fact. A director who was a neighbor of the controlling shareholder was not disabled. *Odyssey Partners, L.P. v. Fleming Cos.*, 735 A.2d 386, 409 (Del. Ch. 1999). Although many of these cases involves interested director transactions and the like, their teachings are instructive for the staffing of an SLC or critiquing it after the fact.

NOTES ON STRIKE SUIT ERA REFORMS

1. *Record Ownership.* Today, for convenience's sake (ease of transfer, margin borrowing, etc.) 99 percent of shareholders hold shares in nominee, or "street," names, that is, they are the beneficial owner while the record owner is the nominee of the brokerage firm (often Cede & Co., a subsidiary of Depository Trust Clearing Corp.

(DTCC)). In fact, the brokerage firm will levy a $25 or so additional charge to "order out" a certificate and transfer ownership into record name. Notwithstanding the reality, a few states retain the requirement that a derivative action plaintiff be a holder of record, mostly as a pitfall for the unwary. *Cf.* MBCA § 7.40(2) (" 'Shareholder' includes a beneficial owner whose shares are held . . . by a nominees on the beneficial owner's behalf.").

2. *Contemporaneous Ownership.* MBCA § 7.41 provides: "A shareholder may not commence or maintain a derivative proceedings unless the shareholder . . . was a shareholder of the corporation at the time of the act or question complained of or became a shareholder through transfer by operation of the law [bequest, intestate succession, marital dissolution] from one who was a shareholder at that time." The requirement dates from *Home Fire Ins. Co. v. Barber*, 93 N.W. 1024 (Neb. 1903). It prevents a speculator who seeks a windfall from buying shares and bringing suit based upon earlier wrongs.

Plaintiffs sometimes seek to blunt the force of the rule by characterizing the acts complained of as a continuing wrong, allowing the plaintiff to bring suit for harm occurring after the time he purchased his shares. *See, e.g., Rosenthal v. Burry Biscuit Corp.*, 60 A.2d 106 (Del. Ch. 1948) (five-year below market price stock option grant to corporate president); *Hanson v. Kake Tribal Corp.*, 939 P.2d 1320 (Alaska 1997) (periodic payment by the corporation on life insurance policies on some but not all shareholders' lives; each payment prolongs the wrong). *Cf. Kaliski v. Bacot (In re Bank of N.Y. Derivative Litig.)*, 320 F.3d 291 (2d Cir. 2003) (rejects continuing wrong exception for contemporaneous ownership rule).

3. *Exception — Double Derivative Actions.* A shareholder in a subsidiary corporation may complain of acts being done in the parent corporation. The plaintiff is a contemporaneous owner of subsidiary but not of parent shares. Alternatively, a shareholder of a parent corporation complains of acts being done in a subsidiary. Most courts allow such a "double derivative action," which in reality is an exception (sort of) to the contemporaneous ownership rule. *See, e.g., Brown v. Tenney*, 532 N.E.2d 230 (Ill. 1988). In theory, a triple (shareholder in a subsidiary complains of wrongdoing in a grandparent corporation) or even quadruple (great grandparent corporation) derivative action is a possibility.

4. *Continuous Ownership.* The plaintiff must not only have owned shares at the time of the wrong complained of: she must maintain her ownership through settlement or trial and appeal(s), if any. *See, e.g., Strategic Asset Mgmt. Inc. v. Nicholson*, 2004 Del. Ch. LEXIS 178 (Del. Ch. Nov. 30, 2004) (plaintiff institutional investor sold stock before settlement presented to court for approval: suit dismissed for lack of standing). This is true even if the corporate defendant enters into a squeeze out merger with the motive of eliminating plaintiff's continuous ownership. *See, e.g., Lewis v. Anderson*, 477 A.2d 1040, 1046–48 (Del. 1984) (merger of Conoco into a Dupont subsidiary, depriving plaintiff Harry Lewis of standing to complain of golden parachutes at Conoco). There may be limited exceptions, to wit, a reorganization that does not really affect plaintiff's ownership, such as formation of a holding company. *Schreiber v. Carney*, 447 A.2d 17, 22 (Del. Ch. 1982). In those cases, plaintiffs may have a new cause of action: for fraud, if the merger documents did not fully disclose the motive(s) for the merger. Or for violation of the duty of loyalty on the grounds that fiduciaries have sanctioned highly unfair, but fully disclosed, acts or practices. Several jurisdictions have abandoned any continuous ownership requirement, holding that contemporaneous ownership is sufficient. *Brown v. Brown*, 731 A.2d 1212, 1215 (N.J. 1999); *Drain v. Covenant Life Ins.*, 685 A.2d 119, 125 (Pa. Super. 1996); *Alford v. Shaw, supra.*

5. *Security for Costs.* A number of states require that, in a derivative action, a plaintiff post a bond or put up other security for costs. *See, e.g.,* N.Y. Bus. Corp. L. § 627; Pa. Stat. Ann. § 15-1516. Although such a requirement may keep certain would-be plaintiffs out of court, they have passed constitutional muster. *Cohen v. Beneficial*

Indus. Loan Corp., 337 U.S. 541 (1949). Court has also trivialized such statutes by holding they are security for costs, not fee shifting statutes. *See, e.g., De Bow v. Lakewood Hotel & Land Ass'n*, 145 A.2d 493, 497 (N.J. App. 1958). Nonetheless, large law firms which defend such actions often attempt to use such statutes in an attempt to force rulings that shareholder plaintiffs must post gargantuan bonds, sufficient to cover substantial defense attorneys' fees. Most courts have resisted, requiring security for costs in amount that are quite modest ($5,000, $10,000, or $25,000). *See* Douglas M. Branson, Corporate Governance § 11.19, at 650–51. Any requirement for security (bond, cash, negotiable securities) has a strong tendency to scare off all but the most dedicated plaintiff, one whose shareholdings, and therefore the benefit of any recovery, are quite large.

6. *Verification.* Under modern pleading rules it is often the attorney who signs the complaint. She prepares the complaint, alleging most or all matters "on information and belief," and files it, thus negating the need for a second or third trip downtown by the named plaintiff. By contrast, one who signs a verified complaint attests that the matters alleged, with limited exceptions, are true. Generally speaking, the attorney can not do this. The plaintiff must have knowledge of the facts, reading and signing the complaint. Verification requirements have all but disappeared from codes of civil procedure but persist in a few delimited areas such as family matters and derivative actions.

The MBCA has eliminated the verification requirement, MBCA § 7.41, but it still exists in many jurisdictions. In *Surowitz v. Hilton Hotels Corp.*, 383 U.S. 363 (1966), Mr. Justice Black upheld a verification requirement but held that it means only some one, not necessarily the plaintiff who verified the complaint, has conducted an investigation of the allegations and found them to be of substance. There, in signing the complaint, the plaintiff, an elderly Polish immigrant who worked as a cleaning person, relied upon her son-in-law, Irving Brilliant, who was a graduate of Columbia Law School, and had served as a prosecutor at the Nuremburg war crimes trials. For the most part, Justice Black thereby de-fanged verification requirements, where they exist. Most courts follow *Surrowitz*, although courts here and there beat up derivative action plaintiffs for having verified complaints with insufficient knowledge. *See, e.g., Brown v. Hart, Schaffner & Marx*, 96 F.R.D. 64 (N.D. Ill. 1982); *Rogosin v. Steadman*, 71 F.R.D. 514, 518 (S.D.N.Y. 1976). *Cf. Lewis v. Curtis*, 671 F.2d 779, 788 (3d Cir. 1982) (sufficient that professional plaintiff had read article in the *Wall Street Journal* before signing). Delaware has never had a verification requirement but exerts a similar loose control under the adequately represents standard *infra.*

7. *Clean Hands.* The plaintiff shareholder must not only have cleans hands, in many instances she must also have taken from a transferor who had clean hands as well. It is "a settled rule of equity that a shareholder may not complain of acts of corporate mismanagement if he acquired shares from those who participated in the alleged wrongful transactions." *Bangor Punta Operations, Inc. v. Bangor & A. R. Co.*, 417 U.S. 703 (1974). "The basis for this rule is that where shareholders have purchased . . . at a fair price, they have personally sustained no injury from wrongs which occurred prior to their purchase." *Courtland Manor, Inc. v. Leeds*, 347 A.2d 144, 147 (Del. Ch. 1975). "Similarly, our courts have recognized the basic principle that one who acquires his stock from a shareholder who participated in or acquiesced in a corporate wrong lacks the capacity himself to complain of it." *Id. See also Ettridge v. TSI Group, Inc.*, 548 A.2d 813, 817–18 (Md. 1988) (" 'he that hath committed inequity shall not have equity.' A purchaser of stock generally acquires the rights that his transferor had.").

8. *Fair and Adequate Representation.* "[I]n order to give a judgment rendered in a derivative action res judicata effect, [courts] impose a requirement of fair and adequate representation on the named plaintiffs. The specter of res judicata, by which a decision is binding on all of the shareholders, makes the named plaintiff in a shareholder derivative suit similar to a representative in a class action." *Palmer v. United States Sav. Bank*, 553 A.2d 781 (N.H. 1989). The determination of whether a plaintiff shareholder is an adequate representative is not a "beauty contest." In *Turner v. Bernstein*, 768 A.2d 24 (Del. Ch. 2000), the trail court rejected shareholder affidavits the CEO had gathered that shareholders did not support the litigation. "Form affidavits of this sort are entitled to very little, if any, weight." *See also Palowsky v. Premier Bancorp, Inc.*, 597 So. 2d 543, 546–47 (La. App. 1992) (existence of several other lawsuits over "notes and other matters" did not disqualify plaintiff shareholder from bringing derivative suit). Rather than ability and experience, the inquiry goes to the existence vel non of disabling conflicts of interest on the shareholder plaintiff's part and to the ability and absence of conflicts on the part of the plaintiff shareholder's counsel. At the plaintiff level, then, courts have disqualified as plaintiffs shareholders who also were competitors, *Roussel v. Tidelands Capital Corp.*, 438 F. Supp. 684, 688 (N.D. Ala. 1977); employees or former employees, *Recchion on behalf of Westinghouse Electric Corp. v. Kirby*, 637 F. Supp. 1309 (W.D. Pa. 1986); and contract claimants who also held shares, *Palmer v. United States Sav. Bank*, 553 A.2d 781, 786 (N.H. 1989). On the counsel's side, "the plaintiff's attorney must be qualified, experienced, and generally able to conduct the proposed litigation." *Wetzel v. Liberty Mut. Ins. Co.*, 508 F.2d 239 (3d Cir. 1975). *See also Brandon v. Brandon Constr. Co.*, 776 S.W.2d 349, 353 (Ark. 1989) ("the plaintiff's attorney must be qualified, experienced, and generally able to conduct the litigation").

PROBLEMS

1. It is 1955. In your office is Patsy Cline, a vocal performance artist, who owns shares in Swift & Co., the publicly held meat packing company. Patsy has a number of complaints. The directors approved the acquisition of a Beefalo ranch from the CEO's nephew. Several directors took for themselves an opportunity to expand in emerging post-war European markets, and the directors have approved a severance package ("golden parachute") for the CEO which is excessive by any measure. In short, she claims numerous breaches of fiduciary duty which may be vindicated, if at all, through a derivative action.

Patsy wishes to proceed if (1) she will not receive adverse publicity, and (2) out-of-pocket costs are not too high. What would you say to her?

2. Saul Steinberg has been a customer and shareholder of South Shore Bank. He has also been a thorn in the bank's side. He has filed three lender liability suits against the bank, all of which settled for nuisance value. Saul waged an unsuccessful proxy campaign to put himself in as a director.

Saul now brings a lawsuit alleging that South Shore's losses over the last two years were the result of gross mismanagement. He is joined by his cousin, Phillip Steinberg, who purchased a large block of South Shore shares last month, which are held in "street name" by his broker, Merrill Lynch. Saul and Philip are represented by Saul's nephew, Avi Steinberg, a newly admitted member of the bar who has, so far, specialized in personal injury litigation.

You represent South Shore Bank. What arguments do you make in your motion to dismiss?

3. First year law student Clarissa received a telephone conversation from her cousin Vinnie, a lawyer. Clarissa owns 100 shares of MCI. Vinnie has prepared a class and derivative action with Clarissa as plaintiff, attempting to block the proposed MCI merger with NPSI, Inc., another telecommunications company. Although she never heard of the merger, or of the proposed lawsuit, Clarissa quickly reads the complaint and signs it.

Several months later, at her deposition, Clarissa testifies that she knew she owned the stock, that she received a call from Vinnie, whom she believes to be "brilliant." She then met with him, asking, "Are you sure about this?," and signed.

The following day the defense firm of Crushem, Bashem & Sanctionem requests that you (you are Vinnie's supervising partner in the firm) see that the complaint is withdrawn or they will seek sanctions against you, Vinnie, and Clarissa. Should you fold the tent?

D. UNIVERSAL DEMAND

IN RE GUIDANT SHAREHOLDERS DERIVATIVE LITIGATION
Supreme Court of Indiana
841 N.E.2d 571 (2006)

SHEPARD, CHIEF JUSTICE.

The U.S. District Court of the Southern District of Indiana has asked us if passage of the Indiana Business Corporation Law in 1986 requires a shareholder commencing a derivative lawsuit to make a written demand on the corporation unless irreparable injury to the corporation would result, or if demand is still excused if it would be futile. . . .

We have accepted this certified question and now hold that the Indiana Business Corporation Law retains the futility standard, but narrows its applicability substantially by authorizing corporations to establish disinterested committees to determine whether the corporation should pursue certain claims.

Defendant Corporation is an Indiana company that develops . . . cardiovascular medical products. Endovascular Technologies Inc. is a wholly owned subsidiary of Guidant. Endovascular designed the Ancure Endograft System to treat abdominal aortic aneurysms and received FDA approval for commercial sale in the United States in 1999. In June 2003, after an investigation into defects in the device, the incomplete handling and reporting of complaints, inadequate corrective actions, and FDA violations, Guidant pled guilty to one felony count of making false statements to a federal agency and nine felony counts of shipping misbranded medical devices in interstate commerce. Guidant also agreed to pay a $43.4 million criminal fine and a $49 million civil settlement.

Six Guidant shareholder derivative actions were filed on behalf of Guidant in response to these events, and they were consolidated in the Southern District of Indiana with Alaska Electrical Pension Fund as the lead derivative plaintiff.

I. Indiana Has Long Recognized Demand Futility

Normally, a shareholder wishing to file a derivative lawsuit to pursue a corporation's rights must first demand that the board of directors take action. Since the late 19th century, Indiana has consistently recognized an excuse from the demand requirement where the shareholder alleges with particularity in a verified complaint that a majority of the board of directors are either the tortfeasors and/or interested in the transaction at issue.

II. The Indiana BCL Does Not Impose Universal Demand

In 1985, the Indiana General Assembly created the Indiana General Law Study Commission to evaluate the viability of completely revising the Indiana General Corporation Act. 1985 Ind. Acts 2490-91. Based on the Commission's recommendations, the General Assembly passed the Indiana Business Corporation Law ("BCL") in 1986.

The Commission based the BCL largely on the 1984 version of the Revised Model Business Corporation Act ("RMA") . . . .

The BCL's demand provision, which has remained unchanged since its enactment, reads as follows: A complaint in a proceeding brought in the right of a corporation must be verified and allege with particularity the demand made, if any, to obtain action by the board of directors and either that the demand was refused or ignored or why the shareholder did not make the demand. Whether or not a demand for action was made, if the corporation commences an investigation of the charges made in the demand or complaint (including an investigation commenced under section 4 of this chapter), the court may stay any proceeding until the investigation is completed.

The BCL reflected Indiana's long-standing demand requirement and the fact that demand may sometimes be excused, but it neither explicitly enumerated nor explained in commentary what constitutes adequate excuse. Some modest explanation is provided in the RMA's comments, which the Commission adopted. They state, "there may be circumstances showing that a demand on the board of directors would be useless, and in those circumstances it should be sufficient to allege the reasons why the plaintiff did not make the demand." Model Bus. Corp. Act § 7.40 cmt. 1(e) (1984). . . .

The Guidant directors . . . say that section 23-1-32-2 must be read in conjunction with section 23-1-32-4, an innovation of the 1986 act that authorizes a corporation board to form a disinterested committee to determine whether the corporation should pursue a possible claim. They contend that these two sections reflect legislative adoption of the "universal demand" standard. . . . A good example of the universal demand standard comes from the current version of the RMA. It requires a shareholder to wait ninety days after a demand is made to file suit unless "irreparable injury to the corporation would result." Model Bus. Corp. Act § 7.42 (1991). . . . Their contentions find support in Boland v. Engle, 113 F.3d 706, 712 (7th Cir.1997), where the Seventh Circuit speculated "that the highest court in Indiana would today be persuaded by the general trend in the law towards narrowing, if not eliminating, the exceptions from the demand requirement." The court went on to note the growing trend of states adopting the universal demand standard.

If anything, the national trend towards the universal demand rule has accelerated since the Seventh Circuit's observation. Boland, 113 F.3d at 712 (noting that eleven states had then adopted universal demand by statute). Since Boland, eleven more states legislatures have passed universal demand statutes. Ariz. Rev. Stat. Ann. § 10-742 (1996); Haw. Rev. Stat. § 414-173 (2000); Idaho Code Ann. § 30-1-742 (1998); Iowa Code § 490.742 (2002); Me. Rev. Stat. Ann. tit. 13-C, § 753 (2003); Mass. Gen. Laws ch. 156D, § 7.42 (2004); R.I. Gen. Laws § 7-1.2-711(c) (2005); S.D. Codified Laws § 47-1A-742 (2005); Tex. Bus. Org. Code Ann. § 21.553 (2006); Utah Code Ann. § 16-10a-740(3) (a) (ii) (2000); Wyo. Stat. Ann. § 17-16-742 (1997). In addition, the Pennsylvania Supreme Court adopted the universal demand rule. Cuker v. Mikalauskas, 547 Pa. 600, 692 A.2d 1042, 1048–49 (1997). . . .

[T]he new universal demand version requires a shareholder to wait ninety days after a demand is made and before filing suit unless "irreparable injury to the corporation would result." Model Bus. Corp. Act s 7.42 (1991). Though the [Indiana] General Assembly has amended other parts of the BCL since 1991, it has left the demand statute unchanged. . . .

. . .

Both section 23-1-32-2 and the comments to the 1984 version of the RMA express a preference for the board of directors to enforce a corporation's rights. . . .

Section 23-1-32-4 of the BCL permits a board of directors to establish a committee of three or more disinterested directors or persons to determine if a corporation has a legal or equitable right or remedy and whether it is in the best interests of the corporation to pursue that right or remedy. This section of our law has no RMA counterpart. To insure that the committee is disinterested, the BCL denies the board the ability to control or terminate the committee. Ind.Code s 23-1-32-4(b). The committee's determination not to pursue a right or remedy through a derivative proceeding is "presumed to be conclusive against any shareholder making a demand or bringing a derivative proceeding with respect to such right or remedy," unless a shareholder can prove the committee was not disinterested or there was no good faith investigation. Ind.Code s 23-1-32-4c). In fact, this statute codifies the "business judgment rule" as applied to a special committee's determination of whether or not pursuit of a legal claim is in the corporation's best interest. See Ind.Code s 23-1-32-4 cmt. c) (specifically rejecting Zapata v. Maldonado) . . .

The Indiana study commission explicitly explained that even though the RMA did not provide for a disinterested committee, it believed that "defining procedures for board actions in this area would benefit Indiana corporations, attorneys and the courts."

Conclusion

A shareholder may be excused under Indiana Code § 23-1-32-2 from making a demand on the board of directors before filing a derivative suit if such demand would be futile. Such a demand is no longer futile, however, simply because the verified complaint names the members of the board, or because it alleges that members of the board are involved in wrongdoing. The availability of the disinterested committee will bar a separate derivative action unless the derivative plaintiff can establish that the committee was not disinterested or that its decision was not undertaken after a good faith investigation.

DICKSON, SULLIVAN, BOEHM, and RUCKER, JJ., concur.

NOTES

1. *Home Grown Statutes.* In advance of, or in lieu of, what the ABA Committee on Corporate Laws did with the MBCA, *see infra,* several states adopted corporate law statutes providing for creation of special litigation committees and for limited review by courts of an SLC's recommendations, as recounted of Indiana in the principal case. *See, e.g., Evans v. Paulson,* 2007 U.S. Dist. LEXIS 38064 (D. Minn. May 24, 2007) (applying Minn. Stat. § 302A.241).

2. *The MBCA and Universal Demand.* As the principal case indicates, the Committee on Corporate Laws did incorporate a universal demand requirement the revised derivative action procedures the Committee inserted into the MBCA in 1990. MBCA § 7.42 provides:

No shareholder may commence a derivative proceeding until:

(1) A written demand has been made upon the corporation to take suitable action; and

(2) Ninety days have expired from the date the demand was made unless the shareholder has earlier been notified that the demand has been rejected by the corporation or unless irreparable injury to the corporation would result by waiting for the expiration of the 90-day period.

Approximately half the Model Act jurisdictions have adopted the universal demand statute. In turn, the statue has its derivation in a universal demand procedure incorporated in ALI Corp. Gov. Proj. § 7.02.

3. *Judicial Interpretation.* Plaintiff owned 20 percent of corporation which owned a horse farm. She objected to the sale at $4 million, when she had an appraisal at $7 million and the board of directors had an appraisal at $6.68 million. Her suit was dismissed for failure to have made a demand under Virginia's adoption of MBCA § 7.41: "Demand is required in every case." Does the new statute thereby emphasize form over substance, leaving corporate law with another instance of "a wrong without a remedy?" *Firestone v. Wiley,* 485 F. Supp.2d 694 (E.D. Va. 2007).

4. *Judicial Attempt at Universal Demand.* Judge Frank Easterbrook, no doubt emboldened by what he had witnessed at ALI meetings he had attended, found universal demand to be on the road to being widely used. He therefore adopted it as a matter of "federal common law." *Kamen v. Kemper Fin. Serv., Inc.,* 908 F.2d 1338 (7th Cir, 1990). In an opinion by Mr. Justice Thurgood Marshall, the Supreme Court reversed, finding that demand, with its three branches, represents a careful allegation of power among the organs of a company (shareholders, directors and officers) worked out over many decades and which, absent authority, a court should not disturb. Moreover, the demand futility branch applies to a money market mutual fund, as a matter of state corporate law, even thought the Investment Company Act of 1940 grants subject a matter jurisdiction to federal courts. Therefore, the demand requirement is substantive. It is not the procedural type incident with which federal common law deals. *Kamen v. Kemper Fin. Servs.*, 500 U.S. 90 (1991).

PROBLEM

In the Happy Days hypothetical, *supra*, assume that Potsie and his attorney decide to proceed directly to court, alleging that demand was excused because most of the directors were related to or dominated by Richie. As Potsie is in his lawyer's office, verifying the complaint, he asks innocently enough, "What about the other shareholders? There are nine of them. Do we have to notify them or something?"

Or, assume further, that Happy Days has become a publicly held corporation. Assume also that instead of nine other shareholders there are 900, or 9000? Is demand upon shareholders required as well?

E. AVOIDING DERIVATIVE CHARACTERIZATION — DIRECT VERSUS DERIVATIVE

TOOLEY v. DONALDSON, LUFKIN & JENREETTE, INC.
Supreme Court of Delaware (en banc)
845 A.2d 1031 (2004)

VEASEY, CHIEF JUSTICE:

. . . .

Plaintiff-stockholders brought a purported class action in the Court of Chancery, alleging that the members of the board of directors of their corporation breached their fiduciary duties by agreeing to a 22-day delay in closing a proposed merger, plaintiffs contend that the delay harmed them due to the lost time-value of the cash paid for their shares. The Court of Chancery granted the defendants' motion to dismiss on the sole ground that the claims were, "at most," claims of the corporation being asserted derivatively. . . .

[Although the trial court's legal analysis of whether the complaint alleges a direct or derivative claim reflects some concepts in our prior jurisprudence, we believe those concepts are not helpful . . . . That issue must turn solely on the following questions: (1) who suffered the alleged harm (the corporation or the suing stockholders, individually); and (2) who would receive the benefit of any recovery or other remedy (the corporation or the stockholders, individually)? . . .

Patrick Tooley and Kevin Lewis are former minority stockholders of Donaldson, Lufkin & Jenrette, Inc. (DLJ), a Delaware corporation engaged in investment banking. DLJ was acquired by Credit Suisse Group (Credit Suisse) in the Fall of 2000. Before that acquisition, AXA Financial, Inc.(AXA), which owned 71% of DLJ stock, controlled DLJ. Pursuant to a stockholder agreement between AXA and Credit Suisse, AXA agreed to exchange with Credit Suisse its DLJ stockholdings for a mix of stock and cash. The consideration received by AXA consisted primarily of stock. Cash made up one-third of the purchase price. Credit Suisse intended to acquire the remaining minority interests of publicly-held DLJ stock through a cash tender offer [100% cash].

The tender offer price was set at $90 per share in cash. The tender offer was to expire 20 days after its commencement. The merger agreement, however, authorized two types of extensions. First, Credit Suisse could unilaterally extend the tender offer if certain conditions were not met, such as SEC regulatory approvals or certain payment obligations. Alternatively, DLJ and Credit Suisse could agree to postpone acceptance by Credit Suisse of DLJ stock tendered by the minority stockholders.

Credit Suisse availed itself of both types of extensions to postpone the closing of the tender offer [from October 5 to November 2]. . . .

Plaintiffs challenge the second extension that resulted in a 22-day delay. They contend that this delay was not properly authorized and harmed minority stockholders while improperly benefitting AXA. They claim damages representing the time-value of money lost through the delay.

The order of the Court of Chancery dismissing the complaint . . . state[s] that the dismissal is based on the plaintiffs' lack of standing to bring the claims asserted therein. Thus, when plaintiffs tendered their shares, they lost standing under Court of Chancery Rule 23.1, the contemporaneous holding rule. The ruling before us on appeal is that the plaintiffs' claim is derivative . . . "Because this delay affected all DLJ shareholders equally, plaintiffs' injury was not a special injury, and this action is, thus, a derivative action, at most."

Plaintiffs argue that they have suffered a "special injury" because they had an alleged contractual right to receive the merger consideration of $90 per share without suffering the 22-day delay . . . . But the trial court's opinion convincingly demonstrates that plaintiffs had no such contractual right that had ripened at the time the extensions were entered into . . . DLJ stockholders had no individual contractual right to payment until November 3, 2000, when their tendered shares were accepted for payment. Thus, they have no contractual basis to challenge a delay in the closing of the tender offer up until November 3. Because this is the date the tendered shares were accepted for payment, the contract was not breached and plaintiffs do not have a contractual basis to bring a direct suit.

. . .

The Court of Chancery correctly noted that "[t]he Court will independently examine the nature of the wrong alleged and any potential relief to make its own determination of the suit's classification. . . . Plaintiffs' classification of the suit is not binding." The trial court's analysis was hindered, however, because it focused on the confusing concept of "special injury" as the test for determining whether a claim is derivative or direct. The trial court's premise was as follows:

> In order to bring a direct claim, a plaintiff must have experienced some "special injury." [citing Lipton v. News Int'l, 514 A.2d 1075, 1079 (Del.1986).] A special injury is a wrong that "is separate and distinct from that suffered by other shareholders, . . . or a wrong involving a contractual right of a share-holder, such as the right to vote, or to assert majority control, which exists independently of any right of the corporation." [citing Moran v. Household Int'l Inc., 490 A.2d 1059, 1070 (Del.Ch.1985), aff'd, 500 A.2d 1346 (Del. 1986 [1985]).]

In our view, the concept of "special injury" that appears in some Supreme Court and Court of Chancery cases is not helpful to a proper analytical distinction between direct and derivative actions. We now disapprove the use of the concept of "special injury" as a tool in that analysis.

The Proper Analysis to Distinguish Between Direct and Derivative Actions

The analysis must be based solely on the following questions: Who suffered the alleged harm-the corporation or the suing stockholder individually-and who would receive the benefit of the recovery or other remedy? . . . [(T)his test is similar to that articulated by the American Law Institute (ALI), a test that we cited with approval in Grimes v. Donald, 673 A.2d 1207 (Del. 1996). The ALI test is as follows:

> A direct action may be brought in the name and right of a holder to redress

an injury sustained by, or enforce a duty owed to, the holder. An action in which the holder can prevail without showing an injury or breach of duty to the corporation should be treated as a direct action that may be maintained by the holder in an individual capacity.

2 American Law Institute, Principles of Corporate Governance: Analysis and Recommendations § 7.01(b) at 17.

A Brief History of Our Jurisprudence

. . . A stockholder who is directly injured . . . does retain the right to bring an individual action for injuries affecting his or her legal rights as a stockholder. Such a claim is distinct from an injury caused to the corporation alone. In such individual suits, the recovery or other relief flows directly to the stockholders, not to the corporation.

. . .

In Lipton v. News International, Plc., this Court applied the "special injury" test. There, a stockholder began acquiring shares in the defendant corporation presumably to gain control of the corporation. In response, the defendant corporation agreed to an exchange of its shares with a friendly buyer. Due to the exchange and a supermajority voting requirement on certain stockholder actions, the management of the defendant corporation acquired a veto power over any change in management.

The Lipton Court concluded that the critical analytical issue in distinguishing direct and derivative actions is whether a "special injury" has been alleged. There, the Court found a "special injury" because the board's manipulation worked an injury upon the plaintiff-stockholder unlike the injury suffered by other stockholders. That was because the plaintiff-stockholder was actively seeking to gain control of the defendant corporation. Therefore, the Court found that the claim was direct. Ironically, the Court could have reached the same correct result by simply concluding that the manipulation directly and individually harmed the stockholders, without injuring the corporation.

In Kramer v. Western Pacific Industries, Inc. [546 A.2d 348, 352 (Del. 1988)], this Court found to be derivative a stockholder's challenge to corporate transactions. . . . The stockholders challenged the decision by the board of directors to grant stock options and golden parachutes to management. The stockholders argued that the claim was direct because their share of the proceeds from the buy-out sale was reduced by the resources used to pay for the options and golden parachutes. Once again, our analysis was that to bring a direct action, the stockholder must allege something other than an injury resulting from a wrong to the corporation. . . . The claim in Kramer was essentially for mismanagement of corporate assets. Therefore, we found the claims to be derivative. . . .

In Grimes v. Donald [673 A.2d 1207, 1213 (Del. 1996)], we sought to distinguish between direct and derivative actions in the context of employment agreements granted to certain officers that allegedly caused the board to abdicate its authority. . . . [T]he plaintiff was seeking a declaration of the invalidity of the agreements on the ground that the board had abdicated its responsibility to the stockholders. Thus, based on the relief requested, we affirmed the judgment of the Court of Chancery that the plaintiff was entitled to pursue a direct action.

. . . .

[A] court should look to the nature of the wrong and to whom the relief should go. The stockholder's claimed direct injury must be independent of any alleged injury to the corporation. The stockholder must demonstrate that the duty breached was owed to the stockholder and that he or she can prevail without showing an injury to the corporation.

Standard to Be Applied in This Case

In this case it cannot be concluded that the complaint alleges a derivative claim. There is no derivative claim asserting injury to the corporate entity. There is no relief that would go the corporation. Accordingly, there is no basis to hold that the complaint states a derivative claim.

But, it does not necessarily follow that the complaint states a direct, individual claim. While the complaint purports to set forth a direct claim, in reality, it states no claim at all. The trial court analyzed the complaint and correctly concluded that it does not claim that the plaintiffs have any rights that have been injured. Their rights have not yet ripened. The contractual claim is nonexistent until it is ripe . . . .

. . . .

Because our determination that there is no valid claim whatsoever in the complaint before us was not argued by the defendants and was not the basis of the ruling of the Court of Chancery, the interests of justice will be best served if the dismissal is without prejudice, and plaintiffs have an opportunity to replead if they have a basis for doing so under Court of Chancery Rule 11 . . . .

[Reversing the order of dismissal with prejudice, remanding for dismissal without prejudice]

NOTES AND QUESTIONS

1. *Avoiding Derivative Litigation.* Experienced shareholder plaintiffs attorneys often seek to avoid derivative litigation whenever possible. They do so because of the many impediments that remain from anti-strike suit reform days and, more recently, because of the near omnipotent power the SLC device has for derailing derivative suits. One primary means to avoid derivative characterization is to bring shareholder claims exclusively as direct rather than derivative actions, which may not always be possible, and having a court uphold the plaintiff's characterization of her claim.

2. *Fundamental Error.* In the principal case, *Tooley v. Donaldson, Lufkin & Jenrette*, the Supreme Court of Delaware agreed with the chancellor below that "this delay affected all DLJ shareholders equally." Ergo, the special injury rule would not lead to a finding that the claim was direct, which it obviously was. Based upon that finding, Mr. Justice Veasey took it upon himself to throw out the special injury rule, devising a new test. But isn't the premise flawed? Wasn't the effect on the two groups of shareholders different, even if their genesis was in the same act (agreeing to a 22-day extension)? As majority shareholder, holding 71% of DLJ's stock, Credit Swiss would be prejudiced as to 30% of the consideration it was to receive (30% in cash). Minority shareholders were prejudiced by the delay as to 100% of consideration they were to receive (100% in cash).

3. *Not One Test but Two.* Courts, including courts in Delaware, have always applied two tests in seriatim (or one test that had two parts). First, a court asked if the shareholder bringing the suit either herself, as part of a group, but less than all, shareholders, had suffered a separate and "special" injury. An example would be a financial benefit (a dividend or other distribution the corporation gives to some but not all shareholders). If the plaintiff could make out a special injury, she could proceed in a direct, rather than derivative action, thereby avoiding anti-strike suit provisions, demand, universal demand where it exists, and an SLC.

If she could not make out a special injury, the plaintiff shareholder would proceed to the second test. Even if she suffered a wrong in common with all other shareholders, was the wrong the consequence of being denied a right associated with share ownership? Thus, in addition to a right to be free of discrimination, a shareholder has a right to disclosure, to votes on certain matters, or to be free of dilution that has no business purpose.

4. *Characterization Is Discretionary.* Thus, absent an abuse of discretion, an appellate court should let stand characterizations of shareholders suits as direct, or as derivative, even though the appellate court might have decided differently in the first place. *See, e.g., Hanson v. Kake Tribal Corp.*, 939 P.2d 1320, 1327 (Alaska 1997) ("Courts generally have wide discretion in interpreting whether a complaint states a direct or derivative claim.").

5. *Pleading Standards.* Besides avoiding demand requirements, special litigation committees, and other hurdles, a direct action plaintiff benefits from a more lenient pleading standard:

> In asserting direct claims, as distinct from shareholder derivative actions, the complaint only need give general notice of the claim asserted. [P]laintiff need only provide a well-pleaded short and plain statement of the claim showing that the pleader is entitled to relief. A requirement that the pleader state facts "with particularity" is reserved for stockholder derivative claims . . . and for fraud or mistake claims under Rule 9(b).

Loudon v. Archer-Daniels-Midland Co., 700 A.2d 135, 140 (Del. 1997).

PROBLEM

In the Roadstar problem, *supra*, before Falconer can even file his claim, he obtains more "bad news." At a Roadstar board meeting, the Manleys declare an extraordinary dividend of $30 per share (the stock sells for $15), but payable only to those shareholders who have held shares for five years or longer. Falconer has held his shares for four years.

The day after the dividend is paid the Manleys sell all the company's assets to Drummond Co., the fabricator. There is no shareholders' meeting or other formal action. There is just an announcement to the local press, prepared on stationery with the Manley family coat of arms.

Falconer now is triply "frosted." What are his claims now?

Chapter 12

SECURITIES LITIGATION

This Chapter focuses on selected key subjects in securities litigation. The Chapter begins with § 11 of the Securities Act which provides a private right of action for materially false or misleading statements contained in a Securities Act registration statement. Second, the most frequently invoked provision in securities litigation — § 10(b) of the Securities Exchange Act — is covered. Third, federal legislation focusing on securities class action reform is examined. The Chapter concludes with coverage of state securities litigation.

A. SECTION 11 OF THE SECURITIES ACT

As discussed in Chapter 5, a registered offering under the Securities Act requires that a registration statement be filed with the SEC. A key policy underlying this requirement is to enable prospective purchasers to make informed investment decisions based upon the disclosure of adequate and truthful information regarding the issuer, its associated persons, and the offering. This policy is frustrated when a registration statement (including the statutory prospectus which comprises part of the registration statement) contains materially false or misleading statements.

In view of the above, investors under certain conditions may recover their losses if they purchase securities pursuant to a registration statement which contains a material misrepresentation or nondisclosure. The federal law provision most likely to be invoked in this context is § 11 of the Securities Act.

Although handed down four decades ago, the seminal case on due diligence in the § 11 context is *Escott v. BarChris Construction Corporation*. While reading the decision, consider whether the court's approach adequately takes into account business realities. Does *BarChris* reflect an accommodation between the interests of entrepreneurs and investors? What due diligence steps should potential § 11 defendants routinely take to help guard against their being held liable for a materially false or misleading registration statement?

ESCOTT v. BARCHRIS CONSTRUCTION CORPORATION
United States District Court, Southern District of New York
283 F. Supp. 643 (1968)

McLEAN, DISTRICT JUDGE.

This is an action by purchasers of 5½ per cent convertible subordinated fifteen year debentures of BarChris Construction Corporation (BarChris). . . .

The action is brought under Section 11 of the Securities Act of 1933 (15 U.S.C. § 77k). Plaintiffs allege that the registration statement with respect to these debentures filed with the Securities and Exchange Commission, which became effective on May 16, 1961, contained material false statements and material omissions.

Defendants fall into three categories: (1) the persons who signed the registration statement; (2) the underwriters, consisting of eight investment banking firms, led by Drexel & Co. (Drexel); and (3) BarChris's auditors, Peat, Marwick, Mitchell & Co. (Peat, Marwick).

The signers, in addition to BarChris itself, were the nine directors of BarChris, plus its controller, defendant Trilling, who was not a director. Of the nine directors, five were officers of BarChris, i.e., defendants Vitolo, president; Russo, executive vice president; Pugliese, vice president; Kircher, treasurer; and Birnbaum, secretary. Of the remaining four, defendant Grant was a member of the firm of Perkins, Daniels, McCormack & Collins, BarChris's attorneys. He became a director in October 1960. Defendant Coleman, a partner in Drexel, became a director on April 17, 1961, as did the other two, Auslander and Rose, who were not otherwise connected with BarChris.

Defendants, in addition to denying that the registration statement was false, have pleaded the defenses open to them under Section 11 of the Act, plus certain additional defenses . . . .

[Some] background facts should be mentioned. At the time relevant here, BarChris was engaged primarily in the construction of bowling alleys, somewhat euphemistically referred to as "bowling centers." These were rather elaborate affairs. They contained not only a number of alleys or "lanes," but also, in most cases, bar and restaurant facilities.

The introduction of automatic pin setting machines in 1952 [when bowling became "kingpin"] gave a marked stimulus to bowling. It rapidly became a popular sport, with the result that "bowling centers" began to appear throughout the country in rapidly increasing numbers. BarChris benefitted from this increased interest in bowling. Its construction operations expanded rapidly. It is estimated that in 1960 BarChris installed approximately three per cent of all lanes built in the United States. It was thus a significant factor in the industry, although two large established companies, American Machine & Foundry Company [AMF] and Brunswick, were much larger factors.

BarChris's sales increased dramatically from 1956 to 1960. According to the prospectus, net sales, in round figures, in 1956 were some $800,000, in 1957 $1,300,000, in 1958 $1,700,000. In 1959 they increased to over $3,300,000, and by 1960 they had leaped to over $9,165,000.

For some years the business had exceeded the managerial capacity of its founders. Vitolo and Pugliese are each men of limited education. Vitolo did not get beyond high school. Pugliese ended his schooling in seventh grade. Pugliese devoted his time to supervising the actual construction work. Vitolo was concerned primarily with obtaining new business. Neither was equipped to handle financial matters.

Rather early in their career they enlisted the aid of Russo, who was trained as an accountant. . . . He eventually became executive vice president of BarChris. In that capacity he handled many of the transactions which figure in this case.

In 1959 BarChris hired Kircher, a certified public accountant who had been employed by Peat, Marwick. He started as controller and became treasurer in 1960. In October of that year, another ex-Peat, Marwick employee, Trilling, succeeded Kircher as controller. At approximately the same time Birnbaum, a young attorney, was hired as house counsel. He became secretary on April 17, 1961.

In general, BarChris' method of operation was to enter into a contract with a customer, receive from him at that time a comparatively small down payment on the purchase price, and proceed to construct and equip the bowling alley. When the work was finished and the building delivered, the customer paid the balance of the contract price in notes, payable in installments over a period of years. BarChris discounted these notes with a factor and received part of their face amount in cash. The factor held back part as a reserve.

. . . .

BarChris was compelled to expend considerable sums in defraying the cost of construction before it received reimbursement. As a consequence, BarChris was in constant need of cash to finance its operations, a need which grew more pressing as operations expanded.

. . . .

By early 1961, BarChris needed additional working capital. The proceeds of the sale of the debentures involved in this action were to be devoted, in part at least, to fill that need.

The registration statement of the debentures, in preliminary form, was filed with the Securities and Exchange Commission on March 30, 1961. A first amendment was filed on May 11 and a second on May 16. The registration statement became effective on May 16. The closing of the financing took place on May 24. On that day BarChris received the net proceeds of the financing.

By that time BarChris was experiencing difficulties in collecting amounts due from some of its customers. Some of them were in arrears in payments due to factors on their discounted notes. As time went on those difficulties increased. Although BarChris continued to build alleys in 1961 and 1962, it became increasingly apparent that the industry was overbuilt. Operators of alleys, often inadequately financed, began to fail. Precisely when the tide turned is a matter of dispute, but at any rate, it was painfully apparent in 1962.

In May of that year BarChris made an abortive attempt to raise more money by the sale of common stock. It filed with the Securities and Exchange Commission a registration statement for the stock issue which it later withdrew. In October 1962 BarChris came to the end of the road. On October 29, 1962, it filed in this court a petition for an arrangement under Chapter XI of the Bankruptcy Act. BarChris defaulted in the payment of the interest due on November 1, 1962 on the debentures.

The Debenture Registration Statement

. . . . [T]he [court found that] various falsities and omissions . . . [in the Debenture Registration Statement were material.]

. . . .

The "Due Diligence" Defenses

Section 11(b) of the Act provides that:

> . . . no person, other than the issuer, shall be liable . . . who shall sustain the burden of proof — . . .
>
> (3) that (A) as regards any part of the registration statement not purporting to be made on the authority of an expert . . . he had, after reasonable investigation, reasonable ground to believe and did believe, at the time such part of the registration statement became effective, that the statements therein were true and that there was no omission to state a material fact required to be stated therein or necessary to make the statements therein not misleading; . . . and (C) as regards any part of the registration statement purporting to be made on the authority of an expert (other than himself) . . . he had no reasonable ground to believe and did not believe, at the time such part of the registration statement became effective, that the statements therein were untrue or that there was an omission to state a material fact required to be stated therein or necessary to make the statements therein not misleading. . . .

Section 11(c) defines "reasonable investigation" as follows: In determining, for the purpose of paragraph (3) of subsection (b) of this section, what constitutes reasonable investigation and reasonable ground for belief, the standard of reasonableness shall be that required of a prudent man in the management of his own property.

Every defendant, except BarChris itself, to whom, as the issuer, these defenses are not available, and except Peat, Marwick, whose position rests on a different statutory provision, has pleaded these affirmative defenses. Each claims that (1) as to the part of the registration statement purporting to be made on the authority of an expert (which, for convenience, I shall refer to as the "expertised portion"), he had no reasonable ground to believe and did not believe that there were any untrue statements or material omissions, and (2) as to the other parts of the registration statement, he made a reasonable investigation, as a result of which he had reasonable ground to believe and did believe that the registration statement was true and that no material fact was omitted. As to each defendant, the question is whether he has sustained the burden of proving these defenses. Surprising enough, there is little or no judicial authority on this question. No decisions directly in point under Section 11 have been found.

Before considering the evidence, a preliminary matter should be disposed of. The defendants do not agree among themselves as to who the "experts" were or as to the parts of the registration statement which were expertised. Some defendants say that Peat, Marwick was the expert, others say that BarChris's attorneys, Perkins, Daniels, McCormack & Collins, and the underwriters' attorneys, Drinker, Biddle & Reath, were also the experts. On the first view, only those portions of the registration statement purporting to be made on Peat, Marwick's authority were expertised portions. On the other view, everything in the registration statement was within this category, because the two law firms were responsible for the entire document.

The first view is the correct one. To say that the entire registration statement is expertised because some lawyer prepared it would be an unreasonable construction of the statute. Neither the lawyer for the company nor the lawyer for the underwriters is an expert within the meaning of § 11. The only expert, in the statutory sense, was Peat, Marwick, and the only parts of the registration statement which purported to be made upon the authority of an expert were the portions which purported to be made on Peat, Marwick's authority.

The parties also disagree as to what those portions were. Some defendants say that it was only the 1960 figures (and the figures for prior years, which are not in controversy here). Others say in substance that it was every figure in the prospectus. . . .

Here again, the more narrow view is the correct one. The registration statement contains a report of Peat, Marwick as independent public accountants dated February 23, 1961. This relates only to the consolidated balance sheet of BarChris and consolidated subsidiaries as of December 31, 1960, and the related statement of earnings and retained earnings for the five years then ended. This is all that Peat, Marwick purported to certify. It is perfectly clear that it did not purport to certify the 1961 figures, some of which are expressly stated in the prospectus to have been unaudited.

I turn now to the question of whether defendants have proved their due diligence defenses. The position of each defendant will be separately considered.

Russo

Russo was, to all intents and purposes, the chief executive officer of BarChris. He was a member of the executive committee. He was familiar with all aspects of the business. He was personally in charge of dealings with the factors. He acted on BarChris's behalf in making the financing agreements with Talcott and he handled the negotiations with Talcott in the spring of 1961. He talked with customers about their delinquencies.

. . . .

It was Russo who arranged for the temporary increase in BarChris's cash [on deposit with] banks on December 31, 1960, a transaction which borders on the fraudulent. He was thoroughly aware of BarChris's stringent financial condition in May 1961. He had personally advanced large sums to BarChris of which $175,000 remained unpaid as of May 16.

In short, Russo knew all the relevant facts. He could not have believed that there were no untrue statements or material omissions in the prospectus. Russo has no due diligence defenses.

Vitolo and Pugliese

They were the founders of the business who stuck with it to the end. Vitolo was president and Pugliese was vice president. Despite their titles, their field of responsibility in the administration of BarChris's affairs during the period in question seems to have been less all-embracing than Russo's. Pugliese in particular appears to have limited his activities to supervising the actual construction work.

Vitolo and Pugliese are each men of limited education. It is not hard to believe that for them the prospectus was difficult reading, if indeed they read it at all.

But whether it was or not is irrelevant. The liability of a director who signs a registration statement does not depend upon whether or not he read it or, if he did, whether or not he understood what he was reading.

And in any case, Vitolo and Pugliese were not as naive as they claim to be. They were members of BarChris's executive committee. At meetings of that committee BarChris's affairs were discussed at length. They must have known what was going on. Certainly they knew of the inadequacy of cash in 1961. They knew of their own large advances to the company which remained unpaid. They knew that they had agreed not to deposit their checks until the financing proceeds were received. They knew and intended that part of the proceeds were to be used to pay their own loans.

All in all, the position of Vitolo and Pugliese is not significantly different, for present purposes, from Russo's. They could not have believed that the registration statement was wholly true and that no material facts had been omitted. And in any case, there is nothing to show that they made any investigation of anything which they may not have known about or understood. They have not proved their due diligence defenses.

Kircher

Kircher was treasurer of BarChris and its chief financial officer. He is a certified public accountant and an intelligent man. He was thoroughly familiar with BarChris's financial affairs. He knew the terms of BarChris's agreements with Talcott. He knew of the customers' delinquency problem. He participated actively with Russo in May 1961 in the successful effort to hold Talcott off until the financing proceeds came in. He knew how the financing proceeds were to be applied and he saw to it that they were so applied. He arranged the officers' loans and he knew all the facts concerning them.

Moreover, as a member of the executive committee, Kircher was kept informed as to those branches of the business of which he did not have direct charge.

Kircher worked on the preparation of the registration statement. He conferred with Grant [the outside counsel] and on occasion with Ballard [underwriters' counsel]. He supplied information to them about the company's business. He read the prospectus and understood it. He knew what it said and what it did not say.

Kircher's contention is that he had never before dealt with a registration statement, that he did not know what it should contain, and that he relied wholly on Grant, Ballard and Peat, Marwick to guide him. He claims that it was their fault, not his, if there was anything wrong with it. He says that all the facts were recorded in BarChris's books where these "experts" could have seen them if they had looked. He says that he truthfully answered all their questions. In effect, he says that if they did not know enough to ask the right questions and to give him the proper instructions, that is not his responsibility.

There is an issue of credibility here. In fact, Kircher was not frank in dealing with Grant and Ballard. He withheld information from them. But even if he had told them all the facts, this would not have constituted the due diligence contemplated by the statute. Knowing the facts, Kircher had reason to believe that the expertised portion of the prospectus, i.e., the 1960 figures, was in part incorrect. He could not shut his eyes to the facts and rely on Peat, Marwick for that portion.

As to the rest of the prospectus, knowing the facts, he did not have a reasonable ground to believe it to be true. On the contrary, he must have known that in part it was untrue. Under these circumstances, he was not entitled to sit back and place the blame on the lawyers for not advising him about it. Kircher has not proved his due diligence defenses.

. . . .

Birnbaum

Birnbaum was a young lawyer, admitted to the bar in 1957, who, after brief periods of employment by two different law firms and an equally brief period of practicing in his own firm, was employed by BarChris as house counsel and assistant secretary in October 1960. Unfortunately for him, he became secretary and a director of BarChris on April 17, 1961, after the first version of the registration statement had been filed with the Securities and Exchange Commission. He signed the later amendments, thereby becoming responsible for the accuracy of the prospectus in its final form.

. . . .

It seems probable that Birnbaum did not know of many of the inaccuracies in the prospectus. He must, however, have appreciated some of them. In any case, he made no investigation and relied on the others to get it right. . . . [H]e was entitled to rely upon Peat, Marwick for the 1960 figures, for as far as appears, he had no personal knowledge of the company's books of account or financial transactions. But he was not entitled to rely upon Kircher, Grant and Ballard for the other portions of the prospectus. As a lawyer, he should have known his obligations under the statute. He should have known that he was required to make a reasonable investigation of the truth of all the statements in the unexpertised portion of the document which he signed. Having failed to make such an investigation, he did not have reasonable ground to believe that all these statements were true. Birnbaum has not established his due diligence defenses except as to the audited 1960 figures.

Auslander

Auslander was an "outside" director, i.e., one who was not an officer of BarChris. He was chairman of the board of Valley Stream National Bank in Valley Stream, Long Island. In February 1961 Vitolo asked him to become a director of BarChris. Vitolo gave him an enthusiastic account of BarChris's progress and prospects. As an inducement, Vitolo said that when BarChris received the proceeds of a forthcoming issue of securities, it would deposit $1,000,000 in Auslander's bank.

. . . .

On March 3, 1961, Auslander indicated his willingness to accept a place on the board. Shortly thereafter, on March 14, Kircher sent him a copy of BarChris's annual report for 1960. Auslander observed that BarChris's auditors were Peat, Marwick. They were also the auditors for the Valley Stream National Bank. He thought well of them.

. . . .

At the May 15 meeting, Russo and Vitolo stated that everything was in order and that the prospectus was correct. Auslander believed this statement.

In considering Auslander's due diligence defenses, a distinction is to be drawn between the expertised and non-expertised portions of the prospectus. As to the former, Auslander knew that Peat, Marwick had audited the 1960 figures. He believed them to be correct because he had confidence in Peat, Marwick. He had no reasonable ground to believe otherwise.

As to the non-expertised portions, however, Auslander is in a different position. He seems to have been under the impression that Peat, Marwick was responsible for all the figures. This impression was not correct, as he would have realized if he had read the prospectus carefully. Auslander made no investigation of the accuracy of the prospectus. He relied on the assurance of Vitolo and Russo, and upon the information he had received in answer to his inquiries back in February and early March. These inquiries were general ones, in the nature of a credit check. The information which he received in answer to them was also general, without specific reference to the statements in the prospectus, which was not prepared until some time thereafter.

It is true that Auslander became a director on the eve of the financing. He had little opportunity to familiarize himself with the company's affairs. The question is whether, under such circumstances, Auslander did enough to establish his due diligence defense with respect to the non-expertised portions of the prospectus.

Although there is a dearth of authority under § 11 on this point, an English case under the analogous Companies Act is of some value. In *Adams v. Thrift*, [1915] 1 Ch. 557, *aff'd*, [1915] 2 Ch. 21, it was held that a director who knew nothing about the prospectus and did not even read it, but who relied on the statement of the company's managing director that it was "all right," was liable for its untrue statements.

. . . .

Section 11 imposes liability in the first instance upon a director, no matter how new he is. He is presumed to know his responsibility when he becomes a director. He can escape liability only by using that reasonable care to investigate the facts which a prudent man would employ in the management of his own property. In my opinion, a prudent man would not act in an important matter without any knowledge of the relevant facts, in sole reliance upon representations of persons who are comparative strangers and upon general information which does not purport to cover the particular case. To say that such minimal conduct measures up to the statutory standard would, to all intents and purposes, absolve new directors from responsibility merely because they are new. This is not a sensible construction of Section 11, when one bears in mind its fundamental purpose of requiring full and truthful disclosure for the protection of investors.

I find and conclude that Auslander has not established his due diligence defense with respect to the misstatements and omissions in those portions of the prospectus other than the audited 1960 figures.

. . . .

Grant

Grant became a director of BarChris in October 1960. His law firm was counsel to BarChris in matters pertaining to the registration of securities. Grant drafted the registration statement for the stock issue in 1959 and for the warrants in January 1961. He also drafted the registration statement for the debentures. In the preliminary division of work between him and Ballard, the underwriters' counsel, Grant took initial responsibility for preparing the registration statement, while Ballard devoted his efforts in the first instance to preparing the indenture.

Grant is sued as a director and as a signer of the registration statement. This is not an action against him for malpractice in his capacity as a lawyer. Nevertheless, in considering Grant's due diligence defenses, the unique position which he occupied cannot be disregarded. As the director most directly concerned with writing the registration statement and assuring its accuracy, more was required of him in the way of reasonable investigation than could fairly be expected of a director who had no connection with this work.

. . . .

It is claimed that a lawyer is entitled to rely on the statements of his client and that to require him to verify their accuracy would set an unreasonably high standard. This is too broad a generalization. It is all a matter of degree. To require an audit would obviously be unreasonable. On the other hand, to require a check of matters easily verifiable is not unreasonable. Even honest clients can make mistakes. The statute imposes liability for untrue statements regardless of whether they are intentionally untrue. The way to prevent mistakes is to test oral information by examining the original written record.

There were things which Grant could readily have checked which he did not check. For example, he was unaware of the provisions of the agreements between BarChris and Talcott. He never read them. . . .

As to the backlog figure, Grant appreciated that scheduled unfilled orders on the company's books meant firm commitments, but he never asked to see the contracts which, according to the prospectus, added up to $6,905,000. Thus, he did not know that this figure was overstated by some $4,490,000.

. . . On the subject of minutes, Grant knew that minutes of certain meetings of the BarChris executive committee held in 1961 had not been written up. . . .

Grant was entitled to rely on Peat, Marwick for the 1960 [audited] figures. He had no reasonable ground to believe them to be inaccurate. But the matters which I have mentioned were not within the expertised portion of the prospectus. As to this, Grant, was obliged to make a reasonable investigation. I am forced to find that he did not make one. After making all due allowances for the fact that Bar Chris's officers misled him, there are too many instances in which Grant failed to make an inquiry which he could easily have made which, if pursued, would have put him on his guard. In my opinion, this finding on the evidence in this case does not establish an unreasonably high standard in other cases for company counsel who are also directors. Each case must rest on its own facts. I conclude that Grant has not established his due diligence defenses except as to the audited 1960 figures.

The Underwriters and Coleman

The underwriters other than Drexel made no investigation of the accuracy of the prospectus. . . . [The other underwriters] all relied upon Drexel as the "lead" underwriter. Drexel did make an investigation. The work was in charge of Coleman, a partner of the firm, assisted by Casperson, an associate. Drexel's attorneys acted as attorneys for the entire group of underwriters. Ballard did the work, assisted by Stanton [a junior associate].

On April 17, 1961 Coleman became a director of BarChris. He signed the first amendment to the registration statement filed on May 11 and the second amendment, constituting the registration statement in its final form, filed on May 16. He thereby assumed a responsibility as a director and signer in addition to his responsibility as an underwriter.

. . . .

After Coleman was elected a director on April 17, 1961, he made no further independent investigation of the accuracy of the prospectus. He assumed that Ballard was taking care of this on his behalf as well as on behalf of the underwriters.

In April 1961 Ballard instructed Stanton to examine BarChris's minutes for the past five years and also to look at "the major contracts of the company."[1] Stanton went to BarChris's office for that purpose on April 24. He asked Birnbaum for the minute books. He read the minutes of the board of directors and discovered interleaved in them a few minutes of executive committee meetings in 1960. He asked Kircher if there were any others. Kircher said that there had been other executive committee meetings but that the minutes had not been written up.

Stanton read the minutes of a few BarChris subsidiaries. His testimony was vague as to which ones. . . . Stanton was a very junior associate. He had been admitted to the bar in January 1961, some three months before. This was the first registration statement he had ever worked on.

As to the "major contracts," all that Stanton could remember seeing was an insurance policy. Birnbaum told him that there was no file of major contracts. Stanton did not examine the agreements with Talcott. He did not examine the contracts with customers. He did not look to see what contracts comprised the backlog figure. Stanton examined no accounting records of BarChris. His visit, which lasted one day, was devoted primarily to reading the directors' minutes.

On April 25 Ballard wrote to Grant about certain matters which Stanton had noted on his visit to BarChris the day before, none of which Ballard considered "very earth shaking." . . .

. . . .

---

[1] [This footnote has been moved to the text. — Eds.]

Ballard did not insist that the executive committee minutes be written up so that he could inspect them, although he testified that he knew from experience that executive committee minutes may be extremely important. If he had insisted, he would have found the minutes highly informative. . . .

Ballard did not examine BarChris's contracts with Talcott. He did not appreciate what Talcott's rights were under those financing agreements or how serious the effect would be upon BarChris of any exercise of those rights.

Ballard did not investigate the composition of the backlog figure to be sure that it was not "puffy." He made no inquiry after March about any new officers' loans . . . . He was unaware of the seriousness of BarChris's cash position and of how BarChris's officers intended to use a large part of the proceeds. . . .

Like Grant, Ballard, without checking, relied on the information which he got from Kircher. He also relied on Grant who, as company counsel, presumably was familiar with its affairs.

The formal opinion which Ballard's firm rendered to the underwriters at the closing on May 24, 1961 made clear that this is what he had done. The opinion stated ([italics] supplied):

> In the course of the preparation of the Registration Statement and Prospectus by the Company, we have had numerous conferences with representatives of and counsel for the Company and with its auditors and we have raised many questions regarding the business of the Company. Satisfactory answers to such questions were in each case given us, and all other information and documents we requested have been supplied. *We are of the opinion that the data presented to us* are accurately reflected in the Registration Statement and Prospectus and that there has been omitted from the Registration Statement no material facts included in such data. *Although we have not otherwise verified the completeness or accuracy of the information furnished to us,* on the basis of the foregoing and with the exception of the financial statements and schedules (which this opinion does not pass upon), we have no reason to believe that the Registration Statement or Prospectus contains any untrue statement of any material fact or omits to state a material fact required to be stated therein or necessary in order to make the statements therein not misleading.

Coleman testified that Drexel had an understanding with its attorneys that "we expect them to inspect on our behalf the corporate records of the company including, but not limited to, the minutes of the corporation, the stockholders and the committees of the board authorized to act for the board." Ballard manifested his awareness of this understanding by sending Stanton to read the minutes and the major contracts. It is difficult to square this understanding with the formal opinion of Ballard's firm which expressly disclaimed any attempt to verify information supplied by the company and its counsel.

In any event, it is clear that no effectual attempt at verification was made. The question is whether due diligence required that it be made. Stated another way, is it sufficient to ask questions, to obtain answers which, if true, would be thought satisfactory, and to let it go at that, without seeking to ascertain from the records whether the answers in fact are true and complete?

I have already held that this procedure is not sufficient in Grant's case. Are underwriters in a different position, as far as due diligence is concerned?

The underwriters say that the prospectus is the company's prospectus, not theirs. Doubtless this is the way they customarily regard it. But the Securities Act makes no such distinction. The underwriters are just as responsible as the company if the prospectus is false. And prospective investors rely upon the reputation of the underwriters in deciding whether to purchase the securities.

. . . .

In a sense, the positions of the underwriter and the company's officers are adverse. It is not unlikely that statements made by company officers to an underwriter to induce him to underwrite may be self-serving. They may be unduly enthusiastic. As in this case, they may, on occasion, be deliberately false.

The purpose of Section 11 is to protect investors. To that end the underwriters are made responsible for the truth of the prospectus. If they may escape that responsibility by taking at face value representations made to them by the company's management, then the inclusion of underwriters among those liable under § 11 affords the investors no additional protection. To effectuate the statute's purpose, the phrase "reasonable investigation" must be construed to require more effort on the part of the underwriters than the mere accurate reporting in the prospectus of "data presented" to them by the company. It should make no difference that this data is elicited by questions addressed to the company officers by the underwriters, or that the underwriters at the time believe that the company's officers are truthful and reliable. In order to make the underwriters' participation in this enterprise of any value to the investors, the underwriters must make some reasonable attempt to verify the data submitted to them. They may not rely solely on the company's officers or on the company's counsel. A prudent man in the management of his own property would not rely on them.

It is impossible to lay down a rigid rule suitable for every case defining the extent to which such verification must go. It is a question of degree, a matter of judgment in each case. In the present case, the underwriters' counsel made almost no attempt to verify management's representations. I hold that was insufficient.

On the evidence in this case, I find that the underwriters' counsel did not make a reasonable investigation of the truth of those portions of the prospectus which were not made on the authority of Peat, Marwick as an expert. Drexel is bound by their failure. It is not a matter of relying upon counsel for legal advice. Here the attorneys were dealing with matters of fact. Drexel delegated to them, as its agent, the business of examining the corporate minutes and contracts. It must bear the consequences of their failure to make an adequate examination.

The other underwriters, who did nothing and relied solely on Drexel and on the lawyers, are also bound by it. It follows that although Drexel and the other underwriters believed that those portions of the prospectus were true, they had no reasonable ground for that belief, within the meaning of the statute. Hence, they have not established their due diligence defense, except as to the 1960 audited figures.

The same conclusions must apply to Coleman. Although he participated quite actively in the earlier stages of the preparation of the prospectus, and contributed questions and warnings of his own, in addition to the questions of counsel, the fact is that he stopped his participation toward the end of March 1961. He made no investigation after he became a director. When it came to verification, he relied upon his counsel to do it for him. Since counsel failed to do it, Coleman is bound by that failure. Consequently, in his case also, he has not established his due diligence defense except as to the audited 1960 figures.

Peat, Marwick

Section 11(b) provides:

> Notwithstanding the provisions of subsection (a) no person . . . shall be liable as provided therein who shall sustain the burden of proof —
>
> . . . .
>
> (3) that . . . (B) as regards any part of the registration statement purporting to be made upon his authority as an expert . . . (i) he had, after reasonable investigation, reasonable ground to believe and did believe, at the time such part of the registration statement became effective, that the statements therein were true and that there was no omission to state a material fact required to be stated therein or necessary to make the

statements therein not misleading. . . .

This defines the due diligence defense for an expert. Peat, Marwick has pleaded it.

The part of the registration statement purporting to be made upon the authority of Peat, Marwick as an expert was, as we have seen, the 1960 figures. But because the statute requires the court to determine Peat, Marwick's belief, and the grounds thereof, "at the time such part of the registration statement became effective," for the purposes of this affirmative defense, the matter must be viewed as of May 16, 1961, [which was the registration statement's effective date] and the question is whether at that time Peat, Marwick, after reasonable investigation, had reasonable ground to believe and did believe that the 1960 figures were true and that no material fact had been omitted from the registration statement which should have been included in order to make the 1960 figures not misleading. In deciding this issue, the court must consider not only what Peat, Marwick did in its 1960 audit, but also what it did in its subsequent "S-1 review." The proper scope of that review must also be determined.

. . . .

The 1960 Audit

Peat, Marwick's work [concerning BarChris] was in . . . charge of a member of the firm, Cummings, and more immediately in charge of Peat, Marwick's manager, Logan. Most of the actual work was performed by a senior accountant, Berardi, who had junior assistants, one of whom was Kennedy.

. . . .

It is unnecessary to recount everything that Berardi did in the course of the audit. We are concerned only with the evidence relating to what Berardi did or did not do with respect to those items which I have found to have been incorrectly reported in the 1960 figures in the prospectus. More narrowly, we are directly concerned only with such of those items as I have found to be material.

. . . .

The burden of proof on this issue is on Peat, Marwick. Although the question is a rather close one, I find that Peat, Marwick has not sustained that burden. Peat, Marwick has not proved that Berardi made a reasonable investigation . . . and that his ignorance of the true facts was justified.

B.   SECTION 10(b) OF THE SECURITIES EXCHANGE ACT

The following material focuses on § 10(b) of the Securities Exchange Act and Rule 10b-5 promulgated thereunder by the SEC (as well as certain related issues). Generally, the antifraud provisions of the securities acts were designed to protect investors, to help ensure fair dealing in the securities markets, and to promote ethical business practices. Consistent with these objectives, § 10(b) makes it unlawful to employ deceptive or manipulative devices "in connection with the purchase or sale of any security." As enacted by Congress, § 10(b) was designed to be a "catch-all" provision and, as such, it encompasses a broad range of practices.

The language of § 10(b) does not create an express private remedy for its violation. Neither does the legislative history reveal that Congress intended to create a private right of action under the statute at the time of its passage. Nonetheless, the federal courts have routinely recognized the existence of a private remedy under § 10(b). As the Supreme Court has recognized, "[t]he existence of this implied remedy is simply beyond peradventure." [2]

In order to establish a successful claim under § 10(b), a plaintiff must prove certain elements. A number of these elements are explored in depth in this Chapter. These

---

[2]   Herman & MacLean v. Huddleston, 459 U.S. 375, 380 (1983).

elements include that the plaintiff must establish (by proof of the preponderance of the evidence):

(1) Establish the *requisite jurisdictional means.* This requirement is normally met without difficulty. For example, as one appellate court has pointed out, "proof of intrastate telephonic messages in connection with the employment of deceptive devices or contrivances is sufficient to confer jurisdiction in a § 10(b) and Rule 10b-5 action."[3]

(2) Have the status as a *purchaser or seller* of the subject securities. Note that the defendant need not be a purchaser or seller.[4]

(3) Prove *"manipulation" or "deception"* and not "merely" breach of fiduciary duty.[5]

(4) Show that a misstatement or nondisclosure of fact is *material,* signifying that a reasonable investor would consider such information important in making an investment decision. The investor need not show that the misstatement or nondisclosure, if accurately disclosed, would have changed the investment decision. Hence, to satisfy the materiality requirement, "there must be a substantial likelihood that the disclosure of the omitted fact would have been viewed by the reasonable investor as having significantly altered the 'total mix' of information made available."[6] Moreover, in the merger context as well as other situations involving uncertain events, the probability/ magnitude standard has been applied. Under this standard, the existence of materiality depends "at any given time upon a balancing of both the indicated probability that the event will occur and the anticipated magnitude of the event in light of the totality of the company activity." [7]

(5) Establish that the defendant acted with *"scienter,"* signifying knowing or intentional misconduct.[8]

(6) Where called for, show that the plaintiff *relied* on the alleged misrepresentation and exercised *due diligence.*[9]

(7) Establish *causation* between the defendant's wrongful conduct and the plaintiff's loss.[10]

(8) Related to the causation requirement, prove that the manipulative or deceptive practice was *"in connection with"* the purchase or sale of a security. Generally, in order to meet this requirement, the proscribed conduct must be integral to the purchase or sale of the security.[11]

---

[3]   Loveridge v. Dreagoux, 678 F.2d 870, 874 (10th Cir. 1982).

[4]   *See* Blue Chip Stamps v. Manor Drug Stores, 421 U.S. 723 (1975); *Accord,* The Wharf (Holdings) Limited v. United International Holdings, Inc., 532 U.S. 588 (2001).

[5]   *See* Santa Fe Industries, Inc. v. Green, 430 U.S. 462 (1977).

[6]   Basic, Inc. v. Levinson, 485 U.S. 224, 232 (1988), *quoting,* TSC Industries, Inc. v. Northway, Inc., 426 U.S. 438, 449 (1976).

[7]   SEC v. Texas Gulf Sulphur Co., 401 F.2d 833, 849 (2d Cir.) (en banc), *cert. denied,* 394 U.S. 976 (1969), *quoted in,* Basic, Inc. v. Levinson, 485 U.S. 224, 238 (1988). *See also* SEC Staff Accounting Bulletin No. 99, 64 Fed. Reg. 45150 (1999) (opining that "exclusive reliance on certain quantitative benchmarks to assess materiality in preparing financial statements and performing audits of those financial statements is inappropriate").

[8]   *See* Aaron v. SEC, 446 U.S. 680 (1980); Ernst & Ernst v. Hochfelder, 425 U.S. 185 (1976).

[9]   *See* Basic, Inc. v. Levinson, 485 U.S. 224 (1988); Affiliated Ute Citizens v. United States, 406 U.S. 128 (1972).

[10]   *See* Dura Pharmaceuticals, Inc. v. Broudo, 544 U.S. 336 (2005). Section 21D(b)(4) of the Exchange Act expressly provides that the plaintiff must prove loss causation in any private action arising under the Exchange Act. *See generally* Fox, *Understanding* Dura, 60 Bus. Law. 1547 (2005); Kaufman, *Loss Causation Revisited,* 32 Sec. Reg. L.J. 357 (2004). In *Dura,* the Supreme Court held that plaintiffs in an action seeking damages under § 10(b) must "allege and prove the traditional elements of causation and loss." 544 U.S. at 346.

[11]   *See* SEC v. Zandford, 535 U.S. 813 (2002) (holding that because "the SEC complaint describes a

(9) Where liability is based upon *silence*, establish that the alleged primary violator had a *duty to disclose*.[12]

(10) Prove the extent of *damages* suffered.[13]

In addition, the plaintiff must bring its action within the applicable *statute of limitations* which is two years after the violation was (or, pursuant to the prevailing view, should have been) discovered by the plaintiff and in no event more than five years after the violation.[14]

Note moreover that the plaintiff also *must plead fraud with particularity* in its Section 10(b) cause of action. Rule 9(b) of the Federal Rules of Civil Procedure provides: "In all averments of fraud or mistake, the circumstances constituting fraud or mistake shall be stated with particularity. Malice, intent, knowledge, and other condition of mind of a person may be averred generally."[15] As applied in the securities law context, Section 21D(b) of the Exchange Act generally requires that a plaintiff must specifically plead each alleged misrepresentation or nondisclosure and why such is misleading, and must allege specific facts as to each such disclosure deficiency supporting a "strong inference" that the subject defendant knew that the misstatement or omission was false. Accordingly, under this pleading requirement, as held by the Supreme Court, "[a] complaint will survive . . . only if a reasonable person would deem the inference of scienter cogent and at least as compelling as any opposing inference one could draw from the facts alleged."[16]

Also, only primary violators are liable in private actions under Section 10(b). In *Central Bank of Denver v. First Interstate Bank of Denver*, the Supreme Court held that in private actions Section 10(b) liability may not be imposed against aiders and abettors. Nonetheless, the SEC may institute enforcement actions against aiders and abettors for alleged violations of Section 10(b).[17]

The *defendant* may assert a number of *defenses*, including *in pari delicto, laches*, and *waiver*.[18]

With respect to *indemnification*, because the Supreme Court has ruled that scienter (e.g., deliberate or perhaps reckless misconduct) is required to state a successful Section 10(b) (and Rule 10b-5) claim under the Exchange Act,[19] it appears that indemnification would frustrate the public policy as well as the statutory underpinnings of the Act and therefore is prohibited in the Section 10(b) context.[20]

The right to *contribution* under Section 10(b) likewise has been resolved. In the

---

fraudulent scheme in which the securities transactions and breaches of fiduciary duty coincide . . . those breaches were therefore 'in connection with' securities sales within the meaning of § 10(b)"); Superintendent of Insurance v. Bankers Life & Casualty Co., 404 U.S. 6 (1971); Black, *The Second Circuit's Approach to the "In Connection With" Requirement of Rule 10b-5*, 53 BROOKLYN L. REV. 539 (1987); Fletcher, *The "In Connection With" Requirement of Rule 10b-5*, 16 PEPPERDINE L. REV. 913 (1989).

[12] See *Chiarella v. United States*, 445 U.S. 222 (1980), discussed in Chapter 13 *infra*.

[13] *See* M. KAUFMAN, SECURITIES LITIGATION: DAMAGES (2007); Thompson, *The Measure of Recovery Under Rule 10b-5: A Restitution Alternative to Tort Damages*, 37 VAND. L. REV. 349 (1984).

[14] *See* 28 U.S.C. § 1658(b) (as enacted pursuant to § 804 of the Sarbanes-Oxley Act).

[15] Rule 9(b) of the Federal Rules of Civil Procedure. *See* Wexner v. First Manhattan Co., 902 F.2d 169 (2d Cir. 1990).

[16] *See* Tellabs, Inc. v. Makor Issues & Rights, Ltd., 127 S. Ct. 2499, 2510 (2007).

[17] *See* § 20(e) of the Exchange Act (granting to the SEC authority to pursue aiders and abettors under the 1934 Act); Central Bank of Denver v. First Interstate Bank of Denver, 511 U.S. 164 (1994) (holding that aiders and abettors not subject to liability in § 10(b) private actions).

[18] *See* Bateman Eichler, Hill Richards, Inc. v. Berner, 472 U.S. 299 (1985); Hecht v. Harris, Upham & Co., 430 F.2d 1202 (9th Cir. 1970).

[19] See cases cited in note 8, *supra*.

[20] *See, e.g.*, Globus v. Law Research Serv., Inc., 418 F.2d 1276 (2d Cir. 1969).

Musick Peller decision, the Supreme Court recognized such a right to contribution under Section 10(b). In the 1995 legislation, Congress codified this right to contribution.[21]

PROBLEM

Kentach Labs, Inc., a high-tech concern with a brief operating history, had its first, and thus far only, public offering in February 2007 raising $60 million. The registration statement filed with the SEC contained, as is required, a "use of proceeds" section. Unknown to the accountants, counsel, and investment bankers, Kentach's "inside" directors (Stevens, Lyle, and Morris) anticipated that roughly 35% of the proceeds would be used to pay off prior debts rather than 90% of the proceeds going toward expansion of the business as the registration statement indicated.

Kentach assumed public reporting obligations pursuant to § 12(g) of the Exchange Act upon its conducting of the registered offering. Since the 2007 public offering, Kentach has timely filed annual and other periodic reports. The company, however, from 2007 through May 2008 never disclosed that 35% of the proceeds received from the offering were used to pay off prior debts. In June 2008, it was revealed that Stevens, Lyle, and Morris had "fudged" or "cooked" Kentach's financial records in order to hide the true use of the proceeds of the 2007 offering.

Kentach is still in business and solvent. The price of its stock, however, has decreased from its initial offering price of $11.00 in February 2007, to a price of $4.50 per share in June 2008. Later in June 2008, after public revelation of the true use of the proceeds, the price of the stock quickly dropped to $1.50 per share.

Nuval, an electronic engineer by trade, always is interested in expanding her stock portfolio. Although, she had never read or seen a Kentach shareholder or other report, she was somewhat familiar with the company through her profession and had a hunch that the stock was undervalued. In March 2008, she called her broker, Mondal, and asked her whether she knew of any information about the company. Mondal replied that she did not "follow" the company. Upon checking the research reports on the company, Mondal conjectured that Kentach's relatively low market price may have been due to the market's recognition of a disappointing earnings history and whether the company would achieve the growth that financial analysts had forecasted when the company went public. Nonetheless, Nuval in April 2008, without having read a Kentach shareholder or other report, decided to purchase 15,000 shares at $5.50 per share. In July 2008, she brings suit under § 10(b) of the federal securities laws (in a class action) against Kentach, Stevens, Lyle, Morris, and the accountants. The price of Kentach stock in July 2008 is $1.50 per share. What result?

---

[21] *See* Musick, Peeler & Garrett v. Employers Insurance of Wausau, 508 U.S. 286 (1993).

1. The "Deception" or "Manipulation" Requirement

SANTA FE INDUSTRIES, INC. v. GREEN
Supreme Court of the United States
430 U.S. 462, 97 S. Ct. 1292, 51 L. Ed. 2d 480 (1977)

Mr. Justice White delivered the opinion of the Court.

The issue in this case involves the reach and coverage of _ 10(b) of the Securities Exchange Act of 1934 and Rule 10b-5 thereunder in the context of a Delaware short-form merger transaction used by the majority stockholder of a corporation to eliminate the minority interest.

I

In 1936, petitioner Santa Fe Industries, Inc. (Santa Fe), acquired control of 60% of the stock of Kirby Lumber Corp. (Kirby), a Delaware corporation. Through a series of purchases over the succeeding years, Santa Fe increased its control of Kirby's stock to 95%; the purchase prices during the period 1968–1973 ranged from $65 to $92.50 per share. In 1974, wishing to acquire 100% ownership of Kirby, Santa Fe availed itself of _ 253 of the Delaware Corporation Law, known as the "short-form merger" statute. Section 253 permits a parent corporation owning at least 90% of the stock of a subsidiary to merge with that subsidiary, upon approval by the parent's board of directors, and to make payment in cash for the shares of the minority stockholders. The statute does not require the consent of, or advance notice to, the minority stockholders. However, notice of the merger must be given within 10 days after its effective date, and any stockholder who is dissatisfied with the terms of the merger may petition the Delaware Court of Chancery for a decree ordering the surviving corporation to pay him the fair value of his shares, as determined by a court-appointed appraiser subject to review by the court.

Santa Fe obtained independent appraisals of the physical assets of Kirby — land, timber, buildings, and machinery — and of Kirby's oil, gas, and mineral interests. These appraisals, together with other financial information, were submitted to Morgan Stanley & Co. (Morgan Stanley), an investment banking firm retained to appraise the fair market value of Kirby stock. Kirby's physical assets were appraised at $320 million (amounting to $640 for each of the 500,000 shares); Kirby's stock was valued by Morgan Stanley at $125 per share. Under the terms of the merger, minority stockholders were offered $150 per share.

The provisions of the short-form merger statute were fully complied with. The minority stockholders of Kirby were notified the day after the merger became effective and were advised of their right to obtain an appraisal in Delaware court if dissatisfied with the offer of $150 per share. They also received an information statement containing, in addition to the relevant financial data about Kirby, the appraisals of the value of Kirby's assets and the Morgan Stanley appraisal concluding that the fair market value of the stock was $125 per share.

Respondents, minority stockholders of Kirby, objected to the terms of the merger, but did not pursue their appraisal remedy in the Delaware Court of Chancery. Instead, they brought this action in federal court on behalf of the corporation and other minority stockholders, seeking to set aside the merger or to recover what they claimed to be the fair value of their shares. The amended complaint asserted that, based on the fair market value of Kirby's physical assets as revealed by the appraisal included in the information statement sent to minority shareholders, Kirby's stock was worth at least $772 per share. The complaint alleged further that the merger took place without prior notice to minority stockholders; that the purpose of the merger was to appropriate the difference between the "conceded pro rata value of the physical assets," and the offer of $150 per share — to "freez[e] out the minority stockholders at a wholly inadequate price," and that Santa Fe, knowing the appraised value of the physical assets, obtained a "fraudulent appraisal" of the stock from Morgan Stanley and offered $25 above that appraisal "in order to lull the minority stockholders into erroneously believing that [Santa Fe was] generous." This course of conduct was alleged to be "a violation of Rule 10b-5 because defendants employed a 'device, scheme, or artifice to defraud' and engaged in an 'act, practice or course of business which operates or would operate as a fraud or deceit upon any person, in connection with the purchase or sale of any security.'" . . .

The District Court dismissed the complaint for failure to state a claim upon which relief could be granted. . . .

. . . .

A divided Court of Appeals for the Second Circuit reversed. 533 F. 2d 1283 (1976). It first agreed that there was a double aspect to the case: first, the claim that gross undervaluation of the minority stock itself violated Rule 10b-5; and second, that "without any misrepresentation or failure to disclose relevant facts, the merger itself constitutes a violation of Rule 10b-5" because it was accomplished without any corporate purpose and without prior notice to the minority stockholders. . . . The Court of Appeals' view was that, although the Rule plainly reached material misrepresentations and nondisclosures in connection with the purchase or sale of securities, neither misrepresentation nor nondisclosure was a necessary element of a Rule 10b-5 action. . . .

We granted the petition for certiorari challenging this holding because of the importance of the issue involved to the administration of the federal securities laws. We reverse.

II

. . . .

To the extent that the Court of Appeals would rely on the use of the term "fraud" in Rule 10b-5 to bring within the ambit of the Rule all breaches of fiduciary duty in connection with a securities transaction, its interpretation would, like the interpretation rejected by the Court in *Ernst & Ernst*, "add a gloss to the operative language of the statute quite different from its commonly accepted meaning." . . .

The language of § 10(b) gives no indication that Congress meant to prohibit any conduct not involving manipulation or deception. Nor have we been cited to any evidence in the legislative history that would support a departure from the language of the statute. . . . Thus the claim of fraud and fiduciary breach in this complaint states a cause of action under any part of Rule 10b-5 only if the conduct alleged can be fairly viewed as "manipulative or deceptive" within the meaning of the statute.

III

It is our judgment that the transaction, if carried out as alleged in the complaint, was neither deceptive nor manipulative and therefore did not violate either § 10(b) of the Act or Rule 10b-5.

As we have indicated, the case comes to us on the premise that the complaint failed to allege a material misrepresentation or material failure to disclose. The finding of the District Court, undisturbed by the Court of Appeals, was that there was no "omission" or "misstatement" in the information statement accompanying the notice of merger. On the basis of the information provided, minority shareholders could either accept the price offered or reject it and seek an appraisal in the Delaware Court of Chancery. Their choice was fairly presented, and they were furnished with all relevant information on which to base their decision.[22]

. . . .

It is also readily apparent that the conduct alleged in the complaint was not "manipulative" within the meaning of the statute. "Manipulation" is "virtually a term of art when used in connection with securities markets." The term refers generally to practices, such as wash sales, matched orders, or rigged prices, that are intended to mislead investors by artificially affecting market activity. . . . Section 10(b)'s general prohibition of practices deemed by the SEC to be "manipulative" — in this technical sense of artificially affecting market activity in order to mislead investors — is fully consistent with the fundamental purpose of the 1934 Act "to substitute a philosophy of full disclosure for the philosophy of caveat emptor. . . . " Indeed, nondisclosure is usually essential to the success of a manipulative scheme. No doubt Congress meant to prohibit the full range of ingenious devices that might be used to manipulate securities prices. But we do not think it would have chosen this "term of art" if it had meant to bring within the scope of § 10(b) instances of corporate mismanagement such as this, in which the essence of the complaint is that shareholders were treated unfairly by a fiduciary.

IV

The language of the statute is, we think, "sufficiently clear in its context" to be dispositive here but even if it were not, there are additional considerations that weigh heavily against permitting a cause of action under Rule 10b-5 for the breach of corporate fiduciary duty alleged in this complaint. Congress did not expressly provide a private cause of action for violations of § 10(b). Although we have recognized an implied cause of action under that section in some circumstances, we have also recognized that a private cause of action under the antifraud provisions of the Securities Exchange Act should not be implied where it is "unnecessary to ensure the fulfillment of Congress' purposes" in adopting the Act. As we noted earlier, the Court repeatedly has described the "fundamental purpose" of the Act as implementing a "philosophy of full disclosure"; once full and fair disclosure has occurred, the fairness of the terms of the transaction is at most a tangential concern of the statute. As in *Cort v. Ash*, 422 U.S. 66, 80 (1975), we are reluctant to recognize a cause of action here to serve what is "at best a subsidiary purpose" of the federal legislation.

A second factor in determining whether Congress intended to create a federal cause of action in these circumstances is "whether 'the cause of action [is] one traditionally relegated to state law. . . . '" The Delaware Legislature has supplied minority shareholders with a cause of action in the Delaware Court of Chancery to recover the fair value of shares allegedly undervalued in a short-form merger. Of course, the existence of a particular state-law remedy is not dispositive of the question whether Congress meant to provide a similar federal remedy, but we conclude that "it is entirely appropriate in this instance to relegate respondent and others in his situation to whatever remedy is created by state law." . . .

The reasoning behind a holding that the complaint in this case alleged fraud under

---

[22] [14] In addition to their principal argument that the complaint alleges a fraud under clauses (a) and (c) of Rule 10b-5, respondents also argue that the complaint alleges nondisclosure and misrepresentation in violation of clause (b) of the Rule. Their major contention in this respect is that the majority stockholder's failure to give the minority advance notice of the merger was a material nondisclosure, even though the Delaware short-form merger statute does not require such notice. . . . But respondents do not indicate how they might have acted differently had they had prior notice of the merger. Indeed, they accept the conclusion of both courts below that under Delaware law they could not have enjoined the merger because an appraisal proceeding is their sole remedy in the Delaware courts for any alleged unfairness in the terms of the merger. Thus, the failure to give advance notice was not a material nondisclosure within the meaning of the statute or the Rule. . . .

Rule 10b-5 could not be easily contained. It is difficult to imagine how a court could distinguish, for purposes of Rule 10b-5 fraud, between a majority stockholder's use of a short-form merger to eliminate the minority at an unfair price and the use of some other device, such as a long-form merger, tender offer, or liquidation, to achieve the same result; or indeed how a court could distinguish the alleged abuses in these going private transactions from other types of fiduciary self-dealing involving transactions in securities. The result would be to bring within the Rule a wide variety of corporate conduct traditionally left to state regulation. In addition to posing a "danger of vexatious litigation which could result from a widely expanded class of plaintiffs under Rule 10b-5," *Blue Chip Stamps v. Manor Drug Stores*, 421 U.S., at 740, this extension of the federal securities laws would overlap and quite possibly interfere with state corporate law. Federal courts applying a "federal fiduciary principle" under Rule 10b-5 could be expected to depart from state fiduciary standards at least to the extent necessary to ensure uniformity within the federal system. Absent a clear indication of congressional intent, we are reluctant to federalize the substantial portion of the law of corporations that deals with transactions in securities, particularly where established state policies of corporate regulation would be overridden. As the Court stated in *Cort v. Ash*: "Corporations are creatures of state law, and investors commit their funds to corporate directors on the understanding that, except where federal law expressly requires certain responsibilities of directors with respect to stockholders, state law will govern the internal affairs of the corporation."

We thus adhere to the position that "Congress by § 10(b) did not seek to regulate transactions which constitute no more than internal corporate mismanagement." . . . There may well be a need for uniform federal fiduciary standards to govern mergers such as that challenged in this complaint. But those standards should not be supplied by judicial extension of § 10(b) and Rule 10b-5 to "cover the corporate universe."[23]

The judgment of the Court of Appeals is reversed, and the case is remanded for further proceedings consistent with this opinion.

So ordered.

Mr. Justice Brennan dissents and would affirm for substantially the reasons stated in the majority and concurring opinions in the Court of Appeals, 533 F.2d 1283 (CA2 1976).

2. Materiality

Materiality under the federal securities laws signifies that the misstated or omitted fact, if accurately disclosed, would have been considered important by a reasonable investor in making his or her voting or investment decision. As stated by the Supreme Court:

> An omitted [or misstated] fact is material if there is a substantial likelihood that a reasonable shareholder would consider it important in deciding how to [invest or] vote. . . . It does not require proof of a substantial likelihood that disclosure of the [misstated or] omitted fact would have caused the reasonable investor to change his [mind]. What the standard does contemplate is a showing of a substantial likelihood that, under all circumstances, the [misstated or] omitted fact would have assumed actual significance in the deliberations of the

---

[23] Cary, *Federalism and Corporate Law: Reflections Upon Delaware*, 83 Yale L.J. 663, 700 (1974) (footnote omitted). Professor Cary argues vigorously for comprehensive federal fiduciary standards, but urges a "frontal" attack by a new federal statute rather than an extension of Rule 10b-5. He writes: "It seems anomalous to jig-saw every kind of corporate dispute into the federal courts through the securities acts as they are presently written."

reasonable shareholder. . . . [T]here must be a substantial likelihood that the disclosure of the [misstated or] omitted fact would have been viewed by the reasonable investor as having significantly altered the total mix of the information available. [*TSC Industries, Inc. v. Northway, Inc.*, 426 U.S. 438, 449 (1976).]

At times, a subject event or circumstance may give rise to difficult materiality determinations. For example, the probability and magnitude in regard to the consummation of certain corporate developments, such as the successful completion of merger negotiations, may be "contingent or speculative in nature."[24] To ascertain whether such contingent developments are material, the probability/magnitude test is utilized. This test postulates that materiality "will depend at any given time upon a balancing of both the indicated probability that the event will occur and the anticipated magnitude of the event in light of the totality of the company activity." [25]

During the past decade, attention has focused on whether materiality is based on solely quantitative valuations. For example, one traditionally followed approach is that if a misrepresentation or omission is less than five percent of the value being assessed, then such disclosure deficiency is not material, absent the presence of self-dealing or similar misconduct.[26] A number of courts continue to adopt this approach. [27] Nonetheless, the prevailing view today embraces the concept of qualitative economic materiality. For example, the SEC staff in Staff Accounting Bulletin (SAB) 99 set forth the following list of considerations that may result in a quantitatively "small" misstatement of a financial statement item being deemed "material":

- Whether the misstatement arises from an item capable of precise measurement or whether it arises from an estimate and, if so, the degree of imprecision inherent in the estimate;

- Whether the misstatement masks a change in earnings or other trends;

- Whether the misstatement hides a failure to meet analysts' consensus expectations for the enterprise;

- Whether the misstatement changes a loss into income or vice versa;

- Whether the misstatement concerns a segment or other portion of the registrant's business that has been identified as playing a significant role in the registrant's operations or profitability;

- Whether the misstatement affects the registrants' compliance with regulatory requirements;

- Whether the misstatement affects the registrant's compliance with loan covenants or other contractual requirements;

- Whether the misstatement has the effect of increasing management's compensation, for example, by satisfying requirements for the award of bonuses or other forms of incentive compensation; and

- Whether the misstatement involves concealment of an unlawful transaction.[28]

Several courts have applied qualitative economic materiality principles to both narrative and financial statement disclosure, thereby rejecting a rigid numerical formula (e.g., less than five percent).[29] According to this view, "[a]ny approach that designates a

---

[24] Basic Inc. v. Levinson, 485 U.S. at 224, 232 (1998).

[25] *Id.* at 238, *citing*, SEC v. Texas Gulf Sulphur Co., 401 F.2d 833 (2d Cir. 1968).

[26] As discussed in Staff Accounting Bulletin (SAB) 99, 64 Fed. Reg. 45,150 (1999).

[27] *See, e.g., In re* SCB Computer Technology, Inc., Securities Litigation, 149 F. Supp. 2d 334 (W.D. Tenn. 2001) (holding misstatements of revenue of less than three percent not material); SEC v. Hoover, 903 F. Supp. 1135 (S.D. Tex. 1995) (holding misstatement of three percent not material).

[28] SAB 99, note 26 *supra*.

[29] *See, e.g.,* Helwig v. Vencor, Inc., 251 F.3d 540 (6th Cir. 2001); Ganino v. Citizens Utilities Co., 228 F.3d

single fact or occurrence as always determinative of an inherently fact-specific finding, such as materiality, must necessarily be overinclusive or underinclusive."[30]

3. The Reliance Requirement

Proof of reliance normally is required to help prove the causal connection between the defendants's wrongdoing and the complainant's loss. Positive proof of reliance has not been demanded of the plaintiff where unnecessary to show causation. In such instances, upon demonstrating materiality (e.g., of the nondisclosure), the complainant enjoys a presumption of reliance which the defendant can rebut (e.g., by showing that the plaintiff would not have acted differently had he/she known of the nondisclosure). As the Supreme Court stated in *Affiliated Ute Citizens v. United States*, 406 U.S. 128, 153–54 (1972):

> Under the circumstances of this case involving primarily a failure to disclose, positive proof of reliance is not a prerequisite to recovery. All that is necessary is that the facts withheld be material in the sense that a reasonable investor [would] have considered them important in the making of this decision. . . . This obligation to disclose and this withholding of a material fact establish the requisite element of causation in fact.

Hence, in cases involving primarily a failure to disclose, the plaintiff's reliance is presumed. On the other hand, in cases of misrepresentation, reliance must be proven by the plaintiff.

Plaintiffs also may enjoy a presumption of reliance by invoking the "fraud on the market" theory. This theory postulates that investors assume that the market price of a security traded in an efficient market is determined by the available material information and that no unsuspected fraudulent conduct has affected the price. The use of this theory to apply a rebuttable presumption of reliance received Supreme Court approbation in the following case — *Basic, Inc. v. Levinson*.

BASIC, INC. v. LEVINSON
Supreme Court of the United States
485 U.S. 224, 108 S. Ct. 978, 99 L. Ed. 2d 194 (1988)

JUSTICE BLACKMUN delivered the opinion of the Court.

This case requires us to apply the materiality requirement of § 10(b) of the Securities Exchange Act of 1934 and the Securities and Exchange Commission's Rule 10b-5 in the context of preliminary corporate merger discussions. We must also determine whether a person who traded a corporation's shares on a securities exchange after the issuance of a materially misleading statement by the corporation may invoke a rebuttable presumption that, in trading, he relied on the integrity of the price set by the market.

I

Prior to December 20, 1978, Basic Incorporated was a publicly traded company primarily engaged in the business of manufacturing chemical refractories for the steel industry. As early as 1965 or 1966, Combustion Engineering, Inc., a company producing mostly alumina-based refractories, expressed some interest in acquiring Basic, but was deterred from pursuing this inclination seriously because of antitrust concerns it then entertained. In 1976, however, regulatory action opened the way to a renewal of Combustion's interest. . . .

Beginning in September 1976, Combustion representatives had meetings and telephone conversations with Basic officers and directors, including petitioners here,

---

154 (2d Cir. 2000); Holmes v. Baker, 166 F. Supp. 2d 1362 (S.D. Fla. 2001).

[30] *Ganino*, 228 F.3d at 162, *quoting Basic*, 485 U.S. at 236.

concerning the possibility of a merger. During 1977 and 1978, Basic made three public statements denying that it was engaged in merger negotiations. On December 18, 1978, Basic asked the New York Stock Exchange to suspend trading in its shares and issued a release stating that it had been "approached" by another company concerning a merger. On December 19, Basic's board endorsed Combustion's offer of $46 per share for its common stock, and on the following day publicly announced its approval of Combustion's tender offer for all outstanding shares.

Respondents are former Basic shareholders who sold their stock after Basic's first public statement of October 21, 1977, and before the suspension of trading in December 1978. Respondents brought a class action against Basic and its directors, asserting that the defendants issued three false or misleading public statements and thereby were in violation of § 10(b) of the 1934 Act and of Rule 10b-5. Respondents alleged that they were injured by selling Basic shares at artificially depressed prices in a market affected by petitioners' misleading statements and in reliance thereon.

The District Court adopted a presumption of reliance by members of the plaintiff class upon petitioners' public statements that enabled the court to conclude that common questions of fact or law predominated over particular questions pertaining to individual plaintiffs. See Fed. Rule Civ. Proc. 23(b)(3). The District Court therefore certified respondents' class. . . .

The United States Court of Appeals for the Sixth Circuit affirmed the class certification. . . .

The Court of Appeals joined a number of other circuits in accepting the "fraud-on-the-market theory" to create a rebuttable presumption that respondents relied on petitioners' material misrepresentations, noting that without the presumption it would be impractical to certify a class under Fed. Rule Civ. Proc. 23(b)(3).

We granted certiorari to resolve the split among the Courts of Appeals as to the standard of materiality applicable to preliminary merger discussions, and to determine whether the courts below properly applied a presumption of reliance in certifying the class, rather than requiring each class member to show direct reliance on Basic's statements.

. . . .

IV

A

We turn to the question of reliance and the fraud-on-the-market theory. Succinctly put:

> The fraud on the market theory is based on the hypothesis that, in an open and developed securities market, the price of a company's stock is determined by the available material information regarding the company and its business. . . . Misleading statements will therefore defraud purchasers of stock even if the purchasers do not directly rely on the misstatements. . . . The causal connection between the defendants' fraud and the plaintiffs' purchase of stock in such a case is no less significant than in a case of direct reliance on misrepresentations. *Peil v. Speiser*, 806 F.2d 1154, 1160–1161 (CA3 1986).

Our task, of course, is not to assess the general validity of the theory, but to consider whether it was proper for the courts below to apply a rebuttable presumption of reliance, supported in part by the fraud-on-the-market theory.

This case required resolution of several common questions of law and fact concerning the falsity or misleading nature of the three public statements made by Basic, the presence or absence of scienter, and the materiality of the misrepresentations, if any. In their amended complaint, the named plaintiffs alleged that in reliance on Basic's statements they sold their shares of Basic stock in the depressed market created by petitioners. . . . Requiring proof of individualized reliance from each member of the proposed plaintiff class effectively would have prevented respondents from proceeding with a class action, since individual issues then would have overwhelmed the common ones. The District Court found that the presumption of reliance created by the fraud-on-the-market theory provided "a practical resolution to the problem of balancing the substantive requirement of proof of reliance in securities cases against the procedural requisites of [Fed. Rule Civ. Proc.] 23." The District Court thus concluded that with reference to each public statement and its impact upon the open market for Basic shares, common questions predominated over individual questions, as required by Fed. Rule Civ. Proc. 23(a)(2) and (b)(3).

Petitioners and their *amici* complain that the fraud-on-the-market theory effectively eliminates the requirement that a plaintiff asserting a claim under Rule 10b-5 prove reliance. They note that reliance is and long has been an element of common-law fraud, see e.g., *Restatement (Second) of Torts* § 525 (1977); Prosser and Keeton on The Law of Torts § 108 (5th ed. 1984), and argue that because the analogous express right of action includes a reliance requirement, § 18(a) of the 1934 Act, . . . so too must an action implied under § 10(b).

We agree that reliance is an element of a Rule 10b-5 cause of action. . . . Reliance provides the requisite causal connection between a defendant's misrepresentation and a plaintiff's injury. . . . There is, however, more than one way to demonstrate the causal connection. Indeed, we previously have dispensed with a requirement of positive proof of reliance, where a duty to disclose material information had been breached, concluding that the necessary nexus between the plaintiff's injury and the defendant's wrongful conduct had been established. See *Affiliated Ute Citizens v. United States*, 406 U.S. at 153–154 [1972]. . . .

The modern securities markets, literally involving millions of shares changing hands daily, differ from the face-to-face transactions contemplated by early fraud cases, and our understanding of Rule 10b-5's reliance requirement must encompass these differences.

> In face-to-face transactions, the inquiry into an investor's reliance upon information is into the subjective pricing of that information by that investor. With the presence of a market, the market is interposed between seller and buyer and, ideally, transmits information to the investor in the processed form of a market price. Thus the market is performing a substantial part of the valuation process performed by the investor in a face-to-face transaction. The market is acting as the unpaid agent of the investor, informing him that given all the information available to it, the value of the stock is worth the market price. *In re LTV Securities Litigation*, 88 F.R.D. 134, 143 (N.D. Tex. 1980).

. . . .

B

Presumptions typically serve to assist courts in managing circumstances in which direct proof, for one reason or another, is rendered difficult. The courts below accepted a presumption, created by the fraud-on-the-market theory and subject to rebuttal by petitioners, that persons who had traded Basic shares had done so in reliance on the integrity of the price set by the market, but because of petitioners' material misrepresentations that price had been fraudulently depressed. Requiring a plaintiff to show a speculative state of facts, *i.e.*, how he would have acted if omitted material information had been disclosed . . . or if the misrepresentation had not been made, . . . would place an unnecessarily unrealistic evidentiary burden on the Rule 10b-5 plaintiff who has traded on an impersonal market.

Arising out of considerations of fairness, public policy, and probability, as well as judicial economy, presumptions are also useful devices for allocating the burdens of proof between parties. . . . The presumption of reliance employed in this case is consistent with, and, by facilitating Rule 10b-5 litigation, supports, the congressional policy embodied in the 1934 Act. In drafting that Act, Congress expressly relied on the premise that securities markets are affected by information, and enacted legislation to facilitate an investor's reliance on the integrity of those markets:

> No investor, no speculator, can safely buy and sell securities upon the exchanges without having an intelligent basis for forming his judgment as to the value of the securities he buys or sells. The idea of a free and open public market is built upon the theory that competing judgments of buyers and sellers as to the fair price of a security brings [sic] about a situation where the market price reflects as nearly as possible a just price. Just as artificial manipulation tends to upset the true function of an open market, so the hiding and secreting of important information obstructs the operation of the markets as indices of real value.

See *Lipton v. Documation, Inc.*, 734 F.2d 740, 748 (CA11 1984). . . .

The presumption is also supported by common sense and probability. Recent empirical studies have tended to confirm Congress' premise that the market price of shares traded on well-developed markets reflects all publicly available information, and, hence, any material misrepresentations. It has been noted that "it is hard to imagine that there ever is a buyer or seller who does not rely on market integrity. Who would knowingly roll the dice in a crooked crap game?". . . . Indeed, nearly every court that has considered the proposition has concluded that where materially misleading statements have been disseminated into an impersonal, well-developed market for securities, the reliance of individual plaintiffs on the integrity of the market price may be presumed. Commentators generally have applauded the adoption of one variation or another of the fraud-on-the-market theory. An investor who buys or sells stock at the price set by the market does so in reliance on the integrity of that price. Because most publicly available information is reflected in market price, an investor's reliance on any public material misrepresentations, therefore, may be presumed for purposes of a Rule 10b-5 action.

C

The Court of Appeals found that petitioners "made public, material misrepresentations and [respondents] sold Basic stock in an impersonal, efficient market. Thus the class, as defined by the district court, has established the threshold facts for proving their loss." 786 F.2d at 751. The court acknowledged that petitioners may rebut proof of the elements giving rise to the presumption, or show that the misrepresentation in fact did not lead to a distortion of price or that an individual plaintiff traded or would have traded despite his knowing the statement was false.

Any showing that severs the link between the alleged misrepresentation and either the price received (or paid) by the plaintiff, or his decision to trade at a fair market price, will be sufficient to rebut the presumption of reliance. For example, if petitioners could show that the "market makers" were privy to the truth about the merger discussions here with Combustion, and thus that the market price would not have been affected by their misrepresentations, the causal connection could be broken: the basis for finding that the fraud had been transmitted through market price would be gone. Similarly, if, despite petitioners' allegedly fraudulent attempt to manipulate market price, news of the merger discussions credibly entered the market and dissipated the effects of the misstatements, those who traded Basic shares after the corrective statements would have no direct or indirect connection with the fraud. Petitioners also could rebut the presumption of reliance as to plaintiffs who would have divested themselves of their

Basic shares without relying on the integrity of the market. For example, a plaintiff who believed that Basic's statements were false and that Basic was indeed engaged in merger discussions, and who consequently believed that Basic stock was artificially underpriced, but sold his shares nevertheless because of other unrelated concerns, *e.g.*, potential antitrust problems, or political pressures to divest shares of certain businesses, could not be said to have relied on the integrity of a price he knew had been manipulated.

V

In summary:

. . . .

5. It is not inappropriate to apply a presumption of reliance supported by the fraud-on-the-market theory.

6. That presumption, however, is rebuttable.

7. The District Court's certification of the class here was appropriate when made but is subject on remand to such adjustment, if any, as developing circumstances demand.

The judgment of the Court of Appeals is vacated and the case is remanded to that court for further proceedings consistent with this opinion.

It is so ordered.

THE CHIEF JUSTICE, JUSTICE SCALIA, and JUSTICE KENNEDY took no part in the consideration or decision of this case.

JUSTICE WHITE, with whom JUSTICE O'CONNOR joins, concurring in part and dissenting in part.

I join Parts I–III of the Court's opinion, as I agree that the standard of materiality we set forth in *TSC Industries* . . . should be applied to actions under § 10(b) and Rule 10b-5. But I dissent from the remainder of the Court's holding because I do not agree that the "fraud-on-the-market" theory should be applied in this case.

Even when compared to the relatively youthful private cause-of-action under § 10(b), see *Kardon v. National Gypsum Co.*, 69 F. Supp. 512 (E.D. Pa. 1946), the fraud-on-the-market theory is a mere babe. Yet today, the Court embraces this theory with the sweeping confidence usually reserved for more mature legal doctrines. In so doing, I fear that the Court's decision may have many adverse, unintended effects as it is applied and interpreted in the years to come.

. . . .

In general, the case law developed in this Court with respect to § 10(b) and Rule 10b-5 has been based on doctrines with which we, as judges, are familiar: common-law doctrines of fraud and deceit. . . . Even when we have extended civil liability under Rule 10b-5 to a broader reach than the common law had previously permitted, we have retained familiar legal principles as our guideposts. . . . The federal courts have proved adept at developing an evolving jurisprudence of Rule 10b-5 in such a manner. But with no staff economists, no experts schooled in the "efficient-capital-market hypothesis," no ability to test the validity of empirical market studies, we are not well equipped to embrace novel constructions of a statute based on contemporary microeconomic theory.

. . . [T]he Court today ventures into this area beyond its expertise, beyond — by its own admission — the confines of our previous fraud cases. Even if I agreed with the Court that "modern securities markets . . . involving millions of shares changing hands daily" require that the "understanding of Rule 10b-5's reliance requirement" be changed, I prefer that such changes come from Congress in amending § 10(b). The Congress, with its superior resources and expertise, is far better equipped than the federal courts for the task of determining how modern economic theory and global financial markets require that established legal notions of fraud be modified. In choosing to make these decisions itself, the Court, I fear, embarks on a course that it does not genuinely understand, giving rise to consequences it cannot foresee. For while the economists' theories which underpin the fraud-on-the-market presumption may have the appeal of mathematical exactitude and scientific certainty, they are — in the end — nothing more than theories which may or may not prove accurate upon further consideration. Even the most earnest advocates of economic analysis of the law recognize this. *See, e.g.*, Easterbrook, *Afterword: Knowledge and Answers*, 85 Colum. L. Rev. 1117, 1118 (1985). Thus, while the majority states that, for purposes of reaching its result it need only make modest presumptions about the way in which "market professionals generally" do their jobs, and how the conduct of market professionals affects stock prices, I doubt that we are in much of a position to assess which theories aptly describe the functioning of the securities industry.

Consequently, I cannot join the Court in its effort to reconfigure the securities laws, based on recent economic theories, to better fit what it perceives to be the new realities of financial markets. I would leave this task to others more equipped for the job than we.

. . . .

NOTE

The Court's decision in *Basic* recognizes the necessity of the class action in § 10(b) litigation. If the majority had required proof of reliance by each individual plaintiff, the class action mechanism apparently would have been unavailable. As stated by a federal district court in a pre-*Basic* decision, "[t]he necessity of individual proof ordinarily precludes a Section 10(b) and Rule 10b-5 claim from being asserted as a class action."[31] Hence, the Supreme Court's recognition of the fraud-on-the-market theory helps to ensure that ordinary investors have a viable remedy when they allegedly are defrauded in the impersonal securities markets.

Characteristics of an "Efficient" Market. In order for the presumption of the efficient market theory to apply, the subject security must be traded in an *efficient* market. In making this determination, the principal focus is on the market for that particular security and not on the location (such as the New York Stock Exchange or the NASDAQ) where such security trades. Hence, for fraud-on-the-market purposes, the market for each security is distinct, leading to the conclusion that a stock exchange (or over-the-counter market) can be efficient for some securities listed on such exchange (or traded on such OTC market) but not for others.[32]

Therefore, what factors generally comprise an efficient market to support the *Basic* presumption of reliance? In *Freeman v. Laventhol & Horwath*, the Sixth Circuit looked to the following five factors:

(1)   a large weekly trading volume,

(2)   the existence of a significant number of reports by securities analysts,

(3)   the existence of market makers and arbitrageurs in the security,

(4)   the eligibility of the company to file an S-3 Registration Statement, and

(5)   a history of immediate movement of the stock price as the result of unexpected corporate events or financial releases.[33]

The foregoing five factors serve as indicia that a company's stock trades in an efficient market. While the satisfaction of all five factors normally should be conclusive, an efficient market nonetheless may be found to exist even if a particular factor may be

---

[31] Gibb v. Delta Drilling Company, 104 F.R.D. 59, 65 (N.D. Tex. 1984).

[32] *See* Harman v. Lyphomed, Inc., 122 F.R.D. 522, 525–26 (N.D. Ill. 1988).

[33] 915 F.2d 193, 199 (6th Cir. 1990).

absent.[34]

4. Forward-Looking Statements

ASHER v. BAXTER INTERNATIONAL, INC.
Court of Appeals of United States
377 F.3d 727 (7th Cir. 2004)

EASTERBROOK, CIRCUIT JUDGE.

Baxter International, a manufacturer of medical products, released its second-quarter financial results for 2002 on July 18 of that year. Sales and profits did not match analysts' expectations. Shares swiftly fell from $43 to $32. This litigation followed; plaintiffs contend that the $43 price was the result of materially misleading projections on November 5, 2001, projections that Baxter reiterated until the bad news came out on July 18, 2002. Plaintiffs want to represent a class of all investors who purchased during that time either in the open market or by exchanging their shares of Fusion Medical Technologies. (Baxter acquired Fusion in a stock-for-stock transaction; plaintiffs think that Baxter juiced up the market price so that it could secure Fusion in exchange for fewer of its own shares.) Bypassing the question whether the suit could proceed as a class action, the district court dismissed the complaint for failure to state a claim on which relief may be granted. The court did not doubt that the allegations ordinarily would defeat a motion under Fed. R. Civ. P. 12(b)(6). Still, it held, Baxter's forecasts come within the safe harbor created by the Private Securities Litigation Reform Act of 1995. The PSLRA creates rules that judges must enforce at the outset of the litigation; plaintiffs do not question the statutes' application before discovery but do dispute the district court's substantive decision.

Baxter's projection, repeated many times (sometimes in documents filed with the SEC, sometimes in press releases, sometimes in executives' oral statements), was that during 2002 the business would yield revenue growth in the "low teens" compared with the prior year, earnings-per-share growth in the "mid teens," and "operational cash flow of at least $500 million." Baxter often referred to these forecasts as "our 2002 full-year commitments," which is a strange elocution. No firm can make "commitments" about the future — Baxter can't *compel* its customers to buy more of its products — unless it plans to engage in accounting shenanigans to make the numbers come out right no matter what happens to the business. But nothing turns on the word; the district court took these "commitments" as "forward-looking statements," and plaintiffs do not quarrel with that understanding. What they do say is that the projections were too rosy, and that Baxter knew it. That charges the defendants with stupidity as much as with knavery, for the truth was bound to come out quickly, but the securities laws forbid foolish frauds along with clever ones.

According to the complaint, Baxter's projections were materially false because (1) its Renal Division had not met its internal budgets in years; (2) economic instability in Latin America adversely affected Baxter's sales in that part of the world; (3) Baxter closed plants in Ronneby, Sweden and Miami Lakes, Florida that had been its principal source of low-cost dialysis products; (4) the market for albumin (blood-plasma) products was "over-saturated," resulting in lower prices and revenue for the BioSciences Division; (5) sales of that division's IGIV immunoglobin products had fallen short of internal predictions; and (6) in March 2002 the BioScience Division had experienced a sterility failure in the manufacture of a major product, resulting in the destruction of

---

[34] *See In re* PolyMedica Corp. Securities Litigation, 432 F.3d 1 (1st Cir. 2005); *In re* Xcelera.com Securities Litigation, 430 F.3d 503 (1st Cir. 2005); Unger v. Amedisys Inc., 401 F.3d 316 (5th Cir. 2005); No. 84 Employer-Teamster Joint Council Pension Trust Fund v. America West Holding Corp., 320 F.3d 920 (9th Cir. 2003); Cammer v. Bloom, 711 F. Supp. 1264, 1287 (D.N.J. 1989); A. BROMBERG & L. LOWENFELS, SECURITIES FRAUD & COMMODITIES FRAUD § 8:6 (2007).

multiple lots and a loss exceeding $10 million. The district court assumed, as shall we, that failure to disclose these facts would create problems but for the statutory safe harbor, though items (2) and (4) at least are general business matters rather than Baxter's secrets, and the securities laws do not require issuers to disclose the state of the world, as opposed to facts about the firm. Item (3) also was public knowledge (Baxter issued a press release announcing the closings and a substantial charge against earnings) — though the cost of products that had been made at these plants may have been secret. Whether all firm-specific non-disclosure add up to a material non-disclosure — and whether Baxter had some non-public information about those matters that seem to be general information — are topics we need not tackle.

. . . The statutory safe harbor forecloses liability if a forward-looking statement "is accompanied by meaningful cautionary statements identifying important factors that could cause actual results to differ materially from those in the forward-looking statement". . . . The fundamental problem is that the statutory requirement of "meaningful cautionary statements" is not itself meaningful. What must the firm say? Unless it is possible to give a concrete and reliable answer, the harbor is not "safe"; yet a word such as "meaningful" resists a concrete rendition and thus makes administration of the safe harbor difficult if not impossible. . . . A safe harbor matters only when the firm's disclosures (including the accompanying cautionary statements) are false or misleadingly incomplete; yet whenever that condition is satisfied, one can complain that the cautionary statement must have been inadequate. The safe harbor loses its function. Yet it would be unsound to read the statute so that the safe harbor never works. . . .

Baxter provided a number of cautionary statements throughout the class period. This one, from its 2001 Form 10-K filing — a document to which many of the firm's press releases and other statements referred — is the best illustration:

"Statements throughout this report that are not historical facts are forward-looking statements.

"These statements are based on the company's current expectations and involve numerous risks and uncertainties. Some of these risks and uncertainties are factors that affect all international businesses, while some are specific to the company and the health care arenas in which it operates.

"Many factors could affect the company's actual results, causing results to differ materially, from those expressed in any such forward-looking statements. These factors include, but are not limited to, interest rates; technological advances in the medical field; economic conditions; demand and market acceptance risks for new and existing products, technologies and health care services; the impact of competitive products and pricing; manufacturing capacity; new plant start-ups; global regulatory, trade and tax policies; regulatory, legal or other developments relating to the company's Series A, AF, and AX dialyzers; continued price competition; product development risks, including technological difficulties; ability to enforce patents; actions of regulatory bodies and other government authorities; reimbursement policies of government agencies; commercialization factors; results of product testing; and other factors described elsewhere in this report or in the company's other filings with the Securities and Exchange Commission. Additionally, as discussed in Item 3 — 'Legal Proceedings,' upon the resolution of certain legal matters, the company may incur charges in excess of presently established reserves. Any such change could have a material adverse effect on the company's results of operations or cash flows in the period in which it is recorded.

"Currency fluctuations are also a significant variable for global companies, especially fluctuations in local currencies where hedging opportunities are unreasonably expensive or unavailable. If the United States dollar strengthens significantly against most foreign currencies, the company's ability to realize projected growth rates in its sales and net earnings outside the United States could be negatively impacted.

"The company believes that its expectations with respect to forward-looking statements are based upon reasonable assumptions within the bounds of its knowledge of its business operations, but there can be no assurance that the actual results or performance of the company will conform to any future results or performance expressed or implied by such forward-looking statements."

The district court concluded that these are "meaningful cautionary statements identifying important factors that could cause actual results to differ materially from those in the forward-looking statement." They deal with Baxter's business specifically, mentioning risks and product lines. Plaintiffs offer two responses. First, they contend that the cautionary statements did not cover any of the six matters that (in plaintiffs' view) Baxter had withheld. That can't be dispositive; otherwise the statute would demand prescience. As long as the firm reveals the principal risks, the fact that some other event caused problems cannot be dispositive. Indeed, an unexpected turn of events cannot demonstrate a securities problem at all, as there cannot be "fraud by hindsight." The other response is that the cautionary statement did not follow the firm's fortunes: plants closed but the cautionary statement remained the same; sterilization failures occurred but the cautionary statement remained the same; and bad news that (plaintiffs contend) Baxter well knew in November 2001 did not cast even a shadow in the cautionary statement.

. . . . That leaves the question whether these statements satisfy the statutory requirement that they adequately "identify[ ] important factors that could cause actual results to differ materially from those in the forward-looking statement."

The parties agree on two propositions, each with support in decisions of other circuits. First, "boilerplate" warnings won't do; cautions must be tailored to the risks that accompany the particular projections. Second, the cautions need not identify what actually goes wrong and causes the projections to be inaccurate; prevision is not required. . . . Unfortunately, these principles don't decide any concrete case — for that matter, the statutory language itself does not decide any concrete case. It is the result of a compromise between legislators who did want any safe harbor (or, indeed any new legislation), and those who wanted a safe harbor along the lines of the old Rule 175 that did not require any cautionary statements but just required the projection to have a reasonable basis. Rule 175 was limited to statements in certain documents filed with the SEC; proponents of the PSLRA wanted to extend this to all statements, including oral declarations and press releases. As is often the situation, a compromise enabled the bill to pass but lacks much content; it does not encode a principle on which political forces agreed as much as it signifies conflict about both the scope and the wisdom of the safe harbor. Compromises of this kind lack spirit. Still, the language was enacted, and we must make something of it.

Plaintiffs say that Baxter's cautions were boilerplate, but they aren't. Statements along the lines of "all businesses are risky" or "the future lies ahead" come to nothing other than caveat emptor (which isn't enough); these statements, by contrast, at least included Baxter-specific information and highlighted some parts of that business that might cause problems. For its part, Baxter says that mentioning these business segments demonstrates that the caution is sufficient; but this also is wrong, because then any issuer could list its lines of business, say "we could have problems in any of these," and avoid liability for statements implying that no such problems were on the horizon even if a precipice was in sight.

What investors would like to have is a full disclosure of the assumptions and calculations *behind* the projections; then they could apply their own discount factors. For reasons covered [elsewhere], however, this is not a sensible requirement. Many of the assumptions and calculations would be more useful to a firm's rivals than to its investors. Suppose, for example, that Baxter had revealed its sterility failure in the

BioSciences Division, the steps it had taken to restore production, and the costs and prospects of each. Rivals could have used that information to avoid costs and hazards that had befallen Baxter, or to find solutions more quickly. . . . Baxter's shareholders would have been worse off. Similarly Baxter might have added verisimilitude to its projections by describing its sales policies and the lowest prices it would accept from major customers, but disclosing reservation prices would do more to help the customers than to assist the investors.

Another form a helpful cautions might take would be the disclosure of confidence intervals. After saying that it expected growth in the low teens, Baxter might have added that events could deviate 5% in either direction (so the real projection was that growth would fall someplace between 8% and 18%); disclosure of the probability that growth will be under 10% (or over 16%) would have done much to avoid the hit stock prices took when the results for the first half of 2002 proved to be unexpectedly low. Baxter surely had developed internally some estimate of likely variance. Revealing the mean, median, and standard deviation of these internal estimates, and pinpointing the principal matters that could cause results to differ from the more likely outcome, could help to generate an accurate price for the stock. Knowledge that the mean is above the median, or that the standard deviation is substantial, would be particularly helpful to those professional investors whose trades determine the market price. Perhaps, however, a firm's data do not permit estimates to be stated in probabilities. If, for example, a major source of uncertainty for Baxter's business was how Congress would resolve the debate about Medicare coverage for prescription drugs, or whether a rival would manage to win the FDA's approval for a product that would compete with one of Baxter's most profitable items, it would be hard to reduce these chances to probabilities. Events such as these are discrete rather than continuous variables, so standard confidence intervals would be meaningless even if probabilities could be attached to the likely outcomes.

Whether or not Baxter could have made the cautions more helpful by disclosing assumptions, methods, or confidence intervals, none of these is required. The PSLRA does not require the *most* helpful caution; it is enough to "identify important factors that could cause actual results to differ materially from those in the forward-looking statement." This means that it is enough to point to the principal contingencies that could cause actual results to depart from the projection. The statute calls for issuers to reveal the "important factors" but not to attach probabilities to each potential bad outcome, or to reveal in detail what could go wrong; as we have said, that level of detail might hurt investors (by helping rivals) even as it improved the accuracy of stock prices. (Requiring cautions to contain elaborate detail also would defeat the goal of facilitating projections, by turning each into a form of registration statement. Undue complexity would lead issuers to shut up, and stock prices could become even less accurate. Incomplete information usually is better than none, because market professionals know other tidbits that put the news in context.) Moreover, "[i]f enterprises cannot make predictions about themselves, then securities analysts, newspaper columnists, and charlatans have protected turf. There will be predictions aplenty outside the domain of the securities acts, predictions by persons whose access to information is not as good as the issuer's. When the issuer adds its information and analysis to that assembled by outsiders, the *collective* assessment will be more accurate even though a given projection will be off the mark."

Yet Baxter's chosen language may fall short. There is no reason to think — at least, no reason that a court can accept at the pleading stage, before plaintiffs have access to discovery — that the items mentioned in Baxter's cautionary language were those that at the time were the (or any of the) "important" sources of variance. The problem is not that what actually happened went unmentioned; issuers need not anticipate all sources of deviations from expectations. Rather, the problem is that there is no reason (on this record) to conclude that Baxter mentioned those sources of variance that (at the time of the projection) were the principal or important risks. For all we can tell, the major risks

Baxter objectively faced when it made its forecasts were exactly those that, according to the complaint, came to pass, yet the cautionary statement mentioned none of them. Moreover, the cautionary language remained fixed even as the risks changed. When the sterility failure occurred in spring 2002, Baxter left both its forecasts and cautions as is. When Baxter closed the plants that (according to the complaint) were its least-cost sources of production, the forecasts and cautions continued without amendment. This raises the possibility — no greater confidence is possible before discovery — that Baxter omitted important variables from the cautionary language and so made projections more certain that its internal estimates at the time warranted. Thus this complaint could not be dismissed under the safe harbor, though we cannot exclude the possibility that if after discovery Baxter establishes that the cautions did reveal what were, *ex ante*, the major risks, the safe harbor may yet carry the day.

Baxter urges us to affirm the judgment immediately, contending that the full truth had reached the market despite any shortcomings in its cautionary statements. If this is so, however, it is hard to understand the sharp drop in the price of its stock. A "truth-on-the-market" defense is available in principle, but not at the pleading state. Likewise one must consider the possibility that investors looked at all of the projections as fluff and responded only to the hard numbers; on this view it was a reduction in Baxter's growth rate, not the embarrassment of a projection, that caused the price to decline in July 2002; again it is too early in the litigation to reach such a conclusion. It would be necessary to ask, for example, whether the price rose relative to the rest of the market when Baxter made its projections; if not, that might support an inference that the projections were so much noise.

Nor has the time arrived to evaluate Baxter's contention that its projections panned out, so there was no material error. Baxter insists that all of the projections dealt with the entire calendar year 2002, and that by year-end performance was up to snuff — close enough to the projections that any difference was immaterial. Once again, it is inappropriate to entertain such an argument at the pleading stage. The district court will need to determine whether all of the forward-looking statements referenced calendar 2002 as a whole, rather than anticipated improvements quarter-by-quarter over the preceding year. It will be necessary to evaluate whether differences between the projections and the outcome were material under the standard of *Basic*. Finally it may be necessary to explore what Baxter's full-year results actually were; plaintiff's reply brief accuses Baxter of using gimmicks to report extra revenue in 2002 at the expense of later years. The implication is that Baxter may have overstated its 2002 results. Whether that is so cannot be determined on the pleadings, even when supplemented with the documents that Baxter has filed with the SEC.

Reversed and Remanded.

5. Primary Liability Exposure for "Secondary" Actors

The Supreme Court has held that aiding and abetting liability may not be imposed in private actions under § 10(b) of the Securities Exchange Act. *See* Central Bank of Denver v. First Interstate Bank of Denver, 511 U.S. 164 (1994). The key issue litigated after *Central Bank* is whether the alleged violator's misconduct gives rise to primary liability under § 10(b). In *Central Bank*, the Court stated: "Any person or entity, including a lawyer, accountant, or bank, who employs a manipulative device or makes a material misstatement (or omission) on which a purchaser or seller of securities relies may be liable as a primary violator under [Rule] 10b-5. . . . " The Supreme Court narrowly interpreted this language in *Stoneridge Investment Partners, LLC v. Scientific-Atlanta, Inc.*, 169 L. Ed. 2d 627 (U.S. 2008). Holding that plaintiffs were unable to prove the requisite reliance with respect to the secondary actors' alleged scheme to defraud, the Court opined: "no member of the investing public had knowledge, either actual or presumed, of respondents' deceptive acts during the relevant time [and that] as a result, cannot show reliance upon any of the respondents' actions except in an indirect claim that we find too remote for liability."

C. CLASS ACTION "REFORM"

PRIVATE SECURITIES LITIGATION REFORM ACT
JOINT EXPLANATORY STATEMENT OF THE
COMMITTEE OF CONFERENCE (1995)

[The Private Securities Litigation Reform Act of 1995] contains provisions to reform abusive securities class action litigation. It amends the Securities Act of 1933 (the "1933 Act") by adding a new section 27 and the Securities Exchange Act of 1934 (the "1934 Act") by adding a new section 21D. These provisions are intended to encourage the most capable representatives of the plaintiff class to participate in class action litigation and to exercise supervision and control of the lawyers for the class. These provisions are intended to increase the likelihood that parties with significant holdings in issuers, whose interests are more strongly aligned with the class of shareholders, will participate in the litigation and exercise control over the selection and actions of plaintiffs' counsel. The legislation also provides that all discovery is stayed during the pendency of any motion to dismiss or for summary judgment. These stay of discovery provisions are intended to prevent unnecessary imposition of discovery costs on defendants.

THE PROFESSIONAL PLAINTIFF AND LEAD PLAINTIFF PROBLEMS

House and Senate Committee hearings on securities litigation reform demonstrated the need to reform abuses involving the use of "professional plaintiffs" and the race to the courthouse to file the complaint.

Professional plaintiffs who own a nominal number of shares in a wide array of public companies permit lawyers readily to file abusive securities class action lawsuits. Floor debate in the Senate highlighted that many of the "world's unluckiest investors" repeatedly appear as lead plaintiffs in securities class action lawsuits. These lead plaintiffs often receive compensation in the form of bounty payments or bonuses.

The Conference Committee believes these practices have encouraged the filing of abusive cases. Lead plaintiffs are not entitled to a bounty for their services. Individuals who are motivated by the payment of a bounty or bonus should not be permitted to serve as lead plaintiffs. These individuals do not adequately represent other shareholders — in many cases the "lead plaintiff" has not even read the complaint.

The Conference Committee believes that several new rules will effectively discourage the use of professional plaintiffs.

Plaintiff certification of the complaint

This legislation requires, in new section 27(a)(2) of the 1933 Act and new section 21D(a)(2) of the 1934 Act, that the lead plaintiff file a sworn certified statement with the complaint. The statement must certify that the plaintiff: (a) reviewed and authorized the filing of the complaint; (b) did not purchase the securities at the direction of counsel or in order to participate in a lawsuit; and (c) is willing to serve as the lead plaintiff on behalf of the class. To further deter the use of professional plaintiffs, the plaintiff must also identify any transactions in the securities covered by the class period, and any other lawsuits in which the plaintiff has sought to serve as lead plaintiff in the last three years.

Method for determining the "most adequate plaintiff"

The Conference Committee was also troubled by the plaintiffs' lawyers "race to the courthouse" to be the first to file a securities class action complaint. This race has caused plaintiffs' attorneys to become fleet of foot and sleight of hand. Most often, speed has replaced diligence in drafting complaints. The Conference Committee believes two incentives have driven plaintiffs' lawyers to be the first to file. First, courts traditionally appoint counsel in class action lawsuits on a "first come, first serve" basis. Courts often afford insufficient consideration to the most thoroughly researched, but later filed, complaint. The second incentive involves the court's decision as to who will become lead plaintiff. Generally, the first lawsuit filed also determines the lead plaintiff.

The Conference Committee believes that the selection of the lead plaintiff and lead counsel should rest on considerations other than how quickly a plaintiff has filed its complaint. As a result, this legislation establishes new procedures for the appointment of the lead plaintiff and lead counsel in securities class actions in new section 27(a)(3) of the 1933 Act and new section 21D(a)(3) of the 1934 Act.

A plaintiff filing a securities class action must, within 20 days of filing a complaint, provide notice to members of the purported class in a widely circulated business publication. This notice must identify the claims alleged in the lawsuit and the purported class period and inform potential class members that, within 60 days, they may move to serve as the lead plaintiff. Members of the purported class who seek to serve as lead plaintiff do not have to file the certification filing as part of this motion. "Publication" includes a variety of media, including wire, electronic, or computer services.

Within 90 days of the published notice, the court must consider motions made under this section and appoint the lead plaintiff. If a motion has been filed to consolidate multiple class actions brought on behalf of the same class, the court will not appoint a lead plaintiff until after consideration of the motion.

The current system often works to prevent institutional investors from selecting counsel or serving as lead plaintiff in class actions. The Conference Committee seeks to increase the likelihood that institutional investors will serve as lead plaintiffs by requiring courts to presume that the member of the purported class with the largest financial stake in the relief sought is the "most adequate plaintiff."

The Conference Committee believes that increasing the role of institutional investors in class actions will ultimately benefit shareholders and assist courts by improving the quality of representation in securities class actions. Institutional investors are America's largest shareholders, with about $9.5 trillion in assets, accounting for 51% of the equity market. According to one representative of institutional investors: "As the largest shareholders in most companies, we are the ones who have the most to gain from meritorious securities litigation."

Several Senators expressed concern during floor consideration of this legislation that preference would be given to large investors, and that large investors might conspire with the defendant company's management. The Conference Committee believes, however, that with pension funds accounting for $4.5 trillion or nearly half of the institutional assets, in many cases, the beneficiaries of pension funds — small investors — ultimately have the greatest stake in the outcome of the lawsuit. Cumulatively, these small investors represent a single large investor interest. Institutional investors and other class members with large amounts at stake will represent the interests of the plaintiff class more effectively than class members with small amounts at stake. The claims of both types of class members generally will be typical.

The Conference Committee recognizes the potential conflicts that could be caused by the shareholder with the "largest financial stake" serving as lead plaintiff. As a result, this presumption may be rebutted by evidence that the plaintiff would not fairly and adequately represent the interests of the class or is subject to unique defenses. Members of the purported class may seek discovery on whether the presumptively most adequate plaintiff would not adequately represent the class. The provisions of the bill relating to the appointment of a lead plaintiff are not intended to affect current law with regard to challenges to the adequacy of the class representative or typicality of the claims among the class.

Although the most adequate plaintiff provision does not confer any new fiduciary duty on institutional investors — and the courts should not impose such a duty — the Conference Committee nevertheless intends that the lead plaintiff provision will encourage institutional investors to take a more active role in securities class action lawsuits. Scholars predict that increasing the role of institutional investors will benefit both injured shareholders and courts: "Institutions with large stakes in class actions have much the same interests as the plaintiff class generally; thus, courts could be more confident settlements negotiated under the supervision of institutional plaintiffs were 'fair and reasonable' than is the case with settlements negotiated by unsupervised plaintiffs' attorneys."

Finally, this lead plaintiff provision solves the dilemma of who will serve as class counsel. Subject to court approval, the most adequate plaintiff retains class counsel. As a result, the Conference Committee expects that the plaintiff will choose counsel rather than, as is true today, counsel choosing the plaintiff. The Conference Committee does not intend to disturb the court's discretion under existing law to approve or disapprove the lead plaintiffs' choice of counsel when necessary to protect the interests of the plaintiff class.

The Conference Report seeks to restrict professional plaintiffs from serving as lead plaintiff by limiting a person from serving in that capacity more than five times in three years. Institutional investors seeking to serve as lead plaintiff may need to exceed this limitation and do not represent the type of professional plaintiff this legislation seeks to restrict. As a result, the Conference Committee grants courts discretion to avoid the unintended consequence of disqualifying institutional investors from serving more than five times in three years. The Conference Committee does not intend for this provision to operate at cross purposes with the "most adequate plaintiff" provision. The Conference Committee does expect, however, that it will be used with vigor to limit the activities of professional plaintiffs.

Limitation on lead plaintiff's recovery

This legislation also removes the financial incentive for becoming a lead plaintiff. New section 27(a)(4) of the 1933 Act and section 21D(a)(4) of the 1934 Act limits the class representative's recovery to his or her pro rata share of the settlement or final judgment. The lead plaintiff's share of the final judgment or settlement will be calculated in the same manner as the shares of the other class members. The Conference Committee recognizes that lead plaintiffs should be reimbursed for reasonable costs and expenses associated with service as lead plaintiff, including lost wages, and grants the courts discretion to award fees accordingly.

IMPROVEMENTS TO SETTLEMENT PROCESS

Restriction on sealed settlement agreements

New section 27(a)(5) of the 1933 Act and section 21D(a)(5) of the 1934 Act generally bar the filing of settlement agreements under seal. The Conference Committee recognizes that legitimate reasons may exist for the court to permit the entry of a settlement or portions of a settlement under seal. A party must show "good cause," i.e., that the publication of a portion or portions of the settlement agreement would result in direct and substantial harm to any party, whether or not a party to the action. The Conference Committee intends "direct and substantial harm" to include proof of reputational injury to a party.

Limitation on attorneys' fees

The House and Senate heard testimony that counsel in securities class actions often receive a disproportionate share of settlement awards.

Under current practice, courts generally award attorney's fees based on the so-called "lodestar" approach — i.e., the court multiplies the attorney's hours by a reasonable hourly fee, which may be increased by an additional amount based on risk or other relevant factors. Under this approach, attorney's fees can constitute 35% or more of the entire settlement awarded to the class. The Conference Committee limits the award of attorney's fees and costs to counsel for a class in new section 27(a)(6) of the 1933 Act and new section 21D(a)(6) of the 1934 Act to a reasonable percentage of the amount of recovery awarded to the class. By not fixing the percentage of fees and costs counsel may receive, the Conference Committee intends to give the court flexibility in determining what is reasonable on a case-by-case basis. The Conference Committee does not intend to prohibit use of the lodestar approach as a means of calculating attorney's fees. The provision focuses on the final amount of fees awarded, not the means by which such fees are calculated.

Improved settlement notice to class members

The House and Senate heard testimony that class members frequently lack meaningful information about the terms of the proposed settlement. Class members often receive insufficient notice of the terms of a proposed settlement and, thus, have no basis to evaluate the settlement. As one bar association advised the Senate Securities Subcommittee, "settlement notices provided to class members are often obtuse and confusing, and should be written in plain English." The Senate received similar testimony from a class member in two separate securities fraud lawsuits: "Nowhere in the settlement notices were the stockholders told of how much they could expect to recover of their losses . . . . I feel that the settlement offer should have told the stockholders how little of their losses will be recovered in the settlement, and that this is a material fact to the shareholder's decision to approve or disapprove the settlement."

In new section 27(a)(7) of the 1933 Act and new section 21D(a)(7) of the 1934 Act, the Conference Committee requires that certain information be included in any proposed or final settlement agreement disseminated to class members. To ensure that critical information is readily available to class members, the Conference Committee requires that such information appear in summary form on the cover page of the notice. The notice must contain a statement of the average amount of damages per share that would be recoverable if the settling parties can agree on a figure, or a statement from each settling party on why there is disagreement. It must also explain the attorney's fees and costs sought. The name, telephone number and address of counsel for the class must be provided. Most importantly, the notice must include a brief statement explaining the reason for the proposed settlement.

MAJOR SECURITIES CLASS ACTION ABUSES

Limits on abusive discovery to prevent "fishing expedition" lawsuits

The cost of discovery often forces innocent parties to settle frivolous securities class actions. According to the general counsel of an investment bank, "discovery costs account for roughly 80% of total litigation costs in securities fraud cases." In addition, the threat that the time of key employees will be spent responding to discovery requests, including providing deposition testimony, often forces coercive settlements.

The House and Senate heard testimony that discovery in securities class actions often resembles a fishing expedition. As one witness noted, "once the suit is filed, the plaintiffs' law firm proceeds to search through all of the company's documents and take endless depositions for the slightest positive comment which they can claim induced the plaintiff to invest and any shred of evidence that the company knew a downturn was coming."

The Conference Committee provides in new section 27(b) of the 1933 Act and new section 21D(b)(3) of the 1934 Act that courts must stay all discovery pending a ruling on a motion to dismiss, unless exceptional circumstances exist where particularized discovery is necessary to preserve evidence or to prevent undue prejudice to a party. For example, the terminal illness of an important witness might require the deposition of the witness prior to the ruling on the motion to dismiss.

To ensure that relevant evidence will not be lost, new section 27(b) of the 1933 Act and new section 21D(b)(3) of the 1934 Act make it unlawful for any person, upon receiving actual notice that names that person as a defendant, willfully to destroy or otherwise alter relevant evidence. The Conference Committee intends this provision to prohibit only the willful alteration or destruction of evidence relevant to the litigation. The provision does not impose liability where parties inadvertently or unintentionally destroy what turn out later to be relevant documents. Although this prohibition expressly applies only to defendants, the Conference Committee believes that the willful destruction of evidence by a plaintiff would be equally improper, and that courts have ample authority to prevent such conduct or to apply sanctions as appropriate.

Attorneys' fees awarded to prevailing parties in abusive litigation

The Conference Committee recognizes the need to reduce significantly the filing of meritless securities lawsuits without hindering the ability of victims of fraud to pursue legitimate claims. The Conference Committee seeks to solve this problem by strengthening the application of Rule 11 of the Federal Rules of Civil Procedure in private securities actions.

Existing Rule 11 has not deterred abusive securities litigation. Courts often fail to impose Rule 11 sanctions even where such sanctions are warranted. When sanctions are awarded, they are generally insufficient to make whole the victim of a Rule 11 violation: the amount of the sanction is limited to an amount that the court deems sufficient to deter repetition of the sanctioned conduct, rather than imposing a sanction that equals the costs imposed on the victim by the violation. Finally, courts have been unable to apply Rule 11 to the complaint in such a way that the victim of the ensuing lawsuit is compensated for all attorneys' fees and costs incurred in the entire action.

The legislation gives teeth to Rule 11 in new section 27(c) of the 1933 Act and new section 21D(c) of the 1934 Act by requiring the court to include in the record specific findings, at the conclusion of the action, as to whether all parties and all attorneys have complied with each requirement of Rule 11(b) of the Federal Rules of Civil Procedure.

These provisions also establish the presumption that the appropriate sanction for filing a complaint that violates Rule 11(b) is an award to the prevailing party of all attorney's fees and costs incurred in the entire action. The Conference Report provides that, if the action is brought for an improper purpose, is unwarranted by existing law or legally frivolous, is not supported by facts, or otherwise fails to satisfy the requirements set forth in Rule 11(b), the prevailing party presumptively will be awarded its attorney's fees and costs for the entire action. This provision does not mean that a party who is sanctioned for only a partial failure of the complaint under Rule 11, such as one count out of a 20-count complaint, must pay for all of the attorney's fees and costs associated with the action. The Conference Committee expects that courts will grant relief from the presumption where a de minimis violation of the Rule has occurred. Accordingly, the Conference Committee specifies that the failure of the complaint must be "substantial" and makes the presumption rebuttable.

For Rule 11(b) violations involving responsive pleadings or dispositive motions, the rebuttable presumption is an award of attorneys' fees and costs incurred by the victim of the violation as a result of that particular pleading or motion.

A party may rebut the presumption of sanctions by providing that: (i) the violation was de minimis; or (ii) the imposition of fees and costs would impose an undue burden and be unjust, and it would not impose a greater burden for the prevailing party to have to pay those same fees and costs. The premise of this test is that, when an abusive or frivolous action is maintained, it is manifestly unjust for the victim of the violation to bear substantial attorneys' fees. The Conference Committee recognizes that little in the way of justice can be achieved by attempting to compensate the prevailing party for lost time and such other measures of damages as injury to reputation. . . . If a party successfully rebuts the presumption, the court then impose[s] sanctions consistent with Rule 11(c)(2). The Conference Committee intends this provision to impose upon courts the affirmative duty to scrutinize filings closely and to sanction attorneys or parties whenever their conduct violates Rule 11(b).

Limitation on attorney's conflict of interest

The Conference Committee believes that, in the context of class action lawsuits, it is a conflict of interest for a class action lawyer to benefit from the outcome of the case where the lawyer owns stock in the company being sued. Accordingly, new section 27(a)(8) of the 1933 Act and new section 21D(a)(9) requires the court to determine whether a lawyer who owns securities in the defendant company and who seeks to represent the plaintiff class in a securities class action should be disqualified from representing the class.

Bonding for payment of fees and expenses

The house hearings on securities litigation reform revealed the need for explicit authority for courts to require undertakings for attorney's fees and costs from parties, or their counsel, or both, in order to ensure the viability of potential sanctions as a deterrent to meritless litigation. Congress long ago authorized similar undertaking in the express private right of action in section 11 of the 1933 Act and in sections 9 and 18 of the 1934 Act. The availability of such undertakings in private securities actions will be an important means of ensuring that the costs under Rule 11 will not become, in practice, a one-way mechanism only usable to sanction parties with deep pockets.

The legislation expressly provides that such undertakings may be required of parties' attorneys in lieu of, or in addition to, the parties themselves. In this regard, the Conference Committee intends to preempt any contrary state bar restrictions that may inhibit attorneys' provision of such undertakings in behalf of their clients. The Conference Committee anticipates, for example, that where a judge determines to require an undertaking in a class action, such an undertaking would ordinarily be imposed on plaintiffs' counsel rather than upon the plaintiff class, both because the financial resources of counsel would ordinarily be more extensive than those of an individual class member and because counsel are better situated than class members to evaluate the merits of cases and individual motions. This provision is intended to effectuate the remedial purposes of the bill's Rule 11 provision.

REQUIREMENTS FOR SECURITIES FRAUD ACTIONS

Heightened pleading standard

Naming a party in a civil suit for fraud is a serious matter. Unwarranted fraud claims can lead to serious injury to reputation for which our legal system effectively offers no redress. For this reason, among others, Rule 9(b) of the Federal Rules of Civil Procedure requires that plaintiffs plead allegations of fraud with "particularity." The Rule has not prevented abuse of the securities laws by private litigants. Moreover, the courts of appeals have interpreted Rule 9(b)'s requirement in conflicting ways, creating distinctly different standards among the circuits. The House and Senate hearings on securities litigation reform included testimony on the need to establish uniform and more stringent pleading requirements to curtail the filing of meritless lawsuits.

The Conference Committee language is based in part on the pleading standard of the Second Circuit. The standard also is specifically written to conform the language to Rule 9(b)'s notion of pleading with "particularity."

Regarded as the most stringent pleading standard, the Second Circuit requirement is that the plaintiff state facts with particularity, and that these facts, in turn, must give rise to a "strong inference" of the defendant's fraudulent intent. Because the Conference Committee intends to strengthen existing pleading requirements, it does not intend to codify the Second Circuit's case law interpreting this pleading standard. The plaintiff must also specifically plead with particularity each statement alleged to have been misleading. The reason or reasons why the statement is misleading must also be set forth in the complaint in detail. If an allegation is made on information and belief, the plaintiff must state with particularity all facts in the plaintiff's possession on which the belief is formed.

Loss causation

The Conference Committee also requires the plaintiff to plead and then to prove that the misstatement or omission alleged in the complaint actually caused the loss incurred by the plaintiff in new Section 21D(b)(4) of the 1934 Act. For example, the plaintiff would have to prove that the price at which the plaintiff bought the stock was artificially inflated as the result of the misstatement or omission.

DAMAGES

Written interrogatories

In an action to recover money damages, the Conference Committee requires the court to submit written interrogatories to the jury on the issue of defendant's state of mind at the time of the violation. In expressly providing for certain interrogatories, the Committee does not intend to otherwise prohibit or discourage the submission of interrogatories concerning the mental state or relative fault of the plaintiff and of persons who could have been joined as defendants. For example, interrogatories may be appropriate in contribution proceedings among defendants or in computing liability when some of the defendants have entered into settlement with the plaintiff prior to verdict or judgment.

Limitation on "windfall" damages

The current method of calculating damages in 1934 Act securities fraud cases is complex and uncertain. As a result, there are often substantial variations in the damages calculated by the defendants and the plaintiffs. Typically, in an action involving a fraudulent misstatement or omission, the investor's damages are presumed to be the difference between the price the investor paid for the security and the price of the security on the day the corrective information gets disseminated to the market.

Between the time a misrepresentation is made and the time the market receives corrected information, however, the price of the security may rise or fall for reasons unrelated to the alleged fraud. According to an analysis provided to the Senate Securities Subcommittee, on average, damages in securities litigation comprise approximately 27.7% of market loss. Calculating damages based on the date corrective information is disclosed may end up substantially overestimating plaintiff's damages. The Conference Committee intends to rectify the uncertainty in calculating damages in new section 21D(e) of the 1934 Act by providing a "look back" period, thereby limiting damages to those losses caused by the fraud and not by other market conditions.

This provision requires that plaintiff's damages be calculated based on the "mean trading price" of the security. This calculation takes into account the value of the security on the date plaintiff originally bought or sold the security and the value of the security during the 90-day period after dissemination of any information correcting the misleading statement or omission. . . .

President Clinton vetoed the Private Securities Litigation Reform Act. Subsequently, Congress overrode the President's veto and the Act became law. The President's Veto Message follows.

PRESIDENTIAL VETO MESSAGE ON THE PRIVATE SECURITIES LITIGATION REFORM ACT

The White House. Office of the Press Secretary. December 20, 1995. Message from President William J. Clinton to the House of Representatives. December 20, 1995.

TO THE HOUSE OF REPRESENTATIVES:

I am returning herewith without my approval H.R. 1058, the "Private Securities Litigation Reform Act of 1995." This legislation is designed to reform portions of the Federal securities laws to end frivolous lawsuits and to ensure that investors receive the best possible information by reducing the litigation risk to companies that make forward-looking statements.

I support these goals. Indeed, I made clear my willingness to support the bill passed by the Senate with appropriate "safe harbor" language, even though it did not include certain provisions that I favor — such as enhanced provisions with respect to joint and several liability, aider and abettor liability, and statute of limitations.

I am not, however, willing to sign legislation that will have the effect of closing the courthouse door on investors who have legitimate claims. Those who are the victims of fraud should have recourse in our courts. Unfortunately, changes made in this bill during conference could well prevent that.

This country is blessed by strong and vibrant markets and I believe that they function best when corporations can raise capital by providing investors with their best good-faith assessment of future prospects, without fear of costly, unwarranted litigation. But I also know that our markets are as strong and effective as they are because they operate — and are seen to operate — with integrity. I believe that this bill, as modified in conference, could erode this crucial basis of our markets' strength.

Specifically, I object to the following elements of this bill. First, I believe that the pleading requirement of the Conference Report with regard to a defendant's state of mind impose an unacceptable procedural hurdle to meritorious claims being heard in Federal courts. I am prepared to support the high pleading standard of the U.S. Court of Appeals for the Second Circuit — the highest pleading standard of any Federal circuit court. But the conferees make crystal clear in the Statement of Managers their intent to raise the standard even beyond that level. I am not prepared to accept that.

The conferees deleted an amendment offered by Senator Specter and adopted by the Senate that specifically incorporated Second Circuit case law with respect to pleading a claim of fraud. Then they specifically indicated that they were not adopting Second Circuit case law but instead intended to "strengthen" the existing pleading requirements of the Second Circuit. All this shows that the conferees meant to erect a higher barrier to bringing suit than any now existing — one so high that even the most aggrieved investors with the most painful losses may get tossed out of court before they have a chance to prove their case.

Second, while I support the language of the Conference Report providing a "safe harbor" for companies that include meaningful cautionary statements in their projections of earnings, the Statement of Managers — which will be used by courts as a guide to the intent of the Congress with regard to the meaning of the bill — attempts to weaken the cautionary language that the bill itself requires. Once again, the end result may be that investors find their legitimate claims unfairly dismissed.

Third, the Conference Report's Rule 11 provision lacks balance, treating plaintiffs more harshly than defendants in a manner that comes too close to the "loser pays" standard I oppose.

I want to sign a good bill and I am prepared to do exactly that if the Congress will make the following changes to this legislation: first, adopt the Second Circuit pleading standards and reinsert the Specter amendment into the bill. I will support a bill that submits all plaintiffs to the tough pleading standards of the Second Circuit, but I am not prepared to go beyond that. Second, remove the language in the Statement of Managers that waters down the nature of the cautionary language that must be included to make the safe harbor safe. Third, restore the Rule 11 language to that of the Senate bill.

While it is true that innocent companies are hurt by frivolous lawsuits and that valuable information may be withheld from investors when companies fear the risk of such suits, it is also true that there are innocent investors who are defrauded and who are able to recover their losses only because they can go to court. It is appropriate to change the law to ensure that companies can make reasonable statements and future projections without getting sued every time earnings turn out to be lower than expected or stock prices drop. But it is not appropriate to erect procedural barriers that will keep wrongly injured persons from having their day in court.

I ask the Congress to send me a bill promptly that will put an end to litigation abuses while still protecting the legitimate rights of ordinary investors. I will sign such a bill as soon as it reaches my desk.

D. STATE SECURITIES REMEDIES

In the last two decades, the U.S. Supreme Court has handed down a number of restrictive decisions under the federal securities laws. Due to this development, the question arises whether investors should consider pursuing their state law actions with greater vigor.

Drawbacks to State Court Suits. In some situations, plaintiffs should pursue their grievances under the federal securities acts. For example, a state such as New York declines to recognize a private right of action for violation of its securities laws.[35] In addition, certain other states in their respective securities statutes provide private redress for purchasers only,[36] and afford a shorter statute of limitations than that prescribed by federal law.[37] Moreover, by premising liability upon the status of the primary violator as a seller, many of these statutes evidently cannot be invoked against a corporate defendant and its fiduciaries in secondary market frauds, such as when a company allegedly issues a deliberately false press release or earnings statement.[38] Adoption of a sufficiently broad definition of "seller" in this context would expand the statute's scope to encompass such situations.[39]

Another significant downside to state law is with respect to class action litigation. Unlike federal law which recognizes the fraud on the market theory to create a presumption of reliance,[40] thereby facilitating use of the class action mechanism, a number of state courts have declined to adopt this doctrine with respect to actions alleging common law fraud.[41] The consequence is that individualized proof of reliance is

---

[35] *See* CPC Int'l v. McKesson Corp., 70 N.Y.2d 268, 519 N.Y.S.2d 804, 514 N.E.2d 116 (1987).

[36] *See, e.g.*, N.D. COMM. CODE § 10-04-17, construed in *Weidner v. Engelhart*, 176 N.W.2d 509, 513 (N.D. 1970); OHIO REV. CODE § 1707.43. *See also* Section 410(a) of the Uniform Securities Act, reprinted in 1 BLUE SKY L. REP. (CCH) ¶ 5500, at 1566 (Adopted 1956).

[37] *See, e.g.*, GA. CODE § 97-114(d); MO. CODE § 409.411(e); N.C. SEC. ACT § 78A-56(f); VA. CODE § 13.1-522(D); Clouser v. Temporaries, Inc., 730 F. Supp. 1127 (D.D.C. 1989) (holding claim was barred by the two-year District of Columbia blue sky statute of limitations, D.C. CODE § 2-2613(e)).

[38] Hence, many states have adopted the section 12(a)(2) counterpart but have declined to provide a private remedy for the Rule 10b-5 counterpart. *Compare* TEX. SEC. ACT Art. 581-33A(2) (Section 12(a)(2) counterpart) *with* Washington Securities Act, RCW 21.20.010 (Rule 10b-5 counterpart).

[39] For example, holding that a company issuing a materially misleading press release aided the sale, played an integral role in the sale, or solicited the transaction for its financial benefit would, depending upon the standard adopted, confer "seller" status upon the entity, thereby subjecting it to liability exposure in secondary open market transactions.

[40] Basic Inc. v. Levinson, 485 U.S. 224 (1988). This case is set forth earlier in this Chapter.

[41] Because many blue sky remedial statutes do not have a reliance requirement, this issue most frequently arises with respect to common law fraud claims. *See, e.g.*, Peil v. Speiser, 806 F.2d 1154, 1163 n.17 (3d Cir. 1986) ("While the fraud on the market theory is good law with respect to the Securities Acts, no state courts have adopted the theory, and thus direct reliance remains a requirement of a common law securities fraud claim.");

required, hence impeding class certification. For example, in rejecting the fraud on the market in cases alleging common-law fraud, the California Supreme Court opined that recognition of the theory would eliminate the reliance requirement.[42] Similarly, the Delaware Supreme Court has held that "[a] class action may not be maintained in a purely common law or equitable fraud case since individual questions of law or fact, particularly as to the element of justifiable reliance, will inevitably predominate over common questions of law or fact."[43]

The Securities Litigation Uniform Standards Act (SLUSA). Enactment of the Securities Litigation Uniform Standards Act (SLUSA or the Uniform Standards Act) severely limits the availability of state law redress. Indeed, *regarding securities class actions* [44] *involving nationally traded securities,*[45] *SLUSA* [46] *generally preempts state law.*[47] Certain important exceptions exist, however, thereby preserving state securities and common law in those situations. For example, derivative actions may be pursued under state law.[48] State law also may be invoked in suits challenging the conduct of a subject issuer, any of its affiliates, or affected corporate fiduciaries with respect to specified actions — namely, going-private transactions, tender offers, mergers, and the exercise of appraisal rights.[49] Importantly, SLUSA declines to preempt in any way the

---

Mirkin v. Wasserman, 5 Cal. 4th 1082, 858 P.2d 568, 23 Cal. Rptr. 2d 101 (1993); Gaffin v. Teledyne, Inc., 611 A.2d 467, 474 (Del. 1992); Antonson v. Robertson, 141 F.R.D. 501, 508 (E.D. 1991). *But see* OHIO REV. CODE § 1707.43 (no reliance requirement); Hurley v. Federal Deposit Insurance Corp., 719 F. Supp. 27, 34 n.4 (D. Mass. 1989); Allyn v. Wortman, 725 So. 2d 94, 101 (Miss. 1998); Arnold v. Dirrim, 398 N.E.2d 426 (Ind. Ct. App. 1979).

[42] Mirkin v. Wasserman, 5 Cal. 4th 1082, 858 P.2d 568, 23 Cal. Rptr. 2d 101 (1993). Importantly, the court recognized that the state securities law provisions discussed at bar contained no reliance requirement.

[43] Gaffin v. Teledyne, Inc., 611 A.2d 467, 474 (Del. 1992).

[44] Pursuant to the Securities Litigation Uniform Standards Act of 1998, a "covered class action" means:

(i) any single lawsuit in which —

(I) damages are sought on behalf of more than 50 persons or prospective class members, and questions of law or fact common to those persons or members of the prospective class, without reference to issues of individualized reliance on an alleged misstatement or omission, predominate over any questions affecting only individual persons or members; or

(II) one or more named parties seek to recover damages on a representative basis on behalf of themselves and other unnamed parties similarly situated, and questions of law or fact common to those persons or members of the prospective class predominate over any questions affecting only individual persons or members; or

(ii) any group of lawsuits filed in or pending in the same court and involving common questions of law or fact, in which —

(I) damages are sought on behalf of more than 50 persons; and

(II) the lawsuits are joined, consolidated, or otherwise proceed as a single action for any purpose.

Section 101 of the Uniform Standards Act, *amending* Section 16(f)(2)(A) of the Securities Act, *and* § 28(f)(5)(B) of the Exchange Act.

[45] The term nationally traded security or "covered security" means a security that meets the standards set forth in section 18(b) of the Securities Act. These securities include those that are listed for trading on the New York Stock Exchange, American Stock Exchange, and the NASDAQ National Market System (NMS). Securities issued by registered investment companies also are defined as nationally traded securities.

[46] Pub. L. No. 105-353, 112 Stat. 3227 (1998). *See* H.R. Rep. No. 105-803, 105th Cong., 2d Sess. (1998).

[47] See Section 101 of the Uniform Standards Act, amending § 16 of the Securities Act and § 28 of the Exchange Act.

[48] See § 101 of the Uniform Standards Act, amending § 16(f)(2)(B) of the Securities Act and Section 28(f)(5)(C) of the Exchange Act (stating that "the term 'covered class action' does not include an exclusively derivative action brought by one or more shareholders on behalf of a corporation"). For the definition of "covered class action," see note 44 *supra*.

[49] See § 101 of the Uniform Standards Act, amending § 16(d)(1) of the Securities Act and § 28(f)(3)(A) of the

authority of the state securities commissions, thereby empowering the states to continue their investigatory and enforcement functions.[50]

The impact of SLUSA is significant. Prior to its enactment, proponents asserted that publicly-held companies were reluctant to disclose forward-looking information,[51] irrespective of the safe harbor provided by the Private Securities Litigation Reform Act of 1995. The concern remained that such disclosure of forward-looking information would subject the applicable company to state court litigation.[52] SLUSA's enactment, generally preempting state law in securities class actions involving nationally traded securities,[53] generally has provided sufficient comfort to induce subject registrants to disclose forward-looking information.[54]

In *Merrill Lynch, Pierce, Fenner & Smith, Inc. v. Dabit*,[55] the Supreme Court construed the "in connection with the purchase or sale" language of SLUSA in the context of a securities class action brought in state court on behalf of those shareholders who held (but did not purchase or sell) the subject securities. In the decision below, the Second Circuit incorporated the *Blue Chip* purchaser-seller standing limitation for section 10(b) private actions[56] into SLUSA. Based on this analysis, fraud is deemed "in connection with the purchase or sale" of securities under SLUSA if such misconduct is alleged by a purchaser or seller. Accordingly, the Second Circuit concluded that holders of the subject securities, who allegedly were fraudulently induced not to sell, fell outside of SLUSA's parameters and were therefore able to pursue their class action claims in state court.[57]

The Supreme Court reversed and held that the holders were precluded from bringing their state class action under SLUSA. Construing SLUSA's "in connection with the purchase or sale" language broadly, the Court opined that "it is enough that the fraud alleged 'coincide' with a securities transaction — whether by the plaintiff or by someone

---

Exchange Act. In addition, the Uniform Standards Act excludes from federal preemption suits instituted by a state, a political subdivision thereof, or a state pension plan provided that such state, political subdivision thereof, or state pension plan is named as a plaintiff in such action and has authorized its participation in such action. See § 101 of the Uniform Standards Act, amending § 16(d)(2) of the Securities Act and § 28(f)(3)(B) of the Exchange Act. As another exception, "a covered class action that seeks to enforce a contractual agreement between an issuer and an indenture trustee may be maintained in a State or Federal court by a party to the agreement or a successor to such party." See§ 101 of the Uniform Standards Act, amending § 16(d)(3) of the Securities Act *and* § 28(f)(3)(C) of the Exchange Act.

[50] See § 101 of the Uniform Standards Act, amending § 16(e) of the Securities Act and § 28(f)(4) of the Exchange Act (stating that "[t]he securities commission (or any agency or office performing like functions) of any State shall retain jurisdiction under the laws of such State to investigate and bring enforcement actions").

[51] See sources cited in Levine & Pritchard, *The Securities Litigation Uniform Standards Act of 1998: The Sun Sets on California's Blue Sky Laws*, 54 BUS. LAW. 1, 12 (1998).

[52] *See* Grundfest et al., *Securities Class Action Litigation in 1998: A Report to NASDAQ from the Stanford Law School Securities Class Action Clearinghouse*, 1070 PLI/Corp 69 (1998) ("Since passage of the Reform Act, a substantial portion of class action litigation has shifted from federal to state court in an apparent attempt to evade the Act's provisions.").

[53] Note, however, that the preservation of state derivative actions along with the Delaware Supreme Court's interpretations relating to a corporate fiduciary's duty of candor may not foreclose state litigation in the general disclosure context. *See, e.g.*, Malone v. Brincat, 722 A.2d 5 (Del. 1998).

[54] *See generally* J. HAMILTON & T. TRAUTMANN, SECURITIES LITIGATION UNIFORM STANDARDS ACT OF 1998: LAW AND EXPLANATION (CCH 1998); Casey, *Shutting the Doors to State Court: The Securities Litigation Uniform Standards Act of 1998*, 27 SEC. REG. L.J. 141 (1999); Painter, *Responding to a False Alarm: Federal Preemption of State Securities Fraud Causes of Action*, 84 CORNELL L. REV. 1 (1998).

[55] 126 S. Ct. 1503 (2006).

[56] *See* Blue Chip Stamps v. Manor Drug Stores, 421 U.S. 723 (1975).

[57] Dabit v. Merrill Lynch, Pierce, Fenner & Smith, Inc., 395 F.3d 25 (2d Cir. 2005), *rev'd*, 126 S. Ct. 1503 (2006).

else."[58] Hence, the requisite showing under SLUSA to show preemption is that the alleged deception occur in connection with the purchase or sale of the security, not that the deception be perpetrated against an identifiable purchaser or seller.[59] The Supreme Court's decision in *Dabit* thus signifies that state class actions brought by holders involving a nationally traded security are preempted under SLUSA. The Court concluded: "For purposes of SLUSA preemption . . . the identity of the plaintiffs does not determine whether the complaint alleges fraud 'in connection with the purchaser or sale' of securities. The misconduct of which [the plaintiffs] complain here — fraudulent manipulation of stock prices — unquestionably qualifies [under SLUSA] as fraud 'in connection with the purchase or sale' of securities . . . ."[60]

Advantages of State Claims

On the other hand, there may be several distinct advantages for plaintiffs to bring state blue sky and common law claims.[61] Importantly, many state securities acts provide that, if appropriate, successful plaintiffs may recover reasonable attorneys' fees and punitive damages.[62]

Another example is that many state securities statutes provide for monetary damages based on negligent material misrepresentations or omissions made in the initial offering context as well as in the secondary trading markets.[63] Under federal law, if section 10(b) is invoked, scienter must be shown.[64]

Also, a number of the state statutes extend liability exposure to those who materially aid in consummating the transaction.[65] This concept of secondary liability is particularly important in view of the U.S. Supreme Court's decision in *Central Bank of Denver* foreclosing aiding and abetting liability in private actions under section 10(b).[66] Indeed, one who materially aids a sale under such a state statute is subject to liability unless he

---

[58] 126 S. Ct. at 1513.

[59] *Id.*

[60] *Id.* at 1515. *See* Loewenstein, Merrill Lynch v. Dabit: *Federal Preemption of Holders' Class Actions*, 34 SEC. REG. L.J. 209 (2006). In a subsequent decision, the Supreme Court held that when a securities class action is remanded to state court by a federal district court under SLUSA, that order is not appealable. Kircher v. Putnam Funds Trust, 126 S. Ct. 2145 (2006). The Court's decision is significant because "[s]ecurities defendants will no longer be able to tie up a case on appeal for years litigating the propriety of a remand when the district court finds that the plaintiff's case does not implicate SLUSA." Coyle, *High Court Makes a Call in 'Removal Wars'*, Nat. L.J., June 19, 2006, at p. 4.

[61] *See* Branson, *Collateral Participant Liability Under State Securities Laws*, 19 PEPP. L. REV. 1027 (1992); Steinberg, *The Emergence of State Securities Laws: Partly Sunny Skies for Investors*, 62 U. CIN. L. REV. 395 (1993).

[62] *See, e.g.*, Uniform Securities Act § 410(a), *supra* note 36, at 1566; ARIZ. REV. STAT. § 44-2001; WASH. REV. CODE § 21.20.430(1), (2). Punitive damages also may be awarded in appropriate situations, such as where malice or egregious fraud is shown. *See* OHIO REV. CODE § 2315.21(B); Price v. Griffin, 359 A.2d 582, 589–90 (D.C. Ct. App. 1976).

[63] For example, the Washington Supreme Court in *Kittilson v. Ford*, 93 Wash. 2d 223, 608 P.2d 264 (1980) (a civil action for damages), rejected the *Hochfelder* scienter standard. In distinguishing *Hochfelder* and holding that negligence is sufficient to impose liability, the *Kittilson* court reasoned:

> We believe the holding in *Ernst & Ernst v. Hochfelder* [425 U.S. 185 (1976)] [is] inapplicable to our Securities Act. First, the "manipulative or deceptive" language of section 10(b) of the 1934 Act is not included in the Washington Act. Secondly, in contrast to the federal scheme, the language of Rule 10b-5 is not derivative but is the statute in Washington. Finally, no legislative history similar or analogous to Congressional legislative history exists in Washington.

[64] Aaron v. SEC, 446 U.S. 680 (1980); Ernst & Ernst v. Hochfelder, 425 U.S. 185 (1976).

[65] *See, e.g.*, ARIZ. REV. STAT. ANN. § 44-2003; OR. REV. STAT. § 59.115(3); OHIO REV. CODE § 1707.43; Sterling Trust Company v. Adderley, 168 S.W.3d 835 (Tex. 2005). *See generally* J. LONG, BLUE SKY LAW § 7.08 (2007).

[66] Central Bank of Denver v. First Interstate Bank of Denver, 511 U.S. 164 (1994).

or she meets the reasonable care defense.[67] In effect, this standard may enable a plaintiff successfully to reach certain parties who would avoid liability under the federal securities laws. For example, those persons who were aiders and abettors rather than primary violators would face state securities law liability exposure.

There are other key advantages for plaintiffs under certain of the state securities provisions. For example, many states hold that reliance is not required to be shown under the applicable blue sky statute,[68] hence facilitating class action certification. Proving loss causation also may be dispensed with by plaintiffs in a number of states.[69] This more relaxed liability framework prompted Professor Cane to poignantly observe:

> It would seem that a plaintiff bringing a suit under [the Florida statute] could rescind [the transaction] without a showing of proximate cause, or any damage, or any scienter on the part of the defendant. . . . Was the intent of the Florida legislature to create a system of investor insurance?[70]

In addition to their state blue sky claims, investors also may emerge victorious when seeking relief on common law fraud, negligent misrepresentation, and breach of fiduciary duty grounds. In some states, even though not a purchaser or seller of stock, a shareholder who held the subject securities may be entitled to bring a common law action for fraud.[71]

In conclusion, provided that SLUSA does not preclude the action, the state securities laws are likely to be invoked by plaintiffs with greater frequency. Due to their more flexible construction, many of the state statutes provide the plaintiff with a right of action where such right may be lacking under federal law. Hence, the effect of the federal courts' restrictive approach to the remedial provisions of the Securities Acts may well be to induce plaintiffs more frequently to file their actions in the state courts. Given the broad relief awarded in some of these state court proceedings, this result in the end may be more detrimental to defendants. Hence, it indeed is ironic that many plaintiffs, by electing to bring suit in state court, may be better off than they were prior to the time that the federal courts embarked on their restrictive approach.

Nonetheless, as discussed earlier, it must be emphasized that pursuant to the Securities Litigation Uniform Standards Act (SLUSA), state law (with certain exceptions) is preempted in class actions involving nationally traded securities. In such circumstances, federal law serves as the sole source for plaintiff redress.

---

[67] For application of the reasonable care standard as an affirmative defense, see, e.g., *Arnold v. Dirrim*, 398 N.E.2d 426, 434–35 (Ind. Ct. App. 1979); *McGarity v. Craighill*, 83 N.C. App. 106, 111–12, 349 S.E.2d 311, 314–15 (1986).

[68] *See. e.g.*, CAL. CORP. CODE §§ 25400, 25500; Mirkin v. Wasserman, 5 Cal. 4th 1082, 858 P.2d 568, 23 Cal. Rptr. 2d 101 (1993); OHIO REV. CODE § 1707.43; Roger v. Lehman Bros. Kuhn Loeb, Inc., 621 F. Supp. 114, 118 (S.D. Ohio 1985) (interpreting OHIO REV. CODE ANN. § 1707.43); TEX. SEC. ACT Art. 581-33A(2); Anderson v. Vinson Exploration, Inc., 832 S.W.2d 657 (Tex. App. 1992).

[69] *See* E.F. Hutton & Company, Inc. v. Rousseff, 537 So. 2d 978, 981 (Fla. 1989).

[70] Cane, *Proximate Causation in Securities Fraud Actions for Rescission*, FLA. BAR BUS. QUART. REP., Vol. 2, No. 2, at p. 14 (Spring 1989).

[71] *See* Small v. Fritz Companies, 65 P.3d 1255 (Cal. 2003) (allowing persons who allegedly were wrongfully induced to hold their stock rather than selling such securities to bring suit based on common law fraud and negligent misrepresentation); Gutman v. Howard Savings Bank, 748 F. Supp. 254, 266 (D.N.J. 1990) (interpreting New Jersey law, standing to bring common law fraud claim granted and reliance may be shown in regard thereto where alleged misstatements were made directly to the complainant).

Chapter 13
INSIDER TRADING

A. INTRODUCTION

1. Overview

The subject of "insider" trading has been the focus of increased judicial scrutiny, vigorous SEC enforcement, and congressional attention. The Supreme Court has decided three major cases in this area. In *Chiarella v. United States*, 445 U.S. 222 (1980), the Court asserted that the imposition of liability under § 10(b) and Rule 10b-5 for trading on material non-public information must be premised upon a duty to disclose. In *Dirks v. SEC*, 463 U.S. 646 (1983), the Court held that the duty of tippers-tippees to disclose or abstain from trading under § 10(b) and Rule 10b-5 depends on "whether the insider personally will benefit [e.g., by receipt of pecuniary gain or reputational enhancement that will translate into future earnings], directly, or indirectly, from his disclosure. Absent some personal gain, there has been no breach of duty to stockholders. And absent a breach by the insider, there is no derivative breach [by the tippee]."[1] And, in *United States v. O'Hagan*, 521 U.S. 642 (1997), the Court upheld the validity of: (1) the misappropriation theory under § 10(b) as well as (2) SEC Rule 14e-3.

The decisions in *Chiarella* and *Dirks*, although embracing certain traditional principles that had been adopted by the lower courts and the SEC,[2] render it more difficult for the SEC and private claimants to emerge victorious. Thus far, however, the SEC generally has met this challenge. In both *Chiarella* and *Dirks*, for example, the Court left unresolved the viability of the misappropriation theory. After *Chiarella*, the SEC and the Department of Justice successfully invoked this rationale. For example, in *United States v. Newman*, 664 F.2d 12, 17–18 (2d Cir. 1981), the Second Circuit upheld an indictment on the grounds that the defendants had allegedly misappropriated valuable non-public information entrusted to them in the utmost secrecy. The court found that the defendants had "sullied the reputations" of their employers, investment banks, "as safe repositories of client confidences" and had deceived the clients of these investment banks "whose takeover plans were keyed to target company stock prices fixed by market forces, not artificially inflated through purchases by purloiners of confidential information." Several other appellate courts adopted the misappropriation theory. Ultimately, the Supreme Court in *United States v. O'Hagan*, 521 U.S. 642 (1997), upheld the misappropriation theory, holding that a person who engages in securities trading, using confidential material information in breach of a fiduciary duty owed to the source of the information, violates § 10(b).

Investors trading contemporaneously in the securities markets in such misappropriation cases initially were left without a remedy. In *Moss v. Morgan Stanley*, 719 F.2d 5 (2d Cir. 1983), the Second Circuit, in affirming the dismissal of an action seeking monetary damages for violations of § 10(b), held that the plaintiffs failed to prove that the defendants breached a duty owed to them. In legislation enacted in 1988, however, Congress provided contemporaneous traders with an express right of action against those on the opposite side of the transaction who allegedly engaged in

---

[1] Another relevant Supreme Court decision is *Carpenter v. United States*, 484 U.S. 19 (1987).

[2] *See, e.g.*, SEC v. Texas Gulf Sulphur Co., 401 F.2d 833 (2d Cir. 1968) (en banc), *cert. denied*, 394 U.S. 976 (1969) (imposing a duty on corporate officers and directors premised on the equal access theory to disclose or refrain from trading on material non-public information); In re Cady, Roberts & Co., 40 S.E.C. 907 (1961) (same).

illegal insider trading of the same class of securities.[3]

Another example of the SEC's response to *Chiarella* was its promulgation, pursuant to § 14(e) of the Williams Act, of Rule 14e-3 which seeks to deter insider and tippee trading in the tender offer setting. Generally, the rule, with certain exceptions, contains broad "disclose or abstain from trading" as well as "anti-tipping" provisions. With certain exemptions, Rule 14e-3 applies the disclose-or-abstain provision where an individual is in possession of material information relating to a tender offer and knows or has reason to know that such information is nonpublic and was obtained directly or indirectly from the offeror, the subject corporation, any of their affiliated persons, or any person acting on behalf of either company.

In the release adopting the rule, the Commission asserted that *Chiarella* did not limit its authority under § 14(e) to prescribe such a mandate regulating insider trading in the tender offer context. Subsequently, the Supreme Court in *United States v. O'Hagan*, 521 U.S. 642 (1997), upheld the validity of Rule 14e-3, at least insofar as applied to the circumstances present in that case.[4]

Congress also has been active in this area by enacting legislation in 1984 and 1988. Due to the difficulty in comprehensively defining "insider trading," Congress elected to leave the further development of this concept to judicial interpretation. Among other provisions, the 1984 legislation amends § 21(d) of the Exchange Act to authorize the SEC to seek the imposition of a civil monetary penalty amounting to three times the profit received or loss avoided due to the violative transaction(s). As provided by the 1988 legislation, under certain conditions, broker-dealers, investment advisers, and others are subject to the treble monetary penalty for illegal inside trades effected by those persons who are under their control.[5]

Given our focus on state corporation law in this course, it perhaps is surprising that insider trading law in this country is generally within the province of federal law. Although a few states (such as New York[6]) allow derivative suits against alleged inside traders based on perceived harm to the corporation or on the basis of unjust enrichment, state law remedies often are unavailable in this context.[7] This lack of state law redress is due to the lack of an insider's disclosure obligation when transactions occur in the impersonal securities markets and the view that such trading activity does not harm the corporation. Indeed, outside of New York and a few other states, even for those states that hold that insiders owe a duty to disclose material information before trading, such "duty attach[es] where the insider and the shareholder trade face-to-face; transactions conducted on anonymous exchanges apparently do not qualify."[8]

It also it bears emphasis that, until recently, many countries did not prohibit insider trading. As an *Economist* survey pointed out in 1989: "West Germany and France

---

[3] For more discussion on *Chiarella, Dirks, O'Hagan*, and their implications, see, for example, A. Bromberg & L. Lowenfels, *Securities Fraud & Commodities Fraud* §§ 7.4–7.5 (2007); D. Langevoort, *Insider Trading: Regulation, Enforcement & Prevention* (1992 & supp.); W. Wang & M. Steinberg, *Insider Trading* (2d ed. 2005 & ann. supp.).

[4] For commentary on Rule 14e-3, see, e.g., W. Wang & M. Steinberg, *Insider Trading* §§ 9.1–9.4 (2d ed. 2005 & ann. supp).

[5] For commentary on the 1984 and 1988 legislation, see, e.g., Aldave, *The Insider Trading and Securities Fraud Enforcement Act of 1988: An Analysis and Appraisal*, 52 ALBANY L. REV. 893 (1988); Friedman, *The Insider Trading and Securities Fraud Enforcement Act of 1988*, 68 N. CAR. L. REV. 465 (1990); Langevoort, *The Insider Trading Sanctions Act of 1984 and Its Effect on Existing Law*, 37 VAND. L. REV. 1273 (1984).

[6] Diamond v. Oreamuno, 24 N.Y.2d 494, 248 N.E.2d 910, 301 N.Y.S.2d 78 (1969).

[7] *See, e.g.*, Freeman v. Decio, 584 F.2d 186 (7th Cir. 1978) (applying Indiana law); Shein v. Chasen, 313 So. 2d 739 (Fla. 1975).

[8] W. Wang & M. Steinberg, *Insider Trading* § 15:2 (2d ed. 2005). See generally Branson, *Choosing the Appropriate Default Rule — Insider Trading Under State Law*, 45 ALA. L. REV. 753 (1994); Hazen, *Corporate Insider Trading: Reawakening the Common Law*, 39 WASH. & LEE. L. REV. 845 (1982).

assumed until recently that insider trading was what financial life was all about."[9] Even today, although technically illegal, insider trading rarely is prosecuted in a number of countries. What significance should be given to the position taken by other countries? Do these countries believe that the discouragement of insider trading through local business norms is sufficient? Or, do some of these countries view insider trading as a legitimate management perk and a means to enhance market efficiency? Nonetheless, given the increasing number of countries that recently have enacted legislation illegalizing insider trading and are actively pursuing alleged violators, evidently the view of insider trading held in the United States is gaining international acceptance.[10]

2. The Meaning of "Material" and "Nonpublic" Information

Under certain conditions, the federal securities laws prohibit the trading of securities (or 'tipping' related thereto) when such person uses *material nonpublic* information. In *SEC v. Mayhew*, 121 F.3d 44 (2d Cir. 1997), the Second Circuit discussed the meaning of *material* and *nonpublic* information:

Nonpublic Information Requirement

Citing articles in the financial press and the fluctuations in the price of Rorer shares prior to his November 1989 conversation with [his source] Piccolino, [defendant] Mayhew argues that the information he received from Piccolino was already public, relieving him of liability.

Of course, trading based on public information does not violate [§ 10(b) or] § 14(e). Information becomes public when disclosed "to achieve a broad dissemination to the investing public generally and without favoring any special person or group," . . . or when, although known only by a few persons, their trading on it "has caused the information to be fully impounded into the price of the particular stock," . . . Moreover, "[t]o constitute non-public information under the act, information must be specific and more private than general rumor." . . . On the other hand, information may be nonpublic within the meaning of the 1934 Act even though it does not reveal all the details of a [particular event or] tender offer.

Mayhew bases his argument on the widespread media speculation, prior to November 15, 1989, that Rorer was a takeover or merger candidate. As early as April 5, 1988, one article predicted that "Rorer itself ha[d] become a takeover candidate" after its stock price dropped following Rorer's failed attempt to acquire another pharmaceutical company. . . . On May 30, 1989, another article placed Rorer on a "hit list" of six pharmaceutical companies that it predicted were vulnerable takeover targets. . . . On July 31, 1989, an article discussed the rise in Rorer stock due to "speculation about the next takeover target" in the pharmaceutical industry. . . . In contrast, another article indicated that Rorer planned to stay independent. . . .

In sum, the aggregate of public information prior to November 15, 1989, was to the effect that Rorer was willing to merge if it found the right partner and that Rorer was discussing this possibility with up to three companies. Privately, Rorer executives took care to keep information about actual merger discussions secret by limiting the persons who knew about specific merger negotiations to top executives and by using codes in related documents.

---

[9] *A Survey of Europe's Internal Market*, Economist, July 8, 1989, at 15.

[10] For scholarship in this area, see, for example, Beny, *Insider Trading Laws and Stock Markets Around the World: An Empirical Contribution to the Theoretical Law and Economics Debate*, 32 J. Corp. L. 237 (2007); Nasser, *The Morality of Insider Trading in the United States and Abroad*, 52 Okla. L. Rev. 377 (1999); Steinberg, *Insider Trading Regulation — A Comparative Analysis*, 37 Int'l Law. 153 (2003); Symposium, 19 Dickinson J. Int'l L. No. 1 (2000).

We agree with the district court that the information Piccolino conveyed to Mayhew went beyond that which had been publicly disseminated. Mayhew learned from Piccolino that Thurman, the president of Rorer's pharmaceuticals business, had confirmed that Rorer was "actually in discussions" toward merger with a candidate or candidates. He also learned that these merger talks were at a "serious" stage — far enough along to warrant PCA's involvement in negotiating a new employment agreement for Rorer's CEO. To a reasonable investor, this combination of new information, acquired privately, transformed the likelihood of a Rorer merger from one that was certainly possible at some future time to one that was highly probably quite soon.

In *Cusimano*, [97 F.3d 663 (2d Cir. 1996),] we held that a corporate insider's confirmation of information on which the financial press had speculated can satisfy the nonpublic requirement in the context of § 10(b). In that case, the *Wall Street Journal* had reported that AT&T and NCR Corporation were discussing ways to integrate their businesses. On the same day that the article was published, an AT&T insider called Cusimano to confirm the contents of the article and predicted that AT&T would acquire NCR. Cusimano subsequently began trading in NCR securities. We held that the tip Cusimano received satisfied the nonpublic requirement of § 10(b) because the confirmation by an insider of the merger speculated in the press made it less likely that nothing would happen. We see no reason to take a different view under similar circumstances in the context of § 14(e), and thus discern no error in the district court's finding that the information passed from Thurman to Piccolino to Mayhew exceeded that in the financial press and, to that extent, was not public.

In the alternative, Mayhew argues that the information he received from Piccolino was public because it was already built into the price of Rorer stock which had risen on speculation of merger and subsequently fallen as rumored mergers did not take place. We agree that the merger rumors in the media, prior to November 15, 1989, had pushed up the price of Rorer shares; however, the fact that, from the investors' perspective, the rumors had not borne fruit was also impounded into the price, causing it to drop. In these circumstances, it was reasonable for the finder of fact to conclude that this new information that (i) serious merger negotiations were actually ongoing, and (ii) had reached the point where the CEO was about to negotiate a new employment contract with the merged entity, had not been impounded into the price of Rorer stock. That conclusion is buttressed by the fact that on January 15, 1989, when the merger discussions were disclosed, the price of Rorer stock rose more than 20 percent from $49.75 to $63 per share.

In sum, we discern no clear error in the district court's finding that the information Mayhew received from Piccolino following the latter's November 15, 1989 luncheon with Thurman, effectively confirming information about which there had been speculation and lending a degree of immediacy to it, was nonpublic.

Materiality Requirement

Mayhew also challenges the district court's materiality finding, arguing that the information he received from Piccolino lacked sufficient specificity to be material. We disagree.

Information is material "if there is a substantial likelihood that a reasonable [investor] would consider it important in deciding how to [invest]." *Basic Inc. v. Levinson*, 485 U.S. 224, 231 (1988). . . . The materiality of information is a mixed question of law and fact. "The legal component depends on whether the information is relevant to a given question in light of the controlling substantive law. The factual component requires an inference as to whether the information would likely be given weight by a person considering that question." . . .

To be material, the information need not be such a reasonable investor would necessarily change his investment decision based on the information, as long as a reasonable investor would have viewed it as significantly altering the "total mix" of information available. . . . Material facts include those "which affect the probable future of the company and those which may affect the desire of investors to buy, sell, or hold the company's securities." . . .

In the context of a merger, where information can be speculative and tenuous, the materiality standard may be difficult to apply. Materiality will, in such cases, depend "upon a balancing of both the indicated probability that the event will occur and the anticipated magnitude of the event in light of the totality of the company activity." . . . Thus, a violation of the securities laws will not be found where "the disclosed information is so general that the recipient thereof is still 'undertaking a substantial economic risk that his tempting target will prove to be a 'white elephant.' " . . . However, because a merger is one of the most important events that can occur for a small company, information regarding a merger "can become material at an earlier stage than would be the case as regards lesser transactions." . . . Moreover, where information regarding a merger originates from an insider, the information, even if not detailed, "takes on an added charge just because it is inside information." . . . And a major factor in determining whether information was material is the importance attached to it by those who knew about it. . . .

In this case, it was reasonable for the district court to conclude the information material to Mayhew's and Piccolino's decisions to invest, in Piccolino's case for the first time in options and for the first time in Rorer securities. Although Mayhew had invested in Rorer prior to November 15, 1989, he had sold all his Rorer shares at a loss by that date. After the Thurman-Piccolino luncheon, Mayhew plunged heavily into Rorer stock and options, committing more than half of his portfolio to the investment. Although Mayhew was not given the specific details of the merger, a lesser level of specificity is required because he knew the information came from an insider and that the merger discussions were actual and serious. . . . We see no basis for disturbing the district court's conclusions that a reasonable investor would find the information to have significantly altered the total mix of available information and that the information was thus, material.

. . . .

Interestingly, the issue of materiality was presented with respect to Martha Stewart's trading of the common stock of ImClone Systems Incorporated (ImClone). Ms. Stewart was criminally convicted for making false statements to government officials and for conspiracy (433 F.3d 273 (2d Cir. 2006)). The alleged insider trading violations were a subject of SEC civil enforcement action but not Department of Justice criminal prosecution. Ms. Stewart settled (without admitting or denying) the SEC's civil action against her for alleged illegal insider trading (38 SEC. REG. & L. REP. (BNA) 1397 (S.D.N.Y. 2006)). See *Martha Stewart's Legal Troubles* (J. Heminway editor 2006); Heminway, *Martha Stewart Saved! Insider Violations of Rule 10b-5 for Misrepresented or Undisclosed Personal Facts*, 65 MD. L. REV. 380 (2006). The issue of materiality thus was not resolved. Serving as an expert witness on behalf of Ms. Stewart, one of the authors of this text opined:

[1] I understand from the Indictment and the Government's opening argument at trial that the Government has insinuated that Ms. Stewart committed insider trading on December 27, 2001 when she sold her shares of ImClone Systems Incorporated (ImClone). As alleged by the Government, one

of her motives, if not her primary motive for allegedly lying, conspiring, and obstructing a governmental investigation, was to cover up the allegedly improper trade. Upon review of testimony concerning the conversation [that Ms. Stewart's stock broker] Mr. Faneuil allegedly had with Ms. Stewart and the surrounding circumstances, I conclude that, accepting the Government's evidence as true, Ms. Stewart did not commit illegal insider trading. Based upon the custom and practice of the SEC and the securities industry, Ms. Stewart would have reasonably believed that she was not engaging in illegal insider trading with respect to her sales of ImClone common stock (stock).

[2] [Ms. Stewart's stock broker] Mr. Faneuil testified that he told Ms. Stewart on December 27, 2001 that Dr. Samuel Waksal, the CEO of ImClone, was trying to sell all of his ImClone stock held at Merrill Lynch & Co., Inc. (Merrill Lynch). He also testified that Ms. Stewart asked for a price quote, he gave a price quote, and then she ordered the sale of her remaining ImClone stock. Accepting this testimony as true, the information Mr. Faneuil gave Ms. Stewart about Dr. Waksal's contemplated sale was not "material" information applying standards of custom and practice as understood under the federal securities laws. Therefore, this information cannot serve as the basis for an insider trading charge.

[3] Corporate executive officers and directors, including CEOs, sell shares of a subject company's stock for a variety of reasons, many of which have nothing to do with the subject company. It is well known that a CEO of a U.S. publicly-held company may sell stock: because he/she needs money to use for personal or business purpose(s); to ameliorate margin dilemmas in his/her securities account(s); to diversify the CEO's portfolio to include a broader number and type of investments; to convey a gift; to generate cash to repay a loan or for some other obligation; or for tax planning purposes (especially at the end of the year). Normally, these reasons are irrelevant to the subject company and communicate no useful information to investors about the subject company.

[4] As testified to by [Ms. Stewart's stockbroker] Mr. Faneuil, the conversation with Ms. Stewart occurred at the end of the year (i.e., December 27, 2001). This testimony constitutes further support that information about Dr. Waksal's selling was not material. End of the year selling by CEOs and other insiders for tax planning purposes or to provide gifts to family members is a common occurrence.

[5] CEOs may sell stock for reasons that may impact (either positively or negatively) the subject company. For example, a CEO may sell a number of his/her shares of the subject company due to a lack of confidence in the company's future projects. As another example, a CEO may sell shares of the company's stock in response to a third party's tender offer. Dr. Waksal, for instance, sold over 800,00 shares of ImClone stock in October 2001 pursuant to a tender offer made by Bristol Myers Squibb Company (Bristol Myers).

[6] Under custom and practice today, a corporate insider, such as a CEO, would not sell company stock based on material non-public information. Because of sophisticated investigative resources, vigorous government enforcement, and self-imposed corporate insider trading "black-out" periods, insiders who trade on or tip material non-public information act at their peril.

[7] The purported significance of an insider's contemplated sales of subject securities recedes further when the information communicated does not include the number of shares or the percentage of the CEO's holdings that are contemplated to be sold. According to [Ms. Stewart's stock broker] Mr. Faneuil's testimony, he did not tell Ms. Stewart how many shares Dr. Waksal wanted to sell or what percent of Dr. Waksal's ImClone holdings were at Merrill Lynch; indeed, Mr. Faneuil testified that he told Ms. Stewart that he was sure

that Dr. Waksal did not have all of his ImClone shares at Merrill Lynch. My understanding is that there is no evidence that Ms. Stewart was aware of either the amount or the percent of ImClone shares that Dr. Waksal had at Merrill Lynch. A review of the Form 4 filed by Dr. Waksal with the SEC on or about November 13, 2001 and the Form 5 filed by Dr. Waksal with the SEC on or about February 15, 2002, which I understand have been admitted into evidence as Stewart Exhibits AC and AD, reveals that although Dr. Waksal attempted to sell and later transferred 79,797 shares of ImClone stock to his daughter, he still owned over 2.9 million shares of ImClone stock after the transfer. Dr. Waksal thus attempted to dispose of approximately 2.6% of his ImClone stock holdings on or about December 27, 2001. As set forth in this Declaration, under custom and practice today, this information was not material. An additional fact negating materiality is that approximately two months earlier, in late October 2001, Dr. Waksal sold 814,676 shares of ImClone stock pursuant to the Bristol Myers tender offer, representing over twenty percent of his ImClone stock holdings. This sale, of which I understand Ms. Stewart was aware, evidenced that Dr. Waksal was receptive (or at least not adverse) to selling shares of his ImClone stock.

[8] After approximately twenty-five years experience in the securities law field, including my work at the SEC, I am aware of no case in the history of the federal securities laws, prior to the litigation against Ms. Stewart, in which anyone was charged with civil or criminal insider trading based solely upon a tip that a CEO or other insider was selling his/her securities of the subject corporation.

[9] Such a charge also is incongruous given the legal regime that existed as of December 27, 2001. In December 2001, any subject insider who sold a subject security generally did not have to disclose that trade to the public until the making of an SEC filing by the tenth day of the month following the trade. Even after Congress' enactment of the Sarbanes-Oxley Act of 2002, this information generally is not required to be filed with the SEC until the end of the second business day following the trade. This regimen evidences that an insider's trade standing alone is not material. If an insider's trade standing alone were material, then a subject insider would be required to publicly disclose his/her contemplated sale of subject securities prior to ordering such sale, not after such sale of subject securities has been effected as existing law generally mandates.

[10] If the fact that a corporate insider (such as a CEO) were seeking to sell his/her stock were itself material information, then every insider trade (such as by a CEO) would itself violate the law. Such a sale transaction under this approach would violate Section 10(b0 and Rule 10b-5 because (among other reasons): (1) the sale was non-public (subject company shareholders and prospective investors were unaware of the contemplated trade); and (2) the trade was itself material. Such a position, as set forth in this Declaration, is contrary to the custom and practice that prevailed in December 2001 and that remains true today.

[11] Based on the foregoing, and accepting the Government's evidence as true, it is my opinion that: Ms. Stewart did not receive material information; and, on December 27, 2001, it would have been reasonable for Ms. Stewart to believe that her sale of ImClone stock was not illegal insider trading.

Declaration of Marc I. Steinberg in *United States v. Martha Stewart* (dated Feb. 19, 2004).

PROBLEMS

1. "Red" Calhounse, Organic State University's football coach, has cocktails with an alumnus and her spouse at an alumni function. The alumnus during cocktails tells her spouse that the corporation, of which she is a director, will announce the receipt of a multi-million dollar contract the following week. Calhounse, being privy to the conversation, thereupon purchases 10,000 shares. He sells them three years later at a profit of $80,000. The SEC brings suit. What result and why?

2. Thomas, a financial analyst for Z.G. Gold, Inc., an investment banking and brokerage firm, calls Gregory, the chief financial officer of Mak-It Corp., seeking information about Mak-It's earnings during the last quarter which will be announced the following week. Gregory says "It looks like our earnings will be down quite a bit." Thomas immediately informs his customers who sell Mak-It stock. The SEC brings suit. Who are "proper" defendants? Result?

3. EZ-Tech, Inc. intends to make a tender offer for the shares of LoMar Corporation, a publicly-held company whose common stock is traded on the New York Stock Exchange. Before the EZ-Tech tender offer is announced, Liz Meriweather, a lawyer working for Nameth, Shields & Davis, a law firm that represents EZ-Tech, has dinner with her husband Ryan. She informs Ryan that she is exhausted because of the long hours she is working in regard to the forthcoming EZ-Tech tender offer for LoMar. She adds that this information is confidential. The next day Liz and Ryan, unaware of the purchases by the other, each acquire a few thousand shares of LoMar common stock. Ryan's broker T.Y. Little also purchases Lo-Mar stock based on "hints" communicated by Ryan. After public announcement of the EZ-Tech offer, Liz, Ryan and T. Y. each sell their LoMar shares for a substantial profit. The SEC and private parties in separate actions institute suit against Liz, Ryan and T.Y. What result and why? Would the result be different if the contemplated transaction took the form of a merger rather than a tender offer?

B. THE "DUTY" THEORY

CHIARELLA v. UNITED STATES
Supreme Court of the United States
445 U.S. 222, 100 S. Ct. 1108, 63 L. Ed. 2d 348 (1980)

MR. JUSTICE POWELL delivered the opinion of the Court.

The question in this case is whether a person who learns from the confidential documents of one corporation that it is planning an attempt to secure control of a second corporation violates § 10(b) of the Securities Exchange Act of 1934 if he fails to disclose the impending takeover before trading in the target company's securities.

I

Petitioner is a printer by trade. In 1975 and 1976, he worked as a "markup man" in the New York composing room of Pandick Press, a financial printer. Among documents that petitioner handled were five announcements of corporate takeover bids. When these documents were delivered to the printer, the identities of the acquiring and target corporations were concealed by blank spaces or false names. The true names were sent to the printer on the night of the final printing.

The petitioner, however, was able to deduce the names of the target companies before the final printing from other information contained in the documents. Without disclosing his knowledge, petitioner purchased stock in the target companies and sold the shares immediately after the takeover attempts were made public.[11] By this method, petitioner realized a gain of slightly more than $30,000 in the course of 14 months. Subsequently, the Securities and Exchange Commission (Commission or SEC) began an investigation of his trading activities. In May 1977, petitioner entered into a consent decree with the Commission in which he agreed to return his profits to the sellers of the shares. On the same day, he was discharged by Pandick Press.

In January 1978, petitioner was indicted on 17 counts of violating § 10(b) of the Securities Exchange Act of 1934 (1934 Act) and SEC Rule 10b-5. After petitioner unsuccessfully moved to dismiss the indictment, he was brought to trial and convicted on all counts.

The Court of Appeals for the Second Circuit affirmed petitioner's conviction. 588 F.2d 1358 (1978). We granted certiorari and we now reverse.

II

Section 10(b) of the 1934 Act prohibits the use "in connection with the purchase or sale of any security . . . [of] any manipulative or deceptive device or contrivance in contravention of such rules and regulations as the Commission may prescribe." Pursuant to this section, the SEC promulgated Rule 10b-5. . . .

This case concerns the legal effect of the petitioner's silence. The District Court's charge permitted the jury to convict the petitioner if it found that he willfully failed to inform sellers of target company securities that he knew of a forthcoming takeover bid that would make their shares more valuable. In order to decide whether silence in such circumstances violates § 10(b), it is necessary to review the language and legislative history of that statute as well as its interpretation by the Commission and the federal courts.

Although the starting point of our inquiry is the language of the statute, § 10(b) does not state whether silence may constitute a manipulative or deceptive device. Section 10(b) was designed as a catchall clause to prevent fraudulent practices. But neither the legislative history nor the statute itself affords specific guidance for the resolution of this case. When Rule 10b-5 was promulgated in 1942, the SEC did not discuss the possibility that failure to provide information might run afoul of § 10(b).

The SEC took an important step in the development of § 10(b) when it held that a broker-dealer and his firm violated that section by selling securities on the basis of undisclosed information obtained from a director of the issuer corporation who was also a registered representative of the brokerage firm. In *Cady, Roberts & Co.*, 40 S.E.C. 907 (1961), the Commission decided that a corporate insider must abstain from trading in the shares of his corporation unless he has first disclosed all material inside information known to him. The obligation to disclose or abstain derives from

> [a]n affirmative duty to disclose material information [which] has been traditionally imposed on corporate "insiders," particularly officers, directors, or controlling stockholders. We, and the courts have consistently held that insiders must disclose material facts which are known to them by virtue of their position but which are not known to persons with whom they deal and which, if known, would affect their investment judgment.

The Commission emphasized that the duty arose from (i) the existence of a relationship affording access to inside information intended to be available only for a corporate purpose, and (ii) the unfairness of allowing a corporate insider to take advantage of that information by trading without disclosure.

That the relationship between a corporate insider and the stockholders of his

---

[11] [1] Of the five transactions, four involved tender offers and one concerned a merger. 588 F.2d 1358, 1363, n.2 (CA2 1978).

corporation gives rise to a disclosure obligation is not a novel twist of the law. At common law, misrepresentation made for the purpose of inducing reliance upon the false statement is fraudulent. But one who fails to disclose material information prior to the consummation of a transaction commits fraud only when he is under a duty to do so. And the duty to disclose arises when one party has information "that the other [party] is entitled to know because of a fiduciary or other similar relation of trust and confidence between them."[12] In its *Cady, Roberts* decision, the Commission recognized a relationship of trust and confidence between the shareholders of a corporation and those insiders who have obtained confidential information by reason of their position with that corporation. This relationship gives rise to a duty to disclose because of the "necessity of preventing a corporate insider from . . . tak[ing] unfair advantage of the uninformed minority stockholders." . . .

The federal courts have found violations of § 10(b) where corporate insiders used undisclosed information for their own benefit. The cases also have emphasized, in accordance with the common-law rule, that "[t]he party charged with failing to disclose market information must be under a duty to disclose it." Accordingly, a purchaser of stock who has no duty to a prospective seller because he is neither an insider nor a fiduciary has been held to have no obligation to reveal material facts.

. . . .

Thus, administrative and judicial interpretations have established that silence in connection with the purchase or sale of securities may operate as a fraud actionable under § 10(b) despite the absence of statutory language or legislative history specifically addressing the legality of nondisclosure. But such liability is premised upon a duty to disclose arising from a relationship of trust and confidence between parties to a transaction. Application of a duty to disclose prior to trading guarantees that corporate insiders, who have an obligation to place the shareholder's welfare before their own, will not benefit personally through fraudulent use of material, nonpublic information.[13]

III

In this case, the petitioner was convicted of violating § 10(b) although he was not a corporate insider and he received no confidential information from the target company. Moreover, the "market information" upon which he relied did not concern the earning power or operations of the target company, but only the plans of the acquiring company. Petitioner's use of that information was not a fraud under § 10(b) unless he was subject to an affirmative duty to disclose it before trading. In this case, the jury instructions failed to specify any such duty. In effect, the trial court instructed the jury that petitioner owed a duty to everyone; to all sellers, indeed, to the market as a whole. The jury simply was told to decide whether petitioner used material, nonpublic information at a time when "he knew other people trading in the securities market did not have access to the same information."

The Court of Appeals affirmed the conviction by holding that "[a]nyone — corporate insider or not — who regularly receives material nonpublic information may not use that information to trade in securities without incurring an affirmative duty to disclose." . . . Although the court said that its test would include only persons who regularly

---

[12] [9] Restatement (Second) of Torts § 551(2)(a) (1976). See James & Gray, *Misrepresentation — Part II*, 37 Md. L. Rev. 488, 523–27 (1978). As regards securities transactions, the American Law Institute recognizes that "silence when there is a duty to . . . speak may be a fraudulent act." ALI, Federal Securities Code § 262(b) (Prop. Off. Draft 1978).

[13] [12] "Tippees" of corporate insiders have been held liable under § 10(b) because they have a duty not to profit from the use of inside information that they know is confidential and know or should know came from a corporate insider, *Shapiro v. Merrill Lynch, Pierce, Fenner & Smith, Inc.*, 495 F.2d 228, 237–238 (2d Cir. 1974). The tippee's obligation has been viewed as arising from his role as a participant after the fact in the insider's breach of a fiduciary duty. . . .

receive material, nonpublic information, its rationale for that limitation is unrelated to the existence of a duty to disclose. The Court of Appeals, like the trial court, failed to identify a relationship between petitioner and the sellers that could give rise to a duty. Its decision thus rested solely upon its belief that the federal securities laws have "created a system providing equal access to information necessary for reasoned and intelligent investment decisions." . . . The use by anyone of material information not generally available is fraudulent, this theory suggests, because such information gives certain buyers or sellers an unfair advantage over less informed buyers and sellers.

This reasoning suffers from two defects. First, not every instance of financial unfairness constitutes fraudulent activity under § 10(b). See Santa Fe Industries, Inc. v. Green, 430 U.S. 462, 474–477 (1977). Second, the element required to make silence fraudulent — a duty to disclose — is absent in this case. No duty could arise from petitioner's relationship with the sellers of the target company's securities, for petitioner had no prior dealings with them. He was not their agent, he was not a fiduciary, he was not a person in whom the sellers had placed their trust and confidence. He was, in fact, a complete stranger who dealt with the sellers only through impersonal market transactions.

We cannot affirm petitioner's conviction without recognizing a general duty between all participants in market transactions to forgo actions based on material, nonpublic information. Formulation of such a broad duty, which departs radically from the established doctrine that duty arises from a specific relationship between two parties, should not be undertaken absent some explicit evidence of congressional intent.

As we have seen, no such evidence emerges from the language or legislative history of § 10(b). Moreover, neither the Congress nor the Commission ever has adopted a parity-of-information rule . . . .

Section 10(b) is aptly described as a catchall provision, but what it catches must be fraud. When an allegation of fraud is based upon nondisclosure, there can be no fraud absent a duty to speak. We hold that a duty to disclose under § 10(b) does not arise from the mere possession of nonpublic market information. The contrary result is without support in the legislative history of § 10(b) and would be inconsistent with the careful plan that Congress has enacted for regulation of the securities markets.

IV

In its brief to this Court, the United States offers an alternative theory to support petitioner's conviction. It argues that petitioner breached a duty to the acquiring corporation when he acted upon information that he obtained by virtue of his position as an employee of a printer employed by the corporation. The breach of this duty is said to support a conviction under § 10(b) for fraud perpetrated upon both the acquiring corporation and the sellers.

We need not decide whether this theory has merit for it was not submitted to the jury. . . .

. . . Because we cannot affirm a criminal conviction on the basis of a theory not presented to the jury, we will not speculate upon whether such a duty exists, whether it has been breached, or whether such a breach constitutes a violation of § 10(b).

The judgment of the Court of Appeals is

Reversed.

MR. CHIEF JUSTICE BURGER, dissenting.

I believe that the jury instructions in this case properly charged a violation of § 10(b) and Rule 10b-5, and I would affirm the conviction.

     . . . .

As a general rule, neither party to an arm's-length business transaction has an obligation to disclose information to the other unless the parties stand in some confidential or fiduciary relation. See W. Prosser, Law of Torts § 106 (2d ed. 1955). This rule permits a businessman to capitalize on his experience and skill in securing and evaluating relevant information; it provides incentive for hard work, careful analysis, and astute forecasting. But the policies that underlie the rule also should limit its scope. In particular, the rule should give way when an informational advantage is obtained, not by superior experience, foresight, or industry, but by some unlawful means. . . .

I would read § 10(b) and Rule 10b-5 to encompass and build on this principle: to mean that a person who has misappropriated nonpublic information has an absolute duty to disclose that information or to refrain from trading.

. . . .

The Court's opinion, as I read it, leaves open the question whether § 10(b) and Rule 10b-5 prohibit trading on misappropriated nonpublic information.[14] Instead, the Court apparently concludes that this theory of the case was not submitted to the jury. In the Court's view, the instructions given the jury were premised on the erroneous notion that the mere failure to disclose nonpublic information, however acquired, is a deceptive practice. And because of this premise, the jury was not instructed that the means by which Chiarella acquired his informational advantage — by violating a duty owed to the acquiring companies — was an element of the offense.

The Court's reading of the District Court's charge is unduly restrictive. Fairly read as a whole and in the context of the trial, the instructions required the jury to find that Chiarella obtained his trading advantage by misappropriating the property of his employer's customers. . . .

In sum, the evidence shows beyond all doubt that Chiarella, working literally in the shadows of the warning signs in the print shop, misappropriated — stole to put it bluntly — valuable nonpublic information entrusted to him in the utmost confidence. He then exploited his ill-gotten informational advantage by purchasing securities in the market. In my view, such conduct plainly violates § 10(b) and Rule 10b-5. Accordingly, I would affirm the judgment of the Court of Appeals.

MR. JUSTICE BLACKMUN, with whom MR. JUSTICE MARSHALL joins, dissenting.

Although I agree with much of what is said in Part I of the dissenting opinion of The Chief Justice, I write separately because, in my view, it is unnecessary to rest petitioner's conviction on a "misappropriation" theory. The fact that petitioner Chiarella purloined, or, to use The Chief Justice's word, "stole," information concerning pending tender offers certainly is the most dramatic evidence that petitioner was guilty of fraud. He has conceded that he knew it was wrong, and he and his co-workers in the print shop were specifically warned by their employer that actions of this kind were improper and forbidden. But I also would find petitioner's conduct fraudulent within the meaning of § 10(b) of the Securities Exchange Act of 1934 and the Securities and Exchange Commission's Rule 10b-5, even if he had obtained the blessing of his employer's principals before embarking on his profiteering scheme. Indeed, I think petitioner's brand of manipulative trading, with or without such approval, lies close to the heart of what the securities laws are intended to prohibit.

The Court continues to pursue a course, charted in certain recent decisions, designed to transform § 10(b) from an intentionally elastic "catchall" provision to one that catches

---

[14] [4] There is some language in the Court's opinion to suggest that only "a relationship between petitioner and the sellers . . . could give rise to a duty [to disclose]." The Court's holding, however, is much more limited, namely, that mere possession of material, nonpublic information is insufficient to create a duty to disclose or to refrain from trading. Accordingly, it is my understanding that the Court has not rejected the view, advanced above, that an absolute duty to disclose or refrain arises from the very act of misappropriating nonpublic information.

relatively little of the misbehavior that all too often makes investment in securities a needlessly risky business for the uninitiated investor. Such confinement in this case is now achieved by imposition of a requirement of a "special relationship" akin to fiduciary duty before the statute gives rise to a duty to disclose or to abstain from trading upon material, nonpublic information. The Court admits that this conclusion finds no mandate in the language of the statute or its legislative history. Yet the Court fails even to attempt a justification of its ruling in terms of the purposes of the securities laws, or to square that ruling with the longstanding but now much abused principle that the federal securities laws are to be construed flexibly rather than with narrow technicality.

I, of course, agree with the Court that a relationship of trust can establish a duty to disclose under § 10(b) and Rule 10b-5. But I do not agree that a failure to disclose violates the Rule only when the responsibilities of a relationship of that kind have been breached. As applied to this case, the Court's approach unduly minimizes the importance of petitioner's access to confidential information that the honest investor, no matter how diligently he tried, could not legally obtain. In doing so, it further advances an interpretation of § 10(b) and Rule 10b-5 that stops short of their full implications. Although the Court draws support for its position from certain precedent, I find its decision neither fully consistent with developments in the common law of fraud, nor fully in step with administrative and judicial application of Rule 10b-5 to "insider" trading.

. . . .

By its narrow construction of § 10(b) and Rule 10b-5, the Court places the federal securities laws in the rearguard of this movement, a position opposite to the expectations of Congress at the time the securities laws were enacted. I cannot agree that the statute and Rule are so limited. The Court has observed that the securities laws were not intended to replicate the law of fiduciary relations. Rather, their purpose is to ensure the fair and honest functioning of impersonal national securities markets where common-law protections have proved inadequate. As Congress itself has recognized, it is integral to this purpose "to assure that dealing in securities is fair and without undue preferences or advantages among investors." . . .

Whatever the outer limits of the Rule, petitioner Chiarella's case fits neatly near the center of its analytical framework. He occupied a relationship to the takeover companies giving him intimate access to concededly material information that was sedulously guarded from public access. The information, in the words of *Cady, Roberts & Co.*, was "intended to be available only for a corporate purpose and not for the personal benefit of anyone." Petitioner, moreover, knew that the information was unavailable to those with whom he dealt. And he took full, virtually riskless advantage of this artificial information gap by selling the stocks shortly after each takeover bid was announced. By any reasonable definition, his trading was "inherent[ly] unfai[r]." This misuse of confidential information was clearly placed before the jury. Petitioner's conviction, therefore, should be upheld, and I dissent from the Court's upsetting that conviction.

C. "TIPPER-TIPPEE" LIABILITY

DIRKS v. SECURITIES & EXCHANGE COMMISSION
Supreme Court of the United States
463 U.S. 646, 103 S. Ct. 3255, 77 L. Ed. 2d 911 (1983)

JUSTICE POWELL delivered the opinion of the Court.

Petitioner Raymond Dirks received material nonpublic information from "insiders" of a corporation with which he had no connection. He disclosed this information to investors who relied on it in trading in the shares of the corporation. The question is whether Dirks violated the antifraud provisions of the federal securities laws by this disclosure.

I

In 1973, Dirks was an officer of a New York broker-dealer firm who specialized in providing investment analysis of insurance company securities to institutional investors. On March 6, Dirks received information from Ronald Secrist, a former officer of Equity Funding of America. Secrist alleged that the assets of Equity Funding, a diversified corporation primarily engaged in selling life insurance and mutual funds, were vastly overstated as the result of fraudulent corporate practices. Secrist also stated that various regulatory agencies had failed to act on similar charges made by Equity Funding employees. He urged Dirks to verify the fraud and disclose it publicly.

Dirks decided to investigate the allegations. He visited Equity Funding's headquarters in Los Angeles and interviewed several officers and employees of the corporation. The senior management denied any wrongdoing, but certain corporation employees corroborated the charges of fraud. Neither Dirks nor his firm owned or traded any Equity Funding stock, but throughout his investigation he openly discussed the information he had obtained with a number of clients and investors. Some of these persons sold their holdings of Equity Funding securities, including five investment advisers who liquidated holdings of more than $16 million.

While Dirks was in Los Angeles, he was in touch regularly with William Blundell, the Wall Street Journal's Los Angeles bureau chief. Dirks urged Blundell to write a story on the fraud allegations. Blundell did not believe, however, that such a massive fraud could go undetected and declined to write the story. He feared that publishing such damaging hearsay might be libelous.

During the two-week period in which Dirks pursued his investigation and spread word of Secrist's charges, the price of Equity Funding stock fell from $26 per share to less than $15 per share. This led the New York Stock Exchange to halt trading on March 27. Shortly thereafter California insurance authorities impounded Equity Funding's records and uncovered evidence of the fraud. Only then did the Securities and Exchange Commission (SEC) file a complaint against Equity Funding and only then, on April 2, did the Wall Street Journal publish a front-page story based largely on information assembled by Dirks. Equity Funding immediately went into receivership.

The SEC began an investigation into Dirks' role in the exposure of the fraud. After a hearing by an administrative law judge, the SEC found that Dirks had aided and abetted violations of § 17(a) of the Securities Act of 1933, § 10(b) of the Securities Exchange Act of 1934, and SEC Rule 10b-5, by repeating the allegations of fraud to members of the investment community who later sold their Equity Funding stock. The SEC concluded: "Where 'tippees' — regardless of their motivation or occupation — come into possession of material 'information that they know is confidential and know or should know came from a corporate insider,' they must either publicly disclose that information or refrain from trading." Recognizing, however, that Dirks "played an important role in bringing [Equity Funding's] massive fraud to light," the SEC only censured him.

Dirks sought review in the Court of Appeals for the District of Columbia Circuit. The court entered judgment against Dirks "for the reasons stated by the Commission in its opinion." . . .

. . . We now reverse.

III

We were explicit in *Chiarella* in saying that there can be no duty to disclose where the person who has traded on inside information "was not [the corporation's] agent, . . . was not a fiduciary, [or] was not a person in whom the sellers [of the securities] had placed their trust and confidence." Not to require such a fiduciary relationship, we recognized, would "depar[t] radically from the established doctrine that duty arises from a specific relationship between two parties" and would amount to "recognizing a general duty between all participants in market transactions to forgo actions based on material, nonpublic information." This requirement of a specific relationship between the shareholders and the individual trading on inside information has created analytical difficulties for the SEC and courts in policing tippees who trade on inside information. Unlike insiders who have independent fiduciary duties to both the corporation and its shareholders, the typical tippee has no such relationships.[15] In view of this absence, it has been unclear how a tippee acquires the duty to refrain from trading on inside information.

A

The SEC's position, as stated in its opinion in this case, is that a tippee "inherits" the *Cady, Roberts* obligation to shareholders whenever he receives inside information from an insider:

> In tipping potential traders, Dirks breached a duty which he had assumed as a result of knowingly receiving confidential information from [Equity Funding] insiders. Tippees such as Dirks who receive non-public material information from insiders become "subject to the same duty as [the] insiders." Such a tippee breaches the fiduciary duty which he assumes from the insider when the tippee knowingly transmits the information to someone who will probably trade on the basis thereof. . . . Presumably, Dirks' informants were entitled to disclose the [Equity Funding] fraud in order to bring it to light and its perpetrators to justice. However, Dirks — standing in their shoes — committed a breach of the fiduciary duty which he had assumed in dealing with them, when he passed the information on to traders.

This view differs little from the view that we rejected as inconsistent with congressional intent in *Chiarella*. In that case, the Court of Appeals agreed with the SEC and affirmed Chiarella's conviction, holding that

> [a]nyone — corporate insider or not — who regularly receives material nonpublic information may not use that information to trade in securities without incurring an affirmative duty to disclose.

Here, the SEC maintains that anyone who knowingly receives nonpublic material information from an insider has a fiduciary duty to disclose before trading.

---

[15] [14] Under certain circumstances, such as where corporate information is revealed legitimately to an underwriter, accountant, lawyer, or consultant working for the corporation, these outsiders may become fiduciaries of the shareholders. The basis for recognizing this fiduciary duty is not simply that such persons acquired nonpublic corporate information, but rather that they have entered into a special confidential relationship in the conduct of the business of the enterprise and are given access to information solely for corporate purposes. When such a person breaches his fiduciary relationship, he may be treated more properly as a tipper than a tippee. For such a duty to be imposed, however, the corporation must expect the outsider to keep the disclosed nonpublic information confidential, and the relationship at least must imply such a duty.

In effect, the SEC's theory of tippee liability in both cases appears rooted in the idea that the antifraud provisions require equal information among all traders. This conflicts with the principle set forth in *Chiarella* that only some persons, under some circumstances, will be barred from trading while in possession of material nonpublic information. . . .

. . . We reaffirm today that "[a] duty [to disclose] arises from the relationship between parties . . . and not merely from one's ability to acquire information because of his position in the market."

Imposing a duty to disclose or abstain solely because a person knowingly receives material nonpublic information from an insider and trades on it could have an inhibiting influence on the role of market analysts, which the SEC itself recognizes is necessary to the preservation of a healthy market. It is commonplace for analysts to "ferret out and analyze information," . . . and this often is done by meeting with and questioning corporate officers and others who are insiders. And information that the analysts obtain normally may be the basis for judgments as to the market worth of a corporation's securities. The analyst's judgment in this respect is made available in market letters or otherwise to clients of the firm. It is the nature of this type of information, and indeed of the markets themselves, that such information cannot be made simultaneously available to all of the corporation's stockholders or the public generally.

B

The conclusion that recipients of inside information do not invariably acquire a duty to disclose or abstain does not mean that such tippees always are free to trade on the information. The need for a ban on some tippee trading is clear. Not only are insiders forbidden by their fiduciary relationship from personally using undisclosed corporate information to their advantage, but they may not give such information to an outsider for the same improper purpose of exploiting the information for their personal gain. Similarly, the transactions of those who knowingly participate with the fiduciary in such a breach are "as forbidden" as transactions "on behalf of the trustee himself." . . . As we noted in *Chiarella*, "[t]he tippee's obligation has been viewed as arising from his role as a participant after the fact in the insider's breach of a fiduciary duty."

Thus, some tippees must assume an insider's duty to the shareholders not because they receive inside information, but rather because it has been made available to them improperly. And for Rule 10b-5 purposes, the insider's disclosure is improper only where it would violate his *Cady, Roberts* duty. Thus, a tippee assumes a fiduciary duty to the shareholders of a corporation not to trade on material nonpublic information only when the insider has breached his fiduciary duty to the shareholders by disclosing the information to the tippee and the tippee knows or should know that there has been a breach. As Commissioner Smith perceptively observed in *Investors Management Co.*: "[T]ippee responsibility must be related back to insider responsibility by a necessary finding that the tippee knew the information was given to him in breach of a duty by a person having a special relationship to the issuer not to disclose the information. . . . " Tipping thus properly is viewed only as a means of indirectly violating the *Cady, Roberts* disclose-or-abstain rule.

C

In determining whether a tippee is under an obligation to disclose or abstain, it thus is necessary to determine whether the insider's "tip" constituted a breach of the insider's fiduciary duty. All disclosures of confidential corporate information are not inconsistent with the duty insiders owe to shareholders. In contrast to the extraordinary facts of this case, the more typical situation in which there will be a question whether disclosure violates the insider's *Cady, Roberts* duty is when insiders disclose information to analysts. In some situations, the insider will act consistently with his fiduciary duty to shareholders, and yet release of the information may affect the market. For example, it may not be clear — either to the corporate insider or to the recipient analyst — whether the information will be viewed as material nonpublic information. Corporate officials may mistakenly think the information already has been disclosed or that it is not material enough to affect the market. Whether disclosure is a breach of duty therefore depends in large part on the purpose of the disclosure. This standard was identified by the SEC itself in *Cady, Roberts*: a purpose of the securities laws was to eliminate "use of inside information for personal advantage." Thus, the test is whether the insider personally will benefit, directly or indirectly, from his disclosure. Absent some personal gain, there has been no breach of duty to stockholders. And absent a breach by the insider, there is no derivative breach. . . .

The SEC argues that, if inside-trading liability does not exist when the information is transmitted for a proper purpose but is used for trading, it would be a rare situation when the parties could not fabricate some ostensibly legitimate business justification for transmitting the information. We think the SEC is unduly concerned. In determining whether the insider's purpose in making a particular disclosure is fraudulent, the SEC and the courts are not required to read the parties' minds. Scienter in some cases is relevant in determining whether the tipper has violated his *Cady, Roberts* duty. But to determine whether the disclosure itself "deceive[s], manipulate[s], or defraud[s]" shareholders, the initial inquiry is whether there has been a breach of duty by the insider. This requires courts to focus on objective criteria, i.e., whether the insider receives a direct or indirect personal benefit from the disclosure, such as a pecuniary gain or a reputational benefit that will translate into future earnings. There are objective facts and circumstances that often justify such an inference. For example, there may be a relationship between the insider and the recipient that suggests a quid pro quo from the latter, or an intention to benefit the particular recipient. The elements of fiduciary duty and exploitation of non-public information also exist when an insider makes a gift of confidential information to a trading relative or friend. The tip and trade resemble trading by the insider himself followed by a gift of the profits to the recipient.

Determining whether an insider personally benefits from a particular disclosure, a question of fact, will not always be easy for courts. But it is essential, we think, to have a guiding principle for those whose daily activities must be limited and instructed by the SEC's inside-trading rules, and we believe that there must be a breach of the insider's fiduciary duty before the tippee inherits the duty to disclose or abstain. In contrast, the rule adopted by the SEC in this case would have no limiting principle.

IV

Under the inside-trading and tipping rules set forth above, we find that there was no actionable violation by Dirks. It is undisputed that Dirks himself was a stranger to Equity Funding, with no pre-existing fiduciary duty to its shareholders. He took no action, directly or indirectly, that induced the shareholders or officers of Equity Funding to repose trust or confidence in him. There was no expectation by Dirk's sources that he would keep their information in confidence. Nor did Dirks misappropriate or illegally obtain the information about Equity Funding. Unless the insiders breached their *Cady, Roberts* duty to shareholders in disclosing the nonpublic information to Dirks, he breached no duty when he passed it on to investors as well as to the Wall Street Journal.

It is clear that neither Secrist nor the other Equity Funding employees violated their *Cady, Roberts* duty to the corporation's shareholders by providing information to Dirks. The tippers received no monetary or personal benefit for revealing Equity Funding's secrets, nor was their purpose to make a gift of valuable information to Dirks. As the facts of this case clearly indicate, the tippers were motivated by a desire to expose the fraud. In the absence of a breach of duty to shareholders by the insiders, there was no derivative breach by Dirks. Dirks therefore could not have been "a participant after the fact in [an] insider's breach of a fiduciary duty."

V

We conclude that Dirks, in the circumstances of this case, had no duty to abstain from use of the inside information that he obtained. The judgment of the Court of Appeals therefore is

Reversed.

JUSTICE BLACKMUN, with whom JUSTICE BRENNAN and JUSTICE MARSHALL join, dissenting.

The Court today takes still another step to limit the protections provided investors by § 10(b) of the Securities Exchange Act of 1934. The device employed in this case engrafts a special motivational requirement on the fiduciary duty doctrine. This innovation excuses a knowing and intentional violation of an insider's duty to shareholders if the insider does not act from a motive of personal gain. Even on the extraordinary facts of this case, such an innovation is not justified.

. . . .

The fact that the insider himself does not benefit from the breach does not eradicate the shareholder's injury.

. . . It makes no difference to the shareholder whether the corporate insider gained or intended to gain personally from the transaction; the shareholder still has lost because of the insider's misuse of nonpublic information. The duty is addressed not to the insider's motives, but to his actions and their consequences on the shareholder. Personal gain is not an element of the breach of this duty.

. . . .

The improper purpose requirement not only has no basis in law, but it rests implicitly on a policy that I cannot accept. The Court justifies Secrist's and Dirks' action because the general benefit derived from the violation of Secrist's duty to shareholders outweighed the harm caused to those shareholders. . . . Under this view, the benefit conferred on society by Secrist's and Dirks' activities may be paid for with the losses caused to shareholders trading with Dirks' clients.[16]

. . . .

Dirks and Secrist were under a duty to disclose the information or to refrain from trading on it. I agree that disclosure in this case would have been difficult. I also recognize that the SEC seemingly has been less than helpful in its view of the nature of disclosure necessary to satisfy the disclose-or-refrain duty. The Commission tells persons with inside information that they cannot trade on that information unless they disclose; it refuses, however, to tell them how to disclose. This seems to be a less than sensible policy, which it is incumbent on the Commission to correct. The Court, however, has no authority to remedy the problem by opening a hole in the congressionally mandated prohibition on insider trading, thus rewarding such trading.

. . . .

In my view, Secrist violated his duty to Equity Funding shareholders by transmitting material nonpublic information to Dirks with the intention that Dirks would cause his

---

[16] [14] This position seems little different from the theory that insider trading should be permitted because it brings relevant information to the market. See H. Manne, *Insider Trading and the Stock Market* 59–76, 111–146 (1966); Manne, *Insider Trading and the Law Professors*, 23 Vand. L. Rev. 547, 565–576 (1970). The Court also seems to embrace a variant of that extreme theory, which postulates that insider trading causes no harm at all to those who purchase from the insider.

Both the theory and its variant sit at the opposite end of the theoretical spectrum from the much maligned equality-of-information theory, and never have been adopted by Congress or ratified by this Court. The theory rejects the existence of any enforceable principle of fairness between market participants.

clients to trade on that information. Dirks, therefore, was under a duty to make the information publicly available or to refrain from actions that he knew would lead to trading. Because Dirks caused his clients to trade, he violated § 10(b) and Rule 10b-5. Any other result is a disservice to this country's attempt to provide fair and efficient capital markets. I dissent.

———

NOTE

Subsequent to *Dirks*, the SEC has responded tenaciously in an effort to maintain a vigilant enforcement program against insider trading. One route has been to embrace the "quasi-insider" principle that received approbation in *Dirks*. Under this rationale, individuals enjoying a special relationship with the corporation, such as accountants, attorneys, consultants, and underwriters, may be viewed as insiders when they trade on material non-public information that they legitimately received during the course of that relationship. As stated by the *Dirks* Court, "[t]he basis for recognizing this fiduciary duty is not simply that such persons acquired nonpublic corporate information, but rather that they have entered into a special confidential relationship in the conduct of the business of the enterprise and are given access to information solely for corporate purposes." Another approach invoked by the Commission has been to make the showing of "benefit," required by *Dirks*, by proving that the insider disclosed the information for financial gain or made a "gift" of material non-public information to the tippee.

In perhaps a surprising decision, *United States v. Evans*, 486 F.3d 315 (7th Cir. 2007), the Seventh Court upheld the conviction of a tippee even though a prior jury had acquitted the tipper of all charges. Given that a tippee's liability is derivative and must be premised on the tipper's breach, the court's decision may be suspect. Nonetheless, the court reasoned that the earlier acquittal of the tipper "did not prevent a properly instructed second jury from finding that [the tipper's] tips were unlawful and that [the tippee,] by knowingly trading on that information, violated the law." For another recent decision involving a former university professor who was criminally convicted for unlawful tipping to his then wife and to his then best friend, see *United States v. Blackwell*, 459 F.3d 739 (6th Cir. 2006).

Nevertheless, as the following case indicates, the Commission's task at times has been rendered more difficult.

SECURITIES & EXCHANGE COMMISSION v. SWITZER
United States District Court, Western District of Oklahoma
590 F. Supp. 756 (1984)

SAFFELS, DISTRICT JUDGE, Sitting by Designation.

This action brought by the Securities and Exchange Commission [hereinafter SEC] was tried to the court on March 19–22, 1984. It involved allegations of violations of Section 10(b) of the Securities Exchange Act of 1934 and violations of Commission Rule 10b-5. On the basis of the following findings of fact and conclusions of law, the court shall enter judgment on behalf of the defendants.

Findings of Fact

The following findings of fact have been stipulated to by all parties and accepted by the court and are set forth as follows.

. . . .

6. Barry L. Switzer resides at 2811 Castlewood Drive, Norman, Oklahoma (73070). At all times mentioned in the complaint, Switzer was the head football coach at the University of Oklahoma in Norman, Oklahoma.

. . . .

13. Texas International Company [hereinafter TIC] is a Delaware corporation with principal offices located in Oklahoma City, Oklahoma. At all times mentioned in the complaint, TIC was engaged in, among other things, exploration for and development of oil and natural gas properties. . . . On or about June 18, 1982, a wholly-owned subsidiary of TIC merged with Phoenix Resources Company [hereinafter Phoenix] and Phoenix became a wholly-owned subsidiary of TIC. At all times mentioned in the complaint prior to the merger, TIC owned in excess of fifty percent (50%) of the common stock of Phoenix, and, by reason of such ownership position, controlled Phoenix through election of three of the five members of the Phoenix Board of Directors.

14. Prior to the merger, Phoenix, the successor to King Resources Company, was a Maine corporation with principal offices located in Oklahoma City, Oklahoma. At all times mentioned in the complaint prior to the merger, Phoenix engaged in, among other things, exploration for and development of oil and natural gas properties. . . .

. . . .

18. On or about Wednesday, June 10, 1981, after the public announcement [of the merger, defendant] Hoover sold all sixteen thousand five hundred (16,500) shares of Phoenix at prices between Fifty-Nine Dollars ($59) and Sixty-Three and 50/100 Dollars ($63.50) per share; the pre-tax profits realized on the basis of trading over this three-day period [June 8–10] amounted to approximately Two Hundred Sixty-Seven Thousand Seven Hundred Twenty-Eight Dollars ($267,728); and the pre-tax profits paid to and divided by [defendants] Switzer and Smith amounted to approximately One Hundred Ten Thousand Four Hundred Ninety-One Dollars ($110,491).

19. [Defendants] Hodges and Amyx agreed to purchase Phoenix stock through the Hodges, Amyx, Cross and Hodges investment partnership account.

20. On or about Monday, June 8, and Tuesday, June 9, 1981, Amyx, on behalf of the Hodges, Amyx, Cross and Hodges investment partnership, purchased thirteen thousand (13,000) shares of Phoenix at prices between Forty-Three and 50/100 Dollars ($43.50) and Forty-Eight and 50/100 Dollars ($48.50) per share.

21. On or about Wednesday, June 10, and Thursday, June 11, 1981, the Hodges, Amyx, Cross and Hodges investment partnership sold all thirteen thousand (13,000) shares of Phoenix at prices between Fifty-Nine Dollars ($59) and Sixty-Five Dollars ($65) per share; the pre-tax profits realized by the investment partnership on the basis of trading over a four-day period amounted to approximately Two Hundred Five Thousand Fifty-Five Dollars ($205,055); and the pre-tax profits from such trading paid to and divided by [defendants] Switzer and Smith amounted to approximately Eighty-Five Thousand Three Hundred Ten Dollars ($85,310).

. . . .

The following additional facts are found by the court:

. . . .

32. Barry Switzer is a well-recognized "celebrity" in Oklahoma and elsewhere. He has an interest in the oil and gas industry, as he is personally involved in various ventures within the industry.

33. Over the past several years, defendants Switzer, Kennedy, Deem, Smith, Hodges, Amyx, and Hoover have acted together in varying combinations of persons (or in various groups of persons) in making investments. They have formed partnerships such as S & H Investments, Waverly Ltd., and Hodges, Amyx, Cross and Hodges, to assist them in their investment ventures. Oftentimes, they trade on rumors or gossip they hear within the investing community. Profits and losses occurring as a result of stock investments made through these partnerships are shared by the members of the partnerships.

34. TIC had been considering various options for either consolidating or separating TIC and Phoenix for some time prior to its approaching Morgan Stanley on June 4 or 5, 1981. Rumors concerning these various options were circulating within the investing oil and gas community prior to June 4 or 5, 1981.

35. On June 6, 1981, four days prior to the public announcement concerning Phoenix, a state invitational secondary school track meet was held at John Jacobs Field on the University of Oklahoma campus. The track meet was a day long event. Several hundred spectators attended, including Barry Switzer, who arrived at the meet between 10:00 and 10:30 a.m. to watch his son compete, and George and Linda Platt, who arrived between 9:00 and 10:00 a.m. to watch their son compete. Soon after Switzer's arrival at the track meet, he and G. Platt recognized and greeted each other. Neither Switzer nor G. Platt knew that the other would be attending the meet. [G. Platt was Chairman of the Board and the Chief Executive Officer of TIC and served as a director on the Phoenix Board of Directors.]

36. G. Platt was a supporter of Oklahoma University football and had met Switzer at a few social engagements prior to June of 1981. TIC was a sponsor of Switzer's football show, "Play Back." G. Platt had had season tickets to the OU football games for approximately five years. G. Platt had obtained autographs from Switzer for G. Platt's minor children, and had had his secretary telephone Switzer to request that his season tickets be upgraded. Upgrading of tickets was extended as a courtesy by Switzer to many season ticket holders. On at least two occasions Switzer had phoned G. Platt requesting continued sponsorship by TIC of Switzer's football television program. These calls were made at the urging of Tom Goodgame, General Manager of the television station which then produced "Play Back." As of June 5, 1981, Switzer knew that G. Platt was Chairman of the Board of TIC and further knew that TIC was a substantial shareholder of Phoenix because Switzer was a stockholder in TIC and thereby knew Phoenix was a subsidiary.

37. Neither G. Platt nor his wife Linda are particularly impressed by Switzer. They view him as "just a nice fellow."

38. Upon first greeting each other at the track meet, G. Platt and Switzer exchanged pleasantries. Switzer then departed and continued on through the bleachers.

39. Throughout the course of the day, G. Platt and Linda Platt generally remained in one place in the bleachers. Switzer, however, throughout the day moved around a great deal, at times speaking with his son or other participants and their families, signing autographs and watching the different events on the field. While moving about, Switzer joined the Platts to visit with them about three to five times. During these visits Switzer and the Platts talked about their sons' participation in the meet, the oil and gas business, the economy, football and their respective personal investments.

40. G. Platt and Switzer did not have any conversations regarding Phoenix or Morgan Stanley, nor did they have any conversations regarding any mergers, acquisitions, take-overs or possible liquidations of Phoenix in which Morgan Stanley would play a part. G. Platt did not make any stock recommendations to Switzer, nor did he intentionally communicate material, non-public corporate information to Switzer about Phoenix during their conversations at the track meet. The information that Switzer heard at the track meet about Phoenix was overheard and was not the result of an intentional disclosure by G. Platt.

41. Sometime in the afternoon, after his last conversation with G. Platt, Switzer laid down on a row of bleachers behind the Platts to sunbathe while waiting for his son's next event. While Switzer was sunbathing, he overheard G. Platt talking to his wife about his trip to New York the prior day. In that conversation, G. Platt mentioned Morgan Stanley and his desire to dispose of or liquidate Phoenix. G. Platt further talked about several companies bidding on Phoenix. Switzer also overheard that an announcement of a "possible" liquidation of Phoenix might occur the following Thursday. Switzer remained on the bleachers behind the Platts for approximately

twenty minutes then got up and continued to move about.

42. At this time Switzer had no knowledge as to whether the information he had overheard was confidential.

43. G. Platt was not conscious of Switzer's presence on the bleachers behind him that day, nor that Switzer had overheard any conversation.

44. G. Platt had returned home late the previous day from his meetings in New York, and his wife was to leave town for an entire week on the following day. Having minor children, it is the Platts' common practice to try to arrange for G. Platt to be at home when his wife is out of town. The day of the track meet provided the Platts with an opportunity to discuss their respective plans for the up-coming week. During this discussion, G. Platt's prior business activities in New York and his resultant obligations and appointments were mentioned. In addition, when G. Platt appears distracted, it is not uncommon for his wife to inquire of him what is on his mind. On these occasions, he will talk to her about his problems, even though she does not have an understanding of nor interest in business matters. On the day of the track meet, Phoenix was weighing upon the mind of G. Platt, as it had been for the past several years, prompting G. Platt to talk to his wife about it.

45. On June 6, 1981, after the track meet, Switzer returned home and looked up the price of Phoenix in the paper. . . .

46. By the end of the evening, Switzer . . . had expressed an intention to purchase Phoenix stock.

. . . .

49. On Sunday, June 7, 1981, Switzer called Lee Allan Smith, a close friend with whom he had previously entered joint investments. Switzer told Smith that he had been at a track meet on Saturday and had overheard some information regarding the possible liquidation or buy-out of Phoenix. Switzer attributed the information to "someone who should know," and said that he had overheard that Morgan Stanley was involved and that something could happen by Thursday of the following week. Switzer and Smith decided to approach . . . Robert Hoover about providing the capital for buying some Phoenix stock with them because Smith and Switzer had insufficient available cash at that time to purchase a significant number of shares on their own. . . . Hoover has known Smith for thirty years and has been a personal friend of both Smith and Switzer. . . .

. . . .

56. On Sunday, June 7, 1981, . . . Switzer and Smith met with Robert Hoover at his home, where he was having a party. Switzer and Smith arrived separately. Smith first discussed the matter with Hoover and did not mention where he had received the information. Switzer also told Hoover something was going to happen with Phoenix, but did not say from whom he had heard the information.

57. Hoover agreed to purchase Phoenix stock jointly with Smith and Switzer. Hoover advanced the capital and purchased the stock for his account, based on an understanding that any losses or profits would be split, fifty percent (50%) to Hoover, and the remaining fifty percent (50%) to be divided between Smith and Switzer.

58. Hoover purchased sixteen thousand (16,000) shares of Phoenix stock on or about Monday, June 8, or Tuesday, June 9, 1981.

59. G. Platt did not learn of Switzer's purchase or sale of Phoenix stock, or of the conversation Switzer had overheard, until on or about March 10 or 11, 1982. On or about March 10 or 11, 1982, Switzer called G. Platt at Platt's condominium in Snow Mass, Colorado, and asked to meet with him because Switzer said something he had inadvertently done would affect Platt. At the time Switzer was also staying in Snow Mass, Colorado. During this meeting, Switzer told G. Platt, for the first time, that Switzer had been sitting behind G. Platt and his wife at the track meet on June 6, 1981,

and had overheard G. Platt's conversation with his wife regarding Phoenix, and that as a result of that overheard conversation, Switzer and other friends of his had subsequently purchased and sold Phoenix stock. G. Platt had heard as early as February of 1982 that Phoenix was under investigation by the SEC. . . .

. . . .

61. G. Platt did not share in the profits made through the transactions in Phoenix stock by Switzer [and others] nor did he receive any other financial benefit as a result of those transactions.

62. G. Platt did not receive any direct or indirect pecuniary gain nor any reputational benefit likely to translate into future earnings due to Switzer's inadvertent receipt of the information regarding Phoenix.

63. G. Platt did not make any gift to Switzer at this time, nor has he ever made a gift to Switzer.

64. Neither Switzer, [nor any other defendant] has ever been employed by or been an officer or director of Phoenix or TIC, nor have any of these defendants ever had any business relationship with Phoenix or with G. Platt personally. None of these defendants is a relative or personal friend of G. Platt.

65. None of the defendants had a relationship of trust and confidence with Phoenix, its shareholders or G. Platt.

. . . .

Conclusions of Law

Based upon the foregoing findings of fact, the court makes the following conclusions of law.

. . . .

7. [O]nly when a disclosure is made for an "improper purpose" will such a "tip" constitute a breach of an insider's duty, and only when there has been a breach of an insider's duty which the "tippee" knew or should have known constituted such a breach will there be "tippee" liability sufficient to constitute a violation of § 10(b) and Commission Rule 10b-5.

8. In *Dirks*, the court held that a disclosure is made for an "improper purpose" when an insider personally will benefit, directly or indirectly, from his disclosure. That court stated: "Absent some personal gain, there has been no breach of duty to stockholders. And absent a breach by the insider [to his stockholders], there is no derivative breach [by the tippee]."

9. G. Platt did not breach a fiduciary duty to stockholders of Phoenix for purposes of Rule 10b-5 liability nor § 10(b) liability, when he disclosed to his wife at the track meet of June 6, 1981, that there was going to be a possible liquidation of Phoenix.

10. This information was given to Mrs. Platt by G. Platt for the purpose of informing her of his up-coming business schedule so that arrangements for child care could be made.

11. The information was inadvertently overheard by Switzer at the track meet.

12. Rule 10b-5 does not bar trading on the basis of information inadvertently revealed by an insider.

13. The information was not intentionally imparted to Switzer by G. Platt, nor was the disclosure made for an improper purpose.

14. G. Platt did not personally benefit, directly or indirectly, monetarily or otherwise from the inadvertent disclosure.

15. As noted above, *Dirks* set forth a two-prong test for purposes of determining whether a tippee has acquired a fiduciary duty. First, it must be shown that an insider

breached a fiduciary duty to the shareholders by disclosing inside information; and, second, it must be shown that the tippee knew or should have known that there had been a breach by the insider.

16. G. Platt did not breach a duty to the shareholders of Phoenix, and thus plaintiff failed to meet its burden of proof as to the first prong established in *Dirks*. Since G. Platt did not breach a fiduciary duty to Phoenix shareholders, Switzer did not acquire nor assume a fiduciary duty to Phoenix's shareholders, and because Switzer did not acquire a fiduciary duty to Phoenix shareholders, any information he passed on to defendant [tippees] was not in violation of Rule 10b-5.

17. Since plaintiff did not meet its burden of proof as to the first prong of the two-prong *Dirks* test, i.e., it was not proved that G. Platt breached a fiduciary duty to the shareholders of Phoenix, tippee liability cannot result from G. Platt's inadvertent disclosure to Switzer.

18. Even if, however, plaintiff had met the first prong of the two-part test, i.e., had proven that G. Platt did disclose material non-public information to Switzer at the track meet in an improper manner, the court would still find no resulting tippee liability to Switzer [or any other defendant] because the court concludes plaintiff failed to prove the second prong of the *Dirks* test as well. These defendants did not know, nor did they have reason to know, that the information they received was material, non-public information disseminated by a corporate insider for an improper purpose, and, thus, under *Dirks*, are not liable as tippees under Rule 10b-5.

. . . .

D. THE "MISAPPROPRIATION" THEORY

UNITED STATES v. O'HAGAN
Supreme Court of the United States
521 U.S. 642, 117 S. Ct. 2199, 138 L. Ed. 2d 724 (1997)

Justice Ginsburg delivered the opinion of the Court.

This case concerns the interpretation and enforcement of § 10(b) and § 14(e) of the Securities Exchange Act of 1934, and rules made by the Securities and Exchange Commission pursuant to these provisions, Rule 10b-5 and Rule 14e-3(a). Two prime questions are presented. The first relates to the misappropriation of material, nonpublic information for securities trading; the second concerns fraudulent practices in the tender offer setting. In particular, we address and resolve these issues: (1) Is a person who trades in securities for personal profit, using confidential information misappropriated in breach of a fiduciary duty to the source of the information, guilty of violating § 10(b) and Rule 10b-5? (2) Did the Commission exceed its rulemaking authority by adopting Rule 14e-3(a), which proscribes trading on undisclosed information in the tender offer setting, even in the absence of a duty to disclose? Our answer to the first question is yes, and to the second question, viewed in the context of this case, no. [Rule 14e-3 is discussed in Part F of this Chapter.]

Respondent James Herman O'Hagan was a partner in the law firm of Dorsey & Whitney in Minneapolis, Minnesota. In July 1988, Grand Metropolitan PLC (Grand Met), a company based in London, England, retained Dorsey & Whitney as local counsel to represent Grand Met regarding a potential tender offer for the common stock of the Pillsbury Company, headquartered in Minneapolis. Both Grand Met and Dorsey & Whitney took precautions to protect the confidentiality of Grand Met's tender offer plans. O'Hagan did no work on the Grand Met representation. Dorsey & Whitney withdrew from representing Grand Met on September 9, 1988. Less than a month later, on October 4, 1988, Grand Met publicly announced its tender offer for Pillsbury stock.

On August 18, 1988, while Dorsey & Whitney was still representing Grand Met, O'Hagan began purchasing call options for Pillsbury stock. Each option gave him the right to purchase 100 shares of Pillsbury stock by a specified date in September 1988. Later in August and in September, O'Hagan made additional purchases of Pillsbury call options. By the end of September, he owned 2,500 unexpired Pillsbury options, apparently more than any other individual investor. O'Hagan also purchased, in September 1988, some 5,000 shares of Pillsbury common stock, at a price just under $39 per share. When Grand Met announced its tender offer in October, the price of Pillsbury stock rose to nearly $60 per share. O'Hagan then sold his Pillsbury call options and common stock, making a profit of more than $4.3 million.

The Securities and Exchange Commission (SEC or Commission) initiated an investigation into O'Hagan's transactions, culminating in a 57-count indictment. The indictment alleged that O'Hagan defrauded his law firm and its client, Grand Met, by using for his own trading purposes material, nonpublic information regarding Grand Met's planned tender offer. According to the indictment, O'Hagan used the profits he gained through this trading to conceal his previous embezzlement and conversion of unrelated client trust funds. . . . A jury convicted O'Hagan on all 57 counts, and he was sentenced to a 41-month term of imprisonment.

A divided panel of the Court of Appeals for the Eighth Circuit reversed all of O'Hagan's convictions. 92 F.3d 612 (1996). Liability under § 10(b) and Rule 10b-5, the Eighth Circuit held, may not be grounded on the "misappropriation theory" of securities fraud on which the prosecution relied. The Court of Appeals also held that Rule 14e-3(a) — which prohibits trading while in possession of material, nonpublic information relating to a tender offer — exceeds the SEC's § 14(e) rulemaking authority because the rule contains no breach of fiduciary duty requirement. The Eighth Circuit further concluded that O'Hagan's mail fraud and money laundering convictions rested on violations of the securities laws, and therefore could not stand once the securities fraud convictions were reversed. . . . We granted certiorari, and now reverse the Eighth Circuit's judgment.

II

We address first the Court of Appeals' reversal of O'Hagan's convictions under § 10(b) and Rule 10b-5. Following the Fourth Circuit's lead, see *United States v. Bryan*, 58 F.3d 933 (1995), the Eighth Circuit rejected the misappropriation theory as a basis for § 10(b) liability. We hold, in accord with several other Courts of Appeals, that criminal liability under § 10(b) may be predicated on the misappropriation theory.

A

[Section 10(b)] proscribes (1) using any deceptive device (2) in connection with the purchase or sale of securities, in contravention of rules prescribed by the Commission. The provision, as written, does not confine its coverage to deception of a purchaser or seller of securities; rather, the statute reaches any deceptive device used "in connection with the purchase or sale of any security."

Pursuant to its § 10(b) rulemaking authority, the Commission has adopted Rule 10b-5 . . . . Liability under Rule 10b-5, our precedent indicates, does not extend beyond conduct encompassed by § 10(b)'s prohibition. . . .

Under the "traditional" or "classical theory" of insider trading liability, § 10(b) and Rule 10b-5 are violated when a corporate insider trades in the securities of his corporation on the basis of material, nonpublic information. Trading on such information qualifies as a "deceptive device" under § 10(b), we have affirmed, because "a relationship of trust and confidence [exists] between the shareholders of a corporation and those insiders who have obtained confidential information by reason of their position with that corporation." *Chiarella v. United States*, 445 U.S. 222, 228 (1980). That relationship, we recognized, "gives rise to a duty to disclose [or to abstain from trading] because of the 'necessity of preventing a corporate insider from . . .

tak[ing] unfair advantage of . . . uninformed . . . stockholders.' " . . . The classical theory applies not only to officers, directors, and other permanent insiders of a corporation, but also to attorneys, accountants, consultants, and others who temporarily become fiduciaries of a corporation. See *Dirks v. SEC*, 463 U.S. 646, 655, n.14 (1983).

The "misappropriation theory" holds that a person commits fraud "in connection with" a securities transaction, and thereby violates § 10(b) and Rule 10b-5, when he misappropriates confidential information for securities trading purposes, in breach of a duty owed to the source of the information. Under this theory, a fiduciary's undisclosed, self-serving use of a principal's information to purchase or sell securities, in breach of a duty of loyalty and confidentiality, defrauds the principal of the exclusive use of that information. In lieu of premising liability on a fiduciary relationship between company insider and purchaser or seller of the company's stock, the misappropriation theory premises liability on a fiduciary-turned-trader's deception of those who entrusted him with access to confidential information.

The two theories are complementary, each addressing efforts to capitalize on nonpublic information through the purchase or sale of securities. The classical theory targets a corporate insider's breach of duty to shareholders with whom the insider transacts; the misappropriation theory outlaws trading on the basis of nonpublic information by a corporate "outsider" in breach of a duty owed not to a trading party, but to the source of the information. The misappropriation theory is thus designed to "protec[t] the integrity of the securities markets against abuses by 'outsiders' to a corporation who have access to confidential information that will affect th[e] corporation's security price when revealed, but who owe no fiduciary or other duty to that corporation's shareholders." . . .

In this case, the indictment alleged that O'Hagan, in breach of a duty of trust and confidence he owed to his law firm, Dorsey & Whitney, and to its client, Grand Met, traded on the basis of nonpublic information regarding Grand Met's planned tender offer for Pillsbury common stock. This conduct, the Government charged, constituted a fraudulent device in connection with the purchase and sale of securities.[17]

B

We agree with the Government that misappropriation, as just defined, satisfies § 10(b)'s requirement that chargeable conduct involve a "deceptive device or contrivance" used "in connection with" the purchase or sale of securities. We observe, first, that misappropriators, as the Government describes them, deal in deception. A fiduciary who "[pretends] loyalty to the principal while secretly converting the principal's information for personal gain," . . . "dupes" or defrauds the principal. See Aldave, *Misappropriation*: A General Theory of Liability for Trading on Nonpublic Information, 13 Hofstra L. Rev. 101, 119 (1984).

We addressed fraud of the same species in *Carpenter v. United States*, 484 U.S. 19 (1987), which involved the mail fraud statute's proscription of "any scheme or artifice to defraud," 18 U.S.C. § 1341. Affirming convictions under that statute, we said in *Carpenter* that an employee's undertaking not to reveal his employer's confidential information "became a sham" when the employee provided the information to his co-conspirators in a scheme to obtain trading profits. A company's confidential information, we recognized in *Carpenter*, qualifies as property to which the company has a right of exclusive use. The undisclosed misappropriation of such information, in

---

[17] [5] The Government could not have prosecuted O'Hagan under the classical theory, for O'Hagan was not an "insider" of Pillsbury, the corporation in whose stock he traded. Although an "outsider" with respect to Pillsbury, O'Hagan had an intimate association with, and was found to have traded on confidential information from, Dorsey & Whitney, counsel to tender offeror Grand Met. Under the misappropriation theory, O'Hagan's securities trading does not escape Exchange Act sanction, as it would under the dissent's reasoning, simply because he was associated with, and gained nonpublic information from, the bidder, rather than the target.

violation of a fiduciary duty, the Court said in *Carpenter*, constitutes fraud akin to embezzlement — " 'the fraudulent appropriation to one's own use of the money or goods entrusted to one's care by another.' " *Carpenter's* discussion of the fraudulent misuse of confidential information, the Government notes, "is a particularly apt source of guidance here, because [the mail fraud statute] (like Section 10(b)) has long been held to require deception, not merely the breach of a fiduciary duty." . . .

Deception through nondisclosure is central to the theory of liability for which the Government seeks recognition. As counsel for the Government stated in explanation of the theory at oral argument: "To satisfy the common law rule that a trustee may not use the property that [has] been entrusted [to] him, there would have to be consent. To satisfy the requirement of the [Exchange] Act that there be no deception, there would only have to be disclosure." . . .

The misappropriation theory advanced by the Government is consistent with *Santa Fe Industries, Inc. v. Green*, 430 U.S. 462 (1977), a decision underscoring that § 10(b) is not an all-purpose breach of fiduciary duty ban; rather, it trains on conduct involving manipulation or deception. In contrast to the Government's allegations in this case, in Santa Fe Industries, all pertinent facts were disclosed by the persons charged with violating § 10(b) and Rule 10b-5; therefore, there was no deception through nondisclosure to which liability under those provisions could attach. Similarly, full disclosure forecloses liability under the misappropriation theory: Because the deception essential to the misappropriation theory involves feigning fidelity to the source of information, if the fiduciary discloses to the source that he plans to trade on the nonpublic information, there is no "deceptive device" and thus no § 10(b) violation — although the fiduciary-turned-trader may remain liable under state law for breach of a duty of loyalty.[18]

We turn next to the § 10(b) requirement that the misappropriator's deceptive use of information be "in connection with the purchase or sale of [a] security." This element is satisfied because the fiduciary's fraud is consummated, not when the fiduciary gains the confidential information, but when, without disclosure to his principal, he uses the information to purchase or sell securities. The securities transaction and the breach of duty thus coincide. This is so even though the person or entity defrauded is not the other party to the trade, but is, instead, the source of the nonpublic information. . . . A misappropriator who trades on the basis of material, nonpublic information, in short, gains his advantageous market position through deception; he deceives the source of the information and simultaneously harms members of the investing public.

The misappropriation theory targets information of a sort that misappropriators ordinarily capitalize upon to gain no-risk profits through the purchase or sale of securities. Should a misappropriator put such information to other use, the statute's prohibition would not be implicated. The theory does not catch all conceivable forms of fraud involving confidential information; rather, it catches fraudulent means of capitalizing on such information through securities transactions.

. . . .

The Government notes another limitation on the forms of fraud § 10(b) reaches: "The misappropriation theory would not . . . apply to a case in which a person defrauded a bank into giving him a loan or embezzled cash from another, and then used the proceeds of the misdeed to purchase securities." . . . In such a case, the Government states, "the proceeds would have value to the malefactor apart from their use in a securities transaction, and the fraud would be complete as soon as the money was obtained." . . . In other words, money can buy, if not anything, then at least many things; its misappropriation may thus be viewed as sufficiently detached from a

---

[18] [7] Where, however, a person trading on the basis of material, nonpublic information owes a duty of loyalty and confidentiality to two entities or persons — for example, a law firm and its client — but makes disclosure to only one, the trader may still be liable under the misappropriation theory.

subsequent securities transaction that § 10(b)'s "in connection with" requirement would not be met.

The dissent's charge that the misappropriation theory is incoherent because information, like funds, can be put to multiple uses misses the point. The Exchange Act was enacted in part "to insure the maintenance of fair and honest markets," and there is no question that fraudulent uses of confidential information fall within § 10(b)'s prohibition if the fraud is "in connection with" a securities transaction. It is hardly remarkable that a rule suitably applied to the fraudulent uses of certain kinds of information would be stretched beyond reason were it applied to the fraudulent use of money.

The dissent does catch the Government in overstatement. Observing that money can be used for all manner of purposes and purchases, the Government urges that confidential information of the kind at issue derives its value only from its utility in securities trading. Substitute "ordinarily" for "only," and the Government is on the mark.

Our recognition that the Government's "only" is an overstatement has provoked the dissent to cry "new theory." . . . Here, . . . Rule 10b-5's promulgation has not been challenged; we consider only the Government's charge that O'Hagan's alleged fraudulent conduct falls within the prohibitions of the rule and § 10(b). In this context, we acknowledge simply that, in defending the Government's interpretation of the rule and statute in this Court, the Government's lawyers have pressed a solid point too far, something lawyers, occasionally even judges, are wont to do.

The misappropriation theory comports with § 10(b)'s language, which requires deception "in connection with the purchase or sale of any security," not deception of an identifiable purchaser or seller. The theory is also well-tuned to an animating purpose of the Exchange Act: to insure honest securities markets and thereby promote investor confidence. . . . Although informational disparity is inevitable in the securities markets, investors likely would hesitate to venture their capital in a market where trading based on misappropriated nonpublic information is unchecked by law. An investor's informational disadvantage vis-a-vis a misappropriator with material, nonpublic information stems from contrivance, not luck; it is a disadvantage that cannot be overcome with research or skill. See Brudney, Insiders, Outsiders, and Informational Advantages Under the Federal Securities Laws, 93 Harv. L. Rev. 322, 356 (1979).

In sum, considering the inhibiting impact on market participation of trading on misappropriated information, and the congressional purposes underlying § 10(b), it makes scant sense to hold a lawyer like O'Hagan a § 10(b) violator if he works for a law firm representing the target of a tender offer, but not if he works for a law firm representing the bidder. The text of the statute requires no such result.[19] The misappropriation at issue here was properly made the subject of a § 10(b) charge because it meets the statutory requirement that there be "deceptive" conduct "in connection with" securities transactions.

---

[19] [9] As noted earlier, however, the textual requirement of deception precludes § 10(b) liability when a person trading on the basis of nonpublic information has disclosed his trading plans to, or obtained authorization from, the principal — even though such conduct may affect the securities markets in the same manner as the conduct reached by the misappropriation theory. Contrary to the dissent's suggestion, the fact that § 10(b) is only a partial antidote to the problems it was designed to alleviate does not call into question its prohibition of conduct that falls within its textual proscription. Moreover, once a disloyal agent discloses his imminent breach of duty, his principal may seek appropriate equitable relief under state law. Furthermore, in the context of a tender offer, the principal who authorizes an agent's trading on confidential information may, in the Commission's view, incur liability for an Exchange Act violation under Rule 14e-3(a).

C

The Court of Appeals rejected the misappropriation theory primarily on two grounds. First, as the Eighth Circuit comprehended the theory, it requires neither misrepresentation nor nondisclosure. As we just explained, however, deceptive nondisclosure is essential to the § 10(b) liability at issue. Concretely, in this case, "it [was O'Hagan's] failure to disclose his personal trading to Grand Met and Dorsey, in breach of his duty to do so, that ma[de] his conduct 'deceptive' within the meaning of § 10(b)."

Second and "more obvious," the Court of Appeals said, the misappropriation theory is not moored to § 10(b)'s requirement that "the fraud be 'in connection with the purchase or sale of any security.'" According to the Eighth Circuit, three of our decisions reveal that § 10(b) liability cannot be predicated on a duty owed to the source of nonpublic information: Chiarella v. United States, 445 U.S. 222 (1980); Dirks v. SEC, 463 U.S. 646 (1983); and Central Bank of Denver, N.A. v. First Interstate Bank of Denver, N.A., 511 U.S. 164 (1994). "[O]nly a breach of a duty to parties to the securities transaction," the Court of Appeals concluded, "or, at the most, to other market participants such as investors, will be sufficient to give rise to § 10(b) liability." We read the statute and our precedent differently, and note again that § 10(b) refers to "the purchase or sale of any security," not to identifiable purchasers or sellers of securities.

Chiarella involved securities trades by a printer employed at a shop that printed documents announcing corporate takeover bids. Deducing the names of target companies from documents he handled, the printer bought shares of the targets before takeover bids were announced, expecting (correctly) that the share prices would rise upon announcement. In these transactions, the printer did not disclose to the sellers of the securities (the target companies' shareholders) the nonpublic information on which he traded. For that trading, the printer was convicted of violating § 10(b) and Rule 10b-5. We reversed the Court of Appeals judgment that had affirmed the conviction.

The jury in *Chiarella* had been instructed that it could convict the defendant if he willfully failed to inform sellers of target company securities that he knew of a takeover bid that would increase the value of their shares. Emphasizing that the printer had no agency or other fiduciary relationship with the sellers, we held that liability could not be imposed on so broad a theory. There is under § 10(b), we explained, no "general duty between all participants in market transactions to forgo actions based on material, nonpublic information." Under established doctrine, we said, a duty to disclose or abstain from trading "arises from a specific relationship between two parties."

The Court did not hold in *Chiarella* that the only relationship prompting liability for trading on undisclosed information is the relationship between a corporation's insiders and shareholders. That is evident from our response to the Government's argument before this Court that the printer's misappropriation of information from his employer for purposes of securities trading — in violation of a duty of confidentiality owed to the acquiring companies — constituted fraud in connection with the purchase or sale of a security, and thereby satisfied the terms of § 10(b). The Court declined to reach that potential basis for the printer's liability, because the theory had not been submitted to the jury. But four Justices found merit in it. And a fifth Justice stated that the Court "wisely le[ft] the resolution of this issue for another day." . . .

Chiarella thus expressly left open the misappropriation theory before us today. Certain statements in *Chiarella*, however, led the Eighth Circuit in the instant case to conclude that § 10(b) liability hinges exclusively on a breach of duty owed to a purchaser or seller of securities. The Court said in *Chiarella* that § 10(b) liability "is premised upon a duty to disclose arising from a relationship of trust and confidence between parties to a transaction," and observed that the printshop employee defendant in that case "was not a person in whom the sellers had placed their trust and confidence." These statements rejected the notion that § 10(b) stretches so far as to impose "a general duty between all participants in market transactions to forgo actions based on material, nonpublic information," and we confine them to that context. The statements highlighted by the Eighth Circuit, in short, appear in an opinion carefully leaving for future resolution the validity of the misappropriation theory, and therefore cannot be read to foreclose that theory.

Dirks, too, left room for application of the misappropriation theory in cases like the one we confront. *Dirks* involved an investment analyst who had received information from a former insider of a corporation with which the analyst had no connection. The information indicated that the corporation had engaged in a massive fraud. The analyst investigated the fraud, obtaining corroborating information from employees of the corporation. During his investigation, the analyst discussed his findings with clients and investors, some of whom sold their holdings in the company the analyst suspected of gross wrongdoing.

The SEC censured the analyst for, inter alia, aiding and abetting § 10(b) and Rule 10b-5 violations by clients and investors who sold their holdings based on the nonpublic information the analyst passed on. In the SEC's view, the analyst, as a "tippee" of corporation insiders, had a duty under § 10(b) and Rule 10b-5 to refrain from communicating the nonpublic information to persons likely to trade on the basis of it. This Court found no such obligation, and repeated the key point made in *Chiarella*: There is no " 'general duty between all participants in market transactions to forgo actions based on material, nonpublic information.' " . . .

No showing had been made in *Dirks* that the "tippers" had violated any duty by disclosing to the analyst nonpublic information about their former employer. The insiders had acted not for personal profit, but to expose a massive fraud within the corporation. Absent any violation by the tippers, there could be no derivative liability for the tippee. Most important for purposes of the instant case, the Court observed in *Dirks*: "There was no expectation by [the analyst's] sources that he would keep their information in confidence. Nor did [the analyst] misappropriate or illegally obtain the information. . . . " *Dirks* thus presents no suggestion that a person who gains nonpublic information through misappropriation in breach of a fiduciary duty escapes § 10(b) liability when, without alerting the source, he trades on the information.

Last of the three cases the Eighth Circuit regarded as warranting disapproval of the misappropriation theory, *Central Bank* held that "a private plaintiff may not maintain an aiding and abetting suit under § 10(b)." We immediately cautioned in *Central Bank* that secondary actors in the securities markets may sometimes be chargeable under the securities acts: "Any person or entity, including a lawyer, accountant, or bank, who employs a manipulative device or makes a material misstatement (or omission) on which a purchaser or seller of securities relies may be liable as a primary violator under 10b-5, assuming . . . the requirements for primary liability under Rule 10b-5 are met." The Eighth Circuit isolated the statement just quoted and drew from it the conclusion that § 10(b) covers only deceptive statements or omissions on which purchasers and sellers, and perhaps other market participants, rely. It is evident from the question presented in *Central Bank*, however, that this Court, in the quoted passage, sought only to clarify that secondary actors, although not subject to aiding and abetting liability, remain subject to primary liability under § 10(b) and Rule 10b-5 for certain conduct.

. . . .

In sum, the misappropriation theory, as we have examined and explained it in this opinion, is both consistent with the statute and with our precedent. Vital to our decision that criminal liability may be sustained under the misappropriation theory, we emphasize, are two sturdy safeguards Congress has provided regarding scienter. To establish a criminal violation of Rule 10b-5, the Government must prove that a person "willfully" violated the provision. Furthermore, a defendant may not be imprisoned for violating Rule 10b-5 if he proves that he had no knowledge of the rule. . . . In addition, the statute's "requirement of the presence of culpable intent as a necessary element of the offense does much to destroy any force in the argument that application of the [statute]" in circumstances such as O'Hagan's is unjust.

The Eighth Circuit erred in holding that the misappropriation theory is inconsistent with § 10(b). The Court of Appeals may address on remand O'Hagan's other challenges to his convictions under § 10(b) and Rule 10b-5.

. . . .

JUSTICE THOMAS, with whom THE CHIEF JUSTICE joins, concurring in the judgment in part and dissenting in part.

Today the majority upholds respondent's convictions for violating § 10(b) of the Securities Exchange Act of 1934, and Rule 10b-5 promulgated thereunder, based upon the Securities and Exchange Commission's "misappropriation theory." Central to the majority's holding is the need to interpret § 10(b)'s requirement that a deceptive device be "use[d] or employ[ed], in connection with the purchase or sale of any security." Because the Commission's misappropriation theory fails to provide a coherent and consistent interpretation of this essential requirement for liability under § 10(b), I dissent.

NOTE ON FAMILY AND OTHER PERSONAL RELATIONSHIPS — SEC RULE 10b5-2

After *O'Hagan*, the applicability of the misappropriation theory in the business setting — such as where an employee purloins material nonpublic information from his or her employer — is well established. In the context of family and other personal relationships, however, the misappropriation theory's impact is less certain.

For example, in *United States v. Chestman*, 947 F.2d 551 (2d Cir. 1991), the Second Circuit rejected the government's reliance on the misappropriation rationale under the facts presented when the wife entrusted inside information to her husband. The court asserted that "a fiduciary duty cannot be imposed unilaterally by entrusting a person with confidential information" and that "marriage does not, without more, create a fiduciary relationship." No such duty arose in the case at bar because the inside information was gratuitously communicated to the husband by the wife with no promise by the husband to keep the information confidential. Further, the court concluded that the husband was not part of the family's "inner circle" (that included the wife's parents), signifying that a fiduciary or comparable duty was not present.

So much for "family values." One can understandably be upset by the law giving greater sanctity to a shareholder's relationship with a director of a publicly-held company (with whom such shareholder has never spoken or met) than to one's spouse, parent, child, or sibling. Evidently by adopting Rule 10b5-2, the SEC agrees with the asserted absurdity of this approach. The Rule provides a non-exclusive list of three situations in which a person is deemed to have a relationship of trust and confidence for purposes of invoking the misappropriation theory when the person receiving the material nonpublic information trades or tips in the following situations: (1) when such recipient explicitly agreed to maintain the confidentiality of the information; (2) when a reasonable expectation of confidentiality existed due to the fact that the persons who had the communications(s) (including the misappropriator) enjoyed a history, practice, or pattern of sharing confidences; and (3) when the source of the information (i.e., the person providing such information) was a spouse, child, parent, or sibling of the person receiving the information, unless it can be established as an affirmative defense that on the facts and circumstances of the particular family relationship that no reasonable expectation of confidentiality existed. *See* Securities Exchange Act Release No. 43154 (2000). Query whether the first situation, namely, when the recipient agreed to maintain the information's confidentiality is unduly broad, thereby exceeding the parameters of the misappropriation theory set forth in *O'Hagen*?

NOTES AND QUESTIONS

Although upholding the validity of the misappropriation theory in *O'Hagan*, the Court's decision imposes certain limitations on the theory's scope. For example, consider the following:

1. Does full disclosure to the source(s) of the material nonpublic information that one intends to trade (or tip) signify that no "deception" exists and, hence, there is no § 10(b) violation? Should it matter whether such person reveals his or her intent to trade (or tip) before or after the receipt of the information from the source to whom such person owes a fiduciary duty? Note that in *SEC v. Rocklage*, 470 F.3d 1 (1st Cir. 2006), even though the wife told her husband she was planning to trade after he revealed material nonpublic information to her, the court found that liability was appropriate due to the wife's preexisting agreement with her brother that she would convey the inside information to him. Hence, the court reasoned that the deceptive conduct occurred prior to the wife's receipt of the information and her brother's trading of the securities.

2. Note that attorneys may incur disciplinary sanctions for trading (or tipping) on inside information. *See generally* Bainbridge, *Insider Trading Under the Restatement of the Law Governing Lawyers*, 19 J. CORP. L. 1 (1993).

3. Is the misappropriation theory applicable when the source of the information reveals such information with no expectation of confidentiality to one who trades (or tips)? (*See Dirks*, at fn. 14.)

4. To violate § 10(b), is it necessary for the trader "to use" rather than merely "to possess" the material nonpublic information? For example, after *O'Hagan*, is it a viable defense that the trader had planned to purchase the subject securities on a certain date prior to the time that he/she came into possession of the inside information? The next section of this Chapter addresses this issue.

E. "POSSESSION" vs. "USE"

When charged with insider trading, a defendant may contend that he/she had planned to purchase or sell the subject securities prior to coming into possession of the inside information. In response, the SEC's position generally has been that mere possession, rather than use, of the material nonpublic information is sufficient to trigger liability under Section 10(b). Likewise, the Second Circuit, endorsing the "possession" standard, opined that "material information cannot lie idle in the human brain." *United States v. Teicher*, 987 F.2d 112, 120 (2d Cir. 1993).

Disagreeing, the Ninth and Eleventh Circuits, held that proof of use rather than mere possession is consistent with Section 10(b)'s scienter requirement. Language in the Supreme Court's decision in *O'Hagan* also supports the "use" approach. 117 S. Ct. at 2208 (stating that, under the misappropriation theory, "the fiduciary's fraud is consummated . . . when without disclosure to his principal, he *uses* the information to purchase or sell securities"). In *SEC v. Adler*, 137 F.3d 1325 (11th Cir. 1998), the Eleventh Circuit held that Section 10(b)'s scienter requirement mandates that the Commission must establish that the defendant when he/she traded actually "used" the material nonpublic information. Phrased somewhat differently, the SEC must show that the defendant's knowledge of such information constituted a substantial factor in his or her decision to purchase or sell the subject securities at the particular price or at the particular time. Importantly, however, the court held that a defendant's knowing possession of material nonpublic information when trading raises a strong inference of use. Such inference may be rebutted by the defendant establishing that he/she had independent, justifiable reasons for engaging in the particular transactions at that time and in the amount traded. Similarly, the Ninth Circuit in *United States v. Smith*, 155 F.3d 1051 (9th Cir. 1998), adopted the "use" rather than "possession" standard. The court, however, declined to adhere to the Eleventh Circuit's inference of use (upon a showing of knowing possession) due to constitutional reasons arising from a criminal prosecution.

Reacting to the Ninth and Eleventh Circuit decisions, the SEC adopted Rule 10b5-1. Securities Exchange Act Release No. 43154 (2000). The Rule triggers liability exposure when a person purchases or sells securities while "aware" of material nonpublic information. Hence, a trade is deemed to be "on the basis" of material nonpublic information under Rule 10b5-1 if the trader was "aware" of such information at the time of the purchase or sale. The Rule reflects the position that one who is aware of inside information at the time of trading will have inevitably made use of such information. While the awareness standard expands the scope of insider trading liability (as compared to the Ninth and Eleventh Circuits' approaches), the SEC posits that Rule 10b5-1 enhances investor confidence and the integrity of the securities markets.

Under Rule 10b5-1, an affirmative defense generally is available if the trader engages in the specified transaction(s) pursuant to a pre-existing plan, contract, or instruction that is binding and specific. Under such circumstances, the inside information was not a factor in the trading decision. More specifically, to establish the affirmative defense, a person must satisfy the following criteria. First, a person must demonstrate that prior to becoming aware of the inside information, he/she had entered into a binding contract to purchase or sell the security, had provided instructions to another person to execute the trade for the instructing person's account, or had adopted a written plan for trading securities. Second, the person must demonstrate that, with respect to the purchase or sale, the contract, instructions, or plan: expressly specified the amount(s), price(s), and date(s); or did not permit the person to exercise any influence over how, when, or whether to execute the trade(s) (and in the event that any other person exercised such influence, that person was not aware of the material, nonpublic information). Third, the person must demonstrate that the trade(s) that occurred were pursuant to the previously established contract, instructions, or plan. This means that the person neither may alter or deviate from the contract, instruction, or plan, nor enter into a corresponding or opposite hedging transaction with respect to those securities. Furthermore, the defense is governed by a good-faith requirement that the person did not enter into the contract, instruction, or plan as part of a scheme to avoid liability under Rule 10b5-1.

Rule 10b5-1 provides another affirmative defense for trading parties the are entities. This defense is available as an alternative to the defense discussed above. Under the provisions of this defense, an entity will not be liable if it demonstrates that the individual responsible for the investment decision on behalf of the entity was not aware of the material inside information, and that the entity had implemented reasonable policies and procedures to prevent insider trading. *See generally*, Horwich, *The Origin Application, Validity and Potential Misuse of Rule 10b5-1*, 62 Bus. Law. 913 (2007); Karmel, *The Controversy of Possession Versus Use*, N.Y. L.J., Dec. 17, 1998, at 3; McLucas & Walker, *Insider Trading Developments: Do the Adler and Smith Cases Portend Tougher Times for SEC Enforcement?*, 32 Rev. Sec. & Comm. Reg. 93 (1999); Nagy, *The "Possession" vs. "Use" Debate in the Context of Securities Trading by Traditional Insiders: Why Silence Can Never Be Golden*, 67 U. Cin. L. Rev. 1129 (1999).

F.   RULE 14e-3

Subsequent to the Supreme Court's decision in *Chiarella*, the SEC, in an effort to regulate insider and tippee trading in the tender offer context, adopted Rule 14e-3 which establishes a "disclose or abstain from trading" rule under § 14(e) of the Exchange Act. As adopted, with certain exceptions, Rule 14e-3 applies this disclose-or-abstain provision to the *possession* of material information relating to a tender offer where the person knows or has reason to know the information is nonpublic and was received directly or indirectly from the offeror, the subject corporation, any of their affiliated persons, or any person acting on behalf of either company. Moreover, the rule contains a broad anti-tipping provision and provides for certain exceptions pertaining to sales to the offeror and to certain activities by multiservice financial institutions. Hence, generally one who possesses material nonpublic information in the tender offer setting cannot trade or tip, irrespective of whether a fiduciary relationship exists.

In the release adopting Rule 14e-3, the Commission asserted that *Chiarella* did not limit its authority under § 14(e) to adopt this broad "parity of information" mandate regulating insider trading in the tender offer context. In *O'Hagan*, 521 U.S. 642 (1997), under the facts presented in that case, the Supreme Court upheld the validity of Rule 14e-3.

G. DAMAGES AND PENALTIES

1. Damages — § 10(b) Actions

The measure of damages for insider trading in open market transactions under § 10(b) has received diverse treatment from the relatively few courts that have considered the issue. *Shapiro v. Merrill Lynch, Pierce, Fenner & Smith, Inc.*, 495 F.2d 228 (2d Cir. 1974), represents an expansive approach. There, the Second Circuit, relying on *Affiliated Ute Citizens v. United States*, 406 U.S. 128 (1972), stated that "[t]he proper test to determine whether causation in fact has been established in a nondisclosure case is 'whether the plaintiff would have been influenced to act differently than he did if the defendant had disclosed to him the undisclosed fact.' " After finding that causation in fact had been established (notwithstanding that all transactions occurred on a national securities exchange), the court formulated a potentially broad measure of damages:

> [W]e hold that defendants are liable in this private action for damages to plaintiffs who, during the same period that defendants traded in or recommended trading in Douglas common stock, purchased Douglas stock in the open market without knowledge of the material inside information which was in the possession of defendants.

Having so held, the Second Circuit, however, left to the district court's discretion the proper measure of damages, noting its concern with the potential for draconian liability.

In *Fridrich v. Bradford*, 542 F.2d 307 (6th Cir. 1976), the Sixth Circuit rejected the *Shapiro* analysis. Disagreeing with the Second Circuit, the *Fridrich* court found that the plaintiffs had failed to show that their loss was caused by the defendants' inside trading. The Sixth Circuit supported its holding by pointing out that an award of damages to contemporaneous traders in the open market would create a windfall for fortuitous investors while being essentially punitive. Although the court recognized that it could limit the amount of recovery to the defendants' profits, it declined to do so.

Subsequently, in *Elkind v. Liggett & Myers, Inc.*, 635 F.2d 156 (2d Cir. 1980), the Second Circuit, although not expressly rejecting the *Shapiro* rationale, greatly limited the potential damages recovery. There, the court considered three alternative measures of damages: (1) out-of-pocket; (2) market-repercussion; and (3) disgorgement. Rejecting the out-of-pocket measure, the court pointed out that this measure is normally directed toward compensating a trader for damages which are directly traceable to the defendant's perpetration of a fraud upon the trader. In an impersonal open market, however, "uninformed traders . . . are not induced by representations on the part of the tipper or tippee to buy or sell." Secondly, the Second Circuit observed that the out-of-pocket measure posed serious proof problems as the "value" of the stock traded during the period of nondisclosure can often be hypothetical. Lastly, the court concluded that the out-of-pocket measure had the potential for the imposition of "draconian, exorbitant damages, out of all proportion to the wrong committed."

The *Elkind* court also rejected the market-repercussion theory of damages. This measure would allow recovery of damages caused by erosion of the stock's market price that is traceable to the defendant's wrongful trading. The rationale underlying the theory is that "if the market price is not affected by the [defendant's] trading, the uninformed investor is in the same position as he would have been had the insider abstained from trading." Upon analysis, the Second Circuit rejected this theory due to the difficult problems of proof it would impose on plaintiffs and that adoption of the theory would frequently preclude recovery for an insider's breach of his or her duty to disclose the confidential information prior to trading.

The *Elkind* court thereupon adopted a third alternative, the disgorgement measure of damages. This measure also is the proper measure of damages under Section 20A for contemporaneous traders who trade on the opposite side of the transaction from the defendant. Under the *Elkind* formulation, the measure of damages is as follows:

> (1) [T]o allow any uninformed investor, where a reasonable investor would either have delayed his purchase or not purchased at all if he had the benefit of the tipped information, to recover any post-purchase decline in market value of his shares up to a reasonable time after he learns of the tipped information or after there is a public disclosure of it but (2) limit his recovery to the amount gained by the [subject violator] as a result of his selling at the earlier date rather than delaying his sale until the parties could trade on an equal informational basis. . . . Should the intervening buyers, because of the volume and price of their purchases, claim more than the [subject violator's] gain, their recovery (limited to that gain) would be shared *pro rata*. [635 F.2d at 172]

2. Penalties

A number of different parties may be subject to a variety of monetary penalties under the federal securities laws for engaging in illegal insider trading. These parties may include actual traders, their tippers, as well as broker-dealers and investment advisers (when they fail to take appropriate steps to prevent the insider trading violation(s) or fail to maintain and enforce policies and procedures reasonably designed to prevent the occurrence of such trading). Penalties that may be levied in this context are (1) requiring the subject party to "disgorge" the ill-gotten profits (or loss avoided) in an SEC enforcement action, (2) subjecting individuals to a criminal fine and imprisonment, and (3) in an SEC enforcement action, within a court's discretion, ordering the subject party to pay into the United States Treasury a treble damages penalty amounting to three times the profit gained or loss avoided. These penalties, together with the imposition of jail terms and the availability of civil damages, are intended to strongly deter insider trading. As an additional measure to combat insider trading, the SEC may award "bounties" (up to ten percent of the amount disgorged or monetary penalty imposed) to persons who provide information concerning insider trading violations.

To recover monetary penalties against "control persons" in the insider trading context, the SEC must show that such control person "knew or recklessly disregarded the fact that such controlled person was likely to engage in the act or acts constituting the violation and failed to take appropriate steps to prevent such act or acts before they occurred." . . .

> If the controlling person is a broker-dealer or investment advisor, [the 1988 legislation] provides the Commission with more potent ammunition for imposing the new monetary penalties. [It] sets forth an affirmative duty on broker-dealers and investment advisors to maintain adequate procedures to protect against insider trading and it defines a separate standard for controlling person liability in reference to that duty. First, [the legislation] added Section 15(f) of the Exchange Act and Section 204A of the Investment Advisors Act of 1940 which impose an affirmative duty on broker-dealers and investment advisors to maintain "written policies and procedures reasonably designed" to prevent insider trading violations. Second, Section 21A(b)(1)(B) subjects broker-dealers

and investment advisors to controlling person liability if they "knowingly or recklessly failed to establish, maintain, or enforce" those procedures and "such failure substantially contributed to or permitted the occurrence" of the insider trading violation.

Steinberg & Fletcher, *Compliance Programs for Insider Trading*, 47 SMU L. Rev. 1783, 1788–89 (1994).

In enacting the 1988 legislation, Congress declined to define the term "insider trading." Some observers believe that, given the stigma and penalties imposed upon those who have engaged in insider trading, the term should be defined by statute. A clear definition, proponents claim, would promote commercial certainty and ease the attorney's burden when advising his or her client. Others contend that a statutory definition is unnecessary. They argue that the court-drawn parameters of insider trading have established sufficiently clear guidelines. Moreover, a statutory definition may well be murky, contain loopholes, and be the subject of frequent judicial interpretation.

What is your conclusion? Should Congress enact a statute defining what conduct constitutes illegal insider trading? If so, what should such a statute provide?

3. Contemporaneous and Option Traders

After the Second Circuit's decision adopting the misappropriation theory in *United States v. Newman*, the question remained whether purchasers and sellers of securities had a cause of action for monetary damages under § 10(b) even though the defrauding parties who misappropriated the inside information owed them no fiduciary duty. In *Moss v. Morgan Stanley, Inc.*, 719 F.2d 5 (2d Cir. 1983), the Second Circuit held that in order to recover under § 10(b) for monetary damages it must be shown that the defendant breached a duty owed to the plaintiff. Relying on *Chiarella*, the court asserted that the relationship giving rise to a duty to disclose must be between the parties to the transaction. Hence, because the misappropriators in *Moss* owed no fiduciary duty to the plaintiff, no § 10(b) right of action was available.

In subsequently enacted legislation, Congress nullified the *Moss* decision in this respect. In the Insider Trading and Securities Fraud Enforcement Act of 1988, Congress enacted § 20A of the Exchange Act to provide an express right of action on behalf of "contemporaneous traders" who were trading the same class of securities on the opposite side of the transaction during the time that the allegedly illegal inside trade(s) occurred. Thus, to recover under this express right of action, the plaintiff must be trading contemporaneously with and on the opposite side of the transaction from the inside trader. Moreover, the damages available in an action instituted under § 20A on behalf of contemporaneous traders are limited to the profit gained or loss avoided by the defendant's illegal trades.

Importantly, § 20A does not limit a complainant's entitlement to private rights of action under other provisions of the Exchange Act, such as § 10(b). In this regard, a private right of action under § 10(b) may be available against inside traders (as well as their tippers) on behalf of certain noncontemporaneous traders. Such a situation may arise when, due to insider trading which has increased the price of the target company's stock, a bidder must pay more to acquire such stock. In the House Report accompanying the 1988 legislation, the Committee took the position that a § 10(b) right of action exists in the above situation and that a plaintiff should be able to recover the full extent of any actual damages incurred.

Moreover, as part of the Insider Trading Sanctions Act of 1984, Congress added § 20(d) to the Exchange Act. That provision states:

> Wherever communicating, or purchasing or selling a security while in possession of, material nonpublic information would violate, or result in liability to any purchaser or seller of the security under any provision of this Act, or any

rule or regulation thereunder, such conduct in connection with a purchase or sale of a put, call, straddle, option, or privilege with respect to such security or with respect to a group or index of securities including such security, shall also violate and result in comparable liability *to any purchaser or seller of that security* under such provision, rule or regulation.

Section 20(d)'s effect is to provide, within the confines of *Chiarella* and *Dirks*, an option-trading plaintiff with a private right of action against an inside trader of options. Note, however, that a distinct issue is presented as to whether an *option* trader has a private cause of action against an inside *stock* trader. Section 20(d) does not resolve this issue. The lower federal courts are divided. *Compare* Deutschman v. Beneficial Corp., 841 F.2d 502 (3d Cir. 1988) (providing a right of action), *with* Laventhall v. General Dynamics Corp., 704 F.2d 407 (8th Cir. 1983) (not permitting suit).

H. SECTION 16 — "SHORT-SWING" TRADING

Section 16 of the Exchange Act applies to directors, officers, and beneficial owners of more than ten percent of any class of equity security of an issuer (other than an exempted security), with such class of equity security having been registered pursuant to § 12(b) or § 12(g) of the Exchange Act. The statute seeks to deter insider trading based on the use of material nonpublic information by such persons. Section 16 contains three key provisions in attempting to meet this objective.

1. Section 16(a) of the Exchange Act requires that, upon becoming an officer, director, or ten percent equity shareholder of a § 12(b) or § 12(g) issuer, such individual must file with the SEC (and with the self-regulatory organization (SRO) with which the stock is listed or traded) a report disclosing the number of the corporation's shares beneficially owned. Subsequent reports must be filed on a timely basis (generally within two business days) to reflect changes in the number of shares beneficially owned.

2. Section 16(c) prohibits such insiders to transact short sales in their issuers' equity securities.

3. Generally, "Section 16(b) is designed to permit the corporation or a security holder bringing an action upon behalf of the corporation to recover for the benefit of the corporation short-swing profits arising from the purchase [and sale or sale and purchase] by insiders within any six-month period of equity securities of the company."[20]

Under § 16(b), an irrebuttable presumption is created when "insiders" engage in such short-swing transactions. The profits that the insider gained from the transaction(s) are recoverable by the issuer in a suit initiated by it, or if it declines to do so, in a properly instituted shareholder's suit expressly authorized by the statute. In view of the broad remedial nature of the statute, a strict formula for computing "profit realized" has been established. Such a formula is designed "to squeeze all possible profits out of stock transactions, and thus to establish a standard so high as to prevent any conflict between the selfish interest of a fiduciary officer, director, or stockholder and the faithful performance of his duty."[21] The formula established matches the lowest price "in" with the highest price "out," thus ensuring recovery of all possible profits. In fact, this formula can yield a profit when in actuality a loss has been suffered.[22]

Moreover, an insider's intent to profit under a transaction that falls within § 16(b)'s scope need not be shown in order for there to be recovery. As the Seventh Circuit (as

---

[20] H. Bloomenthal, *Securities Law* 365 (1966).

[21] Smolowe v. Delendo Corp., 136 F.2d 231 (2d Cir. 1943).

[22] *See* Morales v. Consolidated Oil & Gas, Inc., [1982 Transfer Binder] Fed. Sec. L. Rep. (CCH) 98,796 (S.D.N.Y. 1982).

well as other courts) pointed out, an insider is "deemed capable of structuring his dealings to avoid any possibility of taint and therefore must bear the risks of any inadvertent miscalculation."[23] In some situations, however, the courts, by finding that certain unorthodox transactions do not constitute the predicate purchase or sale, have displayed a judicial reluctance to impose liability under § 16(b) where no congressional purpose would be served.[24]

I. BLACKOUT PERIODS

Under § 306 of the Sarbanes-Oxley Act, officers and directors are prohibited from trading any equity security of the issuer, acquired through the scope of employment, during a blackout period, when at least half of the issuer's individual account plan participants are not permitted to trade in the equity security for more than three consecutive business days. Furthermore, the Act requires that the issuer deliver notice of blackout periods at least 30 days prior to the blackout period, giving proper notice to employees, executives, and the SEC. The SEC has adopted rules governing the prohibition on trading during blackout periods. Under Regulation Blackout Trading Restriction (BTR), during a blackout period, directors and executive officers of domestic issuers, foreign private issuers, banks and savings associations, small business issuers, and their family members, partnerships, corporations, limited liability companies and trusts are prohibited from trading equity securities acquired in connection with the director's or officer's service to an issuer. A violation of § 306(a) of the Sarbanes-Oxley Act will be considered a violation of the Exchange Act and is subject to SEC enforcement action. Furthermore, an issuer or a security holder may bring on behalf of such issuer an action against the director or officer who violated the blackout period, and seek disgorgement of all profits from the sale of such securities acquired in connection with the director's or officer's service to the issuer. The amount disgorged will be calculated, under Regulation BTR, as the difference between the amount paid for the equity security on the date of the transaction and the amount that would have been received for the security if the transaction had taken place outside the blackout period.

J. REGULATION FD

The SEC adopted Regulation FD (Fair Disclosure) in response to the perceived unfairness when companies selectively disclose material nonpublic information to analysts, institutional investors, and other securities market insiders. The Regulation's basic premise provides that "when an issuer, or person acting on its behalf, discloses material nonpublic information to [selective] persons . . . , it must make public disclosure of that information." The timing of when the issuer must make such a public disclosure depends on whether the selective disclosure was intentional or non-intentional.

The SEC sought to address several concerns by promulgating Regulation FD. First, it believed that issuers often disclose important nonpublic information, such as advance warnings of earnings results, to securities analysts and/or institutional investors before making such information available to the general investing public. The Commission warned that as a result of this practice, the investing public might not believe that they are on an equal playing field with market insiders and may thereby lose confidence in the integrity of the securities markets. Second, the SEC stated that selective disclosure closely resembles the "tipping" of inside information, but noted that the current state of insider trading law may not create liability for an issuer's selective disclosure.[25] Third,

---

[23] Bershad v. McDonough, 428 F.2d 693, 696 (7th Cir. 1970). *See* Whiting v. Dow Chemical Co., 523 F.2d 680, 687 (2d Cir. 1975) ("[T]he unwary who fall within [§ 16(b's)] terms have no one but themselves to blame.").

[24] *See, e.g.*, Kern County Land Co. v. Occidental Petroleum Corp., 411 U.S. 582 (1973).

[25] "[I]n light of the 'personal benefit' test set forth in the Supreme Court's decision in *Dirks v. SEC*, 463

the Commission perceived that the integrity of the securities markets was threatened by issuers selectively disclosing information as a means to secure favorable reviews by analysts. Specifically, analysts may feel pressured to report about a company in a positive light or risk losing their access to company personnel. Finally, the SEC opined that recent technological advances, particularly in the communications area, no longer pose undue impediments to timely public disclosure.

As summarized by the SEC:

> *Regulation FD (Fair Disclosure)* is a new issuer disclosure rule that addresses selective disclosure. The regulation provides that when an issuer, or person acting on its behalf, discloses material nonpublic information to certain enumerated persons (in general, securities market professionals and holders of the issuer's securities who may well trade on the basis of the information), it must make public disclosure of that information. The timing of the required public disclosure depends on whether the selective disclosure was intentional or non-intentional; for an intentional selective disclosure, the issuer must make public disclosure simultaneously; for a non-intentional disclosure, the issuer must make public disclosure promptly. Under the regulation, the required public disclosure may be made by filing or furnishing a Form 8-K, or by another method or combination of methods that is reasonably designed to effect broad, non-exclusionary distribution of the information to the public.

Selective Disclosure and Insider Trading, Securities Exchange Act Release No. 43154 (2000). Stated in somewhat different terms:

> Regulation FD prohibits issuers or individuals acting on their behalf from selectively disclosing material nonpublic information to certain enumerated persons (generally securities market professionals and holders of the issuer's securities who may well trade on the basis of the information) without disclosing the information publicly. If the selective disclosure is intentional, then the issuer must publicly disclose the information simultaneously by filing or furnishing a Form 8-K to the SEC or in a manner reasonably designed to provide broad distribution of the information. If the selective disclosure in unintentional, then the issuer must disclose the information to the public promptly, but in no event after the later of 24 hours or the opening of the next day's trading on the New York Stock Exchange. Violating Regulation FD exposes the issuer to SEC administrative and civil enforcement action, but does not by itself impose any Rule 10b-5 antifraud liability on the issuer or establish a private right of action.[26]

U.S. 646 (1983), many have viewed issuer selective disclosures to analysts as protected from insider trading liability." Regulation FD Adopting Release, Securities Exchange Act Release No. 43154 (2000).

[26] M. Steinberg, Understanding Securities Law 478 (4th ed. 2007).

Chapter 14

EXCULPATION, INDEMNIFICATION, AND INSURANCE

A. INTRODUCTION

In *Smith v. Van Gorkom* (Chapter 10), the Delaware Supreme Court shook up the legal and business communities by finding the board of directors of Trans Union liable for violating the fiduciary duty of care in spite of the Business Judgment Rule. Directors became concerned that they might be found personally liable for mere lapses in judgment under circumstances in which indemnification — corporate reimbursement for costs and damages suffered by directors in fiduciary duty litigation —may not be available. At the same time, insurance industry premiums and deductibles were on the rise and coverage was being reduced under corporate and individual policies covering director and officer liability (known as D&O insurance). Although, many blame the Delaware Supreme Court's decision in *Smith v. Van Gorkom* for these increased costs, other factors (including increases in mergers, acquisitions, and bankruptcies, as well as judicial opinions construing the terms of D&O insurance contracts) arguably played a role. *See, e.g.*, Roberta Romano, *What Went Wrong with Directors' and Officers' Liability Insurance?*, 12 DEL. J. CORP. L. 1 (1989) (describing the business conditions and legal conditions that contributed to the perceived D&O insurance crisis at that time). Many believed that qualified persons would refuse to serve as directors for fear of personal monetary liability. Indeed, there is some (albeit limited) evidence that potential directors may have refused service after *Van Gorkom* for liability reasons.

Interestingly, the Trans Union directors who were found liable in *Van Gorkom* did not pay any of the assessed monetary damages for their liability out of their own pockets. In fact, they were indemnified by the company and the acquiror and covered by D&O insurance. Yet, states did begin to react. Indiana and Virginia were front-movers in enacting legislation to limit breaches of the duty of care. Delaware's legislature, spurred on by the fear of losing both qualified directors and corporate charters, enacted DGCL § 102(b)(7), which permits a corporation to include in its charter a provision that exculpates directors for monetary liability for breaches of the duty of care. Other states then rapidly followed suit by enacting statutory exculpation provisions permitting the limitation of director liability for breaches of the duty of care. These statutory exculpation provisions (also known as "opting out," "tender-mercy provisions," and "raincoat provisions") added yet another layer of protection for directors facing breach of fiduciary duty claims like those in *Van Gorkom* (adding to the previously available protections of the Business Judgment Rule, indemnification, and D&O insurance). *See* E. Norman Veasey et al., *Delaware Supports Directors with a Three-Legged Stool of Limited Liability, Indemnification, and Insurance*, 42 BUS. LAW. 399 (1987).

With the enactment of exculpation statutes, four layers of protection may be available for corporate directors and officers facing potential personal liability for their actions or inaction as directors and officers. First, exculpation provides an affirmative defense for directors (but not officers) against claims for monetary damages (but not equitable relief) based on a breach of the duty of care (but not loyalty or good faith). Next, the Business Judgment Rule — the judicial presumption that directors and officers act in the best interest of the corporation, on a fully informed basis, and in good faith — burdens the plaintiff with proof that is hard to obtain. A third level of protection, indemnification, may be available as a means of reimbursing directors or officers for litigation expenses and monetary liability if a director or officer is found personally liable for damages for an alleged breach of fiduciary duty. The final level of protection is D&O insurance. D&O insurance may fill in the liability gaps not covered by exculpation and indemnification (although significant policy exclusions may prevent this from being the case). Insurance also serves as a potential funding source for the corporation's indemnification obligations.

The chart below summarizes the major characteristics of exculpation, indemnification, and insurance under Delaware law and under the Model Business Corporation Act. (You already have studied the nature and operation of the Business Judgment Rule in Chapters 10 and 11.) It is important to understand both the differences among these distinct types of potential statutory protection and the interplay among these layers of protection.

Director and Officer Liability Protections

Which protection?	Exculpation	Indemnification	Insurance
What does it do?	Limits personal monetary liability of directors (as provided, consistent with applicable law) for breaches of the duty of care	Corporation reimburses or pays the personal monetary liability of directors and/or officers (as provided, consistent with applicable law)	Insurer reimburses or pays the personal monetary liability of directors and/or officers (as provided)
Where is it authorized?	DGCL § 102(b)(7); MBCA § 2.02(b)(4)	DGCL § 145; MBCA §§ 2.02(b)(5), 8.50–8.56, 8.58, 8.59	DGCL § 145(g); MBCA § 8.57
Where is it found?	Charter (certificate of incorporation in Delaware or articles of incorporation in an MBCA jurisdiction)	Charter; by-laws; separate agreement between the corporation and its directors and/or officers; or shareholder or director resolution	Policy (contract) taken out by the corporation; individual policies taken out by directors and/or officers
What are some of the key issues?	Exactly what is covered (monetary liability for breaches of the duty of care); in most jurisdictions, if not in the initial charter, requires a director and shareholder vote to approve (in that order), e.g., under DGCL § 242 or MBCA § 10.03 (i.e., the approval process is initiated by the directors)	Must be appropriately authorized/ approved; applicable statutory legal standard must be met; advancement of expenses may be made available; liabilities for indemnification may be covered by insurance	Insurance may be provided for liabilities for which indemnification may not be made or is not available by or from the corporation; significant policy exclusions exist; also may be a funding source for corporate indemnification obligations

Additional, more detailed information about exculpation, indemnification, and D&O insurance is set forth in the remainder of the chapter.

B.   EXCULPATION

Generally, exculpation statutes like those found in DGCL § 102(b)(7) and MBCA § 2.02(b)(4) allow a corporation to include a provision in its charter (e.g., certificate of incorporation or articles of incorporation) that releases directors from personal monetary liability for a breach of the duty of care. At first reading, the express provisions of these statutes allow for the elimination or limitation of liability for breach of fiduciary duty more broadly; however, the statutes also expressly provide that liability may not be eliminated or limited for a breach of the duty of loyalty, a failure to act in good faith, intentional misconduct, a knowing violation of a law, the attainment of an improper personal benefit, or the unlawful authorization of a divided or approval of a stock repurchase (as provided under DGCL § 174 or MBCA § 8.33).

Exculpation protection is not automatic; it must be enabled by an express provision in the corporation's charter. This means that a newly formed corporation must include an exculpation provision in its charter in order to protect its directors, and an existing corporation without an exculpation provision in its charter must amend its charter by the appropriate statutory method (typically involving both board and shareholder approvals) to add an exculpation provision. (Charter amendments are provided for in DGCL § 242 and MBCA § 10.03 and discussed in more detail in Chapter 15.) Although many corporations (and nearly all public corporations) have enacted exculpation provisions to protect directors, this level of protection is optional. A careful transactional lawyer or litigator will review a corporation's charter, as well as the applicable corporate statute, before giving advice to a client on the possible liability of a particular director for a breach of the duty of care.

In *Malpiede v. Townson*, 780 A.2d 1075 (2001), the Delaware Supreme Court addresses the manner in which an exculpation provision is used in litigation to eliminate the personal monetary liability of director for an alleged breach of the duty of care. Specifically, in *Malpiede*, the court affirms the Court of Chancery's dismissal of an action against corporate directors on a Rule 12(b)(6) motion, despite the fact that charter-based exculpation is a matter outside the complaint (although the court notes that presentation of matters outside the pleadings required the court to convert the Defendants' motion to dismiss into a motion for summary judgment).

In dismissing the action, the *Malpiede* court makes certain salient observations about exculpation provisions and their application in litigation.

> [W]e have held that the amended complaint here does not allege a loyalty violation or other violation falling within the exceptions to the Section 102(b)(7) exculpation provision. Likewise, we have held that, even if the plaintiffs had stated a claim for gross negligence, such a well-pleaded claim is unavailing because defendants have brought forth the Section 102(b)(7) charter provision that bars such claims. This is the end of the case.

> And rightly so, as a matter of the public policy of this State. Section 102(b)(7) was adopted by the Delaware General Assembly in 1986 following a directors and officers insurance liability crisis and the 1985 Delaware Supreme Court decision in *Smith v. Van Gorkom*. The purpose of this statute was to permit stockholders to adopt a provision in the certificate of incorporation to free directors of personal liability in damages for due care violations, but not duty of loyalty violations, bad faith claims and certain other conduct. Such a charter provision, when adopted, would not affect injunctive proceedings based on gross negligence. Once the statute was adopted, stockholders usually approved charter amendments containing these provisions because it freed up directors to take business risks without worrying about negligence lawsuits.

> . . .

> Section 102(b)(7) is not, and was not intended to be, a panacea for directors.

> In addition, new section 102(b)(7) does not eliminate the duty of care that is properly imposed upon directors.

> While section 102(b)(7) may not be a panacea, it provides a layer of protection for directors by allowing stockholders to dramatically reduce the type of situations in which a director's personal wealth is put "on the line." Thus, the

"the first leg" of support afforded directors under the Delaware statutory scheme is a reduction in the overall sphere of liability to which a director is otherwise exposed in acting in his capacity as such. The other two "legs" of support — indemnification rights and insurance — operate within this reduced sphere of liability.

Our jurisprudence since the adoption of the statute has consistently stood for the proposition that a Section 102(b)(7) charter provision bars a claim that is found to state only a due care violation. Because we have assumed that the amended complaint here does state a due care claim, the exculpation afforded by the statute must affirmatively be raised by the defendant directors. The directors have done so in this case, and the Court of Chancery properly applied the . . . charter provision to dismiss the plaintiffs' due care claim.

NOTES AND QUESTIONS

1. *Procedural Aspects.* A defense based on an exculpation provision is by its nature an affirmative defense. *See Rothenberg v. Santa Fe Pac. Corp.*, C.A. No. 11749, slip op. at 8 (Del. Ch. May 18, 1992), *citing Boeing Co. v. Shrontz*, C.A. No. 11273, slip. op. at 7 (Del. Ch. Apr. 20, 1992). Therefore, DGCL § 102(b)(7) is not properly before a court on a motion to dismiss, but rather is used to support a motion for summary judgment. If a plaintiff adequately pleads conduct that falls within the statutory exceptions (e.g., loyalty or good faith claims) and there are no other reasons for dismissal, the director-defendants face a full trial on all claims (in which they may interpose their affirmative exculpation defense — which, once presented, allows the directors to avoid damage claims based on any breaches of the duty of care). *See Emerald Partners v. Berlin*, 787 A.2d 85 (Del. 2001). Where, as in *Malpiede*, a plaintiff fails to make cognizable loyalty or bad faith claims, however, the introduction of an exculpation provision on a motion to dismiss will convert the defendants' motion to one for summary judgment.

2. *Disclosures: Are They Care or Are They Loyalty?* Major decisions by the Board of Directors concerning the corporation, especially publicly traded corporations, require disclosure of material information to the stockholders. Faulty disclosures may result not only in claimed violations of the federal securities laws (as and if applicable), but also in asserted breaches of state corporate law fiduciary duties. *See, e.g., Malone v. Brincat*, 722 A.2d 5 (Del. 1998) ("[D]irectors who knowingly disseminate false information that results in corporate injury or damage to an individual stockholder violate their fiduciary duty, and may be held accountable in a manner appropriate to the circumstances."). In *Zirn v. VLI Corp.*, 621 A.2d 773 (Del. 1993), the Delaware Supreme Court held that certain state law claims (related to disclosure by equitable fraud in a third-party merger) involved a breach of the duty of loyalty; therefore, exculpation under DGCL § 102(b)(7) did not shield directors from liability. However, in *Arnold v. Society for Sav. Bancorp.*, 650 A.2d 1270 (Del. 1994), the Delaware Supreme Court found that individual defendants did not violate the duty of loyalty under the facts of the case and the court extended the protections of exculpation to disclosure violations. Do you think claims of disclosure violations should be characterized as a duty of loyalty or duty of care? What cases support your conclusion?

3. *End of Duty of Care Claims.* One of the direct results of the enactment of exculpation statutes was the decline in duty of care violations alleged in legal actions. Exculpation statutes and charter provisions typically do not bar all claims of the breach of the duty of care; only duty of care claims requesting monetary damages; therefore, a plaintiff could prevail on a duty of care claim seeking an injunction or another equitable remedy. However, because most stockholder lawsuits request damages, plaintiffs have been pigeonholed into alleging breaches of the duties of loyalty and good faith in order to recover damages for breach of fiduciary duty. *See, e.g., Brehm v. Eisner*, 746 A.2d 244 (Del. 2000); *In re The Walt Disney Co. Derivative Litig.*, 825 A.2d 275 (Del. 2003). Subsequently, the Delaware Supreme Court characterized directors' failure to act in

good faith as a component of the duty of loyalty where an oversight failure is at issue. *See Stone v. Ritter*, 911 A.2d 362 (Del. 2006). Although a failure to oversee often is understood as a breach of the duty of care, after *Stone v. Ritter*, it is clear that this type of board malfeasance may be conceptualized and litigated as a violation of the duty of good faith or the duty of loyalty — a failure to act with the good faith belief that the actions taken are in the best interest of the corporation. Accordingly, this type of claim is not subject to exculpation.

C. INDEMNIFICATION

If a director is not relieved of personal monetary liability under an exculpation provision (because, for example, the violation relates to an alleged breach of the duty of loyalty or good faith) or if a breach of fiduciary duty claim is brought against an officer, indemnification may step in to protect the director or officer by providing reimbursement for expenses. Also, corporate indemnification may allow for advancement or reimbursement of a director's or officer's litigation costs (including attorneys' fees) by the corporation in connection with threatened or actual litigation against a director or officer for action or inaction taken in a corporate capacity.

Under common law agency principles, an agent is indemnified for expenses incurred by him or her while acting in the scope of the agency. *See* RESTATEMENT (THIRD) OF AGENCY, § 8.14. However, an early New York case, *New York Dock Co. v. McCollum*, 173 Misc. 106 (N.Y. Misc. 1939), found that corporate directors are not agents of the corporation for which they serve and, thus, are not entitled to those common law indemnification rights. As a result, corporate statutes were enacted to afford corporations the authority to indemnify directors if they wished to do so.

In fact, indemnification by a corporation of its directors and officers is both authorized and circumscribed by statute. (Examples include DCGL § 145 and MBCA §§ 2.02(5) and 8.50–8.56.) As implemented, indemnification rights are contractual in nature. A typical arrangement requires the corporation to pay specified costs associated with liability arising from activities undertaken by a person in that person's corporate position, subject to specified exceptions, conditions, and limits. In other words, corporate indemnification of directors and officers is a corporation's promise to cover the director's or officer's litigation expenses and personal liability if the director or officer is sued because he or she is or was a director or officer. Indemnification typically extends to civil, criminal, administrative, or investigative proceedings as long as they relate to the party's participation as a director or officer. Indemnification is not, however, typically available for expenses incurred in connection with shareholder derivative litigation in which a director or officer is found liable to the corporation for monetary damages. *See, e.g.*, DGCL § 145(b) and Note 2, below.

In *Green v. Westcap Corp.*, 492 A.2d 260 (1985), the Delaware Supreme Court describes and applies the Delaware indemnification statute. The case was brought by a director seeking indemnification from the corporation for which he served for his successful defense in a criminal case where a subsequent civil case also was possible.

> 8 Del. C. § 145 is a substantial revision of the former indemnification provision, which appeared as § 122(10) of the former Delaware General Corporation Law, 8 Del. C. (1953) Ch. 1. The present Delaware General Corporation Law is the product of a committee of eminent Delaware lawyers. FOLK, THE DELAWARE GENERAL CORPORATION LAW, p. xii. The portion of the revised corporation law which substantially rewrote an important subject such as director indemnification received careful attention. . . . . Hence, any insertion or omission was done deliberately. Moreover, it is apparent from the completeness of the wording that the philosophy was to overstate rather than understate. Thus, even though the requisites in § 145(a) and § 145(b) are similar, each subsection sets forth the requisites. Therefore, when considering the reference in subsection (c) to "any action, suit or proceeding referred to in subsections (a)

and (b)" the conclusion is that the only portion of subsection (a) and (b) which is incorporated by reference is the portion which defines the type of action, suit or proceeding covered by each section and that that reference does not incorporate the subsequent qualification required for indemnification. The following quotation from the review of the 1967 Delaware General Corporation Law shows the objective of § 145(c):

> In addition to defining the area in which a corporation is permitted to grant indemnity, the new statute adds a provision granting an absolute right of indemnity to any director, officer, employee or agent of the corporation who has been successful, on the merits or otherwise, in the defense of any proceeding, or any claim, issue or matter therein. Such person is entitled to recover his expenses, including attorneys' fees, actually and reasonably incurred by him in connection with that portion of his defense which was successful. . . .

Westcap points out that the judge who directed judgment of acquittal in favor of Green noted that his finding Green not guilty of the criminal charge did not find him innocent and that he believed that he would be punished in the civil courts. Here, Green only seeks indemnification for his successful defense of the criminal charge. This suit goes no further than that criminal defense. It does not establish his right to indemnification for expense incurred in any other litigation. Under § 145 indemnification must be considered as each criminal or civil proceeding arises or is concluded. Presumably each will involve its own expenses and each must meet the statutory qualifications applicable to it. Whether Green is or will be entitled to indemnification for the defense of the Texas civil litigation is, of course, not before the Court in this suit.

. . . Westcap's motion to dismiss or to stay is denied.

NOTES AND QUESTIONS

1. *Independent Determination.* The Delaware Supreme Court's decision in the *Westcap* case explains that under Delaware law, a director's entitlement to indemnification is made on a case by case basis. Success in one proceeding entitles a director to indemnification even if the director may not be successful in another type of proceeding based on the same facts.

2. *Circular Payments?* When a successful action is brought against a director or officer by the corporation or on its behalf by a shareholder in a shareholder derivative action, a liable director or officer cannot be indemnified. DGCL § 145(b); MBCA § 8.51(d)(1). This makes sense; it would be absurd to require a director or officer to pay the corporation damages and then allow the corporation to reimburse the director. However, a corporation can indemnify a director who settles a suit brought by or on behalf of the corporation if the director meets the statutory criteria for permissive indemnification. DGCL § 145(b); MBCA § 8.51(d)(1). Additionally, a court may order indemnification of legal expenses, if fair and reasonable, even though a director is found liable in a derivative suit. DGCL § 145(b); MBCA § 8.54(a)(3). The MBCA even permits a court to order indemnification of settlement amounts in a derivative suit, if fair and reasonable. MBCA § 8.54(a)(3). Do the permissive indemnification rules on settlements and legal expenses make sense when the corporation or a derivative plaintiff is bringing an action against a corporate director or officer?

3. *Mandatory and Permissive Indemnification.* Some indemnification statutes are mandatory in application and some are permissive, requiring implementation in a particular corporation by charter or bylaw provision or individual contract. Typically, mandatory indemnification is available for a director who is wholly successful or, under modern statutes, "successful, on the merits or otherwise." Delaware has a mixed mandatory and permissive statute of this kind. *See* DGCL § 145; *see also* ALA. CODE §§ 10-2B-8.51–8.52. Other states have purely permissive statutes which give complete discretion to the corporation to determine to what extent directors and officers should be indemnified. *See* OHIO REV. CODE ANN. § 1701.13 (2007). Similarly, Indiana allows a corporation to determine the extent of indemnification, but there must be an express provision in the articles of incorporation; otherwise, there is default mandatory indemnification for wholly successful defenses. *See* IND. CODE § 23-1-37-8 to 13. In statutes affording mandatory indemnification for wholly successful defenses, success is defined as success on the merits, such as a suit dismissed for lack of evidence or a finding of nonliability after a trial. Success also may include a resolution in the director's favor on procedural grounds — for example, when a plaintiff lacks standing or the applicable statute of limitations has run. *See, e.g.,* DGCL § 145(c); MBCA § 8.52. But success typically does not include a claim settled out of court. Success under Delaware General Corporation Law § 145(c) extends "to the extent" a defendant is successful, allowing the corporation to indemnify a director for partial success.

4. *Success.* The Delaware Supreme Court interpreted the words "to the extent" in DGCL § 145(c) to require indemnification if the director was partially successful. *Merritt-Chapman & Scott Corp. v. Wolfson,* 321 A.2d 138 (Del. Sup. Ct. 1974). In the *Merritt-Chapman* case, a director was charged with five criminal counts and pled "no contest" to one on the condition the others were dropped. The court found that he was entitled to indemnification reimbursement as a matter of right on the four counts that were dropped. *See also Waltuch v. ContiCommodity Servs., Inc.,* 88 F.3d 87 (2d Cir. 1996) (applying Delaware law to require indemnification of litigation expenses incurred by a director charged with conspiring to corner the silver market, after the company — but not the director — paid to settle lawsuits brought by silver traders). Conversely, the MBCA takes an all-or-nothing approach and requires a director to be wholly successful in order to be indemnified.

5. *Type of Claim Can Determine Success.* An *un*successful director or an officer, employee, or other agent of the corporation may be entitled to indemnification if the applicable corporate statute allows for indemnification and the corporation has acted under the statute to provide that indemnification. Both the type of claim brought and the corporate capacity or status of the defendant may play a role in whether the corporation is able to provide indemnification to these indemnitees. Under some statutes, if a claim is brought by a third party, the indemnitee must prove that he or she acted in good faith and reasonably believed his or her actions were in (or not opposed to) the corporation's best interests. DGCL § 145(a); MBCA § 8.51(a)(1). In general, indemnitees increase their chances of receiving permissive indemnification by settling or plea bargaining because most statutes state that a judgment, order, settlement, or no contest plea is not determinative as to whether the indemnitee meets the criteria for permissive indemnification. Decisions concerning whether a particular indemnitee is entitled to permissive indemnification are usually made by independent directors, a special committee of directors, or (in some cases) independent legal counsel. DGCL § 145(d); MBCA § 8.55(b). An internal finding that an indemnitee is entitled to indemnification is not conclusive; it is subject to judicial review. *See In re Landmark Land Co.,* 76 F.3d 553 (4th Cir. 1996) (applying California's indemnification statute to reverse a decision by independent directors to indemnify fellow directors, since illegal avoidance of federal S&L regulations could not constitute "good faith"). Some critics argue that unlimited corporate indemnification of directors undermines director accountability by nullifying the deterrent effect of potential personal liability under (among other things) securities, environmental, and corporate law.

6. *Exclusivity of Indemnification Statutes.* The MBCA makes the statutory indemnification provisions exclusive. Any indemnification under articles of incorporation or bylaws is permitted only to the extent consistent with the state statute. MBCA §§ 8.58(a), 8.59. In contrast, Delaware law allows corporations to provide indemnification that is outside the statutory scheme, as long as the indemnification is consistent with public policy. DGCL § 145(f). However, courts have held that further indemnification provisions are subject to a "consistency" limitation not unlike that in the MBCA; indemnification bylaws or contract provides must be consistent with the types of indemnification the statute authorizes. Under these decisions, indemnification beyond the limits set by corporate statutes is void as against public policy. Accordingly, non-exclusive indemnification does not mean open-ended indemnification.

7. *Advancement of Expenses.* Because litigation can be very costly and most directors and officers do not have enough money to pay all of the expenses out-of-pocket, the corporation may advance litigation expenses to directors and officers under specific circumstances provided by statute. DGCL § 145(e); MBCA § 8.53. Under the MBCA, a director seeking advancement of expenses must (1) affirm his or her good faith belief that he would be entitled to permissive indemnification or indemnification under the charter provision and (2) undertake to repay the advances if he or she is not entitled to indemnification. MBCA § 8.53(a). Delaware law only requires that an officer or director undertake repayment. DGCL § 145(e); *see Senior Tour Players 207 Mgmt. Co. LLC v. Golftown 207 Holding Co.*, 853 A.2d 124 (Del. Ch. 2004) (stating that the right to advancement is not conditioned on whether indemnification ultimately is appropriate and that the statutory requirement to repay improper advancements does not require a written promise). Under the MBCA, disinterested directors, if there are two or more, or shareholders in the case of interested directors, must authorize the advancement of expenses by the corporation; these decisions are subject to all the fiduciary duties surrounding board decisions. The official comment to MBCA § 8.51 provides that the directors and officers are not entitled to authorize the advancement of expenses to a director if there are "red flags" indicating that the director is not likely entitled to indemnification. Also, the MBCA does not require security for the advancement of expenses so as to not discriminate against directors of modest means. Finally, if a corporation mandatorily indemnifies directors or officers under the MBCA "to the fullest extent of permitted by law," the corporation is then obligated to advance expenses, even in derivative suits, unless advancement is expressly limited. MBCA § 8.58(a). Delaware does not specify who must authorize expense advancements.

8. *Funding Indemnification Obligations.* Corporations should recognize that indemnification involves two decisions: the authorization decision and the funding decision. Much consideration is given to the former but almost none to the latter. A theoretical right to indemnification is worthless in reality, unless a funding source exists and is tapped. This is especially true because indemnification can be costly, and the corporation itself often is under siege (creating significant transaction costs) at the same time shareholders are making claims against directors and officers. Corporations can, of course, self-insure or purchase D&O insurance to cover some or all of their indemnification obligations. Other funding sources include provisions for sinking funds, security interests in identified corporate assets, and other funding mechanisms. *See generally* Douglas M. Branson, Corporate Governance 735–814 (1993). Regardless, corporate consideration should be given to the funding of these obligations at the time indemnification is authorized.

9. *Implementation.* Corporations often draft charter and bylaw indemnification provisions using words akin to "indemnification shall be allowed to the fullest extent allowed by Tennessee (or Missouri or Ohio) law." That wording may be insufficient. One problem is that, after a change in control of the corporation, a new board or management can amend the charter or bylaws to alter indemnification obligations. More sophisticated corporations and directors insist that the corporation grant contractual rights to each director as he or she comes on the board. Typically, the contract will be quite detailed, outlining the means by which the authorization decision will be made, guaranteeing expense advances with a minimum of hassle, requiring insurance with certain policy limits, and possibly mandating the corporation's employment of other funding sources, among other things. In most cases, exculpation, indemnification, and insurance are addressed in some way.

D. INSURANCE

D&O insurance may be purchased by a corporation to cover the risks associated with potential director and officer malfeasance — regardless of any applicable indemnification. In addition, as noted earlier in the chapter, D&O insurance is a frequently adopted funding source for indemnification obligations. Traditional D&O policies provide dual coverage, including reimbursement to the corporation for indemnification payments made to officers and directors and reimbursement to officers and directors for the unindemnified losses. The insurance purchased by a corporation to cover officer and director liability in excess of the corporation's indemnification obligation is considered compensation to those officers and directors. *See* MBCA § 8.57; DGCL § 145(g).

Typically, D&O insurance policies require that the insurer control litigation that may require coverage under the terms of the policy. This control extends to, among other things, agreements to settle the litigation. In some cases, the interests of the insurer and the insured in a proffered settlement may not be the same. For example, an insurer may have an objective to settle cases for no more than a specific percentage of the coverage limits, taking the risk of an unfavorable result in the litigation, but knowing that its responsibility is capped at the coverage limits. As a result, some courts have imposed a duty of care on the insurer in making a decision not to settle a case. *See, e.g., G. A. Stowers Furniture Co. v. American Indem. Co.*, 15 S.W.2d 544, 548 (Tex. App. 1929). Courts also have refereed other contests between insurers and insureds in circumstances where insurers behaved in a similarly recalcitrant manner.

Coverage battles also are fought over the express terms of the insurance contract and its exclusion provisions. D&O insurance policies usually cover both liabilities and defense costs arising from directors' or officers' actions for the corporation. The policies usually exclude coverage for liability associated with certain claims, as alleged or proven under the policy. Typically excluded is, for example, coverage for potential or actual liability associated with: the receipt of improper personal benefits (self-dealing); actions taken in bad faith (including those involving dishonesty); illegal compensation; libel or slander; knowing violations of law; and other willful misconduct. Many current insurance contracts include additional exclusions. Because of these exclusions, insurance often is not as encompassing as indemnification. Claims under D&O insurance policies may be heavily litigated because of the potential applicability of a policy exclusion. The case excerpted below exemplifies this type of litigation.

SPHINX INTERNATIONAL, INC. v. NATIONAL UNION FIRE INSURANCE COMPANY OF PITTSBURGH

Court of Appeals of United States, Eleventh Circuit

412 F.3d 1224 (2005)

TJOFLAT, CIRCUIT JUDGE:

This case is about a directors' and officers' liability policy (D&O policy). More specifically, it's about that D&O policy's "insured vs. insured" exclusion, which acts to bar coverage for claims brought by directors and officers. The district court held on summary judgment that this exclusion bars coverage for claims brought by a former director and officer. We agree and thus affirm.

We divide our opinion in three parts. In Part I, we explain the case's factual and procedural history. In Part II, we apply the law to this history. In Part III, we briefly conclude.

I.

Sphinx International, Inc. was formerly known as Phoenix International Ltd., Inc. Both Sphinx and its predecessor, which we refer to exclusively as Sphinx, design and implement computer software and systems for financial institutions. When Sphinx incorporated in January 1993, Bahram Yusefzadeh became CEO and Chairman of the

Board at Sphinx. Prior to incorporation, Yusefzadeh met George Taylor. Soon after their meeting, Yusefzadeh offered Taylor a job as a director and an officer (along with ten percent of the shares of Sphinx). Taylor accepted. Taylor served in these two positions until his employment was terminated in July 1994. Sphinx states that it terminated Taylor's employment because he did not disclose a covenant not to compete from his former job and he misrepresented his qualifications by falsely claiming that he was an expert in client-server technology for financial institutions.

In July 1996, Sphinx contracted with Genesis Indemnity Insurance Co. for D&O policies. In general, D&O policies indemnify directors and officers from liability for their business decisions. While Sphinx had two D&O policies from Genesis, the particular policy at issue here was to run from July 1, 1996 to July 1, 1999, and it was extended to August 13, 2000. This policy was a claims-made policy, which means that it covered Sphinx for claims made during the policy period, irrespective of when those claims arose. The policy also contained an "insured vs. insured" exclusion that barred claims.

> By or at the behest of . . . any DIRECTOR or OFFICER, or by any security holder of the COMPANY, whether directly or derivatively, unless such CLAIM is instigated and continued totally independent of, and totally without the solicitation of, or assistance of, or active participation of, or intervention of, any DIRECTOR or OFFICER or the COMPANY or any affiliate of the COMPANY.

The policy defined "director" and "officer" to mean "all persons who were, now are, shall be duly elected Directors or duly elected or appointed Officers of the COMPANY."

For a few years Sphinx did well. But it missed its earnings projections in 1998 and 1999. As a result, Taylor filed a securities class action against Sphinx on November 23, 1999. On that same day, Taylor published a notice in a national newswire service soliciting other Sphinx shareholders. Taylor then amended his complaint to add as plaintiffs the shareholders that responded to his solicitation.

In response to Taylor's lawsuit, Sphinx sought D&O coverage from Genesis. Genesis denied that claim, justifying its denial on the "insured vs. insured" exclusion. Specifically, Genesis said that because Taylor was a former director and officer, the exclusion barred coverage.

Sphinx then filed suit in Florida state court against Genesis and National Union Fire Insurance Company of Pittsburgh, PA. (another company with which Sphinx had insurance coverage). The case was removed to the Middle District of Florida on the basis of diversity of citizenship under 28 U.S.C. §§ 1332, 1341. To make a long procedural story short, there were essentially two sets of motions and responses that matter on this appeal. The first set began with Genesis's "Motion To Dismiss or, in the Alternative, For Summary Judgment," which focused in large part on the "insured vs. insured" exception. . . .

[T]he district court granted summary judgment in favor of Genesis and denied everything else. The court wrote that "[s]ince the parties have filed affidavits in support of their positions, the Court will treat [Genesis]'s submission as a motion summary judgment rather than a motion to dismiss." *Sphinx Int'l, Inc. v. Nat'l Union Fire Ins. Co. of Pittsburgh, PA.*, 226 F.Supp. 2d 1326, 1328 n. 1 (M.D.Fla.2002). Sphinx appealed, but because the district court's order did not dispose of the claims against National Union, we dismissed the appeal. Sphinx then settled with National Union, and the district court dismissed the suit against it, in effect making the court's earlier summary judgment decision now final and appealable.

II.

. . . Sphinx makes several arguments, three of which deserve discussion. Sphinx's first argument focuses on the D&O policy's language: it argues that Taylor was not a "duly elected" officer or director and therefore not an "insured." Its second argument focuses on the rationale behind the D&O policy: it argues that the "insured vs. insured" exclusion acts only to prevent collusive suits and therefore does not apply because Taylor and Sphinx were adversarial. Sphinx's third argument is its fallback position: it argues that even if the language and rationale act to deny coverage, we should deny coverage only to that percentage of the claim attributed to Taylor. All of these arguments fail. To explain why, we address each argument in turn.

A.

Sphinx's first argument focuses on the meaning of "duly elected." The "insured vs. insured" exclusion bars claims "brought by or at the behest of . . . any DIRECTOR OR OFFICER." The policy defines directors and officers as "persons who were, or now are, or shall be *duly* elected Directors or *duly* elected or appointed Officers." (Emphasis added). Sphinx contends that Taylor was not a "duly" elected officer or director because he did not disclose a covenant not to compete and misrepresented his qualifications. . . .

[T]he plain language of the policy in general, and the word "duly" in particular, unambiguously includes Taylor as a former director or officer and therefore bars Sphinx's claim for coverage. There are two reasons why this is so: (1) the ordinary dictionary definition of "duly" indicates that Taylor was a director and an officer, and (2) the fact that Sphinx's policy did not expressly define "duly" is not determinative.

First, the district court based its decision in part on the plain meaning of "duly":

As noted by Defendant, the definition of "duly" found in Webster's dictionary is "in a due manner, time, and degree." The use of the term "duly elected" defines and limits the universe of insured to those [that] have attained officer or director statutes in a due manner-that is through regular and proper channels of corporate governance. Based on that "ordinary" definition, Taylor was a "duly elected or appointed" officer or director under the Genesis policy.

Sphinx Int'l, 226 F.Supp.2d at 1332. The district court's reasoning is spot on. . . .

B.

Sphinx's second argument focuses on a perceived conflict between the text and the rationale for the "insured vs. insured" exclusion. The original rationale behind the exclusion was to bar coverage for "collusive suits[,] such as suits in which a corporation sues its officers or directors in an effort to recoup the consequences of their business mistakes." *Level 3 Communications, Inc. v. Fed. Ins. Co.*, 168 F.3d 956, 958 (7th Cir.1999); *see also Harris v. Gulf Ins. Co.*, 297 F.Supp.2d 1220, 1227 (N.D.Cal.2003) (stating that "protection from collusive suits . . . was apparently the primary reason that ['insured vs. insured'] exclusions were adopted"). Sphinx argues that this rationale trumps the text. To support this argument, Sphinx cites several non-Florida cases.

We agree with the district court that the exclusion's rationale does not trump its text. To be sure, there is a genuine split of authority. Some courts look behind an exclusion's text to its rationale. But while there is a conflict, it's fought outside Florida. Part II. A demonstrates that in Florida the rule for interpreting insurance contracts is the plain meaning of its terms.

As a corollary to Florida's plain-meaning rule, Florida courts do not look behind unambiguous policies in search of countervailing rationales. The Florida Supreme Court put it this way: "unless we conclude that the policy language is ambiguous, it would be inappropriate for us to consider the arguments pertaining to the drafting history of the . . . exclusion clause." In the words of a federal district court applying Florida law: "Absent ambiguity in the policy language, however, rules of construction are unnecessary and courts will apply the plain language of the policy."

Florida's plain-meaning rule — and the rule's corollary against searching for countervailing rationales in an otherwise unambiguous insurance policy — means that Sphinx's argument fails. Sphinx essentially asks us to overlook both the rule and its corollary, focusing instead on the policy behind the "insured vs. insured" exclusion. As we are bound by Florida law, we cannot comply. Thus, just like the district court in this case, we will not search for a countervailing rationale in Sphinx's otherwise unambiguous insurance policy. Instead, because the D&O policy's language is unambiguous, we apply it as written.

C.

Sphinx's third argument is its fallback position. Sphinx argues that even if we apply the "insured vs. insured" exclusion to bar coverage, we should only exclude that percentage of the claim attributed to Taylor.

Sphinx is not alone in making this argument: for support, it cites *Level 3 Communications*, 168 F.3d 956 (7th Cir.1999). In that case, the Seventh Circuit dealt with an "insured vs. insured" exclusion that "exclude[d] liability on account of any 'Claim made against an Insured Person' if the Claim is 'brought or maintained by or on behalf of any Insured.'" *Id.* at 957. The policy defined "'Insured Person' . . . to include a 'person who *has been*, now is, or shall become a duly elected director or a duly elected or appointed officer of the Insured Organization.'" *Id.* In that case, six shareholders brought suit; six months later, a former director joined the suit. The insurance company then invoked the "insured vs. insured" exclusion. The Seventh Circuit agreed that the former director's claim was not covered, but the court did not deny coverage for the other claims:

> [The former director] had 16 percent of the shares and so presumably received 16 percent of the settlement, with the rest going to plaintiffs who were not "Insureds" within the meaning of the insurance contract. The coverage of their claims was not barred by the "Insured versus Insured" exemption.

Id. at 960. Sphinx argues that we should similarly segregate Taylor's claim from the claims of the remaining plaintiffs.

Unfortunately for Sphinx, *Level 3 Communications* is too different to be useful. One important difference is that the former-director plaintiff in *Level 3 Communications* was merely a passive shareholder who joined a larger suit. Specifically, the plaintiff was one of eight other plaintiffs and only joined the suit six months after it was filed. Here, in contrast, Taylor *brought* the lawsuit and recruited every other plaintiff. Therefore, this case does not implicate *Level 3 Communications*'s concern that a former director's presence as "an unnamed class member" with a small stake would cause the insured to lose coverage. *Level 3 Communications*, 168 F.3d at 958.

Moreover, the language of the policy in our case differs from *Level 3 Communications*. In that case, the policy excluded coverage for claims "brought or maintained by or on behalf of any Insured." *Level 3 Communications*, 168 F.3d at 957. Here, in contrast, the D&O policy is much broader, barring coverage for claims "By or at the behest of . . . any DIRECTOR or OFFICER . . . unless such CLAIM is instigated and continued totally independent of, and totally without the solicitation of, or assistance of, or active participation of, or intervention of, any DIRECTOR or OFFICER or the COMPANY or any affiliate of the COMPANY." While the language in *Level 3 Communications* gave the court some wiggle room, the language in our case is plain and clear, compelling our conclusion that Genesis need not cover Sphinx for Taylor's lawsuit.

Let us be clear: we are not saying that *Level 3 Communications* was wrongly decided. We are merely saying that its facts are too dissimilar to our own to be decisive.

Because *Level 3 Communications* is not on point, we are left with the perspicuous mandate of several Florida Supreme Court decisions: focus on the plain meaning of the policy unless that policy is ambiguous. And as detailed above, the "insured vs. insured" exclusion in this case is unambiguous. Understood from this perspective, Sphinx is really inviting this court to rewrite the D&O policy at issue to require the segregation of claims based on the percentage attributable to each litigant. We reject its invitation because the Florida Supreme Court would reject it. That court has stated that, "As a court, we cannot place limitations upon the plain language of a policy exclusion simply because we think it should have been written [another] way." *Deni Assocs.*, 711 So.2d at 1139. To illustrate, the court recently rejected an attempt by an insured to change the plain language of its insurance policy. See generally *Swire Pac. Holdings*, 845 So.2d 161. In that case, the court said that while the insured's "reasoning . . . is certainly logical," *id.* at 169, "[i]t [was] inappropriate for [the insured] to attempt to add language to the contract which changes its effect in an attempt to secure coverage." *Id.* at 168.

The Florida Supreme Court would likely be equally suspicious of Sphinx's attempt to secure coverage. Sphinx's D&O policy clearly bars coverage for suits by former directors and officers. Sphinx's request to read the policy differently essentially asks a court to rewrite it, which is something we will not do.

III.

For the reasons stated above, we conclude that the district court did not err in granting summary judgment in favor of Genesis.

AFFIRMED.

NOTES AND QUESTIONS

1. *Text vs. Rationale.* Litigation over D&O insurance policies tends to focus on contract law principles. The *Sphynx International* court makes the argument that the words of the insurance contract trump the rationale for the policy exclusion. Does this make sense? Do you agree with the court that the text should always be followed? Are there contract interpretation principles to the contrary, and if so, could they be operative here to lead to the opposite conclusion?

2. *Suit Initiator.* The *Sphynx International* court makes a distinction between a passive shareholder initiating a suit (as in *Level 3 Communications*) and a former director initiating a suit (as in this case). Do you believe this is a justified distinction or is it merely a distinction that should make no real difference? What legal or policy concerns justify your answer?

3. *Insurance Extends Indemnification.* Many corporate statutes authorize the purchase of insurance even if it covers expenses and liability for which the corporation may not provide indemnification. DGCL § 145(g); MBCA § 8.57. The rationale? The corporation's insurance premiums are considered to be in the nature of compensation to the directors and officers. Accordingly, if the corporation could pay the director or officer cash to purchase a liability policy for his or her own benefit, then the corporation should be able to directly pay for an equivalent policy.

PROBLEM

Target Corp., a Delaware corporation, is being acquired by its majority shareholder, Acquiror Inc., also a Delaware corporation, in a direct merger. Disgruntled, a shareholder of Target, brings a direct action against Target's directors for breach of fiduciary duty, alleging that (a) the Target board did not act on a fully informed basis in approving the merger agreement and the merger and (b) the transaction is tainted by a conflicting interest because of Acquiror's dominant control over Target and Target's board. The suit is properly before the court under *Weinberger*. Disgruntled's complaint requests that the merger be enjoined or, in the alternative, damages for any adjudicated breach. Target's charter includes an exculpation provision that limits a director's liability to the full extent permitted under DGCL § 102(b)(7) and provides mandatory director indemnification and advancement of expenses to the full extent permitted under DGCL § 145.

Target believes that its D&O insurance policy will cover any financial losses (assessed damages and expenses) suffered by the directors as a result of the litigation, but it would prefer to limit those losses to the extent practicable, including by attempting to dismiss all or part of the suit as soon as practicable.

1. Briefly advise Target on the potential availability of exculpation and its potential use in dismissing or otherwise determining the outcome of the suit.

2. Briefly describe your understanding of Target's obligation to indemnify the directors and advance their expenses in connection with the suit.

E. COMPARATIVE PERSPECTIVE

The United States is not the only country that has legally established or permitted corporate and contractual methods of protecting directors from liability for breaches of fiduciary duty. Of course, the laws of each country afford directors and officers different authority, liability, and protections from liability, and these laws change over time in reaction to social forces, including globalization.

> German law does not permit director exculpation and places extreme limits on indemnification. French law permits neither. Admittedly, the formal exposure to liability that these laws sustain for European directors currently may not be especially meaningful. Lawsuits against boards are not very likely when large bank creditors and shareholders also serve on the boards. Notably, however, English law, which also both prohibits immunization and severely limits indemnification to narrow circumstances, has not deterred top directors from joining shareholder market-model corporations in the United Kingdom. Thus, European laws that expose directors to personal liability without indemnification may not mean very much now, but that is likely to change as the forces of globalization continue. Pressure to change these laws is likely to come, but should be resisted.

Lawrence A. Cunningham, *Commonalities and Prescriptions in the Vertical Dimension of Global Corporate Governance*, 84 CORNELL L. REV. 1133, 1185–86 (1999).

F. RECENT DEVELOPMENTS

Although the Trans Union directors were found liable by the court in *Van Gorkom*, as noted at the beginning of this chapter, they did not individually pay out-of-pocket for the damages arising from that violation. Since that time, the enactment of exculpation provisions, combined with well funded indemnification and D&O insurance, has virtually ensured that directors do not have to personally pay for liability associated with their corporate positions. However, settlements of litigation stemming from the WorldCom and Enron scandals changed this landscape a bit. Directors agreed to pay, and in fact paid, monetary settlement amounts out-of-pocket as a result of the negotiations among the parties. It remains unclear whether these negotiated settlement payments signal a change in policy or practice. However, fear of liability may be more real for directors after these settlements than it has been for over 20 years. *See* Michael Klausner et al., *Outside Directors' Liability: Have WorldCom and Enron Changed the Rules?*, 71 STANFORD LAW. 36 (2005).

Chapter 15
BASIC CORPORATE CHANGES

A. OVERVIEW

As the preceding chapters show, once a corporation comes into legal existence, it is not a static organism. The ongoing operations of the firm, the relationships among its constituents, and the exigencies of the markets with which it interacts may make changes in the essential structure and governance of the corporation necessary or desirable. These structure and governance alterations typically enable, effectuate, or represent major corporate transactions. Some of these modifications — which may include actions resulting in the termination of the corporation's existence — are so fundamental that they require filings with the secretary of state in the corporation's jurisdiction of organization that effect or constitute modifications to the corporation's charter (i.e., the certificate of incorporation for Delaware corporations or articles of incorporation for MBCA corporations). Accordingly, like the initial chartering of the corporation, these basic corporate changes are strongly rooted in state corporate statutes.

As a result, the available types of basic corporate changes differ from state to state. In general, however, they may include: (i) charter and bylaw amendments; (ii) statutory business combination transactions like mergers, consolidations, share exchange transactions, and dispositions of all or substantially all of a corporation's assets; and (iii) dissolutions. These basic corporate changes raise a variety of internal governance questions, including most prominently requirements for (and relating to) director and shareholder approval (typically, but not always, involving board approval followed by shareholder approval) and the exercise of director and officer fiduciary duties. As a result, the board's role in recommending basic corporate changes to shareholders has been advisory.

> Directors must in certain circumstances make recommendations to stockholders regarding proposed actions that fundamentally affect the interests of the stockholders, such as mergers, charter amendments, sales of all or substantially all of the corporation's assets, dissolution, or tender offers to acquire stock of the corporation. The allocation to directors of that advisory responsibility has an obvious rationale. As the ultimate repository and source of information about the corporation and its affairs, directors are most efficiently situated to provide information to stockholders when the stockholders are called upon to act on mergers, tender offers, and the like.

Lawrence A. Hamermesh, *Calling Off the Lynch Mob: The Corporate Director's Fiduciary Disclosure Duty*, 49 Vand. L. Rev. 1087, 1144 (1996) (footnotes omitted). Because of the importance of fundamental changes to the corporate form, states may restrict the ability of board committees — as opposed to the board as whole — to act in approving and recommending to shareholders the subject transaction or transactions. *See* DGCL § 141(c); MBCA § 8.25.

The characterization of the board's role as advisory, while correct, belies the fact that the shareholder role typically is *pro forma*, especially in public corporations. Since the right to initiate amendments under modern corporate statutes lies solely with the board, the shareholders cannot implement these basic corporate changes on their own. As a practical matter, shareholder involvement in basic corporate changes is limited to voting to approve a decision already made and recommended by the board. Perhaps this explains why, as we see in other areas of director or shareholder conflict, issues relating to corporate governance in fundamental corporate change transactions most commonly are vetted in direct or derivative shareholder litigation against the corporation or its directors.

In reading the materials in this chapter, it is important to recognize that the United States is not the only country to identify the need for shareholder involvement in basic corporate changes. The laws of many other countries, for example, mandate shareholder approval rights for fundamental corporate change transactions and other actions. *See, e.g.*, Yevgeniy V. Nikulin, *The New Self-Enforcing Model of Corporate Law: Myth or Reality*, 6 D.C.L. J. Int'l L. & Prac. 347, 411 n.74 (1997) (noting, in describing Russian law, "shareholder approval for amendments to the Charter [and] any reorganization including transformations, liquidations, large sales of assets"); Cherie J. Owen, *Board Games: Germany's Monopoly on the Two-Tier System of Corporate Governance and Why the Post-Enron United States Would Benefit From Its Adoption*, 22 Penn St. Int'l L. Rev. 167 (2003) ("Unlike shareholders of American corporations, shareholders of German corporations have the power to amend the articles of incorporation and to declare dividends."). The exact nature of the approvals and the types of transactions that trigger those approvals vary from country to country (as they do from state to state in the United States). Moreover, the litigation environment may differ in other countries, especially to the extent that most other countries are civil law, rather than common law, jurisdictions.

This chapter describes the various different types of basic corporate change in turn, identifies the statutory basis for each type, and highlights the key corporate governance issues that arise in the context of each type. Specifically, the chapter focuses attention on changes to the corporation that alter its basic, organic configuration — transactions that typically are implemented as a means of reorganizing, recapitalizing, or otherwise restructuring the entity. For example, a corporation may need to modify its capital structure (equity or debt) or operations because it is in financial trouble. Alternatively, a corporation may want to take advantage of favorable changes in capital or other markets by changing its capital structure (equity and/or debt) or shedding, acquiring, or realigning operational units. And to do any of the foregoing may require changes to ways in which the board is constituted or takes action. The principle objective of these corporate reorganizations, recapitalizations, and restructurings often is increased efficiency and improved profitability for the corporation. Transactions used to implement these types of corporate changes may include stock splits and reverse stock splits, mergers, acquisitions and dispositions, and spin-offs.

B. CHARTER AND BYLAW AMENDMENTS

As you learned in Chapter 4, a corporation's charter is, in effect, its constitution. The corporate charter establishes the corporation as an entity and sets forth its basic corporate structure. The terms and provisions of the chartering document (both mandatory and permissive) are governed by statutory law. *See, e.g.*, DGCL § 102; MBCA § 2.02. Without a charter, there is no corporation.

A corporation's bylaws institute certain rules for the corporation's ongoing operation as an entity. These rules govern various aspects of corporate existence, including the number, designation, and election of officers, the number and election of directors and the conduct of business at board meetings, the conduct of business at shareholder meetings, and various other general matters, e.g., the location of the corporation's headquarters or principal place or business, whether the corporation will have a corporate seal, how the bylaws may be amended, etc. The existence of the bylaws is mandated, and the content of the bylaws is shaped, by the corporate statutes of the state of incorporation. *See, e.g.*, DGCL § 109; MBCA § 2.06.

Together, the charter and bylaws constitute the two key corporate organizational documents. Many different kinds of changes can be made by altering the terms and provisions of a corporation's charter or bylaws. Some of these changes relate to general corporate governance and are addressed in other chapters of this book (notably Chapters 8 and 9). Moreover, as noted in Chapter 16, modifications to corporate charters and bylaws also may be used to protect the corporation against unsolicited (and unwanted) acquisitions.

For example, corporate reorganizations, recapitalizations, and restructurings frequently require, among other things, additions or modifications to the corporation's organizational documents. A corporation may need to alter its name or its corporate purpose (to the extent that the purpose is set forth in its charter) to effectuate its objectives. More commonly, the corporation may desire to change its authorized equity capital as set forth in its charter (i.e., the class and/or number of shares, par value, terms, etc.). Some of these transactions involve diminishing or changing the rights of then existing corporate shareholders. In all cases, these changes to the corporation's charter and/or bylaws are governed by state corporate law and the terms and provisions of the corporation's charter and bylaws, which require board and, in many cases, shareholder approval. As a general matter, state corporation laws require both director and shareholder approval of charter amendments (with board approval coming first). Typically, bylaw amendments always may be made by shareholders, but sometimes also may be made by the directors. (Sometimes, directors are given a broad, parallel right to amend bylaws by default in the corporate statute; sometimes, the statute only permits directors to have a parallel right to amend bylaws if and to the extent the corporation's charter expressly authorizes director bylaw amendments.)

Specifically, Delaware law requires that the board first approve an amendment to the certificate of incorporation, declaring its advisability, and then put the amendment to a shareholder vote. By default, directors take action by majority vote at a meeting at which a quorum is present (with a majority of the directors constituting a quorum). DGCL §141(b). A vote of holders of a majority of the outstanding shares entitled to vote (and of a majority of the outstanding shares of any class entitled to vote, voting separately) in favor of the amendment constitutes approval. DGCL § 242(b)(1). Class voting is required "if the amendment would increase or decrease the aggregate number of authorized shares of such class, increase or decrease the par value of the shares of such class, or alter or change the powers, preferences, or special rights of the shares of such class so as to affect them adversely." DGCL § 242(b)(2). Numerous cases construe the meaning of "affect them adversely" in this context.

Similarly, the Model Business Corporation Act requires that, for corporations that already have issued shares, proposed amendments to the articles of incorporation first be adopted by the board of directors and then be submitted by the board of directors to the shareholders for their approval. The board's submission of the amendment for shareholder approval must be accompanied by its recommendation for approval (unless the board determines that it should not make a recommendation). *See* MBCA § 10.03. Class voting is required under circumstances enumerated in the statute (generally, circumstances in which the rights of holders of the class are substantially changed). MBCA § 10.04. There are limited exceptions to these rules requiring shareholder approval. Specifically, board approval alone is sufficient for certain ministerial and nominal amendments and, for corporations with only one class of outstanding shares, specified capitalization changes. *See* MBCA § 10.05. By default, director approvals must be obtained by majority vote taken at a meeting at which a quorum consisting of a majority of the directors is present, MBCA § 8.24, and shareholder approval occurs when votes approving the amendment exceed those opposing the amendment at a meeting at which a quorum consisting of a majority of the votes entitled to be cast is present (and for class votes, a majority of the votes entitled to be cast by each voting class). MBCA §§ 7.25 & 10.03(e).

Under both the Delaware General Corporation Law and the Model Business Corporation Act, charter amendments are effectuated by a filing with the Secretary of State of the state in which the charter itself was filed. Under the Delaware General Corporation Law, the filing is denominated a "certificate of amendment," and under the Model Business Corporation Act, the filing is called "articles of amendment." *See* DGCL

§ 242(b)(1); MBCA § 10.06. The best evidence of incorporation or the current terms and provisions of a corporation's charter is a copy of the corporation's charter, certified by the Secretary of State.

Amendment rules for bylaws are different. Under Delaware law, shareholders have the right to amend bylaws, and the board also may be afforded that right by express provision in the certificate of incorporation. DGCL § 109. By default, the vote of holders of a majority of the shares present and entitled to vote at a meeting at which a quorum is present, DGCL § 216(2), or, where applicable, a majority of directors present at a meeting at which a quorum is present, DGCL § 141(b), approves bylaw amendments. Class voting rules also may apply. Under the Model Business Corporation Act, bylaws can be amended or repealed by the shareholders and by the board of directors, unless the articles of incorporation or a shareholder-approved bylaw otherwise provides. MBCA § 10.20. Special rules exist for bylaws that alter director quorum or voting requirements and for specified public company bylaws relating to director elections. MBCA §§ 10.21 & 10.22. By default, once a quorum exists, bylaw amendments are approved by shareholders when the votes favoring the action exceed those opposing the action, MBCA § 7.25, or when a majority of the directors present vote in favor. MBCA § 8.24.

Bylaw amendments are not required to be filed with the Secretary of State to become effective. Rather, the approval of the requisite governing body (shareholders or directors) renders bylaw amendments effective. The best evidence of the terms and provisions of a corporation's bylaws is a copy of the corporation's bylaws, certified by the corporate secretary or other authorized corporate officer.

This modern statutory framework stands in stark contrast to the "vested rights" doctrine that formerly existed under case law. The vested rights doctrine provided a strong check on the establishment of fundamental corporate changes. Under the doctrine, a fundamental corporate change — certain charter amendments, a merger — required unanimous shareholder approval, because shareholders were deemed to have a vested right in corporate participation through their property interest in the equity of the firm. This unanimous approval rule was supplanted by corporate statutes and related case law that permit or impose majority and supermajority shareholder approval of fundamental corporate changes, fiduciary duties of the majority to the minority, and requirements of entire fairness in specified factual circumstances (as we have seen in Chapters 10 and 11), and (for mergers and, in some states, significant asset dispositions) appraisal rights for dissenting shareholders. In fact, the Model Business Corporation Act includes an affirmative disavowal of the vested rights doctrine: "A shareholder of the corporation does not have a vested property right resulting from any provision in the articles of incorporation, including provisions relating to management, control, capital structure, dividend entitlement, or purpose or duration of the corporation." MBCA § 10.01(b). These statutes and cases and the related fiduciary duty principles, are at issue in this chapter. Vested rights reflected a significantly more active governance role for shareholders than exists under current corporate law rules and norms.

1. Charter Amendments

The case set forth below illustrates a series of fundamental corporate changes conducted by amendments of corporate charters and some related approval and governance issues. In essence, the case analyzes the conversion of a for-profit corporation (IOTA) into a non-profit corporation, and the subsequent conversion of that non-profit back into a for-profit corporation (defendant-appellee DCX), all under Delaware law. Note the interesting procedural posture of the case. Also note that otherwise legally valid changes made to charters and bylaws may be invalidated if directors breach their fiduciary duties in approving the changes.

FARAHPOUR v. DCX, INC.
Supreme Court of Delaware
635 A.2d 894 (1994)

. . .

Upon Certification of Questions of Laws from the District of Columbia Court of Appeals.

WALSH, JUSTICE:

This matter is before the Court as the result of the certification of two questions of law pursuant to Article IV, Section 11(9) of the Delaware Constitution and Supreme Court Rule 41. The questions of law have been certified by the District of Columbia Court of Appeals ("the Court of Appeals"), the highest court of that jurisdiction. In the exercise of our discretion to consider questions of law where there are important and urgent reasons for immediate determination, and in view of the fact that the underlying dispute is controlled by Delaware corporate law, we have accepted both certified questions for determination.

The certified questions are the following:

1. Whether, under Delaware law, a corporation, incorporated in the State of Delaware, may make fundamental changes in its structure and purposes, through amendment of its articles of incorporation[1] . . . ?

2. Whether the changes . . . may be accomplished without notification to the corporation's nonvoting members, without a dissolution of the [predecessor] nonprofit corporation, without a merger or consolidation, and without the corporation providing anything of value to the members whose rights have been extinguished? . . .

[W]e believe they may be answered in the affirmative, i.e., the General Corporation Law of Delaware (the "GCL") does authorize a corporation to make the changes outlined in the questions. . . .

II

Before addressing the specific questions posed by the certification, certain general observations are appropriate. A Delaware corporation can "make fundamental changes in its structure and purposes" through amendments to its certificate of incorporation. Section 102(a) of the GCL provides that filed, certificate of incorporation shall set forth, inter alia, the purposes and capital structure of the corporation. Once adopted and properly filed, the certificate may be amended with the scope of the amendments unlimited, so long as the added provision "would be lawful and proper to insert in an original certificate filed at the time of the filing of the amendment." 8 *Del. C.* § 242(a). Of course, the mechanics of the amendatory procedures, as set forth in Section 242, must be followed for the process to be effective and complete.

Regarding the role of the corporation's board of directors in the amendment process, the GCL is equally clear. Normally, a proposed amendment to the certificate of incorporation must be submitted to a vote of the corporation's stockholders entitled to vote thereon. 8 *Del. C.* § 242(b)(1)-(2). There are two exceptions which are pertinent to the present inquiry. First, if a corporation has not yet received payment for its shares, the board of directors may amend the certificate by board action alone. 8 *Del. C.* § 241. Second, if a corporation has no capital stock, the "governing body" may approve a certificate amendment, on its own, in a two step process by (1) adopting "a resolution setting forth the amendment proposed and declaring its advisability," and (2) approving the amendment by majority vote of the members of the governing body at a subsequent

---

[1] The question as certified to the court apparently uses the wrong term (articles of incorporation, rather than certificate of incorporation) for a Delaware corporate charter.

meeting held between 15 and 60 days after the meeting at which the resolution was adopted. 8 *Del. C.* § 242(b)(3).

Against this background of general principles, we separately address the four scenarios which constitute the first certified question.

A.

CONVERSION FROM A FOR-PROFIT, STOCK CORPORATION TO A NONPROFIT, NONSTOCK CORPORATION.

The parties do not dispute that a for-profit, stock corporation may be converted into a nonprofit, nonstock, mutual benefit corporation. This agreement is dictated by Section 242's grant of board power of amendment, including the right to change its corporate power and purposes, § 242(a)(2), to reclassify its authorized capital stock, § 242(a)(3), and to create new classes of stock, § 242(a)(5). These designated powers encompass the right to make the change from a for-profit stock corporation to a nonprofit, nonstock mutual benefit corporation, a status permissible at the time of the filing of the original certificate of incorporation. . . .

The 1928 amendment of ITOA's certificate of incorporation, which converted it to a nonprofit, nonstock corporation, recites that it was approved by the holders of a majority of stock. Thus, it would appear that there was full compliance with Delaware corporate law in the conversion of ITOA from a for-profit corporation to a nonprofit, nonstock corporation.

B.

CONVERSION FROM A NONPROFIT, NONSTOCK CORPORATION BACK INTO A FOR-PROFIT, STOCK CORPORATION.

In 1989, ITOA changed its name to Diamond Cab of D.C., Inc., and altered its corporate status, changing from a nonprofit, nonstock corporation back into a for-profit stock corporation. The appellant contends that Delaware law does not permit such a radical change without express authorization. As with the preceding scenario, the GCL contains no restrictions precluding this type of conversion. Nor is there any requirement that the members of the nonstock corporation approve a conversion amendment unless the certificate of incorporation requires such a vote. 8 *Del. C.* § 242(b)(3).

Section 242(b)(3) permits amendment to be effectuated upon vote of the "governing body" of a nonstock corporation, the equivalent of the board of directors of a stock corporation. In the absence of a certificate requirement, a vote by members generally is not mandated. Additionally, § 257 of the GCL allows for conversion from a nonprofit to a for-profit entity through a merger as long as the nonprofit organization is not charitable in nature § 257(e). Since DCX has never been a charitable organization, nothing in § 257, either explicitly or implicitly, prohibits the change from a nonprofit to a for-profit entity through certificate amendment. Finally, it should be noted that the Third Circuit Court of Appeals applying Delaware law, has held that a nonprofit nonstock corporation may amend its certificate to authorize the issuance of stock. *Plechner v. Widener College, Inc.*, 3d Cir., 569 F.2d 1250 (1977).

We conclude, therefore, that Delaware law authorizes change from a nonprofit, nonstock mutual benefit corporation into a for-profit stock corporation without the vote of its members. Accordingly, this portion of the certified question is answered in the affirmative.

C.

ISSUANCE BY THE RECONVERTED CORPORATION OF NEWLY-AUTHORIZED STOCK SOLELY TO VOTING MEMBERS OF THE CORPORATION.

As a matter of legal authority, it is clear that a board of directors may issue stock to whomever it chooses so long as the constitutionally required consideration is received. See 8 *Del. C.* § 151–53. Such issuance is normally accomplished by board resolution and thus no amendment to the certificate is necessary unless the stock being issued is not yet authorized by the certificate. . . .

If the subject corporation is a stock corporation with some paid-for shares outstanding, it cannot amend its certificate by board action alone under Section 242(b)(1). Of course, if the stock corporation has not yet received payment for any of its stock, it can amend its certificate under Section 241(a) by vote of the directors alone. If the subject corporation is a nonstock corporation, it may amend its certificate by a resolution and vote of its governing body to become a stock corporation, pursuant to Section 242(b)(3), which can then issue stock as it chooses.

D.

ELIMINATION OF TWO CLASSES OF NONVOTING MEMBERS ALONG WITH THEIR RIGHTS TO RECEIVE A DISTRIBUTION OF ASSETS IN THE EVENT OF DISSOLUTION.

In addressing this question, we again assume that the subject corporation is a nonstock corporation since the reference is to classes of "members," not "stockholders." Under this assumption, the amendment in question could be approved without a vote of the members, voting or nonvoting, so long as the governing body of the corporation adheres to the procedures set forth in Section 242(b)(3). We also assume the inquiry concerns the elimination of the "classes" of members, along with any rights attendant upon dissolution of the classes, not with the elimination of members themselves.

Section 102(a)(4) provides that "the conditions of membership of [nonstock] corporations shall likewise be stated in the certificate of incorporation or the certificate may provide that the conditions of membership shall be vested in the by-laws." Again, if it be assumed that there are no certificate provisions otherwise providing, Section 242(b)(3) permits amendments to the certificate, including conditions of membership, without the approval of a class of members, even where such amendments are contrary to the interests of the affected class. By contrast, and significantly, Section 242(b)(2) expressly provides that a class of stockholders is entitled to a class vote on a proposed amendment "whether or not [the class is] entitled to vote thereon by the certificate of incorporation" if the amendment adversely affects the rights of the class. The contrasting provisions reflect a legislative intent to provide fewer voting rights, of pure statutory origin, to members of nonstock corporations in the adoption of amendments to the certificate of incorporation. In sum, such members have neither a right to vote on an amendment generally nor a right to vote on an amendment as a class member unless the certificate of incorporation provides otherwise. . . .

The parties dispute the fairness of the 1989 amendments, but in the context of the corporation's legal authority to effectuate the certificate amendment, the answer to the certified question must be in the affirmative. The equitable aspect of this transaction will be hereafter considered.

III

We next address the second basic inquiry, *viz.*, whether the certificate changes outlined above may be accomplished without: (1) notification to the corporation's nonvoting members, (2) dissolution of the [predecessor] nonprofit corporation, (3) merger or consolidation and (4) providing anything of value to the member whose rights have been extinguished. To the extent that any of the certificate changes can be accomplished by the amendatory process expressly permitted under one section of the GCL, specifically Section 242, the doctrine of independent legal significance provides that such action will not be tested by compliance with other sections of the GCL. Thus, a nonprofit, nonstock mutual benefit association such as IOTA could be reconverted into a for-profit stock corporation without dissolution (and attendant distribution of assets), merger, consolidation or compensation to affected members.

The question of whether nonvoting members are entitled to notice of amendatory actions is, by analogy, controlled by the Section 222(b) standard for stockholders. That section provides that "the written notice of any meeting shall be given not less than 10 nor more than 60 days before the date of the meeting *to each stockholder entitled to vote at* such meeting." (emphasis added). Thus, there is no statutory requirement that notice be given, either before action is taken or afterwards, to nonvoting members, or, in the case of corporations with stock outstanding, to stockholders without entitlement to vote.

The focus of the certified questions is the authority *vel non*, *i.e.* the legal entitlement of a corporation to enact certain certificate amendments under Delaware law. Our answers are necessarily a narrow response to the questions framed. Because the limited factual basis for the questions suggests that a minority or special class of members are disputing the exercise of corporate power by a larger voting class, we add the following caveat to our answers. Strict adherence to the procedures authorized by particular provisions of the GCL does not insure that the result will receive judicial approval in litigation initiated at the behest of disgruntled members or shareholders. The use of the corporate machinery, even in full compliance with Delaware law, does not insulate corporate management or directors from claims of inequitable conduct. Where fiduciary duties arising from management control are implicated, judicial scrutiny may extend to the purpose for which an otherwise lawful course was undertaken and the result achieved. Where inequitable conduct is established, a court will act to correct the inequity.

With the qualification noted, the certified questions are answered in the AFFIRMATIVE.

2.   Bylaw Amendments

Fundamental changes effected through bylaws most often are undertaken as part of restructurings in connection with a change in control of the corporation. In *Frankino v. Gleason*, 1999 Del. Ch. LEXIS 219 (Del. Ch. Nov. 5, 1999), Chancellor Chandler determines the validity of an amendment to corporate bylaws in a control-change context and, in the process, teaches the litigants and others about the importance of protecting a supermajority vote provision from amendment by a mere majority of shareholders.

> Despite being a 55% shareholder, Frankino found himself at odds with NAC's board of directors. In order to regain corporate control over [NAC], Frankino endeavored to expand the size of the board and appoint directors loyal to him. Standing in his path was Article IX of [NAC] bylaws, entitled "Miscellaneous."
>
> Article IX purports to require an 80% supermajority vote to amend Article III of the bylaws. Article III generally governs matters concerning NAC's board of directors including, among other things, board size. In light of Article

IX's supermajority requirement to amend Article III, Frankino's 55% simple majority ownership seemed insufficient to expand the board's size.

Thinking strategically, Frankino sought and indeed found a chink in the armor: there was no language in Article IX that prevented its amendment or wholesale repeal by a simple majority vote. Frankino proceeded to eliminate Article IX's supermajority provision through majority written consent as there was nothing in the bylaws that seemed to prevent him from doing so. Immediately thereafter, he amended Article III, again by simple majority written consent, and elected his nominees to the newly created board seats. Frankino then filed this § 225 action seeking entry of an order confirming (i) the validity of the amendments to the company's bylaws, and (ii) the election of his nominees to the expanded board.

Defendants contend that such an order would render their amendment to the bylaws nugatory, as the provision requiring a supermajority vote would have been amended by a bare majority. They invite me to examine the "self-evident purpose" of the bylaw's supermajority provision and *imply language requiring a supermajority vote to amend Article IX.*

Based on the undisputed evidence, most notably an NAC bylaw recognizing that only "express provisions" can create a requirement for a supermajority vote, I conclude that Frankino's amendments by majority written consent are valid. Accordingly, I direct that Frankino's nominees take their rightful places as members of NAC's board. . . .

NOTES AND QUESTIONS

1. *Potential for Disenfranchisement of Minority Shareholders.* Since the demise of the vested rights doctrine, accountability of the majority to the minority in making fundamental corporate changes principally comes through fiduciary duty analysis rather than through shareholder voting. Yet the modern approach may not always efficiently serve minority shareholder interests.

From 1940 onward, courts in various jurisdictions eliminated vested rights doctrines. The majority of shares could vote to eliminate a preemptive right or a right to cumulative voting for directors. Elimination did not strip an objecting shareholder minority of all protection. Courts held that elimination of basic rights was subject to a fairness analysis. The objecting minority, however, was deprived of the surefire objection to majority action that vested rights doctrines historically had represented.

Elimination of vested rights gave rise to a commonly observed phenomenon in corporate law . . . . In corporate law what one cannot do directly one can do indirectly. What cannot be accomplished in one step may be accomplished in three or four. Form routinely is exalted over substance.

Douglas M. Branson, *Indeterminacy: The Final Ingredient in an Interest Group Analysis of Corporate Law*, 43 VAND. L. REV. 85, 92–93 (1990)[*] (footnotes omitted). Consider this observation in light of the materials on close corporations in Chapter 9 and the materials in the remainder of the chapter.

2. *Analytical Approach Exemplified.* Cases involving charter and bylaw amendments often evidence a hierarchy in the analysis and determination of corporate law questions that can and should be applied to scrutinize both fundamental corporate changes and other corporate law matters. The corporate statute, together with related decisional law, is paramount. Corporate charters are next in the hierarchy. They are governed by, and must be consistent with, that body of corporate statutory and decisional law. Bylaws are governed by and must be consistent with both the corporate law and the corporate charter. Contracts between or among corporate constituents, if any, and specialty laws that may be designed or needed to fill gaps in the corporate law scheme complete the picture. Although courts are not always transparent in employing this hierarchy in their analyses, both litigators and transaction planners should be sensitive to it. *See, e.g., Centaur Partners, IV v. National Intergroup, Inc.*, 582 A.2d 923 (Del. 1990).

PROBLEM

Recap Inc., a Delaware corporation, has one class of common stock authorized in its certificate of incorporation. Each share of common stock entitles the holder to one vote on all matters requiring a shareholder vote. Recap's board and the holder of a majority if its outstanding shares desire to modify its charter to provide that, upon the effectiveness of a certificate of amendment effectuating the modification, each holder of shares of common stock entitles the holder to ten votes per share until the share is transferred, at which time the transferee holder shall be permitted to exercise only one vote per share. A group of minority holders desires to block adoption of the proposed charter amendment. Assuming Recap's certificate of incorporation does not alter the default rules in the Delaware General Corporation Law as to the voting requirements for charter amendments, can the disaffected minority holders block adoption of the recapitalization? Why, or why not? Explain the required approvals in support of your answer.

Now, assume that Recap has both a class of voting common stock and a class of voting preferred stock authorized and that shares of each are issued and outstanding. Also assume that, by its express terms, the preferred stock (a) votes with the common stock as to all matters on which shareholders are entitled to vote and (b) does not vote as a separate class as to any matter on which shareholders are entitled to vote. If the same amendment to the certificate of incorporation (providing for supervoting common stock that reverts back to one-share-one-vote common stock upon transfer of the shares) is proposed for adoption and the majority holder of the common stock, do the holders of the voting preferred stock get a class vote on the amendment? Why, or why not?

C. STATUTORY BUSINESS COMBINATIONS

Businesses conducted through corporations can be acquired in a variety of ways. For example, by purchasing all of the outstanding shares of a corporation, an individual or entity can buy that business. This type of acquisition is a traditional, market-based purchase and sale arrangement, and it is described and explored in more detail in Chapter 16. As such, stock purchase transactions are largely outside the regulation of state corporate law (other than any state tender offer regulation that may be applicable).

There are, however, many other ways to acquire a business conducted through the corporate form. This chapter explores those other ways as further examples of corporate actions that constitute or make fundamental corporate changes. First, some relevant nomenclature must be covered.

When corporations merge or are acquired, we refer to the relevant merger or acquisition transaction as a business combination transaction. When that transaction is either ordained by statute or requires authorization in accordance with statutory provisions, we refer to it as a statutory business combination. Each statutory business combination has different approval requirements and may or may not trigger appraisal rights for dissenting shareholders. These statutory rights are, among other things, bases for choosing among the different types of business combination transaction. A summary of approval and appraisal rights for each type of transaction under the Delaware General Corporation Law and the Model Business Corporation Act is provided below.

Approval and Appraisal Rights for Statutory Business Combinations under the DGCL and the MBCA

DGCL	Merger or Consolidation	Share Exchange	Sale of Assets
Approval Rights (Voting Rights)	***Generally:*** Agreement of merger or consolidation first must be approved by the board of directors of each corporation that desires to merge. [§§ 251(a) and (b)] Stockholders of each constituent corporation then must act upon the agreement and adopt it by majority vote. [§ 251(c)] ***De Minimis Change:*** Mergers meeting certain specified requirements — relating to negligible changes in the charter and capitalization (total equity and voting equity) of the surviving corporation and excluding share issuance transactions covered by § 251(f)(3) — do not require the approval of stockholders of the surviving corporation. [§ 251(f)] Stock exchange rules may call for shareholder approval if there is a significant issuance of stock in the merger. ***Parent/subsidiary (Short-form) Mergers:*** 90% (or more) subsidiary can be merged with its parent (with either surviving) without the approval of the subsidiary's stockholders. [§ 253(a)]	No operative statutory provision. Transaction cannot be done in Delaware.	The board of directors may determine to sell all or substantially all of the corporation's assets only with majority stockholder approval. [§ 271]

DGCL	Merger or Consolidation	Share Exchange	Sale of Assets
Dissenters' Rights (Appraisal Rights)	*Generally,* stockholders in all constituent corporations to a merger or consolidation may dissent if they are entitled to vote on the merger. [§ 262(a); § 262(b)(1)] Proper procedures must be followed (including prior notice and not voting in favor of the merger). [§ 262(d)(1)] Exceptions exist for stockholders of any class or series (i) listed on a national securities exchange or designated as a national market system security by the NASD or (ii) held of record by 2,000 or more stockholders (either being *"liquid shares"*), if the stockholders get cash in lieu of fractional shares, stock of the surviving corporation, liquid shares. [§ 262(b)(1) and (2)] In a § 253 (parent/subsidiary) merger, Delaware subsidiary stockholders may dissent. [§ 262(b)(3)]	See above.	None.

MBCA	Merger or Consolidation	Share Exchange	Sale of Assets
Approval Rights (Voting Rights)	***Generally:*** Plan of merger first must be adopted by the board of directors of each party to the merger. [§ 11.02; § 11.04(a)] Shareholders of each corporation party to the merger entitled to vote also must approve the plan of merger, as submitted and recommended to them. A separate vote of holders of individual classes or series may be statutorily required for approval of the plan of merger. [§ 11.04 (b)—(f)] ***De Minimis Change:*** Mergers meeting certain specified requirements — relating to negligible changes in the charter and capitalization (total equity and voting equity) of the surviving corporation and excluding share issuances covered by § 6.21(f) — do not require the approval of shareholders of the surviving corporation. [§ 11.04(g)] Stock exchange rules may call for shareholder approval if there is a significant issuance of stock in the merger. ***Parent/ subsidiary (Short-form) Mergers:*** 90% (or more) subsidiary can be merged with its parent (with either surviving) or a sister subsidiary without the approval of the subsidiary's shareholders. [§ 11.05(a)]	Same as for mergers, generally. Approval by the shareholders of the acquiring corporation generally is not required. [§ 11.03; § 11.04(a)—(g)] (There are no parent/ subsidiary rules.)	The board of directors may determine to sell all or substantially all of the corporation's assets in the usual and regular course of the corporation's business without shareholder approval. [§ 12.01] The board of directors may determine to sell all or substantially all of the corporation's assets outside § 12.01 (e.g., <u>not</u> in the usual and regular course of the corporation's business) only with shareholder approval, if the corporation would be left without a significant continuing business activity. The board must initiate the process. [§ 12.02]

MBCA	Merger or Consolidation	Share Exchange	Sale of Assets
Dissenters' Rights (Appraisal Rights)	In general, in a § 11.04 merger, if shareholder approval is required, shareholders entitled to vote may dissent, unless the class of stock they hold remains outstanding after the merger. [§ 13.02(a)(1)(I)] Proper procedures must be followed (including prior notice and not voting in favor of the merger). [§ 13.21(a)] Exceptions exist for shareholders of any class or series (i) listed on a national securities exchange or designated as a national market system security by the NASD or (ii) held of record by 2,000 or more shareholders and having a market value of at least $20 million, as calculated under the statute (either being *"liquid shares"*), **if** the shareholders get cash or *liquid shares* in the merger and the transaction does not involve an affiliated shareholder or a corporate director or officer (i.e., pricing is *reliable*). [§ 13.02(b)] In a § 11.05 (parent/ subsidiary) merger, subsidiary shareholders may dissent and seek appraisal, even though they have no voting rights. [§ 13.02(a)(1)(ii)]	In general, shareholders entitled to vote on the share exchange plan whose shares will be acquired in the exchange may dissent. [§ 13.02(a)(2)] Exceptions exist under the same circumstances as they exist for mergers. [§ 13.02(b)]	If shareholder approval is required, those shareholders entitled to vote may dissent. [§ 13.02(a)(3)] Exceptions exist under the same circumstances as they exist for mergers. [§ 13.02(b)]

Although approval and appraisal rights do provide transaction participants with important information relating to the structuring of a business combination transaction, other legal and regulatory issues also are of paramount concern. Tax (especially income tax) and other issues outside state corporate law (among other things, antitrust considerations, other governmental regulation related to the business(es) of the combining parties, and environmental, employment, and employee benefit law concerns) often drive the choice of transactional form in a business combination transaction. Unfortunately, these matters are beyond the scope of this text. A course in Corporate Finance, Mergers and Acquisitions, or Transactional Tax Planning, if your law school offers one, should provide more insights on these other factors. Short of that, because of the heightened importance of federal income tax issues in this area, the brief summary provided below highlights some of those issues. Note that the excerpt covers tax issues concerning share acquisitions (covered in Chapter 16) as well as statutory business combinations.

A. Mergers and Consolidations

. . . . Mergers and consolidations can be structured to be taxable or non-taxable for federal income tax purposes. Simply stated, if stock is the consideration for the acquisition of the non-surviving corporation, the merger can qualify as an A reorganization under Section 368(a)(1)(A) of the Internal Revenue Code of 1986, as amended (the "Code"). Thus, a shareholder of the target corporation receives stock in the purchasing corporation wholly tax-free. However, a shareholder of the target company who receives only boot (i.e., consideration other than purchaser's stock or other purchaser securities under certain circumstances) is normally taxed as if the shareholder had sold his stock in the target corporation in a taxable transaction. Generally stated, a shareholder who receives both stock and boot is not taxed on the stock received but is taxed on the boot. The boot is taxed either as a dividend or as a capital gain, but not in excess of the gain which would have been realized if the transaction were fully taxable.

B. Purchases of Shares

Purchases of shares of the target company can likewise be handled on a taxable or non-taxable basis. In a voluntary stock purchase, the acquiring corporation must generally negotiate with each selling shareholder individually. An exception to this is a mechanism known as the share exchange permitted by certain state business corporation statutes under which the vote of holders of the requisite percentage (but less than all) of shares can bind all of the shareholders to exchange their shares pursuant to the plan of exchange approved by such vote.

Generally speaking, if the purchasing corporation acquires the stock of the target corporation solely in exchange for the purchaser's voting stock and, after the transaction the purchasing corporation owns stock in the target corporation possessing at least 80% of the target's voting power and at least 80% of each class of the target corporation's non-voting stock, the transaction can qualify as a tax-free B reorganization.

Note that one disadvantage of an acquisition of the target corporation's stock is that the purchasing corporation does not obtain a step-up in the basis of the target corporation's assets for tax purposes. If the stock acquisition qualifies as a qualified stock purchase under Section 338 of the Code (which generally requires a taxable acquisition by a corporation of at least 80% of the target corporation's stock within a 12-month period), an election may be made to treat the stock acquisition as a taxable asset purchase for tax purposes. However, after the effective repeal of the *General Utilities* doctrine, discussed *infra*, Section 338 elections are seldom made unless the target is a member of a group of corporations filing a consolidated federal income tax return (or, since 1994, an S corporation) and the seller(s) agrees to a Section 338(h)(10) election which causes the seller to bear the tax on the deemed asset sale, since the present value of the tax savings to the buyer from a stepped-up basis in target's assets is less than the corporate-level tax on the deemed asset sale.

C. Asset Purchases

. . . . A disadvantage involved in asset purchases in recent years . . . has been the repeal, pursuant to the Tax Reform Act of 1986, of the so-called *General Utilities* doctrine. Prior to then, the Code generally exempted a C corporation from corporate-level taxation (other than recapture) on the sale of its assets to a third party in connection with a complete liquidation of the corporation and the distribution of the proceeds to its shareholders. After the effective repeal of the *General Utilities* doctrine, a C corporation generally recognizes full gain on a sale of assets even in connection with a complete liquidation. Thus, if a purchasing corporation buys the target's assets and the target corporation liquidates, the target pays a corporate-level tax on its full gain from the sale of its assets (not merely the recaptured items). The shareholders of the target are taxed as if they had sold their stock for the liquidation proceeds (less the target's corporate tax liability). Absent available net operating losses, if the sale is a gain, the *General Utilities* doctrine repeal thus makes an asset sale less advantageous for the shareholders.

Generally speaking, for a non-taxable acquisition of assets, the purchaser must acquire substantially all of the target's assets solely in exchange for the voting stock of the purchaser. Basically, a C reorganization is disqualified unless the target distributes the purchaser's stock, securities and other properties it receives, as well as its other properties, in pursuance of the plan of reorganization.

Byron F. Egan et al., *Asset Acquisitions: A Colloquy*, 10 U. MIAMI BUS. L. REV. 145, 148–50 (2002)* (footnotes omitted).

1. Statutory Mergers and Consolidations

A merger or consolidation, like the corporation itself, would not exist absent statutory law. Form the standpoint of a corporate lawyer, there is no actual transfer of stock or assets that occurs in a merger or consolidation. Instead, by following the applicable statutory provisions, one or more corporations involved in a merger or consolidation disappear, and the assets, liabilities, and operations of the disappearing corporation or corporations magically reappear in either one of the combining corporations (in the case of a merger) or in a newly constituted corporation (in the case of a consolidation). *See* MBCA § 11.07; DGCL § 259. The combining corporations that are parties to a merger or consolidation often are referred to as "constituent corporations." *See, e.g.,* DGCL §§ 251 & 252. Under the MBCA, a merger may result in the creation of a new corporation that houses the business of all the constituent corporations. *See* MBCA § 11.02(a). Accordingly, what is called a consolidation in Delaware is just another form of merger in jurisdictions that adopt the Model Business Corporation Act.

There are several easily identifiable types of mergers. Prominent among them are direct mergers and triangular mergers. Direct mergers are transactions in which one or more corporations merge with and into another corporation. When one of the corporations owns a significant percentage of the stock of the other or others (typically 90% or more), we call the merger a parent or subsidiary (or short-form) merger. *See* MBCA § 11.05; DGCL § 253. Triangular mergers involve three or more corporations. In a three-corporation triangular merger, the acquiror creates a shell subsidiary (often referred to as the merger subsidiary) — a subsidiary that holds no assets and conducts no business — that becomes a party to a merger with the company to be acquired (target). If the target merges with and into the subsidiary, we call the transaction a forward triangular (or forward subsidiary) merger. If the shell subsidiary merges with and into the target, we call the transaction a reverse triangular (or reverse subsidiary) merger.

Why so many different kinds of merger? Although mergers facilitate in many ways the acquisition of one incorporated business by another, acquirors often do not want to assume all of the target's liabilities. (The only business combination transaction that allows an acquiror to expressly exclude liabilities is an acquisition of all or substantially all of the assets of the target corporation, which, as we will later see, is significantly more cumbersome to execute than a merger.) By using a subsidiary of the acquiror as the constituent corporation in the merger, the acquiror can effectively acquire the

---

target as a wholly owned subsidiary. The veil of limited liability that protects corporate shareholders therefore protects the acquiror from liability for the target's obligations, unless there is a reason to pierce that veil. *See* Chapter 7.

Why two different directions for triangular mergers (forward and reverse)? Forward triangular mergers are more intuitive for most people. In a forward triangular merger, no change in the surviving corporation — e.g., its name or capital structure — is required, although many do change the name of the surviving merger subsidiary to the name of the target corporation in or immediately following the merger, as and if the statute may allow.

However, it is important to note that a merger effectuates a change in the legal ownership of the disappearing corporation's assets (real property, fixtures, intellectual property, licenses and permits, contracts, etc.); the surviving corporation is vested in these assets by operation of law when the merger becomes effective. *See* DGCL § 259; MBCA § 11.07(3). This may create problems where the disappearing corporation has assets that are subject to restrictions on transfer. For example, many regulatory licenses and permits and many private contracts include anti-assignment clauses (or provisions requiring notice or consent upon a transfer of the license, permit, or contract). The transfer, even by operation of law, of these licenses, permits, and contracts may trigger those restrictive provisions, creating significant transaction costs and potentially putting third parties in control of the timing or execution of the merger. In a forward triangular merger, these asset transfers are significant, since the pre-existing operating entity — the target corporation — disappears in the merger. Accordingly, a forward triangular merger has the capacity to create significant transaction costs.

This is why the reverse triangular merger has proven to be such a popular business combination transaction. In a reverse triangular merger, the target (operating) corporation is the *surviving* corporation in the merger, averting the need to transfer of business-critical licenses, permits, and contracts. (They merely stay where they are — in the target corporation — while the merger subsidiary's assets, if any, are transferred to the target by operation of law.)

Mergers and consolidations generally require board approval first and then submission of the transaction for approval by the shareholders of each constituent corporation, except (a) in the event that only specified nominal changes are made to the surviving corporation and its shareholders as a result of the transaction, in which case the surviving corporation's shareholders are not required to vote to approve, or (b) in the event of a short-form merger, in which case the subsidiary's shareholders are not required to vote to approve. DGCL §§ 251 & 253; MBCA §§ 7.25, 7.26, 11.02, 11.04, 11.05.

Mergers and consolidations are consummated by the filing of a certificate of merger or consolidation, DGCL §§ 251(c) & 252(c), or articles of merger, MBCA § 11.06, with the Secretary of State of the jurisdiction or jurisdictions of incorporation of each of the constituent corporations. This filing constitutes an amendment of the corporation's charter. For this reason, a merger or consolidation has a lot in common with the fundamental corporate changes by charter amendment described and discussed earlier in this chapter. In fact, they may be seen as two separate ways of achieving basic changes.

> The contractual rights vested in corporate stockholders by a certificate of incorporation are subject to amendment by vote of those stockholders or by merger. 8 Del. C. § 242(b)(2) (amendments to a certificate of incorporation to alter or change the preferences or special rights of a class of stock may be made with the approval of a majority of the outstanding shares of that class or such greater vote as the certificate requires); . . . 8 Del. C. § 251(e) (upon merger of two corporations, "the certificate of incorporation of the surviving corporation shall automatically be amended to the extent, if any, that changes in the

certificate of incorporation are set forth in the agreement of merger"); Rothschild Int'l Corp. v. Liggett Group, Inc., Del. Supr., 474 A.2d 133, 136–37 (1984) ("where a merger of corporations is permitted by law, a shareholder's preferential rights are subject to defeasance").

In re GM Class H Shareholders Litig., 734 A.2d 611, 615–16 (Del. Ch. 1999).

Like the construction and adoption of charter amendments, the crafting and approval of mergers and consolidations must follow all applicable statutory requirements in the corporate law in order to be valid, and the parties must ensure that all internal governance rules in the corporation's charter and bylaws, as well as related contractual rights and applicable fiduciary duties, are observed. In this statutorily defined environment, drafting and process are incredibly important. Along these lines, two key Delaware cases address shareholder claims that the terms of their preferred stock entitle them to a class vote on a merger — *Elliott Assocs., L.P. v. Avatex Corp.*, 715 A.2d 843 (Del. 1998), and *Warner Communications, Inc. v. Chris-Craft Industries, Inc.*, 583 A.2d 962 (Del. Ch. 1989), which is cited to in *Elliott Associates*. In *Elliott*, Chief Justice Veasey notes:

> The Avatex certificate of incorporation provides that Avatex preferred shares have no right to vote except on matters set forth therein or required by law. This denial of the right to vote is subject to an exception carved out for any "amendment, alteration or repeal" of the certificate "whether by merger, consolidation or otherwise" that "materially and adversely" affects the rights of the preferred stockholders. Such an event requires the consent of two-thirds of the First Series Preferred stockholders voting as a class.

> This appeal, then, reduces to a narrow legal question: whether the "amendment, alteration, or repeal" of the certificate of incorporation is caused "by merger, consolidation, or otherwise" thereby requiring a two-thirds class vote of the First Series Preferred stockholders, it being assumed for purposes of this appeal that their rights would be "materially and adversely" affected. The Court of Chancery answered this question in the negative. Although we respect that Court's craftsmanlike analysis, we are constrained to disagree with its conclusion.

> Relying primarily on *Warner Communications, Inc. v. Chris-Craft Industries, Inc.*, the Court of Chancery held that it was only the *conversion* of the stock as a result of the merger, and not the *amendment, alteration or repeal* of the certificate, that would adversely affect the preferred stockholders. It is important to keep in mind, however, that the terms of the preferred stock in *Warner* were significantly different from those present here, because in *Warner* the phrase "whether by merger, consolidation or otherwise" was not included. The issue here, therefore, is whether the presence of this additional phrase in the Avatex certificate is an outcome-determinative distinction from *Warner*.

> . . . *Warner* held that there it was only the stock conversion, not the amendment that adversely affected the preferred. But . . . the language of the First Series Preferred stock is materially different from the language in *Warner* because here we have the phrase, "whether by merger, consolidation or otherwise." This provision entirely changes the analysis and compels the result we hold today. Here, the repeal of the certificate and the stock conversion cause the adverse effect. . . .

> The path for future drafters to follow in articulating class vote provisions is clear. When a certificate (like the Warner certificate or the Series A provisions here) grants only the right to vote on an amendment, alteration or repeal, the preferred have no class vote in a merger. When a certificate (like the First Series Preferred certificate here) adds the terms "whether by merger, consolidation or otherwise" and a merger results in an amendment, alteration or repeal that causes an adverse effect on the preferred, there would be a class vote.

When a certificate grants the preferred a class vote in any merger or in any merger where the preferred stockholders receive a junior security, such provisions are broader than those involved in the First Series Preferred certificate. We agree with plaintiffs' argument that these results are uniform, predictable and consistent with existing law relating to the unique attributes of preferred stock.

The judgment of the Court of Chancery is reversed and the matter is remanded for further proceedings consistent with this Opinion.

NOTES AND QUESTIONS

1. *Effect of Preferred Stock Terms on Approval Rights.* The express terms of the First Series Preferred stock, as added to Avatex's certificate of incorporation by the filing of a certificate of designation in accordance with pre-existing blank check authority established in Avatex's certificate of incorporation, determined the voting rights of holders of the First Series Preferred stock in the merger. As the court notes, absent the establishment of these class voting rights in the terms of the First Series Preferred stock, holders of First Series Preferred stock would have no right to vote on the Avatex or Xetava merger, whether with the common stock or as a separate class.

2. *Doctrine of Independent Legal Significance.* In an unexcerpted portion of the opinion in *Elliott*, the court references the doctrine of independent legal significance to support its determination that charter amendments under Delaware General Corporation Law § 242 are distinct from, and therefore may not be treated in the same way as, certificates of merger under Delaware General Corporation Law § 251. You may recall that the court in *Farahpour v. DCX, Inc.*, 635 A.2d 894 (Del. 1994), excerpted earlier in this chapter, also references this doctrine, noting that matters undertaken through a properly adopted amendment to a corporation's certificate of incorporation need not also meet the requirements of other, distinct statutory provisions of the Delaware General Corporation Law that could be used to meet the same objectives. The doctrine, also known as the doctrine of equal dignity, essentially provides just that.

> [A]ction taken in accordance with different sections of that law are acts of independent legal significance even though the end result may be the same under different sections. The mere fact that the result of actions taken under one section may be the same as the result of action taken under another section does not require that the legality of the result must be tested by the requirements of the second section.

Orzeck v. Englehart, 195 A.2d 375, 377 (Del. 1963). This doctrine is central to Delaware corporate law in the post-vested rights era. It informs numerous corporate finance issues under Delaware law, especially those involving mergers and other basic corporate changes.

3. *Fiduciary Duty Overlay.* As with charter amendments and other means of effecting fundamental corporate changes, even when a merger or consolidation is valid under the statute and complies with the terms of the corporation's charter (including the embedded terms of its various classes and series of stock), bylaws, and contracts, these transactions often raise claims involving breaches of fiduciary duty (like those we saw in Chapter 10). The court alludes to the existence of these types of claims in its opinion in *Elliott*, but notes that these fiduciary duty claims are not before the court.

2. Statutory Share Exchanges

Given the increasing and sustained popularity of reverse triangular mergers, practitioners, and scholars thought it wise to establishing a statutory business combination alternative that has the approval and appraisal process of a merger, the limited liability effect of a triangular merger, and the preservation of the target's existence and non-transfer of assets that exists in a reverse triangular merger but eliminates the need for (and transaction costs associated with) formation of a shell subsidiary to effectuate the combination. Put another way, what these folks were looking for was a transaction that has the attributes of a share purchase but avoids the need to solicit shareholder participation on an individual basis (allowing, instead, the acquiror and target to negotiate an agreement that looks much like a merger agreement). The statutory share exchange was born by the addition of authorizing provisions in the Model Business Corporation Act.

> In a share exchange, Target and Acquirer enter into an agreement that, with shareholder approval, causes the stock of Target's shareholders to be converted by operation of law to the consideration recited in the share exchange agreement. These share exchange statutes extend the corporate law benefits of a merger to stock acquisitions by enabling Acquirer to secure the stock of recalcitrant Target shareholders by operation of law. Share exchanges are taxed as stock purchases, notwithstanding their substantive similarity to a cash merger.

Jeffrey L. Kwall, *What Is a Merger?: The Case for Taxing Cash Mergers Like Stock Sales*, 32 Iowa J. Corp. L. 1, 29 (2006) (footnotes omitted).

Like mergers, share exchange transactions do not exist at common law and, therefore, are not possible absent express statutory authorization and compliance with applicable statutory rules. Share exchange transactions are not authorized under the Delaware General Corporation Law.

As you may have noted in the charts summarizing "Approval and Appraisal Rights for Statutory Business Combinations under the MBCA and the DGCL" included earlier in this chapter, statutory share exchange transactions are approved in much the same way mergers are approved: the board acts first and recommends that the shareholders approve the plan of share exchange; then the shareholders vote to approve the plan. MBCA §§ 7.25, 7.26, 11.04. Absent another applicable requirement for obtaining a shareholder vote (*see, e.g.*, MBCA § 6.21(f), requiring a shareholder vote for transactions in which more than 20% in voting power of the corporation's shares will be issued other than for cash), only shareholders of the target corporation typically have statutory voting and appraisal rights in share exchange transactions (since the acquiring corporation and its shareholders typically undergo no or little change in connection with a share exchange transaction). MBCA § 11.04(g). Appraisal rights are granted to shareholders on much the same basis as they are in connection with mergers. MBCA §§ 13.01–13.40. Predictably, in light of the foregoing, the shareholder claims relating to share exchange transactions are the same as those made in connection with mergers, although there is little case law on shareholder approval and appraisal rights in share exchange transactions (since they continue to be used less frequently than mergers).

A share exchange transaction is consummated upon the filing of (or as otherwise set forth in) articles of share exchange with the Secretary of State of the jurisdiction of incorporation of the target corporation. MBCA § 11.06.

NOTES AND QUESTIONS

1. *Underuse of Statutory Share Exchanges.* Although the authors are unaware of any empirical work on the subject, anecdotal observation indicates that, despite its apparent efficiencies, share exchange transactions are not widely used in jurisdictions that have adopted the statutory framework supplied by the MBCA. Instead, reverse

triangular mergers continue to be used to achieve the end-result of a statutory share exchange without the need to negotiate individually with each of the target's shareholders. Why might this be the case?

2. *Related Drafting Issues.* In advising clients on transactions that afford rights (including notice and consent privileges, antidilution and antidestruction protections, etc.) based on fundamental corporate changes, it is important for the corporate lawyer to take into account the law of the corporation's jurisdiction of incorporation in the relevant transaction documents. This means, for example, that specified fundamental changes involving Delaware corporations would include consolidations but not share exchange transactions, and fundamental corporate changes for a corporation organized in a jurisdiction that has adopted the MBCA would include share exchanges but not consolidations.

3.   Dispositions of All or Substantially All of a Corporation's Assets

A corporation's sale of all or substantially all of its assets is yet another form of statutory business combination transaction that constitutes a basic corporate change.

An acquisition might be structured as an asset purchase for a variety of reasons. It may be the only structure that can be used when a noncorporate seller is involved or where the buyer is only interested in purchasing a portion of the company's assets or assuming only certain of its liabilities. If the stock of a company is widely held or it is likely that one or more of the shareholders will not consent, a sale of stock . . . may be impractical. In many cases, however, an acquisition can be structured as a merger, a purchase of stock or a purchase of assets.

As a general rule, often it will be in the buyer's best interest to purchase assets but in the seller's best interest to sell stock or merge. Because of these competing interests, it is important that counsel for both parties be involved at the outset in weighing the various legal and business considerations in an effort to arrive at the optimum, or at least an acceptable, structure. Some of the considerations are specific to the business in which a company engages, some relate to the particular corporate or other structure of the buyer and the seller, and others are more general in nature. . . .

Asset transactions are typically more complicated and more time consuming than stock purchases and statutory combinations. In contrast to a stock purchase, the buyer in an asset transaction will acquire only the assets described in the acquisition agreement. Accordingly, the assets to be purchased are often described with specificity in the agreement and the transfer documents. The usual practice, however, is for buyer's counsel to use a broad description that includes all of the seller's assets, while describing the more important categories, and then to specifically describe the assets to be excluded and retained by the seller. Often excluded are cash, accounts receivable, litigation claims or claims for tax refunds, personal assets, and certain records pertaining only to the seller's organization. This puts the burden on the seller to specifically identify the assets that are to be retained.

A purchase of assets also is cumbersome because transfer of the seller's assets to the buyer must be documented, and separate filings or recordings may be necessary to effect the transfer. This often will involve separate real property deeds, lease assignments, patent and trademark assignments, motor vehicle registrations and other evidences of transfer that cannot simply be covered by a general bill of sale or assignment. Moreover, these transfers may involve assets in a number of jurisdictions, all with different forms and other requirements for filing and recording.

Byron F. Egan et al., *Asset Acquisitions: A Colloquy*, 10 U. MIAMI BUS. L. REV. 145, 150–51 (2002)*.

In sum, in the acquisition of a business by acquiring all or substantially all the assets of a target corporation, an acquiror assumes increased transaction costs in the form of additional drafting and documentation, but it gets in return the enhanced flexibility of choosing the assets and liabilities that it actually wants to acquire. In fact, this is the only form of business combination transaction in which an acquiror can simply leave pre-transaction liabilities behind with the target (seller), at least in theory. The tort doctrine of successor liability may force an acquiror to accept responsibility for certain excluded liabilities if, for example, the transaction is merely a means to fraudulently avoid the excluded liabilities, if the transaction constitutes a *de facto* merger (as described later in the chapter), or if the acquisition is a mere continuation of the business of the selling corporation — i.e., more in the nature of a reorganization than an acquisition. Because successor liability rules vary from state to state, the exceptions to the general rule that acquirors of assets are not responsible for pre-acquisition liabilities associated with those assets also varies from state to state. *See* George W. Kuney, *A Taxonomy and Evaluation of Successor Liability*, 3 FLA. ST. U. BUS. REV. 1 (2006) (surveying and commenting on the successor liability laws of the 50 states) and the accompanying annually updated Web site, http://www.law.utk.edu/FACULTY/ AppendixKun.pdf. Moreover, a statute (as written or as judicially interpreted) may impose successor liability on an acquiror, even where the acquiror has contractually excluded that liability from the transaction. *See, e.g., New York v. Westwood-Squibb Pharm. Co.*, 62 F. Supp. 2d 1035 (W.D.N.Y. 1999) (finding that CERCLA imposes successor liability).

Asset dispositions generally are deemed standard commercial transactions that can occur absent statutory authorization. However, when an incorporated entity disposes of all or substantially all of its assets, state corporate law may step in to regulate the conduct of the transferring corporation by requiring shareholder approval of the transaction and, in some jurisdictions, appraisal rights to dissenting shareholders.

Specifically, the Delaware General Corporation Law provides that the board can authorize a sale of all or substantially all of the corporation's assets only with the approval of the holders of a majority of the corporation's outstanding stock entitled to vote. The board must approve the transaction before the matter is put to a vote of shareholders. DGCL § 271. The Model Business Corporation Act provides that the directors may determine to sell any or all of the corporation's assets in the usual and regular course of the corporation's business without shareholder approval. MBCA § 12.01. The directors may determine to sell all or substantially all of the corporation's assets outside the usual and regular course of the corporation's business only with shareholder approval at a meeting at which a quorum is present, if the corporation would be left without a significant continuing business activity. The retention by the corporation of "a business activity that represented at least 25 percent of total assets at the end of the most recently completed fiscal year, and 25 percent of either income from continuing operations before taxes or revenues from continuing operations for that fiscal year" constitutes retention by the corporation of a significant continuing business activity. As in Delaware, the board must approve the disposition before the matter is put to shareholders for approval. MBCA §§ 12.01 & 12.02. Appraisal rights are available to dissenting shareholders under the MBCA, but not under the DGCL. MBCA § 13.02.

No filings with the Secretary of State are required in order to consummate a sale of all or substantially all of a corporation's assets. However, as with other asset transfers, documentation of the asset conveyance (though a bill of sale) and the execution (and, where required or desirable, filing) of related consents, assignments, instruments —

---

including instruments of title — must be undertaken.

As with the other forms of fundamental corporate change described in this chapter, actions undertaken by a corporation to approve sales of all or substantially all of its assets must not only comply with the relevant statutory rules, but also be consistent with applicable fiduciary duties. The case excerpted below illustrates a typical shareholder challenge to an asset disposition in these contexts.

KATZ v. BREGMAN
Court of Chancery of Delaware
431 A.2d 1274 (Del. Ch. 1981)

MARVEL, CHANCELLOR:

The complaint herein seeks the entry of an order preliminarily enjoining the proposed sale of the Canadian assets of Plant Industries, Inc. to Vulcan Industrial Packaging, Ltd., the plaintiff Hyman Katz allegedly being the owner of approximately 170,000 shares of common stock of the defendant Plant Industries, Inc., on whose behalf he has brought this action, suing not only for his own benefit as a stockholder but for the alleged benefit of all other record owners of common stock of the defendant Plant Industries, Inc. . . .

The complaint alleges that during the last six months of 1980 the board of directors of Plant Industries, Inc., under the guidance of the individual defendant Robert B. Bregman, the present chief executive officer of such corporation, embarked on a course of action which resulted in the disposal of several unprofitable subsidiaries of the corporate defendant located in the United States, namely Louisiana Foliage Inc., a horticultural business, Sunaid Food Products, Inc., a Florida packaging business, and Plant Industries (Texas), Inc., a business concerned with the manufacture of woven synthetic cloth. As a result of these sales Plant Industries, Inc. by the end of 1980 had disposed of a significant part of its unprofitable assets.

According to the complaint, Mr. Bregman thereupon proceeded on a course of action designed to dispose of a subsidiary of the corporate defendant known as Plant National (Quebec) Ltd., a business which constitutes Plant Industries, Inc.'s entire business operation in Canada and has allegedly constituted Plant's only income producing facility during the past four years. The professed principal purpose of such proposed sale is to raise needed cash, and thus improve Plant's balance sheets. And while interest in purchasing the corporate defendant's Canadian plant was thereafter evinced not only by Vulcan Industrial Packaging, Ltd. but also by Universal Drum Reconditioning Co., which latter corporation originally undertook to match or approximate and recently to top Vulcan's bid, a formal contract was entered into between Plant Industries, Inc. and Vulcan on April 2, 1981 for the purchase and sale of Plant National (Quebec) despite the constantly increasing bids for the same property being made by Universal. One reason advanced by Plant's management for declining to negotiate with Universal is that a firm undertaking having been entered into with Vulcan that the board of directors of Plant may not legally or ethically negotiate with Universal. But see *Thomas v. Kempner*, C.A. 4138, March 22, 1973.

In seeking injunctive relief, as prayed for, plaintiff relies on two principles, one . . . found in 8 Del. C. § 271 to the effect that a decision of a Delaware corporation to sell ". . . all or substantially all of its property and assets. . . ." requires not only the approval of such corporation's board of directors but also a resolution adopted by a majority of the outstanding stockholders of the corporation entitled to vote thereon at a meeting duly called upon at least twenty days' notice.

Support for the other principle relied on by plaintiff for the relief sought, namely an alleged breach of fiduciary duty on the part of the board of directors of Plant Industries, Inc., is allegedly found in such board's studied refusal to consider a potentially higher bid for the assets in question which is being advanced by Universal, *Thomas v. Kempner*, supra.

Turning to the possible application of 8 Del. C. § 271 to the proposed sale of substantial corporate assets of National to Vulcan, it is stated in *Gimbel v. Signal Companies, Inc.*, Del. Ch., 316 A.2d 599 (1974) as follows:

> "If the sale is of assets quantitatively vital to the operation of the corporation and is out of the ordinary and substantially affects the existence and purpose of the corporation then it is beyond the power of the Board of Directors."

According to Plant's 1980 10K form, it appears that at the end of 1980, Plant's Canadian operations represented 51% of Plant's remaining assets. Defendants also concede that National represents 44.9% of Plant's sales' revenues and 52.4% of its pre-tax net operating income. Furthermore, such report by Plant discloses, in rough figures, that while National made a profit in 1978 of $2,900,000, the profit from the United States businesses in that year was only $770,000. In 1979, the Canadian business profit was $3,500,000 while the loss of the United States businesses was $344,000. Furthermore, in 1980, while the Canadian business profit was $5,300,000, the corporate loss in the United States was $4,500,000. And while these figures may be somewhat distorted by the allocation of overhead expenses and taxes, they are significant. In any event, defendants concede that " . . .National accounted for 34.9% of Plant's pre-tax income in 1976, 36.9% in 1977, 42% in 1978, 51% in 1979, and 52.4% in 1980."

While in the case of *Philadelphia National Bank v. B.S.F. Co.*, Del. Ch., 41 Del. Ch. 509, 199 A.2d 557 (1969) [*sic*], *rev'd on other grounds*, Del. Supr., 42 Del. Ch. 106, 204 A.2d 746 (1964), the question of whether or not there had been a proposed sale of substantially all corporate assets was tested by provisions of an indenture agreement covering subordinated debentures, the result was the same as if the provisions of 8 Del. C. § 271 had been applicable, the trial Court stating:

> "While no pertinent Pennsylvania case is cited, the critical factor in determining the character of a sale of assets is generally considered not the amount of property sold but whether the sale is in fact an unusual transaction or one made in the regular course of business of the seller. . . ."

Furthermore, in the case of *Wingate v. Bercut* (CA9) 146 F.2d 725 (1945), in which the Court declined to apply the provisions of 8 Del. C. § 271, it was noted that the transfer of shares of stock there involved, being a dealing in securities, constituted an ordinary business transaction.

In the case at bar, I am first of all satisfied that historically the principal business of Plant Industries, Inc. has not been to buy and sell industrial facilities but rather to manufacture steel drums for use in bulk shipping as well as for the storage of petroleum products, chemicals, food, paint, adhesives, and cleaning agents, a business which has been profitably performed by National of Quebec. Furthermore, the proposal, after the sale of National, to embark on the manufacture of plastic drums represents a radical departure from Plant's historically successful line of business, namely steel drums. I therefore conclude that the proposed sale of Plant's Canadian operations, which constitute over 51% of Plant's total assets and in which are generated approximately 45% of Plant's 1980 net sales, would, if consummated, constitute a sale of substantially all of Plant's assets. By way of contrast, the proposed sale of Signal Oil in *Gimbel v. Signal Companies, Inc.*, supra, represented only about 26% of the total assets of Signal Companies, Inc. And while Signal Oil represented 41% of Signal Companies, Inc. total net worth, it generated only about 15% of Signal Companies, Inc. revenue and earnings.

I conclude that because the proposed sale of Plant National (Quebec) Ltd. would, if consummated, constitute a sale of substantially all of the assets of Plant Industries, Inc., as presently constituted, that an injunction should issue preventing the consummation of such sale at least until it has been approved by a majority of the outstanding stockholders of Plant Industries, Inc., entitled to vote at a meeting duly called on at least twenty days' notice. Compare *Robinson v. Pittsburg Oil Refining Company*, Del. Ch., 126 A. 46 (1924).

In light of this conclusion it will be unnecessary to consider whether or not the sale here under attack, as proposed to be made, is for such an inadequate consideration, viewed in light of the competing bid of Universal, as to constitute a breach of trust on the part of the directors of Plant Industries, Inc., *Robinson v. Pittsburg Oil Refining Company*, supra.

Being persuaded for the reasons stated that plaintiff has demonstrated a reasonable probability of ultimate success on final hearing in the absence of stockholder approval of the proposed sale of the corporate assets here in issue to Vulcan, a preliminary injunction against the consummation of such transaction, at least until stockholder approval is obtained, will be granted. . . .

NOTES AND QUESTIONS

1. *A Matter of Perspective.* Note that the sale by a parent corporation (like the corporate defendant in *Katz*, Plant Industries, Inc.) of the stock of a subsidiary corporation (like Plant National (Quebec) Ltd., the Canadian subsidiary of Plant Industries, Inc. in the *Katz* case) constitutes a sale of the parent corporation's assets. (In other words, from the perspective of corporate statutes, a corporation holds another corporation's stock as an asset.) Note, however, that as to the subsidiary, the sale of its stock is a disposition of shares (in *Katz*, by the sole shareholder parent corporation), a transaction we will cover in Chapter 16.

2. *"Substantially All" of a Corporation's Assets.* It should be clear when all of a corporation's assets are being sold; but it often is not as clear when substantially all of a corporation's assets are being sold. (How helpful, for example, is the court's recitation of the standard from the *Gimbel* case: a "sale . . . of assets quantitatively vital to the operation of the corporation" that "is out of the ordinary and substantially affects the existence and purpose of the corporation?") The inherent vagueness of the standard causes major problems for transaction planners, including legal counsel, since the need for a shareholder vote hinges on a determination as to whether all or substantially all of the corporation's assets are being sold.

In applying *Gimbel*, the *Katz* court looks at a number of quantitative measures of the importance of the Canadian subsidiary to the parent's operations over a three-year period — attributable asset value, sales revenues, and pre-tax net operating income, as well as the contribution of the Canadian operations to the overall profit of the parent. The court compares these figures to those from the *Gimbel* case in reaching the conclusion that the sale by the corporation of the subsidiary's stock is a sale of substantially all the parent's assets. Finally, the *Katz* court assesses whether the sale of the subsidiary is extraordinary for the parent corporation and what its overall effects are. In this regard, the court concludes that "to embark on the manufacture of plastic drums represents a radical departure from Plant's historically successful line of business, namely steel drums." Do you agree? What other facts support the court's opinion? What facts seem to contravene the court's holding?

PROBLEM

Acquiror, Inc. desires to acquire the business conducted by Target Corp. at the lowest possible transaction costs. Both corporations are organized in jurisdictions that have adopted the MBCA.

Target conducts its business out of new facilities, updated with the most current equipment and technology. Also, Target holds a number of valuable patents. Acquiror wants to ensure that it acquires both Target's facilities and Target's patents when it acquires the business of Target. In addition, in making the acquisition, Acquiror desires to conserve cash, avoid succeeding to Target's existing product liability exposure, and avoid getting the approval of its shareholders for the transaction.

Assess the likelihood that the following transactions will satisfy Acquiror's objectives. Suggest the addition of any appropriate term in each case that may further promote the achievement of Acquiror's objectives.

1.   direct statutory merger

2.   triangular merger

3.   statutory share exchange transaction

4.   asset acquisition

4.   Appraisal Rights

The law review article excerpt included below explains the nature, history, and historic purposes of the statutory appraisal rights remedy afforded to shareholders who dissent from certain fundamental corporate changes.

Mary Siegel, *Back to the Future: Appraisal Rights in the Twenty-First Century*
32 Harv. J. on Legis. 79[*] (1995)
(footnotes omitted)

. . . The appraisal remedy in corporate law evolved from a confluence of contract principles and business exigencies. In the nineteenth century, courts uniformly recognized that the corporate charter gave each shareholder a vested contract right with both the corporation and the state. Each shareholder, as a contracting party, was required to consent to amend the corporate charter. Thus, each shareholder had the power to block any proposed change. As recently as the late nineteenth century, courts protected each shareholder's contract right to veto asset sales, charter amendments and consolidations.

When Justice Story suggested, in the landmark case of *Trustees of Dartmouth College v. Woodward*, that a state could reserve the power to amend its contract with the corporation, the requirement of unanimity for charter amendments began to erode. Beginning with charter amendments in public utilities and railroads, the standard changed from unanimity to majority consent. For private corporations, the notion of majority control seemed equally attractive. Building on Justice Story's theory, private corporations added provisions in their charters authorizing amendments by less than unanimous consent. Such attempts to skirt the unanimity requirement but still remain within the parameters of contract law coincided with the emergence of courts and legislatures more sympathetic to the corporations' perspective. Judges and legislators had begun to consider issues beyond the individual shareholder's contract right, such as the wisdom of allowing one shareholder to block change thought desirable by the majority.

As was the case with charter amendments, the evolution from unanimity to majority control for other major corporate transactions proceeded within the confines of contract law. Mergers, consolidations and sales of all corporate assets originally required unanimous consent. If, however, the corporation was insolvent with no prospect for profit, courts permitted the majority to sell all corporate assets for cash, to wind up the corporation, and to distribute the remaining cash to the shareholders. Such action is consistent with contract law, which permits non-performance of a contract where the purpose of the agreement has been frustrated. This application of contract law, however, quickly gave way to business needs. By the late nineteenth century, courts permitted such asset sales by the majority for marketable stock — and later less marketable stock — when no cash buyers were available. Thus, when the seller dissolved and distributed to its shareholders the buyer's stock, the seller's shareholders

---

became shareholders of the buyer. In short, when the corporation was insolvent, majority rule replaced vested rights and stock replaced cash as acceptable consideration. In effect, these two changes forced minority shareholders to become shareholders of a new corporation.

Courts next relaxed the requirement of insolvency to allow majority rule in situations in which the corporation was not yet insolvent. Soon after, a corporation suffering merely poor prospects could effectuate these asset sales. Eventually, courts permitted what has become today's norm: a corporate sale of all assets for either cash or stock whenever the majority determines that such a sale is in the best interests of the corporation.

With the majority able to effectuate both charter amendments and asset sales for stock or cash, the requirements that mergers and consolidations could be effectuated only for stock consideration and only by unanimous consent became ripe for change. It had not gone unnoticed that the permitted asset sales for cash or stock followed by the dissolution of the seller were de facto mergers. Considering the substance of those transactions, rather than just their form, courts put asset sales and mergers on parallel tracks, eventually permitting both to be carried out by a majority vote for stock or cash.

Once asset sales and mergers could be effectuated for stock or cash consideration, there remained only one gap in the creation of appraisal rights. This missing link was to provide dissatisfied minority shareholders a cash option in stock transactions. Minority shareholders initially secured this cash option through litigation. While shareholders often sued for injunctive relief, courts usually instead awarded shareholders the fair value of their stock, reasoning that their shares had been effectively converted. Such litigation enabled minority shareholders to escape the choice of either forced membership in a new corporation or the acceptance of a pro rata share in cash of the transaction's proceeds; instead, shareholders received the appraised fair value of their shares.

Litigation, however, proved unsatisfactory both for the corporation and for minority shareholders. The corporation feared the possibility of an injunction, and the shareholders disliked the expensive and risky process of judicially resolving their claims. Both the corporation and the shareholders bettered their respective positions when they could settle on a cash payment and avoid judicial intervention, particularly given the likelihood that such litigation would require a cash settlement. Eventually, legislatures began to follow the courts' lead by enacting appraisal statutes. While these statutes sought to ensure that dissenting shareholders received "value" for their shares, courts interpreting these statutes consistently awarded the stock's fair value in cash, rather than simply a cash pro rata share of the transaction's proceeds. By 1927, at least twenty states had adopted appraisal statutes. Today, all jurisdictions include appraisal provisions in their corporate statutes.

The evolution of appraisal rights is important for several reasons. By the time appraisal rights emerged, shareholders no longer enjoyed a vested contract right which could be breached, and majority rule was not perceived as wrongful. As a result, the remedy was not designed as a damage action for breach of contract. Instead of damages, shareholders were awarded the fair value of their stock.

Second, the history helps explain why the corporate statutes differ so widely as to which transactions trigger the remedy. The common feature of charter amendments, asset sales, and mergers is that they all once required unanimous shareholder approval. Once that common link was severed, no unifying aspect remained to distinguish transactions that should offer appraisal rights from those that should not. Today, all corporate statutes recognize appraisal rights for at least some mergers. Almost all statutes also afford appraisal rights for short-form mergers and sales of substantially all assets. Many statutes also provide an appraisal remedy for certain charter amendments and share exchanges, and a few states provide the remedy for a variety of additional transactions.

Most importantly, however, the history of the appraisal remedy is crucial to explaining why the appraisal statutes vary so greatly. While the legislatures could have overruled the rights that the courts had created, legislatures instead chose to codify these rights. Legislatures evidently found the appraisal remedy attractive; unfortunately, they explained neither the reasons for this attraction nor their intended purpose for this new remedy. The result has been a remedy built on quicksand, with shifting premises and purposes.

For example, some commentators look at the remedy's history and conclude that appraisal rights were designed to compensate the minority for the loss of their veto power: while shareholders could no longer veto a transaction, they could "veto" their continuing involvement in a "fundamentally different" corporation by requiring the corporation to cash them out. Others interpret the remedy's history as creating a cash exit, citing either the original requirement that mergers be effectuated only for stock consideration, the common law prohibition against forcing shareholders to become shareholders of another corporation, or the cash exit compromise struck by the majority and minority shareholders. One eminent scholar has a third view of the remedy: Dean Bayless Manning argues that the effect of the appraisal remedy, if not its purpose, was to protect the majority from the tyranny of the minority. This theory posits that the remedy decreased both the minority's incentive to seek injunctions and the courts' willingness to issue them.

With Delphic ambiguity and without explaining whether the appraisal remedy was needed to compensate for the loss of veto power, to effectuate a cash exit, or to protect the majority, the legislatures of all fifty states have incorporated the remedy into their corporate statutes. . . .

There are few reported appraisal cases, despite the theoretical importance of appraisal as a remedy for dissenting shareholders in specified transactions involving basic corporate changes. In some cases, this is because shareholders do not realize that they want to cash out through the appraisal rights process until it is too late for them to exercise their rights. Appraisal statutes are only triggered by certain specified transactions (including mergers and statutory share exchanges, and sometimes, sales of all or substantially all of the corporation's assets, reverse stock splits, or other charter amendments making basic corporate changes), and they typically require that the dissenting shareholder notify the corporation that the shareholder intends to exercise appraisal rights *before* a vote is taken on the transaction. In addition, the shareholder must not vote for (and under some statutes, must vote against) the subject transaction. Other statutory procedures also must be followed. The process is both detailed and complex. Typically, courts require strict compliance with appraisal rights statutes before awarding dissenting shareholders the fair value of their shares. *See, e.g., Pink v. Cambridge Acquisition, Inc.*, 126 Md. App. 61 (1999).

Moreover, even assuming strict adherence to the applicable statutory procedures, the actual process of seeking an appraisal and receiving the cash value of a dissenting shareholder's shares, whether by agreement or (more likely) in a court proceeding, is expensive and time-consuming. Typically, the dissenting shareholder and the subject corporation present markedly different valuations of the corporation, in each case substantiated by models constructed and calculations performed by investment banks or other valuation experts (creating a veritable "battle of the experts"). These models and calculations involve various valuation techniques and assumptions based on the nature and history of the business of the subject corporation. *See, e.g., Montgomery Cellular Holding Co. v. Dobler*, 880 A.2d 206 (Del. 2005). Judges, many of them not highly expert in valuation methodology, typically end up determining the appropriate valuation process and amount.

One of the key cases that interprets the Delaware appraisal rights statute is *Cede & Co. v. Technicolor, Inc.*, 684 A.2d 289 (Del. 1996). This case appeals a Chancery Court valuation in an appraisal action brought by minority shareholders of Technicolor Incorporated ("Technicolor"), dissenters to a reverse subsidiary merger as a result of which MacAndrews & Forbes Group Incorporated ("MAF") obtained a 100% equity interest in Technicolor. As a first step in the transaction, MAF had acquired a controlling interest in Technicolor in a tender offer.

At issue in the case is whether, in its appraisal valuation of Technicolor's stock, the Chancery Court properly excluded the effects of business plans and strategies adopted between the date of the merger agreement and the date of the merger by the controlling shareholder of MAF, Ronald O. Perelman (the "Perelman Plan"), instead valuing Technicolor in accordance with then existing business plans and strategies of Technicolor's Chairman, Morton Kamerman (the "Kamerman Plan"). A key difference between the Perelman Plan and the Kamerman Plan was that the Perelman Plan called for the disposition of a number of businesses, including Technicolor's One-Hour Photo business ("OHP"). The plaintiff minority shareholders argued in the Court of Chancery that elements of value arising from the Perelman Plan (which was "fixed" at the time the merger agreement was signed, but not to be fully implemented until the merger became effective) should be included in a valuation of the Technicolor shares at the time the merger. Technicolor successfully argued in the Chancery Court that the effect of the Perelman Plan on share value should be excluded in the court's valuation, since it was dependent upon, and arose from the expectation of, the merger. *See* DGCL § 262(h).

The Delaware Supreme Court, in an opinion written by Justice Randy Holland, reversed the Court of Chancery on this issue and remanded the case. Justice Holland's opinion makes a number of key points about appraisals and valuation under Delaware law, starting with a summary of relevant principles from the Delaware Supreme Court's "seminal decision" in *Weinberger v. UOP, Inc.*, 457 A.2d 701 (Del. 1983), which is excerpted in Chapter 16.

> In *Weinberger*, this Court broadened the process for determining the "fair value" of the company's outstanding shares by including all generally accepted techniques of valuation used in the financial community. *Weinberger v. UOP, Inc.*, 457 A.2d at 712–13; see *Technicolor I*, 542 A.2d at 1186–87. The result of that expansion was the holding in *Weinberger that* "the standard 'Delaware block' or weighted average method of valuation, formerly employed in appraisal and other stock valuation cases, shall no longer exclusively control such proceedings." *Weinberger v. UOP, Inc.*, 457 A.2d at 712–13.
>
> The Delaware appraisal statute provides that the Court of Chancery:
>
>> shall appraise the shares, determining their fair value exclusive of any element of value arising from the accomplishment or expectation of the merger or consolidation, together with a fair rate of interest, if any, to be paid upon the amount determined to be the fair value. In determining such fair value, the Court shall take into account all relevant factors.
>
> 8 *Del. C.* § 262(h). In *Weinberger*, this Court construed the appraisal statute. That construction required this Court to reconcile the dual mandates of Section 262(h) which direct the Court of Chancery to: determine "fair" value based upon "all relevant factors;" but, to exclude "any element of value arising from the accomplishment or expectation of the merger." In making that reconciliation, the *ratio decidendi* of this Court was, as follows:
>
>> *Only the speculative elements of value that may arise from the "accomplishment or expectation" of the merger are excluded. We take this to be a very narrow exception to the appraisal process*, designed to eliminate use of *pro forma* data and projections of a speculative variety relating to the completion of a merger. But elements of future value, including the *nature of the enterprise*, which are known or susceptible of proof as of the date of the

merger and not the product of speculation, may be considered. When the trial court deems it appropriate, fair value also includes any damages, resulting from the taking, which the stockholders sustain as a class. If that was not the case, then the obligation to consider "all relevant factors" in the valuation process would be eroded. We are supported in this view not only by [*Tri-Continental Corp. v. Battye*, Del. Supr., 31 Del. Ch. 523, 74 A.2d 71, 72 (1950)], but also by the evolutionary amendments to section 262.

Weinberger v. UOP, Inc., 457 A.2d at 713 (emphasis added).

After examining the evolution of the statutory text in Section 262(h), this Court concluded "there is a legislative intent to fully compensate shareholders for whatever their loss may be, *subject only to the narrow limitation that one can not take speculative effects of the merger into account.*" *Id.* at 714 (emphasis added). Therefore, in *Weinberger*, this Court held that the more liberal methodology we had just authorized in appraisal and other stock valuation cases "*must* include proof of value by any techniques or methods which are generally considered acceptable in the financial community and otherwise admissible in court, *subject only to our [narrow] interpretation of [the exclusionary language in] 8 Del. C. § 262(h),*" *i.e.*, requiring that only speculative elements of value, which may arise from the accomplishment or expectation of the merger, be disregarded. #2026;

The Court of Chancery excluded any value that was admittedly part of Technicolor as a going concern on the date of the merger, if that value was created by substituting new management or redeploying assets during the transient period between the first and second steps of this two-step merger, *i.e.*, Perelman's Plan. The Court of Chancery reasoned that valuing Technicolor as a going concern, under the Perelman Plan, on the date of the merger, would be tantamount to awarding Cinerama a proportionate share of a control premium, which the Court of Chancery deemed to be both economically undesirable and contrary to this Court's holding in *Bell v. Kirby Lumber Corp.*, Del. Supr., 413 A.2d 137, 140–42 (1980). Thus, the Court of Chancery concluded "that value [added by a majority acquiror] is not . . . a part of the 'going concern' in which a dissenting shareholder has a legal (or equitable) right to participate."

In *Kirby* and its progeny, including *Technicolor I*, this Court has explained that the dissenter in an appraisal action is entitled to receive a proportionate share of fair value in the *going concern* on the date of the merger, rather than value that is determined on a liquidated basis. Thus, the company must first be valued as an operating entity. . . .

In a two-step merger, to the extent that value has been added following a change in majority control before cash-out, it is still value attributable to the going concern, *i.e.*, the extant "nature of the enterprise," on the date of the merger. The dissenting shareholder's proportionate interest is determined only after the company has been valued as an operating entity on the date of the merger. Consequently, value added to the going concern by the "majority acquiror," during the transient period of a two-step merger, accrues to the benefit of all shareholders and must be included in the appraisal process on the date of the merger.

In this case, the question in the appraisal action was the fair value of Technicolor stock on the date of the merger, January 24, 1983, as Technicolor was operating pursuant to the Perelman Plan. The Court of Chancery erred, as a matter of law, by determining the fair value of Technicolor on the date of the merger "but for" the Perelman Plan; or, in other words, by valuing Technicolor as it was operating on October 29, 1982, pursuant to the Kamerman Plan. By failing to accord Cinerama the *full proportionate value of its shares in the going concern on the date of the merger*, the Court of Chancery imposed a penalty upon Cinerama for lack of control.

The "accomplishment or expectation" of the merger exception in Section 262 is very narrow, "designed to eliminate use of *pro forma* data and projections of a speculative variety relating to the completion of a merger." That narrow exclusion does not encompass known elements of value, including those which exist on the date of the merger because of a majority acquiror's interim action in a two-step cash-out transaction. "Only the *speculative* elements of value that may arise from the 'accomplishment or expectation' of the merger" should have been excluded from the Court of Chancery's calculation of fair value on the date of the merger.

The Court of Chancery's determination not to value Technicolor as a going concern on the date of the merger under the Perelman Plan, resulted in an understatement of Technicolor's fair value in the appraisal action. That result was inevitable when the Court of Chancery valued Technicolor pursuant to a discounted cash flow model with the negative factual input and assumptions from the Kamerman Plan rather than the Perelman Plan. Consequently, the Court of Chancery permitted MAF to "reap a windfall from the appraisal process by cashing out a dissenting shareholder [Cinerama]," for less than the fair value of its interest in Technicolor as a going concern on the date of the merger.

Cinerama has asked this Court to make an appraisal of the fair value of its Technicolor shares on the date of the merger, rather than remand this protracted litigation to the Court of Chancery. This Court will not make an independent determination of value on appeal. This appraisal action will be remanded to the Court of Chancery for a recalculation of Technicolor's fair value on the date of the merger.

Upon remand, it is within the Court of Chancery's discretion to select one of the parties' valuation models as its general framework, or fashion its own, to determine fair value in the appraisal proceeding. The Court of Chancery has properly recognized that its choice of a framework does not require it to adopt any one expert's model, methodology, or mathematical calculations *in toto*. . . .

NOTES AND QUESTIONS

1. *A Need to Simplify Process.* Professor Randall Thomas writes:

> The appraisal remedy is procedurally complex. There are several strict deadlines that a shareholder must satisfy in order to perfect her appraisal right. To begin, the shareholder must deliver a written appraisal demand to the corporation before the vote on the transaction informing the company of her desire to seek appraisal. Failure to do so eliminates the shareholder's ability to seek appraisal. The purpose of this requirement is to ensure that the corporation receives notice of the number of shareholders that will seek appraisal.

> These procedural requirements seem quite burdensome on smaller shareholders. While it is undoubtedly important, for example, for corporations to obtain information about how many of their shareholders intend to dissent from a proposed transaction, might not the corporation, as part of its normal shareholder communications, assume the burden of finding out which shareholders intend to dissent? This could be particularly appropriate where the company will be contacting its shareholders to determine how they are going to vote on the proposed transaction. All of these procedural requirements for perfection of appraisal rights should be reexamined and either eliminated or simplified wherever possible.

Randall S. Thomas, *Revising the Delaware Appraisal Statute*, 3 DEL. L. REV. 1, 30

(2000) (footnotes omitted). Do you agree? Whose burden should it be to identify dissenting shareholders that desire an appraisal remedy? Why?

2. Cede *Case on Remand.* On remand, in an unreported decision, Chancellor Chandler determined that he would retain a court-appointed expert to value Technicolor in accordance with the Delaware Supreme Court's opinion reproduced above. He explains.

> In closing, I note that the Supreme Court granted me the flexibility to fashion my own valuation methodology to appraise Technicolor. It is difficult for a judge with a legal, not finance, background to undertake a complete appraisal. Therefore, I am delegating the creation of an appraisal report to my expert, in line with the Supreme Court's instructions to fashion my own methodology. After the parties have argued their exceptions and other issues before me, I shall issue my own legal and factual findings in this matter.

> I am heeding the spirit of the Appraisal Remand by empowering the expert to construct a new model for valuing Technicolor that factors out Chancellor Allen's tainted findings and that sifts through Cinerama's wideranging reargument of its legal and factual positions. At the same time, I expect the expert's final report to provide a coherent, comprehensible body of issues upon which to focus the parties' arguments and my rulings. The parties will have the opportunity to cross-examine my expert, providing me with their critique of his final report. This will enable me to examine the data and methodology employed by the expert and to assemble a final ruling that is factually accurate, financially sound and in accord with the law of the Appraisal Remand.

> An order appointing the special court-appointed expert witness shall issue after I confer with counsel.

Cede & Co. v. Technicolor, Inc., 24 Del. J. Corp. L. 1039, 1059 (1999). Does this seem like a logical way to handle the appraisal, given the detailed nature of the Supreme Court's opinion?

The Delaware Supreme Court later reversed Chancellor Chandler's decision to appoint a neutral expert (because, in its view, the Chancellor lacked authority to take this action) and remanded the case for a new appraisal. *Cede & Co. v. Technicolor, Inc.,* 758 A.2d 485 (Del. 2000). Eventually, in May 2005, the Supreme Court released its final opinion, valuing Technicolor's shares at $28.41 per share and awarding the plaintiffs prejudgment interest at the rate of 10.32% compounded annually. *Cede & Co. v. Technicolor, Inc.,* 884 A.2d 26 (Del. 2005). Thus, the actual value of the shares was determined more than 22 years after consummation of the cash-out merger at issue in the case (which became effective in January 1983).

3. *The Corporation Itself Is Valued.* Note that the per share appraisal value assigned by the court is arrived at by valuing the entity as a whole and then attributing a value to each share pro rata. This means, among other things, that individualized elements of value (e.g., tax effects to or created by an individual shareholder, transfer restrictions applicable to an individual shareholder, minority holder status, etc.) are not relevant to a shareholder's appraisal valuation. In many cases, this approach is bolstered by provisions in state corporate statutes that require equal treatment of shares of the same class. *See, e.g., Cawley v. SCM Corp.,* 72 N.Y.2d 465, 473–74 (1988).

4. *"All Relevant Factors."* The *Cede* court cites to the language in DGCL § 262(h) that requires courts, in determining the fair value of shares, to "take into account all relevant factors." The *Cede* court notes that, in *Weinberger,* the court uses that language to find that the pre-existing dominant judicial valuation method previously in use in Delaware, the "Delaware Block method," is a nonexclusive valuation model, and that courts must look beyond it to identify other applicable valuation techniques and evidence.

Despite its relative disfavor in Delaware (and other jurisdictions that have adopted the Delaware Supreme Court's approach in *Weinberger*), the Delaware Block method (now sometimes called the "block method") may continue to be a significant valuation model in a number of other states. *See, e.g., Elk Yarn Mills v. 514 Shares of Common Stock of Elk Yarn Mills, Inc.*, 742 S.W.2d 638 (Tenn. Ct. App. 1987). The Massachusetts Supreme Judicial Court simply described this valuation technique almost 30 years ago in a landmark case.

> The Delaware courts have adopted a general approach to the appraisal of stock which a Massachusetts judge might appropriately follow, as did the judge in this case. The Delaware procedure, known as the "Delaware block approach," calls for a determination of the market value, the earnings value, and the net asset value of the stock, followed by the assignment of a percentage weight to each of the elements of value.

Piemonte v. New Boston Garden Corp., 377 Mass. 719, 723–24 (1979). What are the virtues and perils of the modern "all relevant factors" approach over the block method?

5. *Speculative v. Nonspeculative Elements of Value.* In *Cede*, the court attempts to distinguish speculative elements of value arising from a merger from those elements of value that are, like the Perelman Plan in the *Cede* case, nonspeculative. In defining speculative elements of value that may not be included in appraisal valuations under DGCL § 262(h), the *Cede* court references *"pro forma* data and projections." In fact, merger proxy materials typically include *pro forma* financial data — data that attempt to reflect how the survivor or acquiror in a business combination would look, based on certain assumptions and projections, if the merger or acquisition had occurred as of a specified historical date or for a specified historical period for which financial statements of the corporation are available. The creation of *pro forma* financial data is governed by specialized accounting rules, but *pro forma* data is *not* constructed using generally accepted accounting principles (GAAP).

How is *pro forma* financial data different from projected financial data concerning Technicolor that reflects implementation of the Perelman Plan? Is it easy for a court to make this distinction?

6. *Waivability of Appraisal Rights.* Most courts agree that appraisal rights are statutory entitlements that inure to all qualifying holders of capital stock. They cannot be bargained away by contract. *See, e.g., In re Appraisal of Ford Holdings*, 698 A.2d 973, 976 (Del. Ch. 1997) (referring to DGCL § 262 as one of the few "mandatory provisions of Delaware law"). However, shareholders may contractually bargain for appraisal rights in addition to those expressly set forth in statute. *See, e.g.,* DGCL § 262(c); VA. CODE ANN. § 13.1-730(A)(5). Moreover, it may be possible for holders of preferred stock (the terms of which generally are determined by agreement between the holders and the corporation within the parameters set by the statute and, as applicable, the corporate charter) to tailor, but not waive, their statutory appraisal rights, as long as they use clear, unequivocal language to do so. *See In re Appraisal of Ford Holdings*, 698 A.2d 973, 974 (Del. Ch. 1997) ("properly expressed terms of a Certificate of Designation of preferred stock may establish the consideration to which holders of the stock will be entitled in the event of a merger and, when the documents creating the security do so, that the amount so fixed or determined constitutes the 'fair value' of the stock for the purposes of dissenters' rights under Section 262 of the Delaware General Corporation Law"). There is no statutory guarantee of appraisal rights for LLC members in Delaware; the appraisal rights for members of an LLC in Delaware are wholly contractual. *See* DEL. CODE. ANN. tit. 6, § 18-210.

7. *Comparative Appraisal Rights.* The United States is not alone in providing appraisal or buyout rights to shareholders who dissent from fundamental corporate change transactions or are otherwise deemed to need a cash exit strategy. *See, e.g.,* Sofie Cools, *The Real Difference in Corporate Law Between the United States and Continental Europe: Distribution of Powers*, 30 DEL. J. CORP. L. 697, 727 (2005) ("[I]n Belgium, the right to step out with appraisal exists upon proof of well-founded reasons, but not for listed companies." (footnote omitted)); James A. Fanto, *The Role of*

Corporate Law in French Corporate Governance, 31 CORNELL INT'L L.J. 31, 68 (1998) ("In certain cases, . . . CMF regulations create a rough equivalent of appraisal for shareholders in French publicly-owned companies. If a person or group acquires more than one-third of the shares of the surviving company in a nonmerger context . . . , such person or group is required to make a buyout offer for all of the outstanding shares."); Julian Javier Garza, *Rethinking Corporate Governance: The Role of Minority Shareholders — A Comparative Study*, 31 ST. MARY'S L.J. 613, 689 (2000) ("Mexican law provides for a minority shareholder's right that is similar in nature to the dissenter or appraisal right contemplated by United States law. However, the treatment of this right under Mexican law is insufficient and lacks the development, maturity, and thoroughness of United States provisions." (footnote omitted)); Jeffrey N. Gordon, *Pathways to Corporate Convergence? Two Steps on the Road to Shareholder Capitalism in Germany*, 5 COLUM. J. EUR. L. 219, 229 (1999) (referencing "the German equivalent of an appraisal remedy (Spruchverfahren) in which any 'improvement' over the negotiated exchange ratio would have been paid out in cash to all shareholders, not just the dissenters."); Katharina Pistor et al., *The Evolution of Corporate Law: A Cross-Country Comparison*, 23 U. PA. J. INT'L ECON. L. 791, 831 (2002) (noting that under English law, "any merger transaction triggers a mandatory appraisal and minority shareholders are bound by the outsider appraisers' assessment."); *id.* at 858 (referencing Japanese appraisal rights). A number of countries afford these rights in the form of mandatory tender offers (offers to purchase shares described in Chapter 16). Some of the rights in countries outside the United States are included in statutory law; others are applicable to publicly traded companies only through stock exchange regulations. How does the nature of the rule and the rulemaking body impact the availability and efficiency of the process to corporations and shareholders?

8. *Valuation.* An eminent German law professor observes that:

> valuation is not just accounting and mathematics. Valuation is "mathematics in context" and as always, context creates meaning. Yet as lawyers like to say, "it all depends." Attempts to transform appraisals into questions of rationality are doomed. This is particularly true in trans-border appraisals. Differing legal cultures and corporation law color every detail of the valuation process.

Bernhard Grossfeld, *Global Valuation: Geography and Semiotics*, 55 SMU L. REV. 197, 209 (2002) (footnotes omitted). Based on what you have read about valuation under evolving and differing state laws in the United States, how do you think differences in corporate laws and legal systems shape the valuation process and the valuation resulting from that process?

5. *De Facto* Mergers

The decline of the vested rights doctrine and resulting statutory variations in both required approvals and the availability of appraisal rights for different kinds of business combination transactions have together afforded opportunistic corporations the ability to choose forms of business combination that avoid shareholder approval or appraisal or both (while also achieving desired tax and other objectives). For example, based on the law we already have covered in this chapter, a Delaware corporate acquiror can purchase substantially all of the assets of a Delaware target corporation without seeking the approval of its own shareholders and without triggering appraisal rights for the target's shareholders. Accordingly, in certain cases, shareholders who desire a role in the approval process are shut out of that process and often have no alternative exit strategy under state corporate law, the corporation's organizational documents (charter and bylaws), or individual contractual arrangements. Dissatisfied and disgruntled shareholders therefore seek to assert a role through litigation.

We already have seen, in Chapter 11 and elsewhere in this text (including in this chapter), that shareholder derivative litigation claiming a breach of fiduciary duty by directors or officers has its place in vetting shareholder concerns and holding management accountable. However, in transactions involving a fundamental corporate change (especially where no appraisal rights may be asserted and directors and officers have acted in good faith, on a fully informed basis, and in a manner consistent with the best interests of the corporation), another type of claim also is common. Shareholders also may claim that a specific transactional path taken by the corporation (e.g., the sale of substantially all of the assets of a corporation to another corporation, followed by the selling corporation's liquidation) is really another transaction (e.g., a direct merger) because the result is the same. (In other words, the combined asset sale/liquidation transaction is, in fact, a merger, or a *de facto* merger.) This type of claim — and there are examples other than the rather common one covered in the preceding sentences — enables shareholders to argue that they should have approval, appraisal, or other rights in circumstances where the corporation's transactional choice otherwise denies them those rights. *See, e.g., Irving Bank Corp. v. Bank of N.Y. Co., Inc.,* 140 Misc. 2d 363, 530 N.Y.S.2d 757 (N.Y. Sup. Ct. 1988); *Pratt v. Ballman-Cummings Furniture Co.,* 549 S.W.2d 270, 274 (Ark. 1977); *Rath v. Rath Packing Co.,* 136 N.W.2d 410 (Iowa 1965); *Applestein v. United Board & Carton Corp.,* 159 A.2d 146 (N.J. Super. Ct. Ch. Div. 1960), *aff'd,* 161 A.2d 474 (N.J.); *Farris v. Glen Alden Corp.,* 143 A.2d 25 (Pa. 1958) (later overruled by statute).

Some jurisdictions are more open to these equitable claims than others. As you read the following case excerpt, note the determinative role that the doctrine of independent legal significance (equal dignity), first described and discussed earlier in this chapter, plays in Delaware litigation of this kind.

HARITON v. ARCO ELECTRONICS, INC.
Court of Chancery of Delaware
40 Del. Ch. 326 (1962)

SHORT, VICE CHANCELLOR:

Plaintiff is a stockholder of defendant Arco Electronics, Inc., a Delaware corporation. The complaint challenges the validity of the purchase by Loral Electronics Corporation, a New York corporation, of all the assets of Arco. Two causes of action are asserted, namely: (1) that the transaction is unfair to Arco stockholders, and (2) that the transaction constituted a de facto merger and is unlawful since the merger provisions of the Delaware law were not complied with.

Defendant has moved to dismiss the complaint and for summary judgment on the ground that the transaction was fair to Arco stockholders and was, in fact, one of purchase and sale and not a merger.

Plaintiff now concedes that he is unable to sustain the charge of unfairness. The only issue before the court, therefore, is whether the transaction was by its nature a de facto merger with a consequent right of appraisal in plaintiff. . . .

In the summer of 1961, Arco commenced negotiations with Loral with a view to the purchase by Loral of all of the assets of Arco in exchange for shares of Loral common stock. . . . Finally, on October 11, 1961, Loral offered a purchase price based on the ratio of one share of Loral common stock for three shares of Arco common stock. This offer was accepted by the representatives of Arco on October 24, 1961, and an agreement for the purchase was entered into between Loral and Arco on October 27, 1961. This agreement provides, among other things, as follows:

1. Arco will convey and transfer to Loral all of its assets and property of every kind, tangible and intangible; and will grant to Loral the use of its name and slogans

2. Loral will assume and pay all of Arco's debts and liabilities.

3. Loral will issue to Arco 283,000 shares of its common stock.

4. Upon the closing of the transaction Arco will dissolve and distribute to its shareholders, pro rata, the shares of the common stock of Loral.

5. Arco will call a meeting of its stockholders to be held December 21, 1961 to authorize and approve the conveyance and delivery of all the assets of Arco to Loral.

6. After the closing date, Arco will not engage in any business or activity except as may be required to complete the liquidation and dissolution of Arco.

Pursuant to its undertaking in the agreement for purchase and sale, Arco caused a special meeting of its stockholders to be called for December 27, 1961. The notice of such meeting set forth three specific purposes therefor: (1) to vote upon a proposal to ratify the agreement of purchase and sale, a copy of which was attached to the notice; (2) to vote upon a proposal to change the name of the corporation; and (3) if Proposals (1) and (2) should be adopted, to vote upon a proposal to liquidate and dissolve the corporation and to distribute the Loral shares to Arco shareholders. Proxies for this special meeting were not solicited. At the meeting, 652,050 shares were voted in favor of the sale and none against. The proposals to change the name of the corporation and to dissolve it and distribute the Loral stock were also approved. The transaction was thereafter consummated.

Plaintiff contends that the transaction, though in form a sale of assets of Arco, is in substance and effect a merger, and that it is unlawful because the merger statute has not been complied with, thereby depriving plaintiff of his right of appraisal.

Defendant contends that since all the formalities of a sale of assets pursuant to 8 Del. C. § 271 have been complied with the transaction is in fact a sale of assets and not a merger. In this connection, it is to be noted that plaintiffs nowhere allege or claim that defendant has not complied to the letter with the provisions of said section.

The question here presented is one which has not been heretofore passed upon by any court in this state. In *Heilbrunn v. Sun Chemical Corporation*, 38 Del. Ch. 321, 150 A.2d 755, the Supreme Court was called upon to determine whether or not a stockholder of the purchasing corporation could, in circumstances like those here presented, obtain relief on the theory of a de facto merger. The court held that relief was not available to such a stockholder. It expressly observed that the question here presented was not before the court for determination. It pointed out also that while Delaware does not grant appraisal rights to a stockholder dissenting from a sale, citing *Argenbright v. Phoenix Finance Co.*, 21 Del. Ch. 288, 187 A. 124, and *Finch v. Warrior Cement Corp.*, 16 Del. Ch. 44, 141 A. 54, those cases are distinguishable from the facts here presented, "because dissolution of the seller and distribution of the stock of the purchaser were not required as a part of the sale in either case." In speaking of the form of the transaction, the Supreme Court observes:

> "The argument that the result of this transaction is substantially the same as the result that would have followed a merger may be readily accepted. As plaintiffs correctly say, the Ansbacher enterprise [seller] is continued in altered form as a part of Sun [purchaser]. This is ordinarily a typical characteristic of a merger. Moreover the plan of reorganization *requires* the dissolution of Ansbacher and the distribution to its stockholders of the Sun stock received by it for the assets. As a part of the plan, the Ansbacher stockholders are compelled to receive Sun stock. From the viewpoint of Ansbacher, the result is the same as if Ansbacher had formally merged into Sun.

> "This result is made possible, of course, by the overlapping scope of the merger statute and the statute authorizing the sale of all the corporate assets. This possibility of overlapping was noticed in our opinion in the Mayflower case.

> "There is nothing new about such a result. For many years drafters of plans of corporate reorganization have increasingly resorted to the use of the sale-of-assets method in preference to the method by merger. Historically at least, there were reasons for this quite apart from the avoidance of the appraisal right given to stockholders dissenting from a merger."

Though it is said in the *Heilbrunn* case that the doctrine of de facto merger has been recognized in Delaware, it is to be noted that in each of the cases cited as recognizing the doctrine, namely, *Drug, Inc. v. Hunt*, 35 Del. 339, 168 A. 87 and *Finch v. Warrior Cement Corp.*, supra, there was a failure to comply with the statute governing sale of assets. In both cases the sales agreement required delivery of the shares of the purchasing corporation to be made directly to the shareholders of the selling corporation. It was, of course, held in each case that no consideration passed to the selling corporation and that therefore the transaction did not constitute a sale of the assets of the selling corporation to the purchasing corporation. No such failure to comply with the provisions of the sale of assets statute is present in this case. On the contrary, as heretofore observed there was a literal compliance with the terms of the statute by this defendant.

The doctrine of de facto merger in comparable circumstances has been recognized and applied by the Pennsylvania courts, both state and federal. *Lauman v. Lebanon Valley Railroad Co.*, 30 Pa. 42; *Marks v. Autocar Co.*, D.C., 153 F. Supp. 768; *Farris v. Glen Alden Corporation*, 393 Pa. 427, 143 A.2d 25. The two cases last cited are founded upon the holding in the case first cited which was decided on common law principles. The basis for the holding in the Lauman case is not at all clear. . . . The later Pennsylvania cases adopt the de facto merger approach and stress the requirement of dissolution and distribution of the purchaser's stock among the seller's shareholders. The Farris case demonstrates the length to which the Pennsylvania courts have gone in applying this principle. It was there applied in favor of a stockholder of the purchasing corporation, an application which our Supreme Court expressly rejected in Heilbrunn.

The right of appraisal accorded to a dissenting stockholder by the merger statutes is in compensation for the right which he had at common law to prevent a merger. At common law, a single dissenting stockholder could also prevent a sale of all of the assets of a corporation. The Legislatures of many states have seen fit to grant the appraisal right to a dissenting stockholder not only under the merger statutes but as well under the sale of assets statutes. Our Legislature has seen fit to expressly grant the appraisal right only under the merger statutes. This difference in treatment of the rights of dissenting stockholders may well have been deliberate, in order "to allow even greater freedom of action to corporate majorities in arranging combinations than is possible under the merger statutes."

While plaintiff's contention that the doctrine of de facto merger should be applied in the present circumstances is not without appeal, the subject is one which, in my opinion, is within the legislative domain. Moreover it is difficult to differentiate between a case such as the present and one where the reorganization plan contemplates the ultimate dissolution of the selling corporation but does not formally require such procedure in express terms. . . . Arco continued in existence as a corporate entity following the exchange of securities for its assets. The fact that it continued corporate existence only for the purpose of winding up its affairs by the distribution of Loral stock is, in my mind, of little consequence. The argument underlying the applicability of the doctrine of de facto merger, namely, that the stockholder is forced against his will to accept a new investment in an enterprise foreign to that of which he was a part has little pertinency. The right of the corporation to sell all of its assets for stock in another corporation was expressly accorded to Arco by § 271 of Title 8, Del. C. The stockholder was, in contemplation of law, aware of this right when he acquired his stock. He was also aware of the fact that the situation might develop whereby he would be ultimately forced to accept a new investment, as would have been the case here had the resolution authorizing dissolution followed consummation of the sale. Inclusion of the condition in the sale agreement does not in any way add to his position to complain.

There is authority in decisions of courts of this state for the proposition that the various sections of the Delaware Corporation Law conferring authority for corporate action are independent of each other and that a given result may be accomplished by proceeding under one section which is not possible, or is even forbidden under another. For example, dividends which have accrued to preferred stockholders may not be eliminated by an amendment to the corporate charter under § 242, Title 8. On the other hand, such accrued dividends may be eliminated by a merger between the corporation and a wholly owned subsidiary. In *Langfelder v. Universal Laboratories, Inc., D.C.*, 68 F. Supp. 209, Judge Leahy commented upon these holdings as follows:

" . . . *Havender v. Federal United Corporation*, Del. Sup., 24 Del. Ch. 318, 11 A.2d 331 and *Hottenstein v. York Ice Machinery Corp.*, D.C. Del., 45 F. Supp. 436; *Id.*, 3 Cir., 136 *F.2d* 944 hold that in Delaware a parent may merge with a wholly owned subsidiary and thereby cancel old preferred stock and the rights of the holders thereof to the unpaid, accumulated dividends, by substituting in lieu thereof stocks of the surviving corporation. Under Delaware law, accrued dividends after the passage of time mature into a debt and cannot be eliminated by an amendment to the corporate charter under Sec. 26 of the Delaware Corporation Law, Rev. Code 1935, § 2058. But the right to be paid in full for such dividends, notwithstanding provisions in the charter contract, may be eliminated by means of a merger which meets the standard of fairness. The rationale is that a merger is an act of independent legal significance, and when it meets the requirements of fairness and all other statutory requirements, the merger is valid and not subordinate or dependent upon any other section of the Delaware Corporation Law."

In the footnote to Judge Leahy's opinion the following comment appears:

"The text is but a particularization of the general theory of the Delaware Corporation Law that action taken pursuant to the authority of the various sections of that law constitute acts of independent legal significance and their validity is not dependent on other sections of the Act. *Havender v. Federal United Corporation* proves the correctness of this interpretation. Under *Keller v. Wilson & Co.* accrued dividends are regarded as matured rights and must be paid. But, this does not prevent a merger, good under the provisions of Sec. 59, from having the incidental effect of wiping out such dividend rights, i.e., Sec. 59 is complete in itself and is not dependent upon any other section, absent fraud. The same thing is true with most other sections of the Corporation Law."

The situation posed by the present case is even stronger than that presented in the *Havender* and *York Ice cases*. In those cases the court permitted the circumvention of matured rights by proceeding under the merger statute. Here, the stockholder has no rights unless another and independent statute is invoked to create a right. A holding in the stockholder's favor would be directly contrary to the theory of the cited cases.

I conclude that the transaction complained of was not a de facto merger, either in the sense that there was a failure to comply with one or more of the requirements of § 271 of the Delaware Corporation Law, or that the result accomplished was in effect a merger entitling plaintiff to a right of appraisal.

Defendant's motion for summary judgment is granted. Order on notice.

NOTES AND QUESTIONS

1. *De Facto Mergers in Pennsylvania.* In reaction to, among other things, the *Lauman* and *Farris* opinions (referenced in the *Hariton* case), the Pennsylvania legislature eventually expressly revoked the *de facto* merger doctrine. *See* 15 PA. CONS. STAT. §§ 1105, 1904.

2. *Effects on Successor Liability.* As noted earlier, despite the general rule that an acquiror of assets does not assume pre-acquisition liabilities of the seller, an acquiror of assets may assume successor liability for the pre-acquisition obligations of the seller if a court finds that the asset acquisition is a *de facto merger*. *See, e.g., Shannon v.*

Samuel Langston Co., 379 F. Supp. 797, 803 (W.D. Mich. 1974) (applying New Jersey law); *Marks v. Minn. Mining & Mfg. Co.*, 187 Cal. App. 3d 1429 (1986).

3. *Doctrine of Independent Legal Significance (Equal Dignity).* One of the authors writes:

> The Delaware equal dignity rule may find its best expression in the de facto merger cases. In *Farris v. Glen Alden Corp.*, List Corporation desired to achieve two objectives in its acquisition of Glen Alden, a Pennsylvania corporation. First, List wanted Glen Alden to be the surviving corporation in order to preserve and utilize Glen Alden's tax loss carryforward against List's profits. The second objective was preservation of List's store of cash. If Glen Alden shareholders had a right to dissent and receive cash for their shares, a number of them might have done so. A number of dissents would have depleted List's cash hoard. Counsel, therefore, structured the transaction as stock for assets rather than stock for stock and as a reverse transaction. Technically, Glen Alden would be issuing stock to List shareholders and List would be selling assets. In reality, though, the reverse was true. Under Pennsylvania statutory law then in effect, shareholders of a corporation buying assets had no right to dissent and receive cash for the appraised value of their shares. In a statutory merger they would have had such a right.

> The Pennsylvania Supreme Court held that the structure of the transaction between Glen Alden and List was functionally equivalent to a merger. Holding that substance must prevail over form, the court ruled the sale of assets to be a de facto merger. Dissenting shareholders therefore would be entitled to cash for their shares, as in cases of statutory merger.

> The Delaware courts reached the opposite result four years later in Hariton v. Arco Electronics, Inc. The Delaware statutes contained procedures for merger of two corporations. Those procedures created for target company shareholders the right to dissent and seek appraisal and cash for their shares in the Delaware courts. The statutes also contained procedures for a corporation to sell all or substantially all of its assets to another corporation in return for stock or cash. Those procedures did not include a right of shareholders to dissent and seek appraisal.

> The Delaware Vice Chancellor held that the two statutory pathways were independent of each other so that a result may be accomplished by proceeding on a course of action under one section which is not possible, or even forbidden, under another. The courts refrained from saying which of two or more inconsistent procedures was superior to another. That task was for the legislature.

> The Delaware Supreme Court affirmed that the sale-of-assets statute and the merger statute were, and are, independent of one another. They are, so to speak, of equal dignity. The result of decisions like Hariton is that no matter how circuitous a path might be, if in the Delaware statute a corporate lawyer can find a track to his objective, that path or track is of equal dignity with a more direct path, even though the circuitous track has fewer or no shareholder protections. Two or more paths to the same objective are of equal dignity.

> The equal dignity rule emerged as a green light, signaling the Delaware courts' readiness to approve corporate transactions. For the corporate practitioner, the equal dignity rule signals that where there is a will there is a way. And, of course, the Delaware equal dignity rule is not a rule; it is a "non-rule" that permits a corporate lawyer to choose from, and a judge to validate a choice from, seemingly contradictory pathways or norms.

Douglas M. Branson, *Indeterminacy: The Final Ingredient in an Interest Group*

Analysis of Corporate Law, 43 VAND. L. REV. 85, 94–96 (1990)* (footnotes omitted).

Based on what you have read in this chapter, what incentives does the doctrine of independent legal significance afford transaction planners and shareholders? What are the advantages and disadvantages of Pennsylvania's approach in *Farris* over the Delaware approach evidenced in *Hariton*?

PROBLEM

C. Dean Olson and H. Glenn Olson sell off all the capital stock of seven California corporations engaged in the egg business in California to Bellanca Corporation, a Delaware corporation, for a purchase price of $5,150,000 It was agreed among the parties that the purchase price be paid by Bellanca to the Olsons as follows: delivery of 150,000 shares of Bellanca's common stock, $1.00 par value per share at closing; payment of one-half the proceeds recovered by Bellanca in certain specified litigation; and payment of the balance, in cash, over a 12-year period, with interest at 2.5% annually, commencing four years after the date of the purchase agreement. As a result of the transaction, the Olsons controlled the affairs of Bellanca.

After consummation of the asset acquisition, Bellanca effected a short-form (parent/subsidiary) merger under DGCL § 253, merging each of the seven acquired corporations (then wholly-owned subsidiaries of Bellanca) with and into itself and changing its name to Olson Brothers, Incorporated. Bellanca and the subsidiaries each complied with all applicable requirements of Delaware and California law in consummating the short-form merger. Accordingly, Olson Brothers now conducts the egg business in California and is controlled and its affairs directed by the Olson brothers.

A minority shareholder of Olson Brothers (formerly Bellanca) filed a complaint alleging that the series of transactions described above constitute a *de facto* merger and, therefore, that they are unlawful because the applicable merger provisions of the DGCL were not complied with. Specifically, the shareholder complained that she was denied the right to vote on the combined transactions and the right to seek an appraisal of her shares. What should the court likely hold, and what should its reasoning be? How would your answer change if Olson Brothers (formerly Bellanca) were organized under the law of a state that has adopted the holding and reasoning of the *Farris* court?

D. DISSOLUTIONS

In Chapter 9, we learned that dissolution is (among other things) one way of resolving shareholder oppression and disagreements in close corporations. Dissolution, however, is a much more broadly applicable concept in corporate law. It is a statutorily ordained process constituting the most basic of corporate changes: the devolution of the corporation itself. More specifically, dissolution is the statutory event that catapults the corporation toward its termination. *See, e.g.*, MBCA § 14.05. Having come this far in this casebook, you might say that the corporation is born, lives, and dies by virtue of legislative grace.

Note that dissolution often is confused with wind-up and liquidation. While the three terms — dissolution, wind-up, and liquidation — often are used interchangeably in common parlance, the three concepts are best understood as separate but related. Dissolution is the corporate statutory event. As a result of the occurrence of dissolution, the corporation winds up its affairs so that it can formally and finally terminate its existence. As part of the wind-up, the corporation engages in a liquidation of its assets for the purposes of marshaling cash to pay off its creditors and, if there is any residual, its equity holders.

Dissolution is a corporate occurrence that, like charter and bylaw amendments and

---

business combination transactions, constitutes a fundamental corporate change. It therefore is important that we understand the rules by which a corporate dissolution is authorized. One of these rules, in most statutory frameworks, involves the same, ordered process that we have seen in connection with the approval of charter amendments, mergers, and share exchanges; the board must act first, and then the shareholders also must approve. Yet, there are many ways to dissolve a corporation, and they differ from state to state.

The DGCL sets forth a relatively simple dissolution scheme. Under Delaware law, a corporation can:

- judicially dissolve by application of one of its two shareholders if it is a joint venture corporation that has only two shareholders, DGCL § 273;

- voluntarily dissolve if the corporation has not issued shares or has not commenced the business for which the corporation was organized if "a majority of the incorporators, or, if directors were named in the certificate of incorporation or have been elected, a majority of the directors" files a certificate with the secretary of state, DGCL § 274; or

- voluntarily dissolve if the board resolves to dissolve the corporation, holders of a majority of the outstanding stock of the corporation entitled to vote subsequently approve the dissolution, and a certificate is filed with the secretary of state, DGCL § 275.

In addition, under Delaware law, the Court of Chancery can "revoke or forfeit the charter of any corporation for abuse, misuse, or nonuse of its corporate powers, privileges, or franchises" upon application by the Attorney General. The Court of Chancery then administers and winds up the corporation. DGCL § 284. This process is analogous to administrative dissolutions in the MBCA.

Under the more complex scheme set forth in the MBCA, dissolution occurs when:

- a majority of the incorporators or initial directors of a corporation that has neither issued shares nor commenced business voluntarily dissolves the corporation by delivering articles of dissolution to the secretary of state for filing, MBCA § 14.01;

- a corporation's board of directors proposes voluntary dissolution and submits the proposal to the shareholders for approval, after which the shareholders approve (at a meeting at which a majority of the votes entitled to be cast is present) and the corporation delivers articles of dissolution to the secretary of state for filing, MBCA § 14.02;

- the secretary of state administratively dissolves a corporation either because the period of duration for the corporation as stated in its articles has expired or for failure to pay franchise taxes, failure to deliver its annual report, or failure to maintain a registered agent or registered office in the state or give proper notice of changes in the registered agent or registered office, MBCA § 4.20;

- a specified court judicially dissolves a corporation by application of the attorney general because "the corporation obtained its articles of incorporation through fraud" or "the corporation has continued to exceed or abuse the authority conferred upon it by law," MBCA § 14.30(1);

- a specified court judicially dissolves a corporation by application of a shareholder (as illustrated in Chapter 9) because of: a director or shareholder deadlock; an illegal, oppressive, or fraudulent act; or a misappropriation or waste of corporate assets, MBCA §14.30(2);

- a specified court judicially dissolves a corporation by application of a creditor because:

    "(i) the creditor's claim has been reduced to judgment, the execution on the judgment returned unsatisfied, and the corporation is insolvent; or

(ii) the corporation has admitted in writing that the creditor's claim is due and owing and the corporation is insolvent," MBCA § 14.30(3); or

- a specified court judicially dissolves a corporation by application of the corporation to have its voluntary dissolution continued under court supervision, MBCA § 14.30(4).

A corporation may revoke its voluntary dissolution under certain circumstances specified in the statute, usually involving approvals similar to those needed for the dissolution itself and a filing with the secretary of state. DGCL § 311; MBCA § 14.04. Similarly, a corporation that has had its charter revoked or forfeited under the DGCL or a corporation administratively dissolved under the MBCA may make a filing with the secretary of state for reinstatement, revival, or restoration (as the case may be) in accordance with certain specified statutory procedures. DGCL §312; MBCA § 14.22.

As with other forms of fundamental corporate change, shareholders want their say and the benefit of their economic bargain in corporate dissolutions, and (as you can see from the statutory framework) they do not always get it. Among other things, shareholders often claim that they have voting rights under corporate law or the corporation's organizational documents that are additional to or different from those (if any) afforded to the shareholders by corporate management in authorizing the corporation's dissolution. Shareholders also claim that management's actions in dissolving the corporation robbed shareholders of some greater financial benefit the shareholders otherwise would have or could have received. In many cases, shareholder arguments of these kinds are framed similarly to the equitable arguments made in *de facto* merger cases: namely, that a transaction or series of transactions approved and implemented by the corporation's board of directors should, in fact, be recharacterized as a different kind of transaction or transactions that is or are more beneficial to the shareholders (from a voting or financial perspective) than the transaction(s) authorized by the directors. Moreover, shareholders typically assert breach of fiduciary duty claims in litigation over dissolutions, just as they do in cases challenging other fundamental corporate changes. *See, e.g., Elward v. Peabody Coal Co.*, 121 Ill. App. 2d 298 (1970); *Flarsheim v. Twenty Five Thirty Two Broadway Corp.*, 432 S.W.2d 245 (Mo. 1968).

NOTES AND QUESTIONS

1. *Differences in the Ability of Shareholders to Initiate Dissolution.* The DGCL and MBCA vary significantly in the amount of control given to shareholders to affect a corporate dissolution. As we saw in Chapter 9, states using an MBCA-like scheme allow shareholders to initiate dissolution by judicial application in the event of, for example, certain deadlocks or illegal, oppressive, or fraudulent director behavior. *See* MBCA § 14.30(2). Delaware law does not give shareholders this right. Other states permit shareholder initiation of dissolution but on bases that differ from those set forth in the MBCA. For example, under New York law, shareholders can petition for dissolution of the corporation if they "adopt a resolution stating that they find that its assets are not sufficient to discharge its liabilities, or that they deem a dissolution to be beneficial to the shareholders." *See* N.Y. C.L.S. Bus. Corp. § 1103. Moreover, as noted in Chapter 9, a close corporation may be able to opt out of a shareholder-initiated dissolution under the MBCA and specific state statutes if another shareholder or the corporation elects to purchase the shares own by the shareholder-petitioner. *See, e.g.,* MBCA § 14.34; N.Y. C.L.S. Bus. Corp. § 1118.

2. *Corporate Revocation of Shareholder-Initiated Dissolution.* One law professor observes that:

> [s]tates differ on how, if at all, a corporation can revoke a shareholder-initiated dissolution. If the board could revoke the dissolution, it could nullify the shareholders' action. Presumably, a court would eventually stop the board from undoing the shareholders' action, but litigation over the matter is undesirable.

New York and California provide little resistance to shareholder-initiated dissolution. In New York, neither directors nor shareholders can revoke corporate dissolution by normal corporate action. New York does allow a court, upon the petition of the corporation or of certain other third parties, to annul the dissolution. Where the dissolution has not disadvantaged minority shareholders, creditors, or other claimants, though, the court has no reason to intervene. Only if shareholders initiated the petition to annul the dissolution should a court even consider a petition from "the corporation" to annul the dissolution.

In California, revocation is possible but does not threaten shareholder sovereignty over dissolution. While shareholders can revoke dissolutions generally, the board may revoke only board-initiated dissolutions. The statute does not contemplate the board revoking a voluntary dissolution by the shareholders.

The Illinois statute clearly contemplates shareholders initiating and authorizing voluntary dissolution without board action (and, implicitly, against board wishes) and appears to allow shareholders to revoke dissolution once it has been called. Surprisingly, however, Illinois also allows the board, without shareholder action, to revoke a dissolution, a situation that invites management to frustrate shareholders' wishes.

Park McGinty, *Replacing Hostile Takeovers*, 144 U. Pa. L. Rev. 983, 1036–37 (1996)* (footnotes omitted). What approach seems most appropriate? Why?

3. *Corporate Finance Drafting Implications.* Holders of preferred shares often are plaintiffs in litigation over the validity of corporate dissolutions. As a general matter, because of the fact that preferred stock is a contractual equity instrument — where the corporation and the holder bargain for specific rights and responsibilities in a relatively free statutory framework — preferred shareholders have arguments for enhanced voting and financial rights that may emanate from both the corporate statutes and the terms of their equity instrument, as embodied in the corporate charter (or a related certificate or amendment that becomes part of the charter upon filing). Courts tend to place heavy emphasis in these types of cases on the bargained-for terms of the plaintiff's securities. *See, e.g.*, *Elward v. Peabody Coal Co.*, 121 Ill. App. 2d 298 (1970). This set of circumstances places heavy responsibility on the drafters of these terms to foresee potential shareholder arguments (e.g., that a redemption is, in fact, a liquidation — or vice versa — if the alternative transaction is more advantageous to the shareholder). Careful drafting is critical and can forestall or limit future litigation expense. Accordingly, corporate finance lawyers need to have a strong knowledge of the case law on dissolutions and other fundamental corporate changes in order to best serve their clients.

4. *Talking Out of Both Sides of Its Mouth?* The Supreme Court of Delaware states the following in an important and well-cited corporate law opinion discussed in more detail in Chapter 16:

Under the statutory framework of the General Corporation Law, many of the most fundamental corporate changes can be implemented only if they are approved by a majority vote of the stockholders. Such actions include elections of directors, amendments to the certificate of incorporation, mergers, consolidations, sales of all or substantially all of the assets of the corporation, and dissolution. 8 Del. C. §§ 211, 242, 251–258, 263, 271, 275. Because of the overriding importance of voting rights, this Court and the Court of Chancery have consistently acted to protect stockholders from unwarranted interference with such rights.

Paramount Communications v. QVC Network, 637 A.2d 34, 42 (Del. 1994) (footnote omitted).

As we close out this chapter, it seems important to ask whether (and, if so, how) this statement can be squared with the doctrine of independent legal significance in Delaware. State and substantiate your views.

Chapter 16
CHANGE OF CONTROL OF THE CORPORATION

A. OVERVIEW

State corporate laws provide that the corporation is managed by or under the control of its board of directors. This board of directors typically elects or appoints officers to manage the day-to-day business of the corporation, and the members of this board of directors are elected by some or all of the corporation's shareholders. Other constituents, including employees, creditors, suppliers, customers, or clients, also play significant roles in the corporation. Accordingly, there are multiple levels and dimensions of control in the corporate context.

Scholars and others have debated the question "Who controls the corporation?" in many contexts and with sharply differing outcomes, both within specific contexts and on an aggregate basis. Control may be created by statutory rules, corporate organizational documents (including charters and bylaws), or contracts or instruments through which control rights are conferred. Moreover, control may be manifested or exercised in corporate actions taken by officers (or other corporate agents) or in votes taken by corporate shareholders or directors. In fact, the locus of control in corporate decision making may vary based on the context in which decisions are being made. The debate as to the actual and desired locus of control in the corporation has loomed large in recent discussions about public company corporate governance. A number of overlapping and competing models have emerged. A few of the more dominant, overarching models are described in the succeeding paragraphs.

1. Shareholder Primacy

Among the different theories of corporate control, "shareholder primacy," the notion that shareholders are and should be the controlling constituents in the corporation, has received significant support. Since the shareholders elect the directors — the macro-managers of the corporation — to act on their behalf and for their benefit, directors sometimes function like principals in an agency relationship. Under this analogy (which admittedly is an imperfect one) the directors can be seen as agents who are acting on behalf of the shareholders of the corporation. Commentators advocating and describing this theory of corporate control note that, although the board of directors typically owes its duties to the corporation (and not specifically to any of the corporation's individual constituents), decisional law generally supports the view that the board serves shareholder interests first and foremost (if not exclusively). Shareholder primacists also hold the voting rights of shareholders (collectively termed the shareholder franchise) in the highest respect. They believe that the shareholder franchise should be preserved and, in a number of cases, enhanced. For example, it is shareholder primacists who have advocated shareholder selection of director nominees and shareholder approval of executive compensation arrangements.

2. Director Primacy

An alternative view of corporate control is that the directors, as the statutorily ordained managers of the corporation, do and should exert the true power in the corporation. This theory of corporate control typically is described as "director primacy." Director primacists generally view shareholder voting rights as limited and ineffective corporate control tools. This is because directors hand-pick, by committee or board vote, not only the officers of the corporation, but also their own colleagues on the board (by nominating those whose names are put before the shareholders by the corporation for a vote). Similarly, as we saw in Chapter 15, under state corporate law rules, the board generally must approve basic corporate changes that require charter modifications (including charter amendments, mergers, and asset dispositions, for example) and voluntary corporate dissolutions; only after a positive outcome at the board level (if at all) are these basic changes put before the shareholders for a vote. Finally, shareholders have limited recourse against directors when they disagree with board decisions. Under current corporate law, it is difficult to replace directors with shareholder-selected director nominees, and it is difficult for shareholders to hold directors accountable for their decisions. As we have seen, both the business judgment rule and the procedural aspects of shareholder derivative litigation tend to make it difficult for shareholders to control directors through litigation or the threat of litigation.

3.   Managerialism

Promoters of yet a third perspective on corporate control, managerialism, note that high-level officers of the corporation are, in fact, and should be the controlling constituency in many corporate situations. Managerialists point to the fact that, even though the corporation's chief executive officer and other senior executive officers typically are appointed by the board, the chief executive officer of the corporation generally selects director nominees that are considered and approved by the board or a board committee. Of course, corporate officers manage the day-to-day business at the corporation. In the process, the executive officers control and implement important corporate decisions. Moreover, the executive officers of the corporation wield significant influence over the board both through their substantial control over matters that come before the board and through the power of persuasion they can exercise at board meetings based on their comprehensive knowledge of corporate operations. In short: the managers know best. Directors, in fact, endorse or defer to the corporation's officers on many significant questions, including those involving executive compensation and other matters that raise the specter of self-dealing.

This deference largely reflects the widely held view that officers are highly incentivized to act in the best interests of the corporation because of the direct financial rewards (salary and incentive compensation) that they reap from the corporation's success. To the extent that officers are compensated with equity-based incentives and to the extent that shareholders are viewed as the key corporate constituency, officers then may rationally focus their efforts toward maximizing public share values (often in the short term), sometimes to the detriment of other corporate interests. Of course, actions taken by officers of the corporation generally are subject to the same fiduciary duties that govern director actions; however, officers also are shielded by the same business judgment rule and shareholder derivative suit protections that shield director actions, making it difficult for shareholders to hold officers accountable for their actions.

4.   Resulting Theoretical Confusion

With so many theories of corporate control (none of which, alone, is dominant or fully explains actual or desired control in the corporation), it is difficult for the judiciary to decide corporate law cases and for the legislature to fashion new corporate laws. In short, there is:

> a theoretical ambiguity at the base of corporate doctrine. In the classical doctrinal conception, the corporation is an entity and the powers of the board of directors are original and undelegated. Even as the shareholders elect the board, they are not accorded the rights of principals in an agency relationship. Unfortunately for the goal of doctrinal coherence, corporate law also frequently lapses into an agency characterization, the lapses being much encouraged by the economic theory of agency. The ambiguity in the legal model opens the way for an ongoing contest over the line dividing management and shareholder authority within the firm, a contest centered on topics like shareholder access, proxy regulation, and takeover defense.

William W. Bratton, *Welfare, Dialectic, and Mediation in Corporate Law*, 2 BERKELEY BUS. L.J. 59, 63–64 (2005). This chapter explores that dividing line between management and shareholder authority — a dividing line that we also explore throughout Chapter 8 and in various other portions of this text — in the context of the market for corporate control and change of control transactions.

5. Market for Corporate Control

From these observations made in the context of governance-based theories of corporate control, there emerges a more general theory on the market for corporate control. When a publicly traded corporation is undervalued in the market, the corporation becomes ripe for a takeover. An acquiror then can step in to rescue the corporation by unseating its management and realizing the corporation's full potential value for the benefit of the shareholders. The acquiror achieves this objective by succeeding in a proxy fight for control of the board or by acquiring voting control over the corporation's shares (typically, in the case of a public company acquisition target, through a regulated public tender offer) and replacing the board and officers. In this way, the acquiror does not need to negotiate with the board in order to achieve a change of control. In theory, the possibility that such a putative acquiror may emerge to unseat management incentivizes directors and executive officers to take action to preserve their positions with the corporation by increasing the corporation's market valuation (including principally by improving performance). The theoretical market for corporate control recognizes that shareholder primacy, board primacy, and managerialism co-exist in the corporate form.

Yet, management may react differently to the threat of an unsolicited change of control. Directors and officers may attempt to defend the corporate bastion against a change of control at least in part as a means of retaining their corporate positions. Conversely, directors and officers may be incentivized in certain circumstances to approve a change of control of the corporation. For example, in circumstances where directors or officers stand to receive large severance packages or lucrative stock option vesting, they may be motivated to support a change of control in circumstances that otherwise would result in aggressive negotiation (and, potentially, a higher price).

6. A Birds-Eye View of Change-of-Control Transactions

Consistent with these theories, there are a number of distinct strategies and techniques for changing control of a corporation. Often, more than one transaction or approach is used to complete the change of control, and some strategies and techniques cut across more than one category.

Predictably, as activity in this area has increased and become both interstate and international, bodies of applicable federal regulation have been instituted and enhanced. This regulation occurs principally through the federal securities laws and rules in and under the Securities Exchange Act of 1934 (the "1934 Act"), which mandate disclosure and prevent fraud in the conduct of certain change of control transactions, notably those that use the proxy solicitation process to change the control of the board of directors (proxy contests), those that consist of or incorporate direct offers to a public company's shareholders to purchase their shares (tender offers), and those that result in privatizing the market for a public company's shares ("going private" transactions).

Of course, states also have a continuing and critical interest in the nature of transactions that result in changes of corporate control. This sets up a federal-state regulatory competition, which is itself of interest. Among other things, federal law has supplanted and supplemented state regulation of change of control transactions (especially as to public companies), federal securities fraud litigation involving change of control transactions has increased as an alternative or supplement to state actions for violations of directors' and officers' fiduciary duties, and state legislatures have attempted their own statutory solutions. As we shall see, courts have invalidated some state legislative efforts at regulation on the basis that they are preempted by federal regulation.

Changes in corporate control can be negotiated (friendly) or non-negotiated (unfriendly or, more commonly, hostile). Negotiated transactions involve the acquiror bargaining with the target and agreeing on terms. The transaction then is approved by the target's board of directors (as well as, in most cases, the acquiror's board of directors). Non-negotiated transactions involve the acquiror persuading a controlling bloc of the target's shareholders either to vote for the acquiror's director nominees and related proposals or to sell their shares to the acquiror. Non-negotiated changes of control are deemed "hostile" because, in these types of transactions, the acquiror bypasses the target's board of directors — the body that manages or controls management of the target corporation — and deals directly with the target's shareholders. Some change of control transactions begin as hostile bids for control and end as negotiated mergers or acquisitions. As a result (and, as noted above, potentially in conflict with the performance incentives created by the market for corporate control), publicly traded corporations often adopt defensive measures to ward off or stall potential acquisition bids. Courts typically decide controversies involving anti-takeover devices based on claims that directors have breached their fiduciary duties to the corporation and its shareholders in either adopting or using one or more defensive mechanisms. The resulting body of case law is both fascinating and contradictory.

Overall, legal actions relating to change of control transactions may consist of alleged violations of: mandatory disclosure rules or antifraud provisions in and under the federal securities laws (including those described in this chapter); state takeover legislation (described later in this chapter); state law fiduciary duties; state corporate appraisal rights statutes; and other state corporate laws, including statutes providing for board authority and statutes relating to necessary approvals. The remedies available to plaintiffs in these actions vary based on the nature of the action. Accordingly, litigants may choose their desired claims based on their desired remedies or other factors, e.g., the elements of the claim, the burdens and standards of proof, the forum in which the claim may be made, etc.

The U.S system for regulating corporate control has been critiqued on a number of bases, including its complexity (multiple rules, on both a state and federal level, applicable to a single transaction or series of transactions) and lack of predictability (as a result of, among other things, the prominence of indeterminate judge-made standards in fiduciary duty and corporate fraud analyses). Reform proposals abound. Some of these are based on the regulatory systems in effect in other countries.

With all of the foregoing in mind, this chapter categorizes and describes the transactions through which control of a U.S. publicly traded corporation can change and identifies and summarizes the state and federal laws and regulations governing these transactions. The chapter then continues by explaining the mechanics of various defensive tactics — ways in which a potential target corporation may protect itself from putative acquirors through provisions in its corporate organizational documents, through terms in specific contracts and instruments, and through other corporate actions. State anti-takeover statutes are a part of this defensive landscape, deriving from and enhancing individual corporate defensive efforts. Frustrated acquirors and shareholders, among others, have challenged the validity of both corporate-initiated takeover defenses and state anti-takeover statutes, resulting in new law governing fiduciary duties and preemption. The chapter briefly treats the rich jurisprudence in these areas. Finally, in its last two sections, the chapter outlines proposals for reform of the existing U.S. system of regulating change-in-control transactions and describes key issues relating to changes of corporate control under the laws of other countries.

B.   TYPES AND REGULATION OF CHANGE OF CONTROL TRANSACTIONS

As indicated in the Overview provided above, changes in corporate control involve a change in the control of a corporation's board or shareholdings. This portion of the chapter explores different transactions that constitute or comprise a change of corporate control.

1.   Charter Amendments and Business Combinations

As you already may recognize, certain transactions described in Chapter 15 — corporate reorganizations, recapitalizations, and restructurings by way of charter amendment or business combination — may effectuate, alone or together with other transactions, a change in corporate control. As noted in Chapter 15, these transactions (mergers, statutory share exchanges, and asset acquisitions) must be approved by the board of directors before they are put to a shareholder vote, if a shareholder vote is required. Accordingly, these transactions only can be used in a negotiated change of control. The acquiror must come to the target's board of directors first; the target's board is in control. As Chapter 15 indicates, the structuring and approval of these transactions fundamentally are governed by state corporate law.

2.   Proxy Contests (a.k.a. Proxy Fights) and Other Changes in Control of the Board of Directors

Of course, as we earlier explored in Chapter 8, federal law also steps in, as an overlay to state law rules and corporate charter and bylaw provisions, to control aspects of the shareholder voting process for public companies through proxy regulation under § 14(a) of the 1934 Act. As you may recall, proxy contests — battles over director elections waged through dueling proxy materials — are among the regulated activities. Proxy contests (like charter amendments and business combinations, including going private transactions, if successful) result in a change of control of the subject corporation. By gaining control of the board of directors — the corporate constituent that manages or controls the management of the corporation — the insurgent gains control of the corporation itself.

In a proxy contest, a putative acquiror typically creates and files his, her, or its own proxy materials and solicits proxies from the target corporation's shareholders to elect its own nominees as corporate directors. Often, the solicitation also forwards other proposals necessary to effectuate or complete the change of control of the target corporation (including, for example, any proposal needed to defuse an impediment takeover defense). Especially if the solicitation is not for an annual meeting and there are no vacancies on the board, the insurgent's solicitation materials also may need to propose the removal of existing directors or an increase in the size of the corporation's board of directors in order to effectuate a change of control.

Note that the proxy contest process is different from the shareholder proposal process under Rule 14a-8 studied in Chapter 8, where a shareholder uses the corporation's own proxy materials to promote a resolution for approval at a corporation's shareholder meeting. That shareholder proposal process cannot be used for proxy contests. *See* Rule 14a-8(i)(8).

As noted above, although state law authorizes and establishes the conditions for voting by proxy, federal law and rules largely regulate the tournament between the insurgent acquiror and the target corporation. Specifically, § (a) of, and Regulation 14A under, the 1934 Act regulate the form, content, filing, and dissemination of a dissident's proxy statement and proxy card, just as they regulate the form, content, filing, and dissemination of the target corporation's proxy statement and proxy card. Moreover, Rule 14a-7 requires that the target corporation either distribute the insurgent's proxy materials on behalf of the insurgent or supply the insurgent with a current list of the names, addresses, and holdings of each of the target's shareholders so that the insurgent can do its own mailing. The dissident's solicitation, like that of the target, also is governed by applicable antifraud provisions, namely Rule 14a-9.

3.   Tender Offers and Other Share Purchases

In addition to fundamental corporate change transactions (especially mergers and transfers of all or substantially all of a corporation's assets), proxy contests, and going private transactions (described *infra*), the sale of a corporation's shares can result in a change of control of that corporation. Although shareholder control over corporate affairs may be weaker and less direct than the control afforded to the board of directors, shareholders have the ability to elect directors and (in most cases) approve fundamental corporate changes. Because a change in ownership of a corporation's shares can lead to a change in the composition of the board of directors (the statutory locus of corporate control), a change in corporate control can occur through a change in control of the corporation's voting shares.

As a general matter, a simple sale of shares is an individual commercial transaction undertaken by the shareholder. As such, the corporate law does not regulate this type of transaction through its default rules. Absent share transfer restrictions imposed by statutorily authorized provisions in corporate organizational documents or shareholder agreements, under state law, shareholders can buy and sell shares as they may choose.

However, when share sale transactions involve the capital markets (which extend across state and national borders), federal securities law does intervene to regulate the conduct of buyers and sellers as a means of ensuring the protection of investors and the maintenance of market integrity. This regulation principally occurs through the Williams Act in the form of federal regulation of tender offers (codified in a number of different sections in the 1934 Act).

What, exactly, is a "tender offer"? This turns out to be a harder question to answer than one might expect, given that a statutory framework has been created to regulate tender offers. In fact, neither the Williams Act itself nor related Securities and Exchange Commission ("SEC") rules define the term. This means that we depend on case law to supply the definition. A 1999 District Court opinion briefly summarizes the state of the decisional law defining a tender offer.

> [T]he Supreme Court observed that there was no question that "Congress intended to protect investors" in enacting the Williams Act, which insures " 'that public shareholders who are confronted by a cash tender offer for their stock will not be required to respond without adequate information.' " Yet Congress provided more than just disclosure requirements in the Act. "Besides requiring disclosure and providing specific benefits for tendering shareholders, the Williams Act also contains a broad antifraud prohibition. . . ."
>
> While the purpose of the Act is clear, the type of transaction it seeks to regulate does not lend itself to easy definition. . . . One district court established an eight-factor test for determining what constitutes a tender offer. Wellman v. Dickinson, 475 F. Supp. 783 (S.D.N.Y. 1979), *aff'd on other grounds*, 682 F.2d 355 (2d Cir. 1982). The factors are:
>
>> (1) active and widespread solicitation of public shareholders for the shares of issuer; (2) solicitation made for a substantial percentage of the issuer's stock; (3) offer to purchase made at a premium over the prevailing market price; (4) terms of the offer are firm rather than negotiable; (5) offer contingent on the tender of a fixed number of shares, often subject to a fixed maximum number to be purchased; (6) offer open only a limited period of time; (7) offeree subjected to pressure to sell his stock[; and, (8)] public announcements of a purchasing program concerning the target company precede or accompany

rapid accumulation of large amounts of the target company's securities.

The Second Circuit later refused to elevate this list to "a mandatory 'litmus test,'" reasoning that

> in any given case a solicitation may constitute a tender offer even though some of the eight factors are absent or, when many factors are present, the solicitation may nevertheless not amount to a tender offer because the missing factors outweigh those present.

Hanson Trust PLC v. SCM Corp., 774 F.2d 47, 57 (2d Cir. 1985). The applicability of the Williams Act, the court concluded, should be determined by looking to its statutory purpose, that is, "whether the particular class of persons affected need the protection of the Act." Yet this seems, at first blush, more tautology than test. Accordingly, the *Hanson* court found the eight factors "relevant for purposes of determining whether a given solicitation amounts to a tender offer." The court also declared that:

> An offering to those who are shown to be able to fend for themselves is a transaction "not involving any public offering." Similarly, since the purpose of § 14(d) is to protect the ill-informed solicitee, the question of whether a solicitation constitutes a "tender offer" within the meaning of § 14(d) turns on whether, viewing the transaction in the light of the totality of circumstances, there appears to be a likelihood that unless the pre-acquisition filing strictures of that statute are followed there will be a substantial risk that solicitees will lack information needed to make a carefully considered appraisal of the proposal put before them.

Other courts have continued to recognize the *Wellman* eight-factor test in determining whether an outsider's bid for control constitutes a tender offer.

Clearfield Bank & Trust Co. v. Omega Fin. Corp., 65 F. Supp. 2d 325, 337–38 (W.D. Pa. 1999).

Once it has been determined that a tender offer exists, mandatory disclosure rules and anti-fraud protections become applicable to the transaction (just as they do for proxy solicitations and going-private transactions, for example). Key mandatory disclosure rules relate to:

- the "early warning" system required by Section 13(d) of, and Rule 13d-1 under, the 1934 Act (which requires beneficial owners of more than five percent of a firm's publicly traded securities to file a statement reporting their ownership and making certain related disclosures); and

- the tender offer statement (and, as applicable) response system established under Sections 13(e) and 14(d) of, and Rules 13e-4, 14d-3, and 14d-9 under, the 1934 Act (which requires, among other things, (1) a tender offeror/acquiror to file a tender offer statement under cover of Schedule TO disclosing information about itself and the terms and conditions of its offer and (2) the subject/target of that offer to file a recommendation or solicitation statement under cover of Schedule 14D-9).

Key fraud protection rules include § 14(e) of, and Rule 14e-3 under, the 1934 Act.

Unfortunately, the elements of a fraud claim under § 14(e) are unclear. However, a number of courts have endeavored to clarify the area in the context of specific cases, including by reference to the elements of other federal securities law claims.

> Section 14(e) was modeled after the antifraud provisions of § 10(b) and Rule 10b-5. Consistent with the § 10(b) jurisprudence and the language of the statute, I conclude that a plaintiff seeking a permanent injunction must prove that the defendant (1) made misstatements or omissions, (2) of material fact, (3) with scienter, (4) in connection with a tender offer.

Clearfield Bank & Trust Co., 65 F. Supp. 2d at 340. The same court went on to construe the concepts of materiality and scienter in the context of a § 14(e) claim, adopting (unsurprisingly, given the court's reference point) the construction of these concepts under Section 10(b) and Rule 10b-5. *Id.* at 341-44.

4. Going Private Transactions

a. State Law Regulation

State corporate law, through fiduciary duty litigation, regulates transactions in which public company shareholders are cashed out of their publicly traded equity interests. Most of these transactions are analyzed in traditional fiduciary duty actions in which the business judgment rule applies. In many of these transactions, a public company target corporation is acquired by a single acquiror, resulting in the target "going dark" or "going private" — deregistering as a public company. State law issues multiply when a publicly held company is acquired for cash consideration in a two-step transaction. Known variously as two-step mergers, two-tier offers, squeeze-out mergers, and cash-out mergers, these transactions consist of (i) a front-end tender offer in which at least a majority (and ideally more than 90%) of the target corporation's publicly traded shares are acquired followed by (ii) a back-end merger. As you may recall, a two-step transaction was at issue in the *Cede & Co. v. Technicolor, Inc.* case excerpted in Chapter 15 as part of the description of valuation issues in appraisal proceedings.

In fact, one state corporate law issue in these types of transactions is whether shareholders should be able to seek a remedy for breach of fiduciary duty at all, given that shareholders have the statutory right to dissent from the merger and seek an appraisal of their shares. Delaware law has drifted back and forth on this question, having both, at times, allowed actions for breach of fiduciary duty relating to cash-out mergers (at least when the plaintiff alleged that the transaction did not have a valid business purpose) and, at times, determined that appraisal was the exclusive remedy for disgruntled shareholders under these circumstances, and finally (and again) having permitted actions to be brought for breach of fiduciary duty.

A second state corporate law issue in these cases involves the appropriate standard of review. In a two-step transaction, after shares are taken down by the acquiror in the tender offer, the acquiror has a controlling interest in the target. Accordingly, the acquiror then has the ability to elect its own designees as directors and can control the target's board and shareholder votes on the merger. Therefore, the board's approval of the merger is likely to be tainted with potential self-interest. Accordingly, it seems inappropriate to apply the threshold presumptions of the business judgment rule in these circumstances.

The seminal case in this area, *Weinberger v. UOP*, is excerpted below. Note, as you review the opinion, how it addresses:

- the availability of an action for breach of fiduciary duty, and the remedy associated with a successful action for breach of fiduciary duty, in the cash-out merger context; and

- the appropriate standard of — and process for — review of fiduciary duty claims arising out of a cash-out merger.

WEINBERGER v. UOP
Supreme Court of Delaware
457 A.2d 701 (Del. 1983)

MOORE, J.

This post-trial appeal was reheard en banc from a decision of the Court of Chancery. It was brought by the class action plaintiff below, a former shareholder of UOP, Inc., who challenged the elimination of UOP's minority shareholders by a cash-out merger between UOP and its majority owner, The Signal Companies, Inc. Originally, the defendants in this action were Signal, UOP, certain officers and directors of those companies, and UOP's investment banker, Lehman Brothers Kuhn Loeb, Inc. The present Chancellor held that the terms of the merger were fair to the plaintiff and the other minority shareholders of UOP. Accordingly, he entered judgment in favor of the defendants.

Numerous points were raised by the parties, but we address only the following questions presented by the trial court's opinion:

1) The plaintiff's duty to plead sufficient facts demonstrating the unfairness of the challenged merger;

2) The burden of proof upon the parties where the merger has been approved by the purportedly informed vote of a majority of the minority shareholders;

3) The fairness of the merger in terms of adequacy of the defendants' disclosures to the minority shareholders;

4) The fairness of the merger in terms of adequacy of the price paid for the minority shares and the remedy appropriate to that issue; and

5) The continued force and effect of *Singer v. Magnavox Co.*, Del. Supr., 380 A.2d 969, 980 (1977), and its progeny.

In ruling for the defendants, the Chancellor re-stated his earlier conclusion that the plaintiff in a suit challenging a cash-out merger must allege specific acts of fraud, misrepresentation, or other items of misconduct to demonstrate the unfairness of the merger terms to the minority. We approve this rule and affirm it.

The Chancellor also held that even though the ultimate burden of proof is on the majority shareholder to show by a preponderance of the evidence that the transaction is fair, it is first the burden of the plaintiff attacking the merger to demonstrate some basis for invoking the fairness obligation. We agree with that principle. However, where corporate action has been approved by an informed vote of a majority of the minority shareholders, we conclude that the burden entirely shifts to the plaintiff to show that the transaction was unfair to the minority. But in all this, the burden clearly remains on those relying on the vote to show that they completely disclosed all material facts relevant to the transaction.

Here, the record does not support a conclusion that the minority stockholder vote was an informed one. Material information, necessary to acquaint those shareholders with the bargaining positions of Signal and UOP, was withheld under circumstances amounting to a breach of fiduciary duty. We therefore conclude that this merger does not meet the test of fairness, at least as we address that concept, and no burden thus shifted to the plaintiff by reason of the minority shareholder vote. Accordingly, we reverse and remand for further proceedings consistent herewith.

In considering the nature of the remedy available under our law to minority shareholders in a cash-out merger, we believe that it is, and hereafter should be, an appraisal under 8 Del. C. § 262 as hereinafter construed. We therefore overrule *Lynch v. Vickers Energy Corp.*, Del. Supr., 429 A.2d 497 (1981) (*Lynch II*) to the extent that it purports to limit a stockholder's monetary relief to a specific damage formula. But to give full effect to section 262 within the framework of the General Corporation Law we adopt a more liberal, less rigid and stylized, approach to the valuation process than has heretofore been permitted by our courts. While the present state of these proceedings does not admit the plaintiff to the appraisal remedy per se, the practical effect of the remedy we do grant him will be co-extensive with the liberalized valuation and appraisal methods we herein approve for cases coming after this decision.

Our treatment of these matters has necessarily led us to a reconsideration of the business purpose rule announced in the trilogy of *Singer v. Magnavox Co., supra*; *Tanzer v. International General Industries, Inc.*, Del. Supr., 379 A.2d 1121 (1977); and *Roland International Corp. v. Najjar*, Del. Supr., 407 A.2d 1032 (1979). For the reasons hereafter set forth we consider that the business purpose requirement of these cases is no longer the law of Delaware.

I.

. . . Signal became interested in UOP as a possible acquisition. Friendly negotiations ensued, and Signal proposed to acquire a controlling interest in UOP at a price of $ 19 per share. UOP's representatives sought $ 25 per share. In the arm's length bargaining that followed, an understanding was reached whereby Signal agreed to purchase from UOP 1,500,000 shares of UOP's authorized but unissued stock at $ 21 per share.

This purchase was contingent upon Signal making a successful cash tender offer for 4,300,000 publicly held shares of UOP, also at a price of $ 21 per share. This combined method of acquisition permitted Signal to acquire 5,800,000 shares of stock, representing 50.5% of UOP's outstanding shares. The UOP board of directors advised the company's shareholders that it had no objection to Signal's tender offer at that price. Immediately before the announcement of the tender offer, UOP's common stock had been trading on the New York Stock Exchange at a fraction under $ 14 per share.

The . . . resulting tender offer was greatly oversubscribed. However, Signal limited its total purchase of the tendered shares so that, when coupled with the stock bought from UOP, it had achieved its goal of becoming a 50.5% shareholder of UOP.

Although UOP's board consisted of thirteen directors, Signal nominated and elected only six. Of these, five were either directors or employees of Signal. The sixth, a partner in the banking firm of Lazard Freres & Co., had been one of Signal's representatives in the negotiations and bargaining with UOP concerning the tender offer and purchase price of the UOP shares.

However, the president and chief executive officer of UOP retired during 1975, and Signal caused him to be replaced by James V. Crawford, a long-time employee and senior executive vice president of one of Signal's wholly-owned subsidiaries. Crawford succeeded his predecessor on UOP's board of directors and also was made a director of Signal.

By the end of 1977 Signal basically was unsuccessful in finding other suitable investment candidates for its excess cash, and by February 1978 considered that it had no other realistic acquisitions available to it on a friendly basis. Once again its attention turned to UOP.

The trial court found that at the instigation of certain Signal management personnel, including William W. Walkup, its board chairman, and Forrest N. Shumway, its president, a feasibility study was made concerning the possible acquisition of the balance of UOP's outstanding shares. This study was performed by two Signal officers, Charles S. Arledge, vice president (director of planning), and Andrew J. Chitiea, senior vice president (chief financial officer). Messrs. Walkup, Shumway, Arledge and Chitiea were all directors of UOP in addition to their membership on the Signal board.

Arledge and Chitiea concluded that it would be a good investment for Signal to acquire the remaining 49.5% of UOP shares at any price up to $ 24 each. Their report was discussed between Walkup and Shumway who, along with Arledge, Chitiea and Brewster L. Arms, internal counsel for Signal, constituted Signal's senior management. In particular, they talked about the proper price to be paid if the acquisition was pursued, purportedly keeping in mind that as UOP's majority shareholder, Signal owed a fiduciary responsibility to both its own stockholders as well as to UOP's minority. It was ultimately agreed that a meeting of Signal's Executive Committee would be called to propose that Signal acquire the remaining outstanding stock of UOP through a cash-out merger in the range of $ 20 to $ 21 per share.

The Executive Committee meeting was set for February 28, 1978. As a courtesy, UOP's president, Crawford, was invited to attend, although he was not a member of Signal's executive committee. On his arrival, and prior to the meeting, Crawford was asked to meet privately with Walkup and Shumway. He was then told of Signal's plan to acquire full ownership of UOP and was asked for his reaction to the proposed price range of $ 20 to $ 21 per share. Crawford said he thought such a price would be "generous," and that it was certainly one which should be submitted to UOP's minority shareholders for their ultimate consideration. He stated, however, that Signal's 100% ownership could cause internal problems at UOP. He believed that employees would have to be given some assurance of their future place in a fully-owned Signal subsidiary. Otherwise, he feared the departure of essential personnel. Also, many of UOP's key employees had stock option incentive programs which would be wiped out by a merger. Crawford therefore urged that some adjustment would have to be made, such as providing a comparable incentive in Signal's shares, if after the merger he was to maintain his quality of personnel and efficiency at UOP.

Thus, Crawford voiced no objection to the $ 20 to $ 21 price range, nor did he suggest that Signal should consider paying more than $ 21 per share for the minority interests. Later, at the Executive Committee meeting the same factors were discussed, with Crawford repeating the position he earlier took with Walkup and Shumway. Also considered was the 1975 tender offer and the fact that it had been greatly oversub-scribed at $ 21 per share. For many reasons, Signal's management concluded that the acquisition of UOP's minority shares provided the solution to a number of its business problems.

Thus, it was the consensus that a price of $ 20 to $ 21 per share would be fair to both Signal and the minority shareholders of UOP. Signal's executive committee authorized its management "to negotiate" with UOP "for a cash acquisition of the minority ownership in UOP, Inc., with the intention of presenting a proposal to [Signal's] board of directors . . . on March 6, 1978." Immediately after this February 28, 1978 meeting, Signal issued a press release stating:

> The Signal Companies, Inc. and UOP, Inc. are conducting negotiations for the acquisition for cash by Signal of the 49.5 per cent of UOP which it does not presently own, announced Forrest N. Shumway, president and chief executive officer of Signal, and James V. Crawford, UOP president.
>
> Price and other terms of the proposed transaction have not yet been finalized and would be subject to approval of the boards of directors of Signal and UOP, scheduled to meet early next week, the stockholders of UOP and certain federal agencies.

The announcement also referred to the fact that the closing price of UOP's common stock on that day was $ 14.50 per share.

Two days later, on March 2, 1978, Signal issued a second press release stating that its management would recommend a price in the range of $ 20 to $ 21 per share for UOP's 49.5% minority interest. This announcement referred to Signal's earlier statement that "negotiations" were being conducted for the acquisition of the minority shares.

Between Tuesday, February 28, 1978 and Monday, March 6, 1978, a total of four business days, Crawford spoke by telephone with all of UOP's non-Signal, i.e., outside, directors. Also during that period, Crawford retained Lehman Brothers to render a fairness opinion as to the price offered the minority for its stock. He gave two reasons for this choice. First, the time schedule between the announcement and the board meetings was short (by then only three business days) and since Lehman Brothers had been acting as UOP's investment banker for many years, Crawford felt that it would be in the best position to respond on such brief notice. Second, James W. Glanville, a long-time director of UOP and a partner in Lehman Brothers, had acted as a financial advisor to UOP for many years. Crawford believed that Glanville's familiarity with UOP, as a member of its board, would also be of assistance in enabling Lehman Brothers to render a fairness opinion within the existing time constraints.

Crawford telephoned Glanville, who gave his assurance that Lehman Brothers had no conflicts that would prevent it from accepting the task. Glanville's immediate personal reaction was that a price of $ 20 to $ 21 would certainly be fair, since it represented almost a 50% premium over UOP's market price. Glanville sought a $ 250,000 fee for Lehman Brothers' services, but Crawford thought this too much. After further discussions Glanville finally agreed that Lehman Brothers would render its fairness opinion for $ 150,000.

During this period Crawford also had several telephone contacts with Signal officials. In only one of them, however, was the price of the shares discussed. In a conversation with Walkup, Crawford advised that as a result of his communications with UOP's non-Signal directors, it was his feeling that the price would have to be the top of the proposed range, or $ 21 per share, if the approval of UOP's outside directors was to be obtained. But again, he did not seek any price higher than $ 21.

Glanville assembled a three-man Lehman Brothers team to do the work on the fairness opinion. These persons examined relevant documents and information concerning UOP, including its annual reports and its Securities and Exchange Commission filings from 1973 through 1976, as well as its audited financial statements for 1977, its interim reports to shareholders, and its recent and historical market prices and trading volumes. In addition, on Friday, March 3, 1978, two members of the Lehman Brothers team flew to UOP's headquarters in Des Plaines, Illinois, to perform a "due diligence" visit, during the course of which they interviewed Crawford as well as UOP's general counsel, its chief financial officer, and other key executives and personnel.

As a result, the Lehman Brothers team concluded that "the price of either $ 20 or $ 21 would be a fair price for the remaining shares of UOP." They telephoned this impression to Glanville, who was spending the weekend in Vermont.

On Monday morning, March 6, 1978, Glanville and the senior member of the Lehman Brothers team flew to Des Plaines to attend the scheduled UOP directors meeting. Glanville looked over the assembled information during the flight. The two had with them the draft of a "fairness opinion letter" in which the price had been left blank. Either during or immediately prior to the directors' meeting, the two-page "fairness opinion letter" was typed in final form and the price of $ 21 per share was inserted.

On March 6, 1978, both the Signal and UOP boards were convened to consider the proposed merger. Telephone communications were maintained between the two meetings. Walkup, Signal's board chairman, and also a UOP director, attended UOP's meeting with Crawford in order to present Signal's position and answer any questions that UOP's non-Signal directors might have. Arledge and Chitiea, along with Signal's other designees on UOP's board, participated by conference telephone. All of UOP's outside directors attended the meeting either in person or by conference telephone.

First, Signal's board unanimously adopted a resolution authorizing Signal to propose to UOP a cash merger of $ 21 per share as outlined in a certain merger agreement and other supporting documents. This proposal required that the merger be approved by a majority of UOP's outstanding minority shares voting at the stockholders meeting at which the merger would be considered, and that the minority shares voting in favor of the merger, when coupled with Signal's 50.5% interest would have to comprise at least two-thirds of all UOP shares. Otherwise the proposed merger would be deemed disapproved.

UOP's board then considered the proposal. Copies of the agreement were delivered to the directors in attendance, and other copies had been forwarded earlier to the directors participating by telephone. They also had before them UOP financial data for 1974-1977, UOP's most recent financial statements, market price information, and budget projections for 1978. In addition they had Lehman Brothers' hurriedly prepared fairness opinion letter finding the price of $ 21 to be fair. Glanville, the Lehman Brothers

partner, and UOP director, commented on the information that had gone into preparation of the letter.

Signal also suggests that the Arledge-Chitiea feasibility study, indicating that a price
of up to $ 24 per share would be a "good investment" for Signal, was discussed at the
UOP directors' meeting. The Chancellor made no such finding, and our independent
review of the record, detailed *infra*, satisfies us by a preponderance of the evidence that
there was no discussion of this document at UOP's board meeting. Furthermore, it is
clear beyond peradventure that nothing in that report was ever disclosed to UOP's
minority shareholders prior to their approval of the merger.

After consideration of Signal's proposal, Walkup and Crawford left the meeting to
permit a free and uninhibited exchange between UOP's non-Signal directors. Upon their
return a resolution to accept Signal's offer was then proposed and adopted. While
Signal's men on UOP's board participated in various aspects of the meeting, they
abstained from voting. However, the minutes show that each of them "if voting would
have voted yes."

On March 7, 1978, UOP sent a letter to its shareholders advising them of the action
taken by UOP's board with respect to Signal's offer. This document pointed out, among
other things, that on February 28, 1978 "both companies had announced negotiations
were being conducted."

Despite the swift board action of the two companies, the merger was not submitted
to UOP's shareholders until their annual meeting on May 26, 1978. In the notice of that
meeting and proxy statement sent to shareholders in May, UOP's management and
board urged that the merger be approved. The proxy statement also advised:

> The price was determined after *discussions* between James V. Crawford, a
> director of Signal and Chief Executive Officer of UOP, and officers of Signal
> which took place during meetings on February 28, 1978, and in the course of
> several subsequent telephone conversations. (Emphasis added.)

In the original draft of the proxy statement the word "negotiations" had been used
rather than "discussions." However, when the Securities and Exchange Commission
sought details of the "negotiations" as part of its review of these materials, the term was
deleted and the word "discussions" was substituted. The proxy statement indicated that
the vote of UOP's board in approving the merger had been unanimous. It also advised
the shareholders that Lehman Brothers had given its opinion that the merger price of
$ 21 per share was fair to UOP's minority. However, it did not disclose the hurried
method by which this conclusion was reached.

As of the record date of UOP's annual meeting, there were 11,488,302 shares of UOP
common stock outstanding, 5,688,302 of which were owned by the minority. At the
meeting only 56%, or 3,208,652, of the minority shares were voted. Of these, 2,953,812,
or 51.9% of the total minority, voted for the merger, and 254,840 voted against it. When
Signal's stock was added to the minority shares voting in favor, a total of 76.2% of UOP's
outstanding shares approved the merger while only 2.2% opposed it.

By its terms the merger became effective on May 26, 1978, and each share of UOP's
stock held by the minority was automatically converted into a right to receive $ 21 cash.

II.

A.

A primary issue mandating reversal is the preparation by two UOP directors,
Arledge and Chitiea, of their feasibility study for the exclusive use and benefit of Signal.
This document was of obvious significance to both Signal and UOP. Using UOP data, it
described the advantages to Signal of ousting the minority at a price range of $ 21-$ 24
per share. Mr. Arledge, one of the authors, outlined the benefits to Signal:

Purpose Of The Merger

1) Provides an outstanding investment opportunity for Signal — (Better than any recent acquisition we have seen.)

2) Increases Signal's earnings.

3) Facilitates the flow of resources between Signal and its subsidiaries — (Big factor — works both ways.)

4) Provides cost savings potential for Signal and UOP.

5) Improves the percentage of Signal's 'operating earnings' as opposed to 'holding company earnings.'

6) Simplifies the understanding of Signal.

7) Facilitates technological exchange among Signal's subsidiaries.

8) Eliminates potential conflicts of interest.

Having written those words, solely for the use of Signal, it is clear from the record that neither Arledge nor Chitiea shared this report with their fellow directors of UOP. We are satisfied that no one else did either. This conduct hardly meets the fiduciary standards applicable to such a transaction. . . .

Mr. Crawford, UOP's president, could not recall that any documents, other than a draft of the merger agreement, were sent to UOP's directors before the March 6, 1978 UOP meeting. Mr. Chitiea, an author of the report, testified that it was made available to Signal's directors, but to his knowledge it was not circulated to the outside directors of UOP. He specifically testified that he "didn't share" that information with the outside directors of UOP with whom he served.

None of UOP's outside directors who testified stated that they had seen this document. The minutes of the UOP board meeting do not identify the Arledge-Chitiea report as having been delivered to UOP's outside directors. This is particularly significant since the minutes describe in considerable detail the materials that actually were distributed. While these minutes recite Mr. Walkup's presentation of the Signal offer, they do not mention the Arledge-Chitiea report or any disclosure that Signal considered a price of up to $ 24 to be a good investment. If Mr. Walkup had in fact provided such important information to UOP's outside directors, it is logical to assume that these carefully drafted minutes would disclose it. The post-trial briefs of Signal and UOP contain a thorough description of the documents purportedly available to their boards at the March 6, 1978, meetings. Although the Arledge-Chitiea report is specifically identified as being available to the Signal directors, there is no mention of it being among the documents submitted to the UOP board. Even when queried at a prior oral argument before this Court, counsel for Signal did not claim that the Arledge-Chitiea report had been disclosed to UOP's outside directors. Instead, he chose to belittle its contents. This was the same approach taken before us at the last oral argument.

Actually, it appears that a three-page summary of figures was given to all UOP directors. Its first page is identical to one page of the Arledge-Chitiea report, but this dealt with nothing more than a justification of the $ 21 price. Significantly, the contents of this three-page summary are what the minutes reflect Mr. Walkup told the UOP board. However, nothing contained in either the minutes or this three-page summary reflects Signal's study regarding the $ 24 price.

The Arledge-Chitiea report speaks for itself in supporting the Chancellor's finding that a price of up to $ 24 was a "good investment" for Signal. It shows that a return on the investment at $ 21 would be 15.7% versus 15.5% at $ 24 per share. This was a difference of only two-tenths of one percent, while it meant over $ 17,000,000 to the minority. Under such circumstances, paying UOP's minority shareholders $ 24 would have had relatively little long-term effect on Signal, and the Chancellor's findings concerning the benefit to Signal, even at a price of $ 24, were obviously correct.

Certainly, this was a matter of material significance to UOP and its shareholders. Since the study was prepared by two UOP directors, using UOP information for the exclusive benefit of Signal, and nothing whatever was done to disclose it to the outside UOP directors or the minority shareholders, a question of breach of fiduciary duty arises. This problem occurs because there were common Signal-UOP directors participating, at least to some extent, in the UOP board's decision-making processes without full disclosure of the conflicts they faced.

B.

In assessing this situation, the Court of Chancery was required to:

> examine what information defendants had and to measure it against what they gave to the minority stockholders, in a context in which 'complete candor' is required. In other words, the limited function of the Court was to determine whether defendants had disclosed all information in their possession germane to the transaction in issue. And by 'germane' we mean, for present purposes, information such as a reasonable shareholder would consider important in deciding whether to sell or retain stock.

*   *   *

> . . . Completeness, not adequacy, is both the norm and the mandate under present circumstances.

Lynch v. Vickers Energy Corp., Del. Supr., 383 A.2d 278, 281 (1977) (*Lynch I*). This is merely stating in another way the long-existing principle of Delaware law that these Signal designated directors on UOP's board still owed UOP and its shareholders an uncompromising duty of loyalty. The classic language of *Guth v. Loft, Inc.,* Del. Supr., 23 Del. Ch. 255, 5 A.2d 503, 510 (1939), requires no embellishment:

> A public policy, existing through the years, and derived from a profound knowledge of human characteristics and motives, has established a rule that demands of a corporate officer or director, peremptorily and inexorably, the most scrupulous observance of his duty, not only affirmatively to protect the interests of the corporation committed to his charge, but also to refrain from doing anything that would work injury to the corporation, or to deprive it of profit or advantage which his skill and ability might properly bring to it, or to enable it to make in the reasonable and lawful exercise of its powers. The rule that requires an undivided and unselfish loyalty to the corporation demands that there shall be no conflict between duty and self-interest.

Given the absence of any attempt to structure this transaction on an arm's length basis, Signal cannot escape the effects of the conflicts it faced, particularly when its designees on UOP's board did not totally abstain from participation in the matter. There is no "safe harbor" for such divided loyalties in Delaware. When directors of a Delaware corporation are on both sides of a transaction, they are required to demonstrate their utmost good faith and the most scrupulous inherent fairness of the bargain. The requirement of fairness is unflinching in its demand that where one stands on both sides of a transaction, he has the burden of establishing its entire fairness, sufficient to pass the test of careful scrutiny by the courts.

There is no dilution of this obligation where one holds dual or multiple directorships, as in a parent-subsidiary context. Thus, individuals who act in a dual capacity as directors of two corporations, one of whom is parent and the other subsidiary, owe the same duty of good management to both corporations, and in the absence of an independent negotiating structure . . . , or the directors' total abstention from any participation in the matter, this duty is to be exercised in light of what is best for both companies. The record demonstrates that Signal has not met this obligation.

C.

The concept of fairness has two basic aspects: fair dealing and fair price. The former embraces questions of when the transaction was timed, how it was initiated, structured, negotiated, disclosed to the directors, and how the approvals of the directors and the stockholders were obtained. The latter aspect of fairness relates to the economic and financial considerations of the proposed merger, including all relevant factors: assets, market value, earnings, future prospects, and any other elements that affect the intrinsic or inherent value of a company's stock. However, the test for fairness is not a bifurcated one as between fair dealing and price. All aspects of the issue must be examined as a whole since the question is one of entire fairness. However, in a non-fraudulent transaction we recognize that price may be the preponderant consideration outweighing other features of the merger. Here, we address the two basic aspects of fairness separately because we find reversible error as to both.

D.

Part of fair dealing is the obvious duty of candor . . . . Moreover, one possessing superior knowledge may not mislead any stockholder by use of corporate information to which the latter is not privy. Delaware has long imposed this duty even upon persons who are not corporate officers or directors, but who nonetheless are privy to matters of interest or significance to their company. With the well-established Delaware law on the subject, and the Court of Chancery's findings of fact here, it is inevitable that the obvious conflicts posed by Arledge and Chitiea's preparation of their "feasibility study," derived from UOP information, for the sole use and benefit of Signal, cannot pass muster.

The Arledge-Chitiea report is but one aspect of the element of fair dealing. How did this merger evolve? It is clear that it was entirely initiated by Signal. The serious time constraints under which the principals acted were all set by Signal. It had not found a suitable outlet for its excess cash and considered UOP a desirable investment, particularly since it was now in a position to acquire the whole company for itself. For whatever reasons, and they were only Signal's, the entire transaction was presented to and approved by UOP's board within four business days. Standing alone, this is not necessarily indicative of any lack of fairness by a majority shareholder. It was what occurred, or more properly, what did not occur, during this brief period that makes the time constraints imposed by Signal relevant to the issue of fairness.

The structure of the transaction, again, was Signal's doing. So far as negotiations were concerned, it is clear that they were modest at best. Crawford, Signal's man at UOP, never really talked price with Signal, except to accede to its management's statements on the subject, and to convey to Signal the UOP outside directors' view that as between the $ 20-$ 21 range under consideration, it would have to be $ 21. The latter is not a surprising outcome, but hardly arm's length negotiations. Only the protection of benefits for UOP's key employees and the issue of Lehman Brothers' fee approached any concept of bargaining.

As we have noted, the matter of disclosure to the UOP directors was wholly flawed by the conflicts of interest raised by the Arledge-Chitiea report. All of those conflicts were resolved by Signal in its own favor without divulging any aspect of them to UOP.

This cannot but undermine a conclusion that this merger meets any reasonable test of fairness. The outside UOP directors lacked one material piece of information generated by two of their colleagues, but shared only with Signal. True, the UOP board had the Lehman Brothers' fairness opinion, but that firm has been blamed by the plaintiff for the hurried task it performed, when more properly the responsibility for this lies with Signal. There was no disclosure of the circumstances surrounding the rather cursory preparation of the Lehman Brothers' fairness opinion. Instead, the impression was given UOP's minority that a careful study had been made, when in fact speed was the hallmark, and Mr. Glanville, Lehman's partner in charge of the matter, and also a UOP director, having spent the weekend in Vermont, brought a draft of the "fairness opinion letter" to the UOP directors' meeting on March 6, 1978 with the price left blank. We can only conclude from the record that the rush imposed on Lehman Brothers by Signal's timetable contributed to the difficulties under which this investment banking firm attempted to perform its responsibilities. Yet, none of this was disclosed to UOP's minority.

Finally, the minority stockholders were denied the critical information that Signal considered a price of $ 24 to be a good investment. Since this would have meant over $ 17,000,000 more to the minority, we cannot conclude that the shareholder vote was an informed one. Under the circumstances, an approval by a majority of the minority was meaningless.

Given these particulars and the Delaware law on the subject, the record does not establish that this transaction satisfies any reasonable concept of fair dealing, and the Chancellor's findings in that regard must be reversed.

E.

Turning to the matter of price, plaintiff . . . challenges its fairness. His evidence was that on the date the merger was approved the stock was worth at least $ 26 per share. In support, he offered the testimony of a chartered investment analyst who used two basic approaches to valuation: a comparative analysis of the premium paid over market in ten other tender offer-merger combinations, and a discounted cash flow analysis.

. . . [T]he Chancellor perceived that the approach to valuation was the same as that in an appraisal proceeding. Consistent with precedent, he rejected plaintiff's method of proof and accepted defendants' evidence of value as being in accord with practice under prior case law. This means that the so-called "Delaware block" or weighted average method was employed wherein the elements of value, i.e., assets, market price, earnings, etc., were assigned a particular weight and the resulting amounts added to determine the value per share. This procedure has been in use for decades. However, to the extent it excludes other generally accepted techniques used in the financial community and the courts, it is now clearly outmoded. It is time we recognize this in appraisal and other stock valuation proceedings and bring our law current on the subject. . . .

Accordingly, the standard "Delaware block" or weighted average method of valuation, formerly employed in appraisal and other stock valuation cases, shall no longer exclusively control such proceedings. We believe that a more liberal approach must include proof of value by any techniques or methods which are generally considered acceptable in the financial community and otherwise admissible in court, subject only to our interpretation of 8 Del. C. § 262(h), *infra*. This will obviate the very structured and mechanistic procedure that has heretofore governed such matters.

Fair price obviously requires consideration of all relevant factors involving the value of a company. This has long been the law of Delaware as stated in *Tri-Continental Corp.*, 74 A.2d at 72:

> The basic concept of value under the appraisal statute is that the stockholder is entitled to be paid for that which has been taken from him, viz., his proportionate interest in a going concern. By value of the stockholder's proportionate interest in the corporate enterprise is meant the true or intrinsic value of his stock which has been taken by the merger. In determining what figure represents this true or intrinsic value, the appraiser and the courts must take into consideration all factors and elements which reasonably might enter into the fixing of value. Thus, market value, asset value, dividends, earning prospects, the nature of the enterprise and any other facts which were known

or which could be ascertained as of the date of merger and which throw any light on *future prospects* of the merged corporation are not only pertinent to an inquiry as to the value of the dissenting stockholders' interest, but *must be considered* by the agency fixing the value. (Emphasis added.)

This is not only in accord with the realities of present day affairs, but it is thoroughly consonant with the purpose and intent of our statutory law. Under 8 Del. C. § 262(h), the Court of Chancery:

shall appraise the shares, determining their *fair* value exclusive of any element of value arising from the accomplishment or expectation of the merger, together with a fair rate of interest, if any, to be paid upon the amount determined to be the *fair* value. In determining such *fair* value, the Court shall take into account *all relevant factors* . . . (Emphasis added)

. . . It is significant that section 262 now mandates the determination of "fair" value based upon "all relevant factors." Only the speculative elements of value that may arise from the "accomplishment or expectation" of the merger are excluded. We take this to be a very narrow exception to the appraisal process, designed to eliminate use of *pro forma* data and projections of a speculative variety relating to the completion of a merger. But elements of future value, including the nature of the enterprise, which are known or susceptible of proof as of the date of the merger and not the product of speculation, may be considered. When the trial court deems it appropriate, fair value also includes any damages, resulting from the taking, which the stockholders sustain as a class. If that was not the case, then the obligation to consider "all relevant factors" in the valuation process would be eroded. We are supported in this view not only by *Tri-Continental Corp.*, 74 A.2d at 72, but also by the evolutionary amendments to section 262.

Prior to an amendment in 1976, the earlier relevant provision of section 262 stated:

(f) The appraiser shall determine the value of the stock of the stockholders . . . The Court shall by its decree determine the value of the stock of the stockholders entitled to payment therefor . . .

The first references to "fair" value occurred in a 1976 amendment to section 262(f), which provided:

(f) . . . the Court shall appraise the shares, determining their fair value exclusively of any element of value arising from the accomplishment or expectation of the merger. . . .

It was not until the 1981 amendment to section 262 that the reference to "fair value" was repeatedly emphasized and the statutory mandate that the Court "take into account all relevant factors" appeared [section 262(h)]. Clearly, there is a legislative intent to fully compensate shareholders for whatever their loss may be, subject only to the narrow limitation that one can not take speculative effects of the merger into account. . . .

[T]he provisions of 8 Del. C. § 262, as herein construed, respecting the scope of an appraisal and the means for perfecting the same, shall govern the financial remedy available to minority shareholders in a cash-out merger. Thus, we return to the well established principles of *Stauffer v. Standard Brands, Inc.*, Del. Supr., 41 Del. Ch. 7, 187 A.2d 78 (1962) and *David J. Greene & Co. v. Schenley Industries, Inc.*, Del. Ch., 281 A.2d 30 (1971), mandating a stockholder's recourse to the basic remedy of an appraisal. . . .

REVERSED AND REMANDED.

NOTES AND QUESTIONS

1. Weinberger *Case on Remand.* After performing its valuation in accordance with the Supreme Court's opinion, the Chancery Court awarded the *Weinberger* plaintiffs $ 1.00 in monetary damages on top of the merger consideration they already had received. *Weinberger v. UOP, Inc.*, 1985 Del. Ch. LEXIS 378 (Del. Ch. Jan. 30, 1985). This award later was affirmed by the Delaware Supreme Court. *Weinberger v. UOP, Inc.*, 497 A.2d 792 (Del. 1985).

2. *Damages Based on an Appraisal Valuation.* The *Weinberger* court takes pains to note that a shareholder's financial remedy for a breach of fiduciary duty in connection with a cash-out merger is equal to the fair value of the shareholder's shares computed in accordance with DGCL § 262. Does this make sense? Explain your answer. Is the shareholder's remedy in a cash-out merger easier or harder to calculate after *Weinberger*?

3. *A Different Rule for Short-form Mergers.* When a tender offer at the front end of a two-step acquisition results in the acquiror's ownership of more than 90% of the target's outstanding shares, state law typically allows for an abbreviated back-end merger process. Known as a short-form (or parent-subsidiary) merger, this back-end transaction does not require a vote of minority shareholders. *See, e.g.,* DGCL § 253; MBCA § 11.05. After *Weinberger*, questions emerged as to whether the same standard of review would apply in a case involving a short-form merger. In 2001, the Delaware Supreme Court answered that question.

[W]e must decide whether a minority stockholder may challenge a short-form merger by seeking equitable relief through an entire fairness claim. Under settled principles, a parent corporation and its directors undertaking a short-form merger are self-dealing fiduciaries who should be required to establish entire fairness, including fair dealing and fair price. The problem is that § 253 authorizes a summary procedure that is inconsistent with any reasonable notion of fair dealing. In a short-form merger, there is no agreement of merger negotiated by two companies; there is only a unilateral act — a decision by the parent company that its 90% owned subsidiary shall no longer exist as a separate entity. The minority stockholders receive no advance notice of the merger; their directors do not consider or approve it; and there is no vote. Those who object are given the right to obtain fair value for their shares through appraisal.

The equitable claim plainly conflicts with the statute. If a corporate fiduciary follows the truncated process authorized by § 253, it will not be able to establish the fair dealing prong of entire fairness. If, instead, the corporate fiduciary sets up negotiating committees, hires independent financial and legal experts, etc., then it will have lost the very benefit provided by the statute — a simple, fast, and inexpensive process for accomplishing a merger. We resolve this conflict by giving effect the intent of the General Assembly. In order to serve its purpose, § 253 must be construed to obviate the requirement to establish entire fairness.

Thus, we . . . hold that, absent fraud or illegality, appraisal is the exclusive remedy available to a minority stockholder who objects to a short-form merger. In doing so, we . . . reaffirm *Weinberger's* statements about the scope of appraisal. The determination of fair value must be based on *all* relevant factors, including damages and elements of future value, where appropriate. So, for example, if the merger was timed to take advantage of a depressed market, or a low point in the company's cyclical earnings, or to precede an anticipated positive development, the appraised value may be adjusted to account for those factors. We recognize that these are the types of issues frequently raised in entire fairness claims, and we have held that claims for unfair dealing cannot be litigated in an appraisal. But our prior holdings simply explained that equitable claims may not be engrafted onto a statutory appraisal proceeding; stockholders may not receive rescissionary relief in an appraisal. Those decisions should not be read to restrict the elements of value that properly may be considered in an appraisal.

Although fiduciaries are not required to establish entire fairness in a short-form merger, the duty of full disclosure remains, in the context of this request for stockholder action. Where the only choice for the minority stock-holders is whether to accept the merger consideration or seek appraisal, they must be given all the factual information that is material to that decision. The Court of Chancery carefully considered plaintiffs' disclosure claims and applied settled law in rejecting them. We affirm this aspect of the appeal on the basis of the trial court's decision.

Glassman v. Unocal Exploration Corp., 777 A.2d 242, 247–48 (Del. 2001).

4. *A Perplexing Difference in Standards of Review.* Many have questioned the reasoning that resulted in different standards of review being applied in *Weinberger* and *Glassman* (described in Note 3 above). Is there a way in which the different approaches of the *Weinberger* and *Glassman* courts can be harmonized? *See* Clark W. Furlow, *Back to Basics: Harmonizing Delaware's Law Governing Going Private Transactions*, 40 AKRON L. REV. 85 (2007).

5. *At the Intersection of* Weinberger, Glassman, *and* Technicolor. Two scholars highlight the importance of the appraisal remedy in current transaction planning and litigation, while at the same time raising important questions.

> The Weinberger decision in 1983 revolutionized appraisal law, and like many revolutions left an array of messy puzzles that persist to this day. One was its dictum concerning the statutory prohibition against including gains from mergers in calculating the fair value of the firm in appraisal. Despite the literal clarity and breadth of the statutory prohibition, the court opined that the exclusion is "a very narrow exception to the appraisal process, designed to eliminate use of . . . projections of a speculative variety relating to the completion of the merger." It was not until Technicolor that both the Delaware Court of Chancery and the Delaware Supreme Court addressed the Weinberger ruling and its tension with the literal language of the statutory exclusion. While the court of chancery attempted to resolve that tension, the supreme court rejected the Chancellor's reasoning and reaffirmed its earlier ruling, without providing much guidance for resolving the uncertainty as to the scope of the statutory valuation exclusion.

> The issue is a significant one. Appraisal is becoming an increasingly important remedy in light of the growth of going private mergers, the fact that appraisal is the exclusive remedy in short-form mergers after Glassman, and the growing use of tender offers as the mechanism of choice for completing a merger. In all these cases, it is the squeeze-out cash merger (along with the mergers involving a close corporation) that gives rise to most of the appraisal cases. What then to make of the supreme court's ruling in Weinberger? What types of gains that occur after such a merger can be included in valuing a firm in appraisal? Is the line drawn between "speculative" and "nonspeculative" gains, as the court suggested, or should the line be drawn differently?

Lawrence A. Hamermesh & Michael L. Wachter, *The Fair Value of Cornfields in Delaware Appraisal Law*, 31 IOWA J. CORP. L. 119, 121 (2005).

b. Federal Law Regulation

Federal regulators take an interest in change of control transactions when they result in the removal of a corporation's publicly traded shares from the public securities trading markets. Typically, this happens when a fundamental corporate change or business combination transaction concentrates formerly dispersed public shareholdings in the hands of one shareholder or a small number of shareholders. These types of change of control transactions are referred to as "going private" transactions.

Rule 13e-3, adopted by the SEC under Section 13(e) of the 1934 Act, governs these transactions, subject to specified exceptions. Paragraph (a)(3) of the Rule defines going private transactions — known as Rule 13e-3 transactions — using a two-step test that involves classifying both the transaction and its effects. First, the transaction must be of an enumerated type, including:

"a purchase of any equity security by the issuer of such security or by an affiliate of such issuer;"

"a tender offer for or request or invitation for tenders of any equity security made by the issuer of such class of securities or by an affiliate of such issuer;" or

"a solicitation subject to Regulation 14A . . . of any proxy, consent or authorization of . . . , or a distribution subject to Regulation 14C . . . of information statements to, any equity security holder by the issuer of the class of securities or by an affiliate of such issuer, in connection with:"

- "a merger, consolidation, reclassification, recapitalization, reorganization or similar corporate transaction of an issuer or between an issuer (or its subsidiaries) and its affiliate;"

- "a sale of substantially all the assets of an issuer to its affiliate or group of affiliates; or"

- "a reverse stock split of any class of equity securities of the issuer involving the purchase of fractional interests."

Second, the enumerated transaction must cause a class of public equity securities of the issuer to be held of record by less than 300 persons, or cause a nationally listed or quoted class of equity securities of the issuer to cease being listed on any national securities exchange or authorized to be quoted on an inter-dealer quotation system of any registered national securities association. In other words, the transaction must result in the withdrawal of the corporation's publicly traded securities from the public markets.

This two-part definition makes apparent the fact that going private transactions come in many different, well known forms. For example, when a financial buyer acquires control of a publicly held corporation using debt that is secured by the acquired corporation's assets, we call that transaction a "leveraged buyout" or "LBO." And when a leveraged buyout results in management owning a significant interest in the corporation, we call the transaction a "management buyout" or "MBO." In nearly all cases, LBOs and MBOs are going private transactions.

Going private transactions, like other transactions regulated under the federal securities laws, are subject to both mandatory disclosure and anti-fraud regulation under Rule 13e-3. (Rule 13e-3, like the tender offer rules described *supra*, is adopted by the SEC under the Williams Act, legislation enacted by Congress in the late 1960s in response to increasing takeover activity in public companies.) Paragraphs (d), (e), and (f) of the Rule govern mandatory disclosure obligations of the issuer or affiliate engaged in the going private transaction, including the filing with the SEC of a Schedule 13E-3 Transaction Statement and the dissemination of required information to shareholders. Paragraphs (b) and (c) contain the Rule's fraud proscriptions, including (in paragraph (b)(1) of the Rule) an anti-fraud provision that uses language substantially similar to that used in Rule 10b-5 under the 1934 Act, the broad-based federal anti-fraud rule relating to purchases and sales of securities.

Certain going private transactions are not, however, subject to regulation under Rule 13e-3 by its very terms. Paragraph (g) of the Rule governs these exceptions. *See, e.g.,*

Rosenberg v. Nabors Indus., 2002 U.S. Dist. LEXIS 14255 (S.D. Tex. June 14, 2002).

NOTES AND QUESTIONS

1. *Contract Drafting and Risk Allocation in Change of Control Transactions.* In a negotiated change of control transaction, parties can manage regulatory responsibilities and effects, and otherwise adjust the allocation of risks among themselves through careful drafting of the defining agreement. Law school courses in corporate finance, mergers and acquisitions, transaction planning, and the like often offer the opportunity to learn about the structure and drafting of these agreements — merger agreements, asset purchase agreements, and share (or stock) purchase agreements.

Parties to business combination agreements contend with many interesting drafting issues in balancing and allocating risk. Perhaps none are more important than those that involve allocating the risk of non-consummation of the transaction itself (which must be grappled with whenever the closing of the business combination is to occur some period of time after the merger or acquisition agreement is signed and delivered). At what point should a party to a negotiated business combination be able to walk away from the deal (fail to close) without breaching the contract? What are the rights, liabilities, and remedies of the other party or parties when one party exercises a right to walk away? These questions should be asked and answered as the parties negotiate and draft the relevant contract. However, even with clear and comprehensive drafting, the parties may end up in litigation over whether a party to the business combination agreement has appropriately exercised its termination rights under the agreement.

Some of the more interesting cases in this area emanate from conditions to the closing of a negotiated merger or acquisition transaction. Of particular note are cases interpreting "material adverse change" ("MAC") clauses. A closing condition that invokes a MAC clause typically allows an acquiror to walk away from the transaction if there is a material adverse change in the business of the target. Merger and acquisition agreements vary widely in their handling of this type of closing condition. Some attempt to define what is "material" and "adverse" in rather specific terms (by the use of definitions and exceptions); others leave things rather open-ended, allowing courts to define concepts and fill gaps. Both kinds of agreements have resulted in interesting court opinions that attempt to balance the intentions, expectations, and interests of the parties. *See* Kenneth A. Adams, *A Legal-Usage Analysis of "Material Adverse Change" Provisions*, 10 FORDHAM J. CORP. & FIN. L. 9 (2004); Yair Y. Galil, *MAC Clauses in a Materially Adversely Changed Economy*, 2002 COLUM. BUS. L. REV. 846; Kari K. Hall, *How Big is the MAC?: Material Adverse Change Clauses In Today's Acquisition Environment*, 71 U. CIN. L. REV. 1061 (2003); *Bradley D. Peters, Material Adverse Change Clauses Following the* Tyson *Decision*, 3 TRANSACTIONS: TENN. J. BUS. L. 19 (2001). Although the Delaware courts are leaders in this area, other state courts also have issued important opinions construing MAC clauses. *See, e.g., In re IBP S'holders Litig.*, 789 A.2d 14, 21 (Del. Ch. 2001) (Delaware); *Pine State Creamery Co. v. Land-O-Sun Dairies, Inc.*, No. 98-2441, 1999 U.S. App. LEXIS 31529 at *2 (4th Cir. Dec. 5, 1999) (North Carolina); *Allegheny Energy, Inc. v. DQE, Inc.*, 74 F. Supp. 2d 482, 485 (W. D. Pa. 1999) (Pennsylvania); Bradley C. Sagraves & Bobak Talebian, *Material Adverse Change Clauses In Tennessee:* Genesco v. Finish Line, 9 TRANSACTIONS: TENN. J. BUS. L. 343 (2008) (Tennessee).

2. *Linkage to Theories of Corporate Control.* Review the materials at the beginning of the chapter regarding theories of corporate control, including the market for corporate control. How do the types of change of control transactions reflect or use these theories of corporate control? How does the regulation (under state and federal law) of these transactions interact with theories of corporate control?

C. DEFENDING THE CORPORATE BASTION

As earlier noted, both proxy contests and tender offers can accomplish changes in control of a target corporation without consultation with or the consent of the target's board of directors or officers. It is the contact of a third-party acquiror with, and the resultant actions of, the target's shareholders (rather than negotiation with management) that effectuate these types of unsolicited changes of corporate control. Often, in fact, proxy contests (or other uses of the proxy process) and tender offers (or other share acquisitions) are used together to achieve a change of control. For example, an acquiror may acquire shares of the target (through a tender offer or otherwise) and then use the amassed shares to effectuate (perhaps by the call of a special meeting) a removal and replacement of directors in a proxy contest.

Some of the change-of-control scenarios designed and implemented by acquirors are abusive in that they coerce shareholders into accepting a suboptimal price or terms in connection with the sale of their shares. Among other things, acquirors in the acquisition heyday of the 1980s employed two-step transactions (described earlier in this chapter in the discussion of going private transactions) in ways that both corporate management and courts found objectionable. In an abusive, coercive two-tier tender offer, the acquiror typically offers a premium, all-cash price on the front end of the transaction (usually for a bare controlling interest) and a less valuable, less secure form of consideration in the back end. All of this is disclosed to target shareholders up front, at the time the tender offer is made. In this way, shareholders are incentivized to tender all their shares into the front end; but because not all shares will be purchased in the front end, shareholders will have to accept the less desirable back-end consideration for all or a part of their equity interest in the target corporation.

1. Corporate Takeover Defenses

Corporate boards of directors and officers, as the statutory monitors and day-to-day managers of the corporation, respectively, are accustomed to controlling the destiny of the corporation. Proxy contests and tender offers strip them of that level of control when it seems to matter most — in connection with a transfer of control of the corporation. Also, the advent of two-tiered tender offers in the 1980s raised specific concerns in and outside the board room that shareholders might be better off with an intermediary to do their bidding for them in takeover situations where shareholders have little bargaining power and the costs of collective action are high. As a result of these factors, directors and officers typically have not been content to merely stand by and allow a third-party, unsolicited acquiror to take the corporation away from them and the shareholders. Moreover, the directors and officers of the target corporation realize that a change of control of the target corporation may result in replacement of the target's managers — namely, themselves.

Accordingly, as a means of empowerment — and, perhaps, entrenchment — target corporation management and target corporation counsel began to fashion takeover defenses: strategies and techniques for inserting themselves in the process of proxy contests and tender offers. Some of these strategies and techniques increase the cost of a potential acquisition of the target corporation. Others act as delaying mechanisms to give target management time to identify and implement alternative transactions or courses of action. Some takeover defenses make changes of control both more expensive and more time-consuming.

Labeled as shark repellents, porcupine provisions, and other things, takeover defenses are born of no small amount of legal knowledge and creativity. The possibilities are not limitless, but enterprising legal advisors consistently continue to innovate in this area. Each of these defenses builds off one or more of the theories of corporate control set forth in the beginning of this chapter. Moreover, each is constructed based on a detailed knowledge of corporate structure and governance.

Takeover defenses comprise both general corporate transactions used to ward off unsolicited changes in control and specialized anti-takeover devices. In fact, although you may not have recognized them as such, you have seen a number of defensive tools (or components of them) in prior chapters. For instance, charter and bylaw amendments (including those instituting classified — staggered — boards, cumulative voting, blank-check preferred stock, or super-voting stock and those that put conditions on business combination transactions or provide that directors may be removed by shareholders only for cause) and mergers (including reincorporation mergers) all may be used as or in takeover defenses. Take a moment to consider why each of these provisions could delay or prevent an unsolicited acquisition.

Takeover defenses may be adopted by a target on a completely "clear day" — i.e., without knowledge of a specific unsolicited offer for the target — or at a time when a generalized threat exists that the target may be the subject of an unsolicited offer (including upon board approval of a solicited merger or acquisition) or as a defense against a specific unsolicited offer for the corporation. When takeover defenses are erected to shield a target from unsolicited acquisition proposals after execution of an agreement with a friendly acquiror that provides for a negotiated merger or acquisition involving the target, we often refer to those takeover defenses as "deal protection" devices or mechanisms.

The full range of takeover defenses is too large to cover here. However, a brief, summary listing and description of a number of common takeover defenses is set forth below for your reference as you read this chapter. Come back to this list as you read the cases in this part of the chapter and ensure that you understand how the takeover defense at issue in each case works to increase the costs, or delay consummation, of specific forms of change of control transactions.

Supermajority Voting Provisions. Under state corporate law, corporations typically are permitted to adjust the default rules for shareholder voting (often a majority of the shares present or represented by proxy at a meeting at which there is a quorum) on any issue. Supermajority voting provisions generally increase the required vote for specified transactions to at least 66⅔ % of shares presented or represented by proxy at the meeting. In most circumstances, the applicable corporate statute requires that this kind of private ordering be done in the corporation's charter. By increasing the required vote on, for example, a merger transaction, a would-be acquiror may find it more difficult to acquire shares sufficient to approve the merger, even if it acquires enough shares to change control of the board of directors.

Fair Price Provisions. Sometimes combined with supermajority voting provisions (forming what is commonly known as a "fair price supermajority provision"), fair price provisions set a uniform minimum price at which all shares of the corporation must be acquired under given circumstances. Typically, fair price protections apply only to potential acquirors that already have obtained a certain percentage (usually set anywhere from 5% to 20%) of the target's shares. These shares are known as the "control shares." Once the prospective acquiror obtains the control shares, the acquiror must pay at least the same price as it paid for the control shares in acquiring any additional shares of the target corporation. The target's board of directors and shareholders have the power to exempt a share acquisition transaction from the fair price limitations by approving the transaction

Provisions Limiting or Eliminating the Right of Shareholders to Call a Special Meeting. Some state statutory default provisions permit shareholders of a certain specified level of ownership (e.g., 10%) of the corporation to call a special meeting of shareholders (if certain procedural requirements are met). Although many fundamental corporate change transactions require that the directors act first, before the matter is put to a shareholder vote (e.g., charter amendments and mergers), shareholders may desire to call a special meeting to remove and replace corporate directors, amend a corporation's bylaws, or forward a precatory (nonbinding) shareholder proposal. If the threshold level of ownership required to call a special meeting is too high (up to and including unanimity), acquiror shareholders will not be able to wield or acquire sufficient shares to call a meeting on their own, forcing them to wait to take action until the corporation's next annual meeting (or an earlier special meeting called by the corporation).

White Squire Share Purchases. A "white squire" is a person or entity friendly to the target that, in the face of an actual or likely acquisition overture from an unsolicited acquiror, acquires a noncontrolling, but significant, equity interest in the target corporation. Most often, this percentage interest is in excess of the amount needed to block a short-form merger (which requires an 85% or 90% vote in most jurisdictions). Commonly, the white squire acquires convertible preferred shares with favorable voting rights and other valuable terms. When a friendly person or entity acquires a controlling interest in the target's equity, we call that person or entity a "white knight."

Employee Stock Ownership Plans (or "ESOPs"). ESOPs are qualified retirement plans through which corporate employees beneficially own equity interests (most typically common stock) in the corporation for which they work. Used as a takeover defense, an ESOP is, in many respects, a specialized white squire. Typically, to effectuate the ESOP, an employee stock ownership trust is established that acquires (often from the target corporation itself) a significant, but noncontrolling, interest in the target's common stock, which then is allocated among accounts held by the trustee for the benefit of participating employees. In that way, the establishment and funding of the ESOP places a nontrivial amount of the target's equity in (theoretically) friendly hands.

Stock Repurchases (a.k.a. Buybacks). Target corporations often repurchase their own common stock at a premium to the market price and any existing takeover bid as a means of thwarting a potential or actual unsolicited bid for control by increasing the market price of the target's common stock (and therefore increasing the price of a share acquisition). A share repurchase of this kind (also known as a stock buyback) may constitute, and therefore be regulated as, a tender offer under federal law. (These tender offers by corporations for their own shares are known as self-tender offers.) Selective stock repurchases — individually arranged repurchases of shares from one or more key shareholders — are referred to as "greenmail" when the purpose of the stock repurchase is to buy out the interest of a putative acquiror at a premium to the market price of the shares. The *Cheff*, *Unocal*, and *Unitrin* cases excerpted or discussed later in this chapter all involve the use of stock repurchases as takeover defenses.

Golden Parachutes. A target corporation may both incentivize management to stay through the duration of a drawn-out acquisition process and, at the same time, ward off certain potential unsolicited suitors by entering into lucrative severance contracts with its key executives. Severance typically becomes payable upon a change of control of the target (single-trigger plan) or both a change of control of the target and, within a specified period thereafter, the actual or constructive termination of employment of the executive (double-trigger plan). These terms may be memorialized as part of the executive's overall employment agreement or in a separate severance agreement.

Poison Pills (a.k.a. Shareholder or Stockholder Rights Plans). Although many use the term "poison pill" in common parlance to refer to anti-takeover devices more broadly, *see e.g.*, the *Revlon* opinion excerpted later in the chapter, the term most commonly is used to reference a specific type of takeover defense also known as a shareholder (or stockholder) rights plan. The establishment of a poison pill involves the board's declaration of a dividend of rights (which work like call options) to purchase common stock (or fractions of a share of preferred stock with voting and liquidation terms that mimic common stock). These rights attach to and trade with the common stock.

The rights only are exercisable (if at all) after an offer to acquire, or an actual acquisition of, a threshold amount of common stock (typically, about 15%, but sometimes as low as 10%, of the outstanding shares). Any stock purchase rights held by the acquiror who triggers the exercisability of the rights are not exercisable and become null and void. At the same time that the stock purchase rights become exercisable, they separate from the common stock and become tradable (meaning that they can be bought and sold) as a separate instrument. Often, at this stage, it is not economical for a right holder to exercise the rights, because the exercise price is higher than the market price for the underlying shares. The real potency of poison pill rights emerges upon the occurrence of specified change of control events (including acquisitions of a controlling equity interest or the consummation of certain business combination transactions), when the rights become exercisable for common stock of the target (or, after a business combination, the acquiror) at a discounted price. The exercise of these attractive discount stock purchase rights by the holders has the potential to dilute the acquiror's interest in the target corporation (since the acquiror cannot exercise any rights it holds) and therefore make a change of control of the target significantly more expensive.

The poison pill takeover defense was validated under Delaware law in *Moran v. Household Int'l, Inc.*, 500 A.2d 1346, 1355 (Del. 1985). It is important for readers of the case to note, however, that *Household* describes an older generation form of poison pill that no longer is used. A more recent case reaffirming the board of directors' ability to adopt a poison pill is *Account v. Hilton Hotels Corp.*, 780 A.2d 245 (Del. 2001).

Lock-up Options. Lock-up options are a type of deal protection device. They typically are entered into by a corporation as part of a negotiated business combination transaction in order to prevent other potential acquirors from interceding and busting up the negotiated transaction. A stock lock-up option gives the acquiror in the negotiated transaction (who may be a White Knight, as described in the "White Squire Share Purchases" paragraph above) the option to buy a significant amount of newly issued or treasury shares of the common stock of the target corporation (typically, just under 20% of the outstanding common stock of the target, in order to avoid shareholder approval requirements under state corporate law or stock exchange rules). An asset lock-up transaction gives the friendly acquiror an option to purchase a valuable asset of the target at a favorable price and on favorable terms. (Where an asset is especially important to the target's business, the related asset lock-up option may be referred to as a "Crown Jewel" option.) In either case, the lock-up option is not exercisable unless and until a third party acquires a significant amount of the target's common stock (typically, about 25%) or the target corporation agrees to be acquired by a third party (or its board recommends a business combination transaction with a third party). In some circumstances, the exercisability of the lock-up option is tied to and triggered by the same circumstances that trigger payment of a termination fee (described *infra*).

No-shop Provisions. No-shop provisions, another form of deal protection, typically are covenants in a merger or acquisition agreement (although they sometimes comprise stand-alone agreements) that prevent one or more parties to the agreement from soliciting, initiating, encouraging, or assisting in the submission of superior competing acquisition proposals ("topping bids") from third parties (i.e., potential acquirors not party to the merger or acquisition agreement). The penalty for violation of the covenant is contract damages or, in the event that specified termination provisions in the merger or acquisition agreement are triggered, payment of a termination fee, a separate (but sometimes related) deal protection mechanism described *infra*. As such, no-shop provisions (also infrequently referred to as "standstill provisions" — a term that usually refers to restrictions imposed on share acquirors) are deal protection devices that may increase the price of an interloper's topping bid.

Because compliance with a no-shop provision may require the target's board of directors to violate state law fiduciary duties, parties to a merger or acquisition agreement that are bound by no-shop provisions often will negotiate "fiduciary out" clauses that expressly permit the target's board to engage in specified contacts or arrangements with one or more potential third-party acquirors when the board's fiduciary duties otherwise would be in conflict with the no-shop provision. Other exceptions to no-shop obligations constitute or result in "window shopping provisions" (where the board can appropriately respond to, but not solicit or encourage, topping bids) or "market-check provisions" (which give the target a limited period of time to seek topping bids). Finally, it is interesting to note that some recent agreements have begun to reverse the long-standing trend to include no-shop provisions in merger and acquisition agreements by including "go-shop provisions" in their merger and acquisition agreements — covenants that expressly endorse target conduct that seeks out and promotes topping bids.

Termination (or "Bust-up" or "Cancellation") Fees. Termination fees are deal protection mechanisms in the nature of (and sometimes analyzed as) liquidated damages — fixed cash payments required to be made by a target in the event that a negotiated merger or acquisition agreement is terminated for specified reasons, most often including the failure to obtain approval of the transaction from shareholders of the target and the receipt by the target of a topping bid. These provisions, like other deal protection devices, are heavily negotiated parts of merger and acquisition agreements. Payment of the termination fee increases the cost of a competing bid for the target.

## 2.	Applicable Judicial Review Standards

Unsurprisingly, these and other anti-takeover efforts have been contested by putative acquirors and target shareholders. Often, these contests include court challenges to specific takeover defenses on the basis that they violate state corporate statutes governing corporate authority to implement or use instruments that comprise the particular takeover defense. Sometimes, acquiror and shareholder challenges are based on general common law doctrines and principles. Almost always, legal claims brought in court by acquirors and shareholders include claims that the target's board has violated one or more of its fiduciary duties.

These fiduciary duty claims raise questions about the applicability of the business judgment rule in evaluating the legality of takeover defenses as a whole and of specific anti-takeover tactics. The case law in this area is complex and, in some cases, contradictory. Bright-line rules are hard to discern, but standards and trends have developed over the years that offer a framework in which corporations, shareholders, and legal counsel can operate in determining whether particular takeover defenses are valid (or at least unlikely to be invalidated) by a court. The cases described and excerpted in the subsections below illustrate bases for, and key components of, those standards of review and relevant legal trends.

### a.	Use and Decline of a Traditional BJR Analysis

Until 1985, takeover defenses adopted by Delaware corporations were by-and-large reviewed by courts under the business judgment rule analysis described in Chapter 10. In 1964, however, *Cheff v. Mathes*, 199 A.2d 548, 550 (Del. 1964), established a basis for treating the judicial review of board actions in creating or implementing takeover defenses differently than the judicial review of other board actions. *Cheff* involved the repurchase of shares by a corporation, Holland, and some of its affiliates from an unsolicited and unwanted acquiror, Maremont, who had been buying shares of Holland in the market. (As you may know, this kind of selective purchase is referred to as "greenmail.") The court first analyzed the statutory authority of the corporation to make stock repurchases and then analyzed whether the decision of the directors to repurchase the shares was consistent with their fiduciary duties.

> Under the provisions of 8 Del. C. § 160, a corporation is granted statutory
> power to purchase and sell shares of its own stock. Such a right, as embodied in

the statute, has long been recognized in this State. The charge here is not one of violation of statute, but the allegation is that the true motives behind such purchases were improperly centered upon perpetuation of control. . . . [I]f the actions of the board were motivated by a sincere belief that the buying out of the dissident stockholder was necessary to maintain what the board believed to be proper business practices, the board will not be held liable for such decision, even though hindsight indicates the decision was not the wisest course. On the other hand, if the board has acted solely or primarily because of the desire to perpetuate themselves in office, the use of corporate funds for such purposes is improper. . . .

Our first problem is the allocation of the burden of proof to show the presence or lack of good faith on the part of the board in authorizing the purchase of shares. Initially, the decision of the board of directors in authorizing a purchase was presumed to be in good faith and could be overturned only by a conclusive showing by plaintiffs of fraud or other misconduct. [I]n *Bennett v. Propp,* . . . we stated:

> "We must bear in mind the inherent danger in the purchase of shares with corporate funds to remove a threat to corporate policy when a threat to control is involved. The directors are of necessity confronted with a conflict of interest, and an objective decision is difficult. Hence, in our opinion, the burden should be on the directors to justify such a purchase as one primarily in the corporate interest."

. . . To say that the burden of proof is upon the defendants is not to indicate, however, that the directors have the same "self-dealing interest" as is present, for example, when a director sells property to the corporation. . . .

The question then presented is whether or not defendants satisfied the burden of proof of showing reasonable grounds to believe a danger to corporate policy and effectiveness existed by the presence of the Maremont stock ownership. It is important to remember that the directors satisfy their burden by showing good faith and reasonable investigation; the directors will not be penalized for an honest mistake of judgment, if the judgment appeared reasonable at the time the decision was made. . . .

[W]e are of the opinion that the evidence presented in the court below leads inevitably to the conclusion that the board of directors, based upon direct investigation, receipt of professional advice, and personal observations of the contradictory action of Maremont and his explanation of corporate purpose, believed, with justification, that there was a reasonable threat to the continued existence of Holland, or at least existence in its present form, by the plan of Maremont to continue building up his stock holdings. We find no evidence in the record sufficient to justify a contrary conclusion. . . .

Cheff v. Mathes, 199 A.2d 548, 550 (Del. 1964).

b. Enhanced Scrutiny under *Unocal*

As you read the case excerpt below, consider how the approaches to issues of statutory authority and fiduciary duty analysis evidenced in the case emanates from the Delaware Supreme Court's analysis in *Cheff v. Mathes.*

UNOCAL CORP. v. MESA PETROLEUM CO.
Supreme Court of Delaware
493 A.2d 946 (Del. 1985)

MOORE, J.

We confront an issue of first impression in Delaware — the validity of a corporation's self-tender for its own shares which excludes from participation a stockholder making a hostile tender offer for the company's stock.

The Court of Chancery granted a preliminary injunction to the plaintiffs, Mesa Petroleum Co., Mesa Asset Co., Mesa Partners II, and Mesa Eastern, Inc. (collectively "Mesa"), enjoining an exchange offer of the defendant, Unocal Corporation (Unocal) for its own stock. The trial court concluded that a selective exchange offer, excluding Mesa, was legally impermissible. We cannot agree with such a blanket rule. The factual findings of the Vice Chancellor, fully supported by the record, establish that Unocal's board, consisting of a majority of independent directors, acted in good faith, and after reasonable investigation found that Mesa's tender offer was both inadequate and coercive. Under the circumstances the board had both the power and duty to oppose a bid it perceived to be harmful to the corporate enterprise. On this record we are satisfied that the device Unocal adopted is reasonable in relation to the threat posed, and that the board acted in the proper exercise of sound business judgment. We will not substitute our views for those of the board if the latter's decision can be "attributed to any rational business purpose." Accordingly, we reverse the decision of the Court of Chancery and order the preliminary injunction vacated.

I.

The factual background of this matter bears a significant relationship to its ultimate outcome.

On April 8, 1985, Mesa, the owner of approximately 13% of Unocal's stock, commenced a two-tier "front loaded" cash tender offer for 64 million shares, or approximately 37%, of Unocal's outstanding stock at a price of $ 54 per share. The "back-end" was designed to eliminate the remaining publicly held shares by an exchange of securities purportedly worth $ 54 per share. However, pursuant to an order entered by the United States District Court for the Central District of California on April 26, 1985, Mesa issued a supplemental proxy statement to Unocal's stockholders disclosing that the securities offered in the second-step merger would be highly subordinated, and that Unocal's capitalization would differ significantly from its present structure. Unocal has rather aptly termed such securities "junk bonds."

Unocal's board consists of eight independent outside directors and six insiders. It met on April 13, 1985, to consider the Mesa tender offer. Thirteen directors were present, and the meeting lasted nine and one-half hours. The directors were given no agenda or written materials prior to the session. However, detailed presentations were made by legal counsel regarding the board's obligations under both Delaware corporate law and the federal securities laws. The board then received a presentation from Peter Sachs on behalf of Goldman Sachs & Co. (Goldman Sachs) and Dillon, Read & Co. (Dillon Read) discussing the bases for their opinions that the Mesa proposal was wholly inadequate. Mr. Sachs opined that the minimum cash value that could be expected from a sale or orderly liquidation for 100% of Unocal's stock was in excess of $ 60 per share. In making his presentation, Mr. Sachs showed slides outlining the valuation techniques used by the financial advisors, and others, depicting recent business combinations in the oil and gas industry. The Court of Chancery found that the Sachs presentation was designed to apprise the directors of the scope of the analyses performed rather than the facts and numbers used in reaching the conclusion that Mesa's tender offer price was inadequate.

Mr. Sachs also presented various defensive strategies available to the board if it concluded that Mesa's two-step tender offer was inadequate and should be opposed. One of the devices outlined was a self-tender by Unocal for its own stock with a reasonable price range of $ 70 to $ 75 per share. The cost of such a proposal would cause the company to incur $ 6.1–6.5 billion of additional debt, and a presentation was made informing the board of Unocal's ability to handle it. The directors were told that the primary effect of this obligation would be to reduce exploratory drilling, but that the company would nonetheless remain a viable entity.

The eight outside directors, comprising a clear majority of the thirteen members present, then met separately with Unocal's financial advisors and attorneys. Thereafter, they unanimously agreed to advise the board that it should reject Mesa's tender offer as inadequate, and that Unocal should pursue a self-tender to provide the stockholders with a fairly priced alternative to the Mesa proposal. The board then reconvened and unanimously adopted a resolution rejecting as grossly inadequate Mesa's tender offer. Despite the nine and one-half hour length of the meeting, no formal decision was made on the proposed defensive self-tender.

On April 15, the board met again with four of the directors present by telephone and one member still absent. This session lasted two hours. Unocal's Vice President of Finance and its Assistant General Counsel made a detailed presentation of the proposed terms of the exchange offer. A price range between $ 70 and $ 80 per share was considered, and ultimately the directors agreed upon $ 72. The board was also advised about the debt securities that would be issued, and the necessity of placing restrictive covenants upon certain corporate activities until the obligations were paid. The board's decisions were made in reliance on the advice of its investment bankers, including the terms and conditions upon which the securities were to be issued. Based upon this advice, and the board's own deliberations, the directors unanimously approved the exchange offer. Their resolution provided that if Mesa acquired 64 million shares of Unocal stock through its own offer (the Mesa Purchase Condition), Unocal would buy the remaining 49% outstanding for an exchange of debt securities having an aggregate par value of $ 72 per share. The board resolution also stated that the offer would be subject to other conditions that had been described to the board at the meeting, or which were deemed necessary by Unocal's officers, including the exclusion of Mesa from the proposal (the Mesa exclusion). Any such conditions were required to be in accordance with the "purport and intent" of the offer.

Unocal's exchange offer was commenced on April 17, 1985, and Mesa promptly challenged it by filing this suit in the Court of Chancery. On April 22, the Unocal board met again and was advised by Goldman Sachs and Dillon Read to waive the Mesa Purchase Condition as to 50 million shares. This recommendation was in response to a perceived concern of the shareholders that, if shares were tendered to Unocal, no shares would be purchased by either offeror. The directors were also advised that they should tender their own Unocal stock into the exchange offer as a mark of their confidence in it.

Another focus of the board was the Mesa exclusion. Legal counsel advised that under Delaware law Mesa could only be excluded for what the directors reasonably believed to be a valid corporate purpose. The directors' discussion centered on the objective of adequately compensating shareholders at the "back-end" of Mesa's proposal, which the latter would finance with "junk bonds." To include Mesa would defeat that goal, because under the proration aspect of the exchange offer (49%), every Mesa share accepted by Unocal would displace one held by another stockholder. Further, if Mesa were permitted to tender to Unocal, the latter would in effect be financing Mesa's own inadequate proposal.

On April 24, 1985 Unocal issued a supplement to the exchange offer describing the partial waiver of the Mesa Purchase Condition. On May 1, 1985, in another supplement, Unocal extended the withdrawal, proration and expiration dates of its exchange offer to May 17, 1985.

Meanwhile, on April 22, 1985, Mesa amended its complaint in this action to challenge the Mesa exclusion. A preliminary injunction hearing was scheduled for May 8, 1985. However, on April 23, 1985, Mesa moved for a temporary restraining order in response to Unocal's announcement that it was partially waiving the Mesa Purchase Condition. After expedited briefing, the Court of Chancery heard Mesa's motion on April 26.

On April 29, 1985, the Vice Chancellor temporarily restrained Unocal from proceeding with the exchange offer unless it included Mesa. The trial court recognized that directors could oppose, and attempt to defeat, a hostile takeover which they considered adverse to the best interests of the corporation. However, the Vice Chancellor decided that in a selective purchase of the company's stock, the corporation bears the burden of showing: (1) a valid corporate purpose, and (2) that the transaction was fair to all of the stockholders, including those excluded. . . .

After the May 8 hearing the Vice Chancellor issued an unreported opinion on May 13, 1985 granting Mesa a preliminary injunction. . . .

On May 13, 1985, the Court of Chancery certified this interlocutory appeal to us as a question of first impression, and we accepted it on May 14. . . .

II.

The issues we address involve these fundamental questions: Did the Unocal board have the power and duty to oppose a takeover threat it reasonably perceived to be harmful to the corporate enterprise, and if so, is its action here entitled to the protection of the business judgment rule?

Mesa contends that the discriminatory exchange offer violates the fiduciary duties Unocal owes it. Mesa argues that because of the Mesa exclusion the business judgment rule is inapplicable, because the directors by tendering their own shares will derive a financial benefit that is not available to *all* Unocal stockholders. Thus, it is Mesa's ultimate contention that Unocal cannot establish that the exchange offer is fair to *all* shareholders, and argues that the Court of Chancery was correct in concluding that Unocal was unable to meet this burden.

Unocal answers that it does not owe a duty of "fairness" to Mesa, given the facts here. Specifically, Unocal contends that its board of directors reasonably and in good faith concluded that Mesa's $ 54 two-tier tender offer was coercive and inadequate, and that Mesa sought selective treatment for itself. Furthermore, Unocal argues that the board's approval of the exchange offer was made in good faith, on an informed basis, and in the exercise of due care. Under these circumstances, Unocal contends that its directors properly employed this device to protect the company and its stockholders from Mesa's harmful tactics.

III.

We begin with the basic issue of the power of a board of directors of a Delaware corporation to adopt a defensive measure of this type. Absent such authority, all other questions are moot. Neither issues of fairness nor business judgment are pertinent without the basic underpinning of a board's legal power to act.

The board has a large reservoir of authority upon which to draw. Its duties and responsibilities proceed from the inherent powers conferred by 8 Del.C. § 141(a), respecting management of the corporation's "business and affairs." Additionally, the powers here being exercised derive from 8 Del.C. § 160(a), conferring broad authority upon a corporation to deal in its own stock. From this, it is now well established that in the acquisition of its shares a Delaware corporation may deal selectively with its stockholders, provided the directors have not acted out of a sole or primary purpose to entrench themselves in office.

Finally, the board's power to act derives from its fundamental duty and obligation to protect the corporate enterprise, which includes stockholders, from harm reasonably perceived, irrespective of its source. Thus, we are satisfied that in the broad context of corporate governance, including issues of fundamental corporate change, a board of directors is not a passive instrumentality.

Given the foregoing principles, we turn to the standards by which director action is to be measured. In *Pogostin v. Rice*, Del. Supr., 480 A.2d 619 (1984), we held that the business judgment rule, including the standards by which director conduct is judged, is applicable in the context of a takeover. The business judgment rule is a "presumption that in making a business decision the directors of a corporation acted on an informed basis, in good faith and in the honest belief that the action taken was in the best interests of the company." A hallmark of the business judgment rule is that a court will not substitute its judgment for that of the board if the latter's decision can be "attributed to any rational business purpose."

When a board addresses a pending takeover bid it has an obligation to determine whether the offer is in the best interests of the corporation and its shareholders. In that respect a board's duty is no different from any other responsibility it shoulders, and its decisions should be no less entitled to the respect they otherwise would be accorded in the realm of business judgment. There are, however, certain caveats to a proper exercise of this function. Because of the omnipresent specter that a board may be acting primarily in its own interests, rather than those of the corporation and its shareholders, there is an enhanced duty which calls for judicial examination at the threshold before the protections of the business judgment rule may be conferred.

This Court has long recognized that:

> We must bear in mind the inherent danger in the purchase of shares with corporate funds to remove a threat to corporate policy when a threat to control is involved. The directors are of necessity confronted with a conflict of interest, and an objective decision is difficult.

In the face of this inherent conflict, directors must show that they had reasonable grounds for believing that a danger to corporate policy and effectiveness existed because of another person's stock ownership. However, they satisfy that burden "by showing good faith and reasonable investigation. . . . " Furthermore, such proof is materially enhanced, as here, by the approval of a board comprised of a majority of outside independent directors who have acted in accordance with the foregoing standards.

IV.

A.

In the board's exercise of corporate power to forestall a takeover bid our analysis begins with the basic principle that corporate directors have a fiduciary duty to act in the best interests of the corporation's stockholders. As we have noted, their duty of care extends to protecting the corporation and its owners from perceived harm whether a threat originates from third parties or other shareholders. But such powers are not absolute. A corporation does not have unbridled discretion to defeat any perceived threat by any Draconian means available.

The restriction placed upon a selective stock repurchase is that the directors may not have acted solely or primarily out of a desire to perpetuate themselves in office. Of course, to this is added the further caveat that inequitable action may not be taken under the guise of law. The standard of proof established in *Cheff v. Mathes* . . . is designed to ensure that a defensive measure to thwart or impede a takeover is indeed motivated by a good faith concern for the welfare of the corporation and its stockholders, which in all circumstances must be free of any fraud or other misconduct. However, this does not end the inquiry.

B.

A further aspect is the element of balance. If a defensive measure is to come within the ambit of the business judgment rule, it must be reasonable in relation to the threat posed. This entails an analysis by the directors of the nature of the takeover bid and its effect on the corporate enterprise. Examples of such concerns may include: inadequacy of the price offered, nature and timing of the offer, questions of illegality, the impact on "constituencies" other than shareholders (i.e., creditors, customers, employees, and perhaps even the community generally), the risk of nonconsummation, and the quality of securities being offered in the exchange. While not a controlling factor, it also seems to us that a board may reasonably consider the basic stockholder interests at stake, including those of short term speculators, whose actions may have fueled the coercive aspect of the offer at the expense of the long term investor. Here, the threat posed was viewed by the Unocal board as a grossly inadequate two-tier coercive tender offer coupled with the threat of greenmail.

Specifically, the Unocal directors had concluded that the value of Unocal was substantially above the $ 54 per share offered in cash at the front end. Furthermore, they determined that the subordinated securities to be exchanged in Mesa's announced squeeze out of the remaining shareholders in the "back-end" merger were "junk bonds" worth far less than $ 54. It is now well recognized that such offers are a classic coercive measure designed to stampede shareholders into tendering at the first tier, even if the price is inadequate, out of fear of what they will receive at the back end of the transaction. Wholly beyond the coercive aspect of an inadequate two-tier tender offer, the threat was posed by a corporate raider with a national reputation as a "greenmailer."

In adopting the selective exchange offer, the board stated that its objective was either to defeat the inadequate Mesa offer or, should the offer still succeed, provide the 49% of its stockholders, who would otherwise be forced to accept "junk bonds", with $ 72 worth of senior debt. We find that both purposes are valid.

However, such efforts would have been thwarted by Mesa's participation in the exchange offer. First, if Mesa could tender its shares, Unocal would effectively be subsidizing the former's continuing effort to buy Unocal stock at $ 54 per share. Second, Mesa could not, by definition, fit within the class of shareholders being protected from its own coercive and inadequate tender offer.

Thus, we are satisfied that the selective exchange offer is reasonably related to the threats posed. It is consistent with the principle that "the minority stockholder shall receive the substantial equivalent in value of what he had before." This concept of fairness, while stated in the merger context, is also relevant in the area of tender offer law. Thus, the board's decision to offer what it determined to be the fair value of the corporation to the 49% of its shareholders, who would otherwise be forced to accept highly subordinated "junk bonds," is reasonable and consistent with the directors' duty to ensure that the minority stockholders receive equal value for their shares.

V.

Mesa contends that it is unlawful, and the trial court agreed, for a corporation to discriminate in this fashion against one shareholder. It argues correctly that no case has ever sanctioned a device that precludes a raider from sharing in a benefit available to all other stockholders. However, as we have noted earlier, the principle of selective stock repurchases by a Delaware corporation is neither unknown nor unauthorized. *Cheff v. Mathes*, 199 A.2d at 554; *Bennett v. Propp*, 187 A.2d at 408; *Martin v. American Potash & Chemical Corporation*, 92 A.2d at 302; *Kaplan v. Goldsamt*, 380 A.2d 556 at 568; *Kors v. Carey*, 158 A.2d at 140–141; 8 Del.C. § 160. The only difference is that heretofore the approved transaction was the payment of "greenmail" to a raider or dissident posing a threat to the corporate enterprise. All other stockholders were denied such favored treatment, and given Mesa's past history of greenmail, its claims here are rather ironic.

However, our corporate law is not static. It must grow and develop in response to, indeed in anticipation of, evolving concepts and needs. Merely because the General Corporation Law is silent as to a specific matter does not mean that it is prohibited. In the days when *Cheff, Bennett, Martin* and *Kors* were decided, the tender offer, while not an unknown device, was virtually unused, and little was known of such methods as two-tier "front-end" loaded offers with their coercive effects. Then, the favored attack of a raider was stock acquisition followed by a proxy contest. Various defensive tactics, which provided no benefit whatever to the raider, evolved. Thus, the use of corporate funds by management to counter a proxy battle was approved. Litigation, supported by corporate funds, aimed at the raider has long been a popular device.

More recently, as the sophistication of both raiders and targets has developed, a host of other defensive measures to counter such ever mounting threats has evolved and received judicial sanction. These include defensive charter amendments and other devices bearing some rather exotic, but apt, names: Crown Jewel, White Knight, Pac Man, and Golden Parachute. Each has highly selective features, the object of which is to deter or defeat the raider.

Thus, while the exchange offer is a form of selective treatment, given the nature of the threat posed here the response is neither unlawful nor unreasonable. If the board of directors is disinterested, has acted in good faith and with due care, its decision in the absence of an abuse of discretion will be upheld as a proper exercise of business judgment.

To this Mesa responds that the board is not disinterested, because the directors are receiving a benefit from the tender of their own shares, which because of the Mesa exclusion, does not devolve upon *all* stockholders equally. However, Mesa concedes that if the exclusion is valid, then the directors and all other stockholders share the same benefit. The answer of course is that the exclusion is valid, and the directors' participation in the exchange offer does not rise to the level of a disqualifying interest. The excellent discussion in *Johnson v. Trueblood*, 629 F.2d at 292–293, of the use of the business judgment rule in takeover contests also seems pertinent here.

Nor does this become an "interested" director transaction merely because certain board members are large stockholders. As this Court has previously noted, that fact alone does not create a disqualifying "personal pecuniary interest" to defeat the operation of the business judgment rule.

Mesa also argues that the exclusion permits the directors to abdicate the fiduciary duties they owe it. However, that is not so. The board continues to owe Mesa the duties of due care and loyalty. But in the face of the destructive threat, Mesa's tender offer was perceived to pose, the board had a supervening duty to protect the corporate enterprise, which includes the other shareholders, from threatened harm.

Mesa contends that the basis of this action is punitive, and solely in response to the exercise of its rights of corporate democracy. Nothing precludes Mesa, as a stockholder, from acting in its own self-interest. However, Mesa, while pursuing its own interests, has acted in a manner which a board consisting of a majority of independent directors has reasonably determined to be contrary to the best interests of Unocal and its other shareholders. In this situation, there is no support in Delaware law for the proposition that, when responding to a perceived harm, a corporation must guarantee a benefit to a stockholder who is deliberately provoking the danger being addressed. There is no obligation of self-sacrifice by a corporation and its shareholders in the face of such a challenge.

Here, the Court of Chancery specifically found that the "directors' decision [to oppose the Mesa tender offer] was made in the good faith belief that the Mesa tender offer is inadequate." . . . [W]e are satisfied that Unocal's board has met its burden of proof.

VI.

In conclusion, there was directorial power to oppose the Mesa tender offer, and to undertake a selective stock exchange made in good faith and upon a reasonable investigation pursuant to a clear duty to protect the corporate enterprise. Further, the selective stock repurchase plan chosen by Unocal is reasonable in relation to the threat that the board rationally and reasonably believed was posed by Mesa's inadequate and coercive two-tier tender offer. Under those circumstances the board's action is entitled to be measured by the standards of the business judgment rule. Thus, unless it is shown by a preponderance of the evidence that the directors' decisions were primarily based on perpetuating themselves in office, or some other breach of fiduciary duty such as fraud, overreaching, lack of good faith, or being uninformed, a Court will not substitute its judgment for that of the board.

In this case, that protection is not lost merely because Unocal's directors have tendered their shares in the exchange offer. Given the validity of the Mesa exclusion, they are receiving a benefit shared generally by all other stockholders except Mesa. . . . If the stockholders are displeased with the action of their elected representatives, the powers of corporate democracy are at their disposal to turn the board out.

With the Court of Chancery's findings that the exchange offer was based on the board's good faith belief that the Mesa offer was inadequate, that the board's action was informed and taken with due care, that Mesa's prior activities justify a reasonable inference that its principle objective was greenmail, and implicitly, that the substance of the offer itself was reasonable and fair to the corporation and its stockholders if Mesa were included, we cannot say that the Unocal directors have acted in such a manner as to have passed an "unintelligent and unadvised judgment." The decision of the Court of Chancery is therefore REVERSED, and the preliminary injunction is VACATED.

NOTES AND QUESTIONS

1. *The* Unitrin *Gloss.* After *Unocal* was decided, litigants and commentators began to explore the contours of *Unocal's* second prong — the proportionality of the takeover defense as a response to identified threats. What, exactly, does it mean for a takeover defense to be "reasonably related to the threats posed"? *Unocal Corp. v. Mesa Petroleum Co.*, 493 A.2d 946. 956 (1985). In 1995, the Delaware Supreme Court made an attempt at clarifying this element of balance enunciated in the *Unocal* case, focusing in, on (among other things) the *Unocal* court's use of the word "Draconian." *Id.* at 955.

An examination of the cases applying *Unocal* reveals a direct correlation between findings of proportionality or disproportionality and the judicial determination of whether a defensive response was draconian because it was either coercive or preclusive in character. . . .

More than a century before *Unocal* was decided, Justice Holmes observed that the common law must be developed through its application and "cannot be dealt with as if it contained only the axioms and corollaries of a book of mathematics." As common law applications of *Unocal's* proportionality standard have evolved, at least two characteristics of draconian defensive measures taken by a board of directors in responding to a threat have been brought into focus through enhanced judicial scrutiny. In the modern takeover lexicon, it is now clear that since *Unocal*, this Court has consistently recognized that defensive measures which are either preclusive or coercive are included within the common law definition of draconian.

If a defensive measure is not draconian, however, because it is not either coercive or preclusive, the *Unocal* proportionality test requires the focus of enhanced judicial scrutiny to shift to "the range of reasonableness." Proper and proportionate defensive responses are intended and permitted to thwart perceived threats. When a corporation is not for sale, the board of directors is the defender of the metaphorical medieval corporate bastion and the protector of the corporation's shareholders. The fact that a defensive action must not be coercive or preclusive does not prevent a board from responding defensively before a bidder is at the corporate bastion's gate.

The *ratio decidendi* for the "range of reasonableness" standard is a need of the board of directors for latitude in discharging its fiduciary duties to the corporation and its shareholders when defending against perceived threats. The concomitant requirement is for judicial restraint. Consequently, if the board of directors' defensive response is not draconian (preclusive or coercive) and is within a "range of reasonableness", a court must not substitute its judgment for the board's.

Unitrin, Inc. v. American Gen. Corp. (In re Unitrin, Inc.), 651 A.2d 1361, 1387–88 (Del. 1995) (footnote omitted). The *Unitrin* court cited numerous cases in support of its ruling. The combination of *Unocal* and *Unitrin* took hold in the academic and practice communities, to the extent that many commentators labeled the requisite framework the "*Unocal/Unitrin* analysis." How helpful is *Unitrin* in defining *Unocal*'s second prong?

2. *Fashioning a Workable Analytical Framework.* As a result of *Cheff, Unocal,* and *Unitrin*, what is the current framework for analyzing the validity of a takeover defense? What "hints" do the three decisions give us about applying this framework? (Those who are visual learners may want to incorporate the answers to these questions into a flow chart.)

3. *Multiplicity Of, and Interaction Between and Among, Deal Protection Devices.* Courts wrestle with breach of fiduciary duty actions relating to deal protection provisions — components of merger or acquisition agreements that attempt to prevent others from proposing or effectuating competing business combination transactions at higher values or on better terms than those negotiated and agreed to by original merger or acquisition partners. Among the issues are the employment of and interaction among multiple deal protections.

A key case in this area is *Omnicare, Inc. v. NCS Healthcare, Inc.*, 818 A.2d 914 (Del. 2003). In *Omnicare*, the court analyzes a merger agreement that effectively locked up a majority of the votes — enough to approve the merger — while at the same time providing the target's directors with no "fiduciary out" provision. In other words, the directors had no ability to terminate the merger agreement or abrogate its terms to comply with their fiduciary duties (for example, if NCS were to receive a higher offer) without breaching the contract.

Omnicare has interesting and unusual facts. NCS, the target corporation, was experiencing financial difficulties. It had defaulted on a significant amount of debt, and its public stock price was suffering. As a result, it began to look for alternative transactions to rescue it from its possible demise. Eventually, NCS attracted and engaged in protracted negotiations with two bidders, Genesis and Omnicare. After fully vetting a series of increasingly favorable proposals from each, NCS was given an exploding offer from Genesis on very favorable terms. The offer required board approval by NCS within 24 hours and that the transaction be protected from further competing bids.

Based upon the NCS board's evaluation of the Genesis offer and advice from its counsel and financial advisors, the board approved the Genesis offer, executed a merger agreement with Genesis, and recommended that NCS shareholders approve and adopt the merger agreement. The merger agreement contained a provision (authorized by DGCL § 251(c)) requiring NCS to put the Genesis merger agreement before its stockholders for a vote, even if its board no longer recommended approval of the merger, and, as noted above, included no fiduciary out. Simultaneously, as required by Genesis, two board members entered into a voting agreement with Genesis in which they agreed to vote all of their shares in favor of approving and adopting the merger agreement. The shares held by these two board members together constituted over 65% of NCS's outstanding shares—enough shares to guarantee approval and adoption of the Genesis merger agreement at the NCS shareholder meeting.

Omnicare later (after the execution of the Genesis merger agreement and before the NCS shareholder vote) submitted a new bid at a higher price than that offered by

Genesis. The NCS board then withdrew its recommendation that shareholders approve and adopt the Genesis merger agreement. But the voting agreement assured NCS shareholder approval in any case, and the lack of a fiduciary out prevented the NCS board from renegotiating or abandoning the Genesis merger agreement.

Omnicare therefore sued to invalidate the Genesis merger agreement on fiduciary duty grounds. (A separate fiduciary duty suit was brought by minority shareholders of NCS.) The court, in a 3-2 decision using a Unocal/Unitrin analysis, concludes that board approval of a merger agreement that locks up the votes needed for the merger but fails to include a fiduciary out is a violation of the directors' fiduciary duties because it is not reasonable in response to the threat posed.

> Although the minority stockholders were not forced to vote for the Genesis merger, they were required to accept it because it was a *fait accompli*. The record reflects that the defensive devices employed by the NCS board are preclusive and coercive in the sense that they accomplished a *fait accompli*. In this case, despite the fact that the NCS board has withdrawn its recommendation for the Genesis transaction and recommended its rejection by the stockholders, the deal protection devices approved by the NCS board operated in concert to have a preclusive and coercive effect. Those tripartite defensive measures — the Section 251(c) provision, the voting agreements, and the absence of an effective fiduciary out clause — made it "mathematically impossible" and "realistically unattainable" for the Omnicare transaction or any other proposal to succeed, no matter how superior the proposal. . . .

> The defensive measures that protected the merger transaction are unenforceable not only because they are preclusive and coercive but, alternatively, they are unenforceable because they are invalid as they operate in this case. Given the specifically enforceable irrevocable voting agreements, the provision in the merger agreement requiring the board to submit the transaction for a stockholder vote and the omission of a fiduciary out clause in the merger agreement completely prevented the board from discharging its fiduciary responsibilities to the minority stockholders when Omnicare presented its superior transaction. "To the extent that a [merger] contract, or a provision thereof, purports to require a board to act or not act in such a fashion as to limit the exercise of fiduciary duties, it is invalid and unenforceable." [citing to *Paramount Communications Inc. v. QVC Network Inc.*, 637 A.2d 34, 51 (Del. 1993)]. . . .

> Under the circumstances presented in this case, where a cohesive group of stockholders with majority voting power was irrevocably committed to the merger transaction, "[e]ffective representation of the financial interests of the minority shareholders imposed upon the [NCS board] an affirmative responsibility to protect those minority shareholders' interests." The NCS board could not abdicate its fiduciary duties to the minority by leaving it to the stockholders alone to approve or disapprove the merger agreement because two stockholders had already combined to establish a majority of the voting power that made the outcome of the stockholder vote a foregone conclusion. . ..

> Any board has authority to give the proponent of a recommended merger agreement reasonable structural and economic defenses, incentives, and fair compensation if the transaction is not completed. To the extent that defensive measures are economic and reasonable, they may become an increased cost to the proponent of any subsequent transaction. Just as defensive measures cannot be draconian, however, they cannot limit or circumscribe the directors' fiduciary duties. Notwithstanding the corporation's insolvent condition, the NCS board had no authority to execute a merger agreement that subsequently prevented it from effectively discharging its ongoing fiduciary responsibilities. . . .

The NCS board was required to contract for an effective fiduciary out clause to exercise its continuing fiduciary responsibilities to the minority stockholders. The issues in this appeal do not involve the general validity of either stockholder voting agreements or the authority of directors to insert a Section 251(c) provision in a merger agreement. In this case, the NCS board combined those two otherwise valid actions and caused them to operate in concert as an absolute lock up, in the absence of an effective fiduciary out clause in the Genesis merger agreement.

In the context of this preclusive and coercive lock up case, the protection of Genesis' contractual expectations must yield to the supervening responsibility of the directors to discharge their fiduciary duties on a continuing basis. The merger agreement and voting agreements, as they were combined to operate in concert in this case, are inconsistent with the NCS directors' fiduciary duties. To that extent, we hold that they are invalid and unenforceable.

Omnicare, Inc. v. NCS Healthcare, Inc., 818 A.2d 914, 936-939 (Del. 2003). In their dissent, Justices Veasey and Steele argue, among other things, the following:

The Majority invalidates the NCS board's action by announcing a new rule that represents an extension of our jurisprudence. That new rule can be narrowly stated as follows: A merger agreement entered into after a market search, before any prospect of a topping bid has emerged, which locks up stockholder approval and does not contain a "fiduciary out" provision, is per se invalid when a later significant topping bid emerges. As we have noted, this bright-line, per se rule would apply regardless of (1) the circumstances leading up to the agreement and (2) the fact that stockholders who control voting power had irrevocably committed themselves, *as stockholders*, to vote for the merger. Narrowly stated, this new rule is a judicially-created "third rail" that now becomes one of the given "rules of the game," to be taken into account by the negotiators and drafters of merger agreements. In our view, this new rule is an unwise extension of existing precedent.

Although it is debatable whether Unocal applies — and we believe that the better rule in this situation is that the business judgment rule should apply — we will, nevertheless, assume arguendo — as the Vice Chancellor did — that Unocal applies. Therefore, under Unocal the NCS directors had the burden of going forward with the evidence to show that there was a threat to corporate policy and effectiveness and that their actions were reasonable in response to that threat. The Vice Chancellor correctly found that they reasonably perceived the threat that NCS did not have a viable offer from Omnicare — or anyone else — to pay off its creditors, cure its insolvency and provide some payment to stockholders. The NCS board's actions — as the Vice Chancellor correctly held — were reasonable in relation to the threat because the Genesis deal was the "only game in town," the NCS directors got the best deal they could from Genesis and — but-for the emergence of Genesis on the scene – there would have been no viable deal. . . .

In our view, the Majority misapplies the Unitrin concept of "coercive and preclusive" measures to preempt a proper proportionality balancing. Thus, the Majority asserts that "in applying enhanced judicial scrutiny to defensive devices designed to protect a merger agreement,. . . .a court must . . .determine that those measures are not preclusive or coercive. . . ." Here, the deal protection measures were not adopted unilaterally by the board to fend off an existing hostile offer that threatened the corporate policy and effectiveness of NCS. They were adopted because Genesis – the "only game in town" – would not save NCS, its creditors and its stockholders without these provisions. . ..

We respectfully disagree with the Majority's conclusion that the NCS board breached its fiduciary duties to the Class A stockholders by failing to negotiate a "fiduciary out" in the Genesis merger agreement. . ..

In this case, Genesis made it abundantly clear early on that it was willing to negotiate a deal with NCS but only on the condition that it would not be a "stalking horse." Thus, it wanted to be certain that a third party could not use its deal with NCS as a floor against which to begin a bidding war. As a result of this negotiating position, a "fiduciary out" was not acceptable to Genesis. The Majority Opinion holds that such a negotiating position, if implemented in the agreement, is invalid per se where there is an absolute lock-up. We know of no authority in our jurisprudence supporting this new rule, and we believe it is unwise and unwarranted.

Id. at 942-45.

Which of the two analyses — that in the majority opinion or that in the dissent — is more persuasive to you? Revisit this note after reading about *Revlon* and its progeny, *infra*. Consider whether you still hold the same view and whether *Revlon* duties apply.

c. The Need for a Compelling Justification Under *Blasius*

Takeover defenses that have shareholder disenfranchisement as a primary purpose may be valid but are inherently suspect. The key case in this area, cited by Justice Holland in *Unitrin*, is a Delaware Chancery Court case decided in 1988 and excerpted in Chapter 8: *Blasius Industries, Inc. v. Atlas Corp.* Review that excerpt in the context of takeover defenses. Note as you review it both the level of scrutiny and operative standard that the Chancery Court employs in evaluating the validity of a takeover defense that impedes the exercise of shareholder voting power in the context of a proxy contest.

d. Price Maximization under *Revlon* and its Progeny

The need for deal protection devices among the arsenal of takeover defenses responds to the prospect that a target corporation may negotiate a business combination with a desired acquiror and find that another bidder may emerge with a topping bid since the target corporation is deemed to be "on the market" or "in play". The initial, "friendly" acquiror often will demand protection for the benefit of the bargain it strikes with the target through a negotiated lock-up option, a no-shop provision, termination fees, and the like.

As evidenced by negotiated fiduciary out provisions, questions also arise in a competitive bidding context as to when a target's board, in exercising its fiduciary duties, must abandon the target's chosen bidder in favor of an interloper. It seems clear that, as in the other takeover defense situations explored above, the business judgment rule will not initially be applicable. Moreover, absent a duty of loyalty issue, the entire fairness standard is not clearly applicable in this situation. Accordingly, we must ask whether the *Unocal/Unitrin* framework (or, as applicable in disenfranchisement situations, the *Blasius* compelling justification standard) is the appropriate mechanism for judicial review of deal protection devices or whether something else is needed. Three leading cases establish the framework for analysis in this factual context. One is excerpted below; the other two then are summarized.

i. The Emergence of a *Revlon* Duty

The *Revlon* case, excerpted below, represents (to many) a watershed in Delaware corporate law. Note how *Revlon* addresses both deal protection devices and other takeover defenses, all in one opinion. What role does the *Unocal* standard of review serve in *Revlon* in an analysis of the deal protection provisions? Is it the same as the role it serves in a review of the board's actions in adopting other takeover defenses? What is *Revlon*'s overall role in the jurisprudence of takeover defenses?

REVLON, INC. v. MACANDREWS & FORBES HOLDINGS, INC.
Supreme Court of Delaware
506 A.2d 173 (1986)

MOORE, J.

In this battle for corporate control of Revlon, Inc. (Revlon), the Court of Chancery enjoined certain transactions designed to thwart the efforts of Pantry Pride, Inc. (Pantry Pride) to acquire Revlon.[1] The defendants are Revlon, its board of directors, and Forstmann Little & Co. and the latter's affiliated limited partnership (collectively, Forstmann). The injunction barred consummation of an option granted Forstmann to purchase certain Revlon assets (the lock-up option), a promise by Revlon to deal exclusively with Forstmann in the face of a takeover (the no-shop provision), and the payment of a $ 25 million cancellation fee to Forstmann if the transaction was aborted. The Court of Chancery found that the Revlon directors had breached their duty of care by entering into the foregoing transactions and effectively ending an active auction for the company. The trial court ruled that such arrangements are not illegal *per se* under Delaware law, but that their use under the circumstances here was impermissible. We agree. Thus, we granted this expedited interlocutory appeal to consider for the first time the validity of such defensive measures in the face of an active bidding contest for corporate control. Additionally, we address for the first time the extent to which a corporation may consider the impact of a takeover threat on constituencies other than shareholders.

In our view, lock-ups and related agreements are permitted under Delaware law where their adoption is untainted by director interest or other breaches of fiduciary duty. The actions taken by the Revlon directors, however, did not meet this standard. Moreover, while concern for various corporate constituencies is proper when addressing a takeover threat, that principle is limited by the requirement that there be some rationally related benefit accruing to the stockholders. We find no such benefit here.

Thus, under all the circumstances we must agree with the Court of Chancery that the enjoined Revlon defensive measures were inconsistent with the directors' duties to the stockholders. Accordingly, we affirm.

I.

The somewhat complex maneuvers of the parties necessitate a rather detailed examination of the facts. The prelude to this controversy began in June 1985, when Ronald O. Perelman, chairman of the board and chief executive officer of Pantry Pride, met with his counterpart at Revlon, Michel C. Bergerac, to discuss a friendly acquisition of Revlon by Pantry Pride. Perelman suggested a price in the range of $ 40–50 per share, but the meeting ended with Bergerac dismissing those figures as considerably below Revlon's intrinsic value. All subsequent Pantry Pride overtures were rebuffed, perhaps in part based on Mr. Bergerac's strong personal antipathy to Mr. Perelman.

Thus, on August 14, Pantry Pride's board authorized Perelman to acquire Revlon, either through negotiation in the $ 42–$ 43 per share range, or by making a hostile tender offer at $ 45. Perelman then met with Bergerac and outlined Pantry Pride's alternate approaches. Bergerac remained adamantly opposed to such schemes and conditioned any further discussions of the matter on Pantry Pride executing a standstill agreement prohibiting it from acquiring Revlon without the latter's prior approval.

On August 19, the Revlon board met specially to consider the impending threat of a

---

[1] The nominal plaintiff, MacAndrews & Forbes Holdings, Inc., is the controlling stockholder of Pantry Pride. For all practical purposes, their interests in this litigation are virtually identical, and we hereafter will refer to Pantry Pride as the plaintiff.

hostile bid by Pantry Pride. At the meeting, Lazard Freres, Revlon's investment banker, advised the directors that $ 45 per share was a grossly inadequate price for the company. Felix Rohatyn and William Loomis of Lazard Freres explained to the board that Pantry Pride's financial strategy for acquiring Revlon would be through "junk bond" financing followed by a break-up of Revlon and the disposition of its assets. With proper timing, according to the experts, such transactions could produce a return to Pantry Pride of $ 60 to $ 70 per share, while a sale of the company as a whole would be in the "mid 50" dollar range. Martin Lipton, special counsel for Revlon, recommended two defensive measures: first, that the company repurchase up to 5 million of its nearly 30 million outstanding shares; and second, that it adopt a Note Purchase Rights Plan. Under this plan, each Revlon shareholder would receive as a dividend one Note Purchase Right (the Rights) for each share of common stock, with the Rights entitling the holder to exchange one common share for a $ 65 principal Revlon note at 12% interest with a one-year maturity. The Rights would become effective whenever anyone acquired beneficial ownership of 20% or more of Revlon's shares, unless the purchaser acquired all the company's stock for cash at $ 65 or more per share. In addition, the Rights would not be available to the acquiror, and prior to the 20% triggering event, the Revlon board could redeem the rights for 10 cents each. Both proposals were unanimously adopted.

Pantry Pride made its first hostile move on August 23 with a cash tender offer for any and all shares of Revlon at $ 47.50 per common share and $ 26.67 per preferred share, subject to (1) Pantry Pride's obtaining financing for the purchase, and (2) the Rights being redeemed, rescinded or voided.

The Revlon board met again on August 26. The directors advised the stockholders to reject the offer. Further defensive measures also were planned. On August 29, Revlon commenced its own offer for up to 10 million shares, exchanging for each share of common stock tendered one Senior Subordinated Note (the Notes) of $ 47.50 principal at 11.75% interest, due 1995, and one-tenth of a share of $ 9.00 Cumulative Convertible Exchangeable Preferred Stock valued at $ 100 per share. Lazard Freres opined that the notes would trade at their face value on a fully distributed basis. Revlon stockholders tendered 87 percent of the outstanding shares (approximately 33 million), and the company accepted the full 10 million shares on a pro rata basis. The new Notes contained covenants which limited Revlon's ability to incur additional debt, sell assets, or pay dividends unless otherwise approved by the "independent" (non-management) members of the board.

At this point, both the Rights and the Note covenants stymied Pantry Pride's attempted takeover. The next move came on September 16, when Pantry Pride announced a new tender offer at $ 42 per share, conditioned upon receiving at least 90% of the outstanding stock. Pantry Pride also indicated that it would consider buying less than 90%, and at an increased price, if Revlon removed the impeding Rights. While this offer was lower on its face than the earlier $ 47.50 proposal, Revlon's investment banker, Lazard Freres, described the two bids as essentially equal in view of the completed exchange offer.

The Revlon board held a regularly scheduled meeting on September 24. The directors rejected the latest Pantry Pride offer and authorized management to negotiate with other parties interested in acquiring Revlon. Pantry Pride remained determined in its efforts and continued to make cash bids for the company, offering $ 50 per share on September 27, and raising its bid to $ 53 on October 1, and then to $ 56.25 on October 7.

In the meantime, Revlon's negotiations with Forstmann and the investment group Adler & Shaykin had produced results. The Revlon directors met on October 3 to consider Pantry Pride's $ 53 bid and to examine possible alternatives to the offer. Both Forstmann and Adler & Shaykin made certain proposals to the board. As a result, the directors unanimously agreed to a leveraged buyout by Forstmann. The terms of this accord were as follows: each stockholder would get $ 56 cash per share; management would purchase stock in the new company by the exercise of their Revlon "golden parachutes"; Forstmann would assume Revlon's $ 475 million debt incurred by the issuance of the Notes; and Revlon would redeem the Rights and waive the Notes covenants for Forstmann or in connection with any other offer superior to Forstmann's. The board did not actually remove the covenants at the October 3 meeting, because Forstmann then lacked a firm commitment on its financing, but accepted the Forstmann capital structure, and indicated that the outside directors would waive the covenants in due course. Part of Forstmann's plan was to sell Revlon's Norcliff Thayer and Reheis divisions to American Home Products for $ 335 million. Before the merger, Revlon was to sell its cosmetics and fragrance division to Adler & Shaykin for $ 905 million. These transactions would facilitate the purchase by Forstmann or any other acquiror of Revlon.

When the merger, and thus the waiver of the Notes covenants, was announced, the market value of these securities began to fall. The Notes, which originally traded near par, around 100, dropped to 87.50 by October 8. One director later reported (at the October 12 meeting) a "deluge" of telephone calls from irate noteholders, and on October 10 the Wall Street Journal reported threats of litigation by these creditors.

Pantry Pride countered with a new proposal on October 7, raising its $ 53 offer to $ 56.25, subject to nullification of the Rights, a waiver of the Notes covenants, and the election of three Pantry Pride directors to the Revlon board. On October 9, representatives of Pantry Pride, Forstmann, and Revlon conferred in an attempt to negotiate the fate of Revlon, but could not reach agreement. At this meeting Pantry Pride announced that it would engage in fractional bidding and top any Forstmann offer by a slightly higher one. It is also significant that Forstmann, to Pantry Pride's exclusion, had been made privy to certain Revlon financial data. Thus, the parties were not negotiating on equal terms.

Again privately armed with Revlon data, Forstmann met on October 11 with Revlon's special counsel and investment banker. On October 12, Forstmann made a new $ 57.25 per share offer, based on several conditions. The principal demand was a lock-up option to purchase Revlon's Vision Care and National Health Laboratories divisions for $ 525 million, some $ 100-$ 175 million below the value ascribed to them by Lazard Freres, if another acquiror got 40% of Revlon's shares. Revlon also was required to accept a no-shop provision. The Rights and Notes covenants had to be removed as in the October 3 agreement. There would be a $ 25 million cancellation fee to be placed in escrow, and released to Forstmann if the new agreement terminated or if another acquiror got more than 19.9% of Revlon's stock. Finally, there would be no participation by Revlon management in the merger. In return, Forstmann agreed to support the par value of the Notes, which had faltered in the market, by an exchange of new notes. Forstmann also demanded immediate acceptance of its offer, or it would be withdrawn. The board unanimously approved Forstmann's proposal because: (1) it was for a higher price than the Pantry Pride bid, (2) it protected the noteholders, and (3) Forstmann's financing was firmly in place. The board further agreed to redeem the rights and waive the covenants on the preferred stock in response to any offer above $ 57 cash per share. The covenants were waived, contingent upon receipt of an investment banking opinion that the Notes would trade near par value once the offer was consummated.

Pantry Pride, which had initially sought injunctive relief from the Rights plan on August 22, filed an amended complaint on October 14 challenging the lock-up, the cancellation fee, and the exercise of the Rights and the Notes covenants. Pantry Pride also sought a temporary restraining order to prevent Revlon from placing any assets in escrow or transferring them to Forstmann. Moreover, on October 22, Pantry Pride again raised its bid, with a cash offer of $ 58 per share conditioned upon nullification of the Rights, waiver of the covenants, and an injunction of the Forstmann lock-up.

On October 15, the Court of Chancery prohibited the further transfer of assets, and eight days later enjoined the lock-up, no-shop, and cancellation fee provisions of the agreement. The trial court concluded that the Revlon directors had breached their duty of loyalty by making concessions to Forstmann, out of concern for their liability to the noteholders, rather than maximizing the sale price of the company for the stockholders' benefit.

II.

To obtain a preliminary injunction, a plaintiff must demonstrate both a reasonable probability of success on the merits and some irreparable harm which will occur absent the injunction. Additionally, the Court shall balance the conveniences of and possible injuries to the parties.

A.

We turn first to Pantry Pride's probability of success on the merits. The ultimate responsibility for managing the business and affairs of a corporation falls on its board of directors. 8 DEL. C. § 141(a). In discharging this function the directors owe fiduciary duties of care and loyalty to the corporation and its shareholders. These principles apply with equal force when a board approves a corporate merger pursuant to 8 Del.C. § 251(b); and of course they are the bedrock of our law regarding corporate takeover issues. While the business judgment rule may be applicable to the actions of corporate directors responding to takeover threats, the principles upon which it is founded — care, loyalty and independence must first be satisfied.

If the business judgment rule applies, there is a "presumption that in making a business decision the directors of a corporation acted on an informed basis, in good faith and in the honest belief that the action taken was in the best interests of the company." However, when a board implements anti-takeover measures there arises "the omnipresent specter that a board may be acting primarily in its own interests, rather than those of the corporation and its shareholders . . ." This potential for conflict places upon the directors the burden of proving that they had reasonable grounds for believing there was a danger to corporate policy and effectiveness, a burden satisfied by a showing of good faith and reasonable investigation. In addition, the directors must analyze the nature of the takeover and its effect on the corporation in order to ensure balance — that the responsive action taken is reasonable in relation to the threat posed.

B.

The first relevant defensive measure adopted by the Revlon board was the Rights Plan, which would be considered a "poison pill" in the current language of corporate takeovers — a plan by which shareholders receive the right to be bought out by the corporation at a substantial premium on the occurrence of a stated triggering event. By 8 Del.C. §§ 141 and 122(13), the board clearly had the power to adopt the measure. Thus, the focus becomes one of reasonableness and purpose.

The Revlon board approved the Rights Plan in the face of an impending hostile takeover bid by Pantry Pride at $ 45 per share, a price which Revlon reasonably concluded was grossly inadequate. Lazard Freres had so advised the directors, and had also informed them that Pantry Pride was a small, highly leveraged company bent on a "bust-up" takeover by using "junk bond" financing to buy Revlon cheaply, sell the acquired assets to pay the debts incurred, and retain the profit for itself. In adopting the Plan, the board protected the shareholders from a hostile takeover at a price below the company's intrinsic value, while retaining sufficient flexibility to address any proposal deemed to be in the stockholders' best interests.

To that extent the board acted in good faith and upon reasonable investigation. Under the circumstances it cannot be said that the Rights Plan as employed was unreasonable, considering the threat posed. Indeed, the Plan was a factor in causing Pantry Pride to raise its bids from a low of $ 42 to an eventual high of $ 58. At the time of its adoption, the Rights Plan afforded a measure of protection consistent with the directors' fiduciary duty in facing a takeover threat perceived as detrimental to corporate interests. Far from being a "show-stopper," . . . the measure spurred the bidding to new heights, a proper result of its implementation.

Although we consider adoption of the Plan to have been valid under the circumstances, its continued usefulness was rendered moot by the directors' actions on October 3 and October 12. At the October 3 meeting the board redeemed the Rights conditioned upon consummation of a merger with Forstmann, but further acknowledged that they would also be redeemed to facilitate any more favorable offer. On October 12, the board unanimously passed a resolution redeeming the Rights in connection with any cash proposal of $ 57.25 or more per share. Because all the pertinent offers eventually equalled or surpassed that amount, the Rights clearly were no longer any impediment in the contest for Revlon. This mooted any question of their propriety . . . .

C.

The second defensive measure adopted by Revlon to thwart a Pantry Pride takeover was the company's own exchange offer for 10 million of its shares. The directors' general broad powers to manage the business and affairs of the corporation are augmented by the specific authority conferred under 8 Del.C. § 160(a), permitting the company to deal in its own stock. However, when exercising that power in an effort to forestall a hostile takeover, the board's actions are strictly held to the fiduciary standards outlined in *Unocal*. These standards require the directors to determine the best interests of the corporation and its stockholders, and impose an enhanced duty to abjure any action that is motivated by considerations other than a good faith concern for such interests.

The Revlon directors concluded that Pantry Pride's $ 47.50 offer was grossly inadequate. In that regard, the board acted in good faith, and on an informed basis, with reasonable grounds to believe that there existed a harmful threat to the corporate enterprise. The adoption of a defensive measure, reasonable in relation to the threat posed, was proper and fully accorded with the powers, duties, and responsibilities conferred upon directors under our law.

D.

However, when Pantry Pride increased its offer to $ 50 per share, and then to $ 53, it became apparent to all that the break-up of the company was inevitable. The Revlon board's authorization permitting management to negotiate a merger or buyout with a third party was a recognition that the company was for sale. The duty of the board had thus changed from the preservation of Revlon as a corporate entity to the maximization of the company's value at a sale for the stockholders' benefit. This significantly altered the board's responsibilities under the *Unocal* standards. It no longer faced threats to corporate policy and effectiveness, or to the stockholders' interests, from a grossly inadequate bid. The whole question of defensive measures became moot. The directors' role changed from defenders of the corporate bastion to auctioneers charged with getting the best price for the stockholders at a sale of the company.

III.

This brings us to the lock-up with Forstmann and its emphasis on shoring up the sagging market value of the Notes in the face of threatened litigation by their holders. Such a focus was inconsistent with the changed concept of the directors' responsibilities at this stage of the developments. The impending waiver of the Notes covenants had caused the value of the Notes to fall, and the board was aware of the noteholders' ire as well as their subsequent threats of suit. The directors thus made support of the Notes an integral part of the company's dealings with Forstmann, even though their primary responsibility at this stage was to the equity owners.

The original threat posed by Pantry Pride — the break-up of the company — had become a reality which even the directors embraced. Selective dealing to fend off a hostile but determined bidder was no longer a proper objective. Instead, obtaining the highest price for the benefit of the stockholders should have been the central theme guiding director action. Thus, the Revlon board could not make the requisite showing of good faith by preferring the noteholders and ignoring its duty of loyalty to the shareholders. The rights of the former already were fixed by contract. The noteholders required no further protection, and when the Revlon board entered into an auction-ending lock-up agreement with Forstmann on the basis of impermissible considerations at the expense of the shareholders, the directors breached their primary duty of loyalty.

The Revlon board argued that it acted in good faith in protecting the noteholders because *Unocal* permits consideration of other corporate constituencies. Although such considerations may be permissible, there are fundamental limitations upon that prerogative. A board may have regard for various constituencies in discharging its responsibilities, provided there are rationally related benefits accruing to the stockholders. However, such concern for non-stockholder interests is inappropriate when an auction among active bidders is in progress, and the object no longer is to protect or maintain the corporate enterprise but to sell it to the highest bidder.

Revlon also contended that . . . it had contractual and good faith obligations to consider the noteholders. However, any such duties are limited to the principle that one may not interfere with contractual relationships by improper actions. Here, the rights of the noteholders were fixed by agreement, and there is nothing of substance to suggest that any of those terms were violated. The Notes covenants specifically contemplated a waiver to permit sale of the company at a fair price. The Notes were accepted by the holders on that basis, including the risk of an adverse market effect stemming from a waiver. Thus, nothing remained for Revlon to legitimately protect, and no rationally related benefit thereby accrued to the stockholders. Under such circumstances we must conclude that the merger agreement with Forstmann was unreasonable in relation to the threat posed.

A lock-up is not *per se* illegal under Delaware law. Its use has been approved in an earlier case. Such options can entice other bidders to enter a contest for control of the corporation, creating an auction for the company and maximizing shareholder profit. Current economic conditions in the takeover market are such that a "white knight" like Forstmann might only enter the bidding for the target company if it receives some form of compensation to cover the risks and costs involved. However, while those lock-ups which draw bidders into the battle benefit shareholders, similar measures which end an active auction and foreclose further bidding operate to the shareholders' detriment.

Recently, the United States Court of Appeals for the Second Circuit invalidated a lock-up on fiduciary duty grounds similar to those here. . . . [T]he court stated:

> In this regard, we are especially mindful that some lock-up options may be beneficial to the shareholders, such as those that induce a bidder to compete for control of a corporation, while others may be harmful, such as those that effectively preclude bidders from competing with the optionee bidder.

. . . .

The Forstmann option had a . . . destructive effect on the auction process. Forstmann had already been drawn into the contest on a preferred basis, so the result of the lock-up was not to foster bidding, but to destroy it. The board's stated reasons for approving the transactions were: (1) better financing, (2) noteholder protection, and (3) higher price. As the Court of Chancery found, and we agree, any distinctions between the rival bidders' methods of financing the proposal were nominal at best, and such a consideration has little or no significance in a cash offer for any and all shares. The principal object, contrary to the board's duty of care, appears to have been protection of the noteholders over the shareholders' interests.

While Forstmann's $ 57.25 offer was objectively higher than Pantry Pride's $ 56.25 bid, the margin of superiority is less when the Forstmann price is adjusted for the time value of money. In reality, the Revlon board ended the auction in return for very little actual improvement in the final bid. The principal benefit went to the directors, who avoided personal liability to a class of creditors to whom the board owed no further duty under the circumstances. Thus, when a board ends an intense bidding contest on an insubstantial basis, and where a significant by-product of that action is to protect the directors against a perceived threat of personal liability for consequences stemming from the adoption of previous defensive measures, the action cannot withstand the enhanced scrutiny which *Unocal* requires of director conduct.

In addition to the lock-up option, the Court of Chancery enjoined the no-shop provision as part of the attempt to foreclose further bidding by Pantry Pride. The no-shop provision, like the lock-up option, while not *per se* illegal, is impermissible under the *Unocal* standards when a board's primary duty becomes that of an auctioneer responsible for selling the company to the highest bidder. The agreement to negotiate only with Forstmann ended rather than intensified the board's involvement in the bidding contest.

It is ironic that the parties even considered a no-shop agreement when Revlon had dealt preferentially, and almost exclusively, with Forstmann throughout the contest. After the directors authorized management to negotiate with other parties, Forstmann was given every negotiating advantage that Pantry Pride had been denied: cooperation from management, access to financial data, and the exclusive opportunity to present merger proposals directly to the board of directors. Favoritism for a white knight to the total exclusion of a hostile bidder might be justifiable when the latter's offer adversely affects shareholder interests, but when bidders make relatively similar offers, or dissolution of the company becomes inevitable, the directors cannot fulfill their enhanced *Unocal* duties by playing favorites with the contending factions. Market forces must be allowed to operate freely to bring the target's shareholders the best price available for their equity. Thus, as the trial court ruled, the shareholders' interests necessitated that the board remain free to negotiate in the fulfillment of that duty.

The court below similarly enjoined the payment of the cancellation fee, pending a resolution of the merits, because the fee was part of the overall plan to thwart Pantry Pride's efforts. We find no abuse of discretion in that ruling.

IV.

Having concluded that Pantry Pride has shown a reasonable probability of success on the merits, we address the issue of irreparable harm. The Court of Chancery ruled that unless the lock-up and other aspects of the agreement were enjoined, Pantry Pride's opportunity to bid for Revlon was lost. The court also held that the need for both bidders to compete in the marketplace outweighed any injury to Forstmann. Given the complexity of the proposed transaction between Revlon and Forstmann, the obstacles to Pantry Pride obtaining a meaningful legal remedy are immense. We are satisfied that the plaintiff has shown the need for an injunction to protect it from irreparable harm, which need outweighs any harm to the defendants.

V.

In conclusion, the Revlon board was confronted with a situation not uncommon in the current wave of corporate takeovers. A hostile and determined bidder sought the company at a price the board was convinced was inadequate. The initial defensive tactics worked to the benefit of the shareholders, and thus the board was able to sustain its *Unocal* burdens in justifying those measures. However, in granting an asset option lock-up to Forstmann, we must conclude that under all the circumstances, the directors allowed considerations other than the maximization of shareholder profit to affect their judgment, and followed a course that ended the auction for Revlon, absent court intervention, to the ultimate detriment of its shareholders. No such defensive measure can be sustained when it represents a breach of the directors' fundamental duty of care. In that context the board's action is not entitled to the deference accorded it by the business judgment rule. The measures were properly enjoined. The decision of the Court of Chancery, therefore, is AFFIRMED.

ii. Defining the Applicability and Scope of the *Revlon* Duty

In the *Revlon* case, the court found that a break-up of Revlon was "inevitable" and that the board no longer was permitted to deal selectively with putative acquirors. Instead, the board's obligation was to obtain for shareholders the highest price available. This obligation of the directors is known as a "*Revlon* duty" (often referred to in the plural as "*Revlon* duties"). Although most understood from *Revlon* that the duty requires price maximization and applies in an auction context, details about the scope and applicability of the duty were unclear. Moreover, questions arose about the *Revlon* court's reference, at the end of the opinion, to "a breach of the directors' fundamental duty of care." Did the *Revlon* court really mean that the directors had breached their duty of care in failing to act in a manner consistent with price maximization? If so, in what sense? If not, is the *Revlon* duty a new fiduciary or other duty, or is it part of the directors' duty to act in good faith or in the best interests of the corporation? Subsequent case law has begun to answer some of these questions. Two of those cases are particularly important.

Paramount Communications, Inc. v. Time, Inc., 571 A.2d 1140 (Del. 1989), often referred to as the *Time Warner* case, relates to Paramount's attempt to acquire control of Time, Inc. after Time's announcement of a negotiated business combination with Warner Communication, Inc. In that litigation, shareholder plaintiffs argue, among other things, that the business combination negotiated between Time and Warner "resulted in a change of control which effectively put Time up for sale, thereby triggering *Revlon* duties." The shareholder plaintiffs specifically argue that the exchange ratio favored Warner, resulting in Warner's shareholders acquiring a controlling interest in the combined Time-Warner company, and that Time's directors intended to sell the corporation "as evidenced in their statements that the market might perceive the Time-Warner merger as putting Time up 'for sale' and their adoption of various defensive measures." In rejecting this *Revlon* argument, the court describes the circumstances in which it believes that the *Revlon* duty attaches to director actions.

> Under Delaware law there are, generally speaking and without excluding other possibilities, two circumstances which may implicate *Revlon* duties. The first, and clearer one, is when a corporation initiates an active bidding process seeking to sell itself or to effect a business reorganization involving a clear break-up of the company. However, *Revlon* duties may also be triggered where, in response to a bidder's offer, a target abandons its long-term strategy and seeks an alternative transaction also involving the break-up of the company. Thus, in *Revlon*, when the board responded to Pantry Pride's offer by contemplating a "bust-up" sale of assets in a leveraged acquisition, we imposed

upon the board a duty to maximize immediate shareholder value and an obligation to auction the company fairly. If, however, the board's reaction to a hostile tender offer is found to constitute only a defensive response and not an abandonment of the corporation's continued existence, *Revlon* duties are not triggered, though *Unocal* duties attach.

571 A.2d at 1150–51 (citations and footnotes omitted). The court finds that the *Revlon* duty is not invoked under this standard, expressly:

- declining "to extend *Revlon's* application to corporate transactions simply because they might be construed as putting a corporation either 'in play' or 'up for sale;'"

- refusing to find that the adoption of deal protection devices, taken alone, implicate *Revlon*; and

- failing to find that Time's restructuring, from a share exchange to a share purchase, of its business combination with Warner either constituted an abandonment of Time's strategic plan or made a sale of Time inevitable.

As a result, the court the applies a *Unocal* analysis and finds that plaintiffs are not likely to prevail in their overall claim that Time's use of deal protection devices (in this case, a lock-up agreement, a no-shop clause, and "dry-up" agreements) constitute a breach of the directors' fiduciary duties.

The second case, *Paramount Communications v. QVC Network*, 637 A.2d 34 (Del. 1994), involves an attempt by QVC Network Inc. to enjoin deal protection devices (a no-shop provision, a termination fee, and a stock lock-up option) designed to support a "strategic alliance" between Viacom Inc. and Paramount in the wake of an unsolicited, high-value tender offer by QVC for Paramount's outstanding stock. In this case, Paramount argues that *Revlon* duties do not attach to its board's approval of the deal protection provisions adopted in connection with the strategic alliance. Paramount's argument in this regard is rejected by the court. After applying the law from *Revlon* and the first *Paramount* case (*Time Warner*) to the facts, the court holds "that the sale of control in this case, which is at the heart of the proposed strategic alliance, implicates enhanced judicial scrutiny of the conduct of the Paramount Board under *Unocal* . . . and *Revlon*" and "that the conduct of the Paramount Board was not reasonable as to process or result."

In reaching its holding on the *Revlon* claim, the court both further defines the type of transaction that may constitute a sale of control and also further describes the circumstances under which a *Revlon* duty will be deemed to apply to a board's actions in thwarting a potential bidder in a battle for corporate control. In defining change of control transactions, the court begins by noting the importance of voting control, both in general and in this specific case. The court's remarks echo and reinforce Delaware court commentary in *Blasius* and other cases on the value of the shareholder franchise.

> In the case before us, the public stockholders (in the aggregate) currently own a majority of Paramount's voting stock. Control of the corporation is not vested in a single person, entity, or group, but vested in the fluid aggregation of unaffiliated stockholders. In the event the Paramount-Viacom transaction is consummated, the public stockholders will receive cash and a minority equity voting position in the surviving corporation. Following such consummation, there will be a controlling stockholder who will have the voting power to: (a) elect directors; (b) cause a break-up of the corporation; (c) merge it with another company; (d) cash-out the public stockholders; (e) amend the certificate of incorporation; (f) sell all or substantially all of the corporate assets; or (g) otherwise alter materially the nature of the corporation and the public stockholders' interests. Irrespective of the present Paramount Board's vision of a long-term strategic alliance with Viacom, the proposed sale of control would provide the new controlling stockholder with the power to alter that vision.

Because of the intended sale of control, the Paramount-Viacom transaction has economic consequences of considerable significance to the Paramount stockholders. Once control has shifted, the current Paramount stockholders will have no leverage in the future to demand another control premium. As a result, the Paramount stockholders are entitled to receive, and should receive, a control premium and/or protective devices of significant value. There being no such protective provisions in the Viacom-Paramount transaction, the Paramount directors had an obligation to take the maximum advantage of the current opportunity to realize for the stockholders the best value reasonably available. . . .

[S]ome of the methods by which a board can fulfill its obligation to seek the best value reasonably available to the stockholders . . . include conducting an auction, canvassing the market, etc. Delaware law recognizes that there is "no single blueprint" that directors must follow.

Id. at 43–44 (citations and footnotes omitted). These views help to flesh out in more detail the contents of directors' duties under *Revlon*. Paramount disagrees that a *Revlon* duty and enhanced scrutiny apply under the facts of the case (since there is no "break-up" of Paramount as a result of the strategic alliance with Viacom). The court expressly, directly addresses Paramount's arguments in its opinion, further clarifying the circumstances under which a *Revlon* duty attaches to board action taken to protect or favor a particular change of control transaction.

The Paramount defendants' position that *both* a change of control *and* a break-up are *required* must be rejected. Such a holding would unduly restrict the application of *Revlon*, is inconsistent with this Court's decisions . . . , and has no basis in policy. There are few events that have a more significant impact on the stockholders than a sale of control or a corporate break-up. Each event represents a fundamental (and perhaps irrevocable) change in the nature of the corporate enterprise from a practical standpoint. It is the significance of *each* of these events that justifies: (a) focusing on the directors' obligation to seek the best value reasonably available to the stockholders; and (b) requiring a close scrutiny of board action which could be contrary to the stockholders' interests.

Accordingly, when a corporation undertakes a transaction which will cause: (a) a change in corporate control; *or* (b) a break-up of the corporate entity, the directors' obligation is to seek the best value reasonably available to the stockholders. This obligation arises because the effect of the Viacom-Paramount transaction, if consummated, is to shift control of Paramount from the public stockholders to a controlling stockholder, Viacom. Neither *Time-Warner* nor any other decision of this Court holds that a "break-up" of the company is essential to give rise to this obligation where there is a sale of control.

Id. at 47–48. The court then focused on an analysis of the Paramount board's actions taken (and omissions to act) in protection of the strategic alliance between Paramount and Viacom in the face of QVC's competing offers, finding that the Paramount directors had breached their fiduciary duties by failing to fulfill their *Revlon* duties.

In light of *Revlon* and the two Paramount cases, review the Note on the *Omnicare* case at the end of part C.2.b., *supra*, and consider whether a *Revlon* duty applies.

The problems set forth below allow you to reflect on all of the cases and materials you have read in this chapter regarding takeover defenses, including *Revlon* and its case law progeny (as set forth above). Put yourself in the role of the legal advisor to Ski-Me in each case. How would you advise your client?

PROBLEMS

Ski-Me Industries, Inc., a Delaware corporation, owns four ski resorts, two in New England and two in Colorado. Ski-Me's first resort was Ski-Me Village, a ski resort in New Hampshire. Ski-Me has been profitable for fifteen successive years. It has utilized its cash flow to purchase the two Colorado resorts and to modernize all its facilities, which now have new, spacious, energy-efficient lodges and high-speed quad chair lifts on all major ski runs.

Last year there was no snow, other than man-made, at three of Ski-Me's four resorts. Ski-Me was barely profitable. The per share market price of its common stock (the only class of capital stock it has outstanding) has retreated from about $ 19–20 to about $ 13–14, which is the approximate book value per share. Ski-Me has over 300 shareholders of record and over 3,000 beneficial owners. Its common stock is listed on the NASDAQ Capital Market under the symbol SKII. Ski-Me's certificate of incorporation includes a provision that allows directors to adopt, amend, or repeal its bylaws.

1. Worried that Ski-Me had possibly become vulnerable to a hostile takeover bid, the directors (a) amended the corporation's bylaws to stagger the board into three classes, each to serve a three-year term, and (b) instituted requirements that shareholders (i) could remove directors "only for cause" and (ii) could approve mergers only with a vote of two-thirds or more of the shares present and voting (assuming a quorum is present).

Can Ski-Me's directors do these things or will a reviewing court strike them down? Consider both the board's authority to take these actions and the board's fulfillment of its fiduciary duties. Cite to relevant statutes and case law.

2. Now assume that Ski-Me's directors ascertain that, indeed, a bidder is on the scene. National Skiing, Inc. has filed a Statement of Beneficial Ownership on Schedule 13D with the SEC. The Schedule 13D discloses a 12% ownership stake in Ski-Me. At an emergency special meeting, Ski-Me's directors vote to give an option on the two Colorado ski resorts, at a favorable price, to Telluride Ski Resort, Inc., another recreation company. The option is exercisable if any person or group of people acquire beneficial ownership of 20% or more of Ski-Me's common stock.

Ski-Me's directors also approve and announce a defensive self-tender offer for up to 40% of Ski-Me's stock, at a 35% premium over the current market price (i.e., $ 17 per share as opposed to $ 13 per share). The terms of Ski-Me's Offer to Purchase for the self-tender prohibit any shareholder who owns ten percent or more of Ski-Me's shares from participating.

Assess for Ski-Me's management the likelihood that each, or either defense, will withstand judicial scrutiny. (National Skiing has already announced that its attorneys are preparing to seek a preliminary injunction against the implementation of each defense in the Delaware Chancery Court.)

3. Now assume that other bidders come forward. National Skiing makes a formal bid for all outstanding shares of Ski-Me at $ 17.50 per share, in cash. Breckenedge Ski Corp. enters the fray next with combined stock and cash offer valued at $ 19.00 per share. National Skiing then increases its cash bid to $ 19.50 per share, after which Saturday River Mountain Corp. enters with a bid of $ 21.00 per share. National Skiing tops that at $ 21.50 per share in cash. Ski-Me's board of directors then rescinds the "Crown Jewel" option granted to Telluride Ski Resort.

Informally, Saturday River's management lets Ski-Me's officers and directors know that Saturday River's $ 21.00 per share cash bid is a "first and final offer."

Ski-Me's directors consult with you. They wish to tender their own shares to Saturday River. They also wish to recommend the Saturday River bid to their rank-and-file shareholders. Last of all, they wish to grant to Saturday River a "leg up" option on approximately 20 percent of Ski-Me's authorized, but unissued, common stock. Their reasoning is that Saturday River is an experienced ski resort operator who will not make any radical changes in operations or management staffing, while National Skiing is well known to be a corporation that buys up smaller, well-run ski mountains and changes the individual, local character of these resorts by standardizing their look, feel, and overall operations. Can Ski-Me enter into an agreement with Saturday River providing for the acquisition of Ski-Me by Saturday River in a two-step acquisition (tender offer followed by merger), recommend that shareholders tender into the Saturday River offer, and grant Saturday River the desired stock option?

4. Now assume that, instead of the transaction with Saturday River described in Problem 3, *supra*, Ski-Me and Telluride Ski Resort work out a merger in which each of the two companies will have six directors on a twelve-director board. The office of CEO will first go to Ski-Me's current CEO, but after four years will rotate to the much younger Telluride Ski Resort CEO.

The plan of merger also devotes significant resources to preserving the two companies' cultures. Both companies specialize in operating ski resorts that cater to children and families. Both have a philosophy of "groomed and gradual" for maintenance of their ski runs rather than the "steep and deep" philosophy of Saturday River, Breckenedge, and National Skiing, all of whom cater to the jet set and the beautiful people.

The merger agreement also has several "deal protection" measures. It has a "no-shop" clause that prohibits Ski-Me or its directors from soliciting another bidder. It also has a "no talk" provision that, similarly, prohibits furnishing any non-public information to any potential bidder. There is a termination, or "goodbye fee," provision under which Ski-Me must pay to Telluride Ski Resort $40 million (approximately five percent of the value of the transaction) if, for any reason, the merger is not consummated.

The Telluride Ski Resort bid is valued at $19.50 per share and is in stock. Recall that Saturday River has offered $21.00 in cash and National Skiing has offered $21.50 in cash.

Do the Ski-Me directors have a *Revlon* duty to conduct an auction?

3. State Anti-Takeover Statutes

Target corporations and their counsel are not the only actors presenting barriers to unsolicited acquisition transactions. State legislatures, acting to protect target corporations and their various constituencies within the state's jurisdiction, promoted and passed anti-takeover statutes, most of which arise out of, supplement, and reinforce the takeover defenses instituted by corporations. These state statutes raise a number of issues, the most significant of which relate to actual and potential conflicts with the U.S. Constitution and federal takeover regulation.

There are two leading cases in this area: *Edgar v. MITE Corp.*, 457 U.S. 624 (1982), and *CTS Corp. v. Dynamics Corp. of America*, 481 U.S. 69 (1987). The net effect of the two decisions is to limit, but not obviate, a state role in regulating management behavior in takeovers outside the fiduciary duty context. Accordingly, members of corporate management must act in accordance with these state legislative initiatives as well as fiduciary duty principles, any applicable federal regulation, and contractual restrictions (including those in stock exchange listed company rules), when they engage in and respond to transactions that comprise or represent a change of control. As an example, note that Delaware corporate law mandates board (or shareholder) approval of certain transactions involving "interested stockholders" — those who acquire 15% or more (but less than 85%) of the corporation's outstanding voting stock — over the three-year period after the interested stockholder attains that status. *See* DGCL § 203. Some of these state anti-takeover statutes are not embodied in the state general corporation law or corporate code, so it is important to be aware of them and seek them out in a change of control scenario. Former SEC Commissioner Professor Roberta Karmel describes well the overall nature of state legislative activity in this area and its overall impact on management responses to unsolicited change-of-control transactions.

[M]anagement and labor groups were able to persuade state legislatures to pass anti-takeover statutes. Early statutes either unduly delayed the takeover process or permitted state blue-sky commissioners to conclude that takeovers were unfair. Such a statute was struck down by the U.S. Supreme Court as unconstitutional. Later state statutes, which imposed delays in the tender offer process, prohibited control share merger transactions for a period of years, or endorsed the consideration by corporate managers of nonshareholder constituencies in control contests, were upheld by the federal courts.

The refusal of the federal courts to invalidate most state anti-takeover legislation, or to endorse SEC efforts to curb takeover defenses, left the task of articulating how management should behave in control contests to the state courts. Because a majority of U.S. public corporations are incorporated in Delaware, decisions by the Delaware state courts became determinative of how the relevant law developed. The only national standard applicable to contests for corporate control other than the disclosure and specific procedural provisions of the Williams Act are stock exchange listing standards, which have an ambiguous legal footing. Although they originated in state contract laws, they are SRO "rules" under the Exchange Act, subject to SEC review and approval.

Most academics have criticized the impasse that developed between federal and state law with regard to takeovers, believing that takeovers are important mechanisms for protecting shareholders and disciplining corporate managers. But the Main Street interests that question the wisdom of encouraging hostile takeovers are probably at least as powerful as the Wall Street interests favoring hostile takeovers. Therefore, it is unlikely that state anti-takeover statutes or state corporate law giving corporate management considerable leeway in responding to takeover bids will be overturned, unless economic developments create a new consensus with respect to contests for corporate control.

Roberta S. Karmel, *Appropriateness of Regulation at the Federal or State Level: Reconciling Federal and State Interests in Securities Regulation in the United States and Europe*, 28 BROOK. J. INT'L L. 495, 534–35 (2003).* *See also* Manning Gilbert Warren, III, *Developments in State Takeover Regulation: MITE and Its Aftermath*, 40 BUS. LAW. 671 (1985).

D.   REFORM PROPOSALS

The complexity of corporate governance rules and the inherent related tensions among directors, officers, and shareholders of public companies have spawned numerous reform proposals, many of which relate to or have effects on change of control transactions. As you read the excerpt below, consider with respect to each reform proposal the genesis of the proposal, its capacity for achieving the desired effect on corporate governance, its effects on change of control transactions, and its desirability.

Margaret M. Blair, *Reforming Corporate Governance: What History Can Teach Us*
1 BERKELEY BUS. L.J. 1 (2004)* (footnotes omitted)

. . . Corporate governance questions moved into the public policy spotlight during the early 1980s, when the corporate sector suddenly faced a wave of hostile tender offers. Takeover offers often triggered controversial defensive responses by corporate managers and directors, and the resulting debate produced a wave of legal scholarship on the questions of whether takeovers were good or bad for the economy, whether directors and officers should be allowed to resist a hostile offer, and if they do, what tactics were legitimate, both legally and from the perspective of public policy. Some businesspeople and a few legal practitioners and management professors protested that the sudden and pervasive threat of hostile takeover was contributing to unhealthy pressures on businesses from the financial markets to focus on short-term performance at the expense of long-term performance. But the legal and finance faculties of leading universities largely accepted the premise that hostile takeovers were the market's way of correcting bad management — the fulfillment of Henry Manne's argument that the "market for corporate control" would prevent managers from straying too far from their job of maximizing value for shareholders.

A. Some Prominent Proposals Designed to Weaken Takeover Protection

The dominant academic response to the takeover wars of the 1980s, then, has been a continuing stream of reform proposals that would encourage takeovers and weaken the ability of corporate officers and directors to fight off unwanted takeovers. The following is not a comprehensive list, but a sampling of prominent proposals to weaken the ability of corporate directors to resist takeovers:

* Corporate managers should be required to remain passive in the face of a takeover bid, and the decision about whether to accept the tender offer should rest with the shareholders alone.

* Directors should not be allowed to frustrate takeover bids but should advise shareholders as to the fairness of the bid, and seek competing bids.

* Shareholders should be able to adopt bylaws that would allow them to control the use of poison pills in takeover battles.

* Shareholders should be entitled to opt into a body of federal takeover law that would require the board to remove a pill if a majority of outstanding shares vote in favor of a takeover bid.

One puzzle about the intensity and ongoing nature of the debate over takeovers and their defenses is that the underlying premise, that takeovers are the financial market's way of correcting poor management, is rarely challenged. In the early 1980s, scholars produced a large body of evidence that target company share prices rise when a tender offer is announced. To finance scholars, steeped in the belief in efficient capital markets, a rise in the price of the target company stock that is not offset by a decline in the price of some other asset could only be interpreted to mean that the proposed takeover must enhance productivity. But this price-increasing effect could alternatively be explained by the fact that tender offers are nearly always made at a price that represents a substantial premium over the previous price of the stock in order to get existing shareholders to sell. It should hardly be surprising, then, that the trading price of the target stock rises as the market incorporates some estimated probability that the bidder will eventually pay the higher offered price. Furthermore, the fact that the acquiring company's shares do not all immediately fall by an amount sufficient to offset the gains to the target shareholders can be explained by the fact that the market may not be able to tell initially whether the acquiring company will be able to improve the performance of the target company.

The real test comes in the months and years after a takeover, and there is substantial evidence indicating that acquiring companies typically lose money on corporate acquisitions. Meanwhile, there is little or no evidence that takeover targets are poorly performing companies, or that their performance improves after the takeover. Moreover, there is no robust evidence that takeover defenses, such as staggered boards and poison pills, actually impair the performance of companies that have them, nor that they are effective at preventing takeovers. One possible explanation for the absence of clear empirical support for the efficacy of takeovers is that the threat of takeovers actually has a mixed effect on corporate performance. On one hand, takeovers may in some cases discourage wasteful managerial empire-building, but on the other hand, the vulnerability of companies to unwanted takeovers may make it more difficult for corporate managers to foster long-term cooperation and commitment to the corporate enterprise by "team members" other than shareholders.

Nonetheless, the debate goes on, and takeover advocates continue to generate reform proposals that would weaken the power of directors to fight off takeover offers that, in the directors' judgment, would not be in the long-run best interest of the target company.

B. Proposals That Would Enhance Shareholders' Exit Options or Give Them More Direct Control over Corporate Assets

One of the most relentless proponents of the view that agency costs are a severe problem for the corporate sector, and that takeover defenses increase agency costs by entrenching managers, has recently proposed a very aggressive set of corporate governance reforms that would greatly strengthen shareholders' control over corporate assets, even beyond the takeover context. [Professor Lucian] Bebchuk classifies his proposals into three categories, according to how they influence one of three kinds of decisions made within corporations: "(i) 'rules-of-the-game' decisions to amend the corporate charter or change the company's state of incorporation; (ii) 'game-ending' decisions to merge, sell all assets, or dissolve; and (iii) 'scaling-down' decisions to contract the size of the company's assets by ordering a cash or in-kind distribution." I regard his "rules-of-the-game" proposals as proposals that give shareholders a more effective voice, so I consider them in the next section, and here consider only his "game-ending" and "scaling-down" proposals:

(1) Scaling-down proposals:

   * Shareholders should have the power to initiate and approve distributions, in cash or in other corporate assets.

   * Shareholders should have the power to order the distribution of new debt securities to shareholders, compelling management to liquidate assets in order to satisfy the claims of the new securities.

(2) Game-ending proposals:

   * Shareholders should have the power to initiate mergers and/or consolidations with other companies.

   * Shareholders should have the power to initiate a sale of all the assets of a company to a certain buyer (or even to auction the assets to the highest bidder).

   * Shareholders should have the power to initiate the dissolution of the company.

Bebchuk's case for these proposals is based on an argument that apparently assumes that whatever is better for shareholders at any point in time is "better" in some larger social sense. Or he may believe that giving shareholders more power is "better" because it is more consistent with his apparent view of shareholders as "owners" of corporations, and, therefore, serving their interests honors their property rights.

Perhaps Bebchuk would not claim that shareholders are the "owners" of corporations, but he nonetheless considers their situation to be analogous to that of partners in a partnership, except that shareholders lack the degree of influence and control rights over corporations that partners have in partnerships. But if this is Bebchuk's analogy, this line of reasoning suggests its own response: If equity investors in corporations had wanted the same rights of control over corporate assets as partners in a partnership have over partnership assets, then they should have invested in partnership-type organizations rather than in corporations.

As discussed above, unlike shareholders, partners are considered "co-owners" with direct interests in partnership assets, and as such have considerable leeway to influence the use of partnership assets, to withdraw their share of the partnership assets, and to compel dissolution of the partnership. Since those options are available to investors through the partnership organizational form (and can be modified to the precise specifications of any given group of investors through the details of the partnership agreement), then restructuring *corporate* law so that shareholders have similar options by legislative requirement would effectively deny investors the opportunity to commit their assets to ventures that they think might be more effective if capital is locked in. Bebchuk's proposals would reduce the range of investment opportunities now available to investors by eliminating one of the most important factors that distinguishes corporations from partnerships.

C. Proposals That Give Shareholders More Information and More Effective Voice

The corporate scandals of the last few years have made it clear that agency problems in corporations can be severe, but even granting that agency costs can be a problem, it is hard to see how Bebchuk's "scaling-down" proposals or "game-ending" proposals would have helped to prevent the frauds that happened at Enron or WorldCom, or the insider dealing at Tyco, or even the errors in business judgment that might have been behind Time Warner's merger with AOL. The financial markets appeared to love all of those companies right up until their problems were revealed, and by then it was too late to prevent them.

Financial investors, however, may not be able to make optimal investment decisions because they are likely to suffer from limited and/or distorted information about the performance of companies in their portfolios. Presumably, it was bad information and distorted perceptions, rather than stupidity, that led financial investors to invest so much cash in internet and telecom companies in the late 1990s, resulting in the financial market boom of that period, and the subsequent bust since 2000. Hence, corporate governance proposals that are aimed at enhancing investor information, and even giving investors more effective voice, might "improve" corporate governance (in the sense of increasing the wealth-creating potential of corporations) by reducing agency costs and facilitating the allocation of capital toward truly promising investments, while not undermining the features of corporate governance that help to solve the team production problem. A sampling of the reforms that have been proposed (or enacted) are:

(1) Enhancing the quality of information:

   * Enhance oversight of the accounting profession through a new, publicly-chartered oversight board.

   * Enhance the rules for auditor independence.

   * Require CEOs and CFOs to take personal responsibility for the accuracy of reports filed with the Securities and Exchange Commission.

   * Enhance disclosure requirements regarding off-balance sheet arrangements and contractual obligations.

* Reduce the time allowed for companies to report insider transactions.

These reforms have, of course, all been made law by the enactment of the Sarbanes-Oxley Act of 2002. Without analyzing the merits of these reforms (which would be beyond the scope of this Article), we can safely assume that all of them are intended to improve the quality and reliability of information that shareholders have about the corporations in which they are investing. Better information will help shareholders decide whether to buy or sell shares, causing the market price to more accurately reflect the true underlying value of the shares. But better information does not affect the degree of control that corporate directors have over corporate decisions or allocation of corporate assets. Hence, these are the kinds of reforms that could reduce agency costs in ways that are consistent with the "team production" and "locking-in of capital" functions of corporate law.

(2) "Rules-of-the-game" proposals:

     * Shareholders should have the right to vote on all equity-based compensation plans.

     * Shareholders should have the right to nominate directors.

     * Shareholders should have the power to initiate charter amendments as well as bylaw amendments.

     * Shareholders should have the power to initiate actions to reincorporate in another state under different statutory rules.

These proposals all clearly shift power and influence away from directors and toward shareholders, and so I regard them with caution. But they do so in ways that are not *necessarily* inconsistent with the ability of directors to retain ultimate control over "scaling-down" and "game-ending" decisions, which are the types of decisions that, if left to shareholders, would have the greatest potential for undermining the team-production-fostering role of the corporate form. If shareholders were permitted to nominate directors, propose charter amendments, and initiate reincorporations in other states, it would be interesting to see whether they would use these rights to improve their access to information and ability to monitor performance, or whether they would use these additional powers to attempt to extract immediate benefits for shareholders at the expense of other stakeholders or at the expense of the long-run wealth-creating potential of the corporation.

The funds managers at large institutional investors may understand that, to a great degree, the performance of their portfolios is ultimately tied to the performance of the economy as a whole. Although it might benefit individual shareholders from time to time to engage in scaling-down or game-ending strategies that extract wealth at the expense of the long-run performance of a particular firm, it does not serve the interests of shareholders as a class to have weak directors and managers who are unable to elicit the enthusiastic cooperation of other corporate stakeholders in the wealth-creating enterprise of the firm. Thus, to the extent that the large-block shareholders in U.S. companies are widely diversified institutional investors, they might use these new powers in moderation, and would not undermine the strength of boards or compel the premature distribution of corporate assets.

This line of argument does not apply to the game-ending and scaling-down decisions, because the short-term benefits that are available from extracting assets from a corporation can sometimes be attractive enough to motivate individual investors to acquire concentrated holdings and form coalitions with other undiversified and short-term-oriented investors to strip assets out of a corporation. This could occur despite the fact that a widely-diversified institutional investor, with a very long time horizon (such as an indexed pension fund) would not find that the advantage to be gained from pulling assets out of one corporation outweighed the costs in lost credibility of the capital lock-in bargain that would affect its whole portfolio of investments.

D. Proposals That Strengthen the Role and Effectiveness of Boards

The team production approach to understanding corporate law emphasizes the role of strong independent boards of directors in maintaining the right balance among the competing claims and interests in corporations. By contrast, the principal-agent approach to understanding corporate law often conflates the roles of directors and managers. In Bebchuk's article on empowering shareholders, for example, he never even acknowledges that boards of directors might be distinct from managers institutionally, legally, and in terms of the personalities involved. Hence, he acknowledges no role for boards of directors to help address the principal-agent problem by monitoring managers to be sure that they are not self-dealing, and that their actions are directed toward long-run wealth creation by the corporation rather than get-rich-quick schemes by management itself. If the role of boards of directors is properly understood, then it seems clear that any reforms that enhance the independence of boards, that provide them with better information, or that help them to work better and smarter, are likely to enhance both the team production-fostering and the agency cost-reducing functions. A sampling of proposals that I believe have the potential to generate this effect include:

* Boards of directors should consist of a majority of independent directors.

* Boards should have audit, nominating, and governance committees consisting entirely of independent directors.

* Directors and committee members should be required to meet without management, and their responsibilities should be enhanced to include reviewing more closely the goals, objectives, and performance of management, and evaluating compensation in light of these.

Although reforms such as these are not inconsistent with the role of boards in addressing the team production problem, they would not necessarily improve the performance of boards, nor of companies, by themselves. What is also needed is education and acculturation of directors so that they better understand, buy into, and have the tools they need to fulfill their roles.

E.   COMPARATIVE INTERNATIONAL PERSPECTIVES

Since the rules of law applicable to corporations, more broadly, are different from state to state within the United States and from nation to nation around the world, it is unsurprising that legal rules applicable to changes of corporate control vary within a range. Indeed, many proposals for merger, acquisition, and other control-related reform in the United States are based on the legal rules applicable to changes of corporate control in other countries. The excerpts reproduced below compare and contrast U.S. law and the laws of other nations as they may impact change of control transactions. The second excerpt also raises issues with respect to the relationship between supra-national takeover regulation through the Thirteenth Directive of the European Union and the independent regulations of European member states. Use these two excerpts, among other things, to reflect on the desirability of maintaining the existing balance as among corporate directors, officers, and shareholders in U.S. change of control situations. Also, consider the effects of national differences on the growing market for cross-border transactions.

Robert B. Thompson, *Takeover Regulation after the 'Convergence' of Corporate Law*
24 SYDNEY L. REV. 323 (2002)* (footnotes omitted)

Recent scholarship on corporate governance, cutting across law, finance, government and economics[,] has centred around whether or not corporate law is converging toward one dominant model within a competitive global capital market. There seems little doubt about the growing globalization of mergers and acquisitions. In 1985, for example, the great majority of takeovers included at least one American party, a percentage that by 1999 had fallen by more than half to 40 per cent and was below the number of takeovers involving at least one European party. Other factors support the growth of globalization: IPOs have become common across Europe, including civil law systems; and stock markets have grown dramatically outside the United States and the United Kingdom. . . .

Jurisdictions outside the United States have developed somewhat different substantive rules for takeovers and an alternative forum to resolve challenges that arise in a takeovers context. The United Kingdom has been relying on voluntary codes of conduct in the takeover area since the 1950s, through the City Takeovers Code and then the Takeovers Panel. In addition to requirements relating to disclosure and terms of the bid that are covered by the Williams Act in the United States, the City Code goes a good bit farther in terms of restricting defensive tactics that target companies may take. The General Principles state that if an offer has been made or is imminent, the target board cannot take action 'which could effectively result in any bona fide offer being frustrated or in the shareholders being denied the opportunity to decide on its merits.'

Australia's recent changes relating to the Takeovers Panel suggest a move that will mark a greater contrast with the United States in terms of the forum within which conflicts about takeovers and defensive tactics are resolved. Reconstituted as part of the Federal Government's Corporate Law and Economic Reform (CLERP) legislation in March 2000, the Panel has received positive reviews in its first two years. The new law broadened the parties who might refer matters to the panel and it seeks to resolve takeover disputes quickly, informally and effectively. This quasi-private system parallels what has been achieved by government in the United States where the Delaware courts have also been able to combine speed and substantive knowledge now offered by the Takeovers Panel. The majority of America's largest corporations are incorporated under the laws of Delaware so takeover disputes under corporate law are usually taken to its courts. All matters are originally heard by one of five judges who sit on the Delaware Court of Chancery, for whom corporate matters make up the bulk of their workload. These judges necessarily have achieved and are recognized for their expertise in corporate law. Any appeals are taken to the five member Delaware Supreme Court, who also have extensive experience in corporate law issues. Both courts are able to make quick decisions in the heat of a takeovers battle. Other American states have attempted to create special courts that could rival and take business way from Delaware, but have not been able to create a critical mass of casework and expertise in their judiciary on corporate law matters. Australia's [T]akeovers [P]anel, made up of practitioners in business and law and some judges and academics, has achieved notable expertise. Its informality and speed provides substantial appeal in a business context.

The substance of takeover regulation also differs somewhat under the Australian regime as compared to the United States. The question of termination fees as they are frequently called in the [United States] or break fees as they are termed in Australia are resolved by the United States in the context of specific cases within the umbrella of fiduciary duties; in Australia they have been the recent subject of a Panel action. The

---

outcome shows the differences that remain in a convergent world. Break-fees are uncommon in Australia and under the guidelines of the Panel cannot be more than 1 per cent of the value of the target company. In the United States, fees regularly show up in the two to four percent range and have sometimes been higher.

Target shareholders ability to take defensive actions seems more constrained in Australia. Poison pills and other defensive tactics are limited by listing requirements of the Australia Stock Exchange. The Takeovers Panel's ability to provide guidance notes on particular policy issues provides a process for evolution of these rules outside of a government-based system.

The alternative regimes being developed in Australia, the United Kingdom and other common law countries with developed securities markets do a better job of protecting shareholder space to make corporate decision[s] in a takeovers context when the interests of directors may diverge from those of shareholders. We may yet have convergence on one corporate law system, but at the moment the divergence in the discretion permitted shareholders, and who makes takeover decisions, appears to be a welcome characteristic of our global corporate law system.

Marco Ventoruzzo, *Europe's Thirteenth Directive and U.S. Takeover Regulation: Regulatory Means and Political and Economic Ends*
41 TEX. INT'L L.J. 171 (2006)* (footnotes omitted)

. . . .

Somewhat surprisingly given the existence of profound historical, legal, and cultural differences among the several European countries, most of the takeover laws (in particular those of France, Germany, Italy, Spain and the United Kingdom, as well as the European Union's Thirteenth Directive) share a common overall structure. The parts of this structure upon which I shall concentrate are the compulsory tender offer and the restrictions on defensive measures. These are, for our purposes, the distinguishing features of takeover regulation in Europe. Needless to say, there are other important regulatory issues that will not be considered in this analysis, primarily because they are implemented in various manners across Europe, although the variance is relatively minor and the regulations further the larger overarching shared structure.

Following the U.K. experience, most European countries required compulsory tender offers on all outstanding shares when a specified controlling threshold was acquired, converging toward a similar regulatory approach. There are two rationales for adopting a compulsory public offer regime. On the one hand, the technique is designed to favor the distribution of the controlling premium to a large group of investors. In the absence of an obligation to make a compulsory tender offer, controlling shareholders can sell a controlling participation in the company and thus "cash in" the premium for control. The premium for control is the difference between the market price for an individual share and the price of a share that includes participation in control. For example, the percentage difference between the prices of shares with higher voting rights and those with lower voting rights, or between ordinary share price and the price paid for a block that would provide control, is called the voting premium, which — according to some theories — is partially determined by the possibility of extracting from the corporation the private benefits of control.

The extent to which mandating a public offer ensures a broader distribution of the control premium depends on the quantity of shares that the bidder must offer to buy and the price at which the offer must be launched. These variables can be, and are, adjusted by legislatures to serve certain policy goals. For example, the higher the price of the compulsory offer, the greater the benefit for minority shareholders. But the cost of obtaining control is also greater and, consequently, takeovers may be discouraged.

A second goal of compulsory tender offers, which is related to the first but conceptually distinguishable from it, is to provide a fair opportunity for minority shareholders to exit in the event of an undesirable change in the controlling shareholder. This purpose is most evident in "subsequent" compulsory tender offers (as in the European approach I am discussing), in which offers on all outstanding shares must be launched after someone reaches a defined controlling threshold. Ensuring the possibility of exit for every shareholder who dissents from the acquisition turns on the percentage of outstanding shares that the bidder is required to offer to buy. Only an offer for all the outstanding shares allows every investor an unobstructed way out, without the need for pro-rata acquisitions.

A mandatory tender offer system also bears costs and benefits for the development of equity markets more generally, apart from the individual preferences of and price protection for individual minority investors. By ensuring that in any takeover a large number of shareholders will benefit from control premiums, compulsory tender offers strengthen financial markets by providing a systemic protection against exploitation of minority shareholders. On the cost side of the ledger, compulsory tender offer requirements also — almost inevitably — make takeovers more expensive. A bidder might be forced to purchase not only the percentage of shares necessary to control the corporation, but also an additional quantity of shares at a given price, which can exceed the market price. This possibility might discourage takeovers and cause stagnation in the market for corporate control. In addition to the financial expenditure necessary to acquire all the outstanding shares, the need to comply with a complicated body of regulations, which typically also require distributing a tender offer prospectus, increases the administrative and legal expenses associated with the takeover. In this respect, the existence of compulsory tender offer requirements operate similarly to defensive measures by protecting incumbent controlling shareholders and managers from the policing role of corporate raiders.

Even this general sketch suggests that, as a matter of policy, the introduction of compulsory tender offers lies at the edge of a very complex evaluation. These provisions may be particularly desirable in a market that is regarded as not particularly "thick" or efficient, meaning a market in which control of listed corporations is often transferred outside the market, through friendly transactions among insiders able to capitalize control premiums to the detriment of minority investors. This risk is particularly high in corporations with strong controlling shareholders and concentrated ownership structures, a condition present, to varying degrees, in most continental European countries.

The preceding discussion suggests that efficiency arguments are not the only ones driving the introduction of compulsory tender offers. The idea that the premium for corporate control belongs also, at least partially, to non-controlling shareholders relies on a particular idea of distributive justice and a specific political choice. Any sophisticated descriptive account, and clearly any normative account, of takeover regulation cannot ignore the socio-political motivations that inform this rule.

The overall framework is even more complex, given the multi-jurisdictional aspect of the European and U.S. business environments. Resident subjects, including political actors, are able to influence regulatory outcomes. Even without overt lobbying efforts, their interests are naturally considered by policy makers. If there is a significant risk of takeovers initiated by outsiders, and if compulsory bids offer some degree of protection to the incumbent controlling residents, it is neither surprising nor necessarily undesirable that such instruments will also be adopted as a form of protectionism. Along the same lines, in the current European context, in most cross-border takeovers, the bidder is a foreign company, while both the controlling shareholders of a target national corporation, as well as its minority shareholders and its employees are, for the most part, political actors in the system in which the policy makers responsible for regulating the takeovers operate. In an increasingly integrated Europe, the implications of these dynamics should fade. In the meantime, however, this element of nationalism continues to have some force. If compulsory takeovers contribute to strengthen, at least in the short term, the economic positions of important immediate constituencies, policy makers will be inclined to adopt them.

The second founding principle of the European takeover regime deals with limitations to the defensive measures that a target company can implement to resist hostile acquisitions through public offers. An unfriendly acquisition raises a conflict of interest between the incumbents controlling the corporation and, in particular, the directors, as well as the shareholders. The U.S. system addresses this conflict of interest mainly through the fiduciary duties owed by the directors to the shareholders, holding them liable in cases of breach of their duties of loyalty or of care, as developed in takeover case law. On the contrary, the European approach freezes directors' powers once a public offer has been launched and requires any action that might adversely affect the outcome of the takeover to be approved by the shareholders. In addition, some poison pills that might not require any action from the directors, but still prevent the takeover and jeopardize the interests of minority shareholders, are temporarily neutralized through the so-called "breakthrough rule."

In brief, it might be said that the European approach directly empowers shareholders on the issue of defensive measures. The desirability of this approach must be considered in light of the peculiar ownership patterns that prevail in Europe, since it might be argued that Europe has simply replaced the conflict between directors and shareholders with that between controlling and minority shareholders.

Chapter 17
THE ROLE OF COUNSEL

A. INTRODUCTION

The role of the corporate/securities attorney in the advisory and transactional setting is the focus of this Chapter. Undoubtedly, counsel plays an integral part in providing routine legal advice, in the drafting of legal documents, in the issuance of legal opinions, and in the consummation of business transactions. This pivotal role is underscored by the widespread perception that counsel's preparation of the necessary documents and the rendering of the pertinent legal opinions signify that the attorney acts as the "red or green light" to the effectuation of business deals.

B. ENRON AND OTHER CORPORATE DEBACLES: RAMIFICATIONS ON ATTORNEY CONDUCT

Largely due to massive corporate debacles that wreaked havoc on investors and the integrity of the U.S. securities markets, Congress enacted the Sarbanes-Oxley Act of 2002 (Sarbanes-Oxley or SOX). Among its many significant provisions, Congress mandated that the Securities and Exchange Commission (SEC) promulgate a rule focusing on attorney "up the ladder" reporting with respect to a corporate client, when faced with a material violation of fiduciary duty, securities law, or similar violation by a subject corporate constituent (such as a director, officer or employee). Following Congress' directive, the SEC in 2003 adopted standards of professional conduct.

These standards as well as those proposed (but not yet adopted) have generated zealous responses from the practicing securities bar, corporate executives, and academicians. Much of the discussion has dealt with whether the SEC should require counsel to make a "noisy withdrawal" when faced with client fraud (or similar material violation). At this time, the Commission appears unlikely to adopt such a provision.

1. Sarbanes-Oxley and the SEC's Response — A Brief Overview

The following discussion provides an overview of the attorney standards under Sarbanes-Oxley and the SEC's promulgation of applicable standards thereunder. Under Section 307 of SOX, Congress directed the SEC to adopt a rule:

> (1) requiring [a subject] attorney to report evidence of a material violation of securities law or breach of fiduciary duty or similar violation by the company or any agent thereof, to the chief legal counsel or the chief executive officer of the company (or the equivalent thereof); and

> (2) if the counsel or officer does not appropriately respond to the evidence (adopting, as necessary, appropriate remedial measures or sanctions with respect to the violation), requiring [such] attorney to report the evidence to the audit committee of the board of directors of the issuer or to another committee of the board of directors comprised solely of directors not employed directly or indirectly by the issuer, or to the board of directors.

Section 307 and a large part of the SEC's response closely resemble existing ethical standards as set forth by the American Bar Association, the American Law Institute, and the states. Responding to Congress' directive, the SEC adopted standards implementing "up the ladder" reporting and recognized the legitimacy of a Qualified Legal Compliance Committee (QLCC) to serve as an alternative.[1] In its 2003 rule adoption, however, the Commission declined to adopt the attorney "noisy withdrawal"

---

[1] As defined in Section 205.2(k) of the SEC Standards, a Qualified Legal Compliance Committee (QLCC)

provisions as proposed by the SEC in an earlier release. Under this proposal, if the corporate client refused to take appropriate corrective action after counsel dutifully went "up the ladder," counsel was obliged to make a "noisy withdrawal," notifying the SEC that such counsel disaffirmed documents that he or she had prepared during the course of the representation.[2]

The making of a noisy withdrawal, of course, sounds a siren that fraud or other grievous misconduct likely is afoot. Corporate fiduciaries and the securities bar (as well as such groups as the American Bar Association) reacted with alarm, asserting that such a noisy withdrawal mandate would drive a wedge between attorneys and corporate insiders. Afraid that counsel would "blow the whistle" (albeit by action rather than words), constituents of the business enterprise would be reluctant to seek legal advice on troubling subjects. Thus, the proposed provision, according to opponents, would be quite detrimental. Proponents favoring a noisy withdrawal provision, on the other hand,

---

is a committee of a publicly-held issuer (which committee may also be the audit or other committee of the issuer) that:

(1) Consists of at least one member of the issuer's audit committee (or, if the issuer has no audit committee, one member from an equivalent committee of independent directors) and two or more members of the issuer's board of directors who are not employed, directly or indirectly, by the issuer and who are not, in the case of a registered investment company, "interested persons" as defined in section 2(a)(19) of the Investment Company Act of 1940 (15 U.S.C. 80a-2(a)(19));

(2) Has adopted written procedures for the confidential receipt, retention, and consideration of any report of evidence of a material violation under § 205.3;

(3) Has been duly established by the issuer's board of directors, with the authority and responsibility:

(i) To inform the issuer's chief legal officer and chief executive officer (or the equivalents thereof) of any report of evidence of a material violation (except in the circumstances described in § 205.3(b)(4));

(ii) To determine whether an investigation is necessary regarding any report of evidence of a material violation by the issuer, its officers, directors, employees or agents and, if it determines an investigation is necessary or appropriate, to:

(A) Notify the audit committee or the full board of directors;

(B) Initiate an investigation, which may be conducted either by the chief legal officer (or the equivalent thereof) or by outside attorneys; and

(C) Retain such additional expert personnel as the committee deems necessary; and

(iii) At the conclusion of any such investigation, to:

(A) Recommend, by majority vote, that the issuer implement an appropriate response to evidence of a material violation; and

(B) Inform the chief legal officer and the chief executive officer (or the equivalents thereof) and the board of directors of the results of any such investigation under this section and the appropriate remedial measures to be adopted; and

(4) Has the authority and responsibility, acting by majority vote, to take all other appropriate action, including the authority to notify the Commission in the event that the issuer fails in any material respect to implement an appropriate response that the qualified legal compliance committee has recommended the issuer to take.

17 C.F.R. § 205.2(k).

[2] *See* Securities Exchange Act Release No. 46868 (2002) (setting forth proposed § 205.3(d)). As used in the proposed rule, "disaffirm" means:

Disaffirm to the Commission, in writing, any opinion, document, affirmation, representation, characterization, or the like in a document filed with or submitted to the Commission, or incorporated into such a document, that the attorney has prepared or assisted in preparing and that the attorney reasonably believes is or may be materially false or misleading.

assert that counsel must have this leverage in order to better ensure that corrective action is taken, thereby protecting the corporate client, its shareholders, and creditors. Hence, faced with the reality that counsel must make a noisy withdrawal if appropriate steps are not undertaken, corporate insiders will be "persuaded" to act in compliance with the law.

At this time, the SEC appears unlikely to adopt a noisy withdrawal provision or any of the proposed alternatives. One of these alternatives would require the affected company (rather than counsel) to notify the Commission of the attorney's withdrawal from representation on the basis that such counsel did not receive a suitable response to a report concerning a material violation. If the Commission had adopted this latter proposal, the rate of corporate adherence thereto may well have been problematic.

2.   State Ethical Rules

Today, at least 42 states permit or require an attorney to reveal a client's crime or fraud that threatens substantial financial loss. Pursuant to its 2003 amendments, the ABA Model Rules now permit such disclosure. Moreover, many states as well as ABA Model Rule 1.6 allow a lawyer under certain conditions to reveal client confidences in order to prevent, mitigate, or rectify substantial financial harm that "is reasonably certain to result or has resulted from the client's commission of a crime or fraud in furtherance of which the client has used the lawyer's services" (ABA Model Rule 1.6(b)(3)). In this respect, the SEC standards adopted in 2003 generally are consistent with these state ethical standards. They generally will have an impact only in states (such as California) which prohibit counsel's disclosure of client confidences and secrets in situations involving financial harm.[3]

For further literature on attorney responsibility in this "new" era, see, for example, M. STEINBERG, ATTORNEY LIABILITY AFTER SARBANES-OXLEY (2007); Symposium, 52 AM. U.L. REV. No. 3 (2003); Symposium, 8 STAN. J. LAW BUS. & FIN. No. 1 (2002); Symposium, 70 TENN. L. REV. No. 1 (2002); Symposium, 46 WASHBURN L.J. No. 1 (2006); Symposium, 3 WYOM. L. REV. No. 2 (2003); Cramton, *Enron and the Corporate Lawyer: A Primer on Legal and Ethical Issues*, 58 BUS. LAW. 143 (2002); Greenbaum, *The Attorney's Duty to Report Professional Misconduct: A Roadmap for Reform*, 16 GEO. J. LEG. ETH. 259 (2003); Nicholson, *A Hobson's Choice for Securities Lawyers in the Post-Enron Environment: Striking a Balance Between the Obligations of Client Loyalty and Market Gatekeeper*, 16 GEO. J. LEG. ETH. 91 (2002); Simon, *Whom (Or What) Does the Organization's Lawyer Represent?: An Anatomy of Intraclient Conflict*, 91 CALIF. L. REV. 57 (2003); Warren, *Revenue Recognition and Corporate Counsel*, 56 SMU L. REV. 885 (2003).

C.   ATTORNEY LIABILITY BASED ON CLIENT FRAUD

In the Lincoln Savings and Loan debacle, U.S. District Court Judge Stanley Sporkin, former SEC Director of the Division of Enforcement (and former General Counsel of the Central Intelligence Agency), asserted:

> Where were these professionals, a number of whom are now asserting their rights under the Fifth Amendment, when these clearly improper transactions were being consummated?
>
> Why didn't any of them speak up or disassociate themselves from the transactions? Where also were the outside accountants and attorneys when these transactions were effectuated?
>
> What is difficult to understand is that with all the professional talent involved

---

[3] The above discussion derives from an article authored by Professor Steinberg in 3 WYOMING L. REV. 371 (2003).

(both accounting and legal) why at least one professional would not have blown the whistle to stop the overreaching that took place in this case.

Lincoln Savings & Loan Association v. Wall, 743 F. Supp. 901, 920 (D.D.C. 1990).

In the aftermath of Judge Sporkin's assertion, the Washington Post editorialized that "it is a charge to bar associations and accounting boards to consider this enormous failure of their professional standards to protect both clients and the public."[4] The financial fraud debacles of the last few years accentuate this point.

PROBLEM

In the course of her duties as general outside counsel for Abso Property Investments, Inc. (API), a publicly held corporation whose stock is listed on the New York Stock Exchange, Melinda Jacobs has learned that API is the subject of heated litigation regarding one of its premier investment properties. While the lawsuit was filed a number of years ago, it is now reaching the trial phase. Thus far, API has not disclosed the suit and its potentially detrimental financial effects on the company in any of its SEC-filed documents. Damages sought by the plaintiffs exceed ten percent of API's annual revenues. A jury trial is scheduled to commence in three months.

1. What are Jacobs' obligations as API's outside counsel in advising API with respect to disclosure?

2. Assume that Jacobs approaches API's inside general counsel Harry Hairston about this issue. Hairston tells Jacobs, "Thank you for bringing this to our attention. It will be taken care of." Is this a satisfactory result? How should Jacobs proceed?

3. Assume instead that when Jacobs approaches Hairston about the subject, she is told that there is already a committee in place to look into the issue of whether this is a material fact that should be disclosed, and that Hairston will get back to her when a decision is made. Is this a satisfactory result?

4. What result if Hairston has the API board of directors appoint independent outside counsel to investigate the disclosure issue, and that counsel opines that the litigation is not material and, therefore, does not need to be reported?

5. What should Jacobs do if she believes that, after talking to Hairston and "climbing the ladder" all the way to API's board of directors, API declines to provide adequate disclosure in its SEC documents as she concludes is required?

1.   SEC Action

IN THE MATTER OF CARTER AND JOHNSON
Securities and Exchange Commission
[1981 Transfer Binder] Fed. Sec. L. Rep. (CCH) ¶ 82,847 (1981)

[In this Rule 2(e) [now Rule 102(e)] proceeding, two prominent attorneys (Carter and Johnson who practiced with "Wall Street Firms") were charged with having violated the antifraud provisions of the securities laws as well as having violated standards of professional responsibility in connection with their representation of National Telephone Company. The Administrative Law Judge (ALJ) found that the attorneys had assisted National Telephone's management in concealing material facts concerning the company's financial condition and had failed to inform the company's board of directors concerning management's refusal to make adequate disclosures. The ALJ also held that the attorneys had engaged in improper professional conduct, thereby violating Rule 2(e).]

. . . .

---

[4]   Editorial, *Judgment on Lincoln S & L*, Wash. Post, Aug. 8, 1990, at A26.

For the reasons stated more fully below, we reverse the decision of the Administrative Law Judge with respect to both respondents. We have concluded that the record does not adequately support the Administrative Law Judge's findings of violative conduct by respondents. Moreover, we conclude that certain concepts of proper ethical and professional conduct were not sufficiently developed, at the time of the conduct here at issue, to permit a finding that either respondent breached applicable ethical or professional standards. In addition, we are today giving notice of an interpretation by the Commission of the term "unethical or improper professional conduct," as that term is used in Rule 2(e)(1)(ii). This interpretation will be applicable prospectively in cases of this kind.

The Purpose of Rule 2(e). The Commission promulgated Rule 2(e) pursuant to its general rule-making powers in order to protect the integrity of its processes. These powers were not exercised with a view to the creation of new administrative proceedings to fill gaps in the Commission's current statutory panoply of remedies. Rule 2(e) is not intended to provide an administrative remedy as an alternative to our power to seek injunctive relief for violations of provisions of the securities laws which do not already provide for an administrative remedy. For example, it does not reach any of the myriad of non-professionals who may have been involved in violations of the securities laws for which an administrative remedy is not available. It is addressed to a different problem — professional misconduct — and its sanction is limited to that necessary to protect the investing public and the Commission from the future impact on its processes of professional misconduct.

Rule 2(e) represents a balancing of public benefits. It rests upon the recognition that the privilege of practicing before the Commission is a mechanism that generates great leverage — for good or evil — in the administration of the securities laws. A significant failure to perform properly the professional's role has implications extending beyond the particular transaction involved, for wrongdoing by a lawyer or an accountant raises the specter of a replication of that conduct with other clients.

Recognition of the public implications of the securities professional's role does not mean that the Commission has, by rule, imposed duties to the public on lawyers where such duties would not otherwise exist. Accountants, of course, issue audit reports that speak directly to the investing public and publicly represent that the code of conduct embodied in the statements of auditing standards promulgated by the AICPA has been followed. The duty of accountants to those who justifiably rely on those reports is well-recognized. But the traditional role of the lawyer as counselor is to advise his client, not the public, about the law. Rule 2(e) does not change the nature of that obligation. Nevertheless, if a lawyer violates ethical or professional standards, or becomes a conscious participant in violations of the securities laws, or performs his professional function without regard to the consequences, it will not do to say that because the lawyer's duty is to his client alone, this Commission must stand helplessly by while the lawyer carries his privilege of appearing and practicing before the Commission on to the next client.

[Note that Rule 102(e) has been codified in Section 4C of the Securities Exchange Act pursuant to Congress' enactment of the Sarbanes-Oxley Act of 2002.]

The Operation of Rule 2(e). The operation of subparagraphs (i) and (ii) of Rule 2(e)(1) responds to [relevant] policy considerations. . . . Subparagraph (i) provides for sanctions upon a finding that a respondent does "not . . . possess the requisite qualifications to represent others." The motivating concept is clear: the Commission's processes cannot function effectively without the existence of competent professionals who counsel and assist their clients in securities matters. The same focus is evident in subparagraph (ii), which provides for sanctions if a respondent is "lacking in character or integrity or [has] engaged in unethical or improper professional conduct."

The operation of subparagraph (iii) of the Rule reflects the same concerns. This provision provides for suspension or disbarment if the Commission finds, after notice of and opportunity for hearing, that a respondent has "willfully violated, or willfully aided and abetted the violation of any provision of the federal securities laws . . . or the rules and regulations thereunder." Not every violation of law, however, may be sufficient to justify invocation of the sanctions available under Rule 2(e). The violation must be of a character that threatens the integrity of the Commission's processes in the way that the activities of unqualified or unethical professionals do.

Against that background, we turn to an analysis of respondents' conduct. In our judgment, that conduct presents difficult questions under the applicable legal and professional standards.

. . . .

ETHICAL AND PROFESSIONAL RESPONSIBILITIES

A. *The Findings of the Administrative Law Judge*

The Administrative Law Judge found that both respondents "failed to carry out their professional responsibilities with respect to appropriate disclosure to all concerned, including stockholders, directors and the investing public . . . and thus knowingly engaged in unethical and improper professional conduct, as charged in the Order." In particular, he held that respondents' failure to advise National's board of directors of [its executive] Hart's refusal to disclose adequately the company's perilous financial condition was itself a violation of ethical and professional standards referred to in Rule 2(e)(1)(ii).

Respondents argue that the Commission has never promulgated standards of professional conduct for lawyers and that the Commission's application in hindsight of new standards would be fundamentally unfair. Moreover, even if it is permissible for the Commission to apply — without specific adoption or notice — generally recognized professional standards, they argue that no such standards applicable to respondents' conduct existed in 1974–75, nor do they exist today.

We agree that, in general, elemental notions of fairness dictate that the Commission should not establish new rules of conduct and impose them retroactively upon professionals who acted at the time without reason to believe that their conduct was unethical or improper. At the same time, however, we perceive no unfairness whatsoever in holding those professionals who practice before us to generally recognized norms of professional conduct, whether or not such norms had previously been explicitly adopted or endorsed by the Commission. To do so upsets no justifiable expectations, since the professional is already subject to those norms.

The ethical and professional responsibilities of lawyers who become aware that their client is engaging in violations of the securities laws have not been so firmly and unambiguously established that we believe all practicing lawyers can be held to an awareness of generally recognized norms. We also recognize that the Commission has never articulated or endorsed any such standards. That being the case, we reverse the Administrative Law Judge's findings under subparagraph (ii) of Rule 2(e)(1) with respect to both respondents. Nevertheless, we believe that respondents' conduct raises serious questions about the obligations of securities lawyers, and the Commission is hereby giving notice of its interpretation of "unethical or improper professional conduct" as that term is used in Rule 2(e)(1)(ii). The Commission intends to issue a release soliciting comment from the public as to whether this interpretation should be expanded or modified.

B. *Interpretive Background*

Our concern focuses on the professional obligations of the lawyer who gives essentially correct disclosure advice to a client that does not follow that advice and as a result violates the federal securities laws. . . .

While precise standards have not yet emerged, it is fair to say that there exists considerable acceptance of the proposition that a lawyer must, in order to discharge his professional responsibilities, make all efforts within reason to persuade his client to avoid or terminate proposed illegal action. Such efforts could include, where appropriate, notification to the board of directors of a corporate client. . . .

We are mindful that, when a lawyer represents a corporate client, the client — and the entity to which he owes his allegiance — is the corporation itself and not management or any other individual connected with the corporation. Moreover, the lawyer should try to "insure that decisions of his client are made only after the client has been informed of relevant considerations." These unexceptionable principles take on a special coloration when a lawyer becomes aware that one or more specific members of a corporate client's management is deciding not to follow his disclosure advice, especially if he knows that those in control, such as the board of directors, may not have participated in or been aware of that decision. Moreover, it is well established that no lawyer, even in the most zealous pursuit of his client's interests, is privileged to assist his client in conduct the lawyer know to be illegal. The application of these recognized principles to the special role of the securities lawyer giving disclosure advice, however, is not a simple task.

The securities lawyer who is an active participant in a company's ongoing disclosure program will ordinarily draft and revise disclosure documents, comment on them and file them with the Commission. He is often involved on an intimate, day-to-day basis in the judgments that determine what will be disclosed and what will be withheld from the public markets. When a lawyer serving in such a capacity concludes that his client's disclosures are not adequate to comply with the law, and so advises his client, he is "aware," in a literal sense, of a continuing violation of the securities laws. On the other hand, the lawyer is only an adviser, and the final judgment — and, indeed, responsibility — as to what course of conduct is to be taken must lie with the client. Moreover, disclosure issues often present difficult choices between multiple shades of gray, and while a lawyer's judgment may be to draw the disclosure obligation more broadly than his client, both parties recognize the degree of uncertainty involved.

The problems of professional conduct that arise in this relationship are well-illustrated by the facts of this case. In rejecting [the law firm of] Brown, Wood's advice to include the assumptions underlying its projections in its 1974 Annual Report, in declining to issue two draft stockholders letters offered by respondents and in ignoring the numerous more informal urgings by both respondents and Socha to make disclosure, [National Telephone's executives] Hart and Lurie indicated that they were inclined to resist any public pronouncements that were at odds with the rapid growth which had been projected and reported for the company.

If the record ended there, we would be hesitant to suggest that any unprofessional conduct might be involved. [National Telephone's management — Hart and Lurie] were, in effect, pressing the company's lawyers hard for the minimum disclosure required by law. That fact alone is not an appropriate basis for a finding that a lawyer must resign or take some extraordinary action. Such a finding would inevitably drive a wedge between reporting companies and their outside lawyers; the more sophisticated members of management would soon realize that there is nothing to gain in consulting outside lawyers.

However, much more was involved in this case. In sending out a patently misleading letter to stockholders on December 23 in contravention of [the] express advice to clear all such disclosure with Brown, Wood, [and by engaging in a number of other troubling maneuvers,] the company's management erected a wall between National and its outside lawyers — a wall apparently designed to keep out good legal advice in conflict with management's improper disclosure plans.

Any ambiguity in the situation plainly evaporated in late April and early May of 1975 when Hart first asked [the attorney] Johnson for a legal opinion flatly contrary to the express disclosure advice Johnson had given Hart only five days earlier, and when Lurie soon thereafter prohibited the delivery of a copy of the company's April 1975 Form 8-K to Brown, Wood.

These actions reveal a conscious desire on the part of National's management no longer to look to Brown, Wood for independent disclosure advice, but rather to embrace the firm within Hart's fraud and use it as a shield to avoid the pressures exerted by the banks toward disclosure. Such a role is a perversion of the normal lawyer-client relationship, and no lawyer may claim that, in these circumstances, he need do no more than stubbornly continue to suggest disclosure when he knows his suggestions are falling on deaf ears.

C. "Unethical or Improper Professional Conduct"

The Commission is of the view that a lawyer engages in "unethical or improper professional conduct" under the following circumstances: When a lawyer with significant responsibilities in the effectuation of a company's compliance with the disclosure requirements of the federal securities laws becomes aware that his client is engaged in a substantial and continuing failure to satisfy those disclosure requirements, his continued participation violates professional standards unless he takes prompt steps to end the client's non-compliance. The Commission has determined that this interpretation will be applicable only to conduct occurring after the date of this opinion.

We do not imply that a lawyer is obliged, at the risk of being held to have violated Rule 2(e), to seek to correct every isolated disclosure action or inaction which he believes to be at variance with applicable disclosure standards, although there may be isolated disclosure failures that are so serious that their correction becomes a matter of primary professional concern. It is also clear, however, that a lawyer is not privileged to unthinkingly permit himself to be co-opted into an ongoing fraud and cast as a dupe or a shield for a wrong-doing client.

Initially, counseling accurate disclosure is sufficient, even if his advice is not accepted. But there comes a point at which a reasonable lawyer must conclude that his advice is not being followed, or even sought in good faith, and that his client is involved in a continuing course of violating the securities laws. At this critical juncture, the lawyer must take further, more affirmative steps in order to avoid the inference that he has been co-opted, willingly or unwillingly, into the scheme of non-disclosure.

The lawyer is in the best position to choose his next step. Resignation is one option, although we recognize that other considerations, including the protection of the client against foreseeable prejudice, must be taken into account in the case of withdrawal. A direct approach to the board of directors or one or more individual directors or officers may be appropriate; or he may choose to try to enlist the aid of other members of the firm's management. What is required, in short, is some prompt action that leads to the conclusion that the lawyer is engaged in efforts to correct the underlying problem, rather than having capitulated to the desires of a strong-willed, but misguided client.

Some have argued that resignation is the only permissible course when a client chooses not to comply with disclosure advice. We do not agree. Premature resignation serves neither the end of an effective lawyer-client relationship nor, in most cases, the effective administration of the securities laws. The lawyer's continued interaction with his client will ordinarily hold the greatest promise of corrective action. So long as a lawyer is acting in good faith and exerting reasonable efforts to prevent violations of the law by his client, his professional obligations have been met. In general, the best result is that which promotes the continued, strong-minded and independent participation by the lawyer.

We recognize, however, that the "best result" is not always obtainable, and that there may occur situations where the lawyer must conclude that the misconduct is so extreme or irretrievable, or the involvement of his client's management and board of directors in the misconduct is so thorough-going and pervasive that any action short of resignation would be futile. We would anticipate that cases where a lawyer has no choice but to resign would be rare and of an egregious nature. [This case does not involve, nor do we here deal with, the additional question of when a lawyer, aware of his client's intention to commit fraud or an illegal act, has a professional duty to disclose that fact either publicly or to an affected third party. Our interpretation today does not require such action at any point. . . . — moved to text from footnote—editor]

D. *Conclusion*

As noted above, because the Commission has never adopted or endorsed standards of professional conduct which would have applied to respondents' activities during the period here in question, and since generally accepted norms of professional conduct which existed outside the scope of Rule 2(e) did not, during the relevant time period, unambiguously cover the situation in which respondents found themselves in 1974-75, no finding of unethical or unprofessional conduct would be appropriate. That being the case, we reverse the findings of the Administrative Law Judge under Rule 2(e)(1)(ii). In future proceedings of this nature, however, the Commission will apply the interpretation of subparagraph (ii) of Rule 2(e)(1) set forth in this opinion.

An appropriate order will issue.

SEC ADOPTS ATTORNEY CONDUCT RULE UNDER SARBANES-OXLEY ACT
Securities and Exchange Commission
Press Release No. 2003-13 (January 23, 2003)

The Securities and Exchange Commission today adopted final rules to implement Section 307 of the Sarbanes-Oxley Act by setting "standards of professional conduct for attorneys appearing and practicing before the Commission in any way in the representation of issuers." In addition, the Commission approved an extension of the comment period on the "noisy withdrawal" provisions of the original proposed rule and publication for comment of an alternative proposal.

[In] 2002, the Commission voted to propose the standards of professional conduct. That proposal defined who is appearing and practicing before the Commission in the representation of an issuer. Attorneys were required to report evidence of a material violation "up-the-ladder" within an issuer. In addition, under certain circumstances, these provisions permitted or required attorneys to effect a so-called "noisy withdrawal" — that is, to withdraw from representing an issuer and notify the Commission that they have withdrawn for professional reasons.

The rules adopted by the Commission today will

- require an attorney to report evidence of a material violation, determined according to an objective standard, "up-the-ladder" within the issuer to the chief legal counsel or the chief executive officer of the company or the equivalent;

- require an attorney, if the chief legal counsel or the chief executive officer of the company does not respond appropriately to the evidence, to report the evidence to the audit committee, another committee of independent directors, or the full board of directors;

- clarify that the rules cover attorneys providing legal services to an issuer who have an attorney-client relationship with the issuer, and who have notice that documents they are preparing or assisting in preparing will be filed with or submitted to the Commission;

- provide that foreign attorneys who are not admitted in the United States, and who do not advise clients regarding U.S. law, would not be covered by the rule, while foreign attorneys who provide legal advice regarding U.S. law would be covered to the extent they are appearing and practicing before the Commission, unless they provide such advice in consultation with U.S. counsel;

- allow an issuer to establish a "qualified legal compliance committee" (QLCC) as an alternative procedure for reporting evidence of a material violation. Such a QLCC would consist of at least one member of the issuer's audit committee, or an equivalent committee of independent directors, and two or more independent board members, and would have the responsibility, among other things, to recommend that an issuer implement an appropriate response to evidence of a material violation. One way in which an attorney could satisfy the rule's reporting obligation is by reporting evidence of a material violation to a QLCC;

- allow an attorney, without the consent of an issuer client, to reveal confidential information related to his or her representation to the extent the attorney reasonably believes necessary: (1) to prevent the issuer from committing a material violation likely to cause substantial financial injury to the financial interests or property of the issuer or investors; (2) to prevent the issuer from committing an illegal act; or (3) to rectify the consequences of a material violation or illegal act in which the attorney's services have been used;

- state that the rules govern in the event the rules conflict with state law, but will not preempt the ability of a state to impose more rigorous obligations on attorneys that are not inconsistent with the rules; and

- affirmatively state that the rules do not create a private cause of action and that authority to enforce compliance with the rules is vested exclusively with the Commission.

In addition, the final rules modify the definition of the term "evidence of a material violation," which defines the trigger for an attorney's obligation to report up-the-ladder within an issuer. The revised definition confirms that the Commission intends an objective, rather than a subjective, triggering standard, involving credible evidence, based upon which it would be unreasonable, under the circumstances, for a prudent and competent attorney not to conclude that it is reasonably likely that a material violation has occurred, is ongoing or is about to occur.

The Commission voted to extend for 60 days the comment period on the "noisy withdrawal" and related provisions originally included in [the] proposed [standard]. Given the significance and complexity of the issues involved, including the implications of a reporting out requirement on the relationship between issuers and their counsel, the Commission decided to continue to seek comment and give thoughtful consideration to these issues.

The Commission also voted to propose an alternative to "noisy withdrawal" that would require attorney withdrawal, but would require an issuer, rather than an attorney, to publicly disclose the attorney's withdrawal or written notice that the attorney did not receive an appropriate response to a report of a material violation. Specifically, an issuer that has received notice of an attorney's withdrawal would be required to report the notice and the circumstances related thereto [to the SEC], within two days of receiving the attorney's notice. [At this point in time, the SEC has not adopted the proposed rule and appears unlikely to do so.]

NOTE

Under the ethical rules, an attorney retained by a corporation (or other business enterprise) represents such enterprise acting through its duly authorized constituents (such as the board of directors or senior management). *See* Rule 1.13(a) of the American Bar Association's (ABA) Model Rules of Professional Conduct. Pursuant to Model Rule 1.13, if counsel for a corporation knows that an officer, employee, or another individual affiliated with that corporation is engaged in a violation of law that is likely to cause substantial injury to the corporation, then counsel shall use reasonable efforts to prevent the harm. The steps taken by counsel should be designed to minimize disruption and the risk of disclosing confidences. Such steps may include: (1) asking that the matter be reconsidered; (2) seeking a separate legal opinion concerning the matter for review by the appropriate authority in the enterprise; and (3) referring the issue to "higher authority in the organization, including if warranted by the circumstances, to the highest authority that can act on behalf of the organization as determined by applicable law." Provided that after referral to the board of directors or similar authority in the organization, the organization persists in the illegal conduct, counsel should resign from the representation. The Model Rules also permit counsel to reveal information outside the organization that counsel believes is necessary to prevent the client's commission of a fraudulent or criminal act that is likely to cause substantial financial harm.

2. Duty to Disclose Client Fraud

As discussed earlier in this Chapter, the vast majority of state ethical rules permit counsel to disclose client fraud that threatens substantial financial loss. With respect to Section 10(b) liability, the majority of courts decline to impose liability upon lawyers as primary violators for their failure to disclose client fraud. The Seventh Circuit's statement in *Barker v. Henderson, Franklin, Starnes & Holt*, 797 F.2d 490, 496 (7th Cir. 1986), serves as a well-known example:

> The extent to which lawyers and accountants should reveal their client's wrongdoing — and to whom they should reveal — is a question of great moment. . . . We express no opinion on whether the [law firms] did what they should, whether there was malpractice under state law, or whether the rules of ethics (or other fiduciary doctrines) ought to require lawyers and accountants to blow the whistle in equivalent circumstances. We are satisfied, however, that an award of damages under the securities laws is not the way to blaze the trail toward improved ethical standards in the legal and accounting professions. Liability depends on an existing duty to disclose. The securities law therefore must lag behind changes in ethical and fiduciary standards. The plaintiffs have not pointed to any rule imposing on either [law firm] a duty to blow the whistle.

The Supreme Court has held that aiding and abetting liability may not be imposed in private actions under § 10(b) of the Securities Exchange Act. *See Central Bank of Denver v. First Interstate Bank of Denver*, 511 U.S. 164 (1994). The key issue litigated after *Central Bank* is whether the alleged violator's misconduct gives rise to primary liability under § 10(b). In *Central Bank*, the Court stated: "Any person or entity, including a lawyer, accountant or bank, who employs a manipulative device or makes a material misstatement (or omission) on which a purchaser or seller of securities relies may be liable as a primary violator under [rule] 10b-5. . . . " The Supreme Court narrowly interpreted this language in *Stoneridge Investment Partners, LLC v. Scientific-Atlanta, Inc.*, 128 S. Ct. 761 (2008) (holding that plaintiffs were unable to prove the requisite reliance with respect to secondary actors' alleged scheme to defraud, stating: "no member of the investing public had knowledge, either actual or presumed, of respondents' deceptive acts during the relevant times [and that] as a result, cannot show reliance upon any of the respondents' actions except in an indirect claim that we find too remote for liability").

3. Attorney Malpractice

In addition to securities law liability, attorneys may be subject to liability to their clients and to third parties based on state common law concepts of negligence. A number of states still require attorney client privity to state a malpractice action. *See, e.g., Pelham v. Griesheimer*, 92 Ill. 2d 13, 440 N.E.2d 96, 99 (1982) ("The concept of [attorney-client] privity has long protected attorneys from malpractice claims by non-clients."); *Flaherty v. Weinberg*, 303 Md. 116, 492 A.2d 618, 620 (1985) ("[A]bsent fraud, collusion or privity of contract, an attorney is not liable to a third party for professional malpractice.").

Today, several courts permit certain allegedly injured third parties to sue an attorney based on negligence under a number of different theories. This expansion of liability under state law has affected securities counsel. For example, in *Vereins-Und Westbank, AG v. Carter*, 691 F. Supp. 704, 709 (S.D.N.Y. 1988) (applying New York law), a non-client recipient of an opinion letter sued the attorney and his law firm for the negligent rendering of such opinion. The court denied the defendants' motion for summary judgment, reasoning that "liability for negligent misstatements to one not in contractual privity may attach where the statement is made for the principal purpose of having it relied upon by such person, and where its benefit to the party authorizing the statement stems precisely from such reliance by the third party."

An expansive approach holds that any reasonably foreseeable third party may bring suit against an attorney if the attorney's negligence proximately caused the loss. For example, in *Zendell v. Newport Oil Corp.*, 226 N.J. Super. 431, 544 A.2d 878 (1988), the court allowed purchasers of limited partnership interests to sue the law firm for its alleged negligence in the sale of securities in violation of the Securities Act's registration requirements. Even though the plaintiffs did not have an attorney-client or fiduciary relationship with the law firm, they were foreseeable third parties. Consequently, relying on the New Jersey Supreme Court's decision in *H. Rosenblum, Inc. v. Adler*, 93 N.J. 324, 461 A.2d 138 (1983), it was held that the plaintiff-investors could maintain an action for negligent misrepresentation.

Another approach is that of the American Law Institute's (ALI) Restatement (Second) of Torts. Generally, under the Restatement's approach, attorneys may be held liable for negligent misrepresentation to their clients, to intended known beneficiaries, and to any unidentified person of an identified class of beneficiaries. Hence, the Restatement subjects attorneys to liability for negligence to unknown beneficiaries if such beneficiaries are members of a limited, identifiable class for whom the information was intended to be furnished. Broadly interpreted, the ALI Restatement may extend to investors who purchase securities in a limited or public offering.

D. PREDECESSOR-SUCCESSOR COMMUNICATIONS

An important issue is the extent to which an attorney who resigns from a representation because of a client's fraud can inform the prospective successor lawyer of the facts and circumstances relating to the resignation. This issue surfaced in the saga that follows, *In re O.P.M. Leasing Services, Inc.*

IN RE O.P.M. LEASING SERVICES, INC.
Bankruptcy Court of United States
30 B.R. 642 (S.D.N.Y. 1983)

*REPORT OF THE TRUSTEE CONCERNING FRAUD
AND OTHER MISCONDUCT IN THE MANAGEMENT
OF THE AFFAIRS OF THE DEBTOR*

James P. Hassett, Trustee of O.P.M. Leasing Services, Inc., submits this Report under section 1106(a)(4) of the Bankruptcy Code concerning fraud and other misconduct in the management of OPM's affairs.

. . . .

OPM: The Story in Brief

Mordecai Weissman founded his own leasing company in July 1970 at the age of twenty-three in hopes of prospering with a minimum investment of his own capital and effort. He called the new enterprise O.P.M. Leasing Services, Inc., a name whose mysterious initials often sparked curiosity as the company grew. Different explanations offered for the name wryly capture the different facets of the OPM debacle.

OPM's principals often told customers and others in the business and financial communities that "O.P.M." stood for "other people's machines." To the outside world that watched OPM grow into one of the nation's largest computer leasing companies, this explanation seemed to fit OPM's role as intermediary between computer manufacturers and computer users.

But the truth was that the initials stood for "other people's money." The name connoted the plan of Weissman and Myron S. Goodman, his brother-in-law and partner, to rely almost exclusively on funds advanced by others to run the business. But beyond that, the name reflected the pair's cynical, unscrupulous attitude toward financial and personal interests of other people. Seen from the inside, their business relied on corruption and deception from the start to create an illusion of success. Meanwhile OPM actually lost money at ever increasing rates. By the end Weissman and Goodman were able to continue operating only with other people's money they obtained by fraud of record proportions.

The fraud relied heavily on a factor identified in yet another explanation offered for the OPM initials — "other people's mistakes." Numerous financiers, businessmen, and professionals acted through ignorance, carelessness, poor judgment, or self-interest in ways that permitted the fraud to continue for years. This Report is not simply a story of the myth and reality of OPM; it is also a study of how outsiders who dealt with OPM allowed the fraud at OPM to occur.

. . . .

"Other People's Mistakes": The Outsiders

No less noteworthy than the remarkable saga of OPM from the inside is the combination of actions and inactions by various outsiders that permitted the fraud to occur and, in some instances, actively contributed to its success. Accountants, management consultants, lawyers, investment bankers, lessee representatives, bankers, and other businessmen all worked intimately with Goodman and Weissman in ways that exposed them to transactions used for the fraud. In the misguided belief that someone else was checking the bona fides of OPM's transactions or was acting to stop the fraud, all stood by while the fraud continued at an ever increasing pace.

. . . .

Lawyers

Lawyers played a critical role in the massive Rockwell lease fraud. Without their witting or unwitting assistance, the fraud simply could not have occurred.

The law firm of Singer Hutner Levine & Seeman (and its predecessor and successor firms) served as OPM's outside general counsel from 1971 to September 1980 and did not fully sever its relationship with OPM until December 1980. Singer Hutner closed all but seven of the fifty-four financings of fraudulent Rockwell leases.

Singer Hutner acquired OPM as a client in 1971 through Andrew B. Reinhard, the older brother of a close boyhood friend of Goodman. Reinhard was then a Singer Hutner associate and later became a partner. In 1972 Weissman and Goodman elected Reinhard the third director of OPM. As OPM's business expanded, Singer Hutner followed along, more than doubling in size to twenty-seven lawyers in 1980. By 1975 Singer Hutner participated in virtually every facet of OPM's business. Goodman likened the close relationship between OPM and Singer Hutner to a "bondage of the bookends."

From 1976 through 1980 Singer Hutner received legal fees of almost $7.9 million — sixty to seventy percent of its revenues — from OPM. Singer Hutner also received almost $2 million in reimbursement of expenses. While Singer Hutner lawyers, unlike

Goodman, may not have regarded the firm as an adjunct to OPM, their prosperity was tied to OPM's success. The Trustee believes Singer Hutner was not sufficiently alert to the danger that its professional judgment might be impaired by its financial dependence on OPM.

One of the most difficult questions encountered during the Trustee's investigation was whether Reinhard knowingly participated in any of the fraudulent activities at OPM. Although the United States Attorney's Office determined not to seek a grand jury indictment against him, the decision not to prosecute is not dispositive.

The principal witness against Reinhard is Goodman. Goodman testified that, having previously told Reinhard about the early frauds at OPM, he informed Reinhard in early 1979 of his intention to finance three phantom Rockwell leases and successfully enlisted Reinhard's assistance in the fraud. Goodman says he told Reinhard that the financing was necessary to keep OPM in business because of a temporary cash shortage, that he would buy out the financings within several weeks, and that he would never engage in fraudulent financings again. According to Goodman, Reinhard resisted but eventually agreed to help. Goodman testified that Reinhard reluctantly assisted in several subsequent fraudulent financings.

Through his lawyers Reinhard denies he had any knowledge of fraud at OPM apart from information obtained by his firm in June and September 1980. On advice of counsel, Reinhard invoked his Fifth Amendment privilege and refused personally to respond to any questioning by the Trustee concerning the fraud.

Despite a number of internal inconsistencies and anomalies, Goodman's testimony has a ring of truth. Statements by other members of the OPM fraud team and Marvin Weissman tend to corroborate Goodman's testimony. On the other hand, Goodman is an acknowledged master liar and may have hoped implicating Reinhard would endear Goodman to the United States Attorney's Office. While the issue is by no means free from doubt, the Trustee believes there is substantial evidence that Goodman led Reinhard to become, however reluctantly, a knowing participant in the Rockwell fraud.

Apart from Reinhard's probable complicity in the fraud from the outset, Singer Hutner's conduct as OPM's counsel in closing fraudulent Rockwell financings cannot be justified. By early 1979 Singer Hutner had received indications that Goodman and Weissman were capable of serious illegality. Some lawyers were aware that Weissman and Goodman had engaged in lease fraud and commercial bribery, and the firm knew that Goodman had recently perpetrated a $5 million check kiting scheme. Singer Hutner also had knowledge of facts showing that OPM was suffering severe cash shortages that provided a motive for further fraud.

In the sixteen months between the first financing of phantom Rockwell leases in February 1979 and Goodman's first confession to Singer Hutner of serious wrongdoing in June 1980, numerous facts came to Singer Hutner's attention that should have raised suspicions about the bona fides of OPM-Rockwell leases. . . . With all these red flags, Singer Hutner should have exercised extreme caution in closing OPM-Rockwell lease financings. Instead, until June 1980 the firm closed these transactions on a business as usual basis.

On June 12, 1980, Goodman met with Joseph L. Hutner, a Singer Hutner partner, and confessed that he had engaged in past "wrongful transactions" in an amount exceeding $5 million. During a break in the meeting, Goodman somehow retrieved the letter . . . describing the details of the Rockwell fraud. Goodman refused to return the letter or provide additional details of his acknowledged wrongdoing, citing his desire for assurances that Singer Hutner would keep the information secret under the attorney-client privilege.

Singer Hutner promptly retained Joseph M. McLaughlin, then dean of Fordham Law School, and Henry Putzel, III, formerly an associate professor of professional responsibility at Fordham, to advise the firm on its ethical responsibilities in dealing with Goodman's disclosure. Whether or not Singer Hutner's conduct based on their advice was "ethical" (a legal question the Trustee does not address), it was woefully inadequate to prevent further fraud. After June 1980 Singer Hutner closed fifteen additional fraudulent Rockwell transactions totaling $70 million.

Singer Hutner kept Goodman's misdeeds secret and continued closing OPM transactions on the basis of certificates from Goodman attesting to the legitimacy of the transactions. The Trustee believes Singer Hutner was wrong in relying on Goodman's representations that the fraud had stopped and ignoring substantial evidence that it had not. . . . [O]n two occasions in June and July Singer Hutner lawyers noticed peculiarities in title documents used in fraudulent Rockwell lease financings that should have led them to seek to confirm their authenticity with third parties.

For months Goodman resisted pressure to make full disclosure of the fraud to Singer Hutner by a series of gambits including a threat to jump out of a window in OPM's ninth story offices if pressed further. In September 1980 Goodman finally came clean, or so he claimed. At a meeting with the Singer Hutner partners, Goodman described the mechanics of the Rockwell fraud and quantified it at $30 million — only about $100 million short of the truth. Notwithstanding Goodman's continued insistence that the fraud had stopped by June 1980, and Goodman's hysterical threat to "bring down this firm," on September 23 Singer Hutner voted to resign as OPM's counsel.

With Putzel's approval, Singer Hutner agreed to characterize its resignation misleadingly as a "mutual determination of our firm and [OPM] to terminate our relationship as general counsel." Singer Hutner also agreed to continue rendering legal services over a two and one-half month transition period to avoid unnecessary injury to OPM.

In late September or early October Goodman dropped the bombshell that the fraud had in fact continued throughout the summer of 1980. Despite this shocking acknowledgment by Goodman that he had continued to use Singer Hutner as an instrument of fraud even after his initial confession of wrongdoing, Putzel advised Singer Hutner that it could not ethically warn successor counsel of the danger that Goodman would use them to help finance additional fraudulent transactions.

After Singer Hutner's withdrawal, OPM's young in-house lawyers and the law firm of Kaye, Scholer, Fierman, Hays & Handler represented OPM in its lease transactions. Kept in the dark by Goodman and Singer Hutner about the real reasons for the departure of Singer Hutner, OPM's in-house staff unwittingly closed six fraudulent financings of Rockwell leases and Kaye Scholer unwittingly closed one.

Singer Hutner, of course, relies on the advice it received from McLaughlin and Putzel to justify its conduct during the summer and fall of 1980. While the Trustee does not attempt to resolve the question whether that advice was consistent with the legal profession's code of ethics, it is clear that McLaughlin and Putzel could have advised other courses, consistent with Singer Hutner's ethical responsibilities, that would have stopped the fraud. Although McLaughlin and Putzel in good faith considered their advice appropriate in the circumstances, the Trustee believes it was in fact the worst possible advice from the point of view of OPM, the third parties with whom it dealt, Singer Hutner's successor counsel, and Singer Hutner itself. Accordingly, McLaughlin and Putzel must shoulder significant responsibility for their client's conduct.

But Singer Hutner cannot properly shift all blame for its actions after Goodman's first confession of wrongdoing to McLaughlin and Putzel. While Singer Hutner relied on McLaughlin and Putzel for advice on its ethical obligations, McLaughlin and Putzel relied on the firm for the central factual predicate for their advice — whether the fraud was continuing. . . .

Viewed as a whole, the Trustee finds Singer Hutner's conduct nothing short of shocking, given the warnings it received before June 1980 and the remarkable events of the summer and early fall. Although Singer Hutner cites its ethical obligation not to injure its client unnecessarily, the most questionable aspects of Singer Hutner's conduct raise issues beyond professional ethics. Even after learning that Goodman had engaged in major wrongdoing, Singer Hutner continued to close OPM debt financings without obtaining prior disclosure of the nature of the wrongdoing and without independently verifying transaction facts. No rule of professional ethics can or should exempt lawyers from the general legal proscriptions against willful blindness to their clients' crimes or reckless participation in them.

. . . .

NOTE

As seen in *OPM*, predecessor counsel kept a closed-mouth approach, evidently for the purpose of preserving the former client's confidences and secrets. Unfortunately, this approach allows the former client to continue its fraudulent conduct, employing unwitting successor counsel as a resource to achieve its objectives.

An alternative response is as follows:

> Former counsel should not stand idly by acquiescing in the former client's retention of successor counsel, thereby resulting in further injury to innocent victims. In such situations, predecessor counsel should send "red flags" to the inquiring attorney. For example, predecessor counsel may state: "I'm unable by the ethical rules to explain why I resigned unless the former client gives me permission to tell you." If the client refuses to give such permission, this should signal to the inquiring attorney that the prospective engagement should be declined. In any event, and particularly if the representation is undertaken by successor counsel, such counsel should draft a memorandum documenting the results of such inquiry and the information obtained. Moreover, it would be prudent for predecessor counsel to document the contents of communications with prospective successor counsel.

Steinberg, *Attorney Liability for Client Fraud*, 1991 COLUM. BUS. L. REV. 1, 21–22 (1991). *See* Brown, *Counsel with a Fraudulent Client*, 17 REV. SEC. REG. 909 (1984); Comment, *The Client-Fraud Dilemma: A Need for Consensus*, 46 MD. L. REV. 436 (1987).

E.   LEGAL OPINIONS

Legal opinions play an important role for an attorney engaged in a transactional-type of practice. The discussion that follows provides an overview of this significant aspect of securities law practice.

Darrel Rice & Marc I. Steinberg, *Legal Opinions In Securities Transactions*
16. Corp. L. 375 (1991)*

The attorney who represents a client in a securities transaction must ascertain relevant facts, review the law, and provide competent professional advice to the client. In fulfilling his or her professional responsibility, the lawyer must perform the duties that are owed with the requisite degree of care to give informed, prudent, and sound advice. Lawyers are frequently called upon to give legal opinions in securities transactions to their clients and to third parties who are not their clients. Delivery by an attorney of an opinion in the planning or closing of a securities transaction is, in many instances, a crucial part of the lawyer's function and is frequently a condition to the ability of the client to obtain capital.

The form and substance of legal opinions in securities transactions should be carefully considered, and the "due diligence" requirements in securities law

---

transactions should be carefully defined and understood by the opinion giver and the opinion recipient. Any required investigation of facts or law should be performed in a manner necessary both to discharge the professional responsibility of the attorney and to avoid creating any basis for potential liability. An attorney's legal opinion, is in essence, a reflection of his or her professionalism and expertise. Consequently, each attorney who prepares or reviews a legal opinion given in a securities transaction should exercise sound professional judgment and give careful and thoughtful attention to the language and meaning of the opinion, as well as to the factual investigation and legal research that are necessary to support the opinion. Additionally, because the client must ultimately bear the costs of any such legal opinion, the diligence and effort must be sensible and cost effective, and in the final analysis may, in many instances, be determined by agreement between the opinion giver and the opinion recipient.

. . . .

Purposes of Legal Opinions

Legal opinions in securities transactions are most commonly prepared to satisfy a condition to the closing of the transaction. A legal opinion is generally given for the purpose of (a) providing assurance that a proposed course of conduct is lawful or that certain desired legal consequences will result from a proposed action, (b) confirming the existence or creation of certain legal relationships, or (c) providing an independent verification or check on the accuracy of representations and warranties made by parties to a transaction. Legal opinions may also be given to governmental agencies or regulatory authorities to satisfy regulatory requirements, such as opinions of counsel that are required as part of registration statements which are filed with the SEC.

Many types of securities transactions are customarily completed only upon the delivery of legal opinions that are described in or required by the transaction documents. Certain common examples of legal opinions that relate to securities transactions include: (1) opinions as to the valid issuance of securities, (a) in offerings that are registered with the SEC under the Securities Act of 1933 (the "Securities Act"), (b) in "private offerings" that are exempt from registration under the Securities Act by virtue of Section 4(2) thereof, or (c) by virtue of "Regulation D"; (2) opinions to underwriters in public securities offerings; and (3) opinions regarding compliance with applicable exemptions from registration under the Securities Act for resales of unregistered securities by persons other than the issuer. The closing of securities transactions is frequently conditioned upon commonly used legal opinions on such matters as corporate status, corporate power and authority to enter into the transaction, due authorization, execution and delivery of the transaction documents, enforceability of the transaction documents, absence of conflicts created by the transaction under material agreements or governmental regulations or constraints to which the parties are subject, absence of material litigation, and absence of the requirement of governmental or third party consents.

. . . .

Factual Basis for Legal Opinions

. . . [T]he underlying facts and circumstances that relate to any proposed legal opinion must, to the extent that they are not assumed, be established through independent verification, review of documents and certificates or other suitable methods of factual investigation. The results of this investigation are often documented in the files of the attorney or the law firm that renders the opinion prior to the issuance of the opinion.

Although it is not entirely clear, many lawyers would agree that the knowledge of each lawyer in a firm is attributable to the firm itself, and therefore, any information in the firm's files, or in the actual knowledge of an individual attorney in a firm, constitutes part of the "knowledge" of the firm. In complex situations, or in large firms that have multiple attorneys who work on various matters for a single client, some investigation and inquiry among several lawyers in the firm may be necessary. In certain cases, it may be appropriate to conduct a firm-wide investigation that is similar to that conducted in responding to auditors' inquiries in annual audits. The following is a brief discussion of the factual bases for opinions, and some recommendations on how to gather facts for an opinion.

A. Standards for Factual Examinations

Persons who conduct factual investigations that are preliminary to the rendering of a legal opinion should generally comply with the following guidelines:

(i) the factual examination should be performed by a lawyer who possesses sufficient technical training and expertise to perform all phases of the investigative task;

(ii) the lawyer who makes the examination should maintain an independent mental attitude in all matters that relate to the investigation, and should avoid conflicts of interest;

(iii) due professional care should be exercised in the performance of the examination and the preparation of memoranda or other appropriate written evidence that documents the scope and results of the factual investigation;

(iv) the factual investigation should be sufficiently complete to provide appropriate evidential matter as to relevant facts through inspection, observation, inquiries, confirmations, and research, in order to afford a reasonable factual basis for the opinion; and

(v) in a multi-lawyer firm, before completing the examination, the attorney who is involved in the factual investigation should consult with other lawyers in the firm who may have special knowledge about the facts that are under examination, or who may have particular knowledge of certain matters that relate to the business or organization of the client.

B. How to Gather Facts for an Opinion

1. Review of Operative Documents

The basic underlying agreements or operative documents for the securities transaction in question should be reviewed thoroughly by the lawyer in preparation for rendering a legal opinion. This process requires a review of the loan agreement, underwriting agreement, private placement agreement, stock purchase agreement, indenture, or other operative document to determine the nature and extent of the legal opinion that is required of the lawyer. In complex transactions, there will be a number of related documents that will require review, and in some cases more than one opinion of counsel will be required. If reference is made to other documents, such as registration statements or proxy statements that are filed with the SEC, those other documents should also be reviewed carefully to determine the nature of the facts that may have to be investigated as a basis for rendering the opinion.

2. Preparation of Preliminary Checklist

After the lawyer has reviewed the relevant operative documents, it is frequently useful to prepare an outline or checklist for factual investigation, listing the major types of investigation involved, and the key areas of examination. The outline should segregate the legal conclusions required to be given in the opinion, as well as the documents to be reviewed and the factual investigations to be made in order to establish the factual basis for each opinion. In the area of litigation or claims, the lawyer may need to review complaints and correspondence that discuss potential claims, make appropriate inquiries of the client, and obtain appropriate officer's certificates from the client with respect to litigation.

3. Conducting the Factual Investigation

The factual investigation to support an opinion, including any necessary corporate examination of minute books, corporate stock records, and other records, should be conducted as early as possible in the process after the general scope and nature of the inquiry can be determined. If the transaction proceeds over a long period of time, it may be necessary to update certain aspects of the examination at a date relatively near to the closing of the proposed transaction, in order to determine that no new facts have developed, or that no changes have occurred between the date of the original examination and the date of delivery of the opinion.

4. Record of the Factual Investigation

It is important that the factual investigation that has been made is documented appropriately in the files of the opining attorney or law firm. The attorney or attorneys who perform the factual investigation should prepare, for the internal records of the opining counsel, a synthesis or summary of what has been done to support the opinion. This synthesis or summary does not need to set forth the full examination in great detail, but rather should summarize the examination, highlighting any possible problems noted, and if possible, either actions taken to correct the problem, or suggestions as to methods of solution. The summary should be in a form that will be both helpful to the attorney during the investigation, and helpful to the firm later, in the event that it is ever asked to substantiate the factual investigation that supports the opinion. The summary should be in a form that will allow the lawyer to determine what work remains to be done, and to make an estimate of the timing of the investigation and the necessary lawyers, paralegals or other staff personnel necessary to accomplish the investigation. For example, in a corporate examination, the summary may contain the list of all missing documents such as minutes of meetings, notices of meetings, waivers of notices of meetings, or unanimous consents, along with the names of those persons whose services are needed to complete the record.

Procedures and Policies to Maintain Professionalism and Quality Control

Attorneys have a strong personal and professional interest in maintaining professionalism and quality control in the legal opinions that they issue. This section briefly discusses some recommended procedures and policies that may be utilized to promote and maintain professionalism and quality control.

A. Issue Identification: Defining the Scope and Substance of Legal Opinions

In connection with the issuance of legal opinions, the lawyer has a fundamental professional duty to advise the client concerning the legal opinions that should be requested, and to identify the relevant factual and legal questions to be answered in connection with the securities transaction that the client proposes to enter. The attorney has a professional responsibility to competently and diligently make judgments regarding the proposed transaction, and to the extent appropriate, advise the client as to what legal opinions the client should obtain, and from whom such opinions should be obtained, including any that should be obtained from the lawyer rather than or in addition to counsel to other parties to the transaction. Once the relevant issues are identified by the attorney, counsel should, to the extent appropriate, advise the client as to the necessary investigation of facts and law that will be required for any legal opinion that the attorney is rendering. Furthermore, counsel should advise the client as to whether the client appears to be adequately protected in relying upon opinions that are to be received from counsel to other parties in the transaction. All of the foregoing duties require the attorney to exercise sound professional judgment, and to make an inquiry and analysis that is adequate under the circumstances and in the context of the particular transaction in question.

Because one of the main goals of legal opinions is to inform, the attorney should confer with the client and discuss matters that are covered by the legal opinion to the extent necessary to inform the client as to (i) matters that may affect the client's conduct or judgment in the transaction, (ii) the client's needs to enable such client to make "business decisions" that are properly made by the client rather than the attorney, and (iii) matters that may significantly increase the cost of the transaction, through increased legal fees or otherwise. In many situations, the lawyer will bear the ultimate responsibility for identifying the issues, defining the scope and substance of legal opinions required in the transaction, and defining the nature and adequacy of factual and legal review necessary to support the opinion. In certain special situations, an attorney may act upon specific instructions from the client as to factual assumptions or investigations.

B. Standard Opinion Forms

Many attorneys and law firms have developed "standard" opinion forms that are utilized as a basis for negotiating legal opinions in a particular type of transaction. The use of forms of opinions is helpful both for providing instruction and guidance to lawyers within a firm, as well as for avoiding the necessity of "reinventing the wheel," by providing a convenient source of accumulated know-how for rendering opinions. However, discretion should be exercised in the use of opinion forms, because no form can be drafted that is appropriate for all transactions. Every lawyer who negotiates, drafts, or signs a legal opinion should give fair, reasonable, and dispassionate review and consideration to requests for legal opinions that depart from the "standard" opinion forms that are maintained by the particular attorney or firm being requested to render the opinion.

C. Internal Review of Opinions

1. Opinion Committee

Many leading law firms have established opinion committees that are responsible for reviewing all opinions that are issued by the law firm. Typically, this review occurs prior to the signing and delivery of the opinion. Some firms require the approval of both a member of the opinion committee and a partner who is experienced and knowledgeable in the substantive area that is addressed by the opinion.

2. Substantive Review by Experienced Individual Attorneys

Most law firms require that firm opinions be reviewed by a partner before they are delivered to the recipient of the opinion. Although the practice among firms appears to vary widely, the most important aspect of this type of review would appear to be the substantive review by an experienced individual attorney who is knowledgeable in the areas of practice that are addressed in the opinion. The advantage of having opinions reviewed by a single partner, rather than an opinion committee, may be that the process is less cumbersome and more efficient, and perhaps can be accomplished in a more timely manner. Obviously, whether any particular procedure works for a law firm depends upon the personalities, policies, and professional style and approach of the attorneys or firms that are involved.

D. Opinion Manuals or Memoranda of Firm Policy

Some firms have developed manuals of firm policies and procedures that set forth the law firm's policies and procedures concerning the issuance of legal opinions. Preferably, any such manual would be a looseleaf compilation, so that the policies and procedures of the firm could be updated or changed by circulating new materials or changes to policies and procedures to all attorneys in the firm from time to time. The policies and procedures manual or memorandum approach may be used in addition to, or possibly in lieu of, the approval of opinions by an opinion committee. The use of an opinion manual may be particularly desirable for larger firms, since it can be used to encourage uniformity in the giving of opinions, and adherence to policies for rendering opinions based on many years of collective experience.

. . . .

The literature on legal opinions is voluminous. *See, e.g.*, S. FITZGIBBON & D. GLAZER, LEGAL OPINIONS (2d ed. 2004); ABA Task Force on Securities Law Opinions, *Legal Opinions in SEC Filings*, 59 BUS. LAW. 1505 (2004); ABA Committee on Legal Opinions, *Legal Opinion Principles*, 53 BUS. LAW. 831 (1998); Fitzgibbon & Glazer, *Legal Opinions on Incorporation, Good Standing and Qualification to Do Business*, 41 BUS. LAW. 461 (1986); McCallum & Young, *Ethical Issues in Opinion Practice*, 62 BUS. LAW. 417 (2007); Ryan, *Recipient Counsel Responsibilities and Concerns*, 62 BUS. LAW. 401 (2007); Symposium on Legal Opinions, 1989 COLUM. BUS. L. REV. Nos. 2 & 3 (1989).

TABLE OF CASES

[References are to pages]

[References are to pages]

C

D

[References are to pages]

[References are to pages]

[References are to pages]

[References are to pages]

[References are to pages]

INDEX

[References are to pages.]

[References are to pages.]

[References are to pages.]